MODERN RHETORIC

Third Edition

Cleanth Brooks

Robert Penn Warren

MODERN RHETORIC

Third Edition

Harcourt, Brace & World

New York / Chicago / San Francisco / Atlanta

ISBN: 0–15–562807–0

Library of Congress Catalog Card Number: 73–113705

Printed in the United States of America

to **David M. Clay**

Preface

The third edition of *Modern Rhetoric* represents a thorough and systematic reworking. This should not suggest that we have renounced the principles on which the earlier editions were based. We remain convinced that good writing is a natural expression of necessary modes of thought and not merely a matter of rules or tricks. We remain convinced, too, that the best and quickest way to learn to write well is not through a process of blind absorption, or trial and error, or automatic conditioning, but through the cultivation of an awareness of the underlying logical and psychological principles, an awareness to be developed in the double process of constantly analyzing specific examples and constantly trying to write against a background of principle. To look at the matter in a slightly different way, the student learns to write by coming to a deeper realization of the workings of his own mind and feelings, and of the way in which those workings are related to language.

The twenty years that have elapsed since *Modern Rhetoric* first appeared have, we trust, taught us how to present the principles of writing more clearly and how to apply them more practically. Our aim in this edition is to make our book more accessible to the ordinary student by sharpening our formulations, by eliminating certain overfine distinctions, and by omitting certain theoretical niceties that may have tended to blur more fundamental matters. In short, the book is now better organized and better focused, as well as more richly and pertinently illustrated.

We have tried here to draw the student into a fuller participation in the actual process of learning, to encourage an active instead of a passive attitude. To this end, we have completely reworked the first four chapters to emphasize the stage of "prewriting," to show how the act of writing is grounded and how it may be approached rationally. In these chapters, as later, we have undertaken to offer the student more, and more pertinent, things "to do." Again and again, instead of merely describing, or even illustrating, how he should or should not handle a given situation, we have set him concrete problems to solve for himself. With the hope of encouraging this fuller participation we have, also, tried to provide the student with better, fresher, and more interesting examples, in both the Rhetoric section and the Readings.

The whole book has, as we have said, been reworked and rewritten. In addition to the changes in the first four chapters, we should like to indicate other significant developments. The chapter on Exposition has been completely reorganized and rewritten with a considerable amount of new material. That on Argument, though retaining the earlier method of organization, has been carefully rethought and reworked. We have added an entirely new chapter, that on Persuasion, on two assumptions, first, that the chapter on Argument, important as it is, does not cover all the problems the student will meet in winning a reader's assent, and second, that persuasion, rather than argument, is what the student most often encounters in his contact with the world. We call special attention to the chapter on Narration, which has been expanded and pointed up.

Part IV, which concerns itself with the preparation for and the writing of a research paper, has been much expanded. Users of the book had encouraged us to be content with our presentation of the research paper on a historical topic, but it became evident that there was need for a fairly full account of how to write a paper of literary criticism. We have added such a section, and here, as in the treatment of the historical paper, we have tried to take the student, step by step, through the stages of gathering material, locating a true subject, organizing his observations and ideas, developing an actual plan for the paper, converting his plan into words, and—not least important—criticizing and revising his paper. For each step we have provided specific illustrations and examples. We should add that this paper, like the historical paper, is by a student who worked under the supervision of one of the present authors.

We have mentioned our attempt to make the Readings more interesting to the student. In the previous editions, we tried to touch on certain basic issues of the modern world, for example, in the selections by Carl Becker, B. F. Skinner, and C. S. Lewis (the last two of which we have retained). We now add a number of selections that treat more immediate issues, particularly those close to the concerns of the student himself. But we wish to emphasize that mere topicality has not been our basic criterion: we have sought examples that show serious minds seriously at work on topical questions. We have tied this new book of Readings more closely than ever to the Rhetoric proper, incorporating into the text abundant exercises. We should add that there are twenty-seven new items in the Readings and that most of this material has been published in the last five years.

With this edition we are providing, for the first time, an Instructor's Manual, which will make available to the instructor our interpretations of the questions raised in the Applications as well as questions on the Readings.

Whatever improvement appears in this revision of *Modern Rhetoric* is largely due to the criticisms, suggestions, and other contributions made throughout the years by friends of the book. Though these friends are many and all merit our deep gratitude, we wish to make special mention of Mr. Lloyd Bruno of Sacramento Junior College, Mr. Henry Cassady of Hartnell College, Mr. Edward Gordon of Yale University, Miss Mary K. Hill, Mr. Sanford Kahrmann of Columbia University, the Reverend Dennis B. McCarthy, O.P., of Providence College, Mr. Ernest Nagel of Columbia University, Mr. George B. Rodman of the University of Wisconsin, Mr. Gerald A. Smith of the State University of New York at Geneseo, Mr. Marinus Swets of Grand Rapids Junior College, Mrs. Mildred Tackett, the late Richard M. Weaver, Mr. Rulon Wells of Yale University, and Mr. Harold Whitehall of Indiana University.

C. B.

R. P. W.

Contents

PART TWO

THE FORMS OF DISCOURSE

PART THREE

SPECIAL PROBLEMS OF DISCOURSE

PART FIVE

A BOOK OF READINGS

3 / ARTICLES OF PROPAGANDA AND OPINION

4 / ESSAYS FORMAL AND INFORMAL

5 / CRITICISM

6 / HISTORY

7 / BIOGRAPHY

MODERN RHETORIC

Third Edition

PART ONE

MAKING A
BEGINNING

CHAPTER 1

Language, Thinking, Feeling, and Rhetoric

Man may be called the animal with language—the "symbol-making animal." [1] By a little reflection we can see that only by means of language can man create and carry with him the body of concepts, attitudes, and skills that constitute civilization. Only by language can man carry the past with him, understand the present, and project the future. Only by language can he have a clear notion of himself as an individual: "I think, therefore I am," as the great philosopher Descartes put it. And only by language can men forge the bonds of a society—a society as distinguished from some sort of instinctual herd or tribal swarm.

Language and Thought

Ordinarily and superficially, we regard language as merely a convenient device for communicating preexisting ideas or attitudes. It is indeed hard to overestimate the value of language in communication, but it is even harder to overestimate its value in thinking. Language is tied to the very process of thought. This principle is affirmed in a time-worn joke about the old lady who, when asked to say what she meant, replied, "But how can I know what I mean till I say it?" Was the old lady a scatterbrained rattletrap, or was she talking sense?

---

[1] Exactly what is at stake in this description is discussed in this book in "The Reach of Imagination," by Jacob Bronowski (pp. 637–44).

She was talking sense. How often have we felt that we knew our own minds on something, or knew all about something, only to find, when we started to put what we knew into words, that we didn't know our own minds at all, or perhaps didn't even know what we were talking about. When we frame even the simplest sentence, we are forced to establish a set of meaningful relations; that is, we are forced to think more clearly. We instinctively know this, and we imply as much when, in a moment of confusion or doubt, we say, "Let's talk this out."

"Writing things out"—which is the business of this course—is only a more rigorous way of trying to understand a subject and understand oneself in relation to that subject. "Talking out" and "writing out"—both are ways, fundamentally, of "thinking out."

Language and Feeling

We not only think things out, we feel things out too. And language is fundamental, too, to this "feeling out." A human being isn't merely a machine for logical thought. Thought shades off into feeling, and feeling shades off into thought. We cannot exclude feeling from our experience, nor should we wish to do so, but we do want our life of feeling and our life of thought to be consistent with each other, to make some kind of total sense. A person whose feelings run counter to his judgment is bound for considerable unhappiness—and very probably for disaster.

This is not to say that one's judgment is necessarily good and one's feelings are necessarily bad. It may well be the other way around. But if feelings and judgment are not more or less in tune, we will be constantly jangled and disorganized. We want some degree of unity in ourselves, some degree of harmony.

To gain this unity, this harmony, we need not only to think straight but also to understand our own feelings and to see how they are related to each other, to our own general experience, and to the world around us. A considerable part of our use of language involves our instinctive attempt to clarify our feelings, to come to grips with them. We say, "Now that I've talked about it, I feel better." In other words, the talking-out process not only helps us to make up our minds but to "make up our feelings" too.

Language is an instrument for discriminating and expressing shades of feeling. The poet's metaphor and the schoolboy's slang have this purpose in common—and the slang may sometimes serve the purpose better than the metaphor. Later on, we shall discuss the various means that language uses to discriminate feelings—such things as imagery, rhythm, tone, and so on—but for the moment we merely emphasize the fact that language helps us to understand feelings as well as ideas, and thus, in the end, helps us to understand ourselves.

The Immediate Practical Demand: And Beyond

We have been speaking of language in broad, sweeping terms. Let us come closer to home. You are beginning your college career, and no matter what your major interests are, much of your instruction will be in language, and you will be required to respond in language. If you do not understand language well and cannot use it effectively, the chances are that you will not do well in college. And after college, in most occupations, language will become more, not less, important. There are letters and reports to be written, conferences to be held, policies to be drawn up and debated, and many other forms of communication that require skill in language. Even for a man who has great aptitude in one of the occupations in which thinking seems to be nonverbal—even if he is a born musician, painter, physicist, or businessman—there remain those aspects of life outside that occupation, the part of life that involves a man's relation to society and the part of life that is purely inward and personal. Whatever a man's practical success, he will, if he lacks competence in language, spend much of his life fumbling in a kind of twilight world in which ideas, facts, and feelings are perceived only dimly and often in distorted shapes.

So we have come back to our starting point, the notion that through language man discovers his world and himself. This idea is nowhere better put than in Helen Keller's account of her introduction to language. She had been blind and deaf almost from birth, and had never learned to speak. When she was seven, a gifted and imaginative teacher began her education:

> We walked down the path to the well-house, attracted by the fragrance of the honeysuckle with which it was covered. Someone was drawing water and my teacher placed my hand under the spout. As the cool stream gushed over one hand she spelled into the other the word water, first slowly and then rapidly. I stood still, my whole attention fixed upon the motions of her fingers. Suddenly I felt a misty consciousness as of something forgotten—a thrill of returning thought; and somehow the mystery of language was revealed to me. I knew then that "w-a-t-e-r" meant the wonderful cool something that was flowing over my hand. That living word awakened my soul, gave it light, hope, joy, set it free! There were barriers still, it is true, but barriers that could in time be swept away.
>
> I left the well-house eager to learn. Everything had a name, and each name gave birth to a new thought. As we returned to the house every object which I touched seemed to quiver with life. That was because I saw everything with the strange, new sight that had come to me.
>
> —HELEN KELLER: *The Story of My Life.*

A note about this course: rhetoric

What is this course about? Is it concerned with punctuation, figures of speech, and participial phrases? Does it have to do with outlining themes, constructing topic sentences, and studying the principles of unity, co-herence, and emphasis? Obviously, the answer to these questions is yes. But such matters are not studied for their own sake. They are studied be-cause they contribute to the effective use of language.

Rhetoric is the art of using language effectively.

A note about you

We have said that language is at the very center of the life of thought and the life of feeling. This sounds very grand and impressive—and may seem to cast an awesome shadow over the day-to-day business of studying exposi-tion or narration and the rules of punctuation, or of writing themes. Indeed, you may be so impressed that you feel shy of beginning.

But you should realize that you are not beginning at the beginning. You have behind you many years of effort that can be made to apply to your present problems. You are the beneficiary of a long training, and much of that training was not in books.

You began to learn language when you were an infant, and you are still learning. Books have helped you toward an effective use of language, and now they will help you even more, but remember that what books can give is not something separate from what life can give. What books can give is, rather, an extension and refinement of life.

■ APPLICATIONS

The exercises offered below are to suggest some of the questions involved in writing. They constitute a kind of preview of this course. They may give you a chance to feel your way into the work you will be required to do—or bet-ter, to feel your way into the state of mind that will enable you to do that work. Your acquaintance with the types of questions involved here is of more im-portance than the particular answers you may give. But, of course, you will become fully acquainted with the questions only if you conscientiously strug-gle to find satisfactory answers.

I   Here you are to deal with the meanings of individual words. Choose the word in the column that, in your opinion, comes closest to the meaning of the word to the left. Some of the words, of course, are not close, and even in the word you choose you may see important shades of difference in meaning. After you have made your choice, try to state whatever differences in meaning you find. (When you have completed the exercise, consult a dictionary to see what words appearing in the column are regarded as *synonymous* with the word to the left.)

1	inscrutable	dark	2	spite	irritability
		unknown			rancor
		difficult			detestation
		arcane			hate
		mysterious			unforgivingness
		indistinct			mercilessness
		abysmal			revenge
3	subversion	craftiness	4	despair	resignation
		treason			desperation
		substitution			stoicism
		morbidity			failure
		dishonesty			timidity
		overthrow			hopelessness
		defalcation			defeat

II A Read the passage below very carefully several times. Try to sense the overall meaning. Now from Group 1, choose the word that will best fit into the first blank space. And from Group 2, the best word for the second blank space. Be prepared to defend your choices. Remember that you are trying to choose the words that will fit best into the passage taken as a whole. Use a dictionary for the meanings of words you are not absolutely sure of.

> It was a situation so full of shadows, uncertainty, and
> _____(1)_____ that it gave no firm _____(2)_____ on which to
> base a lever of decision.

(1)		(2)	
chagrin	mistrust	point	middle
turpitude	nihilism	basis	fulcrum
distress	assiduity	relation	wedge
ambiguity	melancholy	idea	aspiration
confusion	ambition	religion	intention
solace	mercilessness	hope	morality

In making your choices, you no doubt have determined that for Space 1 you need a word closely related to *shadows* and *uncertainty,* but a word that does something more than merely repeat those notions. You may have vaguely considered the words *nihilism, melancholy,* and *mercilessness,* because they do have a negative quality bearing some relation to *shadows* and *uncertainty.* But *ambiguity* and *confusion* have closer relations. *Confusion* perhaps seems too close to *uncertainty.* So *ambiguity,* which adds a new dimension but one that extends what is already there, seems the best choice of all.

When you come to Space 2, your sense of the overall meaning tells you that the space should be filled with something related to the metaphor of the lever. You may have considered such words as *religion* or *hope,* but they are too general. *Point, basis,* and *wedge* might have some merit. But *fulcrum* is the most precise.

B Repeat the previous exercise with the following example. Now, however, you have a wider choice of words that will make fairly good sense. But you must try to get the words that will most sharply express what you take to be the basic meaning and that will best bind the passage together. One way to go about this would be to select from each group several possible words and then try various combinations. Be sure you know why you reject a word. This may be more important than your reasons for accepting one.

> In that ___(1)___ hour of her disappointment, she was like an alpinist who, without warning, has slipped into a ___(2)___ , and in that isolation feels, because of the absolute ___(3)___ , a sudden burst of relief in being freed from the burden of ___(4)___ that life is.

(1)		(2)	
joyful	mischievous	desolation	mercy
unfortunate	unplanned	finality	perspicuity
icy	unwarranted	fatigue	indirection
unexpected	assimilated	hopelessness	courage
horrible	perfunctory	morass	desuetude
unredeemed	destined	addendum	crevasse

(3)		(4)	
militancy	distress	joy	intensification
complication	aimlessness	hope	duty
mania	blankness	ambition	mortality
hopelessness	mortality	refusal	routine
montage	misery	yearning	consanguinity
remorse	aspiration	aspiration	confusion

For Space 1 we might well use *unfortunate* or even *horrible,* but let us ask whether such a word would be as precise as some other that would tie the whole sentence together. Space 2 should offer no great problem. We sense that Spaces 3 and 4 are closely related and carry some contrast or paradox. We might make *blankness* our choice for Space 3, and *ambition* or *aspiration* for Space 4. These choices would make a certain sense. But can we find another pair to give a sharper and more precise effect?

III Here are two passages, one the work of an eminent writer[2] and the other a garbled version. The context of the scene described is the walk in Venice of a middle-aged man who suddenly finds himself involved in a shameful infatuation that he cannot break out of. With this information as a background, try to decide which is the original version.

[2] *Death in Venice,* by Thomas Mann.

A   There was a hateful sultriness in the narrow street. The air was so heavy that all the manifold smells wafted out of houses, shops, and cook-shops—the smells of oil, perfumery, and so forth—hung low, like exhalations, not dissipating. Cigarette smoke seemed to stand in the air, it drifted so slowly away.

B   In the city, there was, now that morning had passed, an uncomfortable heat. As he passed down a narrow street, he found that all the manifold smells wafted out of houses, shops, and cook-shops—smells of oil, perfumery, and so forth—hung in the air, because now there was no wind off the Adriatic to relieve the heat, which grew more intense every day. Even cigarette smoke hung in the air a moment before it began to drift off, beautifully blue in the sunlight.

IV   The passage below is from a story laid more than a century and a half ago in Mississippi. At the moment when a planter, who has been down to New Orleans to sell his crop, steps ashore a strange storm is blowing up on the Mississippi River. Your assignment is to fix on those words or phrases that give the atmosphere and then to rewrite to destroy the effect. For instance, you might change the beginning of the first sentence to read as follows: "As his feet touched shore, the sun sank into the river, in which its red color was reflected, and at once . . . ." Or in the second sentence you might simply omit "and strained again," a phrase that admirably gives the sense of the uneasy tossing of the river.

> As his foot touched shore, the sun sank into the river the color of blood, and at once a wind sprang up and covered the sky with black, yellow, and green clouds the size of whales, which moved across the face of the moon. The river was covered with foam, and against the landing the boats strained in the waves and strained again. River and bluff gave off alike a leaf-green light, and from the water's edge the red torches lining the Landing-under-the-Hill and climbing the bluff to the town stirred and blew to the left and right. There were sounds of rushing and flying, from the flourish of carriages hurrying through the streets after dark, from the bellowing throats of the flatboatmen, and from the wilderness itself, which lifted and drew itself in the wind, and pressed its savage breath even closer to the little galleries of Rodney, and caused a bell to turn over in one of the steeples, and shook the fort and dropped a tree over the racetrack.
>
> —Eudora Welty: *The Robber Bridegroom.*[3]

V   Here again we are dealing with two passages, one the original [4] and the other a garbled version. Our concern now is with logical order. Which passage do you regard as more satisfactory?

---

[3] From *The Robber Bridegroom*, by Eudora Welty. Reprinted by permission of Harcourt, Brace & World, Inc.

[4] From *The Hero in History*, by Sidney Hook. Reprinted by permission of Humanities Press Inc.

A   In our own time interest in the words and acts of outstanding individuals has flared up to a point never reached before. There is a perennial interest in heroes even when we outgrow the hero worship of youth. The sources of this interest are many and deep. One is that what outstanding people do makes interesting copy for the newspapers, TV, and radio, and this is the age of communications. But laying that aside as not really relevant, the special reasons for this passionate concern vary in intensity from one historic period to another. The passionate concern in our age has reasons which are quite apparent, because we think that what important people do may affect our society. But, as I pointed out, they make good reading or "viewing," in any case.

B   There is a perennial interest in heroes even when we outgrow the hero worship of youth. The sources of this interest are many and deep. But they vary in intensity and character from one historic period to another. In our own time interest in the words and acts of outstanding individuals has flared up to a point never reached before. The special reasons for this passionate concern in the ideas and deeds of the uncrowned heroes of our age are quite apparent. During a period of wars and revolutions, the fate of peoples seems to hang visibly on what one person, perhaps a few, decide.

CHAPTER **2**

The Problem of Making
a Beginning

In the preceding chapter we have tried to answer the question: "What is the ultimate purpose of the study of writing?" The next question is: "Where should the study of writing begin?" Should it begin with the medium—that is, with a study of words? With the subject—that is, with the ideas that one wishes to express? Or with the occasion—that is, with the situation in which the writer finds himself with respect to a particular audience? It is impossible to say that any one of these considerations is more important than the other two, and it is also impossible to say that one of the three should logically precede the others, since they are all intimately related.

We might argue that we should begin with the medium, with the study of words, and then move by easy stages from diction through the next larger units, the sentence and the paragraph, and then on to the general problems of organization to be met in the whole theme.

But we could counter this argument by pointing out that when we choose words, we choose them in relation to other words, in relation to the general subject about which we mean to write, and in relation to our attitude toward our reader (that is, in relation to the occasion). In the same way, we could argue that the study of the sentence, important as it is, should not necessarily precede the study of problems of general organization. For it is the pattern of sentences, the relation of sentences to one another, that defines the progression of our ideas. In writing, we are first concerned—just as we are finally concerned—with our complete utterance, our overall idea, our main purpose. There is something to be said, therefore, for beginning, as we do here, with problems of general organization. Other problems usually take specific form only when the writer attempts to come to grips with his subject.

Finding a Subject

Sometimes in your college work a subject will be assigned to you, but often in this course you will have to choose one from a range of suggestions or find one of your own. What kind of subject is likely to draw forth your best work?

Beginnings are always hard, and this beginning of the very beginning of a piece of writing is often the hardest of all. Hours can be wasted in floundering around this question of choice. You may find some help, however, in asking yourself two questions:

What do I know about?
What am I interested in?

We have said that all your life up to this point has been, in a sense, a preparation for this course, and in the question of choosing a subject this is obviously true. You have had many experiences. You know about many things at first-hand: skiing, dressmaking, movies, swimming, picnics, pets, people, places, carpentry, gardening, fishing, jobs, chess or checkers or bridge, football, friendship, family life, pains and pleasures. And you know about many other things through reading, for instance, the Antarctic or George Washington. Your experience has been rich—far richer, no doubt, than you ordinarily realize.

What makes that experience rich is that it is your own. It represents your life, your reactions and decisions, your evaluations, your interests. Trust those interests. If you are interested in something you can probably make it interesting to others.

When you set out to choose a subject, you are, then, engaged in self-scrutiny, self-exploration, self-evaluation. So we return to the thought that writing is, ultimately, an extension of your own life process.

The subject you choose represents, in one way or another, you.

Finding a true subject: focus

Suppose, out of your experience and your interests, you have settled on a subject, perhaps tennis, your grandmother, rose gardens, or George Washington. Now that you think you have a subject, what do you really have? What, for instance, are you ready to say about tennis?

You are a good tennis player, have followed the game, know a great deal about many high-ranking players, and even know some good competition players personally. So you begin:

> I have played tennis since I could hold a racket, and before that my father made me do strokes with a badminton racket and a light ball. My father was a very good player. He once had a national ranking, and if he had not broken his wrist he might have made a name for himself. Not that he grieves about that, for he has a full life, and as a hobby still follows the game and knows a lot of players. In any case, I have always had my tennis heroes, and I have known——

You stop, suddenly realizing that you are lost. There is no clear line of development here, no control, no forward thrust on which you can depend. You simply don't know where you are going. And certainly your reader would not know.

The trouble is that your subject—tennis—is too inclusive, too shifting. Writing about it is like trying to grab a handful of fog.

You must try, therefore, to be more specific, to find more manageable topics drawn from the general subject matter of tennis. You may even scribble them down:

Why I like tennis.
The strategy of doubles.
History of the game.

Then you look at the last sentence of your trial beginning, and put down another topic:

Players I have known.

That, you decide, may have more general interest than the previous topics, and so you linger on it. Suddenly an idea hits you. What do tennis players—really good tennis players—have in common? What background? What training? What characteristics? What temperament?

You write down another topic:

The tennis temperament.

This is specific. It involves, directly or indirectly, all you know about tennis, but it sharpens that knowledge to a point. It is a topic brought to focus. It is a true subject.

You may not yet be ready to write, but you have a question to control your thinking: What is the tennis temperament? It is conceivable that, after reflection, you may decide that there is no such thing as the "tennis temperament"—that you have no true subject after all. But your question was a real one, and you have at least learned to isolate and explore a topic.

Too bad it did not turn out.

The true subject and the proposition

Let us suppose, however, that it does turn out. On further reflection you decide that, after all, in spite of all the differences among tennis players, there is a similarity of temperament that sets them apart from other athletes, not to mention nonathletes. The fact that you have to struggle to convince yourself that you have a true subject is, you suddenly realize, a great blessing to you. The fact that other people, just as you did for a time, may resist the idea that there is a "tennis temperament" means that you have set up a controversial proposition for your theme: There is a tennis temperament.

You know now that you have to meet objections. You have to prove your point. You have, therefore, a motive and a direction for your theme.

THE PROPOSITION: WHAT IT IS

A proposition is an assertion that may be believed, disbelieved, or doubted. It is, in itself, clear-cut. It can be dealt with.

The proposition is what gives the hard core of your intention. It is what you must demonstrate, or exhibit, to your reader. It is your governing idea—your thesis.[1]

It embodies your fundamental belief about or attitude toward your true subject.

NOTE: THE PROPOSITION AND DRAMATIC CONTEXT

Do not be disturbed if the proposition you arrive at is debatable. A proposition that is universally acceptable will probably result in a very dull theme. A theme based on the proposition that the sun rises in the east will scarcely evoke a passionate response. Resistance is what makes a proposition interesting: no challenge, no interest. It is resistance that provides the dramatic context for your theme. Your job is to overcome the resistance, by logic, by facts, by persuasion, by vividness, by humor, by the authority of your own experience, by the intensity of your own interest.

Remember that it is easier to overcome resistance than to overcome lack of interest.

A writer is, in one way, like a judo expert. He uses the reader's resistance to throw the reader.

● CAUTION: LOOK TWICE AT HIGHFALUTIN SUBJECTS

There is always a temptation to choose grand, high-sounding, highfalutin, general subjects, such as patriotism, democracy, religion, justice, and education. Such subjects are, at first glance, attractive because they seem easy—easy because they have accumulated around themselves a body of generally accepted and conventionally approved interpretations and

---

[1] We shall return to the nature of the proposition in considerable detail when we come to the subject of Argument (pp. 172–78).

arguments, and a set of respectable and pious attitudes. The writer thinks that he can merely rehash the interpretations, arguments, and attitudes and have his theme.

He is wrong, and on three counts.

First, such topics are usually so sweeping and general that the writer—certainly the beginner—has trouble getting down to a true subject, down to specifics, down to a sense of experience, down to concrete illustrations.

Second, as a corollary of the first difficulty, a topic of this kind tends to encourage dependence on abstract words, which stand for general qualities, relations, ideas, and concepts. We are not implying that such words should be struck from the language; they are essential for thought. But dependence on such words commonly makes for vagueness, dullness, and irrelevance. The interplay of the abstract and the concrete is the very life of language and thought. (See pp. 398–404.)

Third, the writer who takes refuge in grand, highfalutin subjects is wrong because such subjects, having accumulated around them generally accepted ideas and respectable attitudes, are usually lacking in the dramatic resistance spoken of above. The reader knows what to expect. He is bored before he begins.

There is, however, a way to beat the game of the dull, abstract subject, to awaken the reader to the reality that has been lost in the mossy growth and encrustation of conventional ideas and attitudes. You have to scrape off the moss, break the crust. The reader must be shocked into rethinking his attitudes, into sorting out the merely conventional from the vital aspects of the subject.

When Samuel Johnson, the famous eighteenth-century writer, said that "patriotism is the last refuge of the scoundrel," he was not denying the value and nobility of patriotism, but paradoxically, he was shocking the reader into contrasting true patriotism with the shabby self-serving substitutes. The great Justice Oliver Wendell Holmes of the Supreme Court once said: "All I mean by truth is what I can't help thinking." James Russell Lowell said that "democracy is nothing more than an experiment in government . . . which must stand or fall on its own merits as others have done before it." Holmes and Lowell are scraping off the moss, breaking the crust. They force us to take another look at truth, at the sanctity of democracy.

A theme that begins with a statement like that of Johnson, Holmes, or Lowell would wake the reader up.

■ APPLICATIONS

I Here is a list of general subjects. Select five from the list, and frame three true subjects for each.

Marijuana	Military service	Wiretapping
Alcoholic beverages	Shakespeare's plays	Morality in the year 2000
The jury system	Space exploration	Robert E. Lee
George Washington	A professional army	Abraham Lincoln
Your grandmother	Public education	The generation gap
Amateurism in sports	Love on the campus	The revolver

II For each of five of the true subjects you have framed, write a proposition that you think would lead to an interesting theme.

The Discourse: Main Divisions

Once you have found your true subject and have framed your proposition, you must consider the general organization into which your theme will fall. You know that there will be an introduction, a discussion, and a conclusion—that is, a beginning, a middle, and an end. Very probably, in trying to settle on your true subject and frame the proposition, you have already been thinking, however vaguely, of these divisions. They are, in fact, the natural divisions for the treatment of any subject; they represent the way the mind works. (See Narration, pp. 323–25.)

Now you should try to think your whole scheme through, to firm up the structure and flesh out each division with the main points involved in it. Some writers find that the best way to start is to jot down ideas almost at random, letting the mind wander over the subject, following the free association of ideas, jumping here and there, if necessary, without trying to state all the logical connections. What comes out of this process will look like a hodgepodge, but the process may catch on the wing certain things that might have eluded a more systematic approach.

You cannot, of course, leave the ideas caught in this free fashion in the order in which they came. You must sort them out under the three main divisions. Having done this, you should try to arrange in logical order the ideas in each division. To guide you in this process, you will find in Chapter 14 a discussion of the Outline. After consulting this, you are prepared to make a more or less complete projection of what you now think your theme will be—a topic outline or a sentence outline.

Example of preparation for a theme

A student who had chosen from the previous Application "Morality in the year 2000" as a general subject came up with a true subject in the form of the following proposition: The change of forms of morality will not change the essential basis of morality. Here are his running notes on that topic:

RUNNING NOTES ON "MORALITY IN THE YEAR 2000"

Bible—revealed morality
   other religions had revealed morality too
Hemingway: "morality is what you feel good after." Why?
Because what you have done squares with your own values? Or because you feel in accord with other people—society—in what you have done

Social values of morality vs. idea of revealed values.

Idea that morality of a society is what that society needs for survival—raise children, defend economy, defend country, etc. This means family, whatever economic system, and patriotism. But different from country to country.

Overpopulation example of conflict between social morality (birth control) and revealed morality (many churches were against, some yet, Pope still is against).
   Ditto in regard to property.

Patriotism changing. A hundred years back a person here was patriotic about his state, like Lee about Virginia, etc. Nobody thinks about his state now. People move around too much for that. What will mobility do for patriotism by 2000? United Europe, etc.

Back to over-pop. Birth control is gaining ground. Social morality gaining. But a religious person might still justify this—if he didn't just hang on words.

Property sense changing. More of attitude that property has to "pay its way" socially speaking. Business in ghettos, etc. Not mere profit or there won't be any profit someday.

Sex morality. Divorce. Churches giving ground on divorce. In Sweden sex for adolescents accepted. Is this trend here? But Sweden stable society. Need for family. People like families. Affection and common interests. Don't see state raised children.

Morality has to satisfy majority of people or won't last—I mean a particular system. What does satisfy mean. Short run vs. long run.

The notes above are simply a random set of ideas, put down as they came into the student's head. Here is the next stage in his preparation, in which he sorted out the running notes according to the major divisions:

Beginning [Introduction]
Definition of morality—two views.

Middle [Discussion]
Prediction of morality in 2000 A.D. that will result from changing needs.
1. Sexual morality based on family needs.
   Overpopulation and conflict with revealed morality.
   O–P and sex: more frequent divorce?
   Change and sexual freedom for young.
   The pill. General unrest in schools and colleges. Example of other societies, especially Sweden, where anything goes.
2. Business morality, business, and long-range view of profit.

3. Patriotism. Change of focus with century. Direction from this toward internationalism.

End [Conclusion]
Same needs will continue for individual and group in spite of change in forms.

The last stage of preparation was to make a sentence outline, which is here offered. Observe that certain items in the running notes are dropped, and that certain things are added, for instance, the references to Margaret Mead and Susan Sontag. The points of support for the basic proposition, too, are developed in the outline. Observe, also, that the divisions of the outline do not follow the three divisions of the second stage, but we can easily see the relation: Beginning—I; Middle—II, III, and IV; End—V.

OUTLINE OF THEME ON "MORALITY IN THE YEAR 2000"

Proposition: The change of forms of morality will not change the essential basis of morality.
  I. We should begin by defining morality.
     A. There are two views: revealed morality vs. morality as an outgrowth of social needs.
        1. Revealed morality is seen in Old Testament and Koran, came from a divine source.
        2. Morality as an outgrowth of social needs is seen in the practices that help a society survive: raise family, promote economic system, defend country.
        3. Revealed morality can be seen, too, as what was effective for survival: morality of Jews made a small tribe survive and conquer.
     B. The problem of predicting morality in the year 2000 is to see how definition will change with changing social needs.
 II. Changes in the nature of the family mean change in sex morality.
     A. Most obvious problem is overpopulation.
        1. There is conflict between revealed morality and social need in relation to birth control—churches that were against now accept theory of social need; even Catholic Church is now split on question, in spite of Pope.
        2. Will fewer children and less economic pressure mean weakening of family structure, with more and easier divorce?
        3. Famous anthropologist Margaret Mead argues that the mate for one period of life is not necessarily right for whole life; this suggests increase of divorce, etc. (Supported by number 2, above.)
     B. Various changes in society make for sexual freedom among the young.
        1. The "pill" has made sex common among adolescents.
        2. Sexual freedom is supported by general unrest of young people in high school and college.
        3. Example of other countries, particularly Sweden, has effect

here: in Sweden adolescent sex generally accepted; marriages not too uncommonly begin with one or more children already. (Quote article on Sweden by Susan Sontag in *Ramparts* magazine.)

III. Morality is related to our system of free enterprise.
  A. Class and race unrest have changed our property sense and business morality.
    1. Business must "pay its way" socially speaking, having an obligation to ghetto, etc.
    2. Mere profit is not enough for business; it must help reform society, or there won't be any profit.
  B. One obligation of business is to help educate the young.
    1. There is an increase in the amount of support for education at all levels.
    2. Self-interest of business is a form of the new morality.
IV. Morality of patriotism is based on definition of fatherland.
  A. Patriotism has been changing over the past century.
    1. Up to the Civil War the individual state was felt to be fatherland, example of Robert E. Lee.
    2. Northern victory in Civil War changed nature of fatherland.
  B. Mobility now makes state loyalty idiotic.
    1. Corporations move men everywhere, and there is much other job mobility.
    2. Travel has been greatly increased by automobiles, etc.
    3. Network of friendships and business connections is now more important than loyalty to place.
  C. Next change is in spreading loyalties beyond the nation.
    1. This process now seen in the United Nations, United States of Europe, Common Market, etc.
    2. How far will process go by 2000?
  D. What effect does fear of the bomb, etc., have in creating loyalties above the nation?
V. In spite of changes in forms, the morality of the future will have to serve the same human needs.
  A. In one form or another, family will survive through affection for children and mate, common experiences, fear of loneliness.
  B. New business morality will be based on more enlightened view of profit, not death of profit motive.
  C. People need loyalties for a new "patriotism" even if base is broader.

■ APPLICATION

Do you think that you could tighten this outline? Do you have any ideas on the subject of morality? This outline might lead you to do a theme on the same topic, especially if you disagree with the present writer.

Never feel bound to an outline. The actual process of writing may give you something much better than what the outline promises. In other words, though your outline is a useful guide, you must submit it to the complicated process of thinking things through, word by word, as you begin the actual process of writing. And this sort of thinking a subject through results, almost inevitably, in a more or less thorough reorganization of the structure.

The outline is, you must remember, only a step in your thinking.

The introduction

An introduction must really introduce.

The reader is entitled to know what you are going to write about. Your title presumably tells him something, but now, in the introduction, you must fix the subject more precisely. You must state, or at least suggest, your proposition, and it is sometimes good to indicate how you intend to present your discussion.

Here is the introduction of a student theme:

> Everyone knows the importance of jet propulsion today, but not everyone knows the history of how it was developed. That history is a good example of how important and complicated inventions can be worked out from the simplest of ideas. We can start by stating the simple idea from which jet propulsion developed.

Whatever its shortcomings, this introduction does state the subject (the history of jet propulsion), gives hints of a context that may be developed to make the subject interesting, and indicates the method the writer will follow in tracing the germ idea, stage by stage, to the modern mechanism. The introduction is simple and downright, and does not compare too unfavorably with the introduction to an article called "Causation of Ice Ages," written by two research scientists:

> Beneath the oceans lie clues to many basic questions regarding not only the earth's dominant features, the continents and ocean basins, but also the evolution of life, the climatic history and chronology of the Pleistocene, and one of the most tantalizing of all geological problems, the cause of the ice ages. —DAVID B. ERICSON AND GOESTA WOLLIN:
> in the *Columbia Forum* (Winter 1968).

The two scientists, like the student writing on jet propulsion, are setting out to give a direct objective account of the subject (the relation of oceanographic data to the problem of the ice ages), which they place in the context of clues to other important questions. In both introductions the subject treated demands little more than the bare statement and the minimum of context because the author is giving a report. Even if a report involves vas⟩

information, the fact that it is objective and impersonal means that certain demands are not made on the writer in framing his introduction. In other words, the nature of the introduction is likely to be modified by the subject and the occasion.

For instance, examine the following introduction:

> Contrary to current fears, there is little evidence, I believe, to support the notion that man is simply the passive creature of technology. Moreover, there is considerable unclarity as to how technology got to be the way it is in the first place.   —SEYMOUR MELMAN: "Who Decides Technology?"
> *Columbia Forum* (Winter 1968).

Here the writer is going to present a body of objective facts, but his motive is not merely to give a report. He is going to try to persuade his reader, who may be subject to "current fears," that he should adopt a certain attitude based on those objective facts; the proposition that he wishes the reader to accept is that man is not "the passive creature of technology." The fact that the author is going to offer an argument against immediate and significant fears means that here the proposition—what he is specifically trying to establish—comes to the fore. It is the chief concern of the introduction, as of the whole article.

With the following introduction, again from a student theme, we encounter another concern:

> The textbook says that you write best about something you are interested in, and I am more interested in drag-racing than in anything else except my girl, who right here shall be nameless. So, since I cannot write about her, I'll write about drag-racing. To be more specific, and state my true subject, as the textbook advises, I am going to write about why I am interested in drag-racing—though *interested* is a very weak word for what I feel when I drop into the old bucket, latch the belt, and inhale that first dizzy whiff of burned high octane.

Our previous examples have been objective and impersonal. This last is intensely personal. It is effective, in fact, only in so far as we get some feeling for the author's personality—that of a vigorous, extroverted, adventurous, happy-go-lucky lad, wrapped up in his girl, speed, and machinery, and possessed of a bright mind and a sense of humor. He even makes a sort of joking, high-spirited game of writing his theme. He has a relish for the immediate experience of things; one manifestation of this is the concreteness with which he writes. He does not say, "when I get ready to begin a race," but says, "drop into the old bucket" and "inhale that first dizzy whiff of burned high octane."

The specific, the concrete, the immediate, the flavor of the moment, come naturally to him, and these qualities are what catch us and remind us that the theme is about *him* and why *he* likes drag-racing. It is not merely about drag-racing objectively considered.

"Specifics"—of the concrete and the particular—are not confined, however, to themes that are strongly personal in tone. In objective factual accounts they may also appear, and appear most effectively, to give vividness and immediacy. For instance, here is the introductory paragraph of a news report in *Time* (March 21, 1969) about the relief flights over the Nigerian blockade of Biafra, sponsored by various charitable organizations.

COME ON DOWN AND GET KILLED

By day, Sao Tomé Island drowses in tropic torpor. Toward evening, however, the diminutive Portuguese colony off West Africa's underbelly in the Gulf of Guinea suddenly rouses. Along its single airport's runway can be seen a motley squadron of DC-6s, a C-46, a Super Constellation, and lately bigger but nonetheless obsolete C-97 stratofreighters, wheezing into readiness. Trucks dash up, hauling crates of food and medicines. Eventually, crews as varied as their airplanes—Swedes, Finns, Americans, a stolid Yorkshireman, a not so dour Scot—screech up in cars and climb aboard. One by one, at 20 minute intervals, the cargo planes lumber down the runway, turn northward toward the Nigerian coast. Late afternoon sunlight splashes on little blue and gold fish, the fuselage emblems of the interfaith airlift organized by the World Council of Churches and the Catholic relief organization Caritas to shuttle food to starving Biafra.[2]

The reporter does not want merely to give us the facts; he wants us to have some of the "feel," the atmosphere, of the island waking from the "tropic torpor" of daylight to the bustle of the preparations, the excitement and danger. Notice, too, how a piece of mere information, the names of the sponsoring organizations, is presented visually—as though we had seen the little symbols and had inquired for their meaning.

As we realize from the news story on Biafran relief, the visual impression is worth more than any amount of generalized description. Seeing is believing, and the thing in motion catches the eye:

Toward the end of the second quarter of the Super Bowl game, Jim Turner of the New York Jets ambled onto the grass to try a medium-long field goal. A Baltimore sports columnist traced a finger down the printed roster, located Turner's name, squinted as he sought to recall if he had ever heard it before and then turned to the man in the next seat.
"This fellow Turner," said the columnist, "he any good?"
"Well, he kicked more field goals this season than anybody in history."
"Oh," said the columnist.
— EDWIN SHRAKE: "Now the AFL Owns the Football,"
Sports Illustrated (January 27, 1969).

The passage quoted here does not complete the introduction, but it has fixed our attention on Turner and told us that he has the all-time record for field goals. This fact, as we discover if we continue with the article, leads to the general proposition that the American Football League, once regarded as inferior to the NFL, has come into its own.

---

[2] Reprinted by permission; Copyright Time Inc. 1969.

● CAUTION

Do not think that we have listed all the ways of writing an introduction. Indeed, a mere list would be useless. What you must do is to get the feel of the process. Ask yourself the question: What kind of introduction does my subject demand? How long should it be? One paragraph or more?

■ APPLICATIONS

I Read the introductory section of each of the following selections: "The Reach of Imagination," by Jacob Bronowski (pp. 637–44), "The Age of Over-kill," by Benjamin DeMott (pp. 692–98), "Conflict of Generations," by Lewis S. Feuer (pp. 699–711), and "Making It: The Brutal Bargain," by Norman Podhoretz (pp. 647–58). If the proposition is stated, point it out. If it is merely implied, frame a statement of it. In each instance decide if the introduction suggests that the article will be merely an objective presentation or if the author expects some resistance to his views.

II Skim through several current magazines, reading the introductory sections of articles. Select two that strike you as especially effective, copy them out, and bring to class. Be prepared to explain your choice.

III Turn to the discussion of the Paragraph (Chapter 10). Now write an introductory paragraph (or paragraphs, if necessary) for one of the true subjects you have framed in the Application on pp. 15–16.

INTRODUCTION: TO WHOM?

We have been discussing the introduction primarily in relation to what it introduces, but inevitably we have had to suggest, at certain moments, the presence of the reader. Let us turn more specifically to that question. Here we are concerned with what we may call the *occasion:* the kind of reader you are writing for, his attitude toward your subject and toward you, and, naturally, your attitude toward him.[3]

Before you set down your first word, you should ask yourself some questions about the occasion, questions that will serve not only as a guide for the introduction but for the development of the whole theme:

1 Does the reader have any interest in my subject, or must I try to attract his attention?
2 If I have to attract his attention, how do I do it?
3 How ignorant is he of my subject? How much do I have to explain to give him a background for my discussion?
4 Am I merely trying to present something to him, or am I trying to convince him of something? If, in other words, he has a re-

---

[3] With regard to audience, see Tone, pp. 466–73.

sistance to the view I am presenting, what attitude shall I take toward him?

Here is the introduction to a theme entitled "The Nature and Use of the Spinnaker," written by a student with a passionate interest in sailing:

> Anybody who has never sailed couldn't possibly be interested in what I am going to say about spinnakers, and in fact, probably wouldn't even know what one is. Anybody who has sailed at all, however, knows what a spinnaker is, and knows the thrill that comes when it first snaps out and bellies with wind and you hear the new hiss of water at the bow. That person will know, too, that there is a lot to know about the spinnaker, and will know that it is worth discussing and investigating. I am writing for him. Let landlubbers sheer off.

The writer here has put his cards on the table. He is writing strictly for readers who have some interest in sailing, and who are willing to dwell on its finer points. He is humorous about his warning to landlubbers—but he means it.

Consider the following example from the essay "Wordsworth in the Tropics," in which much more subtly the author has warned off certain readers:

> In the neighbourhood of latitude fifty north, and for the last hundred years or thereabouts, it has been an axiom that Nature is divine and morally uplifting. For good Wordsworthians—and most serious-minded people are now Wordsworthians, either by direct inspiration or at second hand—a walk in the country is the equivalent of going to church, a tour through Westmorland is as good as a pilgrimage to Jerusalem. To commune with the fields and waters, the woodlands and the hills, is to commune, according to our modern and northern ideas, with the visible manifestations of the "Wisdom and Spirit of the Universe."
>
> —ALDOUS HUXLEY: *Do What You Will.*

Readers who don't know anything about Wordsworth, or what a "good Wordsworthian" is, need not apply for admittance to this essay. For those who have some acquaintance, however, this introduction does some well-mannered coaching: to commune with nature is to commune "with the visible manifestations of the 'Wisdom and Spirit of the Universe.'" The coaching is politely unobtrusive, a gentle nudge as it were, and the reader says to himself, "Yes, of course, I knew that all the time." He has been won over by the author's courtesy and concealed flattery.

This introduction has, we may point out as an aside, another important element: in the very first sentence it prepares the reader for a shock, implying that his cherished notion about the uplifting qualities of nature is merely an accident of history and of "latitude fifty north." The body of the essay will develop the nature of this shock. We shall return to shock as a device for introduction.

Aldous Huxley, like the young sailor in his introduction, has warned off certain readers. The problem is different when the writer can assume that any reasonably intelligent general reader may take an interest in a topic, even though he has no general background for it. In a theme entitled "Jet Pilots Are Human, and Space Men Too," a student deals with that problem:

> As new planes fly higher and faster every day, and as men take off for the moon, we begin to feel that there is no limit to what the designers and engineers can do. But we tend to forget one thing. There are no new designs for the human body and there are no new models being built in the hush-hush atmosphere of the experimental shop. The pilot is the old model, and we have to think of what speed and altitude do to his "liver and lights" and how much sloshing around he can stand. And spacemen are old models too.

What has the writer done in this paragraph? He has corrected a misconception that the general reader may well have—the idea that design and engineering are the only important factors in the future of aviation and space exploration. And he has given a preliminary, general statement of the problem of the human body in flight, the central idea he intends to develop. He has built his introductory paragraph around an important fact, that the reader, however intelligent, may have failed to consider. The assumption here is that the reader, once he has the fact pointed out to him—politely, of course—will want to pursue the topic.

The Uninterested Reader   Up to this point we have been assuming readers with special interests (sailors, Wordsworthians) or readers with general curiosity who merely need some special information (about the human body and jet flight). But what about the reader who brings no predisposition at all to your subject?

On many occasions you yourself have been the uninterested reader who, idly thumbing through a magazine or newspaper feature section, has been caught by the first few sentences of an article and has gone on to read the whole piece. In his opening sentences, the skillful writer has shown that something previously uninteresting to you bears on your welfare, your health, your ambitions and aspirations, your pocketbook, your prejudices, your patriotism, your religion, your education. Or he may simply have shown the general human interest in a subject that you had thought abstract and dull.

The author of the following paragraph is making a bid for the reader's attention by showing how his subject, "The Alaskan Islands," might affect the personal life of his reader:

> There was a time when I thought that geography was the boring subject that happened in the first period after the noon recess or that it was the pictures in the old *National Geographic* magazines in the dentist's office which you thumbed through while you were waiting for a new filling. But

now I know that what the Arabs eat in Mecca or the Burmese get as take-home pay affects our national security and our tax bill. This fact was brought home to me last summer when I went to Alaska and had the good fortune to be asked to go on a ten-day cruise through the Aleutian Islands in a private boat. Those islands are steppingstones between America and Asia, and you know that you can go two ways on steppingstones.

Having challenged the reader to accept his point of view about geography, the writer concludes his paragraph with what will become the chief point to be developed in his theme: the military importance of the Aleutians.

The appeal in the introduction above is basically to self-interest: the reader ought to be concerned with military security. But there is another fundamental appeal, in a way contradictory to self-interest: the appeal to human sympathy. Here is the introduction to a theme on coal mining in Kentucky, which makes ordinary human interest—putting yourself in another man's place—the bait for the reader:

To a man who works in the mines, coal isn't just a dirty black substance that you shovel into the furnace. It is life itself—and sometimes it is death. Like most people, I had never understood the real meaning of coal until I spent two summers in eastern Kentucky. Then I met old Thad Holloway, and I learned about his life in the mines (and out, when there wasn't any work), and I heard the tales he told in his dry, mountaineer way. If you knew Thad, you knew about coal. And you knew, too, a lot that you had never known before about courage, endurance, and human will-power.

If we turn to the actual theme written by the tennis enthusiast mentioned earlier in this chapter (pp. 12–14), entitled "A Different Breed of Cats," we find another kind of appeal:

Have you ever thought of a bear playing tennis? Or an elephant? Or a horse? Or a dog? If you ever did think of one of these whacking a ball, it would be strictly for laughs. Even a chimpanzee playing tennis—in spite of his resemblance to humans, or perhaps because of it—would seem funny. But somehow it isn't funny to think of a cat playing tennis. At least, it isn't funny long, for the cat—I mean any member of what the biologists call the genus *felis*, pumas, leopards, tigers, housecats, even lions—has certain qualities that really do make us think of tennis players. They have the speed, terrific coordination, the power in grace, the timing, and the hard, honed-up, self-sufficient loneliness, that a really good tennis player has. They have what I'll call the tennis temperament, and I'll try to explain what I mean.

Here the author is trying to appeal to readers beyond the world of tennis, to anyone interested in human psychology. He uses a startling, fantastic, humorous approach and a play on the slang meaning of the word *cat* in the title to catch the reader's attention. As in the theme on drag-racing, the appeal here also lies, in part at least, in the personality and fresh point of view of the writer.

The Hostile Reader The best long-range method for dealing with the hostile reader is to find a common ground with him to show that, in the end, you and he have sounder reasons for agreement than disagreement. Later in this book you will find a discussion of this method, and a look at it now would be helpful (pp. 167–70). Another effective approach is to establish that the hostile reader's position actually works against his self-interest or is inconsistent with some other of his more deeply held convictions. In all of these methods the reasonable, friendly tone is extremely important— more important, perhaps, than any logical argument that could be mentioned in an introduction.

What we have been talking about here involves some of the most complicated questions to be treated in this book, and we are not ready to develop them now.[3] You can, however, begin to think seriously in your own way about these matters and consider them when you come to actual writing. The student who wrote the following introduction was trying to win over a hostile reader.

> In my senior year in high school I was what is known as a "student leader," and one thing I led was the nearest thing to a riot that Silas Morton High School ever had—and I hope ever will have. I am giving this information not as a way of boasting or as a horror story in which I beat my breast and explain how my experience made me decide to "go straight"—that is, suck up to anybody who happens to be running the show. I simply want anybody who reads this to know that I have had a real experience with what for most college freshmen is purely theoretical, and that I do understand what it means to be in a school as full of faults as Swiss cheese is of holes and Limburger is of perfume. Our grievances were really real, and I sympathize with any student who feels powerless against a situation like that. It is not that "bad" people have ganged up on you. It is that there is a kind of gray, greasy, smothering fog over everything and you can't do anything about it. It is nobody's responsibility any more than the weather is, it just happens. I know what that feeling is, and I am all in favor of doing something about it. The "what" is what I am writing about.

The tone of the introduction above is soothing. It aims to promote sweet reasonableness. But shock can also be a method for dealing with the hostile reader—the assumption being that only through shock, through making him fully aware of his hostility, can he be brought to reconsider his position. An excellent example is in this introduction to a magazine article on the race question in America, entitled "Black-White: Can We Bridge the Gap?" (Patricia Coffin, *Look,* January 7, 1969). Here are the first few sentences of the opening paragraph:

---

[3] See Persuasion (pp. 238–74), Metaphor (pp. 435–65), and Tone (466–505).

> Black Power is Beautiful! Does that shock you? If so, you are one of
> millions of Americans, black and white, who haven't a clue to what is
> happening here. Does it puzzle you? Then you do not comprehend that
> the black man inherited the American dream with Lincoln's Emancipation
> Proclamation. . . .

An even greater shock—this time to whites only—appears in the opening
lines of another introductory paragraph on the same subject of race in
America:

> You lied. You tried to hide the shame of slavery by calling Africans
> lazy and uncivilized. You taught the lie; you murmured it over tea. You
> created Tarzan and Amos 'n' Andy. And now you reap the darkness of it.
> In truth, man's sunrise glowed first in Africa. . . .

Now substitute the word "we" for each use here of the word "you." [4]
"You lied" gives a direct shock to the white reader. "We lied" keeps something of the shock, but it combines the shock tactic with the tactic of the
common ground: you lied, but I lied too, and we must share the guilt and the
consequences. As a matter of fact, it was this latter version (Jack Shepherd,
"Black America's African Heritage"), with "we" always for "you" to give
the double tactic, that appeared in an article in the same issue of *Look* as
the foregoing excerpt.

NO FORMULA

There is no formula for the introduction of a theme. Certainly, keep your
eyes open as you read to see various possibilities. The main thing, however,
is to cultivate your common sense and imagination. Try to put yourself in
the reader's place. Ask yourself what information you would need to follow
the discussion. Ask yourself how you would respond if some deep conviction of yours were being affronted by a theme. Ask what would make you
reconsider—give a second thought to—a long-held belief.

● CAUTION

You may find that your introduction is running away with you, that it is
becoming a theme in itself. If so, you may have failed to limit and fix your
subject closely enough. Think again. Or perhaps the idea in your introduction is your real subject, and it should be expanded to a whole theme. Think
over that possibility.

INTRODUCTION: DELAY IT?

We have given a good deal of space to discussing the introduction, and
it is of extreme importance. We shall now make a suggestion, however, that
may seem to contradict what has just been said. Sometimes the way to write
a good introduction is not to begin the actual process of writing with the

---

[4] This change involves a matter of the attitude of the writer toward the subject and his audience.
(See chapter on Tone.)

introduction. It may be a good idea to plunge straight into the body of the theme and follow through to the end. Then ask yourself what you have accomplished, what needs to be said in the introduction to give the reader his bearings for what you have already put down. As we saw earlier in Chapter 1, often it occurs that we know what we want to say only after we have tried to express it in words.

This introduction-in-reverse process should not be used regularly, but it may help give you a better sense of the relation between the introduction and the body of the theme. When the introduction is written before the rest of the theme, it may be well to reconsider it after the body of the theme has been completed. In the light of the completed theme, you may be able to make very useful revisions.

■ APPLICATIONS

I   Read the introductions to "The Abolition of Man," by C. S. Lewis (pp. 652–57), "Adolescence: Self-Definition and Conflict," by Edgar Z. Friedenberg (pp. 712–21), "Hipsters Unleashed," by David McReynolds (pp. 728–34), "The Anatomy of Academic Discontent," by Bruno Bettelheim (pp. 734–45), and "It Was a Stable World," by Robert Graves (pp. 803–810). Which one particularly caught your interest? Try to analyze the reason. Then read through the piece. Does the body of discussion fulfill the promise of the introduction?

II   Examine the introductory paragraphs of "The American Civilization Puzzle" (pp. 814–26). What appeals to interest does the author try to make? Does he really convince you that his subject is "important"? Even if you already think it important, has he given adequate reasons for its importance?

III   Write an introduction of 75 to 100 words addressed to a hostile reader. Be careful to choose a subject that would offer some real provocation.

The body of the discussion and the conclusion

For the present, we shall take very little space to discuss the body of the discourse and the conclusion. There is a good reason for this, for, from this point on, everything we shall be doing in this course will be a way of studying how to develop the main body of the discussion. Suffice it to say here that the body of the discussion should not betray the promise of the introduction. You have promised the reader to develop a fixed and limited subject along a certain line. Having made this promise, keep it.

There are one or two things that ought to be said about the conclusion. A short theme often does not need a formal conclusion. The paragraph making the last important point, or the climactic point, may constitute a thoroughly adequate conclusion, provided always that the theme has a sound general organization.

But whether your concluding paragraph is elaborate or simple, it occupies one of the two naturally emphatic positions in the composition. Moreover, it constitutes your last chance at your reader. Failure at this point may well mean failure for the whole piece of writing. You must avoid two things: (1) merely trailing off or (2) taking refuge in vague generalities and repetitious summaries. The conclusion must really "conclude" the discussion. Put your finger on your main point, on what you want to bring to focus. Then write your conclusion on that point.

■ APPLICATION

Return to the first Application on page 29, where you were asked to read through one of the selections listed and say whether the discussion fulfilled the promise of the introduction. Now examine again the conclusion of the same selection. What is the main point? What effect does the author wish to leave on the reader? What kind of reader is he writing for?

CHAPTER 3

Organizing the Composition

The introduction, body, and conclusion—or, if you like, the beginning, middle, and end—are the natural divisions of a discourse. But there is another threefold set of terms natural to any process of composition. They are unity, coherence, and emphasis.

Any sound piece of writing will exemplify these three principles, and to study them is the first step toward understanding how to develop the discussion and how to relate the main body of the composition to the introduction and the conclusion.

Unity

Common sense tells us that the basic interest determining the writer's subject must permeate the whole composition. The composition must be *one* thing—not a hodgepodge. We have, of course, already encountered the demands of unity in the problem of fixing on a true subject—that is, of limiting our interest to a single dominant topic—and in organizing a theme through notes or an outline.

But unity is not arbitrary, a limitation imposed from the outside. It is inherent in the subject. If we decide that "George Washington" is too general and vague to give us a true subject for a theme—that is, that it lacks unity—and settle on "What the Frontier Taught George Washington," we can do this only because the frontier *did* teach Washington something, and because, no matter how deeply related this fact is to Washington's whole career, it can be thought about as separate; it has a natural unity.

● CAUTION

We recognize unity. We do not impose it.

How to recognize unity: three tests

Unity, however, is not always easy to recognize. If you are scatter-brained you will not recognize it. To recognize it you must put your powers of logic to work. You must be able to do three things:

1 Define your dominant topic—that is, your true subject.
2 Distinguish what is relevant to the main topic from what is irrelevant to it.
3 Keep the minor topics subordinated to the main topic, and do not allow any one of them a disproportionate amount of space.

A bad example

This theme, written on an assigned topic, is by an intelligent and serious-minded student, but it is defective in several respects, chiefly in regard to unity. The teacher's comments accompany the theme:

WHAT DO I WANT OUT OF COLLEGE?

The subject assigned for this theme is, I know, one of the standard ones for generations of freshmen. It is as old as the hills, and when I saw the assignment, I was tempted to adapt the standard joke, and say: "Yes, old as the hills and not half as grassy," for there didn't seem to be anything fresh and green about it. Then it occurred to me that maybe it was fresh. What I mean is, fresh to me, fresh because I was the one trying to answer the question: "What do I want out of college?"

> Unity: I applaud what you are trying to do here—an easy, humorous way into a stodgy subject, but I fear that this is distracting—and wordy. I don't know the joke, I confess. But even so?

To break down and confess, this is a question that has never really crossed my mind. I have been a kind of day-to-day fellow, doing what came my way, whether it was play or work. But I never had much tendency ~~to see~~ the overall scheme of things, and that means, I suppose, ~~that I am sort of~~ average, for I have noticed that a large number of people tend to lead their lives this way, hacking along as best they can or happen to. I hadn't even bothered to

> Unity: Is the idea of your "averageness" relevant to the main idea?

notice this fact until I went to the funeral last spring of my Uncle Gilbert. He had been a fine athelete, a pro baseball player, until he sprung his knee and had what you might call an inforced retirement. He had just enjoyed things as they came and had made no plans for his life after baseball. He stumbled into a good job given him in the business of one of his fans, but it didn't last, he went steadily downhill, and died before his time, broke, beat-up, and suffering from alcoholism.

So I am ready to try to think about the question which is the subject of this theme and see what it means to me. And I have an answer. I know it will sound either trite or flip or what they call hedonistic, but I do not mean it exactly any of those ways. I have really thought about it. For what it is worth, here it is, "I want happiness out of college."

I have said "trite" about the answer because anybody will say they want to be happy. And I have said "flip," because saying this can be taken as a way of just being offhand. I have said "hedonistic," because it might sound like I was just out to have a good time in college. But, to begin with, the assignment says "out of college" and not "in college"—which I take to mean what you have got to take away when you finish, and which means that I want the happiness I can take with me afterwards, so it is not just the good times I may happen to have in college, even remembering them the way Uncle Gilbert would remember his hell-raising days. The question is to find out while I am in college what will make me happy later.

But now I do not know what kind of work I want to do for my lifework. So one thing I want out of college is to try to decide. I like math, and I have even thought of being a mathematician, but I now think of business administration to get some action in the real world—and some money too. I want to shop around in courses. This may sound like I just want to dabble, but I know that if I don't work reasonably hard at a course, I won't know what the subject might have to offer me for a decision. My father has the habit of saying that you get out of a thing what you put into it. I have heard that often enough to begin to believe it, especially when I see how much my father has put out for his success.

There is another thing I want out of college. You do not live just in your job, and I want to know a

Unity: Is this paying its way?

Repetition: You have been over-working this word throughout, sometimes unnecessarily. Check back!

Diction: The word is *Romance*. Check your dictionary.

Diction: In what sense? To make money as a politician? To give idealistic ideas a practical form? Or what?

Repetitious and wordy, again: Why not have simply a one-sentence paragraph for the conclusion—the last sentence in the theme? Have you more to say?

general sense of values. I don't *mean* this to sound like *Sunday School,* which, to tell the truth, I never got much out of. I *mean* I want to find out what might satisfy a man beyond just making money and providing for his family, and going fishing now and then. One of my friends teaches in a slum school, and he says this makes him feel he is connected with something bigger than he is. My brother, who is a whiz at languages and has a big scholarship to Columbia University, was in the student strikes there. He is getting more and more interested in politics, and is about to give up the idea of being a professor of *Romantic* Languages. He says in politics you have a chance to mold society into more decent forms and make idealism *pay off.* I do not know what I want, but I intend to experiment and find out.

A person has one life to lead and he can't take anybody's word. He has to experiment and try to find out. What I want out of college is a chance to do that.

General remarks: You have a sound idea, but there are serious faults in execution, all connected, I think. (1) *Proportion:* You take three—really four—paragraphs for the introduction. It seems that you feel you will not have enough to say and so pad out as much as possible. Or have you merely failed to think your subject through before beginning? (2) *Unity:* This defect may spring from the same impulse to pad, or again, from a failure to plan ahead. In any case, it gives an impression of being scatterbrained. You simply do not stay on the main line of thought, and you keep bringing in competing interests. (3) *Wordiness:* This, again, is padding, but padding in a merely local way. Try to think what you really mean to say. It is better to be accurate than graceful—if that hard choice arises. But don't think that multiplying words means grace.

The theme is basically good but badly needs rewriting. This means rethinking. Outline the whole thing from scratch to clarify your line of thought. In this process think about proportion. Use a sentence outline, for this will help you discard the irrelevant—though often interesting—things. By the way, the theme is far longer than the assignment. Rewrite it and reduce to essentials.

■ APPLICATION

After carefully studying the theme above, follow the teacher's suggestion. Make a sentence outline of what you think the theme should be, and then rewrite it in about 400 words.

Coherence

As an effective discourse must have unity, it must have coherence; that is, the elements of the discourse must stick together. This may seem to be simply another way of saying that a discourse must have unity. Unity and coherence are, indeed, related, but it is worth making a distinction between them.

Let us take the example of a "hashed" paragraph—one in which the order of sentences is shuffled.

> The second is the slowness of its operation even when he believes the majority is right. But sooner or later he finds himself straining against two features of the democratic process. The hero in a democratic community—the potentially event-making man—may sincerely believe that he accepts its underlying philosophy. The first is the principle of majority rule, especially when he is convinced that the majority is wrong on a matter of great import.[1]

From even a most casual reading, it is clear that this paragraph has a kind of unity, however unfocused: every sentence either mentions the word *democratic* or refers to the question of majority rule. But the paragraph lacks coherence. With the very first sentence we are in a fog, for we don't know what the "second" referred to is or the antecedent of the "he." In the second sentence, we don't know to what the "but" stands in opposition, and though we assume that the "he" is the same as the "he" in the first sentence, we still don't have an antecedent. Worse, we see no connection between this sentence and the first. In the third sentence we feel—"feel" because we cannot be sure—that the "hero" is the antecedent of the "he," but this sentence has no demonstrable continuity with the previous sentences. In the last sentence we suspect that the "first" refers to one of the "two features" of the second sentence and are fairly certain, again, that the antecedent of "he" is, as throughout, the "hero."

Even though, after our close analysis, we begin to sense a continuous line of thought, it is because we are fumbling at a reconstruction of the paragraph, not because there is coherence in the present form. The paragraph lacks logical order.

The word *order* is the key to the distinction between unity and coherence. In unity, the emphasis is on the relation of the various elements of a discourse to the dominant topic. In coherence, the emphasis is on the order—the continuity—of the elements.

---

[1] Drawn from *The Hero in History*, by Sidney Hook. Reprinted by permission of Humanities Press Inc.

I Put the four sentences of the "hashed" paragraph above into their logical order. To do this, you will merely have to push a little further into the process we have outlined in the discussion.

II Choose the introductory paragraph from any of the selections in Readings, and "hash" it so that there remains some sense of unity but a minimum of coherence. Give it to a classmate to be restored to the original order. You should try the same thing with a "hashed" paragraph prepared by a classmate.

Kinds of order

The kind of order that will give coherence to the description of, say, a woman's face would not serve for giving an account of a baseball game, for arguing for the abolition of Greek-letter fraternities, or for explaining the causes of the Russian Revolution. Different subjects demand different principles of order.[2] In a broad general way, we may say that there are four kinds of order that may, singly or in combination, be involved in establishing coherence:

1 order of logic
2 order of time
3 order of space
4 order of feeling[3]

ORDER OF LOGIC

Logic is, the dictionary says, the science of reasoning. At the very center of the reasoning process is the order in which relations are established between one thing and another: one thing is connected with or leads to another. We inspect cause and effect, evidence and conclusion.

The coherence established by logical order depends, fundamentally, on the clarity with which (1) the steps in the reasoning process are distinguished from each other, and (2) the interrelations are established among the steps. To put it simply, one thing must lead to another; each "thing" must be recognizably "one," and the process of "leading" must be convincingly indicated. Later we shall study this process in considerable detail, but for the moment, in a rough-and-ready way, we can dwell on the fact that the language itself offers many connective words and phrases with the function of indicating structure. If we can recognize the function of such

---

[2] We must not confuse these kinds of order with the four modes of discourse—exposition, argument, description, and narration—that we shall later be studying. The kinds of order involved here flow into and interpenetrate the modes of discourse. For example, though it is true that the order of logic is most obviously fundamental to exposition and argument, it is also found in all but the most rudimentary form of narration—that of mere sequence. See p. 39 and Narration (pp. 313–52).

[3] The discussion of this question will be postponed. See Description (pp. 272–312), Narration (pp. 313–52), Metaphor (pp. 435–65), and Tone (pp. 466–506).

"controls," we have gone a long way toward understanding how to achieve coherence in a discourse.

Below is a section from a theme by a student defending his choice of a profession; he intends to take a teacher's certificate after college and teach in a slum high school. In this section we have underscored the "controls"—the words or phrases that help us grasp the relations involved in the discourse.

> I know that there are objections to my choice of a lifework. Specifically, there is the big one my father points out: money. I know, of course, that a man has to make a living, that money makes the mare go, to use the old saying; but, as I tell him, a man doesn't need more than his tastes require. He says, in good nature, that I don't know how expensive my tastes are, that I have had lots of privileges I don't even recognize as such, for example coming to this kind of college. It doesn't do much good to reply that, even though I have had it easy, I want something beyond that easiness of life. You see, he cuts me off here, and says that I have a good hard logical mind and a man isn't happy unless he is using his best talents, and that, consequently, I should go into law or something like that to use mine. Undoubtedly, my father is right, generally speaking. He himself, in fact, has used his talents; for he is one hell of a good corporation lawyer, and is happy in his business. But I am me.
>
> When I say that I am me, I know that I'm taking the risk of thinking I know myself. But I think I know two things.
>
> First, even if I happen to have that logical mind (and maybe I haven't), I get bored in dealing with general rules and abstractions, and in logic-chopping. It is too impersonal, and that is what law is, logic-chopping—for me, anyway. I have to have something personal. For one thing, I like to deal with people directly, to try to know how they respond, as individual people. I have the feeling that I myself get more real when this is going on. Feeling real is what I call living, and therefore anything I do must give me that feeling.
>
> Second, when it comes to a profession, I want something that society seems to need bad right now. Even if it does sound sappy to say I know that this will make me happier than the law. It would make me, to repeat, feel more real. I have this philosophy of life, and so I am going to act on it.
>
> To sum up, my decision depends . . .

Let us list the underscored items and state the function of each:

specifically: introduces an illustration, one of the "objections."

of course: makes a concession, here to the general idea the father proposes.

but: introduces a contradiction, here of the father's general proposition as applied in particular cases.

for example: introduces an illustration.

even though: admits a concession that is to be reversed.

consequently: announces the conclusion of a line of reasoning, here about the use of a man's best talents.

undoubtedly: admits a concession, the father is right.

generally speaking: modifies the concession.

in fact: introduces an illustration of the father's proposition, here working as an additional concession.

but: makes a contradiction of the father's proposition.

when: introduces and emphasizes the key argument of the son, by repetition binding this paragraph to the preceding one.

first (second): signals for division and order.

anyway: makes a concession in general, but actually emphasizes the personal nature of the son's idea.

for one thing: introduces illustration.

therefore: introduces a logical conclusion, the decision.

even if: makes a concession, to be reversed in following statement, and therefore emphasizes the son's position.

to repeat: device of binding and emphasis.

so: introduces the consequence of the philosophy of life.

to sum up: device of binding and focus for conclusion.

Logical Order: Other "Controls" The section of the theme presented above is basically an argument: the student is arguing in defense of his choice of profession. But many of the controls merely assist in indicating the structure of thought and do not specifically refer to the process of reasoning, which is the moving from evidence to conclusion or from cause to effect. We notice that only three controls here do that: *consequently, therefore,* and *so.* But there are available other controls that help to pinpoint reasoning, and a list of them may be helpful. Since reasoning may be presented as going forward or backward (evidence-conclusion, cause-effect; conclusion-evidence, effect-cause), we shall divide the controls into two groups.

Controls that announce a conclusion (effect) after evidence (cause) has been given:

> thus
> hence
> proves that
> implies that
> leads one to conclude that

Controls that announce evidence (cause) after a conclusion (effect) has been given:

> because
> since
> as
> as shown by
> for [4]

---

[4] The control *for* may be used *only* after the conclusion or result has been given. It should be observed that we refer here to *for* used as a conjunction and not as a preposition.

Such a list need not be memorized, but you should familiarize yourself with it and in your reading, you should be constantly aware of the words and phrases that indicate relations. You want to cultivate precision in indicating relations, and you want to avoid monotony.

■ APPLICATIONS

I Can you think of any other words or phrases that might be added to the list having to do with cause-effect and evidence-conclusion?

II In the excerpt from the theme above, the author, working hard to give his work coherence, may have put in unnecessary controls. Read the excerpt, omitting all the underscored items. Is the line of thought clear without the controls? If it is not, which do you think should be restored?

III Study the first three paragraphs of "Making It: The Brutal Bargain," by Norman Podhoretz (pp. 847–58), and of "The Inscrutability of History," by Arthur Schlesinger, Jr. (pp. 826–38). Mark all the controls you find there, and state the function of each.

ORDER OF TIME

The order of logic depends on the way the mind works in moving from a cause to an effect, a piece of evidence to a conclusion—that is, in establishing a certain kind of connection between the two things. The order of time depends on our natural perception of sequence in our experience. We perceive that one thing simply comes after another thing. That is the only relation with which we are concerned in simple perception—not cause and effect, not evidence and conclusion. We may, of course, add such ideas to the sequence to interpret it, but they are not necessary to the fact of sequence. Look at this passage of pure sequence:

> Lying on the bed, in the dark room, he heard the flow of the strange language from the street below. He heard footsteps in the hall, outside his door. Somebody was going down into the street. He lay on the cot and felt the hard lumps in the mattress. Somewhere in the hotel, a phonograph was playing American jazz. He tried not to hear it. He began reciting the multiplication table. Then he saw, against the purple sky of the night, the first long finger, far off, of a searchlight, moving majestically. He shut his eyes. He tried not to listen to the phonograph. The phonograph stopped. It was in the middle of a record.

This is in pure sequence. Nothing is explained or interpreted. We do not know who the man is, where he is, what he is doing there. But the next paragraph runs:

The *alerte* came. He began to sweat. He knew he would have to vomit soon. At least, he had last night. He shut his eyes and waited for the first explosion.

We now have an interpretation grafted onto the sequence. We now know that the man has been clinging to the mere fact of sequence, even to reciting the multiplication table (a mechanical sequence) in order to overcome his fear of an impending air raid. We can guess that if he tries not to listen to the jazz, it is because the association may divert him from the sequence in which he takes refuge. Even with the addition of this explanation and interpretation the time order remains the basic order of the passage.

Time is the basic order of all narration. It is the order that underlies even the most complicated novels, for on the order of time we find the interpretations erected. But the order of time appears in many other forms of writing.

Here are some common controls of time:

since	the following day (or whatever)
when	having completed that (or whatever)
while	(so and so) being begun
as	having met success (or failure)
afterwards	
after	
before	
then	
henceforward	

■ APPLICATIONS

I What are the meanings of the word *as?* Use the dictionary, then make up a sentence exhibiting each meaning.

II Discriminate between the meanings of *when* and *while.*

III One of the important controls of the order of time is the tense of verbs. Are you satisfied with the verb forms used in the following sentences? When not satisfied, correct them.

1   If he did not do it, he would have been successful.
2   Running up the steps, he found his mother in the hall.
3   He finished the pie when the clock struck.
4   He had finished the pie before the clock struck.
5   Did you finish yet?
6   Hoping for the best, he lay down and waited.
7   She thought she will do it tomorrow.

IV Try to add some items to the above list of the controls of time.

The order of space, like that of time, is based on the way we perceive the world in which we live. When the eye moves we are aware of a spatial sequence—left to right, near to far, or whatever the case may be. If we recount the sequence in which the eye perceives objects, we have a principle of coherence that the reader instinctively recognizes and accepts. In its simplest form, such a principle of organization may be found in the literal movement of the eye from one object to another, as in the following passage:

> The train toils slowly round the mountain grades, the short and powerful blasts of its squat funnel sound harsh and metallic against the sides of rocky cuts. One looks out the window and sees cut, bank, and gorge slide slowly past, the old rock wet and gleaming with the water of some buried mountain spring. The train goes slowly over the perilous and dizzy height of a wooden trestle; far below, the traveller can see and hear the clean foaming clamors of rock-bright mountain water; beside the track, before his little hut, a switchman stands looking at the train with the slow wondering gaze of the mountaineer. The little shack in which he lives is stuck to the very edge of the track above the steep and perilous ravine. His wife, a slattern with a hank of tight drawn hair, a snuff-stick in her mouth, and the same gaunt, slow wondering stare her husband has, stands in the doorway of the shack, holding a dirty little baby in her arms.
>
> It is all so strange, so near, so far, terrible, beautiful, and instantly familiar, that it seems to the traveller that he must have known these people forever, that he must now stretch forth his hand to them from the windows and the rich and sumptuous luxury of the pullman car, that he must speak to them. And it seems to him that all the strange and bitter miracle of life—how, why, or in what way, he does not know—is in that instant greeting and farewell; for once seen, and lost the minute that he sees it, it is his forever and he can never forget it. And then the slow toiling train has passed these lives and faces and is gone, and there is something in his heart he cannot say. —THOMAS WOLFE: *Of Time and the River.*[5]

There are, of course, many patterns more subtle, complex, and imaginative that can be derived from spatial order. We shall come to study these in the section on Description, but meanwhile, as need arises, you should try to develop your own variations from the simple, literal pattern.

● CAUTION

Any pattern based on the order of space should come from our natural ways of perceiving things. But the ways of perceiving vary according to circumstances. If we are in motion we find one pattern; at rest, another. Moreover, the interest we bring to bear determines what is at the center of our perception. (See Description, pp. 297–305.)

---

[5] Reprinted with the permission of Charles Scribner's Sons from *Of Time and the River* by Thomas Wolfe. Copyright 1935 Charles Scribner's Sons; renewal copyright © 1963 Paul Gitlin, Administrator C.T.A. Reprinted by permission of William Heinemann Ltd.

■ APPLICATIONS

I Assume that, on coming into a strange room, your eye fixes on some single striking or interesting particular and then discovers other things in relation to that. Write a paragraph of description, of 100 words, using this principle. Or write a paragraph based on some other principle of perception of which you are aware.

II Make a short list of controls for the order of space.

OTHER CONTROLS

We have made some fairly sharp distinctions of kinds of controls in terms of cause and effect and evidence and conclusion, time, and space. But there are many others that somewhat less specifically indicate relationships. For example, for adding or continuing we have such controls as the following: *and, or, but, moreover, likewise, also, in fact, indeed.* For opposition and contrast we have, for example: *but, nevertheless, still, notwithstanding.* For concession: *although, whereas.* Then there are all sorts of words and phrases of reference that give lines of connection through a discourse. For instance, pronouns that cast back to antecedents, including relative and demonstrative pronouns, and phrases like *all of them, some of them, as we have said, as we have pointed out, as will be seen, as will be clear in the sequel, that is to say, that is, to anticipate,* and *remembering that.*

Equally important, and even more flexible and subtle, are the controls that the author may develop in the text for logical, temporal, spatial, or other relations. Let us glance at a few examples, chosen almost at random:

> . . . When you read what New England intellectuals were saying about the common people early in the nineteenth century you are reminded of what British and French colonial officials were saying about the natives when the clamor for independence rose after the last war: "Wait and see what a mess these savages will make of things."
> A resemblance between intellectuals and colonial officials strikes us at first sight as incongruous . . .   —ERIC HOFFER: *The Temper of Our Time.*[6]

Observe that the second paragraph begins with a restatement in different words ("resemblance") of the comparison between the New England intellectuals and the colonial officials, this restatement as preparation for the development of the discussion.

> . . . they must one and all remember that the Algerian people is today an adult people, responsible and fully conscious of its responsibilities. In short, the Algerians are men of property.
> If we have taken the example of Algeria to illustrate our subject, it is

---

[6] From pp. 74–75 in *The Temper of Our Time* (Hardbound Ed.) by Eric Hoffer (Harper & Row, 1965). Reprinted by permission of Harper & Row, Publishers.

not at all with the intention of glorifying our own people, but simply to show the important part played by war . . .

—FRANTZ FANON: *The Wretched of the Earth.*

Here another type of repetition acts as a "binder," the repetition of a word—*Algerian, Algeria*—which serves to introduce a summarizing justification for the preceding discussion: "to show the important part played by war . . ."

. . . it is a literature of combat because it assumes responsibility, and because it is the will to liberty expressed in terms of time and space.

On another level, the oral tradition—stories, epics, and songs of the people—which formerly were filed away as set pieces are now beginning to change. —FRANTZ FANON: *The Wretched of the Earth.*

Here the "binder" is a phrase, "on another level," which introduces another example of the idea of the previous paragraph, the effect on literature of a revolutionary situation.

. . . I threw off an overcoat, took an armchair by the crackling logs, and awaited patiently the arrival of my hosts.

Soon after dark they arrived, and gave me a most cordial welcome . . .

—EDGAR ALLAN POE: "The Gold-Bug."

This is an example on continuity by pure sequence: "Soon after dark . . ."

. . . He caught her eyes only as she went, on which he thought them pretty and touching.

Why especially touching at that instant he could certainly scarcely have said; it was involved, it was lost in the sense of her wishing to oblige him . . . —HENRY JAMES: *The Wings of the Dove.*

The repetition of a single word here provides the continuity: the word *touching* leads to the development in the second paragraph of the idea that brings the former paragraph into focus.

No Formula There is no formula for using such transitions to give coherence. But you should observe constantly the variations you encounter and stock your mind with them. The point of this is not so much to repeat accepted devices as to master the principle—the necessity for maintaining continuity while indicating shifts in meaning and emphasis. You can then develop devices of your own that carry the impression of freshness and spontaneity. The real point is to cultivate a feeling for coherence. Your work must be considered under two aspects: that of a structure with parts, and that of a stream that flows. Keep this in mind.

● THREE CAUTIONS

First, whatever the main order of controls appropriate to a particular piece of writing (for instance, of time), controls of other orders may be incidentally useful. For example, observe the variety of controls in the theme by the student who wants to teach in a slum school (pp. 37–38).

Second, you should not depend merely on controls and devices of transition to establish coherence. You should aim at a continuity embodied as fully as possible in the actual writing—continuity from sentence to sentence, paragraph to paragraph, and division to division. Then, when such intrinsic continuity is not immediately obvious, you may resort to the controls.

Third, the controls are not for ornament. They should be used *only* when necessary.

● ANOTHER CAUTION

In every instance, analyze to your own satisfaction the exact function you wish a control to perform.

■ APPLICATION

In the following passage fill in the controls that you feel appropriate to establish the coherence.

_____ we had come out of the gorge, the snow stopped, and now, as a _____, we could see the great opening out of the prairie beyond. _____ the sun was near setting, we could see with great clarity, in the distance _____ the expanse of new snow, the Indian village in the cottonwood grove at the bend of the river. _____ there was no wind, the smoke from the tepees stood straight up, gray-blue in the gold light of sunset. We looked to our firearms, _____ there was no way to know of what tribe they were. _____ we were thus engaged, François, the trapper, was peering across the distance. "Blackfeet!" he suddenly exclaimed. My heart sank, _____ I knew that he was rarely mistaken in such matters. I gave the order to proceed across the prairie toward the village, hoping, _____ against my better judgment, that a bold show was the best policy.

Emphasis

A piece of writing may be unified and coherent and still not be effective if it does not observe the principle of emphasis. When this principle is properly observed, the intended scale of importance of elements in the discourse is clear to the reader. All cats are black in the dark, but all things should not look alike in the light of a reasonable writer's interest in his subject. To change our metaphor, there is a foreground and a background of interest, and the writer should be careful to place each item in its proper location. Like unity and coherence, emphasis is a principle of organization.

Emphasis by flat statement

How does the writer emphasize an element in a piece of writing?

The first and most obvious way is to make a flat statement of his own view on the importance of a matter. In an article by the editors of *Time,* the first sentence reads "Crime in the U.S. is a national disgrace." In the *New York Times Magazine* ("The Great Society Is a Sick Society," August 20, 1967), Senator J. W. Fulbright concludes an article by writing:

> If I had to bet my money on what is going to happen, I would bet on this younger generation—this generation of young men and women who reject the inhumanity of war in a poor and distant land, who reject the poverty and sham in their own country, who are telling their elders what their elders ought to have known—that the price of empire is America's soul and that the price is too high.

The editors of *Time* and Senator Fulbright have insisted on the importance of what they have to say. The editors start with their proposition and proceed to develop it in detail. Senator Fulbright moves toward his through the body of discussion. But in both instances the cards are on the table. There is no question as to the focus of importance.

The statement is the most obvious device of emphasis. But if the statement is unsupported, it will not achieve its purpose. You must be sure, when you resort to stating the emphasis outright that the statement proceeds from, or will be justified by, the line of thought you have developed.

Be sure you really believe your own statement.

Emphasis by position

A second way to emphasize is by position. "First or last" is a fairly sound rule for emphasis by position. This rule corresponds to two general methods for treating a subject. The main idea can be presented and then discussed or proved, or discussion or proof can lead up to the main idea. Ordinarily the second method is better, and the end is the most emphatic position, for the last impression a reader receives is what counts most. But some rather conventionalized forms of writing, such as news stories, put the most important material first. In any case, the middle is the least emphatic position.

Emphasis by proportion

Proportion in itself is a means of emphasis. The most important topic in a discussion reasonably receives fullest treatment. This principle, however, is more flexible than the preceding statement would indicate. In some writing the last and most important topic may have been so well prepared for by the foregoing discussion that it does not require elaborate treatment.

The writer must decide each case on its own merits and be sure that he is not indulging in elaboration merely for the sake of elaboration.

Other devices of emphasis

Flat statement, order of importance, proportion, and style (to be discussed in Chapter 13) are major means of expressing emphasis, but there are certain minor ones. For instance, repetition of an idea can give it prominence. The danger here is that the repetition may become merely mechanical and therefore dull. To be effective, repetition must be combined with some variety and some progression in the treatment of the subject. Then there is the device of the short, isolated paragraph. The idea set off by itself strikes the eye. But not all short paragraphs are in themselves emphatic. The content and the phrasing of the short paragraph must make it appear worthy of the special presentation. Obviously if many paragraphs are short, all emphasis disappears.

Faulty devices of emphasis

Certain common devices of emphasis are worse than useless. Irresponsible exaggeration always repels the reader. Catchwords and hackneyed phrases, such as *awfully, terribly, tremendously, the most wonderful thing I ever saw, you never saw anything like it, I can't begin to tell you*—these make a claim on the reader's attention that he is rarely prepared to grant. Random underlining and italicizing and the use of capitals and exclamation points usually defeat their own purpose. Writers use these devices when they are not sure that what they have to say will stand on its own merits. To insist that what you have to say is important does not prove the point. As the writer, you must prove it.

In applying any of the means of emphasis the writer must first of all be sure that the thing emphasized is worth emphasizing. Common sense must help him here. Nothing else can.

A theme: he tries again

The student who wrote the theme entitled "What Do I Want out of College?" that was so deficient in unity tried again with the theme below. The assigned topic was, again, a standard one, "An Interesting Person." Wisely enough, he thought over people he knew well and settled on a member of the family, his uncle, for whom he had affection and respect. But Uncle Conroy, if taken in the lump, would, he knew, be too general and uncontrolled a subject, and so he set about trying to define for himself the reasons for his feelings about the old man. Having arrived at a fairly clear notion, he focused his subject in the title "The Person I Admire Most."

Having failed so dismally at unifying his previous long theme and giving it satisfying proportion, he was determined to overcome his tendency to be scatterbrained; so he jotted down some of the things he could remember about his uncle, and some of the reasons for his feelings about him. Then he tried to organize them in an outline. His outline ran as follows:

Statement of the Subject   Why I admire my Uncle Conroy

Introduction
 I. My uncle as he now appears—apparent failure and real success

Body
 II. The background of my uncle's achievement
   A. His worldly success and ruin
   B. His illness and despair
 III. The nature of my uncle's achievements
   A. His practical achievements
     1. Help with the children
     2. Help with my father's business
     3. Help with my mother's illness
   B. His achievement in self-control
     1. Naturalness of his actions
     2. Cheerfulness in the face of pain
   C. His greatest achievement, an example to others—the summary of his other achievements

Conclusion
 IV. My uncle as a type of success and my admiration for him

When he had written the note for the conclusion, he decided that the title was too vague and did not really suit the theme. So now, even before he began to write, he scratched it out and substituted "Success and Uncle Conroy."

Actually, the student did not follow his outline slavishly in writing his theme about Uncle Conroy. We shall discuss a little later some of the ways in which he departed from it. But first, let us look at his theme.

SUCCESS AND UNCLE CONROY

 1   I suppose that my Uncle Conroy is the person I admire most in the world. This statement would probably seem strange to anyone who happened to visit our home and see the old man sitting, hunched over and shabbily dressed, at a corner of the hearth, not saying much, with his old meerschaum pipe left over from his early days stuck in his mouth, but not lit, probably. He looks like the complete failure, and by ordinary standards he is. He has no money. He has no children. He is old and sick. But he has made his own kind of success, and I think he is happy.

 2   At one time in his life he was a success by ordinary standards. He was the son of a poor Methodist minister (my mother's father), but he ran away from home in Illinois to Oklahoma, back in the days when things

were beginning to boom out there. He had a fine house in Oklahoma City and a ranch. He was hail-fellow-well-met, and men and women liked him. He was a sportsman, kept good horses, and took long hunting trips to Mexico and Canada. Then one day, on his own ranch, his horse stumbled in a gopher hole and threw him. He was badly hurt and was in the hospital for two years. While he was in the hospital a partner to whom he had given power of attorney, either through dishonesty or stupidity (my uncle would never discuss this) ran everything into the ground and broke it off. So he came back to Illinois, and my mother and father took him in.

3   It must have been an awful comedown for a man like that to be living on charity. But the worst was yet to happen, for while he was still convalescing, he developed arthritis in a very painful form, and it became clear he could never work again. I remember the first year or so, even though I was a very small child. He even tried to commit suicide with gas from the stove. But my mother saved him, and after that he began to change.

4   The first thing was that he began to take an interest in us children. He would read to us and talk to us. He helped us with our lessons. That relieved mother a great deal and made her life easier. My father was an insurance man and had a lot of paper work to do. It got so that my uncle took an interest in that, and before long he was helping my father by doing reports and writing letters. Then when my mother was ill for a long time, he learned to do some of the housework, as much as his strength would permit, and even dressed the two smaller children.

5   What he did was important, but more important was the way he did things. He was so natural about it. You never got the impression he was making any effort or sacrifice. We all got so we didn't notice what he did, and I am sure that that was what he wanted.

6   As I look back now, or when I go home and see Uncle Conroy, his biggest achievement, however, seems to be the kind of example he gave us all. He was often in pain, but he was always cheerful. If he felt too bad, he simply hid away from the family for a while in his room—what he called his "mope-room." He even made a joke out of that. And he didn't act like a man who had failed. He acted like a man who had found what he could do and was a success at it. And I think that he is a success. We all admire success, and that is why I admire my Uncle Conroy.

This theme is unified and coherent, and builds to an effective emphasis in the summarizing conclusion. Let us examine the general pattern of the work.

First, by way of introduction, the author gives a brief sketch of the uncle as he now appears—the man who is to be interpreted by the theme. The appearance of failure (even the detail of the burned-out pipe) in contrast to the reality of success gives dramatic interest and excites the reader's curiosity. The introduction implies a proposition, a thesis, a leading idea, which we may state: This man embodies a success beyond his practical failure. The proposition is expressed in the image of the old man in his failure, and this image suggests a question that leads the reader into the body of the theme: How can this old man be a success? In other words, the proposition gives the focus for the unity of the theme, and the question provides the principle of coherence: the whole theme demonstrates the proposition, but the process of answering the question is what carries us from point to point. It must be remembered, to be sure, that the unity and coherence here, as always, are intimately related.

Although the question gives a general coherence, with paragraphs 2, 3, and 4 (which with paragraph 5 form the body of the theme) the author brings in another method of maintaining coherence, one not suggested in the introduction: the order of time. He does not analyze the character of Uncle Conroy; he tells the story of his development over the years, and this story provides a frame of continuity. It provides, however, more than a frame, for the story involves a contrast between the rich past and the poor present, and this contrast between the two kinds of success gives a continuing reference to the unifying proposition. Let us look at this section in more detail.

In the second paragraph the writer tells of his uncle's days of outward success. This topic does not get into the theme merely because the uncle, as a matter of fact, had such success. Many things that happened to him are certainly omitted here. Instead, it gets in because the taste of worldly success makes more impressive the uncle's achievement in being able to shift his values in the face of adversity.

The third paragraph presents the despair of the uncle—a normal response to bankruptcy and illness. This topic has a place in the general organization, for it states the thing that the uncle must fight against. Paragraph 4, still in terms of narrative, gives, without comment, the picture of Uncle Conroy as a "success." With paragraph 5 the author leaves the order of time as a principle of coherence, and gives a general interpretation, but one still tied to the scene: "we didn't notice."

Paragraph 6 provides a summary with emphasis on the overall interpretation. The implied proposition of the introduction is now stated. We may notice that the author places his main interpretation in the position of emphasis at the very end of the last paragraph; it serves as the climax of the whole composition.

In discussing the relation of part to part in the foregoing theme, it may be well also to review briefly the relation of the theme to the student's preliminary outline. Paragraph 1 corresponds to I (Introduction); paragraph 2, to II:A; paragraph 3, to II:B; paragraph 4, to III:A:1, 2, 3; paragraph 5, to III:B:1; and paragraph 6, to III:B:2, III:C, and IV.

Topic III:B:2, now in paragraph 6, should probably be in paragraph 5; and the writer of the theme should probably have made topic IV into a separate paragraph, which would give a statement of the writer's definition of success and the application of the definition to his uncle's case. Nevertheless, the student has written a theme that is fundamentally systematic. It builds continuously toward a climax. It has a sound structure, which was developed in the outline before the actual writing was begun.

I In the theme "Success and Uncle Conroy," indicate the kinds of controls used to maintain coherence. Explain the function of each. Indicate the devices of emphasis, and explain them.

II You are now ready to write your longest theme to date, a theme of some 750 words about yourself. Remember that you have a particular audience, the instructor. That person is almost a stranger to you, but he is friendly and interested. He wants to know you better. For one thing, he wants to know the basic facts of your life. These facts are bound to be part of your story. But he wants to know a good deal more, something of the inside "you," your character, your training, your ambitions, your view of yourself.

But "yourself" is a big topic. Begin by thinking about it, by exploring it. Try to answer honestly, in your own mind, such questions as the following:

1   What kind of family do I have?
2   What kind of intellectual and moral training have I received?
3   What would I criticize about that training?
4   What people have had the greatest influence on me?
5   Has that influence been for good or bad?
6   What important experiences have I had? Why were they important to me?
7   What have I done that I am most proud of?
8   Have I made the most of my opportunities?
9   What is my own character like?
10   What are my strong points? Weak points?
11   What do I enjoy most?
12   What do I dislike most?
13   Did I get good training in high school?
14   Who were my good teachers? Why were they good for me?
15   Why did I come to college?
16   Did I drift to this college or have I some reason for being here?
17   What is my ambition?
18   What is my best talent? How does it relate to the career I plan?
19   What other questions should I answer to arrive at some estimate of my-self?
20   Have I answered these questions thoughtfully and honestly?

You now have a large body of material laid out for your theme. You will not be able to use it all. In the first place, your theme will not be long enough. In the second place, if you try to use it all, you will end up with a lot of un-organized facts and remarks. But attempting to answer these questions may give you some perspective on yourself and may lead to some line of interest to serve as the central idea of your theme and the spine for its organization.

In trying to see how you can relate various facts and ideas to one another, you may find certain further general questions helpful. For instance:

1 To what extent have circumstances (heredity, family situation, certain persons, and experience) made me what I am?
2 To what extent do I feel myself responsible for what I am?
3 How do I assess myself and my possibilities at this moment?
4 What do I want to do with myself?

Having pondered these questions, you may come up with such thematic statements as: "I am of a decayed New England stock," "My grandparents arrived in America stony broke," "I have to live down my father's fame," or "I am that monster, the completely average person," or "I know what I want to do." If these questions have not led you to a controlling idea about yourself—a true subject—frame some new questions and pursue them—and pursue them as honestly as possible. If you have trouble in striking on a subject, try to tell the story of your life to yourself. Do you see any thread running through it?

When you have a subject, begin to jot down notes, almost at random, trying to feel your way into your theme. Next, try to sort out what you have assembled, establishing relations to the main idea. But—and perhaps fortunately—you may have struck on another idea. If so, inspect it. Don't feel wedded to the first one.

Your next stage is to make an outline, a topic outline to start with. This done, you should try to convert your outline into a sentence outline, using sentences that really say something, that really indicate content and stages of development.

Now write. But when you actually begin composition, keep an open mind. If new ideas come, as they almost certainly will, think them over on their merits, even if this means a change in your plan.

After you have finished the first draft of your theme, check it by the outline. If the theme seems good and systematic but does not match the outline, revise the outline to conform to the theme. But if the theme does not seem satisfactory and the outline does, revise the theme to conform to the outline. Attach your rough note jottings and the outlines to the theme before you hand it in.

PART TWO

THE FORMS
OF DISCOURSE

CHAPTER 4

The Main Intention

Thus far we have discussed three key topics: (1) the true subject and how to arrive at it; (2) the divisions of a discourse, and their special functions and interrelations; and (3) unity, coherence, and emphasis, what they are and how to achieve them. Looking back on these topics, we see that they are closely related, and that the discussion of each represents a stage in a larger, continuing discussion that is concerned with a deep, general question—the relationship between form and function, shape and point.

Form and Function

A piece of writing has, presumably, been composed to accomplish some purpose, perform some function, make some point. If the writer is a good writer, all the elements in his composition will contribute, directly or indirectly, to fulfilling that function, making that point. The form is determined by the function, the shape by the point. But function, too, is determined by form, point by shape. This idea lies behind everything that you will be studying in this book.

    The reciprocal relationship between form and function, shape and point, appears in the very process of composition. Certainly, your purpose—the function you wished to see fulfilled—conditions what you put down on paper. But in the process of putting ideas into words, the words themselves tend to generate new ideas, and so the function intended may be constantly modified in the very act of embodying it in a form.

The Main Intention

The reciprocal modification of form and function in the process of composition is, however, limited by what we may call the main intention appropriate to the occasion. When a lawyer, with the obligation to prepare a brief to present to the court, sits down to write, he may well come on new points that will enrich his thought or new objections that will deflect it into new channels. But he is not likely to drift off into writing a poem, a short story, or even a letter to his aged mother. There may be other occasions on which he writes a poem, a short story, or a letter to his aged mother, but not on this one. Now he will stick to his main intention. In the same way, a fiction writer at work on a novel may change his characters and plot a half dozen times along the way, and what had started as a comedy may end as a tragedy, or vice versa, but it is highly improbable that this writer will drift off into a legal brief, a poem, or even a letter to his own aged mother.

The main, the underlying, purpose of the lawyer is to write the brief. That of the novelist is to write a novel. The purpose underlies and conditions the process of the writing. It determines the kind of form and the kind of force appropriate in each instance. The form and force of a brief are different from those of a novel. The form and force of the brief are those appropriate to an argument. The form and force of the novel are those appropriate to a narrative.

The Four Kinds of Discourse

There are four basic natural needs that are fulfilled in discourse. We want to explain or inform about something. We want to convince somebody. We want to tell what a thing looked like—or sounded like, or felt like. We want to tell what happened.[1] These natural needs determine the four forms of discourse. Each need represents, then, an intention that is fulfilled in a particular kind of discourse.

The four kinds of discourse are exposition, argument, description, and narration.[2] Let us linger a little longer on the kind of intention that each represents.

In the first of these, exposition, the intention is to explain something,

---

[1] Somebody may well object that there are more than four natural needs—that when you hit your finger with a hammer you cry "ouch" or swear. But your exclamation is not discourse, it is an utterance. To look at the question from another angle, a discourse aims at communication, the utterance aims at mere expression. When you cry "ouch," you blow off steam without necessary reference to an audience.

[2] Persuasion, to which a separate chapter is given in this book, is commonly thought of under the mode of argument.

for instance, to make some idea clear to the reader, to analyze a character or situation, to define a term, to give directions. The intention, in short, is to inform.

In argument, the intention is to make somebody change his mind, his attitude, his point of view, or his feelings.[3]

In description, the intention is to make the reader as vividly aware as possible of what the writer has perceived through his senses (or in his imagination), to give him the "feel" of things described, the quality of a direct experience. The thing described may be anything that we can grasp through the senses, a natural scene, a city street, a cat or a racehorse, the face of a person, the sound of a voice, the texture of bark, the odor of an attic, a piece of music.

In narration, the intention is to present an event to the reader—what happened and how it happened. The event itself may be grand or trivial, a battle or a ball game, a presidential campaign or a picnic; but whatever it is, the intention of the writer is to give the impression of movement in time, to give some immediate impression of the event, the sense of witnessing an action.

Mixture of the kinds of discourse

We have commented on the four kinds of discourse as traditionally described in their pure form. We do, now and then, encounter an example in a relatively pure form. The excerpt from the theme whose author plans to be a teacher in a slum high school (p. 37) is primarily an argument, an argument between the student and his father. But more often we find the forms mixed, for instance, in the theme "Success and Uncle Conroy." There paragraph 1 is chiefly description, giving the picture of the old man as he now is. Paragraphs 2, 3, and 4 are primarily narration, and bits of narration appear even in paragraph 6, the conclusion. But is the main intention descriptive or narrative?

No, it is neither. If we look at paragraph 1, we find a question implied: Why should I admire the apparent failure, Uncle Conroy? The body of the theme answers that question, and the intention of doing so is what controls the description and narration. When we get to the conclusion we find that the author admires Uncle Conroy because he is a "success," but further, we find that the theme has been concerned with a distinction between what we may call a false success and a true success, the kind that Uncle Conroy has attained in the midst of his worldly failure.

In other words, the main intention of the theme is expository, and the descriptive and narrative elements are subordinate to that intention.

At this point the student may well ask: "What becomes of the notion of a kind of discourse as the main intention if the kinds are so mixed up in

---

[3] But see also Persuasion, pp. 238–74.

ordinary practice?" This is a reasonable question, and the answer to it is fundamental. In a good piece of writing the mixing of the kinds of discourse is never irresponsible. The class report will always be, by its very nature, a piece of exposition. The novel, no matter how much exposition, description, or argument it may contain, will always be primarily an example of narration. Certain instances, it is true, may not be as clear-cut as these. A magazine article on international affairs may seem to be primarily expository, but it may, in the end, aim to convince the reader of the need for a certain policy—and thus, by the main intention, be an argument. In fact, exposition and argument easily blend. Exposition is often the best argument, or exposition may have to resort to the kind of reasoning characteristic of argument, the reasoning from cause to effect or from evidence to conclusion.[4]

Sometimes we may even have to go outside a particular discourse and look at its context before we can be sure of the main intention. Let us suppose that a certain scientist is lecturing to his students. To them the chain of reasoning he presents is expository. Its purpose is to inform, to explain. But we can imagine the identical discourse, word for word, being given in a scientific congress with the purpose of argument. To label the discourse, then, we would have to know the occasion and context, and the motive.

Method of study

Though most writing does involve a mixture of the kinds of discourse, we can best study them in isolation, one by one, as we shall do in the five succeeding chapters.[5] We will analyze relatively pure examples in order to observe the types of organization appropriate to each kind of discourse. It is only after one understands the kinds of discourse in pure form that one can make them work effectively together in unity in a larger composition.

■ APPLICATIONS

I Try to label the dominant kind of discourse in each of the following selections. When there are intentions subordinate to the main intention, try to label them too.

A How can there fail to be unity in the achievement of all life, as there is in its chemical basis? Flowers have evolved their perfection of color, shape, and scent, insects their brilliance and intricacy of bodily form, birds their plumage and song, animals their strength and grace. Man has evolved his noble cultures and his troubled, imperfect soul, nourishing them upon the rest of creation.

---

[4] As we shall see, description and narration also naturally flow together.
[5] Argument and persuasion are usually lumped together as one form of discourse, but they are treated here in separate chapters.

If, as I believe, evolution has a purpose to achieve in the sense that the acorn is purposeful, then clearly there is an underlying power behind it of which all these manifestations are related parts. In the total picture there can be no absolute division between the feathers put out by a bird of paradise and the canvases filled in by painters; all are equally reactions of life expressing itself through the finest organizations of matter. I am certainly not inclined to minimize the importance of the human mind and its creative power; for me it is supreme so far as this small planet is concerned; but there is no impassable barrier between it and the rest of existence . . .

—Jacquetta Hawkes: *Man on Earth.*[6]

B   By reason of this tender rapport between commander and men, Lee is a greater legendary hero than the stern Stonewall Jackson, the brusque Sherman, the stolid Grant who sacrificed his hecatombs at Cold Harbor. Again, the only true analogy with Lee is Lincoln. The story of the sleeping sentinel had its Southern parallel. A private deserted the ranks to go home, after getting a distressful letter from his wife; he was arrested and sentenced to be shot. Lee pardoned him. And tradition said that the man later fell bravely in action, the last survivor at his gun. This final detail cannot be proved, but the popularity of the story is significant. It reveals that Lee, like Lincoln, became a symbol of clemency softening the horror of war. To the General, military discipline was more important than to the Union President; it is probable that sentiment has tended to exaggerate the gentleness of Lee. In the main, he regretted "the sad necessity" of shooting deserters, but agreed to that punishment—and saw it meted out more and more often, from the autumn of 1864 to the end of the war. Yet Lee did believe in giving deserters the benefit of the doubt, and once got up at 2:00 a.m. to intervene with President Davis because it had just occurred to Lee that a German deserter might not have understood the published orders. Also, in the early spring of 1865, sensing the imminent close of the war, Lee held up indefinitely the execution of Federal spies.

—Dixon Wecter: *The Hero in America.*[7]

C   Another, more ingenious theory, is that before the progenitor of man became a hunting ape, the original ape that had left the forests went through a long phase as an aquatic ape. He is envisaged as moving to the tropical sea-shores in search of food. There he will have found shellfish and other sea-shore creatures in comparative abundance, a food supply much richer and more attractive than that on the open plains. At first he will have groped around in the rock pools and the shallow water, but gradually he will have started to swim out to greater depths and dive for food. During this process, it is argued, he will have lost his hair like other mammals that have returned to the sea. Only his head, protruding from the surface of the water, would retain the hairy coat to protect him from the direct glare of the sun. Then, later on, when his tools (originally developed for cracking open shells) became sufficiently ad-

---

[6] From *Man on Earth*, by Jacquetta Hawkes. Reprinted by permission of A. D. Peters & Co.
[7] Reprinted with the permission of Charles Scribner's Sons from *The Hero in America*, pages 291–292, by Dixon Wecter. Copyright 1941 Charles Scribner's Sons; renewal copyright © 1969 Elizabeth Farrar Wecter.

vanced, he will have spread away from the cradle of the sea-shore and out into the open land spaces as an emerging hunter.

—Desmond Morris: *The Naked Ape.*[8]

D   This sea-marsh stretched for miles. Seaward, a grayness merging into sky had altogether rubbed out the line of dunes which bounded it that way: inland, another and darker blurred grayness was all you could see of the solid Welsh hills. But near by loomed a solitary gate, where the path crossed a footbridge and humped over the big dyke, and here in a sodden tangle of brambles the scent of a fox hung, too heavy today to rise or dissipate.

The gate clicked sharply and shed its cascade as two men passed through. Both were heavily loaded in oilskins. The elder and more tattered one carried two shotguns, negligently, and a brace of golden plover were tied to the bit of old rope he wore knotted about his middle: Glimpses of a sharp-featured weather-beaten face showed from within his bonneted sou'wester, but mouth and even chin were hidden in a long weeping mustache. The younger man was springy and tall and well-built and carried over his shoulder the body of a dead child. Her thin muddy legs dangled against his chest, her head and arms hung down his back; and at his heels walked a black dog—disciplined, saturated, and eager.   —Richard Hughes: *The Fox in the Attic.*[9]

II   Read "Adolescence: Self-Definition and Conflict," by Edgar Z. Frieden-berg (pp. 712–21). This essay is basically expository, but some attitude is being argued for. State the argument in your own words. What evidence does Friedenberg offer?

---

[8] From *The Naked Ape* by Desmond Morris. Copyright 1968. Used with permission of McGraw-Hill Book Company. Reprinted by permission of Jonathan Cape Ltd.
[9] Reprinted from *The Fox in the Attic*, by Richard Hughes, by permission of David Higham.

CHAPTER 5

The Methods of Exposition

The word *exposition* quite literally means to set forth a subject. It appeals to the understanding. Argument also appeals to the understanding, but it does so, not to explain something, but to convince the reader of the truth or desirability of something. Description and narration may, of course, lead to understanding, but their special appeal is to the imagination, to the reader's capacity for re-creating in his mind the immediate qualities of an object or event.

Exposition is the most common kind of writing, for it is applicable to any task that challenges the understanding—the definition of a word, the way to a street address, the structure of a plant, the mechanism of a watch, the cause of a historical event, the motive of an act, the meaning of a philosophy.

When we study the methods of exposition, we are simply studying some of the ways our minds naturally work. We are not following an arbitrary scheme; we are following the ways in which we ordinarily observe and reason about our world. We are doing systematically something that ordinary living, in its hit-or-miss, unsystematic fashion, forces on us, quite naturally, all the time.

Interest

A piece of exposition may be regarded as the answer to a question. If a specific question has been asked—"Why are you majoring in chemistry?" or "What were the causes of the American Revolution?"—it is rather easy to frame an answer that does not waver too badly from the point. The question controls the answer.

If, however, we set out to write a piece of exposition simply because we feel that a subject is engrossing or important, we are very likely to give a wandering and confused account. Our vague feelings will not be enough to guide us. Much in the way we went about locating a "true subject" in a general one (pp. 12–13), we must decide what specific question may be taken as our concern. The question sharpens to a focus the *interest* the subject holds for us.

The question will govern our answer.

Let us draw up an informal list to suggest at least some of the kinds of interests that exposition may satisfy:

1   What is it?
2   What does it mean?
3   What does it do?
4   How is it put together?
5   How does it work?
6   What was it intended to do?
7   How did it come to be this way?
8   When did it occur, or exist?
9   Why, or how, did it occur, or exist?
10   What is it good for?
11   What is its importance?
12   How well does it fulfill its function, or purpose?

Naturally, not all of these questions would be appropriate for the same subject. If we are trying to explain the nature of a triangle, we would scarcely ask when it occurred, since the nature of a triangle—what makes a figure a triangle and not something else—has no reference to time at all. Or if we are discussing a railroad wreck, we would scarcely ask how well it fulfilled its purpose. It would be appropriate, however, to ask how or why it occurred.

At first glance, we may add, some of these questions may seem too obvious or trivial to provide the basis for a discussion. For instance, the questions "What is it?" and "When did it occur?" ordinarily demand only the briefest answer. But if we ask the former question with reference to a complicated concept such as democracy, we may wind up with a book. Or if we ask the latter question with reference to the existence of the dinosaur, we may well have to go into an elaborate account of methods of geological dating.

Question and proposition

In a discussion of any length we commonly find more than one question involved. There is the main question, which represents the main interest, but to get a satisfactory answer to that, perhaps other questions must be asked and answered along the way. So we encounter again the problems of unity and coherence.

The main question must govern the whole. And we may think of the answer to the main question as giving the proposition, the thesis, the governing idea of the discussion. For instance, a historian, in answering the question "Why did it occur?" about the American Revolution, might come up with this answer to serve as his proposition: "The causes of the American Revolution were primarily economic." He might proceed to do a book offering a very elaborate analysis of the background of the event, but this proposition would control the whole work.

● CAUTION

The list of questions offered above must not be taken as complete. It merely suggests the kinds of interest that exposition may be used to satisfy—or, to put it differently—the kinds of question that a "thing," anything, an idea, an object, an event, may provoke in our minds.

More emphatically, these questions are not to be taken as necessarily corresponding to particular methods of exposition—though some of them may happen to do so.

The purpose of the list is to suggest ways in which you may regard a general subject and bring it to focus.

■ APPLICATIONS

I Can you add to the list of guiding questions given above?

II Below is a list of general subjects. What questions, including, if relevant, some from your additional list, would you think appropriate for any five of these subjects:

Going steady	Fraternities
College reformers	The honor system
Drinking	Abraham Lincoln
The Catholic (or other) Church	The San Francisco earthquake
The theory of relativity	The "new mathematics"
The concept of justice	Dogs

An example: dogs

A student who is particularly fond of dogs takes that subject as one to frame questions about. His questions are:

1 What is a dog?
2 How did it come to be as it is today?
3 What is it good for?

When he comes to write a theme, he toys with the idea of making the first question his topic, thinking that he might use a zoological classification as the basis of his work. But this seems too mechanical and dull. Then he thinks he might answer the question with some such title as "Man's Best Friend," but this strikes him as even duller. The second question appears more promising. He is really a fanatic about dogs and has read everything he can get his hands on; so he considers the possibility of writing on the evolution of the dog and the development of the two basic types, the wolf-dog and the jackal-dog. But he decides that this would not give him much opportunity for originality, for any personal touches. The third question leads him to consider the various kinds of work that dogs may be bred or trained to do. He is about to drop this subject, when suddenly, he gets his idea. He will write on training. He begins to jot down his ideas as a basis for an outline.

His preliminary jottings begin like this:

> where start—name, come, stand, heel, sit, wait
> time factor—when puppy—repetition—patience—

The word *patience* gives him another idea. He sees how boring a theme would be that merely lists the methods of teaching a dog, for there would be little variety in the actual process of teaching. But with the idea of patience, interest switches to the teacher. He now jots down:

> patience—imagination—put self in dog's place—be fair—be consistent—

He knows that he now has the true subject for his theme: the qualities necessary to a good trainer. He sets up a scratch outline:

I. *Introduction*
II. *Body*
    A. Sympathy—friendliness—start early to gain his confidence
    B. Patience—dog learns only by repetition—not lose temper
    C. Imagination—put self in dog's place
    D. Consistency—signal always same—never change mind—firmness in demands
    E. Fairness—most important—dog wants appreciation most of all—not bribery—no irrational punishment—*never lose temper*

III. *Conclusion*
   Training brings out best in dog

The student has no idea for the introduction and therefore starts with the main discussion. Having finished that to his satisfaction, he returns to the introduction. After several false starts, he decides simply to give a personal background for the theme. He writes that introduction, then jumps to the end and flings down his one-sentence conclusion. So we have:

TRAINING A DOG

I have always liked dogs. I come by this naturally, for my father is crazy about them too, not only his hunting dogs, but other kinds as well. We have always had a half dozen or so around the house, and my father and I like nothing better than talking about dogs, or reading about them, or going to dog shows. Dogs are a fascinating subject to us. One of the most fascinating things is to raise and train a dog. You really feel, then, that it is yours.

For the best results you have to start to train a dog young. I always feel, as a matter of fact, that you ought to start when the dog is only a puppy. It is true that the puppy can't learn, but you set up some kind of confidence, and the puppy gets to recognize and like you. This makes things easier later.

To train a dog you need several qualities. You must be patient. You must put yourself in the dog's place. You must be consistent. You must be fair.

A dog can learn only by constant repetition. It is boring for a human being to go over and over the same simple thing, but you have to realize that this boredom is the price you pay for a good dog. You have to be patient and never let your boredom show. And you must never lose your temper.

This leads to the second thing, putting yourself in the dog's place. You have to sympathize with him. If you do, you will not be irritated. You will feel how hard it is for the animal to understand your wishes and how dependent he is on you.

It is obvious why you have to be consistent. The dog understands you only when your word or signal is exactly the same as before. If you are inconsistent, he gets confused. For the same reason you must never change your mind. Once you give an order, stick to it, even if it was a bad order. Your word must be law, or you are wasting your breath.

Fairness is important always, but especially in training. You have to show the dog that you appreciate him, and once he gets this point, he wants nothing more than to please you. There is no use bribing a dog to obey. You have to make him want to please you, and the only way is by fairness. As for punishment, there is no use in punishing the dog if he doesn't know why he is being punished. You should always punish him immediately after the misbehavior, and you should always use the same punishment for the same kind of misbehavior. But don't lose your temper.

Training brings out the best in a dog and is worth all the time it takes.

On reflection, the student finds the conclusion skimpy and graceless. He wants something rather similar in tone to the introduction, which he now looks at again. The word *father* in the first sentence reminds him of something else his father has said and suggests his conclusion. The new conclusion is personal; it balances the introduction and is directly tied to the introduction by the reference to the father. The conclusion now reads:

> Training brings out the best in a dog and is worth all the time it takes. But my father says something else in addition. He says that when you train a dog you are training yourself, too. You teach yourself more than you teach the dog. My father says that you cannot learn too much patience and sympathy, consistency and fair play, and so you ought always to be training a dog just to learn to control yourself.

The theme has some repetitiousness, the phrasing is occasionally vague, and the organization in the next to last paragraph is a little fuzzy. But the writer has intelligently located his true subject, which gives his theme unity; he has a clear system of organization for the main body (the listing and discussion of the qualities of the trainer), which gives his theme coherence; and he has a sensible conclusion, which carries a little agreeable surprise with it (not the dog but the man learns most from the training process).

Multiple interests

The author of the theme on the training of dogs located and followed through one interest in his theme about dogs. This *main interest* gave him his subject. A writer may, however, appeal to more than one interest in the same composition, and in any extended discussion he is almost certain to do so. But in so doing he must be careful to keep the interests distinct. He must develop each interest at a different stage in his overall treatment. He must be sure that all the interests to which he appeals are related to the main interest of the composition and are subordinated to it. He must be sure that the main interest dominates and permeates the whole.

Here is a student theme involving several interests:

LINDBERGH: BEING OR DOING

When I was a senior in high school, I was interested in nothing but space. While the first moon-landing was on TV, I couldn't eat or sleep. Later, when the splashdown came, even my father let out a deep breath and said: "Lord, that's as great as Lindbergh!"

I asked who Lindbergh was.

"He flew the Atlantic," my father said.

That didn't sound so big right then with the moon-landing, but I was polite enough to ask whether the Atlantic had been flown before. When my father said

1. This introduction may be out of proportion, but it is systematic. The first interest is merely in the short scene between father and son, but this leads to the main interest, that is, the meaning of the title: "being or doing."

yes, I said that I didn't see what was so great about this Lindbergh.

"There's such a thing as being as well as doing," my father said, and looked at me as though he couldn't decide why I was so stupid. Then he walked out of the room.

That is how I came to investigate Lindbergh, and got hooked on him. It is true that he wasn't the first to fly the Atlantic. There had been sixty-seven men before him, even though nobody had soloed. In 1927 a prize of $25,000 was offered for a solo flight, and six men had died trying. As a matter of fact, it took some nerve to fly at all in those days, and Lindbergh, only twenty-five years old, had already had to bail out four times. But he became a hero not just because he was brave. The six dead men had done a brave deed, too, and a week later nobody knew their names. They were heroes, but what you might call heroes in a strictly private way. Something else went into making Lindbergh a hero to all the world.

One thing, of course, was that he did fly the Atlantic. Doing that was important, for a hero has to "do." But it was important, too, that he was a "sleeper" or "dark horse." Admiral Byrd, who was already famous, was all set and waiting for good weather. Then all at once there was a young fellow up in the air heading out. He was from somewhere in the Middle West; nobody had ever heard of him a week before; he lived off stale sandwiches and chocolate bars; he was grease monkey to his own plane. There he was out over all that water, by himself, wearing his good suit, an old blue serge that needed cleaning and pressing, the sort a poor farmer keeps to wear to church and funerals.

It looked for a while as though there might be a funeral back in the Middle West, but without the guest of honor. The plane was sighted over Newfoundland. Then there was no more news. Lindbergh was heading along the Great Circle, as they call the Northern route, and fog and sleet had settled in. But on the second day, late, he picked up the coast of Europe, and at 10 P.M., he was getting out of his plane at the Paris airport and trying to explain that he was Lindbergh. As though that howling mob there didn't know!

All Europe went wild, and there he was in his beat-up blue serge and his hair needed combing. He hadn't even brought pajamas, and the Ambassador had to lend him some. America went wild, too, and sent

2. With this paragraph, we have, as a threshold interest, the state of aviation at the time of Lindbergh's flight, but it leads to another concern: What beyond courage is required of a hero?

3. This paragraph begins to answer the question asked above: it introduces an element of dramatic surprise, the "sleeper," the "dark horse," as opposed to the expected performance of Byrd. Also, we are following bit by bit the interest in the Lindbergh story. Meanwhile, the reference to the "old blue serge" prepares for a return to the theme of "being" versus "doing."

4. Primarily narrative interest, but ending with the world's appreciation of the "dark horse."

5. More of the "dark horse" interest, the blue serge suit, and so forth, but moving toward the statement in the conclusion. The details of narrative interest continue.

a cruiser to bring him home. He was made a colonel in the Air Force, and a dress uniform was sent out three hundred miles to meet the cruiser. When he stepped on the pier at New York, he was wearing the old blue serge.

That told the story. He was himself. There were $5,000,000 in offers waiting for him, but he took only straight, legitimate offers concerned with aviation, for that was his passion. This gets back to "doing" and "being." Lindbergh had done a lot for himself with his hard work, study, and self-discipline, and he had done a lot for his country and aviation. Certainly he was brave. But what sticks in your mind is the fellow alone in the fog and the sleet—just himself. And the fellow stepping down from the plane in his old blue serge. This sense of Lindbergh as a human being—as a man who was not afraid just to be himself—is what we remember. And this fact of being "yourself," as somehow over against and separate from what the world is and expects, may be the biggest thing necessary to being remembered, in the end, as a real hero.

6. The conclusion continues the narrative interest, but focuses more on the character of Lindbergh, thus setting up the final statement: the significance of "being"— over against and separate from the world.

■ APPLICATIONS

I Read "Conflict of Generations," by Lewis S. Feuer (pp. 699–711) or "The Anatomy of Academic Discontent," by Bruno Bettelheim (pp. 734–45). What is the main interest of the article you have chosen? What are the subsidiary interests? Can you state how each subsidiary interest is related to the main interest?

II Below is a list of general subjects. Select three that seem fruitful to you (or take three of your own), and for each state an interest that might give you a true subject. Then take one of the true subjects you have prepared and try to work out the pattern for a theme with the true subject as the main interest and other subjects as subsidiary interests. Try to specify the relations the subsidiary interests would bear to the main interest. Now prepare a full sentence outline for such a theme.

Space exploration
Popular music of today and yesterday
Television
Camping
The crisis in the cities
The variety of religious beliefs

Cooking: art or science?
Newspapers
Women's fashions
Basketball versus football as a
    national sport

The methods of exposition

We shall now study the methods of exposition: identification, comparison and contrast, illustration, classification, definition, and analysis. These are the ways in which we go about answering questions that demand exposition. But as we have pointed out above, this statement does not mean that there is a method to correspond to each question on our list. Some methods may be used in answering more than one question, and the answer to a single question may sometimes be arrived at by a combination of methods.

Almost any discourse—for example, an editorial, an essay, a theme, a chapter in a textbook—will probably use more than one expository method. As a matter of fact, we rarely find a method in its pure state. But here, where we are trying to understand the nature of each method, we shall be concerned with relatively pure examples.

The First Method: Identification

Identification is the simplest way of answering the question: "What is it?" It is a kind of pointing by means of language. "Who is Mrs. Bertrand Smith?" somebody asks, and the answer is, "Oh, she is the blond woman in the black dress, sitting to the right of the white-haired old man." The reply has in effect pointed a finger at Mrs. Smith. But perhaps Mrs. Smith is not there to be pointed at. In that case, the answer may be, "She is the woman who won the city golf tournament last year and then married the son of old Jason Smith, the banker." In either case the answer places the subject, Mrs. Smith, in a context so that she can be identified.

We constantly use such casual forms of identification in conversation. But we can use the same method in writing. For example, we can begin an article on the Carmel Mission by writing: "The Carmel Mission stands just outside the village of Monterey, California. It was founded by Padre Junipero Serra, who had come up from San Diego in the year 1770." We have thus identified the subject. Such a method might be considerably elaborated, though in this process it would tend to absorb, or be absorbed by, other methods of exposition. The main thing to remember is that in using identification the writer makes a kind of frame or chart in which to locate the item that needs to be identified.

The Second Method: Comparison and Contrast

It is natural for us, in confronting an unfamiliar object, to set it against the familiar. We instinctively want to know in what ways it is like the familiar and in what ways different. This is a simple, and essential, way of sorting out our experience of the world.[1]

A child asks, "What is a zebra?" We reply, "Oh, a zebra—it's an animal sort of like a mule, but it's not as big as a mule. And it has stripes like a tiger, black and white stripes all over. But you remember that a tiger's stripes are black and orange." Here we have used both comparison and contrast. We have compared the shape of the zebra to that of the mule, but have contrasted the two animals in size. And we have compared the stripes of the zebra to the stripes of a tiger, but have contrasted them in color. If the child knows what mules and tigers are like, he now has a pretty good idea of a zebra.

The informal, instinctive use of comparison and contrast, as in the answer to the child's question, is useful; but we can make the method infinitely more useful in thinking and expressing ourselves, if we are systematic.

Kinds of purpose

To be systematic means, first of all, to understand the kinds of purpose for which comparison or contrast may be made.

We may distinguish three types of purpose. First, we may wish to present information about one item and may do so by relating it to another item with which our audience is familiar. For example, if we wish to explain the British Parliament to a fellow American, we may do so by comparing it with our Congress, which he does know about.

Second, we may wish to inform about both items, and proceed to do so by treating them in relation to some general principle that would apply to both and with which our audience is presumably familiar. For example, if we are reviewing two novels, neither of which our audience is acquainted with, we may compare and contrast them by reference to what we assume our audience knows about the principles of fiction.

Third, we may compare and contrast items with which our audience is familiar for the purpose of informing about some general principle or idea. For instance, if we want to give a notion of what religion is, we may compare and contrast several kinds, say Protestantism, Catholicism, Buddhism, and the religion of the Aztecs, to show what elements they have in common. In fulfilling this last purpose, we are, of course, using comparison and contrast as a way of proceeding from our examples to a general description of the class to which these examples belong. (See Argument, pp. 206–10.)

---

[1] Here we are speaking of comparison and contrast strictly as a method of exposition, but we should recognize that the instinctive need to make comparisons reaches in many other directions. For example, a poet making a comparison in a poem or a painter contrasting two forms in planning the composition of a picture would not be concerned at all with exposition as we are discussing it here. He would be acting from an appreciative or artistic motivation, as compared with an expository or scientific one. Again comparison and contrast are rich sources of humor. For these and related matters, see Metaphor (pp. 435–65) and Tone (pp. 466–506).

Area of interest: class

There is an amusing little scene (III, 2) in Shakespeare's play *Hamlet* in which the Prince baits the foolish old Polonius:

> HAMLET: Do you see yonder cloud that's almost in shape like a camel?
> POLONIUS: By the mass, and 'tis like a camel, indeed.
> HAMLET: Methinks it is like a weasel.
> POLONIUS: It is backed like a weasel.
> HAMLET: Or like a whale?
> POLONIUS: Very like a whale.

Part of the humor of the little scene comes from the fact that the comparisons Hamlet suggests and that the old simpleton accepts so seriously are meaningless and random. And this leads to our point that mere random similarities and differences are not very instructive. Our minds, in the casual exercise of the tendency toward comparisons, do throw off many casual and merely fanciful notions of resemblance or difference, and such notions may be humorous or poetic, but we learn no more from them than we learn about clouds, camels, weasels, and whales from Hamlet's baiting of Polonius.

We have said that comparison, to be useful, must be systematic; and one way to be systematic is to start with the realization that to be significant a comparison or contrast must be between two or more items within a special area of interest, two members, that is, of a group or class that is defined by a special interest brought to the material.[2] A zoologist, for example, may profitably compare and contrast a hawk and a garter snake, for he can place them both in the significant class of living creatures. An aeronautical engineer may compare the hawk and an airplane by putting them in the class of things that fly. But it isn't likely that he would find much profit in putting an airplane and a garter snake together, even for contrast.

Contrast, like comparison, is significant only when some common ground is recognized between the things contrasted—when they belong to the same significant class, the significance of the class depending upon the purpose of the contrast. For instance, it is not instructive to say that John's dog is wicked and is therefore in contrast to John, who is virtuous. The dog, unlike John, does not belong to the class of morally responsible creatures in which such a contrast would be significant. It would be nonsense to contrast them on this basis, for, in fact, a dog cannot be said to be wicked. But we can make sense of the contrast between the virtuous John and his wicked brother James.

---

[2] The idea of *class* in this sense will recur throughout this chapter, for we shall find thinking by classes a basic method in exposition.

Let us look at this as a picture:

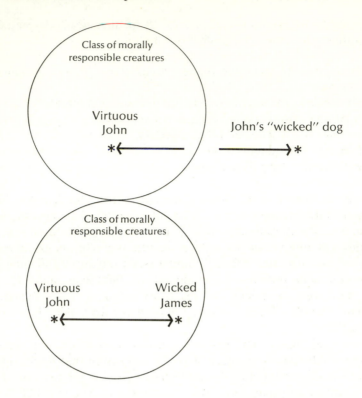

The nature of a class significant for a comparison or contrast is determined, we must always remember, by some interest we ourselves bring. Our interest defines the class. A farmer looking at a field thinks of the quality of the soil, the drainage, the exposure, and so on. That is, he puts the field in the class *arable land* and, on this basis, compares or contrasts it with other tracts he is acquainted with. But suppose that an infantry officer comes along and looks at the same field. He may well think of how a defensible position might be found here. That is, he would put the field in the class *defensible position*—a class determined by his special interest— and set it against other "positions" in the class.

We bring an interest to bear on an object or situation, but interests, of course, are variable. The military man, for example, may also be a farmer, and one moment he may regard the field as in the class *defensible position,* and the next, as in the class *arable land.* Or he may also be interested in painting, and at a particular moment, may think neither of crops nor of machine-gun emplacements, but of the color relations of the landscape.

Kinds of method

When we come to use comparison and contrast in extended form, we find that there are, broadly speaking, four ways of presenting material.

By the first method, we may fully present one item and then fully present the other, making continuous reference to the points of comparison or contrast. This method is, in general, appropriate when the points to be set against each other are fairly broad and obvious. By the second method, we present a part of one item and then a part of the second in relation to the corresponding part of the first item, until we have touched on all relevant parts. When a great many details are involved, this method is likely to be more useful than the first. By the third method, we present one item fully, and then, in presenting the second, refer, part by part, to the first item. Finally, by the fourth method, when a general principle is involved (as in the second and third of the types of general purpose mentioned on page 70), we can move from a statement of the principle to the process of comparison or contrast, or reversing the method, move through the process toward the principle. Sometimes, as we shall see, there may be a mixture of the methods.

■ APPLICATIONS

I Put five of the following sets of items into one or more significant classes, and give a few points of comparison or contrast for each set.

> Chess, bridge, and poker
> Mussolini and Julius Caesar
> Carpentry and writing verse
> President Andrew Johnson and President Lyndon B. Johnson
> The pictures an artist may see under the influence of drugs and those
>   he paints on his canvas
> Abraham Lincoln and John F. Kennedy
> New York and ancient Rome
> The poet and the advertising man

II Give five different sets of items for comparison or contrast and state your reasons for making each grouping.

III Look again at "The Reach of Imagination," by Jacob Bronowski (pp. 637–44), or "Conflict of Generations," by Lewis S. Feuer (pp. 699–711). In both you will find examples of comparison and contrast. For each instance what class is assumed? For what purpose is each comparison or contrast being made?

Examples of methods of organization

Here is a student theme written according to the first method:

MY CHILDHOOD

My father died when I was a small child, and I do not even remember him. I was raised by my mother and my maternal grandfather, in whose home we lived until I came to college. My mother loved her father, and I have no reason to think he did not love her, but they were so different that I was aware from the first of a conflict between them. Or, if it was not a direct conflict between them, it was a conflict between what they stood for. And both of them exerted a strong influence over me. Therefore, as I grow up, I think more and more about their contrasting personalities and values and try to detect in myself the traces of each of them. I do this because I am trying to understand myself.

My grandfather, whose name was Carruthers McKenzie, was of Scotch-Irish blood and belonged to the Presbyterian Church. He had a long, bony face, sunken cheeks, and a straggly beard. He was a man with an iron will if I ever saw one, and all of his way of life was one long discipline for himself and everybody about him. But it was a discipline chiefly for himself. He never spent a day in bed in his life until his last illness, and yet he was probably ill a good part of his life. After he died—and he died of a cancer of the stomach—the doctor told us that he could not understand how any man could keep on his feet so long without giving in to the pain.

There was discipline enough left over for my mother and me and the two hired hands who worked about the place. We had morning prayers and evening prayers. I had to read the Bible an hour a day and learn long passages by heart. My grandfather was a prosperous man, but I never had a nickel to spend which I had not earned, and his rates of payment for my chores were not generous. From the time I was eight, I had to study three hours in the afternoon and at least two hours at night, except for weekends. My grandfather never uttered a word of praise to me except now and then the statement, "You have done your duty." As one could guess, my grandfather never told jokes, was scrupulous about all kinds of obligations, never touched an alcoholic beverage or even soft drinks, and wore sober black, winter and summer.

My mother must have taken after her own mother, who was of South-German parentage and a Catholic by training. My mother's mother had given up her religion to marry my grandfather and had taken on his way of life, but she died very young. My mother was rather short in stature and had a rather full but graceful figure, the kind they call "partridge-y." She had round, pink cheeks and a complexion like a child's. She had blue eyes, very large. She loved to laugh and joke. My mother was a good mother, as the phrase goes; she loved me and she was careful of all my wants. But she also liked idleness. She would sit on the veranda half the afternoon and look across the yard, just rocking in her chair and enjoying the sunshine. And she went to bridge parties and even took an occasional glass of wine or, as I imagine, a highball. She was made for a good time and noise and people, and when my grandfather was out of the house, she used to romp and play with me or take me on long walks in the country back of our place.

When I was eighteen and went off to college, she got married. She married the kind of man you would expect her to pick. He is big and strong-looking, with a heavy, black mustache with a little gray in it. He smokes cigars and he likes fine whisky. He has a Cadillac agency in the city, and he keeps a little plane out at the airport. He loves sports and a good time. My mother has married exactly the man for her, I think, and I am enough like my mother to think he is fine, too. But as I look back on my grandfather—he died three years ago, when I was seventeen—I have a great admiration for him and a sneaking affection.

Here, in an excerpt from a discussion of English and American sportsmanship, is an example of the second method, which proceeds by a series of contrasts on different points of the items under discussion:

> Thanks to this universality of athletic sports, English training is briefer and less severe. The American makes, and is forced to make, a long and tedious business of getting fit, whereas an Englishman has merely to exercise and sleep a trifle more than usual, and this only for a brief period. Our oarsmen work daily from January to July, about six months, or did so before Mr. Lehmann brought English ideas among us; the English varsity crews row together nine or ten weeks. Our football players slog daily for six or seven weeks; English teams seldom or never "practice" and play at most two matches a week. Our track athletes are in training at frequent intervals throughout the college year and are often at the training table six weeks; in England six weeks is the maximum period of training, and the men as a rule are given only three days a week on the cinder track. To an American training is an abnormal condition; to an Englishman it is the consummation of the normal.
>
> —JOHN CORBIN: *An American at Oxford.*

The third method of organization appears in the following selection. First, one item of the comparison, General Grant, is given in full. Then General Lee is compared and contrasted, point by point, with Grant.

> Grant was, judged by modern standards, the greatest general of the Civil War. He was head and shoulders above any general on either side as an over-all strategist, as a master of what in later wars would be called global strategy. His Operation Crusher plan, the product of a mind which had received little formal instruction in the higher art of war, would have done credit to the most finished student of a series of modern staff and command schools. He was a brilliant theater strategist, as evidenced by the Vicksburg campaign, which was a classic field and siege operation. He was a better than average tactician, although, like even the best generals of both sides, he did not appreciate the destruction that the increasing firepower of modern armies could visit on troops advancing across open spaces.
>
> Lee is usually ranked as the greatest Civil War general, but this evaluation has been made without placing Lee and Grant in the perspective of

military developments since the war. Lee was interested hardly at all in "global" strategy, and what few suggestions he did make to his government about operations in other theaters than his own indicate that he had little aptitude for grand planning. As a theater strategist, Lee often demonstrated more brilliance and apparent originality than Grant, but his most audacious plans were as much the product of the Confederacy's inferior military position as of his own fine mind. In war, the weaker side has to improvise brilliantly. It must strike quickly, daringly, and include a dangerous element of risk in its plans. Had Lee been a Northern general with Northern resources behind him, he would have improvised less and seemed less bold. Had Grant been a Southern general, he would have fought as Lee did.

Fundamentally Grant was superior to Lee because in a modern total war he had a modern mind, and Lee did not. Lee looked to the past in war as the Confederacy did in spirit. The staffs of the two men illustrate their outlooks. It would not be accurate to say that Lee's general staff were glorified clerks, but the statement would not be too wide of the mark. Certainly his staff was not, in the modern sense, a planning staff, which was why Lee was often a tired general. He performed labors that no general can do in a big modern army—work that should have fallen to his staff, but that Lee did because it was traditional for the commanding general to do it in older armies. Most of Lee's staff officers were lieutenant-colonels. Some of the men on Grant's general staff, as well as on the staffs of other Northern generals, were major and brigadier generals, officers who were capable of leading corps. Grant's staff was an organization of experts in the various phases of strategic planning. The modernity of Grant's mind was most apparent in his grasp of the concept that war was becoming total and that the destruction of the enemy's economic resources was as effective and legitimate a form of warfare as the destruction of his armies. What was realism to Grant was barbarism to Lee. Lee thought of war in the old way as a conflict between armies and refused to view it for what it had become— a struggle between societies. To him, economic war was needless cruelty to civilians. Lee was the last of the great old-fashioned generals; Grant, the first of the great moderns.

—T. HARRY WILLIAMS: *Lincoln and His Generals.*[3]

Here is another example of the second and third method of organization, in an extended contrast between two types into which the author would divide humanity, the "Red-bloods" and the "Mollycoddles."

We have divided men into Red-bloods and Mollycoddles. "A Red-blood man" is a phrase which explains itself; "Mollycoddle" is its opposite. We have adopted it from a famous speech by Mr. Roosevelt [Theodore Roosevelt], and redeemed it—perverted it, if you will—to other uses. A few examples will make the notion clear. Shakespeare's Henry V is a typical Red-blood; so was Bismarck; so was Palmerston; so is almost any business-

[3] From *Lincoln and His Generals,* by T. Harry Williams. Copyright 1952 by Alfred A. Knopf, Inc. Reprinted by permission of the publisher. Reprinted by permission of Hamish Hamilton, Ltd.

man. On the other hand, typical Mollycoddles were Socrates, Voltaire, and Shelley. The terms, you will observe, are comprehensive and the types very broad. Generally speaking, men of action are Red-bloods. Not but what the Mollycoddles may act, and act efficiently. But, if so, the Mollycoddle acts from principle, not from the instinct for action. The Red-blood, on the other hand, acts as the stone falls, and does indiscriminately anything that comes to hand. It is thus that he carries on the business of the world. He steps without reflection into the first place offered him and goes to work like a machine. The ideals and standards of his family, his class, his city, his country, his age, he swallows as naturally as he swallows food and drink. He is therefore always "in the swim"; and he is bound to "arrive," because he has set before him the attainable. You will find him everywhere in all the prominent positions. In a military age he is a soldier, in a commercial age a businessman. He hates his enemies, and he may love his friends; but he does not require friends to love. A wife and children he does require, for the instinct to propagate the race is as strong in him as all other instincts. His domestic life, however, is not always happy; for he can seldom understand his wife. This is part of his general incapacity to understand any point of view but his own. He is incapable of an idea and contemptuous of a principle. He is the Samson, the blind force, dearest to Nature of her children. He neither looks back nor looks ahead. He lives in present action. And when he can no longer act, he loses his reasons for existence. The Red-blood is happiest if he dies in the prime of life; otherwise, he may easily end with suicide. For he has no inner life; and when the outer life fails, he dies too. Nature, who has blown through him, blows elsewhere. His steps are numb; he is dead wood on the shore.

The Mollycoddle, on the other hand, is all inner life. He may indeed act, as I said, but he acts, so to speak, by accident; just as the Red-blood may reflect, but reflects by accident. The Mollycoddle in action is the Crank; it is he who accomplishes reforms; who abolished slavery, for example, and revolutionized prisons and lunatic asylums. Still, primarily, the Mollycoddle is a critic, not a man of action. He challenges all standards and all facts. If an institution is established, that is a reason why he will not accept it; if an idea is current, that is a reason why he should repudiate it. He questions everything, including life and the universe. And for that reason Nature hates him. On the Red-blood she heaps her favors; she gives him a good digestion, a clear complexion, and sound nerves. But to the Mollycoddle she apportions dyspepsia and black bile. In the universe and in society the Mollycoddle is "out of it" as inevitably as the Red-blood is "in it." At school, he is a "smug" or a "swat," while the Red-blood is captain of the Eleven. At college, he is an "intellectual," while the Red-blood is in the "best set." In the world, he courts failure while the Red-blood achieves success. The Red-blood sees nothing; but the Mollycoddle sees through everything. The Red-blood joins societies; the Mollycoddle is a non-joiner. Individualist of individualists, he can stand alone, while the Red-blood requires the support of a crowd. The Mollycoddle engenders ideas, and the Red-blood invents. The whole structure of civilization rests on foundations laid by Mollycoddles; but all the building is done by Red-bloods. The Red-blood despises the Mollycoddle, but, in the long run, he does what the Mollycoddle tells him. The Mollycoddle also despises the Red-blood, but he cannot do without him. Each thinks he is master of the other, and, in a sense, each is right. In his lifetime the Mollycoddle may be the slave of the Red-blood; but after his death, he is his master, though the Red-blood may know it not.

Nations, like men, may be classified roughly as Red-blood and Mollycoddle. To the latter class belong clearly the ancient Greeks, the Italians, the French and probably the Russians; to the former the Romans, the Germans, and the English. But the Red-blood nation *par excellence* is the American; so that in comparison with them, Europe as a whole might almost be called Mollycoddle. This characteristic of Americans is reflected in the predominant physical type—the great jaw and chin, the huge teeth, the predatory mouth; in their speech, where beauty and distinction are sacrificed to force; in their need to live and feel and act in masses. To be born a Mollycoddle in America is to be born to a hard fate. You must either emigrate or succumb. This, at least hitherto, has been the alternative practiced. Whether a Mollycoddle will ever be produced strong enough to breathe the American atmosphere and live, is a crucial question for the future. It is the question whether America will ever be civilized. For civilization, you will have perceived, depends on a just balance of Red-bloods and Mollycoddles. Without the Red-blood there would be no life at all, no stuff, so to speak, for the Mollycoddle to work upon; without the Mollycoddle, the stuff would remain shapeless and chaotic. The Red-blood is the matter, the Mollycoddle the form; the Red-blood the dough, the Mollycoddle the yeast. On these two poles turns the orb of human society. And if, at this point, you choose to say that the poles are points and have no dimensions, that strictly neither the Mollycoddle nor the Red-blood exists, and that real men contain elements of both mixed in different proportions, I have no quarrel with you except such as one has with the man who states the obvious. I am satisfied to have distinguished the ideal extremes between which the Actual vibrates. The detailed application of the conception I must leave to more patient researchers.

—G. LOWES DICKINSON: "Red-bloods and Mollycoddles," *Appearances*.[4]

For an excellent example of comparison according to the fourth method (the purpose being to treat a number of items to arrive at a general principle) see "America's New Culture Hero," by Robert Brustein (pp. 139–41). The fact that this essay is used there as an example of analysis suggests how the methods of exposition often overlap.

■ APPLICATIONS

I We have distinguished the various methods of organization for comparison and contrast (p. 73). In the selection that discusses "Red-bloods" and "Mollycoddles," each of the first two paragraphs is a fairly clear example of

[4] From *Appearances* by G. Lowes Dickinson. Copyright 1914 by G. Lowes Dickinson. Reprinted by permission of Doubleday & Company, Inc.

a simple method. Define the method of each. But how is the third paragraph organized? Do you think that the third paragraph is an example of clear organization, or do you find it somewhat confused?

II Work out in the form of sentence outlines the points of comparison or contrast for three of the following pairs. (Or use some pairs of your own making.) Be sure to make clear the purpose of each comparison or contrast you set up and the significant class involved in each.

> Catholicism and Protestantism
> Two novels
> Two people you know
> Jack Uptight and Joe Downloose
> Poor relations and rich relations
> Schools for boys (or girls) only and coeducational schools
> A student's life at home and in a dormitory
> My mother's temperament and my father's
> Nicotine and alcohol
> The value of a liberal arts education and that of a scientific education

III In a single paragraph not shorter than 150 words, develop each of the outlines you have prepared. In each use a different method of presentation.

IV Return to "Freedom and the Control of Men," by B. F. Skinner (pp. 644–51) and "The Abolition of Man," by C. S. Lewis (pp. 651–57). Write a paragraph in which you contrast the basic ideas of the two essays.

The Third Method: Illustration

Our conversation is full of phrases like "for example" and "for instance" and "for illustration." Our use of illustration is as instinctive as that of comparison and contrast. But in illustration the mind operates somewhat differently. Both comparison and illustration, it is true, involve thinking in terms of class and particular items, but the characteristic relations are different. In comparison and contrast, as we have seen, two or more particular items in a significant class are set against each other. In illustration, we cite the particular item (or items) to clarify the nature of a class in which it is included.

Here, "for example," is how the method works:

> If anyone wants to exemplify the meaning of the word "fish," he cannot choose a better animal than a herring. The body, tapering to each end, is covered with thin, flexible scales, which are very easily rubbed off. The taper head, with its underhung jaw, is smooth and scaleless on the top; the large eye is partly covered by two folds of transparent skin, like

eyelids—only immovable and with the slit between them vertical instead of horizontal; the cleft behind the gill-cover is very wide, and, when the cover is raised, the large red gills which lie underneath it are freely exposed. The rounded back bears the single moderately long dorsal fin about its middle.   —THOMAS HENRY HUXLEY: "The Herring."

We may indicate by a diagram what Huxley has done:

Bass
Trout   Pickerel
Bream   Perch
Salmon
Weakfish
Flounder, etc.
Herring

"to exemplify the meaning of the word fish,
he cannot choose a better animal than a herring"

We have said that the relation of the particular to the class is fundamental to the process of illustration. But what of the fact that here the species *herring* (which of course is a group, or class, of fish) appears as a particular? The point is that though *herring* is a class, it is being used to explain a more inclusive class *fish:* the characteristic movement from the particular to the general, to the class, is observed. What is important is that the particular— be it individual or group—must be truly included in the class and must truly represent the relevant qualities of that class.

The particular and its irrelevant qualities: interest

When Huxley uses a species as his particular, it is implied that any individual herring would possess the relevant qualities. Certainly, there are differences among individual herring—size, weight, and so forth—but these differences are not among the essential characteristics that set off the species herring from other species of fish. So Huxley, for all practical purposes, is referring to any herring.

But let us jump from fish to men. We think of the class *man,* but we also recognize the individuality of any member of that class we encounter— the postman, our sister, a stranger on the street, anybody. In addition to the qualities any individual member of the class *man* must have in order to be a member of that class, he has an infinite number of other qualities that are irrelevant to the class but constitute aspects of his individuality.

If, then, we are to use Mr. Jones as an illustration of the class *banker,* we have to think of him as Mr. Jones—the individual—at the same time that we think of him as a typical banker. Otherwise we are not using Mr. Jones as an example, we are merely using an abstract scheme that we happen to label Mr. Jones. The individualizing—and irrelevant—qualities contribute essentially to what we may call the dramatic tension at the heart of the intellectual act of illustration. The interest of an illustration lies in a tension between the relevant and the irrelevant. As writer or reader, we may become enthralled with the particular for its very particularity, but at the same time we must maintain our concern for the relations of the particular to the class.

● CAUTION

Writing a good piece of illustration is like walking a tightrope. You can fall on either side.

Notice how the author of the following selection about the great Western gunman Billy the Kid has balanced, and interwoven, relevant and irrelevant qualities to create a greater interest:

The secret of Billy the Kid's greatness as a desperado—and by connoisseurs in such matters he was rated as an approach to the ideal desperado type—lay in a marvellous coordination between mind and body. He had not only the will but the skill to kill. Daring, coolness, and quick thinking would not have served unless they had been combined with physical quickness and a marksmanship which enable him to pink a man neatly between the eyes with a bullet, at, say, thirty paces. He was not pitted against six-shooter amateurs but against experienced fighters themselves adept in the handling of weapons. The men he killed would have killed him if he had not been their master in a swifter deadliness. In times of danger, his mind was not only calm but singularly clear and nimble, watching like a hawk for an advantage and seizing it with incredible celerity. He was able to translate an impulse into action with the suave rapidity of a flash of light. While certain other men were a fair match for him in target practice, no man in the Southwest, it is said, could equal him in the lightning-like quickness with which he could draw a six-shooter from its holster and with the same movement fire with deadly accuracy. It may be remarked incidentally that shooting at a target is one thing and shooting at a man who happens to be blazing away at you is something entirely different; and Billy the Kid did both kinds of shooting equally well.

His appearance was not unprepossessing. He had youth, health, good nature, and a smile—a combination which usually results in a certain sort of good looks. His face was long and colorless except for the deep tan with which it had been tinted by sun, wind, and weather and was of an asymmetry that was not unattractive. His hair was light brown, worn usually rather long and inclined to waviness. His eyes were gray, clear, and steady. His upper front teeth were large and slightly prominent and to an extent disfigured the expression of a well-formed mouth. His hands and feet were remarkably small. He was five feet eight inches tall, slender and well proportioned. He was unusually strong for his inches, having for a small man quite powerful arms and shoulders. He weighed, in condition, one hundred and forty pounds. When out on the range, he was as rough looking as any other cowboy. In towns, among the quality folk of the frontier, he dressed neatly and took not a little care in making himself personable. Many persons, especially women, thought him handsome. He was a great beau at fandangos and was considered a good dancer.

He had an air of easy, unstudied, devil-may-care insouciance which gave no hint of his dynamic energy. His movements were ordinarily deliberate and unhurried. But there was a certain element of calculation in everything he did. Like a billiardist who "plays a position," he figured on what he might possibly have to do next. This foresightedness and forehandedness even in inconsequential matters provided him with a sort of subconscious mail armor. He was forearmed even when not forewarned; forever on guard.

Like all the noted killers of the West, Billy the Kid was of the blond type. Wild Bill Hickok, Ben Thompson, King Fisher, Henry Plummer, Clay Allison, Wyatt Earp, Doc Holliday, Frank and Jesse James, the Youngers, the Daltons—the list of others is long—were all blond. There was not a pair of brown eyes among them. It was the gray and blue eyes that flashed death in the days when the six-shooter ruled the frontier. This blondness of desperados is a curious fact, contrary to popular imagination and the traditions of art and the stage. The theater immemorially has portrayed its unpleasant characters as black-haired and black-eyed. The popular mind associates swarthiness with villainy. Blue eyes and golden hair are, in the artistic canon, a sort of heavenly hallmark. No artist has yet been so daring as to paint a winged cherub with raven tresses, and a search of the world's canvases would discover no brown-eyed angel. It may be remarked further, as a matter of incidental interest, that the West's bad men were never heavy, stolid, lowering brutes. Most of them were good-looking, some remarkably so. Wild Bill Hickok, beau ideal of desperadoes, was considered the handsomest man of his day on the frontier, and with his blue eyes and yellow hair falling on his shoulders, he moved through his life of tragedies with something of the beauty of a Greek god. So much for the fact versus fancy. Cold deadliness in Western history seems to have run to frosty coloring in the eyes, hair, and complexion.

—WALTER NOBLE BURNS: *The Saga of Billy the Kid*.[5]

Method of presentation

Although illustration is, in its main intention, expository, we observe that in actual presentation other forms of discourse may be used. For instance, description appears in both the illustration of the herring and of Billy the Kid. In the next example, narration will be the method of pres-

---

[5] From *The Saga of Billy the Kid* by Walter Noble Burns. Copyright 1925, 1926 by Doubleday & Company, Inc.

entation. But before the narrative begins, the author indicates that he is basically concerned with the method of illustration, that his intention is expository. Before the narrative of the bear hunt by Eskimos begins, we find this conversation between the two hunters as they confront the bear:

> Shivering with the lust of the hunt Ernenek knelt beside him. "Let us set the dogs on him and finish quickly."
> Anarvik shook his head. "He might kill many dogs, and we have none to spare. No, Ernenek. Somebody [we] will get the bear in the usual, proven fashion."

Here Anarvik asserts, as it were, that the hunt will be an illustration of the "usual, proven fashion" of bear hunting. Let us chart the process:

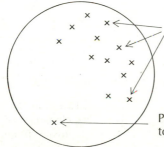

x ← All bear hunts not of the "usual, proven
x ← fashion"—not relevant, rejected by Anarvik
x ←
x ←

CLASS
All bear hunts using the
"usual, proven fashion"

All other bear hunts by Eskimos
using the "usual, proven fashion"

Particular hunt by Anarvik and Ernenek
to illustrate the usual fashion

Now the narrative begins:

> Circling and sniffling, the bear was slowly moving closer.
> With his flint knife Anarvik had carved a long splint from his whalerib bow and sharpened the ends. He coiled the splint in his hand and released it suddenly to test its resilience. Then he pulled out a chunk of blubber he had been warming within his clothes, against his stomach. He kneaded the blubber into a ball, swiftly, before it could freeze, and pressed the tightly coiled whalebone splint into it. The blubber ball hardened instantly on the ice.
> He began moving forward on all fours and the bear withdrew growling, with little jumps, throwing up his shaggy hindquarters and leering over his

shoulder. Anarvik stopped and called to him with motions and cooing sounds, and the bear returned tentatively, in a half-circle. Anarvik's sparse mustache quivered as he rolled the spring bait forcefully over the thin blanket of snow.

The yellow ball came to a halt a few paces from the bear. Puzzled, he approached cautiously, stretching out his nose forward and whimpering a little in uncertainty. Hunger told him to eat; another instinct, deeper and more mysterious, told him to distrust whatever came from those little beings, so frighteningly purposeful.

Anarvik waited flat and motionless, arms and legs spread out. Behind him Ernenek breathlessly watched the bear put out a long blue tongue and lick the bait, retire, lick again, and staunchly retire again. But it was impossible to resist temptation forever. Bears are only human. With a billowy movement, his snout suddenly shot forward and engulfed the bait, dropping it into the bottomless pit of his belly.

Simultaneously, Anarvik and Ernenek leaped to their feet with cheers and laughter, for the bear was theirs.

Almost.

At the men's sudden outburst the bear backed up. Mystified, he began to circle, then sat down on his haunches and studied them for a while. Finally, he began closing in.

The men were preparing to retreat when suddenly he jumped up and gave a long anguished moan that ran unchecked over the great sea, silencing the dogs, then bucked about and growled savagely.

"In his stomach the blubber has melted," cried Anarvik triumphantly. "And the blade has sprung open!"

All at once the bear turned on his heels and shuffled off yammering.

Dusk was dimming already, for day was short as yet, lighting the roof of the world for but a few hours with each turn of the sun. Without a word Anarvik and Ernenek gripped their spears and started after their quarry, glancing at each other and laughing, just laughing with the glee of the hunt, everything else forgotten.

Stumbling and wailing the bear drifted coastward, as the men moved to cut off his retreat toward the sea fields, his element and abode. After reaching the first foothills of the land he began to stop frequently and look over his shoulder to see if the chase was still on, threads of spittle dangling on his chest. His lair must be nearby, but he wouldn't lead the hunters there. Reluctantly he moved on, up the frozen hillsides.

The soles of his feet, covered with close-set hair, enabled him to walk securely on the ice, while the men's boots had a poor grip on the slippery slopes. And they had to take heed not to work themselves into a sweat, which meant freezing to death. But the bear's course was wayward and erratic and the men could keep up with him covering only half as much ground.

It grew colder on the heights, fifty or sixty below, and the beloved gale blew, and Anarvik and Ernenek were happy because they hunted. Never for an instant did they worry about the forsaken provisions, and the dogs and the woman. They were not hungry at the moment; the dogs were always hungry anyhow, whether they were fed or not; and the woman would manage somehow as women always did. This was the Hunt—the very essence of life.

They ate nothing but the bear's droppings that were streaked with blood, and after the beast was gutted of everything but fear and pain, and hunger came knocking at the walls of their stomachs, Ernenek said:

"Somebody is hungry." These were the first words spoken since the chase had started.

Anarvik nodded his agreement.

But never for a moment did they consider turning back.

When day had once more risen tentatively, a gale pouring from the Glacial Ocean churned up the shallow snow, turning the pallid heaven a murky gray, and for a space they lost sight of their quarry in the blinding blizzard and plunged forth in sudden alarm.

They were led back to the bear by his laments and almost crashed into him, and both men contrived to give him a good poke in the ribs with their horn-tipped spears to let him know he wasn't dreaming. A snarl of rage rose from the huge shadow fumbling upright in the snow swirl and drowned off in the wind, and from there on they stuck so close to their quarry that they could smell it—smell the bitter odor of fear emanating from its pelt.

A few times the bear wheeled about in rage and charged; they then waddled off in a hurry, whining in terror, stumbling and slipping down-hill, until the bear sat down on his haunches, wagging his head; and the instant danger was past, the men laughed.

The second night was the worst. The blizzard thickened, forcing them to follow the bear too close at the heels for comfort, and the pangs of hunger hammered with mounting intensity, weakening their knees and increasing the danger of perspiration, while the bear, that seemed to have a hundred lives, kept trekking his furious trek up and down the forbidding slopes. . . .

Once they came within a brief march of one of the meat caches which they kept scattered on land and sea.

"Maybe he goes off that way," Anarvik said. "Then one of us can get provisions."

They tried to drive the bear in the right direction, without success. He knew nothing about the cache. . . .

By this time the bear was very sick. In his lumbering fashion he jogged on laboriously, dragging on the ground a head that had grown too heavy.

Sometimes slipping and stumbling to their knees the men followed stonily, their laughter gone, the lines of strain marking their greased faces, their eyes red and rimmed with rime. Hunger had departed. Stomachs had gone to sleep. They did not even scoop up handfuls of snow any longer. Their mouths were set, their bellies forgotten, and in their very minds all thoughts and memories had perished. Between skin and flesh, fat had been burning away incessantly, unreplaced, their motion no longer warmed them and they shivered a little, the cold knifing noticeably down their throats with every breath.

And still, could there be anything greater than this—chasing the white bear over the top of the world?

The end came suddenly. All at once the bear gave up. As though he had decided that if he had to die he might as well die with dignity, he squatted on his hindquarters, put his forepaws in his lap, and waited. Round his neck was a pink napkin of frozen froth. He held his ears flat and his teeth bared as in a sneer. No longer did he cry. Only the white clouds of respiration came fast and raspy and his little bloodshot eyes moved helplessly.

The two men closed in slowly, Ernenek from the front and Anarvik from the side, ready to jump if he pawed. The bear grabbed Anarvik's spear and broke it like a straw the instant Ernenek speared him clean through the top of the throat, below the jaw, where the pelt was thinnest. . . .

—HANS RUESCH: *Top of the World*.[6]

In the following selection, which illustrates the concept of "neighborliness," narration is again the basic method:

A good neighbor, as the term was understood in the days when as a little girl I lived on a farm in Southern Michigan, meant all that nowadays is combined in corner store, telephone, daily newspaper, and radio. But your neighbor was also your conscience. You had to behave yourself on account of what the neighbors would think.

A good neighbor knew everything there was to know about you—and liked you anyway. He never let you down—as long as you deserved his good opinion. Even when you failed in that, if you were in trouble he would come to your rescue. If one of the family was taken sick in the night, you ran over to the neighbor's to get someone to sit up until the doctor arrived. Only instead of sending for the doctor, you went for him. Or one of the neighbors did.

The Bouldrys were that kind of neighbors. Lem Bouldry was a good farmer and a good provider. Mis' Bouldry kept a hired girl and Lem had two men the year round. They even had a piano while the most the other neighbors boasted was an organ or a melodeon. Mis' Bouldry changed her dress every afternoon (my mother did too; she said she thought more of herself when she did), and they kept the front yard mowed.

But the Covells were just the opposite—the most shiftless family the Lord ever let set foot on land. How they got along my father said he didn't know, unless it was by the grace of God. Covell himself was ten years younger than my father, yet everybody called him "Old Covell." His face and hands were like sole leather and if his hair had ever been washed, it was only when he got caught in a rainstorm. Father said Old Covell would borrow the shirt off your back, then bring it around to have it mended; Mother said, well, one thing certain, he wouldn't bring it around to be washed.

Yet the time Mis' Covell almost died with her last baby—and the baby did die—Mis' Bouldry took care of her; took care of the rest of the children too—four of them. She stayed right there in the Covell house, just going home to catch a little sleep now and then. She had to do that, for there wasn't so much as an extra sheet in the house, much less an extra bed.

And Mis' Bouldry wasn't afraid to use her hands even if she did keep a hired girl—she did all the Covells' washing herself.

But even Old Covell, despite his shiftlessness, was a good neighbor in one way: he was a master hand at laying out the dead. Of course, he wasn't worth a cent to sit up with the sick, for if it was Summer he'd go outside to smoke his pipe and sleep; and if it was Winter he'd go into the kitchen and stick his feet in the oven to warm them and go to sleep there. But a dead man seemed to rouse some kind of pride and responsibility in him. There was no real undertaker nearer than ten miles, and often the roads were impassable. Folks sent for my mother when a child or woman died, but Old Covell handled all the men. Though he never wore a necktie himself, he kept on hand a supply of celluloid collars and little black bow ties for the dead. When he had a body to lay out, he'd call for the deceased's best pants and object strenuously if he found a hole in the socks. Next, he'd polish the boots and put on a white shirt, and fasten one of his black ties to the collar button. All in all, he would do a masterly job.

Of course, nobody paid Old Covell for this. Nobody ever thought of paying for just being neighborly. If anybody had offered to, they'd have been snubbed for fair. It was just the way everybody did in those half-forgotten times. —DELLA T. LUTES: "Are Neighbors Necessary?"

Summary

1 The nature of the general governs the nature of the particular.
2 The particular must really belong to the class in question.

■ APPLICATIONS

I What touches in the bear hunt and in the illustration of neighborliness give vividness? Which of these touches are "irrelevant" (that is, are there merely for vividness), and which also indicate some relation to the class being illustrated?

II In the second selection, why do you think that the most worthless fellow in the community is used as the chief illustration of the idea of neighborliness?

III Make a diagram of the method used in the illustration of neighborliness.

An aside: humor and satire

Illustration is a method of exposition, and exposition has the purpose of explaining. But illustration, like some of the other methods of exposition, may also be used for fun—for humor or satire.

Here is a student theme using illustration. It takes Al Capone, the famous Chicago gangster of the prohibition era, as an example of the "great man."

A GREAT MAN

When I started to select a figure to illustrate the notion of a great man, I ran over a list including Alexander the Great, Julius Caesar, George Washington, Napoleon, and Abraham Lincoln, but decided against them all. Too dull, I thought. Everybody knows they are great, so what? The list needs fresh blood.

To be sure of my ground, I drew up the qualifications for a spot on the ticket of greatness. To really qualify you have to be something of a surprise, to upset expectations. The cash customer loves that. The ugly duckling story, that's what we all want, for we figure ourselves as the ugly duckling just not quite ready to turn into a swan. That is why "poppa's boy" can never be quite tops in greatness. It upsets the script. That's why Alexander the Great never really comes to a boil on my stove. Poppa Philip had got the phalanx all fixed and ready for him. Some may object that Caesar also started in a great family. But everybody thought he was just a playboy, with perfume on his hair. Nobody expected him to deliver. This ugly duckling act, this is where Napoleon shines—the little bow-legged runt alone down in the corner of the school yard, not even able to speak proper French, not a sou in his pocket, every centimeter a born loser, a joke.

So along this line, I remembered Al Capone, whose acquaintance I first made on a TV rerun of a great old movie, "Scarface." Well, Al was born in a Sicilian slum in NYC, nothing but a tin spoon in his mouth, and that with a bent handle; he grew up with not a dime in his pocket, and his non-"good-looks" were spoiled early before he got proficient at knife-dodging. A knife took a slice off one cheek and gave him the name Scarface. A perfect ugly duckling.

Having a sense of history, they say, is another qualification for greatness. Al had it. Prohibition became the law, and he said that if the law makes booze illegal, somebody will have to make and market a lot of illegal booze. The man and the hour had met.

Al had another qualification for greatness: vision, as they call it. He did not see any percentage in just controlling the market in half of Chicago. Why not all Chicago? And then, like Alexander, Lenin, and Hitler, tomorrow the world? He dreamed big.

A cause bigger than the self, that is necessary for greatness, and nobody can say Al Capone, alias "Scarface," didn't have a cause bigger than he was. He had it, and he stood ready to give his all for it. In contrast to Al's devotion to his cause, Abraham Lincoln's passion for the Union would pale to a small boy's affection for washing behind the ears. What was Al's great cause? Nothing less than the health, well-fare, and solvency of Al. And since what Al thought Al was, was a lot bigger than Al really was, this was a cause bigger than the self. *N'est-ce pas?*

Courage goes without saying, and Al had the courage to get into a game he knew could turn rough. But the great man does not confuse courage with foolhardiness, and Al never did. Not after that early piece of bad footwork involving the knife. Later, when anything seemed on the verge of happening, he had the courage of his convictions and was somewhere else.

A sense of realism stands high on the list for greatness. Caesar once said to somebody who got in his way that it was easier for Caesar to act than to threaten. Ditto for Al. He never threatened the guys at the Saint Valentine Day's Massacre. He just stood them up against the wall and let them have it. Realism: he knew they had to go.

The Saint Valentine Day's party reminds me of another qualification, the capacity to inspire loyalty. Think of Caesar and the 10th Legion! Think of the Old Guard at Waterloo! Well, Al inspired loyalty. Nothing inspires loyalty like being nervous about having a hole in the head.

A great man does not fear odds. Here is where Al takes the cake. He first took on the Chicago Police Force, almost single-handed. This did not satisfy his almost insatiable appetite for odds. So he took on the G-men. He took on the Internal Revenue Department. He took on the Woman's Christian Temperance Union. In fact, he took on the whole U.S.A.

But Al did not win, you say. Well, victory has never been a criterion of greatness. Caesar got stabbed. Napoleon wound up on the Island of St. Helena. Al did time at Alcatraz. What's the dif?

Somebody is going to object that I have left being good out of the list of qualifications for greatness.

Well, gentlemen, make me a list of your ten "great men," and put a star beside every one who was good, then turn the paper in after class.

Next question, please.

This theme is a burlesque. Part of the fun is in applying a method commonly used for serious purposes to a trivial subject. But that is not the only source of the humor. There is also what we may unhumorously call the discrepancy between the ordinary notion of greatness and the man that the author sets out to prove is great by the ordinary criteria. This sort of humor succeeds best when done with a straight face, and if the author of the theme had maintained a pretense of gravity he might have made his piece funnier. As it is, the slapdash style and the tone of burlesque give the impression of nudges and winks at the reader. Do you remember how blandly serious is the effect of Swift's satire in *Gulliver's Travels*?

■ APPLICATIONS

I Most people would think Old Covell, with his celluloid collars and little black ties, funny. If you think so, what do you regard as the source of the humor?

II You are now to write a theme of 500 words using the method of illustration. You have two obligations: your particular example must truly represent the class, and it must be in itself as interesting and vivid as you can make it.

In fulfilling the first requirement, you must be sure you know what the essential qualities of the class really are, as contrasted with the merely individual qualities of your particular item. If the qualities of the class are fairly numerous and complicated, be sure that you are systematic in establishing the relation between your example and those qualities. Here an outline can be useful.

In fulfilling the second requirement, hunt for details that catch the attention. Use your imagination. Visualize the illustration. What you want are details like the scales of the herring, Billy the Kid's crooked teeth, the pink napkin of foam around the neck of the dying polar bear, the little black ties Old Covell kept on hand.

There are various ways of organizing such a theme, as you have no doubt observed, but two obvious ones should be mentioned. You can set up a generalized presentation of your subject, say the "Campus Go-getter," and then introduce your example. Or you can present an individual "go-getter" and indicate, one by one, how the qualities of the class are embodied in him. Go back to the examples given earlier and see what method has been used in each. Then read "The Age of Overkill," by Benjamin DeMott (pp. 692–98), and see what method is used there.

Be sure that your theme has a shape.

If none of the following topics attracts you, use one of your own.

The Campus Reformer	Laziness Pays
The Campus Go-getter	The American Town
The Campus Beauty Queen	Honor
The Campus Rebel	The Young Executive
The True Square	

Write a funny theme if you like.

The Fourth Method: Classification

Like comparison and contrast and illustration, classification is a natural process, and like them, it is a process of bringing order out of experience. Like them, too, it is concerned with the relation of a class to a particular item (or particular items, as the case may be). Classification, however, is concerned with systems of classes, ranging from the least inclusive class up to the most inclusive. When we place a particular item in any given class in the system, we can immediately know its relation up and down the system. Classification is a fundamental way of organizing knowledge. It is a filing system. But it is more, it is also a method for arriving at new knowledge.

Let us linger a moment to say what is at stake here. A class is not a mere sum of the items that fall within the class. It is, rather, the idea, the concept, of the qualities that any particular item must have in order to fall within the class. If we think of the class *cat* we do not think of an endless parade of particular cats. We think of what qualities a creature—any cat— must have in order to be termed a cat. A cat is not a cat because it is black or white, big or little, long-haired or short-haired. A cat is a cat because of its "catness." The qualities that constitute "catness" define the class *cat*.

A class, to state matters more technically, is determined by a complex of significant characteristics shared by all members of the class.[7]

Significant characteristics: interest

When we say "significant characteristics," we must ask the question, "Significant to whom?" What constitutes a significant characteristic *may* vary according to the person and his special interest. For example, a maker of cosmetics may think of women in classes determined by complexion, and the secretary of the YWCA, in classes determined by religious affiliation. The registrar of a college and the gymnasium instructor would classify the same body of students according to different systems—one by grades, the other by athletic ability.

The maker of cosmetics and the other classifiers are all dealing with the human race. They have been subdividing the class *man* according to their special interests. But how do we set the class *man* in a larger system of classes? A zoologist would do this by treating man as a subclass far down in a system based on the interpretation of life forms.

ANIMAL KINGDOM

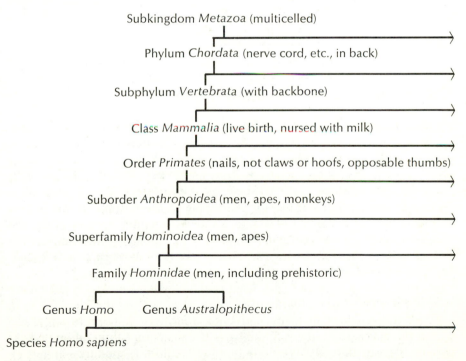

Subkingdom *Metazoa* (multicelled)

Phylum *Chordata* (nerve cord, etc., in back)

Subphylum *Vertebrata* (with backbone)

Class *Mammalia* (live birth, nursed with milk)

Order *Primates* (nails, not claws or hoofs, opposable thumbs)

Suborder *Anthropoidea* (men, apes, monkeys)

Superfamily *Hominoidea* (men, apes)

Family *Hominidae* (men, including prehistoric)

Genus *Homo*   Genus *Australopithecus*

Species *Homo sapiens*

---

[7] See Analysis, Classification, and Structure, pp. 130–31.

Because the same group of items may be classified according to different interests, and because the classifier chooses the basis on which a classification is to be made, do not think that classification is arbitrary or whimsical. To approach the matter negatively: if you merely break up a group of one hundred persons into groups of ten, you are not classifying, you are merely dividing. No individual will be in any particular group because of any qualities he possesses; he merely counts as one of the ten. But if you divide the group of one hundred persons by religious affiliations or by complexion, then you have a classification. It is a classification because the quality that provides the basis of the classification inheres *objectively* in the items—the particular persons—being classified.

It is true that the basis of a classification is subjectively chosen, as when the maker of cosmetics decides to classify ladies on the basis of complexion. But his choice is significant only in so far as differences in complexion actually exist.

Keep this distinction in mind.

SIMPLE SYSTEM

The president of the Young Republican Club in college makes the following classification of the student body:

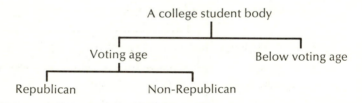

This system, we observe, indicates only two classes at any one stage: voting age and below voting age, Republican and non-Republican. Such a system, called *dichotomous,* is a method of splitting each group into a positive and a negative—those who have as against those who do not have a certain characteristic. In its simplicity, this system is well adapted to certain purposes. For instance, it is suitable to the purpose of the Young Republican Club in that it isolates the students who may vote and who may be expected to vote Republican. But such a system has one obvious limitation. It tells nothing about the "negative" groups—those below voting age and those non-Republican.

COMPLEX SYSTEM

At the opposite end of the spectrum from this simple system is, for example, the enormously complicated zoological classification that, in theory, aims at indicating the relationships of all forms of animal life. Or to think of something somewhat less complex, there is the classification of the books of a great library, which, presumably, would hold all types of books.

The most obvious difference between the simple system above and these systems is the fact that at no stage is there simple splitting. For instance, the class *voting age* is merely split into Republicans and non-Republicans, as contrasted with the treatment of *suborder* **Anthropoidea** (monkeys, apes, and men) in the zoological classification:

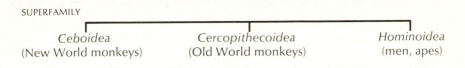

SUPERFAMILY

Ceboidea	*Cercopithecoidea*	*Hominoidea*
(New World monkeys)	(Old World monkeys)	(men, apes)

Or if we subdivide the class *history* in a library classification, we do not get:

History

American history   Non-American history

Instead, we would get a very complicated breakdown like this:

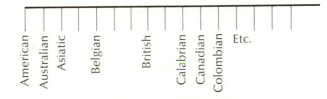

American   Australian   Asiatic   Belgian   British   Calabrian   Canadian   Colombian   Etc.

The point is that in such complex classifications, all distinguishable subgroups are, at each stage, accounted for specifically.

● CAUTION: CROSS-RANKING

The great trap in making a classification is what is called cross-ranking. Suppose you need to work out a classification with reference to more than one interest. You are a member of the Young Republican Club who has been assigned the task of finding out how many Republican coeds have done volunteer teaching in the slums. There are, obviously, three interests to be considered in the classification: (1) political affiliation, (2) sex, and (3) volunteer teaching in slums. Each interest must be confined to a single stage. A moment ago, we reduced the classification to "Republican" and "non-Republican." And now, under "Republican" we can distinguish "male" and "female." Having done that, we can distinguish the "teachers" from the "nonteachers."In this acceptable classification, each stage deals with one, and only one, principle of division. So we have:

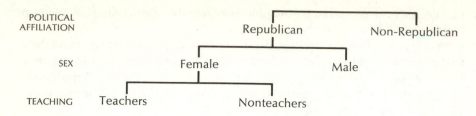

POLITICAL AFFILIATION	Republican	Non-Republican
SEX	Female	Male
TEACHING	Teachers	Nonteachers

But here is an example of absurd classification in sorting out a student body:

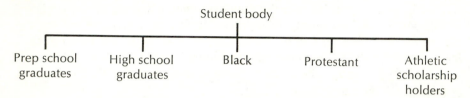

Student body

| Prep school graduates | High school graduates | Black | Protestant | Athletic scholarship holders |

This example of what is called "cross-ranking" in classification is absurd because the groups involved (prep school graduates, high school graduates, blacks, Protestants, and athletic scholarship holders) are not mutually exclusive. That is, a prep school graduate might also be a black Protestant who holds an athletic scholarship. How, then, could you proceed to place him in this scheme? It would be impossible.

■ **APPLICATIONS**

I Construct a classification that would locate the prep school graduates who are black, Roman Catholic, and athletic scholarship holders.

II Here is a classification from the first sentence of a student theme: "The people connected with this college fall into the following groups: the board of trustees, the officers of the administration, the staff, meaning clerical workers, maintenance personnel, and so forth, the faculty, the boys, and the coeds."

What is wrong with this?

Classification: how you use it

Classification helps us organize things, ideas, experiences. It is a way of coming to grips with a subject. Classification places a subject in relation to a system. It gives it a logical context.

You may ask, however, of what use are such things as the zoological classification or the library classification in writing ordinary exposition? They are only rarely of direct use, but they are often of great indirect use because they show the principle of classification in a highly elaborated and precise form. If you have grasped the principle they illustrate, you are ready to adapt it to your special purposes.

A classification, remember, is always determined by an interest—by a purpose—and you must adapt the principle to your own purpose, instance by instance.

PURPOSE

Classification, in many instances, serves the purpose of increasing your understanding of a subject, but such an understanding is only a preparation for writing a piece of exposition. A chart, in short, is not a theme. However, a classification may serve as an outline, and often can provide the structure of a discussion. Furthermore, a classification may need explanation, and the placing of any particular item in the scheme may need justification; thus the classification itself becomes subject matter.

Classification may, then, serve three distinguishable, though related, purposes:

1 It may serve as preparation for a theme.
2 It may provide the structure of a theme.
3 It may contribute to the subject matter of a theme.

In the following example, an essay from a college magazine, we can easily detect the scheme of classification underlying the discussion and at the same time see that without the discussion the scheme would not be very interesting.

FOR WOMEN MOSTLY

With all the controversy about the relative uselessness of Penn men and Penn women, there seems to be a need for a certain amount of field work in the subject. Apparently each side is judged by the most objectionable of its kind, so—girls—here is submitted a carefully compiled report on Penn Men You Need to Avoid. If referred to before you accept dates, it may save you a lot of bitterness and gnashing of teeth.

Type 1. The Party-Boy. This one simply isn't himself until he gets outside of a little alcohol. Then he manages to be so much himself that you are bored to death. His conversation is either quiet or loud; when quiet, it consists of long accounts of drinking bouts, in which he took part: and when loud, it is usually carried on with his buddy across the room who wants everybody to sing the "Whiffenpoof Song," while our joyboy favors "Roll Me Over in the Clover." For these occasions he is conveniently equipped with a foghorn voice that makes everybody turn around and look. If you happen to be sitting next to him you cringe and wilt and feel about two inches high. You gaze up at him with a sick smile that you hope will make everybody think you're having as much fun as he is.

There may be occasions in the course of the evening when he feels like dancing. Dancing, to him, consists of zooming around ricocheting off walls, other couples, moose heads, etc. They ought to jail him for flying low.

Then the fire-eater creeps up on him and he commences to be morose.

In the life of every party-boy there is an unrequited love; and furthermore given even less than half a chance, he will tell you all about it. It sounds vaguely like *True Confessions*. But because you have nothing better to do at the moment, you listen, and sympathize—outwardly, with him; inwardly, with the girl.

Finally he quietly passes out, wrapped comfortably around a chandelier or something, and one of his less enthusiastic brothers takes you home. All this is very interesting, provided you can hold him up long enough to get through the party. And he really isn't useless; he always makes a good bar rag.

Type 2. The Lover. He is a ball of fire with the women—the sultry, slow-burning kind, of course. He overwhelms you with attentions. He leans so close to you when you talk that you get the impression he is concerned about the condition of your wisdom teeth. He has a special hungry sick-dog look which he uses for gazing deeply into eyes. When you go away and talk to somebody else, he sulks. He may even follow you and turn you around to face him, and look silently at you. He is hurt. You have crushed him. You are ashamed. You monster.

An evening with him is like a nice quiet session with a boa constrictor. No amount of hinting around that, as far as he's concerned, you are of the let's-just-be-friends school of thought, will do; you have to pick up a bottle or something and slug him before he gets the idea. Then, kid, you're washed up. Your name is mud. Not only are you nasty, ungrateful, and a terrible date—but to top it all off, you're an icebox—and this is the sin unforgivable.

Type 3. The Great Mind. You have to prepare ahead of time for a date with one of these. If you're not read up on your Nietzsche and Schopenhauer, you've got two strikes against you before you start. You and Junior will sit down together, cozy-like, in a corner and solve world problems. Then for the sake of variety you might go on to metaphysics. You toss Absolutes and Causes and Effects back and forth for a whole evening. I won't say any more on this subject. There's nothing more to say.

Type 4. The Bohemian. This one's theme song is "I Don't Care." He dreams of a garret for two on the Left Bank and a Jug of Wine, a Loaf of Bread—and Thou; and if Thou isn't crazy about the idea, Thou is inhibited, repressed, suppressed, a slave to convention, a conformist, and a louse. The boy knows he's a genius, but just because he dyes his hair pale green and wears a purple satin shoestring for a necktie, people don't appreciate him.

He has moods. Blue moods, black moods, red moods—all kinds. If he's having mood number 157E, keep away from him. Keep away from him anyway. Unless you've reserved a bunk at Byberry, that is.

Type 5. The Dud. He gives you a fleeting impression of a horrible, sticky, gray nothingness. He doesn't smoke, drink, dance, drive, stay out late, or raise his voice. He isn't funny—he isn't interesting—he isn't clever. You talk into a vacuum. He is probably very good to his mother, but every time he comes out with that slightly hysterical giggle you feel like slapping him. He sits there like a rock in mid-stream and the party eddies around him. He has a wonderful time. You go home and get a nice big ax and go hunting for the person who got you the date.

Watch the aftereffects of this. He'll call you up, sure as next week. He'll call you again. He'll call you nine or ten times more. If you happen to be wandering around on campus with somebody whom you'd like to impress, he'll pop up out of his hole in the lawn and greet you like a long-lost sister. He's the world's best argument for mercy killing.

Type 6. The Missing Link. Not that we object to muscles, but there is a type that has too much of a good thing. He has an amazing supply of every kind of matter but gray. He looks like something out of the Old Stone Age—and talks surprisingly like it, too. His knuckles drag on the ground. He grunts occasionally to show he's alive. You expect him to stand up and hammer on his chest at any minute. He majors in-duh-phys ed, and takes Advanced Pencil Sharpening on the side.

He's a charming date if you're taking anthropology. Or if you have to write a criticism of *The Man with the Hoe* or *Of Mice and Men.* You couldn't find a better case study.

Of course you have to watch these creatures. If he gets playful you're liable to end up mashed into dog food. It's best to take along a whip and a light metal chair and be able to say "Back, Sultan," in an authoritative voice. Once your nerve fails, you're done.

Well, there they are. Now the object of the game is to go out and find one that doesn't fall into one of these categories. Then, if it's got blood and skin and if it moves around, you're set. Hang onto it. It must be a man.

—BARBARA JONES.[8]

The general purpose of the college coed who wrote "For Women Mostly" was not to do a sociological survey or a term paper for a psychology course, or even a handy guide to dating. She was having fun, much in the way that the author of the theme taking Al Capone as an illustration of the "great man" was having fun. And part of the fun in both instances lies in taking a method usually reserved for sober-sided purposes and using it for something considerably less pretentious.

Part of the humor, too, is that, in both cases, hidden in the fun, is a sharp satirical thrust. Just as the author of the theme on Capone takes a telling dig at ordinary notions of greatness, so the coed here makes some shrewd assessments of the male ego and male frailty.

● CAUTION

Notice that even in the article "For Women Mostly," which contains a classification made with a humorous intention, the classification is real. The divisions are not mere divisions, they are not arbitrary. They are made with reference to a principle.

Exhaustive classification

We have said that dichotomous classification (p. 92), though limited in its usefulness, does, by the very nature of its formula of division by x and

---
[8] From *Penn Pics,* a Franklin Society publication of the University of Pennsylvania.

non-x, give an exhaustive scheme. We have also said that complex schemes such as that made by the zoologist or used in the great library aim to be exhaustive. But what about exhaustiveness when you are settling down to the practical business of writing a theme?

Let us examine a theme:

TEACHERS I HAVE KNOWN

STAGE I

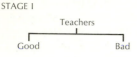

STAGE I (second version)

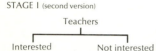

STAGE II

STAGE II

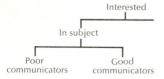

STAGE III

In my thirteen and a half years at school, I have, of course, known many teachers; I have made rather a hobby of studying my teachers because I hope one day to become a teacher myself. There are many kinds of teachers, but they can all be classified under one of two headings—good and bad. Fortunately for students there are many more teachers under the first heading than under the second.

Actually, it does not mean much to say that teachers are good or bad—the same can be said of people in any profession. A better way of separating the teachers that really teach from those that just stand up in front of a class is to ask how they got to be teachers in the first place. Did they become teachers because they were really interested in their subject and in young people, or did they just drift into the profession through indifference or necessity?

I should like to dispose of the second category first. There is little need to say much about such teachers; every student has known a few of them. Either they are indifferent toward their job, in which case the class is terribly boring, and the students fool around; or they actively hate teaching. Then watch out! The best thing to do in a class like that is to keep quiet and do only as much work as necessary to avoid the teacher's notice.

The other teachers are much more interesting, and there are many more kinds of them. Some become teachers because of an intense interest in their subject. They may be great teachers or well-known researchers; particularly in college, they may be outstanding men in their field. Some of them do not have the ghost of a notion how to put their subject across; they may not even try particularly, for students simply don't exist for them. All that matters is the subject. Even so, the student can get a lot out of his courses if he puts some effort into understanding them. Other teachers in this category do have a gift for organizing and communicating their subject. Their classes are a constant challenge—the teacher is not likely to make his subject easy!—and a delight.

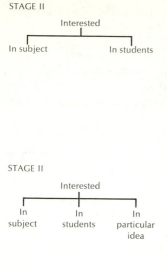

Another variety of teacher with a purpose is the kind who is interested in his students. He is not a scholar; his main motivation is to help students. That is his mission in life. At the college level you probably find fewer of these teachers than in elementary or high school. I remember particularly my seventh-grade arithmetic teacher. It was a bad year for me; more than once I got into trouble with the school authorities. But this teacher was so decent to me that I became better, and I even learned some arithmetic. Miss Jones may not have been a great mathematician, but she did me some good and taught me more than many other teachers I have had.

I should mention one other kind of interested teacher, a kind to be careful of. That is the teacher who wants to indoctrinate his students about something. He believes fanatically that all automobile engines should be limited to 60 horsepower, and he wants you to believe that, too. He is apt to spend lots of time preaching about this *idée fixe,* and that time will be largely wasted for you. But otherwise he may be a good teacher. Be tolerant of the bee in his bonnet, and remember that the teacher is human, too.

This theme is based on a classification, as we have indicated along the left margin. If we assemble these notes, we find a scheme like this:

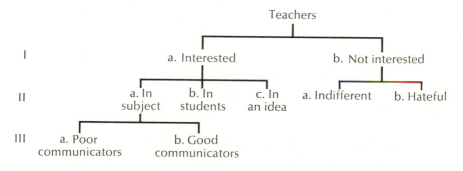

Is this scheme adequate for the student's purpose? Does it exhaust the kinds of teachers he has known? Doesn't common sense suggest some types that are not mentioned? Or does the author mean to imply that, though he knows other kinds exist, he is dealing only with types that he has actually observed in the classroom?

There is still another problem with the classification in this theme: in the first paragraph the author says that he expects to be a teacher himself, and we therefore expect that at the end of the theme he will present some type of "good" teacher whom he will take as a model. A classification should be governed by the purpose for which it is undertaken, but we are never quite sure of this writer's purpose.

The writer's uncertainty about his purpose accounts, no doubt, for some of the fuzziness in the classification. In Stage I, the classification is dichotomous, and therefore exhaustive; it might be argued that Stage III is also exhaustive in so far as it develops IIa. But Stage II is not developed according to a clear-cut principle, and as we have said, we don't know whether it is supposed to be exhaustive.

It may be objected that the theme "For Women Mostly" is not exhaustive either, that there are many other types of dates. But for the writer's purpose, which is to write a light-hearted piece of satire, her classification is adequate. She has chosen her types shrewdly and with enough variety. They give good targets for her fun—and ours. What more should we ask?

The kind of classification—that is, the criteria by which the sorting out is made—and the degree of exhaustiveness are determined by purpose. Your first step in making a classification is to know what your purpose is.

■ APPLICATION

Write a theme of some 500 words based on classification. Make it funny, whimsical, satirical, serious—whatever tone you wish. Do not feel limited to the following topics:

Liars (or Liars I Have Known)	Choosing a Shotgun
Trout Flies	Wives
Classmates	Mothers
Bleeding Hearts	Saturday Night on Campus
College Reformers	What Girl for the Prom?
Success Boys	Sensitive Souls

The Fifth Method: Definition

A dictionary will give you two different definitions of the word *definition:* (1) "a statement of what a thing is" and (2) "a statement or explanation of what a word or phrase means or has meant." In the strict sense, a definition, as we shall use the word here, is not of a thing but of a word.[9]

---

[9] The dictionary tells the generally accepted usage of a word. For a word in common use the dictionary reports as a standard what is acceptable among educated people. For a word of some specialized use, such as technical terms, it reports what is acceptable among the specialists who use the word—say, engineers or zoologists. The dictionary may, of course, give other information too, but this is basic: to report usage within a certain "linguistic community."

If we define *cat,* we are telling how to use the word *cat.* A definition sets the limits or bounds within which a term can be used, as the derivation of the word *definition* implies (it comes from two Latin words: *de,* meaning "with relation to," and *finis,* meaning "limit").

This sense of the word *definition* is quite natural to us, for we speak of "looking up a word in the dictionary," we talk of the "precise definition of a word," and we say to the opponent in an argument, "define your terms"—a term being any key word or phrase that constitutes a unit of meaning in his argument.

The process of making a definition is not, however, a mere game of words. It is clear that we cannot make a useful definition without knowledge of the thing (that is, object, event, idea, etc.) to which the word (or term) refers. And it is equally clear that the definition of a word communicates knowledge about the thing. A definition does give knowledge of "what a thing is," and equally important, may lead the maker of a definition to clarify his own thoughts on the nature of the "thing."

In fact, a description can often serve as a definition: by enlightening us about a thing, it enlightens us about the use of the term that refers to the thing. For example, we find later in this chapter (pp. 137–38) a theme describing the mechanism used to make maple syrup, and when we have finished reading that, we know how to define the term *syrup cooker.*[10] But for the moment, we are not concerned with description as a form of definition, nor concerned with certain other kinds of definition (for instance, what is known as *recursive definition* in arithmetic and grammar). We are, instead, concerned with traditional, or classic, definition, which goes back as far as Aristotle. Our discussion in the immediately following pages is confined to that form.

● CAUTION

A definition is not a synonym. If, in the dictionary, you find the word *sacred* after the entry *holy,* this does not mean that *sacred* is a definition of the word *holy.* It is merely a word with approximately the same meaning as *holy.* This fact becomes immediately clear if you do not know the meaning of *sacred.* You must have a definition, after all.

Parts of a definition: convertibility

A definition has two parts, two terms: the *to-be-defined (definiendum)* and the *definer (definiens).* The terms appear as an equation. For example, if we define *slave* as a human being who is the legal property of another, then we can set up the equation:

Slave	is	human being who is the legal property of another
The *to-be-defined*	=	the *definer*

---

[10] See also Metaphorical Language, pp. 113–14.

We know that the terms of an equation are interchangeable. So if we make a statement using the word that is the *to-be-defined,* we may substitute the *definer* for that word without any change of sense. The statement "To be a slave is worse than death" has exactly the same meaning as the statement "To be a human being who is the legal property of another is worse than death." The terms are, as we say, *convertible.*[11]

DEFECTS OF DEFINITION: TOO BROAD AND TOO NARROW

Let us take another proposition: "A slave is a man." This statement is, clearly, true. But is it a definition? Let us consider the question by thinking of two classes, *slave* and *man.* The class *man* is, clearly, a larger group than the class *slave;* that is, there are men who are not slaves. Our original proposition, "A slave is a man," affirms that the class *slave* will be included in the class *man.*

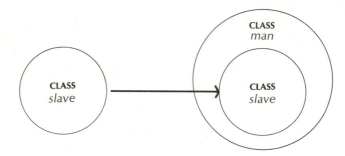

It is obvious that any statement we make about man as a class (that is, any statement that is true of all men) will necessarily be true of slaves, for the class *slave* is included in the class *man.* But no statement about slaves is *necessarily* true of all men. It may be true (as when we say, "Slaves have

[11] Students sometimes challenge the idea that the terms of a definition can "really" be convertible. To challenge this is, of course, to challenge the possibility of making a "really" good definition. We recognize the difficulty of making precise definitions, but we should distinguish between what is demanded by the principle of definition and the failure in certain attempts at definition. For example, the definition of *slave* given above has been challenged along the following lines: "A big league baseball player is owned, too, and who would say that to be a big league baseball player is worse than death? So you can't convert the terms."

The problem here lies in what is meant by the term *owned.* The baseball team owns a contract with a player, and the contract states the limits of the control over the player, including a time limit. The owner of a slave, on the other hand, held more or less unlimited control of the slave. Some dictionaries use the idea of absolute control in defining slavery, but this idea might be challenged, too. Many societies have existed in which the law specified limits of control over a slave; for example, in certain Catholic countries a slave might not be denied the sacraments.

In any case, we may say that the control over a slave approached the absolute, while the baseball player has normal freedom of action in areas not covered by his contract.

The whole problem here is, as we have said, due to confusion in interpreting the word *owned.* In framing definitions we must try to use language as precisely as possible. Furthermore, as this discussion has illustrated, knowledge (here of baseball contracts and systems of slavery) may be crucial.

two legs"), but there are many reasonable statements about slaves (such as our statement above, "To be a slave is worse than death") that are not applicable to all men (for we can scarcely substitute *man* for *slave* in our last statement and say, "To be a man is worse than death"). In other words, our proposition, "A slave is a man," does not have convertible terms (pp. 206–08). The definer is larger than the *to-be-defined* and includes it. The definition is, we say, too broad.

We can also go wrong in the other direction. We can have a *definer* that is smaller than the *to-be-defined*. We make that error, for instance, if we say that a table is a piece of furniture on which we serve meals. The *definer* ("a piece of furniture on which we serve meals") is too small, because it will not cover the many other classes of tables—study tables, bedside tables, sewing tables, billiard tables, and so on. Here the definition is too narrow. So we get the following picture:

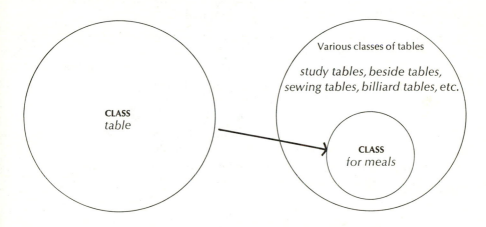

To sum up, the *to-be-defined* and the *definer* must, if we think of them graphically as one superimposed on the other, be the same size; they must be *coterminous*.

And this, of course, is only another way of saying that the terms of a definition are convertible.

■ APPLICATION

None of the following statements is a correct definition. Some are too broad and some are too narrow. You must distinguish one kind from the other.

For example, if we say "A belt is what a man puts around his waist to hold his trousers up," our *definer* is too narrow. There are, of course, belts not worn by men. Furthermore, belts may be used for purposes other than holding up trousers: women use them to hold up skirts. Some belts are used for carrying weapons. Some are purely ornamental. And so on. Or suppose we say, "Lacrosse is a game played with a ball and a kind of racket." Our definer here is too broad. Tennis, too, is played with a ball and racket. So is squash. If we modify "racket" by saying "a kind of racket laced with thong and called a stick," we begin to narrow the definer, although such a formulation may not yet give an adequate definition of lacrosse. But making an adequate definition is not your present problem. You are to determine only whether each definition given here is too broad or too narrow or perhaps both.

1   Baseball is a game played with a clublike wooden instrument called a bat, and a rather small, leather-covered ball.
2   An automobile is a vehicle propelled by an internal combustion engine.
3   An automobile is a four-wheeled self-propelling vehicle.
4   A hero is a man who is useful to society.
5   Democracy is the form of government we have in the United States.
6   A collar is the thing a man wears around his neck.
7   Leisure is that free time during which you can rest.
8   A patriot is the man who serves the best interests of his country.
9   A cat is a member of the zoological genus *felis*.

The structure of definition

A definition locates its subject in a class and then proceeds to point out the characteristics that make it differ from other items in that class and that, therefore, allow it to be assigned to a subclass. This process is, it is clear, a special variant of the process of classification. A definition simply sets its subject in a limited scheme of classification.

The process of definition is, like classification, a natural way the mind works. It is no more arbitrary than other methods of exposition we have studied. We make definitions constantly, and instinctively. Let us examine a very simple example of how the process works.

A small child who has never seen a cat receives one as a pet. The father tells the child that the animal is a cat—a kitty. The proud parent now assumes that the child knows what the word *cat* means. But he is surprised one day to find the child going up to a Pekingese and saying "Kitty, kitty." It is obvious that the child is using the word to mean any small, furry animal.

When the father takes him to the park, the child is very likely to call a squirrel a kitty, too.

The father now undertakes to give the child a definition of *cat*. To do so, he must instruct the child in the differences between a cat, a Pekingese, and a squirrel. In other words, he undertakes to break up the class, or group, that the child has made (all small, furry animals) into certain subgroups (cats, Pekingese, squirrels) by focusing attention upon the differences (the differentiae) that distinguish one subgroup from another.

If the child understands his father, he can then give a questioner a definition of the word *cat*—an inadequate definition, of course, but nevertheless one arrived at by the proper method and exhibiting the characteristic structure.

QUESTIONER: What does *cat* mean?

CHILD: It's a little animal, and it's got fur.

QUESTIONER: But dogs have fur, too, and dogs aren't cats.

CHILD: Yes, but dogs bark. Cats don't bark. Cats meow. And cats climb trees.

QUESTIONER: But squirrels have fur, and they climb trees and are little.

CHILD: Yes, but squirrels don't just *climb* trees like cats. They live in trees. And they don't meow like cats.

The child has put *cat* into a class or group (small, furry animals), and then has distinguished the subgroup *cat* from the other subgroups, *dog* and *squirrel*.

If we chart the child's reasoning, we get a diagram like this:

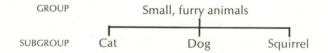

Whenever we make a definition, we go through the same process as the child trying to tell what a kitty is. We locate the *to-be-defined* as a species in relation to a group (genus) that includes several different species and then try to say what quality or qualities (differentia or differentiae) distinguish the *to-be-defined* from the other species in the genus. So we get the formula:

Definition of species	=	*genus + differentiae*
The *to-be-defined*	=	the *definer*

The pattern of the child's attempt to define *cat* is the pattern of all definition of the classic type, but the definition that the child gives will not serve us in our adult world. It will not serve us, because the genus and differentiae that the child adopts are not significantly distinguished for our adult purposes.

A zoologist, for instance, would go about the business very differently. He might begin by saying: "A cat—*Felis domestica,* we call it—is a digitigrade, carnivorous mammal of the genus *Felis,* which includes the species tiger (*Felis tigris*), the species ocelot (*Felis pardalis*), the species lion (*Felis leo*), the species cougar (*Felis concolor*), and several other species. All the species of the genus *Felis* have lithe, graceful, long bodies, relatively short legs, with soft, padded feet, strong claws, which are retracted into sheaths when not in use, powerful jaws with sharp teeth, and soft, beautifully marked fur. The cat is the smallest of the genus, usually measuring so-and-so. It is the only species easily domesticated. . . ."

Like the child, the zoologist has set up a group, which he calls a genus, and has given the characteristics of the group. Then he has broken up the group into several subgroups, each of which he calls a species. Last, he has set about pointing out the differences between the species *cat* and the other species of the same genus.

Diagrammed, his thinking has this form:

GENUS   Felis

SPECIES   *Felis domestica* (cat)   *Felis tigris* (tiger)   *Felis leo* (lion)   *Felis concolor* (cougar)   Etc.

The form used by the zoologist is, we see, the same as that used by the child. The difference is that the zoologist thinks in *significant* classes. We should note, too, that the zoologist uses the words *genus* and *species* with somewhat different meanings from ours. For him the word *genus* means not only a group including smaller groups called species but also a group of species closely related structurally and by origin; and the word *species* means a subgroup whose members possess numerous characteristics in common and interbreed to preserve those characteristics. In other words, the zoologist has a specialized significance for the words *genus* and *species,* a significance dictated by the materials he is dealing with—living forms. Despite this specialized significance, he uses the words in his pattern of definition just as we do, for instance, in setting up the formal scheme for the definition of *bungalow:*

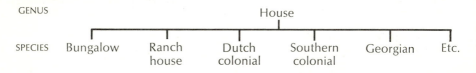

GENUS   House

SPECIES   Bungalow   Ranch house   Dutch colonial   Southern colonial   Georgian   Etc.

Though genus and species are part of all definition, we do not ordinarily use technical language in giving a casual definition. For *bungalow* we are likely to say: "Oh, it's a kind of house. It differs from Dutch colonial, Southern colonial, Georgian, and some other styles in that it has only one story. The best way to distinguish the bungalow from other one-story houses is by the floor plan. For instance, if we compare it with a ranch house, we find . . ." Here, in an informal way, we are giving the differentiae. Let us analyze a dictionary definition:

> hammer, "a tool for pounding, usually consisting of a metal head and a handle." [12]

Here "tool" is clearly the genus and "for pounding" is a differentia. But on a moment's reflection we see that the single differentia "for pounding" would be too broad: there are tools other than the hammer that are used for pounding, for instance, pestles and tampers. So we should know what distinguishes a hammer from a pestle or tamper. To help us here the dictionary adds "usually consisting of a metal head and a handle." Set up as a scheme this runs:

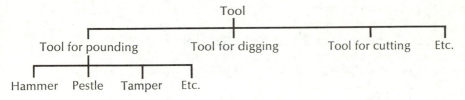

differentia: metal head and handle [13]

The dictionary definition has, we see, compressed three stages of classification, but the experienced reader of dictionaries learns to sort out the various stages in question. The dictionary gives a kind of short-hand.

■ APPLICATION

Below are a group of definitions drawn from the same dictionary as that of *hammer*. Set up each in the following form. For example, here is the definition of a triangle ("A triangle is a geometrical figure having three angles and three sides."):

To-be-defined	genus	differentiae
Triangle	geometrical figure	three angles and three sides

The main problem is to be sure you have the genus right. Here is the dictionary's definition of *hammock:* "a length of netting, canvas, etc., swung

---

[12] *Webster's New World Dictionary of the American Language,* College Edition, 1953.

[13] A student may well object that "usually consisting of a metal head and a handle" does not really distinguish a hammer from a tamper or a pestle. He would be right. He might also object that the metal head would not indicate the class *hammer,* but a subclass under *hammer,* for there are hammers with stone heads and, even, rubber heads. Again he would be right. For further discussion see pp. 108–10.

from ropes at both ends and used as a bed or couch." Which is the genus—"length of netting, canvas, etc." or "bed or couch"? This question would, in all likelihood, never arise if you were framing your own definition. Almost certainly the first thing to pop into your head about a hammock is that you lie in it. Your response would be correct: a hammock is something you lie in, made in a certain way. Set up the scheme.

1 *chasm:* "a deep crack in the earth's surface; abyss; crevasse; narrow gorge."
2 *ravine:* "a long, deep hollow in the earth's surface, worn by the action of a stream."
3 *oligarchy:* "a form of government in which the ruling power belongs to a few persons."
4 *lend:* "to let another use or have (a thing) temporarily and on condition that it, or its equivalent, is to be returned."
5 *fog:* "a large mass of water vapor condensed to fine particles, at or just above the earth's surface."
6 *ax:* "a tool for chopping trees and splitting wood: it has a long wooden handle and a metal head with a blade usually on only one side."
7 *hatchet:* "a small ax with a short handle for use with one hand."

Necessary and sufficient characteristics

We have seen from our formula that the definer specifies at least two conditions, that of the genus and that of the differentia (or differentiae) determining the species. The definition will not apply, that is, to something that satisfies merely the requirement of the genus or merely that of the species. To state it another way, a characteristic may be necessary and yet not sufficient to fulfill the requirement of a definition.

Let us look at what is probably the most famous definition ever made, Aristotle's definition of *man:*

Man is a rational animal.

The formula might be set up as:

To-be-defined	genus	differentia
man	animal	rational

Being an animal is the condition specified in the genus, and being rational, that in the species. Both are *necessary* characteristics for qualifying as a member of the class *man.* For example, there are numberless species of animals that are nonrational (all nonmen). And there are creatures conceived as rational but nonanimal—like the gods of Greece or the angels of Christian theology.

Neither of the necessary characteristics is, taken alone, *sufficient.* Taken together they are sufficient. They fulfill all the conditions of the definition.

Only two conditions are proposed in Aristotle's definition of *man,* but in some cases several may be involved. Looking back at our discussion of the definition of *hammer* (p. 107), we see that, though being a tool and being for pounding (the requirements proposed by genus and species) are necessary conditions for fulfilling the definition of *hammer,* they are not, strictly speaking, sufficient. There are, as we have mentioned, tools for pounding that are not hammers. To distinguish hammers from such tools we should have to add the characteristic of having a heavy head and handle, and perhaps that of having a certain relation between the handle and the head. Then we should have *all* the necessary conditions—and, as we have seen, we must have *all* the necessary conditions if we are to have a sufficient definition.

Definition and generalization: supportive characteristics

It is clear that if we have a definition of *hammer* we want it to be good for all hammers. That is, the definition must be a general statement, applicable to all members of the class tagged by the word being defined. In dictionaries, however, we often find definitions like the one we have quoted for *hammer:* "a tool for pounding, usually consisting of a metal head and a handle." What is the word *usually* doing here?

When the dictionary-maker adds the *usually,* he is getting away from a truly generalized definition: there are, for instance, stone hammers in museums, and perhaps some are still being used in, say, New Guinea. But the dictionary-maker's aim is not necessarily to give a universal definition; he simply tries to provide a helpful description of a common type of modern hammer, one that most people have seen. He is trying to be helpful, again, when he adds (as he does in the rest of the definition): "one end of the head may be a pronged claw for pulling nails."

Having a metal head, or a claw on one end of the head, or a magnetized head for tacks—none of these attributes, let us insist, is necessary to the basic quality of "hammerness," but they may be incidentally useful in identifying the object. We shall call such characteristics *supportive,* in contrast to those that are necessary or sufficient. Some such distinction is what the dictionary-maker has in mind when he says "usually," or, as in connection with the claw hammer, "may be."

Supportive characteristics may be helpful in a definition, even if they are not strictly a part of it, not only in that they remind us of relevant examples we are likely to have seen and pinpoint the application of the definition, but in that they indicate a subgroup, or subgroups, under the species. Under the species *hammer,* the reference to the metal head sets up a subgroup, the reference to the claw head sets up another, subsumed under "metal head." Thus a supportive characteristic boxes in the definition, as it were; by extending the classification, it broadens the base of information. In fact, an understanding of the relation of supportive characteristics to the necessary and the sufficient will help us immeasurably in learning how to frame a definition.

■ APPLICATIONS

I In each of the following "definitions" indicate necessary and sufficient characteristics and those that are merely supportive. The question is not whether a definition is acceptable or not. Simply try to follow the instruction as best you can.

1 *ducking stool:* a chair, attached to a pole or plank balanced on a fulcrum, to which a convicted person was tied and then ducked into a pool or stream: a practice common in early New England, where the culprit was usually a woman known as a common scold: a cucking stool.

2 *electron:* an elementary particle that is a fundamental constituent of matter, having a negative charge of 1.602×10^{-19} coulombs, a mass of 9.108×10^{-31} kilograms, and spin of $\frac{1}{2}$, existing independently or as the component outside the nucleus of an atom.

3 Man is a featherless biped.

4 Faith is the evidence of things not seen.

5 *lugsail:* a four-cornered sail, with no boom or lower yard, suspended from an upper yard hung obliquely on the mast: the name probably in reference to the lugging, or hauling, of the sail around the mast in order to change course.

6 War is legalized murder on a large scale, without, it may be added, the usual rational justifications for murder.

7 *quarterdeck:* the afterpart of the upper deck of a ship, by tradition reserved for officers: so called because originally it lay between poop and mainmast and was one half the length of the half deck.

II One way—and a rather good way—to begin making a definition is to assemble the characteristics associated with the to-be-defined, even the most random ones. When they are assembled, you can begin to weed out those that you decide are merely random, that do not enlighten one about the essential meaning of the to-be-defined. Suppose, to make a definition of *stockbroker,* you come up with the following list:

> sells stocks
> Wall Street
> makes lots of money
> fleeces widows and orphans
> jumps out of high windows when market crashes
> wears a dark gray suit and conservative tie
> drinks too much
> went to an Ivy League college

has had a divorce
plays bridge well
sails
votes Republican
is good at statistics
has good manners and a persuasive personality
advises clients
takes orders from clients
has handsomely furnished office
has ticker-tape machine in office
entertains lavishly
buys stocks, too
commutes to wealthy suburb
tends to cultivate wealthy people
will die of heart attack or ulcers

You may now begin to sort out the items that are not significant. True, widows and orphans have been fleeced, but how relevant is this to your purpose, even in a supportive way? What about heavy drinking? Even if drinking does run high among stockbrokers, is this characteristic specifically related to that occupation?

Certainly a broker does buy and sell stocks. You seem on firm ground here. But is this fact sufficient for a definition? You remember that trust companies and insurance companies also buy and sell stocks.

Having made your survey of the list, you may want to add other characteristics. Do so, if you wish. Now check your list with the notations *NS* (necessary, sufficient), *S* (supportive), and *I* (irrelevant). Then try to frame your definition, but frame it as a statement, as full as you think necessary.

If you feel you don't know enough about stockbrokerage to write a definition, find out more about the business.

III Following the pattern in Application II, develop a definition of a word chosen from the list below. Hand in all your notes along with the finished definition.

freedom	tyranny
lassitude	personality
conscience	administrator
sport	psychiatrist
capitalism	

● CAUTION: DEFINITION AND THE COMMON GROUND

We shall soon discuss the more complex kind of definition known as extended definition, but before we embark on that, there are three important cautions to be given, one concerning the common ground, one concerning metaphorical language, and one concerning what is called circular definition.

Suppose, history and language permitting, that we try to give our definition of *bungalow* to an American Indian of the old days. He probably would not let us get past the first sentence, "Oh, it's a kind of house," for he would immediately want to know what a house is. In other words, if we give a definition, we assume that our audience knows the genus we are going to work in. If the audience does not know the genus, we must go back to a more inclusive group, a group including our genus as a subgroup, and try again, hoping now to have a common ground. So, if our Indian does not understand what a house is, we may try again and begin by saying, "A house is a kind of shelter—but a shelter you make, and so on." Our Indian knows what a shelter is, and he can get a notion of manmade shelter, for he has a tepee or lodge or hogan. We now have a common ground.

What we have developed by implication is a scheme something like this:

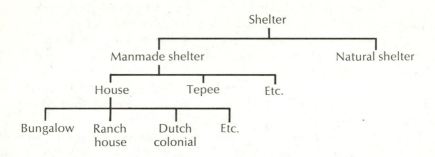

The Indian has pushed us back a couple of stages, and we now have a common ground and can define *house*. It is not likely that we'll get down to *bungalow,* for the Indian probably will not understand our necessary differentiae under the now-established genus *house*.

Not only with our Indian but with everyone, a common ground is necessary for an effective definition. This principle of the common ground is very important, for it implies that a definition is not only *of some term* but is *for somebody*. The giver of the definition can define only by reference to what his particular audience already knows or is willing to learn for the purpose at hand.

This necessary knowledge must be of two kinds: of words and of things. It must be of words, for a definition is in words. The giver of the definition must use words that his audience can understand or can readily become acquainted with. For instance, when the zoologist refers to the cat as a "digitigrade mammal," he is using a word that most of us would not know. For the general reader, the zoologist would need to explain further that *digitigrade* means "walking on the toes," as a cat does, as opposed to "walking on the whole foot" (*plantigrade*), as a man does. In this way the zoologist would provide the common ground of language.

The second kind of knowledge is, as we have said, of things. For instance, there is no use in trying to define the color beige to a man blind from birth. If you say that beige is a light, brownish color, the natural color of wool, you have really said nothing to him, for he has had no experience of color. If you go on and give the physicist's definition of color, referring to wavelengths of light, you run into the same difficulty. He can grasp the notion of wavelength, but he has no basis for knowing what light is. You run into a defect in his experience, in his knowledge. There is always the possibility of running into some defects in our audience's knowledge, and, in so far as possible, we must work with what is known.

● CAUTION: METAPHORICAL LANGUAGE

The language of definition should be as logically precise as possible. The purpose of a definition is, as the derivation indicates, to limit the meaning of a word in an acceptable way. For this purpose metaphorical language is especially dangerous, for the essence of metaphor is not to limit meaning but to extend meaning by developing new and complex ranges implicit in the literal base.[14]

It is true that metaphor and simile, as forms of comparison, may be used for expository purposes. Herman Melville, in a passage quoted later in this book (p. 135), compares the try-works of an old whaling ship to a brick kiln lifted from a field and set on the deck, and thus gives a sharp visual image of what he is trying to describe. So a heart may be compared to a pump (p. 135). This second instance does not sharpen the reader's idea of what a heart looks like (as would be the case if we said "A heart is like a large, somewhat misshapen apple"); it gives the reader a notion of what a heart does.

These comparisons are effective for exposition primarily because the literal spread between the two things compared is very narrow: the structure of a try-works and that of a brick kiln *are* much alike, and a heart is, in fact, a kind of pump. We might even say that the second is, in the strict sense, no comparison at all. The statement that the heart "is a muscular pump" is, as a matter of fact, a definition: "pump" is simply the genus, and the differentia specifying the species is "muscular."

Let us set the statement "the heart is a muscular pump" against that made in a famous poem by Robert Burns: "My love is like a red, red rose." We recognize immediately that Burns is not using the comparison for expository purposes. He is certainly not giving a definition. Even if he said of his beloved, "My love is a red, red rose," he would still not be giving a definition.

What Burns is doing is setting up an interplay of qualities (or of connotations) between girl and rose so that the qualities of the two interfuse in

---
[14] See Metaphor, pp. 435–65.

the reader's imagination. If anything is being defined here, it is neither the girl nor the rose; it is the nature of the poet's feeling for the girl (real or fictional). The language of logic cannot describe the experience of love (and of many other experiences); it cannot "define" love in any fashion that really enlightens us. Only poetry (in the broadest as well as the narrowest sense) can do that.

To take one more example, the author of the Epistle to the Hebrews, in the Bible, traditionally thought to be Saint Paul, says: "Faith is the substance of things hoped for, the evidence of things not seen." This passage has the form of a definition, or rather of two parallel definitions: the genus of the first is "substance," with "hoped for" as the differentia; the genus of the second is "evidence," with "things not seen" as the differentia. Now substance and evidence are contradictory to faith; they are the things that logic deals with and the very things that faith leaps beyond. What the author of the Epistle says, by putting the contradiction in the form of a definition, is that faith has an overriding "logic" of its own. The author is making a powerful and paradoxical metaphor that enriches our understanding of, and feeling for, the experience of faith; but he is not defining it.

● A STRONG CAUTION: CIRCULAR DEFINITION

We cannot define a word by repeating the word itself in the definition. If, for example, we define the word *statistician* by saying that it means anybody who makes a profession of compiling and studying statistics, we have committed this error. The real question: "What kind of thing does a statistician do?" has been left unanswered. The pretended definition does not enlarge anybody's knowledge, because it merely repeats the term to be defined: *statistics, statistician*. It is also possible to make the error of circular definition without repeating a word, but merely by repeating an idea, as, "The causes of war are the several factors that result in armed conflict." (Observe that here we have, in another form, the error of a definition by synonym. See p. 101.)

■ APPLICATIONS

I None of the following statements is an acceptable definition. What is wrong with each? Is it metaphorical, too broad, too narrow, circular? Or what? If you lack the information necessary to judge some of the statements, use a dictionary or an encyclopedia, or some other reference work. For example, Number 10 uses the word *anthropology*. If you do not know what anthropology is, find out. If it studies more than morality, then the statement here is not acceptable.

1   A god is a divinity.
2   Poetry is what is written by poets.

3   Poetry is the breath and finer spirit of all knowledge.
4   A soiree is a social function that does not take place in the afternoon.
5   The French word *cheval* means "horse."
6   Her hair is a woman's crowning glory.
7   A protuberance is a thing that protrudes.
8   To inhume is to put something into the ground.
9   To inhume is to inter.
10 Anthropology is the science that studies morality.
11 Love is a tender sentiment.
12 Cricket is a game played with a wooden instrument called a bat and a rather small, leather-covered ball.
13 Democracy is that form of government founded on the assumption that a popular error is more desirable than an unpopular one.
14 Patriotism is the last refuge of a scoundrel.
15 Patriotism is a holy sentiment.
16   'Home is the place where, when you have to go there,
       They have to take you in.'
                           'I should have called it
  Something you somehow haven't to deserve.'   —Robert Frost.
17   Duty is the 'Stern daughter of the voice of God.'   —William Wordsworth.

II Amend as many as possible of the above statements to make acceptable definitions. For instance, you cannot well amend a mere synonym or a metaphor given as a "definition." You would have to start over. Confine your efforts to the statements that are definitions, however inadequate.

Extended definition

Thus far we have been dealing with relatively brief definitions of the kind that commonly appear in themes of exposition. We might, for instance, begin a theme on drag-racing by defining the term for the uninformed reader. Sometimes, however, particularly when we are thinking seriously about a complicated concept, such as democracy, we use a definition as the basis for an entire theme; that is, we write what may be called an *extended definition*. The method is often the best way for us to come to our own understanding of such a term—and of such a subject; and it is often the best way of explaining the term, or subject.

The basic problem with a word such as *democracy* is that no commonly available short definition is sufficient to give us an understanding of the full implications of the word. For such understanding we would have to go into the history lying behind the word and into the complex systems of ideas involved in it. For instance, as a basis for understanding the term *democracy*, we might find ourselves not only referring to the origin of the word in Ancient Greek, but also using the history of Athens, even including the development of techniques and crafts that preceded the rise of popular government. Or we might find ourselves using the beginnings of Christianity, with its idea of the worth of the individual human soul, in relation to the democratic impulses in subsequent history. We would have to feel our way along, trying out different ideas to see where they lead us, discarding some and trying again. We can use whatever will help us to understand, including other forms of exposition or other modes of discourse—description, narration, or argument.

This sort of treatment may seem to lead us far from the purpose of definition—which is to limit the meaning of a term. It may, that is seem to confuse the mere explanation of the meaning of a word for some "linguistic community" (or communities) with the explanation of when, how, and why the term came to be so used. True, both purposes may be present in an extended definition, but there will be no confusion if we can clearly use the second purpose to support the first—that is, if all the material concerning when, how, and why is directed toward giving a fuller understanding of the term in question. We shall soon be dealing with certain examples that make this process clear, for instance, the two extended definitions of *wealth*, to which we now come, and the even more elaborate definition of *academic freedom* (pp. 122–24).

The formula of definition as frame

The most obvious way to organize an extended definition is to use the standard formula as a frame, taking genus, species, and differentiae as a basis for the development of a discussion. Here an economist sets out to define *wealth* by this method:

> There is a certain desirable thing which is and must be the subject of political economy. Whether avowed or not, a definite conception is, in reality, under discussion in every treatise on this science. For this conception the term *wealth,* if used in accordance with history and etymology, is an accurate designation. The Saxon *weal* indicated a condition of relative well-being, the state of having one's wants well supplied as compared with a prevailing standard. No possession common to all men can constitute such relative well-being. The limitless gifts of nature do not produce it, since they are indiscriminate in their ministrations; air and sunlight make no differences among men and, though creating absolute well-being, cannot create that social condition indicated by the term *wealth*. This relative condition can be produced only by that which, besides satisfying wants, is capable of appropriation.
>
> It is by a transfer of meaning that the term which primarily designated a condition of life has been applied to the things which produce the condition. But not all causes of comparative happiness are included in the meaning of the word. Wealth, as historically used, signified the well-being resulting from outward rather than inward causes. Health and contentment may make a shepherd happier than the owner of flocks; yet the owner only is "well off." Reserving a broader term to designate well-being in general,

usage has employed the word *wealth* to signify, first, the comparative welfare resulting from material possession and, second, and by a transfer, the possessions themselves.

Wealth then consists in the relative weal-constituting elements in man's material environment. It is objective to the user, material, useful, and appropriable. . . .   —JOHN B. CLARK: *The Philosophy of Wealth.*

Here the author starts with the derivation of the word, just as a dictionary might do, and then shows how the meaning has become specialized by the addition of differentiae that distinguish wealth from other kinds of weal, or well-being. Since the differentiae are somewhat complicated, he does not simply list them, but explains each one.

Below is another, somewhat more elaborate definition of *wealth,* in which the author uses a different approach to definition. Whereas Clark builds his definition by *including* the differentiae properly belonging to the term, Hilaire Belloc, the author of the definition to follow, begins by *excluding* the *differentiae* that do not properly belong.

The economic definition of Wealth is subtle and difficult to appreciate. . . . First, we must be clear as to what Wealth is *not.*

Wealth is never properly defined, for the purpose of economic study, by any one of the answers a person would naturally give off-hand. For instance, most people would say that a man's wealth was the money he was worth. But that, of course, is nonsense: for even if there were no money used, his possessions would still be there, and if he had a house and cattle and horses, the mere fact that money was not being used where he lived would not make him any worse off.

Another and better, but still wrong, answer is: "Wealth is what a man possesses." For instance, in the case of this farmer, his house and his stock and his furniture and implements are what we call his "wealth." In ordinary talk that answer will do well enough. But it will not do for the strict science of Economics, for it is not accurate.

For consider a particular case. Part of this man's wealth is, you say, a certain gray horse. But if you look closely at your definition and make it rigidly accurate, you will find that *it is not the horse itself which constitutes his wealth, but something attaching to the horse,* some quality or circumstance which affects the horse and gives the horse what is called its *value.* It is this *value* which is wealth, not the horse. To see how true this is consider how the value changes while the horse remains the same.

On such and such a date any neighbor would have given the owner of the horse from 20 to 25 sacks of wheat for it, or, say, 10 sheep, or 50 loads of cut wood. But suppose there comes a great mortality among horses, so that very few are left. There is an eager desire to get hold of those that survive in order that the work may be done on the farms. Then the neighbors will be willing to give the owner of the horse much more than 20 to 25 sacks of wheat for it. They may offer as much as 50 sacks, or 20 sheep, or 100 loads of wood. Yet the horse is exactly the same horse it was before. The wealth of the master has increased. His horse, as we say, is "worth more." *It is this Worth, that is, this ability to get other wealth in exchange, which constitutes true Economic Wealth.*

I have told you that the idea is very difficult to seize, and that you will find the hardest part of the study here at the beginning. There is no way to make it plainer. One has no choice but to master the idea and make oneself familiar with it, difficult as it is. *Wealth does not reside in the objects we possess, but in the economic values attaching to those objects.*

We talk of a man's wealth or a nation's wealth, or the wealth of the whole world, and we think at once, of course, of a lot of material things: houses and ships, and pictures and furniture, and food and all the rest of it. But the economic wealth which it is our business to study is not identical with those *things*. Wealth is the sum total of the *values* attaching to those things.

That is the first and most important point.

Here is the second: Wealth, for the purposes of economic study, *is confined to those values attaching to material objects through the action of man, which values can be exchanged for other values.*

I will explain what that sentence means.

Here is a mountain country where there are few people and plenty of water everywhere. That water does not form part of the *Economic Wealth* of anyone living there. Everyone is the better off for the water, but no one has *wealth* in it. The water they have is absolutely necessary to life, but no man will give anything for it because any man can get it for himself. It has no *value in exchange*. But in a town to which water has to be brought at great expense of effort, and where the amount is limited, it acquires a value in exchange, that is, people cannot get it without offering something for it. That is why we say that in a modern town water forms part of *Economic Wealth*, while in the country it usually does not.

We must carefully note that wealth thus defined is *not* the same thing as well-being. The mixing up of these two separate things—well-being and economic wealth—has given rise to half the errors in economic science. People confuse the word "wealth" with the idea of well-being. They say: "Surely a man is better off with plenty of water than with little, and therefore conditions under which he can get plenty of water for nothing are conditions under which he has *more wealth* than when he has to pay for it. He has more wealth when he gets the water free than he has when he has to pay for it."

It is not so. Economic wealth is a separate thing from well-being. Economic wealth may well be increasing though the general well-being of the people is going down. It may increase though the general well-being of the people around it is stationary.

The science of Economics does not deal with true happiness nor even with well-being in material things. It deals with a strictly limited field of what is called "Economic Wealth," and if it goes outside its own boundaries it goes wrong. Making people as happy as possible is much more than Economics can pretend to. Economics cannot even tell you how to make people well-to-do in material things. But it can tell you how exchangeable Wealth is produced and what happens to it; and as it can tell you this, it is a useful servant.

That is the second difficulty at the very beginning of our study. *Economic Wealth consists in **exchangeable** values, and nothing else....*

Let us sum up this first, elementary, part of our subject, and put it in the shortest terms we can find—what are called "Formulae," which means short and exact definitions, such as can be learnt by heart and retained permanently.

We write down, then, two Formulae:

1. Wealth is made up, not of things, but of economic values attaching to things.

2. Wealth, for the purpose of economic study, means *only* exchange values: that is, values against which other values will be given in exchange.

—HILAIRE BELLOC: *Economics for Young People.*

The maker of this definition of *wealth* starts by ruling out certain common misconceptions. Wealth is not money. Wealth is not what a man possesses. But merely to rule out these errors requires discussion and illustration, through which we arrive at the notion that the "ability to get other wealth in exchange" is the key to the definition, that wealth resides not "in the objects we possess, but in the economic values attaching to those objects."

This statement gives us, of course, a genus (*value*) and differentiae (summed up under the term *economic*). We have a notion what the genus *value* means, but the differentiae are not clear to us. The writer, then, sets about explaining that economic value is exchange value, "values attaching to material objects through the action of man, which can be exchanged for other values." He discusses this idea by illustration, the illustration of water in the country and water in the town. This discussion leads him to make a sharp distinction between wealth and well-being, thus making a definition exactly opposite that of the previous writer. Having completed his explanation, Belloc is prepared to set up what he calls his formulae, which embody both his definition of wealth as economic value and a summary of his explanation of economic value, which amounts to another definition. So here, to understand one definition we have to have another.

To return to our preliminary discussion of extended definition (pp. 115–16), we must remember that, no matter how elaborate an extended definition may be, everything in it should be subordinate to the purpose of defining the term in question. A term referring to a complex concept may need a complex discussion, but the dominant purpose must be kept clear.

■ APPLICATION

The second of the definitions of *wealth* is from a book called *Economics for Young People*. The title of the book defines its audience (or pretends to do so). For what kind of book do you think the first definition was written? A professional work? A textbook? A general magazine? Or what? And why do you think so?

The following is a student theme of extended definition:

WHAT IS A GOOD COACH?

Ever since I went to high school, I have wanted to be an athletic coach for my life work—I mean a good coach. A coach is a trainer, but he is a special kind of trainer, not like the trainer who gets a squad in condition. The coach assumes that the squad is in good condition before he begins his special work. What he does, it seems to me, has two parts, one concerning the body, the other the mind.

For the first part, he has to bring the body into the proper relation to the particular sport involved. This means that he has to analyze the various factors of a peak performance for each boy on the team, on one hand things like speed and timing in general, and on the other, special aspects of the action belonging to the sport, such as passing, line backing, broken field running. For the requirements of the game (and the position the boy is to play) the coach has to analyze the elements and then weld them back together in a fluid performance.

I have been talking about the requirements of the sport, whatever sport it is, but even if a coach has a group perfectly prepared in this respect, he has to do another welding job along the way; he has to weld the individuals together into a team, and that means to make them all understand the overall purpose of the game, how every individual player, and every individual act, is part of a pattern that is pointed like a pistol at the goal line or basket or whatever. He has to make each boy realize that no matter how great he is, he is expendable. That is, the game doesn't exist just to make him shine. The purpose is to punch the ball over.

For the second part, the mind. A coach has to instill the fighting spirit, sure. But to make this mean anything, he has to be able to inspire confidence of two kinds. The first is confidence in him, not just as a guy who is expert at the game, but as a guy who understands every fellow and has his good at heart. Then he has to inspire the fellows with confidence in themselves. Each fellow has to know that he has something to give, but more important, he has got to feel that he stands a little above winning or losing. If a fellow can't stand losing one Saturday, for instance, he probably won't have the bounce to come back and win the next time. Sure, it feels good to be winning, to be the guy who pushed the ball over and got the cheers, to feel tuned up and with a skill you can depend on. But there's something more in knowing how to live a sport without reference to winning or losing, to feel that the sport has its own value somehow. A coach has to get this across. Call it character-building, like they do in the college catalogue. Even that won't spoil it.

It is what made our team at school carry Coach Hadley around the field on their shoulders after we lost the championship—on our own field. The poor old guy looked as though he were going to cry.

Here the author has made a real effort to think through his definition, and he has tried to be systematic in the same way as Clark in his definition of *wealth*. He has moved through a number of distinctions, setting up the differentiae for each, trying to close in on his subject. This theme has two features not found in the examples by Clark and Belloc, for here the author gives a specific setting to explain the need for definition, and in the last paragraph he deserts the method of definition for that of illustration, using the illustration to sum up all he has been talking about. Let us notice, too, that the illustration is not simply exposition; it contains a hint of narrative, the reference to an episode.

■ APPLICATIONS

I Outline the method of extended definition in "What Is a Good Coach?" For example in the first paragraph, the author begins with the class *trainer*, which he subdivides into two smaller classes, one of which indicates what he means by *coach*. Then he makes another kind of distinction between the two kinds of things, generally considered, that the coach must work on: body, mind. Proceed with the analysis of the theme. Use diagrams if you find them useful. Do you find any blurs or confusions? If so, comment on them. Another point: Is the title accurate for this theme? When you make a definition of *nail*, are you thinking about bad nails, or nails characteristically considered? Ponder this awhile.

II Analyze the structure of the following definition. How is the method of genus and differentiae used? Indicate the distinctions made. Are there any merely descriptive elements here? Any supportive characteristics?

> Chemistry is that branch of science which has the task of investigating the materials out of which the universe is made. It is not concerned with the forms into which they may be fashioned. Such objects as chairs, tables, vases, bottles, or wires are of no significance in chemistry; but such substances as glass, wool, iron, sulfur, and clay, as the materials out of which they are made, are what it studies. Chemistry is concerned not only with the composition of such substances, but also with their inner structure. Further, these materials are constantly undergoing change in nature: iron rusts, wood decays, sugar ferments, coal burns, limestone rock is eaten away by water, and living organisms digest their foods and build up their structures. Chemistry investigates such changes—the conditions under which they occur, the mechanism by which they take place, the new substances that are formed as their result, and the energy that is liberated or absorbed by them. Chemistry also studies the way in which these and similar changes can be carried out in the laboratory or on a larger scale in the chemical plant. As a result of investigations along these lines, chemistry has found how metals can be extracted from their ores; how impoverished fields can be made fertile again; and how the materials that are found in nature can be converted into thousands of new substances to help feed the race, to cure the sick, and to provide such comfort and even luxury for the common man as was not enjoyed by the wealthy of an earlier generation.
>
> —John Arrend Timm: *General Chemistry*.

III Write a theme of extended definition of 300 to 400 words. The list below may suggest a subject to you:

Political Equality   Student Power
The Square   The Good Citizen
The Hippie   Physics
Human Rights
Sportsmanship
Heroism
The Liberal
Cynicism

You may find it necessary to investigate your subject before writing. Use the library.

ELABORATION IN EXTENDED DEFINITION

The following example, an examination of the term *academic freedom* by a well-known philosopher, is not only longer than those we have been looking at, it has much greater variety of method. But observe how closely the whole discussion is related to the dominant purpose: to define the term. And observe how relevant each detail is to Hook's conception of the term.

What is academic freedom? This freedom is a very recent acquisition in this country. It is less than a century old. It is an un-American import from Imperial Germany, a country which was at the time not politically democratic but which nonetheless was the first country in the history of the world to develop what we understand today as "academic freedom." In Germany "academic freedom" was originally defined as *Lehrfreiheit* and *Lernfreiheit,* freedom to teach and freedom to learn. When "academic freedom" was first introduced, or rather bruited about, in this country nobody paid attention to *Lernfreiheit* or the freedom to learn. The founding fathers of the American Association of University Professors, John Dewey and Arthur Lovejoy, were only concerned with the freedom to teach which was imperiled (or hardly existed) in the U.S. until Johns Hopkins was established as a regular graduate university. To this day, when we speak of academic freedom we normally mean freedom to teach. Freedom to learn which today is at the basis of most claims for "student academic freedom" has only recently received attention in the United States. The phrase "student academic freedom" would have been considered a neologism a few short years ago.

The shortest and most adequate definition I know of academic freedom (*Lehrfreiheit*) is the one I proposed a few years ago in the interests of economy of space and time. I defined academic freedom as "the freedom of professionally qualified persons to inquire, discover, publish, and teach the truth as they see it in the field of their competence, subject to no control or authority save the control and authority of the rational methods by which conclusions are established in their disciplines." There are several important implications of this definition. First of all, this definition doesn't say that academic freedom is the right or freedom to teach the truth. It asserts only that academic freedom is the right or freedom *to seek* the truth. Does this mean that error has the same rights as truth? No, not when it is revealed as error; yes, until the issue is decided in the light of evidence and argument. Even if we granted Augustine's dictum that "error has no rights," on my definition there would still be a right to be wrong. After all, no one can properly claim to be infallible or to possess the absolute truth. All we can ask of him is that he honestly seek the truth. If academic freedom is the right not *to teach* the truth but *to seek* the truth, then teachers must enjoy freedom from any ecclesiastical or religious or economic or political dogma which would bar the road to further inquiry.

Another very important implication of my definition is that the right to academic freedom is not a civil right, not a "human right." Notice that we have defined it as the right of *professionally qualified* persons. The right of academic freedom is a right that must be earned, whereas a civil right, or a human right, is something which doesn't have to be earned. It is possessed by every human being because he's a member of a community. You don't have to earn your right to speak freely. It's yours because you are a member of a democratic community. You don't have to earn your right to a fair trial. It's yours because you are a member of a civilized community, and it is intrinsic to your status as man and citizen. Anybody has a civil right to talk nonsense in any field he pleases. But on my definition, one must be professionally qualified to talk nonsense in a university! Of course what you may think is nonsense may turn out to be the higher part of wisdom. If my definition is accepted, it also follows that the qualified teacher has the right honestly to reach any conclusion in the field of his competence. That is to say, academic freedom carries with it the right to heresy whether it's in biology, literature, or . . . politics! If a teacher honestly in pursuit of an argument comes to a conclusion that others regard as fascist or communist or racist or whatnot, once he has been certified as competent by his peers, he merits protection by the community against those who would punish him for his heresy. Not only the community of scholars but the general community, if it supports academic freedom must support his right to be wrong, subject, of course, to the criticism of his peers. Academic freedom does not mean immunity from criticism, vigorous criticism. Many people feel uncomfortable when I maintain that there is a right to heresy, but if one reflects upon the fact that the heresy of today may be the truth of tomorrow, that no one can plausibly claim infallibility or absolute truth for any theory, he will realize that the very nature of free academic activity implies an openness to all points of view provided only that they express the result of honest inquiry.

Does this mean that anything goes in a university or college, that a teacher can say or do anything he pleases? No. The right to heresy must not be confused with conspiracy, and by "conspiracy" in this connection I mean a deliberate act in violation of the canons of professional ethics and integrity. You will recall that I said academic freedom is the right of *professionally qualified* persons to inquire, discover, publish, and teach in the field of their competence. If a professor of mathematics does not teach mathematics to his classes but insists upon teaching sociology or denouncing sin or a professor of English concerns himself mainly with a defence of Lysenko or other subjects which are unrelated to his field and in which he has no competence, he cannot plead the right of heresy. He is violating the ethics of his profession. More important. Suppose a teacher were discovered to be on the payroll of a corporation under instructions of its public relations office to propagandize for positions that are not reached as a result of his free inquiry but are dictated to him, we would rightly say that he has surrendered his professional integrity, that he has given hostages to the enemies of free inquiry, and therefore rendered himself *prima facie* professionally unfit. The question of his fitness would be raised not on doctrinal grounds but solely on grounds of professional ethics. He would be entitled to a hearing by his peers, but the burden of proof would rest on him to show why he should not be dismissed if the facts were as stated and he had undertaken to teach according to directives received from without.

Similarly, suppose an individual were a member of a political party or group, whatever its ideological affiliation or complexion, that explicitly gave him instructions to angle or slant his position in the classroom, and "without exposing himself" to indoctrinate for the "party line." Whether it was the line of a church, a political party or a cultist sect, we would emphatically deny that such conduct fell under the right to heresy. This would be conspiracy, and render him presumptively unfit on grounds of professional ethics to continue teaching. His actions would be comparable to that of a physician who had agreed to recommend unnecessary operations to his patients in order to split fees with the surgeon or of a lawyer who had planned to throw his client's case for a higher fee. All would be guilty of unprofessional conduct.

If there is no right to conspiracy, then no member of any group which prescribes unprofessional conduct in the classroom or on campus as among the duties of its teacher-members is entitled to the protection of academic freedom which he is sure to invoke when he is exposed as a member of such a group. Nor is it necessary to prove that he has actually carried out the official instructions of the group any more than it is necessary to prove that a person who has voluntarily joined a ring to commit a crime must carry it out before we are justified, after a hearing in which he would have an opportunity to rebut the evidence, in barring him from the position that would enable him to act on his instructions and abuse his professional trust.

This conception of academic freedom is notably and eloquently expressed in the Declaration of the Graduate School of the New School for Social Research which was founded by exiles from Hitler's Germany:

> "The New School knows that no man can teach well, nor should be permitted to teach at all, unless he is prepared 'to follow the truth of scholarship wherever it may lead.' No inquiry is ever made as to whether a lecturer's private views are conservative, liberal, or radical; orthodox or agnostic; views of the aristocrat or commoner. Jealously safeguarding this precious principle, the New School stoutly affirms that a member of any political party or group which asserts the right

to dictate in matters of science or scientific opinion is not free to teach the truth and thereby is disqualified as a teacher."

—SIDNEY HOOK: *Academic Freedom and Academic Anarchy.*[15]

Here the author does not begin—as does J. B. Clark in defining wealth—with the etymology of the term *academic freedom,* but by giving the historical setting in which the idea arose, first in Imperial Germany, and then in the United States. Having provided the historical setting, Hook then does frame a short definition of the standard sort:

To-be-defined	=	*Definer*	
Academic freedom	is	the "freedom"	(*genus*)
		1 of professionally qualified persons	(*differentiae*)
		2 to inquire, discover, publish, and teach the truth as they see it in fields of their competence	
		3 subject only to the control and authority of the rational methods by which truth is established	

But this definition needs discussion. So we have the supporting ideas.

1 Academic freedom is *not* the right to *teach* the truth: only to seek truth.[16]
2 It is *not* a civil right, or human right; it is a right only of the professionally qualified person.
3 It is not contingent upon the "truth" (or social acceptability) of a conclusion reached: "heresy" may be taught—but taught only in the context of criticism by other "professionally qualified persons."
4 The right to heresy is *not* the right to conspiracy.

Having set forth his supporting ideas, Hook then proceeds to give, by way of summary, the Declaration of the Graduate School of the New School for Social Research. Hook has a very good reason for quoting it—a reason that he does not state, but merely suggests. The New School was founded by exiles from Hitler's Germany: therefore they should understand and value more deeply academic freedom than we do, who tend to accept it as natural.

---

[15] Reprinted by permission of Sidney Hook and the Institute for the Comparative Study of Ideologies and Political Systems at the University of Colorado.

[16] It may be argued that there is a contradiction here, that in the second differentia (above) the right to "teach the truth" is specified. But the author might resolve this difficulty by saying that the "truth" is not, except in rare instances, to be settled absolutely and that the "seeking" is a constantly on-going process—that what one sees as the truth is subject to criticism.

■ APPLICATIONS

I   Would you disagree with any element of this definition? The points about heresy and conspiracy are likely to provoke controversy. If you disagree on these or other matters, try to revise Hook's definition to make it conform to your ideas.

II   Read (or review) "Adolescence: Self-Definition and Conflict," by Edgar Z. Friedenberg (pp. 712–21) and "Hipsters Unleashed," by David McReynolds (pp. 728–34). What definition of an adolescent is developed in the first, and of a hipster in the second? Summarize each definition in a paragraph of about 150 words.

VARIETY IN EXTENDED DEFINITION

We have seen how the author of the theme about coaching leaves, at the end, the ordinary method of definition and resorts to illustration. The purpose of a definition is, after all, elucidation, explanation, and clarification, and so in extended definition we often find a great variety of methods. The writer uses any tool necessary to make us know what the limits of his term are. For instance, the contrast of "Red-bloods" and "Mollycoddles" (pp. 76–78) amounts to an extended definition of both, and the short essay on "Neighborliness" (pp. 86–87) amounts to a definition by means of illustrations that in themselves employ description and narration. By the same token, definition, in either a strict or a broad form, is often a useful device to lead to or support other forms of exposition, or other modes of discourse. For instance, the two definitions of *wealth* given above are merely preliminary to long studies of economics that involve argument as well as exposition.

It definition may be used so loosely, why, you may ask, have we dwelt in such detail on definition in the strict sense?

We have done so, because a grasp of that process is the greatest help possible to clarity in free-flowing discussion in which the formal structure of definition is absorbed and blended with other methods. For instance, look at the following selections as examples of such absorption or of methods other than definition used for the purposes of definition.

> Snobbery is not the same thing as pride of class. Pride of class may not please us but we must at least grant that it reflects a social function. A man who exhibited class pride—in the day when it was possible to do so—may have been puffed up about what he *was*, but this ultimately depended on what he *did*. Thus, aristocratic pride was based ultimately on the ability to fight and administer. No pride is without fault, but pride of class may be thought of as today we think of pride of profession, toward which we are likely to be lenient.
> Snobbery is pride in status without pride of function. And it is an uneasy

pride of status. It always asks, "Do I belong—do I really belong? And does he belong? And if I am observed talking to him, will it make me seem to belong or not to belong?" It is the peculiar vice not of aristocratic societies which have their own appropriate vices, but of bourgeois democratic societies. For us the legendary strongholds of snobbery are the Hollywood studios, where two thousand dollars a week dare not talk to three hundred dollars a week for fear he be taken for nothing more than fifteen hundred dollars a week. The dominant emotions of snobbery are uneasiness, self-consciousness, self-defensiveness, the sense that one is not quite real but can in some way acquire reality.

—LIONEL TRILLING: *The Liberal Imagination.*[17]

I think it is legitimate to say . . . that the Beat Generation's worship of primitivism and spontaneity is more than a cover for hostility to intelligence; it arises from a pathetic poverty of feeling as well. The hipsters and hipster-lovers of the Beat Generation are rebels, all right, but not against anything so sociological and historical as the middle class or capitalism or even respectability. This is the revolt of the spiritually underprivileged and the crippled of soul—young men who can't think straight and hate anyone who can; young men who can't get outside of the morass of self. . . .

—NORMAN PODHORETZ: "The Know-Nothing Bohemians,"
Doings and Undoings: The Fifties and After in American Writing.[18]

■ APPLICATIONS

I Write a point-by-point contrast between Podhoretz's definition of the Beats and your summary of McReynolds's definition of the hipster. Then read (or review) "Slouching Towards Bethlehem," by Joan Didion (pp. 658–72) and compare, in a paragraph, her implied definition of the hipster with that of McReynolds.

II The following quotation is from Albert Einstein, the great physicist and the father of the theory of relativity. It is his way of answering the question of what religion is, and it is therefore intended as a definition. The passage includes an example of the standard formula of definition (though it deals with the "religious person" and not with "religion"). Try to isolate it and state it. Then specify the stages in Einstein's discussion. What does he add to the formula?

At first, then, instead of asking what religion is, I should prefer to ask what characterizes the aspirations of a person who gives me the impression of

---

[17] From *The Liberal Imagination* by Lionel Trilling. Copyright 1948 by Lionel Trilling. Reprinted by permission of The Viking Press, Inc. and Martin Secker & Warburg, Ltd.
[18] Reprinted from "The Know-Nothing Bohemians," from *Doings and Undoings: The Fifties and After in American Writing*, by Norman Podhoretz, by permission of Norman Podhoretz. This essay first appeared in *Partisan Review*, vol. 25, no. 2 (Spring 1958).

being religious: a person who is religiously enlightened appears to me to be one who has, to the best of his ability, liberated himself from the fetters of his selfish desires and is preoccupied with thoughts, feelings, and aspirations to which he clings because of their super-personal value.

It seems to me that what is important is the force of this super-personal content and the depth of the conviction concerning its overpowering meaningfulness, regardless of whether any attempt is made to unite this content with a Divine Being, for otherwise it would not be possible to count Buddha and Spinoza as religious personalities.

Accordingly, a religious person is devout in the sense that he has no doubt of the significance and loftiness of those super-personal objects and goals which neither require nor are capable of rational foundation. They exist with the same necessity and matter-of-factness as he himself. In this sense religion is the age-old endeavor of mankind to become clearly and completely conscious of these values and goals and constantly to strengthen and extend their effects.

—Albert Einstein: "Science and Religion," *Science News Letter.*

III Here are seven statements about religion. Some may be metaphorical, some are definitions that are too narrow or too broad. Perhaps you might interpret one or more as acceptable. The point here is for you to discuss these "definitions" as thoughtfully as you can. Do indicate what limitations you find. But also try to see which of these statements might be drawn into a proper definition of religion—that is, into one that you yourself would accept. Furthermore, try to see what led the maker of each statement to say what he did.

For this exercise, as for many other exercises in this book, there is no clear-cut right or wrong, yes or no, with the answer in the back of the book. Simply try to reflect seriously on what is at stake here.

A Religion, after trying to see as best I could what various religions and religious people had in common, I felt impelled to define as the reaction of the personality as a whole to its experience of the Universe as a whole.
—Sir Julian Huxley.

B Religion is 'morality tinged with emotion.' —Matthew Arnold.

C Religion is the 'belief in spiritual beings.' —E. B. Tylor.

D Religion is 'that voice of the deepest human experience.'
—Matthew Arnold.

E Religion is the 'opium of the people.' —Karl Marx.

F Religion is 'a propitiation or conciliation of powers superior to man which are believed to direct or control the course of nature and of human life.'
—Sir James Frazer.

G Pure religion and undefiled before God is this, to visit the fatherless and widows in their affliction, and to keep himself unspotted from the world.
—Saint James.

H Being religious means asking passionately the question of the meaning of our existence and being willing to receive answers, even if the answers hurt.
—Paul Tillich: "The Lost Dimension in Religion,"
Adventures of the Mind.

IV   You have read "The Reach of Imagination," by Jacob Bronowski (pp. 637–44) and "The Abolition of Man," by C. S. Lewis (pp. 652–57). What definition of imagination is implied in the first, of man in the second? What term or terms has each author been concerned to define? For what purpose? How has he proceeded? Read "Politics of the Non-political," by Stephen Spender (pp. 722–27). What definition of a university does Spender give, by statement or implication? Write a brief summary of the definition. Compare the definition in Spender's essay with the definition of a university implied in the discussion of academic freedom by Sidney Hook (pp. 122–24).

V   You are now to write a long theme (at least 800 words) of extended definition. This will differ from your earlier theme of definition not only in length, for here you should aim to use a variety of methods, including straight description or even narration. In preparing for the actual writing, you might use the following questions to guide you, making notes as you go along:

1   Derivation of the word—does the origin enlighten us?
2   History of the application of the word—do earlier applications differ from the present application?
3   Genus and differentiae in present application—how can the species be distinguished from other significant species?
4   Analysis of species—does it have any "subspecies," and if so, how are they to be distinguished from one another?
5   Application of the definition to individual instances—does the definition really meet this test, and does it enlighten us about the individual instances?
6   Can you think of any contrasts or comparisons that would help pinpoint the subject?
7   Looking back over your notes, do you feel that your major interest is to frame a definition or to use the method of definition (in the broad sense) as a way to control a discussion?

The topics below may serve as suggestions. You will notice that some of them have appeared before. You may even have written a theme on one. If you have, do not let that keep you from using it again; this will be a different theme. It should be the most ambitious and interesting you have done.

How I Define Personal Liberty	Love
Leisure: Fun or Fulfillment?	The Role of a Parent
Black Power	Tragedy (in the literary sense)
Sexual Freedom	Comedy (in the literary sense)
The Duty of the Individual to Society	Education
Emotional Depression	Patriotism
War	Social Obligation

The Sixth Method: Analysis

In studying the methods of exposition thus far we have been often concerned with the relation of the particular to the general, of the individual item to the class. Now, when we turn to analysis, we treat the individual item, whatever it may be, not in relation to something more general or inclusive, but in relation to its own parts.

Analysis is the method of dividing into component parts. (The word *analysis* actually means "loosening into parts.") It can be applied to anything that can be thought of as having parts. We can analyze an object, such as a dog, a house, a tree, a picture. We can analyze an intangible, such as the character of a person, or an idea, such as "goodness." We can analyze an organization, such as a church or a corporation. We can analyze a process, such as baking bread, or an event, such as the French Revolution.

Analysis, classification, and structure

You may ask how analysis differs from classification. A class may, it is true, be said to include the items in that class, but a class, as ordinarily conceived, has no structure in relation to the particular items that fall within it. That is, particular items are not *parts* of the class.[19]

A thing (object, mechanism, idea, or whatever) is an analyzable structure when its components are organized and have a mutually supporting function in determining the nature of the structure. A brick wall is a structure, for the individual bricks supporting one another are necessary to one another and to the wall. The human body is a structure, for the parts are mutually necessary and necessary to the whole.

A class does not have such characteristics. A class exists as the *idea* of the qualities shared by a number of individual items. But no one item or set of items belonging to the class is necessary for the existence of the class. We can destroy one individual book, or a million, and the class *book,* the idea of what constitutes a book, is not impaired. But we cannot knock many bricks from a wall or do much cutting on a human body. Nor can we omit an act from a play or a logical step from an argument, unless we can assume that the hearer knows it already. For here, too, we are dealing with structures—as common usage recognizes, for we refer to the structure of a play, or the structure of an argument.

An analysis cannot take place except in accordance with the principle of the structure of the thing being analyzed. A small boy beating on an alarm clock with a hammer is not analyzing the mechanism, no matter how many things get knocked loose. Even if he carefully takes the clock apart

---

[19] There are "ordered classes," for instance, in mathematics, but they do not concern us here.

with a screwdriver and not a hammer, he is still not making an analysis—unless he grasps the principle of the relation among the parts.

Interest and method

Analysis represents a rational interest on the part of the person making the analysis. Therefore it must be conducted by some method, not hit-or-miss. The method used depends on the nature of the structure under consideration.

But here we must remember that the same object may, according to the different kinds of interest brought to bear on it, be regarded as more than one kind of structure. For example, the botanist would regard an apple as a botanical structure and therefore would analyze it into stem, skin, flesh, seeds, and so forth; whereas a chemist would regard it as a chemical structure and would analyze it into certain elements, or a painter would regard it as an aesthetic structure and would analyze it into a pattern of color. Each man would perform his analysis in terms of a particular interest, and the interest prompting his analysis would decide the kind of structure that he took the object to be. The kind of structure would in turn determine what might be regarded as the parts of the structure.

In illustrating the fact that a particular object may be regarded as having different kinds of structure, we have used an example having physical existence, an apple. But what we said may also apply to something with no physical existence, say a short story. We may regard it as a grammatical structure, for it is made up of words. Or we may regard it as a fictional structure, that is, as being composed of plot, of characters, of theme—elements that we can think of and discuss separately. An institution may also be regarded as having different kinds of structure. For instance, we may regard the family as a biological structure, or as an economic structure, or as a moral structure. Each of these structures focuses attention on different kinds of relationships among the members of a family.

● CAUTION

Do not confuse analysis with classification. For example, in the exercise that follows it is not relevant for you to place your mother in a religious, ethnic, or financial classification. But you could regard her as, for instance, a chemical structure. What other structures would be applicable to her? Or suppose love were an item on our list. It is not relevant to place it among the emotions or sentiments. It would be relevant, however, to try to discriminate what motives or feelings merge to give us what we call love. For instance, William Wordsworth was said, by his friend Coleridge, to regard love as a mixture of lust and esteem. Wordsworth had performed an analysis of love—good or bad, that is not the point.

■ **APPLICATION**

Can you think of more than one kind of interest by which an analysis of the following items might be executed? Be specific. List the kinds of interest, and indicate certain parts that might appear in each kind of analysis.

Your mother	Generosity
A poem	Radar
A helicopter	The human heart
American sectionalism	A corporation
A picture	The American party system

Analysis and technical (or expository) description

Analysis is the form of description achieved by distinguishing the parts of the thing described. This kind of description, which we shall presently contrast with ordinary description, is called *technical* (or *expository*) *description*.

We can contrast technical description and ordinary description by considering the different types of occasion from which each arises. Technical description arises from the demand for *information about* the thing described; ordinary description, from the demand for an *immediate sense impression* of the thing described. The first kind of description is expository in that it attempts to enlarge the understanding. The second kind, ordinary description, aims to give us an experience of the object through imagination. (See Description, pp. 275–81, for a fuller discussion.) We shall call it *suggestive description*.

Let us take two examples and contrast them:

TECHNICAL DESCRIPTION:

For Quick Sale
Attractive Cape Cod cottage, lge. liv. rm., 13 x 25, knotty pine, stone fireplace; din. rm., sunny, 12 x 14; small den or libr., fireplace; kitchen, modern, elec. stove, lge. gas refrig., dishwasher, all practically new; med.-size, concrete basement, gas furn., ht. water; 2 bedrms., 14 x 16, 15 x 18; 2 baths, lge. and small; roof white oak shingle. Lot well planted, landscaped, brook, 2 acres; heated garage, 2 cars; small greenhouse. Built by owner, 1936. Excellent condition. Take reasonable offer. Call: BE–1632.

SUGGESTIVE DESCRIPTION:

Dear Mother:
We have found a place at last, and we love it, Jack just as much as I. I must tell you about it, so you can have some notion before you come to see us here. Well, you don't see it from the highway, for there is a high hedge with just a little gap that lets you into the lane, a winding lane among a grove of white oaks, like a lane going down to a pasture on

somebody's farm, a million miles away from town. When you pass the oaks you see a dip down to a brook, lined with willows, a stone bridge, and just beyond the bridge the house on a slight rise. The house is white and trim, two stories, but rather low, just seeming to crop out of the ground. You have the feeling that once you cross that bridge and enter that door you'll be safe and sound and the world will never come to bother you.

When you do enter, you know that your feeling is right. There is a long room with a big fireplace, and windows to the east for the morning sun. It is a perfect room for the furniture that Grandmother left me, just the sort of room she would have loved, peaceful and old-fashioned. The instant you come in, you think of a fire crackling on the hearth, and a kettle humming to heat water for tea, and you see the copper glinting on the andirons. . . .

The motives behind the two pieces of description are very different. The seller of the house wants to give information about the house. The buyer of the house, writing to her mother, wants to give the feel, the atmosphere, of the house. (Note that we are here using the method of contrast, with illustrations, to drive home the difference between the two kinds of descriptions.)

The advertisement, which is an analysis of the house, is an instance of technical description. Except in so far as we know the general type of Cape Cod cottage, we have no basis for visualizing the actual house. The writer of the advertisement has not been concerned that we should get a direct impression of the house; the only attempt in this direction is his use of the word *sunny* about the dining room. But if the writer has not been concerned with giving us the picture and atmosphere of his house, he has been greatly concerned with giving us a fairly complete body of information about the house considered, from a technical point of view, as a shelter and a mechanism for living.

We should find the same motive behind a naturalist's description of a species of bird, a mechanic's description of the ignition system of an automobile, or a physiologist's description of the structure of the human brain. In none of these examples would there be any attempt to make us perceive the thing described except in so far as that attempt would enlarge our understanding of the object's structure.

In the excerpt from the letter above, however, the situation is reversed. The writer is concerned with making an appeal to her reader's senses in order to establish the impression of the house, its quietness and isolation, its old-fashioned charm. The details she has selected all contribute to this impression. The suggestive description does not, as does the technical, give a systematic and relatively complete body of information concerning the subject: it does not analyze the subject. Instead, it simply presents the details that support the sensory and emotional effect the writer wishes to communicate. The technical description *tends* to be enumerative; the suggestive description *tends* to be selective and impressionistic.

There is another and very important distinction between technical and suggestive description. In strictly technical description there is no place for interpretation by the writer. The description is concerned only with the facts about the object, facts that can be observed by anyone. For example, when the writer of the advertisement of the Cape Cod cottage lists six rooms, or says that the living room is of knotty pine, he is stating a fact, something objective and beyond dispute. He is being strictly technical. But when he says that the cottage is "attractive," he is not being technical, but subjective; that is, he is interpreting the object according to his personal tastes. The letter of the buyer, though it lists certain objective facts about the house, is primarily subjective; she is trying to explain why she finds the house peaceful and charming. The subjective bias becomes clear when we think that to another person the house might be depressing rather than peaceful.

GENERALIZED DESCRIPTION

In the above example of technical description a specific house has been the subject. Often, however, technical description analyzes the characteristics of a *type*, a class, and not of a specific thing. For instance, here is a technical description that is generalized:

> Chestnut oak is the big tough-looking tree with bark in heavy ridges. At the bottom of the furrows between ridges, bark is cinnamon-red. Chestnut oak has the largest acorns known on oaks—1½ or even 2 inches. This is the acorn to roast and eat. It's the sweetest of all the northern oaks. Look for orange-brown twigs that are not round but angled in an interesting way. Name comes from resemblance to chestnut leaves—large ovals with wavy edges; one of the most beautiful of oak leaves.
>
> —RUTHERFORD PLATT: *A Pocket Guide to the Trees.*

This description gives the characteristics of a species of oak, not of a particular tree one has known—the tree at the corner of the yard that once sheltered childhood play, or the tree on the ridge blasted by lightning to a peculiar shape, weird in moonlight.

THE DEVELOPED ANALYSIS

The two examples of technical description, the advertisement for the Cape Cod cottage and the description of the species of oak, are very brief. They are little more than listings of parts. But many occasions for analysis demand more development. For one thing, we want to indicate the relation among the parts, to give an overall concept of the thing analyzed. In a book on fly-fishing, the following paragraph introduces an analysis of that sport:

> Fly-fishing has three elements: equipment, knowledge of stream life, and presentation. The equipment centers on the artificial fly; the knowledge

of stream life encompasses insects and trout; presentation is skill, acquired and magical, in presenting the fly to the trout. Fly-fishing argument, which is fabulous, revolves around the comparative values of these elements.

—JOHN MC DONALD: Introduction to *The Complete Fly Fisherman, The Notes and Letters of Theodore Gordon.*

This example differs, as we can readily see, from the two previous examples in that it systematically indicates the relation among the elements and thereby gives the basis for a detailed discussion. We shall never be at a loss to fit any detail into the overall structure here outlined.

Not only should we establish the relation among the parts, but we should, to make understanding easier for our reader or listener, settle on some single governing idea by reference to which, for the purpose of the description, the parts can be charted. In the following exposition of the try-works (the great kettles in which whale blubber was cooked down) of an old whaler, we notice how our understanding of the parts is governed by the strange image of a brick kiln set on the deck of a ship:

> Besides her hoisted boats, an American whaler is outwardly distinguished by her try-works. She presents the curious anomaly of the most solid masonry joining with oak and hemp in constituting the completed ship. It is as if from the open field a brick-kiln were transported to her planks.
>
> The try-works are planted between the foremast and mainmast, the most roomy part of the deck. The timbers beneath are of a peculiar strength, fitted to sustain the weight of an almost solid mass of brick and mortar, some ten feet by eight square, and five in height. The foundation does not penetrate the deck, but the masonry is firmly secured to the surface by ponderous knees of iron bracing it on all sides, and screwing it down to the timbers. On the flanks it is cased with wood, and at top completely covered by a large, sloping, battened hatchway. Removing this hatch we expose the great try-pots, two in number, and each of several barrels' capacity. When not in use, they are kept remarkably clean. Sometimes they are polished with soapstone and sand, till they shine within like silver punch-bowls.
> —HERMAN MELVILLE: *Moby Dick.*

In the following passage the comparison of the heart to a pump gives us the basis for understanding the relation among the parts:

> The heart is a complicated mechanism. Essentially it is a muscular pump composed of four chambers and their incoming and outgoing blood vessels. The action of these chambers is coordinated and controlled by an intricate nervous mechanism. The chambers are paired into a right half and a left half. The upper chamber on each side is called the auricle; the lower, the ventricle. Each auricle is separated from its ventricle by a muscular valve which permits the flow of blood downward but prevents the leakage of blood backward.
> —LOUIS I. DUBLIN: *The Problem of Heart Disease.*

■ **APPLICATION**

Write a short theme (250 words) of generalized description, being sure to bring your subject to focus by a single governing idea, or image. Avoid a merely random list of parts. Indicate the relation of the parts constituting the thing analyzed.

Functional analysis

The kind of analysis we have been discussing thus far answers the question: "How is it put together?" A tree, we say, is composed of roots, trunk, branches, and leaves, attached to each other in a certain way. A radar set is composed of a modulator, a radio-frequency oscillator, an antenna with scanning mechanism, a receiver, and an indicator. But with the tree or the radar set (or almost anything else), as soon as we begin to explore the idea of the relation among parts, we come to another question: "How does it work?" It is not merely the parts, but the function of the parts in relation to a characteristic function of the whole that now concerns us. The explanation of how the parts of anything relate to one another in action we may call functional analysis.[20]

In the passage about the heart the use of the comparison with a pump makes us think of the parts in action. As we continue to read the paragraph, we see that the writer has moved from analysis of parts into functional analysis: What does the pump do?

> Venous blood arriving from all parts of the body in the right auricle passes from the auricle through the valve into the right ventricle. It is then pumped through the pulmonary arteries to the lung where it is aerated. The blood then returns to the left auricle, passes down through the valve on that side into the left ventricle, whence it is pumped out through the aorta to be distributed to all parts of the body.

We might list and describe all the parts of a radar set, and this would give us a certain amount of information about radar. But to make a thorough analysis, we must say what function the parts perform. Such an analysis might go something like this:

> While the physical form of each of these components may vary widely from one kind of radar set to another, each radar must have the following complement of parts in order to function:

---

[20] We may, strictly speaking, distinguish between function and purpose. If we are discussing a university, we can treat the subject in terms of purpose, for it is an institution created by men to achieve certain ends. But if we are discussing the circulation of the blood, we can treat the subject only in terms of a characteristic function. We cannot say that purpose is involved. In both instances, however, we observe a relation of parts in terms of a characteristic action, and for the present purpose we use the term *functional analysis* for either. The distinction can be important, however, when it comes to understanding what sort of structure is involved in a particular case.

1. The *modulator* is a device for taking power from the primary source (which may be the commercial power line, a special engine or motor-driven generator, or storage batteries) and forming suitable voltage pulses to drive the radio-frequency oscillator in its bursts of radio-frequency oscillations. In other words, the modulator turns on the radio-frequency oscillator to oscillate violently for a millionth of a second or so, turns it off sharply, and keeps it in repose until time for the next burst.

2. The *radio-frequency oscillator* is a vacuum tube of suitable design, or a group of such tubes, which will oscillate at the desired radio frequency and give the desired bursts of radio-frequency power when connected to the modulator. . . .

We could go on listing all the components, with an explanation at each stage of the function of the part in the operation of the whole apparatus.

Here is a student theme analyzing the parts of an apparatus in relation to function:

COOKING SYRUP

There is one mechanical contraption that I know well—that for making maple syrup. I ought to know it well, for I was raised on a farm in Vermont, the last one in the neighborhood that made syrup. The season for syrup-making was for us kids, all five of us, about as fine as Christmas, and I think it was that way for our parents and grandparents, too.

To describe the mechanism, I'll have to explain the process. Maple sap as it comes out of the tree is very clear, weakly sweet in taste, and as thin as water. People used to call it "sugar water," in fact. To get syrup this sap has to be boiled down at about a ratio of forty to one. You can, if you want to, just boil some down in a pot on the stove, and get syrup. And the early settlers used a big "cauldron" kettle over a wood fire. The process is so simple that the Indians did it long before the paleface came, and they didn't have metal for cooking, just threw hot rocks in a container of wood or bark.

But the paleface gave up the cauldron system as soon as he had learned to tap the trees on a large scale and had a sled to haul sap. So the evaporator was developed. That is the key to the syrup set-up—a big flat container where the syrup can spread thin and get the most even heat. In the old days the evaporator, just a big metal pan, was set on a brick arch that held the fire. That was the kind my grandfather, who liked old things, had, and we didn't get the new system until I was a boy.

The pan of the modern evaporator is of galvanized iron, tin sheet, or copper. The size depends on the size of the "sugar-bush," as you call the grove, allowing about ten square feet of pan for every hundred good trees. The evaporator is divided into two sections, the front and the back, the back getting more heat. In our sugar house the back pan is eight-and-a-half feet long, and the front is five feet and two inches, and both are five-and-a-half feet wide. The rim is seven-and-a-half inches high. The back pan has a corrugated bottom, for this exposes the sap to more heat, and you want the heat at the back where the sap enters. The front pan has a flat bottom.

At one corner of the back pan is a door for letting the sap in, and at each front corner of the front pan is a "draw-off" door. You can take your choice of draw-off door according to which settling pan is full. But I'll be coming to that. The pans have partitions to maintain an even flow.

Under the pans is the firebox, made of galvanized iron sheets lined with firebrick and protected with brick. It is still called the "arch" in memory of the time when it was just that. Inside, it has a grating for the wood (you use hardwood to build the heat) and a slope backward toward the chimney for draft.

There are two other basic parts to the set-up, one leading in, the other out. The "in" is a storage tank, ours being outside the sugar house on the north wall, with a pipe and automatic control for the evaporator. You have to have a storage tank, for the syrup in the pan should be about one inch deep always, and you have to be ahead of the game to keep it so.

The "out" apparatus consists of one or more settling tanks, made of galvanized iron and equipped with felt filters for their outlet pipes. Our tanks have three filters each. Below the filters is the lead for filling cans or bottles. We never use bottles. My father has fine fresh new cans that have bright labels on them, with a picture of our sugar house and the name "Joshua Millbank," and under that: "If you want the best." Then comes the grade of the syrup. I forgot to say that there are several grades, with the best grade called "fancy."

So you see we have come a long way from the poor Indian, or even Miles Standish.

The author of the theme has thought out the mechanism. He might have been tempted to describe the mechanism and build in the comment on function as he went along, but he is probably right in stating the principle underlying the process before embarking on the analysis of the structure. It is not as clear, however, that the arrangement of the rest of the theme is the best possible. Having set up the principle, the author might have started with the storage tank, the lead pipe, and the automatic control, and then proceeded step by step to explain the rest of the apparatus. This organization might have been more economical and achieved a tighter composition. Even so, the present system is acceptable.

As for faults, perhaps there is some disproportion between the part of the theme that deals with the evaporator proper and the parts concerned with the storage tank, settling tanks, and firebox. The lack of proportion is not so much a matter of length (after all, the evaporator is the central part of the mechanism), as a failure to give a few relevant details in treating the subsidiary parts. How big should a storage tank be? How does the automatic control work? What, in fact, is a sugar house like? He merely mentions one. Adding such details would not necessarily have made the theme too long, for some close revision could reduce what we now have.

The next to the last paragraph is rather miscellaneous, and throughout the sentence structure tends to be loose.

The student theme analyzes the mechanism for boiling maple syrup.

Robert Brustein, in an essay "America's New Culture Hero," analyzes the way in which the characteristic hero of a cycle of movies embodies certain qualities of our current society. Below is an extended and self-explanatory excerpt from this essay:

I do not think we can escape the conclusion that [Marlon] Brando's spectacular film success rests to a large extent on his being one of the images (he was the original image) of the inarticulate hero. It is, in other words, to the inarticulate hero that the mass audience responds.

The most conspicuous thing about the inarticulate hero as a movie figure is that he is invariably an outcast or a rebel, isolated from friends, from parents, from teachers, from society. This is emphasized by his shabby, careless appearance; in a world of suits and ties, the leather jacket and open collar are symbols of alienation and rebellion. The main character in *On the Waterfront* is, until he is beaten up by labor hoodlums, befriended by neither police nor peers and finds consolation only in homing pigeons. Although the hero of *The Wild One* begins as the leader of a group of cyclists who terrorize a small town, he repudiates his vicious companions and is, in turn, assaulted by the furious townspeople. The young boy (James Dean) of *Rebel Without a Cause* cannot gain acceptance by his adolescent contemporaries nor can he come to terms with his family until he is attacked by a juvenile gang revenging themselves for the death of their leader. The son in *East of Eden* is a pariah, doomed like Cain (with whom he is identified) to be despised by his father and rejected by the town in which he lives. The hero of *Edge of the City,* on the run from the police and alone until befriended by a paternal Negro dock worker, gets involved in a vicious hook fight with a sadistic dockyard foreman. The schoolboy in *Careless Years,* anxious to marry before he is old enough, isolates himself from everybody's love and friendship until he is soundly whipped in a fist fight with his father. The oil worker of *Giant* lives alone in a dilapidated shack, building a fortune so that he can revenge himself on the smug and settled families of the area. In *Jailhouse Rock,* the hero spends a year in jail for manslaughter, where he learns to play the guitar; upon being released, he becomes rich as a rock-and-roll singer, alienating his closest friends until he is beaten up by his best friend. In each case, although the hero is a rebel against established authority, he is not necessarily identified with the lawless elements of society. He is in the middle, isolated and alone, a victim of forces he cannot understand. Frequently involved with the police, he is often in jail. Society itself is viewed as the outside of a prison, mechanical, forbidding, inhibitive, and repressive, but curiously enough, the hero is trying to enter this prison, for it offers warmth and security on the inside. The obstacle is his own rebellion and before he can enter he must get involved in violence, as if in expiation for some sin. Before he can become a member of society, he must first be beaten up. In order to win—to be accepted—he first must lose.

The pattern of all these films, then, is the same: although the hero starts off on the wrong side, he is almost always converted to righteousness before the end. This is usually accomplished with the aid of his one ally in society, the girl who loves him. The girl (her face is that of Julie Harris,

Natalie Wood, Eva Marie Saint, or Elizabeth Taylor, but her character doesn't vary) is frequently an adolescent and invariably virtuous and understanding. Unlike the boy, she speaks coherently (and interminably), attends school regularly, gets good grades, and is accepted from the outset by her family and friends. Most significant, she exhibits a maternal protectiveness that belies her adolescent appearance and tends to make the hero extremely dependent on her (a situation reflected in much of our popular music where the recurring motif is "I want you, I need you, I love you"). The boy's actual mother has little personality, little influence on his life, and even less of a role, while the girl friend is the only one who can control him. The disguised family romance usually found in these movies becomes, in *Giant,* more explicit. One of the main objects of dispute between Rock Hudson and James Dean is Hudson's wife, Elizabeth Taylor. Only she offers the boy understanding and tenderness, and it is primarily for frustrated love of her that the boy fashions his revenge on the moneyed families of the town.

The antagonism which the boy feels toward society, convention, law and order is, of course, merely an extension of hostility toward his father. While Brando's films are not concerned much with family life (the isolation of the character he plays is complete), most of James Dean's films center on the family situation, a fact which accounts for a good deal of his posthumous popularity. In *East of Eden, Rebel Without a Cause,* and *Giant,* Dean is found in violent combat with his father or father figure. In *Rebel Without a Cause,* for example, the crucial scene occurs when the boy lashes his father for his weakness and for having no effective advice to offer him in time of trouble. In *East of Eden,* the boy is alienated by his father's indifference to him and his inability to see that his best son is not Abel, the conventional good boy, but Cain, the unconventional rebel. The boy's feelings toward his father, however, are, as we might expect, ambivalent. In one scene in *East of Eden,* the boy, whipped to indignation by his father's coldness, begins to pummel and ends by embracing him. The boy's acceptance by society at the end of these films is usually a symbol of filial reconciliation. The greatest reward the hero can achieve is acceptance by the group and the love of his father. And here we have a glimpse into the meaning of the hero's inarticulateness, for we are led to believe that his original alienation arose out of misunderstanding. Conflict is caused by a failure in communication; the boy cannot express his true feelings and therefore the father thinks him hostile. In the final scene of *East of Eden,* the father has suffered a paralytic stroke and is dying. He lies mutely on his bed (the camera shooting from above emphasizes his helplessness), his arms and lips paralyzed, able to signify assent or denial only with his eyes. Only then, when the parental authoritative voice of the father is quiet, when there can be no interruptions from him, when the fear he has instilled has been dispelled by his powerlessness, only then can the boy speak truly, coherently, and clearly, and effect understanding and reconciliation.

Ambiguous feelings toward the father (leading to hostility toward society in general) is, of course, a classic juvenile dilemma, and there can be little doubt that the inarticulate hero is fostered and cherished by the juvenile elements of our society. The striking thing to note is how effectively adolescents have been able to persuade our culture today to conform with their views of it (a recent ad for *Look* magazine promises the life of Jesus as seen "through the troubled eyes of a teen-ager"). It is significant that not only Marlon Brando and James Dean have become spokesmen for the adolescent generation, but Elvis Presley as well; for Presley is the musical counterpart of the inarticulate hero. In Elvis Presley, the testament of Stanley Kowalski is being realized, for, besides the physical resemblances and the explicit sexuality they share, both prophesy the ruin of culture. It is no accident that the costume of the inarticulate hero (blue jeans, T-shirts, sneakers) is primarily the same as that of the proletarian hero. The burden of protest has been handed down, as a heritage, from the one to the other. Denied the social and political outlets rebellion once was permitted to take, the adolescent is now seeing dramatized, in his music and in the movies and TV, the only rebellion left him, the Freudian protest. Although this rebellion often has an apparently happy ending with the hero securely ensconced in the bosom of his family, in reality nothing has been resolved; the hero is never seen in a mature action. The adolescent rebel never grows up; when James Dean grows to middle age, in *Giant,* he merely has some powder added to his hair.

These films, then, give the hero an appearance of growth but derive their success from catering to the anarchic impulses of the young. Inarticulateness is a sympton of this anarchy because speech is an instrument of control. To teach children to speak is to teach them to frustrate their sexual and aggressive desires. To accept this speech is to accept all the difficulties as well as all the glories that speech entails: the teachings of the father, the complexity of the world, the discipline of a developing intelligence, the gifts of tradition, history, science, and art. To reject it is to find consolation in raw feeling, in mindlessness, and in self-indulgence, to seek escape in sex and violence. In the hero's inarticulateness, we find represented the young American's fears of maturity, for to speak out—to be a speaker—is to be a man. It is to replace his father, to take the consequences of his hostility toward him, symbolically to kill him. The unnamed sin for which the hero is beaten, at the end of most of these films, is the sin against the father. When this is expiated by physical punishment, then the hero finds his way home, not to independent manhood but to the kind of security which breeds conformity and complacency.

—ROBERT BRUSTEIN: *The Third Theatre.*[21]

■ APPLICATION

Write a theme of 500 words, or more, analyzing a mechanism, organization, or institution. In doing so, consider the following points:

1 Identify or define the structure to be analyzed.
2 Explain the basic function or purpose of the structure.

3 Specify what principle of structure determines the characteristic operation.
4 Indicate the parts, relating each to its characteristic operation as a part.
5 Be sure that all parts are clearly related to the overall structure and the basic function or purpose.

Remember that these points are *not* to be taken as an outline of your theme. You must develop what you consider an appropriate way of presenting your material.

The following list may suggest a topic:

A newspaper office	An insurance company
A tank corps	A poem
A political party	A hospital
A church	A factory
A bank	An athletic team
A department store	A television set

FUNCTIONAL ANALYSIS AND PROCESS

Thus far we have been putting the emphasis on the parts of a structure as explained by their characteristic function. That is, we have been concerned, by and large, with mechanism. But we may switch the emphasis to the analysis of a process. A process may involve a mechanism—the human heart or a legislature—but our chief concern here is with the stages of the process and not with the parts of the mechanism. The parts, then, are interesting only in so far as they help explain the stages.

Functional analysis is the method by which we distinguish the stages in a process that may be regarded as having a characteristic function or purpose.

EXPOSITORY NARRATION

Once we are concerned with the stages of a process, we are dealing with a sequence of events in time. That is, we have narration, but narration used for an expository purpose.

As we can make a distinction between technical (or expository) description and ordinary description (pp. 132–34), so can we make one between expository narration and ordinary narration. Ordinary narration, as we shall see when we come to discuss it as a basic kind of discourse (in Chapter 9), is concerned with presenting an action. It aims to give the sense of the event as experienced, and it involves an appeal to the imagination. But expository narration merely gives information to enlarge the understanding. If we give directions as to how to build a boat or make a cake, we are treating a sequence of events in time, and we are forced to use a form of narration. If we tell how radar works, we are again using a kind of narration. An instructor in military history lecturing on the First Battle of the Marne in World War I is concerned with making his class understand the stages of the event and the problems of tactics, but he is not necessarily concerned with bringing the event into the imagination of his audience. So he, too, is using expository narration.

By analogy with generalized description, we can see that when expository narration deals with a type of process or type of event, instead of a unique and particular event, we call it generalized narration. For example, if we give the steps that we went through in baking our first pie, we are writing expository narration; we are dealing with the stages of a particular event. But if we are giving directions for making apple pie, we are dealing with stages in a type of process, and hence with generalized narration.

Let us glance at a section from a handbook on repairing antique furniture:

GLUING FELT TO WOOD

You may occasionally wish to glue thin felt to wood, as when replacing it on an old desk top. Other occasions are applying felt to a lamp base or to the bottom of legs of heavy furniture so that floors will not be scratched.

Thin felt for such purposes may usually be purchased in a variety of colors at department stores. The most popular colors are green and brown. Measure the size needed and buy a piece larger than required, as it may shrink somewhat when applied and the glue dries.

Use either the "Synthetic Resin Waterproof Glue" mixed a bit thick or "Old Fashioned Glue" as it comes from the container.

Proceed as follows:

1. When the surface is prepared, by removing any old glue, scratch or roughen it with coarse abrasive paper and clean off. Then apply a generous and even coat of the glue. Allow this to dry until it becomes very sticky and is not too liquid. Otherwise, it might soak through the felt.

2. Apply an oversize piece of felt to the surface, starting on one side and laying it carefully in correct position with no wrinkles. The felt must overlap on all sides. The hands must be clean and free from dust.

3. The felt must now be rolled or patted into the glue. This is best done with a photographer's roller. If a roller is not available, hold a lintless clean cloth around a small wood block and pat the entire surface. It is best not to rub it for fear of moving or stretching the felt.

4. Allow to dry for 24 to 48 hours in a warm room.

5. If the felt goes beyond the edges, trim off closely with sharp scissors. Should it be used on a piece such as a desk top which has a wood border around the surface to which it is applied, the excess felt material is best cut off with a safety razor blade against a straight edge as a guide. (A carpenter's large steel square is good for this purpose.)

—RALPH KINNEY: *The Complete Book of Furniture Repair and Refinishing.*[22]

---

[22] Reprinted with the permission of Charles Scribner's Sons from *The Complete Book of Furniture Repair and Refinishing* by Ralph Kinney. Copyright 1950 Charles Scribner's Sons.

This is a very clear and systematic account of a simple process. It has a single point—to tell us how felt is glued—and it never wavers from that intention. It is complete; it tells us everything we can reasonably want to know, assuming nothing on our part, not even that we know where to get the felt or what kind of glue is best. And it uses very simple language. Technical terms known only to expert cabinetmakers are not used; any amateur of furniture repairing can understand the directions given.

The organization is systematic. It falls into three sections, which correspond to the order in which questions will arise:

I   Type of situation that demands gluing felt to wood
II   Identification of materials
III The process—"proceed as follows" with stages in strict chronological order, and numbered. Notice that there are certain interpolated cautions and suggestions, but that these appear at points where they may be needed in the process.

We see that the directions are little more than an expanded outline, a skeleton that is to be fleshed out, not by words but by the actual doing. But often we are concerned with the explanation of a process, not in order to carry it out, but merely to satisfy curiosity and to enlarge the understanding. In such instances the strict schematic method used for giving directions will scarcely satisfy us or our readers.

Here is an account of the method of planting dark tobacco in Tennessee and Kentucky, written as part of an introduction to an American novel translated into French. The account is thus intended for a reader who knows nothing of farming in those states and is expected to have only the casual interest provoked by the novel itself, and certainly no intention of going out and raising a crop.

> The work begins in January, when winter breaks a little and the soil thaws. On the sunny side of a patch of woodland, where the soil is thick and rich, the farmer piles up some dry wood, mixed with a little green, on a space about twenty feet wide by fifty to a hundred feet long. At evening he sets fire to his big woodpile, and sometimes in a sort of ritual picnic all the family comes down to watch, for this is the beginning of a new year of work and hope. Next day the soil, mixed with the ashes of the bonfire, is turned up, pulverized and raked to prepare a bed for the little seeds of tobacco which the farmer then treads into the soil and ashes. Long ago the farmers used to place boughs over the bed to protect it, but in later times they stretch over the bed, on a frame, a cheap white cloth, very light, called canvas, light enough to allow sun and rain to come through. In this protected bed the fragile plant of tobacco develops until the time when it will be replanted in the open field.
>
> The time of setting out the plants comes in May or June. The farmer has prepared his field. He has plowed and harrowed the soil to pulverize it as perfectly as possible, and he has laid it out in squares. When the rain comes and the soil is well soaked—that is to say, when the farmer gets

what he calls a "season"—the tender plants are drawn from the bed. Now every available person turns out, women and children, to carry the plants in baskets across the field, letting one fall at the exact center of each square. Behind the "droppers," the women and children with the baskets of plants, come the men, the "setters," who with one hand pick up the plant and with the other drive a sharpened stake of wood, called a "dibble," into the earth to make a hole for the plant. The setter presses down the damp earth around the plant, and without straightening up, takes another step forward, to the next square and the next plant. This setting out process is grinding work; in May or June, the sun of Kentucky is already powerful, and you can't interrupt yourself, even to straighten an aching back, for every moment is precious as long as the soil is damp enough to receive the plants.

Here the writer has tried to fill out the skeleton of the exposition with just enough material—the family coming down to watch the fire, the heat of the sun, the aching back, and so on—to make the French reader have some immediate sense of the process. In other words, there are certain elements in the passage that belong to suggestive narration or description. But the intention here is primarily expository—to analyze the process of tobacco setting for the French reader.

● CAUTION: GENERALIZED NARRATION AND INTENTION

In cases where generalized narration is used not for a practical purpose (to tell us how to glue felt to wood) but simply to satisfy curiosity and enlarge our understanding, we may be tempted to wander, in either writing or reading, from the main intention. But we should remember that our intention is expository; this intention should provide the spine, as it were, about which the discussion must be developed.

■ APPLICATIONS

I   In the Readings, study "The American Civilization Puzzle," by George P. Carter (pp. 814–26). What is the author's view of the process of the diffusion of ideas? Write a paragraph summarizing the process.

II   Below is a list of possible subjects for themes, some that may well be treated as directions, some more properly adapted to the account of a process to satisfy curiosity. Select one of the subjects that interests you (or think up one of your own). First decide whether your subject suggests a particular or generalized form of narration. The two examples given above are generalized; the directions for gluing felt are, of course, supposed to be applicable in general, as is the account of setting tobacco. But if you take the last football game, you will be explaining a specific event.

If you are giving a generalized treatment, you must remember that you are trying to present the essential pattern that never varies significantly from one instance to another. If you are giving the explanation of an event—for instance, the last football game—you are concerned with its particularity and must make clear why your team won or lost under the special circumstances.

Having decided whether you are concerned with a particular or general treatment, make your outline, breaking the process or event down into its stages, in chronological order. Then write a short theme, say about 500 words, to develop the outline. Remember that you are supposed to be giving information to a person relatively ignorant of the subject, that you should leave nothing of consequence to his surmise, and remember, too, if you are writing directions, to include any appropriate cautions or suggestions. But always stick to your main point; do not let your cautions or suggestions lead you away from it.

The curing of tobacco in
    your section
How the news story gets to
    the front page
How to lay out a vegetable
    garden
A beaver dam
Space exploration

A chemical experiment
Baking a deep-dish apple pie
Horse breeding
How to train a bird dog
How to organize a charity drive
The Battle of ——
Slalom racing

Causal analysis

In dealing with processes we often want to go beyond the mere account of the stages in time sequence. In fact, in expository narration we naturally find ourselves concerned with what makes one stage lead to the next. In other words, we find ourselves making a causal analysis.

Causal analysis concerns two questions:

1   What caused this?
2   Given this set of circumstances, what effect will follow?

In answering the first question we must reason from effect back to cause, and in answering the second, from cause forward to effect.

CAUSE

We all have a rough-and-ready notion of what cause is. We must in order to get through the day. The burnt child who doesn't shun the fire may well get incinerated, and even the stupidest cat does not make a habit of sitting on hot stove lids.

Indeed, the cat that has once sat on a hot stove lid will probably give up the idea of sitting on *any* stove lid. The cat has achieved a notion of cause and effect, but the notion is too rough-and-ready to be useful except in a negative way: no stove lid to be sat on. The cat has not gone far enough in causal analysis to see that it is not stove lids as such that are unsittable, but stove lids that have, or have recently had, fire under them.

The cat has made a connection between events: stove lid and hot behind, but the connection has not been fully analyzed.[23]

RULES OF CONNECTION

Cause is the kind of connection between events that conforms to the following rules:

I   Without event *A*, event *B* would not have come about.
II   Whenever there is *A* there will be *B*.

Keep these rules firmly in mind. Everything that follows in this chapter is related to them.

CONDITIONS: REMOTE AND IMMEDIATE

No event takes place in isolation. It always involves a complicated set of circumstances spreading in all directions. Tennyson, in the poem "Flower in the Crannied Wall," states the notion:

> Flower in the crannied wall,
> I pluck you out of the crannies,
> I hold you here, root and all, in my hand,
> Little flower—but *if* I could understand
> What you are, root and all, and all in all,
> I should know what God and man is.

Since there is in the world an almost infinitely extended texture of relations, if the poet could know the complete "cause" of the flower—that is, all the conditions determining its existence—then he would know the universe.

In a famous passage by Tolstoy, from the novel *War and Peace,* we find the same principle more elaborately stated and carried over into human behavior:

> When an apple has ripened and falls, why does it fall? Because of its attraction to the earth, because its stalk withers, because it is dried by the sun, because it grows heavier. because the wind shakes it, or because the boy standing below wants to eat it?
> Nothing is the cause. All this is only the coincidence of conditions in which all vital organic and elemental events occur. And the botanist who finds that the apple falls because the cellular tissue decays and so

---

[23] The use here of the word *event* may be objected to. It may be said that the word *thing* is more appropriate, at least in some circumstances. But suppose, for example, we say that a nail is the cause of the fact that a picture hangs on the wall. A nail is, of course, a thing, but it is not the nail as a *thing* that sustains the picture. It is the nail's state of being in the wall that causes the picture to be sustained, and being in the wall is an event. Things must exist, of course, for events to exist, but the event is what we are concerned with. The state of a thing is an event in our meaning of the word.

forth is equally right with the child who stands under the tree and says the apple fell because he wanted to eat it and prayed for it. Equally right and wrong is he who says that Napoleon went to Moscow because he wanted to, and perished because Alexander desired his destruction, and he who says that an undermined hill weighing a million tons fell because the last navvy struck it for the last time with his mattock. In historic events, the so-called great men are labels giving names to events, and like labels they have but the smallest connection with the event itself.

Every act of theirs, which appears to them an act of their own will, is in an historical sense involuntary and is related to the whole course of history and predestined from eternity.

—LEO TOLSTOY: *War and Peace.*

Clearly, when we are making a causal analysis, we cannot be concerned with the notion of cause in the way Tennyson and Tolstoy have referred to it. We must be concerned with the more or less *immediate* connection between an event and its conditions. We need a workaday, usable conception.

Let us look at a simple experiment. To a rod is attached a little bell. The rod, in turn, is attached to an electric mechanism that will make it sway back and forth when a button is pushed. The whole affair, except the control button, is rigged up in a hermetically sealed jar connected with a vacuum pump. Somebody pushes the button, the rod sways, the bell rings. We hear the sound of the bell. What is the cause of the sound?

One person says it is caused by the clapper striking the inside of the bell. Another says it is caused by the movement of the rod. Another says: "No, Jack pushed the button." And common sense tells us that everybody is right and everybody is wrong. In each case the person answering has fixed on some particular factor and assumed the other factors.

We can see more clearly how much assumption is involved in our talk about cause if we pump the air entirely out of the jar and then push the button. The mechanism works, the bell clapper strikes metal, but there is no sound. We know why. For sound to exist, there must be a medium, in this instance air, in which the sound waves can travel.

The first three people who specified a cause for the sound forgot all about the necessity for a medium for the sound waves. But now a fourth person says: "Ah, it was the air that caused the sound." Again, he is both right and wrong. The air is a "cause" in the sense that without air there is no sound, but the air is only one of several factors that must be present: the bell, the clapper striking it, the person pushing the button, and the air for the sound waves. All these factors are necessary. *A necessary factor is called a condition.*

● CAUTION

In considering the problem of cause in any situation, it is essential to distinguish between the *necessary factors*—the *conditions*—and the *incidental factors*. In our experiment here, for example, the bell may be brass or steel, the insulation on the wire may be silk or rubber, the person who pushes the button may be male or female, red-haired or black-haired. None of these factors is crucial—that is, none is a condition. They are merely incidental.

In thinking of causality we are concerned with conditions.

CAUSE AND INTEREST

Since there is a necessary interrelation among the conditions of an event, we may, strictly speaking, maintain that cause is always complex, and we shall return to this idea. But for the moment, let us ask in what sense can we say that a particular condition is *the* cause of an event?

The choice of any particular condition as *the* cause is always *provisional* and *selective*. The choice is determined by a special interest brought to bear on the event.

Let us take the instance of the death of a small child. We must confine ourselves, we remember, to conditions having a more or less immediate connection with the event: we rule out as too remote, for example, the birth of a certain grandfather, even though that birth is necessary to the existence of the child. Among the immediate conditions, various choices might be made. A neighbor telling the news says, "Little Willie got killed from falling off a stepladder." The bereaved mother takes her own carelessness as the cause: she had left the ladder standing on the edge of the back porch instead of putting it in the closet where it belonged. The family doctor, making out the death certificate, records that death was the result of a fracture of the skull.

Each person has brought a special interest to bear on the event, a special interpretation, and each statement is, in itself, true. At the same time, each is incomplete. The point is to be aware of what we are about when we select a particular condition in the light of a special interest. We must know what conditions are being rejected, and why.[24]

REASONING ABOUT CAUSE

The fallacy of post hoc, ergo propter hoc   Let us turn again to *War and Peace:*

> Whenever I see the movement of a locomotive I hear the whistle and see the valves opening and wheels turning; but I have no right to conclude

---

[24] You may well ask how selection of *the* cause from among a set of conditions squares with the Rules of Connection for causality with which we started.

Since by definition a condition is a necessary factor, Rule I is fulfilled. Restating the rule, we have: without the "necessary factor" *A*, event *B* would not have come about. No argument is possible here.

Rule II is fulfilled *only* if we are properly aware of the limitation of the act of selection. Restating the rule, we would say: whenever there is the "necessary factor" *A* (in conjunction, of course, with the complex of other, unspecified conditions), there will be *B*. Here the awareness of the nature of the act of selection is crucial. Thus, the fact that the mother left the stepladder on the porch is a necessary factor only because little Willie climbed the ladder and fell on his head.

that the whistling and the turning of wheels are the cause of the movement of the engine.

The peasants say that a cold wind blows in late spring because the oaks are budding, and really every spring cold winds do blow when the oak is budding. But I do not know what causes the cold winds to blow when the oak buds unfold, I cannot agree with the peasants that the unfolding of the oak buds is the cause of the cold wind, for the force of the wind is beyond the influence of the buds. I see only a coincidence of occurrences such as happens with all the phenomena of life, and I see that however much and however carefully I observe . . . the valves and wheels of the engine, and the oak, I shall not discover the cause of . . . the engine moving, or of the winds of spring. To do that I must entirely change my point of view and study the laws of the movement of steam . . . and of the wind.

—LEO TOLSTOY: *War and Peace.*

Here the peasant who thinks that the cold wind comes because the oak leaves are out is committing one of the most common errors in thinking about cause, the fallacy of *post hoc, ergo propter hoc*—"after this, therefore because of this."

The trouble here is that the peasant has in his mind a false generalization about cause. He ties event *A* and event *B* together in time sequence and then, because sequence is a *necessary* feature in causality, assumes that it is a *sufficient* feature.

The mind of the peasant, however, is not unsimilar to that of the modern educated citizen. This fallacy, for instance, is the stock in trade of most politicians on the hustings and of many historians when they take pen in hand. If it could be abolished, there would be vast stretches of silence on the airwaves at election time, and the shelves of libraries would be decimated. Needless to add, among advertising agencies bankruptcy would set in like the Black Death. (See Persuasion, pp. 238–74.)

■ APPLICATIONS

I In terms of causality, how would you analyze the pictures described below?

1 In the advertisement of a certain airline, we see, on what seems to be the terrace of a luxurious tropical hotel, pairs of handsome young men and women engaged in delightfully intimate conversation.

2 In the advertisement of the manufacturer of a certain well-known medicament, we see a woman's face contorted in pain and despair. Next to this distressing picture we see the same face now smiling in beautiful and blissful relief.

II The following statements are among the clichés of our time. Study them.

1 If Abraham Lincoln had not been assassinated, a peaceful and just Reconstruction would have ensued in the South.
2 If President Kennedy had not been assassinated, there would have been no escalation of the war in Vietnam.
3 Student unrest can be traced back to the bomb, ultimately.
4 The terrible condition of the world can be traced back to the fact that America dropped the bomb on Hiroshima.
5 The terrible weather in recent years can be traced back to the bomb.
6 America beat Japan by dropping the bomb on Hiroshima.
7 The automobile destroyed old-time American sexual morality.
8 The pill is destroying old-time American sexual morality.
9 The "new affluence" is the cause, basically, of campus disorders.

Having studied these statements, try to say how each might be discussed as an example of reasoning about cause and effect.

There is no yes-or-no answer here. Use your common sense, your acquaintance with logic, and whatever information you possess.

Generalization and Uniformity   We have remarked that Tolstoy's peasant was guilty of a false generalization. What generalization should he have made?

When we say that *A* is the cause of *B*, we are not merely referring to the particular case of a particular *A* and a particular *B*. We are implying that a general principle exists, that under the same circumstances any *A* would cause a *B*. We imply a principle of uniformity behind the particular case. To arrive at a true principle of uniformity, Tolstoy's peasant should have studied the "laws of the movement . . . of the wind."

In other words, the peasant should have studied what we call the laws of nature.

The Laws of Nature   The principle of uniformity is most clearly seen in what we call a law of nature. A chemist says that when we ignite hydrogen in the presence of oxygen we will get water (H_2O). Under specified conditions the element hydrogen and the element oxygen always behave in the same way. At least, we believe that they will so behave because they have always behaved that way in the past. We appeal to experience and to a number of instances for our principle. We assume that there will be no exceptions.

Here we must emphasize the word *assume*. We base our scientific operations, as well as our decisions of ordinary life, on this assumption. But, as the eminent philosopher and mathematician Bertrand Russell put it, we have, even in science, only a probability:

> It must be conceded . . . that the fact that two things have often been found together and never apart does not, by itself, suffice to *prove* demonstratively that they will be found together in the next case we examine.

The most we can hope is that the oftener things are found together, the more probable it becomes that they will be found together another time, and that, if they have been found together often enough, the probability will amount *almost* to a certainty.

—BERTRAND RUSSELL: *The Problems of Philosophy*.

● CAUTION: ESSENTIAL CHARACTERISTICS

The principle of uniformity, we must remember, refers only to the essential characteristics of a situation. For instance, it does not matter whether the laboratory worker igniting hydrogen in the presence of oxygen is a Catholic or a Jew, a Republican or a Democrat, a Chinese or a Greek. The boy who, in Charles Lamb's essay, accidentally discovered how to roast a pig by burning down a house, had not isolated the essential characteristic of the situation: he had not learned that he did not need to burn down a house every time he wanted roast pig. He had not recognized, as we have earlier put the same idea, the incidental factors, and then discarded them.

Never appeal to the principle of uniformity without analyzing the circumstances to determine the relevance of characteristics involved.

Controlled Circumstances   In the laboratory a scientist can control the circumstances of his experiments and repeat them over and over, without variation. But outside the laboratory it is difficult to control circumstances with any certainty, and many events that we want to explain—for instance, a political election—cannot be repeated at will and identically. When we want to understand the causes of an event that we cannot repeat, we must examine similar events, that is, the various political elections we know about, and try to make sense of them. In other words, we must try to see what is uniform in them in the hope that this process will lead to the discovery of a cause. When we try to find the cause of a particular effect, we must look for uniformities beyond the particular situation.

An Example from the Ordinary World   Let us take an example, applying the principle of uniformity, not from a laboratory, but from the ordinary world:

TOM: Why did Jane speak so curtly at dinner last night?
JACK: Because she was angry with her husband.
TOM: How do you know?
JACK: That's the way she always behaves when she's angry with him.
TOM: You must have been around the family a lot.
JACK: Sure. I lived in the house for a year.

When Jack says that the cause of Jane's conduct was her anger with her husband, he is not merely commenting on the particular instance. And Tom's further question elicits the fact that a principle of uniformity is involved: Jane behaves this way *every* time she gets angry with her husband. The principle here may not be one we can depend on with any great degree of certainty. On some future occasion she may not be short with her husband at dinner but may kick the cat, get a divorce, or shoot her husband. But past observation gives us some degree of probability that when Jane is angry with her husband, she usually behaves in a certain way at dinner—that is, a principle of uniformity is involved. In fact, a second and broader principle of uniformity is involved: not only do we have a generalization that when Jane becomes angry with her husband she displays a bad temper and forgets her manners, but another generalization that any person who becomes angry with a spouse may then display a bad temper in general and forget his manners, simply because temper and anger tend to spill over.

Hypothesis   In answering Tom's question, Jack has offered what is known as a hypothesis. He confronts a problem—"What made Jane curt last night?" He assembles evidence in terms of a principle of uniformity. Then he asserts that the question at hand is to be regarded as an instance of a general principle.

■ **APPLICATION**

Read "The Method of Scientific Investigation," by T. H. Huxley (pp. 619–25). Now write a short theme, say 250 words, illustrating the principle of hypothesis. It may be an episode treated in dialogue, as in the discussion of Jane's manners, or it may be a description of an experiment. Or you may devise some other form of presentation. But it must involve a particular case, an illustration of the principle.

Samples   When Tom says to Jack that he must have been around Jane's house a lot, he is implying that, to establish a principle of uniformity, you must have a certain number of relevant samples in agreement. Jack gets this point, for he immediately says that he has lived in Jane's house for a year—that is, he has many samples of her conduct.

Certainly a year is better than a month for observing Jane and her husband, but as we have suggested, no matter how many samples are obtained, they can lead only to an assumption about cause, not a certainty.

Negative Instances and Control   Suppose that often when Jane quarrels with her husband she does not lose her manners, and that Bill, who hears the conversation between Jack and Tom, is aware of this fact. That is, Bill knows negative cases that impair the generalization Jack has made.

To go further, let us take it that Bill, who is often in Jane's house, has observed that Jane loses her manners after a quarrel *only* when these circumstances occur: (1) when she has quarreled with her husband because the husband insists that Jack remain as a guest in the house; and (2) when, at dinner after the quarrel, Jack is at the table.

Here Bill knows what we may call control instances—that is, that Jane does not lose her manners merely from quarreling with her husband. These instances suggest that there must be another factor—Jane's dislike for Jack's presence.

Competing Hypothesis   Let us assume that Jane does not dislike Jack, and assume that another person, Sam not Bill, is listening to the original conversation. Sam is Jane's physician, and he thinks that Jack's hypothesis is wrong. He knows that Jane is a secret drinker and always sneaks a few extras before dinner, and that she has come to him worrying about her habit. His hypothesis is that the drinking, with associated guilt and self-contempt, accounts for Jane's bad manners at dinner. Of course, his professional ethics forbid him to offer his hypothesis to Jack and Tom, but it may be preferable to either of theirs.

When possible, consider competing hypotheses.

Assessing Hypotheses: Simplicity and Statistics   How do we choose between competing hypotheses? There is no rule of thumb. But within limits, certain principles are useful.

For instance, there is an old logical principle that the simple explanation is to be preferred over the complex. The idea that Oswald independently assassinated President Kennedy has the appeal of simplicity over the various theories that invoke conspiracy as an explanation. But the appeal of simplicity is never decisive in the face of contrary evidence. It is merely a starting point.

There is, also, the principle of statistical frequency—the simple notion that the more frequently a certain kind of event occurs the more likely it is to occur again. For instance, the night watchman of a bank finds a man wandering around in the basement of the building where the vaults are at about 3 A.M. He puts in an alarm, and the police arrive. The man is taken to the station house and rigorously questioned. He has no identification and is not entirely coherent, but he claims that he had been passing the bank, had been taken by a fit of dizziness, had entered and gone down to the wash rooms, had fainted, and had only come to in the dark. He explains that he must have lost his wallet and papers when he fell.

The police, acting on the principle of statistical frequency (most people caught in the vault section of banks at 3 A.M. are up to no good), regard him with deep suspicion. But statistical frequency can be misleading: investigation absolves the unfortunate man. The wallet is found. He is a respected clergyman, has recently had fainting fits because of ear trouble, and had been seen in a dazed condition on the street just outside the bank, toward closing time.

Nature of Observer   To return to the competing hypotheses of Jack, Bill, and Sam, we may mention another factor that may influence us to accept Sam's version of Jane's behavior. He is a doctor. But the relevance of this is based not merely on the fact that, as a doctor, he has had access to certain information (Jane drinks and is worried), but on the fact that, as a doctor, he has been trained to make certain kinds of observation. By reason of such training, he is, we assume, prepared to work out the psychological generalization (drinkers tend to suffer from guilt and self-contempt) that he theorizes is applicable to Jane.

Remember that the nature of the reporter may affect the weight to be given his evidence (pp. 195–98).

■ APPLICATION

How would you assess the reasoning about causality in the following instances?

1 James knows that Jack is allergic to ham. After they have dined out together, Jack gets sick. James says: "There must have been ham in that meat loaf."
The wife of Jack, who is with them, says: "Yes, I think you are right."

2 Bill says: "All the best shots have light eyes. Billy the Kid had them, and Wild Bill Hickock, Wyatt Earp, and Jesse James."
Ralph says: "But my Uncle Josh is a great shot and he has brown eyes."

3 Isaac says: "Poetry is written by people who simply can't deal with the world."
Jim: "What makes you think that? You haven't studied literature."
Isaac: "Good Lord, look at a guy like Shelley, the mess he was always in, or Hart Crane committing suicide."

4 Louise: "I have always said that it is the lowering of moral standards in the family that causes so much juvenile delinquency in the slums."
Lucy: "What makes you think that?"
Louise: "My aunt was a social worker for years, and she ought to know."
Lucy: "I didn't know she ever had a job."
Louise: "Well, it wasn't exactly a job. She was a volunteer when she had time."

5 The treachery of the Japanese caused the United States to get into World War II.

6 John comes into the kitchen and sees the dog eating hamburger out of a burst package wrapped in butcher's paper. He kicks the dog. His wife enters, followed by the cat, and exclaims, "Don't do that, the package was on top of the refrigerator." "Damn it," the husband retorts, "just because it's your dog doesn't keep him from eating it!" He kicks the dog again.

Complex Cause Even in a simple event—the bell ringing in the jar, say— we find a number of conditions, necessary factors as we have called them; and we have discussed what is at stake when, in terms of a special interest, we select one of the necessary factors as *the* cause. We know that the event takes place as the result of a number of factors (the clapper striking the bell, Jack pushing the button, the presence of air in the jar, etc.), and that none of these factors, though *necessary,* can be taken as *sufficient.* Knowing this, we often wish to analyze a number of the conditions involved in an event; we wish to get, in other words, as full and rounded a picture as possible of the "causes," or, if we wish to put it another way, of the complex cause. Many events, if they are to be understood at all, must be considered in this way. For instance, how can we have any notion of the meaning of World War II if we do not try to sort out a number of factors in the context of the event and try to understand in so far as possible, their interrelations? We know that it is idiotic to say "Hitler caused the war" or "The Treaty of Versailles caused the war." Or, "The fact that Germany was allowed to occupy the Ruhr caused the war." Or, "The British caused the war by the appeasement at Munich." All these factors have a place in the picture, along with a number of others. For a century—or for centuries—historians will be trying to assess them, and there will never be an easy and definitive answer to the problem of what caused World War II.

Events involving human behavior—even relatively simple events—are always difficult to treat in terms of cause and effect, but we are all committed to the attempt. Many occupations and professions—advertising, teaching, psychiatry, politics, poker playing, fiction writing, sociology, history—are fundamentally concerned with cause and effect. Aside from such special and highly organized instances, we are all inevitably involved in trying to understand the causes of human behavior. If we don't try to understand the people we live among, and don't try to understand ourselves, we are very likely to make a mess of our lives, and the only rug under which to sweep such messes is usually the turf. The turf in the cemetery.

● CAUTION

There is no easy rule for determining causes in the tangled situations of life—in society, in history, in medicine, in politics, and so forth. But we can begin to think constructively about cause if we steadfastly refuse to accept easy and simplistic solutions and insist on trying to analyze situations to discriminate between necessary factors (conditions) and merely incidental factors, and between what is necessary and what is sufficient. For instance, when someone says "The Treaty of Versailles caused World War II," he is taking as sufficient what is, at the most, only necessary. If an event is the result of a set of conditions, no single condition, much less an incidental factor, can be taken as sufficient. And of course an incidental factor can never be a cause. Yet attributing cause to one condition or incidental factor is one of the commonest of errors.

Here are two handy rules of thumb to apply in order to distinguish between conditions and incidental factors:

1 *A* cannot be the cause of *B* if *A* is ever absent when *B* is present.
2 *A* cannot be the cause of *B* if *B* is ever absent when *A* is present.

These rules are relatively easy to apply in a laboratory. They are very far from easy to apply out in the world. But you must try to apply them.

● **A LAST CAUTION**

In the foregoing discussion of cause many of the principles involved have probably struck you as familiar. They are familiar. You have been making judgments of cause and effect all your life—in fishing and hunting, in games, in gardening, in laboratory work, in crossing the street. Being acquainted with the principles, however, is not quite enough. You must make a practice of applying them systematically, as occasions demand. If you can think straight about a problem of cause and effect, then it will be easy for you to write well about it. And to think straight, you must be systematic in analyzing events and in applying principles. (For further study, see Appendix 1, Causal Analysis, pp. 591–95.)

■ **APPLICATIONS**

I Read "Jackdaws," by Konrad Lorenz (pp. 629–37) and "On the Inscrutability of History," by Arthur Schlesinger, Jr. (pp. 826–38). Both essays are concerned, in one way or another, with questions of cause and effect. What particular examples of reasoning about cause and effect do you find? Summarize the content of each example.

II Read the following passage by the noted scientist Robert A. Millikan:

> When in 1825 my grandfather loaded into a covered wagon his young wife, his Lares and Penates, and all his worldly goods, and trekked west from Stockbridge, Massachusetts, first to the Western Reserve in Ohio, and again in 1838 to the banks of the Rock River in western Illinois, the conditions of that migration, the motives prompting it, the mode of travel of the immigrants, their various ways of meeting their needs and solving their problems, their whole outlook on life, were extraordinarily like those which existed four thousand years earlier when Abraham trekked westward from Ur of the Chaldees. In a word, the changes that have occurred within the past hundred years, not only in the external conditions under which the average man, at least in this Western world, passes his life on earth, but in his superstitions, such as the taboo on the number thirteen or on Friday sailings (why, my own grandmother carried a dried potato in her pocket to keep off rheumatism), in his fundamental belief, in his philosophy, in his concept of religion, in his whole world-outlook, are probably greater than those that occurred during the preceding four thousand years all put together. Life seems to remain static for thousands of years and then to shoot forward with amazing speed. The last century has been one of those periods of extraordinary change, the most amazing in human history.

If, then, you ask me to put into one sentence the cause of that recent, rapid, and enormous change and the prognosis for the achievement of human liberty, I should reply, *It is found in the discovery and utilization of the means by which heat energy can be made to do man's work for him.* The key to the whole development is found in the use of power machines, and it is a most significant statistical fact that the standard of living in the various countries of the world follows closely the order in which so-called labor saving devices have been most widely put to use. In other words, the average man has today more of goods and services to consume in about the proportion in which he has been able to produce more of goods and services through the aid of power machines which have been put into his hands. In this country there is now expended about 13.5 horsepower per day per capita—the equivalent of 100 human slaves for each of us; in England, the figure is 6.7, in Germany 6.0, in France 4.5, in Japan 1.8, in Russia 0.9, in China 0.5. In the last analysis, this use of power is why our most important social changes have come about. This is why we no longer drive our ships with human slaves chained to the oars, as did the Romans and the Greeks. This is why we no longer enslave whole peoples, as did the Pharaohs, for building our public structures and lash them to their tasks. This is why ten times as many boys and girls are in the high schools today in the United States as were there in 1890—more than five million now, half a million then. This is why we have now an eight-hour day instead of, as then, a ten-, twelve-, or sometimes a fourteen-hour day. This is why we have on the average an automobile for every family in the country. This is why the lowest class of male labor, i.e., unskilled labor, gets nearly twice as much in real wages in the United States as in England, three times as much as in Germany or France, and thirteen times as much as in Russia, and this is why the most abused class of labor in the world, domestic service, is even better off relatively in this country, though completely unorganized, i.e., through the unhampered operation of economic laws, than is any other class of labor, skilled or unskilled, in other countries.

—Robert A. Millikan: "Science, Freedom and the World of Tomorrow," in *Freedom: Its Meaning.*[25]

1   The author has here said that the discovery and utilization of means of developing power have caused an increase in "human liberty." Some of his facts are out of date, but can you think of any current facts to support his view?

2   Even while Dr. Millikan wrote this essay, "whole peoples" were being enslaved by countries that possessed modern machines. What caused such enslavement in Germany or Russia? To what extent, do you think, has modernization increased "human liberty" in the United States? How do you feel about Millikan's general conclusion?

III   You are going to be asked to write a theme in causal analysis, but before you begin, here is a student theme to consider. It is not complete; it is only the

---

[25] From *Freedom: Its Meaning*, edited by Ruth Nanda Anshen. Reprinted by permission of Harcourt, Brace & World, Inc.

first part of a long research theme for late in the course. But the writer has chosen a subject involving causal analysis. (The footnotes proper to a research theme are dropped here. We will take up the problems of the research paper in Chapters 14 and 15.)

CAUSES OF THE TEXAS REVOLUTION

In this paper, I intend to do three things: First, to list the causes of the Texas revolution and define each one. Second, to show how these causes combined to bring about the revolution. Third, to sort out the causes in some order of importance. It is all a little bit like trying to keep three Indian clubs in the air at one time. But since I can't do everything at once, I shall list and define the causes first, then try to tell the story, and then, by way of a conclusion, line them up in importance, or what to me seems to be their importance.

The first cause was simply the difference in civilization between the Mexicans who owned Texas and the Americans who came there. I don't mean in the amount of civilization; I mean in the kind of civilization they had. The Mexicans had a Spanish and Catholic civilization, and they believed in power and authority and tradition. The Americans believed in democracy and self-reliance. You might say that this difference was the thing underlying all the trouble that followed. But perhaps it would not have been enough of a thing to make the revolution if certain other things had not been the way they were.

The second cause was the fact that the Mexicans couldn't get rid of a fear of American adventurers coming in to seize Texas. There had been a lot of adventurers coming in to filibuster far back in the Spanish times, and the Mexicans didn't really trust the Americans that they themselves invited in and who took out citizenship and honestly tried to be good and loyal Mexicans.

The third cause is related to the second. There were a good many adventurers in Texas, and you might go so far as to say that some of the leaders, like Sam Houston, were adventurers and were seeking to take Texas from Mexico.

The fourth cause was bad Mexican policy and administration. After they had called in American settlers to develop the country they couldn't develop and fight off the Indians they hadn't been able to control, the Mexican government turned around and tried to block the prosperity of these people. They used heavy custom duties, passed laws to prevent further immigration, and failed to establish coastwise trade with Mexico proper.

The fifth cause was violation of civil rights when a dictatorship was set up, the sending in of troops to hold down the people, sometimes convict troops, and Santa Anna's flinging Austin into jail.

Another cause was the United States policy in trying to buy Texas. The United States government had very bad judgment in the choice of diplomats. A man like Butler tried to bribe high Mexican officials and wrote anonymous letters to stir up rebellion.

It was the big financial panic of 1819 that drove so many Americans to Texas, especially frontiersmen of Kentucky and Tennessee. The self-reliance of the frontiersman was . . .

This theme is written in a dull, pedantic style. But the writer has tried to be systematic, and his concern with being systematic makes this theme one for the student to analyze. He can see another writer wrestling with the problem of organization. Basically the way the writer of the theme solves his problem is sensible. The difficulty is merely that he is somewhat awkward in applying the solution.

For your own theme in causal analysis you may take some historical event that you already know something about or an event that you have observed or experienced. You should try to make your theme more than a dull and slightly expanded outline, such as we find in the theme above. Try to apply the various principles of reasoning about cause that we have been studying. For instance, when you sort out various conditions, distinguish them clearly from incidental factors, and at the same time indicate, when possible, the interrelations among the conditions. The line of hard reasoning must be constantly available to your reader, but remember that you are analyzing a process in life and should try to make the account lively. Flesh out your discussion of cause with illustrations and comparisons, and with vivid detail. Your subject is, in one sense, a narrative, and so try to give it the thrust and suspense of narrative. It deals with human experience. How did the human beings feel who were involved? How would you feel?

Here is a list of topics that may be suggestive:

Why I Failed to Make the Grade
What Caused the Vietnamese War?
Why Did Benedict Arnold Become a Traitor?
Was It Good Luck or Bad?
My Aunt's Character
Why _____ Lost the Election
A Triumph of Character over Circumstance
If Stonewall Jackson Had Not Been Killed, Then What?
Can Democracy Survive in the Large Modern City?
Why Are the Young Alienated?
Would You Want a Flower Child for a Father?
Would You Want a Flower Child for a Child?
Would You Want the President of a Great Corporation for a Father?
Will Technology Bring Human Freedom?
What Forces Made Your Home Town What It Is?

CHAPTER **6**

Argument

We commonly think of argument as arising in conflict. "Why did Mr. Smith shoot Mr. Jones?" we ask. And somebody answers, "Oh, they had an argument." We think of formal debate between two college teams as a sporting event, of the confrontation on television between two presidential candidates as something akin to a gladiatorial combat, and of the encounter of two lawyers before a jury as, to use the phrase lawyers themselves often use, a joust.

Much of our time is spent, in fact, in listening to, or participating in, arguments that do arise, quite obviously, in conflict. It is only natural, then, that when we try to prove a point to a stupid or recalcitrant friend, or try to justify an opinion in class, we should think in terms of attack and defense. We think in terms of "winning" and "losing."

Argument and Doubt

When we think of argument as between two persons, the element of conflict is very often clear. Even when we think of it as between two ideas, or two points of view, the element of conflict is present, as is indicated in the phrase "a conflict of opinions" or "a conflict of values." But once we shift the emphasis from persons to views, we introduce another factor.

Look at it this way. A person, we say, wins an argument. How does he win? He wins in that his opponent says, "I was wrong, you are right," or that a third party (or parties), in the role of judge, says, "You win, you are right." In short, at the inception of the argument somebody (a participant, a judge, a mere bystander) has had the option of two opposing views. There had been a doubt as to which was "right."

Argument may, and frequently does, arise in conflict. But underlying this notion is another notion, more inclusive and philosophical—the notion of doubt. A party to the conflict is thus merely supporting a view of the matter that hangs in doubt.

This is not to say that a person in an argument may not be passionately certain of the rightness of his view. His passionate certainty is not, however, a guarantee that his view is not false, and some of the greatest errors in history have been the most ardently and ably defended. When we say that argument arises in doubt, we refer, not to the depth of commitment or the degree of skill of the participants, but to the objective fact that if one view were *obviously* right, there could be no argument.

Antagonists, in fact, are not even necessary to argument. This is clearly indicated by the fact that when you are in doubt about something you will probably say that you are "arguing" with yourself, or that you are "debating" your decision. In your own mind, you are, it is true, alternately playing two roles, now defending one option, now the other; but the key fact of this process is your doubt about which is the right one.

Doubt may often be the dynamic of argument.

Life is full of doubts. You, a premed student, do not know whether an elective in English literature or one in European history, which you like equally well, would best serve your career. In the spring of 1863, General Lee, facing a superior force under General Hooker, at Chancellorsville, Virginia, had to decide whether to retreat, to assemble his forces and fight a head-on battle, or to run the risk of dividing his already inferior army by detaching one part to strike Hooker in the rear, by surprise. In Shakespeare's play, Hamlet does not know whether to believe the ghost and kill King Claudius. Every day, in fact, is a tissue of decisions and choices, great or small, and every decision is an attempt to resolve a doubt.

How do we resolve these doubts?

The appeal to reason

Thus far we have been primarily concerned with the situations—those of conflict or doubt—in which argument ordinarily develops, those in which we most commonly feel the need to argue. We have been concerned, that is, with what we may call the *psychological context* of argument.

A little reflection shows us, however, that there are kinds of occasions other than those of conflict or doubt that involve argument. For instance, even though we may not be in conflict or doubt concerning a certain theorem of geometry, we may be interested in the process by which the theorem was established. We may even want to see, as students not infrequently do, if a theorem can be proved by a process not given in the textbook. Here we would be concerned to analyze and evaluate the reasoning involved in the proof, or to construct a new and different line of reasoning to make a proof. In such a situation we have turned from the *psychological context* to the *logical process*—that is, to the nature of the argument.

To approach the matter in another way, we may ask how conflict or doubt may be resolved.

A conflict between persons may be settled by threats, deception, cajolery, or force. Doubt may be settled by an act of faith, an instinctive decision, or a desperate leap in the dark. But either conflict or doubt may, sometimes, be settled by argument.

To settle a matter by argument means to settle it by the appeal to reason.

By reason we mean the mental operation by which we move from what we take as the starting point—the *data,* the *premises,* the *evidence*[1]—to the more or less firm conviction that, with such a starting point, a certain *conclusion* will follow. To state it differently, to reason is to make an *inference*— to accept the conclusion as a consequence of having accepted the particular starting point.

The end of reason is to reach a conclusion which we can accept, in which we can believe, which is dependable, or which we can, at least, gamble on. Through reason we seek "truth." Ideally, since argument implies the appeal to reason, it also implies that the parties involved will accept the findings of reason.

When a person is "arguing with himself," he will presumably accept the findings of reason—if he can override, that is, whatever irrational preferences he may consciously, or unconsciously, have. Similarly, men of good will, seriously bent on finding truth, will seek to resolve by reason, within the limits of their capacities, whatever differences divide them. But there are "arguments" that are purely situations of conflict, and in such cases, to win, not to find truth, is the object. A lawyer defending a man accused of murder has not been hired to seek the truth, he has been hired to save his client's neck. A debating team is not seeking truth, it is trying to score points. A congressman may not be seeking truth, either; he may be trying to satisfy a lobby, consolidate his constituency, or attract enough national attention to be put on the ticket for vice president. What, in such cases, happens to the appeal to reason?

The lawyer, the debater, the congressman *may,* in fact, be distorting reason, trying to confuse issues, and appealing to emotion or prejudices,

---

[1] The *data* is, literally, what is given. It is all the relevant material available at the inception of the argument. It is a broad, general term, including the *premises* and the *evidence.* In the strict sense of the word, in deductive reasoning, a *premise* is a proposition which is assumed to be true and on which the argument is based (pp. 168 and 173–74). *Premise* is also used with the wider meaning of whatever the parties to a dispute take as an assumption they share and can use as a basis for the argument. *Evidence* is whatever can be used to support an argument (pp. 193–98).

but they all *claim* to be offering an argument—that is, they *claim* to be following the dictates of reason.

Even though reasoning may be used to defeat the natural end of reason, truth, the *claim* to reasonableness defines a discourse as belonging to the category of argument. Reason, however distorted, dubious, or devious, remains the crucial substance of argument.

SUMMARY

Argument is the form of discourse characterized by the claim that one thing (the conclusion) merits belief because certain other things (data, premises, evidence) merit belief.

Argument: emotion and reason

If argument implies the appeal to reason, what, then, of the appeal to emotion that we find in the course of many arguments?

This question, so commonly asked, can be answered only by pointing out that, in the question above, the word *argument* is used in two quite different senses. The first time it appears in the question, it is used in a very restricted and technical sense: the form of discourse with the intention of convincing by the appeal to reason. By definition, *argument* in this sense would leave no room for the appeal to emotion. The second time the word appears, it is used quite loosely to indicate a discourse seeking to gain assent by a combination of logical and other appeals.

Throughout the following pages, we shall use the word *argument* in the more limited sense. But this usage is not merely arbitrary. We often say quite spontaneously, "He didn't really have an argument (that is, an appeal to reason), he merely carried the audience by appealing to their emotions." And quite commonly, too, we make a distinction between argument (as strictly considered) and persuasion (as an emotional appeal). What the question we started with is really asking is: What is the relation between *argument* and *persuasion?*

This is a question of great importance and great complexity, and we cannot tackle it until we have clearly limited the nature of argument. When we come to the question of persuasion, we come to the question of argument in its human context, and that is where trouble and fascination inextricably intertwine. (See Persuasion, pp. 238–74.)

Argument, exposition, and logic

Despite distortions of reasoning that often appear in argument[2] and the intrusion of emotional appeals, the study of argument is, at root, the

---

[2] Such distortions are called fallacies; we have already considered one (pp. 149–50), and others will be considered later (pp. 221–25).

study of the principles of reasoning—that is, of logic. We are already familiar with many of these principles, for the study of exposition, too, involves them—as we have seen in classification, definition, and analysis.

What, then, is the difference between exposition and argument?

The act of inference accounts for the crucial difference. In exposition, the nature of a thing—whatever the "thing" may be, object, mechanism, process, idea—is set forth in certain logical forms. In argument, particular starting points are set forth and a particular conclusion is drawn from them.

Here it may be objected that we have treated causal analysis as a form of exposition; but, for example, doesn't a discussion of cause involve inference?

True, but the primary intention in making a causal analysis is to set forth the order and structure of the situation involving causality. The motive, the intention, makes the difference.

But exposition and argument are often, and characteristically, intertwined. For example, the statement of a premise may well involve definition. You state your premise, and somebody asks, "What do you mean by that?" You have to tell him before the argument can proceed, and to do so you may have to resort to the process of definition. Or determining what elements in a situation may be taken as evidence may well involve analysis. It is important in a discourse to distinguish between the elements of exposition and argument, for to fail to do so may mean blurring and confusion; and it is also important to keep firmly in mind the dominant intention of a discourse, for it is the intention that determines the overall organization.

■ APPLICATIONS

Which of the following examples are pure argument, which are pure exposition, and which are mixed? In the examples that are mixed, distinguish the elements of exposition from those of argument.

Let us examine such an example:

> A great many of the kids now looking at the Vietnam war and having just confronted the reality of the bomb for the first time are acting the way English schoolboys behaved in the last days of World War I. The war was taking a terrific death toll then, and the boys who were just under military age all expected to be killed. There are quite a few young people who are doing that now, saying there is no use in going to class, we'll all get drafted and we'll all be killed. So you get this behavior of dancing on the eve of Waterloo, except that now the young men are not dancing.
>
> —Margaret Mead: "We Must Learn to See What's Really New," *Life*.[3]

---

[3] From "We Must Learn to See What's Really New," by Margaret Mead and Irene Neves, *Life* Magazine, August 23, 1968 © 1968 Time Inc.

In the first sentence Margaret Mead announces a comparison between the way young Americans confronting the bomb behave and the way "English schoolboys behaved in the last days of World War I." We take the main intention to be expository—the making of the comparison that is supposed to clarify the present situation. The next two sentences develop the parallel, the behavior of the two different groups of young people in the face of the expectation of death. But in these two sentences, there is, too, an argument partly stated and partly implied: ". . . there is no use in going to class, we'll all get drafted and we'll all be killed." If we develop this argument, we see something like this:

> The only reason for going to class is to get ready for the future.
> But there isn't going to be any future.
> So I'm not going to class.

Then in the last sentence of the excerpt we get a new element in the argument, the dancing instead of class attendance. This implies another development of the argument, which we may state as follows (though this is not the only way to state it):

> If there isn't any future, then I'm going to enjoy the present.
> There isn't going to be any future.
> So I'm going to enjoy the present (that is, dance).

But another element has entered with the last sentence. The reference to the ball before Waterloo implies another comparison (young people now, young people in World War I, and young people at the time of Napoleon—perhaps with the implication of "young people always in the face of great danger"). Then, in the second half of the last sentence we find a contrast developed from the comparison: the young now do not resort to dancing. We may ask, then, what do they resort to? The unstated answer is "protest." Let us make one more observation on the last sentence. It returns us to the main intention, the expository intention that underlies the argument.

In analyzing the following examples, remember that you are not dealing with something as simple as the yes-or-no answer of a problem in arithmetic. There may be discussable margins. There will certainly be different ways of stating things. Furthermore, in handling the methods of argument, you are, in a sense, on your own; you have not yet studied this chapter. But you have argued all your life. Bring to bear now what you have in the way of logical capacity and training. This will be one way for you to approach the study of this chapter.

A
                              THE SURGE IN WAGES
        The seeds of today's trouble were sown three years ago. In 1965, Lyndon
        Johnson decided that the nation could simultaneously support the Viet Nam
        buildup and the Great Society. Critics insisted that such policies would push
        up prices unless taxes were raised. Johnson refused to propose higher taxes.
        Such a move would almost certainly have prompted Congress to cut back

some of his favorite spending programs. Later, faced with soaring federal deficits, Johnson changed his mind and urged a tax increase. But Congress dallied for 18 months—and thus lost an opportunity to halt inflation before it took deep root.[4]

B   AIR–RIDE PROTECTS YOUR POSSESSIONS ON ANY ROAD

We have replaced stiff, hard springs with Air-Suspension on our Mayflower long-distance moving vans. Now we float your fragile, delicate belongings over any road on big, soft cushions of air. It's our million dollar difference that gives your goods *a ride that's twice as gentle,* yet costs you not a nickel more.

Mayflower takes no chances with your belongings.

That's why we have pioneered the major improvements in long-distance moving: the first complete drivers' school . . . the first standardized quality packing service . . . first to remove tailgates from every van . . . the first exclusive, qualified agents' organization to help you. These are just a few, and we're always trying to come up with more. Let *your* nearby Mayflower agent give you the complete Mayflower story next time you move long distance. He'll take the load off your mind! He's listed in the telephone Yellow Pages.   —An advertisement.

C   Because he was such a firm democrat, Thomas [Norman Thomas] found no interest or enchantment in Soviet-style Communism. "The thing which is happening in Russia," he said after a visit during the 1930s, "is not socialism, and it is not the thing which we hope to bring about in America, or in any other land." On another occasion, he noted: "I daresay I have denied Communism, fought against it, more than most people, because at my end of the political spectrum one must make it clear that standing for democratic socialism is quite another thing from standing for Communism."[5]

D   There are two methods of curing the mischiefs of faction: the one, by destroying its causes; the other by controlling its effects.

There are again two methods of removing the causes of faction: the one by destroying the liberty which is essential to its existence; the other, by giving to every citizen the same opinions, the same passions, and the same interests.
—James Madison: *The Federalist* (no. 10).

Argument and the Common Ground

We have said that argument, in the strict sense of the word, represents an appeal to reason. The willingness to accept the dictates of reason is, ideally,

---

[4] From "The Surge in Wages," *Time*, December 27, 1968. Reprinted by permission; Copyright Time Inc. 1968.

[5] From "An American Crusade," *Time*, December 27, 1968. Reprinted by permission; Copyright Time Inc. 1968.

the common ground on which the parties to an argument meet—just as it is the implied promise to the self when you argue with yourself and are trying to make a "reasonable" decision. In other words, the appeal to reason is the broadest and deepest assumption made for argument. It underlies the whole process.

The question of common ground may, however, be considered somewhat more narrowly. Though the parties to an argument accept the standard of reason, they still need to accept (consciously or unconsciously) other things in common on which to erect the structure of reason.[6] If they cannot find some such basis, then they cannot, in any true sense of the word, argue.

Let us take an example:

> Suppose that a Mr. Brown has strong anti-Semitic views and a Mr. Smith is arguing with him. Now the fact that they are arguing at all indicates, as we have said, that they accept, momentarily anyway, a common ground in reason. But clearly, in the conversation below, Mr. Smith is trying to find a more specific common ground to work from. If there is no starting point possible, argument is not possible.
>
> SMITH: Look here, I know how you feel, but I'm just curious to know how it squares with your other views. It just doesn't seem consistent with what I know about you.
>
> BROWN: What do you mean?
>
> SMITH: Well, just the way you manage your affairs, the way you treat people.
>
> BROWN: What's that got to do with it?
>
> SMITH: Well, nobody ever said you aren't a straight shooter, or don't believe in justice, or any of these things. Like that time when you——

---

[6] We have already mentioned data, premises, and evidence as things from which an argument starts, and we have tried to indicate what they are (p. 163). The common ground is, as we have been saying, a thing that must also exist if argument is to exist. How do we distinguish it from the other things? Particular assumptions on which an argument *immediately* depends, we call *premises*. On the basis of immediacy we may also distinguish data and evidence from common ground in our sense. Common ground refers to the more remote and general assumptions.

The willingness to rest on the dictates of reason is, as we have pointed out, the most general assumption for argument, the thing that is usually assumed more or less unconsciously. But there are always other assumptions more or less remote and general. Often we proceed in argument without specifying, or even thinking about, such assumptions. Sometimes, however, we are forced to go back to find a common ground, and to specify it, in much the same way that we had to go back several stages when we tried to define the word *bungalow* for the Indian (pp. 111–13).

When you do have to go back stage by stage in an argument, what was remote and general becomes immediate and can be regarded as a premise. In the example of Smith and Brown, in the argument about anti-Semitism that we are about to explore, we see Smith, under pressure from Brown, trying to find a common ground. When he does find the common ground ("the question just boils down to what a man's interests are"), the common ground can then serve as a premise for a stage in the argument.

We have to think, in other words, what we mean by a term like *common ground,* and in what context it comes.

BROWN: That hasn't got anything to do with it.

SMITH: You don't deny that you believe in people getting justice.

BROWN: Sure, I don't deny that, but——

Smith has tried to locate the more specific common ground in the notion of justice. He has made Brown admit that he has a notion of justice. Now he has the job of making Brown see what justice would mean in a given situation. That may be a hard job, but at least there is a starting point in the common agreement that justice is desirable. But suppose that Brown denies that he is interested in justice:

BROWN: Look here, I know justice is all right, by and large. But, buddy, this is a tough world, and a man's got to look out for himself. He's got to watch his interests.

SMITH: O.K., let's forget that justice stuff. A man's got to watch his own interests. That's right. It's a good practical point of view.

BROWN: I'm a practical man.

SMITH: Well, the question just boils down to what a man's interests are, doesn't it?

BROWN: Sure.

SMITH: Now on the Jewish question, maybe our interests aren't as simple as they sometimes seem——

Smith has here dropped the common ground of justice and accepted the common ground of practical self-interest. Now his job is to show that in the light of self-interest, anti-Semitism may be a shortsighted policy in any society. Again, he may not convince his friend, but at least he has a starting point.

When we are sure about our common ground, we can say to our readers or listeners: "We disagree about the question before us, but we really agree on a more important question than this one, on something that lies deeper. And since we do agree on that deeper question, I can show you that we ought reasonably to agree on the present question." We may not say this in so many words, but it is what we mean to convey.

● CAUTION

This same principle applies when you are writing a theme. Although you do not face an actual person, such as Mr. Brown, whom you wish to convince, you must try to imagine what that unseen audience would accept in common with you. If there is no common ground, your work will be in vain.

This does not mean that you must, in your theme, go back and back, and trace every stage. It does mean that, at the least, you should try to know what unspecified things you yourself are assuming, and should think of these assumptions in the context of the theme you are writing and the audience you are writing for.

The necessity for this becomes obvious when you are dealing with a highly controversial topic. For instance, if you are writing on the population explosion, you (whatever your own religious beliefs) would not assume that a conservative Catholic, a liberal Catholic, a Baptist, and an atheist would share the same common ground. If you are writing about foreign policy, you cannot readily assume the same common ground with both a pacifist and a nonpacifist.

How does this principle apply when you are arguing with yourself—trying to reach a decision?

In each such instance, you must try to state to yourself as precisely as possible the point, or points, from which you start. Try to see how the question at stake is related to your general sense of values and to your sense of your own deepest interests. And be sure that you really know what you assume you know, believe what you assume you believe.

This is nothing but common sense. Look before you leap. Think before you write.

■ APPLICATION

Read "Freedom and the Control of Men," by B. F. Skinner (pp. 644–51) and "The Abolition of Man," by C. S. Lewis (pp. 652–57). What is the common ground for author and reader assumed for each? Is it stated or implied? Write a paragraph (say, 100 words) explaining the relation of the common ground to the body of one of the essay.

What Argument Cannot Profitably Be About

Argument represents an appeal to reason, but in a given context, certain matters cannot be settled by reason alone. To illustrate:

> John comes upon a group obviously engaged in a heated argument and asks: "What are you arguing about?"
>
> JACK: Football!
> JOHN: What about football?
> JACK: About who won the Army-Navy game in 1962.
> JOHN (*laughs*):   You idiots, what are you wasting your breath for? Why don't you telephone the information bureau at the newspaper and find out?

John is saying, in substance, that the resort to verification rather than to argument is appropriate when reliable evidence is available. But an argument may well arise about the reliability of the evidence appealed to for verification. For instance, a man puts up a large bet to back his memory that

Navy won the Army-Navy game in 1962. Would he be willing to accept as final the statement by an anonymous voice on the telephone that Army had won? Might not the person who answers the telephone, even assuming that he is actually in the reference department of a newspaper, misread the record of the game? Or might not a printer's error have crept into the record? The man with the money at stake might challenge the evidence offered and call for further investigation, for new evidence.

But let us be clear on the general point. If there is readily available an *acceptable* means of verification, the resort to argument is not, to say the least, grounded in common sense. If you have a ruler handy, why argue about the length of a piece of string?

The question of what constitutes acceptability may, however, remain. The parties to the argument about a piece of string may well accept the resort to a ruler. But we can imagine a situation in which a party to a dispute about measurement might refuse the ruler as too gross and call for a machinist's calipers. In general, the situation—the nature of the question at stake— determines the nature of acceptability. But of course the parties to a dispute may agree beforehand on the means of verification; then their agreement, not the degree of reliability of the evidence, is what is crucial.

Let us turn to another example of what argument cannot profitably be about. Suppose, again, that John comes upon the group and asks the same question, and Jack again replies, "Football!"

JOHN: What about football?

JACK: Which is the better game, football or basketball?

JOHN (*laughs*):   For the Lord's sake, what are you wasting your breath for? You can't settle that. A guy just likes the game he likes. Take me, I like tennis better than either of them.

John is right again. An argument about a matter of mere taste is useless, and in so far as the word *better* [7] in the above conversation merely means what one happens to like, there is no proper matter for argument.

---

[7] In ordinary usage, expressions such as *better, more desirable, to be preferred, greater, good, acceptable,* and so forth may indicate mere preference, an unarguable question of taste. When dealing with such an expression in an argument, one should ask questions that will determine whether or not the word has an objective content. Take the simple statement: "That is a good horse." We immediately have to ask, "Good for what?" For draying, for racing, for the bridle path, for the show ring, for the range? Or does the speaker merely mean that the horse is gentle, responsive, and affectionate, a sort of pet? By forcing the question we may discover the real meaning behind the original statement. Sometimes there is no meaning beyond the question of taste. Somebody says, "Jake is a good guy." If you force the question here and get the reply, "Oh, he's just regular. I like to be around him," you discover that the statement has no objective content. It tells you nothing about Jake. As the philosopher Spinoza would put it, Paul's opinion about Peter tells more about Paul than about Peter.

Useful forcing questions to apply to such expressions are: What is it good, desirable, useful for? What is it good in relation to? Is the standard invoked objective and therefore worth discussing?

In other words, a matter of absolute taste is not a matter for argument; only a judgment about matters concerning which one may be mistaken is a subject for argument.

We must remember, however, that there is no single hard and fast line between matters of taste and matters of judgment. Between the obvious extremes are a vast number of questions about which it is difficult to be sure. Each such question must be examined on its own merits.

Let us take, for example, an argument about whether Wordsworth or Longfellow is the finer poet. Are we dealing with a matter of taste or a matter of judgment?

If one person says, "I don't care what other people think, I just like Longfellow better," he is treating the question as a matter of taste. He is making no appeal to reason. But if another person tries to set up a standard for poetic excellence in general and tests the poets by that standard, he is making an appeal to judgment. He may say, for instance, that Wordsworth has greater originality in subject matter, has more serious ideas, has had more influence on later poets, and uses fresher and more suggestive metaphors. He may not win agreement, but he is at least using the method of argument; he is trying to appeal to reason in terms of an objective standard, and the argument is now about what constitutes such a standard. The fact that such an objective standard for literary excellence is difficult to devise does not alter the nature of his intention.

The Proposition

We have decided that, ordinarily, argument cannot be about a readily verifiable matter or a mere matter of taste. But before we say what it can be about, let us go back to the "argument" about football. When Jack says that he and his friends are arguing about football, John quite naturally asks: "What about football?"

So we have the following dialogue:

JACK: Oh, about the Michigan-Purdue game last Saturday.
JOHN: Gosh, but you are thickheaded. What *about* the game?
JACK: About Randall and Bolewiensky.
JOHN: Well, I give up!

John is outdone by his friend's stupidity because he knows that one cannot reasonably argue about something just in general—about the game, for instance, or *about* Randall and Bolewiensky. So John now says: "What about Randall and Bolewiensky?"

JACK: About which is the more useful player. I think Randall is.
JOHN: Well it's sure time you were telling me.

John's thickheaded friend has finally managed to state what the argument is about. Jack is prepared to declare: "Randall is a more useful player than Bolewiensky." Somebody denies this, and the argument ensues. The argument is, then, about Jack's declaration. That declaration is *the* proposition of the argument.

A proposition is the declaration of a judgment. As such, it may be believed, doubted, or disbelieved. It is the only thing an argument can be about, for the end of argument is to establish belief or disbelief—or, we may add as a third possibility, to define the ground of continuing doubt.

● CAUTION: <u>THE</u> PROPOSITION

When, as above, we use the phrase "the proposition of the argument," we are using the term *proposition* in a special and restricted sense: the statement of what is to be established by the argument. This is perfectly clear in formal debate, where the proposition is embodied in a resolution. For example: *Resolved,* That the Electoral College should be abolished. Or: *Resolved,* That the language requirements for the B.A. degree should be abolished.

We must, however, distinguish this restricted use of the term from its more general use: any declaration of a judgment is a proposition. In other words, a proposition may be used for many purposes other than that of stating what is to be established by an argument. For instance, a proposition may be the premise of an argument, or the conclusion. Let us go back to the argument about football—or rather, about the proposition that, according to Jack's judgment, Randall is a more useful player than Bolewiensky. This judgment is disbelieved by John. So we have the following interchange:

JOHN: I don't believe that.
JACK: Well, why not, he made that great run?
JOHN: Sure he made a great run, but you said he was more useful.
JACK: Well, a great run is always useful.
JOHN: It sure is. But if we're going to argue about being useful, we ought to know what useful means. Well, here is what I take it to mean. It means being really good and dependable in more than one department. Will you accept that idea?

Here John has offered a proposition about what constitutes usefulness. If Jack accepts this statement as John intends it, they have a premise for their argument; for, clearly, to decide which of the two players is more useful, the arguers must settle on some notion of what usefulness is. Suppose that Jack does accept John's proposition as a premise, and, then, after some discussion, says: "OK John, you win. Even if Randall is a great runner, he isn't more useful than Bolewiensky." So the conclusion of the argument is that Randall is not more useful than Bolewiensky, and this conclusion is also a proposition.

In other forms of discourse, and indeed in argument itself, propositions may appear with many different functions, but we must distinguish from all others *the* proposition, which asserts what is to be established in argument.

So we may say that the premise is a statement accepted as the starting point for the line of reasoning that will lead to a conclusion.

To look at matters another way, an argument is provoked by a proposition, it proceeds with the affirmation of a premise (premises), and ends with an affirmation about the original proposition (belief, disbelief). The affirmation about this proposition, consequent upon the appeal to reason, is the conclusion.

Locating the proposition

Formal debate, as we have said, clearly presents a proposition. But formal debate makes up a very small fraction of all argument, and ordinarily the proposition underlying argument is not formally stated—and, in fact, may not be stated at all. If we want to think straight, however, and want to be effective in argument, we ought to be able to state whatever proposition underlies our argument. We must know what is at stake, and the best way to know that is to frame the proposition, at least for ourselves.

When we come to writing a theme in argumentation, we shall find that the proposition provides our subject. If we don't know what the proposition is, we shall be floundering or wandering; the theme will lack point and unity; it will have poor organization. Even if argument is only a subordinate part of a theme that is primarily expository, descriptive, or narrative, we should make sure that we can state the proposition relevant to that part of the theme.

■ APPLICATIONS

I Review "Freedom and the Control of Men" (pp. 644–51) and "The Abolition of Man" (pp. 652–57). State the proposition basic to each essay. What premises do you find involved?

II What proposition do you think is involved in each of the following excerpts? What premises?

A   I would like first to point out that it is not right to suppose that all the poor live miserable, scarred lives. I don't hold any romantic notions about the poor, but I once was poor myself, and I believe there is a kind of subculture that they live in; they have a kind of confidence in themselves, a kind of completeness, as long as they are not driven to the bare edge of subsistence. My family was not very poor while I was growing up; it had been previously. In any case, I would say we lived a comparatively happy life.
                            —Paul Weiss and Jonathan Weiss: *Right & Wrong*.[8]

[8] From *Right and Wrong* by Paul Weiss and Jonathan Weiss, Basic Books, Inc., Publishers, New York, 1967. Reprinted by permission of Basic Books, Inc., Publishers.

B   The thing that worried me about the prospective 20 to 30 million unemployed was not that they would starve. I assumed that the superfluous population would be given the wherewithal for a good living, even enough to buy things and go fishing. What worried me was the prospect of a skilled and highly competent population living off the fat of the land without a sense of usefulness and worth. There is nothing more explosive than a skilled population condemned to inaction. Such a population is likely to become a hotbed of extremism and intolerance, and can be receptive to any proselytizing ideology, however absurd and vicious. In pre-Hitlerian Germany a population that knew itself to be admirably equipped for action was rusting away in idleness, and gave its allegiance to a Nazi party which offered unlimited opportunities for action.   —Eric Hoffer: *The Temper of Our Time.*[9]

C   A modest but original Frenchman, Cagniard de la Tour, in 1837 poked around in beer vats of breweries. He dredged up a few foamy drops from such a vat and looked at them through a microscope and noticed that the tiny globules of the yeasts he found in them sprouted buds from their sides, buds like seeds sprouting. "They are alive, then, these yeasts, they multiply like other creatures," he cried.   —Paul de Kruif: *Microbe Hunters.*[10]

III State three propositions. (Look carefully again at the definition of a proposition.) For each proposition try to state what premises you think would be necessary for an argument about it. Now for one of the propositions write a short theme (250 words) embodying your argument. (You are, of course, undertaking this without having studied the principles of logic in this chapter. Do the best you can.)

The proposition: two kinds

For present purposes, as we have indicated (p. 173), we will refer only to the proposition that states what is to be established in argument. This proposition may take either of two forms.[11] The first states that something is a fact. The second states that something should be done. Even if we state a proposition negatively and say that something is *not* a fact, or that something should *not* be done, the basic type remains. We have merely turned it upside down.

Let us illustrate. When a lawyer states that his client has an alibi, he is dealing with a proposition of fact: his client *was* at a certain place, at a certain time—or so the lawyer declares. When a car salesman tries to sell a car, he says that the prospect *should* buy that car. These are the propositions that the lawyer and the car salesman must, respectively, argue.

There is an important distinction between the kinds of argument that are

---

[9] From pp. 20–21 in *The Temper of Our Time* (Hardbound Ed.) by Eric Hoffer (Harper & Row, 1965). Reprinted by permission of Harper & Row, Publishers.

[10] From *Microbe Hunters,* by Paul de Kruif. Reprinted by permission of Harcourt, Brace & World, Inc.

[11] For other purposes, propositions may, of course, be treated according to other classifications. For instance, as singular, general, affirmative, negative, and so on.

appropriate for these propositions. For the proposition of fact, you have *only* to establish the key fact. For the proposition of action, you have to work from facts ("this car will save you money, etc.") to the desirability of action.

● CAUTION

There is a temptation to blur the distinction between the proposition of fact and that of action by saying that a fact leads to action. A fact often does lead to action, but this does not affect the distinction.

For example, I am looking at poor John lying abed. I say: "That fellow has typhoid fever." This is a proposition of fact. It says no more than what it says: "The fact is that John has typhoid fever."

Now it is quite likely that if I announce to alarmed relatives that John has typhoid, somebody is likely to exclaim: "Call a doctor!" The exclamation, if put into the form of a proposition, would be: "A doctor should be called." This is a proposition of action: it recommends a certain action.

Let us grant that this second proposition does flow from the first. We set up a logical connection when we say: "John is sick, therefore a doctor should be called." But they are distinct, as we can see even from the foregoing statement, in which the first is given as ground for the second.

This may become clear if we point out that though the second does flow from the first as we have narrated the event, this logical connection is not a *necessary* one. We can have either proposition, that is, without the other. For example, assume that I myself am a doctor. Then we get:

> ME: John has typhoid.
> ALARMED RELATIVE: Is he bad off?
> ME: Yes.
> ALARMED RELATIVE: Call the priest!
> SECOND ALARMED RELATIVE: No, John is an atheist.

Or take another example:

> SMITH: The house is on fire!
> JONES: Call the fire department.
> BROWN: Don't be a fool. Hand me that fire extinguisher.

But suppose Smith, Jones, and Brown are talented young arsonists at work. Then we get:

> SMITH: The house is on fire!
> JONES: Hurrah!
> BROWN: Let's set that old pile next door, it'll go with a bang.

The point is this. A certain fact may indeed lead to action. But to what action? Circumstances alter cases, and the context determines the action. The fact and the action are clearly distinguishable. For argument they must be treated separately.

■ APPLICATION

Which of the following propositions are of fact and which of action? (We are not talking about truth or falsity, merely about the type.)

1   You should vote in every election.
2   Tom Brown did not vote for a Republican in the last election.
3   Leisure is the basis of culture.
4   The capacity for work distinguishes the civilized man from the savage.
5   The civilized man should seek to recapture the sense of the wholeness of life that characterized earlier periods of man's development.
6   If you are going to be an engineer, you do not need to study history.
7   Wealth corrupts morals.
8   We ought not to make the pursuit of wealth our main concern.
9   The present system of welfare payments works inequities.
10   The present system of welfare payments should be changed.
11   Rioting is a legitimate form of social protest.
12   Rioting is a legitimate form of social protest only if other means of protest have been exhausted.
13   The word *legitimate* is improperly used when applied to any action that is against the law.
14   The ground of liberty must be gained by inches.   —Thomas Jefferson.
15   A little rebellion now and then is a good thing, and as necessary in the political world as storms in the physical.   —Thomas Jefferson.

The clear proposition

A proposition should state clearly what is at stake. But it is not always easy to state matters clearly. For one thing, most words, as we ordinarily use them, do not have very precise limits. Even words that refer to an objective, physical situation may be vague. How "tall" is a tall man? Five feet eleven? Six feet? Six feet three? Any of these men is well above average height, but should all be considered "tall"? We may use "tallish," "tall," and "very tall" to indicate the scale, but even then we might hesitate about the choice of a word. Or take the word bald. How much hair must be lacking before we can say that a man is bald? The word does not fix an objective standard, although it does refer to an objective situation.

The problem is even more complicated when we come to such words as *good, cute,* or *progressive,* which do not refer to easily measurable attributes. If we hear, "Mr. Black is a progressive citizen," what are we to understand? That Black works hard, pays his taxes, treats his family decently, saves money, and stays out of jail? Or that he is interested in improving the local school, bringing new factories to town, and planting flowers in the park? Or that he has a certain political philosophy? The word seems to indicate some general approval on the part of the speaker, but we do not know exactly what, and the odds are that he does not know either. The word is vague.

Let us take another example of vagueness, the proposition, "Soviet Russia is more democratic than England." A person defending this proposition might argue that Russia is more democratic than England because in its system there are no hereditary titles, because great fortunes cannot be accumulated, and because the worker is glorified. A person attacking the proposition might argue that England is more democratic because actual political power is in the hands of leaders chosen by the majority of voters in free elections, because there is freedom of speech, and because a man can choose his occupation.

The word *democratic* is vague. It is also ambiguous that the two disputants are using it in different senses—and ambiguity, like vagueness, is an enemy of clarity. In any case, the disputants can have no argument on the original proposition until they have agreed on a definition of *democracy*. And this, of course, may mean that the argument will shift to a new proposition: "Democracy is so-and-so." To proceed they must find a common ground in a definition.

● CAUTION

We cannot expect a proposition to be clear in the same way a good argument is clear. We may very well make such a proposition as "Soviet Russia is more democratic than England," if we know what is at stake in the statement. The meaning of the word *democratic* is at stake, for the first thing. The concept is complex and requires a great deal of defining. In fact, there is no generally accepted definition, and so we should have to scout the various definitions. The problem is that there would be no way to put the content of our process of definition into the proposition. Sometimes we have to accept what we may call a *clue term* in the proposition—a term that points to the line of investigation but does not solve it. The word *democratic* in the proposition about Russia and England is such a clue term. We cannot make that proposition clearer. We simply have to recognize two things: the unsatisfactoriness of its meaning and the direction in which it points. Then we can proceed to clarify the proposition.

Though we often have to accept the inevitability of certain kinds of vagueness, this does not imply that we can accept any kind of vagueness. For instance, the proposition, "People should be good," is rather idiotic. That is, it is both obvious and vague. Certainly the word *democratic* is vague, too. But it is a much more effective clue than the word *good* to a line of fruitful discussion.

HISTORY OF THE QUESTION AND OCCASION OF THE DISCUSSION

Thus far we have been discussing the clarity of a proposition by thinking of the meaning of the words that compose it. Sometimes, however, we need to go beyond this and try to see the meaning of the proposition in some general context. One of the best ways to do this is to investigate what handbooks of debating call the *history of the question*. To do this is to inform ourselves about the circumstances that brought the argument about. For example, if we are arguing that such-and-such a bill to raise tariffs should be passed, we cannot know what is at stake in the proposition unless we know something of how tariffs have affected our economy in the past and what situations, and motives, generally lead to the raising of tariffs. And it is equally important, of course, to investigate the particular situation behind the present bill—what we may call the *occasion of the discussion*.

For almost any truly important subject some knowledge of the history and of the occasion is essential if we are to grasp what is at stake. Topics do not exist in a vacuum.

■ APPLICATIONS

I Are any of the following propositions not to be profitably argued—for instance, are any mere matters of taste? Are any vague? If so, discuss the nature of the vagueness.

1   The dog is man's best friend.
2   A good book is the best friend a man can have.
3   No good Democrat will vote for a Republican.
4   No good citizen will be a slave to his party.
5   The atomic bomb is the most important invention since the steam engine.
6   The atomic bomb is the most useful invention since the steam engine.
7   Space exploration is (is not) important.
8   Square dancing is more interesting than ballroom dancing.
9   Marilyn Monroe was the most attractive actress the screen has ever presented.
10   War is necessary to maintain the manhood of the race.
11   Bourbon is better for you than marijuana.
12   There is a good deal of human nature in man.   —Samuel Clemens.

II Frame an unclear proposition and a proposition you consider acceptable for six of the following topics:

Religion	Tennis
Intoxicants	Patriotism
Reading habits	College
United Nations	Education
War	Filial piety
Motherhood	Democracy
Black Power	Illegitimacy

The single proposition

An argument must have a main point if it is to make sense. That main point is what the proposition of the argument should state, and the proposition should state only the *main* point. In other words, the proposition behind an argument should be single.

Let us take an example. A college student named George is in a very depressed condition, is lacking energy, has headaches and poor digestion, and doesn't seem to be able to study. A friend says: "You should see a doctor."

There are many factors in the situation behind the proposition—George's depression, lack of energy, and so forth—but the proposition is single. It involves a single decision, a single act: to go or not to go to the doctor.

George does go to a doctor, who says: "You ought to take more exercise and study harder." This, clearly, is two propositions, and the fact that they occur in the same sentence doesn't make any difference. True, the reasons that make the doctor decide on more exercise and the reasons that make him decide on more study may be intimately related. They must be intimately related, for they have to do with George's total condition and the causes of that condition. But there are two independent propositions: (1) exercise more and (2) study harder.

We see this fact immediately if we think of George going to another doctor, who says that George should get a job on a pick-and-shovel gang to build up his strength and should, for the time being, forget study altogether. And another doctor may say: "Take no exercise at all, for your heart is very bad, but try to develop an interest in your studies."

We don't know anything about George, and we don't know which doctor is right, but we do see, by common sense, that to accept one of the ideas, that about exercise, doesn't necessarily mean that we have to accept the other one, that about study. They are independent propositions; we may accept one and not the other. And if they are independent, then two arguments, not one, are involved.

Here is a student theme that illustrates the looseness and poor organization one is likely to fall into when trying to argue a double proposition.

COED DORMITORIES

The single most progressive thing this college could do would be to go coed and house male and female students in the same dormitories. I know, I think, most of the arguments against having women on campus, for my father is dead set against it. In fact, one reason I am here today and not at the University of Michigan (where my girl goes) is that this place is not coed, and my father picked it, and, you might say, sort of bribed me. The chief argument, aside from bribery, that he has is that college is a place to get an education and that campus love affairs and education don't mix, for on campus a love affair, he says, runs twenty-four hours a day, seven days a week. What my father doesn't get is that an education is more than a Phi Beta Kappa key (he has one, and a string of degrees), and that part of it is to get ready to live a full life in the modern world.

What my father thinks is that in a coed college you would find the same frantic atmosphere every day that he found here when he was a student and you only saw girls once a term, when they came for a prom—like angels from On High wearing haloes. He doesn't really get it that in a coed place, in fact in any place now, boys and girls are much more casual, they take each other more for granted. It is true that things do get pretty frantic here on a visiting weekend, but that is only because we aren't coed, and they would simmer down if the girls were here all the time, especially if they were in the same dormitories with us.

What my father doesn't realize is that if boys and girls were in the same dormitories they would accept each other so completely that there wouldn't be much distraction or novelty. Friendship could exist in a frank way not now possible, for we could regard each other as people. Then, if two people happened to fall in love, they would be able to judge each other on a sounder basis.

As for girls getting into what used to be called trouble, any parent who worries about that could start worrying no matter where the girl is. People say that college should be *in loco parentis*. Well, it usually is in place of the parent. But what does the parent manage to do in his place? Young people are going to do whatever their own values dictate. Rules don't change that, at home or in college.

Quite clearly this theme involves two propositions: (1) the college should go coed and (2) male and female students should be housed in the same dormitories. That these are quite separate notions (though they involve overlaps) we can see if we remember that the joint-dormitory system is not the only alternative to the all-male college. But the author thinks of the two propositions as one. He even begins: "The single most progressive thing this college could do . . . ." It is this impulse to lump the two propositions together that accounts for the general confusion of the argument.

If he had been systematic, and had kept the two propositions quite distinct, he might well have begun by outlining the defects of the present system. Then having established the need for change, he could have tested the most obvious solution (proposition one). If he had decided that co-education in itself would not solve the problem, then he could have discussed the joint-dormitory system. But he should, all the way through, have been aware of problems that his proposal might entail, and then should have weighed these against the advantages of a change, with each topic considered individually and in a logical sequence.

● CAUTION

1   The fact that two ideas appear in one sentence does not mean that they are one proposition. They are still two.
2   The fact that two ideas relate to the same situation (such as the presence of women on campus) does not mean that they are one proposition. They are still two.
3   If there are two (or more propositions), each has to be argued individually.

The main proposition and supporting points

To say, as we have been saying, that an argument must have a main point, a main proposition, is not to say that more than one idea may not well appear in the course of the argument. In support of the main proposition the arguer may make a number of different individual points, and each point will, in itself, represent a proposition and will have to be argued individually. But if the argument is to have unity and coherence, such supporting points must be subordinated to the main proposition and have a significant relation to it.

Below is a rewriting done by the student who was arguing for coeducation *and* joint dormitories. The assignment for rewriting not only involved a reorganization of the theme in terms of a single main proposition, but a marginal commentary indicating the relation of minor points to the main point.

WHY I AM FOR JOINT DORMITORIES

Our college has not yet gone coed, but it is certain that, in the face of the local pressure from students and with the example of dozens of places, including Princeton and Yale, the day is not far off. The arguments for coeducation are well known, and it would be old hat to go into them now except for one thing. If those arguments are worth considering in the first place, they point beyond the simple fact of coeducation. What I mean to say is that student pressure here should not be just for coeducation but for joint dormitories as well. This is what is going to be at stake as soon as we get coeducation, and the administration might just as well face it now.

I am going back over some of the old arguments, but I must do this to make myself clear on my main point: joint dormitories. The purpose of education is to prepare for life, as I don't think anybody will deny. Now, I am certainly willing to admit that a big part of that preparation is to get knowledge and skills in a systematic way. In the world coming up, a person without those is beat before he starts. This much for the intellectual side. But I want to insist that a person has to have more than intellectual equipment. My family has a friend who graduated from Columbia University at seventeen, and had a Ph.D. in math by the time he was twenty-one; but his life is a mess, with three bad marriages, a hard time holding any job, and being an alcoholic. He was always a kind of baby, as my father, who was a classmate of his, says. He is an extreme case, but my idea is that you have to live with people, and half of them are female.

Marginal notes:

1st Minor Proposition: Arguments for coeducation support joint dormitories.

Main Proposition: Joint dormitories are desirable; implication that they prepare for life.

2nd Minor Proposition: Purpose of education is to prepare for life.

3rd Minor Proposition: Part of preparation is to get knowledge.

4th Minor Proposition: Nonintellectual preparation also important: illustration.

5th Minor Proposition: Part of nonintellectual preparation is to know women.

This idea leads to two points. One is that having girls around actually helps the intellectual side of things. They do look at things differently, and open up new ideas and what you may call perspectives. You might say that with girls in a class, the play *Othello* would always look different. Girls help to educate boys, just as boys help to educate them, for half of the population is us, after all. When somebody like my father objects to coeducation on the grounds that it distracts from intellectual effort, he forgets that the distraction really used to come from the fact that they only saw girls once a term at a prom, when everyone got frantic because of being deprived. If you have them around, you don't get frantic just seeing one or dancing with her, and in class she helps your intellectual broadening. The presence of girls would also make you feel that what you were learning belonged to the real world outside.

The other big point is that the regular presence of girls makes you look at them as people, and so helps prepare you for life. The world is moving in that direction anyway, with more mixing up of the sexes in general activity, and away from the dream-girl kind of romance, as you can tell by the way some students now think that Hemingway's *A Farewell to Arms* is silly. (I do for one, in the girl part.) With girls around, you can have friendships and get to know them. I am not saying that girls are the same as boys, but I am saying that you can appreciate that fact without making it a sex issue—or maybe I should say sexual. Then if two people happen to fall in love, they are able to judge each other on a sounder basis. I have recently read a long article by a professor of psychology who says that most divorces are the result of disillusionment about some childish idea of romance.

I have been over the old arguments to show that they really lead to joint dormitories. If the administration accepts these arguments as reasons for going coed, how can they not accept them for joint dormitories?

I know what the objections are, and I'll say that if any of the objections makes sense, I lose the game. But I don't think I will.

First, there is the old one of distraction. I hate to repeat myself, but the administration uses it again for this after dropping it for coeducation. This thing is really generational. When my father came here to college, the boys were always frantic to even see a girl, and he thinks that that would go on right now twenty-four hours a day if a girl were around to be seen. But it is clear that at the colleges that are coed, nobody is frantic, any more than they are in the supermarket. As soon as coeducation gets established, nobody notices it. People get on with their work.

12th Minor Proposition: Objection on moral grounds not consistent with present rules.

But, second, the big objection is morality. And here I can start by asking a question. Right now girls are allowed in our rooms till ten o'clock two nights a week and till eleven-thirty on Saturday. Would there be any difference on the ground of morality if people living in the same dorm visit each other's rooms? Or can you weigh or count morality? I think, too, that morality depends on a lot of factors, and definition is one of them. It is always getting a new definition. Anyhow, joint dorms would not create a new kind of morality.

13th Minor Proposition: Morality depends on definition, which changes.

Their moral standards would be the result of whatever morality was around, in society in general, I mean. I read in an article in *Ramparts* magazine that in Sweden university dormitories are coed, and nobody thinks anything of it. Isn't Sweden supposed to be one of the most enlightened and progressive countries in the world?

14th Minor Proposition: Sweden, an advanced country, accepts joint dormitories without question.

This reminds me of another objection. The parents would object, the administration says. The parents, they say, want the college to stand *in loco parentis*. Well, as far as I can see, the college *is* in the place of the parents. But what do the parents manage to do in their places? Young people are going to behave, in the end, according to their own values. Rules can't change that, at home or at college. What parents can do is to help the child build his values. If he hasn't got decent ones by the time he is in college, the parents have flunked the course.

15th Minor Proposition: Rules by college can control behavior no better than rules by parents.

16th Minor Proposition: Values of the individual are crucial.

ANALYSIS OF THEME

Here we have the main proposition and sixteen minor propositions (two repeated) that, presumably, support the main proposition. Each minor proposition can be discussed independently, and taken together they support the main proposition, they constitute the discussion.

Some of the minor propositions are directly supportive of the main proposition, for instance, (1), which affirms that the arguments for coeducation support joint dormitories, and (2). Other minor propositions indirectly support the main proposition in various ways. The following chart will illustrate the relationships.

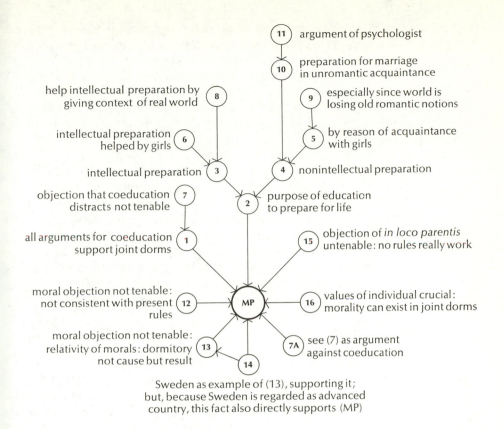

11 — argument of psychologist

10 — preparation for marriage in unromantic acquaintance

8 — help intellectual preparation by giving context of real world

9 — especially since world is losing old romantic notions

6 — intellectual preparation helped by girls

5 — by reason of acquaintance with girls

3 — intellectual preparation

4 — nonintellectual preparation

7 — objection that coeducation distracts not tenable

2 — purpose of education to prepare for life

1 — all arguments for coeducation support joint dorms

15 — objection of *in loco parentis* untenable: no rules really work

12 — moral objection not tenable: not consistent with present rules

MP

16 — values of individual crucial: morality can exist in joint dorms

13 — moral objection not tenable: relativity of morals: dormitory not cause but result

7A — see (7) as argument against coeducation

14 — Sweden as example of (13), supporting it; but, because Sweden is regarded as advanced country, this fact also directly supports (MP)

Let us interpret the chart:[12]

All arguments for coeducation (1) support the main proposition (MP), as will be shown. Meanwhile, note that the objection that coeducation distracts students (7) is not tenable. To proceed: the basic educational purpose of preparing for life (2) supports the main proposition (MP), for the joint dormitories prepare for life intellectually (3) and nonintellectually (4). The intellectual preparation is assisted by girls (6) in that they open up new ideas and perspectives, but also by the very fact of their presence, which sets the learning process in the broader context of the outside world (8). The nonintellectual preparation is accomplished by the mere fact of association in learning, and so forth, for the world is changing to a more realistic relation between the sexes (5), as is shown by the death of the old

---

[12] As a preliminary to interpreting this chart, observe that it is *not* concerned with a chain of cause and effect. It is, instead, concerned with a chain of reasons for having made a statement. For instance, (1) points to (MP), not because (1) *causes* (MP), but because (1) is a reason for holding (MP); that is, one should believe in joint dormitories (says the author) as a consequence of having accepted the arguments for coeducation. Or we could read back from (MP) through (2) to (3) and (4) as follows: we accept the joint dormitories, for, the purpose of education being to prepare for life, the joint system fulfills this requirement, in both intellectual and nonintellectual terms.

romantic notions (9). A related kind of preparation for life is given by the friendly comradeship, which provides a firm basis for marriage, unobscured by false romantic notions (10), as is attested by an eminent psychologist (11). None of these arguments would be forceful, however, if the particular objections to joint dormitories were accepted. The first objection is that of distraction and confusion in the joint dorms, which is really an old objection to coeducation (7) repeated in regard to the dormitories (7A). The moral objection is not tenable on three grounds: it is not consistent with present rules in the college (12), which already allow privacy in rooms; it is not tenable, for the behavior in the joint dormitories would really reflect the world outside (13); Sweden is cited as an example of this, and also as a subsidiary argument for joint dormitories, in that Sweden is regarded as a very advanced country (14); to return to the main line of thought, the objection of *in loco parentis* is not tenable, for the parents themselves do not control behavior even at home (15); the general objection is not tenable, for values of the individual are crucial in morality, and in joint dormitories people will merely enact their values, already fixed (16).

■ APPLICATIONS

I Examine carefully the points in the argument for joint dormitories. Can you think of any additional points that might have been made in favor of the arrangement? Can you think of any additional points against the arrangement that the author has not thought of? If so, can you answer such objections? Remember that the question here is not whether you yourself approve or disapprove of joint dormitories. It is to inspect the argument.

II Read "The Reach of Imagination," by Jacob Bronowski (pp. 637–44). State the main proposition and the minor propositions. Work out the relations among the propositions and draw a chart embodying them.

III Settle on some proposition you think may provide you with the subject of a theme later on. Work out a number of relevant minor propositions and embody them in a chart. Then make a sentence outline in which the logical connections are specified.

An issue

To treat the main proposition in an argument will, as we have seen (from the theme on joint dormitories), involve minor propositions that must be argued individually. When one such minor proposition (or more than one) *must* be proved in order to win the argument, that minor proposition is called an *issue*. An issue, then, is a proposition crucial to the argument: if you defeat it, you defeat the argument. If there happens to be more than one issue in an argument (as there usually is), the defeat of *only* one still spells defeat for the argument. For instance, in the theme on joint dormitories, the author accepts both the matter of distraction and the matter of morality as issues: if the situation distracts from work, the argument is lost, *or* if the situation entails immorality (to be defined), the argument is lost.

Let us take another, and simpler, example. The constitution of a certain college honor society, the Corinthians, specifies that to be eligible for membership a student must (1) have a scholastic average of B or above, (2) have won a letter in at least one college sport, (3) have made some substantial contribution to the general good of the college community, and (4) have conducted himself as a gentleman during the period of his college career. William Smith is proposed for election. His sponsor argues that Smith has made an A average, has won the state junior championship in swimming, has brought about a reform of the student council system by his editorials in the college paper, and is a person of high character and good manners. Smith seems certain of election until one Corinthian refers to the constitution and regretfully points out that Smith cannot fulfill requirement 2. "But he is an excellent athlete," the sponsor retorts. "He can out-swim anybody in this school."

"That's not the point," the other Corinthian replies. "The constitution explicitly states that to be eligible a student must have won a letter in at least one sport. Our college has no swimming team and therefore does not give a letter for swimming."

If the constitution is taken seriously, Smith's eligibility must be denied. The proposition is that Smith is eligible for membership in the Corinthians, and the constitution is the source of authority for the requirements for eligibility.

Each of the four requirements implies a proposition: "Smith has an average of B or above," for example. Each of those propositions is a minor one in the argument, the proposition of which is, "Smith should be elected to the Corinthians." Each is, also, an issue; that is, to fail one means that Smith is not eligible. But here we come to an important distinction. About three of the issues—1, 3, and 4—there is no debate. Such issues outside debate by general consent are called *admitted* issues. An issue (or issues) not admitted is *crucial*. In the case of the eligibility of Smith, the issue of the college letter is crucial: all hinges on this.

But suppose somebody says, "Well, Smith ought to be elected, and if a man like Smith can't get in, what's the meaning of the Corinthians?"

This remark may be true and just—in a general sense. Smith may be the sort of man the college would willingly honor. But—and here is the rub—eligibility isn't based on a general notion of suitability, but on the constitution. Perhaps someone else then says, "The constitution of the Corinthians ought to be changed." Maybe it should, but this is a new proposition and would start a new argument.

This situation is similar to that in certain cases at law in which one may feel that the letter of the law defeats justice. For example, a defending lawyer in a first-degree murder case may argue that his client had suffered intolerable provocation, that the victim had grievously slandered the defendant's wife, and that the defendant, a simple man, raised in rather primitive surroundings, had thought killing the slanderer to be the only course of honor and decency. The prosecution argues that these facts are not issues in the case, because the legal definition of murder is such-and-such and makes no recognition of the provocation of slander or of the personal background of the accused. The prosecution is, of course, right. The law defines the issues by which the proposition that the defendant is guilty of murder in the first degree must stand or fall. If the jury does acquit the defendant, it does so out of sentiment, prejudice, or some notion of justice that is inconsistent with the law.

We must keep firmly in mind the distinction between law (or rules, e.g., the constitution of the Corinthians) and justice. This question is perennial in all institutions of society; the most famous instance in our history arose from the legal status of slavery as opposed to the injustice of the institution. To turn to the ordinary workings of law, we know how, with a conviction, a jury may recommend clemency, or a judge may suspend sentence, or give a light one.

Analysis of the proposition

In the case of William Smith and the Corinthians, or of the murderer mentioned above, the issues are handed us on a silver platter: in the first case the constitution of the society defines eligibility; in the second, the law defines murder. But ordinarily, things are not that simple, and we must locate the issues for ourselves. We must, in other words, analyze the proposition.

To analyze the proposition means simply to apply the method of analysis that we have discussed under the chapter on Exposition. We try to sort out the various elements involved in a situation. This is one of the more obvious instances in which the method of one mode of discourse, here exposition, is intertwined with another, here argument.

It is important, in this connection, to remember that there are, as we have seen, two kinds of proposition, the proposition of fact and that of action. The method for analyzing one is not the same as that for analyzing the other.

ANALYSIS AND PROPOSITIONS OF FACT

Let us take some propositions of fact and see how we should go about analyzing them to determine the issues.

We shall begin with a very simple instance, one in which there can be only a single issue. Two men in the wilderness wish to cross a stream. One of them proposes that they drop a tree across it, but the other objects that the available tree is too short. Though they can establish the height of the tree, they cannot establish the width of the stream. Therefore the proposition that the tree is long enough is a matter of judgment and is subject to argument. Several arguments, good or bad, may be offered on either side, but there is only one issue: Is the tree long enough? In such cases of simple fact, the proposition itself establishes the issue. But in other cases the fact may not be simple.

Let us take the proposition: "John did right in leaving his fortune to the Ashford Medical Foundation."

First, is this a proposition of fact? It may look like a proposition of action, for John did perform an action. Certainly this would be a proposition of action if it were stated: "John will do right to . . ." Or: "John should leave . . ." But in its original form, the proposition concerns an action that has *already* taken place and concerns a judgment of the value of the event. This becomes clear if we translate the proposition into the standard form: "John's conduct in leaving his fortune to the Ashford Medical Foundation *is* (or *was*) right."

Second, how can we establish the issues? To do so, we must decide what we mean by the word *right*—a vague word in the predicate of the proposition. Suppose the opponents agree that a deed is ethically right *only* if it fulfills *all* of the following requirements: (1) the doer is responsible; (2) the doer undertakes the deed for a laudable motive; and (3) the consequences of the deed are beneficial. The issues then become:

1 Was John of sound mind when he made his will?
2 Was his motive laudable?
3 Was the money to be used for a beneficial activity?

The affirmative must establish *all* of these issues in order to win the argument. Suppose that there is no doubt of John's sanity and no doubt that the money will be used for a good purpose. Suppose that these facts or issues are admitted. The second issue then becomes crucial. If the negative establishes that John, in a fit of fury at his daughter for making a marriage without his consent, changed his will to leave his money to the foundation, his motive is a bad one, and the proposition is lost.

Where a fact is complex, as in the proposition above, the locating of the issues becomes a matter of analyzing the fact. In practice this may mean defining the key word (or words) in the proposition, as *right* was defined above.

■ APPLICATIONS

I Study "Politics of the Non-political," by Stephen Spender (pp. 722–27). State the main proposition and the minor propositions of the essay taken as a whole. Now study the "argument" between Kennan and King as reported by Spender, and line up the issues involved. Which are admitted and which are crucial?

II Analyze several of the following propositions of fact into minor propositions and issues:

Big-time college football destroys sportsmanship.
Air travel is safer than automobile travel.
Christianity is the basis of American democracy.
The doctrine of state rights caused the defeat of the Confederacy.
Democracy makes for military inefficiency.
Preparedness prevents war.
The study of literature is useless for a man who plans to go into business.
Industry now attracts the best brains in the country.
Politics has ceased to be attractive to our best men.
Security is the basis of happiness.
Sex education courses should be part of the high school curriculum.

ANALYSIS AND PROPOSITIONS OF ACTION

To analyze a proposition of action effectively, to be certain that we understand all sides of an argument and can anticipate and answer positions taken by possible opponents, or simply to clear our own minds, we should systematically set up all the propositions we can think of on each side of the main proposition. The minor propositions will tend to go in pairs, one for and one against.

Then we should examine the propositions with these questions in mind:

1 Are the propositions all significant?
2 Do they cover the subject?
3 Do they overlap one another?
4 Does any proposition really include more than one idea?

Example A farmer wants to convince his wife to move to town. He jots down some reasons to give her.

1 Better income
2 Better schools
3 House on farm not convenient
4 Social life fuller
5 Better library facilities
6 Theater and movies
7 Music
8 Cultural facilities
9 Hard to get farm labor
10 Everybody is moving to town
11 Daughter Susie needs a long course of dental work.

Then, being a logical man, he recasts the list. He realizes that 5, 6, and 7 really go together under 8, and so scratches them. Next, with some embarrassment, he looks at 10—a man, he then decides, shouldn't consider what other people do; he should make up his own mind. So he scratches 10 as not significant, not even relevant, and makes his new list:

1 Better income
2 Better schools
3 House on farm not convenient
4 Social life fuller
5 Better cultural facilities
6 Difficulty of getting farm labor
7 Susie's dental work

That evening he takes the matter up with his wife. On 1, she immediately counters by saying that in the country their expenses are much less than they would be in town, and adds that he will be coming into a nice inheritance, and therefore they don't need the extra income, anyway. On 2, the matter of schools, she replies that schools are not all of education, that getting acquainted with nature and developing one's own resources in solitude are important, too. She grants that the schools in town are better, but reminds him that he has agreed to send the children east to a prep school. So, by her argument, this question is, finally, not significant. As for 3, she admits that the house is not convenient, but says that it has great charm and the heating system can be fixed. For 4, she replies that they now have more guests than they really want, especially in the summer; then she brings in a new proposition, that they both love the outdoors, and horses and hunting. On the matter of cultural facilities, 5, she says she would like some of the concerts in Smithville, but can make do with radio and hi-fi. As for labor, 6, he can get more machinery to make up for the difficulty of finding labor. She agrees that the dental work for the girl, 7, is important, but she can drive to Smithville once a week to a good dentist there.

From the discussion, the husband now discovers that in 1 he had involved two ideas, not one, omitting to specify the question of need for added income, which in part would arise from the plan to send the children away to school in the East. This need would, in general, raise another subject for debate. He confesses to himself, too, that 2 puts forward a not very significant point, in the light of the plan for prep schools; and as for the matter of outdoor life, he had failed to consider the subject at all. On reflection, he agrees with his wife about the social life and so drops that topic.

But there are still points of disagreement. He does want more money. His farm is not suited to mechanization. So the systematic husband scribbles down a new summary of the problem.

	Husband		*Wife*
1	need more money	1	no—inheritance, lower expenses on farm
2	better income in town	2	admitted—but not significant
3	admitted	3	schools not relevant

4	house on farm not convenient	4 admitted—but charming
5	admitted	5 love of outdoor life
6	admitted	6 social life now satisfactory
7	admitted	7 cultural life satisfactory
8	farm not suited to machinery	8 buy machinery
9	Susie's dental work	9 will drive to town

Here we see two sorts of changes.

First, the husband has brought his list into better order. He has now divided his first minor proposition into two propositions. And he has better covered the subject, in that the love of outdoor life is considered.

For the second kind of change, we see that both parties have made certain admissions. The husband does not now see 6 and 7 as important. He admits 5, too; outdoor life is important to him, but in admitting this he merely indicates that he must weigh this value against other values. The wife makes admissions on 2 and 4, but with reservations; she does not think that what she admits is very important to her final position: that in 2 the increased income would be offset by added expenses, and in 4 the charm offsets inconvenience, to a degree anyway.

As things now stand, we cannot be sure how the couple will finally decide. But we can see that now the argument has been brought to much sharper focus. The husband will, it would seem from the last summary, argue on the matter of money, 1 and 2, and on the matter of labor and mechanization, 8, with, no doubt, some deep thought on 5 as balanced against his idea of moving to town.

What we have been really doing thus far is to follow the process by which an argument might be brought to essential focus. We have been analyzing what is at stake in the proposition "We should move to town."

But suppose the husband, in the middle of the discussion, suddenly confesses to his wife that he has not laid all the relevant facts before her, that his doctor has just told him of a bad heart condition and strongly advises him to reduce his physical activity. He had, he confesses, been trying to conceal this fact behind the other arguments. Presumably now the whole complexion of the discussion changes. The matter of the husband's health becomes the crucial issue, and the family would probably move to town.

■ APPLICATION

In the Application on page 186 you were asked to settle on some topic that you thought might later be good for a theme, to state the main proposition and develop the minor ones, and then to work out the chart and the sentence outlines. Go back to that material, and in the light of what you have learned since, criticize it. If it is not acceptable, revise it. Now write a theme of 500 words.

Evidence

What we have been studying thus far is really preparatory to the joining of battle in argument. We have been deciding what kind of game we are to play—draw poker, stud, or seven-card stud—and have been deciding what the stakes will be. The next step is to assemble the evidence and start reasoning from it. Here we are playing our cards. Here we win or lose.

When you get into an argument, your opponent will be from Missouri. To him, seeing is believing, and what he wants to see is evidence. Without evidence, you can offer only your unsupported views, which you already know your opponent will not accept—for if they had been acceptable to him, there would have been no argument in the first place.

What constitutes evidence?

There are two kinds of evidence, of *fact* and of *opinion*.

The most obvious and natural appeal is to the facts. We appeal, we say, to the "facts of the case," and we take facts as hard and decisive.

But we also appeal to the opinion of other people who are supposed to have some special authority. In the courtroom "expert testimony" is called evidence—the testimony of the psychiatrist, the medical examiner, the ballistics expert, the handwriting expert, and so on. Presumably the expert bases his testimony on facts, but what the jury is asked to consider is his *opinion*—his judgment of the facts. An expert may be wrong, and experts often disagree among themselves, but what they disagree about is ordinarily not the facts themselves, but their interpretation of the facts.[13]

This expert opinion is not, however, the only kind that may appear as evidence. The law also recognizes, as does common sense, what is called the "character witness," an ordinary person who is called on to offer his opinion as to the character of the defendant.

What tests can we apply to evidence?

Fact as evidence

A fact must be a fact. Direct observation by a reliable witness (what constitutes reliability we shall come to) is a powerful indication of fact, but is not infallible. What is offered as observed fact may, on occasion, turn out to be merely a mistaken opinion. We well know this pattern from

---

[13] It may be held that there is no hard and fast distinction between evidence of fact and that of opinion—that what we take as fact (say, that ice melts at 32 degrees Fahrenheit, or that the Declaration of Independence was signed on July 4, 1776) is held to be fact by the assertion of a person (or persons) of special competence, that is, of an expert. By this line of thought the distinction between evidence of fact and that of opinion would become a distinction between items of evidence supported very persuasively and those supported less persuasively —that is, by "experts" of greater or lesser authority. A fact, then, is evidence about which there is no reasonable doubt and hence general agreement, while opinion signifies matters about which even admittedly competent and informed men *may* differ. The distinction, as originally given, is nevertheless useful for practical purposes, and is commonly made.

detective stories. A "fact" points to the guilt of a certain character, who is arrested by the stupid police sergeant. The clever detective proves that the "fact"—that Miss Perkins was observed near the scene of the crime at a certain hour—is not a fact at all: the true criminal, the beloved old butler, had taken Miss Perkins' hooded raincoat and worn it while committing the murder on the moor. But justice is done: Miss Perkins is exonerated and the murderer brought to book.

A fact must be (1) verified or (2) attested by a reliable source.

VERIFICATION

Sometimes observed "facts" may be established by reference to some mechanism of observation more accurate than human perception. For instance, the camera is a more dependable device than the human eye for determining which race horse's nose pokes first over the finish line. And many a football referee has been embarrassed by a camera.

Verification may come, however, not by the recording of an event, but by the appeal to some regularity in nature such as we have encountered in studying causal analysis: that a certain type of cord will not support a certain weight, that potassium permanganate will explode under certain conditions, that the robin's egg is a certain shade of blue with brown markings, that *rigor mortis* sets in at a certain time after death. Each such fact belongs to a pattern in nature that is observable, and to test a particular fact we refer it to the pattern. We have an example in a story of one of Abraham Lincoln's law cases. A witness testified that he had observed a certain event. Lincoln asked him how, and he replied that he had seen it by moonlight. By producing an almanac, Lincoln showed that there had been no moon on the night in question. Lincoln tested the fact by referring it to a natural pattern.

FACT ESTABLISHED BY TESTIMONY

Suppose, however, that the testimony offered cannot be tested against such a natural pattern. What questions may be asked to determine the reliability of the evidence offered by the witness? Four questions are relevant in such a case:

1 Was there opportunity for the witness to observe the event?
2 Is the witness physically capable of observing the event?
3 Is the witness intellectually capable of understanding the event and reporting it accurately?
4 Is the witness honest?

The first question is clear enough, but the others are a little more complicated. For instance, if a blind newsman attests that Bill Sims was present in a railway station at such a time, how good is his evidence? Was he capable of observing the event? If it can be demonstrated that the blind man is capable of recognizing a familiar step and is acquainted with the step of Bill Sims, who stopped at this newsstand every day to buy cigarettes, then it can be assumed that the newsman is capable of recognizing Bill Sims' presence. If, furthermore, it can be accepted that the blind newsman has common sense, is not given to delusions, flights of fancy, or exaggeration, and has a good memory, then it can be assumed that he is intellectually able to understand and report the event. What remains is the question of honesty. If the blind newsman has no connection with the case, if no malice, profit, or other special interest is involved, then it can be assumed that his report is an honest one. But if some motive that might make him color or falsify the report can be established, then his report probably would not be readily accepted, especially by a person who is hostile or indifferent.

The case we have given here for reliability—the blind newsman's testimony—is a relatively simple one, but it illustrates the kind of questions that must be raised in all situations involving testimony. A historian trying to determine the truth about an event long past, a congressional committee conducting a hearing on an economic situation, a farmer shopping for a new tractor, all are engaged in assessing the reliability of testimony and must ask the same questions. And so must you, on occasion after occasion, in daily life as well as in your college reading and writing.

● CAUTION

Never admit as fact what cannot be (1) verified or (2) reliably attested.

Opinion as evidence

Parallel to tests for the admission of fact as evidence, we can set up tests for the admission of opinion. Corresponding to verifiability—the first requirement for the admission of a fact—we find the authority for an opinion. There is no use in introducing an opinion to support an argument if the opinion will carry little or no weight. For instance, no lawyer would want to introduce as expert a witness who had no reputation for competence in his particular field. The manufacturer of athletic supplies wants a champion, not a dud, to endorse his tennis racket, and the manufacturer of cosmetics wants a lady of fashion or a famous actress to give a testimonial for his facial cream. We should be as sure as possible that an authority we invoke in an argument is a real authority: a second-rate navy is no navy, when the moment of combat comes, and a second-rate authority is no authority.

AUTHORITY AND THE TEST OF EXPERIENCE

How do we find out if an authority is real authority? "Ask the man who owns one," a famous automobile advertising slogan suggests; and the maker of a washing machine shows the picture of a happy housewife standing by her prized appliance. The advertisers here appeal to authority on the principle that the proof of the pudding is in the eating: ask the eater, for he is an authority. This is a kind of rough-and-ready authority based on experience, useful but very limited in the degree of conviction that it can carry. Very probably the automobile buyer has not used many different makes of car, and the housewife has not used many different kinds of washing machine. The opinion of an impartial technical expert who had tested many makes of car or washing machine for efficiency, durability, and so forth, would carry much more authority. Here we appeal to experience, too, but to the experience of the expert. And here we are again concerned with principles we have met in studying causal analysis, that of a uniformity in nature and that of the number of samples from which one can reason (pp. 151–54 and 201–02). The expert knows the principles involved, and he has a wide acquaintance with "samples" of cars, washing machines, or whatever.

AUTHORITY AND THE APPEAL TO SUCCESS

Authority is very often based on an appeal to success. The rich man is supposed to know how to make money, the famous painter how to paint pictures, the heavyweight champion how to fight. Success carries prestige and predisposes us to accept the pronouncement of the successful man.

But we should still scrutinize success as a criterion for authority. Perhaps the rich man got rich by luck—he happened to get into business at a time of expansion and rising markets. No doubt he himself attributes his success to his own sterling character, shrewdness, and indefatigable industry, but we may be more inclined to trust the evidence of the economic situation of his time. Or, the famous painter may have been lucky enough to hit upon a popular fashion; history is littered with the carcasses of artists of all kinds whose success was the accident of the moment. The heavyweight gives us a better instance, for it is a simpler one—he merely had to square off with one man and slug it out. But perhaps a granite jaw, a fighting heart, and an explosive punch gave him the championship, and all that he has to say about training, footwork, and strategy may be wrong. He didn't succeed by luck, as did the businessman or the painter; he really did flatten the opponent by his own force—but he may give the wrong reasons for his success.

The fact of success doesn't mean that the successful man really knows the conditions of his success. And he can speak with authority only if he does know. Many successful people are like the man who lived to be a hundred and revealed his secret for long life: "I never read less than one chapter of the Holy Writ a day or drink more than three slugs of likker a night."

AUTHORITY AND TRANSFERENCE

Not infrequently we encounter an appeal to what, for lack of a better phrase, we may call authority by transference. Because a man is considered an authority in one field, it is assumed that he is an authority on anything. The famous musician is used as an authority on statesmanship, the great mathematician is appealed to as an authority on morality, and the great physicist on religion. The All-American fullback endorses a certain break-fast food, and a famous actress prefers such-and-such a face cream. This sort of reasoning is obviously nonsensical and often pernicious, for it is simply a means of imposing on the gullibility of the audience.

AUTHORITY AND TIME

Authority, too, may have some relation to time. What was acceptable as authority at one time may not be acceptable at another. In any field where the body of knowledge is constantly being enlarged and revised, timeliness is very important. A book on chemistry or physics written ten years ago may now lack authority in certain respects, or a history of the American Civil War written in 1875 may now be considered very misleading. Should George Washington's views on foreign policy influence our own?

We want the best authority of *our* time.

CHOOSING AN AUTHORITY

Finding the man who might know is, of course, different from finding out for ourselves what he knows. If we are dealing with authority presumably based on experience, we can ask about the breadth of experience (one wash-ing machine or ten?) and the intelligence and training of the person who has had the experience. If we are dealing with authority based on success, we may inquire into the nature of the success (how much was luck?) and into the capacity of the successful person for analyzing the means to success. And we should not forget to ask if the authority of the successful person is being used as authority by transference. Furthermore, we must ask if the authority is timely.

Let us suppose, for example, that we wish to find an authority on some point of American history. It will not do to go to the library and take down the first book on the subject. The mere fact of print bestows no authority, for every error is somewhere embalmed between boards. We have to find out something about the author. Is his book of recent date? (That is, would he have available the latest research on the subject?) Does he have any special bias or prejudice which must be discounted? Does he occupy a responsible position or has he had other professional recognition? (That is, is he on the faculty of some good college or university, have his works been favorably reviewed, and so forth?) How do his views compare with the views of other historians of recognized importance? To answer these questions means that we have to find out something about American history, even though we are not capable of settling the particular point in question by our own investigation.

AUTHORITY AND THE AUDIENCE

One more thing must be considered. The authority we use must convince a particular audience. Effective authority is authority that is acceptable to the particular audience. The Mohammedan *Koran* carries no authority to a Catholic, the Pope carries no authority to a Methodist, and the first chapter of Genesis carries no authority to a geologist. If we can use an authority that our audience already knows and respects, we have an initial advantage. It this is not possible, then we must establish the prestige of the authority. We can sometimes do this merely by informing the audience, but sometimes we must resort to persuasion. As we have said, the discussion of persuasion will be taken up in the next chapter.

■ APPLICATIONS

I   In the trial of the case described below, what elements would be taken as evidence? Which would be evidence of fact, and which of opinion? Which elements, without being evidence, might be used to influence a jury?

> Percival Jones, a young instructor in Sullivan College, while driving down an icy street at 1 A.M., got into a skid, struck a pedestrian, and killed him. The accident occurred in a 35-mile zone, and neither of two witnesses testified that Jones was going faster—or much faster—than that. But a block before the spot where the accident occurred there was a traffic sign warning against the pavement when wet. After the accident, Jones walked to an all-night diner and called the police.
>
> When they arrived, his manner was cool, detached, and apparently unconcerned. The police discovered that his driver's license, recently expired, had not been renewed. There was no indication of alcohol on his breath, but it developed that two years earlier he had been arrested for driving while intoxicated. With him in the car on the present occasion was a young woman, a student of his, who was out of the girls' dormitory without permission, after hours. It developed that she was in possession of a pass key that Jones, some weeks earlier, had deviously procured.
>
> At the college, Jones was regarded as a brilliant teacher, but a "troublemaker," as the dean put it, and was irregular about turning in grades and attending faculty meetings. But he devoted a good deal of his own time to coaching the student dramatic club. He was the son of a respected Episcopal clergyman in an upstate parish, well known for his work among the poor.
>
> The victim of the accident was identified as one Leo Morris, aged 69, of no certain address or employment. Autopsy showed that at the time of his death there was, in his blood, a concentration of alcohol of .10 percent. One of the two witnesses, both companions of Morris, testified that Jones had not sounded his horn, and that when he inspected the body he said, "Gee, I've cool-cocked the old twirp."

II   Read carefully "How to Detect Propaganda" (pp. 686–91). Then analyze and criticize the evidence offered in five advertisements of common commodities, for instance, a toothpaste, a breakfast food, an automobile or truck, a movie, a face powder, a soap, and a magazine or newspaper.

III   Analyze and criticize the evidence offered in an editorial of your own choosing.

IV Analyze the evidence you have offered in your last theme. Would you care to revise it now?

Reasoning

Once we have assembled our evidence and tested its acceptability, we need to find out for ourselves, and show to others, what the evidence means in relation to the argument, how the evidence will lead to our conclusion. This is not a new process for us. The whole business of living, from first to last, is a long education in the use of reason. Fire burns, cats scratch, pulling things off tables brings a frown or a spanking—we learn these great truths early. Later on we learn other truths—a stitch in time saves nine, honesty is the best policy, to be good is to be happy. We say we learn from experience (or from somebody else's experience), but that is not quite true. Experience would teach us nothing if we could not reason about it.

Reasoning, as we have said earlier, is not something learned from books. Man learned it the hard way a long time ago, over a long period: if your powers of reasoning failed you once too often, you were liquidated by a falling tree, a sabertoothed tiger, or a neighbor who had *reasoned* out that a sharp stone tied to the end of a stout stick gave him a certain advantage in a dispute.

Reasoning is the process by which the mind moves from certain data (evidence) to a conclusion. We can make this progress to a conclusion— we make this inference—because we recognize some regularity in our world. We are back, in other words, to the principle of uniformity, which we talked about in connection with cause (see pp. 151–52 and also Appendix 1, Causal Analysis, pp. 591–95).

This is the process by which we put the particular case up against the general principle to see whether it fits. By inspecting many green apples, we arrive at the conclusion that green apples are sour; therefore we do not eat green apples no matter how invitingly they hang on the bough before us. We know that heavy drinkers tend to have unsteady hands; therefore we don't want Dr. Lush to take out our tonsils.

Induction: generalization

The kind of reasoning by which we arrive at the conclusion that green apples are sour is called *induction*. Let us examine two examples of this kind of reasoning.

A businessman has, at different times, hired five boys from the Hawkins School and has found them all honest, well-mannered, and well-educated. Therefore, when the sixth boy comes along for a job, the man will be inclined to hire him. In other words, the man has generalized from the five instances to the conclusion that all boys from Hawkins School are honest, well-mannered, and well-educated. The man has made a generalization, moving from a number of particular instances to the general conclusion that all instances of the type investigated will be of this same sort.

To take a second example of generalization: after long observation men have concluded that water always freezes at a certain temperature, 32 degrees Fahrenheit. We assume that the same kind of event in nature always happens in the same way under the same conditions—metal expands when heated; in a vacuum, falling bodies, no matter what their mass, move at the same rate. Without this assumption of uniformity we could not accept the conclusions based on the examination of a number of individual instances. And, in fact, all science is based on this assumption.

But even if the same principle of uniformity is applied in reasoning about the boys of Hawkins School that is applied in reasoning about the freezing point of water, the two conclusions compel different degrees of assent. We scarcely doubt that the next pail of water we leave out will freeze at a certain temperature, but we do doubt that absolutely all graduates of Hawkins School are models of education, manners, and honesty. We recognize here that the principle of uniformity in human nature is scarcely as dependable as the principle of uniformity in nature.

THE INDUCTIVE LEAP

The conclusion about the boys of Hawkins School is offered, as we have said, as a generalization—that is, as a proposition presumably applicable to *all* the boys of the school. But again, as we have suggested, the proposition is *only probable on the evidence.* When we argue by induction, our argument is not demonstrative; our conclusion, that is, does not *necessarily* follow from the premises, the premises being the number of instances considered in making the generalization. The fact that all the instances investigated—all the premises—agree in indicating a particular conclusion does not guarantee the truth of that conclusion.[14] We see this readily enough when we consider the proposition about the boys from Hawkins School, but students of logic tell us that from the strictly logical standpoint the conclusion that water always freezes at 32 degrees Fahrenheit is also only probable on the evidence. This is true because no argument that moves from *some* to *all* can give more than a probability. Undoubtedly millions of instances of water freezing at that temperature have been observed, but *all* instances—past, present, and future—have not been observed. After examining a certain number of instances, we take the leap from the some to the all, the inductive leap—another word for the process of *generalization.* We cannot be sure about all possible instances (pp. 151–52).

---

[14] For further discussion of argument that is demonstrative, see Deduction, pp. 205–10.

What tests can we apply to reduce the risk of error in making the inductive leap?

Suppose somebody says: "All Chinese are short and slender. Why, I used to know one out in Wyoming, and he wasn't more than five feet tall and I bet he didn't weigh more than a hundred pounds." Or: "All boys from St. Joseph's College are snobs. There was a fellow from home . . ." We all know this type of reasoning and can see that it proves nothing. A fair number of instances have not been examined. Moreover, there is no way to determine with certainty what is a fair number of instances. We must consider all the evidence available in the given circumstances and remember that only the untrained mind is rash enough to leap without looking.

Second, the instances investigated must be typical. If it can be established that the samples being investigated are indeed typical, then very few are needed. Multiplicity would be superfluous. The problem, then, may often be to determine the typicality of samples. In a laboratory the scientist may be able to test a substance to be sure it is typical of its kind. He can, for example, detect alcohol in a sample of water and therefore will not use that sample in an experiment to demonstrate the freezing point of water.

But sometimes we have to assume, without testing the fact, that the instances available are typical. For example, the businessman who has hired five boys from Hawkins School assumes that they are typical, that other boys from the school will be like them. At other times, however, when we can choose from among a number of instances for our investigation, we must make choices on the basis of typicality. Let us consider the problem of a sociologist who, for some purpose, wishes to give a description of life in the southern Appalachians. The sociologist picks three settlements, investigates the pattern of life there, and concludes that life (in general) in the southern Appalachians is such-and-such. But a rival sociologist may point out that the settlements chosen are not typical, that the people in them, unlike most natives of Appalachia, are of Swiss descent and maintain certain Swiss attitudes. The first sociologist's generalization, then, may be worthless because his instances are not typical.

Third, if negative instances occur they must be explained. Obviously, any negative instance among those that we are using as a basis for generalization will reduce the force of the generalization unless we can demonstrate that the negative instance is *not* typical and therefore need not be considered. For example, if the businessman who has hired five Hawkins boys and found them all honest hires a sixth and finds that he is pilfering in the stockroom, he may decide that he must give up the generalization that the Hawkins graduates are desirable employees. But he may discover that the boy who did the pilfering is a very special case, that he is really unbalanced, is a kleptomaniac, and that consequently he cannot be taken as typical.

Therefore, the businessman returns to his generalization that Hawkins graduates are desirable employees.

SUMMARY: TESTS FOR GENERALIZATION

1 A fair number of instances must be investigated.
2 The instances investigated must be typical.
3 All negative instances must be explained.

INDUCTION: ANALOGY

Induction by analogy is the type of reasoning based on the idea that if two instances are alike on a number of important points, they will be alike on the point in question. For example, a board of directors might argue that Jim Brown would make a good corporation executive because he has been a colonel in the army. The analogy here is between the requirements for a good army officer and a good business executive. The points of similarity might be taken as the ability to deal with men, the ability to make and execute policy, the willingness to take responsibility. Thus, if Brown has been successful as a colonel, it is assumed that he will be successful as a business executive.

We can arrive at certain tests for analogy similar to those for generalization:

1 The two instances compared must be similar in important respects.
2 Differences between the two instances must be accounted for as being unimportant.

In addition to these tests, we must remember that increasing the number of similar instances tends to strengthen our argument. For example, if Brown, the man being considered for an executive position in the corporation, has been a successful division chief in a government bureau as well as a successful colonel, his case is strengthened in the eyes of the board. But with analogy, as with generalization, even true premises do not guarantee a true conclusion.

■ APPLICATIONS

I In the introduction and the first two sections of "Freedom and the Control of Men," by B. F. Skinner (pp. 644–51), locate at least eight examples of generalization and five of analogy. Do you accept them?

II Consider the following problems in the light of the principles of generalization and analogy:

1 You are in charge of hiring for a big industrial concern. You have to choose between a young engineering graduate with a college average of C and a

young graduate who majored in history with an average of A—. Which would you take? How would you defend your decision?

2 I am not going to marry Susie, her mother is always sick and complaining. Look at what happened to Jack Carton after he married Elizabeth.

3 That man has had two accidents. I won't ride in his car. He's jinxed.

4 Our last three wars were entered into while we had a Democratic president. That proves that the Democratic party is certainly the war party.

III Here is another student theme of argument. It gives examples of induction, both by generalization and by analogy. Study it as a first step toward writing a theme of your own. The comments on the left margin may help you in seeing the general organization and the uses made of induction.

WHY I CHOSE _____ COLLEGE

Before I decided on coming here to _____ College, I had to do a lot of arguing with myself and with my family and some friends. But first, I had better say what the argument was about. All my family are doctors, all the men, that is—my father, two uncles, and a first cousin—and all of them are good at the business. When I was a kid, it just never crossed my mind to be a policeman or cowboy. It was doctor all the way, to use the language of the racetrack, where my father takes me now and then when he gets any time off. He once said to me that it was just as well that being a doctor takes so much time, for otherwise he might be a tout.

> The proposition, which is never fully stated but given informally, is: "I should go to _____ College." This is, of course, a proposition of action. The analysis, which is also given informally, involves the three ways in which _____ College could contribute to the student's medical preparation. These are the issues.

My marks in school were good enough for me to have some choice in the college I could go to. Naturally, the first thing I wanted to know about any college was whether you could get good premed work. Everybody knows that you can get good premed training at Harvard or the other big universities, and I am aiming at the Harvard Medical School, but a smaller college like this one has to be investigated. I did investigate, and I found out that in the last ten years, 22 percent of the graduates of _____ College have gone into medicine, and most of them have studied at medical schools in the top ten or so. Only two men failed to finish, and one of them had a physical breakdown. This record seems to settle the case for _____ College as a good place for premed work. I knew, too, that a lot of older men from here had become very successful doctors.

> Here the writer is assembling facts as evidence for the college as a place for premed work. Here is an inductive argument, a generalization: Men from _____ College are well-prepared for medical school. True, there are two negative cases, but one of those can be explained on grounds of poor health.

> More evidence; in fact, another generalization: Many men from here have done well in medicine.

On the faculty here, too, is a famous biologist. In a small place like this you can work pretty close to a big man and watch how he does things and thinks about problems. You see, I think I have learned a lot already, just hearing my father and the family talk about cases

> Here an argument by analogy comes in: The famous biologist is accessible in this small college and will provide an opportunity for observation similar to that the boy enjoys with his father and family.

and medical problems, and I calculated that the same process of what you might call learning by osmosis could continue for me in a smaller college better than in a big one.

This last paragraph sounds as if I were tied to my family and dependent on them. I admire them, but I don't want to be dependent. That is one reason I didn't go to college near home, or to Stanford, where my family all went and are well remembered for studies and athletics. I wanted to get far away and be on my own so that I would become grown-up. A doctor has to learn responsibility early, or he is no good. The senior honors course here at ____ also teaches responsibility, because it requires you to work out a big problem on your own.

Here again are facts used as evidence: Distance from home and the honors course will help the student gain a sense of responsibility.

There was another reason why I chose ____, in addition to its good premed record and the distance from home. It has a well-known English department. I don't mean this to sound like flattery, because everybody knows it is true. When I mentioned this reason to my cousin, Dr. Bob Mathews, he laughed at me and said I had better leave that English alone and get in some extra science. "Son," he said, "all the writing you will have to do if you are a good doctor is filling out prescriptions and signing your income tax return." I know that my cousin sort of laughs, too, at Uncle Bob, his father, in a friendly way and kids him for reading so much and writing a lot of articles, some of them not straight-through professional, but just for the layman.

The fact of a good English department will help in medical training. But this statement needs explaining. The explanation is made necessary by the cousin's objection.

I asked my uncle about Cousin Bob's point of view, and he said about Cousin Bob: "That's what you can expect from a surgeon. A surgeon is like a car mechanic. He just gets into the machine and patches it up. Except for what is wrong with the mechanism, every patient looks alike to him. That may be true for a surgeon, but you plan to be a general practitioner. I'm one myself, and I wouldn't be anything else. It's the kind of medicine that has the human quality in the fullest way."

The opinion in opposition to the cousin's view comes with some weight of authority, for here another successful doctor, the uncle, speaks. But the uncle uses analogy in presenting his argument. Or rather, he attacks the cousin's implied analogy: The body is like a machine. This analogy will not hold for general medicine.

My father agrees with my uncle and says that literature is one way of studying human nature—and a good way. He says, too, that in general practice human nature plays a big part. You have to understand the patient all the way through, not just the patient as a machine with a broken part. He says that you have to know how the driver of the machine is, and when he says that, he touches his forehead. "Lots of times it is bad driving that busts the axle, no fault in the steel."

More opinion as corroborative evidence, with weight of authority, for the father is a good doctor. The father is attacking the cousin's implied analogy, but he uses one of his own: The body isn't just a machine, but a machine with a driver.

Then my father winks at me and says, "Don't forget poker. That's a pretty good way to understand human nature, too. Why do you think I strip all these lawyers

Poker gives another analogy. How good an analogy is this?

around here in my biweekly game? Hell, they're being so logical about everything, and I'm just looking at their faces for symptoms." My father kids a lot, but he is supposed to be one of the best poker players in Santa Barbara, as well as one of the best doctors.

The conclusion sets out to be a mere summary of the three issues as resolved in the discussion, but the writer trails off rather unsystematically into an observation about his personal interest in literature and the use of a hobby for a doctor.

To sum up, I know that _____ is a good place for pre-med work, that it is a good place for me to try to be independent, and that it is a good place for me to study literature for the purpose I have in mind (though I mean to study it, too, because I like it, and a doctor needs some sort of relaxation, such as my father's racing and occasional poker).

IV   By now you have become acquainted with many items in the Readings. Choose one that you find particularly interesting and that is basically an argument, or contains an important element of argument. (For instance, "Freedom and the Control of Men," by B. F. Skinner, is basically an argument; "Adolescence: Self-Definition and Conflict," by Edgar Z. Friedenberg, though basically expository, contains an important element of argument.) Having chosen your item from the Readings, write a précis of it (p. 600). Next, if it is basically an argument, state *the* proposition and list the supportive propositions; if it is not an argument, do the same for the element that is. Last, whether you agree or not with the view of the argument that you are treating, assume that you are to write an essay attacking it, and in preparation draw up a list of propositions countering the supportive propositions of the original argument. What are the issues?

V   Write a theme in argument (about 700 words), using in the course of your discussion both generalization and analogy. Indicate, however briefly, the "occasion of the question," and, if it seems necessary, the "history of the question." In other words, give an introductory setting for your argument. One of the following topics may suggest a subject to you:

There ought to be a required course in English composition (or in American history or some other subject).
College students should not have cars on campus.
Hemingway is a better novelist than Faulkner (or vice versa).
Despite modern appliances, housewives today are worse off than housewives of fifty years ago.
Television violence is a cause of juvenile delinquency.
The dead ball should be restored to baseball.
Love makes the world go round.
Human nature can be changed.
Youth has (has not) a new role in society.
No revolution has ever achieved the end it sought.
One of the greatest threats to world peace is the multiplicity of small new nations.
What this college needs is a basic three-year degree, with additional time when required.

Deduction

In concluding our discussion of induction, we said that in both generalization and analogy we do not get certainty, only probability. This was not to say that generalization and analogy are not useful. In fact, they are indispensable, for many of our most important questions can be dealt with only in terms of probability. But there is a type of reasoning that can be distinguished from induction on the basis of probability. Deductive argument does not, indeed, guarantee the truth or certainty of its conclusion, but it does guarantee that *if* the premises are true, then the conclusion will necessarily be true. With a valid deductive argument, the one situation that is impossible to have is true premises and a false conclusion.[14]

We are already familiar with the process of deduction from our study of geometry in high school. We remember that geometry starts with certain axioms—self-evident statements that are accepted without discussion or demand for proof. For instance: "Things that are equal to the same thing are equal to each other." Or: "If equals are added to equals, the results are equal." Once having accepted the axioms, we use them as the basis for working out the first theorem. Then, from that we can prove—or deduce—the second, and so on through the whole system thus generated by the original axioms.

Once we have the axioms, the whole system will, *necessarily,* follow.

LIMITS OF CERTITUDE: PREMISE

The word *deduction* comes from two Latin words, *de,* meaning "from," and *ducere,* meaning "to lead." To deduce, then, is to lead from something to a conclusion. What is led from is, of course, the premise. A premise is a proposition that, for the purpose in hand, is accepted without demand for proof. The axioms are the premises of geometry.

We have said that "within proper limits," deduction gives "certitude." Those proper limits are always what the particular premises will permit. If, consciously or unconsciously, we accept bad premises, our conclusion may well be bad. *What we are concerned with here, however, is not the selection of premises, but the process of reasoning from them to their necessary conclusion.* (See p. 210.)

DEDUCTION AND REASONING BY CLASSES

What is the process by which we move deductively from premises? How do we think deductively?

One common form of deduction involves thinking by classes. We have already made some acquaintance with this process in studying certain

---

[14] The situations that are possible are: (1) true premises and a true conclusion, (2) false premises and a true conclusion, and (3) false premises and a false conclusion. As for what is meant by validity, see p. 210.

methods of exposition, especially classification and definition. For instance, in discussing the notion of convertibility as a test for definition we found that the statement, "A slave is a man," is not a definition. It is a true statement, but that does not make it a definition. In a definition we must be able to substitute either term for the other in any form of the statement. We accepted the definition that a slave is a person who is legally held as the property of another because we can substitute the term *person legally held as property of another* in any context in which the term *slave* is acceptable. Take the statement, "To be a slave is worse than death." Here we can make the substitution—can *convert* the terms—and we get exactly the same sense: "To be a person legally held as the property of another is worse than death" (pp. 101–03).

We cannot, however, convert the terms of the statement "A slave is a man." If we try it in the statement above, we get, "To be a man is worse than death," a notion that will find few takers.

Why are the terms *man* and *slave* not convertible, since they are linked in a true statement? The answer is simple: the term *man* indicates a class more inclusive than the term *slave*. In fact, *slave* is just one of many subclasses under the class *man*. We can indicate this by drawing a circle:

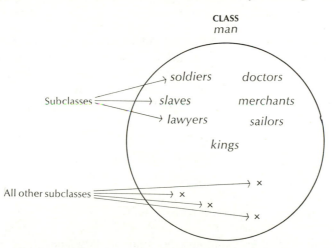

It is clear that much we might say about the class *slave* is not necessarily true about the class *man;* that is, about men in general. But it is also clear that whatever we can say about the class *man* is necessarily true about the class *slave,* for the class *slave* is included in the class *man*. And what we say about the class *man* would be applicable, too, to doctors, lawyers, soldiers, and all other kinds of men. For instance, once we say, "God loves all men," we can clearly say, "God loves slaves." We have stated a premise, "God loves all men," and the other statement, the conclusion, necessarily follows from it. It follows necessarily because we accept as another premise the notion that slaves are men.

If we put these premises into circles, we will have a little circle, the class *slave,* which is in a larger circle, the class *man,* which we now have in a still larger circle, the class *what God loves,* which, of course, includes more than men.

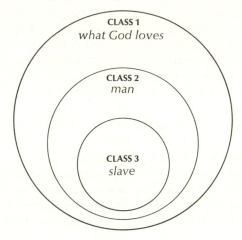

Behind the simple statement that God loves slaves, we have the reasoning indicated in our circles. This, then, is the process of deduction. There are two premises. The first, "God loves man," indicates the relation between Class 1 and Class 2. The second premise, "A slave is a man," indicates the relation between Class 2 and Class 3. From those two premises we deduce the conclusion, "God loves slaves." In other words, if Class 3 is in Class 2, and Class 2 is in Class 1, then Class 3 is in Class 1.

We may set this in the following scheme: [15]

(1st Premise)	God loves man.
(2nd Premise)	A slave is a man.
(Conclusion)	∴ God loves slaves.

Let us take another example, the statement "Even kings die." What argument would support the statement? We have the class *king* included in the class *man,* and the class *man* included in the larger class *things that die;* and so we can attach the meaning *(to die)* of the biggest class to the smallest class *(king),* or to any member, to come down a stage, of that class. We can say, "No matter how proud King William is, he will die like the rest of us." Charted it looks this way:

---

[15] The form of argument embodied in this scheme is called the *syllogism.* It was first discussed by Aristotle.

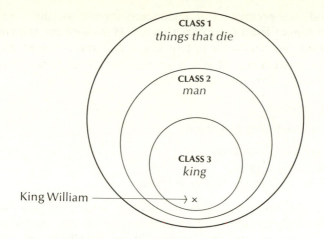

CLASS 1
things that die

CLASS 2
man

CLASS 3
king

King William ———————→ ×

Let us look at another statement: "John simply cannot learn from experience, and anyone who cannot learn from experience is a fool." In this case, all we have given are the two premises, the relation between John and Class 2 (John is in the class of those who cannot learn by experience), and the relation between Class 2 and Class 1 (the class of those who cannot learn by experience is in the class *fool*). But we *necessarily* conclude that John is a fool (that John is in Class 1). If we chart it, we get this picture:

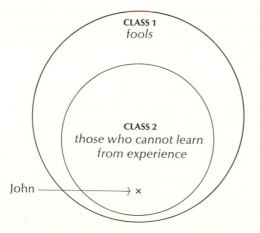

CLASS 1
fools

CLASS 2
those who cannot learn from experience

John ———————→ ×

It does not matter whether we start with the conclusion (as in the statement "King William will die like the rest of us") and have to work back to the chain of reasoning, or whether we start with the premises (as in the statement "John simply cannot learn from experience, and anyone who cannot learn from experience is a fool"); the kind of picture we get is the same, a picture of the relation of classes, and in these two instances, of the relation of an individual to classes. The same is true if we are given the conclusion and one premise. For instance, suppose we say, "John is an awful fool, he cannot learn from experience." Here we have the conclusion and one premise, but we immediately know that the unstated premise is, "People who cannot learn from experience are awful fools." And again we have the picture above.[16]

TRUTH AND VALIDITY

Examine the following syllogism:

> All men have green hair.
> Your father is a man.
> Therefore your father has green hair.

This is a valid syllogism. That is, it conforms to the process by which the mind moves from the premises to the conclusion. In this kind of argument *if* the premises are true, the conclusion will necessarily be true. Here the premise, "All men have green hair," is clearly false, and the conclusion is therefore false; but this does not affect the validity of the syllogism. This syllogism is as valid as the following one that does have true premises and therefore has a true conclusion:

> Every man has a heart.
> Your father is a man.
> Therefore your father has a heart.

Truth refers to the premises of an argument, and its conclusion. *Validity* refers to the nature of the argument, as described above. Truth and validity must be distinguished. The assumption is that *true* premises and a *valid* argument will give a *true* conclusion.

● CAUTION

You may attack the last statement by saying that sometimes a bad argument does give truth. For instance, you may suggest the following:

> Violence is bad.
> War is bad.
> Therefore war is violence.

The reasoning here is invalid, but the conclusion is true. It is true, however, only by accident, as we can intuitively grasp by setting up another syllogism in the same way:

> Men are living creatures.
> Dogs are living creatures.
> Therefore dogs are men.

---

[16] When either a premise or the conclusion is not stated but left to be assumed, the form of syllogism is called an *enthymeme*. We have just been dealing with such instances, as: "John simply cannot learn from experience, and anyone who cannot learn from experience is a fool."

Remember that what is at stake is truth *necessarily*, not accidentally, arrived at.[17]

■ APPLICATIONS

I Below you will find a list of statements. For each you are to decide whether you have a conclusion and a premise or two premises. Chart each item as a fully rendered piece of deductive reasoning. For a guide let us consider: "If you want to cut expenses, better buy an Acme typewriter." We have a general proposition, "You want to cut expenses," and a particular suggestion, "Buy an Acme typewriter." We can chart the statement by a circle with an X in it:

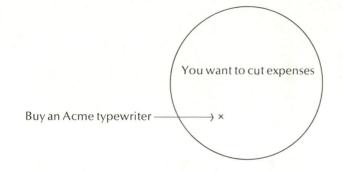

But on what grounds is the X placed in the circle? Obviously one premise is missing—which we may indicate by an intermediate circle that will be in the big one and will include the X. Of course, this circle would be, "Acme typewriters cut expenses." So we would have the picture:

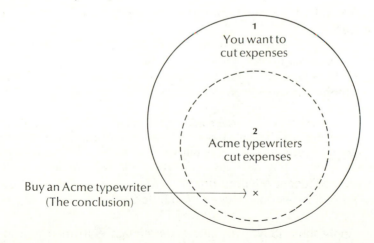

---

[17] In the two syllogisms just given we have been anticipating the discussion of *fallacy* (pp. 221–25). By way of further anticipation, make a chart of the syllogisms above. Do you see why the reasoning is not valid?

For another guiding illustration, consider: "Maybe people with lots of money can get by with dodging taxes, but you cannot." If we diagram the reasoning here, clearly we must draw a large circle for the class of people who have lots of money and a smaller circle for those who are able to dodge taxes with impunity. Our statement declares that the smaller circle falls within the larger, thus:

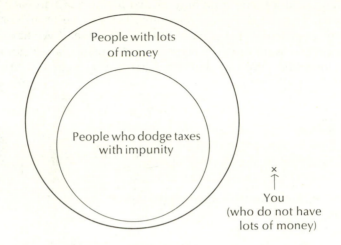

"You" would be represented by an X. The statement denies that X can be placed within the circle including people who dodge taxes with impunity, for it cannot be placed within the larger circle of people with lots of money.

Here is the list of statements to be analyzed:

1 One cannot afford to be careless of health forever. Sam has been careless a long time.
2 Why do you, who enjoy the citizenship of this country, think you should be exempt from the draft?
3 At the Battle of Gettysburg, an old woman called out to a detachment of Federal troops who were retreating: "What are you afraid for? They're only men!"
4   I am an aristocrat. I love justice and hate equality.   —John Randolph.
5   Fools say they learn from their own experience. I have always contrived to get my experience at the expense of others.   —Bismarck.
6 Nobody respects a boy who runs with the pack. No wonder you weren't elected to the Student Advisory Board.
7 You've missed another day's work. You'll be fired.

II In the Application above we have taken certain enthymemes (see footnote, p. 210) and tested them. Now you are to take a number of formal syllogisms and reduce them to enthymemes. Try to compose the enthymemes as they might appear in ordinary conversation or running argument.

1   All Southerners like hominy grits for breakfast.
    Jim Hathaway is a Southerner.
    Jim Hathaway likes hominy grits for breakfast.

2   You should give a guest what he likes.
    Jim Hathaway is going to be our guest.
    You should give Jim Hathaway hominy grits for breakfast.

3   Mortgagees who do not make the monthly payment by the 15th are fined.
    I have not made my payment by the 15th.
    I am going to be fined.

4   Boys who do not study fail this course.
    You have not studied.
    You fail this course.

5   Senators must surrender business interests that conflict with their official obligations.
    Senator Jones has an interest in the All-Western Petroleum Company, which hopes to extend off-shore drilling.
    Senator Jones must divest himself of his holdings in the company.

6   Investment in real estate is the best protection against inflation.
    Inflation will continue.
    I am going to buy real estate.

III   Construct two syllogisms with true conclusions and faulty reasoning.

IV   Here is a very famous piece of argument, a legal opinion written by Justice Oliver Wendell Holmes, of the Supreme Court. Sort out the various individual arguments appearing here as inductive or deductive, and set up each individually.

> Persecution for the expression of opinions seems to me perfectly logical. If you have no doubt of your premises or your power and want a certain result with all your heart you naturally express your wishes in law and sweep away all opposition. To allow opposition by speech seems to indicate that you think the speech unimportant, as when a man says that he has squared the circle, or that you do not care wholeheartedly for the result, or that you doubt either your power or your premises. But when men have realized that time has upset many fighting faiths, they may come to believe even more than they believe the very foundations of their own conduct that the ultimate good desired is better reached by free trade in ideas—that the best test of truth is the power of the thought to get itself accepted in the competition of the market, and that truth is the only ground upon which their wishes safely can be carried out. That at any rate is the theory of our Constitution. It is an experiment, as all life is an experiment. Every year if not every day we have to wager our salvation upon some prophecy based upon imperfect knowledge. While that experiment is part of our system I think we should be eternally vigilant against attempts to check the expression of opinions that we loathe and believe to be fraught with death, unless they so imminently threaten immediate interference with the lawful and pressing purposes of the law

that an immediate check is required to save the country. I wholly disagree with the argument of the Government that the First Amendment left the common law as to seditious libel in force. History seems to me against the notion. I had conceived that the United States through many years had shown its repentance for the Sedition Act of 1798, by repaying fines that it imposed. Only the emergency that makes it immediately dangerous to leave the correction of evil counsels to time warrants making any exception to the sweeping command, "Congress shall make no law . . . abridging the freedom of speech." Of course I am speaking only of expressions of opinion and exhortations which were all that were uttered here, but I regret that I cannot put into more impressive words my belief that in their conviction upon this indictment the defendants were deprived of their rights under the Constitution of the United States.

—Abrams versus United States, 250 U.S. 616, 1919.

● CAUTION: STATEMENT OF PREMISES

Sometimes the form of the statement of a premise is confusing. The most ordinary cause of such confusion is the use of a restrictive or exclusive element in the proposition, an expression such as *all but, all except, none but.* For example, the proposition "None but the brave deserve the fair" seems at first glance to mean, "All the brave deserve the fair." But a little reflection shows that such is not the case, and that it really means, "All who deserve the fair are included in the class of the brave," and this does not exclude the possibility that "Some of the brave may not deserve the fair" for various reasons. In the picture we indicate that some of Class 1 (the brave) may not be in Class 2 (those who deserve the fair).

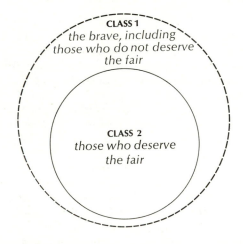

Or, to take another example: "Only students willing to work will pass this course." This does not mean, "All who work will pass this course." Rather, it means, "All who do pass this course will be in the class of those who are willing to work." So we have the picture:

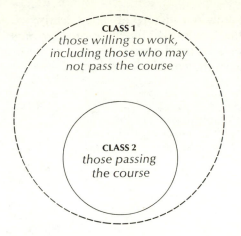

In other words, it is quite possible that some students who work very hard will fail, because they are, let us say, badly prepared or stupid or in poor health.

■ APPLICATION

Interpret and draw the picture for each of the following propositions:

1 None but a fool fails to learn from experience.
2 Only the brave deserve the fair.
3 Only women bear children.
4 Democracies alone can afford mistakes.
5 All but the foolish seek to know God's will.

SLIPS IN REASONING

We have just seen that confusion may arise from misunderstanding the statement of a premise. But it can also arise from a slip in the process of reasoning itself.

Suppose that a lawyer defending a client accused of murder argues: "We know that all good men strive to provide well for their families. They work day after day for that purpose. All good men strive to be considerate and win the love and esteem of their families. They are beloved by their families. Well, I point out to you this man's long record of devotion to his family, and their devotion to him." What is the lawyer up to? He is clearly trying to indicate to his jury that Mr. X is a good man; that is, a man who could not commit murder. If we boil this argument down, it comes out like this:

> Good men are devoted to their families, and so forth.
> Mr. X is devoted to his family.
> Mr. X is a good man, and so forth.

Let us start to draw our picture of this. Clearly, we get the class *good men* included in the larger class *men devoted to their families*. We can readily see this, for a criminal sometimes is a devoted family man, as for example, Jesse James, the notorious outlaw.

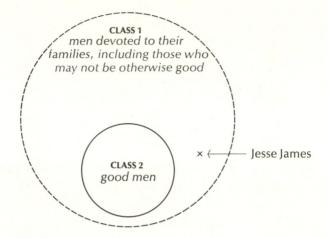

Now the lawyer wants us to put Mr. X in the class *good men*. But we see that we do not have to. All we have to do, according to our second premise, is to put him in the class *men devoted to their families*. Since that class may be larger than the class *good men,* we are able to put him there without putting him in the class *good men*—that is, men who could not commit murder. There is no *necessity* to put him in the class *good men,* and the necessity is what counts, not the possibility.

It is obvious that the chain of reasoning has slipped. In this case, we presume that the lawyer hoped the jury would not notice the slip and would vote for acquittal. But sometimes we slip without meaning to and deceive even ourselves.

Let us try another example. A political candidate says, "Every congressman who voted for the Jones-Higgins Bill betrayed this state. But I did not vote for it. I am no traitor to your interests, but would fight to the death for them."

We do not have to be impressed. The candidate has not offered any convincing reasoning that he is not a traitor to the public interest. Voting for the Jones-Higgins Bill would not be the only way a congressman could betray the public interest.

What the candidate *wants* his conclusion to look like is this picture:

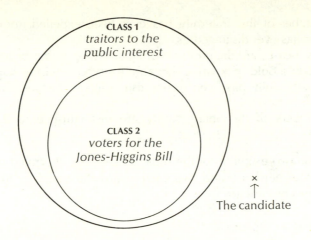

But all we are sure of is that the candidate belongs outside Class 2 (voters for the Jones-Higgins Bill). For all we know, he may still be inside Class 1 (traitors to the public interest). So our figure should indicate that he may fall either inside Class 1 or outside it:

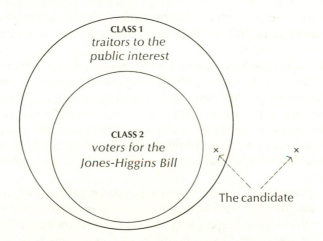

A good check on your own reasoning or on that of other people is to try to look behind the words and see what is *necessarily* included in what. The *maybe* or *perhaps* does not count. To be convincing, the conclusion *must* follow from the premises.

■ APPLICATIONS

I Which of the following arguments would you accept and which not? Draw a picture to show why.

1 No member of this fraternity has ever been expelled from college. No member has ever disgraced us.
2 We, like beasts, are the products of Nature. We are no better than beasts.
3 Everybody should seek virtue, because everybody wishes happiness.
4 The Stuart family has been distinguished in our history, and Joseph is a Stuart.
5 All members of the Stuart family are distinguished, and Joseph is a Stuart.

II Compose two examples of the slips of reasoning illustrated by the lawyer defending the murderer, and two of the slips illustrated by the politician's appeal to his constituency.

REASONING BY *EITHER–OR*

There are two other kinds of deductive reasoning, one of which is characterized by the use of the terms *either-or* and the other by *if-then*.

Let us set up an example of reasoning by *either-or* (the *disjunctive syllogism*). Upon going into the kitchen and finding the steak on the floor under the sink, we think that either the cat or the dog has pulled it down. Then we discover that the cat is locked in the barn to catch rats. Therefore the dog must have committed the crime. The formula is simple. We decide on two possibilities. We exclude one. Naturally the other becomes our conclusion.

To get a true conclusion, we must be sure, as with the usual process of deduction, that our starting point is dependable. The *either-or* premise must really cover the case. The alternatives must be exhaustive. In the example of the cat and dog, if the cat is locked in the barn and the dog is out chasing rabbits, the premise simply does not cover the case. We must investigate further to discover all the possibilities. We find that, after all, it was curly-headed little Willie who pulled the steak off the table and deserves the punishment.

In the example of the disjunctive syllogism just given, the pattern of reasoning may be described as follows: *A* or *B*, not *B*, therefore *A*. (The cat or dog was the culprit; the cat was not the culprit; therefore it was the dog that took the steak.) But can we also reason using this pattern: *A* or *B*, *B*, therefore not *A*? The validity of such reasoning will depend upon what we mean by *either-or*. We may mean (1) *A* or *B*, but not both (that is, *or* used exclusively), or (2) *A* or *B*, or both (that is, *or* used inclusively). If we are using *or* in an exclusive sense, the pattern represented by *A* or *B*, *B*, therefore not *A* yields a valid conclusion. If the cat or the dog, but not both, could have got the steak, and if we can be sure that the dog did get it, then it is valid to conclude that the cat did not. But suppose that we are using *or* in an inclusive sense; then the pattern of reasoning involved in *A* or *B*, *B*, therefore not *A* may yield a nonsensical conclusion. For example: "The man who said that is either a fool or a liar. Now I know that he is a liar;

therefore he is not a fool." The truth of the matter may be that the man is foolish as well as guilty of false statement. (It is unlikely that we mean he is a fool or a liar but *not both*.) In a case so simple as the last, there is not much danger of our getting into trouble, but in more complicated cases we may very well get into trouble unless we check very carefully the sense in which we are using *or*. There is a real opportunity for equivocation (p. 221). But note that in the *negative* pattern of reasoning (*A* or *B*, *not B*, therefore *A*) it does not matter whether we are using *or* in an exclusive or inclusive sense. The negative pattern of reasoning is valid for both.

■ APPLICATIONS

I   Discuss the following instances of reasoning by *either-or:*

1   What is not animal must be vegetable or mineral.
This is not animal.
Therefore this must be vegetable or mineral.

2   Bankruptcies are caused either by dishonesty or by idleness.
John Sutter's bankruptcy was not caused by idleness.
Therefore John Sutter must be dishonest.

3   If Williams revealed our plans, he is either a coward or a traitor.
We know he is a coward.
Therefore he is no traitor.

II   From each of the following syllogisms construct an enthymeme:

1   Either you pay me now or I sue.
So you won't pay me.
Therefore I am going to sue.

2   You will either stop seeing that rat John or stop seeing me.
You will stop seeing him.
Therefore you need not stop seeing me.

REASONING BY *IF–THEN*

Reasoning by *if-then* (the *conditional syllogism*) deals with a condition and a result. *If* the condition is fulfilled, *then* the result necessarily follows.

We constantly use reasoning of this kind, as in the statement "You haven't been watering the lawn, it will be awful for the party." Set out fully, the argument would run:

If you do not water the lawn, the grass will die.
You did not water the lawn.
Therefore the grass will die.

This reasoning is correct. We have affirmed the *if* (which is called the antecedent), and therefore the result necessarily follows. But the reasoning is also correct, if we deny the consequent, as we do below when we state that the grass has not died:

> If you do not water the lawn, the grass will die.
> The grass has not died.
> Therefore you did water the lawn.

The following example does not, however, give us correct reasoning:

> If you do not water the lawn, the grass will die.
> The grass has died.
> Therefore you did not water the lawn.

The result here is not *necessarily* acceptable. The grass may have died, not because the lawn was not watered, but because grub worms are at the roots or too much fertilizer had been applied. For the reasoning in an example like the last to be valid, the *if* would have to mean *only if*. Most errors in reasoning of this type occur because we incorrectly interpret an *if* as an *only if*.

Of course, there are instances in which the *if* should legitimately be interpreted as *only if*. But this is a matter of the truth of the premise we start with, and if we mean *only if* we should say so in the premise.

■ APPLICATIONS

I Examine the pieces of reasoning below. Which are acceptable as they stand? Which could be accepted if the *if* were to be taken as *only if*?

1 If there is smoke, there must be fire.
  There is no smoke.
  Therefore there is no fire.

2 If you leave bounds, you will be expelled from school.
  You have not been expelled from school.
  Therefore you did not leave bounds.

3 If you leave bounds, you will be expelled from school.
  You have not left bounds.
  Therefore you will not be expelled from school.

4 If you leave bounds, you will be expelled from school.
  You have been expelled from school.
  Therefore you did leave bounds.

5 If you do not catch this car, you will be late.
  You did not catch this car.
  Therefore you will be late.

6 If you do not catch this car, you will be late.
  You are late.
  Therefore you did not catch this car.

II Construct enthymemes of the syllogisms above that you consider valid.

III Compose two faulty examples of the conditional syllogism. Compose two acceptable examples of the conditional syllogism of the *if-only* type.

We have already indicated certain characteristic errors in reasoning; for example, in induction a generalization based on too few instances or an analogy based on instances different in important respects, or in deduction the failure to relate classes properly. Such an error we call a fallacy. There are, however, other fallacies not yet touched on, at least not directly, that are common in argument. Those we shall discuss are equivocation, begging the question, ignoring the question, and *non sequitur*—Latin for "It does not follow." (Certain other fallacies appear in the chapter on Persuasion; see pp. 238–74.)

Equivocation   Equivocation is the fallacy of using the same term with different meanings. Here is a well-known example:

> Even scientists recognize a power beyond nature, for they speak of "natural law"; and if there is law, there must be a power to make the law; such a power beyond nature is called God; therefore scientists believe in God.

Here the word *law* is used equivocally, that is, in two meanings. In the sense in which scientists use it when they speak of "natural law," it means the recognition of regularity in natural process—the law of gravity, for example. Here the sense is descriptive. But in the second sense it means what is ordinarily meant in government, a command given by a superior authority. Here the sense is prescriptive. Since the whole argument is based on the word *law,* the argument does not make sense *as an argument* if the word shifts its meaning. It may be true that a number of scientists do believe in God, but that does not make this a good argument.

Begging the Question   Begging the question occurs when an arguer assumes as a premise the conclusion to be proved—or when he assumes as a premise a proposition that can be proved only with the help of the conclusion that he proposes to prove. Suppose that someone offers the proposition: "The unsanitary condition of the slaughter pens is detrimental to health." (See Circular Definition, p. 114.)

What we are supposed to argue, if there is to be an argument, is whether the condition of the slaughter pens is detrimental to health. But the word *unsanitary* means "detrimental to health," and that word has been put into the original proposition. The question that is supposed to be at stake has been begged. In the example above, the begging of the question is basically a matter of language in the proposition.

When we encounter such a proposition, we should restate it and try to see exactly what is being argued.

But the same principle may appear on a larger scale, as in this example of arguing in a circle.

A: I admire Rembrandt's painting "The Night Watch."
B: Why?
A: Because it is a great painting.
B: How do you know?
A: All the best critics say it is.
B: How do you know who the best critics are?
A: Why, the best critics are those who recognize great painting.

Here speaker A has given circular proof. He sets out to prove that the painting is great by appealing to the best critics and then identifies the best critics as those who recognize great painting. This instance is a very simple one, but sometimes the begging may be concealed in a very elaborate argument. We must always be on the watch for it, for such question-begging is an attempt to establish a thing *by itself*.

Ignoring the Question   An arguer ignores the question when he introduces any consideration that will distract from what is really at stake. There are numberless ways of doing this. A competing question may be set up that shifts the argument to new ground, or an appeal may be made to some emotional attitude having nothing to do with the logic of the case. For instance, if a man arguing for a Republican candidate shifts the issue from the candidate's qualification to the praise of Lincoln, the great hero of the party, he is ignoring the question. Or if a Democrat leaves a present question of party policy and begins to discuss the glorious achievements of Thomas Jefferson, he is ignoring the question. Or if a lawyer defending a man accused of murder does not deal with the question of guilt, but argues that the victim was a wicked man or that the family of the accused is worthy of pity, he is likewise ignoring the question.

One of the commonest forms of ignoring the question is to shift from the question to the character or personality of the opponent. For instance, a husband criticizes his wife, and she replies, "Well, you aren't so perfect yourself!" She has ignored the rights and wrongs of the question, her own burnt bread or bad arithmetic or overbid at bridge, and has begun to discuss his shortcomings. We find another instance when we argue that we cannot endorse a certain political measure because the congressman who proposes it has been divorced or drinks whisky. We have shifted from the measure to the man. The Latin name of this famous and frequent fallacy is *argumentum ad hominem*.

Either-Or, All-or-Nothing   This fallacy is related to the disjunctive syllogism (pp. 218–19) in that it involves two possibilities that are presented as mutually exclusive. There are, of course, situations in which such an absolute dichotomy does exist and must be recognized. The surgeon says: "The choice lies between this operation and death." He may well be speaking the truth. Again, when you enter the polling booth, you have chosen one option in the absolute dichotomy of vote and nonvote. Once inside, you again face a clear-cut choice, with no middle ground, between voting for Jim Jones and not voting for Jim Jones. When you stand before the altar and say "I do" to the question in the marriage ceremony, you have gone beyond discussion. Life does present such yes-no decisions, and often such decisions cannot be postponed. The surgeon says the cancer cannot wait on your convenience, and election day drops the boom on political debate.

But life is also full of situations in which thinking in dichotomies falsifies actuality. A situation may be very complex, with many different possibilities. When you look down at a chess board before your first move, you cannot think in dichotomies. But many people, facing the variables of life and its complexities of option and value, will do just that. For example:

SUSIE: It's too bad Jane is so impulsive, she does get herself and others into messes.

MARY: But I thought you were her friend.

SUSIE: Of course, I'm her friend! Whoever said I wasn't. I love her, and——

MARY: But you just said she is too impulsive.

SUSIE: Sure, she is, but she's warm-hearted and generous and loyal and intelligent. She has a hundred great qualities and I love her, and I'm her friend.

MARY: That's a funny kind of friend.

Here Mary is committing the fallacy of either-or, all-or-nothing. "People are either friends or not," she would say, and for her, friendship means a total blindness to any defects. She has no idea that friendship, affection, and love can accept defects in terms of the value of the whole person. This lack of realism on Mary's part means that she herself will make such absolute demands on friendship that she can never have a friend—except some bemused half-wit.

In everyday life, this fallacy is a common and peculiarly repulsive device to dominate other people by making them take sides. For example, a lady, just divorced, says to a person who has been an intimate of the family: "If you are going to be friends with that rat John, you can't be a friend of mine."

INTIMATE OF FAMILY: But look here, I've always liked you both; you're being unreasonable.

DIVORCED LADY: Reasonable, reasonable! You're just wishy-washy, that's what you are. You have no backbone. Make up your mind—that rat or me.

The fallacy is, too, a common device in propaganda. The revivalist, the reformer, and the politician know the value of what may be called crisis psychology. "Now is the time, this may be the last chance, tomorrow is too late, don't be a coward, stand up and be counted"—these are, in one form or another, the constant exhortations. There are, indeed, great moments of crisis, occasions when, without delay, a man should stand up and be counted. But there are also moments when to sit and think is of more value to all concerned. The fallacy occurs when the occasion does not warrant the urgency or when the options proposed are false.

In propaganda this fallacy, we may add, implies a certain condescension toward the audience. The assumption is that the mass of people do not like to analyze issues, that they tend to think by easy disjunctions, by either-or. That great master of propaganda Hitler discusses this matter in *Mein Kampf,* the work in which he drew the blueprint for Nazism. Propaganda should not, he says, "inquire objectively into truth." It must recognize that popular thinking is "not complicated, but very simple and conclusive." To sum up, in popular thinking there "are not many differentiations, but a positive or a negative, love or hate, right or wrong, truth or lie, but never half so and half so . . . ."

Non Sequitur   *Non sequitur,* as we have said, means "it does not follow." In one sense, of course, any fallacy is a *non sequitur,* because by the very nature of the case the conclusion does not follow from fallacious reasoning. But here we shall use the term to cover certain more special kinds of argument.

For instance, it may be argued: "William Brown doesn't drink or smoke, and so he ought to make a good husband." But it is obvious that a man who does not drink or smoke may still make a poor husband. He may gamble, or loaf, or beat his wife. To take another example, it may be argued: "Harry Thompson would make a good governor because he belongs to the upper [or lower] class." We know, however, that belonging to a certain social class proves nothing about a man's ability or integrity. So the conclusion that Thompson would make a good governor does not follow. A connection has been asserted that does not exist.

A somewhat more complicated form of *non sequitur* appears in a piece of parental reasoning like this: "As soon as I increased Billie's allowance, his grades at school began to fall. Therefore we ought to reduce his allowance, since having extra money makes him idle." But Billie may have been suffering from eyestrain, or may have fallen in love, or may now be beginning a subject for which he is badly prepared. Let us take another example: "Just after Herbert Hoover was elected President we had the greatest depression in history. How can you respect a man like that?"

In the argument about Billie and the argument about Hoover the same error occurs. It is argued that because *A* (an increase in Billie's allowance or the election of Hoover) precedes *B* (Billie's bad grades or the depression), *A* must necessarily be the cause of *B*. The arguer does not understand the nature of a cause or has not taken the trouble to analyze the situation. He simply assumes that if one thing precedes another, the first is the cause of the second. This is, of course, the fallacy of *post hoc, ergo propter hoc,* which we have previously discussed (pp. 149–50).

Fallacies and Refutation   Many people who have never heard the word *fallacy* can reason straight or locate defects in the reasoning of another person. When we meet an example of a fallacy in cold type on the page of a textbook, we are inclined to say, "Nobody with common sense would commit such an error." That is true. But common sense is not, after all, so common, and sometimes we have to work for it. An understanding of fallacies is useful in helping us to reason straight, but it is also useful in helping us to locate defects in an opposing argument. If we can point out a fallacy in an opposing argument, we can refute that argument, and refutation is a powerful secondary weapon for maintaining our own position. Even when we are not engaged in a debate nor forced to refute arguments made by an opponent, but are simply writing a piece of argument, we often find that we have to refute certain arguments—arguments that we can anticipate in turning a question over in our minds.

■ **APPLICATIONS**

I   The selection "How to Detect Propaganda" (pp. 686–91) is really an analysis of certain fallacies, but fallacies used quite deliberately to deceive the public. Which of the false appeals analyzed there correspond to fallacies that we have studied here under other names? Which are new to you?

II   Identify the unacceptable premises or arguments in the following instances, and explain the fallacy, or fallacies, involved in each:

1   The holder of one hand in this poker game is bound to win. Jack holds one hand. Therefore he is bound to win.
2   On the seacoast a dying man usually breathes his last just as the tide begins to ebb because the going out of the water takes his strength with it.
3   You should not read the poetry of Byron, because his private life was immoral.
4   Telegrams bring bad luck.
5   No man can live without faith. Faith is the mark of a good Christian. Therefore all men are inherently Christians.
6   I am strongly opposed to our participation in any European war, because Washington, the father of our beloved country, warned us against foreign entanglements.
7   The Irish love whisky, and so I am not going to hire Pat McGoon.
8   After taking several bottles of Lightfoot's Liver Syrup, Mrs. Jones felt much better. So Mrs. Smith immediately bought a bottle.
9   Nothing is better than peace of mind. But half a loaf is better than nothing. Therefore half a loaf is better than peace of mind.
10   This unjust tax should be repealed.
11   I won't hire Pat McGoon because he is a drinking man, and no alcoholic is trustworthy.

12   The North fought the Civil War ostensibly to free the slaves, but they got rich doing it. What does that tell you?

III   Compose two examples of each of the fallacies studied in this section.

IV   Look back over editorials or articles in recent newspapers and magazines. Locate fallacious arguments, copy them down, analyze them, and bring them to class for discussion.

V   Below is an excerpt from an article on the repeal in Denmark of laws against pornography. Analyze it along the following lines:

1   What kinds of evidence are offered? When opinion is being offered here, with what weight does it come?
2   Sort out the arguments into inductive and deductive. Extract each argument and restate it. Do you accept all the arguments? What mutual support do the individual arguments give?
3   What position would you take on this question in this country? Outline your own position.

> The advocates of repeal of laws against pornography make five major arguments in favor of the new laws:
>
> 1. The Medical-Legal Council was right when it predicted that removing the ban would not stimulate sex crimes. After two years' experience, Sven Ziegler says, "There is no evidence that this liberalization is leading to any increase in the number of sex crimes."
>
> Dr. Anders Groth, psychiatrist in the Sankt Hans Hospital, the largest mental hospital in Denmark, says, "We find there has been a steady decline in sex crime since the beginning of the 60's, and between the years 1966 and 1967, there was a decline of at least 25 percent in Copenhagen." Comparing the last half of 1966 against the last half of 1967, he found sex crime in Copenhagen down 34 percent, and, he says, the reduction has held at that level. "The general fear has been that pornography gives rise to uncontrolled impulses or acts. If it did, then there would have been a rise of sex crime. There hasn't been." He points out that sex crimes are declining at the same time other forms of criminality are increasing. In reply to a police officer's question, Dr. Groth wrote: "Pornography seems to give a relaxation of passions rather than stimulate uncontrolled impulses."
>
> 2. Since the law was changed, sales of pornographic books are down, the association of book publishers reports. Denmark has been a prime producer of pornography. But with taboos lifted and free publicity from police seizures and court cases eliminated, publishers have had to cut prices; several have been forced out of the business. Now, producers of visual porno material fear a similar reaction.
>
> One of the most successful producers of such pictures, Jens Theander, who with his brother Peter owns the firm of Rodox-Trading, says, "The Danes are fed up with porno. It's been legal here too long. The curious people disappear."
>
> Rodox-Trading does about $500,000 a year in porno magazines, pictures and films. One magazine, for example, *Color Climax,* sells for $3 a copy and

has a circulation of 30,000, only one-third in Denmark. Rodox has customers in 70 countries. Most numerous are the Germans; it also has many customers in the United States. By all reports, pornographic materials enter the U.S. most easily through Baltimore.

To keep them buying pornography, Jens Theander says, "It has to be strong, it has to show everything, it has to have close-ups, it has to be nice girls, and it has to be in color . . . The story is the same every time." These days, he adds, there is a great demand for material showing group sex.

Hans Hessellund, a researcher at the Psychological Laboratory at the University of Copenhagen, has analyzed mail orders for pornography from 10,000 German, 3,000 American and 6,557 Danish customers. "American customers seem most interested in big breasts. Danish customers are more interested in nice behinds," he judges. From various studies, he concludes that most customers are middle class and upper middle class, most are at least 35 years old, and nearly all are men. The vast majority order only a few times, confirming Dr. Groth's prediction: "As soon as the appetite is satisfied, the market will dwindle to a very small one."

3. The supporters of the new laws expect the quality of pornographic materials to improve. "Good pornography," says Dr. Groth, "is erotic art where people are people with human feelings. Bad pornography is pornography where people act mechanically and where they have feelings only concerned with sex . . . Hard-core pornography is not a thing with a useful effect on people. It is anti-erotic to most people, but most people are curious about what it is. When this material is suddenly available, they will be curious but not aroused."

Dr. Hertoft agrees: "If it is not against the law, you will get better pornography. It may be possible for people with talent to make some films that are artistic."

4. Those who favor the new laws realize that the greatest concern is whether pornography has a bad effect on children. The Medical-Legal Council concluded that the psychosexual development of children is determined by the intimate family circle and later by friends their own age, teachers and others. Its report said, "It is inconceivable that coarse external influences such as pornography should be of any significance in the sexual development of children and adolescents." Hessellund agrees: "What's bad for young people is their parents' attitude toward sex—their feelings that sex is dirty."

Thomas Sigsgaard, who is a professor of child psychology and chairman of the Film Censorship Committee, says, "As far as I know, there is no basis for believing the showing of sexual relations (to children and young people) is harmful. Of course, you can't be sure there will never be any harm." He supports banning pornographic movies for young children because some "can provoke anxieties and attitudes toward sex I consider harmful." He adds, "I think it is strange that some people regard birth as offensive while they do not mind portrayal of violent death at the other end of the life story."

Professor Sigsgaard sums up his view of when pornography can be harmful to children: "If you combine sex and violence and sadism, it might be harmful to many children. If you combine sex with extremely violent emotional reactions as hate and extreme unhappiness, this could be harmful. But lack of any knowledge of sexual matters is harmful too. Sexual matters shown in a story and film in, might I say, a decent way, showing the beautiful side of sexual matters, is not harmful to the great majority of children. I think it can be beneficial to the child. They all know there is something called sex, but if they don't know what it is all about, they will have fantasies of anxiety. Lack of knowledge and fear from the banning of sex is a real danger."

Dr. Groth makes a similar point: "In Denmark, we try to give children through sex education an understanding of reality so they can compare." His landmark study of Danish female sexuality found no relationship between sexual knowledge and the beginning of intercourse.

Dr. Hertoft urges that pornography be explained to children: "We have to accept that many children will get pornography. We have to tell them it is like science fiction. The man is sexual Batman, always potent. The women always do what he wants. The women are not women in daily life. They are only interested in sex, always have orgasm. The point is it is a peculiar world with its own rules."

5. Finally, the Danish advocates of legalizing pornography argue that sometimes pornography actually serves a positive function. The Medical-Legal Council says of adolescents who develop sexual phobias, "Conversations with sexual neurotics will almost invariably reveal that in their childhood any mention of sexual subjects was tabooed in their homes. One gets the impression that they have been told too little about sex life and that they have read too little rather than too much erotic literature."

—J. Robert Moskin: "The Danes' Bold Experiment: Legalized Pornography," *Look,* July 29, 1969.[18]

DEDUCTION AND EXTENDED ARGUMENT

When we finished discussing inductive reasoning, it was relatively easy and natural to set up an extended discussion embodying what had been learned. But often deductive reasoning seems limited and niggling, not suited to a full discussion of a subject. It seems useful only for hacking away at some small point.

Throughout the last several pages we have been hacking away at small points, which is the only way to illustrate what is involved in deductive reasoning. But once we have assimilated the principles, we constantly use them, without self-consciousness, in the development of a discussion.

In much ordinary argumentative prose, we find a series of limited bits of argumentation absorbed and used, step by step. We have already seen how the full chain of inductive reasoning may be indicated by, say, one premise and the conclusion, or the two premises with the conclusion left to the logical sense of the audience—that is, by enthymemes. In this way much argument proceeds, without taking time to develop each piece of reasoning in full. The basic lines of reason may be embedded in the midst of incidental evidence, examples, and other material. Here, for example, is a paragraph from an editorial:

---

[18] By permission of the editors. From the July 29, 1969 issue of *Look* Magazine. Copyright 1969 by Cowles Communications, Inc.

Nobody denies that our tax situation is desperate and that we are facing a crisis, and nobody denies that there is great need for wise legislation in all matters affecting the business of the nation. We must scrutinize with redoubled attention every bill which comes before Congress and try to see what its effect will be in this sphere of activity. This is undoubtedly necessary with the present bill to lower taxes. If it is passed, it will have an inflationary effect. What attitude shall we take toward the present bill?

The main point here concerns a tax-reduction bill. It is assumed as background that the present situation is desperate and that good legislation is needed. The argument that follows can be divided into two chains of reason linked together:

> Tax reduction promotes inflation.
> The present bill would reduce taxes.
> Therefore the present bill would promote inflation.

The conclusion of this chain provides a premise for the next one, a link in the argument:

> Whatever promotes inflation is bad.
> The present bill would promote inflation.
> Therefore the present bill is bad.

The writer of the editorial feels that his reader knows that inflation is bad, and he says only that the present bill is inflationary. Nor does he bother to state the conclusion that this bill is, therefore, bad. He feels that the conclusion will strike the reader more powerfully if the reader is forced to come to it himself. The reader will himself answer the question: "What attitude shall we take toward the present bill?"

● CAUTION: THE WEAKEST LINK

When we are treating the stages of an extended argument, those stages, we readily see, are related, sometimes so closely related that they form what is called a chain of reasoning. No matter how deeply embedded a stage in the chain may be, each one is essential. A chain is not stronger than its weakest link.

The best insurance against putting weak links into our own work is to get the habit of stating each individual piece of reasoning to ourselves, and then criticizing it.

Development of a Theme   Below we shall follow the development of a theme in argument, step by step. The argument is in favor of manned space flights, with the title "Shoot the Moon."

Here is what the first sheet of notes looked like, mere jottings of ideas, not in any order:

> what a vast co-op effort can do—model of way—similar to war but this in peace—first time in peace

comic books—dream before fact

open-ended world suggested by space—
   new hopes and ideas

literal resources in space?

condition of this world now—
   psychological depression, no new frontiers—overpopulation, starvation,
   loss of faith

death of individual in big organization—answer in picture of spacemen

picture or dream, importance   example of human quality (1) intellect and
                                   know-how (2) moral courage, steadiness,
                                   etc. Proud to be.

   research values   astro-observatory on moon

guys as individuals—pictures as kids—single-mindedness—not just overgrown bus drivers with a little math

military motivation—instrument flight vs. manned flight

man out of nature now—conservation, etc.

These notes are obviously nothing more than a suggestive assemblage of uninterpreted ideas. They mean something to the author, but little to us. But then comes his attempt to line up arguments. The letter *F* before the number reference means "For," and the letter *A* means "Against." You will notice, too, that *A–1,* which is the first argument offered "Against," is countered by a whole series of arguments "For," running from *F–1A* to *F–1G*.

For

F–1A. Money spent on space would not necessarily go for social reform.

F–1B. No social program to justify money; unlike space programs, where there is great organization for planning and control.

F–1C. Psychology of space: modern world of technology, no static condition possible: Toynbee and challenge: space most obvious challenge.

F–1D. Meaning of "man" in space —picture.

F–1E. Space as shot in arm to society: like Renaissance and America, new ideas.

F–1F. Modern man said to be cut off from Nature: not in space.

Against

A–1. Desperate need in society for social reform: space money could do this.

F–1G. Individual swamped in modern world, big organizations, etc.: space exploration puts emphasis back on individual, but in team: new picture.

F–2. Don't know: some scientists say great resources possible and can be habitable: see available oxygen on moon to be chemically released. Science never progresses by assumptions of negative sort.

A–2. Space can bring no practical gains: not habitable, no resources.

F–3. See *1D*. Also scientific curiosity makes man want to "go and see." Science cannot progress by negative assumptions. See *1A* and *1B* for money question.

A–3. Scientific gains can be made with instrument flights: manned flights vastly more expensive, money for reform.

F–4. Military objection not really relevant. Tensions already exist. Work on peace at central point, not at margin. Withdrawal from space no answer.

A–4. Space flights, because of military motivation, increase international tension.

F–5. Solution of problem like space flight by great co-op effort may be model for solving social problem.

F–6. Generation gap idea.

When the student prepared his theme in the final form, he was requested to code it with his final set-up of the arguments for and against. He was also requested to draw the arguments used in the theme to the margin and set them up formally.

When you study the theme, you should work with both these sets of references in mind. Try to follow the process of the student's thinking. You will see, for one thing, that the order of the arguments in the original set-up is not strictly an outline of the theme.

SHOOT THE MOON

For as long as I can remember, I have been fascinated by space. Before I could really read I was looking at Buck Rogers and Superman and Batman, which for a kid was space. Then it was science fiction. Now it is not fiction at all. It is truth, and space is full of whizzing hardware with real flesh-and-blood men inside dressed up like Buck Rogers, the way we kids used to do. I have read that everything has to be a dream before it can be real, and so even those comic books were part of the dream. I am going to come back to this dream business later.

When I first began to realize that lots of people were against the space program, I was honestly shocked. It was like hearing that somebody was against football and BLTS (bacon, lettuce and tomato sandwiches, my favorite) and chocolate malt shakes, for I was then just getting into high school and going out for the freshman squad. As I got older, I began to understand their argument. I should say arguments, plural, for if I am going to answer those who oppose manned space exploration, I have to analyze what is at stake.

The first and most general objection is that our country is in a desperate condition, with the troubles of poverty and race, and that all possible money should be spent there. The second is an attack on the program from what claims to be a scientific view; it says there is no practical value in space, space has no resources. Furthermore this objection states that to explore by manned flight is unnecessary, for instrument exploration is just as good or better, and very much cheaper. This objection still has to do with using money for social betterment, but the next one brings in another factor, the military motive of space exploration. This objection states that space exploration, because it has military meaning, tends to increase international tensions.

To take the first argument first, I'll say that I admit the need for social reform. But there is little likelihood that the dollars spent for space would, if the program got dropped, be spent for social reform. There is one big difference here, not to mention some smaller ones. You don't just spend money for space in some loose general way, as people talk about spending it for social betterment. The space dollar gets spent in a very tightly worked-out program, with every detail tucked in. After all, people do get to the moon and on schedule. The program has a target in sharp focus. But there is no controlled plan for social betterment. It is a shambles. And until there is a sharp focus in

1. If you are to argue, you must analyze.
I am going to argue.
* I must analyze.

2. Money should be spent where most needed.   A-1
Money is most needed for social reform.
* Money should be spent for social reform.   A-2

3. If there is no practical value in space, it should not be occupied.
There is no practical value.
* Therefore don't occupy.   A-3

4. If two methods equally effective, use cheaper.
Instrument equally effective.
* Use instrument flight.

5. Military expansion increases   A-4
tension.
Space exploration is military expansion.
* Abandon space exploration.

6. If money saved from space   F-1A
would not go for reform, this argument not relevant.
The money would not go for reform.
* This argument not relevant.

7. If social reform does not offer a   F-1B
hard program, it cannot get big money like space.
It has not been able to offer hard program.
* It cannot get the money.

8. Hard program required to solve social problems.
Space can give model for program.
* Space helps solve social problems.

social programs, there won't be big money for them.

F–5   Right here I'll get a little ahead of myself and say that perhaps the space program will solve the social trouble. The space program has shown that we can put together a big organization of all sorts of experts, all concentrating on a particular problem. The only previous example of this was in World War II, when the atomic bomb was developed and when all the resources of the country were geared for war. This is the first time that such a program has been developed in peace, and it may provide a model for handling social problems.

F–1C   Now I shall come to my main point in answer to the first objection. A country that didn't have the will and the imagination to respond to what is called a challenge would probably not be able to survive long, much less reform itself. They say that a society has to be dynamic and psychologically expanding or die, especially in the age of technology. No business, even, can just coast, or it will go bankrupt. It is like what my history teacher says about the Maginot Line psychology in France before World War II. Space is the most obvious challenge of today: you look up and there it is. My history teacher has talked about a historian named Arnold Toynbee, who has gone back over all civilizations and worked out the principle that civilization depends on challenge and response.

9. A civilization must expand or die.
We do not want death.
* Therefore choose space.

10. Argument by analogy:
Maginot Line.

11. Toynbee uses induction: examine many civilizations to find principle.

F–1D   My next point continues my answer to the first objection, but it also refers to the second, about instrument flight. The fact that a man goes up in space is very important. That is when your imagination becomes involved. A man is accepting the challenge. It is true that instrument flight would give you a sense of what man's brain can do, but when a man goes up you get a new feeling about brain *and* steadiness, nerve, courage, and self-discipline. You suddenly feel proud to belong to the human race, and I don't mind admitting it. You are even proud of all the technicians down to the grease monkeys, for you know that they feel they are part of the ad-

12. Civilization requires pictures of courage, etc.
Space gives these pictures.
* Civilization requires space exploration.

13. You cannot suppress human curiosity.
Space exploration is human curiosity.
* You cannot suppress space exploration.

F–3

14. To deny that practical good can come from space is a negative approach.
A negative approach is anti-scientific.
* To assume that no good can come is not a scientific approach.

F–1E

15. Argument by analogy: Renaissance and America in space age.

F–2

16. Modern man needs to regain touch with nature.
Space gives contact with nature.
* We need space exploration.

F–1F

17. Modern man needs sense of identity.
Space exploration gives this sense.
* Modern man needs space exploration.

F–1G

venture. As for the astronaut in the space ship, he gives you a picture like a dream to remind you of what people can be like. Speaking of what people can be like, one important human quality is plain curiosity, and one form of this is scientific curiosity. Man wants to "go and see." This takes me back to the argument for human flight as against instrument flight, for man wants to see and what he sees is always a little different from what a machine records. This point also answers the objection that there are no practical gains in space, for the "go-see" philosophy requires an open mind. It does not make negative judgments. It assumes the possibility of a big breakthrough.

I have read that half the trouble with our country is a sense that things are running down and closing in, with the frontiers gone, and the possibility of overpopulation and crowding and starvation, and man getting out of tune with nature. The space idea can be a great inspiration to us. It is like the discovery of America, which as everybody knows, helped bring about the exciting era in Europe known as the Renaissance. I will bet that the psychology of space will stir us up the same way.

Also, there's a practical side to space exploration. Some scientists say that some planets may be habitable. And as for modern man getting out of touch with nature, there's plenty of that up there, just a different kind.

Again, it is said that the individual gets lost in the great modern world, and feels that he has no identity. The idea is that you cannot have the big organization that the modern world is and at the same time have individuals with a sense of freedom. It seems to me that the space thing gives us a different image to think about. It *is* a big organization, the most terrific, in a way, ever assembled. But it is individual, too. Those astronauts are individuals; they all started out feeling like themselves and setting out to do what they wanted to do, and paying the price to do it. But they are also team-spirited, and know that a man doesn't just decide to grow wings and take off.

F–4

18. World permeated by military motive.
Space exploration part of the world.
* Space exploration involves military motives.

19. If the problem of war is not attacked at root, peace will not be found.
Refusal of space is not an attack at root.
* Refusal of space does not give peace.

20. To disarm (unilaterally) is not to gain peace.
To refuse space is to disarm.
* To refuse space is not to gain peace.

F–6

I have not yet spoken about the third objection, the one having to do with the military motive for space exploration. I admit that there is some military motivation. It would have to be so when we are living in a world of military motivation. Any sensible man knows we have to work toward reducing tensions, but I say "work" and not simply sit back. I don't have the particular answer, but I know it is not just to withdraw from space and watch the astronauts of other nations flying over. I say do anything to get to the root of the war question, but be sure that what you do is not an empty gesture.

One more general point: I will guess, from my own observation, that kids of the generation that has grown up with space don't have much objection to it. They may not want to turn space into a shooting gallery full of floating missile sites, but they still believe in occupying it. This generation accepts space exploration as natural. It is older people, judging from some I know, who feel shocked and left out by the space developments. They are afraid of the new world they cannot fit into. They don't put it that way, but you can tell.

Maybe I am prejudiced about all this. You see, what I want to be is an astrophysicist. If I can make the grade. Well, back to the logarithms.[19]

■ APPLICATIONS

I Study the original line-up of arguments for and against space exploration. At this stage what arguments would you add to either column? Remember that you are not being asked to state your personal opinions. You are being asked to cover the case from both sides, in order to round out the argument. What matters would be issues in the new list?

II Criticize the pieces of reasoning that the author of the theme outlines in the left margin. Do you find any that are invalid? Be sure that you strictly interpret the word *invalid* (p. 210). Now make any general criticism you wish of the reasoning in the theme. Write a discussion embodying your criticism, including any material you think necessary to support your views. Observe that now, in

---

[19] For another side of this argument see an article by the scientist and novelist C. P. Snow in *Look* (February 4, 1969).

the face of this theme, you are discussing your own views. If you agree with the author, you may develop further material in support of the position. If you disagree you will be systematically saying why.

III Read "Freedom and the Control of Men," by B. F. Skinner (pp. 644–51), "The Anatomy of Academic Discontent," by Bruno Bettelheim (pp. 734–45), or "The Inscrutability of History," by Arthur Schlesinger, Jr. (pp. 826–38) with the purpose of locating five individual pieces of deductive or inductive reasoning embedded in the discussion. Criticize each of these. Do you find any that you consider "weak links"? Write an evaluation of the essay you choose. Do you accept the main idea of the essay? If so, can you add any supporting evidence and argument to it? If not, why don't you?

IV You are now to undertake your most ambitious theme up to this time. After choosing a topic, work out as full a survey of scratch notes as possible, on both sides of the question you are preparing to argue. Now sort out as systematically as you can the points you have raised, trying to pair them. (But, as the author of "Shoot the Moon" found out, you may find many particular points on one side related to one on the other.) What points raised do you regard as issues? Which are admitted, which crucial? Prepare a sentence outline, embodying the material you have assembled. Without concerning yourself with an introduction or conclusion, compose the body of the theme. Do not be disturbed if you find you must abandon at some points the outline you have prepared. The body of the theme should run some 800 to 900 words. Finally, add an introduction and a conclusion. Turn in all your preliminary material with the theme.

As for your subject, you have had a large number of suggestions in earlier Applications. If none of these appeals to you, try to review your own convictions. What do you feel strongly about? It does not have to be a world-shaking subject, merely something that evokes a conviction in you. But be sure that your subject is one that is truly arguable.

Here are a few more suggestions:

1 This college should accept any high school graduate, on a first-come-first-served basis, without reference to grades.
2 All grading should be on a pass-fail basis.
3 In the junior and senior years all students in this college should be housed in coed dormitories.
4 Coed dormitories should be governed by a body of students elected by residents of the dormitory in question.
5 Athletic competition with other institutions should be abolished.
6 Between the ages of 17 and 21, all persons not physically incompetent should be required to serve one year in some nonprofit organization devoted to conservation, social service, medical assistance, or poverty relief.
7 The results of the Mexican War have, in the end, served civilization.
8 The Spanish-American War should not have been fought.

9 War is always a mistake.
10 Bar examinations, examinations for architectural licenses, and state medical examinations should take into account inequalities in educational opportunity.
11 Admission to the bar, to the practice of architecture, and to the practice of medicine should be on a basis of ethnic quota.
12 The United States should unilaterally disarm, except for such forces as might be needed for internal police.

CHAPTER 7

Persuasion

Persuasion is the art, primarily verbal, by which you get somebody to do what you want and make him, at the same time, think that this is what he had wanted to do all the time.

It may be objected that the person persuaded—the persuadee, shall we call him?—may not be persuaded actually to "do" anything, but merely to accept an opinion or adopt an attitude. Within certain limits this objection is reasonable, but there is no clear-cut line between belief, attitude, and feeling on the one side and an action on the other. Furthermore, as soon as we look at the characteristic occasions on which persuasion takes place, we see that the process is usually targeted, at short or long range, toward action. You persuade your friend to lend you five dollars until Saturday, you persuade the child to be good and go to bed, you persuade the policeman not to give you the ticket, you persuade the prospect to buy the car, you persuade the sinner to repent and join the church, you persuade the girl to marry you, you persuade the voter to vote for you.

The persuader wants something that can be granted by the persuadee, and if he is successful, it is granted and the persuadee is happy in the granting. Persuasion is the "engineering of consent." It is a way of exercising power without creating resentment.

Persuasion and Power

Persuasion represents power. Perhaps the highest compliment ever paid the power of oratory, the prime form of persuasion in the world of ancient

Greece and Rome, is embodied in the story of the death of Cicero. After Mark Antony had caused Cicero to be assassinated, and his head and hands were exposed in the Forum, Fulvia, Antony's wife, stuck a gold pin through the tongue of the dead man to take vengeance on its power.

In that world oratory was the instrument that swayed the Athenian electorate, the Senate of Republican Rome, or the street mob of the Roman Empire. From Aristotle, in the fifth century B.C., onward to Cicero and beyond into the Empire, schools of oratory flourished, and an ambitious young man would travel any distance to study with a famous master. Up to a few generations ago, even in this country the ambitious young man studied his Greek and Latin, and the halls of Congress rang with speeches imitated from Demosthenes or Cicero.

If the desire for power was once the spur that drove the young American to a study of the classics, it still remains the fundamental motive for the exercise of persuasion. In that earlier and less sophisticated America, the occasions of public persuasion—the sermon, the college oration, the speech on the hustings, the newspaper editorial, the debate in the state house or in the Capitol at Washington—were not numerous. Today such occasions are multiplied a thousandfold, but numerous as they are, they are lost in the more massive manifestations of persuasion that pour from printing presses, crowd the television screen, fill the airwaves, and blot out the landscape as our automobiles whirl down the highways. Demosthenes and Cicero have been replaced as the masters of persuasion by courses in salesmanship and psychology, charm schools, and other implementations of Dale Carnegie's famous formula "How to Win Friends and Influence People."

The engineering of consent is central to our democratic, industrial society. We live in the age of the advertising man, propaganda expert, and motivation analyst. What was once a sporadic and limited exercise is now incessant and universal, and the stakes played for go higher every day. The political, psychological, social, and moral consequences are not yet fully clear. Even so, some observers are beginning to feel that there is serious cause for concern that the responsible forms of persuasion will be driven out by the irresponsible. That, however, is a question we shall come to later (pp. 264–70).

Differences Between Argument and Persuasion

Argument and persuasion are often lumped together, and their interrelation is indeed intimate. We cannot, however, understand this interrelation unless we sharply distinguish them. It is true that we sometimes say, "I am not persuaded of the truth of that argument." But in that case, we are using the word *persuade* (or the word *argument*) in a more general sense than is intended here (p. 164). The characteristic end of argument, strictly conceived, is truth—truth as determined by the operation of reason. The end of persuasion, on the other hand, is assent—assent to the will of the persuader.

This distinction between the end of argument and that of persuasion is crucial, but to profit fully from it we must realize another distinction. The end of argument is achieved in *only one way,* by the operation of reason; but the end of persuasion may be achieved in a *number of ways,* sometimes used singly, but more often in combination. For instance, Aristotle, in his *Rhetoric,* remarks on three modes of persuasion, the first dependent on the character and credibility of the persuader, the second on the persuader's ability to stir the emotions of those whom he aims to persuade, and the third on the proof of "a truth or an apparent truth."

We may take these three modes as useful guidelines, even though they do not constitute a strict outline for our following discussion.

Identification

To return to the difference between argument and persuasion, we may say that the characteristic end of each implies a different germ situation.

The germ situation out of which argument grows is doubt, and argument usually involves some form of conflict (pp. 161–62). When conflict is involved in argument, the conflict cannot be resolved unless those contending share some common ground; and the minimal requirement for such a common ground is an agreement to accept the dictates of reason (pp. 167–69).

In persuasion, on the contrary, the persuader earnestly seeks to eliminate conflict from the germ situation, and if doubt exists he maintains that it must be shared and resolved in a joint effort marked by mutual good will. The persuader's characteristic assertion is that any difference between his point of view and that of the persuadee is the result of only a slight misunderstanding that can readily be cleared up by a little friendly discussion, for they are two persons of essentially identical interests.

In other words, what the persuader seeks is the broadest possible common ground with the persuadee, something far beyond the ground necessary for argument. What he seeks is much more, even, than an identity of interests objectively regarded. As the eminent critic Kenneth Burke has put it in *A Grammar of Motives:* "You persuade a man only in so far as you can talk his language by speech, gesture, tonality, order, image, attitude, idea, *identifying* your ways with his." *Identification,* not conflict, is what the persuader seeks. An attempt at identification is the key to his method.

This concept of the process is nowhere better put than in the *Autobi-*

ography of Benjamin Franklin, a notable persuader of men in halls of state and of women in more retired quarters:

> I made it a rule to forbear all direct contradiction to the sentiments of others, and all positive assertion of my own. I even forbid myself . . . the use of every word or expression in the language that imported a fixed opinion, such as *certainly, undoubtedly,* etc., and I adopted, instead of them, *I conceive,* or *I imagine* a thing to be so or so; or it *so appears to me at present.* . . . The modest way I proposed my opinions procured them a readier reception and less contradiction; I had less mortification when I was found to be in the wrong, and I more easily prevailed with others to give up their mistakes and join with me when I happened to be in the right.
>
> And this mode, which I at first put on with some violence to natural inclination, became at length so easy, and so habitual to me, that perhaps for these fifty years past no one has ever heard a dogmatical expression escape me. And to this habit (after my character of integrity) I think it principally owing that I had early so much weight with my fellow-citizens when I proposed new institutions, or alterations in the old . . .

To blur conflict, delay inimical contact, blunt the thrust of aggression— these are the basic tactics of the persuader.

The next time you go to a public meeting on a controversial issue try to heckle the speaker. If he is expert in his business, he will have diagnosed his audience and will know what attitude the majority will take to your attack. If he thinks you have support, or feels that he has not yet found a sympathetic relation with the audience, he will almost certainly say: "Now that is a very good question, let's try to think it through together." Or: "I'm glad you brought that up. Perhaps we can pool our efforts and . . ." Or: "That's an interesting way to go at the problem. I've been trying to state it, but you have done it so much better than I ever could."

Even when the speaker feels that he already has sympathetic relations with the audience, he may so value his role as a conciliator that he will pay you, the heckler, this deference. If, on the other hand, he is secure in his audience and chooses to answer your aggression with aggression of his own, trying wittily to make a monkey of you for the public delight, he is still seeking identification with his audience by provoking and entering into their sadistic pleasure in your humiliation.

To sum up, identification is the basic preparation for persuasion. One can go further and say: it is the first stage of persuasion, whether the main appeal is to be emotional or logical or some combination of these qualities.

The ground of identification: knowledge of the audience

Clearly the persuader cannot achieve identification or exploit the persuadee's relation to a group unless he knows the audience. From the time of Aristotle's *Rhetoric* on, writers on persuasion have tried to classify audiences with the hope of establishing basic appeals. Aristotle made a basic and very shrewd classification by age. The young, he said, are optimistic, energetic, brave, loyal, idealistic, quick to love or anger, but they lack calculation, are prey to fads, have no steady goals, and overestimate their own knowledge. The old are skeptical, suspicious, avaricious, dispassionate, comfort-loving, and doubtful of aspiration. But men in the prime may combine the best qualities of youth and age.

Since Aristotle's day, many other writers on persuasion have suggested many other classifications, and such classifications are essential to the operations of publishing, advertising, public relations, and politics. A glance at a magazine rack in a newsstand indicates the variety of groups defined by special interests: there are magazines for people interested in fashion, humor, pornography, business, child-rearing, gardening, dog breeding, woodworking, cockfighting, horse racing, literature, hunting and fishing, sailing, politics, and so on. An advertising man makes classifications in relation to his product, and it is not likely that he will advertise mink coats in a magazine concerned with poetry. Politicians temper their speeches to their audiences: what gets applause in a silk-stocking congressional district in New York City might be suicide in the corn belt. Abraham Lincoln, in his famous debates with Stephen A. Douglas in 1858, altered his pronouncements about slavery according to the latitude of Illinois in which he was speaking. A trial lawyer, too, classifies possible jurors according to the kind of case he is handling; for instance, if his case is to depend on emotional appeals rather than logic, he is very likely to use every effort to keep prospective jurors with college degrees from being seated—on the perhaps naive assumption that a college degree indicates a training in, and respect for, logical thought.

Any persuader instinctively classifies audiences. You are not an editor, advertising man, politician, or lawyer, but in your themes, you, too, must think of the nature of the audience. In the very beginning of this course we have spoken, in general terms, about this matter (pp. 23–28). With persuasion, this principle demands special application.

Identification and the character of the persuader

We have pointed out that Aristotle bases the first mode of persuasion on the character and credibility of the persuader. The persuader may have, of course, a prestige that precedes his utterance and predisposes the audience to accept him; but there is also the immediate effect, the quality of the person on the platform, on the television screen, or behind the printed page. If the personality of the persuader is not acceptable, identification will be granted grudgingly, or not at all. The courses in salesmanship echo Aristotle with brutal simplicity: the first thing you have to sell is yourself.

Over the centuries, vats of ink have been spilt analyzing this process, but common sense remains the best guide. There are certain qualities that tend to detract from the appeal that the speaker might have for most listeners or readers. The man with little self-confidence can expect to win little confidence. The man eaten up by self-admiration can expect little admiration. The man who does not respect others can expect little respect. The man who does not know his own mind can scarcely control the minds of others. The man who cannot give sympathy rarely gets it—and certainly cannot arrive at identification with his audience. The man who has not thought through his subject cannot lead others into that subject. Nobody trusts a blunderer.

We see the face on the platform or on the television screen, the face of the insurance salesman courteously offering his fountain pen as he holds out the application form, or the face of a friend who wants us to go fishing with him. But what of the writer behind a page? We cannot see him. We cannot even hear his voice. How does his personality enter into persuasion?

We should realize, to begin with, that in a broad, general sense, the question of personality is involved in all kinds of writing, not merely in persuasion. We have touched on this very early in this text, for instance in discussing introductory paragraphs (pp. 20–21) and in connection with certain student themes (pp. 26–27). Style, in fact, has long been understood as an index of personality; the style is the man (p. 499). This whole book is, in a way, an attempt to develop the implications of that saying, but for the purpose of understanding persuasion, parts of the chapters on Diction (pp. 396–434) and on Tone (pp. 466–506) are especially important. At this point you should be sure that you have come to grips with the principles discussed there.

■ APPLICATIONS

I In the light of your reading on Diction and Tone, go back to the themes you have written thus far in this course. What impression do they give of your personality? Do you think you have done yourself justice? What response would you expect from your readers? What kinds of readers have you been writing for?

II Here are two samples of introductions. In each, try to state what tone is characteristic, what attitude, in other words, the writer takes toward his audience. What does the writer reveal of his personality? Is he likely to be persuasive? Be sure that you consider questions of diction and rhythm.

A   Dear Mary:
     I have decided to start this book with a letter to you. You know that the idea came to me when I offered to help Johnny with his reading. It's really his book—or yours. So the only proper way to start it is with the words "Dear Mary."
     You remember when I began to work with Johnny half a year ago. That was when he was twelve and they put him back into the sixth grade because he was unable to read and couldn't possibly keep up with the work in junior high. So I told you that I knew a way to teach reading that was altogether different from what . . .   —Rudolf Flesch: *Why Johnny Can't Read.*[1]

[1] Reprinted from *Why Johnny Can't Read,* by Rudolf Flesch, by permission of Harper & Row.

B William Faulkner, the author of the following selection, was not only one of the most famous writers of this century, but also a farmer. He had an intimate knowledge of all levels of life in his native state of Mississippi and is celebrated for the realism of the dialogue in his fiction. At the same time his personal style in fiction is often complex, with an elaborate vocabulary. Many Mississippians felt that in his books he had traduced the people of his native state, and many disagreed with him on the question of race. With this background, consider this introduction to a speech he made in 1952 to an organization called the Delta Council, in the small town of Cleveland, Mississippi. His audience here was a cross section of farmers, planters, and businessmen of the section of North Mississippi called the Delta. The speech was entitled "Man's Responsibility to Fellow Man" and had certain overtones of controversy.

> When the invitation to be here today first reached me, it came from Mr. Billy Wynn. It contained one of the nicest compliments anyone ever received. Mr. Wynn said, we not only want to honor this particular fellow Mississippian, we want him to honor us.
>
> You can't beat that. To reverse a metaphor, that is a sword with not only two edges, but with both edges on the same side; the receiver is accoladed twice with one stroke. He is honored again in honoring them who proffered the original honor. Which is exactly the sort of gesture which we southerners like to believe that only another southerner could have thought of, invented. And sure enough, it happens so often as to convince us that we are right.
>
> He also gave me the council's permission to speak on any subject I liked. That subject won't be writing or farming either. In my fan mail during the past year there was a correspondence with another Mississippi gentleman, who takes a very dim view of my writing ability and my ideas both. He is a Deltan, he may be here today, and can ratify this. In one of his last letters having reviewed again his opinion of a Mississippian who could debase and defile his native State and people as I have done, he said he not only didn't believe I could write, he didn't even believe I know anything about farming either. I answered that it wasn't me who made the claim about my degree as a writer, and so I would agree with him on that one; and after 15 years of trying to cope not only with the Lord but with the Federal Government, too, to make something grow at a profit out of the ground, I was willing to agree with him on both of them.
>
> So I shan't talk about either writing or farming. I have another subject. And, having thought about it, maybe I don't know very much about this one either, for the reason that none of us seem to know much about it any more, that all of us may have forgotten one of the primary things on which this country was founded.
>
> —William Faulkner: "Man's Responsibility to Fellow Man." [2]

III Suppose that you are about to write a piece of persuasion—perhaps a letter or an editorial in the college newspaper. The occasion for this attempt

---

[2] Reprinted from *Essays, Speeches, and Public Letters*, by William Faulkner (Random House, Inc., 1965).

at persuasion may be real or imaginary; but whatever it is, you are to establish clearly in your own mind the general situation, the nature of the audience you are to address, and the kind of attitude you think you should take toward them. You are to decide, in other words, what kind of an introduction would be appropriate. Now write the introduction. (The length may be from 150 to 200 words.)

Logic versus psychology in identification

We may further elaborate our discussion of the distinction between argument and persuasion by saying that the former is based on logic, the latter on psychology.[3] Persuasion begins, as we have said, with the persuader's act of identification and ends with the persuadee's act of assent, and both of these are psychological rather than logical events. That is, they involve the total man, not merely the mind working objectively and logically. The act of identification involves, as fully as possible, all the extralogical aspects of the persuader: he must, as Kenneth Burke puts it, take on all the "ways" of the persuadee. And the act of assent in persuasion requires far more than the logical conviction of the persuadee. As the old saying goes, "A man convinced against his will is of the same opinion still," but with the act of assent, the first thing the persuadee submits to the persuader is his will. His will is the determining fact of his being, of his identity, and when he *willingly* assents, the assent implies his total being.

What happens in between the act of identification and the act of assent is a psychological event of fascinating complexity. It is a process of a paradoxical transformation: though by identification the persuader apparently surrenders his will to the persuadee, in the process he actually seizes the will of the persuadee. No, he does not seize the will of the persuadee; he lulls it, bemuses it, beguiles it, and he does so by appealing to the desires of the persuadee. And here we have another paradox: the persuadee, in the process of seeming to fulfill his own desires, surrenders his will.

When the target of the persuader is not an individual but a group, another psychological dimension develops. Merging with a group, the individual tends to slough off something of his identity—and often he does so with relief. The persuader fosters this process, in the expectation that in so far as the individual sheds the qualities that make him an individual and sinks himself into the group, he becomes more and more malleable and his willing submission to the persuader becomes more and more likely.

The most obvious example of this process is seen in mob action: we all know that a mob may commit acts of violence and brutality that no individual present would commit if not caught up in the "mob spirit." But the same principle applies in certain religious services, patriotic meetings, political

---

[3] This is true even when the persuader uses logic; the logic is presented in a "psychological context" (pp. 253–58).

rallies, protest demonstrations, and the cheering section at football games. The point here is that the same psychological process may occur for either a good or a bad end.

Such persuasion of groups physically assembled together may seem very remote from your concerns in a chapter that has to do with the writing of themes embodying the principles of persuasion. But the same principles that govern the psychology of a group physically assembled have application to the individual privately reading words on a page.

An editorial in a college paper may suggest that "students" behave in a certain way, and the individual student, if he identifies himself with the writer's definition, is susceptible to the persuasion; that is, the individual student wants to "belong," and if certain attitudes and values are assumed to be necessary to belonging, then he may adopt those values. This principle is, of course, pervasive in advertising. For instance, a clothier runs an advertisement in a college paper with the heading "What The Student Will Wear This Fall"—the implication is clear that if you don't wear *that,* you will not be a typical student, will not "belong." Or to take another example, a fashionable store in New York City runs weekly advertisements in a famous national weekly magazine, with the recurring slogan: "For a Certain Kind of Woman"—the kind being, of course, the woman of breeding, good looks, good taste, education, sensibility, glowing health, and ample means. The implication is clear: if you buy an article from the store in question, you belong to such a group; or to put it more subtly, since you do belong to such a group, you will of course shop in that particular store.

■ APPLICATIONS

I Examine some newspapers and magazines to find examples, in editorials, articles, and advertisements, of the technique of persuasion that works by sinking the individual into a group.
II Write a short paragraph (150 words) that would serve as the opening of an editorial or article embodying this principle.

Persuasion and the Emotions

The second mode of persuasion according to Aristotle's analysis is through the emotions. Cicero, the master advocate, declared that all emotions "must be intimately known [by the orator], for all the force and art of speaking as a persuader must be employed in allaying or exciting the feelings of those who listen." This, clearly, is where the arts of the propagandist, politician, advertising man—and even the poet—intersect.

This is the point, too, that most radically distinguishes persuasion from strict argument (pp. 164 and 239–40). We have seen that, in the very first phase of the process of persuasion, the phase of identification, emotional attitudes rather than logic are essential, and that emotional attitudes are involved in the psychological maneuver by which an individual is reduced to a member of a group. But in the second mode of persuasion we move beyond those two preliminary considerations and consider emotion as the prime fact in the body of the persuader's discourse. Our key question, then, becomes: If assent is the end aimed at by the persuader, how does the mere stirring of emotion bring that about?

The answer lies in the psychological fact, long ago discovered, that an emotion, however aroused, seeks a justification and a target. The man who has an angry nature goes through life seeking excuses for his anger and targets on which to vent it. The man with a loving heart, likewise, goes about seeking justifications and targets. Furthermore, emotional agitation makes a person vulnerable to suggestion. "Emotional occasions," said William James, one of the founders of modern psychology, "especially violent ones, are extremely potent in precipitating mental rearrangements." And Freud later pointed out that we are not used to feeling strong emotions "without their having ideational content," and therefore, when content is lacking, "we seize as a substitute upon another content . . ." Thus the persuader, having worked up the emotion, of whatever nature, goes on to provide the content suitable to his intentions; and this content defines the target for the action he desires. Emotion always craves its appropriate fulfillment.

The persuader may work up a powerful particular emotion in his audience and manipulate it, as done in the sermon of a revival preacher or in the harangue of the leader of a lynch mob. Two famous examples of such arousal, which we shall soon study, are in Winston Churchill's address to the House of Commons that focused the British will to win against Nazi Germany (pp. 252–53) and in Mark Antony's speech in the Forum from Shakespeare's play *Julius Caesar* (pp. 270–74).

But the persuader may also work, and sometimes most effectively, with long-term emotional attitudes that may represent desires and needs of which the persuader may be scarcely conscious—or which he may even deny. The advertisement for the expensive Cadillac shows the vehicle against the background of a baronial establishment, and the gloating owners are, of course, a young, elegant, and beautiful couple, almost as much in love with each other as they are with the car. Thus all the hidden, unrealistic yearnings of some balding, no-longer-young but still minor executive—the yearnings for lost youth, good looks, fashion, social standing, ample means, sexual conquest, and true love, and the need to express aggressive impulses on the highway with 350 horsepower—all flow together to guide the hand that signs the contract for the convenient time-payment plan. Or to take an example from a very different area, there is the picture of the preternaturally wide stare of a starving child, and that stare triggers the suppressed and half-forgotten generosity that sends the CARE package on its way.

Human motives are infinitely complex and paradoxical, and for this reason the motivation analyst is important in mapping out an advertising campaign. One writer analyzing the analysts writes as follows:

Another area where guilt feelings on a large scale presented a challenge to marketeers was with the easy-does-it, step-saving products devised for the modern housewife. The wives, instead of being grateful for these wonderful boons, reacted in many cases by viewing them as threats to their feelings of creativeness and usefulness. Working wives (numbering about 10,000,000) could welcome these short-cut products, such as appliances, but regular house-wives, in large numbers, showed unexpected resistance.

The "creative" research director of an ad agency sadly summed up the situation in these words: "If you tell the housewife that by using your washing machine, drier, or dishwasher she can be free to play bridge, you're dead! The housewife today, to a certain extent, is disenfranchised; she is already feeling guilty about the fact that she is not working as hard as her mother. You are just rubbing her the wrong way when you offer her more freedom. Instead you should emphasize that the appliances free her to have more time with her children and to be a better mother."

Our small fears and anxieties, like our guilt feelings, offered many openings for the depth manipulators to map successful campaigns for enterprising merchandisers. It was found, for example, that some products repelled us in a small but measurable way because they filled us with a mild uneasiness.

The trouble that befell Jell-O is an example. Over the years Jell-O was a familiar sight in millions of households because it was established in the public mind as a simple, easy-to-make, shirt-sleeve type of dessert. Then in the early fifties its mentors, ambitious for it to look nice in ads, began showing it in beautiful, layered, multi-color creations with elaborate decorative touches. The ads were spectacular but did not produce the expected sales. Jell-O was in trouble without knowing why. Dr. Dichter [the motivation analyst] was asked to depth-probe the situation. His investigators in talking at length with wives soon pin-pointed the trouble. The wives felt a vague sense of inferiority when they saw the beautiful creations advertised. They wondered if they would fail if they tried to duplicate it, and they vaguely resented the idea of someone watching over their shoulder and saying, "It's got to look like this." So many started saying to themselves when they saw a Jell-O ad, "Well, if I've got to go to all that trouble I might as well make my own dessert."

After Dr. Dichter made his diagnosis Jell-O went back to being a simple, relaxed, shirt-sleeve dessert without fancy trimmings. In 1956, for example, it was typically shown in a simple one-color mound amid amusing fairytale drawings that created widespread comment and admiration for the dessert. . . .

Our relationship with banks is another area where the depth probers have isolated a definite fear factor and have devised techniques for reducing that fear. An ad agency in Rochester, New York, turned to motivation research to try to find out how to broaden the clientele of a leading bank in that city. Its probers turned up in the people sampled a large variety of fears concerning banks: fear of being rejected for a loan, fear of the banker finding out how untidy their family financial affairs really are, or fear of signs of disapproval. The agency concluded that people subconsciously see their bank as a kind of parent, a parent capable of scolding or withholding approval, and constantly scrutinizing. With that subconscious cowering before the parent symbol in mind, the agency designed an ad for the bank, showing a man standing at the bank door saying "How I hated to open that door!" and then relating in the text his story of the warm welcome he got. . . .

Finally, merchandisers began learning to play expertly on our hidden feelings of loneliness, which, as Dr. Harry Stack Sullivan, the famed psychiatrist, once said, is perhaps the most unbearable of all human emotions. A major greeting-card company in the Midwest became curious to learn why people really bought greeting cards, so that it could merchandise more expertly. One thing that had puzzled company officials was that year after year one of its best sellers showed a barren, gnarled tree standing alone on a windswept and often snow-covered hill. It was scarcely cheerful, yet it had tremendous pulling power. In the motivation study the company conducted it found out why: a key factor in the sale of greeting cards is loneliness. The most frequent buyers tend to be widows, spinsters, and divorcees who apparently often feel gnarled and lonely and still are trying to be graceful. Freudian analysis also turned up the fact that many of the more successful greeting cards were loaded with sexual symbolism: artistic moons, candles, ovals, circles. Harry Henderson reported in *Pageant* magazine that the greeting-card company, armed with these discoveries, gave a summary of the study to its artists "to help them design more popular cards and cut down production of cards that lacked unconscious symbols."   —VANCE PACKARD: *The Hidden Persuaders.*[4]

We are not concerned here with motivation research or advertising for their own sakes, but merely as fairly simple illustrations of the range and depth of attitudes that may be appealed to in persuasion. We have said "simple," for what is involved in selling Jell-O or greeting cards is simple in comparison to the complexity of an even moderately successful literary work. And we say "literary work" because a poem (say "Ode to Autumn," by Keats, or a sonnet by Shakespeare) or novel (say *Bleak House,* by Dickens, or *War and Peace,* by Tolstoy) is as much a work of persuasion as a successful speech or an advertising campaign. The crucial difference—and the one on which the greater value of the literary work depends—is in the way the psychological factors are used.[5]

But what relation does all this have to you and your writing?

What is important for you is to cultivate your awareness of the psycho-

---

[4] From *The Hidden Persuaders,* by Vance Packard. Reprinted by permission of David McKay Company. Reprinted by permission of A. P. Watt & Son.

[5] A work of literature is not concerned with "selling" anything. It is concerned with an identification with other men and a sympathy with even the evil aspects of human nature—that is, with a knowledge of the human heart.

logical appeals of literature and to study its techniques of persuasion. More is to be learned about persuasion from Shakespeare or Keats or Dickens (if properly studied) than from Dr. Dichter. Furthermore, you can learn more from the study of yourself than from Dr. Dichter. You should constantly scrutinize your own responses, in your reading and in your daily life. You are your own best laboratory and reference library.

Slanting and suggestion

The evoking and manipulating of emotional attitudes that we have discussed often involve methods known as slanting and suggestion. By slanting we mean the method by which, without violating facts in any narrow sense, the persuader suggests such interpretations as are desired by the persuader. Slanting can be seen in its crudest form in single words or phrases used for connotative values. For example, Mr. X is, literally considered, a politician and a senator. The editorial in a newspaper supporting him refers to him as a "statesman" or a "dedicated public servant." But an editorial in an opposition newspaper prefers to call him a "party hack" or a "politico." The literal referent—Mr. X—is the same in both cases, but the aura of connotation is, clearly, not. (Read the section "How Associations Control Meanings" in Diction, pp. 414–420.)

This control of connotation is one of the devices determining the tone of any discourse, and tone, as we have pointed out, is of the greatest importance in persuasion. The instance of Senator X above is simple and obvious, but the principle can be applied with great complexity and subtlety. The "smuggling in" of emotion, as the critic I. A. Richards has called it, and the control of attitudes by this means are fundamental to all literature, especially to poetry. And this leads us from the general question of connotation in persuasion to that of metaphor; for metaphor, too, involves the smuggling in of emotion and the control of responses.

Let us take an example, the insult visited upon Edward Livingston, an extremely able politician of the early nineteenth century, by John Randolph of Roanoke, another politician and a famous wit. Livingston, said Randolph, "is a man of splendid qualities, but utterly corrupt. Like rotten mackerel in the moonlight, he shines and stinks." The insult converts Livingston's very reputation for brilliance into a liability. The brilliance becomes, in the metaphor, an index to the corruption: the same rotting fish that shines also stinks —the putrescence that it exudes adds to the glitter. And consider the use of the word *moonlight,* which implies that the rotting fish would not seem so brilliant by the light of day; then it would be recognized simply for what it is. The metaphor has condensed a range of meanings into the startling image, an image deep, paradoxical, and memorable.[6]

---

[6] The insult is sometimes reported, erroneously, to have been addressed to Henry Clay. For another famous insult (and a more complex one) see Whittier's poem on Daniel Webster called "Ichabod."

The method used by Randolph does not differ essentially from that in the following passage from Shakespeare's *Antony and Cleopatra* (V, ii, 82–92), which has an entirely different purpose. Here Cleopatra, after the death of Mark Antony, is speaking to an emissary of Octavius Caesar, the victor, trying to persuade him of the greatness of Antony:

> His legs bestrid the ocean: his reared arm
> Crested the world: his voice was propertied
> As all the tuned spheres, and that to friends;
> But when he meant to quail and shake the orb,
> He was as rattling thunder. For his bounty,
> There was no winter in't: an autumn 'twas
> That grew the more by reaping: his delights
> Were dolphin-like: they showed his back above
> The element they lived in: in his livery
> Walked crowns and crownets: realms and island were
> As plates dropped from his pocket.

Through metaphor Cleopatra tries to persuade the emissary to accept Antony as superhumanly great. But the suggestions do more; by implication they convert the victory of Octavius into a kind of defeat, and the defeat Antony has suffered into a transcendent victory. But let us look at another detail in the passage. Take the smuggling in of emotional elements in the lines beginning with "For his bounty . . ." and ending with ". . . element they lived in." The whole world of the imagination and senses is involved in Cleopatra's praise of Antony. We say of some men that they are "sunk in sensuality" or "drowned in pleasure," and some such idea would seem to underly the passage. But Antony is shown as able to live in that world of the senses and imagination and yet rise undamaged above it. More specifically, these lines may be taken as a celebration of the superb sexual vigor of Antony that "grew the more by reaping"; the image of the dolphin suggests the heaving motion of the sexual embrace. This glorification of Antony as a lover again serves, by implication, as a sexual disparagement of the victor Octavius.

■ **APPLICATIONS**

I What emotions are appealed to in the examples that follow? Does the speaker (or the reported speaker, as in A) use the emotional appeal as a way of sinking the individual into a group? Does he insist on his own identification with the audience? Examine the language for elements that suggest unstated emotional appeals. Consider rhythm as a factor. In preparing to do this work, you might look over again the chapters on Diction (pp. 396–434), Metaphor (435–65), and Tone (466–506).

A   In 1843, at a political meeting in Fayette County, Kentucky, Cassius M. Clay, who was an antislavery man, became embroiled in a fight with a certain Brown. It is hard to know who was, in point of fact, the aggressor, but Brown was armed with a pistol against Clay's bowie knife. Brown got off one shot, which struck Clay in the chest, before Clay was upon him. Brown lost an eye, an ear, part of his nose, and a piece of his skull to the bowie knife and then was thrown over a bluff into a creek. Clay, it developed, was unhurt, the pistol ball having been deflected by the silver case of the bowie that he wore under his frilled shirt. Clay was indicted for mayhem and tried in a county that was prevailingly proslavery. But he was defended by his kinsman Henry Clay, who had not lost a criminal case for forty years. The famous lawyer again won an acquittal. He made no defense of the political views of the accused. He first told the jury that the defendant had been "acting in his constitutional and legal right." Then he developed this idea: "Was the defendant 'aggressive,' " he demanded, "standing, as he did, without aiders or abettors, and without popular sympathy; with the fatal pistol of conspired murderers pointed at his heart, would you have him meanly and cowardly fly? Or would you have him to do just what he did . . .?" Then, indicating his kinsman, he declared to the jury, "And if he had not, he would not have been *worthy* of the name which he bears!"

B   The following passage is an excerpt from what is perhaps the most famous sermon ever preached in America, "Sinners in the Hands of an Angry God" (1741). The author was Jonathan Edwards, a Puritan minister famous for his piety and learning.

O sinner! Consider the fearful danger you are in: it is a great furnace of wrath, a wide and bottomless pit, full of the fire of wrath, that you are held over in the hand of that God, whose wrath is provoked and incensed as much against you, as against many of the damned in hell. You hang by a slender thread, with the flames of divine wrath flashing about it, and ready every moment to singe it, and burn it asunder; and you have no interest in any Mediator, and nothing to lay hold of to save yourself, nothing to keep off the flames of wrath, nothing of your own, nothing that you ever have done, nothing that you can do, to induce God to spare you one moment.

C   This passage occurs at the end of the speech made by Winston Churchill on June 4, 1940, to the House of Commons, after the defeat of the French and British armies and the evacuation of the remnant of the British forces from Dunkirk. The speech leading up to this conclusion is rather flat and factual, an account of events and an exposition of the desperate military situation.

I am myself full of confidence that if all do their duty, if nothing is neglected, and if the best arrangements are made, as they are being made, we shall prove ourselves once again able to defend our island home, to ride out the storm of war, and to outlive the menace of tyranny, if necessary for years, if necessary alone. At any rate, that is what we are going to do. That is the resolve of His Majesty's Government—every man of them. That is the will of Parliament and the nation. The British Empire and the French Republic, linked together in their cause and their need, will defend to the death their native soil, aiding each other like good comrades to the utmost of their strength. Even though large tracts of Europe and many old and famous States have fallen or may fall into the grip of the Gestapo and all the odious apparatus of Nazi rule, we shall not flag or fail. We shall go on to the end. We shall fight in France, we shall fight on the seas and the oceans, we shall fight with growing confidence and growing strength in the air, we shall defend our island, whatever the cost may be. We shall fight on the beaches, we shall fight on the landing grounds, we shall fight in the fields and in the streets, we shall fight in the hills; we shall never surrender, and even if, which I do not for a moment believe, this island or a large part of it were subjugated and starving, then our Empire beyond the seas, armed and guarded by the British Fleet, would carry on the struggle, until, in God's good time, the New World, with all its power and might, steps forth to the rescue and the liberation of the old.

II   In the first and second sets of Applications in this chapter (pp. 244–45 and 247) you were asked to write an introduction to a piece of persuasion. Return to those introductions and choose the one that you now consider more successful. What emotional appeals might be useful for developing the subject of the introduction you have chosen? Make an outline for such a development. Then write the section (not less than 300 words).

Persuasion and logic: rationalization

We have been studying the relation of persuasion to emotion and certain methods of manipulating emotion in persuasion. We now turn to Aristotle's third mode of persuasion, that of achieving assent by proving "a truth or an apparent truth." [7] The psychological phenomenon known as *rationalization* provides a sort of bridge between emotion in persuasion and logic in persuasion. Rationalization is the use of reason not to seek truth but to justify desires, attitudes, belief, decisions, or actions already determined on emotional grounds. In rationalization the forms of reason are used to work either or both of two kinds of deception: to deceive the self or to deceive others.

Man cannot bear very much reality," the poet T. S. Eliot says in "Burnt Norton," and rationalization is man's built-in medicine against reality. We live by self-flattering illusions and self-exculpating alibis. When we catch the ball, we say: "Look, *I* caught the ball!" When we miss the ball, we say: "My *hand* slipped." Furthermore, we commonly live by decisions that we consider to be reasonably made and reasonably acted on, but that actually are determined by motives that are unconscious, or that we choose to avoid considering. The same is true of beliefs and attitudes. How much, for instance, does jealousy of the sexual vigor of the young contribute to the belief on the part of a number of the middle-aged that repressive measures in

---

[7] We should clearly distinguish between two different relations of persuasion and logic. The first is the use of logic by the persuader in making his private preparation for the act of persuasion. For example, when the persuader analyzes his audience or the occasion, he is performing a logical operation, but one that is strictly for his own private use in preparing his discourse. The second relation between persuasion and logic appears in the discourse that is actually offered to the audience. It is with the use of logic in such a discourse that we are now concerned.

schools and colleges are essential to maintain law and order? How much does the "idealism" of the young spring from a desire for uninhibited sex and the automatic resentment against the authority of parents?

Although the rationalizer pretends otherwise, rationalization characteristically *follows* action, decision, attitude, or belief. Its function is to make the past comfortable to live with. Its role is not to initiate but to justify.

Not only the life history of an individual may reveal such rationalizations, but also the history of a nation. When the Nazis went to war, they went with Hitler's rationalization that Germany was being encircled and that they were acting in self-defense. When the Civil War in America is referred to as a crusade to free the slaves (which is very different from saying that slavery was a *necessary condition* of the war), some historians, remembering Lincoln's statement that the war was to save the Union, are likely to detect here the sweet smell of rationalization. When slaveholders comforted themselves with the reflection that slavery brought the benighted African into contact with the Christian religion, the same odor began to rise. Europeans, and some Americans, remembering that the participation of the United States in World War I made us a rich and powerful country, look with suspicion on the slogan created to justify that war—"To Make the World Safe for Democracy."

Although it is true that much rationalization shows itself to be wildly illogical, illogicality is not the inevitable hallmark of rationalization. Rationalization, in fact, may express itself in what may seem to be very acceptable logic. To sum up, what distinguishes rationalization from valid reasoning is the *motive* from which it springs. Even a maniac may be faultlessly logical in argument, but we have to inspect his premises and his obsessions.

What use, you may ask, does an understanding of rationalization have for persuasion? The answer is that if you know the needs, desires, attitudes, and beliefs of the audience, then you know their most vulnerable points. A frequently successful stratagem is to provide the audience with an appropriate rationalization; in other words, the persuader may succeed by giving a mask of logic to the impulse of the audience that he wishes to exploit. Conversely, in order to defend yourself, you need to become aware of what rationalizations of your own a persuader may try to exploit.

To take another example from motivation research:

> .... the producers of sugar-tooth items were confronting a public suffering from massive guilt feelings of another sort [different from the guilt feelings of cigarette smokers]. The public was starting to shun anything conspicuously sweet and sugary. Not only were Americans suffering their persistent guilt feelings about indulging themselves, but they were made doubly uneasy by all the publicity about the dangers of overweight and tooth decay, both widely attributed to rich, sugary foods. (Consumption of confectionery items fell more than 10 per cent from 1950 to 1955.) Much of the publicity, it should be added, was generated by the makers of low-calorie products and dentifrices. (Consumption of low-calorie soft drinks

multiplied three hundred times from 1952 to 1955!) The candy manufacturers were reported losing customers in a "sticky market." Producers of sugary foods such as candy raised more than half a million dollars to tell their "story." More important, perhaps, the candymakers hired Dr. Dichter.

He chided them for not countering blow for blow and for meekly accepting the role "imposed on candy by propaganda as being bad for the teeth and fattening instead of being widely known as a delightful, delicious, wholesome, and nourishing food . . . ." He mapped for them a strategy for getting us back to candy-munching on a mass basis in spite of all the propaganda. The real deep-down problem they had to cope with, he advised, was this guilt feeling about self-indulgence. One of the tactics he urged the candymakers to adopt was to emphasize bite-size pieces within the present large-size candy package. That, he advised, would appeal to us as self-indulgence in moderation. He confided: "You will be providing the excuse the consumer needs to buy a bar of candy—'After all, I don't have to eat all of it, just a bite and then put the rest away.' Seriously, we doubt whether the rest will be put away. However, the consumer will be left with the feeling that candy manufacturers understand him and the bite-size piece will give him the 'permission' he needs to buy the candy because the manufacturers are going to 'permit' him to eat in moderation."

—VANCE PACKARD: *The Hidden Persuaders.*[8]

Fallacy

Persuasion, as Aristotle points out (p. 240), has not only to do with "truth," but with "apparent truth," and indeed the most obvious connection of persuasion with logic is its connection with the distortions of logic that we call fallacies. In studying persuasion, as in studying argument, one of the most fruitful fields to explore is that of fallacies. With one difference, however: in studying fallacies for argument, you study what you want to avoid in your own argument and to detect in that of others; in studying them for persuasion, you study what, unless you have moral scruples, you may sometimes profitably use. Certainly, if you want to study fallacies in persuasion, there are God's plenty of examples in advertising, political speeches, sermons, and commencement addresses.

Reasoning for Truth and Reasoning for Assent

We now turn to the relation between persuasion and valid reasoning.

The simplest examples of this relationship have either of two forms. The first is the persuasive appeal used merely as an introduction to an argument,

---

[8] From *The Hidden Persuaders,* by Vance Packard. Reprinted by permission of David McKay Company. Reprinted by permission of A. P. Watt & Son.

or to the presentation of facts that are a basis for argument. Here the persuader is merely trying to gain fair attention; he trusts the force of the argument (or the facts) to achieve, by the logical process, the assent desired. The second form is the use of persuasion, after the argument or facts have been presented, to convert the logical conviction into emotional assent. A famous example of the latter form is to be found in the speech of Churchill after Dunkirk. The conclusion, which we have already seen above (pp. 252–53), follows the low-keyed body of the speech, in which emphasis is not even on argument but on the exposition of the situation; and the conclusion comes all the more forcefully in that plain context, the emotional burst being, as it were, the answer to the question implied in the exposition: What, in such dire peril, shall we do?

The relations just discussed are, as we have said, simple. In more complicated instances, reasoning appears in the main body of the discourse, not as straight argument, but especially adapted to the demands of the persuasive act. And this leads us to a distinction between *reasoning for truth* (as in straight argument) and *reasoning for assent* (as in persuasion). Reasoning for truth is directed to the subject, reasoning for assent to the audience— to the truth *about* the subject, to the assent *of* the audience. The first type of reasoning is characteristic of argument, the second, of persuasion.

Argument tends to the elaboration of reasoning; it aims to cover the case, to prove as much as possible. Persuasion tends to reason minimally, that is, only in so far as is necessary for assent; it aims to focus on one or more points, not to cover the whole case. Persuasion offers as little proof as necessary, for the simple reason that an elaboration of logical detail might, in the end, distract from the emotional commitment that persuasion seeks to evoke.

The amount of proof necessary for any particular instance varies according to the nature of the subject, the audience, and the occasion, but the accomplished persuader knows that even with the most logical audience you can "overargue." You can win the argument, but lose the audience. Therefore, when he resorts to logic, his problem is to be both minimal and effective. To be so, he must locate the *key point* (or *points*) to be argued and present them so that the argument *seems* to be definitive and comprehensive.

For a better understanding, we may regard this aspect of persuasion in relation to the issues of argument that we have discussed earlier (pp. 186–88). Logically considered, an issue is, as we have explained, a point that *must* be proved if the arguer is to win his case; there may, of course, be more than one issue involved, and when that is so, then to win the argument *all* issues must be proved.

With this in mind, let us look at the relation between an issue and what we here call a key point. In this matter we can distinguish two different strategies. The first dictates that the persuader, instead of arguing *all* the issues, as the strictly logical procedure would dictate, choose one or more as his key points and argue only on them. The persuader thus selects, shall we say, Issue A as the key point, and tries to argue it so compellingly that the audience forgets Issues B and C. Thus the persuader is using logic locally applied (merely to Issue A, the key point) to distract his audience from the demands of logic for complete proof. The second basic strategy dictates that the persuader select as the key point a matter that is *not* an issue and undertake to prove it. Here the persuader is using logic to distract from the logical demands of any real issue.

For an example of this second strategy, let us turn back to the argument between the husband and wife about moving to town (pp. 190–92). Suppose that the husband tries not to argue with his wife but to persuade her. To accomplish this, he might take as his key point the wife's love of music, arguing quite logically that her opportunities for hearing music would be much greater in town, for a symphony is being organized there, and so on. On this key point the husband may win the wife's assent to the move—though we know, from our previous analysis, that the availability of music is not really an issue.

Here is another common, though wildly illogical, example of fixing on a key point that is not an issue: the spoiled child (or husband or wife), trying to get something, says, "If you won't give it to me, that proves you don't love me!" Here "proving that you love me" becomes the key point, and the poor persuadee, if he falls for it, will give in to the blackmail to prove "love" —even though love has nothing to do with the rights and wrongs of the situation. The spoiled child has here employed an *illusion* of logic—to prove love—to gain his end.

We must remember, however, that certain occasions, by their very nature, permit no more than the illusion of logic; and in such instances this handling of logic may be legitimate. Let us examine the Gettysburg Address by Abraham Lincoln, which is justly admired as a noble utterance.

> Fourscore and seven years ago our fathers brought forth on this continent a new nation conceived in liberty and dedicated to the proposition that all men are created equal. Now we are engaged in a great civil war testing whether that nation, or any nation so conceived and so dedicated, can long endure. We are met on a great battlefield of that war. We have come to dedicate a portion of that field as a final resting-place for those who here gave their lives that that nation might live. It is altogether fitting and proper that we should do this. But, in a larger sense, we cannot dedicate, we cannot consecrate, we cannot hallow this ground. The brave men, living and dead, who struggled here have consecrated it far beyond our poor power to add or detract. The world will little note nor long remember what we say here, but it can never forget what they did here. It is for us the living rather to be dedicated here to the unfinished work which they who fought here have thus far so nobly advanced. It is rather for us to be here dedicated to the great task remaining before us—that from these honoured dead we take increased devotion to that cause for which they gave the last full measure of devotion—that this nation under God shall have a new birth of freedom, and that government of the people, by the people, for the people, shall not perish from the earth.

Matthew Arnold, one of the most important critics of the nineteenth century, as well as a fine poet, flung aside the newspaper report of this address after he got to the word *proposition*. He felt, presumably, that this hard, factual, almost technical word destroyed the eloquence appropriate to the occasion—the dedication of a cemetery on the field of a great battle. But was he right?

We maintain that Lincoln, not Arnold, was right. The word is appropriate and powerful, and for the very reason that Arnold found it offensive. No speech for such an occasion could undertake to argue the issues of the war, step by step. Lincoln could, in fact, only hint at his key point, for his purpose was simply to evoke a certain emotional attitude toward a particular desired end—the prosecution of the war.[9] But the word *proposition* belongs to the world of argument, debate, and logic, and as such it smuggles into the occasion, as would a metaphor, the sense of rigor and precision associated with its origin. The word serves to say: "We have not time here to argue the whole meaning of the war, but I remind you that it has already been satisfactorily argued, and so we may now proceed to the present concern, our attitude as dictated by that meaning." The word serves to give the illusion of logic—more precisely, an "allusion"[10] to logic—as a basis for persuasion. This effect is continued in the next sentence by the word *testing*, which suggests that even the war itself may be taken metaphorically at least—as a final stage in a logical process.

The following speech, by Senator George McGovern of South Dakota, is a rather complicated example of the use of an allusion to logic, an immediate use of logic, and a mounting intensity of emotional appeal. To understand it, we must know something of its background. In 1963 there had been increasing racial tension with outbreaks of violence in many localities, culminating in the murder of Medgar Evers, a leader in Mississippi of the National Association for the Advancement of Colored People, and in the murder, a little later, of three young civil rights workers near Philadelphia, Mississippi. The Civil Rights Bill was still pending in June of 1964. Senator McGovern's speech came near the end of the protracted debate on it, and the detailed arguments for and against the bill are the assumed background of his speech. His whole speech involves, in fact, an allusion to these arguments. He presents certain new arguments, but never in full detail, using suggestion rather than full development, and often relies on emotional appeal. Notice how the emotional appeal intensifies toward the end of the speech. The speech is, in fact, an effort to convert a large number of arguments, some merely assumed or alluded to, into emotional assent.

Here is the text as given in the Senate on June 4, 1964:

---

[9] The address can be taken as directed not only toward the prosecution of the war, but toward the establishing of a certain kind of peace based on a sense of community. (See Carl Sandburg's *Abraham Lincoln: The War Years*.) Lincoln's policy did not, of course, survive him.

[10] In other words, it is assumed that the argument has already occurred, and all that is now required is a reference to it to establish a context, an "allusion."

Mr. President, the status of the Negro in American life is the most serious moral crisis facing the Nation today.

That crisis has come to a head in the Senate of the United States during these long weeks of argument and struggle centering on the civil rights bill. We have examined in microscopic detail every section, every phrase, every word, and every conceivable interpretation of this bill.

Every feature of the proposed legislation has been hammered by charges, questions, and criticisms. Every one of the arguments against the measure have been patiently and painstakingly evaluated and answered. Nearly all of them were exaggerated, distorted, or largely false. Those that had even a shred of merit have been carefully weighed and in some cases incorporated in the proposed amendments to the bill.

But for the most part, the charges against the bill have been groundless. Most groundless of all is the repeated charge that the bill is unconstitutional. Actually, it seeks to guarantee basic constitutional and moral rights long denied to a minority of our citizens which the rest of us take for granted. As the late President Kennedy put it:

> We are confronted primarily with a moral issue. It is as old as the Scriptures and is as clear as the Constitution.

The Constitution does not limit the benefits of freedom to those born of white parents. Nor does the history of freedom in America leave any doubt on this issue. No one need fear this bill who really accepts the concept of equal dignity, equal freedom and equal opportunity under the law for all our citizens. No one need fear this bill who really practices the implications of Judeo-Christian tradition. That tradition rests on the twin foundation of the fatherhood of God and the brotherhood of man. That tradition does not confine itself to whites or Baptists or rich men or the native born; it proclaims: "All men are brothers."

As we used to sing in Sunday school:

> Jesus loves the little children,
> All the children of the world, red, or yellow, black or white,
> They are precious in His sight,
> Jesus loves the little children of the world.

If we could just accept the message of that simple little Sunday school song, we would have embraced this civil rights bill months ago. Indeed, there would be no need for the bill if we truly believed in our hearts and practiced in our daily lives the simple truths of brotherhood.

But the facts are that we have not fully accepted brotherhood in our hearts or in our land. The proof of our unfinished business is in the black ghettos of our great cities of the North where millions of human beings are living on the edge of despair. They live in stinking, ugly, overcrowded tenements. Their children grow up on the sidewalks and in the alleys where the law of the jungle prevails. Their schools, churches, businesses, and recreational facilities deteriorate while the whites head for the suburbs.

The proof of our unfinished business is also in the South where the cold-blooded killer of Medgar Evers runs free; where the brutal murderers of four little Alabama Sunday school girls still are on the loose spreading their message of hate and death; where ministers of the Gospel are beaten and clubbed because they have had the courage to stand up for the rights of Negro Americans.

The proof of our unfinished business is in Indiana, and Wisconsin, and Maryland where a crusading demagog whose career rests on discrimination against his fellow man was able to secure a sizable vote in his incredible bid for the Presidency.

Nor can we justify our unfinished business with the excuse that we have not yet had time to act.

Last year marked the 100th anniversary of the Emancipation Proclamation, whose unfulfilled hope continues as our most conspicuous failure in the cause of human dignity, both at home and abroad. . . .

So, some of us have been amazed to find that in spite of progress, we have misjudged the cry of the Negro for full citizenship. But it is now clear that we must swiftly muster all the wisdom and courage we can and then act quickly on a moral revolution based on the Judeo-Christian ethic and the politics of Jefferson and Lincoln. That is the power of the democratic ideal which in the long run cannot be denied. It can be resisted, and clubbed, and shot at from ambush, but it cannot be contained, and each new advance will feed new demands until every American is fully free.

As Walter Lippmann puts it:

> There is, so to speak, a point of no return in a movement for the redress of grievances. That point is where gradual reform and token appeasement become suddenly not only insufficient but irritating. Then, instead of putting up with a little done slowly, there is a demand that much must be done suddenly.

This is one of the enduring lessons of the American Revolution. That Revolution was not born of the cruelest oppression in British Imperial history. Indeed, the Colonies enjoyed a comparatively high degree of freedom and independence. Yet, in a condition far better than others had endured, there suddenly came from the ferment of freedom a demand for independence—a willingness to stake lives, fortunes, and sacred honor on the gamble for liberty. Why?

Certainly, the idea was not born in 1776. It had long been affirmed in the ancient scriptures which the colonial fathers knew so well. Likewise, for centuries prior to 1776, the political and legal expression of the brotherhood of man and the sanctity of the individual had been growing in Anglo-Saxon thought. When Jefferson penned the Declaration of Independence, he borrowed heavily from the earlier words of the Englishman John Locke.

The day before our forefathers were Americans, they were Englishmen steeped in English traditions of law and government. Yet, they severed the ties with the mother country. They insisted on the full measure of their heritage. They insisted on being better Englishmen and truer practitioners of English philosophy than King George III desired. Their demands and demonstrations—of which the Boston Tea Party is only the most celebrated—reached a point of no return, the revolution was on, and Englishmen along the eastern shore of this continent became Americans.

I think if we can understand the spirit of 1776, we can better appreciate the rising expectations that are convulsing the American Negro community and the developing continents of the globe.

The American Revolution and countless other historic demands for a redress of grievances all indicate that the cause of freedom is fired by its own gains. The Negro's march toward full acceptance will accelerate rather than diminish with the victories of each passing day.

Roy Wilkins, A. Philip Randolph, Martin Luther King, James Farmer, James Meredith, Medgar Evers, and others have, without question, moved the Negro's demand for full citizenship to the point of no return.

Passage of the civil rights legislation now before the Senate is the next order of business. The alternative is a rising tide of racial unrest and disturbance.

I think it is quite possible that, if the Senate were to reject this long-awaited charter of rights, the people of the United States will be plunged into racial strife that will tear apart the fabric of our society. We would then see infuriated minority leaders and inflamed mobs and sulking killers on an unprecedented scale.

The Negro moderates who have counseled patience and legal redress would be swept aside by the radicals who preach hate and violence. We would then see the Bible of Martin Luther King and the long-suffering patience of Roy Wilkins replaced by the dangerous direct action of Malcolm X and his kind. Race riots, night bombings, assassinations would rage until blood flowed in the streets.

Make no mistake about it: The Negro militants are waiting in the wings, hoping that this bill will be defeated, thus discrediting the moderates and opening the way for a radical takeover of the Negro leadership. Malcolm X recently said:

> I intend to prove that you can't get civil rights in this country. The black man is maturing, he is waking up. That is why I say that we shall have real violence.

I know that there are some Senators who want this bill defeated, but they are not hoping for its defeat as ardently as the radical Negro extremists who are hungrily waiting for a chance to prove that the moderates are wrong.

If I were living in the South or in a great northern city with a sizable Negro population, I would be on my knees praying for the safety of my family if the Senate spurned the reasonable, patient Negro and white leadership that most earnestly supports this bill.

The legislation now pending before the Senate calls for:

First.   Extension of the Civil Rights Commission.
Second. Strengthening of Negro voting rights.
Third.   Empowering the Attorney General to file school desegregation suits.
Fourth. Prohibition of racial discrimination in public places, restaurants, stores, hotels and theaters.
Fifth.   Prevention of discrimination in federally assisted programs; and

Sixth.   Establishment of a Commission on Equal Employment Opportunity.

The bill before us would incorporate a full charter of civil rights in the law of the land.

We are going to enact this bill because the American people will not tolerate the only remaining alternative, which is a massive suppression on a mounting scale of the Negro and his white friends. . . .

Even this is not the whole issue in the Negro's challenge, however, and perhaps not the most fundamental. The late President Kennedy referred to a "moral problem" rooted in our hearts where laws cannot reach. This is the longing of every human being to be accepted as a person of worth, not because it is the law, but because it is right.

I think that in their own way, the Negro demonstrator and his spokesmen are trying to reach this deeper dimension of the racial problem. . . .

The Negro, in short, is echoing the words which Adams and Paine and Jefferson dispatched to King George nearly two centuries ago.

I do not press the analogy to suggest that the American Negro wants to withdraw from the Union. The Black Muslim may talk this way, but in so doing, he stands outside the mainstream of Negro life—both religiously and politically; thus, his leadership of his own people is limited to a small fragment.

The American Negro longs to be an American first and a Negro second. He has been schooled in the doctrine of freedom and has died for it on foreign battlefields. The Negro revolution is different from other revolutions in that it does not seek to upset the established government or the economic system. It does not seek to burn the palace or cut off the king's head or storm the walls. Instead, it says in effect, "the American system is wonderful; let us in on it."

The nonviolent resistance of Martin Luther King—the lunch counter sit-ins, the bus rides, the street parades—have been associated with Gandhi. But Gandhi borrowed the idea from Henry David Thoreau and the New Testament.

The Negro's capacity to refrain from violence even when he is being kicked in the face stems from the religious and cultural traditions of his American past. It came first from the slave balconies of the churches, then from the segregated "colored church" and from preachers barely literate enough to read Scriptures and sing the gospel hymns. They were sensitive to the longings of the soul, however, and beyond some doctors of divinity they were attuned to that "man of sorrows, acquainted with grief." Out of the depths of his spirit the Negro created indigenous American art—the spiritual, the blues, and jazz.

In this spirit the Negro writer is saying that the frustration which drives the Negro into the streets, the lunchrooms, and the bus terminals is a desperate act of caring about the American ideal. He has been carrying on an unrequited love affair with America until his heart has burst its bounds.

Many voices may be heard in the Negro writer, but I would illustrate with James Baldwin who has been poignant on the theme of the estrangement of both Negro and white in America from each other and from their past. Baldwin was rebel enough and like many a white American who became an expatriate to Europe after World War I, he sought out Paris after World War II.

He found out what the best of his predecessors did—that he had to come home. It is more remarkable in him, though, for he did not know he had a home. From the vantage point of Europe, he found his country. He found out how profoundly American he was. He develops the theme in many places in his "Notes of a Native Son," the very title being significant. One brilliant essay develops his confrontation with a native African with whom he had tried to identify in order to recover his racial past. He finds it cannot be done. He is too deeply an American. A hybrid American perhaps, physically and in every other aspect of life which is dominated by the memory of the auction block, but still American and linked to his white brother:

> Dimly and for the first time there begins to fall into perspective the nature of the roles they have played in the lives and history of each other. Now he is bone of their bone, flesh of their flesh; they have loved and hated and obsessed and feared each other and his blood is in their soil. Therefore he cannot deny them, nor can they ever be divorced..

Baldwin goes on to say that he just cannot explain this to the African. Of course, he must establish himself in relation to a past, but he knows that it must be an American one:

> What time will bring Americans—

he writes—

> is at last their own identity. It is on this dangerous voyage and in the same boat that the American Negro will make peace with himself and with the voiceless many thousands gone before him.

In a recent television spotlight on the Negro in Washington, a colored minister said of his people:

> They are too sophisticated to pray, and too angry to laugh.

I thought in response that the white man is also "too sophisticated to pray and too anxious to laugh." The way back will not be easy for either of us, either to the petition for grace on both sides, or the facing of his guilts by the white and the disciplining of his anger by the Negro. It will take us a while to meet and talk and pray as equals. We do not necessarily need to agree upon all matters. Dignity and reason and hopefully a little humor will show the way.

I believe that as both of us review our heritage, as we relearn our history and tradition, we shall together relearn freedom. The great Goethe once wrote:

> What you have inherited from your fathers, earn it, in order truly to possess it.

The Reverend S. D. Whitney, Negro minister of Jackson, Miss., speaking at a memorial service for the slain Medgar Evers, said:

Somewhere in the dark a sniper waited to play his part as the coward. But bullets do not destroy ideas. Nothing destroys an idea but a better idea. And the best idea is freedom. That is what he was fighting for.

And that is what we are called to do. If we heed that call, old words will be born anew and we will indeed become "one nation, under God, indivisible, with liberty and justice for all."

Mr. President, I yield the floor.

—SENATOR GEORGE MC GOVERN: "The Point of No Return."

■ APPLICATIONS

I List the actual arguments in the speech by Senator McGovern, and try to indicate how far each is developed. What is the main proposition? How do other propositions relate to it? Does the main proposition merely concern the passage of the bill, or does it go beyond that question? How would you define the emotion—or emotions—involved in the conclusion of the speech?

II In the last set of Applications you wrote a section of a theme in persuasion, developing emotional appeals (p. 253). Now, for the same theme, develop a section of some 250 words, embodying an appropriate use of logic for persuasion.

III Look back over the last theme you wrote while studying Argument. Can you now see what issues might best be taken as key points in a theme of persuasion on the same topic? Take a key point that is *not* an issue and develop it in about 200 words.

Persuasion and Ethics

Does the mere ability to persuade entitle a man to the uninhibited use of the power that persuasion gives? This question, which is a fundamental one, appears as early as Plato's attack on the school of Sophists, in Athens, who were concerned with persuasion purely as a technique without reference to the ends to which it might be applied. The question is very much alive today. To take a few examples from among many possible ones: Has a politician running for office the right to inflame prejudice and passion on the matter of race? Has the manufacturer of cigarettes, which are presumably harmful, the right to persuade the public to smoke?

The particular question of ethics in persuasion turns on the general question of the relation of ends and means. Here we encounter two extreme views. The first, which we shall call the *technical*, holds that persuasion is merely a matter of technique. By this line of thought the power of persuasion is like, say, the power of nuclear fission: it can be used for good or ill, but is neutral in itself. Or it is like the power of a surgeon: he operates on flesh and bone laid before him without making any moral evaluation of the person whose flesh and bone are to be operated upon. The second view, which we shall call the *purposive*, holds that persuasion is directed toward ends and is therefore responsible for its ends.

In addition to the technical and the purposive views of the ethics of persuasion, we need to take into account another pair of perspectives: the *social* and the *personal*. What are the effects on society of different kinds of persuasion? And what kinds of persuasion are you, with your personal standards, willing to practice?

The social perspective

We must realize that the winning of assent has always had a fundamental role in the working of any society. Even the most tyrannical government has to gain some degree of assent, if merely from the palace guard. In modern democracies the base of necessary assent has been immeasurably broadened, and the achieving of assent is the essence of democratic government; it is also the essence of business. The crucial factors in today's world are the amount of control possible, the degree of the concentration of that control, and the responsibility of that control.

As recently as a generation ago, the novelist and philosopher Aldous Huxley could write that, though there was something "not far removed from a science of advertising," the propagandist still had to "draw bows in the dark." In the period since then, we have seen such developments in advertising as to make that primordial "science of advertising" look like nothing better than bows drawn in the dark. More shockingly, we have seen the staggering achievements of the propaganda of Hitler and Stalin, not to mention those of our own experts of the free world.

Within this century, there has been, as a result of technological development, and as a result of the concentration of financial control, a constant diminution of local and individual channels of expression and debate. Furthermore, public relations experts have tended to narrow the ground of thought and debate—that is, to fix on key points that have immediate impact and propaganda value rather than long-range significance. Moreover, the experts tend to reduce differences between persons and platforms, on the theory that in the clarification of issues more persuasive power is lost than gained. For example, various observers have noted that the opinions of candidates for office tend to get more alike as election day approaches. The world in which Abraham Lincoln and Stephen A. Douglas could seriously debate fundamental matters of the public interest has all but disappeared—or perhaps has already disappeared.

What is called the "image" of a man is more important than the man himself or what he stands for, in politics or in other activities. Raymond K.

Price, one of the architects of President Nixon's election in 1968, is reported to have declared in the early stages of the campaign that rational arguments would "only be effective if we can get people to make the *emotional* leap . . ."

The report, written by a member of the campaign staff, continues:

> To do this, Price suggested attacking the "personal factors" rather than the "historical factors" which were the basis of the low opinion so many people had of Richard Nixon. "These tend to be more a gut reaction," he wrote, "unarticulated, nonanalytical, a product of the particular chemistry between the voter and the *image* of the candidate. *We have to be very clear on this point: that the response is to the image, not to the man . . .*"
> —JOE MC GINNISS: *The Selling of the President 1968.*[11]

This question of the image versus the man was discussed subsequent to the campaign in a conference of experts in the field of communication. Here is a news report on the event:

HOW TO GET THAT GOOD "MEDIA IMAGE"

> On the 1968 Presidential ballot the choice was clear: Hubert Humphrey or Richard Nixon. Or was it? Were the voters really choosing between the ad agencies of Lennen & Newell, on the one side, and Fuller & Smith & Ross on the other? And today, in New York City, the mayoral contestants for City Hall are John Lindsay, John Marchi and Mario Procaccino—or is the Young & Rubicam ad agency really running?
>
> The relationship between candidate and ad man—or puppet and puppeteer, as some would have it—was a topic of serious debate last weekend in New York during the first conference of the American Association of Political Consultants—the media men, advertising executives, copy chiefs, film producers, advance men, creative supervisors and political scientists whose careers depend, at least in part, on the politician's felt need for a "media image." The topics included creative image-making, computer planning of television campaigns, media planning and time buying, television-production techniques, news conferences and over-all campaign guidance. But the unspoken topic was: can candidates be sold on TV like cigarettes and beer?
>
> Tony Isadore of Young & Rubicam, who is supervising Lindsay's re-election campaign,[12] said that the first problem faced by a TV consultant is to overcome the voter's cynicism about "paid political announcements." "People have a filter through which they put all advertising," he said. Accordingly, the idea is to present a political candidate's TV pitch in a nonpolitical setting. "Always run ads next to newscasts if possible," advised Walter De Vries, a former George Romney aide and now a Michigan political science professor. He also advised designing the campaign spot so that it appears like a network news item rather than a campaign pitch by the candidate's staff.

---

[11] From *The Selling of the President 1968,* by Joe McGinniss. Reprinted by permission of Trident Press. Copyright © 1969 by JoeMac, Inc. Reprinted by permission of the Sterling Lord Agency.

[12] John Lindsay, who was reelected Mayor of New York in the fall of 1969.

Voice: TV-campaign aides realize that sometimes a candidate will be hurt by media exposure. "If you know from the beginning that the public doesn't want to hear this man," said adman Eugene Case, "you have to find another way to do it." One other way is the "voice-over," which Case used in Nelson Rockefeller's 1966 bid for re-election as governor of New York State. The screen showed a political problem—such as a polluted river—and a resonant, inoffensive voice quietly recited the governor's past efforts to reduce water pollution. Not once was the candidate's face seen or voice heard.

Some participants admitted that for some candidates, there wasn't anything a "packager" could do to help, agreeing with the now-famous media dictum that a candidate who has a "hard" or "hot" TV image is doomed to lose in a major election. "You just couldn't change George Romney by TV advertising," said Frederic Papert, of Papert Koening Lois. Added another consultant: "Romney was the instance where we applied every technique and none of them worked."

Hubert Humphrey, the conferees agreed, was a hopeless TV performer. For most of them the former Vice President came across on the "cool" medium as a "hot" salesman with a tendency to overplay his pitch. Said one of his TV aides: "The biggest mistake of his campaign may have been that he never learned to use television right." Richard Nixon, on the other hand, was regarded as a successful—if reluctant—convert to the powers of the cool medium. "The hardest job on the past campaign was not selling Nixon to the U.S.," said Joe McGinniss, "but selling Nixon on TV."

McGinniss's new book, "The Selling of the President 1968," will be published next week. It is a detailed look at the way in which Nixon aides carefully prepared Nixon for every TV news conference, "spontaneous" panel show, and spot ad to overcome the candidate's well-known inability to come across on TV as a "cool" performer. . . .

Faults: McGinniss argues that such tactics are fundamentally dishonest. "Humphrey, for all his faults," he said, "was, on TV, an extension of his real self. The TV spots on Nixon were dishonest—they tried to create something that wasn't there." Other participants strongly disagreed. "The qualities that make a good President may make a bad TV performer," said a GOP consultant. "So, is it not the height of morality to create an image to put the good man across?" Many, in any event, agreed with Eugene Case: "It's impossible to live under idealistic rules, and I don't think [we] have."

And, by the end of the conference, some participants began to hedge their bets about the power of their profession. "No one can say," said Alan Gardner, who worked on Humphrey's 1968 campaign, "that X amount of advertising weight on product Y will produce Z sales." Nixon adviser Ailes, however, countered that packaging was becoming so important that the roles of the TV producer and the campaign manager were merging. Clifton White had the last word. "No one can make a President," he said. He should know; he worked for Goldwater in '64 and Reagan in '68.[13]   —*Newsweek,* September 29, 1969.[14]

[13] Barry Goldwater was defeated for the presidency in 1964 by Lyndon B. Johnson; Ronald Reagan's bid for the Republican nomination in 1968 came to nothing.
[14] Reprinted by permission of *Newsweek.* Copyright Newsweek, Inc., September 29, 1969.

The fundamental danger in the massive process of persuasion as we now know it, the danger that all criteria of thought and judgment will be eroded or perverted, is most clearly revealed in what is called saturation techniques, which depend on slogans rather than ideas, repetition rather than discussion, on hypnosis rather than awareness. This danger to thought and judgment is, of course, aggravated by the contempt for, or at least condescension toward, the public that characterizes at least a segment of the professional persuaders, an attitude fairly well indicated by the following remarks of the Whitaker of the famous public relations firm of Whitaker and Baxter:

> The average American, when you catch him after hours, as we must, doesn't want to be educated; he doesn't want to improve his mind; he doesn't want to work, consciously, at being a good citizen.
> But there are two ways you can interest him in a campaign, and only two that we have ever found successful.
> Most every American loves a *contest* . . . So *you can interest him if you put on a fight.* . . .
> Then, too, most every American likes to be entertained. He likes the movies, he likes mysteries; he likes fireworks and parades. . . .
> So if you can't fight, PUT ON A SHOW! . . .
> —PATRICK O. MARSH: *Persuasive Speaking.*[15]

As Aldous Huxley has pointed out, in the early optimism engendered by general literacy and a free press, people were naive enough to believe that there were only two kinds of propaganda, the true and the false. They "did not foresee what in fact has happened, above all in our Western capitalist democracies—the development of a vast mass communication industry, concerned in the main neither with the true nor the false, but with the unreal, the more or less totally irrelevant." [16] And we may add another thing that was not foreseen: in the end, the contempt for, or condescension toward, the public affects the public's own view of itself; it becomes cynical toward its own opinions, more or less dimly realizing that those opinions may be a product of manipulation and are lacking in both intellectual and moral content.

The final contempt, and condescension, is to assume that it does not matter by what process assent is achieved if the assent is to a "good" thing—a good product, show, book, firm, candidate, or idea. This, of course, is a version of the notion referred to earlier that the end justifies the means, a notion that in most circles is not—at least, when baldly stated—regarded as respectable. When applied to persuasion the question becomes this: In what way and to what extent do the techniques devoted to achieving success debauch the capacity for judgment? When the persuadee is persuaded without reference to the grounds of assent, what Jacques Elluel, in *Propaganda: The Formation of Men's Attitudes,* calls the "elimination of individualizing

[15] Reprinted from p. 67 in *Persuasive Speaking* by Patrick O. Marsh (Harper & Row, 1967) by permission of Harper & Row, Publishers.
[16] "Propaganda in a Democratic Society," in *Brave New World Revisited* (New York, 1958).

factors" has occurred. That is, the person has ceased to be a person and has become a thing.

We cannot infer from the foregoing remarks that there ever was a time when rationality and high-mindedness generally reigned in human affairs, but today's expertly organized persuasion has raised doubts that the "examination of opinion," which Walter Lippmann, in *The Public Philosophy,* has called "one of the necessities of man," can survive without dangerous impairment. If there is a ground for optimism, it is that the disease may generate its own cure. The researches that arm the professional persuaders cannot be kept secret, and in so far as they become public knowledge they forewarn the public—unless, of course, the engendering of self-contempt in the public has passed the point of no return. And, too, education in general encourages—or is supposed to encourage—a critical attitude. That some change has been taking place, that there is an increase of awareness in the audience, is indicated by the increasing sophistication of advertising, chiefly in a strain of self-humor, a wink, as it were, at the audience that implies that "we both know this is a game we have to play."

But perhaps even advertising men can be victims of advertising, and politicians, of their own rhetoric. Then what?

The individual perspective

The question of persuasion in the social perspective is, of course, far more complicated than we have been able to suggest, but it is no less so in relation to the individual. He is torn between two roles. He is continually in the role of persuadee, exposed to the lure and benumbing of persuasion, to which he must bring what awareness and self-awareness he can muster. At the same time, to a greater or lesser degree, he plays the role of persuader. And both roles are complicated further by the fact that the ethical criteria applicable to one form of persuasion may not be, within certain limits, applicable to another. For instance, the illogic in much current advertising would not be ethically acceptable—or at least should not be— in a speech on a serious public issue.

What is acceptable to you? To you personally—not to a particular audience or in a particular form of persuasion? You are alone, then, with the question—and with yourself.

A note on rhetoric and persuasion

If the arts of rhetoric can be put to destructive uses when practiced by unscrupulous men, one may well ask: Should they be taught at all?

But clearly nothing is to be accomplished by trying to suppress the knowledge of rhetoric—as if it were a black art like witchcraft. The only remedy is for as many people as possible to learn something about how words work so that they will be armored against unscrupulous attacks on their minds and on their pocketbooks. The best defense against being over-powered by the rabble-rouser or bilked by the unethical advertiser is to become thoroughly aware of the power of words and to learn to distinguish legitimate appeals from illegitimate ones. Indeed, one function of the textbook that you are now reading is to help you become less vulnerable to the come-on of the demagogue and the manipulator of opinion.

■ **APPLICATIONS**

I Here is an excerpt from Shakespeare's play *Julius Caesar* (III, ii, 57–266). It comes just after Brutus, who with Cassius and other conspirators has assassinated Caesar, has made a speech to the Roman mob, explaining the purity of his motives. Mark Antony's speech is a classic example of persuasion (by emotional appeals). Analyze the speech, observing how the mob, bit by bit, changes its attitude. Relate these changes to stages of the speech.

> *Bru.*   My countrymen,—
> *Second Pleb.*   Peace, silence! Brutus speaks.
> *First Pleb.*   Peace, ho!
> *Bru.*   Good countrymen, let me depart alone,
> And, for my sake, stay here with Antony.
> Do grace to Cæsar's corpse, and grace his speech
> Tending to Cæsar's glories, which Mark Antony,
> By our permission, is allow'd to make.
> I do entreat you, not a man depart
> Save I alone, till Antony have spoke.   *Exit.*
> *First Pleb.*   Stay, ho! and let us hear Mark Antony.
> *Third Pleb.*   Let him go up into the public chair;
> We'll hear him. Noble Antony, go up.
> *Ant.*   For Brutus' sake, I am beholding to you.   *Goes into the pulpit.*
> *Fourth Pleb.*   What does he say of Brutus?
> *Third Pleb.*   He says, for Brutus' sake,
> He finds himself beholding to us all.
> *Fourth Pleb.*   'T were best he speak no harm of Brutus here.
> *First Pleb.*   This Cæsar was a tyrant.
> *Third Pleb.*   Nay, that 's certain:
> We are blest that Rome is rid of him.
> *Second Pleb.*   Peace! let us hear what Antony can say.
> *Ant.*   You gentle Romans,—
> *All.*   Peace, ho! let us hear him.
> *Ant.*   Friends, Romans, countrymen, lend me your ears!
> I come to bury Cæsar, not to praise him.
> The evil that men do lives after them,
> The good is oft interred with their bones;
> So let it be with Cæsar. The noble Brutus
> Hath told you Cæsar was ambitious;
> If it were so, it was a grievous fault,

And grievously hath Cæsar answer'd it.
Here, under leave of Brutus and the rest—
For Brutus is an honourable man;
So are they all, all honourable men—
Come I to speak in Cæsar's funeral.
He was my friend, faithful and just to me;
But Brutus says he was ambitious,
And Brutus is an honourable man.
He hath brought many captives home to Rome,
Whose ransoms did the general coffers fill;
Did this in Cæsar seem ambitious?
When that the poor have cried, Cæsar hath wept;
Ambition should be made of sterner stuff:
Yet Brutus says he was ambitious,
And Brutus is an honourable man.
You all did see that on the Lupercal
I thrice presented him a kingly crown,
Which he did thrice refuse. Was this ambition?
Yet Brutus says he was ambitious,
And, sure, he is an honourable man.
I speak not to disprove what Brutus spoke,
But here I am to speak what I do know.
You all did love him once, not without cause;
What cause withholds you then to mourn for him?
O judgement! thou art fled to brutish beasts,
And men have lost their reason. Bear with me;
My heart is in the coffin there with Cæsar,
And I must pause till it come back to me.
    First Pleb.   Methinks there is much reason in his sayings.
    Second Pleb.   If thou consider rightly of the matter,
Cæsar has had great wrong.
    Third Pleb.   Has he, masters?
I fear there will a worse come in his place.
    Fourth Pleb.   Mark'd ye his words? He would not take the crown;
Therefore 't is certain he was not ambitious.
    First Pleb.   If it be found so, some will dear abide it.
    Second Pleb.   Poor soul! his eyes are red as fire with weeping.
    Third Pleb.   There 's not a nobler man in Rome than Antony.
    Fourth Pleb.   Now mark him, he begins again to speak.
    Ant.   But yesterday the word of Cæsar might
Have stood against the world; now lies he there,
And none so poor to do him reverence.
O masters, if I were dispos'd to stir
Your hearts and minds to mutiny and rage,
I should do Brutus wrong, and Cassius wrong,
Who, you all know, are honourable men.
I will not do them wrong; I rather choose
To wrong the dead, to wrong myself and you,
Than I will wrong such honourable men.

But here 's a parchment with the seal of Cæsar;
I found it in his closet; 't is his will.
Let but the commons hear this testament—
Which, pardon me, I do not mean to read—
And they would go and kiss dead Cæsar's wounds
And dip their napkins in his sacred blood,
Yea, beg a hair of him for memory,
And, dying, mention it within their wills,
Bequeathing it as a rich legacy
Unto their issue.
    Fourth Pleb.   We 'll hear the will. Read it, Mark Antony.
    All.   The will, the will! we will hear Cæsar's will.
    Ant.   Have patience, gentle friends, I must not read it;
It is not meet you know how Cæsar lov'd you.
You are not wood, you are not stones, but men;
And, being men, hearing the will of Cæsar,
It will inflame you, it will make you mad.
'T is good you know not that you are his heirs;
For, if you should, O, what would come of it?
    Fourth Pleb.   Read the will; we 'll hear it, Antony.
You shall read us the will, Cæsar's will.
    Ant.   Will you be patient? Will you stay a while?
I have o'ershot myself to tell you of it.
I fear I wrong the honourable men
Whose daggers have stabb'd Cæsar; I do fear it.
    Fourth Pleb.   They were traitors; honourable men!
    All.   The will! the testament!
    Second Pleb.   They were villains, murderers. The will! read the will.
    Ant.   You will compel me, then, to read the will?
Then make a ring about the corpse of Cæsar,
And let me show you him that made the will.
Shall I descend? and will you give me leave?
    All.   Come down.
    Second Pleb.   Descend.
    Third Pleb.   You shall have leave.

                        Antony comes down from the pulpit.
    Fourth Pleb.   A ring; stand round.
    First Pleb.   Stand from the hearse, stand from the body.
    Second Pleb.   Room for Antony, most noble Antony.
    Ant.   Nay, press not so upon me; stand far off.
    All.   Stand back; room; bear back!
    Ant.   If you have tears, prepare to shed them now.
You all do know this mantle; I remember
The first time ever Cæsar put it on.
'T was on a summer's evening in his tent,
That day he overcame the Nervii.
Look, in this place ran Cassius' dagger through;
See what a rent the envious Casca made;
Through this the well-beloved Brutus stabb'd,

And as he pluck'd his cursed steel away,
Mark how the blood of Cæsar followed it,
As rushing out of doors, to be resolv'd
If Brutus so unkindly knock'd, or no;
For Brutus, as you know, was Cæsar's angel.
Judge, O you gods, how dearly Cæsar lov'd him!
This was the most unkindest cut of all;
For when the noble Cæsar saw him stab,
Ingratitude, more strong than traitors' arms,
Quite vanquish'd him: then burst his mighty heart;
And, in his mantle muffling up his face,
Even at the base of Pompey's statuë
Which all the while ran blood, great Cæsar fell.
O, what a fall was there, my countrymen!
Then I, and you, and all of us fell down,
Whilst bloody treason flourish'd over us.
O, now you weep, and I perceive you feel
The dint of pity: these are gracious drops.
Kind souls, what, weep you when you but behold
Our Cæsar's vesture wounded? Look you here:
Here is himself, marr'd, as you see, with traitors.
   First Pleb.   O piteous spectacle!
   Second Pleb.   O noble Cæsar!
   Third Pleb.   O woeful day!
   Fourth Pleb.   O traitors, villains!
   First Pleb.   O most bloody sight!
   Second Pleb.   We will be revenged!
   All.   Revenge! About! Seek! Burn! Fire! Kill! Slay!
Let not a traitor live!
   Ant.   Stay, countrymen.
   First Pleb.   Peace there! hear the noble Antony.
   Second Pleb.   We 'll hear him, we 'll follow him, we 'll die with him.
   Ant.   Good friends, sweet friends, let me not stir you up
To such a sudden flood of mutiny.
They that have done this deed are honourable.
What private griefs they have, alas, I know not,
That made them do it; they are wise and honourable,
And will, no doubt, with reasons answer you.
I come not, friends, to steal away your hearts.
I am no orator, as Brutus is;
But, as you know me all, a plain blunt man
That love my friend; and that they know full well
That gave me public leave to speak of him;
For I have neither wit, nor words, nor worth,
Action, nor utterance, nor the power of speech
To stir men's blood; I only speak right on.
I tell you that which you yourselves do know;
Show you sweet Cæsar's wounds, poor, poor, dumb mouths,
And bid them speak for me: but were I Brutus,

And Brutus Antony, there were an Antony
Would ruffle up your spirits, and put a tongue
In every wound of Cæsar, that should move
The stones of Rome to rise and mutiny.
    All. We'll mutiny.
    First Pleb. We'll burn the house of Brutus.
    Third Pleb. Away, then! come, seek the conspirators.
    Ant. Yet hear me, countrymen; yet hear me speak.
    All. Peace, ho! hear Antony, most noble Antony!
    Ant. Why, friends, you go to do you know not what.
Wherein hath Cæsar thus deserv'd your loves?
Alas, you know not; I must tell you, then.
You have forgot the will I told you of.
    All. Most true. The will! Let 's stay and hear the will.
    Ant. Here is the will, and under Cæsar's seal.
To every Roman citizen he gives,
To every several man, seventy-five drachmas.
    Second Pleb. O noble Cæsar! We'll revenge his death.
    Third Pleb. O royal Cæsar!
    Ant. Hear me with patience.
    All. Peace, ho!
    Ant. Moreover, he hath left you all his walks,
His private arbours and new-planted orchards,
On this side Tiber; he hath left them you,
And to your heirs forever, common pleasures,
To walk abroad, and recreate yourselves.
Here was a Cæsar! When comes such another?
    First Pleb. Never, never! Come, away, away!
We'll burn his body in the holy place,
And with the brands fire the traitors' houses.
Take up the body.
    Second Pleb. Go fetch fire.
    Third Pleb. Pluck down benches.
    Fourth Pleb. Pluck down forms, windows, anything.
                          Exeunt Plebeians with the body.
    Ant. Now let it work. Mischief, thou art afoot,
Take thou what course thou wilt!

II You are now to write a theme in persuasion of some 700 words or more. If you like, you may use the material you have worked up for the previous Applications. In this theme you should try to use what you consider ethical methods of persuasion. Having written it, you are to take the same subject and write another version using whatever unethical appeals and devices may suggest themselves for the subject.

CHAPTER **8**

Description

Description, as we shall understand the word here, is the kind of discourse concerned with the impression that the world makes on our senses. It presents the qualities of objects, persons, conditions, and actions. It aims to suggest to the imagination the thing as it comes immediately to an observer. We call this kind of description *suggestive* to distinguish it from technical description, which is really a form of exposition. We have already discussed (pp. 132–35) the difference between technical description and suggestive description, but let us return to it, with new and more elaborate examples.

TECHNICAL:

The West Indies stand in a warm sea, and the trade winds, warmed and moistened by this sea, blow across all of them. These are the two great primary geographic facts about this group of islands, whose area is but little larger than that of Great Britain.

These trade winds, always warm, but nevertheless refreshing sea breezes, blow mostly from the east or northeast. Thus one side of every island is windward, and the other side is leeward. The third great geographical fact about these islands is that most of them are mountainous, giving to the windward sides much more rain than the leeward sides receive. This makes great differences in climate within short distances, a thing quite unknown in the eastern half of the United States, where our slowly whirling cyclonic winds blow in quick succession from all directions upon every spot of territory. Thus both sides of the Appalachian Mountains are nearly alike in their rainfall, forest growth, and productive possibilities. On the contrary, the West Indian mountains have different worlds on their different slopes. The eastern or windward side, cloud-bathed and eternally showered upon, is damp and dripping. There are jungles with velvety green ferns, and forests with huge trees. The rainbow is a prominent feature of the tropic landscape. On the windward side one receives a striking impression of lush vegetation. On the leeward side of the very same ridge and only a few miles distant there is another kind of world, the world of scanty rainfall, with all its devastating consequences to vegetation. A fourth great geographic fact is the division of these islands into two great arcs, an outer arc of limestone and an inner arc of volcanic islands. The limestone areas are low. The volcanic areas are from moderately high to very high. Some islands have both the limestone and the volcanic features.

—J. RUSSELL SMITH and M. OGDEN PHILLIPS: *North America.*

SUGGESTIVE:

Take five-and-twenty heaps of cinders dumped here and there in an outside city lot; imagine some of them magnified into mountains, and the vacant lot the sea; and you will have a fit idea of the general aspect of the Encantadas, or Enchanted Isles. A group rather of extinct volcanoes than of isles; looking much as the world at large might, after a penal conflagration. . . .

It is to be doubted whether any spot on earth can, in desolation, furnish a parallel to this group. Abandoned cemeteries of long ago, old cities by piecemeal tumbling to their ruin, these are melancholy enough; but like all else which has once been associated with humanity they still awaken in us some thought of sympathy, however sad. Hence, even the Dead Sea, along with whatever other emotions it may at times inspire, does not fail to touch in the pilgrim some of his less unpleasurable feelings. . . .

In many places the coast is rock-bound, or more properly, clinker-bound; tumbled masses of blackish or greenish stuff like the dross of an iron furnace, forming dark clefts and caves here and there, into which a ceaseless sea pours a fury of foam; overhanging them with a swirl of grey, haggard mist, amidst which sail screaming flights of unearthly birds heightening the dismal din. However calm the sea without, there is no rest for these swells and those rocks, they lash and are lashed, even when the outer ocean is most at peace with itself. On the oppressive, clouded days such as are peculiar to this part of the watery Equator, the dark vitrified masses, many of which raise themselves among white whirlpools and breakers in detached and perilous places off the shore, present a most Plutonian sight. In no world but a fallen one could such lands exist.

—HERMAN MELVILLE: "The Encantadas,
or Enchanted Isles," *The Piazza Tales.*

The first of these passages, from a geography of North America, lists four "great geographic" facts and then indicates their influence on climate, vegetation, and appearance of the landscape. Occasionally there are feeble attempts to make the reader see the islands, as in the phrases "cloud-bathed" and "velvety green ferns," but the tendency is to give generalized information. For instance, concerning the rainbow, instead of giving us images that would stir our imaginations, the writers simply say, "The rainbow is a prominent feature of the tropic landscape." Or, instead of picturing for us the arid slopes of the leeward side of the mountains, the writers simply offer the phrase "all its devastating consequences to vegetation." Here the purpose of description is to present information; the chief structural features of the islands are identified, so that we may understand various other facts about the islands.

The second passage, like the first, is the description of a group of tropic islands. But Melville, the author, is not concerned with giving us a list of the great geographic facts and their consequences. His description naturally involves some of these facts, but the passage is not organized about an enumeration of them. It is organized in such a way as to return the reader continually to the sense of loneliness, ruin, and desolation that characterizes the islands. He wants to give the reader an impression of the islands, a feeling for them, rather than a systematic analysis of their characteristics.

The passage begins with the comparison of heaps of cinders in a dumping ground, associating the islands with the used-up, the finished, the dreary. The first paragraph ends with the phrase "penal conflagration," which implies ideas not merely of ruin and waste but also of sin and punishment—sin and punishment on a universal scale. The next paragraph is based on the ideas of the unhuman desolation, the blankness. In the last paragraph the image of the wasteland of cinders appears again in the phrases "clinker-bound" and "like the dross of an iron furnace," and again that of punishment, as suggested by the constant tumult of the sea, in the phrase "lash and are lashed." The idea of punishment and suffering becomes explicit in the last sentence, "In no world but a fallen one could such lands exist."

In other words, the whole passage is based on two things: the image of the cinder heap and the idea of sin and punishment, which combine to give the notion of a world after the Judgment, the final desolation. And it is this notion that provides the organizing principle for the description. It is the key to the interpretation that Melville gives to his facts.

We do not aspire to write like Melville, but if we examine some of the principles used by a great writer, we may be able to adapt them to our own more modest needs. The principles of a good theme are the same as those used by Melville, or by any of the other famous writers whom we shall look at. It is the principles we are concerned with, not mere imitation. Imitation, in fact, is useful only in so far as it makes us aware of principles.

Description: Scientist and Artist

In our study of exposition, we say (p. 132) that technical description is concerned with providing information *about* things, and we distinguish it from suggestive description, which is concerned not with information *about* things but with the direct presentation *of* things. These two kinds of description correspond, we may say, to the two kinds of motive that may underlie our use of description.

We may think of this distinction as the fundamental distinction between the motive of the scientist and the motive of the artist. The scientist appeals to our interest *about* the world and to our interest in explanations *of* the world. He is concerned with the general laws of nature. But the artist (of any kind—painter, poet, novelist, musician, and so on) appeals to our interest in the direct experience *of* the world. He is concerned with particulars as they strike him—particular experiences, particular objects. This is not to say that the artist may not be also concerned with generalizations—generalizations, for example, about human behavior. But the artist tends to approach even generalizations through the presentation of particulars. The novelist, for example, embodies his generalizations about human conduct in a particular story about a particular man.

This distinction between the two kinds of motive means that we find technical description characteristically in scientific writing and suggestive description characteristically in the work of literary artists—poets or essayists or fiction writers. For instance, the geographers describing the West Indies in our first example are writing as scientists. They want to give *information about* the climate, vegetation, and so on, of the islands. Melville, describing his islands, is writing as an artist; he wants to give us the direct *impression of* the place and to indicate to us how we might feel if we saw it.

Most of us are neither scientists nor artists, but we all have a little of the scientist and a little of the artist in us. We want to know about the world, and we want to extend our experience of the world. These two kinds of interest lead us to the use of both kinds of description.

We are not to assume that we find technical description only in scientific works and suggestive description only in artistic works. Technical description may occur in a letter, an essay, a guidebook, a history, an advertisement—wherever and whenever the impulse appears to give information about an object. By the same token, suggestive description may occur in any piece of writing at any point where the impulse for immediacy and vividness comes into play. Sometimes, both types appear in the same piece of writing.

■ APPLICATIONS

I At the end of this chapter (pp. 306–12), there is a group of examples of description. Read them carefully. Do you find any examples of technical description? In examples that are prevailingly suggestive, do you find any elements that might appear in technical description?

II Turn back to the chapter on Exposition and read the realtor's advertisement of a house and the corresponding piece of suggestive description of the house in the letter (pp. 132–33). Also, glance again at the section on comparison and contrast in which we discussed how a thing may be regarded as belonging to different areas of interest—how, for example, a field may be regarded by a farmer, an infantry officer, and a painter (p. 72). Here, clearly, the farmer and infantry officer, if they had to write descriptions, would give us technical description. But the painter would be concerned with the appearance of the field, with the kind of description that might appear in a familiar letter or in a short story if the field were the setting of an episode.

Now select some object, such as the house, or some spot, such as the field, and write one paragraph—say 150 words—of technical description about it, in whatever area of interest you prefer. Then write a paragraph of suggestive description about the same thing.

Suggestive Description and the Senses

Suggestive description tells what impression the world makes on our senses. An apple is red, tweed is rough, lilies are fragrant. But these are crude and general bits of description and do not make us vividly aware of apple, tweed, or lily. A good writer would not be satisfied with this kind of description. He would want to make sharper discriminations. But to do so, he would have to cultivate his powers of observation. Even when writing of an imagined object rather than a real one before his eyes, he would have to call on his store of impressions drawn from real life. Observation gives us our sense of the world, and a person who wishes to become a good writer should make a real effort to train his powers of observation.

Powers of observation, however, are not useful to a writer if he has not trained himself to put his perceptions into words. Discriminations among perceptions must be embodied in discriminations among words. Each sense absorbs an infinite variety of data, and each sense demands that we struggle toward a vocabulary of subtlety and precision. One way to train yourself is to focus attention, even for days at a time, on trying to discriminate among the data that one sense offers. Try to find the word for a particular sound, a particular color, a particular odor. Such an exercise will not only sharpen your sense of the relation of impression to word but will also train you in a basic method of description, the method of making one sense dominant in developing a general effect.

For example, here are three descriptive passages, each primarily concerned with impressions from a single sense. Note the discriminations made in each passage and the language used to record the observation.

> To tell when the scythe is sharp enough this is the rule. First the stone clangs and grinds against the iron harshly; then it rings musically to one note; then, at last, it purrs as though the iron and stone were exactly suited. When you hear this, your scythe is sharp enough; and I, when I heard it

that June dawn, with everything quite silent except the birds, let down the scythe and bent myself to mow.

—HILAIRE BELLOC: "The Mowing of a Field," *Hills and the Sea.*

The thing I chiefly remember about my grandfather's barn is the way it smelled. I reckon this is because when I was there I was often lying with my eyes closed, on the hay in the loft, with only the smell coming to me, or I was down in my little workshop and so preoccupied that I was only aware of the smells. Up in the loft, when I lay there on a rainy day, all I had to do was close my eyes, and there was the impression of a hayfield on a hot summer day, one of the days when I had had such a good time, the kind of dry, sweet smell you get from the hay. When I was down in my workshop, there was the smell like ammonia from the stalls on one side, a clear, sharp sort of smell that makes your nose tingle. There was also the smell of good leather and saddle soap from the tackroom.   —From a theme.

When I think of hills, I think of the upward strength I tread upon. When water is the object of my thought, I feel the cool shock of the plunge and the quick yielding of the waves that crisp and curl and ripple about my body. The pleasing changes of rough and smooth, pliant and rigid, curved and straight in the bark and branches of a tree give the truth to my hand. The immovable rock, with its juts and warped surfaces, bends beneath my fingers into all manner of grooves and hollows. The bulge of a watermelon and the puffed-up rotundities of squashes that sprout, bud, and ripen in that strange garden planted somewhere behind my finger tips are the ludicrous in my tactual memory and imagination.

—HELEN KELLER: *The World I Live In.*

In the first of these passages the sense of hearing is dominant; in the second, the sense of smell; in the third, the sense of touch. But in this third passage, which comes from a remarkable book written by a woman blind and deaf almost from birth, we also find temperature and pressure and strain: the coolness of water and the "upward strength" of the hill.

Thus far we have been speaking as though description depended on sorting out single words that are neatly matched to varieties of sense impressions. Within limits this is true. We hear the loud noise, and if we are to record the noise in a piece of description, the "loud noise" must become the crash, the bang, the thud, the boom, the bong, the clang, the howl, the wail, the scream—or whatever word most accurately presents the sound heard.

But often there is no word right for the occasion. Then we instinctively ask: "What was the sound *like?*"

Like the dry, echoless, air-cushioned report of a heavy board falling absolutely flat on cement? Like the cottony sound of a shotgun fired in distant woods, in fog? Like the anguished shriek of a saw in a sawmill when it strikes the pine knot? Like the dying suck and inhalation of the last greasy water going out of a sink? What was the sound *like?* We have to find some way to re-create the sound in the imagination of the reader.

So here we see in descriptive writing the natural tendency toward metaphor. For the vivid, for the specific, for the concrete—for all the things that it must present, description strains toward metaphor. Even in our brief examples above the interfusion of observation and language occurs only in metaphor: the sound of the shotgun is "cottony," and the saw utters an "anguished shriek."

Massiveness of perception

Ordinarily, we do not depend on one sense exclusively to give us our feeling of the world, and in description we aim for the same massiveness we find in experience. If we say, "The apple is red," we are not giving a very good description of the apple, certainly nothing like our immediate impression of it. The apple is not only red; it is slick-looking and juicy-looking and fragrant. Our response to the apple is massive, involving several sense impressions, blending them into the impression of "appleness." Sometimes a single word may condense a whole series of qualities. If we say, "The ice is glassy," we evoke, with the word *glassy*, the slickness, the hardness, the transparency, and the brightness of glass. Or when we said above that the sound of the distant shotgun in the woods, in fog, was "cottony," we evoked a massive impression.

■ **APPLICATIONS**

I 1 Among the examples at the end of the chapter do you find any that are, for the most part, based on one sense?
   2 Do you find any instances of the attempt to give the massiveness of impression that we have been talking about?
   3 Locate uses of metaphorical language. In each case, try to specify what purpose is served by the use.

II Read "91 Revere Street," by Robert Lowell (pp. 867–76). What descriptive elements do you find here? To these elements apply the questions in the preceding Application.

III For use in the chapters on Description and Narration (description and narration, as you will see, are intimately intertwined), you should keep a little notebook. For a time you should work with each sense individually, trying to make all the discriminations possible. In this process try to enlarge your vocabulary of single words, but also try to think in metaphors. (At this point review the chapter on Metaphor, pp. 435–65, as a supplement to Description.) Then move on from such exercises to record observations and impressions of people, places, and events. Jot down your ideas quickly while they are fresh in your mind, but later try to revise them for greater effectiveness. Now and then, at times specified by your instructor, you should turn in the notebook for his comment.

IV   After you have made entries in your notebook concentrating on individual senses, you should write a long paragraph of description focused on one sense. The paragraphs above will provide models, and your notebook should be a little mine of suggestions.

Description and the Other Kinds of Discourse

Not infrequently we encounter pieces of technical description in isolation— an article for a specialist or a technician of some kind—and we often find technical description as an extended part of long works of exposition and argument, or even in narration. But, aside from a limited number of works— for instance, certain essays and books of travel—we ordinarily find suggestive description subordinated to some other mode of discourse.

Does this mean that description is, therefore, a kind of discourse that we may dismiss lightly? No, for though it rarely stands alone and is often brief, the effect may be great. The vivid stroke, small in itself and seemingly unimportant, may give the touch of reality, the stimulus to the imagination.

Here is a piece of narrative that has been stripped of all its descriptive elements:

> The other waved the cigar, the other hand, in Horace's face. Horace shook it and freed his hand. "I thought I recognized you when you got on at Oxford," Snopes said, "but I—May I set down?" he said, already shoving at Horace's knee with his leg. He flung the overcoat on the seat and sat down as the train stopped. "Yes, sir, I'm always glad to see any of the boys, any time. . . ." He leaned across Horace and peered out the window at a station. " 'Course you ain't in my county no longer, but what I say a man's friends is his friends, whichever way they vote. Because a friend is a friend, and whether he can do anything for me or not. . . ." He leaned back, the cigar in his fingers.

The passage in its original form follows, with the descriptive elements italicized. Note how they give the sense of reality, of the immediately observable world, to what otherwise would be a bare and bleached-out synopsis of events.

> The other waved the cigar, the other hand, *palm-up, the third finger discolored faintly at the base of a huge ring,* in Horace's face. Horace shook it and freed his hand. "I thought I recognized you when you got on at Oxford," Snopes said, "but I—May I set down?" he said, already shoving at Horace's knee with his leg. He flung the overcoat—*a shoddy blue garment with a greasy velvet collar*—on the seat and sat down as the train stopped. "Yes, sir, I'm always glad to see any of the boys, any time. . . ." He leaned across Horace and peered out the window at a *small dingy station with its cryptic bulletin board chalked over, an express truck bearing a wire chicken*

coop containing two forlorn fowls, at three or four men in overalls gone restfully against the wall, chewing. " 'Course you ain't in my county no longer, but what I say a man's friends is his friends, whichever way they vote. Because a friend is a friend, and whether he can do anything for me or not. . . ." He leaned back, the *unlighted* cigar in his fingers.

—WILLIAM FAULKNER: *Sanctuary.*

Here, in a student theme, is an example of an almost completely bare narrative:

GETTING ENGAGED

It had been such a lovely day. There was bright sun and the ocean as still as the ocean ever gets. Joseph had taken me out in his little putt-putt to the island to fish and have a picnic. We fished from the boat, and then came ashore to eat lunch. We ate, then got in the shade of the rocks and sort of dozed off. At least, I did. I woke up with a start. Joseph had called me, I guess. It was easy to tell why. Off yonder, beyond where the sun was still shining, you could see the clouds piling up high.

It fascinated you to watch it. I couldn't take my eyes off it, and then I took a look at Joseph. He was looking at the clouds, too. It was a funny expression, sort of rapt and awe-struck, you might say. And suddenly he seemed so much younger than I had thought of him. It was like a little boy's face, with eyes wide while he looked at the clouds.

He came out of his trance. "Gosh," he said, "gosh, did you ever!" He suddenly went toward the boat, fast as a basketball player catching the ball and turning toward the basket for a shot. (Joseph is a wonderful basketball player.) "Grab the stuff, girlie, and come on!" he said.

I got in, and he shoved off and climbed over the side. He began to pull the lanyard to start the motor. He was nervous, not under control. Then the lanyard broke. I looked into his face and knew what had happened. We were in trouble.

Then he grinned. He looked somewhat scared, but he grinned. "Girlie," he said, "I got you into it, and that sticks me with getting you out."

Then he stopped grinning. He picked up the oars and put them in the oarlocks, not in a hurry. His face was different from what I had ever seen it to be. It looked like a man's face now, and I knew the way he would look at forty or forty-five, or a thousand. I thought that that was a face I wouldn't mind looking at for a long time.

To make a long story short, we did manage to get in, but it was a tough trip. That evening I got engaged.

Here is the same theme as revised after discussion with the instructor. Some of the changes are, it is obvious, to improve paragraph and sentence structure, but by and large, the revision has been directed toward making the description of the scene and the actions more vivid.

GETTING ENGAGED

It had been such a lovely day, perfectly lovely, with bright sun and the ocean as still as the ocean ever gets, a slow swell like somebody breathing in an easy sleep, and instead of waves a lazy rippling now and then that made you think of a cat waking up and stretching in the sunshine, and then dozing off again. Joseph had taken me out in his little putt-putt to the island to fish and have a picnic. After we had fished and come ashore to eat our lunch, we lay in the shade of the rocks and sort of dozed off. At least, I did. I woke up with a start. Joseph had called me, I guess. It was easy to tell why.

Off yonder, beyond the glitter of the water where the sun still struck, you could see the clouds piling up like a cliff, black and slate-colored, streaked with purple. I said like a cliff, but it was like a cliff that somehow, momentarily, grew taller while you stared at it, looking awfully solid but somehow swelling and coiling upward at the same time, as though there were an interior force collecting itself for effort.

It fascinated you to watch it. I couldn't take my eyes off it, and then I sneaked a look at Joseph. He was staring at it, too. He had a funny expression, sort of rapt and awe-struck. And suddenly he looked so much younger than I had thought of him. It was a little boy's face, round and tanned, with eyes so wide suddenly that, against the tan of his face, the whites seemed to leap out at you. There was a smudge of oil on his left cheek, and some white sand stuck untidily in the oil against the brown skin. It was like the face of a little boy you wanted to tell, "Go and wash your face, you're a sight!"

But I didn't have time to say anything, for all at once he jerked out of his trance.

"Gosh," he said, "gosh, did you ever!" He suddenly swung toward the boat, fast as a basketball forward snagging the ball and swinging toward the basket for a shot. (Joseph is a wonderful basketball player.) "Grab the stuff, girlie, and come on!" he yelled.

I grabbed it, and in a numb blur of motion, I fell into the boat, and he shoved off and piled over the side, already reaching for the lanyard of the motor. Then, angrily, he was jerking the lanyard. It was a nervous motion, not steady and controlled, with the right pause, like a count, between tries. The lanyard snapped.

There was Joseph looking blankly down at the piece of cord hanging from his hand, his jaw loose and stupid. Then he looked at me, appealingly, as though I could do something about it. One look at his face, and I knew that we were in bad trouble. I felt sick, just looking at him.

Then he grinned. He grinned twistedly, with the lips tightening and a little white showing splotchily at the corners of the mouth, even under the tan. But it was a grin. "Girlie," he said, "Old Joe got you into this, and I reckon he will have to get you out." All at once, like the edge of a knife blade coming down, the grin was cut off. He grabbed the oars, fast all right, but he set them competently into the oarlocks, without any jiggling, and the first stroke was as slow and steady. Lots of power but no hurry, as though he were on the crew following the count, and the blades came out clean from the water. We felt the oily lift and heave as the first swell took us, but the stroke didn't change.

Then I saw his face.

His face was different from what I had ever seen before. And all at once

I knew it was a man's face, and I knew the way he would look when he was forty years old, or forty-five, or a thousand. I thought that that was a face I wouldn't mind looking at for a long time.

To make a long story short, we did manage to get in, but it was a tough trip. That evening we got engaged.

■ APPLICATIONS

I Make a detailed study of the revision of the theme above. Perhaps the best way would be to underscore all the changes in the revised version, and then, item by item, to try to read the mind of the author who made the revisions. What, in each instance, is at stake?

II Revise the following theme to improve its descriptive elements.

WHAT I FIGURED OUT

It was a surprise to me, when I got home for summer vacation, to hear my father say, "Old Mitch Talley has been sick all spring, and I think you ought to go see him." My father was the kind of man who wants everybody to toe the line. For him you have to do things right, or you'll catch it. But he is also the kind of man who tries to understand other people, and he is fair.

What surprised me at this time was just part of an old surprise. Since my father always demanded that things get done right, it was not natural for him to put up with Mitch Talley, who had never done anything exactly right in his life and who was half-drunk more than half the time. But Mitch had been a hired man on our place from long before I was born. My father had known him since they were kids together. When my mother got down on Mitch, my father would shake his head and say, "Well, there're just some things in life you have to live with. You get stuck now and then."

I did not want to see Mitch. I never had liked him. He was not clean, for one thing. So I said to my father, did I have to go. "I think you ought to," he said. "Well, he's never done anything right in his whole life," I said. He waited a minute, looking at me. Then he said, "Maybe that's the reason you ought to go." I said, "I don't get it." He looked at me some more, then said, "Maybe you will later."

So I went down to the shack where Mitch lived, just off our land, on a couple of acres that belonged to his wife, an old Irish lady. I knocked at the door, and she let me in. The place was just what I had expected: dirty. He was piled up in bed. He knew I didn't like him, but he seemed awfully glad to see me. We talked some about old times, and he boasted a little about this job or that he had done. I had to sit there and agree with him, saying, yes, yes. His wife kept agreeing with him too. After he got tired, then she thought up something to pretend she was remembering, how he had saved the hay crop once. I even made one contribution before I escaped.

That night, my father asked me if I had seen Mitch. I nodded. "He's a goner, I guess," my father said, "the poor old no-good." Then he looked at me. "Are you glad you went to see him?" he asked. I started to say no. Then, just as I was about to say that, to my surprise, I suddenly did feel sort of glad. So I said yes. My father kept looking at me in that way he has. Then he said, "Can you figure out why?"

I hadn't then, but maybe I have now.

III Read "The Fire Next Time," by James Baldwin (pp. 858–67). Underscore the descriptive elements. Now read the selection omitting those elements. How would you define the difference in the effect?

The Dominant Impression

Even when description is used to support some other general intention, as in fiction, history, or reportage, it sometimes appears in a more or less extended form, with its own structure and development. We turn now to a study of the principles of that structure and development. And let us emphasize that we must have some grasp of them in order to make effective use of description even in its more incidental and supportive uses.

Often when we are trying to tell a friend how to recognize somebody we say something like this: "Just watch for that nose; it's the only nose like it in the state. Just think of W. C. Fields and his nose, and you won't miss Jack Purden." Or: "No, Susie isn't good-looking, not if you look close. But you never look close, for she has those wonderful blue eyes. That's all you notice. They're so big and expressive."

When we speak this way, we are illustrating an important principle of description: the principle of the *dominant impression.* Jack Purden's big, bulbous nose (probably with grog blossoms, too) and Susie's wonderful, expressive eyes are dominant features. We recognize the individual by the dominant impression he makes. But the same thing may be true of a place or of anything else. Here, for example, is a paragraph from a student autobiography.

> I was born and went to school in Cheyenne, Wyoming, but I never cared much about the town. What Easterners think romantic about it was just ordinary to me. What I cared about was the place we had for summers, not terribly far from Shoshone Falls. It is a valley with a river, and the valley and river suddenly widen out there with some alfalfa fields and trees and our place. But the big thing, the thing you always are conscious of, is the cliff on the west side. They call it Drum Mountain, because it looks like a drum, round-shaped, squat, and flat on top, an unusual shape for a mountain in that region. The first thing you look at in the morning is the sunlight hitting it and making the black rock glitter. It glitters then like it had fool's gold in it (iron pyrites, that is), but of course it hasn't. If it doesn't glitter, you think it won't be much of a day today, and the fishing will be rotten.

Toward the middle of the afternoon, you suddenly know that the shadow of Old Drum is coming across everything. It makes a night down in the valley long before night comes, and it is peculiar to see bright sky off yonder, high up, when it is already getting dark in the valley. When there is going to be a full moon, the whole family will wait up to see when the moonlight first hits Drum Mountain. Then you go to bed, and I bet in some way Old Drum is always with you even when you are sound asleep.

Drum Mountain dominates the paragraph, provides the main impression, the unifying idea, even as it dominates the valley where the student spends his summers.

A prominent thing catches the eye. But sometimes the mere prominence of an object is not what is important, is not what catches our interest. Some mood or feeling provoked by the object, even though we find it hard to pin down to a particular detail, may strike us more strongly than any single physical feature, however prominent. So when we describe something, we may be concerned not so much with making it merely recognizable, with indicating salient features, as with indicating how we feel about it, how we interpret it. Of course, since we are using description, we must present the object, but the dominant impression that we strive to give may be a feeling provoked by the object—the mood, the atmosphere. We will select those elements in the object that contribute to the dominant impression.

We have already seen how Melville, in describing the Encantadas, keeps emphasizing the ruined, wasted, and tormented aspects in his impression of the islands, the aspects that point to his basic interpretation of the scene. True, the actual physical impression of the islands is strongly rendered. They are "clinker-bound," are like "the dross of an iron furnace." There are dark clefts and caves overhung by "a swirl of grey, haggard mist, amidst which sail screaming flights of unearthly birds." But this objective description constantly emphasizes Melville's own interpretation of the island as an image of ruin and punishment, as when, in the quotation above, he calls the birds "unearthly," and as when, in the last sentence of the piece, he winds up with an explicit statement, "In no world but a fallen one could such lands exist."

We do not need to be as explicit as Melville, however, to convey very strongly a dominant mood for a thing described. Look at the following description by Dickens of a country estate in England:

The waters are out in Lincolnshire. An arch of the bridge in the park has been sapped and sopped away. The adjacent low-lying ground, for half a mile in breadth, is a stagnant river, with melancholy trees for islands in it, and a surface punctured all over, all day long, with falling rain. My Lady Dedlock's "place" has been extremely dreary. The weather, for many a day and night, has been so wet that the trees seem wet through, and the soft loppings and prunings of the woodsman's axe can make no crack or crackle as they fall. The deer, looking soaked, leave quagmires where they pass. The shot of a rifle loses its sharpness in the moist air, and its smoke moves in a tardy little cloud towards the green rise, coppice-topped, that makes a background for the falling rain. The view from my Lady Dedlock's own windows is alternately a lead-coloured view, and a view in Indian ink. The vases on the stone terrace in the foreground catch the rain all day; and the heavy drops fall, drip, drip, drip, upon the broad flagged pavement, called, from old time, the Ghost's Walk, all night. On Sundays, the little church in the park is mouldy; the oaken pulpit breaks out into a cold sweat; and there is a general smell and taste as of the ancient Dedlocks in their graves.   —CHARLES DICKENS: *Bleak House.*

All the details are selected to reinforce the impression of dampness, depression, and gloom. The river is "stagnant," the blows of the ax make only "soft loppings," the report of the rifle "loses its sharpness in the moist air," the church is "mouldy," and the pulpit "breaks out into a cold sweat." Note how the phrase "breaks out into a cold sweat," though applied quite literally to the damp wood of the pulpit, actually serves to remind us of a situation that would make a human being do the same thing and leads us up to the "general taste and smell as of the ancient Dedlocks in their graves."

Items that might contradict the impression that Dickens wants dominant are left out. For example, if Dickens had presented the roaring fires on the hearths of the Dedlock mansion and the steaming roasts and puddings, he would have distracted from the impression he wished to make. The Dedlock family undoubtedly would have had roaring fires and steaming roasts, but that is beside the point.

Dickens, as we have seen, depends primarily on the piling up of details supporting the main impression. Only twice does he use a word that is explicitly interpretive: *melancholy* (once) and *dreary* (once).

Let us turn to a piece of description that uses even less explicit interpretation, a passage from a student autobiography:

> You know, in the country, what the middle of an afternoon in summer can be. Maybe a rooster crows, far off, down back of the barn, and you hear it, but it seems as though it is lost in the stillness. As soon as the sound is gone, you don't believe it ever happened. That was the way it was, day after day, at my aunt's house, in summer. If I walked down the road toward the pike, just to see if anything might be passing, the dust was so thick in the lane I didn't make any more sound than a ghost, and if some bird or animal moved back in the brush by the field, it would scare me. This was, of course, when I was little, say about eight. Maybe I would be down at the pike a half hour, and nothing would pass, and then I would come back to the house, an old-fashioned white farmhouse, and go in. It was always dim in the house, and for coolness I might go in the shut-up parlor and lie on the floor, where a little light came in under the blinds, and read. It was as quiet as being under water, and you thought no time could be passing anywhere. You thought it would be a big, important event if a leaf fell off the white oak outside the window.

Atmosphere and feeling

In the passage above, the author, like Dickens, has undertaken to create what we call an atmosphere—the mood, the temper, the general feeling associated with the thing described. We have the atmosphere of gloom and dampness and decay in the description by Dickens and that of peace in the student theme.

We know, however, even as we use these words to define the atmosphere of this or that piece of description, that the labels we put on the passages are too vague and loose to define the effect that they give. Our defining words do not really define the atmosphere; they merely give a kind of crude indication, a not very dependable hint, of the effect that we find in the actual description.

Our inability to define atmosphere in general terms indicates the importance of the way the author himself goes about presenting it to us. He knows that he cannot create the desired mood or atmosphere simply by using loose, general words. Therefore, he undertakes to give us such concrete details, such aspects of his object, as will stir our imaginations not only to grasp the appearance of the object (or the sound, the color, and so forth) but to adopt a certain feeling toward the object. And here, again, the language of metaphor is of prime importance. For example, notice how the last sentence of the passage from Dickens brings to focus the feeling of the whole, and how that sentence is dominated by the metaphor of the pulpit breaking "into a cold sweat."

We have said earlier that suggestive description aims *not to tell* us about its object, but *to give* us the object. It also can be said that it aims *not to tell* us what feelings to have about the object and what attitudes to take toward it, but *to create* those feelings and attitudes within us. Vividness and immediacy, not only in regard to the physical qualities of the object but in regard to the feelings and attitudes involved, are what the writer desires.

■ APPLICATIONS

I From the examples of description at the end of this chapter (pp. 306–12), select two that give a dominant impression by emphasizing some prominent feature of the thing described. Then select two that seem successful in creating a dominant impression of mood. In this second pair of examples, underscore the details that contribute to the dominant atmosphere. Do you find any contradictory details? Try to explain the effect of any examples of metaphor that you think help create the atmosphere.

II Think of some place that impresses you as having a definite atmosphere. In your notebook make an informal list of the items belonging to the place that contribute to this dominant impression. Make another list of items that seem contradictory. Now make a list of comparisons that might be used to support the dominant mood. In the future, as you encounter or remember some interesting subject, do the same thing.

Selection

In discussing the dominant impression, we made a distinction between features of an object that are impressive in themselves and features that are important because they contribute to the mood or atmosphere. We might say, then, that details in description are important for either vividness or significance. The power of observation, as we have said, is essential, but we cannot merely accumulate details. We must choose the telling ones. Description works by *selection,* and when we are reading description, we should get the habit of asking ourselves, over and over again, "Why did he select this detail?" Or, "Why that one?" Or, "Why does this detail stir my imagination, and why does that one fail to do so?"

With these questions in mind, let us look at a few examples.

Here is the description of a town as approached from the sea. The most obvious quality of what is emphasized, the blinding brilliance of light, strikes the observer at the first moment.

> But when at last we anchored in the outer harbor, off the white town hung between the blazing sky and its reflections in the mirage which swept and rolled over the wide lagoon, then the heat of Arabia came out like a drawn sword and struck us speechless. It was midday; and the noon sun in the East, like moonlight, put to sleep the colors. There were only lights and shadows, the white houses and black gaps of streets; in front, the pallid lustre of the haze shimmering upon the inner harbors; behind, the dazzle of league after league of featureless sand, running up to an edge of low hills, faintly suggested in the far away mist of heat.
>
> —T. E. LAWRENCE: *Seven Pillars of Wisdom.*[1]

Vividness, however, may be gained by indicating some detail that might escape ordinary observation. In such a case, it is the precision and subtlety of the description that makes the thing being described come alive for us. John Burroughs, the naturalist, in a passage on the art of observation, gives a list of details that would escape most observers but that sharply evoke a series of scenes and moments:

> His [the naturalist's] senses are so delicate that in his evening walk he feels the warm and cool streaks in the air, his nose detects the most fugitive odors, his ears the most furtive sounds. As he stands musing in the April twilight, he hears that fine, elusive stir and rustle made by the angleworms reaching out from their holes for leaves and grasses; he hears the whistling wings of the woodcock as it goes swiftly by him in the dusk; he hears the call of the killdee come down out of the March sky; he hears far above

---

[1] From *Seven Pillars of Wisdom* by T. E. Lawrence. Copyright 1926, 1935 by Doubleday & Company, Inc. Reprinted by permission of the publisher.

him in the early morning the squeaking cackle of the arriving blackbirds pushing north; he hears the soft, prolonged, lulling call of the little owl in the cedars in the early spring twilight; he hears at night the roar of the distant waterfall, and the rumble of the train miles across country when the air is "hollow"; before a storm he notes how distant objects stand out and are brought near on those brilliant days that we call "weather-breeders." When the mercury is at zero or lower, he notes how the passing trains hiss and simmer as if the rails or wheels were red-hot.

—JOHN BURROUGHS: *Leaf and Tendril.*

The rustling of the angleworms gives a vivid and immediate sense of the stillness, more vivid and immediate than any number of the usual and easily observable details. Or take the "squeaking cackle" of the blackbirds; it is the absolutely right phrase to describe the sound, and because of the accuracy of the observation, our imagination fills the sky with the flock of birds passing over. Or think how striking is the "hiss and simmer" of the train on the rails!

■ APPLICATIONS

I Return to the examples at the end of the chapter and select details that strike you as effective. Try to distinguish those that seem to be chosen primarily for vividness from those that seem chosen for significance. To do this, you will, of course, have to know what the dominant impression of each example is.

II Review the selections by Baldwin (pp. 858–67), and Lowell (pp. 867–76) and repeat the process suggested above.

Caricature

The word *caricature* comes from the Italian word *caricatura,* which means a satirical picture; but the derivation of the Italian word is from a word meaning "to load," and so the satirical effect in caricature is associated with the idea of overloading, that is, with exaggeration. Caricature, then, comes from the forcing, the exaggeration, of the basic principle of good description—the principle of the dominant impression. We see this most obviously in the work of many cartoonists: the strong chin of the luckless politician becomes as big as a shovel, the strong nose becomes a bulbous potato. But the same principle is an old resource of literature. Here is a famous example from Dickens, who delighted in the method:

Mr. Chadband is a large yellow man, with a fat smile, and a general appearance of having a good deal of train oil in his system. Mrs. Chadband is a stern, severe-looking, silent woman. Mr. Chadband moves softly and cumbrously, not unlike a bear who has been taught to walk upright. He is very much embarrassed about the arms, as if they were inconvenient to him, and he wanted to grovel; is very much in a perspiration about the head; and never speaks without first putting up his great hand, as delivering a token to his hearers that he is going to edify them.

—CHARLES DICKENS: *Bleak House.*

Here the impression of oiliness and fattiness dominates the picture, first in a quite literal sense, but the literal oiliness becomes an interpretation of the character of Chadband; the smile is "fat," and his general manner is unctuous too, like that of a hypocritical preacher. In the following passage, the writer takes the trivial detail of Miss Plimsoll's nose—and the little drop of moisture at its tip—as the main feature of the comic and at the same time pitiful portrait of the poor old maid:

Miss Plimsoll's nose was sharp and pointed like that of Voltaire. It was also extremely sensitive to cold. When the thermometer fell below 60° it turned scarlet; below 50° it assumed a blue tinge with a little white morbid circle at the end; and at 40° it became sniffly and bore a permanent though precarious drop below its pointed tip. I remember with what interest I watched that drop as we drove from the station at Sofia. My parents went in front in the first carriage and Miss Plimsoll and I followed in the brougham. The night was cold and we drove along an endless windswept boulevard punctuated by street lamps. With the approach of each successive lamp Miss Plimsoll's pinched little face beside me would first be illuminated frontways, and then as we came opposite the lamp, spring into a sharp little silhouette, at the point of which the drop flashed and trembled like a diamond.

—HAROLD NICOLSON: "Miss Plimsoll," *Some People.*

■ APPLICATIONS

I   From the examples at the end of the chapter pick out one or more instances of caricature. Do the physical details suggest an interpretation of character?
II   Write a theme of some 400 words using the method of caricature. The following titles may offer an idea:

The Banker Who Is Every Inch a Banker
The Man Who Never Got Over Being a Major in the Marine Corps
The Perfect Professor
The Campus Big Shot
The Campus Revolutionary
The Novelist (or Poet) To-Be
Miss Grimes, of the Third Grade
A Lady Gym Teacher
The Perfect Gentleman
The Grind

The Phi Beta Kappa
The Little Charmer
The Campus Lover

Look into the sketches in your notebook for suggestions.

Choice of words [2]

The inexperienced writer tends to make adjectives bear the burden in description. He tends to overload his description with adjectives, thinking that he should specify all the qualities of the thing being presented. Such a writer forgets that suggestion is often better than enumeration and that the mere listing of qualities is not the best method of evoking an image in the reader's mind. Let us look at the following portrait:

> The woman's face was fat and shapeless, so fat that it looked very soft, flabby, grayish, and unhealthy. The features were blurred because her face was fat. But her small, black, glistening eyes had a quick inquisitive motion as they moved from one face to another while the visitors stated their errand.

In that description the writer has piled up the adjectives, trying to specify each of the qualities of the woman's face and eyes. The result is a rather confused impression. Let us now take the passage as William Faulkner originally wrote it (before we tampered with it):

> Her eyes, lost in the fatty ridges of her face, looked like two small pieces of coal pressed into a lump of dough as they moved from one face to another while the visitors stated their errand.
>
> —WILLIAM FAULKNER: "A Rose for Emily."

Here the writer has managed to dispense with most of the adjectives, for the word *dough* implies *soft, flabby, grayish, shapeless, blurred,* and (when associated with flesh) *unhealthy,* and the word *coal* implies *black* and *glistening.* The use of a comparison will frequently enable the writer to dispense with adjectives. But when the writer does use adjectives, he should be sure that each adjective really adds something essential to the description. Rather than give the list of adjectives above, one could simply say that the face was "fat and doughy."

The discussion above really returns us to the question of selection. But here we are talking about diction—the selection of words rather than details. Although adjectives are an essential part of every writer's equipment, one can frequently get greater vividness by using nouns, adverbs, verbs, and verbals. For instance, note the descriptive force of the italicized nouns in the following examples:

---

[2] See Diction, pp. 396–434.

The very smoke coming out of their chimneys was poverty-stricken. Little *rags* and *shreds* of smoke, so unlike the great silvery *plumes* that uncurled from the Sheridans' chimneys.

—KATHERINE MANSFIELD: "The Garden Party."

They crept up the hill in the twilight and entered the cottage. It was built of *mud-walls,* the surface of which had been washed by many rains into *channels* and *depressions* that left none of the original flat *face* visible: while here and there in the thatch above a rafter showed like a *bone* protruding through the *skin.* —THOMAS HARDY: "The Withered Arm."

And a wind blew there, tossing the withered tops of last year's grasses, and *mists* ran with the wind, and ragged *shadows* with the *mists,* and *mare's-tails* of clear *moonlight* among the *shadows,* so that now the boles of birches on the forest's edge beyond the fences were but opal *blurs* and now cut *alabaster.*

—WILBUR DANIEL STEELE: "How Beautiful with Shoes."

We can see that in these passages the nouns are of two kinds. First, there are those that simply point to some parts of the thing described, such as *channels, depressions, mists, shadows, moonlight.* Second, there are those that involve comparisons, such as *rags, shreds, alabaster, bone,* and *skin.*

When we turn to adverbs, we find that this part of speech sometimes enables a writer to get an effect with great economy by fusing the quality of a thing with its action. When Dickens writes, in describing Chadband, that he "moves softly and cumbrously, not unlike a bear who has been taught to walk upright," the adverbs *softly* and *cumbrously* give a much more vivid and immediate effect than would be possible if we broke up the description in the following fashion: "Mr. Chadband is soft, heavy, and awkward-looking. When he walks his motion is not unlike that of a bear that has been taught to walk upright." But adverbs, like other parts of speech, are subject to misuse. Vague, overworked "intensifiers" like *very, so,* and *really* often actually weaken the effect of a passage.

In the following description of a Mexican revolutionist who is (as we could know from the whole story from which the paragraph comes) both sentimental and cruel, energetic and self-indulgent, lazy and sinister, note how the details selected are expressive of that character:

Braggioni catches her glance *solidly* as if he had been waiting for it, leans forward, *balancing* his paunch between his spread knees, and sings with tremendous emphasis, *weighing* his words. He had, the song relates, no father and no mother, nor even a friend to console him; lonely as a wave of the sea he comes and goes, lonely as a wave. His mouth opens round and *yearns sideways,* his balloon cheeks grow oily with the labor of the song. He *bulges marvellously* in his expensive garments. Over his lavender collar, crushed upon a purple necktie, held by a diamond hoop; over his ammunition belt of tooled leather worked in silver, buckled *cruelly* around his gaping middle; over the tops of his glossy yellow shoes

Braggioni *swells* with ominous ripeness, his mauve silk hose stretched taut, his ankles bound with the stout leather thongs of his shoes.

When he *stretches* his eyelids at Laura she notes again that his eyes are tawny yellow cat's eyes.

—KATHERINE ANNE PORTER: "Flowering Judas."

We have italicized the adverbs, verbs, and verbals that seem expressive. Think how right and unexpected the word *solidly* is as applied to the way Braggioni catches the girl's glance—the sense of his massiveness and imperviousness and, perhaps, brutality, and the sense, too, as indicated in the clause, "as if he had been waiting for it," of his being braced in calculation. Or think of the sense of theatricality in the image of the fat man twisting his mouth sideways in his sentimental song, a song unlike his real nature. If the writer had merely said that he had opened his round mouth in song, we wouldn't have much to stir our imagination, the description would lack expressiveness. Or take *marvellously* and *cruelly*, and consider what they imply not only about the visual image but about the personality of the man.

In the use of verbs, the same concentration of effect is possible; for frequently the right verb can imply something about the nature of the thing or person performing an action as well as about the nature of the action. For instance, the verbs *yearns* and *bulges* are extremely important. *Yearns* implies the sentimental expression on the fat revolutionist's face, and *bulges* implies the brute heft of the man, in contrast to the sentimental song he sings. So the two verbs here really indicate the contrast in his nature as well as in his appearance. What is the significance of the other verbs?

In the following passage, which describes a herd of wild horses corralled in a barn lot, note how the variety and accuracy of the italicized verbs and verbals give the impression of furious, aimless motion and define the atmosphere of violence of the scene:

"Come on, grab a holt," the Texan said. Eck grasped the wire also. The horses *laid* back against it, the pink faces *tossing* above the *backsurging* mass. "Pull him up, pull him up," the Texan said sharply. "They couldn't get up here in the wagon even if they wanted to." The wagon moved gradually backward until the head of the first horse was *snubbed* up to the tail-gate. The Texan took a turn of wire quickly about one of the wagon stakes. "Keep the slack out of it," he said. He *vanished* and *reappeared,* almost in the same second, with a pair of heavy wire-cutters. "Hold them like that," he said, and *leaped.* He *vanished,* broad hat, *flapping* vest, wire-cutters and all, into a kaleidoscopic maelstrom of long teeth and wild eyes and *slashing* feet, from which presently the horses began to burst, one by one like partridges *flushing,* each wearing a necklace of barbed wire. The first one crossed the lot at top speed, on a straight line. It *galloped* into the fence without any diminution whatever. The wire *gave, recovered,* and *slammed* the horse to earth where it lay for a moment, *glaring,* its legs still *galloping* in air. It scrambled up without having ceased to gallop and crossed the lot and *galloped* into the opposite fence and was *slammed* again to earth. The others were now freed. They *whipped* and *whirled* about the lot like dizzy fish in a bowl. It had seemed like a big lot until now, but now the very idea that all that fury and motion should be transpiring inside any one fence was something to be repudiated with contempt like a mirror trick.   —WILLIAM FAULKNER: *The Hamlet.*

We see from these examples that the choice of words for descriptive effect can be extremely complicated; and it is especially important to realize that the interaction of the parts of speech, this interpenetration of function, is not merely to give variety but is related to the very nature of perception. When the author looked at the horses surging in the lot, he perceived the scene totally. He did not see a horse, then add color to it, and then add motion, and then add a description of the motion. He perceived everything at once. This interaction and interpenetration of which we speak in reference to the use of language is simply a way of rendering the unity—what we have earlier called the massiveness—of perception (p. 281). This rendering conforms to the nature of the experience, to its vividness and immediacy.

■ APPLICATIONS

I Write a brief description (250 words) of some action to illustrate the unity of perception.

II In the passage by D. H. Lawrence (p. 307) at the end of this chapter, locate some adjectives, nouns, adverbs, and verbs that you think are used with strong descriptive effect. In each case try to explain what makes the word effective. How would you characterize the atmosphere of the passage? Repeat this process for the selection from Baldwin (pp. 858–67).

Texture and Pattern in Description

Thus far in this chapter we have been concerned with the observation of details, the relation of such details to a dominant impression of the thing described, and the choice of words in giving a description. We may call the combination of these three things the *texture* of description.

In so far as the details of description relate to the dominant impression, they have some principle of order, and in the last analysis the relation of details to the dominant impression is the most important single consideration. But we must also think of the way details are grouped in relation to the structure of the thing described—whatever that thing is, a landscape, an object, a human face. We cannot simply list details at random, even when they do contribute to a dominant impression. There must be some principle of *pattern*.

Pattern and point of view

If one observes a person, an object, or a scene, one notes that each has its proper unity—in a flash we recognize a friend, a tree, a familiar room, a meadow with woods beyond. But if, when we set out to describe one of these things, we give a mere catalogue of unrelated details, a mere enumeration of this, that, and the other, the sense of vital unity is gone.

The reason is clear. When we look at something, even though our attention is focused on some one aspect, we are constantly aware of the totality; it is all there before us at one time. In description, however, the details are presented to us one after another; instead of the simultaneous presentation that we find in actuality, we now have presentation in sequence. Since simultaneous presentation is impossible in description, if the writer is to give the details a proper unity, he must provide some pattern into which the reader can fit them.

When we are dealing with visual description, which is by far the most common kind, it helps to give an impression of unity if we think of whatever is being described as seen by an observer. We need not specify the observer literally in the description; we may merely imply such a presence by the way we present the details. We simply ask how, under such-and-such conditions and from such-and-such a location, an observer would see the details.

FIXED OBSERVER

The most obvious and simple pattern is to assume an observer at some fixed point from which he views the whole scene or object and then reads off the details from left to right, from foreground to background, from bottom to top, or in some such way. In other words, we simply take the details as they come in the object itself, starting from some arbitrary point. Here is an example from a theme:

> When I went home from college for Christmas, I got in on the night train, and as soon as the excitement wore off, I went straight upstairs to bed in my old room, where I had been ever since my baby days. I was so sleepy I didn't see a thing. I just tumbled in. But I woke up early. I couldn't hear a sound in the house, and so I lay there idly just looking around. Suddenly I felt as though this were the first time I had ever been in that room, it was so strange.
>
> Way at the left of my range of vision was the closet, with the door open, the way I must have left it the night before. Inside I could see my summer dresses hanging up in covers, all neat as a pin, and my shoes on racks. I remembered how untidy I had left things and thought that my mother must

have done that for me. Next was my dressing table, almost bare, for I had taken a lot of things with me to college, but what was there was in order, laid out to the quarter of an inch on the glass top. Around the mirror were still stuck some invitations and things, keepsakes from my last year in high school. Then on the wall was a water color I had done in art class, and it was awful—a river too blue, I knew now, and a sunset like a fried egg with catsup.

Then I looked out the window, turning my head on the pillow just a little toward the wall opposite the bed, and I could see the blue patch of sky, no clouds at all, and the snow on the steep, jumbled-up roofs of the Madison place, which is very Victorian, with sharp roofs and little turrets, with lightning rods and weathervanes. You know the kind of place, for every town has a few left. I wondered about Jack Madison, for on the wall just to the right of the window was the Harvard pennant he had given me last summer because he was going to be a freshman at Harvard. I thought now that he was probably ashamed of that, as kid stuff.

Beyond the pennant was my high school picture, the ordinary kind, with the boys looking awful stiff and trying to be grown-up, and the girls all cocking their heads trying to look glamorous like movie stars. I sort of smiled, looking at them, they were so kid-looking and unsophisticated, you might say. Then, all at once I thought that I was in the picture, too, and the silliest one of the lot. I blushed to think how silly. Then suddenly I felt sad. It was as though I had died, that was why everything was so tidy in the room, and I was somebody else who happened to be sleeping in a strange room where somebody else used to live and had died.

The girl who writes the theme has a general idea, of course. She is now grown-up and away at college, and she wants to tell how she feels when she comes back home for the first time. This idea provides the dominant impression she is trying to give: the sense of strangeness and, also, the awareness of a kind of loss. But what we are concerned with at the moment is not the impression she wants to convey, but the way the details that produce the impression are put into order. The order she uses is almost the simplest possible: as she lies on her pillow her glance moves from left to right, and she simply lists the things she sees.

Here is another example, written not by a student this time, but by a famous writer. He is addressing an imaginary companion—the reader— who is supposed to stand by his side looking up at an English cathedral. But the author here, though his description is much more elaborate than that in the girl's theme, uses the same basic pattern, listing items in the simple order of observation, this time from bottom to top.

And so, taking care not to tread on the grass, we will go along the straight walk to the west front, and there stand for a time, looking up at its deep-pointed porches and the dark places between their pillars where there were statues once, and where fragments, here and there, of a stately figure are still left, which has in it the likeness of a king, perhaps indeed a king on earth, perhaps a saintly king long ago in heaven; and so higher

and higher up to the great mouldering wall of rugged sculpture and confused arcades, shattered, and grey, and grisly with head of dragons and
mocking fiends, worn by the rain and swirling winds into yet unseemlier
shape, and coloured on their stony scales by the deep russet-orange lichen,
melancholy gold; and so, higher still, to the bleak towers, so far above
that the eye loses itself among the bosses of their traceries, though they are
rude and strong, and only sees, like a drift of eddying black points, now
closing, now scattering, and now settling suddenly into invisible places
among the bosses and flowers, the crowd of restless birds that fill the whole
square with that strange clangour of theirs, so harsh and yet so soothing,
like the cries of birds on a solitary coast between the cliffs and sea.

—JOHN RUSKIN: *The Stones of Venice.*

MOVING OBSERVER

The two pieces of description above have been given from a fixed point—
the girl's pillow when she wakes up and the open space at the west front of a
cathedral in England. But often we find it useful to think of a moving observer—either a specified observer or one not specified, merely assumed.
In the following example a person (the author) is climbing up a gorge in
Arabia, over a pass, and down the other side. He reports things simply as
he comes to them.

> Our path took us between the Sakhara and the Sukhur by a narrow gorge
> with sandy floor and steep bare walls. Its head was rough. We had to scram-
> ble up shelves of coarse-faced stone, and along a great fault in the hill-side
> between two tilted red reefs of hard rock. The summit of the pass was a
> knife-edge, and from it we went down an encumbered gap, half-blocked
> by one fallen boulder which had been hammered over with the tribal marks
> of all the generations of men who had used this road. Afterwards there
> opened tree-grown spaces, collecting grounds in winter for the sheets of
> rain which poured off the glazed sides of the Sukhur. There were granite
> outcrops here and there, and a fine silver sand underfoot in the still damp
> water-channels. The drainage was towards Heiran.
>
> —T. E. LAWRENCE: *Seven Pillars of Wisdom.*[3]

In the excerpt above, the observer is specified. But the same method, of
course, may be used with an implied observer in motion, as in this theme:

> The approach to ——— is anything but attractive, and it is made worse
> by the contrast with the nice hilly country the road has just passed through,
> where there are lots of woods and streams. The first thing one sees on the
> approach is a paper mill, where they convert the pulp. It is a big, sprawly,
> disorderly looking mass of buildings, two of them very high. They are
> drab colored. The smell is awful, and what they do to Techifaloo River is
> a caution, for the waste goes in there.
> After the paper plant come the real slums of the town. They are mostly
> shacks, but farther on are quite a few very nice houses, with good lawns

---

[3] From *Seven Pillars of Wisdom,* by T. E. Lawrence. Copyright 1926, 1935 by Doubleday
& Company, Inc. Reprinted by permission of the publisher.

and flowerbeds. This is where the skilled workers live. Next comes the new hospital, a really fine brick structure.

The warehouse section begins not far beyond the hospital, for here is where the railroads from the east cross the Techifaloo. . . .

There is some incidental comment and opinion here, along with the description, but the description itself is patterned by the eye of an unspecified observer assumed to be entering the town by the highway.

In the following description of the main street of a small Midwestern town, no observer is specified. The details are pointed out, one after another, not even put in complete sentences, merely listed, jotted down as they appear. (This loose method, the use of jottings as a style of presentation, is called *impressionistic*.) The whole effect is as though a movie camera has simply swung over the street, picking up a detail here, a detail there.

> From a second-story window the sign, "W. P. Kennicott, Phys. & Surgeon," gilt on black sand.
> A small wooden motion-picture theater called "The Rosebud Movie Palace." Lithographs announcing a film called, "Fatty in Love."
> Howland & Gould's Grocery. In the display window, black, overripe bananas and lettuce on which a cat was sleeping. Shelves lined with red crepe paper which was now faded and torn and concentrically spotted. Flat against the wall of the second story the signs of the lodges—the Knights of Pythias, the Maccabees, the Woodmen, the Masons.
> Dahl & Oleson's Meat Market—a reek of blood.
> —SINCLAIR LEWIS: *Main Street.*

The pure impressionistic method, the use of jottings as a style of presentation, seems easy, and therefore tempting—not only are we free of the problem of the order of presentation of detail, we don't have to bother with sentence structure or even with paragraph structure. But the very easiness is a danger. It is easy to be tedious, to accumulate too many details, to lose all sense of structure and of a dominant impression. To be effective in this method we have to be very careful that the details are telling, are sharp, and we must not pile up so many details that the sense of a whole is lost.

Here is a modified example of the impressionistic method, with the details of the modern city of Morelia, in Mexico, mixed with a series of impressions. But observe how the details are subtly related to the notion of the history of the place and to the comparison with Spain. The last detail, the white face powder, sums up the history.

> Under next morning's sun, Morelia does not look like Avila and autumnal Castille. All the same it is very Spanish. A town of under fifty thousand, architecturally homogeneous, of long lines of arcades and seventeenth-century façades, compact, grey, handsome, dwindling into

mud huts, ending abruptly in unbroken countryside. It is quiet after Mexico City, serene by day and melancholy by night. There is nothing particular to see. From the hotel roof, the view over the plain is enchanting. The inside of the Cathedral is decorated to the last square inch in eighteen-ninety polychrome. Christ wears a wig of real hair, the Saints' tears are pearly beads, the Martyrs' blood lozenges of crimson wax, and all the images are kissed to a high polish. Before Independence, Morelia was called Valladolid, Valladolid of Michoacán. Yes, it is very Spanish, but it is not Spain. Like the Puritans on New England, the Spaniards impressed themselves on Mexico. Both settled in a part of the continent whose climate and countryside was familiar and congenial. Both established their language, their religion and a style of building. However, unlike the Puritans, the Spaniards did not eliminate the Indians. In fact, the Indians have about eliminated them. There are now supposed to be only some forty thousand Whites left in a population of three million pure Indians and seventeen million Mestizos, and many of even these Whites are white only by courtesy or the use of face powder.

—SYBILLE BEDFORD: *The Sudden View*.[4]

Pattern by interest

Thus far, except when dealing with the impressionistic method, we have been talking of unifying a description by assuming an observer who sees the details of the object in some physical order—say from left to right, or as he comes to them while moving. But let us assume an observer who is less passive, who brings some strong interest to the thing described. This interest then gives us the unity for describing the object. Here is a soldier inspecting a bridge he is about to dynamite. The structure of the bridge and the location of the enemy defenses give focus to the description.

> The late afternoon sun that still came over the brown shoulder of the mountain showed the bridge dark against the steep emptiness of the gorge. It was a steel bridge of a single span and there was a sentry box at each end. It was wide enough for two motor cars to pass and it spanned, in solid-flung metal grace, a deep gorge at the bottom of which, far below, a brook leaped in white water through rocks and boulders down to the main stream of the pass.
>
> The sun was in Robert Jordan's eyes and the bridge showed only in outline. Then the sun lessened and was gone and looking up through the trees at the brown, rounded height that it had gone behind, he saw, now that he no longer looked into the glare, that the mountain slope was a delicate new green and that there were patches of old snow under the crest.
>
> Then he was looking at the bridge again in the sudden short trueness of the little light that would be left, and studying its construction. The prob-

[4] Reprinted from p. 82 in *The Sudden View* by Sybille Bedford (Harper & Row, 1953) by permission of Harper & Row, Publishers. Reprinted by permission of Sybille Bedford.

lem of its demolition was not difficult. As he watched he took out a note-book from his breast pocket and made several quick line sketches. As he made the drawings he did not figure the charges. He would do that later. Now he was noting the points where the explosive should be placed in order to cut the support of the span and drop a section of it back into the gorge. It could be done unhurriedly, scientifically and correctly with a half dozen charges laid and braced to explode simultaneously; or it could be done roughly with two big ones. They would need to be very big ones, on opposite sides and should go at the same time.

—ERNEST HEMINGWAY: *For Whom the Bell Tolls*.[5]

Here the dynamiter's interest in the bridge holds the passage together. In the passage below, the comparison that Huckleberry Finn draws between houses in town and the house of the Grangerford plantation provides the unifying interest.

It was a mighty nice family, and a mighty nice house, too. I hadn't seen no house out in the country before that was so nice and had so much style. It didn't have an iron latch on the front door, nor a wooden one with a buckskin string, but a brass knob to turn, the same as houses in a town. There warn't no bed in the parlor, nor a sign of a bed; but heaps of parlors in towns has beds in them. There was a big fireplace that was bricked on the bottom, and the bricks was kept clean and red by pouring water on them and scrubbing them with another brick; sometimes they washed them over with red water-paint that they call Spanish-brown, same as they do in town. They had big brass dog-irons that could hold up a saw-log. There was a clock on the middle of the mantel piece, with a picture of a town painted on the bottom half of the glass front, and a round place in the middle of it for the sun, and you could see the pendulum swinging behind it.

—SAMUEL CLEMENS: *The Adventures of Huckleberry Finn*.

● CAUTION

Remember that, sometimes, the mood itself may serve as the device for unifying a description, as for instance in Dickens's description of the Ded-lock estate.

Frame image

So far we have been concerned with unifying description by reference to an observer, specified or unspecified, but the use of an observer is not the only possibility. For instance, a writer may compare the rather complicated object he is describing with something simpler and more easily visualized. This simpler object is then imagined as providing a kind of frame image into which we can fit the details of the original thing to be

---

[5] Reprinted with the permission of Charles Scribner's Sons from *For Whom the Bell Tolls* (Copyright 1940 Ernest Hemingway; renewal copyright © 1968 Mary Hemingway). Reprinted by permission of Jonathan Cape Ltd. and the Executors of the Ernest Hemingway Estate.

described. Here is the image of an arm used to give unity to an impression of Cape Cod:

> Cape Cod is the bared and bended arm of Massachusetts; the shoulder is Buzzard's Bay; the elbow, or crazy-bone, at Cape Mallebarre; the wrist at Truro; and the sand fist at Provincetown,—behind which the state stands on her guard, with her back to the Green Mountains, and her feet planted on the floor of the ocean, like an athlete protecting her Bay,— boxing with northeast storms, and, ever and anon, heaving up her Atlantic adversary from the lap of earth,—ready to thrust forward her other fist, which keeps guard while upon her breast at Cape Ann.
>
> —HENRY DAVID THOREAU: *Cape Cod.*

In this example, the writer has begun by providing the frame image; he then gives the details that are to be set in the frame. But sometimes the writer will reverse the process; that is, he will first give the details, perhaps a swarm of them, which stimulate and baffle the reader's imagination, and then give the frame image, which will suddenly reduce all to order. Here is a very simple example of the method in a student theme. The fact that an observer is involved is not relevant to the use of the frame image.

> My roommate is very fat and sort of bleared-looking. His eyes are large and round. They are the palest blue you ever saw, and they tend to be watery and blinking. His nose is shapeless, just a kind of aimless blob of putty stuck on his face, and his lips are so thick and sort of loose that his small mouth looks as though he is about to whistle or has just tasted a dill pickle and didn't like it too well. His hair is pale blond, almost albino but not quite, and it never lies in place. It isn't thick, but it is always scruffed up in all directions. He is the sort of person who is always sleepy, and when I wake him up in the morning and he lifts his head off the pillow, with that bleared look and his face so round, I always think of a moon coming up in a watery haze that blurs its shape and makes it lose its outline.

It is clear what the writer has done. He has given the details—eyes, nose, mouth, hair—and then absorbed them into one image, the round rising moon blurred in a watery haze. Of course, the image of the watery moon does contribute something to the dominant impression, the blurred, slow, confused appearance of the roommate, but it also gives a frame for putting the details in place; it pulls them together.

Mixed patterns

We have been trying to distinguish several ways of unifying description and have given examples of relatively simple and unmixed methods. But the methods can be mixed, and sometimes the most effective description does combine the methods, as in this passage:

About four in the morning, as the captain and Herrick sat together on the rail, there arose from the midst of the night, in front of them, the voice of the breakers. Each sprang to his feet and stared and listened. The sound was continuous, like the passing of a train; no rise or fall could be distinguished; minute by minute the ocean heaved with an equal potency against the invisible isle; and as time passed, and Herrick waited in vain for any vicissitude in the volume of that roaring, a sense of the eternal weighed upon his mind. To the expert eye, the isle itself was to be inferred from a certain string of blots along the starry heaven. And the schooner was laid to and anxiously observed till daylight.

There was little or no morning bank. A brightening came in the east; then a wash of some ineffable, faint, nameless hue between crimson and silver; and then coals of fire. These glimmered awhile on the sealine, and seemed to brighten and darken and spread out; and still the night and the stars reigned undisturbed. It was as though a spark should catch and glow and creep along the foot of some heavy and almost incombustible wall-hanging, and the room itself be scarcely menaced. Yet a little after, and the whole east glowed with gold and scarlet, and the hollow of heaven was filled with the daylight.

The isle—the undiscovered, the scarce believed in—now lay before them and close aboard; and Herrick thought that never in his dreams had he beheld anything more strange and delicate. The beach was excellently white, the continuous barrier of trees inimitably green; the land perhaps ten feet high, the trees thirty more. Every here and there, as the schooner coasted northward, the wood was intermitted; and he could see clear over the inconsiderable strip of land (as a man looks over a wall) to the lagoon within; and clear over that, again, to where the far side of the atoll prolonged its pencilling of trees against the morning sky. He tortured himself to find analogies. The isle was like the rim of a great vessel sunken in the waters; it was like the embankment of an annular railway grown upon with wood. So slender it seemed amidst the outrageous breakers, so frail and pretty, he would scarce have wondered to see it sink and disappear without a sound, and the waves close smoothly over its descent.

—ROBERT LOUIS STEVENSON: *The Ebb Tide.*

In this passage it is clear that we have a location and an observer specified. At one time, in the course of the description (the view across the atoll), we find the method of simple spatial ordering used, the method of the fixed point of view. At another time, the principle of sequence comes into play, the method of the moving point of view. In fact, it comes into play in two different ways. First, we have the principle of sequence in time, in the coming of dawn, and then we have it in space, as the schooner coasts northward along the island. But we also find the frame image used to give us a clearer notion of the island: Herrick, the observer, "tortured himself to find analogies," and to describe the atoll we find the frame images of the "rim of a great vessel sunken in the waters" and of the "embankment of an annular railway grown upon with wood." We may note that there is an organization in terms of climax, for only at the end of the passage as given here do we get the full statement of the frame image and of the basic mood, Herrick's response to the fragile and dreamlike beauty of the island, which is the dominant impression.

The use of a mixed method, certainly of a mixed method that employs as many individual methods as the above passage, offers certain difficulties to the inexperienced writer. By and large, it is better for the inexperienced writer to try the simpler approaches to his material, at least until he is confident that he understands the principles involved in the various methods and has acquired some skill in adapting them. But in reading it is useful to be aware of what more experienced writers have done. Intelligent observation is the basis of all our learning.

■ APPLICATIONS

I At the end of this chapter there are a number of descriptive passages. List the different types of patterns that are illustrated in them.

II Here are three exercises in description:

1 You are now sitting in a room. Look at your extreme left, then turn your eyes slowly from left to right. What do you see? Describe what you see, nothing more, nothing less, in order, in perhaps 150 to 200 words. What impression, what mood if any, seems dominant as you read your paragraph? What mood or impression strikes you as you look about you again? With this in mind, revise what you have written.

2 Think of your home town, the block you live on, or some familiar spot. Imagine that you are approaching it. What do you see, item by item, and in what order? What feelings and ideas suggest themselves as you imagine approaching the scene? Write a paragraph or two of description, with the objects and your feelings in mind.

3 You have some special interest. You hunt, you fish, you play baseball, you collect postage stamps, you watch birds, you watch people. Think of some scene or occasion that appealed to your special interest. Then write a description of that, using your interest as the device for giving the scene unity.

III This exercise comes later, perhaps a day or a week. You now have your grade on the work requested above. Read over what you have written, and at the same time try to remember your imagined subject and your feelings about your subject. Do the words now before you give you an impression of that subject and of your feelings about it? Be honest with yourself. If you are dissatisfied with what you have written, how would you now improve it?

Selections

On the following pages are a number of examples of description. These have already been referred to in Applications in this chapter, and your instructor may frame new problems for investigation. For review, however, the following suggestions may be helpful:

1   Locate instances of appeals to different senses. What words, phrases, and comparisons make such appeals?
2   Find instances of several types of pattern.
3   Are there any instances of caricature?
4   In instances in which description is used to suggest a character, an atmosphere, or a state of feeling, try to state in your own words what the character, atmosphere, or state of feeling is. What details contribute to your impression?
5   Locate a number of comparisons. Which are used for vividness? Which are used for interpretive significance? Are there any that seem too strained to be effective? Are there any that seem stale?

A   A knot of country boys, gabbling at one another like starlings, shrilled a cheer as we came rattling over a stone bridge beneath which a stream shallowly washed its bank of osiers.

    —WALTER DE LA MARE: *Memoirs of a Midget.*

B   Charmian is a hatchet faced, terra cotta colored little goblin, swift in her movements, and neatly finished at the hands and feet.

    —GEORGE BERNARD SHAW: *Caesar and Cleopatra.*

C   Without being robust, her health was perfect, her needlework exquisite, her temper equable and calm; she loved and was loved by her girlfriends, she read romantic verses and select novels; above all, she danced. That was the greatest pleasure in life for her; not for the sake of her partners— those were surely only round dances, and the partners didn't count; what counted was the joy of motion, the sense of treading lightly, in perfect time, a sylph in spotless muslin, enriched with a ribbon or flower, playing discreetly with her fan, and sailing through the air with feet that seemed scarcely to touch the ground.

    —GEORGE SANTAYANA: *Persons and Places.*

D   Leaning over the parapet, he enjoyed, once more, the strangely intimate companionship of the sea. He glanced down into the water, whose uneven floor was diapered with long weedy patches, fragments of fallen rock, and brighter patches of sand; he inhaled the pungent odor of sea wrack and listened to the breathings of the waves. They lapped softly against the rounded boulders which strewed the shore like a flock of nodding Behemoths. He remembered his visits at daybreak to the beach—those unspoken confidences with the sunlit element to whose friendly caresses he had abandoned his body. How calm it was, too, in this evening light. Near at hand, somewhere, lay a sounding cave; it sang a melody of moist content. Shadows lengthened; fishing boats, moving outward for the night-work, steered darkly across the luminous river at his feet. Those jewel-like morning tints of blue and green had faded from the water; the southern cliff-scenery, projections of it, caught a fiery glare. Bastions of flame. . . .

The air seemed to have become unusually cool and bracing.

—NORMAN DOUGLAS: *South Wind.*

E   So the day has taken place, all the visionary business of the day. The young cattle stand in the straw of the stack yard, the sun gleams on their white fleece, the eyes of Io, and the man with the side-whiskers carries more yellow straw into the compound. The sun comes in all down one side, and above, in the sky, all the gables and grey stone chimney-stacks are floating in pure dreams.

There is threshed wheat smouldering in the great barn, the fire of life: and the sound of the threshing machine, running, drumming.

The threshing machine, running, drumming, waving its steam in a corner of a great field, the rapid nucleus of darkness beside the yellow ricks: and the rich plough-land comes up, ripples up in endless grape-colored ripples, like a tide of procreant desire: the machine sighs and drums, wind blows the chaff in little eddies, blows the clothes of the men on the ricks close against their limbs: the men on the stacks in the wind against a bare blue heaven, their limbs blown clean in contour naked shapely animated fragments of earth active in heaven.

Coming home, by the purple and crimson hedges, red with berries, up hill over the heavy ground to the stone, old three-pointed house with its raised chimney-stacks, the old manor lifting its fair, pure stone amid trees and foliage, rising from the lawn, we pass the pond where white ducks hastily launch upon the lustrous dark grey waters.

So up the steps to the porch, through the doorway, and into the interior, fragrant with all the memories of old age, and of bygone, remembered lustiness.   —D. H. LAWRENCE: *Letters.*[6]

F   When I say they [the gondoliers of Venice] are associated with its [the city's] silence, I should immediately add that they are associated also with its sound. Among themselves they are extraordinarily talkative company. They chatter at the *traghetti* [landings], where they always have some sharp point under discussion; they bawl across the canals; they bespeak your commands as you approach; they defy each other from afar. If you happen to have a *traghetto* under your window, you are well aware that they are a vocal race. I should even go farther than I went just now, and say that the voice of the gondolier is, in fact, the voice of Venice. There is scarcely any other, and that, indeed, is part of the interest of the place. There is no noise there save distinctly human noise; no rumbling, no vague uproar, no rattle of wheels and hoofs. It is all articulate, personal sound. One may say, indeed, that Venice is, emphatically, the city of conversa-

---

[6] From *The Letters of D. H. Lawrence* edited by Aldous Huxley. Copyright 1932 by the Estate of D. H. Lawrence, copyright © renewed 1960 by Angelo Ravagli and C. Montague Weekley, Executors of the Estate of Frieda Lawrence Ravagli. Reprinted by permission of The Viking Press, Inc. Reprinted by permission of Laurence Pollinger Limited and the Estate of the late Mrs. Frieda Lawrence.

tion; people talk all over the place, because there is nothing to interfere with their being heard. Among the populace it is a kind of family party. The still water carries the voice, and good Venetians exchange confidences at a distance of half a mile. It saves a world of trouble, and they don't like trouble. Their delightful garrulous language helps them to make Venetian life a long *conversazione*. This language, with its soft elisions, its odd transpositions, its kindly contempt for consonants and other disagreeables, has in it something peculiarly human and accommodating.

—HENRY JAMES: "Venice," *Portraits of Places*.

G   The dress of the rider and the accouterments of his horse, were peculiarly unfit for the traveller in such a country. A coat of linked mail, with long sleeves, plated gauntlets, and a steel breastplate, had not been esteemed sufficient weight of armor; there was also his triangular shield suspended round his neck, and his barred helmet of steel, over which he had a hood and collar of mail, which was drawn around the warrior's shoulders and throat, and filled up the vacancy between the hauberk and the headpiece. His lower limbs were sheathed, like his body, in flexible mail, securing the legs and thighs, while the feet rested in plated shoes, which corresponded with the gauntlets. A long, broad, straight-shaped, double-edged falchion, with a handle formed like a cross, corresponded with a stout poniard on the other side. The Knight also bore, secured to his saddle, with one end resting on his stirrup, the long steel-headed lance, his own proper weapon, which, as he rode, projected backwards, and displayed its little pennoncelle, to dally with the faint breeze, or drop in the dead calm.

—WALTER SCOTT: *The Talisman*.

H   Say that I had walked and wandered by unknown roads, and suddenly, after climbing a gentle hill, had seen before me for the first time the valley of Usk, just above Newbridge. I think it was on one of those strange days in summer when the sky is at once so grey and luminous that I achieved this adventure. There are no clouds in the upper air, the sky is simply covered with a veil which is, as I say, both grey and luminous, and there is no breath of wind, and every leaf is still.

But now and again as the day goes on the veil will brighten, and the sun almost appear; and then here and there in the woods it is as if white moons were descending. On such a day, then, I saw that wonderful and most lovely valley; the Usk, here purged of its muddy tidal waters, now like the sky, grey and silvery and luminous, winding in mystic esses, and the dense forest bending down to it, and the grey stone bridge crossing it. Down the valley in the distance was Caerleon-on-Usk; over the hill, somewhere in the lower slopes of the forest, Caerwent, also a Roman city, was buried in the earth, and gave up now and again strange relics—fragments of the temple of "Nodens, god of the depths." I saw the lonely house between the dark forest and the silver river, and years after I wrote "The Great God Pan," an endeavor to pass on the vague, indefinable sense of awe and mystery and terror that I had received.

—ARTHUR MACHEN: *Far Off Things*.

I   Ratmiroff gazed gloomily after his wife—even then he could not fail to observe the enchanting grace of her figure, or her movements—and crushing his cigarette with a heavy blow against the marble slab of the chimney-piece, he flung it far from him. His cheeks suddenly paled, a convulsive quiver flitted across his chin, and his eyes wandered dully and fiercely over the floor, as though in search of something. . . . Every trace of elegance had vanished from his face. That must have been the sort of expression it had assumed when he flogged the White Russian peasants.

—IVAN TURGENEV: *Smoke.*

J   He was a Mr. Cornelius Vanslyperken, a tall, meagre-looking personage, with very narrow shoulders and very small head. Perfectly straight up and down, protruding in no part, he reminded you of some tall parish pump, with a great knob at its top. His face was gaunt, cheeks hollow, nose and chin showing an affection for each other, and evidently lamenting the gulf between them which prevented their meeting. Both appear to have fretted themselves to the utmost degree of tenuity from disappointment in love; as for the nose, it had a pearly round tear hanging at its tip, as if it wept.

—FREDERICK MARRYAT: *The Dog Fiend.*

K   Her heart seemed so full, that it spilt its new gush of happiness, as it were, like rich and sunny wine out of an overbrimming goblet.

—NATHANIEL HAWTHORNE: *The Marble Faun.*

L   But I eat. I gradually lose all knowledge of particulars as I eat. I am becoming weighed down with food. These delicious mouthfuls of roast duck, fitly piled with vegetables, following each other in exquisite rotation of warmth, weight, sweet and bitter, past my palate, down my gullet, into my stomach, have established my body. I feel quiet, gravity, control. All is solid now. Instinctively my palate now requires and anticipates sweetness and lightness, something sugared and evanescent; and cool wine, fitting glove-like over those finer nerves that seem to tremble from the roof of my mouth and make it spread (as I drink) into a domed cavern, green with vine leaves, musk-scented, purple with grapes. Now I can look steadily into the mill-race that foams beneath. By what particular name are we to call it? Let Rhoda speak, whose face I see reflected mistily in the looking-glass opposite; Rhoda whom I interrupted when she rocked her petals in a brown basin, asking for the pocket-knife that Bernard had stolen. Love is not a whirl-pool to her. She is not giddy when she looks down. She looks far away over our heads, beyond India. —VIRGINIA WOOLF: *The Waves.*

M   The nether sky opens and Europe is disclosed as a prone and emaciated figure, the Alps shaping like a backbone, and the branching mountain-chains like ribs, the peninsular plateau of Spain forming a head. Broad and lengthy lowlands stretch from the north of France across Russia like a grey-green garment hemmed by the Ural mountains and the glistening Arctic Ocean.   —THOMAS HARDY: *The Dynasts.*

N   I studied M. de Charlus. The tuft of his grey hair, the eye, the brow of which was raised by his monocle to emit a smile, the red flowers in his buttonhole formed, so to speak, the three mobile apices of a convulsive and striking triangle.   —MARCEL PROUST: *The Guermantes Way.*

O   In search of a place proper for this, I found a little plain on the side of a rising hill, whose front towards this little plain was steep as a house-side, so that nothing could come down upon me from the top; on the side of this rock there was a hollow place, worn a little way in, like the entrance or door of a cave; but there was not really any cave, or way into the rock at all.

On the flat of the green, just before this hollow place, I resolved to pitch my tent. This plain was not above an hundred yards broad, and about twice as long, and lay like a green before my door, and at the end of it descended irregularly every way down into the low grounds by the seaside. It was on the NNW. side of the hill, so that I was sheltered from the heat every day, till it came to a W. and by S. sun, or thereabouts, which in those countries is near the setting.   —DANIEL DEFOE: *Robinson Crusoe.*

P   We live on a large farm in southern Tuscany—twelve miles from the station and five from the nearest village. The country is wild and lonely; the climate harsh. Our house stands on a hillside, looking down over a wide and beautiful valley, beyond which rises Monte Amieta, wooded with chestnuts and beeches. Nearer by, on this side of the valley, lie slopes of cultivated land—wheat, olives, and vines. Among them still stand some ridges of dust-colored clay hillocks, the *crete senesi,* as bare and colorless as elephants' backs, as mountains of the moon. The wide riverbed in the valley holds a rushing stream in the rainy season, but during the summer a mere trickle, in a wide desert of stones. Then, when the wheat ripens and the alfalfa has been cut, the last patches of green disappear from the landscape. The whole valley becomes dust-colored—a land without mercy, without shade. If you sit under an olive tree you are not shaded; the leaves are like little flickering tongues of fire. At evening and morning the distant hills are misty and blue, but under one's feet the dry earth is hard. The cry of the cicadas shrills in the noonday.   —IRIS ORIGO: *War in Val d'Orcia.*

Q   The drover waved his staff and scrabbled away over the rocks like a thin gnome. Holme sat for a while and then rose and followed along the ridge toward the gap where the hogs were crossing.

The gap was narrow and when he got to it he could see the hogs welled up in a clamorous and screeching flume that fanned again on the far side in a high meadow skirting the bluff of the river. They were wheeling faster and wider out along the sheer rim of the bluff in an arc of dusty uproar and he could hear the drovers below him calling and he could see the dead gray serpentine of the river below that. Hogs were pouring through the gap and building against the ones in the meadow until these began to buckle at the edges. Holme saw two of them pitch screaming in stiff-legged pirouettes a hundred feet into the river. He moved down the slope toward the bluff and the road that went along it. Drovers were racing brokenly across the milling hogs with staves aloft, stumbling and falling among them, making for the outer perimeter to head them from the cliff. This swept a new wave of panic among the hogs like wind through grass until a whole echelon of them careering up the outer flank forsook the land and faired into space with torn cries. Now the entire herd had begun to wheel wider and faster along the bluff and the outermost ranks swung centrifugally over the escarpment row on row wailing and squealing and above this the howls and curses of the drovers that now upreared in the moil of flesh they tended and swept with dust had begun to assume satanic looks with their staves and wild eyes as if they were no true swineherds but disciples of darkness got among these charges to herd them to their doom.

Holme rushed to higher ground like one threatened with flood and perched upon a rock there to view the course of things. The hogs were in full stampede. One of the drovers passed curiously erect as though braced with a stick and rotating slowly with his arms outstretched in the manner of a dancing sleeper. Hogs were beginning to wash up on the rock, their hoofs clicking and rasping and with harsh snorts. Holme recoiled to the rock's crown and watched them. The drover who had spoken to him swept past with bowed back and hands aloft, a limp and ragged scarecrow flailing briefly in that rabid frieze so that Holme saw tilted upon him for just a moment out of the dust and pandemonium two walled eyes beyond hope and a dead mouth beyond prayer, borne on like some old gospel recreant seized sevenfold in the flood of his own nether invocations or grotesque hero bobbing harried and unwilling on the shoulders of a mob stricken in their iniquity to the very shape of evil until he passed over the rim of the bluff and dropped in his great retinue of hogs from sight.

Holme blinked and shook his head. The hogs boiled past squealing and plunging and the chalky red smoke of their passage hung over the river and stained the sky with something of sunset. They had begun to veer from the bluff and to swing in a long arc upriver. The drovers all had sought shelter among the trees and Holme could see a pair of them watching the herd pass with looks of indolent speculation, leaning upon their staves and nodding in mute agreement as if there were some old injustice being righted in this spectacle of headlong bedlam.

When the last of the hogs had gone in a rapidly trebling thunder and the ochreous dust had drifted from the torn ground and there was nothing but quaking silence about him Holme climbed gingerly from his rock. Some drovers were coming from the trees and three pink shoats labored up over the rim of the hill with whimpering sounds not unlike kittens and bobbed past and upriver over the gently smoking land like creatures in a dream.

—CORMAC MC CARTHY: *Outer Dark*.[7]

R   The Prince's dark blue eyes were of the finest, and, on occasion, precisely resembled nothing so much as the high windows of a Roman palace, of an historic front by one of the great old designers, thrown open on a feast-day to the golden air. His look itself, at such times, suggested an image—that of some very noble personage who, expected, acclaimed by the crowd in the street and with old precious stuffs falling over the sill for his support, had gaily and gallantly come to show himself; always moreover less in his own interest than in that of spectators and subjects whose need to admire, even to gape, was periodically to be considered. The young man's expression became, after this fashion, something vivid and concrete—a beautiful personal presence, that of a prince in very truth, a ruler, warrior, patron, lighting up brave architecture and diffusing the sense of a function. It had been happily said of his face that the figure thus appearing in the great frame was the ghost of some proudest ancestor. Whoever the ancestor now, at all events, the Prince was, for Mrs. Assingham's benefit, in view of the people. He seemed, leaning on crimson damask, to take in the bright day.   —HENRY JAMES: *The Golden Bowl.*

CHAPTER **9**

Narration

Narration is the kind of discourse concerned with action, with events in time, with life in motion. It answers the question "What happened?" It tells a story. As we use the word here, a story is a sequence of events—historically true or false—so presented that the imagination is stimulated. This is not a full account of what we mean by narration, but it is enough to start with.[1]

The kind of narration we are concerned with here is to be sharply distinguished from expository narration, which characteristically appeals to the understanding (pp. 142–43). Let us, for an extreme contrast, set the directions for gluing felt to wood, which we have earlier given as an example of expository narration (p. 143), against a fairy tale, say Hans Christian Andersen's "The Tinder Box." After reading this piece of expository narration, anyone will understand how to glue felt to wood: he can really go ahead and do it. If we read the fairy tale we learn what happened to the little soldier, how he met the witch and how, by a series of marvelous adventures, he married the king's daughter and possessed the kingdom; but it certainly cannot be said that we have come to "understand" how to get possession of a kingdom—or how to win any other success in life. We cannot even see how the success of the little soldier has any logic. He didn't succeed because he was intelligent, industrious, or honest, or because he embodied

---

[1] We ordinarily think of storytelling as the special province of fiction. But fiction is only one kind of narration. There is, for example, history or sports reporting. Here we are concerned with narration in general—as a mode of discourse—though later we shall touch on some of the special problems of fiction.

any virtue whatsoever. Success merely "happened" to him—wonderfully, marvelously, and that was that. Now, to follow this thought, can it be said that the tale is directed to making us "understand" that life often seems illogical, and that success may come by accident—as we know it may? No, the tale makes the child (or the adult, who always retains something of the child deep in him) live imaginatively in the world of wonder and marvel, where success comes with the effortlessness of a dream. In fact, the tale is a kind of dream, in which we escape from the hard logic of the world into the realm of unthwarted desire.

Intention

The contrast between these two examples—the directions for gluing felt to wood and the fairy tale—is, as we have said, extreme. In actual practice we rarely find the distinction so clear-cut. Let us look at another piece of narration, from a book about wolves:

> One factor concerning the organization of the family [of wolves] mystified me very much at first. During my early visit to the den I had seen *three* adult wolves; and during the first few days of observing the den I had again glimpsed the odd wolf several times. He posed a major conundrum, for while I could accept the idea of a contented domestic group consisting of mated male and female and a bevy of pups, I had not yet progressed far enough into the wolf world to be able to explain, or to accept, the apparent existence of an eternal triangle.
>
> Whoever the third wolf was, he was definitely a character. He was smaller than George, not so lithe and vigorous, and with a gray overcast to his otherwise white coat. He became "Uncle Albert" to me after the first time I saw him with the pups.
>
> The sixth morning of my vigil had dawned bright and sunny, and Angeline and the pups took advantage of the good weather. Hardly was the sun risen (at three A.M.) when they all left the den and adjourned to a nearby sandy knoll. Here the pups worked over their mother with an enthusiasm that would certainly have driven any human female into hysterics. They were hungry; but they were also full to the ears with hellery. Two of them did their best to chew off Angeline's tail, worrying it and fighting over it until I thought I could actually see her fur fly like spindrift; while the other two did what they could to remove her ears.
>
> Angeline stood it with noble stoicism for about an hour and then, sadly disheveled, she attempted to protect herself by sitting on her tail and tucking her mauled head down between her legs. This was a fruitless effort. The pups went for her feet, one to each paw, and I was treated to the spectacle of the demon killer of the wilds trying desperately to cover her paws, her tail, and her head at one and the same instant.
>
> Eventually she gave it up. Harassed beyond endurance she leaped away

from her brood and raced to the top of a high and sandy ridge behind the den. The four pups rolled cheerfully off in pursuit, but before they could reach her she gave vent to a most peculiar cry.

The whole question of wolf communication was to intrigue me more and more as time went on, but on this occasion I was still laboring under the delusion that complex communications among animals other than man did not exist. I could make nothing definite of Angeline's high-pitched and yearning whine-cum-howl. I did, however, detect a plaintive quality in it which made my sympathies go out to her.

I was not alone. Within seconds of her *cri-de-coeur*, and before the mob of pups could reach her, a savior appeared.

It was the third wolf. He had been sleeping in a bed hollowed in the sand at the southern end of the esker where it dipped down to disappear beneath the waters of the bay. I had not known he was there until I saw his head come up. He jumped to his feet, shook himself, and trotted straight toward the den—intercepting the pups as they prepared to scale the last slope to reach their mother.

I watched, fascinated, as he used his shoulder to bowl the leading pup over on its back and send it skidding down to the lower slope toward the den. Having broken the charge, he then nipped another pup lightly on its fat behind; then he shepherded the lot of them back to what I later came to recognize as the playground area.

I hesitate to put human words into a wolf's mouth, but the effect of what followed was crystal clear. "If it's a workout you kids want," he might have said, "then I'm your wolf!"

And so he was. For the next hour he played with the pups with as much energy as if he were still one himself. The games were varied, but many of them were quite recognizable. Tag was the steady, and Albert was always "it." Leaping, rolling and weaving amongst the pups, he never left the area of the nursery knoll, while at the same time leading the youngsters such a chase that they eventually gave up.

Albert looked them over for a moment and then, after a quick glance toward the crest where Angeline was now lying in a state of peaceful relaxation, he flung himself in among the tired pups, sprawled on his back, and invited mayhem. They were game. One by one they roused and went into battle. They were really roused this time, and no holds were barred— by them, at any rate.

Some of them tried to choke the life out of Albert, although their small teeth, sharp as they were, could never have penetrated his heavy ruff. One of them, in an excess of infantile sadism, turned its back on him and pawed a shower of sand into his face. The others took to leaping as high into the air as their bowed little legs would propel them; coming down with a satisfying thump on Albert's vulnerable belly. In between jumps they tried to chew the life out of whatever vulnerable parts came to tooth.

I began to wonder how much he could stand. Evidently he could stand a lot, for not until the pups were totally exhausted and had collapsed into complete somnolence did he get to his feet, careful not to step on the small, sprawled forms, and disengage himself. Even then he did not return to the comfort of his own bed (which he had undoubtedly earned after a night of hard hunting) but settled himself instead on the edge of the nursery knoll, where he began wolf-napping, taking a quick look at the pups every few minutes to make sure they were still safely near at hand.

His true relationship to the rest of the family was still uncertain; but as far as I was concerned he had become, and would remain, "good old Uncle Albert." —FARLEY MOWAT: *Never Cry Wolf.*[2]

This account is the work of a scientist, a biologist employed by the Canadian government to make a study of *canis lupus* to determine whether the creature should be exterminated. The overall intention of the biologist is, then, expository, or perhaps argumentative. The first paragraph is basically expository: Mowat wants us to understand the structure of the family of *canis lupus,* the type of family organization characteristic of the species. But we can sharply distinguish this intention, and that of the whole book, from the fact that this account, considered in itself, is a rounded piece of narrative appealing to the imagination, a charming and humorous little tale.

In the following anecdotes we see even more sharply this distinction between the nonnarrative frame (exposition in these instances) and the narrative illustration.

There are men of all nations who feel the fascination of a life unequally divided between months of hardship and short days of riot and spending; but in the end it is the hardship that holds them. The Chinese, taking them as they come, are not like this. They frankly detest hard work. A large belly among them is an honorable thing, because it means that the owner of it does not swink for his living. I never met a Chinese outside of the caravans who was what we should call sentimental about his work. Camel pullers alone have a different spirit, a queer spirit. Time and again when the men were talking around the fire and cursing the weather, the bad taste of the water, or the dust blown into their food, I have heard one ask, rhetorically, "What is a camel puller?" . . .

Then another would say, "Yes, but this is the good life—do we not all come back to it?" and be approved in a chorus of grunts and oaths. Once a veteran said the last word: "I put all my money into land in the newly opened country Behind the Hills, and my nephew farms it for me. My old woman is there, so two years ago when they had the troubles on the Great Road and my legs hurt I thought I would finish with it all—defile its mother! I thought I would sleep on a warm *k'ang* and gossip with the neighbors and maybe smoke a little opium, and not work hard any more. But I am not far from the road, in my place, and after a while in the day and the night when I hear the bells of the *lien-tze* go by, *ting-lang, ting-lang,* there was a pain in my heart—*hsin-li nan-kuo.* So I said, "Dogs defile it! I will go back on the Gobi one more time and pull camels."
—OWEN LATTIMORE: *The Desert Road to Turkestan.*

In the first paragraph, the discussion of the attitude of the Chinese toward hard work is pure exposition; it is generalized. But with the second para-

[2] From *Never Cry Wolf* by Farley Mowat, by permission of Little, Brown and Co. Copyright © 1963 by Farley Mowat.

graph and the particular "camel puller" who, in speaking for himself, speaks for all, we enter upon narrative.

In the same fashion, the two anecdotes that follow illustrate the "bitter passages" in undergraduate life at Harvard in an earlier period.

> Undergraduate life at Cambridge [Massachusetts] has not lacked for bitter passages, which compel notice from any anatomist of society. On the one hand there has long been a snobbery moulded of New England pride and juvenile cruelty which is probably more savage than any known to Fifth Avenue and Newport. Its favorite illustration is the time-worn tale of the lonely lad who to feign that he had *one* friend used to go out as dusk fell over the yard and call beneath his own windows, "Oh, Reinhardt!" And on the other it has moments of mad, terrible loyalty—exampled by the episode which is still recalled, awesomely without names, over the coffee and liqueurs when Harvard men meet in Beacon Street or in the South Seas. It is the true story of a Harvard senior at a party in Brookline, who suddenly enraged by a jocular remark made concerning the girl whom he later married, publicly slapped the face of his best friend—and then in an access of remorse walked to an open fire and held his offending hand in the flame until it shrivelled away to the wrist.
>
> —DIXON WECTER: *The Saga of American Society*.[3]

Each of these three anecdotes, that of the "camel puller" and those of Harvard undergraduate life, serves perfectly as the illustration of a general idea (pp. 79–87). But each is, in itself, a well-organized little narrative. We can readily see how any of them might be the germ of a fully developed short story.

Interest and method

We have seen that a piece of narrative may be found in a context that has an overall nonnarrative intention. But let us take a case in which precisely the same materials may be treated with different methods, one being exposition, the other narration.

> George Barton, a poor boy about twelve years old, was forced to sell the mastiff, which he had reared from a puppy and was much attached to, for two reasons. First, having lost his job, he could no longer buy proper food for a dog of such size. Second, after it had frightened a child in the neighborhood, he was afraid that someone would poison it.

This paragraph involves an action, the fact that the boy sells the dog, but its primary concern is with the causes of the action rather than with the immediate presentation of the action in time. Let us rewrite the passage:

> George Barton owned a mastiff, which he had reared from a puppy. He loved it very much. But he lost his job and could no longer buy proper

---

[3] Reprinted with the permission of Charles Scribner's Sons from *The Saga of American Society* by Dixon Wecter. Copyright 1937 Charles Scribner's Sons; renewal copyright © 1965 Elizabeth Farrar Wecter.

food for it. Then the dog frightened a little child of the neighborhood, who was eating a piece of bread. George was afraid that someone would poison the dog. So he sold it.

Here, as before, the causes of the action are given, but now the emphasis is different, and they are absorbed into the movement of the action itself. When we wrote in the first version that George sold the dog for two reasons, we violated the whole nature of narrative—the movement in time—because we made the causes of the action, not the action itself, the primary interest. The first piece of writing is primarily expository; it explains why the boy sold the dog. The second is primarily narrative; it tells us what happened.

Narration and absorbed forms of discourse

Just as narration can be a part of a larger piece of writing that is a different mode of discourse, so narration can absorb other modes to its dominant intention. To take a simple instance, a novel involving a bank robbery might well include expository narration in presenting the method used by the robbers. The same novel, in giving the psychological background of a robber, might also tell how childhood circumstances had warped his character, and this would be an example of causal analysis. When writing about the black sedan careening down the dark street, the author would, no doubt, use some descriptive touches. And after the gang had made its getaway, the members might well fall into an argument, or one robber, in a fit of conscience, thinking of his dear, gray-haired old mother, might argue with himself as to whether he should give himself up.

● CAUTION

To discriminate and tag the various forms of discourse involved in a piece of narration, as we have just done with the hypothetical story of the bank robbery, is not, in itself, an end, but is merely a way to understand more clearly the relation of other forms of discourse to the narrative intention. Remember:

1   Subordinate intentions must fulfill their own functions.
2   Subordinate intentions must be significantly related to the main function.

Furthermore, the end effect of a piece of narration involving subsidiary intentions should be one of easy absorption and not of jagged differences.

■ APPLICATION

Read "Making It: The Brutal Bargain," by Norman Podhoretz (pp. 847–58) and return to "The Fire Next Time," by James Baldwin (pp. 858–67). Distinguish the forms of discourse involved in each. Can you specify the function served by the subordinate forms?

Summary

Narration gives us a moving picture, objects in motion, life in its flow, the transformation of life from one moment to the next. It does not *tell about* a story. It *tells* a story.

It aims to give immediacy, a sense of the event before our eyes, involving us, our interest, and perhaps our sympathy. Description, too, aims to give immediacy, but its purpose is to give the quality of an action, not the movement of the action itself.

Action is what narration presents.

Action and Sequence

Action is motion, and narration gives us this motion in time. But mere sequence does not constitute an action.

Suppose we should read:

> President Wilson presented his war message to Congress on April 6, 1917. War was declared. Thus the United States embarked on its first great adventure in world affairs. On April 8, 1917, just two days later, Albert Mayfield was born in Marysville, Illinois. He was a healthy baby and grew rapidly. By the time of the Armistice he weighed 22 pounds. On December 12, 1918, the troopship *Mason,* returning to New York from Cherbourg, struck a floating mine off Ireland and sank. Two hundred and sixteen men were lost.

Several events are chronologically recounted in this passage, but as they are presented to us, nothing holds those events together. They have no significant relation to one another. Merely a sequence in time, they do not constitute an action. But suppose we rewrite the passage:

> President Wilson presented his war message to Congress on April 6, 1917. War was declared. Thus the United States embarked on its first great adventure in world affairs. On April 8, 1917, just two days later, Albert Mayfield was born in Marysville, Illinois. Scarcely before the ink had dried on the headlines of the extra of the Marysville *Courier* announcing the declaration of war, Albert embarked on his own great adventure in world affairs. He was a healthy baby and grew rapidly. By the time of the Armistice he weighed 22 pounds. On December 12, 1918, the troopship *Mason,* returning to New York from Cherbourg, struck a floating mine off Ireland and sank. Two hundred and sixteen men were lost. Among those men was Sidney Mayfield, a captain of artillery, a quiet, unobtrusive, middle-aged

insurance salesman, who left a widow and an infant son. That son was Albert Mayfield. So Albert grew up into a world that the war—a war he could not remember—had defined. It had defined the little world of his home, the silent, bitter woman who was his mother, the poverty and the cheerless discipline, and it had defined the big world outside.

Now we are moving toward an action. The random events are given some relationship to one another. We have unity and meaning. We may want to go on and find out more about Albert and about the long-range effects of the war on his life, but what we have is, as far as it goes, an action in itself as well as part of a bigger action, the story of Albert's life.

We have said that an action must have unity of meaning. This implies that one thing leads to another or that both things belong to a body of related events, all bearing on the point of the action. For instance, in the paragraph about Albert Mayfield, the declaration of war by the United States did not directly cause the floating mine to be in a particular spot off Ireland, but both events belong in the body of events contributing to the formation of Albert's character.

An action is, to sum up, a structure.

We shall speak of the structure of action under the categories of *time, logic,* and *meaning.*

Time

An action takes place in time. The movement of an event is from one point in time to another. But narration gives us a *unit* of time, not a mere fragment of time. A unit is a thing that is complete in itself. It may be part of a larger thing, and it may contain smaller parts, which themselves are units, but in itself it can be thought of as complete. A unit of time is that length of time in which a process fulfills itself.

We must now emphasize, not the mere fact of movement in time, but the movement from a beginning to an end. We begin a story at the moment when something is ripe to happen, when one condition prevails but is unstable, and end it when something has finished happening, when a new condition prevails and is, for the moment at least, stable. In between the beginning and the end are all the moments that mark the stages of change, that is to say, the process of the event.

We move, as it were, from A to Z, A the beginning, Z the end; and every item in between has a necessary order in time. We can make a little chart to indicate this natural sequence in time:

NATURAL
ORDER   A B C D E F G H I — etc. — U V W X Y Z
IN TIME

But we recall narratives that do not begin with the first moment when something was ripe to happen, that is, with our A. For instance, a narrative *may* begin with a man in the very midst of his problems, say on the battlefield, in a moment of marital crisis, or at a time when he hears that he has lost his fortune, and then it may cut back to his previous history and experience to explain how he came to be in such a situation. Such a narrative does not move in an orderly fashion from A to Z. It may begin, instead, with G, H, and I and then cuts back to A, B, and C. But we must distinguish here between two things: how the narrator treated the sequence in time and how the sequence existed in time. The narrator may have given us G, H, and I first in order to catch our interest. He may have thought that A, B, and C would not be interesting to us until we knew what they were to lead to. But when he does finally cut back to A, B, and C, we become aware of the full sequence in time and set it up in our imaginations, thus, A, B, C, . . . G, H, I, ... In other words, we must distinguish between the *way* (G, H, I—A, B, C, . . .) in which the narrator presents an action to us and the *action* (A, B, C, D, E, F, G, . . .) which he presents.

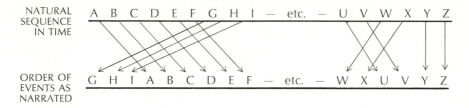

This is a distinction that we easily grasp, for we have long been acquainted with it in all sorts of narration, from conversation, newspaper stories, novels, and so on. But it is an important distinction, because when we talk about *action,* as we use the word here, we are referring to the events in the *natural order* in time and not in the *narrative order* unless the two orders happen to coincide, as they often do.

To repeat: an author confronts the *natural order* in the action that he is going to relate. In his narrative, he may keep it. But he may, for any number of different reasons, change the natural order—to build suspense, to develop a character, to make an interpretation. The simplest and most obvious example of this is in the ordinary news story. The standard practice is to summarize the basic facts in the beginning of the story and then to go back and present the events leading up to the discovery of the body, or the landing on the moon, or whatever event is central to the news story. And all sorts of distortions of the natural order are common in fiction.

Logic and causality

We have said that an action is not a mere sequence of events. It is a sequence in which "one thing leads to another." This is the very essence of narration, and here, as several times before, we are dealing with the notion of causality.

But what causes what? If "one thing leads to another," what is the "thing" that leads or is led to? We say that one event leads to another, and so it does. But in most narratives that hold our interest we are dealing with human beings in the process of living, and so matters of human motive and human character are involved. It is obvious that motive or character leads to an event. Jim embezzles from the bank where he works because he cannot bear to see his aged grandmother lose the old home place. Jack kills Mr. Tracy because Mr. Tracy filed the complaint that led to his arrest and conviction. Jim's motive and Jack's motive can be stated precisely. But motive blends back into character. A person is capable of having a particular motive only if it is consonant with his character. Jim's motive would not be comprehensible to Jack, nor Jack's motive to Jim. The point is, however, that action in life, or in narrative, is significant and interesting only in so far as it represents human agency.

We know, too, that events lead to character and motive. One of the most common ideas is that the individual's character is, to a considerable degree, molded by accidents of birth, social background, education, and all the other factors that we lump together as environment. This idea is necessarily important when we consider the logic of narrative. For a simple example, look back at the passage on the birth of Albert Mayfield (p. 319). The death of his father, when the troopship *Mason* is sunk by a floating mine, condemns the infant to poverty, bad education, and the bitterness of the woman who is his mother. His character, and in turn particular motives developed from that character, are to be understood as "caused" by the loss of the troopship, ironically after the war was over. There are, of course, an infinite number of other illustrations. Almost all fiction is concerned with the causes of human behavior, as are history and biography. Pick up any biography of George Washington, and the frontier will be discussed as an element in the molding of his character.

This concern with the *why* of things is at the very center of narration. If the writer of narrative is concerned with *what* happens and *how* it happens—with rendering the immediate texture of events, and their vividness, even as they come into being—he must be equally concerned with the *why*. He may give a certain immediacy and vividness merely by rendering the *what* and the *how,* but he cannot give a sense of life if he omits the *why.* No matter how immediately and vividly an event may be presented, it does not long hold our attention if we do not sense that it adds up to something, that it has some meaning. One of our deepest concerns is to find, or to create, some pattern in our own living. The question of *why* is intertwined with all our feeling for life.

Narrative does not *necessarily* undertake to deal with the *why* in general terms. It characteristically aims to embody the *why* in the *what* and *how,* to give a sense of the depth and massiveness of experience. But the logic of the *why* is, always, the dynamic of narrative. *What brings on what?*

What we have been saying about logic in narration may seem to contradict what we said in the opening paragraphs of this chapter when we used the example of the fairy tale. We said, there, that the fairy tale merely presents what "happens" without regard to character, moral worth, or logic—that the appeal is that of a dream in which desires are fulfilled effortlessly. This fairy tale, like many other fairy tales dressed up as novels and movies, does offer an escape from the hard logic of the world, an escape into fantasy, but the "escape" would not be possible, or appealing, unless there were this hard logic to escape from. In this sense, logic is the ground of fantasy.

However, the logic of the world is not easily grasped. The industrious are not always rewarded, the good do not always live happily, the evil are not always punished, and so on. All philosophy, all religion, and a great deal of literature have been ultimately concerned with this question of the logic of the world. We sense the logic, even if it is hard to define.

DIVISIONS OF ACTION

In narration, logic manifests itself as structure as well as causality. We feel action as an unbroken flow through time. But we can think of action in terms of a series of stages, divisions in time, each having its own function in a structure. For action is a structure as well as a flow. Aristotle, more than two thousand years ago, divided the action of tragedy into the beginning, middle, and end; and though that division seems too obvious to be worth a comment, it has profound consequences for the discussion of any kind of action. For when we move from the notion of action as a mere flow in time to action as composed of significant stages in a structure, we are moving toward the notion of meaning as embodied in action. We are discussing the structure, the pattern, of an action, and a structure implies meaningful order, not arbitrary arrangement.

Beginning   An action does not spring from nothing. It arises from a situation. The situation, however, must be an unstable one, ready to lead to change and containing in it the seeds of future developments.

A situation may be very simple or very complicated. In the joke we begin, "Two Irishmen met on a bridge at midnight in a strange city. The first Irishman said . . ." We have a minimum of information here, but all we may need for the joke. The situation could not be simpler. But the principle is the same as that in an enormously complicated situation; for instance, the situation from which German Nazism developed, a situation that contained more elements than we can enumerate here. There was the conflict between capital and labor, the insecurity of the lower middle-class, the fear of Communism, the economic collapse and the inflation of the currency, the tradition of German militarism, the demand for revenge after the defeat in World War I, the example of Italian Fascism, the personality of Hitler, his bitterness and frustration. An interaction of these elements and many others characterized the unstable situation that worked itself out in Nazism.

Given this material, the writer of an account of Nazism must first present the situation clearly enough for the reader to see a logic in what follows. In dealing with matters of fact, as such a writer of history would be doing, the first task would be to analyze the material to be sure of what was really significant for the understanding of future developments; and the second task would be to present the material so that the reader could grasp the relation among the various elements, and grasp the nature of the instability of the situation.

It is true that the reader may not grasp the significance of the situation when it is first presented, but he must have enough to go on; the material must feed his curiosity and create suspense. And he must be given enough material for him to feel, when he comes to look back over the whole narrative, that the action is really a logical development from the original situation.

The problem is essentially the same for a writer who is dealing with imaginary events. The only difference is that he does not have to analyze factual material, but has to create his materials. If we glance at Act I of Shakespeare's *Romeo and Juliet,* we find an excellent example of a beginning. There is the feud between the houses of Capulet and Montague, bloodshed and violence are imminent, Romeo is an idealistic young man anxious to fall truly in love. We are given enough information to account for future events.

The beginning, the presentation of the situation, enables us to understand the subsequent narrative. Therefore, that part of the narrative—the beginning—is often given the name of *exposition.* But we must keep this special sense of this word distinct from the more general sense in which it applies to one of the modes of discourse.

Though the exposition of a narrative seems to be merely preliminary, it is not to be regarded as a kind of mere make-ready, a necessary evil to be passed over, a body of dull information. There is a great art to managing exposition, to trapping the reader's interest. The exposition need not consist of explanatory or descriptive material in isolation or a colorless summary of the situation from which the action stems. Instead, the exposition may appear as an episode, a fragment of action, interesting in itself. If we think back on the opening scene of *Romeo and Juliet,* we remember that in it we see a street fight. We are not *told about* the feud between the rival houses of Capulet and Montague, we actually see it in operation. Not all kinds of exposition can take a direct form, but in general it can be said that whenever possible exposition should be dramatically presented, that is, directly presented.

Middle The middle is the main body of the action. It is a series of stages in the process. It involves the points of mounting tension, or increasing *complication,* developing from the original situation. *Romeo and Juliet* will again illustrate. In spite of the hostility of their two families, Romeo and Juliet meet, pledge their love to each other, and are secretly married by Friar Laurence. But the action receives a most important complication when Romeo kills Juliet's kinsman and is banished from the city; and further complication still when Juliet's father decides to force her into marriage with the young nobleman, Paris. In this crisis of tension, Friar Laurence sees only one way out: Juliet must take the potion that will put her into a deathlike sleep. She will then be placed in the tomb—from which Romeo will rescue her. Juliet's resolution to take the risk might be regarded by many readers as the climax of the play; that is, the point of greatest intensity or greatest suspense. The climax is the focal point, the turning point of the narrative.

History as well as fiction may be used to illustrate the nature of the "middle" of an action. To return to our example of the rise of Nazism, we would find such points of mounting tension as the beer hall *Putsch* in Munich, Hitler's imprisonment and the writing of *Mein Kampf,* the street fights against the German Communists, the election of Hitler as Chancellor, the Reichstag fire, the purge of the party, the claims on Sudetenland. Looking back on those events, we can see the points of crisis, the stages at which new tensions emerged. If a historian were writing an account of those years, he might center his attention on those stages. They might provide him with natural chapter divisions.

The same principle of development applies in any narrative, the simple joke or the elaborate novel—and, of course, in any drama. But a mere drift of events is death to the reader's interest. It is the sense of an unfolding structure that demands attention and evokes emotional response.

End The end of an action is not simply the point at which the action stops. It is, rather, the point at which the forces implicit in the situation have worked themselves out. Whether it is the gag line of a joke or Berlin shattered under British and American bombs and Russian shells, the principle is the same. The end of an action, however, is not necessarily the physical victory of one set of forces over another. It may be the reconciliation of forces, or it may be the fusion of previously opposing forces to create a new force. As a matter of fact, the end of an action may simply be a new awareness on the part of a person involved, directly or indirectly, in the action. We know that often we can look back on an experience and recognize the point at which an attitude we held was changed by it.

When we come to writing a narrative, we regard the end as the point where the action achieves its full meaning. It is the point at which the reader is willing to say, "Oh, yes, I see what it is all about." It is the point where the structure as well as the meaning is fulfilled. To put it another way, it is the point where we most fully sense that structure and meaning are aspects of the same thing: they are the thing itself.

The technical name for the end of a narrative is *denouement.* The word means an "untying." With the denouement, the complications are finally untangled and resolved. In *Romeo and Juliet,* for example, the lovers consummate in death their ill-starred love, and their families remorsefully give up the enmity that has destroyed their children.

The relation of the parts of a narrative to one another raises the question of proportion. In one way this term is misleading, for it implies a mere mechanical ratio in the size of the parts. Actually, we cannot look at the question in that way. We cannot say, for instance, that the complication should be three times longer than the exposition or five times longer than the denouement.

We need to ask, rather, whether the parts are adequate to the needs of the special narrative we are dealing with. What would be a satisfactory proportion for one narrative might be quite unsatisfactory for another. In any given instance, does the exposition give all the information necessary to establish the situation for the reader? Is it burdened with information that is unnecessary and distracting? Does the complication clearly present the essential stages of the development of the action? Does it confuse the reader by presenting material that does not bear on the development of the action? Does the denouement give the reader enough information to make the point of the narrative clear? Does it blur the point by putting in irrelevant material or by so extending relevant material that a clear focus is lost?

EXAMPLES OF NARRATIVE PATTERN

Let us look at a few examples of narrative with the idea of indicating the structure, or pattern, of each. The first is the account of how Robinson Crusoe, who fancied himself absolutely alone on his desert island, found a footprint:

> It happened one day about noon, going towards my boat, I was exceedingly surprised with the print of a man's naked foot on the shore, which was very plain to be seen in the sand. I stood like one thunderstruck, or as if I had seen an apparition: I listened, I looked around me, but I could hear nothing, nor see anything. I went up to a rising ground, to look farther; I went up the shore and down the shore, but it was all one; I could see no other impression but that one. I went to it again to see if there were any more, and to observe if it might not be my fancy; but there was no room for that, for there was exactly the print of a foot, toes, heel, and every part of a foot; how it came thither I knew not, nor could I in the least imagine; but, after innumerable fluttering thoughts, like a man perfectly confused and out of myself, I came home to my fortification, not feeling, as we say, the ground I went on, but terrified to the last degree; looking behind me at every two or three steps, mistaking every bush and tree, and fancying every stump at a distance to be a man. Nor is it possible to describe how many various shapes my affrighted imagination represented things to me in, how many wild ideas were found every moment in my fancy, and what strange unaccountable whimsies came into my thoughts by the way.
>
> —DANIEL DEFOE: *Robinson Crusoe*.

Though a piece of narrative could scarcely be simpler than this, we see that it follows the basic pattern. The situation is given, as are the time and place. The complication follows on the discovery of the print—the first reaction, the looking about and listening, the going to higher ground for a wider view, the returning to verify the existence of the print. Then come the flight and the terror consequent upon the discovery. And it is this terror, changing the whole aspect of the familiar landscape, that constitutes the denouement. Crusoe's life cannot be the same again. This fact is not specified, but it is strongly implied.

Our next example makes its point more explicitly:

> And also Mohammet loved well a good Hermit that dwelled in the Deserts a Mile from Mount Sinai, in the Way that Men go from Arabia toward Chaldea and toward Ind, one Day's journey from the Sea, where the Merchants of Venice come often for Merchandise. And so often went Mohammet to this Hermit, that all his Men were wroth; for he would gladly hear this Hermit preach and make his Men wake all Night. And therefore his Men thought to put the Hermit to Death. And so it befell upon a Night, that Mohammet was drunken of good Wine, and he fell asleep. And his Men took Mohammet's Sword out of his Sheath, whiles he slept, and therewith they slew this Hermit, and put his Sword all bloody in his Sheath again. And at the Morrow, when he found the Hermit dead, he was fully sorry and wroth, and would have done his Men to Death. But they all, with one accord, said that he himself had slain him, when he was drunk, and showed him his Sword all bloody. And he trowed that they had said Truth. And then he cursed the Wine and them that drink it. And therefore Saracens that be devout drink never any Wine.
>
> —SIR JOHN MANDEVILLE: *Travels*.

This, too, falls into the pattern. The exposition is a little less simple here than in our earlier example, for now we are concerned not only with the physical facts but with human motives leading up to the action—Mohammet's love of the hermit, his custom of listening to the sermons, the irritation of the men. The complication falls into three divisions—the killing of the hermit, the discovery of the deed and Mohammet's anger, the lie and the bloody sword in his own scabbard. The denouement has two divisions —Mohammet's curse on wine and, as the main point, the result among devout followers in later times.

Our next example is an anecdote told about an argument between the Duke of Windsor and Winston Churchill before World War II. We have here merely a clash of opinion:

> The Windsors' dinner was very grand, and the guests consisted of assorted notables from up and down the coast, mostly English people of high rank who were holidaying in the South. My Lords Rothermere and Beaverbrook had been prevented from attending by colds. (Lord Beaverbrook's cold did not prevent his attendance at the Casino, where we saw him afterward.) When some of the more overpowering guests had departed, after

the long and stately meal in the white-and-gold dining room, the Duke of
Windsor and Mr. Churchill settled down to a prolonged argument with the
rest of the party listening in silence. The Duke had read with amazement
Mr. Churchill's recent articles on Spain and his newest one (out that day,
I believe) in which he appealed for an alliance with Soviet Russia. "You
of all people, Winston," was the gist of his argument, "you cannot wish to
make friends of these murderers and thieves." At one point Mr. Churchill,
who was defending his point of view stubbornly and with undiplomatic
vigor, said: "Sir, I would make a friend of the devil himself, if it would save
England." It resulted plainly from the statements on the two sides that the
self-willed, pleasure-loving little Prince, filled to the fingertips with royal
prejudice, had no conception of the deadly danger to England involved in
his dalliance with Hitler, while Mr. Churchill, disliking the Bolshevik theory
and practice as much as ever, was so thoroughly aware of England's peril
that he would seek the alliance of Stalin at once. We sat by the fireplace,
Mr. Churchill frowning with intentness at the floor in front of him, mincing
no words, reminding H.R.H. of the British constitution, on occasion—
"when our kings are in conflict with our constitution we change our kings,"
he said—and declaring flatly that the nation stood in the gravest danger of
its long history. The kilted Duke in his Stuart tartan sat on the edge of the
sofa, eagerly interrupting whenever he could, contesting every point, but
receiving—in terms of the utmost politeness so far as the words went—
an object lesson in political wisdom and public spirit. The rest of us sat
fixed in silence; there was something dramatically final, irrevocable about
this dispute.   —VINCENT SHEEAN: *Between the Thunder and the Sun.*[4]

This is scarcely a narrative at all, simply a little incident almost buried
in the comment with which the author has surrounded it. But the author
has hinted at the action and has given enough for us to grasp its natural
structure and order (as contrasted with the way he has told it, for he has
not stuck to the chronological order of events).

SITUATION:

Dinner with Windsors. Nature of gathering. World of pleasure and privilege. Churchill and his articles on Spain.

COMPLICATION:

Prolonged argument. The Duke's amazement at Churchill's articles, especially his demand for an alliance with Russia. The Duke's stubbornness.
He eagerly leans forward from sofa, contesting every point. Churchill's
remarks on relation of kingship to English constitution, the danger to England, and so forth. The Duke's argument: "You of all people, Winston, you
cannot wish to make friends of these murderers and thieves."

DENOUEMENT:

Churchill's reply: "Sir, I would make a friend of the devil himself, if it
would save England."

---

[4] From *Between the Thunder and the Sun* by Vincent Sheean. Reprinted by permission of
Curtis Brown, Ltd. Copyright © 1943, by Vincent Sheean.

We do not know all that occurred at that conversation. We do not need to know it to have a notion of the action, in our sense of the word. For, in this connection, *action* is the word we apply to a meaningful event, and the things that merely happened and have no bearing on the meaning of the event are not, properly speaking, a part of the action. The writer has omitted them from his account.

Here is a more fully developed narrative, the story of Andrew Jackson's most famous duel, the duel with Charles Dickinson, who had made some remarks reflecting on the character of Rachel, Andrew Jackson's wife.

EXPOSITION:

On Thursday, May 29, 1806, Andrew Jackson rose at five o'clock, and after breakfast told Rachel that he would be gone for a couple of days and meanwhile he might have some trouble with Mr. Dickinson. Rachel probably knew what the trouble would be and she did not ask. Rachel had had her private channels of information concerning the Sevier affray. At six-thirty Jackson joined Overton at Nashville. Overton had the pistols. With three others they departed for the Kentucky line.

Mr. Dickinson and eight companions were already on the road. "Goodby, darling," he told his young wife. "I shall be sure to be home tomorrow evening." This confidence was not altogether assumed. He was a snap shot. At the word of command and firing apparently without aim, he could put four balls in a mark twenty-four feet away, each ball touching another. The persistent tradition in the countryside, that to worry Jackson he left several such examples of his marksmanship along the road, is unconfirmed by any member of the Dickinson or Jackson parties. But the story that he had offered on the streets of Nashville to wager he could kill Jackson at the first fire was vouchsafed by John Overton, the brother of Jackson's second, a few days after the duel.

Jackson said he was glad that "the other side" had started so early. It was a guarantee against further delay. Jackson had chafed over the seven days that had elapsed since the acceptance of the challenge. At their first interview, Overton and Dr. Hanson Catlett, Mr. Dickinson's second, had agreed that the meeting should be on Friday, May thirtieth, near Harrison's Mills on Red River, just beyond the Kentucky boundary. Jackson protested at once. He did not wish to ride forty miles to preserve the fiction of a delicate regard for Tennessee's unenforceable statute against dueling. He did not wish to wait a week for something that could be done in a few hours. Dickinson's excuse was that he desired to borrow a pair of pistols. Overton offered the choice of Jackson's pistols, pledging Jackson to the use of the other. These were the weapons that had been employed by Coffee and McNairy.

As they rode Jackson talked a great deal, scrupulously avoiding the subject that burdened every mind. Really, however, there was nothing more to be profitably said on that head. General Overton was a Revolutionary soldier of long acquaintance with the Code. With his principal he had canvassed every possible aspect of the issue forthcoming. "Distance . . . twenty-four feet; the parties to stand facing each other, with their pistols down perpendicularly. When they are READY, the single word FIRE! to be given; at which they are to fire as soon as they please. Should either fire before the word is given we [the seconds] pledge ourselves to shoot him down instantly." Jackson was neither a quick shot, nor an especially good one for the western country. He had decided not to compete with Dickinson for the first fire. He expected to be hit, perhaps badly. But he counted on the resources of his will to sustain him until he could aim deliberately and shoot to kill, if it were the last act of his life.

COMPLICATION:

On the first leg of the ride they traversed the old Kentucky road, the route by which, fifteen years before, Andrew Jackson had carried Rachel Robards from her husband's home, the present journey being a part of the long sequel to the other. Jackson rambled on in a shrill voice. Thomas Jefferson was "the best Republican in theory and the worst in practice" he had ever seen. And he lacked courage. How long were we to support the affronts of England—impressment of seamen, cuffing about of our ocean commerce? Perhaps as long as Mr. Jefferson stayed in office. Well, that would be two years, and certainly his successor should be a stouter man. "We must fight England again. In the last war I was not old enough to be any account." He prayed that the next might come "before I get too old to fight."

General Overton asked how old Jackson reckoned he would have to be for that. In England's case about a hundred, Jackson said.

He spoke of Burr. A year ago, this day, Jackson had borne him from the banquet at Nashville to the Hermitage. He recalled their first meeting in 1797 when both were in Congress. Jackson also met General Hamilton that winter. "Personally, no gentleman could help liking Hamilton. But his political views were all English." At heart a monarchist. "Why, did he not urge Washington to take a crown!"

Burr also had his failings. He had made a mistake, observed Jackson, with admirable detachment, a political mistake, when he fought Hamilton. And about his Western projects the General was none too sanguine. Burr relied overmuch on what others told him. Besides, there was Jefferson to be reckoned with. "Burr is as far from a fool as I ever saw, and yet he is as easily fooled as any man I ever knew."

The day was warm, and a little after ten o'clock the party stopped for refreshment. Jackson took a mint julep, ate lightly and rested until mid-afternoon. The party reached Miller's Tavern in Kentucky about eight o'clock. After a supper of fried chicken, waffles, sweet potatoes and coffee, Jackson repaired to the porch to chat with the inn's company. No one guessed his errand. At ten o'clock he knocked the ashes from his pipe and went to bed. Asleep in ten minutes, he had to be roused at five in the morning.

The parties met on the bank of the Red River at a break in a poplar woods. Doctor Catlett won the toss for choice of position, but as the sun had not come through the trees this signified nothing. The giving of the word fell to Overton. Jackson's pistols were to be used after all, Dickinson taking his pick. The nine-inch barrels were charged with ounce balls of seventy caliber. The ground was paced off, the principals took their places. Jackson wore a dark-blue frock coat and trousers of the same material; Mr. Dickinson a shorter coat of blue, and gray trousers.

"Gentlemen, are you ready?" called General Overton.

"Ready," said Dickinson quickly.

"Yes, sir," said Jackson.

"Fere!" cried Overton in the Old-Country accent.

DENOUEMENT:

Dickinson fired almost instantly. A fleck of dust rose from Jackson's coat and his left hand clutched his chest. For an instant he thought himself dying, but fighting for self-command, slowly he raised his pistol.

Dickinson recoiled a step horror-stricken. "My God! Have I missed him?"

Overton presented his pistol. "Back to the mark, sir!"

Dickinson folded his arms. Jackson's spare form straightened. He aimed. There was a hollow "clock" as the hammer stopped at half-cock. He drew it back, sighted again and fired. Dickinson swayed to the ground.

As they reached the horses Overton noticed that his friend's left boot was filled with blood. "Oh, I believe that he pinked me," said Jackson quickly, "but I don't want those people to know," indicating the group that bent over Dickinson. Jackson's surgeon found that Dickinson's aim had been perfectly true, but he had judged the position of Jackson's heart by the set of his coat, and Jackson wore his coats loosely on account of the excessive slenderness of his figure. "But I should have hit him," he exclaimed, "if he had shot me through the brain."

—MARQUIS JAMES: *The Life of Andrew Jackson.*[5]

The event narrated above is historically true. It had causes running back before the episode of the duel (Dickinson had insulted Jackson's wife) and was to have consequences long after the duel. But the writer is not immediately concerned with causes or effects. He is concerned with rendering the episode itself, the duel, and through the duel, something of the character of Jackson. We can see that in doing so he naturally gives his account in three sections—the exposition, the complication, and the denouement.

The exposition describes the attitudes of the two duelists as they make ready and gives the terms of the duel. The complication seems to have a good deal of material off the point—Jackson's long conversation about politics—but we can see that even this apparent digression is related to the point the author wishes to make in his narrative: Jackson's cool certainty and confidence. Then the complication gives the details as the opponents face each other and Dickinson fires. The denouement falls into two related parts, Jackson's self-command when hit and his shooting of Dickinson, and his remark after the event.

Both Vincent Sheean and Marquis James are using narrative to make a

[5] From *The Life of Andrew Jackson,* copyright 1933, 1937, 1938 by Marquis James, reprinted by permission of the publishers, The Bobbs-Merrill Company, Inc.

point in much the same way that narrative is used as illustration in, say, the account of the bear hunt by the Eskimos (pp. 83–86) and the account of the wolf family by Farley Mowat (pp. 314–16). This kind of point—Sheean's wish to show an aspect of the political background of World War II, and James's wish to exhibit the iron will of Jackson—is somewhat different from the kind of point we characteristically find in fiction. This is a distinction we shall come to later. For the moment, what should be emphasized is that though both Sheean and James are using narrative for the purpose of illustration, they work within the basic structure: that is, each narrative fulfills itself as narrative.

■ APPLICATIONS

I Read the theme "Getting Engaged" (pp. 283–85) and the essay "Making It: The Brutal Bargain," by Norman Podhoretz (pp. 847–58). Indicate the general divisions of each. In the middle of each selection, how many stages of complication can you distinguish? Does the denouement of either have more than one element? What point, what meaning, do we find in the denouement?

II You are now to begin work toward writing a narrative. Cast around for your subject, real or imaginary. Here the notebook you began to keep for description and narration should be of great help as a source of suggestions for narratives and for bits of description to flesh out narratives. But you should not follow the notebook slavishly. Look there for starting points rather than for passages that may be transferred as a block.

Once you have settled on a subject, real or imaginary, you should make a set of informal notes, perhaps in your notebook. Follow almost at random whatever ideas and impressions begin to assemble themselves about your subject. This process, by the way, may take several days. Some of your best ideas may come while you are brushing your teeth or walking down the street. Keep the notebook handy. Be alert to trap any fleeting notion. You cannot tell where it may lead. It may even lead you to an entirely new subject, one more exciting than what you have chosen.

When you have assembled your material and begun to feel at home with the subject, ask yourself if your narrative has, first, a point, and then, a structure. Organize your notes into a sentence outline. Is the point clear? Is the structure clear? If not, rethink your material. Perhaps you have tried to draw into your plan irrelevant material simply because it was interesting in itself. This would blur the point and confuse the structure. Or perhaps your material is not adequate for your needs. Again, the trouble may not lie in the material but in your organizing of it. Test each division. Does the beginning really serve as an exposition? Does the middle offer complications that, stage by stage, move toward a climax? Does the end really "untie" the complications and bring the narrative to a significant fulfillment?

When you have satisfied yourself as best you can, lay the outline aside. But continue to think about it. Take out the notebook for a little while every day and read over your work. You should have more and better thoughts before you begin to write. Let the narrative grow in your imagination.

Meaning in narrative

AN EXAMPLE

We shall now trace the development of a narrative from the simple germ situation to the end. The purpose here is not, however, to study further the divisions of narrative. Rather, it is to probe into the process by which narrative achieves meaning—that is, the third aspect of the structure of action.

Let us repeat the paragraph about George Barton and his dog, which we have at the beginning of this chapter:

> George Barton owned a mastiff, which he had reared from a puppy. He loved it very much. But he lost his job and could no longer buy proper food for it. Then the dog frightened a little child of the neighborhood, who was eating a piece of bread. George was now afraid that someone would poison it. So he sold it.

This is a very poor, dull, and incomplete piece of narration. For one thing, it can scarcely be said to *present* an event at all. It gives us little sense of the immediacy of the event. It is so bare of detail that the imagination of the reader finds little to work on. For another thing, we do not know what it means. It has no point.

Let us rewrite it to try to answer the first objection:

> George Barton was a nondescript little boy, scarcely to be distinguished from the other boys living in Duck Alley. He had a pasty face, not remarkable in any way, eyes not blue and not brown but some vague hazel color, and a tangle of neutral-colored hair. His clothes were the drab, cast-off things worn by all the children of Duck Alley, that grimy street, scarcely a street at all but a dirt track, which ran between the bayou and a scattering of shanties. His life there was cheerless enough, with a feeble, querulous father, a mother who had long since resigned herself to her misery, and a sullen older brother, with a mean laugh and a hard set of knuckles, who tormented George for amusement when he was not off prowling with his cronies. But this home did not distinguish George from the other children of Duck Alley. It was like many of the others. What distinguished George was his dog.
>
> One day two years back—it was the summer when he was ten—George had found the dog. It was a puppy then, a scrawny, starving creature with absurd big paws, sniffing feebly in the garbage dump at the end of Duck Alley. No one could have guessed then that it would grow into a sleek, powerful animal, as big as a pony.
>
> George brought it home and defended it against the protests and jeers

and random kicks of the family. "I'll feed him," he asserted. "He won't never eat a bite I don't make the money to pay for." And he was as good as his word. There was no job too hard for him, for he could look forward to evening when he would squat by the old goods box that served as a kennel and watch Jibby gnaw at the hunk of meat he had bought.

Suppose we begin the narrative in that way. We have added several elements to the bare synopsis given before. We know now why the dog is so important to the boy. There is no direct statement on this point, but we see that he lives an isolated and loveless life and that the dog satisfies a craving in his nature for companionship and affection. We also see that now George has a reason for his efforts, a center for his life. In other words, we can imaginatively grasp his state of mind. The reason for George's attachment to the dog, as we have just stated it, is given as explanation, as exposition, but in the narrative itself this expository element is absorbed into situation and action. Similarly, the little bits of description are woven into the narrative to help us visualize the scene and George himself.

What should be emphasized here is that the narrative is concerned to make us sense the fullness of the process, to make us see, hear, feel, and understand the event as a unit. Description alone might make us see or hear some aspect of the event. Exposition might make us understand its meaning, its causes, or results. But narrative, when it is fully effective, makes us aware directly of the event as happening. The sharp detail is the life of narrative.

To return to our little narrative: suppose we should carry on our suggested revision to the moment when George sells his dog. Would there be anything still lacking to make the narrative fully satisfactory? Perhaps there would be. Perhaps the meaning of the action would not be very clear. Let us pick it up at a point after George has lost his job and the dog has frightened the child.

> George sold the dog to John Simpson, a boy who lived in one of the big brick houses on the hill back of town. John Simpson's father was rich. John could feed Jibby. John could take care of him. No one would poison Jibby up at John Simpson's house, behind the high iron fence. George comforted himself with these thoughts.
>
> Sometimes, however, these thoughts did not comfort him enough, and he felt the old loneliness and emptiness that he had felt before Jibby came. But he was getting to be a big boy now, big and tough, and he put those feelings out of his mind as well as he could. He did not work regularly now, but hung around with the Duck Alley gang in the railroad yards. He almost forgot Jibby.
>
> One day on the main street of town he met John Simpson and the dog, such a big, powerful, sleek dog now that he scarcely recognized him. He went up to the dog. "Hi, Jibby! Hi, boy!" he said and began to pull the dog's ears and scratch his head as he had done three years before, in the evenings, back by the goods box, after Jibby had bolted his supper. The

dog nuzzled him and licked his hands. George looked up at the other boy and exclaimed, "Jeez, look at him. Look at him, will ya. Ain't he smart? He remembers me!"

John Simpson stood there for a moment and did not utter a word. Then he said, "Take your hands off that dog. He belongs to me."

George stepped back.

"Come here, Blaze," John Simpson ordered, and the dog went to him. He fondled the dog's head, and the dog licked his hands.

George stood on the pavement and watched John Simpson and the dog disappear down the street.

Neither looked back.

This is somewhat more extended than the previous version. If we stop with the sale of the dog, we have an example of narration, but the reader no doubt is somewhat confused about the exact meaning of the event presented. Perhaps the reader feels sorry for the boy. Perhaps he is aware that poverty is the cause of the boy's loss of the dog. Those reactions may be taken as meanings of the piece of narration, but these meanings are not brought to focus. The reader may not be sure exactly what is intended. He is certain to feel that the narrative is rather fragmentary. With the addition of the section dealing with the meeting of George and John Simpson, the reader, however, is somewhat more certain that the narrative does have a direction, is moving toward a meaning. In fact, the contrast between John Simpson, who owns the dog, and George, who merely loves it, is in itself significant—though the significance is rather too general to be fully satisfying as an end.

We sense that more is at stake than is offered in the mere fact of the contrast. When the dog licks John Simpson's hands, just as he had licked George's, we realize that the act was for George a kind of betrayal. But a hardheaded reader may find this rather sentimental; he may ask, "What did George expect the dog to do? Is he just standing there enjoying his self-pity?"

Let us suppose that, aware of this sort of criticism, we continue:

George continued to stand there, filled with rage, which was not new for him, but with something else that was new, a peculiar, disorienting sickness in his heart. Then he discovered that the rage was, all at once, as much against himself as it was against John Simpson or the dog—or even against the world. The rage was against himself for being weak enough to have that strange feeling of weakness and loss.

"A dog," he said out loud, standing there looking down the street, which was now empty. "Nothing but a God-durn dog." Then, "Anybody give him a hunk of meat, and he'll slobber all over him."

He let the spit gather slowly in his mouth, then, very deliberately, he spat on the spot where the dog had come and fawned on him. He set his foot on the spit and smeared it with a quick movement of disgust. He walked away, not looking back.

We have, now, another stage. George has gone beyond his old feeling. Jibby is now just another "God-durn dog," ready to slobber on anybody who has a hunk of meat. But this realization is, again, vague. We want a sharper focus. And so we try once more:

> The next day George hunted for a job. He found one at the lumberyard where he had worked before, when Jibby was a puppy. He worked as steadily now as he had worked in the old days when he looked forward to getting home to feed the dog and squat by him in the dusk, or, if it were winter, in the dark. But he was through with that sort of thing now.
>
> If now he worked with a grim and driving energy, it was because he had learned one lesson. It was a lesson he was never to forget. He had learned that even love was one of the things you cannot get unless you have the money to pay for it.

These paragraphs give us a positive conclusion. They give the effect of the event on George, not merely the first reaction of resentment or hurt feelings, but the effect that prevails over a long period of time. Neither the reader nor the writer may agree that what George learns is the truth—that money is the basis of everything, even of such things as love and loyalty and kindness—but what George learns is the "truth" for him, the rule by which he will conduct his life for a time to come.

The important thing to understand here is that a point is made. For our present purposes the question is not whether the point is universally true. It is whether the point is psychologically credible. That is, whether, given the sequence of events, George may come to feel it as true. If we accept this, we can accept the narrative as complete. George has reached a significant point in his life, a point at which he recognizes a difference in his feelings about himself and the world he lives in.

The narrative is not complete merely because a summarizing statement has been made by the writer. Certainly, the summarizing statement by itself would not make the narrative complete if what it says did not grow convincingly out of the events. Many narratives, in fact, imply rather than state their meaning. The crucial question is always this: Does the meaning, given the persons involved and the full context, really develop from the events?

We have just said that the narrative is complete. This, however, does not mean that George will never change his mind about the meaning of the experience he has had. The narrative might well be part of a long story or novel that showed how for thirty years George conducted his life by the hard, materialistic "truth" he had learned and then found, even in the moment of his practical success, when he had grown rich and powerful, that his "truth" was really a profound mistake and that he had to learn a new truth. But the particular action given here is, in its own terms, complete.

INTERPRETATION

The meaning of this action is what George takes it to be. Meaning, in the sense we are talking about, is never mathematically absolute. It is what some particular person takes it to be. The meaning is an interpretation.

But what of the author's interpretation? He wrote the narrative, didn't he? This question raises another important matter. We must always distinguish between meaning for a person, real or imaginary, in a narrative, and what we take to be the author's interpretation. Let us suppose that the author of this unwritten novel about George Barton did not accept the hard materialistic "truth" that George had arrived at. The point of his novel—the final interpretation proposed by the author—might be that nobody can live by that "truth." So the novel might go on to show that this philosophy brought George Barton, in the end, to ruin; or that he came to realize his error in some other way. The point is, of course, that the attitude of a character and that of the author do not necessarily coincide. The attitude of the author must be sought in the overall meaning of a work.[6]

The story of George is a made-up story, a simple little piece of fiction, but what we say about interpretation here would apply to other types of narration. Though historians or biographers, for instance, work with facts, the facts have to be evaluated and interpreted. Facts do not automatically make the narrative, or give the meaning of the narrative. The writer does that. It is no wonder, then, that no two biographers ever agree exactly about, say, Queen Elizabeth, or no two historians about the American Civil War. And many men, instead of seeing Andrew Jackson as the man of heroic will described by Marquis James, have seen him as "that blood-thirsty old murderer in the presidential chair."

Though variation in interpretation of the same subject is inevitable, this does not mean that interpretation is whimsical, that anything goes, that one interpretation is as good as another. Each writer confronts afresh the necessity of convincing the reader. The historian, for instance, must assemble as much data as possible; he must be able to assess the meaning of his facts as evidence; and he must have the imagination and intuition to understand personality and motive. And he must, in the end, be able to subordinate his own prejudices, feelings, and even personal convictions to what he finds to be the logic of his investigations. That is, he should try, even while recognizing the personal element, to minimize it. He aims at a "truth" that can be objectively sustained, in so far as that is possible.

It is here that the matter of the difference between the meaning of fiction and that of other forms of narration arises. To take some of the examples we have read earlier, the narrative of the bear hunt fulfills its function only if it is an accurate account, for the purpose is to instruct us about life among the Eskimos. The same is true for the little episode of the wolves, in which the writer is reporting on events he has observed. In the narrative about Andrew Jackson it is harder to be sure of objective truth, but the purpose

---

[6] Let us pursue the question of interpretation a little further: the interpretation by a character is part of the content of the work; it may or may not coincide with the meaning of the work, which is the author's interpretation. But there is also the interpretation arrived at by the reader, which may or may not coincide with that of the author. The author intends to convince the reader of his view of things—of the experiences related in his work and of life in general, but he may fail. Thus, the reader's interpretation must also be considered in making any assessment of a work.

of the episode is to illustrate a character trait, and this fact points, objectively, to a concern beyond the narrative itself. Also, as a piece of history, the episode has another objective reference: the facts of the episode are subject to external review.

When we come to the account of George Barton, or any piece of fiction, however powerful, we find that, in the end, the reference is more subjective. This is not merely to say that the piece of fiction is "made up." Many pieces of fiction report the objective world with great accuracy, or even draw their stories from the world of fact. Certainly, and more importantly, fiction cannot violate our objective sense of human psychology: we expect the character in fiction to behave in accordance with our observations of human behavior, or if what is presented falls beyond our observation, we expect the psychological process leading to the behavior to conform to what we are acquainted with.

These remarks lead to two considerations.

First, the writer of fiction treats the inner life of a character in a depth never possible in other forms of narration. Having "created" his character, he claims to know all. The fact that he may not tell all is not what is at stake. He may or may not tell all, according to his fictional needs. But in contrast with, say, the historian or biographer, his resources are complete; the historian or biographer finds his greatest gaps of knowledge at the most crucial points, those points where action depends on the deepest workings of the soul and where motive is most veiled or ambiguous. This fullness of subjectivity as regards the characters appearing in the work is crucial in distinguishing fiction from other forms of narration.

Our second consideration also involves subjectivity, but subjectivity in relation to the author. In spite of all the objective materials that enter into fiction, the work of fiction, taken as a whole, represents the author's personal vision of life. It is true that we may find such a vision repellent, inadequate, or stupid. We do criticize it, consciously or unconsciously, and our criticism is external and objective. But the validity of the work depends on the internal coherence: does it make sense taken in its own terms? So we often find compelling works that lie very far from our own values and preconceptions. Within certain limits, the "vision" the fiction writer offers us is self-validating—justifies itself by its own inner coherence, by the conviction that it carries an authentic experience.

We have said "within certain limits." There is no automatic way to establish such limits. We may find a work of beautiful inner coherence that is unacceptable to us. It may spring, like a Japanese novel, from a civilization so remote from our own that we cannot enter into it. It may present a level of experience too far beyond us; young students, for instance, respond readily to *Romeo and Juliet* but are often cold to *King Lear*. It may embody values that we find trivial or offensive. We should remember, however, that we do not read—or live—simply to corroborate what we already know or believe. We should seek to expand imaginatively our range of experience and ideas, to feel into and understand even possibilities that we cannot accept. Certainly, a dogmatic approach to reading—or, again, to life—is stultifying.

What we have been discussing is one of the deepest and most difficult of all literary questions. You will continually confront this question, in one form or another, in all your dealings with literature, whether serious or casual. And all your future experience of reading and of life will simply flesh out the question for you and give you further material for thinking about it. As we have said, there is no automatic answer here.

● CAUTION

Remember that a feeling is an interpretation. This would be true of an interpretation made by a character in a narrative, by the author, or by the reader. For the moment, however, we are primarily concerned with the question of the author's interpretation as embodied in a work; we are concerned with the "feeling" a work may convey to the reader.

If a work of narration brings you to a new attitude—or merely to a new feeling—that is an interpretation. If the episode of the wolves (pp. 314–16) makes you change your feeling about wolves, that is an interpretation. When the novel *Uncle Tom's Cabin,* by Harriet Beecher Stowe, changed the feeling of many readers toward slavery, that was an interpretation. In fact, in almost all good narrative there is the element of the awakening and modifying of feeling, even when the author seems to use the narrative merely for purposes of exposition. For instance, look back at the anecdote of the "camel puller" or that of the lonely Harvard student (pp. 316–17).

■ APPLICATIONS

I Try to state the meaning—or meanings—of each of the following selections. Try to define what feelings are appealed to by them. It will be useful to know that the first selection is an excerpt from the autobiography of a young black who grew up in the slums of Harlem. His mother and father had come from the rural South and could never accept the values of their new environment. Pimp is the younger brother of the author; he has already entered a life of crime but is trying to free himself from it.

A   The real reason I wanted to be in Harlem was to spend more time with Pimp. But I couldn't. There just wasn't enough time. I couldn't take him to live with me. He was still too young. I couldn't have him hang out with me. I couldn't go back home. I'd just see him sometimes and talk to him.

       He got in trouble once with some kids, something childish like snatching a pocketbook. It didn't seem too important at the time. I was a little bothered about it, and I spoke to him. He said they'd just done it for kicks. I was trying real hard to keep a check on him from a distance. I knew what he was doing.

       He had started shooting craps, but this was nothing, really. All the young

Narration 339

boys shot craps and gambled. This was what they were supposed to do. But Mama was worried about it. I suppose she and Dad were getting kind of old. She used to tell me, "Oh, that boy, he stays out real late." It seemed as though they were trying to throw their burden of parenthood on me, and I kind of resented that, but I cared about Pimp. I wanted to do something for him.

The only trouble was that I had set such a high standard for him, such a bad example, it was hard as hell to erase. People knew him as my brother. The boys his age expected him to follow in my footsteps. He was my brother, and I had done so much, I had become a legend in the neighborhood. They expected him to live up to it.

I used to try to talk to him. I'd say, "Look, Pimp, what do you want to do, man?" I tried to get him interested in things. He used to like to play ball and stuff like that, but he wasn't interested in anything outside of the neighborhood. He wasn't interested in getting away. He couldn't see life as anything different. At fourteen, he was still reading comic books. He wasn't interested in anything except being hip.

I was real scared about this, but I knew that I couldn't do anything. He was doing a whole lot of shit that he wasn't telling me about. I remember one time I asked him, just to find out if he had started smoking yet, if he wanted some pot. He said, "No, man, I don't want any, and if I wanted some, I'd have it. I know where to get it." I was kind of hurt, but I knew that this was something that had to come. He would've known, and I suppose he should've known. When I was his age, even younger, I knew.

I couldn't feel mad about it, but I felt kind of hurt. I wanted to say, "Look, Pimp, what's happenin', man? Why aren't we as tight as we were before?" He still admired me, but something had happened. It was as though we had lost a contact, a closeness, that we once had, and I couldn't tell him things and get him to listen any more the way he used to do. I felt that if I couldn't control him, nobody could, and he'd be lost out there in the streets, going too fast, thinking he was hip enough to make it all by himself.

I'd take him to a movie or something like that. I'd take him downtown to the Village, and we'd hang out for a day, but I noticed something was missing. We didn't talk about all the really intimate things that we used to talk about. He wouldn't share his secrets with me any more, and this scared me, because I didn't know how far he'd gone. I wanted to say, "Pimp, what happened to the day that you and I used to walk through the streets with our arms around each other's shoulder? We used to sleep with our arms around each other, and you used to cry to follow me when I went out of the house." I wanted to say it, but it didn't make sense, because I knew that day had gone.

—Claude Brown: *Manchild in the Promised Land.*[7]

B   Zach was a big man, . . . he was six feet tall and weighed 190 pounds. This Richard remembered from Zach's account of that day. He had heard the story from others, too; it was famous in Leah [the town]. What had happened was this: the buck, when Zach came up to it, was down, and looked to be dead.

[7] Reprinted with permission of The Macmillan Company from *Manchild in the Promised Land* by Claude Brown. Copyright © Claude Brown, 1965. Reprinted by permission of Jonathan Cape Ltd.

Zach put down his rifle and was about to stick the buck in the sticking place just above the brisket, when the buck came to life. It merely had a broken hind leg and had been in what was, most likely, shock. Zach grabbed the antlers and decided he wasn't going to let the buck go. Even with one broken leg the buck could have run right out of the country. When telling about it, Zach had said, "He soon took that knife away from me."

Zach and the buck, who weighed as much as Zach, wrestled all morning. The buck would have finished Zach except that when he went to rear up in order to stab with his front hoofs, Zach could wrestle him over against his bad leg, and down they'd both go. This way they progressed, a yard or so at a time. Somewhere along the way Zach's jacket and shirt were torn right off him, but he wouldn't let go. When they came to a brook Zach tried to drown the buck, but he couldn't hold the head under water long enough. He tried to wedge the buck in the notch of a tree, but got caught himself and nearly snapped an ankle. He tried to break the buck's neck, but couldn't twist hard enough. All morning the two of them thrashed through the woods, face to face, snorting and glaring at each other. The buck bit his own tongue, and his blood and Zach's blood got all over both of them. Zach wouldn't let go, though, and finally they came to the plowed road. Then somebody came along in a T-model Ford, as Zach told it, and stunned the buck with a tire iron—stunning him long enough so Zach could let go and they could stick the big neck vein with a pocket knife.

—Thomas Williams: *The Night of Trees.*[8]

II   Reread the bear hunt (pp. 83–86). Compare it to the selection above. What feelings are appealed to in each selection? Whose side, for instance, are you on? Or do you have to make a choice? Ask your instructor to talk a little about the nature of tragedy. Both the bear hunt and the struggle with the buck can be thought of as examples of tragedy—though in its simplest terms.

III   Compare the following selection, a student theme, with the bear hunt and with the fight with the buck. What elements do all three have in common? How would you describe your reaction to this narrative? Do you think that the last line of the theme is adequate, or would an analysis of the feeling— not merely the statement "We felt bad about leaving him"—have helped the effect? Sometimes it is more effective to use *understatement,* as is done here, than to analyze and state the desired reaction. But you must judge each instance on what you take to be its merits. What do you think about this one?

A TRUE EPISODE

I live in New Orleans, which is getting to be a big industrial town, but which is still a good-time place and center for tourists. The biggest attraction for tourists is, of course, the old part, called French Town. It is full of bars and night clubs and antique shops and restaurants, with the bars well out ahead, about one per capita for the regular population of the city. Some-

---

[8] From *The Night of Trees* by Thomas Williams. Copyright 1960, 1961 by Thomas Williams. Reprinted by permission of Harold Matson Co., Inc.

thing strange happened to me there this last Christmas when I went home for the holidays.

I have two good friends I went to school with in New Orleans. Both of them now go East to school, one of them to Amherst and the other to Princeton. We had been having a big reunion that first afternoon home, just wandering around, going to a movie, taking on a little beer, but mostly just talking about what had been happening all fall and planning our vacation. Along about six-thirty we were on our way home, passing down Royal Street toward Canal Street. Outside a bar I saw a man on crutches leaning against a lamp post. He was not a man who just happened to be recovering from an injury. You could tell that he was a real cripple, a victim of polio or something like that. He was a well-dressed man, about thirty-five.

Just as we passed him, his crutches slipped, or something, and down he came, every which way. We did what anybody expects to do in a case like that. We found he wasn't hurt, just shaken a little. He sort of grinned, and said, "No bones broken, boys." We assembled his things and got him back on his crutches and propped against the lamp post. He thanked us very politely and wished us a Merry Christmas.

The fumes of whiskey on his breath almost knocked you down.

We had not gone more than six feet away, when we heard it again. He had slipped down again. Naturally we did a repeat performance on our Good Samaritan act. He made some kind of joke about how the city ought to provide foam-rubber curbstones for the tourist trade. I don't want to imply that he was drunk. He had had something to drink, of course, but if it hadn't been for the smell and the falling down, you would never have guessed it. We put him back together, and he again wished us Merry Christmas.

This time we got all of ten feet away. We ran back to him. He wasn't hurt, but he was worse shaken than before. He waited a little longer before he made his new joke. We were about to lift him up to his feet and prop him against the lamp post when he said, "Boys, maybe that will be above my standard of living. Just let me stay down here. Put me against the post where it's nice and comfortable."

We tried everything. We wanted to get a cab for him. We wanted to call somebody. But he would not let us. He was as bright and casual about it all as he could be. "Boys," he said, "it's just three days till Christmas. You don't want to be so worn out by then that you'll oversleep Christmas morning."

So we finally left him. He was whistling "Jeannie with the Light Brown Hair" as we went on away. We felt bad about leaving him, but there didn't seem anything we could do by then.

IV You are now to write the theme for which you have been preparing notes. But first, ask yourself if, in the light of what you have studied since you began to make your notes, you are still satisfied with your idea and your outline. If not, start over. Remember that you are to write a fully rounded narrative—of some 600 to 700 words or more if you wish.

If you are not satisfied with what you have done, perhaps you may find a suggestion for a subject in this list:

My First Love
My First Hate
The First Animal I Ever Shot
Brave—If You Can't Help It
Why Girls Leave Home
Hot Rod
Why I Hung onto the Job
Bark and Bite
The Funniest Thing That Ever Happened to Me

Don't be afraid of writing a funny theme.

How Interest Determines Action

Both the narrative by Vincent Sheean (pp. 327–28) and that by Marquis James (pp. 329–31) are self-contained and tidy examples of narrative structure. Both are drawn from fact, Sheean's from an evening he spent with Churchill and the Duke of Windsor, and James's from historical records. This circumstance raises a question: Did the facts come to either Sheean or James in this tidy structure? Can we expect the world to offer us action so conveniently ready for packaging?

Sometimes the world of fact does offer us an action in nearly perfect form, but this is rare. The world is enormously complex and experience enormously fluid, and there is constant interfusion of events. Think of how many things must have happened at that dinner party that Sheean attended, how many different things were said. There must have been a dozen other "actions" to be found on the same occasion—even actions involving Churchill and the Duke of Windsor—based, perhaps, on a clash of personalities and not on a political issue. But Sheean, being a political reporter, seized on what conformed to his interest. His interest, that is, determined the action. So we return here to an idea that we have already expressed (p. 337), but somewhat differently: the meaning of an event—the same event —may vary with the kind of interest brought to bear on it.

In connection with the narrative of Jackson's duel, we have already mentioned the long and complicated history leading to it. Jackson's marriage had provoked slanderous accusations of bigamy against Rachel, and these had been entwined with the rancorous political struggles of Jackson's career; the duel with Dickinson sprang, in fact, from a remark he had made about Rachel.

In the full-length biography of Jackson from which this episode is excerpted, the author, Marquis James, gives an elaborate treatment of this background; but when he gets to the duel itself, he focuses on what the action demonstrates about Jackson's character. James is not writing a tract against dueling. He is not concerned with the pathos of the death of a promising young man. He is not trying to evoke our sympathy for the young Mrs. Dickinson. All of these considerations may be implicit in the situation. (A little after our excerpt, in fact, James tells how Mrs. Jackson exclaimed, "Oh, God have pity on the poor wife—pity on the babe in her womb!") But the main intention never wavers—to exhibit in action the iron will of Jackson.

Since James has based his structure on this intention, we can lift his account out of its context and find it complete and unified as an action. Again, an interest has determined an action.

Selection

We have already seen how important the principle of selection is for description (pp. 290–91), and that same principle, under another name, is what we have been considering in our discussion of how interest determines an action. Sheean, for instance, selects the material relevant to his interest and to the point he intends to make.

Even in a narrative dealing with fact the author may heighten the interest by leaving out merely casual material. In treating the episode of Jackson's duel, Marquis James may know that after his opponent was hit Jackson actually said more than is given here. The author, however, presents just those remarks that contribute to our awareness of Jackson's character. In dealing with matters of fact, a writer does not want to distort the truth by omissions, but neither does he want to lose the significance of the action by obscuring it behind a screen of mere facts. Certainly, the narrator is concerned with facts, but primarily with significant facts. When he is dealing with imaginary events, the writer has a freer hand and a greater responsibility; for now he cannot rely on the interest that mere fact as fact can sometimes evoke in the reader. With the imaginary narrative a detail can never pay its way simply because it is interesting in itself. It must be relevant.

Relevance

The kind of relevance we have been discussing concerns the main interest, the meaning, the point of the action. Let us call this the "relevance of theme." But there is another sort of relevance that makes its own demands—demands sometimes contradictory to those of theme. These demands spring from the fact that narrative, to be effective, must be, in large part, an immediate presentation of events. Therefore, there must be selection in terms of vividness—the detail, the small gesture, the trivial word that can stir the imagination. And the details that, strictly speaking, are descriptive may be absorbed into the narrative effect. For instance, the cut and color of Jackson's and Dickinson's clothes, the kind of woods by which the meeting took place, and the Irish accent of General Overton when he gave the command to fire contribute to the impression of reality. Marquis James is much concerned to give an immediate presentation. But if we turn back to Vincent Sheean's anecdote of Churchill and the Duke of Windsor, we find that immediacy is not very important to the author. His chief concern is to present a clash of opinions. Even here, however, we do get the details of the Stuart tartan that the kilted Duke wears, his posture on the sofa, and Churchill's position staring at the floor. These are examples of what we may call the "relevance of immediacy." They make us see the event—and seeing is believing. (See Description, pp. 275–312, and Diction, pp. 396–434.)

● CAUTION

The effectiveness of a narrative often depends on skillful interweaving of details dictated by relevance of theme with those dictated by relevance of immediacy.

Consider the function of each detail you use.

Be sure that the details are not offered in solid blocks—one block of one kind and one of another. Weave details into a unified texture, with the action and with each other, so that the reader, without stopping for analysis, may feel the significance of the narrative as it progresses. The narrative, in other words, must have unity of impact.

■ APPLICATIONS

I   Go back over "The Fire Next Time," by James Baldwin (pp. 858–67) and "91 Revere Street," by Robert Lowell (pp. 867–76) to locate details of special effectiveness.

II   Make a criticism of your last theme on the basis of relevance of detail. Revise it where you think desirable.

Point of View

We have used the term *point of view* in connection with description (pp. 297–301) to indicate the physical relation of a spectator to the thing observed. In connection with narration, the phrase has a somewhat different meaning, a meaning that implies some of the more important problems of narration. In narration, point of view involves a person who bears some relation to the action, either as observer or participant, and whose intelligence serves the reader as a kind of guide to the action. Point of view, then, concerns two questions:

1   Who is the narrator?
2   What is his relation to the action?

In general, there are two possible points of view, the first person and the third person. When we read, "That summer when we were staying at Bayport, I had the most astonishing experience of my life," we know that we are dealing with the first-person point of view. When we read, "When Jake Millen, at the age of sixty, surveyed the wreck of his career, he knew that only one course was left open to him," we know that we are dealing with a third-person point of view. That is, in the first example, an "I," real or fictitious, is telling us about an experience in which he himself was involved; in the second example, an author, writing impersonally, is telling us about an experience in which another person was involved.

There are, however, certain shadings and variations possible within these two broad general divisions of point of view. In actual practice, such shadings and variations may be of the greatest complication and subtlety, and it must be held in mind that any attempt to schematize them can only be crudely indicated.

What are the variations possible within the first person? The distinctions here are to be made on the basis of the relation of the first-person narrator to the action that he narrates. Two extreme positions can be taken. First, the narrator may tell of an action in which he is the main, or at least an important, participant. That is, he tells his "own story." We are all familiar with this type of treatment. Most autobiographies are of this kind; for example, the selections from Podhoretz and Yeats. Occasionally, we encounter a piece of informal history using this method; for example, T. E. Lawrence's *Seven Pillars of Wisdom.* Many short stories and novels create an imaginary "I" who is the main character of the story and who tells the story; for example, Daniel Defoe's *Robinson Crusoe* and Ernest Hemingway's *A Farewell to Arms.*

At the other extreme, the narrator, either real or imaginary, recounts in action of which he is merely an observer. This, also, is a familiar type of treatment. Memoirs tend to take this form, for frequently the writer of memoirs has not played a conspicuous role in affairs but has been in a position to observe important events. Theodore Sorensen, in *Kennedy,* and Arthur Schlesinger, Jr., in *A Thousand Days,* have both given accounts of President John F. Kennedy's administration. These are good examples of this type, as is *Between the Thunder and the Sun,* from which we have taken the episode concerning Churchill and the Duke of Windsor. The same type of treatment occurs, naturally, in fiction. Poe's "The Fall of the House of Usher" is a notable instance, and Ring Lardner's story "Haircut" is another.

Thus we may have the two types of the first-person point of view: *narrator-main character* and *narrator-observer.* But in between these two extremes many variations are possible, narratives in which the narrator participates directly in the action and has something at stake in its outcome but is not the main character. We may call this the method of *narrator-involved observer.*

A set of pictures may be helpful:

CIRCLE OF ACTION

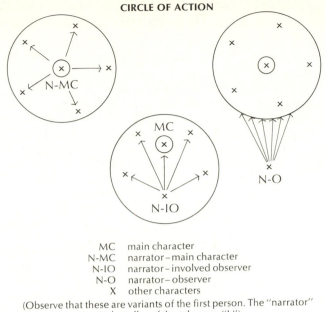

MC   main character
N-MC   narrator – main character
N-IO   narrator – involved observer
N-O   narrator – observer
X   other characters

(Observe that these are variants of the first person. The "narrator"
in each instance is the teller of the tale as an "I.")

But what of the variations possible within the third-person point of view?

In this point of view the narrative is given by an author writing impersonally, that is, as a kind of disembodied intelligence before whom the
events are played out. What is the relation of this impersonal author, this
disembodied intelligence, to the action? In the first place, he does not participate in the action; he is merely an observer. The question then becomes
this: "How much of the action does the author observe?" And here, as in
dealing with the first-person point of view, we can define two extreme
positions.

One extreme we may call the *panoramic*—or *omniscient*—point of view.
In this method the author may report any aspect or all aspects of an action
and may go into the head of any or all of the characters involved in the action. His eye, as it were, sweeps the entire field and he reports whatever is
interesting or relevant. In an imaginary narrative there is no necessary
limit to what may be seen or reported according to this method; the most
private acts and the most secret thoughts or sensations of any or all of the
characters may be reported, for the author is the creator of the whole. But
when a writer is using this method in presenting a nonimaginative narrative,
say a piece of history, he is, of course, limited by what facts or plausible
deductions are available to him. He cannot be as thoroughgoing in applying
the method as the writer of an imaginary narrative, though within the limits
of the facts available to him he may do so. Many pieces of historical and
biographical writing use this method, and, of course, it is common in fiction.
For instance, it appears in the following scene from Thackeray's novel

Vanity Fair, presenting the city of Brussels when the false news comes that Napoleon has won the Battle of Quatre Bras, an engagement just before Waterloo:

> Crowds rushed to the Namur gate, from which direction the noise proceeded, and many rode along the level *chaussée,* to be in advance of any intelligence from the army. Each man asked his neighbor for news; and even great English lords and ladies condescended to speak to persons whom they did not know. The friends of the French went abroad, wild with excitement, and prophesying the triumph of their Emperor. The merchants closed their shops, and came out to swell the general chorus of alarm and clamor. Women rushed to the churches, and crowded the chapels, and knelt and prayed on the flags and steps. The dull sound of cannon went on rolling, rolling. Presently carriages with travellers began to leave the town, galloping away by the Ghent barrier. The prophecies of the French partisans began to pass for facts. "He has cut the army in two," it was said. "He is marching straight on Brussels. He will overpower the English, and be here tonight." "He will overpower the English," shrieked Isidor to his master, "and will be here tonight." The man bounded in and out from the lodgings to the street, always returning with some fresh particulars of disaster. Jos's face grew paler and paler. Alarm began to take entire possession of the stout civilian. All the champagne he drank brought no courage to him. Before sunset he was worked up to such a pitch of nervousness as gratified his friend Isidor to behold, who now counted upon the spoils of the owner of the laced coat.
>
> The women were away all this time. After hearing the firing for a moment, the stout Major's wife bethought her of her friend in the next chamber, and ran in to watch, and if possible to console, Amelia. The idea that she had that helpless and gentle creature to protect, gave additional strength to the natural courage of the honest Irishwoman. She passed five hours by her friend's side, sometimes in remonstrance, sometimes talking cheerfully, oftener in silence, and terrified mental supplication.
>
> —WILLIAM MAKEPEACE THACKERAY: *Vanity Fair.*

At the other extreme from the panoramic point of view we find what we may call the point of view of *sharp focus.* The author does not sweep the entire field of the action, but keeps his, and the reader's, attention focused on one character and on that character's relation to the action; he does, however, "know all" about the character on whom he has chosen to focus his interest. Accordingly, the parts of the action not directly participated in by the selected character are not reported by the author. To use a figure of speech, the character may be regarded as a kind of prism through which the action is refracted. Here is an example of this method:

> He was hungry, for, except for some biscuits which he had asked two grudging curates to bring him, he had eaten nothing since breakfast-time. He sat down at an uncovered wooden table opposite two work-girls and a mechanic. A slatternly girl waited on him.
>
> "How much is a plate of peas?" he asked.

"Three halfpence, sir," said the girl.

"Bring me a plate of peas," he said, "and a bottle of ginger beer."

He spoke roughly in order to belie his air of gentility, for his entry had been followed by a pause of talk. His face was heated. To appear natural he pushed his cap back on his head and planted his elbows on the table. The mechanic and the two work-girls examined him point by point before resuming their conversation in a subdued voice. The girl brought him a plate of grocer's hot peas, seasoned with pepper and vinegar, a fork and his ginger beer. He ate his food greedily and found it so good that he made a note of the shop mentally. When he had eaten all the peas he sipped his ginger beer and sat for some time thinking of Corley's adventure. In his imagination he beheld the pair of lovers walking along some dark road; he heard Corley's voice in deep energetic gallantries, and saw again the leer of the young woman's mouth. This vision made him feel keenly his own poverty of purse and spirit. He was tired of knocking about, of pulling the devil by the tail, of shifts and intrigues. He would be thirty-one in November. Would he never get a good job? Would he never have a home of his own? He thought how pleasant it would be to have a warm fire to sit by and a good dinner to sit down to. He had walked the streets long enough with friends and with girls. He knew what those friends were worth: he knew the girls too. Experience had embittered his heart against the world. But all hope had not left him. He felt better after having eaten than he had felt before, less weary of his life, less vanquished in spirit. He might yet be able to settle down in some snug corner and live happily if he could only come across some good simple-minded girl with a little of the ready. —JAMES JOYCE: "Two Gallants," *Dubliners*.[9]

Between the extremes of the panoramic point of view and the point of view of sharp focus there are, of course, all sorts of gradations and mixtures of the two methods. The choice of one of the methods or the mixing of the two is not a matter to be settled arbitrarily, for the method should reflect a special interest involved in the narrative. For instance, the panoramic point of view is well suited to the rendering of some large and complicated action —a battle, a mob scene, the burning of a city—in which the interest lies in the sweep of events. The point of view of sharp focus is suited to a narrative in which the interest is primarily in the psychology of a single character. A narrative may well involve both such interests, and then the writer may mix his methods according to the needs of the moment.

But the use of the panoramic point of view is not restricted to action that covers a physically broad field, such as a battle. Take, for example, this section from a student theme:

The family sat around, waiting for Jack to come home. He was the youngest, and they were all partial to him. And now he was the first ever

---

[9] From *Dubliners* by James Joyce. Originally published by B. W. Huebsch, Inc. in 1916. Copyright © 1967 by the Estate of James Joyce. All rights reserved. Reprinted by permission of The Viking Press, Inc. Reprinted by permission of Jonathan Cape Ltd. and the Executors of the James Joyce Estate.

to be picked up by the police, and the family didn't even know what it was about. They had to sit there and wait for news.

Waiting had never been easy for the father. He paced around, picking up a newspaper, glancing at it as though nothing had happened, then throwing it down. He chewed his underlip, the way he did when something was building up inside him. *He kept telling himself not to blow up, but misery was welling up in him till he felt sick.* He was a man built for action, and waiting was not his dish.

The mother sat in the rocking chair. She pretended to sew, but all the time her mind was on Jack. She was a religious woman, sincere and without any exhibitionism, and if her lips were moving now, she was praying. *But her prayer consisted only of the name of her son, "Jack, Jack," over and over again.* She finally said to her husband, "John, why don't you sit down? You're wearing out the carpet." It was an old joke between them.

Susie, the daughter of the family, came in about nine, wearing her usual air of self-satisfied virtue. When they told her what had happened, that look of self-satisfied virtue became even more obvious, and she got out a few dramatic sobs, saying, "Poor Jackie, poor Jackie, I've always cautioned him about that car." Then she began to rearrange flowers, humming to herself the gayest little tune as she passed close to her brother Bill. *She felt great and full of energy, as if she were going to a party.*

"You're damned pleased about it, aren't you?" he demanded, in his savage way, and she flounced out of the room. But she came back in a minute and wanted to know if she couldn't get a glass of milk and some cake for "poor Father."

"For God's sake," Bill said, in disgust, and rose from his chair.

"Don't swear, son," the mother said.

"It's enough to make you swear," he said. "When she comes in with that saintly look and wants to do somebody a favor, you know she is getting ready to pull a fast one."

He was right.

Here the event is rendered in the third person, as it would appear to a mere observer. The scene is restricted, but it is treated with a sweeping, panoramic view; that is, we seem to stand back from the scene while the family is waiting. We see them all, one after another, as if a movie camera were slowly sweeping the room, catching each person in some significant gesture or word. But notice that we do have certain intimate glimpses of the minds and feelings of several characters (the passages set in italic in the text). If these passages were omitted, the panorama would be purely objective, not omniscient.

■ APPLICATIONS

I What point of view is used in the following selections?

1 "The Dog That Bit People," by James Thurber (pp. 754–59)
2 The episode of Churchill and the Duke of Windsor (pp. 327–28)

II We have seen two examples of the panoramic method using the third person. This method need not, however, be confined to the third person. Here is the episode of the waiting family transposed, still with the panoramic method, into the first person—though now, as a piece of first-person narrative, it cannot be omniscient. This change might have been made in several ways, for instance by setting an observer in the scene and making him relate it. But here another brother, who has received news of the event, simply reconstructs the scene in his mind, as though he were present.

> It isn't hard for me to imagine how the family was sitting around waiting for my brother to come home. My brother was the youngest of us children, and in a way they were all partial to him. And now he was the first of us ever to get picked up by the police, and the family didn't even know what it was about. They had to sit there and wait for the news.
>
> Waiting wasn't ever very easy for my father, to begin with. I bet he was pacing around, picking up a newspaper, glancing at it as though nothing was on his mind, then throwing it down. He was probably chewing his underlip the way he does when something is building up inside him. He is a man built for action, and waiting is not his dish. He was probably about to lose his temper, too, at some little trifle.
>
> My mother was sure to be in the rocking chair. She would pretend to be sewing, but all the time her mind would be on Jack. She is a religious woman, but not in any sickening way, and, if her lips were moving, she was praying. Then she would finally say to my father, "John, why don't you sit down; you're wearing out the carpet," which is an old joke between them.
>
> Susie, my sister, came in about nine. She is a goodie-good if there ever was one. When they told her, she cried, and said, "Poor Jackie, poor Jackie, I've always cautioned him about that car." Then she began to rearrange flowers, and Bill says she was humming the gayest little tune to herself under her breath. She came too close and he heard her.
>
> "You're damned pleased about it all, aren't you?" he said, and she flounced out of the room. But she came back in a minute and wanted to know if she couldn't get a glass of milk and some cake for my father. That is always a bad sign, a sign she is cooking up one of her fast ones. She was sure getting ready to pull a fast one that night.

With the narrative above as a model, transpose a panoramic scene into one treated in the first person. To find a panoramic scene that may be transposed, browse in a collection of short stories or through some magazines. Be sure, when you make the transposition, to try, by the use of language and by other touches, to indicate a personality for the narrator.

Alternatively, if you cannot find a panoramic scene to be transposed, work the other way around. Take a scene handled in sharp focus and convert it into panoramic treatment, either omniscient or nonomniscient.

III   You are now to do your final theme of this section. You may make it either a piece of reportage or a short story. It should not be shorter than 750 words.

If you make it reportage, you are required to use some incident that you have actually witnessed. If you want to do something in this form and think nothing in your recent experience satisfactory as a subject, go out and cover an event that you think might prove fruitful. In writing your report use as fully as possible the material you have studied up to this point, again with reference to your notebook.

If you decide to try your hand at fiction, it might be a good idea to reread several stories that you have found interesting in the past. In rereading them, try to define as clearly as possible the meaning the story has for you. Then decide how the author has conveyed his meaning. What methods has he used? Does his practice sharpen for you the principles that you have been studying? And again refer to your notebook.

Now write.

PART THREE

SPECIAL PROBLEMS
OF DISCOURSE

CHAPTER 10

The Paragraph and the Sentence

Thus far in this book we have been talking about the writing of whole themes. We have considered how one might go about describing the process of training a dog (p. 65); or how one might outline to another person the steps to be followed in gluing a piece of felt to wood (p. 143). Such problems demand extended solutions and require writing several hundred words. We have been thinking in terms of whole compositions and only incidentally in terms of paragraphs and sentences.

But the process of writing is, of course, a double one: though the writer must constantly keep in mind the developing shape of the composition as a whole, nevertheless, he proceeds by writing individual sentences and paragraphs. The process of revision also requires attention to particular paragraphs and sentences.

In any case, the student is not encountering the problems of paragraph construction for the first time. In his precollege work he has studied the paragraph and the sentence as rhetorical structures—and the sentence as a grammatical structure as well. Many high schools stress the writing of paragraphs. The student who has had sound training of this sort may well regard what follows as simply an intensive review.

The Paragraph as a Convenience to the Reader

The paragraph, since it is a unit of thought, has a certain structure, and like the larger composition of which it is part, it is bound to embody (or fail to embody) the principles of unity, coherence, and emphasis.

When the writer divides his composition into paragraphs, he is indicating to his reader that each of the subdivisions so marked off constitutes a unit of thought. (The normal way of marking off a paragraph is to indent the first sentence; but occasionally this is indicated by putting an extra space between the paragraphs. In manuscript, the beginning of a paragraph may be indicated by the paragraph sign, ¶.) The writer thus undertakes to make his thought structure visible upon the page itself. To do so is surely a courtesy to the reader, and since communication between writer and reader is difficult enough at best, the writer who wants his reader to understand him will make his best use of this device.[1]

Obviously, paragraphing can be of no help to the reader if the paragraphs so set off are not really meaningful segments of the writer's thought. If they pretend to be units of thought but are in fact simply formless blobs arbitrarily divided from each other, they can only mislead the reader. *For a paragraph undertakes to discuss one topic or one aspect of a topic.*

How long should a paragraph be? Common sense dictates that the ordinary paragraph will neither be reduced to a single sentence nor include a hundred sentences. To turn every sentence into a paragraph would be as bad as having no paragraphs at all; and very long paragraphs would tell the reader almost as little as a series of one-sentence paragraphs. In neither case would the writer have provided a means for readily distinguishing the stages of his developing discourse.

Yet this is not to say that an *occasional* very short paragraph may not tell the reader a great deal, for the very shortness of the paragraph—if the brevity is justified—gives special emphasis. Turn back to page 84 and read the account of the Eskimos' attack on the bear. The bear finally yields to temptation and swallows the tallow bait. "With a billowy movement, his snout suddenly shot forward and engulfed the bait, dropping it into the bottomless pit of his belly." Then the author presents the next sentence as a separate paragraph:

> Simultaneously, Anarvik and Ernenek leaped to their feet with cheers and laughter, for the bear was theirs.

Here, obviously the narrator is helping his reader to follow the drama of the chase. With the bear's quiet action of swallowing the bait, the climax of the hunt has now—surprising though it may seem to the reader—occurred, for though the bear may live on for several days, he is doomed and is now effectually in the hunters' power. By setting off as a separate paragraph the sentence that describes the hunters' cheers and laughter, the writer stresses this point.

---

[1] A special convention with reference to the paragraph needs to be noted. When there is direct quotation of a conversation, the change of speakers is normally indicated by a new paragraph. Thus:

"How much is a plate of peas?" he asked.
"Three halfpence, sir," said the girl.
"Bring me a plate of peas," he said, "and a bottle of ginger beer." (See p. 348.)

Yet, much hard work for the hunters still remains. The great bear, though internally wounded, will escape unless they are able to endure the cold and keep following him until they can finish him off. So the writer adds the single word "Almost," and because in this context it is a very important word, he sets it off too as a paragraph in itself.

Even a single word, then, may sometimes warrant being treated as a paragraph. Conversely, in some special circumstances, an abnormally long paragraph may sometimes be justified. The young writer, however, will do well to avoid either of these extremes, and particularly he will do well to avoid very long paragraphs. Long paragraphs, as thoughtful reconsideration may reveal, are often nothing more than large blobs of words, not organized, or if organized, needing to be marked off into two or three shorter paragraphs.

The Structure of the Paragraph

A well-conceived and well-constructed paragraph is a unit, and often this unity is indicated by a key sentence—what is called the *topic sentence*. The topic sentence states the central thought, which the rest of the paragraph develops. We can think of the topic sentence as a kind of backbone, a spine, which supports the body of the paragraph and around which the rest of the structure is formed. Here is an example:

> *The reader of a novel—by which I mean the critical reader—is himself a novelist; he is the maker of a book which may or may not please his taste when it is finished, but of a book for which he must take his own share of the responsibility.* The author does his part, but he cannot transfer his book like a bubble into the brain of the critic; he cannot make sure that the critic will possess his work. The reader must therefore become, for his part, a novelist, never permitting himself to suppose that the creation of the book is solely the affair of the author. The difference between them is immense, of course, and so much so that a critic is always inclined to extend and intensify it. The opposition that he conceives between the creative and the critical task is a very real one; but in modestly belittling his own side of the business he is apt to forget an essential portion of it. The writer of the novel works in a manner that would be utterly impossible to the critic, no doubt, and with a liberty and with a range that would disconcert him entirely. But in one quarter their work coincides; both of them make the novel.   —PERCY LUBBOCK: *The Craft of Fiction.*

In this paragraph the first sentence (which we have italicized) is the topic sentence. There are obvious advantages in presenting at the very beginning of the paragraph a brief statement of the thought that the paragraph is to develop. But the topic sentence need not open the paragraph. Consider the following example:

> The artistic temperament is a disease that afflicts amateurs. It is a disease which arises from men not having sufficient power of expression to utter and get rid of the element of art in their being. It is healthful to every sane man to utter the art within him; it is essential to every sane man to get rid of the art within him at all costs. Artists of a large and wholesome vitality get rid of their art easily, as they breathe easily, or perspire easily. But in artists of less force, the thing becomes a pressure, and produces a definite pain, which is called the artistic temperament. Thus, very great artists are able to be ordinary men—men like Shakespeare or Browning. There are many real tragedies of the artistic temperament, tragedies of vanity or violence or fear. *But the great tragedy of the artistic temperament is that it cannot produce any art.*
>
> —G. K. CHESTERTON: "On the Wit of Whistler," *Heretics.*

The final sentence of this paragraph (italicized) makes a generalized statement about the point developed in the paragraph as a whole. Thus in this instance, the topic sentence serves as a kind of summary. Though a topic sentence frequently occurs at the beginning or at the end of a paragraph, it may in fact occur at any point within the paragraph.

■ APPLICATIONS

I   The following paragraphs contain topic sentences. Point them out.

A   "The Rebuilding of London" proceeds ruthlessly apace. The humble old houses that dare not scrape the sky are being duly punished for their timidity. Down they come; and in their place are shot up new tenements, quick and high as rockets. And the little old streets, so narrow and exclusive, so shy and crooked—we are making an example of them, too. We lose our way in them, do we?—we whose time is money. Our omnibuses can't trundle through them, can't they? Very well, then. Down with them! We have no use for them. This is the age of "noble arteries."

—Max Beerbohm: *Yet Again.*

B   Such was the man who, at the age of thirty-three, became headmaster of Rugby. His outward appearance was the index of his inward character: everything about him denoted energy, earnestness, and the best intentions. His legs, perhaps, were shorter than they should have been; but the sturdy athletic frame, especially when it was swathed (as it usually was) in the flowing robes of a Doctor of Divinity, was full of an imposing vigour; and his head, set decisively upon the collar, stock and bands of ecclesiastical tradition, clearly belonged to a person of eminence. The thick, dark clusters of his hair, his bushy eyebrows and curling whiskers, his straight nose and bulky chin, his firm and upward-curved lower lip—all these revealed a temperament of ardor and determination. His eyes were bright and large; they were also obviously honest. And yet—why was it?—was it the lines of the mouth or the frown on the forehead?—it was hard to say, but it was unmistakable—there was a slightly puzzled look upon the face of Dr. Arnold.

—Lytton Strachey: "Dr. Arnold," *Eminent Victorians*.

C It is odd that American men are so frequently presented in European caricatures of the type, in fiction, plays, and films, as being extremely ill-mannered, loud, rough customers. Such Americans exist, of course, just as sneering Englishmen, bullying Teutons, insolent Latins also exist. But it has always seemed to me that American manners in general tend to err on the side of formality and solemnity. They are rather like those of elderly English dons and clergymen. The ordinary English are much more casual. We do not take enough trouble, for example, with our introductions. Terrified of appearing pompous, we hastily mumble names or hastily accept a mumble of names, so that our introductions do not serve their purpose, and often, not knowing to whom we are talking, we saunter into the most dreadful traps. The deliberate ceremony that most Americans make of introductions protects them from these dangers and errors.   —J. B. Priestley: *Midnight on the Desert*.

II Look back at the student theme "Training a Dog" (p. 65). How many of its eight paragraphs may be said to contain topic sentences?

III Construct paragraphs that will incorporate as topic sentences four of the following:

1 Students should have a part in granting permanent tenure and in the promotion of university professors.
2 Football rather than baseball is now our national sport.
3 The draft should be abolished, and the Army of the United States should be a voluntary army.
4 Television is bringing about the death of the imagination.
5 The medium is indeed the message.
6 The prime problem of civilization today is overpopulation.
7 The prime problem of civilization today is the atomic bomb.
8 Set a thief to catch a thief.

Though every true paragraph is a unit, not every paragraph includes a topic sentence. Sometimes the idea or emotion or aspect of experience with which the paragraph is principally concerned need not be summed up in such fashion. Consider the following paragraph from G. M. Trevelyan's *History of England:*

As Drake entered Plymouth Sound after nearly three years' absence from Europe, his first question to some passing fishermen was whether the Queen were alive and well. Yes, in spite of all her enemies, she was still alive, and well enough to come next year and knight him on board his ship at Deptford. It was the most important knighthood ever conferred by an English sovereign, for it was a direct challenge to Spain and an appeal to the people of England to look to the sea for their strength. In view of this deed, disapproved by her faithful Cecil, who shall say Elizabeth could never act boldly? Her bold decisions are few and can be numbered, but each of them began an epoch.[2]

Few readers would contend that this paragraph is not unified, but there is no clear topic sentence. One might try to make a case for the third sentence, but then one might make an equally good case for the fourth sentence, or even the fifth. Narrative prose (such as this is) and descriptive prose abound in paragraphs without topic sentences. The student might, for example, look at the paragraphs quoted on page 280 (from *The World I Live In*); pages 287–88 and 291–92 (from *Bleak House*); page 290 (from *Seven Pillars of Wisdom*); page 300 (from *Main Street*); pages 306–07 (from *South Wind*); page 348 (from *Vanity Fair*); and page 309 (from *The Waves*).

Methods of Paragraph Organization

Whether or not the writer makes use of a topic sentence, he faces, nevertheless, the problem of organizing his paragraphs. What are some of the typical structural principles that can be employed? Not surprisingly, they turn out to be, by and large, the same as those that govern the composition as a whole. In the chapter on Exposition, we described various methods of organization, such as classification, comparison and contrast, illustration, and definition. These are methods that may be used to shape the smaller as well as the larger units of composition.

By illustration

On pages 79–80 we offered a single paragraph of T. H. Huxley's "The Herring" as an instance of organization by illustration. Though we printed the whole of the selection from *The Saga of Billy the Kid* (pp. 81–82) to show this same principle of organization at work, inspection will make it clear that the opening paragraph itself manifests organization by illustration.

■ APPLICATION

The selection from Della Lutes's "Are Neighbors Necessary?" (pp. 86–87) was offered as another example of exposition achieved through the method of illustration. Which of the individual paragraphs also make use of this method? Are there any that do not?

---

[2] From *History of England* by G. M. Trevelyan. Reprinted by permission of Longmans Group Ltd.

By comparison and contrast

Comparison and contrast, a method often used for building up the whole essay, may also serve to shape an individual paragraph. See the paragraph quoted from John Corbin's *An American at Oxford* (p. 75).

■ **APPLICATION**

Reread G. Lowes Dickinson's "Red-bloods and Mollycoddles" (pp. 76–77) and answer the following questions:

1 How many of the individual paragraphs employ comparison and contrast as their principle of organization?
2 Point out the topic sentences, if any.

By syllogistic pattern

We remarked in Chapter 3 (p. 36) that the "order of logic" was one of the four general modes for achieving coherence and that in "exposition and argument, the order is always that of logic." But in some paragraphs this logical arrangement becomes very strict, sometimes approaching that of a formal syllogism. (See pp. 208–10.) Here is an example:

> A really great pitcher must have control. Charles Ramsey had wonderful speed and a curve that broke as sharply as any that I have ever seen. He dazzled opposing batters with his fireball or made them break their backs reaching for pitches that broke sharply away from the plate. Charles had nearly everything—he even fielded his position brilliantly—but he lacked control. Even on his best days his control was less than certain. Shrewd batters learned this, and waited him out, frequently successfully, for a base on balls. On his worst days he simply couldn't find the plate. A pitcher without control cannot win close games. For this reason I do not consider Ramsey a great pitcher.

Analysis shows that we have here a *major premise* ("A really great pitcher must have control"), a *minor premise* ("Charles Ramsey lacks control"), and a *conclusion* ("Therefore Charles Ramsey is not a great pitcher"). This method of organization is, however, rare, and in general the more complex methods of organization discussed in the chapters on Exposition and Argument, such as functional analysis or causal analysis, do not occur in single paragraphs, for paragraphs are relatively short and their structures necessarily simple.

By sequence in time

To tell what happened first and then what happened next constitutes the most primitive of all the ways of organizing prose. Though it can be as simple as a child's narrative, it can also be put to uses as sophisticated as those in a Henry James novel. It is an indispensable mode of expressing our experience as human beings, for we live in a world of time and are constantly involved in actions and processes. We construct paragraphs in terms of time sequence, then, not only when we attempt fiction (see pp. 313 and 606–16) but also when we describe a process like that of training a dog (see p. 65) or gluing felt to wood (see p. 143).

By arrangement of objects in space

Some of the simplest and most natural ways of organizing a paragraph are found in descriptive prose (see p. 275) in the various schemes by which visible objects may be ordered. (The student might at this point review what has been said earlier in "Texture and Pattern in Description," pp. 296–305.) Consider a paragraph from Joseph Conrad's story, "The Secret Sharer":

> On my right hand there were lines of fishing-stakes resembling a mysterious system of half-submerged bamboo fences, incomprehensible in its division of the domain of tropical fish, and crazy of aspect as if abandoned for ever by some nomad tribe of fishermen now gone to the other end of the ocean; for there was no sign of human habitation as far as the eye could reach. To the left a group of barren islets, suggesting ruins of stone walls, towers, and blockhouses, had its foundations set in a blue sea that itself looked solid, so still and stable did it lie below my feet; even the track of light from the westering sun shone smoothly, without that animated glitter which tells of an imperceptible ripple. And when I turned my head to take a parting glance at the tug which had just left us anchored outside the bar, I saw the straight line of the flat shore joined to the stable sea, edge to edge, with a perfect and unusual closeness, in one levelled floor half brown, half blue under the enormous dome of the sky.

Here we have a fixed observer. He tells us what he sees on his right hand, then on his left, and finally, turning his head, what he sees behind him. (There is even an implied look upward: "the . . . dome of the sky.") The order of composition is simple and even mechanical, though the writing itself is not mechanical. Note, for example, the sense of finality and completeness given by the last sentence. The observer's survey comes to rest in "the straight line" of shore and sea "under the enormous dome of the sky." The paragraph thus rounds out and completes its chosen topic. It is thoroughly unified, though it does *not* contain a topic sentence.

We may also have a paragraph describing a scene through the eyes of an observer who is shifting his position. The paragraph from T. E. Lawrence's *Seven Pillars of Wisdom* (p. 299) furnishes an illustration of this. Or a scene may be described in terms of an image that provokes a frame of reference. Thomas Hardy, for example, describes the continent of Europe through the figure of a human being (see p. 309).

By mood or dominant interest

Various other ways in which descriptions of a scene may be organized have been discussed in Chapter 8. The description may be keyed to some sense, hearing or touch or sight; dominated by a special mood; focused upon a particular detail; and so on. All these methods of describing a scene apply to descriptive *paragraphs* as well as to the larger units of description. In fact, the examples that we used in Chapter 8 to illustrate methods of presenting description turn out to be, almost without exception, distinct paragraphs. The student can learn from them, therefore, a great deal about paragraph development (see especially pp. 272–89).

Unity and Coherence in the Paragraph

Unity implies coherence. As we have pointed out (pp. 35–36), the various elements in a unified piece of writing must cohere—that is, they must have a meaningful relation to each other. Yet though unity implies coherence, the inexperienced writer may discover that unity does not guarantee it. Even though he may have carved out a paragraph that is related to *one* idea and does *one* job within the composition, the parts of that paragraph may not actually hang together. Consider the following paragraph, which does have unity of a sort—it's all about one thing, the herring—but which is scarcely coherent:

> The body, tapering to each end, is covered with thin, flexible scales, which are very easily rubbed off. The taper head, with its underhung jaw, is smooth and scaleless on the top; the large eye is partly covered by two folds of transparent skin, like eyelids—only immovable and with the slit between them vertical instead of horizontal; the cleft behind the gill-cover is very wide, and, when the cover is raised, the large red gills which lie underneath it are freely exposed. If anyone wants to exemplify the meaning of the word "fish," he cannot choose a better animal than a herring. The rounded back bears the single moderately long dorsal fin about its middle.

■ **APPLICATION**

Rearrange the sentences in this paragraph so as to restore full coherence. (After you have made your best effort, you might turn back to pages 79–80 to see how the author actually arranged them.)

Consider what happens to the coherence of the paragraph quoted from Chesterton on page 358 when we rearrange it to read as follows:

Artists of a large and wholesome vitality get rid of their art easily, as they breathe easily, or perspire easily. It is healthful to every sane man to utter the art within him; it is essential to every sane man to get rid of the art within him at all costs. The artistic temperament is a disease that afflicts amateurs. It is a disease which arises from men not having sufficient power of expression to utter and get rid of the element of art in their being. Thus, very great artists are able to be ordinary men—men like Shakespeare or Browning. But in artists of less force, the thing becomes a pressure, and produces a definite pain, which is called the artistic temperament. There are many real tragedies of the artistic temperament, tragedies of vanity or violence or fear. But the great tragedy of the artistic temperament is that it cannot produce any art.

The paragraph as rearranged is "about" one general topic, the nature of the artistic temperament. But a careful comparison of the rearranged paragraph with the original (p. 358) will illustrate how much blurring of thought occurs when we do not think out the relation of sentence to sentence within the paragraph. (It is only fair to observe that an author often achieves much of the finer articulation of part with part only with revision. See Chapter 15.)

■ APPLICATION

The sentences in the paragraphs that follow (three of them from selections in the Readings and one not) have been hashed.

1   Attempt to restore what you take to be the original order.
2   List the words in these sentences that helped you most in restoring the original order.

A   Literature is alive to us because we live in its images, but so is any play of the mind—so is chess: the lines of play that we foresee and try in our heads and dismiss are as much a part of the game as the moves that we make. John Keats said that the unheard melodies are sweeter, and all chess players sadly recall that the combinations that they planned and which never came to be played were the best. Almost everything that we do that is worth doing is done in the first place in the mind's eye. Nor is [the gift of imagination] just a literary gift; it is, I repeat, characteristically human. The richness of human life is that we have many lives; we live the events that do not happen (and some that cannot) as vividly as those that do; and if thereby we die a thousand deaths, that is the price we pay for living a thousand lives. (A cat, of course, has only nine.)

B   Another traced its genesis to the expansion of literacy. Contemporary observers who maintained critical detachment from the new fashion, and sought to define its relations with the past, turned up several notions that still possess interest. One writer theorized that Overkill was an extension of the American tall-tale tradition. Still another theorist sought to connect the rise of Overkill histories like Susan Sontag's with the educational philosophy of the time— in particular, the successful struggle for "immediacy" and "relevance" as against knowledge and the sense of the past. (The ability to write, once a mark of the élite, had come to belong to Everyman; impatient with this lowbrow company, élitists taught themselves to write *extravagantly*, hoping thus to stand out.)

C   Wolves and lions hunt mostly at night, while antelopes and wild cattle graze at night, or in the evening when colors are dim. For nearly all wild mammals are nocturnal or crepuscular. Color-blindness in mammals, other than monkeys, is comprehensible when one considers the lives of the animals in a wild state. But monkeys, in the forests where they live, are awake and about in the daytime, and there are abundant colors for them to see in the bright tropical light.

D   The most elaborate filing systems of library catalogues are arranged by author, subject, and sometimes date of publication, with cross references between these files. The human brain, with one million times as many cells, is unique not only for its ability to store vast amounts of information in a small storage space and for requiring vanishing amounts of operating power, but also for the speed and ease with which any remembered item can be produced. The human file of ideas, however, classifies each idea in an infinite variety of ways; the word "red" can be connected with "green" or "hot" or "blush" or "Skelton" or "Communist" or "blood" or "herring," to mention only a few. Computers can refer to their memories only in a systematic fashion well planned and explained beforehand but cannot create new cross indexing for themselves.

Emphasis in the Paragraph

In Chapter 3 (pp. 31–51) we have discussed unity, coherence, and emphasis at some length. In this chapter we have applied the first two terms to the special problems of paragraph organization. It remains to say something about emphasis as it relates to the paragraph. In general, emphasis is a function of coherence; that is, only when we have made our thought truly coherent can we expect that it will express a proper scale of emphasis. (The rewriting of Chesterton's paragraph, for example, destroys the emphasis as well as the coherence of his thought.)

In a paragraph, the beginning and the end are the places of greatest emphasis. It is no accident that topic sentences—obvious devices for emphasis within the paragraph—tend to occur at the beginning or the end of the paragraph.

Yet topic sentences are not necessarily required for emphasis any more than they are required for unity (p. 359). Look again at the paragraph from Conrad's "The Secret Sharer" (p. 362). Conrad has found a way to bring his hero's panoramic vision of sea and sky to a definite point of reference and the paragraph to a satisfying conclusion.

Clearly this handling of emphasis is not at all a matter of set formula or of the application of a mechanical rule. Moreover, one quickly realizes that it is not determined merely by structural considerations. The content is also highly important. For example, how much of the emphasis in the paragraph quoted on page 309 from Frederick Marryat depends upon the fact that the author has found a startling image with which to complete his portrait of Cornelius Vanslyperken? Or how much of the emphasis in the paragraph beginning "The five-year-old's name is Susan," on page 671, comes from the shocking incongruity presented by the concluding sentences: we don't expect to hear five-year-olds talking about getting "stoned."

● CAUTION

The writer who raises certain expectations in a topic sentence at the beginning of a paragraph must fulfill them as the paragraph is developed. Suppose he writes: "George is cowardly and cruel." If the paragraph then devotes itself to George's cowardice and gives no attention to his cruelty, it is lopsided in emphasis—unless, of course, the author means to deal with George's cruel nature in a subsequent paragraph or paragraphs. In that case, he might do well to state the fact of George's having cowardly and cruel traits—either as necessarily related to each other or as a rather startling paradox—in a short paragraph devoted to that issue and then subsequently devote a paragraph or more to each of George's two salient traits.

Summary

A review of these schemes for paragraph development serves to reinforce a point made earlier. There is no formula by which either the length or the structure of a paragraph may be determined. The student must use his best judgment, his common sense, and his taste. Unless he is very sure of his ground, he will tend to employ paragraphs of medium length and to use the more conventional paragraph structures. But in following these common-sense rules he must not conceive of paragraphs as mechanical units of even length and of homogeneous make-up. He should feel free, on occasion, to formulate paragraphs of "felt unity," relying upon his own impression of the "rightness" of the structure. For the student must never forget that the paragraph is a part—a meaningful part—of a larger structure and therefore cannot be formulated mechanically any more than can the larger structure of which it is a part.

■ APPLICATIONS

I Reread the essay "The Method of Scientific Investigation" (Readings, pp. 619–25), which is organized as an extended definition. How are the paragraphs related to this general function? Are any of them constructed as definitions? Do any provide illustrations?

II What structural principles are to be found in each of the following paragraphs? If you judge that the paragraph has no real structure, say so and indicate why.

1   The second of the two paragraphs from Leo Tolstoy's *War and Peace* quoted on pp. 147–48
2   The first paragraph from Melville's "The Encantadas" quoted on p. 276
3   The paragraph from John Burroughs' *Leaf and Tendril* quoted on pp. 290–91
4   The second paragraph from Millikan's "Science, Freedom, and the World of Tomorrow" quoted on pp. 157–58
5   The second paragraph from Melville's *Moby Dick* quoted on p. 135
6   The paragraph from Vincent Sheean's *Between the Thunder and the Sun* quoted on pp. 327–28

III   Reread the student theme "Training a Dog" (p. 65) or "Shoot the Moon" (p. 231). Attempt to state the structural principle of each of the paragraphs in the theme chosen.

Linking Paragraph with Paragraph

By transitional words and phrases

Since paragraphs are parts of a whole work, elements in an ordered sequence, it is important that they be properly linked together. Even when the chain of development embodied in the series of paragraphs has been thought out carefully, the reader will still be grateful for signposts to direct him. The judicious use of transitional words and phrases, such as *therefore, consequently, hence, thus, accordingly, on the contrary, however, nevertheless, furthermore, finally, in the same way,* and *moreover,* constitutes one way of helping the reader. The writer may also make use of the coordinate conjunctions *for, and, but, or,* and *nor* as signs of connection between paragraphs. Since, however, we ordinarily use these conjunctions to join the parts of a sentence, or to join sentence with sentence, we employ them less frequently to tie a paragraph to a preceding paragraph.

In carrying on an argument it is particularly important that these "controls," as we have called them, should be used accurately and responsibly. In this connection the student might reread pages 36–39.

● CAUTION

If we do provide the reader with transitional words as signposts, obviously we must use them accurately. We must not begin a paragraph by writing

"In the same way" unless what follows *is* "in the same way"; we must not write "Consequently" unless what follows is in fact a consequence of the preceding paragraph.

By the repetition of key words and phrases

The repetition of a key word or phrase is a useful device for linking paragraphs, especially if we wish to avoid the formality of style suggested by the employment of transitional words and the abruptness occasioned by the use of *and, but,* or *or.* To illustrate: T. H. Huxley in "The Method of Scientific Investigation" (p. 622) effects the transition between his eighth and ninth paragraphs in the following manner (we have italicized the key words here and in the examples that follow):

> You mean to say exactly what you know; but in reality you are giving expression to what is, in all essential particulars, an hypothesis. You do not know it at all; it is nothing but an hypothesis rapidly framed in your own mind. And it is an *hypothesis* founded on a long train of *inductions* and *deductions.*
>
> What are those *inductions* and *deductions,* and how have you got at this *hypothesis?* You have observed in the first place. . . .

The exact word or phrase, of course, need not be repeated if the idea is carried over. Here is Huxley's transition from paragraph five to six:

> He sees that the experiment has been tried under all sorts of conditions, as to time, place, and people, with the same result; and he says with you, therefore, that the law you have laid down must be a good one, and he must believe it.
>
> In science we *do the same thing.* . . .

Here is a series of three paragraphs from a story in *Time* magazine:

> *A buzzard coasting* high in the air over Central America last week would have seen nothing unusual. The mountainous, forest-matted isthmus lay quietly in the greasy November sun. Among the many human realities invisible to the buzzard were the boundary lines—the imaginary but very actual barriers that said: "This is Costa Rica; this is Guatemala; this is Nicaragua."
>
> Far below the *coasting buzzard,* in the gray-green jungles of northern Nicaragua, more was stirring than his great bird's-eye view could catch. Snaking through the scrub, *guerilla riflemen made short, sharp little raids* against government outposts. In and out of the piny mountain country on Nicaragua's northern flank, armed, machete-toting *men filtered mysteriously.* In Guatemala and Costa Rica dusty little *companies,* in faded denim and khaki, *marked time in the tropic heat.*
>
> *All this scattered activity* added up to one gathering purpose. That purpose called itself the Caribbean Legion.[3]

---

[3] Reprinted by permission; Copyright Time Inc.

A variant of the key-word device for linking paragraphs is the use of synonyms. As an illustration, consider the following passage.

> *Mary* walked slowly along the street, pondering the character of her interview. It had been more difficult than she had supposed it would be. Mr. Jones had almost glared at her—or so it seemed to her at the time—as he inquired about her speed in typing and her experience in handling business forms. True, he had not said in so many words that she would not be hired. But he had certainly not been very encouraging, nor had he been very mannerly in his questioning.
>
> *The girl* was nearly on the point of tears, but she . . .

■ APPLICATION

Here is a sequence of two paragraphs and the beginning of a third from Dorothy Sayers' *The Mind of the Maker*. What devices does Miss Sayers use to link these paragraphs? Underscore any transitional words and phrases, key terms that are repeated, or synonyms.

> It is for this reason that I have prefixed to this brief study of the creative mind an introductory chapter in which I have tried to make clear the difference between fact and opinion, and between the so-called "laws" based on fact and opinion respectively.
>
> In the creeds of Christendom, we are confronted with a set of documents which purport to be, not expressions of opinion but statements of fact. Some of these statements are historical, and with these the present book is not concerned. Others are theological—which means that they claim to be statements of fact about the nature of God and the universe; and with a limited number of these I propose to deal.
>
> The selected statements are those which aim at defining the nature of God, conceived in His capacity as Creator. They were originally . . .

By the use of demonstrative pronouns

Another device for linking paragraphs is the use of the demonstrative (pointing) pronouns: *this (these), that (those);* but such a method must be used with care. The writer is sometimes tempted to a vague use of the demonstrative pronouns. He assumes that the context will make plain the idea or object to which they refer. But often the reference is not clear, and instead of a tight and neat coupling of the two paragraphs, we have only the vague and clumsy suggestion of a tie. For example, consider the following passage in which the author has been describing an experiment to determine whether bees can distinguish colors. He first puts out a red card and a blue card. He baits the blue card with syrup. After the bees have discovered the syrup and continue to return to the blue card, he puts out fresh blue and red cards; but this time he puts no syrup on the blue card. The author then writes:

After we have arranged these new cards, we have not long to wait. Very soon bees arrive again, and it can be seen that they fly straight on to the blue card; none go to the red card.

—H. MUNRO FOX: "The Colors That Animals Can See," *The Personality of Animals.*

A young writer might be tempted to begin his next paragraph with: "This seems to indicate two things. The first is . . ." But what the author actually wrote was: "This behavior of the bees seems to indicate two things. . . ."

A little reflection will indicate that his judgment was sound. He intends to state clearly a process of proof. In this context, *this* would be a pronoun with a very vague antecedent. The author has, therefore, wisely employed *this* as a demonstrative adjective modifying a specific noun, *behavior.*

● CAUTION

The fault of indefinite antecedent is so common in student themes that the student ought to check each composition he writes in order to make sure that any *this* or *that* standing at the beginning of a paragraph or at the beginning of a sentence refers unmistakably to some specific person, thing, or action.

Paragraphs of Specialized Function

Since paragraphs are parts of a larger structure of meaning, individual paragraphs will often have specialized functions. Thus, the opening paragraph (or paragraphs) must introduce the whole essay;[4] the final paragraph (or paragraphs) must bring the essay to a suitable conclusion. Within the essay itself, individual paragraphs may have specific jobs to do: one paragraph states a particular argument, another provides an illustration, a third makes a transition between two sections of the essay, and so on.

For example, consider the first five paragraphs of Robert Graves's "It Was a Stable World" (pp. 803–05). The first paragraph introduces the essay and states Graves's basic thesis: that the Roman Empire was a stable Mediterranean world with Rome as its hub. Paragraph 2 describes the lands on the perimeter of the Roman world. Paragraph 3 discusses the Romans' basic motive for conquering other lands. Paragraph 4 outlines the Roman technique for conquest and subjugation. Paragraph 5 describes the city of Rome as stuffed with loot from the subjugated lands.

Graves has employed various methods for organizing his individual paragraphs: in general, he makes much use of illustration and comparison and contrast. But paragraph 2 gives us a disposition of details from a fixed point

---

[4] On pages 20–22 we have discussed a series of typical introductory paragraphs.

of view (pp. 803–04), looking out from Rome around the perimeter of the Empire; and paragraph 5 makes use of a "frame" image (p. 805): Rome is compared to a great jackdaw's nest.

Paragraph function determined by context

To repeat by way of summary what has been said earlier: the make-up of any particular paragraph is so much determined by the part the paragraph plays in the whole composition that there is only a limited and provisional value in studying it in isolation. The overriding consideration will rarely be the neatness or the force of the paragraph viewed in isolation; it will be rather what the paragraph contributes to the composition as a whole. Thus, valuable as it is to study the paragraph in isolation, we must never lose sight of its place in, and contribution to, the larger structure of the composition.

■ APPLICATIONS

I   In the following paragraphs from the selections in the Readings, indicate the topic sentences (if any) and the devices for connecting one paragraph with another.

1   The first five paragraphs of "The Age of Overkill" (pp. 692–93)
2   The first six paragraphs of "Jackdaws" (pp. 629–31)
3   The first five paragraphs of "Homage to Hemingway" (pp. 786–87)

II   The paragraphs referred to below exemplify some of the following structures: (a) illustration, (b) comparison and contrast, (c) causal analysis, (d) frame image, and (e) description organized by a dominant impression. Which method of organization is exemplified in each of the following paragraphs?

1   Paragraph 3 of "The Written Word" (p. 750)
2   Paragraph 6 of "Dickens" (p. 775)
3   Paragraph 1 of "The Age of Overkill" (p. 692)
4   Paragraph 1 of "Jackdaws" (p. 629)

Rhetoric and Grammar of the Sentence

A sentence is primarily a grammatical construction, and since it is, we may usefully say a brief word here about the relation of grammar to rhetoric. The grammar of a language is a systematic account of how that language functions to provide intelligible discourse.[5] But rhetoric also is concerned with intelligible discourse and the choice and arrangement of words in such discourse. What is the distinction between grammar and rhetoric? Perhaps it can be put most clearly by using an analogy with the game of football. The rules that govern the play of football may be called the grammar of the game. Thus, a forward pass caught beyond the sideline does not count; if a team in possession of the ball does not gain ten yards in four downs, the ball goes over to the other team; a touchdown is worth six points; a field goal, three; and so forth. These rules are conventional and conceivably can be changed; indeed, occasionally they are changed.[6]

In order to play the game of football, one must observe the rules; but a mere keeping of the rules would not insure that the team necessarily played well or that it won any games. The rhetoric of football, then, would be a knowledge of strategy and maneuver that leads to effective play and a winning game. To play the game correctly would not *necessarily* be to play it effectively, though effective play would have to conform to the rules of the game.

What has just been said, however, does not mean that there is a sharp division between grammar and rhetoric. In fact, there is a large area of overlap. For example, if someone writes: "Laughing through her tears, we heard the hysterical girl try to tell her story," we say (grammatically speaking) that "Laughing through her tears" constitutes a *dangling participle* and is thus an error in grammar (see p. 380); but the sentence is also rhetorically defective, for the statement is garbled and even ludicrous. We are not, of course, really confused about what the writer is trying to say; but we do smile at his bungling: to hear him tell it, *we* were the ones laughing while the girl wept.

The fixed word order of the normal sentence

An important practical application of rhetorical principles to the individual sentence has to do with the arrangement of elements within the sentence. For, as we shall see, the expressiveness of English depends heavily on the order in which the various elements of the sentence succeed each other.

When the Anglo-Saxons came into the island of Britain in the fifth century, they spoke a rather highly inflected language. By Chaucer's time, however, many of the original inflections had been lost, and by the end of the Middle Ages, English had relatively few inflections. Instead of relying

---

[5] Grammar has to do with such matters as the inflection of words and their syntactic arrangement. In his preparation for college, the student has presumably acquired a working knowledge of English grammar. The student's possession of such knowledge is assumed by the authors of this textbook, for their primary concern here is not with grammar but with rhetoric.
[6] Since grammar is based ultimately on usage, and since usage changes, the rules of grammar are subject to change too, though the changes tend to be very gradual.

primarily on inflections for indicating grammatical relations, modern English makes use of the *position* that words occupy in the sentence pattern. Indeed, the change of position can result in a radical change in meaning. Thus, "The boy hit the ball" means something very different from "The ball hit the boy." [7] The shift of position here produces a direct reversal of meaning. Though other rearrangements of normal word order alter the meaning less drastically, they do change it, and if we value the clarity and force of our writing, we shall want to be able to manipulate the arrangement of sentence elements so as to achieve a precise shading of meaning.

The normal order of the English sentence [8] may be diagrammed as follows:

SUBJECT	+	VERB	+	INNER COMPLEMENT (IF ANY)	+	OUTER COMPLEMENT (IF ANY)
John		stood				
He		is				John
He		is				tall
John		gave				a book
John		gave		me		a book

The verb *stood* does not require anything to complete its meaning and here takes no *complement.* The verb *is* acts here as a linking verb and has its meaning completed by *John,* a predicate nominative. In the third sentence the linking verb has its meaning completed by *tall,* a predicate adjective. In the fourth sentence, *book* (which indicates what John gave and is the outer complement) is a direct object. In the fifth sentence we have, in

---

[7] We still have considerable inflection in our pronouns. Thus, in spite of the word order, "Him I hit" means that I delivered the blow and "Me he hit" means that I received it. Yet so strong is our sense of the normal word order (which requires us to say "I hit him" and "He hit me") that though there is no possibility of mistaking their meaning, "Him I hit" and "Me he hit" sound to us intolerably archaic and pretentiously "literary." Thus, "Me he hit" is *grammatically* correct but in most contexts it would be *rhetorically* inept.

[8] One can easily demonstrate how powerfully embedded in our consciousness is this normal word order. We may not know precisely what the word *meniscus* means, but if we read a sentence saying "The meniscus was clearly visible," we know at once that it must be the name of something that is capable of being seen. We may be hazy about the meaning of *fibrillate,* but if we read "The patient's heart began to fibrillate," we know that *fibrillate* is a verb and describes some action performed by the heart or some condition in which the heart became involved.

The power of normal English sentence structure to convey syntactic relations can be even more forcibly illustrated by constructing a sentence out of what are frankly nonsense words. For example, suppose we write: "The snory womped the ogly glomp." Meaningless as this "sentence" is, it does convey *syntactic* relationships. We know, for example, that "snory," preceded as it is by the article *the,* must be a noun, the name of something, and that this snory, whatever it is, did something (in the past, since *-ed* is a sign of the past tense of the verb) to a "glomp," whatever *that* is. We know also that "ogly" describes the glomp; that is, that ogly is an adjective. So strongly ingrained is the sense of normal English structure that even an English speaker who had never studied formal grammar would know all this simply from the position that these words take in relation to each other.

addition to the outer complement (direct object), an inner complement (indirect object, the word that indicates to whom John gave the book).

Use of the Passive Voice Although it is a sound rule for the writer to use normal English word order unless there is a compelling reason to do otherwise, such reasons do exist. There are occasions on which one very properly varies the order. Suppose, for example, that we want to stress *what* it was that John gave. By using a passive construction, we can move into emphatic position at the beginning of the sentence what is normally an outer complement, *book,* and so put lighter stress on John (normally the subject) or even leave John out of account altogether. Thus we can write: "A book was given by John" or perhaps simply "A book was given." [9]

Let us consider another example of the passive construction used properly and naturally. Turn to James Thurber's account of "The Dog That Bit People" (pp. 754–59). The author tells how the dog Muggs on one occasion had him cornered in the living room.

> I managed to get up onto the mantelpiece above the fireplace, but it gave way and came down with a tremendous crash throwing a large marble clock, several vases, and myself heavily to the floor. Muggs was so alarmed by the racket that when I picked myself up he had disappeared.

Why not the normal order: "The racket so alarmed Muggs," and so forth? Because Muggs is the center of attention here—of the reader's attention as well as that of the terrified boy. Muggs clearly comes *first* in this sentence.

● CAUTION

Note that normal word order can sometimes give a false emphasis. A newspaper article describing physical exercises that office workers can do on the job mentions several to be done while sitting at the desk. "Many of these," the article reads, "you can do and no one will know. Perhaps you should do two of these [i.e., two exercises involving arm motion] when the boss is not looking." But the second sentence ought to read: "Perhaps two of these should be done when the boss is not looking." The intended emphasis is on the two exercises; and since it is, the passive construction gives the proper stress.

Expletive Constructions Another device for emphasizing a particular word (whether the normal complement or the normal subject) is the so-called expletive construction, in which we begin the sentence with "It is" or

---

[9] Imagine that someone says "John gave her a book," but so mumbles his words that his companion has to ask: "Did you say John gave a book or a box?" Here there is no question as to who the giver was. What is in question is the gift; and so the first speaker says: "A book was given." Or, since in such conversation "was given" would be understood, the first speaker simply says "A book."

"There is." Thus, we can write: "It was a book that John gave" (or simply "It was a book"). But we can also write, throwing stress on the normal subject: "It was John who gave the book."

To take an example: Alexander Smith, in an essay entitled "A Lark's Flight," writes:

> It is taken for granted that the spectators of public executions—the artizans and country people who take up their stations overnight as close to the barriers as possible, and the wealthier classes who occupy hired windows and employ opera-glasses—are merely drawn together by a morbid relish for horrible sights.

Normal word order would call for something like this:

> Everyone takes for granted that a morbid relish for a horrible sight draws together the spectators of public executions—the artizans, etc.

The normal word order, as a matter of fact, gives us a reasonably effective sentence. Why, then, did the author, almost instinctively, one supposes, use the expletive construction (with the passive) in this sentence? Because here the normal subject requires no emphasis. The normal subject is everybody and anybody. What is important here is not *who* takes it for granted but *what is taken for granted:* the character of the spectators.

● CAUTION

Be on your guard against drifting into expletive or into passive constructions. Obviously we achieve no emphasis if, out of sheer thoughtlessness, we begin a good half of our sentences with "It is" or "There is" or if we use passive constructions indiscriminately, sometimes for no better reason than that we are too lazy or vague to think who or what the true subject is. All emphasis or haphazard emphasis is no emphasis.

■ APPLICATIONS

I Examine the following paragraph in which Helen Keller, blind and deaf from early childhood, tells of how she learned her first word:

> There was a well-house, covered with honeysuckle, and attracted by the smell of the honeysuckle we took a walk down the path to it. There was someone who was drawing water there and my hand was placed under the spout by my teacher. So there was a cool stream gushing over my hand and the word *water* was spelled out into the other hand by my teacher, first slowly and then rapidly. I stood still, because my whole attention was fixed upon the motions of her fingers. Suddenly there was a misty consciousness that came over me as of something forgotten—there was a thrill of returning thought; and somehow the mystery of language was revealed to me. The wonderful cool something that was flowing over my hand was the

thing that was meant by "w-a-t-e-r." My soul was awakened by the living words; it was given light, hope, joy, and it was set free! There were barriers still, it is true, but these were barriers that could in time be swept away.

Compare this garbled rewriting with the version that Helen Keller actually wrote (p. 5). The original version contains one instance of expletive and three of passive construction. Can you say why they are justified, if you think that they are, and why those that we have introduced into the garbled rewriting are not?

II The following paragraphs are from a review of a recently published life of Mary, Queen of Scots.

Mary seemed to possess charm rather than character. She was young and beautiful; she loved festivities and wished to enjoy them without interruption by troublesome state affairs. When she had to make important decisions she was too easily influenced by others. This probably came about at least partly because Mary was a person of great importance when she was only a child and was quite naturally easily influenced by adults at this early age. Unfortunately it became a habit.

Mary was born Queen of Scotland but spent her childhood in the court of Henry II of France. Charles's advice to Mary was always based on what was beneficial to him personally and to the powerful Guise family, never considering Mary's welfare. This was to be the story of her life. Almost everyone surrounding Mary sought to use her for their own interests, ignoring what would be best for her. In fact, Mary is seen as a victim in a net of endless power intrigues.

Rewrite this paragraph, making any improvements that seem necessary to you. Note in particular two faults: (a) the vague reference of the word *this* (which opens two sentences) and of the word *it* and (b) the overuse of the passive construction.

III Convert the following sentences to normal word order; that is, reestablish the pattern of *subject, verb, inner and outer complements,* and, where necessary, eliminate *expletive* and *passive* constructions.
1   Icebergs, he could see wherever he looked.
2   There was a man once that was bored with his life.
3   The arrival of five cruisers and twenty destroyers was reported.
4   The great bear was surrounded by a horde of yapping, excited dogs.
5   It was a great bear that was surrounded by the horde of yapping, excited dogs.
6   When I was five years old, I was given my first book by my grandmother.
7   My first book was given to me by my grandmother when I was five years old.
8   It was a book that was my first present.
9   Books, he had treasured from the earliest period of his life.
10 Ways and means for handling the peak late-afternoon traffic through Westville and Lakeville were discussed.

We have been considering the normal order of subject, verb, and the complements. But modifiers also have their normal positions in the order of the sentence. Adjectival modifiers are relatively fixed in position. Individual adjectives come immediately before the substantive that they modify. Consequently, variations from this normal position constitute a means of emphasizing the modifier. Ordinarily we write "three houses" or "three lakes" or "three soldiers." But when Kipling came to choose a title for one of his books, he called it *Soldiers Three.* By departing from the normal order he emphasized, as he wanted to do, the word *three.* Normally, we would write "a great queen," but we refer to a certain Russian empress as Catherine the Great. The adjective *great* is placed in an emphatic position because it serves to distinguish her from the other Catherines. We usually speak of a "beautiful house," but John Bunyan in his *Pilgrim's Progress* has Christian come upon an edifice which is called "The House Beautiful."

Variations of the normal position of the adjective, like other emphatic devices, are to be used sparingly and with discretion. But so used, the variations can sometimes be quite effective:

> An automobile, *shabby and mud-splashed,* rounded the corner.
> A small face, *dirty,* appeared at the window.

Though single-word adjectives normally come before the word that they modify, phrases and clauses that function as adjectives come *after* the word they modify. Thus:

> The man *to see* is Jim. (infinitive used as an adjective)
> The house *in the country* was charming. (prepositional phrase used as an adjective)
> The house *that I saw* was of red brick. (relative clause used as an adjective)
> The house *I saw* was of red brick. (relative clause, not headed by a relative pronoun, used as an adjective)

Though the position of single adjectives raises few problems for the writer, the position of adjectival *phrases* does; for they almost seem to invite careless positioning, and when carelessly placed, they can sometimes cause confusion. For example, a newspaper published the following advertisement:

> Bird cage and parrot offered by refined young lady, having green feathers and a yellow beak.

"Having green feathers and a yellow beak" is a participial phrase that obviously is meant to modify *parrot,* not *young lady.* Accordingly, the phrase ought to be shifted to a position immediately after the word *parrot.*

Here is another example:

> A two-story house was for sale with green shutters.

A moment's reflection will show that the phrase "with green shutters" is an adjectival phrase describing the particular house that was for sale. Hence the sentence is much clearer if one places the phrase immediately after the word *house* and makes the sentence read "A two-story house with green shutters was for sale."

■ APPLICATION

In the following sentences, some of the adjectival modifiers are awkwardly placed. Rearrange the modifiers and, where necessary, rewrite the sentences to improve clarity and effectiveness.

1 A man in the army that I served with gave me this book.
2 It was the man I knew whom I now saw.
3 The lady whom I knew from Boston has not returned.
4 Boy is missing in first pair of long pants.   —The Detroit *Free Press.*
5 Rex Parsons laid an egg on our table that had been previously laid on the nest by a little white Leghorn hen that was 3 inches in length and $6\frac{1}{2}$ inches in circumference the smallest way.
                                        —The Farmington *Franklin Journal.*
6 The ducks on the pond with ringed necks swam in lazy circles.
7 The ducks were still undisturbed on the pond; those in the nearby meadow quacked noisily.
8 Walking sedately before the bride, came her small nephew George Slaughter 3rd, carrying the ring and two little nieces of the groom.
                                        —The Roswell *Dispatch.*
9 The man in the automobile that I recognized was Jim.
10 The jumbled-up awards system has caused bitter criticism in the past, and taking on the job of revising it doesn't require a bit more courage than tackling a hungry tiger armed with a dull toothpick.
                                        —Los Angeles *Examiner.*

THE POSITION OF ADVERBIAL MODIFIERS

Adverbs that modify adjectives or other adverbs normally are placed immediately in front of the adjective or the adverb that they modify. Thus, we write: "The screen was *intensely* white" or "The horse ran *very* swiftly." But adverbs that modify *verbs,* and all adverbial phrases and clauses, are rather freely movable. Clumsy and inept placing of these can obscure thought and even plunge the whole sentence into absurdity. Consider the following advertisement for a television show:

> Joan Fontaine plays a European countess who returns to her home town in Ohio and charms a young married man tonight at 9 on G.E. Theater.

Surely the writer intended to say:

On G.E. Theater at 9 tonight, Joan Fontaine plays a European countess who returns to her home town in Ohio and charms a young married man.

Consider the following piece of rather turgid prose. Having referred to the wreck of one of his grandfather's ships and his grandfather's narrow escape from death, the grandson writes:

Eight men were drowned, however, and from that memory my grandfather had at intervals all his life suffered and never read anything but the shipwreck of St. Paul if asked to read family prayers.

What William Butler Yeats actually wrote was the following:

Eight men were, however, drowned and my grandfather suffered from that memory at intervals all his life, and if asked to read family prayers never read anything but the shipwreck of St. Paul.

When we remember that adverbial modifiers tell us *when,* or *where,* or *how,* or *why* some action took place and that subordinate clauses, such as those beginning with *since, although, because, if, in order that,* and so forth, have an adverbial function, it becomes easier to understand why adverbial modifiers can take so many positions in the sentence. The writer who can place them skillfully has found an important means for making fine shadings and discriminations of his thought.[10] Conversely, the writer who makes a clumsy disposition of his adverbial modifiers often obscures his thought.

Here are three ways of saying the same thing—or do these sentences say *quite* the same thing?

At ten o'clock, when I heard the news, I felt a pang though I had assured myself that I would be prepared for it.

Though I had assured myself that I would be prepared for it, when, at ten o'clock, I heard the news, I felt a pang.

I felt a pang when I heard the news at ten o'clock, though I had assured myself that I would be prepared for it.

Which arrangement of the modifiers do you prefer? Which seems most natural? Which, most clumsy?

■ APPLICATIONS

I Max Beerbohm describes his first sight of the poet Algernon Swinburne. Which of the following versions would you guess to be the one that he actually wrote?

A   Sparse and straggling though the grey hair was that fringed the immense pale dome of his head, and venerably haloed though he was for me by his

---

[10] To put the matter in terms of unity-coherence-emphasis: proper attention to the disposition of the movable modifiers constitutes one of the most effective means to achieve coherence and proper emphasis within the sentence.

greatness, there was yet about him something—boyish? girlish? childish, rather; something of a beautifully well-bred child.

B   Though the grey hair that fringed the immense pale dome of his head was sparse and straggling, and though for me he was venerably haloed by his greatness, there was yet about him something—boyish? girlish? childish, rather; something of a beautifully well-bred child.

II Grammar demands that adjectival phrases modify some substantive but not that adverbial phrases do so. When a confused writer treats an adjectival phrase as if it were an adverbial phrase and leaves it unattached to any substantive, he produces what is called a "dangling" modifier. The following sentences contain dangling modifiers. Remove them (a) by rewriting the sentence so that the modifier is provided with a substantive to modify or (b) by converting the dangling modifier into a subordinate clause. For example, the following sentence contains a dangling modifier: "Singing merrily, our music put the whole company into a jolly mood." We can correct it to read: (a) "Singing merrily, we put the whole company into a jolly mood." Or (b) "As we sang merrily, we put the whole company into a jolly mood." Revise the following sentences so as to eliminate the dangling modifiers.

1   Hurrying and out of breath, scurrying up the depot stairs, the 9:01 for Grand Central swept past us.
2   The afternoon drowsed on to an end, sipping lemonade and listening to records.
3   Reading the thrilling ghost story, the grandfather clock ticked insistently in our ears.
4   Hanging on for dear life, the car careened to the edge of the road.
5   Walking up the last steps of the drive, the first mutterings of thunder were heard.
6   Thinking as hard as we could, the answer still could not be found.
7   Turning the corner, the gigantic skeleton of New York's newest and the world's highest building comes into view.—The New York *Herald Tribune*.

III In the following sentences, the modifiers that are printed in italics have been shifted out of the order in which they were originally written. Try to restore what you believe to be the proper order.

1   Though the Greek scientist Eratosthenes had, *with only a small error,* calculated the distance of the sun from the earth and the earth's circumference at the equator, this theory of a global world was received by men of common sense *with polite scorn.*
2   In myriad private hotel rooms of myriad hotels the Alumni Weekly Lunch is, *today,* being celebrated, *as every day.*
3   *Because their maxims would not have expressed their hearts,* they would not have been perfect moralists *then, even if their theory had been correct* (which, I think it was, *though not in statement, in intention*).

4   There can be no miracles *unless there exists something else which we may call the supernatural, in addition to Nature.*

5   There are wild woods and mountains, marshes and heaths, even in England. But *only on sufferance* are they there, *because we have chosen to leave them their freedom, out of our good pleasure.*

6   For Nature is always alien and inhuman, *even in the temperate zone,* and diabolic *occasionally.*

7   *For at least some of them* the fun was not over *when the grownups gave the children the order to retire.* . . .

8   The matriarch, *in this eerie light, her head upright under her white night-cap,* looked down on the world as from a throne of snow.

9   A poet, *when talking about poetry,* would generally be wise, *because of his limited knowledge,* to choose either some general subject upon which his conclusions must be true in most cases, *if they are true in a few,* or some detailed matter which only requires the intensive study of a few works.

Some special patterns of sentence structure

PARALLELISM

We have thus far examined the structure of the sentence with reference to one principle: the arrangement of its basic constituents (subject, predicate, and complements) and the arrangement of the various kinds of modifiers. But other principles may determine the make-up of a sentence. One of these is parallelism. Parallelism is a method of adjusting grammatical pattern to rhetorical pattern. In its simplest terms, parallelism means that *sentence elements of like grammatical order or function should be put in like constructions.*

The Balanced Sentence   The general idea that parallel construction may be used to emphasize parallel ideas seems simple enough, but in practice, an enormous variety of effects is thus made possible. Let us begin with some rather simple examples:

1   I like blondes; Bill likes brunettes. We both like red-heads.
2   Jack Sprat could eat no fat;
    His wife could eat no lean. . . .
3   Some books are to be tasted, others to be swallowed, and some few to be chewed and digested. . . .   —SIR FRANCIS BACON.

Here follow some more elaborate instances:

1   As the hart panteth after the water brooks, so panteth my soul after Thee, O God.
2   He was sick of life, but he was afraid of death; and he shuddered at every sight or sound which reminded him of the inevitable hour.

3   To examine such compositions singly cannot be required; they have doubtless brighter and darker parts; but when they are once found to be generally dull, all further labor may be spared; for to what use can the work be criticized that will not be read?

The parallel elements may be represented in the following scheme:

1	as	so
	hart	soul
	panteth	panteth (repetition)
	water brooks	Thee
2	sick	afraid
	life	death
3	singly	generally
	required	spared
	once found	all further
	be criticized	be read

Sentences like the foregoing, especially those that show a rather elaborate balancing of item against item, are called "balanced sentences."

Parallel constructions can, of course, be combined with other rhetorical devices. In the example that follows (from Edmund Burke's speech "On Conciliation with America") the antitheses (e.g., "Ægypt and Arabia and Curdistan" as against "Thrace," or "in his centre" as against "in all his borders") are used primarily to enforce a dominant comparison: "the circulation of power" is likened to the circulation of the blood—most powerful at the *heart* of the empire rather than at its extremities.

> In large bodies the circulation of power must be less vigorous at the extremities. Nature has said it. The Turk cannot govern Ægypt and Arabia and Curdistan as he governs Thrace; nor has he the same dominion in Crimea and Algiers which he has in Brusa and Smyrna. Despotism itself is obliged to truck and huckster. The Sultan gets such obedience as he can. He governs with a loose rein, that he may govern at all; and the whole of the force and vigour of his authority in his centre is derived from a prudent relaxation in all his borders.

The following rather elaborate example (from G. K. Chesterton's *Heretics*) uses parallel structure to enforce contrasts—the contrast between the earth-shaking accomplishments of the scientist and his gentle and harmless demeanor, and between the awesome consequence of his acts and the guilelessness of his motives. (Chesterton writes of the splitting of a grain of *sand* [by the chemist?], for at the time of his writing the physicist had not yet split the *atom:* subsequent events have given more rather than less consequence to what he then had to say.)

> Men find it extremely difficult to believe that a man who is obviously uprooting mountains and dividing seas, tearing down temples and stretch-

ing out hands to the stars, is really a quiet old gentleman who only asks to be allowed to indulge his harmless old hobby and follow his harmless old nose. When a man splits a grain of sand and the universe is turned upside down in consequence, it is difficult to realize that to the man who did it, the splitting of the grain is the great affair, and the capsizing of the cosmos quite a small one. It is hard to enter into the feelings of a man who regards a new heaven and a new earth in the light of a by-product. But undoubtedly it was to this almost eerie innocence of the intellect that the great men of the great scientific period, which now appears to be closing, owed their enormous power and triumph. If they had brought the heavens down like a house of cards, their plea was not even that they had done it on principle; their quite unanswerable plea was that they had done it by accident.

The musician Igor Stravinsky comments on musical snobs:

> Artists have often told me, "Why do you complain about snobs? They are most usefully menial to new movements. If not from conviction, at any rate from their character as snobs. They are your best clients." And I always reply that they are bad clients, false clients, because they are as menial to the false as they are to truth. By serving every cause, they hurt the best, because they confuse it with the worst.
>
> —IGOR STRAVINSKY: *Poetics of Music.*[11]

G. Lowes Dickinson in his essay "Red-bloods and Mollycoddles" makes considerable use of balanced sentences. (See pp. 76–78.)

● CAUTION

The balanced sentence, like every other deviation from the normal pattern, is emphatic (see p. 381 above) and therefore should be used sparingly. All emphasis is no emphasis: a succession of balanced sentences might first impress the reader as artificially shrill but finally would be merely monotonous.

■ APPLICATION

In the passages quoted above from Burke and Chesterton indicate the parallel elements, pointing out which element "balances" which.

More Succinct Uses of Parallelism   Short utterances may be rendered forceful by a judicious use of parallelism. Here are a few instances:

> The superior man understands what is right; the inferior man understands what will sell.
> The superior man loves his soul; the inferior man loves his property.

---

[11] From *Poetics of Music* by Igor Stravinsky. Reprinted by permission of Harvard University Press.

> The superior man always remembers how he was punished for his mistakes; the inferior man always remembers what presents he got.
>
> The superior man is liberal toward others' opinions, but does not completely agree with them; the inferior man completely agrees with others' opinions, but is not liberal toward them. —CONFUCIUS.

Two of the most widely celebrated statements of the last few years take the form of balanced sentences.

> Never ask what your country can do for you; ask rather what you can do for your country. —PRESIDENT JOHN F. KENNEDY.
>
> That's one small step for a man; a giant leap for mankind.[12]
> —NEIL ARMSTRONG, on first setting foot on the moon.

Here is a statement by a famous seventeenth-century prose writer:

> If we begin with certainties, we shall end in doubts; but if we begin with doubts, and are patient in them, we shall end in certainties.
> —SIR FRANCIS BACON.

Note that in Bacon's sentence, the arrangement of key terms is as follows: certainties-doubts, doubts-certainties. In the older rhetoric this pattern was called *chiasmus* (that is, a "criss-cross" like the Greek letter chi, *X*). The rather fancy term doesn't matter, but the device does, for it has its usefulness in heightening emphasis by reversing the arrangement of the key terms. Consider these rather simple examples:

> Love's fire heats water, water cools not love.
> —SHAKESPEARE, Sonnet 154.
>
> He [Christ] saved others; himself he cannot save.—ST. MATTHEW 27:42.

Note that in the criss-cross pattern, the paired terms need not be identical. In the first example we get fire-love, heats-cools, and water-water; in the second, he-he, saved-save, and others-himself. What is essential to the criss-cross is that the wording of the second clause should reverse that of the first.

■ APPLICATION

Using the scheme employed with reference to the three passages on page 382, indicate the parallel elements in the passages quoted on pages 383–84.

Violations of Parallelism The very richness of the English language tempts us to violate parallelism. We have, for example, two noun forms of the verb,

---

[12] In the newspapers (including the *New York Times*) this statement was first printed as "That's one small step for man; a giant leap for mankind." Can you see why "for *a* man" improves the "balance" of the sentence? (In terms of sense and "balance" is there something to be said for "a giant leap" instead of "one giant leap"?)

the infinitive (*to swim*) and the gerund (*swimming*). Consequently, the careless writer may blunder into a sentence like this: *"To swim* and *hunting* are my favorite sports." But here the distinction between infinitive and gerund awkwardly distracts the reader from what is really a coordinate relation. He ought to write: *"Swimming* and *hunting* are my favorite sports." Or: "I like best *to swim* and *to hunt."*

It is, however, our great variety of movable modifiers that most tempts us to violate parallelism. We may carelessly write: "Being lazy by nature and because I am clumsy, I have never liked tennis." A more vigorous sentence would read: "Being lazy by nature and also clumsy, I have never liked tennis." Or: "Because I am clumsy and am naturally lazy, I have never liked tennis." Violations of parallelism such as these easily creep into first drafts—even into the first drafts of a good writer. Careful rewriting is the obvious remedy.

COORDINATION AND SUBORDINATION

It is possible to regard coordination as an aspect of parallelism, and it may be convenient to do so here. In preceding pages we have been considering the rhetorical effectiveness of putting elements of like grammatical function into like constructions and the confusion that often results from our failure to do so. But we must also take care not to treat as parallel any elements that are not really parallel; that is, we must not treat as coordinate sentence elements that are not coordinate. The less important elements must be made subordinate to the more important.

Someone was ill and he stayed at home. If he writes: "I stayed at home; I was ill," he has merely juxtaposed the two ideas. He has not defined the relationship of one statement to the other. It is possible to define that relationship in various ways:

> Because I was ill, I stayed at home.
> While I was staying home, I was ill.
> Although I stayed at home, I was ill.
> Feeling ill, I stayed at home.
> I stayed at home, quite ill.

The precise form of subordination that is used will, of course, depend upon the writer's specific meaning.

Simple uncritical writing, such as that done by a child, tends to present a succession of coordinate units: "Then the bear got hungry. He came out of his den. He remembered the honey tree. And he started walking toward the honey tree." The mature writer indicates the relation of his statements, one to another, by subordination. Thus he writes: "The hungry bear came out of his den, and remembering the honey tree, started walking toward it." The amount of subordination will naturally depend upon a number of things: the circumstances to be discussed or told about, the nature of the audience whom the writer means to address, and the writer's own temperament. A novelist like Henry James is famous for the intricate patterns of subordination that he employs. The following is an example:

> The two ladies who, in advance of the Swiss season, had been warned that their design was unconsidered, that the passes would not be clear, nor the air mild, nor the inns open—the two ladies who, characteristically, had braved a good deal of possibly interested remonstrance were finding themselves, as their adventure turned out, wonderfully sustained.
>
> —*The Wings of the Dove.*

Contrast with the James passage Ernest Hemingway's characteristic pattern of light subordination:

> Before daylight it started to drizzle. The wind was down or we were protected by mountains that bounded the curve the lake had made. When I knew daylight was coming I settled down and rowed hard. I did not know where we were and I wanted to get into the Swiss part of the lake. When it was beginning to be daylight we were quite close to the shore. I could see the rocky shore and the trees.
>
> —ERNEST HEMINGWAY: *A Farewell to Arms.*[13]

Subordination as a Means for Interpretation The writer who, instead of simply leaving relationships to be inferred by the reader, points them up, obviously makes the reader's task easier. He not only gives facts but supplies an interpretation of the facts: the pattern of subordination constitutes an interpretation. If, however, the writer does assume this burden of interpretation, he must be sure that his use of subordination correctly expresses the relation of idea to idea. Unless he does so, he may end up by writing sentences like this: "My head was feeling heavy when I took an aspirin." Such a sentence turns matters upside down and confuses the reader with a subordination that inverts the real relationship. Rather than do that, the writer might have done better simply to write: "My head was feeling heavy; I took an aspirin." (The proper subordination, of course, is obvious: "Because my head was feeling heavy, I took an aspirin." Or "When my head began to feel heavy, I took an aspirin.")

Here are two further examples of improper subordination:

> The workman snored loudly and he had a red face.

Alter to:

> The workman, who had a red face, snored loudly.

Or to:

> The red-faced workman snored loudly.

> Mr. Jones is our neighbor and he drove by in a large automobile.

---

[13] Reprinted with the permission of Charles Scribner's Sons from *A Farewell to Arms* by Ernest Hemingway. Copyright 1929 Charles Scribner's Sons; renewal copyright © 1957 Ernest Hemingway. Reprinted by permission of the Executors of the Ernest Hemingway Estate and Jonathan Cape Ltd.

Alter to:

Mr. Jones, who is our neighbor, drove by in a large automobile.

Or to:

Mr. Jones, our neighbor, drove by in a large automobile.

Though subordination is important as a means for tightening up a naïve and oversimple style, the student ought not to be browbeaten into constant subordination. In certain contexts a good writer might actually prefer:

The workman snored loudly. He had a red face.

This way of saying it has the merit of bringing into sharp focus the detail of the red face. It might even suggest a leisurely observer, looking on with some amusement. For instances of some other effects secured by a simple and uncomplicated style, the student might look at pages 301–02.

Summary   We may sum up this topic as follows: grammatical subordination must conform to the rhetorical sense; it must not mislead by inverting it. On the positive side, subordination is an important means for securing economy. Careful subordination tends to give the sense of a thoughtful observer who has sifted his ideas and arranged them with precision.

WORD ECHO AND JINGLING REPETITION

Before leaving the related topics of parallelism and coordination, we must mention the problems of word echo, repetition, and rhyme. Perhaps these problems seem out of place here and would be more appropriately treated under some such heading as euphony or vowel harmony. That they do bear upon the problem of parallelism, however, can speedily be made evident.

Look at this passage from a recent newspaper story on the golden retriever breed of dogs:

> The golden retriever made his first American appearance before the first World War. Interest flagged for quite a *spell;* then several American sportsmen fell under their *spell* and brought in top stock for breeding. [*Italics ours.*]

Two paragraphs further on we find:

> . . . it is relatively easy for [golden retrievers] to pick up honors in *field* and obedience, *field* and *show,* and some have *shone* in all three. [*Italics ours.*]

The echo of *spell* is somewhat disconcerting when the reader realizes that the echo is pointless and meaningless. The partial echo of *show-shone* is just as pointless, and the defect is much more noticeable by being associated with a repetition (*field-field*) that *is* meaningful.

Though we may be tempted to dismiss these verbal echoes as merely inconsequential, we shall learn something about written discourse if we ask ourselves why they are disconcerting. It is because they seem to promise a parallelism of meaning that is not there. W. K. Wimsatt, Jr.,[14] is illuminating on this point. He quotes the sentence: "To read his tales is a baptism of optimism. . . ." and goes on to comment upon the nasty jingle of "-ptism" and "-ptimism." The jingling effect is, as he says, nasty "just because the two combinations so nearly strive to make these words parallel, whereas they are not; one qualifies the other." That is, the style is bad because the diction ("baptism . . . optimism") suggests a parallelism between terms that are not really parallel, just as in the paragraph about the golden retriever, *spell* and *spell* are not parallel. The reader feels that what pretended to be an expressive element—the *-ism* link between the terms—has turned out to be misleading. (The reader may not, of course, necessarily make this analysis consciously; he will probably merely *feel* it, hearing the *-ism* repetition as an irritating jingle.)

The reporter writing about the golden retriever was probably not experimenting with vowel harmony; he was simply careless and did not revise his copy. One must depend on revision to rid his style of such blunders. The best way to avoid irritating jingles is to read the manuscript aloud. Meaningless verbal echoes then make themselves apparent, and awkwardly misplaced modifiers usually betray their presence by the very awkwardness of the heard rhythms.

TAUTOLOGY AND REPETITION OF IDEA

Repetition of idea may seem even less relevant to "parallelism" than is "jingling repetition." Yet when a student writes "We *pre*planned the meeting *in advance* so that we would be ready" or writes "I propose to discuss the *whole* question *in its entirety,*" we can fairly charge him with misusing parallel elements. He is saying the same thing twice without any gain in emphasis thereby.

One can, to be sure, properly employ repetition for emphasis: for example, "I propose to discuss the whole question; I propose to discuss it in its entirety; I propose to give attention to every aspect of it." This sentence is emphatic, though it may pay too heavy a price for its emphasis. (It has something of the flavor of old-fashioned oratory.) But at least it leaves no doubt that the repetition is calculated, not thoughtless. Most repetition within a sentence is thoughtless, however, the product of confusion or carelessness. Be prepared, therefore, to trim down your sentences: eliminate tautologies and in general all unnecessary words.

■ APPLICATION

Strike out all unnecessary words, including pointless instances of repetition in the following sentences. If you feel that some of the repetitive words and phrases can be justified, state why you think so.

---

[14] *The Prose Style of Samuel Johnson,* Yale University Press, 1941, p. 13.

1   I am not against women as such.
2   I swear to tell the truth, the whole truth, and nothing but the truth.
3   I sort of believe, in a manner of speaking, that Jim thought he was doing well by his country.
4   This is a brilliant and shining example of what one good citizen and patriotic American can accomplish.
5   In the last analysis my first impression of Jones was that he was rather shy in a way.
6   By far the most dry and arid moments of family life for Strachey were public holidays and anniversaries.
7   Only time in my considered opinion will judge the validity and authenticity of these claims and whether they really make sense.
8   Is not our flag the zenith of achievement, the goal to which generations expired have aspired and by which generations unborn will be inspired?

9   [From a Quit Claim deed] ". . . I do remise, release, and forever Quit Claim unto the said grantees and unto the survivors of them and unto such survivors' heirs and assigns forever, all the right, title, interest, claim, and whatsoever as I have. . . ."

10 It depends on the fashion that is in vogue.
11 If he had discovered that he had wronged anyone unfairly, he immediately called that person to apologize. (Heard over the radio on the death of a newspaper columnist.)

LOOSE SENTENCES AND PERIODIC SENTENCES

Sentence structure can be viewed in still another way. We can distinguish between those sentences in which the sense is held up almost until the end (periodic sentences) and those in which it is not held up (loose sentences). Holding up the sense creates suspense: we do not know how the sentence is "coming out" until we have reached, or nearly reached, the end of it. Here are some examples:

> It was partly at such junctures as these and partly at quite different ones that with the turn my matters had now taken, my predicament, as I have called it, grew most sensible.　　　　—HENRY JAMES.

If we convert the sentence to loose structure (that is, to normal English word order), we get something like this:

> With the turn my matters had now taken, my predicament, as I have called it, grew most sensible, partly at such junctures as these and partly at quite different ones.

Here is another example of the periodic sentence:

> But of all those Highlanders who looked on the recent turn of fortune with painful apprehension the fiercest and most powerful were the Macdonalds.　　　　—LORD MACAULAY.

Converted to loose structure, the sentence reads:

> But the Macdonalds were the fiercest and the most powerful of all those Highlanders who looked on the recent turn of fortune with painful apprehension.

The loose sentence is the normal sentence in English; the structure of the periodic sentence is abnormal. As we have noted above, deviation from the norm always tends to be emphatic. The periodic sentence, in skillful hands, is powerfully emphatic. By inversion, by use of the "It was" construction, or by interposition of movable modifiers between subject and predicate, the sentence and its primary statement are made to end together. But like all deviations from the norm, the periodic sentence—and the balanced sentence—are somewhat artificial. Overused, such sentences will soon weary the reader.

Sentence length and sentence variation

How long should a sentence be? It may be as short as one word. "Go!" is a perfectly good sentence; it has a predicate with subject implied. On the other hand, a sentence may be forty or fifty words long. In fact, by tacking together elements with *and*'s and *but*'s, we can construct sentences of indefinite length. These are the possible extremes. But with the sentence, as with the paragraph, common sense and taste set reasonable limits. A succession of very short sentences tends to be monotonous. Extremely long sentences tend to bog the reader down in a quagmire of words.

This is not, of course, to say that the writer should not feel free to use a one-word sentence whenever he needs it or a succession of short sentences to gain special effects (see pp. 658–59 and pp. 693–94). According to the same reasoning, he ought to feel free to use very long sentences in order to gain special effects. The following sentence from Lytton Strachey's *Queen Victoria* will illustrate:

> Perhaps her fading mind called up once more the shadows of the past to float before it, and retraced, for the last time, the vanished visions of that long history—passing back and back, through the cloud of years, to older and ever older memories—to the spring woods at Osborne, so full of primroses for Lord Beaconsfield—to Lord Palmerston's queer clothes and high demeanour, and Albert's face under the green lamp, and Albert's first stag at Balmoral, and Albert in his blue and silver uniform, and the Baron coming in through a doorway, and Lord M. dreaming at Windsor with the rooks cawing in the elm-trees, and the Archbishop of Canterbury on his knees in the dawn, and the old King's turkey-cock ejaculations, and Uncle Leopold's soft voice at Claremont, and Lehzen with the globes, and her mother's feathers sweeping down towards her, and a great old repeater-watch of her father's in its tortoise-shell case, and a yellow rug, and some friendly flounces of sprigged muslin, and the trees and the grass at Kensington. —LYTTON STRACHEY: *Queen Victoria*.

Strachey is imagining what may have passed through the old Queen's dying mind as she slipped from consciousness. He imagines the succession of memories as going backward in time, from those of adult life to those of youth, and on back to the memories of childhood. The loosely linked series of clauses that constitute the sentence can be justified on two counts: the memories are presented as those of a dying mind, and, as the memories go backward in time, they become those of a child. Dramatically considered, the jumping from scene to scene (as suggested by the dashes) and the loose tacking on of additional scenes (by *and*'s) make sense. This long sentence, which closes Strachey's book with what amounts to a recapitulation of Victoria's life, is thus used to gain a special effect.

The normal limitations and requirements of the human mind dictate how much can be taken in satisfactorily "at one bite." Unless the writer is striving for some special effect, he ought to regard with suspicion very short and—most of all—very long sentences.

VARIETY IN SENTENCE LENGTH

The human mind requires variety: sentences should not all be monotonously of the same length. Let us consider a particular case. Look back at the paragraph from Virginia Woolf quoted on page 309. These thirteen sentences range in length from three words to fifty-two. The fourth sentence is quite long; the seventh sentence, very long. But three short sentences lead up to the fourth sentence, and two short sentences separate the fourth and seventh sentences.

Close study of Santayana's "Dickens" (pp. 771–81) will reveal great skill in the maintenance of sentence variety. Santayana's sentences tend to be long. They are carefully constructed and are frequently quite complex. But he is careful not to tire the reader. The following passage will illustrate:

> Having humility, that most liberating of sentiments, having true vision of human existence and joy in that vision, Dickens had in superlative degree the gift of humour, of mimicry, of unrestrained farce.

But after this sentence, we are given the simple statement:

> He was the perfect comedian.

And having had time to catch our breaths, we are ready to go on with:

> When people say Dickens . . .

Alternation of long and short sentences is but one means, however, by which to secure variety. Another, and a most important, means consists in varying the structure of the sentence. The examples from Santayana will illustrate: the sentence "He was the perfect comedian" is not only shorter than the sentence that precedes it; it represents, after the quite complex structure of the preceding sentence, a return to the simplest type of structure (subject + predicate + predicate complement).

Sentences that repeat a pattern become monotonous. Here is an example:

> I was twenty that April and I made the glen my book. I idled over it. I watched the rhododendron snow its petals on the dark pools that spun them round in a swirl of brown foam and beached them on a tiny coast glittering with mica and fool's gold. I got it by heart, however, the dripping rocks, the ferny grottos, the eternal freshness, the sense of loam, of deep sweet decay, of a chain of life continuous and rich with the ages. I gathered there the walking fern that walks across its little forest world by striking root with its long tips, tip to root and root to tip walking away from the localities that knew it once. I was aware that the walking fern has its oriental counterpart. I knew also that Shortia, the flower that was lost for a century after Michaux found it *"dans les hautes montagnes de Carolinie,"* has its next of kin upon the mountains of Japan. I sometimes met mountain people hunting for ginseng for the Chinese market; long ago the Chinese all but exterminated that herbalistic panacea of theirs, and now they turn for it to the only other source, the Appalachians.

The "I was—I idled—I gathered" formula is relieved somewhat by the long descriptive phrases and relative clauses. Even so, it is irritatingly monotonous. Here is the way in which Donald Culross Peattie actually wrote the passage:

> The glen was my book, that April I was twenty. I idled over it, watching the rhododendron snow its petals on the dark pools that spun them round in a swirl of brown foam and beached them on a tiny coast glittering with mica and fool's gold. But I got it by heart, the dripping rocks, the ferny grottos, the eternal freshness, the sense of loam, of deep sweet decay, of a chain of life continuous and rich with the ages. The walking fern I gathered there, that walks across its little forest world by striking root with its long tips, tip to root and root to tip walking away from the localities that knew it once, has its oriental counterpart; of that I was aware. And I knew that Shortia, the flower that was lost for a century after Michaux found it, *"dans les hautes montagnes de Carolinie,"* has its next of kin upon the mountains of Japan. Sometimes I met mountain people hunting for ginseng for the Chinese market; long ago the Chinese all but exterminated that herbalistic panacea of theirs, and now they turn for it to the only other source, the Appalachians.
>
> —DONALD CULROSS PEATTIE: *Flowering Earth.*[15]

There are many ways in which to vary sentence structure. Nearly everything said earlier in this chapter can be brought to bear on this problem. We can invert the normal pattern or rearrange the pattern to throw emphasis on what is normally the subject or complement; we can subordinate severely

---

[15] From *Flowering Earth* by Donald Culross Peattie. Reprinted by permission of Noel R. Peattie and his agent, James Brown Associates, Inc. Copyright © 1939 by Donald Culross Peattie.

or rather lightly. Most of all, we can dispose the modifiers, particularly the movable modifiers, so as to vary the pattern almost indefinitely.

The effort to secure variety should never, of course, become the overriding consideration. A sentence should take the structure best adapted to its special job. The writer will usually find that he is thoroughly occupied in discharging this obligation. Moreover, it is well to remind ourselves here once again of the claims of the whole composition. We never write a "collection of sentences"; we write an essay, a theme, a total composition. The good sentence honors the claims exerted upon it by the total composition. And in our writing, and especially in our *rewriting*, we need to see that we have avoided monotony of sentence length or of sentence structure.

■ APPLICATIONS

I A Do you think that some of the paragraphs in Lewis S. Feuer's "Conflict of Generations" (pp. 699–711) are too long? If you do, try to subdivide the first, second, sixth, and tenth paragraphs of his essay. If you think that any of them are not too long, write a brief justification of why you think so.

B Analyze the length of the paragraphs in Bruno Bettelheim's "The Anatomy of Academic Discontent" (pp. 634–45). Can you make a sensible subdivision of his first, second, and fourth paragraphs? If you think these paragraphs are not overlong, write out an account saying why.

II Try to determine which of the following sentences are periodic in structure and which are loose. Rewrite the periodic sentences into loose sentences, and the loose into periodic. Pick out the balanced sentences, if any.

1   The power, and the restriction on it, though quite distinguishable when they do not approach each other, may yet, like the intervening colors between white and black, approach so nearly as to perplex the understanding, as colors perplex the vision in marking the distinction between them.
                                                            —John Marshall.

2   Peace cannot be secured without armies; and armies must be supported at the expense of the people. It is for your sake, not for our own, that we guard the barrier of the Rhine against the ferocious Germans, who have so often attempted, and who will always desire, to exchange the solitude of their woods and morasses for the wealth and fertility of Gaul.   —Edward Gibbon.

3   The night, the earth under her, seemed to swell and recede together with a limitless, unhurried, benign breathing.   —Katherine Anne Porter.

4   And it is precisely because of this utterly unsettled and uncertain condition of philosophy at present that I regard any practical application of it to religion and conduct as exceedingly dangerous.   —Charles S. Pierce.

5   If we begin with certainties, we shall end in doubts; but if we begin with doubts, and are patient in them, we shall end in certainties.
                                                            —Sir Francis Bacon.

6   The mania for handling all the sides of every question, looking into every

window, and opening every door, was, as Bluebeard judiciously pointed out to his wives, fatal to their practical usefulness in society.   —Henry Adams.

7   Bubbling spontaneously from the artless heart of a child or man, without egoism and full of feeling, laughter is the music of life.   —William Osler.

8   Every night I pulled my flag down and folded it up and laid it on a shelf in my bedroom, and one morning before breakfast I found it, though I had folded it up the night before, knotted around the bottom of the flagstaff so that it was touching the grass.   —W. B. Yeats.

9   The hunger and thirst for knowledge, the keen delight in the chase, the good-humored willingness to admit that the scent was false, the eager desire to get on with the work, the cheerful resolution to go back and begin again, the broad good sense, the unaffected modesty, the imperturbable temper, the gratitude for any little help that was given—all these will remain in my memory, though I cannot paint them for others.   —F. W. Maitland.

10   If he be my enemy, let him triumph; if he be my friend, as I have given him no personal occasion to be otherwise, he will be glad of my repentance. It becomes me not to draw my pen in the defense of a bad cause, when I have so often drawn it for a good one.   —John Dryden.

III   The following paragraphs are taken from *Time*. *Time* style has for long been celebrated for its inversions of, and its drastic departures from, normal sentence order. The motive, presumably, is a desire for condensation and emphasis. Rewrite these paragraphs so as to restore normal sentence order. Can you justify the departures from normal order? Is emphasis intelligently used? Or does too much emphasis result in no emphasis?

An abandoned lime quarry at Makapangsgat, Transvaal, yielded two bones last year to Dart's diggers: part of an occiput (the back part of the skull) and a lower jaw, from a pygmy moppet who had died while still getting his second teeth. Near by were many baboon skulls, bashed in from above or behind with a club which had a ridged head (the distal end of the humerus).

Most startling was Dart's evidence, from a number of charred bones, that the little man had learned to use fire. He lived in the early Ice Age, from 300,000 to 500,000 years before Peking Man, hitherto the earliest known user of fire. In honor of both his fire-bringing record and his prophetic skills, the new little man was named *Australopithecus prometheus*.[16]

IV   The passage from *Time* quoted above dates from the 1950's. Some people think that they have observed of late a return to more normal word order in *Time*. Do the following paragraphs (from the July 25, 1969, issue) seem to you to bear this out?

The ghostly, white-clad figure slowly descended the ladder. Having reached the bottom rung, he lowered himself into the bowl-shaped footpad of *Eagle*, the spindly lunar module of Apollo 11. Then he extended his left foot, cautiously, tentatively, as if testing water in a pool—and, in fact, testing a wholly new environment for man. That groping foot, encased in a heavy multi-layered boot (size 9½B), would remain indelible in the minds of millions

---

[16] Reprinted by permission; Copyright Time Inc.

who watched it on TV, and a symbol of man's determination to step—and forever keep stepping—toward the unknown.

With a cautious, almost shuffling gait, the astronaut began moving about in the harsh light of the lunar morning. "The surface is fine and powdery, it adheres in fine layers, like powdered charcoal, to the soles and sides of my foot," he said. "I can see the footprints of my boots and the treads in the fine, sandy particles." Minutes later, Armstrong was joined by Edwin Aldrin. Then, gaining confidence with every step, the two jumped and loped across the barren landscape for 2 hrs. 14 min., while the TV camera they had set up some 50 ft. from *Eagle* transmitted their movements with remarkable clarity to enthralled audiences on earth, a quarter of a million miles away. Sometimes moving in surrealistic slow motion, sometimes bounding around in the weak lunar gravity like exuberant kangaroos, they set up experiments and scooped up rocks, snapped pictures and probed the soil, apparently enjoying every moment of their stay in the moon's alien environment.[17]

If you feel that there is a distinct difference try to rewrite the preceding paragraphs in the earlier *Time* style; if not, then rewrite these paragraphs in a more conventional style of normal word order.

V The following paragraph is from Ring Lardner's *You Know Me, Al,* which purports to be a series of letters from Jack, the rookie pitcher, to his friend. As a revelation of character and of speech "in character," it is quite perfect. But rewriting it may provide us with a useful exercise in sentence structure and proper subordination. Put it into formal English.

We was to play 2 games here and was to play 1 of them in Tacoma and the other here but it rained and so we did not play neither 1 and the people was pretty mad a bout it because I was announced to pitch and they figured probily this would be there only chance to see me in axion and they made a awful holler but Comiskey says No they would not be no game because the field neither here or in Tacoma was in no shape for a game and he would not take no chance of me pitching and may be slipping in the mud and straneing myself and then where would the White Sox be at next season. So we been laying a round all the p.m. and I and Dutch Schaefer had a long talk to gether while some of the rest of the boys was out buying some cloths to take on the trip and Al I bought a full dress suit of evening cloths at Portland yesterday and now I owe Callahan the money for them and am not going on no trip so probily I wont never get to ware them and it is just $45.00 throwed a way but I would rather throw $45.00 a way then go on a trip a round the world and leave my family all winter.

[17] From *Time* magazine, July 25, 1969. Reprinted by permission; Copyright Time Inc. 1969.

CHAPTER

Diction

Good diction is the result of the choice of the right words. Accurate, effective expression obviously requires the right words, the words that will represent—not nearly, not approximately, but exactly—what we want to say. This is a simple rule; but to apply it is far from simple. The good writer must choose the right words, yes; but how does he know which are the right words?

Diction would be no problem if there existed for each object and each idea just one word to denote specifically that object or idea—if there were one name and one name only for each separate thing. But language is not like that. Most words are not strictly denotative, that is, they do not merely point to a specific object. Some words in English, it is true, particularly scientific words, do represent the only name we have for a specific object or substance. *Lemming,* for example, is the only name we have for a certain mouselike rodent; *purine* is the only name of a compound, the chemical formula of which is $C_5H_4N_4$. The language of science ideally is a language of pure denotation. But this constitutes a special case, and its problems are different from those of more ordinary language.

Actually, instead of one word and only one word for each thing, the writer often finds several words competing for his attention, all of them denoting more or less the same thing. Moreover, even those words that explicitly refer to the same thing may have different associations—different shades of meaning.

For example, *brightness, radiance, effulgence,* and *brilliance* may be said to have the same general denotation, but there is a considerable dif-

396

ference in what they connote, or suggest. *Radiance* implies beams radiating from a source, as the words *brilliance* or *brightness* do not. *Brilliance,* on the other hand, suggests an intensity of light that *effulgence* and *brightness* do not. Again, *brightness* is a more homely, everyday word than are *radiance, brilliance,* and *effulgence.* These are only a few suggested contrasts among the connotations of these words, all of which describe a quality of light.

Varying connotations in words of the same denotation may also be illustrated from the names of common objects. To most people, *firefly* seems more dignified than *lightning bug; taper,* than *candle.* The relative dignity of *bucket* and *pail* is not so easily settled. But for many modern Americans *bucket* is more likely to seem the ordinary word, with associations of everyday activity; whereas *pail* will seem a little more old-fashioned and endowed with more "poetic" suggestions. It connotes for some readers a bygone era of pretty milkmaids in an idyllic setting. But *bucket,* too, may have sentimental associations, someone will exclaim, remembering the song entitled "The Old Oaken Bucket." For words change in meaning from period to period, and their associated meanings change, as a rule, much more rapidly than do their primary meanings.

Words, then, are not static, changeless counters but are affected intimately, especially on the level of connotation, by the changing, developing, restless life of the men who use them.

As Justice Oliver Wendell Holmes said: "A word is not a crystal, transparent and unchanging, it is the skin of a living thought and may vary greatly in color and content according to the circumstances and time in which it is said." [1] Some words wear out and lose their force. Some words go downhill and lose respectability. Other words rise in the scale and acquire respectability. In 1710, Jonathan Swift, the author of *Gulliver's Travels,* poked fun at some of the clipped and slang forms of English that were coming into vogue in his day. Some of these words—for example, *mob* (a clipped form of *mobile*) and *banter* (origin unknown)—have since acquired respectability and now perform useful functions in our language. But other words upon which Swift cast scorn, such as *pozz* (for *possible*), *plenipo* (from *plenipotentiary,* "big shot" in modern slang), and *phiz* (from *physiognomy,* that is, *face*), have disappeared, as Swift hoped they would. One can observe a similar process at work in our own day. Some of the slang of fifty years ago—indeed, some of ten years ago—may now seem oddly quaint.

■ APPLICATION

Do you know, or can you figure out, the origin of the instances of current slang that appear on the next page?

---

[1] Decision, *Town versus Eisner.*

the fuzz	drip
dig	turn on
groovy	cop out
uptight	rap
freak out	

The process of growth and decay in language is so strong that many words in the course of generations have shifted not only their associations but their primary meanings as well; some have even reversed their original meanings.[2]

The fact that what was once merely a secondary meaning may sometimes oust the old primary meaning and become the new primary meaning tells us something about the power of secondary meanings and associated meanings. If we want to write effectively, we have to take the associations of a word into account. We have to control not one but two dimensions of our language—that is, not only the prime meaning but the cluster of sub-meanings surrounding it. Thus, in a romantic tale (or perhaps for ironic or humorous effect) one might appropriately use the word *steed* because of its special associations. But in most contexts, one would call a horse a *horse*. Yet there are still other contexts in which the writer might choose a word with negative associations. If the animal in question was particularly ill-favored or was obviously the worse for wear, he might call it a *plug* or a *nag*. If the man were especially disgusted with it—he had placed a big bet on the horse and it had come in eighth—he might even refer to it as *crow-bait*.[3]

Two Distinctions: General and Specific; Abstract and Concrete

We call a word "general" when it refers to a group or a class; "specific," when it refers to a member of that class. *Tree* is a general word, but *oak, elm, poplar* are specific. We must remember, however, that the terms *general* and *specific* are relative, not absolute, in their reference. *Coat,*

---

[2] Later in this chapter we shall have occasion to return to the history of words when we discuss the use of the dictionary. (See also pp. 406–09.)

[3] *Nag* and *plug,* incidentally, illustrate the way in which the associations of words may change. *Nag* originally meant merely "a small riding horse or pony," and there are hints (see the Oxford English Dictionary) that even *plug* once conveyed no sense of marked inferiority. Moreover, the processes of change have not ceased. A recent newspaper story (1969) reported that a man had been kicked in the chest by the "rear hooves of a mule." In an earlier day the reporter would have written "hind feet of a mule," but in this age in which mules are rare and automobiles numerous, he thought of the animal as if it had "rear" wheels. But the reverse can be found: a radio broadcaster, warning motorists of slippery roads, sometimes advises them to "watch their step."

for example, is more specific than *garment,* for a coat is a kind of garment. But *coat* is itself more general than *hunting jacket,* for a hunting jacket is a kind of coat. So with our trees above. *Oak* is more specific than *tree* but more general than *black oak* or *water oak* or *post oak.*

The specific word tends to give color and tang, tends to appeal to the imagination. Suppose we write: "He saw a ship on the horizon." What can our reader's imagination do with that? It can put some sort of floating object, large, manmade, and designed for transportation, on the imagined horizon. But what is the shape of the object? Will there be a smudge of smoke or the glint of white sail? The word *ship* is a general word and, therefore, cannot give a vivid image in that split second in which the reader's eye rests upon the sentence. Suppose we substitute *liner, schooner, brig, tanker, brig-schooner, junk,* or some other specific word. Then there is something for the imagination to seize on. There is no blur on the horizon; there is a shape.

But suppose, one may object, that we write *brig* and that the reader does not know what sailing-rig such a craft carries. Does he then have a shape on the horizon? Most readers would get the glint of sail and not the smudge of smoke, for their information might go that far. Yet the mere fact of the use of the specific word gives some sort of nudge to the imagination, gives some sense of knowingness, makes the reader kid himself a bit. If we use the word *brig,* even the reader totally ignorant of nautical matters, as most of us are, feels, just for the moment, a little like an old salt.

There is another distinction that is important in our choice of words. It has to do with concreteness and abstraction. *Peach, pear, quince, apple,* and *apricot* are *concrete* words. The word *peach* implies certain qualities: a certain shape, a certain color, a certain kind of sweetness. But *peach* implies these qualities as "grown together," as we should actually find them embodied in a peach. (The Latin word from which *concrete* derives means literally "grown together.") We can, of course, *abstract* (this word literally means "take away") these qualities from the actual peach and refer to them in isolation: *sweetness, fuzziness, softness.* Isolating these qualities, we get a set of *abstract* words. *Sweetness* isolates a quality common to peaches, and common, of course, to many other things; *sweetness* is thought of as an idea in its own right.

Words that refer to ideas, qualities, and characteristics *as such* are usually abstract. Words that name classes of objects and classes of actions are usually general. Words that refer to particular objects and particular actions are usually both concrete and specific. These are, on the whole, our most vivid words; they reflect immediately the world of things known to our senses. This comment is not meant to imply that concrete and specific words are somehow "better" than abstract and general words. For some purposes they are indeed better, but for others, not. The world of ideas and concepts requires its terms just as urgently as does the world of particular things.

I List nouns that are both concrete and specific in the descriptive passages on pages 294–95 and 298–99. (Thus, with reference to the Ruskin passage that begins on p. 298: "And so, taking care not to tread on the *grass,* we will go along the straight *walk* to the west *front* [the context indicates that it is the front of a cathedral], and there stand for a time, looking up at its deep-pointed *porches.* . . ." [*Italics ours.*] If you are in any doubt about when the noun is both concrete and specific—*time,* for example—omit it.)

II Arrange the sentences in the following groups in ascending order of specificity, putting the sentence with the most general word first and the one with the most specific word last. (Your concern in Groups A and C will be with nouns and noun phrases; in B, with verbs.)

A 1 She wore an Yves Saint Laurent evening gown.
   2 A rather shapeless garment enveloped her.
   3 She put on a neat print dress.

B 1 The old crone put herself in motion.
   2 The child skipped along the path.
   3 The youth walked briskly forward.

C 1 She bought a large head of Boston lettuce.
   2 I saw that we needed greens of some sort for salad.
   3 I am not fond of lettuce.

III The following is a passage describing planes in a dogfight over Britain in World War I. We have rewritten the passage to "generalize" it.

> Those Stuka pilots who did get back made it back by only a small margin. Oberleutnant Karl Hentze saw the effect in terms of smoke as his bombs fell on Ford airfield, but somehow, try as he might, he couldn't get his diving-brakes to come back to normal position: the first attack by British planes had removed most of his hydraulic system. The Stuka seemed not in proper equilibrium and exhibited a bumpy reaction—"like riding over bumps"— and he knew that whoever could manage to take good aim at him would probably hit him.
>
> Suddenly two Spitfires approached him from behind, flying around and making movements toward him like birds of prey; a bullet struck his radio telephone, then ricocheted back, cutting a line in his skin at the back of his hand. Momentarily, he became unconscious, then a call from his gunner brought him back to consciousness; the plane was almost touching the water like a big sea-bird and in one second of great fear he felt the wheels go under the surface of the water.[4]

Rewrite this passage to make it more vivid and dramatic. Use your imagination and your dictionary. Replace general terms with more specific terms.

---

[4] Paraphrased from the book *Eagle Day* by Richard Collier. Copyright, ©, 1966 by Richard Collier. Used by permission of E. P. Dutton & Co., Inc. Reprinted by permission of Curtis Brown, Ltd., London.

Here, for a start, are the first two sentences as written by the author:

> Those Stuka pilots who did get back made it *by a hair's-breadth.* Oberleutnant Karl Hentze saw the *powdery black spirals* of smoke as his bomb *struck* Ford airfield. . . . [*Italics ours.*]

IV Compare, in the matter of abstract-general and concrete-specific diction, the passage quoted from *Far Off Things* (p. 308) with that quoted from *Robinson Crusoe* (p. 310). Can you account for the choice of diction in terms of what each author is trying to do? About which of the two scenes described do you have more facts? Which do you visualize more vividly?

V In the following paragraph William Faulkner describes a woman in her sixties, who lives in a shabby-genteel house on what was years ago the best street of a small Southern town. She lives alone, quite cut off from society, and she is a known eccentric. We have omitted a good many words from Faulkner's description. How would you fill the blanks? Use your imagination: try to make your reader *see* this woman. (Whether or not you manage to reconstruct Faulkner's precise description is not the main concern here.)

[The parlor] was furnished in heavy, leather-covered furniture. When the Negro opened the blinds of one window, [the callers] could see that the leather was _____, and when they sat down, a faint _____ rose _____ about their thighs, _____ with _____ motes in the _____ sun-ray. On a _____ gilt easel before the fireplace stood a _____ portrait of Miss _____'s _____.

They rose when she entered. [She was] a _____ woman in _____, with a _____ gold chain _____ to her waist and _____ into her belt, leaning on an ebony cane with a _____ gold head. Her skeleton was _____ and _____; perhaps that was why what would have been merely _____ in another was obesity in her. She looked _____, like a body long submerged in _____ water, and of that _____ hue. Her eyes, lost in the fatty ridges of her face . . .[5]

The student may derive some useful hints by looking back at another section of this passage quoted on page 293.

VI Assume that, in an account of a motor trip through one of the New England states, you have written the following paragraphs:

> We stopped the car beside the stone wall near the gate that had led to the farmhouse door. The house was gray and unpainted. It must have been unlived in for years. Some of the windows were broken. The roof was in disrepair.
> The house was set in what had been a thriving apple orchard, and now on this October day, the old trees were worth looking at. A majority of them were

---

[5] From "A Rose for Emily" from *Collected Stories of William Faulkner* by William Faulkner. Reprinted by permission of Random House, Inc. Reprinted by permission of Curtis Brown Ltd.

filled with fruit. The sun was shining, and the sight was very pretty, even though some of the trees were rotted. A lot of them had vines growing up their trunks, and Jim said it was poison ivy.

Rewrite this passage so as to make the reader see the scene. Your revision will certainly call for changes in diction, but do not hesitate to make more extensive changes.

The misuse of abstract and general words

Writing that is woolly with abstractions is usually ineffective and may not even make much sense to the reader. For example:

> Quite significantly, the emphasis is being placed upon vocational intelligence, which is based upon adequate occupational information for all pupils in secondary schools.... This emphasis upon vocational guidance for the purpose of making young people intelligent concerning the world of occupations and the requirements for entering occupations need not conflict seriously with other views of guidance that take into account everything pertaining to the education of the pupil.

There are a number of things wrong with this flabby statement, among them, the large number of abstract words. The author might have written:

> High schools today insist that the student learn enough about jobs to choose his own job wisely. The student needs to learn what various jobs pay, what training they require, and what kinds of people find them interesting. He can learn these things while he is learning the other things that schools are supposed to teach. Both kinds of learning are preparations for life, and one need not interfere with the other.

The rewritten version still makes use of general and abstract words (*training, preparation,* and so on); but some of the cloudiest of the abstractions (*vocational intelligence, occupational information*) have been removed, and the rewritten version is not only simpler but has more force.

● CAUTION

Abstract-general diction is not necessarily to be avoided. The student is not to conclude that concrete and specific words are somehow "better" than abstract and general words. Sometimes we need to name qualities and classes. If, for example, we lacked the word *sympathy,* how would we say something so simple as "A child needs sympathy"? We can make an attempt: "A child does not like frowns. Cold looks scare him. He flinches from harsh words," and so forth. But trying to convey the notion of sympathy in this way is as awkward as trying to pick up a pin with a gloved hand.

We do need abstract terms and we need general terms. For example, compare "He lived in a house of medium size" with "His home did not have the suburban air of a bungalow, and it certainly had nothing of the rustic style of a lodge. It was much smaller than a mansion, but somewhat larger than a cottage." *Mansion, cottage, bungalow,* and *lodge* (not to mention *cabin, hut, villa,* and *chateau*) are *overspecific* for the writer's purpose here; he needs the simple, general term *house.*[6]

Though the writer cannot, and need not try to, avoid abstract and general words, he ought not to fall into the slovenly habit of using them thoughtlessly. In any case, he should remember that a sprinkling of concrete and specific words can be used to lighten the numbing weight of piled-up abstractions. To illustrate, compare:

> 1 A child needs sympathy. Tolerance of his mistakes and the sense of understanding and comradeship provide the proper stimulus for his developing personality. Conversely, an environment defective in sympathy and understanding can be positively thwarting; it can lead to repressions and thus lay the foundation for ruinous personality problems.

> 2 A child needs sympathy. He didn't intend to smash the vase or to hurt the cat when he pulled its tail. Tolerance of mistakes and some understanding are necessary if he is to feel that he is a comrade. Acceptance as a comrade stimulates him to become a better comrade. He grows and develops toward responsibility. For he finds it hard to grow normally in a cold and repressive atmosphere. The meaningless spanking—meaningless to him, since he had no intention of breaking the vase—drives him in on himself. He becomes confused and repressed. Some of these confusions and repressions may linger into adult life.

In choosing our words, the overriding consideration, of course, will always be the particular effect that the writer wishes to obtain. Description and narration, for example, thrive on the concrete and the specific. Note the number of concrete and specific terms in the following passage:

> He knew the inchoate sharp excitement of hot dandelions in young Spring grass at noon; the smell of cellars, cobwebs, and built-on secret earth; in July, of watermelons bedded in sweet hay, inside a farmer's covered wagon; of cantaloupe and crated peaches; and the scent of orange rind, bitter-sweet, before a fire of coals.
> —THOMAS WOLFE: *Look Homeward, Angel.*[7]

Exposition and argument, on the other hand, by their very nature, call for a diction in which general and abstract words are often important.

---

[6] The clumsy expressions into which we are sometimes forced by overspecific terms is well illustrated from the English personal pronouns, which for some purposes are overspecific. It would, for example, be very convenient if our language possessed a pronoun that could mean either "he" or "she" (and have neutral terms for "his" or "her," "his" or "hers," "him" or "her"). Since we don't have such a pronoun, we have to write "Someone has left his or her pen" or "Someone has left his pen," with the understanding that "his" in this context can also mean "her."

[7] Reprinted with the permission of Charles Scribner's Sons from *Look Homeward, Angel,* page 401, by Thomas Wolfe. Copyright 1929 Charles Scribner's Sons; renewal copyright © 1957 Edward C. Aswell, C.T.A. and/or Fred W. Wolfe. Reprinted with permission of William Heinemann Ltd.

Marx's interpretation of the past is explicit and realistic; his forecast of the future seems to me vague and idealistic. I have called it utopian, but you object to that word. I do not insist on it. I will even surrender the word "idealistic." But the point is this. Marx finds that in the past the effective force that has determined social change is the economic class conflict. He points out that this economic class conflict is working to undermine our capitalistic society. Very well. If then I project this explanation of social changes into the future, what does it tell me? It seems to tell me that there will be in the future what there has been in the past—an endless economic class conflict, and endless replacement of one dominant class by another, an endless transformation of institutions and ideas in accordance with the changes effected by the class conflict.

—CARL BECKER: "The Marxian Philosophy of History,"
Everyman His Own Historian: Essays on History and Politics.

Language Growth by Extension of Meaning

We have said that a word has not only a primary meaning but also implied meanings. The implied meanings are obviously less definite than the primary meaning, and therefore less stable and more amenable to change. In scientific language the specific meanings are rigidly stabilized, and the hazy and shifting implied meanings are, in so far as possible, eliminated. In a colorful and racy use of everyday language, just the reverse is the case. The implied meanings are rich and important. We are often tempted to use a word, not *literally* (that is, adhering strictly to the specific meaning), but *figuratively,* stressing the associations of the word. It is through such a process that words have shifted their meanings in the past; but this process of extension of meaning is constantly at work even in our own time. Let us consider an illustration of the process.

The casual view of language sees each word as fastened neatly and tightly to a certain specific object: *weasel* means a certain kind of small, furry mammal of slender body, which moves furtively, preys on birds, rats, and rabbits, sucking their blood, and occasionally also sucking eggs; *cooking* means the preparation of food by exposing it to heat; *spade* means an instrument for digging in the earth. But words are not actually so neatly fastened to the objects for which they stand. Even when we are determined to speak forthrightly and "call a spade a spade," we rarely do so. It is against the nature of language that we should be able to do so.

For example, Bob, who is determined to call a spade a spade, says: "Well, Joe has weaseled out on us again. Yesterday when I told him the Collins deal was finally cooking, he pretended he had never heard of it and said he wouldn't buy a pig in a poke." But obviously one is not calling a spade a *spade* when he attributes to another human being the actions of a weasel, describes the preparation of a business deal as a piece of cookery, and makes the agreement to be signed the purchase of a pig enclosed in a bag.

Weasel and *cooking*—not to mention the pig—are not being used literally here; their meanings have been extended through analogy. In the case of *cooking* the extension of meaning is very easy to grasp: one sort of preparation—cooking—is extended to mean another and more general sort of preparation. *Weaseling* is more difficult. There may be some implication of "weasel words," that is, words that have had the substance sucked out of them, like eggs sucked by a weasel; but the more probable analogy here is that between Joe's wriggling out of his promise and the weasel's bodily movements as it glides through apparently impossibly small apertures.

The situation we have just considered is thoroughly typical. Many common words have been extended from their original meanings in just this fashion. We speak of the *eye* of a needle, the *mouth* of a river, the *legs* of a chair, the *foot* of a bed. The hole in the end of a needle might have been given a special name; instead, men called it an *eye* because of its fancied likeness to the human eye. So, too, with examples such as these: a *keen* mind, a *bright* disposition, a *sunny* smile, a *black* look. Someone saw an analogy between the way in which a keen blade cut through wood and the way in which a good mind cut into the problem with which it was concerned. The smile obviously does not really shed sunlight, but it may seem to affect one as sunlight does, and in a way quite the opposite of a black look.

But the point to be made here does not concern the basis for the analogy, whether of physical resemblance (the *jaws* of a vise), similarity of function (the *key* to a puzzle), similarity of effect (a *shining* example), or anything else. The point to be made is, rather, that people normally use words in this way, extending, stretching, twisting their meanings, so that they apply to other objects or actions or situations than those to which they originally applied. This is the metaphorical process, about which we shall have more to say in the next chapter. The essence of metaphor inheres in this transfer of meaning, in the application of a word that literally means one thing to something else. (See Chapter 12, pp. 435–38.)

Development of complex words out of simple words

Thus far we have taken our illustrations from common words. But less common words and learned words will illustrate the same process of extension of meaning. Indeed, most of our words that express complex ideas and relationships have been built up out of simpler words. For example, we say, "His generosity caused him to overlook my fault." *Overlook* here means to "disregard or ignore indulgently." But *overlook* is obviously made up of the simple words *look* and *over*. To look over an object may imply something more cursory than a minute inspection of it; for example, one *looks over* an assignment. *Overlook,* then, in the sense of "disregard" is an extension and specialization of one of the implied meanings of *look over*. We have said "one of the meanings," for *look over* obviously implies other possible meanings. Consider the nearly parallel expression "to see over." From it we get the word *oversee*. This word normally means today *to direct, to supervise*—something quite different from "overlook." *Supervise* is built out of the same concepts as *oversee,* for *super* in Latin means "over," and *-vise* comes from the Latin verb *videre* (past participle *visus*), which means "to see." Thus we hope that an alert supervisor will not overlook matters that he ought to take note of. A bishop, by the way, is literally an *overseer*. For *bishop* comes originally from two Greek words: *epi,* which means "over," and *skopein,* which means "to look." Thus, such diverse words as *overlook, oversee, overseer, supervise,* and *bishop* represent particular extensions of much the same primitive literal meaning.

The dictionary: a record of meanings

The etymology (that is, the derivation and history) of a word is not only highly interesting but also useful. The full mastery of a particular word frequently entails knowing its root meaning. By learning that meaning, we acquire a firm grasp on its various later meanings, for we can see them as extended and specialized meanings that have grown out of the original meaning.

Here, for example, is the entry in the *Standard College Dictionary* for the word *litter:* [8]

> **lit·ter** (lit′ər)   *n.*   **1.** Waste materials, scraps, or carelessly dropped objects strewn about; clutter.   **2.** Untidy or chaotic condition; mess.   **3.** The young brought forth at one birth by any mammal normally having several offspring at one time.   **4.** A stretcher used for carrying sick or wounded persons.   **5.** A vehicle consisting of a couch carried between shafts by men or beasts of burden.   **6.** Straw, hay, etc., spread in animal pens, or over plants as protection.   **7.** The uppermost layer of a forest floor, consisting of slightly decomposed leaves, twigs, etc.   — **Syn.** See FLOCK.   — *v.t.* **1.** To make untidy or unsightly by strewing or carelessly discarding trash, etc.   **2.** To drop or scatter carelessly.   **3.** To provide with litter, as for bedding, covering, etc.   **4.** To give birth to (pups, kittens, whelps, etc.)   — *v.i.* **5.** To give birth to a litter of young.   **6.** To drop or scatter refuse, especially in public places.   [< OF *litiere* < Med.L *lectaria* < L *lectus* bed]

The word is first listed as a noun (*n.*). Seven meanings of the noun are given. But the word is also a transitive verb (*v.t.*), for which four meanings are given. For *litter* as an intransitive verb (*v.i.*), two meanings are given.

---

[8] By permission from *Funk & Wagnalls Standard® College Dictionary,* copyright 1968 by Funk & Wagnalls, A Division of Reader's Digest Books, Inc.

The word comes from an Old French word (OF *litiere*), which was derived from Medieval Latin *lectaria* (Med. L *lectaria*) and goes back ultimately to the Latin word for bed (L *lectus* bed). Synonyms (words of nearly the same meaning) for *litter* will be found under *flock* (**Syn.** See FLOCK.).

Let us consider the various meanings given for *litter*. At first glance there seems little to connect meaning 2, "Untidy or chaotic condition," with meaning 3, "The young brought forth at one birth," and even less with meaning 4, "A stretcher used for carrying sick or wounded persons." But once we grasp the fact that *litter* comes originally from a Latin word meaning "bed," it is fairly easy to see how its various apparently unconnected meanings developed. Meanings 4 and 5 obviously refer to special sorts of portable beds; and meaning 6 ("Straw, hay, etc., spread in animal pens") and meaning 3 of *litter* as a verb ("To provide with litter, as for bedding, covering, etc.") also derive (note the idea of *bedding*) from the original Latin root. Primitive human beds did not differ too much from animal beds, for they consisted of straw or rushes heaped together. Such being the case, it is easy to see how any scattering of straw or hay might come to be called a *litter,* and the process of strewing it, a process of *littering*. Meanings 1 and 2 of *litter* as a noun and 1 and 2 of *litter* as a verb are obvious further extensions of the root idea of bed, but in these meanings the emphasis has been shifted from the purpose of making a bed to an aimless and untidy strewing about.

Meanings 3 of the noun and 4 and 5 of the verb derive from the original meaning "bed" by another chain of development. The mother animal frequently makes a sort of rude bed in which she lies to give birth, and by association the rude bed (*litter*) comes to be used for what is found in the bed, the young animals themselves.

Let us consider another example, this time from *Webster's New Collegiate Dictionary*. Here is the dictionary entry for the common word *sad:* [9]

> **sad** \'sad\ *adj* **sad·der; sad·dest** [ME, fr. OE *sæd* sated; akin to OHG *sat* sated, L *satis* enough] **1 a :** affected with or expressive of grief or unhappiness **:** DOWNCAST **b** (1) **:** causing or associated with grief or unhappiness **:** DEPRESSING ⟨~ news⟩ (2) **:** DISMAYING, DEPLORABLE **c :** INFERIOR **2 :** of a dull somber color **:** DRAB — **sad·ly** *adv*

The word is an adjective (*adj*). The forms for the comparative and superlative degrees are given; then comes the derivation: *sad* occurs in Middle English (ME), but comes from the Old English *sæd,* meaning "sated" (fr. OE *sæd* sated). Sad is related to Old High German *sat,* meaning "sated" (OHG *sat* sated) and to Latin *satis,* meaning "enough" (L *satis* enough). The dictionary lists two principal meanings of the word, the first having to do with the emotion of grief or unhappiness; the second, with

---

[9] By permission. From *Webster's Seventh New Collegiate Dictionary* © 1969 by G. & C. Merriam Co., Publishers of the Merriam-Webster Dictionaries.

color. Meaning 1 is subdivided into three submeanings: 1a, 1b, and 1c. Under submeaning 1b two sub-submeanings are distinguished, (1) and (2). This dictionary prints in small capitals what it calls "synonymous cross-references." For example, under b(1), DEPRESSING, as in "depressing news" $<$ ~ news $>$. The synonymous words are called cross-references to indicate to the student that they may be looked up in the dictionary on their own account. Finally, the dictionary notes the form of the adverb derived from *sad* (sad-ly *adv*).

Even so brief a notice as the foregoing hints at a history of developing meanings. Inspection of a larger dictionary, such as *Webster's New International Dictionary* or the *Oxford English Dictionary* (also known as *A New English Dictionary*), with its fuller information as to the derivation of the word and its finer discrimination of meanings (including the various earlier meanings), enables us to make out a detailed history of the meanings of the word.

As we have seen, the German and Latin cognates of *sad* indicate that the basic root from which all meanings are descended must have meant something like "sated with food." Now, a man who has had a big dinner is torpid and heavy, not lively or restless, and so *sad* came to carry the suggestion of "calm," "stable," "earnest." Shakespeare frequently uses it to mean the opposite of "trifling" or "frivolous." But a person who seems thus sober and serious *may* be so because he is grieved or melancholy, and the word thereby gradually took on its modern meaning of "mournful" or "grieved." But we must not end this account without mentioning other lines of development. The sense of "torpid" or "heavy" was extended from animate beings, which can eat to repletion, to inanimate things, which cannot—to bread, for example, that fails to rise, or to a heavy laundry iron (sad-iron). *Webster's New Collegiate Dictionary,* in its definition of *sad-iron,* tells us that the word is made up of *sad* (in the sense of "compact" or "heavy") plus *iron.*

Meaning 2 ("of a dull somber color") represents still another extension of *sad* in the sense of "stable" or "sober." It means the kind of color that a sobersides (as opposed to a gay and sprightly person) would wear: that is, dull, sober colors.

Has the process of extension now ceased? Hardly. In the phrase "sad sack" (U.S. Army slang) a related meaning of *sad* gained wide temporary currency just after World War II, but most speakers now have returned to *sorry* (rather than *sad*) to express the meaning of "inferior" (note 1c above with its synonymous cross-reference INFERIOR) or "worthless": we say "a sorry team," "a sorry outfit," "a sorry job."

Here is a third example of a dictionary listing, this time from *Webster's New World Dictionary:* [10]

---

[10] From *Webster's New World Dictionary of The American Language, Second College Edition.* Copyright 1970 by The World Publishing Co., Cleveland, Ohio.

de·grade (di grād′, dē-) *vt.* -**grad′ed**, -**grad′ing** [ME. *degraden* < OFr. *degrader* < LL. *degradare*, to reduce in rank < L. *de-*, down + *gradus:* see GRADE] **1.** to lower in rank or status, as in punishing; demote **2.** to lower or corrupt in quality, moral character, value, etc.; debase **3.** to bring into dishonor or contempt **4.** *Chem.* to convert (an organic compound) into a simpler compound by removal of one or more parts of the molecule; decompose **5.** *Geol.* to lower (a land surface) by erosion —*vi.* [Rare] to sink to a lower grade or type; degenerate —**de·grad′a·ble** *adj.* —**de·grad′er** *n.*
SYN.—**degrade** literally means to lower in grade or rank, but it commonly implies a lowering or corrupting of moral character, self-respect, etc.; **abase** suggests a loss, often merely temporary and self-imposed, of dignity, respect, etc. [he *abased* himself before his employer]; **debase** implies a decline in value, quality, character, etc. [a *debased* mind]; to **humble** is to lower the pride or increase the humility, esp. of another, and, unqualified, suggests that such lowering is deserved [*humbled* by the frightening experience]; to **humiliate** is to humble or shame (another) painfully and in public [*humiliated* by their laughter] —**ANT.** exalt, dignify

The word is a transitive verb (*v.t.*). Its derivation is traced through Middle English (ME. *degraden*), Old French (OFr. *degrader*), Late Latin (LL. *degradare*), back to Latin (*de* + *gradus*). Five meanings are distinguished; and since *degrade* may also appear as an intransitive verb (*vi.*), one further intransitive meaning. There is a discussion of the differences in meaning between *degrade* and four of its synonyms. Two antonyms (words of opposed meaning) are listed.

The definition of a word is, then, a somewhat more complex business than one might suppose. It consists frequently not just of *the* meaning, but of interrelated sets of meanings, some of which are current and some of which are not, and some of which have been accepted into good society and some of which are merely clinging to the fringes of society. A word that is appropriate in one context obviously might be thoroughly out of place in another.

■ **APPLICATIONS**

I Look up in the *Oxford English Dictionary* or *Webster's International* the origins of the following words:

nostril	enthusiasm	fast (adj.)
aristocracy	urbane	egregious
plutocracy	Bible	sympathetic
complicate	fine (adj.)	malaria
thrilling	infant	starboard
vivid	silly	melancholy
gerrymander	laconic	bourgeois
cheap	stupid	muscle

Does knowledge of its origin clarify the meaning of any of these words? Does it help you understand the relationship between current discrepant mean-

ings (that is, "He made a *fast* trip," and "The boat was made *fast* to the pier";
or "This *fine* print hurts my eyes" and "He was a big, *fine*, upstanding man")?
Does knowledge of the origin of the word help account for such uses as
"legal *infant*" and "the Book" (as applied to the Bible)?

II   With the help of the dictionary discriminate as carefully as you can among
the words in the following groups:

1   sulky, petulant, peevish, sullen, morose, crabbed, surly
2   skeptic, infidel, atheist, freethinker, agnostic
3   reasonable, just, moderate, equitable, fair-minded, judicial
4   rebellion, revolt, insurrection, revolution
5   belief, faith, persuasion, conviction, assurance, reliance
6   sneak, skulk, slink
7   trick, fool, hoodwink, bamboozle, deceive, beguile, delude, cheat,
     mislead
8   brave, daring, courageous, fearless, valiant, dauntless
9   dawdle, idle, loiter, linger, lag
10 solemn, sober, serious, grave, reverential, earnest

Does a knowledge of the origin of the word throw light upon the special
connotations of any of these words?

The Company a Word Keeps:
Informal (Colloquial) and Formal

Earlier, in discussing the implied meanings of words, we touched briefly
upon the way in which these meanings may determine the appropriateness of
a word for a particular context (pp. 396–98). The word *steed*, we saw, would
be proper for some contexts, *nag* for others, and *horse* for still others. But
the problem of appropriateness is important and deserves fuller treatment.

In the first place, there is what may be called the dignity and social standing of the word. Like human beings, a word tends to be known by the
company it keeps. Words like *caboodle* and *gumption* are good colloquial
words and perfectly appropriate to the informal give-and-take of conversation. But they would be out of place in a dignified and formal utterance.
For example, a speech welcoming a great public figure in which he was
complimented on his "statesmanlike gumption" would be absurd. To take
another example, many of us use the slang term *guy*, and though, like much
slang, it has lost what pungency it may once have had, its rather flippant
breeziness is not inappropriate in some contexts. But it would be foolish
to welcome our elder statesman by complimenting him on being a "wise
and venerable guy." It is only fair to say that the shoe can pinch the other

foot. Certain literary and rather highfalutin terms, in a *colloquial* context, sound just as absurd. We do not praise a friend for his "dexterity" or for his "erudition," not, at least, when we meet him on the street or chat with him across the table.

The fact that words are known by the company they keep does not, however, justify snobbishness in diction. Pretentiousness is, in the end, probably in even worse taste than blurting out a slang term on a formal occasion. Words must be used with tact and common sense. But the comments made above do point to certain areas of usage of which most of us are already more or less aware.

The various kinds of diction (and their necessary overlappings) are conveniently represented in the following diagram: [11]

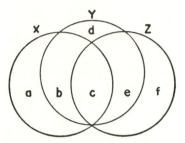

The three circles X, Y, Z, represent the three sets of language habits indicated above.

X—formal literary English, the words, the expressions, and the structures one finds in serious books.

Y—colloquial English, the words, expressions, and the structures of the informal but polite conversation of cultivated people.

Z—illiterate English, the words, the expressions, and the structures of the language of the uneducated.

b, c, and e represent the overlappings of the three types of English.

c—that which is common to all three: formal literary English, colloquial English, and illiterate English.

b—that which is common to both formal literary English and colloquial English.

e—that which is common to both colloquial English and illiterate English.

a, d, and f represent those portions of each type of English that are peculiar to that particular set of language habits.

Modern slang, for example, falls into segment *e*—and possibly *d*. It would be properly available for colloquial and informal writing. (But segments *d* and *e*, of course, include more than slang: they include colloquial terms of all kinds that do not occur in formal literary English.) Segment *a* includes the terms that occur only in formal literary English, but the overlap of formal literary English with colloquial and illiterate English is large—

---

[11] From *The American College Dictionary*. Copyright 1969 by Random House, Inc. Reprinted by permission.

so large that most of the words used in writing of the most formal style are to be found in writings at the other extreme of style.

It would be misleading, therefore, to suggest that there is a mechanical rule for selecting the diction that one uses in an informal essay, or in a formal treatise, or to express the dialogue of "low characters" in a novel. The degrees of height and lowness of style and shadings of formality and informality are so many—and vary so much even within one work—that we cannot hope to find our appropriate diction segregated for us in one compartment. But our chart should make plain that in this matter of levels of diction, the dictionary can be of real help. It marks, as such, colloquial words, slang, technical words, and so on. Yet recourse to the dictionary is not a substitute for the student's developing a feeling for language. The dictionary can help, but wide reading and practice in writing can help even more.

The student already has a more sensitive feeling for language than he realizes. It would not occur to the student—except as a joke—to remark to a friend: "I am trying to ascertain the assignment for next week in English. The amiable pedagogue who directs our labors was inaudible to me, though I think he must have mumbled something. Can you advise me?" Though in his conversation the student is not likely to err in the direction of the pretentious and the highfalutin, he may do so in his writing. Yet for many students the common fault will be not a too precise formality but an inappropriately slangy colloquialism. The student *might* write for his history instructor: "I think that Andrew Johnson got a raw deal from Congress. He was a pretty cantankerous customer, I have to admit, and mighty stubborn. But lots of folks just didn't like his lingo, his accent, or where he came from, for that matter. I guess you could say that people just didn't like the cut of his jib—sort of instinctively. But I think he was honest as hell and it's a great pity that he got himself stuck with such a poor image."

● CAUTION

Avoid both pretentiousness and inappropriate slanginess.

■ APPLICATIONS

I Rewrite the short passage about Andrew Johnson above in order to make it more formal.

II Rewrite the following sentences, removing (a) any stilted diction and (b) any slang or illiterate diction. In general try to make the diction fit an informal standard. (In setting up this exercise, we are not forgetting that the absurdities in such instances as these may be intentional; writers often use disparities of this sort for humorous effect. In this general connection, notice the comment on the Robert Graves passage printed on page 416.)

1 We approached Emporium City from Route 60, driving like a bat out of hell.
2 Miss Warner was a young creature of patrician elegance and of disdainful hauteur but really pretty dumb.
3 It sure was picturesque! Titanic vistas solicited our view. It was all mighty grand.
4   I am the true nonpareil. All others are but tawdry copycats.

                                        —From a fan-dancer's advertisement.

III The following passage is quite informal—even colloquial—in diction and expression. Rewrite the passage so as to make it as formal as possible.

> I could recognize big changes from Commerce down. Beaver Dam Rock was out in the middle of the river now, and throwing a prodigious "break"; it used to be close to the shore, and boats went down outside of it. A big island that used to be away out in mid-river has retired to the Missouri shore, and boats do not go near it any more. The island called Jacket Pattern is whittled down to a wedge now, and is booked for early destruction. Goose Island is all gone but a little dab, the size of a steamboat. The perilous "Graveyard," along whose numberless wrecks we used to pick our way so slowly and gingerly, is far away from the channel now, and a terror to nobody. One of the islands formerly called the Two Sisters is gone entirely; the other, which used to lie close to the Illinois shore, is now on the Missouri side, a mile away; it is joined solidly to the shore, and it takes a sharp eye to see where the seam is—but it is Illinois ground yet, and the people who live on it have to ferry themselves over and work the Illinois roads and pay Illinois taxes: singular state of things!
>
> —Samuel L. Clemens: *Life on the Mississippi*.

IV This passage is much more formal than that by Clemens. Attempt to rewrite the passage so as to make it less formal.

> The reader has been informed, that we were running along the coast, within a mile of it, to enable us to keep sight of the land. The object of this was to make the proper landfall for running into the Gulf of Paria, on which is situated the Port of Spain, in the island of Trinidad, to which we were bound. We opened the gulf as early as nine A.M., and soon afterward identified the three islands that form the *Bocas del Drago,* dragon's mouth. The scenery is remarkably bold and striking at the entrance of this gulf or bay. The islands rise to the height of mountains, in abrupt and sheer precipices, out of the now muddy waters—for the great Orinoco, traversing its thousands of miles of alluvial soil, disembogues near by. Indeed, we may be said to have been already within the delta of that great stream.
>
> Memory was busy with me, as the *Sumter* passed through the Dragon's Mouth. I had made my first cruise to this identical island of Trinidad, when a green midshipman in the Federal Navy. A few years before, the elder Commodore Perry—he of Lake Erie memory—had died of yellow fever when on a visit in one of the small schooners of his squadron up the Orinoco. The old sloop-of-war *Lexington,* under the command of Commander, now Rear-Admiral Shubrick, was sent to the Port of Spain to bring home his remains. I was one of the midshipmen of that ship. A generation had since elapsed.

An infant people had, in that short space of time, grown old and decrepit, and its government had broken in twain. But there stood the everlasting mountains, as I remembered them, unchanged!
—Admiral Raphael Semmes: *Service Afloat.*

How Associations Control Meanings

Thus far we have seen how associated meanings determine what may be called the social tone of a word. But we must go on to consider the very important way in which these meanings actually determine, though sometimes subtly, the effect of the word, that is, the way in which they actually determine meaning. In our time especially, propaganda and advertising have made this whole matter very important. So also has much of the polemical writing of our day. Benjamin DeMott's essay entitled "The Age of Overkill" (pp. 692–97) points out that a feature of our time is the use of an almost hysterical rhetoric. Instead of a biting epithet calculated to strike down an enemy, the writer fires a rhetorical atomic bomb with blast enough to destroy whole institutions, classes, and races. Thus, we read that "The family is the American fascism"; that "The white race is the cancer of history"; and that "We can learn more from any jail than we can from any university," and so forth. We live in an age of inflamed rhetoric. Far from using precise and exact terms, the writers of our "scientific" and rational society often exaggerate, overstate, and caricature. But the student will want to read DeMott's essay, and judge for himself whether DeMott himself overstates the situation.

Another manifestation of the exaggerated rhetoric of our age is the tendency to play up the emotional impact of a word at the expense of accurate reference. The associations that surround a word may actually become more important than its primary meaning. Not long ago, the verb *involved* became very fashionable with people who wished to indicate a sensitive response to social conditions. Taking advantage of the favorable associations that had gathered around the word, an advertising copywriter argued that since South America was "a very involved continent," visitors to South America ought to get there by means of "a very involved airline." If any reader had been tempted to ask with what or in what either the continent or the airline was involved, it is doubtful that an answer would have been forthcoming. Evidently *involved* had become such a favorable term that the writer felt it was sufficient recommendation merely to say someone or something was "involved." Like virtue, involvement was its own reward and its own excuse for being. (It is amusing to note that only a few years previously *involved* had quite other associations: if it was whispered that a woman had been "involved," the implication was that she was mixed up in a scandalous affair; or if a man was said to be "involved," the reference was generally taken to be to a shady financial deal.)

Yet, whether used responsibly or simply abused, the connotations of a word are important, and the writer who hopes to be effective must take them into account. A group of words that point to more or less the same thing may range in their associations from highly favorable to highly unfavorable. For example, we may call an agriculturist a "farmer," a "planter," a "tiller of the soil," or, in more exalted fashion, "the partner of Mother Nature" but we can also refer to him as a "peasant," a "rube," a "hayseed," or a "hick." Many of our words do more than merely *name* something. They imply a judgment about its value as well. They make a favorable or an unfavorable evaluation. Consider, for example, these roughly synonymous terms:

Favorable	Neutral	Unfavorable
secret agent	informant	stool pigeon
cherub	child	brat
self-control	discipline	regimentation

■ APPLICATIONS

I   Can you fill the blanks in the table below with appropriate "synonymous" terms (more than one if you like)?

Favorable	Neutral	Unfavorable
	policeman	
		political boss
	society reporter	
idealist		
	status quo	
	publicity agent	

II   For the following words, try to find synonyms of differing or even opposite associations:

rebellion	harsh	dictator
tycoon	reformer	liberal
elegant	conventional	ward leader
discrimination	diplomacy	theoretical
freedom	practical	aroma
academic	vacillating	radical
esoteric	strait-laced	canard

By choosing terms with the right associations, we can easily color our whole account of a man or a happening or an idea. Much of the effectiveness of this method depends upon the fact that the writer ostensibly is only pointing to certain things, only naming them: the damaging (or ennobling) implications are, as it were, smuggled in surreptitiously. This was the method frequently used a few years ago by such writers as Westbrook Pegler and H. L. Mencken or recently by a writer like Drew Pearson. Notice how heavily the following passage from one of Mencken's essays leans upon this device. (Italics supplied by the editors.)

> "The Ride of the Valkyrie" has a certain intrinsic value as pure music; played by a competent orchestra it may give civilized pleasure. But as it is commonly performed in an opera house, with a *posse* of fat *beldames* throwing themselves about the stage, it can produce the effect of a dose of ipecacuanha. The sort of person who actually delights in such spectacles is the sort of person who delights in plush furniture. Such half-wits are in a majority in every opera house west of the Rhine. They go to the opera, not to hear music, not even to hear bad music, but merely to see a more or less obscene *circus*.   —H. L. MENCKEN: "Opera," *Prejudices: Second Series*.

As a matter of fact, Mencken has here so clearly expressed his attitudes that the use of damaging implications may be obscured. With such a trumpeting of his prejudices, the phrase "smuggled in surreptitiously" may seem a misnomer, even though the effect depends upon implications as well as upon denunciation.

In the following passage, Graves presents Rome as adorning itself with art treasures from the "more ancient and beautiful cities" of Greece.

> Rome was now a great *jackdaw's* nest, with temples and mansions newly built in solid, vulgar, imitation-Greek architectural style—much of it concrete with a thin marble facing—*stuffed* with *loot* from more ancient and beautiful cities. Typical scenes of "the grandeur that was Rome" at the sack of Corinth. A group of smoke-blackened Roman infantrymen, *squatting* on a priceless old master—Aristides's "The God Dionysus"—and *shooting craps* for possession of sacred chalices looted from Dionysus's temple. Others *hacking* souvenirs from the most famous relic of antiquity, the stern of the ship "Argo" which had brought back the Golden Fleece from the Caucasus more than a thousand years before. The Army commander impressing on the transport captains detailed to convey unique works of art back to Rome—"Mind you, my men, anything you lose you'll have to replace." [*Italics ours.*]
> —ROBERT GRAVES: "It Was a Stable World," *Occupation: Writer*.[12]

■ APPLICATION

Graves's attitude toward what the Romans did is expressed quite explicitly. But note the effect of the italicized terms in strengthening and filling out the quality of his judgment.

---

[12] From "It Was a Stable World" from *Occupation: Writer* by Robert Graves. Reprinted by permission of Collins-Knowlton-Wing, Inc. Copyright © 1950 Robert Graves. Reprinted by permission of Robert Graves and A. P. Watt & Son.

1   Discuss the specific associations of each italicized word or phrase.
2   What is the point of stressing the commander's admonition to his men? What makes this the "punch line"? Do the italicized words help to "set up" this line?

The power of association is also illustrated by our recourse to euphemisms. Certain words, even necessary words, which refer to unpleasant things, are avoided in favor of softening expressions or indirect references. In many contexts *bastard* is felt to be too brutal; so *illegitimate* is substituted for it. Even a word like *died* may be shunned in favor of *deceased* or *passed away* or *went to his reward.* Undertakers have taken to calling themselves *morticians,* and butchers in some parts of the country prefer to be known as *meat-cutters.* Whatever one may think of the substitutions, they at least testify to the power of past associations and the desire of men to avoid words with unpleasant or disparaging associations.

The power of association is illustrated positively in our tendency to disparage human beings by associating them with unpleasant animals or insects. Thus, we express contempt by calling a man a *rat,* a *louse,* or a *worm;* a certain admiration for his cleverness, by calling him a *fox;* hatred (and perhaps fear), by calling him a *snake.* In general, the animal creation is a rich source of expressions of attitude toward other human beings, particularly of hostile or contemptuous attitudes. But we may use associations drawn from all sorts of areas: "He is a tower of strength"; "He is as hard as flint"; "She is as neat as a pin." In the next chapter (see pp. 436–37), we shall discuss in detail the uses of figurative language of this sort.

Here follows the account of an incident as it might be reported by a relatively impartial writer:

> Democratic (or Republican) Senator Briggs expressed surprise at being met by reporters. He told them that he had no comment to make on the "Whitlow deal." He said that he had not known that Whitlow was in the employ of General Aircraft and observed that the suggestion that he had received favors from Whitlow was an attempt to discredit him.

How might a hostile reporter describe the incident? He would perhaps give an account something like this:

> Senator Briggs, Democratic (or Republican) wheelhorse, was obviously startled to find himself confronted by newspapermen. He stubbornly refused to comment on what he called the "Whitlow deal" and professed not to have known that Whitlow was a lobbyist. The Senator complained that he was being smeared.

The second account seems to be substantially the same as the first. The "facts" are not appreciably altered. But the emotional coloring and, with it, the intended effect on the reader have been sharply altered. The senator is now a "wheelhorse," with its suggestions of a hardened and (probably) calloused political conscience. Whitlow is a "lobbyist," and again suggestions of political corruption are insinuated. Moreover, the senator's actions and speech ("obviously startled," "stubbornly refused," "professed not to have known," and "complained") are made to suggest guilt.

The attitudes expressed in any piece of writing are extremely important and are, indeed, an integral part of its "meaning." (In this general connection, the student should read "How to Detect Propaganda," pp. 686–91.)

■ **APPLICATIONS**

I Alter the diction of the following passages in order to present (a) a more favorable view; (b) a less favorable view. (The sample sentence, with its optional terms, will illustrate the kind of alteration that the student is to make.)

The veteran (*still-youthful, aging*) movie star walked (*swept, minced*) into the strong (*brilliant, harsh*) light and paused for a moment to look at (*glance at, ogle*) the crowd.

A   The old woman walked up to the counter and priced the scarf. She hesitated, seemed to think for a moment, and then opened her black purse, and extracted a five-dollar bill. She laid it on the counter and began to finger the bright piece of cloth.

B   The mayor, a stocky man of middle age, stepped forward to the microphone with a sheaf of papers in his hand. He placed these on the lectern and cleared his throat. His face was serious as he began his speech.

C   The two boys, fifteen and seventeen, were ill at ease when they appeared before Judge Baker, who regarded them impersonally from the bench. An atmosphere of tension prevailed in the courtroom as lawyers began shuffling their papers.

II   In one of our more picturesque cities debate arose as to whether to build an expressway that would skirt the oldest part of the city. The following account appeared on the editorial page of a newspaper.

> The Metropolitan Area Committee last week urged construction of the proposed Riverfront Expressway at ground level. The organization's views on the long-simmering issue will be transmitted to John A. Volpe, secretary of transportation. The resolution had been proposed by the MAC executive committee, which had been convoked March 5 after the President's Advisory Council on Historic Preservation had announced it was recommending to Volpe that the expressway be relocated or, in the alternative, that it be constructed as a depressed roadway. MAC is a biracial, nonpartisan citizens action group consisting of more than 500 members from many fields. The

ground level concept has been under relentless attack from so-called preservationists who maintain that it would desecrate the French Quarter.
—The New Orleans *Times-Picayune,* March 16, 1969.

Judging by its editorial comment, would you say that this newspaper was for the ground-level expressway or against it?

III A The following excerpt is taken from a novel. In the novel it appears as a note scrawled on the back cover of a copy of *Life* "around all four edges of the Winston ad." We learn that the author of the note is a brilliant, eccentric physician, much given to drinking and wenching. Where a choice of words is indicated, can you determine which word was actually used by the author? Or, if you feel that an author may not be infallible, which word would *you* choose in this context?

[J. F.] Kennedy. With all the campaign biographies, praise for him, hogwash, no one has said what

he was. The reason he was a great man / statesman / politician was that his ironic manner / self-deprecation / derisiveness

kept pace with his charm / beauty / handsome face and his dedication to / love of / affection for country. He

is the only public man / politician / statesman I have ever believed. This is because no man now

is credible / convincing / believable unless he deprecates himself. In him I saw the old is derisive. / is ironic.

eagle virtue / beauty / integrity of the United States of America. I admired / worshipped / loved him.

They, the _____ (unreadable: bourgeois? burghers? bastards?) wanted him dead. Very well, it will serve them right because now——

B The following passage is also taken from a novel: the hero is describing —with what tone and intention?—one of his teachers at college. Again, try to determine which words are the author's.

By far the most distinguished / interesting / outstanding of his teachers this first year was Mr. Edward

Pettigrew ("Buck") Benson, the Greek professor. Buck Benson was a small / little / slight man in the middle forties, a bachelor, somewhat

                                                                                effete,

dapper, but

dandified,

old-fashioned   plump

dated   in his dress. He wore wing collars, large heavy

unmodish   rich-textured

                                   bushy,

cravats, and suede-topped shoes. His hair was stiff, heavily greyed,

                                   thick,

beautifully   courteously aggressive, alert,

neatly   kept. His face was pleasantly belligerent, fierce, with

elegantly   blandly pugnacious, grim,

         bulging   folded

large yellow protruding eyeballs, and several jowled pleatings around

         popped   bulldog

                          handsome uncouthness.

the mouth. It was an altogether distinguished ruggedness.

                                  winning ugliness.

Worn-out Words and Clichés

We began this chapter by saying that the problem of diction is that of finding the right words, the words that will say exactly what the writer wants to say. But we have seen that exactness in language cannot be attained simply and mechanically, that words work on a number of levels in a number of different ways. Words are not static. They have a history; they have biographies; and even have, one is tempted to say, personalities. Most of all, since they are not changeless and inflexible, but to some extent plastic, changing their shape a little under the pressure of the context in which they occur, they offer a continual stimulus and challenge to the imagination of the writer.

Language, as we have seen, changes, develops, grows, and, by the same token, language wears out. We are not thinking, however, of the normal sloughing off of words that have died natural deaths and now either do not occur in a modern dictionary at all or, if they do occur, are marked *obsolete* (*shoon* for *shoes*) or *archaic* (*e'en* for *even*). We are thinking rather of words that have been thoughtlessly used in certain contexts so often that they have lost nearly all their force. We call these threadbare expressions "trite" or "hackneyed" or term them "stereotypes" and "clichés."

■ **APPLICATION**

Consult the dictionary for the etymology of *trite* and *hackneyed*. What do the terms mean precisely? Check also the origin (or literal meaning) of *stereotype* and *cliché*. Does a knowledge of the origin of these terms help you to understand why the qualities they name are to be avoided?

Common stereotypes, including slang

Clichés are produced by writers who do not think out what they want to say but find a worn groove in the language into which they let their thoughts slide. Books on rhetoric sometimes supply lists of threadbare expressions against which the student is warned: "the more the merrier," "last but not least," "to trip the light fantastic toe." Hackneyed phrases of this sort have probably by now become too literary, too old-fashioned, to offer much temptation to a modern student—even to a lazy one. But stereotyping continues, and much of the writing and conversation to which we are constantly exposed is a tissue of trite expressions. Society-page editors have their own brand of stereotypes: "social function," "gala affair," "making one's bow to society," and so forth. The sports page also yields stereotypes in abundance. Mr. Frank Sullivan amusingly exhibits some of these in question-and-answer form:

Q. If [the teams] don't roll up a score what do they do?
A. They battle to a scoreless tie.
Q. What do they hang up?
A. A victory. Or, they pull down a victory.
Q. Which means that they do what to the opposing team?
A. They take the measure of the opposing team, or take it into camp.
Q. And the opposing team?
A. Drops a game, or bows in defeat.
Q. This dropping, or bowing, constitutes what kind of blow for the losing team?
A. It is a crushing blow to its hopes of annexing the Eastern championship. Visions of the Rose Bowl fade.
Q. So what follows as a result of the defeat?
A. A drastic shakeup follows as a result of the shellacking at the hands of Cornell last Saturday.
Q. And what is developed?
A. A new line of attack.
Q. Mr. Smith, how is the first quarter of a football game commonly referred to?
A. As the initial period.   —FRANK SULLIVAN: "Football Is King."

Howard Jacobs provides a neat list of political clichés in the following skit.

QUIZ KIDS DENOUNCE 'BLOATED PLUTOCRATS'

With the mayoral race in the offing and since political spellbinders soon will be loose on the land, it behooves us to review the entrance exams for Professor Chick Hannery's School of Political Science. Let us mosey to the school with the Quiz Kids, Flotsam and Jetsam.

Says the professor: "Now I'm going to ask you some questions to determine your aptitude. First, if your opponent has been defeated in a previous election, how can you best capitalize on the fact?"

"We would always refer to him as discredited, or repudiated," replies Flotsam.

"What makes you think 'discredited' or 'repudiated' are synonymous with 'defeated'?" demands the professor.

"Because we are studying political science, not Webster's definitions," responds Jetsam.

"Very good," remarks the professor. "Now, what should any move of the opposition make our blood do?"

"Boil."

"And what should any move of our own faction give us a solemn sense of?"

"Pride."

"All right," says the professor, "now, how should you refer to our own faction?"

"An organization."

"And that of the opposition?"

"A gang, or a machine, or 'that crowd.'"

"And how would you describe the opposition when at least one of their candidates has completed the payments on his automobile?"

"Bloated plutocrats."

"Excellent. And what would you call a compromise between two different factions opposing you?"

"A sellout."

"And what about a compromise between your faction and one of the opposition?"

"An understanding."

"Good. And what body of water is the opposition always going to sell the people down?"

"The river."

"Perfect. Now suppose you are in office and want to get reelected, at what would you point the finger of pride?"

"The record."

"And if you were out of office and wanted to get in, at what would you point the finger of scorn?"

"The record."

"And what would you call one of your candidates with original ideas?"

"A man of vision."

"And one of the opposition who has original ideas?"

"A visionary."

"One last question. Who is supporting your side?"

"A sturdy coalition of decent, self-respecting citizens."

"And that of the opposition?"

"An unholy alliance of politicians and others of their ilk wishing to feed at the public trough."

"O.K.," says the professor. "You can report for elementary training next week and I'll put a cross by your names. On second thought you should be ready for the advanced course, so we'll make it a double cross."

—HOWARD JACOBS: The New Orleans *Times-Picayune,* April 27, 1969.[13]

To come still closer home, there is slang. Some slang expressions may once have been pungent and colorful. The sportswriter who first described the strike-out of a slugging batter by saying "he made three dents in the atmosphere" conveyed the scene sharply and humorously. When slang is thus "tailor-made" for the occasion, it may be bright and perceptive, though, if it is still fresh and vivid, one could question whether it ought to be viewed as "slang" at all. But, as most of us use it, slang is a worn and impoverished language, not bright and irreverent and lively, but stale and dead: "the party was a washout"; "I'm fed up"; "he crabbed a lot"; "he blew his top." The real sin committed here is not so much that of bringing slang's flippant associations into a serious context. We do not often commit this fault. The real sin in using slang consists in using a thin and inexpressive language—slang that has lost its edge.

Jargon: the degenerative disease of prose

We have to step up, however, to a somewhat more exalted plane to find the stereotypes that most damage modern prose and that are likely to do the student most harm. These stereotypes are such expressions as "along the lines of," "in the last analysis," "socioeconomic considerations," "the world of business affairs," "according to a usually reliable source." Such locutions puff out many an official document, many a political speech, and it must be admitted, many a professor's lecture or article.

This wordy, murky style is sometimes called "officialese." Congressman Maury Maverick called it "gobbledygook," submitting as a horrible sample the following extract:

> Whereas, national defense requirements have created a shortage of corundum (as hereafter defined) for the combined needs of defense and private account, and the supply of corundum now is and will be insufficient for defense and essential civilian requirements, unless the supply of corundum is conserved and its use in certain products manufactured for civilian use is curtailed; and it is necessary in the public interest and to promote the defense of the United States, to conserve the supply and direct the distribution and use thereof. Now, therefore, it is hereby ordered that . . .

---

[13] Reprinted from the New Orleans *Times-Picayune,* April 27, 1969, by permission of the New Orleans *Times-Picayune.*

Here follows a paragraph of jargon with a more academic smack:

> This relationship would define certain linkages between the social and physical structure of the city. It would also provide a precise definition of the commonalities among several spatial distributions. By the same token, the correlation between the residential desirability scale and the continuum of socio-economic status would provide an estimate of the predictive value of aerial photographic data relative to the social ecology of the city.

Mr. Malcolm Cowley, who garnered the specimen of jargon just quoted, comments as follows:

> Mr. Green has used 160 words—counting "socio-economic" as only one —to express an idea that a layman would have stated in thirty-three. As a matter of fact, he has used many more than 160 words, since the whole article is an elaboration of this one thesis. Whatever may be the virtues of the sociological style, or Socspeak, as George Orwell might have called it— it is not specifically designed to save ink and paper.
> —"Sociological Habit Patterns in Linguistic Transmogrification,"
> *The Reporter,* Sept. 20, 1956.

George Orwell himself has written on the subject of the sociological style:

> Prose (nowadays) consists less and less of *words* chosen for the sake of their meaning, and more and more of *phrases* tacked together like the sections of a prefabricated henhouse. . . . There is a huge dump of wornout metaphors which have lost all evocative power and are merely used because they save people the trouble of inventing phrases for themselves. . . . Modern writing at its worst . . . consists in gumming together long strips of words which have already been set in order by someone else.

By using apt comparisons ("sections of a prefabricated henhouse," "dump of worn-out metaphors," "gumming together long strips of words") Orwell vividly makes the two points of his indictment: the jargon writer's careless and slovenly craftsmanship and the secondhand quality of his materials.

Orwell goes on to illustrate his point by suggesting how a modern writer of hand-me-down phrases would express the following passage from Ecclesiastes: "I returned, and saw under the sun, that the race is not to the swift, nor the battle to the strong, neither yet bread to the wise, nor yet riches to men of understanding, nor yet favor to men of skill; but time and chance happeneth to them all."

Such a writer, says Orwell, would probably turn it out like this: "Objective consideration of contemporary phenomena compels the conclusion that success or failure in competitive activities exhibits no tendency to be commensurate with innate capacity, but that a considerable element of the unpredictable must invariably be taken into account."

But whether we call it officialese when it emanates from some government bureau, or gobbledygook, or simply jargon, its empty wordiness is characteristic. Here are two somewhat more respectable samples culled from *College English*—a fact that should warn us that anyone can fall prey to jargon, even a writer who undertakes to teach others how to write effective English.

> 1   If we start at one of the extremes of the continuum, we shall find a grouping around a point of great vitality and wide appeal. Keenly aware of the painstaking scholarship and of the high creative effort that over the centuries has accumulated the body of subject matter we call "English," a group of our ablest teachers conceive their role to be to transmit this product of human endeavor, this hard-won store of learning and of art, this rich portion of man's heritage of culture, to the oncoming generations, and to imbue them with some perception of its worth.
>
> 2   But whether we are trained statisticians or not, we can improve the results of our examination speeches and themes. First of all, we can, without great difficulty, develop better controlled problems. There are various degrees of control possible in examination speeches and themes, and, within reasonable limits, it would seem as though the greater the control the more meaningful the test results. Complete freedom of choice of topic and material puts a premium upon accidental inspiration and upon glibness rather than thoughtfulness. A single assigned topic is palpably unfair since it may strike the interest and experience of some and yet leave others untouched.

We have taken these passages out of context, and the subject matter is admittedly difficult. Even so, the symptoms of jargon are present. Consider the second excerpt: both "puts a premium upon" and "palpably unfair" are clearly stereotypes. Moreover, what does the author gain by specifying "without great difficulty" and "within reasonable limits"? Are these specifications necessary? Could they not be assumed? Has not the writer put them in for rhetorical purposes, that is, to "dress up" his statement rather than to make necessary qualifications?

Consider the following paragraph from Eric Hoffer's *The True Believer*. Hoffer makes the point that discontent by itself does not create a desire for change.

> Those who are awed by their surroundings do not think of change, no matter how miserable their condition. When our mode of life is so precarious as to make it patent that we cannot control the circumstances of our existence, we tend to stick to the proven and the familiar. We counteract a deep feeling of insecurity by making of our existence a fixed routine. We hereby acquire the illusion that we have tamed the unpredictable. Fisherfolk, nomads and farmers who have to contend with the willful elements, the creative worker who depends on inspiration, the savage awed by his surroundings—they fear change. They face the world as they would an all-powerful jury. The abjectly poor, too, stand in awe of the world around them and are not hospitable to change. It is a dangerous life we

live when hunger and cold are at our heels. There is thus a conservatism of the destitute as profound as the conservatism of the privileged, and the former is as much a factor in the perpetuation of a social order as the latter.

—ERIC HOFFER: *The True Believer.*[14]

Though the writing here has a certain vigor, it shows a number of the signs of jargon. The writing is cloudy, and the thought is not clearly articulated. An attempt to restate Hoffer's argument in a somewhat more direct way follows.

> Men avoid change when they fear that any change may be for the worse. This fear has a special hold on those who, like the savage, cannot understand the environment in which they live, and on those who, like the nomad, the fisherman, or the farmer, are powerless to change the weather which controls their very lives. Even the creative artist, in so far as his success depends upon an inspiration that cannot be invoked by an act of will, may feel himself at the mercy of an irrational force. Such men are deeply insecure and, since they are, they may cling to familiar patterns of behavior because a fixed routine gives them the illusion of having tamed the unpredictable; that is, if they cannot make the environment predictable, they will at least make their own behavior predictable.
>
> The abjectly poor also fear to change the conditions under which they live, even though those conditions render them miserable. It is indeed their very misery that makes them inhospitable to change. There is thus a conservatism of the destitute that is as profound as the conservatism of the privileged. Both the abject poor and the complacent rich are afraid to alter the status quo.

The student who ponders this rewritten version may object that it does not contain everything that Hoffer says. This version, for instance, leaves out the allusion to a man's facing an all-powerful jury. Moreover, we have added things not in Hoffer's paragraph. Yet if the student ponders further, he will realize that these omissions and additions are incidental to our attempt to discover what it is that Hoffer was trying to say and to rearrange the steps in his argument so as to make his statement more nearly coherent. For example, on inspection it becomes plain that Hoffer offers two quite separate circumstances that inhibit change: the savage does not understand his environment; the nomad, the fisherman, and the farmer do—at least well enough to know that they are powerless to change the weather, that aspect of the environment that affects them most.

This attempt to sort out Hoffer's thoughts raises a question about his third instance. Ought the creative writer to be classed with the savage or with the farmer or with neither? The writer's inspiration is, like the farmer's weather, unpredictable, but is the typical writer therefore fearful of change? Many writers do often make changes in the conditions under which they write—changes as minor as rearranging a desk or as major as moving from

---

[14] From pp. 7–8 in *The True Believer* (Hardbound Ed.) by Eric Hoffer. Copyright, 1951 by Eric Hoffer. Reprinted by permission of Harper & Row, Publishers.

the mountains to the seashore, or from Manhattan to Barbados—in the hope that with the change they can regain access to their "inspiration." Furthermore, a high percentage of serious writers tend to be critical of the society in which they happen to live and advocate changes in it.

Our rewritten version—assuming that it is more coherent—may in fact raise a serious general question about Hoffer's principal argument. Do men who cannot understand, and men who cannot control, their environment insist on making their own conduct predictable? And if they do so, is their act to be interpreted as an irrational response to their uncertainty about the forces around them? Some men do adopt such a routine as a kind of "magic." The savage who clearly believes in sympathetic magic does so. But one wonders whether this reaction and the motive that prompts it are as nearly universal as Hoffer would like to have his reader believe. There may, for example, be a great difference between the conduct of a superstitious farmer and an educated farmer.

If good prose is designed to inform and persuade the reader, then jargon, which befogs the reader's comprehension, has no place in it. Jargon may also befog the writer himself—may deceive him into thinking that he has stated a forceful argument when he may in fact have done no more than present a few insights that, however interesting, do not make up an argument.

The persistence of jargon and the way in which it obscures thought are powerfully demonstrated in Joseph Warren Beach's rewriting of a paragraph by the philosopher John Dewey. Mr. Beach records his sympathy with many of Dewey's opinions and recognizes his very great reputation as a philosopher; nevertheless, he finds him a careless writer. Beach cites the following passage from *Human Nature and Conduct* as an instance of Dewey's muddy and confused style:

> But no matter how much men in authority have turned moral rules into an agency of class supremacy, any theory which attributes the origin of rule to deliberate design is false. To take advantage of conditions after they have come into existence is one thing; to create them for the sake of an advantage to accrue is quite another thing. We must go back to the bare fact of social division into superior and inferior. To say that accident produced social conditions is to perceive that they were not produced by intelligence. Lack of understanding of human nature is the primary cause of disregard of it. Lack of insight always ends in despising or else unreasoned admiration. When men had no scientific knowledge of physical nature they either passively submitted to it or sought to control it magically. What cannot be understood cannot be managed intelligently. It has to be forced into subjection from without.

Here follows Beach's rewriting of the passage, with the changes indicated in italics:

> But no matter how much men in authority have turned moral rules into an agency of class supremacy, *it would be a mistake to suppose that these rules were created originally with the* deliberate design *of using them for*

this purpose. It is one thing to take advantage of conditions after they have come into existence; it is quite another thing to create them for the sake of an advantage to accrue. *To understand a system of morals, we must go back to the division into classes—into superior and inferior. We shall find that social conditions grew up spontaneously, and that is as much as to say that they were not the product of deliberate thought. Just the contrary, they were the product of a want of intelligence in interpreting human nature. Human nature was disregarded in framing moral rules because it was not understood.* Lack of insight *into anything* leads to its being despised or else admired unreasonably. *It is so with* physical nature; when men had no knowledge of it, they either passively submitted to it or sought to control it magically. What cannot be understood cannot be understood intelligently. It has to be forced into subjection from without.

Let us look at Beach's revision of Dewey's first sentence. The phrase "origin of rule" is so vague as to be puzzling. The origin of moral rule? Of all rule? Of that of men in authority? Or what? If, as Beach does, we expand this phrase to read "these rules were created originally," connecting Dewey's "rule" with his "moral rules," it becomes plain that "any theory" is too general. What is wanted in this context is a reference to a particular, mistaken theory. Hence Beach substitutes "it would be a mistake to suppose that" and so forth.

■ APPLICATIONS

I Study Beach's other revisions. Do you think they are improvements? If you think so, be prepared to say why.

The student might consult Beach's *Outlook for American Prose* [15] for further revisions that he makes in Dewey's *Human Nature and Conduct* and for his own account of why he made these particular revisions.

II In Hoffer's *True Believer* the paragraph quoted on pages 425–26 above is followed, a half page later, by a paragraph in which Hoffer makes the point that those who attempt vast changes believe that they possess some irresistible power. Hoffer writes:

> Offhand one would expect that the mere possession of power would automatically result in a cocky attitude toward the world and a receptivity to change. But it is not always so. The powerful can be as timid as the weak. What seems to count more than possession of instruments of power is faith in the future. Where power is not joined with faith in the future, it is used mainly to ward off the new and preserve the status quo. On the other hand, extravagant hope, even when not backed by actual power, is likely to generate a most reckless daring. For the hopeful can draw strength from the most ridiculous sources of power—a slogan, a word, a button. No faith is potent

---

[15] University of Chicago Press, 1926, pp. 44–49.

unless it is also faith in the future; unless it has a millennial component. So, too, an effective doctrine: as well as being a source of power, it must also claim to be a key to the book of the future.[16]

Attempt your own rewriting of this paragraph. (If you feel that no rewriting is required, be prepared to say why.)

JARGON: SOME ANTIDOTES

Jargon, of course, involves more than stereotypes. Jargon is nearly always compounded of clusters of words that are general and abstract. Though there is no certain prescription against jargon, it is easy to state some practical antidotes.

1   Use words that are as specific and concrete as possible; that is, never use a word more general and indefinite than is called for. Hazy and indefinite expressions represent the easy way out for a writer who is too timid to commit himself or too lazy to think through what he wants to say.

2   Avoid stereotypes of all kinds—prefabricated phrasings that come easily to mind but that may not represent precisely your own ideas and emotions. But note this carefully: you should never avoid a word because it seems simple and common. If the sense calls for a simple, common word, it is generally best to repeat the word, if necessary, again and again. There is little to be said in favor of what is sometimes called elegant variation, that is, the substitution of some synonym in order to avoid repetition. Here is an example: "Mr. Jones was a powerful *financier*. As a *tycoon* he had a deep suspicion of socialism. He shared the feelings of his associates who were also *bankers*." The variations are irritating and can be confusing. Either recast the sentence or repeat *financier*.

You should, on the other hand, learn to be suspicious of *strings of words* —phrasings—that are common and therefore probably stereotyped. Though they are not to be prohibited, inspect them all carefully, especially in revising your work. If you really need to say "along the lines of" or "in consideration of" or "in the last analysis," do so. But make sure that what you are talking about really is *along the lines of* whatever it is you refer to or that the matter of *consideration* is uppermost or that the "analysis" you mention is really the ultimate one.

The rule of thumb would be: (1) never shy away from an individual word merely because it is frequently used, but (2) always be chary of frequently used *phrases*.

3   Use live words, remembering that finite verbs are the most powerful words that we have. In the second sentence of the first excerpt quoted on page 425 we can find an instance of vagueness resulting from the failure to use finite words.

---

[16] From pp. 8–9 in *The True Believer* (Hardbound Ed.) by Eric Hoffer. Copyright, 1951 by Eric Hoffer. Reprinted by permission of Harper & Row, Publishers.

> Keenly aware of the painstaking scholarship and of the high creative effort that over the centuries has accumulated the body of subject matter we call "English," a group of our ablest teachers conceive their role to be to transmit this product of human endeavor, this hard-won store of learning and of art, this rich portion of man's heritage of culture, to the oncoming generations. . . .

This sentence is packed with ideas, but the only finite verb in it (aside from *has accumulated* and *call,* in the two subordinate clauses) is the verb *conceive.* A participle, *aware,* is made to carry the weight of the first twenty-six words; and the whole latter part of the sentence hangs from two successive infinitives, "to be" and "to transmit." The sentence has so little stamina that it sprawls. It sprawls because the writer has starved it of finite verbs. The author might better have written:

> Our ablest teachers realize what effort has gone into the making of that body of subject matter we call "English." They know it is a precious thing, for it embodies the effort of painstaking scholars and of great poets and novelists. They want to transmit this heritage of culture to the oncoming generations.

Finite verbs are more powerful than strings of participles, gerunds, or infinitives. A specific verb is usually stronger than a more general verb qualified by modifiers. Compare "He walked along slowly" with "He strolled," "He sauntered," "He dawdled," "He lagged." Frequently, it is true, we need the qualifiers. But we ought not to forget the wealth of concreteness that the English language possesses in its great number of verbs that name specifically, and therefore powerfully, certain modes of action. In this general connection, see the chapter on Description (pp. 295–96).

4 Use as the staple of your discourse simple sentences in normal sentence order (see p. 373). These rarely degenerate into jargon. An essay so written may be childishly simple, and it can become monotonous; but it will seldom collapse into the spineless flabbiness of jargon.

● CAUTION

Jargon cannot be dealt with summarily. It is our most pervasive kind of "bad" style, and, like style in general, it is the product of the interplay of many elements. We shall have to recur to this topic in the chapters that follow, especially in the discussion of metaphor.

■ APPLICATIONS

I The following passages are badly infected with jargon. Try to determine what the author in each case means to say, and then put it into English for him. (You might apply the four antidotes to jargon described on pages 429–30.)

A   The chemical age gives every highly technical nation a choice between self-sufficiency and trade on whatever barter or bargaining basis it desires, thus upsetting time-honored geographical alignments of monopolies of certain natural products and altering the whole concept of imperialism. This is an entirely new situation for agriculture. For centuries the threat of eventual scarcity of food and land hung over the world. Within a few decades the march of science has brought about a complete reversal. On the one hand the chemist and the technologist have made possible the production of greater and greater quantities of products on less and less land, resulting in enormous surpluses of acreage, crops, and labor. At the same time, ironically enough, the chemist is removing one product after another from the soil into the laboratory, throwing still more land out of cultivation and further reducing the amount of labor needed.

B   The maintenance of democracy will, I believe, require not only a deflation of executive power and its restoration to popular control but a public vigilance greater than that heretofore manifest. Whether it is possible to expect private citizens to make the necessary sacrifices of time and effort to see to it that representative government is not frustrated, only time can tell. But if the electorate will not insist upon congressional control of public policy, executive government will come by default and the historical cycle through which other countries have passed may well be reflected here.

As a way of life our people have heretofore valued the freedom and respect for the human personality which the Constitution was designed to insure. Even that has suffered inroads, necessarily because of legitimate legislative restraints but unnecessarily also because the protection of civil liberties lies for the most part with the local communities, and many elements of our population are becoming indifferent to the fundamental importance of civil liberties. Some people insist that economic well-being explains the luxury of democracy, and that hard times and insecurity promote the surrender of freedom. This only means that the effort to maintain democracy is now more difficult. It should not be allowed to go by default.

II List the clichés and stereotyped phrasings in the following letters. Attempt to rewrite Dorothy Dix's answer in simple, clear English, free of slang and hackneyed expressions.

Dear Miss Dix:
    The time has come when I feel that I need some personal advice. I am a woman 32 years old. A little more than a year ago I met a man 45 years old and fell madly in love with him. I gave him his meals and was thrilled to do it. But now I wonder if I have just had a case of infatuation, for this man never pays any of the bills, or takes me to any place of amusement, or does anything to make me happy.
    He says he loves me and wants to marry me some time, but when I suggest that we settle on a date, he always postpones it. Will a man who does nothing for me before marriage support me after marriage?

Perplexed

Answer:

> Of course, he won't. The dumbest woman in the world would know that a man who grafted his living off a woman before marriage would continue his deadbeat tactics after marriage, if she only would give her brains a chance to function now and then.
>
> Strange and unaccountable are the ways a woman's mind works its wonders to perform. Of all loathsome human beings, the worst is the male parasite who lives on women, instead of working and supporting himself, and how any woman can find anything to love in such a creature, passes all comprehension.
>
> Don't deceive yourself into thinking that this man will ever marry you. He hasn't the slightest intention of doing so. He will leave you as soon as some woman who works a little harder and makes a little more money and is a little better graft comes along. Yet there are thousands of women who fall for this racket.
>
> You ask if I think what you feel for this man is "infatuation"? I'd say that what ails you is just lack of plain, ordinary common sense.

III The author of the following passage is attempting to treat with a light touch a subject which for most people is abstruse and painfully dry. Is he successful? If so, how does his choice of diction contribute to his success? How many concrete words does Hogben use? How many abstract words? How does Hogben avoid the sense of formality? Illustrate from his choice of diction. What are the connotations of *bowling, petrol, car, tank,* and *motorcycle?* What are the connotations of *Greeks, abacus,* and *counting frame?* Does Hogben actually want the contrast between the associations of the two groups of words? If so, what purpose does it serve? Do the associations of *Good Friday* and *All Fools' Day* clash? What purpose is served by this clash?

> [Euclid] was limited by the social culture in which he lived. The Greeks did not live in a world of interest and petrol consumption and bowling analysis. Ratios were not familiar quantities. They represented a process of division which was carried out with a very stiff instrument, the abacus. Proportion did not sit lightly on Euclid's pupils. You can easily see the difficulty of Euclid's pupils. Suppose I know that the petrol consumption of a car is 35 miles to the gallon. I can get the number of miles I can run before filling up by multiplying the number of gallons in the tank by 35. I can get the number of gallons I require by dividing the number of miles I intended to run by 35. The two processes are equally easy in our arithmetic. The arithmetic of the counting frame is different. Multiplying one proper number by another always gives you an exact result which you get by repeated addition. Dividing one proper number by another means finding how many times you can take one away from the other. Usually you have some beads left over on the counting frame. You rarely get an exact answer. So division was a much more difficult process to grasp when people thought that all real numbers were proper numbers. Euclid had to devote a whole book (Book V) to illustrate the simple rules of proportion which are all summed up in the diagonal rule given in the last

chapter. Draw two right-angled triangles, one with the two shorter sides 3 and 4 centimetres long, the other with the two shorter sides of 1½ and 2 inches; compare them, and you will see without difficulty that two triangles having corresponding sides whose lengths are in the same ratio is a situation no more difficult to grasp than the fact that a motorcycle has the same petrol consumption on Good Friday and All Fools' Day.

—Lancelot Hogben: *Mathematics for the Million.*[17]

IV The student will probably conclude that the writing in the following passage is quite effective. It is, on the whole, rather straightforward prose. The sentences are simple in structure. How much of the effectiveness of the passage depends upon the choice of diction? How many hackneyed or slang expressions does it contain, if any? Are any of these expressions justified? Why?

Dutchmen don't get excited over nothing. I was in an airliner over Holland, when the Dutch aboard started crowding each other at the windows: below us, green and shining, was a farm landscape that has only just recently come out of the sea. It is the first piece of a whole new province (a new state, we would say) that Holland is adding to itself: "Flevoland."

I went back later, by car, by boat, by Piper Cub, and looked into this land-making operation. It's the pride of the Dutch. It's what makes their eyes shine.

The main method is this: you build an earthen dam from shore out into the shallow sea and back to shore, so as to fence in part of the sea. Then you pump the water out. You wait a few years for the rains to wash the salt out of the soil. Then you start farming! Such a piece of land—saucer-shaped, lying below sea level, is called a "polder." It's a necessary word, and not translatable. Nobody has polders but the Dutch. They have been making them for five hundred years—small ones—and now, with big money and big machines, they make them big.

I drove out on a dyke that is fencing off one future piece of Flevoland. You drive on the top of the dyke, and you do sixty. We went out of sight of land, and still the road kept going. I thought: "This is big." You hold it against the American scale of things—Hoover Dam, TVA, Empire State Building—and it is still big. You hold it against the size of Holland—six Hollands wouldn't fill the State of Kansas—and it becomes colossal. It's as if we wanted to push the Gulf of Mexico back and build a second Texas. . . .

And this is what makes Holland Holland. Windmills, for instance: land below sea level doesn't drain. You have to keep pumping the rain out. The windmills do that—still do it, though most of the pumping now is electric, or diesel. And those wooden shoes? (You still see them quite a bit.) Why? Much of the soil is always wet, and wooden shoes are watertight and warm. You can't run in them—but then, a Dutchman is well organized; he starts early and has no need to run. Little boys who feel like running have a special Dutch boys' gesture: you take your shoes off and carry them both in your left hand, and run.   —J. Wolfgang Langewiesche: "The Dutch Hustle," *Harper's Magazine*, April, 1956.

---
[17] Reprinted from *Mathematics for the Million* by Lancelot Hogben. By permission of W. W. Norton & Company, Inc. Copyright 1937 by W. W. Norton & Company, Inc. Copyright renewed 1964 by Lancelot Hogben. Reprinted by permission of George Allen & Unwin Ltd.

V In the passage quoted from *Service Afloat* (p. 413), Semmes uses the term *disembogues*. Consult the dictionary for the etymology of this word. Does the root meaning of the word indicate why Semmes chose it rather than some other for the particular passage in which it occurs?

VI In the passage quoted from *Life on the Mississippi* (p. 413), an island "has retired," another island is "booked for early destruction," the division between still another island and the mainland is a "seam." What are the literal or normal meanings of "retire to," "book for," and "seam"? Are the metaphorical extensions involved here justified? Attack or defend them.

CHAPTER 12

Metaphor

In metaphor there is a transfer of meaning[1]—the Greek word from which metaphor is derived means "to transfer." A word that applies literally to one kind of object or idea is applied by analogy to another. Thus a ray of sunshine *cuts* the gloom (as if it were a knife); a ship *courses* the seas (its motion likened to that of a greyhound); a man *weasels* out of his promise (as a ferretlike animal wriggles through a small hole).[2]

In the preceding chapter we considered some of the simpler kinds of metaphor. Thus on page 405 we spoke of the *eye* of a needle, the *legs* of a chair, the *bed* of a river. As we have seen (pp. 404–09), language normally grows by a process of metaphorical extension; we extend old names to new objects. But when, in this process of extension, a metaphor is completely absorbed into the common language (as in the *bed* of a river), it loses its metaphorical force; it becomes a dead metaphor. Compare, for example, "the bed of a river" with "the dance of life." The first phrase carries no suggestion that the bed is a place of repose or that the river is sleepy! We use "the bed of a river" as a pure denotation from which the associated meanings that apply to *bed* in its usual senses are quite absent. But it is very different with the

---

[1] Refer to the second paragraph of the Clark selection on pp. 116–17. Language normally develops through a series of such transfers.

[2] In this chapter we have used *metaphor* in the largest and most inclusive sense. We have not distinguished metaphor proper from *simile* (an *explicit* comparison, usually introduced by *like* or *as:* "she glided into the room *like a swan*," "he was as bald *as an egg*"), or *metonymy* (the use of a part to designate the whole: "he employed twenty *hands* on his farm"), or other such specializations of the metaphoric principle. Such classifications are, in our considered opinion, of little practical importance to the writer.

phrase "the dance of life." This metaphor is still alive. (At least, when a certain writer, Havelock Ellis, used it as the title of one of his books, he must have hoped that it would seem alive.) Here the suggestions, the associations, are thoroughly relevant to Ellis's purpose. The suggestions (of something rhythmic, of patterned movement, even, perhaps, of gaiety and happiness) are meant to be associated with life.

The term *dead metaphor* can itself illuminate the problem now being considered. With "dead" metaphors, we can say *rigor mortis* has set in: they have no flexibility; they have stiffened into one meaning. Metaphors that are still alive prove that they are alive by their flexibility; and because they are still alive, they can be used to give color and life to a piece of writing. They are concrete and particular; they reflect the world of the senses. They can still excite the imagination.

In metaphors that are still recognizably such, there are, of course, varying degrees of life. The following examples are not very lively, but they do show that metaphor is a perfectly natural and important part of our normal speech: we say, for example, "John is a square"; "Jane is a doll"; "He ran out on the deal"; "That remark threw him for a loss." Such expressions are rather worn and faded. But their original metaphorical character is plain enough, and we still think of them, and use them, as metaphors. The list of expressions that are badly shopworn but are still recognizably metaphors could be extended almost indefinitely: "hot as the devil," "independent as a hog on ice," "lazy as a dog," "crazy as a bat," and so on.

■ **APPLICATION**

Draw up a list of a dozen dead (or nearly dead) metaphors.

Importance of Metaphor in Everyday Language

Our preference for the concrete and the particular, as these examples show, is not only normal, it is deeply and stubbornly rooted in the human mind. Consider the following situation: It is a hot day. We can say, "It is hot" or "It is very hot," or, piling on the intensives, we can say, "It is abominably and excruciatingly hot." But most of us, afflicted with heat, will resort to a metaphor of some kind: "It's hot as hell," or more elaborately, "It's hot as the hinges of hell." Evidently metaphor is felt to add forcefulness, and evidently the forcefulness has some relation to sharpness of detail and concreteness of expression.

That is one point, then: in metaphor, force and sharpness of detail, especially of sensory detail, tend to go together. Indeed, we are usually attracted to metaphor in the first place because ordinary language seems worn and stale. A second point to be made is this: metaphor tends to accompany the expression of emotions and attitudes. If we want to give a precise account of the weather, all we need to say is that the temperature is 97.6 degrees Fahrenheit, the relative humidity is 92 percent, and the wind a bare two miles an hour from the southwest. But this cool statement of the facts doesn't begin to express our feelings of discomfort on a muggy afternoon in midsummer.

Let us consider another simple case. Suppose we feel a special kind of happiness and try to express our feelings. We can say, "I feel happy." Or we can try to find a word that more accurately pinpoints this special feeling: *merry, gay, ecstatic, cheerful, glad, jolly,* or *joyous.* There are many synonyms for *happy,* as the dictionary will quickly reveal, and they differ in their shades of meaning. For example, *jolly* suggests the heartiness and good humor that go with comfortable living; *ecstatic* suggests an elevating rapture; *gay* suggests sprightliness, a nimble lightheartedness. We shall do well to consult a dictionary to learn (or remind ourselves of) the wealth of resources at our disposal. Even so, we rarely find an adjective that exactly expresses our feelings. We tend to resort to metaphor. We say, "I'm happy as a June bug," or "I feel like a million dollars," or "I'm walking on air this morning," or "I feel like a colt in springtime." Writers of popular songs, for instance, are constantly trying to devise fresh comparisons in order to express the singer's delirious happiness (or maybe his desolating sadness).

If the feeling is very special or complex, we are usually *forced* to resort to metaphor. Here are the ways in which two writers of fiction express the special kind of happiness that each of their characters experiences.

The first is the happiness of a young soldier when the brilliant woman who has dazzled him shows him a small attention:

> She regarded him with her kindly glances, which made something glow and expand within his chest. It was a delicious feeling, even though it did cut one's breath short now and then. Ecstatically he drank in the sound of her tranquil, seductive talk full of innocent gaiety and of spiritual quietude. His passion appeared to him to flame up and envelop her in blue fiery tongues from head to foot and over her head, while her soul appeared in the center like a big white rose. . . .
> —JOSEPH CONRAD: "The Warrior's Soul," *Tales of Hearsay.*

The author tries to do justice to the intense emotion that the young soldier feels, and in doing so, he twice resorts to metaphor. The first is a rather simple and even conventional metaphor of a feeling of warmth within his chest—something that seems to "glow" and to "expand." The second attempts to interpret as well as present the quality of the emotion—the lady is encircled in flame, but the flames, though fierce ("blue fiery tongues"), do not injure her and may even be said to protect her. The white rose, which in his ecstatic vision stands for her soul, is not scorched or shriveled.

The second example has to do with the experience of a little girl in a Maine village sixty years ago:

> It was a day in spring, and it must have been in early spring, for we had not as yet been allowed to cast off our winter underwear, and as the warmth of the morning increased, it felt cumbrous and uncomfortable. I have no remembrance of where I had been when the peculiar and essential meaning of the day stole over me, but probably on some errand to the village. I know that I was coming up the board sidewalk which led past the picket fence surrounding our orchard when all at once I felt an odd quickening within me.
>
> There had been a white mist in the early morning from a heavy rainfall during the night, and the sun was just then breaking through it in long rays of light. I felt suddenly surrounded by light and half frightened by the equally sudden perception of it. I walked slowly up the sidewalk until I reached the white gate, where I stopped, for I was puzzled and bewildered.
>
> Light to me before this had been absence of darkness, the assurance of safety, of the ordinary and the familiar; and I could not understand why these rays of light dispelling the mist, this unexpected, sudden effulgence, seemed so different from daylight in its usual sense. I felt as though something were happening inside me, for I seemed all at once incomprehensibly alive and new, even as if I had just been born.
>
> —MARY ELLEN CHASE: *The White Gate.*

Again, this passage is made effective by the re-creation of the scene in our imagination. The writer is careful to have us visualize the scene in all its detail. If the reader can be made to see what the little girl saw, he is on the way to understanding the experience. But ultimately the writer has to resort to metaphor in order to tell us what the experience was. It was like a transfiguration—it was like a rebirth.

■ **APPLICATION**

Choose metaphors that will describe *how you feel* in the following situations. Do not necessarily take the first metaphor that comes to mind; try to avoid worn-out metaphor; try to find a metaphor that describes as accurately as possible your own feelings.

1 On getting an A when you would have been happy to settle for the grade of C.
2 On getting well splashed by a passing car when on your way to an appointment.
3 On your first experience of stage fright.
4 On seeing a serious accident.

5 On first discovering that a close friend has betrayed your friendship.
6 On coming to realize that you have been guilty of a serious fault.

Slang and metaphor

While we are discussing metaphor, it will be useful to consider once more slang and jargon, two abuses of language that we have already touched on in the preceding chapter (pp. 421–30). The general impulse to use slang springs from a perfectly respectable motive, our preference for the concrete and the particular. Most slang expressions originated as metaphors, and the misuse of slang cannot be dealt with apart from the more general problem of the use and the abuse of figurative language. For that reason, it doesn't do much good for the instructor to tell the student—or for the student to tell himself—to stop using slang. Most of us want to make our writing warm, colorful, and lively. To substitute abstract expression for such figurative language as we have would be the wrong thing to do.

The student ought not to discard his figurative language, but to improve it. He should try to eliminate all metaphors that are worn and trite, all comparisons that seem pretentious, and all analogies that are not valid or that jangle with the rest of the composition. On the positive side, the student ought to seek out fresh and accurate metaphors. The practical result of such procedures will be that most of the slang will be sloughed off, but sloughed off *because it proves to be poor and ineffective metaphor,* not because an abstract statement is "better."

The truth of the matter is that few writers are able to avoid the use of metaphor, even if they try to do so. But the writer should want his metaphors to be alive rather than dead, responsible and controlled rather than random and irresponsible.

Jargon and worn-out metaphor

So much for the relation of slang to metaphor. As for jargon, though it is a mishmash of trite expressions of every sort, a great number of these are dead or all-but-lifeless metaphors. One can illustrate by citing a passage from a recent popular book, which in a few years has sold far more than a million copies.

> Poets, novelists, and philosophers throughout the centuries have written their most somber and frightening lines when dealing with the menace of death. They grow bitter at the shears of fate which ruthlessly sever the thread of being. They draw vivid word portraits of the unbearable pain of separation, the unfairness of destiny which too frequently plunges its dagger into the pulsating bodies of lovers even as they drain the cup of ecstasy. Poets weep, and make us weep, at the fate of young lives cut short while senility stumbles meaninglessly along its blind highway. They rebel, and make us rebel, at the dark magic of the universe which in the twinkling of

an eye can transform the breathing, laughing, creating artist, scientist, son, mother, wife, into a silent, unoccupied tenement of clay, a shroud of darkness, a crumbling clod of earth.

—JOSHUA LOTH LIEBMAN: *Peace of Mind.*[3]

This passage is, indeed, to use Orwell's phrase on page 424 "a dump of worn-out metaphors." There is, for example, the reference to the shears of fate. The Greeks had a myth about the three Fates, sister goddesses, one of whom spun the thread of a man's life, one of whom measured it, and one of whom snipped it. An allusion to this well-known myth is appropriate in this context, but unless the writer can reinvigorate the story, perhaps he should play it down rather than up. As used here, the figure of the shears is at once perfunctory and yet elaborate and so shows all too clearly how worn it is.

A few lines later, after turning fate into "destiny," the writer does make an attempt at a vigorous and even violent image: destiny "plunges its dagger into the pulsating bodies of lovers." But to say that the lovers "drain the cup of ecstasy" is to drop back into old-fashioned grandiloquence. Modern lovers don't "drain" glasses of champagne when they toast each other, just as they don't "drain" cocktails at a cocktail party. "Cup of ecstasy" is itself a rather faded piece of the highfalutin style. When the writer has villainous destiny plunge its dagger into the bodies of these throbbing lovers as they toss off their cups of ecstasy, the reader finds it hard to take the expression seriously: it is not much more than a needlessly roundabout way of saying that destiny kills them at the height of their pleasure. (If the reader *does* take the expression seriously, he finds himself looking at an unbelievable and therefore unconsciously funny scene from an old-fashioned melodrama.)

The statement that "senility stumbles meaninglessly along its blind highway" may raise as a primary question: What does the metaphor—whether dead or alive—mean? Does the writer mean that the eyes of old age are too dim to see the highway? Thus, is the adjective *blind* applied to the highway as a kind of transferred epithet? Or is the highway literally blind (*cf.* blind alley) in that it proves to be a dead end? But if the writer's point is that the highway of life leads only to death, isn't youth's course along the highway quite as meaningless as senility's? If both youth and age are headed for the dead end of death, there isn't much choice between stumbling or skipping one's way to it: it's a blind highway in either case.

Finally, we get another metaphor, or rather a cluster of them. The corpse is compared to "a silent, unoccupied tenement of clay." ("Tenement of clay" is, by the way, another piece of faded grandiloquence.) Not many of us today think of the body as a tenement (that is, a house) that has the soul for its occupant, and the writer has done nothing in this context to re-

---

[3] Reprinted from *Peace of Mind* by Joshua Loth Liebman by permission of Simon & Shuster, Inc. Reprinted by permission of William Heinemann Ltd.

stress this idea. (Incidentally, a more careful writer would have stated that it was the *body* of the son, mother, wife, etc., that was transformed into an "unoccupied tenement of clay.")

Perhaps the writer's suspicion that all was not well with his tenement comparison prompted him to add, as an appositive phrase, "a shroud of darkness." But the new comparison brings up its own problems. Literally, the dead body is "shrouded" (dressed in burial clothes); yet to write "transform . . . the wife . . . into . . . a shroud of darkness" suggests that the body *itself* becomes a shroud enclosing "darkness." (In that case, the conversion of the body into a shroud may seem to be *too* lively—too bold a metaphor.) Or does "shroud of darkness" as used here mean no more than "shroud composed [made up] of darkness"? Perhaps the writer would have done well to scratch out both the tenement and the shroud figures and to retain only his third and least ambitious phrase: "a crumbling clod of earth." For the three comparisons do not really support each other, and they may even conflict with one another. What is the relation of the clod of earth to the shroud of darkness? And what is the relation of the shroud to the tenement? It would be hard to say, and this lack of precision is one of the characteristics of jargon: the writer has not come to terms with his own thought; he moves from one murky concept to another without articulating any clear relation between one item and the next. The moral would seem to be that even when one is writing about death, he should use metaphors that are alive.

■ APPLICATION

Rewrite the paragraph from *Peace of Mind* (pp. 439–40). Give special attention to removing not only confused metaphors but other bits of jargon as well. Try first to make plain, simple sense of it. Then, if you feel you can, improve it by the use of appropriate metaphor.

Confused metaphor: further instances

The following passage is an excerpt from the advertisement of a savings-and-loan association:

> The little squirrel, with a God-given instinct to prepare for tomorrow, stores away nuts and has plenty to eat . . . when winter comes.
> Is he smarter than *you* are? Think about this.
> Now, today, is the time to start "salting away" that nest egg you'll need sure as fate.

In this advertisement the writer has not been content to compare the savings that the human being puts away with the nut that the squirrel buries for winter food. He insists on finding two more analogies: salting away meat and leaving a nest egg.

Before modern refrigeration methods came into being, meat was laid down in salt to preserve it through the winter and other times of scarcity. The phrase *salt away* was then extended to all sorts of things that were to be reserved and preserved for future use. A "nest egg" was the egg left in the hen's nest so that she would continue to lay. Again, by analogy the term has been extended to other sorts of things that a person, in the hope of getting something more, delays gathering for present use. But the three metaphors, already trite, are here woefully mixed and jostle against one another. You don't *salt away a nest egg*. A human being ought not be asked to attempt what a squirrel has better sense than to try. Of course, we *know* what the copywriter means to say. But that is not the point. The point is the ineffectiveness of the way he chooses to say it.

A newspaper reviewer writes of a ballet performance:

> When the first dancers came on for "After Eden" [a ballet about Adam and Eve], the matter of human possibility became breeched as far as unsuspecting spectators were concerned. . . . Wilson's delineation of a jagged turmoil going through Adam's mind was virtually a sculpturing of space. Miss Archer pointed our way through all the shapes of a woman's psyche. She would evolve from a creature of limp submission into one of terrifying dominance—capable of destruction; ready to populate the world.

The writer evidently responded enthusiastically to the performance, and he meant to write about it with gusto. But can a "possibility" be breached? That is, have a fissure opened in it? ("Breeched," i.e., have breeches put on it, is presumably the typesetter's contribution to this embroglio!) Can a turmoil be said to be "jagged"? How does one point a "way" through "shapes," whether of the psyche or of anything else? And what about the sets of antitheses in the last sentence: submission-dominance and capable of destruction-ready to populate? Which goes with which? Can they be lined up in any significant pattern?

Sportswriters quite often refer to football coaches' "taking their hair down" as a more vivid way of saying that they were willing to state their true opinions. In doing so, they choose a particularly unfortunate cliché. ("The coach leveled with me" or "He finally came clean" are clichés too, but at least they are not absurd.) For if we try to *visualize* the scene, we have an image of the coach removing his hairpins and letting down his tresses.[4] If we *don't* visualize the scene—if the metaphor is completely dead, stone cold—then there is not much point in using it anyway.

One sportswriter has actually written—with reference to a professional football team—that "their slips were showing." Again, this is a figure taken from the world of women and looks very odd when imported into the locker

---

[4] The first sportswriter to use the expression may have meant to be funny. But if so, subsequent repetition has worn out the joke.

room. The context indicates that the writer was not trying to be funny; he had taken this metaphor to be a cliché, a metaphor safely dead. And perhaps for some readers, it remained so. But if it comes to life, its resurrection proves more embarrassing for the writer than the embarrassment that he alleges was suffered by the football warriors.

Newspaper reviewers and journalists in a hurry are not, however, the only writers who bungle their metaphors or who have the misfortune to have one of their "dead" metaphors unexpectedly come alive. Robert Graves, in *Reader Over My Shoulder,* quotes an amusing instance from a book by a distinguished Cambridge University professor of English literature. The professor argues that we ought to be willing to admit new words into the English language because by doing so "we infuse new blood into a tongue of which ... our first pride should be that it is flexible, alive, capable of responding to new demands of man's untiring quest after knowledge and experience." By "tongue" he means, of course, "language." But the metaphor of blood transfusion is likely to wake up the dormant physical image in *tongue,* all the more so when the writer goes on to describe that tongue as "flexible" and "alive." (Even if this grotesque image doesn't arise in the reader's mind, the author's management of metaphor is still not very happy, for the image of performing a blood transfusion on a "language" is itself mildly grotesque.)

■ APPLICATION

The following passages are taken from reputable books and magazines. Make a criticism of the use of metaphor in these passages. Where the metaphors seem garbled or inappropriate, rewrite the passage, substituting more appropriate metaphors.

1 As his fame was slowly ascending, partly because of this social skill of his, into more illustrious circles, so was it trickling down among the more numerous obscure.
2 . . . the writers [of our day] want to be against the *status quo,* but it can't be done. The *status quo* changes too quickly for them. And in changing it buys them off: it salves their wounds with money; it stuffs those cultural gaps with hard cash.
3 It's not the hurt the other fellow does you that keeps on rankling; it's the hurt you do yourself by your own remembering. That sticks in your skin and infects your mind. I guess that's the secret of all successful forgetting. Don't let it break through your insulation at the start. Don't let it make a deep and lasting brand on the sensitive recording plate of your consciousness.
4 A century and a half ago English poetry left those formal gardens brought to perfection by Dryden and Pope, where now their successors seemed

able only to raise forced blooms and artificial flowers, and went out to the wilderness for a change of air, a transfusion of blood.

5   Therefore, when he championed his middle class, he instinctively set his face against everything that threatened to substitute quantity for quality—against the encroachments of commerce and the new imperialism which the progressively minded among both Whigs and Tories were imbibing from Chatham. And the caveat against the dangers lurking in materialistic panaceas is not without implications that carry beyond the time and the place.

6   By kindling and fanning violent passions in the hearts of their followers, mass movements prevent the settling of an inner balance.

The Function of Metaphor

Thus far we have stressed the abuses of figurative language. Aside from some references to metaphor as a means for making language more colorful and for expressing our emotional responses, we have said little about the positive function of metaphor. Yet if we are to understand why metaphor constitutes one of the great resources of the writer, we shall need to define much more clearly what its essential function is.

It is all the more important to do so in view of the conventional ways of stating the uses of metaphor, for they tend to be misleading. Thus, we often hear it said that the purpose of metaphor is to provide an illustration or to give an emotional heightening. But either of these explanations suggests that metaphor is a kind of "extra" that may be a useful or pleasant addition to a statement but that does not constitute an essential part of it. Certainly one practical use of metaphor is to provide a concrete illustration of a point that has been stated more abstractly. In the pages that follow we shall consider examples of such illustrations. But illustration is not its primary or essential use. Still less essential is the use of metaphor to provide a sort of rhetorical decoration—as if the metaphor were a silk ribbon tied around a box of candy.

Metaphors used for the sake of illustration are indeed "extras." They can be left off. Yet if we think of metaphor as something that can be left off, we shall never come to understand why the proper control of metaphor is essential to good writing.

Why strictly notational statement does not require metaphor

There is, to be sure, one very special kind of discourse in which metaphor is indeed inessential. If we wish to say "$2 + 2 = 4$" or that "the square of the hypotenuse of a right triangle is equal to the sum of the squares of the other two sides," we shall not require metaphor. Metaphor would in fact be in the way. Such statements as these, however, are very special; the terms used in them are (or aspire to be) pure denotations. Thus, as was implied in the preceding chapter (p. 496), if such terms have associations at all, the associations are irrelevant. For the "words" employed are not being used as words in the usual sense; whereas most words are capable of metaphorical extension, these "words" are not. They are, as scientific terms, frozen to one specific meaning, and the purest scientific statements are able to dispense with ordinary words altogether: thus $2 + 2 = 4$, or $H_2SO_4 + Fe \rightarrow FeSO_4 + H_2\uparrow$.

But important as such statements are, they represent a stringently specialized discourse. Most of the discourse that interests us as human beings and that we must use as writers goes far beyond abstract relationships of this kind. Most of our discourse has to do with the "full" world of our human experience, not with the colorless, soundless, abstract world of physics, say, or of mathematics.[5]

Metaphor as illustration

Yet though metaphor is not necessary to purely scientific statement, the scientific writer very often needs to go beyond such stringently limited discourse, and then for him too, metaphor, employed as illustration, may be highly useful. The following passage from Bertrand Russell's *The Scientific Outlook* will illustrate this point. The book is addressed to a general audience, and Russell is attempting to convince his reader that "what is actually experienced is much less than one would naturally suppose." He proceeds to analyze a typical experience for us—what happens scientifically when we "see" someone:

> You may say, for example, that you see your friend, Mr. Jones, walking along the street: but this is to go far beyond what you have any right to say. You see a succession of coloured patches, traversing a stationary background. These patches, by means of a Pavlov conditioned reflex, bring into your mind the word "Jones," and so you say you see Jones; but other people, looking out of their windows from different angles, will see something different, owing to the laws of perspective: therefore, if they are all seeing Jones, there must be as many different Joneses as there are spectators, and if there is only one true Jones, the sight of him is not vouchsafed to anybody. If we assume for a moment the truth of the account which physics gives, we shall explain what you call "seeing Jones" in some such terms as the following. Little packets of light, called "light quanta," shoot out from the sun, and some of these reach a region where there are atoms of a certain kind, composing Jones's face, and hands, and clothes. These atoms do

---

[5] This is not, of course, to question the importance or the reality of such worlds. The scientist can deal with his material only in this abstract way. His language is neither more nor less real than the language of the poet or the novelist. It is merely different. In this connection, the student might reread the discussion of abstract and concrete words (pp. 398–404).

not themselves exist, but are merely a compendious way of alluding to possible occurrences. Some of the light quanta, when they reach Jones's atoms, upset their internal economy. This causes him to become sunburnt, and to manufacture vitamin D. Others are reflected, and of those that are reflected some enter your eye. They there cause a complicated disturbance of the rods and cones, which, in turn, send a current along the optic nerve. When this current reaches the brain, it produces an event. The event which it produces is that which you call "seeing Jones." As is evident from this account, the connection of "seeing Jones" with Jones is a remote, round-about causal connection. Jones himself, meanwhile, remains wrapped in mystery. He may be thinking about his dinner, or about how his invest-ments have gone to pieces, or about that umbrella he lost; these thoughts are Jones, but these are not what you see. . . .

—BERTRAND RUSSELL: *The Scientific Outlook.*

The passage may be regarded as an instance of exposition by use of illustration. (See pp. 79–90.) Notice that Russell has completed his analysis with the last statement of the passage; yet apparently he feels that the account may prove too technical and that his reader may fail to understand. Therefore, he adds a concluding illustration: "To say that you see Jones is no more correct than it would be, if a ball bounced off a wall in your garden and hit you, to say that the wall had hit you. Indeed, the two cases are closely analogous." Most readers will be grateful for the analogy. Most minds find abstractions so alien to them that they need a concrete statement such as this analogy provides. Even if the writer is able, as Bertrand Russell is able here, to state his analysis directly, the extra illustra-tion—the concrete analogy drawn from daily experience—is helpful.

■ APPLICATIONS

I The authors of the following passages have supplied illustrative or sum-marizing comparisons to make clearer or more emphatic what they had to say. We have printed here the author's comparison along with two alternate comparisons. Can you pick out the author's own? Try to justify your choice.

A   These molecules move with very high speeds; in the ordinary air of an ordi-nary room, the average molecular speed is about 500 yards a second. This is roughly the speed of a rifle-bullet, and is rather more than the ordinary speed of sound. As we are familiar with this latter speed from everyday ex-perience, it is easy to form some conception of molecular speeds in a gas. It is not a mere accident that molecular speeds are comparable with the speed of sound. Sound is a disturbance which one molecule passes on to another when it collides with it, rather like

1 an infection that one human being passes on to another.

2 relays of messengers passing a message on to one another, or Greek
   torchbearers handing on their lights.
3 a set of box-cars when the locomotive's engineer suddenly applies the
   brakes and each car passes on the jolt to the next.
        —Sir James Jeans: "Exploring the Atom," *The Universe Around Us*.[6]

B An insect, therefore, is not afraid of gravity; it can fall without danger, and
can cling to the ceiling with remarkably little trouble. It can go in for elegant
fantastic forms of support like that of the daddy-long-legs. But there is a force
which is as formidable to an insect as gravitation to a mammal. This is surface tension. A man coming out of a bath carries with him a film of water of
about one-fiftieth of an inch in thickness. This weighs about a pound. A wet
mouse has to carry about its own weight of water. A wet fly has to lift many
times its own weight and, as everyone knows, a fly once wetted by water or
any other liquid is in a very serious position indeed. An insect going for a
drink is in as great danger as

1 a man leaning out over a precipice in search of food.
2 a New Yorker trying to cross 42nd Street at Madison Avenue.
3 a gazelle approaching a waterhole where lions may lie in wait.
        —J. B. S. Haldane: "On Being the Right Size," *Possible Worlds*.

II In the following passages the authors have made much use of illustrative
metaphor. Try to restate what is said in language as unmetaphorical as you
can devise. Do not be surprised if you find that the rewritten version requires
a good many more words than the original passage.

A We, then, the animals, consume those stores in our restless living. Serenely
the plants amass them. They turn light's active energy to food, which is potential energy stored for their own benefit. . . .
    Animal life lives always in the red; the favorable balance is written on the
other side of life's page, and it is written in chlorophyll. All else obeys the
thermodynamic law that energy forever runs down hill, is lost and degraded.
In economic language, this is the law of diminishing returns, and it is obeyed
by the cooling stars as by man and all the animals. They float down its Lethe
stream. Only chlorophyll fights up against the current. It is the stuff in life
that rebels at death, that has never surrendered to entropy, final icy stagnation.
It is the mere cobweb on which we are all suspended over the abyss.
        —Donald Culross Peattie: *Flowering Earth*.[7]

B We should be careful to get out of an experience only the wisdom that is in
it—and stop there; lest we be like the cat that sits down on a hot stove lid.
She will never sit down on a hot stove lid again—and that is well; but also
she will never sit down on a cold one. . . .
        —Mark Twain: *Following the Equator*.

---

[6] Reprinted from "Exploring the Atom" from *The Universe Around Us* by Sir James Jeans
by permission of Cambridge University Press.
[7] From *Flowering Earth* by Donald Culross Peattie. Reprinted by permission of Noel R. Peattie and his agent, James Brown Associates, Inc. Copyright © 1939 by Donald Culross Peattie.

Metaphor as essential statement

In strict scientific statement, then, metaphor has no place, and in less strict scientific discussion it would seem to be auxiliary and optional. But in most of what we read—political speeches, articles on international affairs, letters to friends, expressions of opinion, fiction, poetry, drama, attempts to persuade and convince, essays in which we invite other people to share our experiences and evaluations of life—and in nearly everything that we write, metaphor is a primary device of expression. It is no mere decoration, no "extra." It often represents not only the most compact and vigorous way of saying a thing but also the only way in which the particular thing can be said at all. This last remark holds especially true when "the thing to be said" involves an interpretation or evaluation. Metaphor is indeed an indispensable instrument for interpreting experience.

Let us illustrate. In the sentence that follows, Helen Keller describes what tactile sensation means to a person who has always been blind and deaf: "The immovable rock, with its juts and warped surface, bends beneath my fingers into all manner of grooves and hollows." The rock, of course, does not literally bend; it is "immovable." But under her sensitive fingers, which do duty for eyes, the rock itself seems to respond dynamically to her touch. For what is being described is not the fumbling of an ordinary person who is blindfolded. We are, rather, being let into Helen Keller's "world," a world of exciting qualities that most of us do not know at all. Metaphor here is the only means by which it may be made known to us, since this world does not exist in our experience and cannot be pointed to; it can only be created for us. (The student should compare Helen Keller's account of touch, as given in fuller detail on page 280, with Bertrand Russell's account of sight, pages 445–46. They are radically different in purpose, and therefore in method.)

Consider what metaphor does in the following two verses from Ecclesiastes. "It is better to bear the rebuke of the wise, than for a man to hear the song of fools. For as the crackling of thorns under a pot, so is the laughter of the fool: this also is vanity."

This comparison, as we see, uses the dry, crackling sound of burning thorn branches to describe the laughter of a fool. Now, there is a certain realistic basis for the comparison, but the metaphor is far more than a phonetic description. It makes a value judgment, too: the fool's laughter, it implies, is brittle, hollow, meaningless; it is such a noise as attends the going up in smoke of something quite worthless, the rubbish of dried thorn branches. This implication is the justification for the last clause, "this [the fool's laughter] also is vanity." But the metaphor does much more than "illustrate" the vanity. It is the metaphor itself that defines vanity and realizes it for us—its specious brightness, its explosive chatter, its essential emptiness.

Consider further what metaphor accomplishes in the two following passages.

> In rivers the water that you touch is the last of what has passed and the first of that which comes: so with time present.   —LEONARDO DA VINCI.

This figure may seem to be no more than mere illustration; yet there are other elements. What is being described is not an object but a metaphysical concept, the imaginary boundary—itself without duration—that divides time past from time future. Da Vinci finds the image he requires in the analogy of a moving stream: time present is like the moving water that cannot be caught and held for inspection but at the moment of touching us is already hurrying away. The analogy, in spite of its vividness, preserves in itself something of the mystery that it undertakes to reveal to us. It has "poetic" character—not in the sense that it is pretty or sentimental, but in the sense that it makes a profound revelation.

Thoreau also likens the passage of time to a moving stream and goes on to develop explicitly certain related metaphysical implications: eternity as a concept in our experience of time.

> Time is but the stream I go a-fishing in. I drink at it; but while I drink, I see the sandy bottom and detect how shallow it is. Its thin current slides away, but eternity remains. I would drink deeper; fish in the sky, whose bottom is pebbly with stars.   —*Walden*.

Time is impermanent, thin, "shallow," necessary for men (they must drink of it) and providing them with pleasure and sport ("go a-fishing in"); but the speaker yearns for a deeper draft and more sublime sport than time can provide.

■ APPLICATION

Has Thoreau used his metaphors responsibly? Is his figure strained? Badly mixed? What is the relation of stream bed to sky? Pebbles to stars? How are all the subsidiary metaphors related to each other? Can you fill in the gaps among them? Through this complicated figure, what is Thoreau trying to "say"?

In the following passage E. B. White comments upon the way in which the true Christmas has all but disappeared beneath the commercialized Christmas. Note the extended comparison through which he makes his point:

> To perceive Christmas through its wrapping becomes more difficult with every year. There was a little device we noticed in one of the sporting-goods stores—a trumpet that hunters hold to their ears so that they can hear the distant music of the hounds. Something of this sort is needed now

to hear the incredibly distant sound of Christmas in these times, through the dark, material woods that surround it. "Silent Night," canned and distributed in thundering repetition in the department stores, has become one of the greatest of all noise-makers, almost like the rattles and whistles of Election Night. —E. B. WHITE: *The Second Tree from the Corner.*

One of the most effective things about this passage is that White's main metaphor and the subsidiary metaphors that flank it are taken from the literal details of the commercialized Christmas—the shops, the gift wrappings, the blare of Christmas hymns and carols from advertising loudspeakers. There is a visual image: we have concealed Christmas almost too well beneath its gaudy wrappings—we see the colored paper and not the true gift. Then White shifts to what will be his main image, the hunter's hearing trumpet, which might itself be on display in some exclusive shop as a Christmas present for a sportsman. An analogous device is required to hear the spiritual music of Christmas because we have got so far away from it ("distant sound . . . in these times") and because its sound is blocked off by "dark, material woods." And, finally, another detail from Christmas shopping is used to give a further twist to this last figure: what might be thought to be the very music of Christmas ("Silent Night") has become one of the noises (the hymn "canned and distributed in thundering repetition") that makes it impossible to hear Christmas's true music.

This sequence of related images seems to mirror the very scene that it judges; a faithful description of the commercialized Christmas is made to contribute to a searching criticism of it. This economy of means has its counterpart in forcefulness of effect. Again, the student might try to say all that White is saying *without* benefit of such comparisons. The attempt will show how much this chain of metaphors accomplishes.

We must not, however, allow our choice of examples to make the process of using metaphor seem too complicated and "literary." Consider a passage from a student theme, which was quoted in full on pages 283–85:

> Off yonder, beyond the glitter of the water where the sun still struck, you could see the clouds piling up like a cliff, black and slate-colored, streaked with purple. I said like a cliff, but it was like a cliff that somehow, momentarily grew taller while you looked at it, looking awfully solid but somehow swelling and coiling upward at the same time as if there were an interior force collecting itself for effort.

The comparison to a swelling and coiling cliff enables the reader to visualize what the storm cloud looked like as it boiled up. But it does more; it goes far to suggest the awe and fright that the storm cloud excited in the mind of the girl who describes it.

One more example, this one again selected to combat the conventional notion that metaphor is somehow "literary." Here is the way in which "Bugs" Baer describes the collapse of a prize fighter: "Zale folded as gracefully as the Queen's fan and fell on his battered face alongside the ropes.

His seconds carried him to his corner like three window-dressers packing a melted dummy off during a heat wave on the sunny side of Broadway." This description may be judged good writing or bad, but it is easy to see why Baer used figurative language. He was not trying to "tell" us about the scene; he was trying to make us *see* the scene—vividly, freshly, fully, as a somewhat cynical but highly interested observer might have viewed it.

The nature and function of metaphor can be further illustrated from passages quoted in the earlier chapter on Description. It might be useful for the student to go back and review some of the descriptive passages quoted there. He may well be struck with the amount of metaphor in these passages and also with the *amount of work* that the metaphors actually do. For a starter, the student might reread the description of the Arabian town on page 290 where the heat is "like a drawn sword," or the account of Mr. Chadband on pages 291–92, a man who "moves softly and cumbrously, not unlike a bear who has been taught to walk upright."

A few paragraphs above we cited a passage written by Helen Keller in which she gives an account of her sense of touch. We must admit that the world of Helen Keller's experience is a special world that can be conveyed to us only through suggestion and analogy. Yet, a little reflection will show us that the world of experience belonging to each of us is far more special than we may think, for our world is to a great extent determined by our values, moods, and emotional biases. The world as seen by the girl watching the storm cloud is special in this sense, and so too is that of the Hebrew preacher who speaks in Ecclesiastes. If we are to communicate our experience with any accuracy, figurative language is frequently the only way by which we can do so. By means of metaphor we grasp not only the experience as an entity but its "meaning," its value, to us as well.

■ APPLICATIONS

I The author of the following passage comments on some of the personality traits necessary to a good general and then cites an extended comparison made by Winston Churchill with reference to the British Commander in Chief in World War I.

> There is no question but that one of the requisites of a successful general is a certain indifference to the suffering of his troops. In war it is inevitable that many will be killed or maimed, and the commander responsible for launching his troops into battle cannot concern himself with this to the point where his powers of decision or judgment are crippled by the thought of the suffering of his men. It is for this reason that generals should live in a certain seclusion, protected from seeing too much of the awful human debris of battle. But, of course, this can be carried to an extreme, and the endless slaughter of World War I tended to breed too great an indifference to casualties on the part of the upper levels of command. Winston Churchill, in a not unsympa-

thetic portrait of Sir Douglas Haig, wrote that the British Commander in Chief "presents to me in those red years the same mental picture as a great surgeon before the days of anaesthetics, versed in every detail of such science as was known to him; sure of himself, steady of poise, knife in hand, intent upon the operation; entirely removed in his professional capacity from the agony of the patient, the anguish of relations, or the doctrines of rival schools, the devices of quacks, or the first fruits of new learning. He would operate without excitement, or he would depart without being affronted; and if the patient died, he would not reproach himself."

—Richard M. Watt: *Dare Call It Treason.*[8]

Would you agree with Watt that Churchill's portrait of Haig is "not unsympathetic"? Does the comparison of the general to the surgeon make the necessary "indifference to suffering" seem less brutal and inhuman? Is the analogy between general and surgeon a just one? On what assumption does it rest? If you think the analogy has insufficient basis in fact, would you still give Churchill high marks as a rhetorician? Write a very brief discussion of this extended figure, showing its utility for expressing with exactness Churchill's attitude toward Haig and toward war.

II In the following passage, the author is describing the changes that have occurred in a small town as "progress" takes over.

> Apartment houses—regular flat buildings, with elevator service and all that—shoved their aggressive stone and brick faces up to the pavement line of a street where before old white houses with green shutters and fluted porch pillars had snuggled back among hackberries and maples like a row of broody old hens under a hedge. The churches had caught the spirit too; there were new churches to replace the old ones. Only that stronghold of the ultra conservatives, the Independent Presbyterian, stood fast on its original site, and even the Independent Presbyterian had felt the quickening finger of progress. Under its gray pillared front were set ornate stone steps, like new false teeth in the mouth of a stern old maid, and the new stained glass memorial windows at either side were as paste earrings for her ancient virginal ears. The spinster had traded her blue stockings for doctrinal half hose of a livelier pattern, and these were the outward symbols of the change.
>
> —Irvin Cobb: "Black and White," *Back Home.*

Is the comparison of the "ornate stone steps" to "new false teeth" an effective figure? Is it merely visual? Or does it do something more? Does it tell us anything about the members of the Independent Presbyterian Church? Their taste? Their attitude toward progress? Their attitude toward religion? Notice that the comparison of the church to an old maid develops into an extended analogy. Is the extension of the figure successful? Write a brief account describing what this figure accomplishes (or fails to accomplish).

---

[8] Reprinted from *Dare Call It Treason* by Richard M. Watt by permission of Simon & Shuster, Inc. Reprinted by permission of Chatto & Windus Ltd.

What Makes a "Good" Metaphor?

In judging the value of a metaphor, the physical similarity of the items compared is easily overestimated. In many finely effective comparisons the degree of physical similarity is not very great. Of course, there must be some element of resemblance. But a good comparison is not necessarily one in which there is close resemblance, since "illustration," as we have seen, is not the primary purpose of metaphor.

The element of similarity in metaphor

To realize this last point, let us consider one of the tritest comparisons of all: "Her eyes were like stars." Far from seeming strained or overingenious, the comparison will seem to most of us entirely too simple and easy. Yet even in this well-worn analogy the objects compared are really very dissimilar. Certainly the human eyeball and the flaming mass of elements that make up the stars have very little in common. If this examination, which compares the two objects as scientifically considered, seems somewhat unfair, we can go on to point out that the eyes, even those of a lovely woman, do not much resemble the glinting points of light that are the stars as we see them. The truth of the matter is that what supports this oldest and most hackneyed of comparisons is not the physical resemblances so much as the associations: the associations of stars with brilliance, with the high and celestial. It is these associations that make the stars seem "like" the glances of the eyes of someone loved.

Thus every comparison has a very important subjective element in it; its proper task is to interpret, to evaluate—not to insist upon physical analogies. Its proper function is, as we have said, to define attitude.

Let us consider one of the celebrated comic comparisons in English literature. In his satire "Hudibras," Samuel Butler describes the rosy sky of dawn:

> . . . like a lobster, boyl'd, the morn
> From black to red began to turn.

We think of this as an absurd comparison, and so it is—appropriately so—for "Hudibras" is a humorous poem, and Butler is casting good-humored scorn upon his hero. Yet it is worth asking why the comparison strikes us as absurd. We are likely to say that it is absurd because the dawn does not in the least resemble a boiled lobster. But the colors to be seen in the shell of a boiled lobster may very closely resemble the exact shade of red to be seen on some mornings. The absurdity does not come from any lack of physical resemblance; it comes from the absurd contrast of the small with the large, the commonplace and homely with the beautiful and grand, the grotesque creature in the steaming pot with the wide, fresh expanse of the dawn sky. Butler has, for humorous effect, deliberately played these elements against each other.

The element of contrast in metaphor

Though we commonly call metaphors (and related figurative expressions) "comparisons," it is plain that we might just as accurately call them "contrasts." For the elements of dissimilarity between the terms of a metaphor may be of quite as much importance as the elements of likeness. One can go further still: in an effective metaphor there must be *some degree of contrast*. If we say "the river roared like a flood" or "the dog raged like a wild beast," we feel that the metaphor is weak or nonexistent. A river is already too much like a flood, and a dog, though a tame beast, too nearly resembles a wild beast. If, on the other hand, we say "the fire roared like a flood" or "the fire raged like a wild beast," we begin to feel some metaphoric force. Even though these are rather poor metaphors, fire and flood or fire and beast are sufficiently dissimilar for us to feel that a degree of metaphorical transfer occurs; in these expressions one discerns the "new namings" that constitute metaphor.

We are usually taught to reject what are rather awkwardly called "farfetched" comparisons. (The term is awkward because it suggests that the terms of a good comparison are close together, though we have seen that even "eyes" and "stars" are not really very close.) But if comparisons must not be too "farfetched," neither must they be too "nearly fetched." They have to be fetched some distance if we are to have a recognizable metaphor at all.

The criteria for good metaphor

Because figurative language is such an essential part of effective discourse, it is, as we have seen, easier to indicate what is wrong with a metaphor than what is right with it. Indeed, a brief description of the value of an apt metaphor amounts to little more than the remark that it is properly expressive and plays its due part in the total context. (If we want to say more, and say it in some detail, we shall probably find ourselves discussing the relation of the metaphor to the whole context.) There is no handy list of short rules for determining a good metaphor.

In view of these limiting considerations, perhaps our best procedure is to examine in some detail a variety of metaphors that seem appropriate and successful, plus one or two problem cases that may stimulate us to think further about what makes an acceptable metaphor.

Here is a somewhat extended analogy from a novel about college life.

> The teachers of Benton were like sheep, where money was concerned, and the President was their shepherd: he had to scramble around looking, and worrying, and leading them to greener pastures if he could see any, while they walked on munching their scanty feed and baaing—piteously, but contentedly and accustomedly, too. Sometimes the President seemed to me not a shepherd but a scapegoat, and a willing one: the sheep had all the inconveniences and vexations of doing without money, but all the guilt of getting it had been put on his own . . . shoulders.
>
> —RANDALL JARRELL: *Pictures from an Institution.*

The relationship between the typical president of a college and the typical faculty is here put neatly and wittily. One may also be inclined to add, rather justly. The faculty, for all their complaints, are really glad not to have the responsibility of raising money for their salaries. And though at times they may baa piteously, they are not so sheeplike in their devotion to their shepherd that they cannot feel resentment and occasionally regard him neither as a shepherd nor even as a fellow sheep but as a goat. The passage draws on a rich tradition of pastoral literature and not least from the Scriptures—from the story of the Good Shepherd and his careful charge of his flock and from the account of the scapegoat driven into the wilderness to carry away with him the sins of the people. There may even be a hint of the Last Judgment, in which the sheep will be separated from the goats, the sheep to stand in the place of honor on the right hand of God, while the goats are placed on the left. (The sheepish faculty do know their worth.)

The faculty-administration relationships described so amusingly in this concrete figure have obviously been observed from the inside, but this account has been written with a good deal of detachment. The author is aware of both sides of a complicated relationship and, if we are to enjoy fully the novel from which this brief excerpt is taken, we will have to be able to share in his attitude. In fact, it might be said that one of the most important things that metaphor does is to suggest—forcefully, but often with delicate discrimination—particular attitudes. (This whole matter of the writer's attitude will be discussed fully in the chapter on Tone, which follows.)

Here is Robert Lowell's picture of the "bleak Revere Street dining room" in which he sat through family Sunday dinners, "absorbing cold and anxiety from the table." (For a related section of his account of his early life, see Readings, pp. 867–76.)

> Here, table, highboy, chairs, and screen—mahogany, cherry, teak— looked nervous and disproportioned. They seemed to wince, touch elbows, shift from foot to foot. High above the highboy, our gold National Eagle stooped forward, plastery and doddering. The Sheffield silver-plate urns, more precious than solid sterling, peeled; the bodies of the heraldic mermaids on the Mason-Myers crest blushed a metallic copper tan. In the

harsh New England light, the bronze sphinxes supporting our sideboard looked as though manufactured in Grand Rapids. All too clearly no one had worried about synchronizing the grandfather clock's minutes, days, and months with its mellow old Dutch seascape-painted discs for showing the phases of the moon. The stricken, but still striking gong made sounds like steam banging through pipes. Colonel Myers' monumental Tibetan screen had been impiously shortened to fit it for a low Yankee ceiling. And now, rough and gawky, like some Hindu water buffalo killed in mid-rush but still alive with mad momentum, the screen hulked over us . . . and hid the pantry sink. —ROBERT LOWELL: *Life Studies*.[9]

In this highly personal account, the very furnishings and decorations behave like human beings: they "look nervous"; they "wince, touch elbows, shift from foot to foot"; they "blush." In short, they reflect all the anxieties of the boy who used to look at them and who now, much later, is describing them. These anthropomorphic metaphors also make vivid the sense of clutter arising from crowding too many heterogeneous pieces into one room. Lowell's climactic figure illustrates this "disproportioned" quality of the décor. (He has said that the furnishings "looked nervous" *and* "disproportioned.") The most imposing piece, the Tibetan screen, has been cut down to fit the "low Yankee ceiling." Now, "like some Hindu buffalo killed in mid-rush but still alive with mad momentum," it "hulked over us." The comparison does a number of things at once: it gives a dramatic instance of the "disproportioned" quality; it presents the screen as an exotic trophy, captured and maimed though still alive; and it suggests the vague menace that seems to emanate from it.

Metaphor, then, plays an important part in suggesting to the reader the special character and atmosphere of this particular room. Lowell is obviously interested in giving more than a mere factual description of the pieces of furniture and the various *objets d'art*. He presents a *state of mind*—no mere arrangement of domestic possessions.

The last two examples of metaphor that we have considered are elaborate and complicated, but a brief, condensed figure can also be thoroughly effective. The hero in one of Reynolds Price's novels clasps the hand of a friend of his mother's. He tells us that it was like touching "a hot little plush unused pincushion." The metaphor is vivid and evocative. It suggests a plump little woman with smooth skin. For some of us it will also suggest the kind of woman who dotes on plush pincushions and has around the house unused, spare ones, never stuck by a pin. (We find out as we read the novel that the character is sixtyish, voluble, kindly, lives alone in her little house, and spends most of her time watching television programs.)

Here is another brief comparison from another piece of fiction (Eudora

---

[9] Reprinted with the permission of Farrar, Straus & Giroux, Inc. from *Life Studies* by Robert Lowell, copyright © 1956, 1958, 1959 by Robert Lowell. Reprinted by permission of Faber and Faber Ltd.

Welty's "The Optimist's Daughter"). The scene is a hospital. A woman notices an ordinary old man in the hospital who has been prepared to be taken into the operating room. She observes that he was "baldheaded as an infant, hook-nosed and silent—they had taken away his teeth." The comparison is slightly shocking and is meant to be. The writer wants us to feel the contrast between the tired and ill old man and a newborn baby. But the likeness is there too: many infants are born without hair, and they are also toothless—like the old man, now that his false teeth have been removed. What is the importance of the hook nose here? This, the man's most prominent feature, is one feature in which he does *not* resemble the infant. Babies have small or snub noses. Emphasis upon the nose therefore points the contrast and triggers the ironic perception: the last of the seven ages of man, so different from the first, is after all rather horrifyingly like the first.

The old-man–infant comparison is, on the surface at least, introduced casually. It does not call much attention to itself, but the following metaphor does. We read in one of Faulkner's early novels that when, toward evening, one of the characters opened the street door, "twilight ran in like a quiet violet dog. . . ." The image of the violet dog is incongruous. True, the general idea does make a kind of sense: dogs do sometimes wait quietly outside a familiar door in the hope that someone will open it and give them the chance to slip in. The twilight in this old city is waiting too, and when the door is opened, it seems to rush quietly into the room. Yet the comparison will probably strike the average reader as "contrived," and not quite worth the effort that has been expended in working it up.[10]

Another metaphor in the same novel, however, will probably win the reader's acceptance. Faulkner describes September as "a month of languorous days as regretful as woodsmoke." Is woodsmoke regretful? That will depend on the reader's own experience and on his own past associations. But the comparison at least makes a strong invitation to the reader's imagination to associate the bluish haze of a September day with the blue of woodsmoke, and the woodsmoke itself with the pensive, even sad, coming of the fall and the ebbing of the year.

As the last two examples probably suggest, metaphor is the particular instrument of poetry. But, as we have seen, it is by no means confined to poetry and, in fact, it is one of the most important resources for the prose writer. It is the best means by which to intimate a mood, to imply the shading

---

[10] Why isn't this comparison worth the effort? Why should it be labeled "contrived"? These are proper questions and the student has a right to decide them for himself. But in that case he must look at the context in which the image occurs (*Mosquitoes*, pp. 13–14) and ask himself such questions as these: How does Faulkner lead up to the image? Is it appropriate to Mr. Talliafero (the character in the novel past whom the violet dog runs)? What does the image tell us about Talliafero? What does it accomplish? In terms of setting the atmosphere and mood? The student's final judgment will be in part a subjective one; but so is ours. There is no set formula for deciding the success of a metaphor. (For the importance of the context in deciding the worth of a metaphor, see p. 453 and p. 458.)

of an attitude, and, most of all, to stimulate and involve the imagination of his readers.

Metaphor: the importance of the context

Effective metaphor suits the context in which it occurs. Moreover, an effective metaphor pays its own way—that is, justifies itself by making a real contribution to the writer's total expression. As we have remarked, the violet-dog metaphor may ask more of the reader's attention than it contributes to the meaning of the work. Not every fresh and piquant metaphor is good: contrariwise, not every tame and familiar metaphor is poor. What counts is the "work," in the given context, that each figure performs.

Here is an example. Eudora Welty, in an essay entitled "How I Write," tells us that the inspiration for a story is like "a pull on the line . . . the outside signal that has startled or moved the creative mind to complicity and brought the story to active being. . . ."

Her figure obviously derives from fishing, probably not fly-fishing, but old-fashioned fishing with a baited hook. The tug on the line means that the fisherman has a bite. The metaphor is not new, but the implied analogy is a thoroughly just one. The story lies hidden in the depths of the mind just as the fish lies concealed in the pool. The tug on the line signals no more than a possibility, which may not be fulfilled. In any case, both the fisherman and the fiction writer must exercise skill and have luck in the bargain, if either fish or story is to be landed. One must not jerk the line too quickly and scare the fish away. One has to set the hook and, if the fish is a big fellow, play him carefully before the fish (or story) can be pulled up into the light, seen for what he is, and drawn up safely onto the bank.

Miss Welty merely alludes in passing to this rather complex analogy.[11] But that is, for her purposes, all that she needs to do. The perceptive reader will get the point, probably without any conscious working out of the terms. If he wants to work them out, or if he needs to do so, there is nothing to deter him: the analogy has been honestly used and it supports fully Miss Welty's argument. Why should its familiarity debar it from her use? She hasn't pretended that it was a novel analogy, as her rather glancing reference to it makes plain.

This last example provides an opportunity to stress one more time the supreme importance of the context. Metaphors are related to a total context and contribute to it or fail to do so. They accord with it or they strike a dissonance. Good metaphors contribute their strength to, and draw their ultimate justification from, the whole body of the discourse. They are not isolated sugarplums that have been thrust into the pudding by the writer

---

[11] One does not have to make a *conscious* elaboration of the pull-on-the-line figure in order to feel it as effective. Moreover, the pull on the line may just possibly suggest to some readers not a hooked fish but the pull of a full bucket in the well or the pull exerted by a fellow mountain-climber on the safety rope.

in the hope that the alert reader will from time to time put in his thumb and triumphantly bring them out with a flourish to prove the writer's ingenuity and his own skill in finding them. They are rather an integral part of a total meaningful discourse or dramatic rendering of an experience.

■ APPLICATIONS

1 Consider carefully the metaphors in Santayana's "Dickens" (Readings, pp. 771–81). What is the justification of the author's using so much figurative language? (In this connection one might observe that B. F. Skinner in "Freedom and the Control of Men," pp. 644–51, uses comparatively little metaphor. Do you see why the one writer should use so much, the other so little?)

II The following metaphors may seem to be primarily *illustrative,* that is, the metaphor makes something plain by comparing it with a simpler or more familiar thing. But are they *merely* illustrative? Are any of the metaphors used to *state* a meaning as well as to *illustrate* a meaning? Test them on this point by trying to restate precisely "the thing said" in nonmetaphorical language.

A   On each side of the [bee's] abdomen are four little wax-pockets situated in the joints of the hard-surfaced body; and here the supply of wax may be seen issuing, the flat, light-colored wax appearing somewhat like a letter which a man has tucked up under his waistcoat.
    —Charles D. Stewart: "The Bee's Knees."

B   Intellectual assimilation takes time. The mind is not to be enriched as a coal barge is loaded. Whatever is precious in a cargo is taken carefully on board and carefully placed. Whatever is delicate and fine must be received delicately, and its place in the mind thoughtfully assigned.
    —Arlo Bates: "Reading on the Run," *Talks on the Study of Literature.*

C   Bed is the perfect laboratory—just the right degree of withdrawal from the world, yet with the comforts at hand, and errands delegated to someone else. The toast crumbs, accumulating among the sheets, set up the irritation inside the shell and start the pearl growing.
    —E. B. White: "Peavy, Book and Guitar."

D   When I am dead, the chance that my bones will become fossilized is very remote. Bones decay away like the rest of our bodies unless a lot of very unlikely things happen. First of all, a dead body will not leave any permanent remains in the form of a fossil unless it happens to be covered up and thus protected from decay. That is fairly easy in the case of animals in the sea. Rivers are always carrying sediment out and depositing it, and tides and currents shift the sediment and cover up the bodies of dead animals. But even in this case it is by no means likely that the bones will be fossilized. Much more probably they will gradually dissolve away and leave no trace of themselves. Fossilization is rather a complicated process. It involves the replacement of each particle of bone, as it dissolves away, by a less soluble and therefore more permanent substance. When that has happened, the chances are still very remote that anyone will find the fossil thousands or millions of years later. Our quarries and mines and cuttings are mere scratches on the surface of the earth. With terrestrial animals the chances of fossilization are still less than with marine ones. They are likely to die and decay without being covered up. It would be quite absurd to look with any great hopefulness for the fossil remains of the ancestors of any given animal. It would not simply be like looking for the proverbial pin in a haystack, for then you are supposed to have the advantage of knowing that the pin is there. But in this case you are looking for a soluble pin in a haystack in a thunderstorm, and you always have at the back of your mind the disconcerting thought that perhaps it is no longer there.

—John R. Baker: "Missing Links," *Science in a Changing World.*[12]

E   . . . [the ship's] middle structure was like a half-tide rock awash upon a coast. It was like an outlying rock with the water boiling up, streaming over, pouring off, beating round—like a rock in the surf to which shipwrecked people cling before they let go—only it rose, it sank, it rolled continuously, without respite and rest, like a rock that should have miraculously struck adrift from a coast and gone wallowing upon the sea.   —Joseph Conrad: *Typhoon.*

III   Do the authors of the following passages avoid drifting into jargon? In this connection, observe carefully their use of dead metaphor and confused metaphor.

A   Despite the precept that man cannot pull himself up by his bootstraps, psychology shows us that we can make consistent and gratifying gains in the direction of love, warmth, and tolerance.

—Joshua Loth Liebman: *Peace of Mind.*

What is the writer trying to say? That the precept is wrong since it is possible for a man to lift himself toward *love,* merely by using his own resources? Or that to move oneself in the direction of love is not a matter of lifting oneself up by his bootstraps? Or what does he mean? Try to determine what he is trying to say and frame a sentence (with proper metaphors, if possible) that will express his thought.

B   Even with the most virtuous *at the levers,* how can control be exercised for the good of all when there are so many voices emerging from different conditions, inheriting different traditions, committed to different ideals, and demanding different solutions? Every man wants to realize the opportunities of human knowledge, but each is inclined to believe that all will benefit if knowledge is *mobilized* in the service of his ideals and his traditions. Though their own powers are universal, men's values are local and *mired in the mud of history.* Power is too often *untamed by* responsibility to the world.

Few want to *turn back the clock of science and technology.* Most approve the trend toward an integration of the world so that its resources, its experience, its knowledge will be available to everyone, but they do not want to

[12] Reprinted from "Missing Links" by John R. Baker, in *Science in a Changing World,* ed. by Mary Adams, by permission of Appleton-Century-Crofts, Inc.

turn their backs entirely on the customs, the morals, the language, the institutions which they have inherited from their ancestors. . . . [*Italics ours.*]
—Quincy Wright: "The Universities and the World Order,"
A.A.U.P. Bulletin.

Consider the italicized phrases. Are the metaphors that Wright uses doing any constructive "work"? Or do they obscure the thought? Compare this passage with C. S. Lewis's discussion of this problem in the last paragraph on page 657. What metaphors does Lewis use? Are they more or less effective than Wright's?

C George F. Carter, in "The American Civilization Puzzle" (Readings, pp. 814–26), writes the following passages:

1 Pandora's box was open. The moat was crossed. The Independent Interventionists' vessel had sprung a leak.

2 But this was an uneasy peace. For facts are a bit like the fires of a volcano. They may lie dormant, but actually they are smoldering away, awaiting only the touch of an investigator's hand to spring into life, capable of destroying the most elaborate of philosophical structures.

Are these mixtures of metaphors justified? Has the author made any preparation for them?

D Due to the great increase in the importance of social and economic problems during the past generation, philosophy is giving more attention than heretofore to the social and economic aspects of life. Also, esthetics is receiving greater consideration as the problem of civilization's goal becomes more pressing.
—John Geise: *Man and the Western World.*

IV Santayana's prose will repay careful reading for its treatment of metaphor. The student might look carefully for three things in particular: (1) the occasional extended metaphor, which may dominate a whole section of the essay; (2) the revivification of what would ordinarily be dead metaphor; and (3) the constant pointing up of abstractions by some concrete detail. For example, the passage beginning "In his love of roads" (p. 775) and ending "love and laughter" (p. 776) is rather abstract in its ideas. Moreover, Santayana has risked using such apparent clichés as "never see the wood for the trees," "pendulum soon swings back," and the "vain tides" of things. Mark the metaphors in this passage, and attempt to state how the metaphors are related to one another. Are there any actual clichés? If there are not, what prevents some of the expressions from affecting us as clichés do? What is the relation to the whole pattern of the two or three extended metaphors that occur?

V Do any of the following metaphors seem farfetched and extravagant? Do any seem tame and flat? What principle, if any, seems to determine the matter of acceptability?

Are any of the passages ineffective because the metaphors are "mixed"? Is it possible to shift rapidly from one metaphor to another without producing confusion? Are we never to mix metaphor? What principle, if any, seems to determine this matter?

A   The chickens he raised were all white meat down through the drumsticks, the cows were tended like children, and the big ram he called Goliath had horns with a curl like a morning-glory vine and could butt through an iron door. But Dan'l wasn't one of your gentleman farmers; he knew all the ways of the land, and he'd be up by candlelight to see that the chores got done. A man with the mouth of a mastiff, a brow like a mountain and eyes like burning anthracite—that was Dan'l Webster in his prime.

—Stephen Vincent Benét: *The Devil and Daniel Webster.*

B   A smile lit the eyes of the expiring Kentuck. "Dying!" he repeated; "he's a-taking me with him. Tell the boys I've got the Luck with me now"; and the strong man, clinging to the frail babe as a drowning man is said to cling to a straw, drifted away into the shadowy river that flows forever to the unknown sea.   —Bret Harte: "The Luck of Roaring Camp."

C   Over in the corner Zale was rounding as slowly as the Queen Mary docking in the Hudson. He had taken a beating that would have busted the light in a night club bass drum. . . . In the sixth both sluggers were plugging away like a thirty-six cylinder car at a gasoline pump with the motor running. Neither the car nor the pump had gained an inch. . . . The seventh was as tough a spelling bee as ever missed out on cat. They were moving around like a Fiji fire dancer wearing celluloid sox. And banging both hands to the equator.

—"'Bugs' Baer Says."

D   Take the instant way;
For honor travels in a strait so narrow,
Where one but goes abreast: keep then the path;
For emulation hath a thousand sons,
That one by one pursue: if you give way,
Or hedge aside from the direct forthright,
Like to an enter'd tide they all rush by,
And leave you hindmost:—
Or like a gallant horse fallen in first rank,
Lie there for pavement to the abject rear,
O'er-run and trampled on: Then what they do in present,
Though less than yours in past, must o'ertop yours:
For time is like a fashionable host,
That slightly shakes his parting guest by the hand;
And with his arms out-stretch'd, as he would fly,
Grasps in the comer: Welcome ever smiles,
And farewell goes out sighing.

—Shakespeare: *Troilus and Cressida.*

E   [From a novel: a young man thinks bitterly of modern-day misuses of the word *love*.]

So much the worse for prosperous America, sick with the failure built into its own dream (that men are equal, can be equally good); barnacled already, past scraping, with deceit; sinking slowly from the sheer weight of hot air but savagely swelling, a wallowing balloon.

—Reynolds Price: *Love and Work.*

F   But perfection has one grave defect: it is apt to be dull. Swift's prose is like a French canal, bordered with poplars, that runs through a gracious and undulating country. Its tranquil charm fills you with satisfaction. . . . Dryden flourished at a happy moment. He had in his bones the sonorous periods and the baroque massiveness of Jacobean language and under the influence of the nimble and well-bred felicity that he learnt from the French he turned it into an instrument that was fit not only for solemn themes but also to express the light thought of the passing moment. He was the first of the rococo artists. If Swift reminds you of a French canal, Dryden recalls an English river winding its cheerful way round hills, through quietly busy towns and nestling villages, pausing now in a noble reach and then running powerfully through a woodland country. It is alive, varied, windswept; and it has the pleasant open-air smell of England.   —Somerset Maugham: *The Summing Up.*

G   And he shall be like a tree planted by the streams of water,
        That bringeth forth its fruit in its season,
        Whose leaf also doth not wither;
        And whatsoever he doeth shall prosper.
        The wicked are not so,
        But are like the chaff which the wind driveth away.

—Psalms 1:3–4.

H   We must be vigilantly on our guard to protect our sacred institutions against the boring from within of subversive elements, those blood-thirsty termites who like to fish in troubled waters.   —From a commencement address.

I   Mark but this flea, and mark in this,
        How little that which thou deniest me is;
        It suck'd me first, and now sucks thee,
        And in this flea our two bloods mingled be.
        Thou know'st that this cannot be said
        A sin, nor shame, nor loss of maidenhead;
            Yet this enjoys before it woo,
            And pamper'd swells with one blood made of two;
            And this, alas! is more than we would do.

—John Donne: "The Flea."

VI   What is the analogical basis for each of the following metaphors? Do you think that the element of likeness is adequate? What is the function of each of these metaphors? What, in other words, does the metaphor accomplish?

A   The furnished room received its latest guest with a first glow of pseudo-hospitality, a hectic, haggard, perfunctory welcome like the specious smile of a demirep.   —O. Henry: "The Furnished Room," *Strictly Business.*

B   [A young man looks at a picture of his mother.]

    . . . her large head tipped back, bright eyes on the flashbulb, mouth wide to laugh or to launch a small joke with a fresh-painted dinghy any moment now, to sweeten the day.   —Reynolds Price: *Love and Work.*

C   [An old woman is dying.]

> Her bones felt loose, and floated around in her skin, and Doctor Harry floated like a balloon around the foot of the bed. He floated and pulled down his waistcoat and swung his glasses on a cord.
> —Katherine Anne Porter: "The Jilting of Granny Weatherall."

D   The Medium shows its People what life is, what people are, and its People believe it: expect people to be that, try themselves to be that. Seeing is believing; and if what you see in *Life* is different from what you see in life, which of the two are you to believe? For many people it is what you see in *Life* (and in the movies, over television, on the radio) that is real life; and everyday existence, mere local or personal variation, is not real in the same sense.   —Randall Jarrell: *A Sad Heart at the Supermarket.*[13]

E [Stephen Dedalus has an experience that commits him to be an artist.]

> A girl stood before him in midstream: alone and still, gazing out to sea. She seemed like one whom magic had changed into the likeness of a strange and beautiful seabird. Her long slender bare legs were delicate as a crane's and pure save where an emerald trail of seaweed had fashioned itself as a sign upon the flesh. Her thighs, fuller and softhued as ivory, were bared almost to the hips where the white fringes of her drawers were like feathering of soft white down. Her slate-blue skirts were kilted boldly about her waist and dovetailed behind her. Her bosom was a bird's, soft and slight, slight and soft as the breast of some dark-plumaged dove. But her long fair hair was girlish: and girlish, and touched with the wonder of mortal beauty, her face.
> —James Joyce: *A Portrait of the Artist as a Young Man.*[14]

F   The truth, as everybody knows, is sometimes complicated or hard to understand; is sometimes almost unrecognizably different from what we expected it to be; is sometimes difficult or, even, impossible to accept. But literature is necessarily mixed up with truth, isn't it?—our truth, truth as we know it; one can almost define literature as the union of a wish and a truth, or as a wish modified by a truth. But this Instant Literature is a wish reinforced by a cliché, a wish proved by a lie: Instant Literature—whether it is a soap opera, a Broadway play, or a historical, sexual best-seller—tells us always that life is not only what we wish it, but also what we think it.
> —Randall Jarrell: "The Taste of the Age," *A Sad Heart at the Supermarket.*[15]

VII Discuss in detail the function of the basic metaphor in

A The fifth paragraph from the end in "Adolescence: Self-Definition and Conflict" (pp. 720–21)
B The next-to-last paragraph of "The Reach of Imagination" (pp. 643–44)
C Paragraphs 1 and 2 of "The Age of Overkill" (p. 692)

Material for further exercises on metaphor may be found in the Applications at the end of Chapter 8, pp. 306–12.

VIII Examine in detail the metaphors in two paragraphs in the excerpt from *The Fire Next Time* (the paragraph beginning "As I look back . . ." [pp. 863–65] and the one immediately following that). In your examination do not neglect the metaphors barely hinted at (e.g., "vertical saints") or the metaphors usually allowed to remain dormant in terms like "saved" (pp. 442–43).

CHAPTER **13**

Tone and Other Aspects of Style

Tone as the Expression of Attitude

Every piece of discourse implies a particular situation. A politician is attempting to convince a hostile audience; a mother is attempting to coax a child into doing something that the child dislikes; a legislator who can assume agreements on ends is trying to persuade his colleagues that certain procedures constitute the best means by which to secure these ends. (Even technical treatises, which attempt no persuasion, do imply a special situation; the writer assumes that he is writing for people whose interest in the truth is so absorbing that rhetorical persuasions would be unnecessary and even positively irritating.)

Just as every discourse implies a situation in which the writer is related to his audience, so every discourse also implies a certain tone. This term *tone* is based frankly on a metaphor. We all know how important in speech the tone of voice may be in indicating the precise meaning of the words. For instance, the words *very well* uttered in a certain tone of voice imply enthusiastic agreement, but spoken in another tone of voice they indicate nothing more than surly compliance. The "tone" of a piece of writing, in the same way, may show the writer's attitude, and in so doing may heavily qualify the literal meaning of the words.

The importance of tone is easily illustrated by the misunderstandings that personal letters so often provoke. In conversation, even a rather clumsy and inadequate knowledge of language can be so supplemented by the actual tone of the voice that little serious misunderstanding will occur.

But when such a speaker writes a letter—where, of course, the "tone of voice" cannot be actually heard but has to be implied by the words themselves—all sorts of misunderstandings can, and frequently do, occur. The practiced writer, however, is able even in this medium to control what we have called the "tone."

Although we have rarely used the word, we have been dealing with the problem of tone throughout this book. For example, when in the chapter on Persuasion (pp. 241–45), we talked about the occasion of an argument and the right way to present it, we were concerned with the problem of tone. In the chapter on Diction (pp. 414–18) we touched upon the problem of tone when we discussed the associations of words and the way in which certain words are colored by our attitude—the word *cop,* as used to refer to a police officer, and *rube,* as used to refer to a farmer. Again, we saw in the chapter on Metaphor (p. 436) the ways in which comparisons—"He's a square," "She's a doll," "He's a nut"—express our attitudes. All such devices represent means for controlling tone. But tone is more than these devices; it is a pervasive quality that characterizes the whole composition, and it is a matter so important in its own right that it deserves special discussion.

The importance of tone

In most of our writing an important part of what we are trying to "communicate" is our own attitude. This is certainly true of poetry and fiction, but it is also true of most essays, sermons, orations, and letters. It is true too of much of what we are inclined to regard as pure exposition. For even in expository writing the author is rarely content to give us mere facts, or mere propositions. He feels that to do this is to be painfully and technically "dry."

Konrad Lorenz's "Jackdaws" (Readings, pp. 629–37) will provide a good example. Lorenz is a distinguished scientist. Sir Julian Huxley, a former Director-General of UNESCO, calls him "one of the outstanding naturalists of our day," remarking that it is to Lorenz "more than any other single man that we owe our knowledge of the existence of the strange biological phenomena of 'releaser' and 'imprinting' mechanisms."

In writing *King Solomon's Ring* (the book from which "Jackdaws" is excerpted), Lorenz evidently thinks of himself as a scientist—not as a popularizer and certainly not as a literary artist. In his Preface he tells us, ". . . my only chance of writing something not entirely devoid of charm lies in strict adherence to scientific fact." Yet sticking to scientific fact doesn't require either holding his reader at arm's length or leaving out the personal delight he took in his jackdaws. Though a scientific report on the mechanisms governing bird behavior, "Jackdaws" takes the form of a friendly conversation about a personal experience.

Lorenz's discussion of the "imprinting mechanism" is typical of his manner. On page 631 he writes:

> [In] a bird that has been reared by hand, the natural harmony of [the design of inherited and acquired elements of behavior] is necessarily somewhat disturbed. All those social actions and reactions whose object is not determined by inheritance, but acquired by individual experience, are apt to become unnaturally deflected. In other words, they are directed toward human beings, instead of fellow-members of the bird's species, . . . so Jock [a jackdaw that Lorenz had reared], had he been able to speak, would certainly have called himself a human being. Only the sight of a pair of flapping black wings sounded a hereditary note: 'Fly with us.' As long as he was walking, he considered himself a man. . . .

This account of "imprinting," though not put in technical language, is accurate and quite as precise as the occasion demands.

What attitude does Lorenz adopt toward his reader? How does he envisage his reader? Clearly he does not expect him to be a professional zoologist—nor even a member of the Audubon Society or a semiprofessional birdwatcher. He aims at a general, nonprofessional reader who does not require special rhetorical accommodation as a fellow scientist might (or as might, in a very different way, a city official bent on eliminating jackdaws from city buildings).

Yet though Lorenz does not expect his reader to have technical knowledge, he does obviously assume that the reader is generally well informed about the world that scientists and laymen alike share. If he knows nothing about the behavior of jackdaws, he does know something about the behavior of dogs and other domesticated animals. He has intelligence and common sense. He can follow a clearly stated argument, though with unfamiliar material he will benefit from concrete illustrations.

The text of "Jackdaws" reveals that Lorenz makes one further assumption: he expects his reader to be at least moderately well read in literature and history. It is taken for granted that the reader knows Rudyard Kipling's story about the boy Mowgli, who was brought up by wolves, and that, whether or not he has ever read the poem that Catullus wrote on the death of his mistress's pet sparrow, he has probably at least heard of Catullus and can be reminded of his poetry and "the loose-living ladies of Roman society."

To reconstruct the kind of person for whom Lorenz is writing is to suggest Lorenz's attitude toward him. Lorenz does not preen himself on his own superior knowledge. He does not "talk down" to his reader; rather, he proceeds to share with him a delightful and rewarding personal experience, and one that, as Lorenz tells us, may give us all some "inkling of the infinite beauty of our fellow creatures. . . ." Such is the spirit in which Lorenz addresses his reader. The tone of his discourse may be described as one of friendly and relaxed informality.

Attitude toward subject

There are, of course, subjects that scarcely permit informality of tone, even when being presented to intimates. To take an extreme case, here is a quotation from a sermon by the great seventeenth-century poet and preacher John Donne:

> Make haste to have these spiritual graces; to desire them is to begin to have them: But make not too much haste in the way. Do not think thy self purer than thou art because thou seest another do some such sins as thou hast forborne.
>
> Beloved, at last, when Christ Jesus comes with his scales, thou shalt not be weighed with that man, but every man shall be weighed with God: *Be pure as your Father in heaven is pure,* is the weight that must try us all; and then, the purest of us all that trusts to his own purity must hear that fearful *Mene Tekel Upharsin,* Thou art weighed, thou art found too light. . . .

Donne addresses his congregation intimately and directly. He even calls them "beloved," but no matter how close a relation the preacher assumes to exist, the urgency of the subject forbids informality. He uses simple and realistic language, that is true; but the seriousness of the subject pervades his language.

One is apt to think of death as a subject that always requires seriousness of tone. Banter about a mother's grief for the loss of her son or jesting at the plight of a man condemned to death would indicate that the jester was silly or callous. Yet this is not to say that humor and wit are incompatible with the presentation of even so serious a subject as death. A standard joke is that which tells how a condemned man, being led out to the gallows in the cold dawn, asks for a handkerchief to put around his neck to keep from catching cold. When Mercutio, in Shakespeare's *Romeo and Juliet,* makes a joke about his death wound and says that it is "not so deep as a well, nor so wide as a church door; but 'tis enough, 'twill serve," we are not offended. The condemned man and Mercutio are making light of their own distress. This is a very different matter from someone's making fun of another's agony. Moreover, Mercutio's ability to joke at his own plight has something gallant about it. It works as a kind of understatement, undercutting the expected note of seriousness.

Levity about serious subjects, then, is acceptable when somehow the writer recognizes his own share, directly or merely by sympathy, in some human situation, and through humor rises above it. For example, jokes, and humor in general, about sex and death are universal; but these are subjects for humor only because they are of universal importance and concern us all. Because we have, with reference to these subjects, enormously complicated attitudes, a well-calculated, humorous thrust can sometimes resolve the emotional complication, strike through to a simple attitude, and provide a sudden sense of release in laughter.

Yet we must remember that humor on a serious subject always requires tact and discrimination. It may help us understand the need for tact if we will think of our "writing situation" as analogous to a social situation. (See pp. 21–27.) What kind of reader are we addressing? What can we assume about him? Is he a person who can respond to the humor or is he a person who will be shocked by it? Sometimes, of course, the writer wants to shock. But then he should ask himself whether he wants to shock just to show off, or whether the shock is to make a point, to bring some new awareness to the reader. And always we can recognize that there are certain situations in which levity can only be offensive and, worse, silly. To take a most extreme instance, it is hard to imagine a person who would show levity in discussing the Passion of Christ. Blasphemy would be, in a sense, comprehensible, for, in a backhand way, blasphemy always recognizes the seriousness of the thing blasphemed. It is like an inverted prayer, we might say. But levity would be incomprehensible.

We have been dealing with an extreme instance simply because the extreme case makes the principles involved readily clear. When we come, however, to ordinary subjects we can still see how tone may be related to subject. The material dealt with in the excerpt from C. S. Lewis's "The Abolition of Man" (Readings, pp. 652–57) cannot be treated breezily if one believes, as Lewis does, that the threat to man is a serious one. Or if the writer should treat it breezily, he would have to set the lightness, the humor, against the basic seriousness of his intention.

■ APPLICATIONS

I   Student unrest is a serious issue. It is certainly so for university administrators and faculties and of course for most students. Important principles are at stake and passions have run high. (See the articles by Lewis S. Feuer, Edgar Z. Friedenberg, Stephen Spender, David McReynolds, and Bruno Bettelheim in the Readings, pp. 699–745.) Here is the way in which Art Buchwald treats the student revolt in his newspaper column for February 27, 1969.

SON OFF TO CAMPUS WARS; PARENTS SOB

"You'd better get over to the Diamonds' right away," my wife said when I came home the other night.

"What's the trouble?"

"I don't know, but they sounded terribly upset."

I dashed over to the Diamond house and found Larry and Janet in the living room looking as if the world had fallen apart.

"What is it?" I asked.

"Billy got his draft notice," Janet said.

"He's been drafted?"

"It's worse," Larry said. "He's just been accepted for college."

"That couldn't be so bad."

"He's been accepted at the University of Wisconsin," Janet cried.

I didn't know what to say.

Larry shook his head. "You work all your life for your children and then one day, out of the blue, they grab them and that's it."

"But even if they accepted him, he doesn't have to go," I said.

"You don't understand," Janet said. "He wants to go. He said he can't sit at home doing nothing when so many college kids are sacrificing so much on the campuses."

Larry said, "He wants to be where the action is."

"Billy always had a sense of duty," I said.

"I tried to talk him into going into the Army instead," Larry told me. "But he said, 'Dad, I would be shirking my responsibilities. That's the coward's way out. I have to go where my friends are fighting.'"

Janet sobbed, "I told him to go into the Army for four years and then perhaps the fighting on the campuses would be over. But he said, 'Mother, I could never face my children if they asked me some day what I did during the war on campus and I had to tell them I was in the Army while it was going on.'"

"You have to be proud of him," I said.

"What do you mean, proud?" Larry said. "It's foolhardy. He doesn't know what he's getting into. All he sees is the glamor of it. The blue jeans and the dirty sweater and the beard. But I told him there's more to going to college than that. College is a dirty, miserable business, and it isn't just bands playing and flags waving and girls kissing you in the dormitories."

Janet nodded her head sadly. "I guess he saw too many TV programs about college riots and it went to his head."

Larry said, "Even as a little boy he always had his heart set on college. He used to stage sit-ins in the kitchen, and he picketed our bedroom at night, and once he locked his grandfather in the bathroom because his grandfather wouldn't grant him amnesty for using a naughty word."

"I thought it was a stage all kids go through, so I didn't take it seriously. If I had known he was truly thinking of going to college, I certainly wouldn't have encouraged it."

I tried to cheer my friends up. "Maybe he'll be all right. Don't forget, not everybody who goes to college gets arrested. If he comes out of it without a criminal record, it could be a very broadening experience. Why, some kids even get an education from college."

Janet was really crying. "You're just saying that to buck us up. You really don't believe it, do you?"

I looked at the distraught couple. "I have friends at the University of Wisconsin," I told them. "Perhaps I could use my influence to get Billy into night school. Then, at least, he'll be safe." [1]

What is the tone of this short narrative? Does Buchwald take a frivolous attitude toward what is really a matter of grave concern? Does this bit of fantasy strike you as funny or as reprehensible? If you do find it funny, why? Might it seem funny even to an activist student? Why might such a student see

[1] "Son off to Campus Wars; Parents Sob" by Art Buchwald, *Washington Post*, February 27, 1969. Reprinted by permission of Art Buchwald.

the humor in it? What has Buchwald done to ensure that the reader takes it "in the right way"?

II Read Art Buchwald's "Prof 'Understanding' Right Up to the End" (Readings, pp. 765–67). Buchwald is here writing jokingly about a man about to be lynched. This is the sort of situation that we said on page 469 could hardly be treated humorously. In your opinion does Buchwald get away with his joke? If he does, why?

So much for possible treatments of an essentially serious issue. For a light subject a light treatment is obviously appropriate. We do not want deadpan solemnity—unless, of course, that solemnity is indeed part of the joke. Thurber's "dog that bit people" (pp. 754–59) is a semifabulous creature whose story has to be told with a certain lightness of touch. The charm of the story depends upon the preposterousness of the subject matter coupled with the calm precision of Thurber's way of talking about it. Or to look ahead (p. 475), observe the mock-serious, almost mock-heroic, elements in the passage from "Farewell, My Lovely," Lee Strout White's essay on the Model T. Ford.

Thus far we have concerned ourselves with two extremes: seriousness and levity. Needless to say, there are hundreds of shadings between these extremes. The possible variations of tone are almost infinite.

Attitude toward the audience

Up to this point, we have, for the most part, emphasized tone as indicating the writer's attitude toward his subject, or the attitude that the subject might demand from the writer. But the writer's attitude toward the audience is equally important. It is so important that one can scarcely talk about the attitude toward the subject without drifting over into a discussion of the audience. (See p. 489.)

Let us suppose that we are writing in support of (or maybe attacking) our country's present policy toward Red China. The subject itself would, of course, allow certain different kinds of tone. We know that there is no merely mechanical equation between subject and tone. But the subject is a serious one, and though humor and satire might enter, flippancy could not. The demands of the subject would, however, be only one consideration in our attempt to find a proper tone. Our presentation of the topic to a friendly audience, one that tended to agree with the basic policy that we were advancing and that merely wanted further clarification, would scarcely be adequate for a hostile audience. We might want to persuade the hostile audience and lead them bit by bit to agreement. We might want to find the common ground (pp. 167–69) and try to show that once they recognize it they will have to follow, step by logical step, to the policy we advocate. We might want to shock the audience into an awareness of the necessity of that policy. We might, in fact, try any number of approaches, and each approach, or combination of approaches, would imply a different tone. And each possible tone would, of course, be different from the tone appropriate to mere explanation that we might use with a friendly audience.

Considerations of friendliness and hostility are, however, not the only ones that determine the writer's attitude toward his audience. The knowledge that a special audience possesses and their interests and concerns are also determining factors. It will make a difference if our essay about our China policy is to appear in a technical journal edited for specialists in political science; or in *Fortune* magazine edited for prosperous businessmen; or on a newspaper editorial page; or in *Harper's Magazine*. It will make a difference if we read a paper on the subject before a college forum, or a California audience with its keen awareness of the Orient, or a midwestern chamber of commerce dinner. The same tone would not necessarily serve for all.

The advertising page will furnish another example of the way in which a writer's attitude toward his audience determines tone. Advertising puts a special premium on catching and holding the interest of the reader. The advertising copywriter who did not understand some of the elementary principles of the control of tone would soon be on his way to the nearest government unemployment relief office.

Consider the following advertisement. It is printed in full color and depicts a young woman on a luxurious bed looking dreamily at a handsome blanket. The caption begins: "For you to whom beauty is a necessity. . . . Yours is a nature that thrives on beauty. . . . Seize it as a vital factor in your daily living. To you a blanket should be more than a source of warmth. Exquisite colors, luxuriously deep nap, rich, virgin-wool loveliness— these awaken in you an emotional response far beyond the material."

These statements, of course, are not addressed merely to the young woman pictured in the advertisement. They are addressed to the reader as well, and they make certain flattering assumptions about the reader: that she is a young woman of means who is at home with the luxurious and who has a soul that deserves and requires beauty as a necessity. Coarser natures may buy blankets simply for warmth, but you, dear and lovely reader, require aesthetic pleasure as well.

■ APPLICATIONS

I   Here are the leads into four advertisements in a recent issue of *The New Yorker:*

A   In Palm Beach, the important people will live at The Sun and Surf. . . .

B   Norman Hilton isn't everywhere. Just at the stores that are accustomed to catering to the clothing needs of a select clientele. . . .

C   Countess Mara designs for "one man in a million." Just as women look forward to the new couture collections, many men watch for the new Countess Mara ties. . . .

D   Sophisticated people like the simplest things. Like the table shown [below], for instance. (Or is it a desk?) It's just a basic rectangle of steel and rosewood. Simple. . . .

What is the basis of the appeal made in each of these advertisements? What attitude toward the reader is implied by this appeal?

II   Tom Cat. A man's cologne for a tiger state of mind. A prestige collection of manly lotions. . . .

Does this advertisement flatter the reader? Promise anything? Capitalize on his sense of inadequacy? Try to state the attitude taken toward the reader.

III Select five advertisements from current magazines and state the primary basis of the appeal made to the reader. What attitude is taken toward the reader? What statements or devices in the advertisement suggest this attitude?

IV What kind of audience does T. H. Huxley address in "The Method of Scientific Investigation" (Readings, pp. 619–25)? How do you infer this from the tone of the essay? What adjustments to a particular audience are indicated by the style of his essay?

V   Reread the student theme "Teachers I Have Known" (pp. 98–99) and imagine that you are writing it for a teacher who you think probably knows something about his subject but who is quite dull in the classroom. Perhaps you might turn in this draft to him as it stands. Perhaps it will not hurt his feelings, or the hurt may actually be good for him. But with him in mind, could you render this theme more persuasive? Try rewriting some sections of it, particularly paragraphs 3 and 4, to see whether you can improve the tone as directed toward the special reader we have described.

Tone as a Qualification of Meaning

We began our discussion of tone with special emphasis on tone as a reflection of the author's attitude—his specification as to how we are to "take" what he is saying. But it should be apparent by now that tone also represents a qualification of meaning—a shaping of what is to be said. Indeed, a little reflection will show that full meaning is rarely conveyed by merely literal statement. In order to understand a letter we find that we must "read between the lines," and we usually discover that if we are to understand fully a conversation with a friend it helps to take into account his tone of voice and facial expression. Tone as a guide to meaning is particularly important in essays that deal with valuations and judgments.

For example, consider the importance of the tone in the following passage describing the old Model T Ford:

> I see by the new Sears Roebuck catalogue that it is still possible to buy an axle for a 1909 Model T Ford, but I am not deceived. The great days have faded, the end is in sight. Only one page in the current catalogue is devoted to parts and accessories for the Model T; yet everyone remembers springtimes when the Ford gadget section was larger than men's clothing, almost as large as household furnishings. The last Model T was built in 1927, and the car is fading from what scholars call the American scene— which is an understatement, because to a few million people who grew up with it, the Old Ford practically *was* the American scene.
>
> It was the miracle God had wrought. And it was patently the sort of thing that could only happen once. Mechanically uncanny, it was like nothing that had ever come to the world before. Flourishing industries rose and fell with it. As a vehicle, it was hard-working, commonplace, heroic; and it often seemed to transmit those qualities to the persons who rode in it. My own generation identifies it with Youth, with its gaudy, irretrievable excitements; before it fades into the mist, I would like to pay it the tribute of the sigh that is not a sob, and set down random entries in a shape somewhat less cumbersome than a Sears Roebuck catalogue.
>
> The Model T was distinguished from all other makes of cars by the fact that its transmission was of a type known as planetary—which was half metaphysics, half sheer friction. Engineers accepted the word "planetary" in its epicyclic sense, but I was always conscious that it also means "wandering," "erratic." Because of the peculiar nature of this planetary element, there was always, in Model T, a certain dull rapport between engine and wheels, and, even when the car was in a state known as neutral, it trembled with a deep imperative and tended to inch forward. There was never a moment when the bands were not faintly egging the machine on. In this respect it was like a horse, rolling the bit on its tongue, and country people brought to it the same technique they used with draft animals.
>
> —LEE STROUT WHITE: "Farewell, My Lovely." [2]

To enjoy the passage just quoted one must be aware that the author laments the passing of the Model T with mock seriousness. The game that the author plays is to invest with literary allusions and sentimental clichés a piece of machinery that seems to belong to a nonliterary and nonsentimental world. Suppose we remove the tone of mock lament and simply state the facts literally and directly. Here is what we might have if we treated the first paragraph in this fashion.

> The new Sears Roebuck catalogue indicates that one may still purchase an axle for a 1909 Model T Ford. But this possibility, though interesting, does not mean that the Model T Ford is any longer an important factor in American transportation. The section of the catalogue devoted to Ford

---

[2] "From "Farewell, My Lovely," by Lee Strout White, *The New Yorker,* May 16, 1936. This is part of the essay which originally appeared in *The New Yorker.* Reprinted by permission. Copr. © 1936, 1964 The New Yorker Magazine, Inc.

parts, once larger than that devoted to men's clothing, has now shrunk to a single page. No Model T's have been built since 1927, and this model is rapidly disappearing from the American highway.

The rewriting, by altering the tone, destroys the humor. It does something more. It destroys a good deal of what the passage "says." For the real content of the passage is the presentation of a certain complex attitude toward some aspects of American life. The author's real concern is with American social history, and he presents that history, not clinically and "sociologically," but affectionately and a little whimsically. The tone, then, is a most important element in "what" the author is saying.

■ APPLICATION

"The Age of Overkill" (Readings, pp. 692–98) purports to be written by a historian of about the year 2000, looking back at our troubled period. How would you describe the tone of this essay? How would you go about altering the tone to one of contemporary approval, say, or one of real clinical detachment? Rewrite the first three paragraphs to effect such a change in tone.

Lest the importance of tone in "Farewell, My Lovely" be thought a special case, consider the importance of tone in the following definition of a weed:

> What is a weed? I have heard it said that there are sixty definitions. For me, a weed is a plant out of place. Or, less tolerantly, call it a foreign aggressor, which is a thing not so mild as a mere escape from cultivation, a visitor that sows itself innocently in a garden bed where you would not choose to plant it. Most weeds have natal countries, whence they have sortied. So Japanese honeysuckle, English plantain, Russian thistle came from lands we recognize, but others, like gypsies, have lost all record of their geographic origin. Some of them turn up in all countries, and are listed in no flora as natives. Some knock about the seaports of the world, springing up wherever ballast used to be dumped from the old sailing ships. Others prefer cities; they have lost contact with sweet soil, and lead a guttersnipe existence. A little group occurs only where wool waste is dumped, others are dooryard and pavement weeds, seeming to thrive the more as they are trod by the feet of man's generations. Some prized in an age of simpler tastes have become garden *déclassés* and street urchins; thus it comes about that the pleasant but plebeian scent of Bouncing Bet, that somewhat blowsy pink of old English gardens, is now one of the characteristic odors of American sidewalk ends, where the pavement peters out and shacks and junked cars begin.
>
> —DONALD CULROSS PEATTIE: *Flowering Earth.*[3]

---

[3] From *Flowering Earth* by Donald Culross Peattie. Reprinted by permission of Noel R. Peattie and his agent, James Brown Associates, Inc. Copyright © 1939 by Donald Culross Peattie.

We could describe a weed as follows:

> A weed may be defined as a plant that, though growing in cultivated ground, is economically useless and is a detriment to the crop being cultivated. Yet, it must be conceded that this definition is somewhat subjective, for a plant considered useless by one person might be counted useful by another, and a plant ordinarily cultivated for its own sake might be regarded as a nuisance when found in a field planted to some other crop. But there is general agreement on most of the plants that we call weeds. Some examples would be dog fennel, dock, mullein, and ragweed.

This paragraph may be thought to give substantially the same definition as that given in the paragraph by Peattie. But it is relatively toneless. The author is not visualizing any particular audience, and he does not seem to have a particular attitude toward his subject. As a consequence, this paragraph is quite without personality.

Notice how much of the writer's personality comes through in the original passage. Peattie is obviously familiar with the various "flora" and knows which plants are listed in them and which are not. But his discussion is not intended to be a technical description; rather it is a more desultory and amiable account of weeds. Peattie is a man of perception, with keen senses ("the pleasant but plebeian scent of Bouncing Bet," "the characteristic odors of American sidewalk ends"). He evidently has a sense of humor. He is aware of current politics ("foreign aggressor"). He has a sense of history.

In short, in this passage we get the play of an informed and sensitive mind—a mind that special knowledge has not made stuffy—and of a personality that savors, with evident enjoyment, the varied and amusing world. In this connection notice how a central metaphor that treats the weed as a human being who has broken bounds runs through the whole passage, and how this metaphor is varied through the passage to express the varying aspects of weeds in general and of certain weeds in particular. One weed may be like a "foreign aggressor" to be resisted; another, like an immigrant or colonist from another land; still another, like a gypsy whose original homeland is lost in obscurity. Some weeds, like groups of immigrants, remain near the seaports where they made their first entry. Other weeds have migrated from country to city. They have moved in from the provinces and have become citified and now lead a "guttersnipe" existence. Still other weeds are like human beings who have come down in the world and, having lost pride of class and dignity, are now happily and frowsily plebeian. The general comparison of the weed to the human migrant is flexible enough to provide quite specific illustrations of the various kinds of weeds. The metaphor not only renders the abstract definition concrete, but it suggests Peattie's own attitude toward weeds and, in fact, the world in general—an attitude of genial and good-humored amusement.

Notice, too, how the diction unobtrusively but powerfully supports the variations of the basic metaphor. "Foreign aggressor" is pointed up by the use of the word "sortied." (The word *sortie* means a sally of troops, a military raid.) "Guttersnipe existence" sharpens the hint given by "others prefer cities." "Plebeian" and "somewhat blowsy" support and extend the suggestions made by *"déclassés."*

The diction, of course, does something more. Though Peattie is willing to use a technical term like *flora,* most of his words are specific and concrete. Moreover, he does not hesitate to use colloquial expressions like "knock about" and "peters out." Peattie is not at all like the fabled scholar who knew all the pedantic terms but could not address a dog in his own dialect. He accommodates his diction to the wholesome vulgarity of his subject.

The preceding discussion of Peattie's paragraph may seem overelaborate, but it is usually difficult to define a particular tone without using many more words than the author himself used to achieve it. There is, moreover, a justification for the attention that we have given to this one paragraph. We have wanted to illustrate the fact that a particular tone depends upon various factors—diction and metaphor as well as the larger principles of composition. Tone, indeed, represents a kind of final integration of all the elements that go into a piece of writing. Writing that is toneless or confused in tone is usually bad writing.

■ APPLICATIONS

I Art Buchwald ends a protest against a proposal to ground airline stewardesses at the age of thirty-two with the following paragraphs:

> Younger stewardesses also have a tendency to upset the passengers. Many times I've witnessed wives becoming furious at their husbands because the husbands were watching a pretty young thing in uniform strut down the aisle. I've also seen grown men upset trays of food, just because some young hostess leaned over to adjust their safety belts. But nothing happens with the older, more mature hostesses. They have the air of a professional nurse about them. Your eyes don't have to stray from your magazine every time they walk by. You can keep your thoughts on where you're going and what you're going to do.
>
> And one more thing. Older hostesses know how to cook better. Have you ever compared a meal prepared on board a plane by a twenty-one-year-old hostess with one prepared by a thirty-two-year-old hostess?
>
> There is just no comparison.
>
> There are many of us flying today who are not interested in looking at a young, pretty, sexy girl in uniform. We believe in chic older women in their thirties.
>
> I sincerely hope American Airlines reconsiders its policy almost as much as I hope my wife reads this.[4]

---

[4] Reprinted by permission of The World Publishing Co. from *I Chose Capitol Punishment* by Art Buchwald. Copyright © 1962, 1963 by Art Buchwald. Reprinted by permission of Art Buchwald.

How would you describe the tone? What are some of the ways in which Buchwald lets you know that his "protest" is very much tongue-in-cheek?

II For what audience is the following paragraph written? Has the audience been visualized by the writer? Could it be said that the writing is "toneless"? If so, is its tonelessness a defect or a virtue?

> Before intelligent criteria can be developed for the selection of superimposed leaders, the organization, through its professional staff, must first clearly define the objectives of its group program and establish qualifications for group leadership. Second, these objectives must be made clear to the leaders. In group work terminology the concept *socialization* appears as the central objective, but in the experience of the writer little effort has been made to define this concept so as to be understandable to the leader.
>
> —From a magazine of social research.

III What kind of audience is the author addressing in the passage below? How do you know? Compare the tone of this paragraph with the tone of the fifth and sixth paragraphs of "The Method of Scientific Investigation" (Readings, pp. 620–22).

> When the quest is for a material of inexplicable behavior, of unique and spectacular qualities, water has all other chemicals licked for first place. True, it is the most abundant material on the Earth's surface. If suddenly all the water on the Earth could be broken into its constituent gases and released into the air, the atmospheric pressure (now 15 pounds) would become 6,000 pounds to the square-inch. That's how much water there is. And its quantity is increasing continually. Every fire we light, every explosion we set off, every puff of a cigarette, combines some particles of oxygen to build new water and release it to the air. Yes, water is common, and continually becoming more so. —George W. Gray: "Little Drops of Water."

Literal statement and ironical statement

Irony always involves a discrepancy between what is said literally and what the statement actually means. On the surface the ironical statement says one thing, but it means something rather different. In a lighthearted, laughingly ironical statement, the literal meaning may be only partially qualified; in a bitter and obvious irony (such as sarcasm), the literal meaning may be completely reversed. An example of rather lighthearted and affectionate irony occurs in the discussion of the Model T Ford by Lee Strout White (see p. 475). The little car is treated in almost mock-heroic style ("It was the miracle God had wrought. . . . it was patently the sort of thing that could only happen once. . . . before it fades into the mist, I would like to pay it the tribute of the sigh that is not a sob. . . ."). The informal essay frequently makes use of some form of gentle irony such as this.

A sample of ordinary sarcasm might be represented by a student's outburst at his roommate: "A fine friend you turn out to be, borrowing my car and taking my girl on a date." The literal meaning that proclaims the roommate to be a fine young man is just the opposite of what his irate friend means to say about him.

Between the more delicate ironical qualifications and the sarcastic reversal there are a thousand shadings possible, and it may seem a pity that we do not have specific terms by which to describe them. Yet, on second thought, our lack of such terms may be no real handicap. We can develop these qualifications of meaning without in the least needing to give them a label. Having a glossary of terms is not important; what is important is to be aware of the fact of ironical qualification.

In the following passage the novelist Saul Bellow argues that, contrary to the usual suppositions, New York City is not the literary capital of the United States.

> New York is a publishing center, the business center of American culture. Here culture is prepared, processed, and distributed. Here the publishers with their modern apparatus for printing, billing, shipping, editing, advertising, and accounting, with their specialized personnel wait for manuscripts. Their expenses are tremendous, they cannot afford to wait too long; they must find material somewhere, attract writers or fabricate books in their editorial offices. New York, of course, includes Washington and Boston. Some of its literary mandarins actually live in Cambridge, in New Haven, Bennington, New Brunswick, Princeton, a few are in London and Oxford. These officials of high culture write for the papers, sit on committees, advise, consult, set standards, define, drink cocktails, gossip—they give body to New York's appearance of active creativity, its apparently substantial literary life. But there is no substance. There is only the *idea* of a cultural life. There are manipulations, rackets, power struggles, there is infighting, there are reputations, inflated and deflated. Bluster, vehemence, swagger, fashion, image-making, brain-fixing. These are what the center has to offer.
>
> —SAUL BELLOW: "Skepticism and the Depth of Life." [5]

Notice the ironic flavor given to this passage by the use of business terms like "processed," "distributed," "fabricate," and so forth. What are some of the other devices that Bellow uses to expose New York's false pretensions to creativity and literate culture?

Max Beerbohm's "The Decline of the Graces" (Readings, pp. 759–64) is an informal essay on the education of young women nearly a century and a half ago. Here is part of his first paragraph:

> Have you read *The Young Lady's Book?* You have had plenty of time to do so for it was published in 1829. It was described by the two anonymous Gentlewomen who compiled it as "A Manual for Elegant Recreations, Exercises, and Pursuits." You wonder they had nothing better to think of? You suspect them of having been triflers? They were not, believe me. They were careful to explain, at the outset, that the Virtues of Character were what a young lady should most assiduously cultivate. They, in their day, laboring under the shadow of the eighteenth century, had some-

---

[5] Reprinted by permission of the author.

how in themselves that high moral fervor which marks the opening of the twentieth century, and is said to have come in with Mr. George Bernard Shaw. But, unlike us, they were not concerned wholly with the inward and spiritual side of life. They cared for the material surface, too. They were learned in the frills and furbelows of things.

How seriously would you say Beerbohm takes the old-fashioned education of young women? He certainly *pretends* to take it seriously. What is his tone, and how does he at once establish it? What is Beerbohm's attitude toward his reader? At what kind of reader is Beerbohm aiming?

The following passage is from a review of Gertrude Stein's account of her own life in a book entitled *Everybody's Autobiography*. The review was written by Katherine Anne Porter, the short-story writer and novelist.

> Still earlier she was a plump solemn little girl abundantly upholstered in good clothes, who spent her allowance on the works of Shelley, Thackeray, and George Eliot in fancy bindings, for she loved reading and *Clarissa Harlowe* was once her favorite novel. These early passions exhausted her; in later life she swam in the relaxing bath of detective and murder mysteries, because she liked somebody being dead in a story, and of them all Dashiell Hammett killed them off most to her taste. Her first experience of the real death of somebody had taught her that it could be pleasant for her, too. "One morning we could not wake our father." This was in East Oakland, California. "Leo climbed in by the window and called out that he was dead in his bed and he was." It seems to have been the first thing he ever did of which his children, all five of them, approved. Miss Stein declared plainly they none of them liked him at all: "As I say, fathers are depressing but our family had one," she confessed, and conveys the notion that he was a bore of the nagging, petty sort, the kind that worries himself and others into the grave.
>
> Considering her tepid, sluggish nature, really sluggish like something eating its way through a leaf, Miss Stein could grow quite animated on the subject of her early family life, and some of her stories are as pretty and innocent as lizards running over tombstones on a hot day in Maryland.
>
> —KATHERINE ANNE PORTER: *The Days Before*.

In this passage there is, to be sure, a certain amount of perfectly direct commentary. But what gives the passage its biting power is the calm assumption by the author that what she is describing in Miss Stein's conduct is somehow perfectly characteristic of her. The tone of detached, clinical commentary sets up an ironic contrast with the material that is actually under discussion and so becomes powerfully expressive. (Incidentally, is "sluggish" a pun? If you judge that it is intended to be one, do you think it is justified here?)

● CAUTION

The effectiveness of writing in which the tone is skillfully controlled by a master of style may so impress a young writer that he will try to exercise the same kind of subtlety. And well he may, in aspiration at least, for skillful management of tone is an ideal toward which he should strive. But a successful manipulation of tone does not come easy, and in his early efforts at more subtle tonal effects the novice may blunder into awkwardness or into an irony that seems too contrived and "cute." He must be cautious about going beyond his own resources at the beginning. Even so, it will not hurt for him to begin to experiment with indirection and the oblique approach. Besides, he is no stranger to irony as a mode. He has been using it in conversation all his life. Slang and college repartee, for example, are full of irony and sarcasm.

■ APPLICATIONS

I The following paragraph occurs in Thackeray's novel *Vanity Fair:*

> Being an invalid, Joseph Sedley contented himself with a bottle of claret, besides his Madeira at dinner, and he managed a couple of plates full of strawberries and cream, and twenty-four little rout cakes, that were lying neglected in a plate near him, and certainly (for novelists have the privilege of knowing everything), he thought a great deal about the girl upstairs. "A nice, gay, merry young creature," thought he to himself. "How she looked at me when I picked up her handkerchief at dinner! She dropped it twice. Who's that singing in the drawing-room? Gad! shall I go up and see?"

What is Sedley's attitude toward himself? Toward food? Toward girls? Has Thackeray, by pretending to take Sedley's invalidism seriously, given us an insight into what kind of young man he is?

II The scene described below is a British club in India, some decades ago. The orchestra has just played "God Save the King." What is the author's attitude toward his fellow countrymen? The passage is obviously ironic, but what is the precise shading of irony? Is the author indignant? Mocking? Bitter? Or what?

> Meanwhile the performance ended, and the amateur orchestra played the National Anthem. Conversation and billiards stopped, faces stiffened. It was the Anthem of the Army of Occupation. It reminded every member of the club that he or she was British and in exile. It produced a little sentiment and a useful accession of will-power. The meager tune, the curt series of demands on Jehovah, fused into a prayer unknown in England, and though they perceived neither Royalty nor Deity they did perceive something, they were strengthened to resist another day. They poured out, offering one another drinks.
> —E. M. Forster: *A Passage to India.*

What does Forster mean by the "series of demands on Jehovah"? (Are you familiar with the words of "God Save the King"?)

III Here is a piece of advice on how to go about social climbing:

Even Emily Post offers a few demure suggestions to the "outsider": "The better, and the only way if she [a woman with social ambition] has not the key of birth, is through study to make herself eligible. Meanwhile, charitable or civic work will give her interest and occupation as well as throw her with ladies of good breeding, by association with whom she cannot fail to acquire some of those qualities before which the gates of society always open." The patronage of charity, church settlement work (Episcopalian), the financial support of hospitals, clinics, and opera are probably the safest route which the newcomer can travel. After she has given her cheque for a substantial sum and shown her eagerness to work for the cause, she will be asked to become a sustaining member and sit on the board with women she has wanted to know. Probably they will begin to ask her to tea, then to large parties and luncheons, and finally to dinner. If fortune has blessed her with a small daughter, let her be sent to a fashionable day school, where she will have classmates to be invited to a birthday party, and given expensive souvenirs; in this way a little child may lead them. No climber should overlook the broadening influences of travel; in crossing the Atlantic, cruising the Mediterranean, or circumnavigating the globe, one may get a good table by generous tipping and promptness, and then maneuver eligible acquaintances and celebrities into sitting there. Deck stewards also can do much for one, since during the course of a long voyage propinquity is almost irresistible.

—Dixon Wecter: *The Saga of American Society.*[6]

What is the quality of the irony employed in this passage? Define it as precisely as you can. What are some of the ironical devices employed?

IV In Application V (p. 474), you were asked to rewrite sections of the student theme "Teachers I Have Known" (pp. 98–99), in order to make the theme more persuasive. Now let us consider the possibility of making the tone ironical. As it now stands, the theme shows traces of irony. For example, the student asks: "Did they become teachers because they were really interested in their subject and in young people, or did they just drift into the profession through indifference or necessity?" But in general, the judgments are given directly and explicitly. Would there be any advantage in presenting the judgment against such teachers indirectly and ironically? Try rewriting this theme, making use of an ironical approach. Pretend, for example, that you are praising all teachers; or try to give a deadpan account of the teachers' faults as if you did not realize that they were faults.

V Compare and contrast the quality of irony in the following essays in the Readings:

A 1 Baker's "The Miniature Adults" (pp. 769–70)
2 Lowell's portrait of Commander Billy Harkness (pp. 873–74)
3 DeMott's "The Age of Overkill" (pp. 692–98)

[6] Reprinted with the permission of Charles Scribner's Sons from *The Saga of American Society* by Dixon Wecter. Copyright 1937 Charles Scribner's Sons; renewal copyright © 1965 Elizabeth Farrar Wecter.

Perhaps you think that one or another of the foregoing does not make use of irony. If so, indicate why.

B 1 Is there any irony in Laurie Lee's portrait of Alf (pp. 839–40)?
    2 In the portrait of Milliken in "Love in Paris" (pp. 766–68)?

C How would you characterize the irony in "Sandburg's 'The Cool Tombs' " (pp. 782–83)?

D Irony of situation is to be distinguished from irony of statement. The former is inherent in the situation itself and does not derive from the writer's manner of presentation. But obviously the two modes overlap, and usually it is the writer who makes his reader *aware* of the irony that is inherent in the situation. Do we find irony of situation or irony of statement (or both) in *Slouching Towards Bethlehem* (pp. 658–72)?

Overstatement and understatement

We have been occupied with the distinction between a literal and a nonliteral (including an ironic) use of words. But it is also useful to consider the problem of tone in the light of another distinction, that between overstatement and understatement. Overstatement, as the term implies, is redundancy: one says more than he needs to say. The term connotes gushiness —a straining after effects. In Bret Harte's story "The Outcasts of Poker Flat," a gambler and two prostitutes rise to heroism as they try to shelter and protect an innocent girl who has fallen into their company when they are overtaken by a severe snowstorm in the mountains. The gambler and the older prostitute starve themselves in order to provide more food for the young woman. In the last two paragraphs of the story, which follow, Harte describes the last days of the innocent girl and the younger prostitute.

> The wind lulled as if it feared to waken them. Feathery drifts of snow, shaken from the long pine boughs, flew like white-winged birds, and settled about them as they slept. The moon through the rifted clouds looked down upon what had been the camp. But all human stain, all trace of earthly travail, was hidden beneath the spotless mantle mercifully flung from above.
>
> They slept all day that day and the next, nor did they waken when voices and footsteps broke the silence of the camp. And when pitying fingers brushed the snow from their wan faces, you could scarcely have told from the equal peace that dwelt upon them which was she that had sinned.

Here the author, in his eagerness to describe the pathos of the scene and the redemption of the fallen woman, is not content to let the scene speak for itself. The wind lulls the two women; the moon looks down upon them; a "spotless mantle" is "mercifully flung from above." The pseudo-poetic language, the suggestion that nature mercifully hides "all human stain," the general absence of restraint and reserve—all indicate that the tone here is one of *sentimentality;* that is, emotion in excess of the occasion.

What was Bret Harte's own attitude? One has to conclude that either he himself was "soft" (that is, that he was taken in by his own attempt to "work up" an effect), or else he was cynically trying to seduce his reader into an emotional response that is not justified by the dramatic occasion that he provided. Whatever Harte's attitude, most sensitive readers will feel that the tone is sentimental. Sentimentality usually betrays itself by a straining to work up the reader's feelings. In a sense, of course, any appeal to our emotions represents an attempt to "work up" an effect. But it is one thing to do this legitimately by presenting a scene with imaginative power, and it is quite a different thing to try to bully or trick the reader into the desired emotional response. Readers may disagree on whether a particular response has been sought legitimately or illegitimately, but the principle involved is crucial. Otherwise any writer, however tawdry or mawkish, could demand our response simply by making a direct assault on our feelings.

The student may feel that in the kind of writing that he does there is little danger of his falling into sentimentality; and it is quite true that the particular temptations to which Bret Harte yielded are not likely to entrap him. But student themes present their own opportunities for overwriting. The theme in which a student tries to describe his grandfather and his mother (pp. 74–75) will illustrate. A few phrases like "the dearest Mom in all the world" would alter the effect much for the worse. The student's affection for his mother emerges quite clearly, but he lets us infer it from the way in which he writes about her. (The student themes quoted earlier in this text are in general admirably free from gush.)

We must not, however, associate overwriting merely with the softer emotions of love and pity. It can show itself in a strained attempt at humor or a hectic gaiety or a pretentious heartiness. Advertising copy will provide obvious instances (see pp. 473–74 and 489).

■ **APPLICATION**

The following is a paragraph from a late Victorian novel. A little boy who has brought a ray of sunshine into his wicked uncle's life has been asked by the dying man to watch beside his bedside.

> When the first faint streaks of early morning entered slowly at the half-curtained window, and chased away the shadows of the night, they fell upon a strange sight in the great silent room! An old man with motionless and pallid features, lying with his head turned a little to the light, and his hands crossed upon his breast,—the pitiful remnant of a worn-out and bootless life; and near him, in the deep arm-chair, a beautiful sleeping child, with bright hair falling loosely about his neck, and rosy rounded cheeks, and warm, moist dimples,—a soft, living, breathing creature, in the full flush of health

and youth; the very symbol of Life, as it lay there side by side with Death!
—Marguerite Bouvet: *A Little House in Pimlico.*

Count the adjectives and adverbs in this passage. Why are so many used? Could it be that the author is straining for an emotional effect not really warranted by the occasion? What other evidences of sentimentality are present?

THE VIRTUES OF UNDERSTATEMENT

Overstatement usually suggests a writer's lack of confidence in himself or in his reader. He is afraid to let his account speak for itself. Understatement, by contrast, assumes that the reader is sufficiently sensitive to make the proper response. Consequently, in skillful hands, understatement can become a powerful device for securing certain effects. One may illustrate by a passage from *Seven Pillars of Wisdom* in which T. E. Lawrence describes an incident that occurred in Arabia during World War I while he was serving with the Arabs in their revolt against Turkey. The incident took place while Lawrence was leading a raiding party of Arab tribesmen.

My followers had been quarrelling all day, and while I was lying near the rocks a shot was fired. I paid no attention; for there were hares and birds in the valley; but a little while later Suleiman roused me and made me follow across the valley to an opposite bay in the rocks, where one of the Ageyl, a Boreida man, was lying stone dead with a bullet through his temples. The shot must have been fired from close by; because the skin was burnt about one wound. The remaining Ageyl were running frantically about; and when I asked what it was, Ali, their head man, said that Hamed the Moor had done the murder. I suspected Suleiman, because of the feud between the Atban and Ageyl . . . but Ali assured me that Suleiman had been with him three hundred yards further up the valley gathering sticks when the shot was fired. I sent all out to search for Hamed, and crawled back to the baggage, feeling that it need not have happened this day of all days when I was in pain.

As I lay there I heard a rustle, and opened my eyes slowly upon Hamed's back as he stooped over his saddle-bags, which lay just beyond my rock. I covered him with a pistol and then spoke. He had put down his rifle to lift the gear; and was at my mercy till the others came. We held a court at once; and after a while Hamed confessed that, he and Salem having had words, he had seen red and shot him suddenly. Our inquiry ended. The Ageyl, as relatives of the dead man, demanded blood for blood. The others supported them; and I tried vainly to talk the gentle Ali round. My head was aching with fever and I could not think; but hardly even in health, with all eloquence, could I have begged Hamed off; for Salem had been a friendly fellow and his sudden murder a wanton crime.

Then rose up the horror which would make civilized man shun justice like a plague if he had not the needy to serve him as hangmen for wages. There were other Moroccans in our army; [Hamed the Moor was a Moroccan] and to let the Ageyl kill one in feud meant reprisals by which our unity would have been endangered. It must be a formal execution, and at last, desperately, I told Hamed that he must die for punishment, and laid the burden of his killing on myself. Perhaps they would count me not qualified for feud. At least no revenge could lie against my followers; for I was a stranger and kinless.

I made him enter a narrow gully of the spur, a dank twilight place overgrown with weeds. Its sandy bed had been pitted by trickles of water down the cliffs in the late rain. At the end it shrank to a crack a few inches wide. The walls were vertical. I stood in the entrance and gave him a few moments' delay which he spent crying on the ground. Then I made him rise and shot him through the chest. He fell down on the weeds shrieking, with the blood coming out in spurts over his clothes, and jerked about till he rolled nearly to where I was. I fired again, but was shaking so that I only broke his wrist. He went on calling out, less loudly, now lying on his back with his feet towards me, and I leant forward and shot him for the last time in the thick of his neck under the jaw. His body shivered a little, and I called the Ageyl; who buried him in the gully where he was. Afterwards the wakeful night dragged over me, till, hours before dawn, I had the men up and made them load, in my longing to be set free of Wadi Kitan. They had to lift me into the saddle.   —T. E. LAWRENCE: *Seven Pillars of Wisdom*.[7]

What is Lawrence's attitude toward Hamed? Toward the Arabs and their blood feuds? Most of all, toward himself? Is he ashamed of himself? Proud of himself? Complacent and untroubled about himself?

The incident is told with detachment and with studied restraint. But it is evident that Lawrence is not glossing over the incident casually and briefly. He develops it fully, giving us even minute details, for example, "bullet through his temples," "as he stooped over his saddle-bags," "shot him for the last time in the thick of his neck under the jaw." Even the scene of the execution, the gully, is described carefully and precisely: "Its sandy bed had been pitted by trickles of water down the cliffs in the late rain."

The narrator evidently remembers the whole incident vividly and knows how to make the incident vivid to his reader. Why, then, is he not more explicit about his own feelings and attitudes? Would anything have been gained if Lawrence had added a long paragraph describing his feelings as he decided that he must act as executioner? Would anything have been lost? Notice that Lawrence is willing to use the word "horror," but he does not write, "As a civilized man I was overwhelmed with horror," but rather, "Then rose up the horror which would make civilized man shun justice like a plague if he had not the needy to serve him as hangmen for wages." Why does Lawrence, in this most explicit account of his own feelings, prefer the generalized statement?

A little meditation on these questions is likely to result in some such conclusion as this: that Lawrence, far from remaining cool and detached, was indeed terribly shaken by the experience, but that, nevertheless, he preferred to make his *account* of the experience as detached and objective as he could. He chose to give a restrained description of his actions, leaving his reader to infer from the actions themselves what his feelings must have been.

This restraint has in itself an important effect on the tone: it implies a certain modesty (his own mental anguish is not allowed to dominate the story as if he thought his anguish the important thing in the episode), and it implies a certain confidence in the reader's maturity and sensitiveness— the reader need not be "told" what Lawrence was feeling. But the restraint here is of still further importance; the restraint manifested in Lawrence's *account* of his action is a reflection of, and a type of, the disciplined control that he imposed on his followers and on himself in the desert. The man who relates the action is the man who acted, and his manner of writing about the event suggests his attitude toward the event itself.

The foregoing incident may seem a little too special to be of much service to the student writer. But the rhetorical device of understatement is one that the student will constantly be using in his own work. It has already appeared in some of the student themes that we have read in earlier sections of this book. (See pp. 47, 74, and 333.) For example, in the student theme "Getting Engaged" (p. 283), the basic technique is that of understatement. The writer's fear at the coming of the storm and her excitement at the dangerous trip from the island to the mainland are merely implied. The writer has preferred to "understate" both of them. She has chosen to convey her own emotions about the former by giving us a detailed description of the storm cloud and then a detailed description of Joseph's face as he watches it. About her excitement at the perils of the trip home, she writes merely this:

> To make a long story short, we did manage to get in, but it was a tough trip. That evening we got engaged.

The engagement is the climax of the events of the day. Therefore, the writer has quite properly insisted upon putting it into sharp focus. But the mere announcement of the engagement is all that we need to know, for obviously it was the experience of real danger shared that made the young people realize that they wanted to spend the rest of their lives together.

The foregoing remarks should not leave the student with the feeling that he ought not to write as vividly as he can about exciting experiences. But first things should come first, and underplaying certain aspects of a composition may be a necessary way of putting certain other aspects into proper focus. Understatement is, among other things, a means of bringing about a proper proportioning of the various elements of the composition.

● CAUTION: SOME PRACTICAL DON'TS

The problem of tone, then, is most important. There are obviously too many shadings of tone for us to be able to set down elaborate rules for achieving the proper tone. But it is possible to set down a few "don'ts" that have very general application.

1 WRITING DOWN One must not "write down" to his audience. The sense of oversimple statement and painfully careful explanation can disgust the reader as quickly as any offense of which the writer is capable. Prose that is properly suited to an audience of eight-year-olds would prove completely tiresome or, on the other hand, unintentionally funny, to a mature audience. Take into account your reader's lack of special knowledge of your subject, but never underestimate your reader's intelligence. Don't explain your jokes.

2 FALSE ENTHUSIASM The reader is also likely to resent any hint of artificial breeziness and false camaraderie. Modern advertising leads the way in perpetuating this fault. Bug-eyed young matrons oo-la-la-ing over the purchase of sheets or toothbrushes and the synthetic joviality of super-salesmen more and more fill the advertisements. The student obviously wishes to gain a kind of liveliness and warmth in his style, but an artificial concoction of informality and sprightliness can be more depressing than a rather painful dryness.

3 SENTIMENTALITY This third fault is hardly likely to appear in most simple expository writing, but as we have seen in earlier chapters, there is very little writing that is "simply expository." Sentimentality may show itself as pure gushiness or as a kind of hair-trigger emotional sensitiveness. But whatever form it takes, sentimentality always involves an implied demand on the part of the writer for a greater emotional response than the situation warrants; and it implies, on the part of the sentimental reader, a willingness to respond emotionally when the response is not actually justified.

The Special Audience and the Ideal Audience

Earlier in this chapter (pp. 470–73) we spoke of tone as reflecting the author's attitude toward his audience *and* toward his material, but the student may well ask: "When should the attitude toward the audience dominate, and when the attitude toward the material?"

Writing that demands that the author take into account his particular audience is, as we have seen, always "practical" writing—writing designed to effect some definite purpose. The advertiser is trying to persuade the housewife to buy something. The politician hopes that his speech will induce citizens to vote for him. Or, to take a more exalted case (for there need be no self-interest), a statesman urges a nation (through his writing and his speeches) to adopt a certain course of action. (See Persuasion, pp. 238–39.) Yet these cases all have one thing in common: they are designed to secure a practical end. An audience is to be won to agreement or urged to action.

If such writing is to be effective, the author must, of course, keep his specific audience constantly in mind. An approach calculated to win the suffrage of one audience may very well repel another. The age, the intelligence, the amount of education, the interest, the habits and prejudices of the audience, must all be taken into account. The skillful management of such problems is, of course, an aspect of rhetoric.

The scientist may be thought to escape the need for using rhetoric. The scientist writing strictly as a scientist does not try to persuade his reader; he "just tells him." In purely technical writing the facts are allowed to speak for themselves. But they speak fully only to a specially trained audience. In a work like "The Method of Scientific Investigation" (pp. 619–25), Thomas Huxley is writing for an audience that is not so trained, and the tone that he adopts toward his readers quite properly takes that fact into account.

If the scientist can afford to write for an ideal reader, for whom he has to make no special allowances, so too can the literary artist. Just as the scientist, in his purely technical writing, assumes that his reader has the technical equipment to follow his mode of presentation and requires no inducement to accept a theory beyond the fact that it is clearly true, so the artist assumes that his ideal reader has sufficient intelligence, sensitivity, and general discrimination to grasp his artistic presentation in its totality. There is an important difference, to be sure: purely technical writing has no room for or need of a concern for tone; but for the literary artist as such, the tone is everything. In a sense the tone is the most important thing about his work: it embodies the very spirit of his work.

One can illustrate this latter point by going back to the passage quoted from *Seven Pillars of Wisdom* (pp. 486–87). The passage, as we have seen, tells us a good deal about Lawrence's character, and it makes a commentary on a number of things: on the Arabs, on justice, and on capital punishment. But as we have already observed, such writing makes its points by implication, and it assumes that the reader is mature. For the *ideal* reader, no alteration of tone is required, and Lawrence has managed his problem of tone in probably the most satisfactory way possible.

But let us suppose that Lawrence were relating the episode to an audience that was complacent in its contempt for the "barbarian" Arabs. Unless his attitude toward the Arabs were to be completely distorted, Lawrence would have to alter the tone to take the prejudices of his audience into account. In particular, he would have to make much more explicit the fact that the Arabs honestly face up to their imposition of the death penalty as the more sentimental, but ultimately more callous, citizen of England or America does not.

Or suppose that Lawrence were running for political office and a garbled account of the incident were being used against him. He might be content to rely upon the account that he has given in *Seven Pillars*. Properly read, it shows him to be anything but callous and insensitive. But the politician rarely can afford to risk what the artist can. The objectivity of his account might have to be qualified. In a political context, what his feelings and attitudes were could not safely be left to inference. Lawrence would have to state them explicitly. In general, the rewritten account would be focused not on the drama of the scene itself, but on Lawrence's personal feelings and his struggle with duty.

Yet the student may wonder: What is the bearing of all this on *my* practical problem? Am I to write for an "ideal reader"? The answer is, yes: most student papers, except for the occasional one aimed at a special audience, will be addressed to a general reader who, one hopes, will prove also to be the ideal reader.

Yet it may be well for the student to try to visualize a target audience, for the idea of an ideal reader may be too shadowy to furnish him with something definite at which to aim. It may be useful for him to imagine himself writing for some particular person—the most intelligent and discriminating person that he knows. If he can be convincing to that person, the problem of tone will probably have been taken care of quite adequately.

There is another practical way of considering the problem: whatever the particular audience for which an author writes, he also writes for himself. There is his own sense of fitness that must be satisfied. The writer thus himself becomes the audience at which he aims. The question that he asks himself is not, "Have I made this convincing to Tom, or to Dick, or to Harry?" but rather, "Have I made this convincing to myself?"; or, to put the matter more succinctly still, "Have I made this convincing?"

In writing for this "ideal" reader, then, the author can transpose all problems of tone into the problem of properly handling his material. The necessity for a special tone arises only when the writing is addressed to a specific reader and the degree to which he differs from the ideal reader is taken into account.

Rhythm and Clarity of Meaning

Earlier in this chapter (p. 466) we pointed out that the term *tone* itself is derived from the speaking voice. We said that the tone of one's voice frequently qualifies the literal meaning of what is being said—sometimes can even reverse it—and that in general the tone of voice constantly indicates how the hearer is to "take" the meaning of the statement. Prose rhythm, too, is closely related to the living voice and, as we shall see, like the voice itself can make important qualifications of meaning. The pauses we make and the stresses we place upon particular words affect meaning.

In committing his thoughts to writing a man deprives himself of the resources of gesture, facial expression, tone of voice, natural pause, and emphasis—all of which are part of actual conversation. Yet, as we have remarked in connection with the discussion of tone (p. 467), this deprivation need not be crippling. Nor need it be so with reference to rhythm. By a sound choice and arrangement of the words that he sets down, the writer may achieve an expressive management of this important element. But before we get to the subject of rhythm, let us look at some examples of what the living voice can achieve in the way of emphasis. Consider the following simple sentence: "Are you going to town?" If we stress the word *are*, the sentence becomes an emphatic question; and if we stress it heavily, it may even suggest surprise. But if we stress *you*, the question then centers on whether it is *you* who are going rather than someone else. If we stress *town*, we get a third variation; the question now has to do with the destination.

Thus the rhythmic inflection of a sentence, with its lighter or heavier stresses on particular words, is a very important way in which we express our meanings. When we put the sentence on paper, we can, of course, indicate some of this stress by underlining the words to be emphasized. But mere underlining is a relatively crude substitute for the living voice, and it is the mark of a clumsy writer to have to rely upon constant underlining. The writer, by his control of the rhythms of his sentences, should be able to suggest where the proper emphases are to fall. Rhythm also suggests pauses in the sentences. Punctuation (as we learn from grammar school onward) is another device for signaling pauses, but punctuation is effective only when it follows the natural pauses coincident with rhythm and emphasis. Punctuation that denies, and even contradicts, the natural units of thought —the natural pauses—is badly done even when it is "grammatically" correct.

Like tone, rhythm is the result of the interplay of various elements. On page 392 we suggested some of the ways in which Donald Peattie varied his sentence patterns to avoid monotony and thus achieved—though we did not there use the term—a more varied rhythm. (We might compare this passage with another paragraph by the same author on page 476. There we pointed out Peattie's management of diction and metaphor to establish a particular tone.) Because both tone and rhythm involve the simultaneous control of diverse elements, there is no neat set of rules, the applications of which will guarantee an appropriate tone or a harmonious rhythm. In fact, tone and rhythm come close—each in its own way—to embodying the very spirit of the work in question. They represent characteristic ways in which the inner unity of a piece of prose asserts itself. Rhythm in particular resists complete analysis, though a reader with any fineness of discrimination can readily sense it.

Nevertheless, control of rhythm, difficult though it may be to achieve by mere rule, is very important for clarity of meaning. This fact is illustrated by the muddled and monotonous rhythms of technological jargon. Look back at Maury Maverick's example of gobbledygook (p. 423) and at the examples of academic jargon on page 424. Prose of this sort is, for a variety of reasons, difficult to read. It is fuzzy, abstract, and dull. It lacks flavor. But it lacks clarity as well; for there are no natural emphases, no obvious points of primary stress, and often no natural pauses.

Compare with the passage quoted by Maverick the following sentence from Santayana's essay on Dickens (Readings, pp. 771–81):

> Nor had Dickens any lively sense for fine art, classical tradition, science, or even the manners or feelings of the upper classes in his own time and country: in his novels we may almost say there is no army, no navy, no church, no sport, no distant travel, no daring adventure, no feeling for the watery wastes and the motley nations of the planet, and—luckily, with his notion of them—no lords and ladies.

Santayana's sentence is long and relatively complex, but it is rhythmical. The heavy stresses come where they should, on words like "Dickens," "lively," "fine," "classical," "even." Moreover, phrase balances phrase: "no distant travel" balances "no daring adventure"; "watery wastes" sets off "motley nations." Even the parenthetical phrase "with his notion of them" is prepared for. (Notice that the rhythm is destroyed if we alter the ending to read "and—with his notion of them—luckily no lords and ladies.")

We have observed that lack of rhythm is frequently a symptom of disordered discourse; an easily grasped rhythm, on the other hand, is often the sign of good order and proper disposition of words and phrases. But rhythmic quality is much more, of course, than a mere index of clarity.

The great artist can exploit rhythm for special and sometimes intricate effects. In general, emphatic rhythms tend to accompany emotional heightening. It is no accident that eloquent prose—prose that makes a strong appeal to the feelings—tends to use clearly patterned rhythms, or that poetry has traditionally been written in the systematized rhythm that we call *verse*. The association of formal rhythm with emotional power is based on a perfectly sound psychological fact. Fervent expression of grief, rage, or joy tends to fall into rhythmic patterns—whether it be the sobbing of a grief-stricken woman or the cursing of an irate cab driver.

It is easy to find examples of exalted prose in which the formality of the rhythms comes very close to verse. Consider the following sentence from Sir Thomas Browne's *Religio Medici:*

> If there be any truth in astrology, I may outlive a jubilee; as yet I have not seen one revolution of Saturn, nor hath my pulse beat thirty years, and yet, excepting one, have seen the ashes of, and left under ground, all the kings of Europe; have been contemporary to three emperors, four grand-signiors, and as many popes: methinks I have outlived myself, and begin to be weary of the sun; I have shaken hands with delight in my warm blood and canicular days; I perceive I do anticipate the vices of age; the world to me is but a dream or mock-show, and we all therein but pantaloons and anticks, to my severer contemplations.

Here is an example of elaborately cadenced prose from more recent times: the poet W. B. Yeats uses the sculptured heads of four civilizations to point up the differences in the spiritual quality of those civilizations.

> Those riders upon the Parthenon had all the world's power in their moving bodies, and in a movement that seemed, so were the hearts of man and beast set upon it, that of a dance; but presently all would change and measurement succeed to pleasure, the dancing-master outlive the dance. What need had those young lads for careful eyes? But in Rome of the first and second centuries, where the dancing-master himself has died, the delineation of character as shown in face and head, as with us of recent years, is all in all, and sculptors, seeking the custom of occupied officials, stock in their workshops toga'd marble bodies upon which can be screwed with the least possible delay heads modelled from the sitters with the most scrupulous realism. When I think of Rome I see always those heads with their world-considering eyes, and those bodies as conventional as the metaphors in a leading article, and compare in my imagination vague Grecian eyes gazing at nothing, Byzantine eyes of drilled ivory staring upon a vision, and those eyelids of China and of India, those veiled or half-veiled eyes weary of world and vision alike.
>
> —W. B. YEATS: *A Vision.*[8]

The student may feel that "poetic" or heightened prose of this sort is far removed from his purposes. He is not likely to aspire to write in this fashion, and he may feel that even in the hands of a master like Yeats it risks becoming mannered and precious. Moreover, the student may feel that any conscious attempt to achieve a particular rhythm—let alone that of heightened prose—is simply out of his range.

The student may well be right. In any case, we have full sympathy for any shrinking from the artificial and the mannered. Our concern in *Modern Rhetoric* is practical: we assume that most readers of this text want to form a simple natural style—not a highfalutin style.

Yet a concern for rhythm is in one important aspect thoroughly practical. As we have already remarked, a too monotonous rhythm or a limping rhythm signals that something is amiss with the structure of one's prose. The student should test his composition by reading it aloud, and as he reads it, listen for the jangling discord or the halting rhythm that signals something in the sentence is awry.

This test of reading aloud is particularly useful in the proper disposition of modifiers, adverbial phrases, and the like. (See pp. 377–81.) The student may find that reading his composition aloud and "listening" to it may be the most practical way of detecting sentence elements that have not been placed in their best order. The following sentence will illustrate:

> Oriental luxury goods—jade, silk, gold, spices, vermillion, jewels— formerly had come by way of the Caspian Sea overland; and a few daring

---

Greek sea captains, now that this route had been cut by the Huns, catching the trade winds, were sailing from Red Sea ports and loading up at Ceylon.

The sentence is passable, and is perhaps not noticeably unrhythmical. But if we read this sentence in the form in which Robert Graves actually wrote it (Readings, p. 803), we shall find that it is not only clearer, it is much more rhythmical and much easier to read:

> Oriental luxury goods—jade, silk, gold, spices, vermillion, jewels—had formerly come overland by way of the Caspian Sea and now that this route had been cut by the Huns, a few daring Greek sea captains were sailing from Red Sea ports, catching the trade winds and loading up at Ceylon.

On pages 440–41 we discussed the incoherence of a passage occurring in Liebman's *Peace of Mind*. We commented in particular on the number of dead and all-but-dead metaphors. But the passage is also incoherent rhythmically. The theme is serious, the subject matter suffused with emotion, and the passage is obviously intended to appeal to our emotions, but the rhythm is broken and halting.

■ APPLICATIONS

I The following paragraph describes the author's trip down the Yangtze River in China:

> . . . there were still the rapids, though the more dangerous rocks had now been blasted. The dreadful sucking water, with its visible, audible sucks and hisses, was still the most fearfully alive water I have seen. From what seemed most hideous depths came another skin of water, welling up and swishing itself upon the surface into a carapace design, like a turtle's back, an outline of diamond shapes, and at each angle a hole formed and sucked back into itself, sucking back the dissolving diamond; a little farther bubbles pouted, pouting, spurting, then breaking open; and up welled and surfaced out another hexagonal animal skin. It took little time to be persuaded that one was riding the back of a prehistoric monster, whose skin wrinkled and relaxed while the monster shuffled about. A faint froth, a scarcely perceived rock just breaking the surface; and there were the whirlpools and the sudden notion that water and sky were swivelling round an almost unperceived centre of light delicate froth, which softly, softly, began its inward funnel, sucking one back into the depths from where all this came up; and this went on all the time, for two hundred kilometres of the gorges.
>
> —Han Suyin: *The Crippled Tree*.[9]

Do you find this passage difficult to read aloud? Does it seem rhythmically disordered? Has the author tried to imitate the sounds of the rapids? Are the

---

[9] From *The Crippled Tree* by Han Suyin. Reprinted by permission of G. P. Putnam's Sons, publishers. Reprinted by permission of Jonathan Cape Ltd.

rhythms of the prose calculated to suggest the chaotic flow of the stream? If you think this was the writer's intention, was she, in your opinion, successful?

Is sentence 3 improved by rewriting it as follows?

> Out of what seemed most hideous depths arose another skin of water, welling up, swishing around, and forming upon its surface an outline of diamond shapes, a carapace design, like the shell of a turtle. At the angle of each diamond shape, a hole opened, a funnel-shaped whirlpool, that sucked back into the depths of the stream the dissolving diamond. A little further on, bubbles pouted—pouting, spurting, then breaking open—once more turning the surface of the stream into a hexagonal-figured beast's shell or skin.

Has the rewritten sentence a smoother rhythm? Is it easier to understand? Is it better organized—grammatically and rhetorically?

Try to rewrite the rest of the passage.

II   The following passage is from Alexander Smith's *Dreamthorp*.

> There are some men who have no individuality, just as there are some men who have no face. These are to be described by generals, not by particulars. They are thin, vapid, inconclusive. They are important solely on account of their numbers. For them the census enumerator labours; they form majorities; they crowd voting-booths; they make the money; they do the ordinary work of the world. They are valuable when well officered. They are plastic matter to be shaped by a workman's hand; and are built with as bricks are built with. In the aggregate, they form public opinion; but then, in every age, public opinion is the disseminated thoughts of some half a dozen men, who are in all probability sleeping quietly in their graves. They retain dead men's ideas, just as the atmosphere retains the light and heat of the set sun. They are not light—they are twilight. To know how to deal with such men— to know how to use them—is the problem which ambitious force is called upon to solve.
> —Alexander Smith: "On the Importance of a Man to Himself," *Dreamthorp*.

Though Smith is celebrated as a stylist and the passage printed above is in many respects "well written," some readers will be repelled by the monotony of the sentence pattern: "There are . . . ," "These are . . . ," "They are . . . ," and so forth. Can you think of any reason for Smith's insistence on this pattern? Is he trying to achieve emphasis? A kind of straightforward simplicity? Or do you think he has merely been careless? Rewrite the passage in order to vary the sentence pattern.

III   Nigel Dennis's review of Sinclair's *The Last of the Best* appears in the Readings ("Lordships Observed," pp. 784–86). Sinclair's book is a serious study, but Dennis adopts a bantering tone in his review. His second paragraph will illustrate:

> Like their pedigrees, aristocrats exist only in the imagination. Left to themselves, they would wither away, but the common man sees to it that they are not left to themselves. His common mind leaps up when he reads: DUKE'S SON ON FRAUD CHARGE; EARL BEAT MODEL, SAYS CONSTABLE. "There, but for the grace of God, go I," he mutters enviously.

There are at least two literary echoes: Wordsworth's "The Rainbow" contains the line "My heart leaps up." "There but for the grace of God go I" echoes the remark made by John Bradford (1510?–55) on seeing some criminals: "There but for the grace of God," he said, "goes John Bradford."

Notice that the rhythm also contributes to the tonal quality. Suppose we suppressed the characteristic rhythm by altering the passage to read: "Aristocrats, very much like the pedigrees that appertain to them, have only an imaginary existence. They would wither up if they had to subsist upon themselves; but the common man" and so forth. If we slow down the pace and kill the brisk irreverent run of the sentences, we do a great deal to alter the tone.

Read the whole review and indicate (with illustrations)

1   The various devices that Dennis uses to set and sustain the bantering tone
2   The role that rhythm plays in sustaining the tone

(In illustrating your answer to the second part you may want to rewrite passages to show the way in which an altered rhythm alters the tone.)

IV   Turn back to pages 427–28 and compare, *on the basis of rhythm,* the passage quoted from John Dewey with Joseph Warren Beach's rewritten version. Which version reads more smoothly? For example, compare Dewey's second sentence with Beach's rewriting of it. Or, compare Dewey's fifth and sixth sentences with the sixth and seventh sentences in the rewritten version. The reader's difficulty in comprehending clearly what is being said makes the sentences seem halting as he reads them aloud—if he reads silently, they still make their awkwardness felt on his inner ear. All of which may explain why reading our prose aloud and listening for the breaks in rhythm is a useful device for sensing that something is wrong in the rhetorical structure.

Style

The reader of this text may be surprised to find that the term *style* is now appearing for the first time. He might well have expected a long discussion of style much earlier in the book. But though the term is mentioned here for the first time, actually, from the very first page of this book, we have been discussing style. The plan for conducting an argument or presenting a piece of exposition, the means for connecting paragraph with paragraph, the choice of diction, the handling of tone—all are aspects of style. Style is an overall effect: the style of a piece of prose is determined by the interplay of all sorts of elements—sentence structure, descriptive patterns, figures of speech, rhythm, and so forth. Indeed it is not always easy to pick out of a particular passage just those elements that are most important in giving the style of the writer its special quality. Such elements cannot be measured out by formula: it's quite impossible for a writer to produce a given quality of style by mechanically blending so much of this element with so much of that. A modern author puts the matter in this way: "Style is not an isolable quality of writing; it is writing itself."

So far in this chapter we have seen how difficult it is to isolate and determine the specific value of each of the factors that control tone and rhythm. And it would be much more difficult to accomplish this with respect to style in general, which is a larger concept and represents the interplay of all sorts of elements, including tone and rhythm themselves. There is no one proper shape for a sentence or length for a paragraph nor one "correct" diction. The "correctness" will depend on the occasion and the writer's purpose and the context in which the word or sentence is placed. Sometimes, as we have seen earlier, a sentence consisting of one word or a paragraph of one sentence or, with reference to diction, a slang phrase or a worn cliché may actually be the proper choice. As we have said many times in the preceding pages, it is the particular context that determines what is appropriate, and style itself is a harmonious interplay of all the elements and devices of writing.

Yet, though "style is not an isolable quality of writing," there are, nevertheless, a few *general* comments that may be worth putting on record. First, style is never to be thought of as a mere veneer, a decorative surface laid over the content. In a piece of writing, form and content interpenetrate each other and are finally inseparable.

Thus, we do not put the case accurately when we say that a writer's task is to seek a proper form—that is, a proper "container" into which to put what he wants to say. For a writer often does not know precisely what he wants to say until he has found the proper form in which to put it. (At the very beginning of this book [p. 3] we recalled the story of the old lady who, when asked to say what she meant, replied: "But how can I know what I mean till I say it?") Form and content are indeed closely related—change "how" a thing is said and you have changed, even if only so slightly, "what" is said.

Second, just because in a good style the thing said and the way of saying it are inseparable, a defective style—what we call a "bad" style—always reveals itself in some cleavage between the thing said and the saying— the content and the form. There is a disharmony between what the writer has actually put on the page and what we infer—from the existing discrepancies and disharmonies—he actually meant to say. In other words, the discordant elements call attention to themselves—they "stick out." [10] (See, for example, our discussion of the Hoffer passage [Diction, pp. 426–27].)

---

[10] One must be careful to distinguish between the contradictions and confusions of a defective style and the discrepancies that one notices in an ironic statement. As we observed earlier (pp. 479–81), irony does involve a discrepancy between what is apparently said and what is actually meant. But any confusion in the reader's mind usually lasts only for a moment. He catches on that the writer is speaking ironically, and the ironic discrepancy, thus, proves to be a device under the writer's control—not an ineptitude. The ironic writer knows very well what he wants to say, but he is getting at his meaning *indirectly* and *obliquely*.

Originality

Finally, we ought to say something about originality. For we are constantly told that originality is the hallmark of a good style, and we are further told that the writer ought to be himself—to express his own personality—in all that he writes. One recalls Buffon's famous remark that "the style is the man." This is all very true: but the student needs to be warned against any excessive straining for originality. Instead of urging the novice writer to try to impress his unique self on his work, it is better to remind him that he will find not only what he really wants to say but also his true self through a process of exploration. Fortunately, the right kind of originality, the impress of one's unique personality, can be left to take care of itself provided that the writer manages to take care of what he can consciously control in his composition. For a style, as we have earlier remarked, is not a mere veneer; it is rather the informing principle of content. Thus a good style is bound to carry the impress of the writer's personality. Every tree in the forest has its own grain and the special quality of that tree—its unique grain pattern—will show through any honest piece of furniture made from its wood.

■ APPLICATIONS

I The following are general questions that the student should ask himself as he considers the passages quoted below.

1 What is the author's attitude toward the reader? In what way is this shown?
2 What is the author's attitude toward his material?
3 Are there any instances of sentimentality? In what way is it revealed? Are there any instances of other kinds of overstatement? Is the overstatement justified or unjustified?
4 Which of the passages, if any, makes use of understatement?
5 Do any of the passages make use of irony? Try to characterize the kind of irony in each case—sarcasm, light mocking irony, bitter irony, gay irony, and so on.
6 Are there any passages that are relatively toneless? Are there any that are confused in tone?

A [The mate] felt all the majesty of his great position, and made the world feel it, too. When he gave even the simplest order, he discharged it like a blast of lightning, and sent a long reverberating peal of profanity thundering after it. I could not help contrasting the way in which the average landsman would give an order with the mate's way of doing it. If the landsman should wish the gang-plank moved a foot farther forward, he would probably say: "James, or William, one of you push that plank forward, please"; but put the mate in his place, and he would roar out: "Here, now, start that gang-plank for'ard! Lively, now! What're you about! Snatch it! There! There! Aft again! aft again!

Don't you hear me? Dash it to dash! are you going to sleep over it! 'Vast heaving. 'Vast heaving, I tell you! Going to heave it clear astern? *Where're you going with that barrel!* for'ard with it 'fore I make you swallow it, you dash-dash-dash-*dashed* split between a tired mud-turtle and a crippled hearse-horse!" I wished I could talk like that.

—Samuel L. Clemens: *Life on the Mississippi*.

Characterize the tone of the mate's speech. Characterize the author's attitude toward the mate. Be as specific as you can.

B   It wasn't the bully amateur's world any more. Nobody knew that on armistice day, Theodore Roosevelt, happy amateur warrior with the grinning teeth, the shaking forefinger, naturalist, explorer, magazine writer, Sundayschool teacher, cowpuncher, moralist, politician, righteous orator with a short memory, fond of denouncing liars (the Ananias Club) and having pillowfights with his children, was taken to the Roosevelt hospital gravely ill with inflammatory rheumatism.

     Things weren't bully any more;

     T. R. had grit;

     he bore the pain, the obscurity, the sense of being forgotten as he had borne the grilling portages when he was exploring the River of Doubt, the heat, the fetid jungle mud, the infected abscess in his leg.

     and died quietly in his sleep

     at Sagamore Hill,

     on January 6, 1919

     and left on the shoulders of his sons

     the white man's burden.

—John Dos Passos: "The Happy Warrior," *1919*.[11]

C   No man could have been more bitter against opponents, or more unfair to them or more ungenerous. In this department, indeed, even so gifted a specialist in dishonorable controversy as Dr. [Woodrow] Wilson has seldom surpassed him. He never stood up to a frank and chivalrous debate. He dragged herrings across the trail. He made seductive faces to the gallery. He capitalized his enormous talents as an entertainer, his rank as a national hero, his public influence and consequence. The two great law-suits in which he was engaged were screaming burlesques upon justice. He tried them in the newspapers before ever they were called; he befogged them with irrelevant issues; his appearances in court were not the appearances of a witness standing on a level with other witnesses, but those of a comedian sure of his crowd. He was, in his dealings with concrete men as in his dealings with men in the mass, a charlatan of the very highest skill—and there was in him, it goes without saying, the persuasive charm of the charlatan as well as the daring deviousness, the humanness of naiveté as well as the humanness of chicane.

[11] From *1919*, second volume of *U.S.A.* by John Dos Passos. Published by Houghton Mifflin Company.

He knew how to woo—and not only boobs. He was, for all his ruses and ambuscades, a jolly fellow.

—H. L. Mencken: "Roosevelt: An Autopsy," *Prejudices: Second Series.*[12]

Both Dos Passos and Mencken exhibit definite attitudes toward Theodore Roosevelt; compare and contrast them. How does the attitude in each case color the writer's account? Cite specific instances.

II A The worst experience I ever had was being trapped in a cave. The idea of being all alone and in the dark and unable to move is enough to make most grown men afraid, and I was only fourteen. Even though the chances were I'd be found soon, I couldn't be dead sure. But I kept my head and this probably saved me from serious injury. The doctor said later that if I had tried to pull my foot loose I probably would have injured it severely. It was bad enough as it was, and the sprained ankle kept me on crutches for several weeks. My friends began kidding me about them after a while, but I think it's better to be safe than sorry. The doctor had told me to use the crutches as long as I wanted to.

B Getting trapped in a cave is no fun, but it's not the worst thing that can happen to you if you keep your head. After telling myself over and over "Keep your head, now," it struck me that it wasn't my head I was in danger of losing, it was my foot. I had to laugh, even in the fix I was in, and started telling myself, "Keep your foot, now." It sort of cheered me up and kept me from doing anything stupid.

When it was all over, people kept saying, "I'll bet you were scared to death." And my mother, after she got over her crying spell, would say, "Jimmie's not scared of anything." They were both wrong. I was scared, all right, but I kept seeing the funny side of it.

How would you characterize the tone of the first version? Of the second? Finish the account of the experience, continuing the tone of the first or the second version. Attempt to rewrite this account, giving it still another tone—say one that might be used by a much younger child, or by a philosophical old man.

III A Dear Phyllis,

Laura tells me that you are thinking of joining us on our trip through the South. I hope you can, though I wish you could have decided earlier. I will write Aunt Agnes and Mrs. Stillwell and ask them if they can find a bed for you, too. But I hope you're not expecting a deluxe suite!

I can't imagine why your mother and father should have any objections. After all, we're old enough to take care of ourselves, though our parents are a little stuffy about admitting it. I'm really looking forward to being off on our own for once.

If you do decide to come, please try to be polite to Doris. I know she gets

---

[12] From "Roosevelt: An Autopsy" by H. L. Mencken. Reprinted from *Prejudices: Second Series* by H. L. Mencken, by permission of Alfred A. Knopf, Inc. Copyright 1920 by Alfred A. Knopf, Inc. Copyright 1948 by H. L. Mencken.

in your hair, but after all, she's my cousin and there's no use starting trouble for me.

Love,
Evelyn

How would you characterize the writer of this letter, judging from the tone? Would the letter persuade Phyllis to go on the trip? Would it persuade her parents? Can you rewrite the letter, using a more persuasive tone?

B   Dear Phyllis,

Laura tells me that you are thinking about joining us for our trip through the South. I gather that you are all for it and it's just a question of whether your parents approve. Knowing them as I do, I'm sure they will not decide this arbitrarily. My mother, too, was a little leery at first, but after I had gone over all our plans with her, she agreed that they were perfectly sound.

The fact that we have a new car, which should eliminate any road trouble, and the fact that we'll be staying with relatives or friends every night convinced her that we'll be perfectly safe.

I remember so well the trip I made with you and your family when we were children. The old Chevrolet may have had its weak moments, but your father's ingenuity and good spirits kept us all going merrily along—to say nothing of your mother's unerring ability to spot the perfect place for stopping each night. I hope our trip turns out to be half as much fun as that one. Please give my love to everyone.

Evelyn

Compare the tone of this letter with that in the letter above. How would you characterize the tone here? What objections is it designed to overcome? Is it designed to be shown to Phyllis's parents? If there were no parental objection to be overcome, how differently could the ideas of the letter be expressed? Try to rewrite it.

IV Here are two accounts of the formation of Reelfoot Lake in the northwest corner of the state of Tennessee. The first is from a magazine article; the second from the opening pages of a novel.

A   December 15, 1811, had been a peaceful day for the 800 inhabitants of the frontier Mississippi River town of New Madrid, Mo. Although the air was sultry, fishermen went out on the river, hunters and trappers into the forests. Except for members of the French community, who were dancing, everyone went to bed early, as usual.

At two o'clock in the morning, the inhabitants were roused by a violent, thunderous shock. Houses rocked, tables and chairs jumped, chimneys crashed. Terrified folk fled their collapsing homes only to find themselves reeling across land that waved like the ocean and threw them to the ground, making them seasick. Shocks came every few minutes.

Half an hour after the first awful thunder, there was an ear-shattering concussion. Black clouds of sulphurous vapor shut out the bright new moon and wrapped the earth in total darkness. The sulphur smell, flashes of lightning, and falling pieces of coal spewed up from chasms yawning at their feet made many think the world was ending in fire and brimstone. One hysterical woman ran until her strength gave out, then died of exhaustion.

By daylight more shocks occurred, and people saw as well as felt the incredibly rolling land. Houses, people and trees were lifted and let down as the long, low swells passed beneath them. Entire forests bowed and fell in order, "like battalions of soldiers grounding their rifles at the word of command," as one observer reported. At a crest of a few feet, the dry waves burst open with a raucous roar, shooting out 6- to 40-foot geysers of sand, water and black bituminous shale.

Where the waves broke, great fissures gaped. Merchant A. N. Dillard had stored a boatload of castings from Pittsburgh in his basement. The ground opened under the house and swallowed cellar and contents, which were never seen again.

From its center in New Madrid, the eruption vibrated north and south along the Mississippi Valley. It terrified Indians far up in the north woods of Canada, frightened residents of Washington, D.C., drove people from their homes in Lebanon, Ohio. Not a family slept in Cincinnati. Chimneys fell in many places in Tennessee, Kentucky and Missouri; bricks were knocked loose in Georgia and South Carolina; bells rang, clocks stopped and houses shuddered in Virginia; beds and chairs clattered in Indiana, and mild tremors were felt in Boston.

The mighty Mississippi was never so violent. It boiled, foamed and roared. Thickened with mud and silt thrown up from its bed, it churned and rolled and tore at its banks. About 3 A.M. a phenomenon occurred which lives in legend in the South as "the time the Mississippi flowed backward." The tremendous force originating from pressures deep underground exploded through the riverbed in one mammoth bank-to-bank upheaval, hurling back a mountainous wall of water. Giant waves raced upstream. . . .

The most remarkable feature of the entire disturbance was the formation of Reelfoot Lake, on the Tennessee side of the Mississippi. Now a joy for naturalist and sportsman, the lake appeared during the quake when a swampy area fed by creeks suddenly sank, and an adjacent area to the south thrust upward, cutting off the streams' outlet. The rising tide created in time a body of water ten miles long, three miles wide and 5 to 20 feet deep.

—Blake Clark: "America's Greatest Earthquake,"
Shreveport Magazine, March, 1969.[13]

B   Reelfoot Lake is one of the largest fresh-water lakes south of the Ohio. It is the weirdest and the strangest, the most mysterious and the most sinister. Also it's the newest. It occurred in 1811, which is practically day before yesterday, as the scientists space off such mundane miscellany.

In that year of 1811, Creation certainly was cutting up its didoes. For instance, it was the year "when the stars fell." Night after night, for week on week, the blazing meteors dropped so fast and so thick they did more than streak the sky. They cross-hatched it; they fairly scrim-shawed it with

[13] "America's Greatest Earthquake" by Blake Clark. Reprinted with permission from *Shreveport Magazine* (March '69). Copyright 1969 by The Reader's Digest Assn., Inc. Condensed in the April '69 Reader's Digest. Reprinted by permission of the author.

livid flame. So divers people got religion, thinking the world was to be at an end and all peoples whatsoever got good and scared.

Furthermore, it was the year of Great Shakes; a time that coined a proverb and reshaped a whole slice of the hemispheric contours. It was the time when the mountains seemed to skip like ram-goats and the valleys quivered like proud flesh; which daunting things continued for months on top of months so that men got used to the feel of a formerly dependable planet rolling and heaving in swells beneath their feet. But others, and they a thousand miles from seaboard, were made most horribly seasick.

In the midst of this, with the stars, mind you, still fetching loose from their sockets, and the air full of sounds like thunderclaps, and great seams opening in the soil one day and slamming shut again the next, there came a culminating hour of dread while epileptic nature had the almightiest conniption fit of all. It is recorded that for a longish spell, which to the survivors probably seemed longer, she made the surfaces of the earth to shiver as a galled horse flinches the loose skin on his flanks to drive off the gadflies.

From fright then, many persons lost years off their lives but very few lives actually were lost, by reason that the worst of these seismic convulsions befell along what was the mid-continental frontier of this young republic, afflicting an isolated fringe of game-trails and scattered cabins and wood-landings, a land of unexplored timber and unplumbed bottoms. Nowhere was the crowning upheaval so severe as in the extreme western end of Tennessee and in the neighboring westernmost tip of Kentucky.

Thereabouts in particular the Big Quake played hoss with existing topography. There was one shock that shifted the course of the Mississippi River, and that must have taken some shifting. There came a second which practically made over the Madrid Bend country. Then there was a third, or perhaps merely a continuation of the first two, which crumpled down and depressed an area roughly sixty-five miles in length and of an average width, say, of seven miles, and likewise split a fissure through to the Mississippi, so that for three days the Mississippi ran north through the funnel, to fill up that gaping hollow and overflow the sunken lands bordering it.

Three days and three nights, by the olden accounts, the befuddled Father of Water galloped unwillingly backward. When the lake was brimful and therefore finished, its splayed toes and bloated amidships lay on the Tennessee side; its narrow heel indented the state-line, projecting up into the sister commonwealth of Kentucky. —Irvin S. Cobb: "The Lake of Tragedy." [14]

How would you describe the tone of Clark's account? Obviously, he wants to make his story of the earthquake vivid, and he has tried to fill it with colorful detail. Even so, would you agree that the tone is basically that of an objective historian trying to give a straightforward account of what happened? How does the tone of Cobb's account differ? What is Cobb trying to do? Establish a kind of speaking voice? Imply a speaker of a certain kind of personality? In this connection note such phrases as "cutting up its didoes," "the almightiest conniption fit," and "played hoss with." Is Cobb trying to use the idiom of

---

[14] From *Judge Priest Turns Detective* by Irvin S. Cobb, copyright 1937, reprinted by permission of the publisher. The Bobbs-Merrill Company, Inc.

someone who lived in one of "the scattered cabins" of the mid-continent in 1811? Is Cobb's manipulation of tone successful? Or do you think it is too elaborately cute? (For "the mountains seemed to skip like ram-goats," see Psalm 114.)

Write a brief account of the differences between Cobb's style and Clark's.

V Select one of the following four subjects and write a theme of 500 to 700 words, imitating the style of the selection listed. The imitation should not be slavish, but the student should attempt to apply to his own writing all that he can learn from his model.

A The present state of the United States (depicted as one of stability or instability) on the model of "It Was a Stable World" (Readings, pp. 803–10)

B An essay on a favorite pet on the model of "The Dog That Bit People" (Readings, pp. 754–59)

C A topic of campus interest on the model of Art Buchwald or Russell Baker (Readings, pp. 765–70)

D A piece of reportage on the model of Joan Didion or Norman Mailer (Readings, pp. 658–82)

VI Try to describe the tone (being as specific as you can and using concrete illustrations) of

A Dwight MacDonald's "Ernest Hemingway" (Readings, pp. 794–802)

B Benjamin DeMott's "The Age of Overkill" (Readings, pp. 692–98)

C Robert Lowell's "91 Revere Street" (Readings, pp. 867–76)

VII The two passages that follow describe scenes in the Arabian desert. The scenes are different: that by Hichens pictures a minaret and palm trees caught in a windless noon; that by Lawrence, a desert landscape, now green from recent rains. Yet the descriptions do have certain things in common, including a curiously similar way of describing the wind: "The slight winds were not at play" and "Playful packs of winds came crossing . . ." What decisively differentiates the two passages is the quality of mood, atmosphere, and tone.

Write a brief essay in which you compare and contrast the style of these two passages. Does either author make you *see*, vividly and clearly? Does either of them try to add a mystical element to the scene? How? Is the effort successful? Is there any straining for particular effects? Does either writer exploit suggestion? Is either passage "sentimental" and overstated? Compare the use of metaphor and rhythm in the two passages. Compare also the attitude taken toward the subject and toward the reader. In your essay be specific and give examples.

A   It was noon in the desert.
          The voice of the Mueddin died away on the minaret, and the golden silence

that comes out of the heart of the sun sank down more softly over everything. Nature seemed unnaturally still in the heat. The slight winds were not at play, and the palms of Beni-Mora stood motionless as palm trees in a dream. The day was like a dream, intense and passionate, yet touched with something unearthly, something almost spiritual. In the cloudless blue of the sky there seemed a magical depth, regions of color infinitely prolonged. In the vision of the distances, where desert blent with sky, earth surely curving up to meet the downward curving heaven, the dimness was like a voice whispering strange petitions. . . .   —Robert Hichens: *The Garden of Allah.*

B   . . . every hollow [was] a standing pool, and the valley beds of tall grass [were] prinked with flowers. The chalky ridges, sterile with salt, framed the water-channels delightfully. From their tallest point we could look north and south, and see how the rain, running down, had painted the valleys across the white in broad stripes of green, sharp and firm like brush-strokes. Everything was growing, and daily the picture was fuller and brighter till the desert became like a rank water-meadow. Playful packs of winds came crossing and tumbling over one another, their wide, brief gusts surging through the grass, to lay it momentarily in swathes of dark and light satin, like young corn after the roller. On the hill we sat and shivered before these sweeping shadows, expecting a heavy blast—and there would come into our faces a warm and perfumed breath, very gentle, which passed away behind us as a silver-grey light down the plain of green. Our fastidious camels grazed an hour or so, and then lay down to digest, bringing up stomach-load after stomach-load of butter-smelling green cud, and chewing weightily.
—T. E. Lawrence: *Seven Pillars of Wisdom.*[15]

[15] From *Seven Pillars of Wisdom,* by T. E. Lawrence. Copyright 1926, 1935 by Doubleday & Company, Inc. Reprinted by permission of the publisher.

PART FOUR

THE RESEARCH PAPER

CHAPTER **14**

Preparation and Note-Taking

Most of the longer papers that the student will be asked to write in his college courses will be research papers.[1] That is, the student will be asked to make a study of some particular subject, to assemble materials, organize them, and incorporate them into a unified composition, with footnotes to indicate his authority for the various statements that he makes.

The research paper is a form, and a most important form, of expository discourse. We may want to investigate hydroponics or the architecture of Crusader castles or the history of a literary movement of the Battle of Hastings or the present-day do-it-yourself vogue or a thousand and one other things. But at the end of our research, after we have read our books and magazines or have gone on our field trips or carried out our experiments in the laboratory, there remains the problem of organizing the results. Our facts and opinions need to be organized so as to present their meaning as lucidly and as tellingly as possible. Even if our investigation has been extensive and thorough, it may be wasted if we present its fruits in a muddled and confusing form.

Such a muddled presentation may indeed mean that we ourselves do not know what to make of the facts we have discovered. For facts do not automatically crystallize about a meaning. We have to find what the facts mean, and this involves thinking about them, analyzing them, and working out their implications. The problems to be faced then are those that we have already studied in earlier chapters. We shall need all we have learned about exposition and argument, with their discussion of definition, classification, comparison and contrast, the various kinds of analysis, the nature of evi-

---

[1] For a discussion of the Book Report, Summary, and Précis, see Appendix 2, pp. 596–600.

dence, and the principles of induction and deduction. Sometimes a piece of description may be called for; or we may need to narrate the story of a man, an event, a process, or a development. We should, therefore, by this time already know a great deal about the methods involved in working out a research paper; and by the same token, the research paper should provide us at this point with a fine opportunity to review what we have learned.

Sources

The aim of the research paper is to assemble facts and ideas from various sources, and by studying them, to draw new conclusions or to present the material in the light of a new interest. For instance, a military historian who wanted to understand why General Lee lost the Battle of Gettysburg would study the written records of orders and events, the correspondence and memoirs of witnesses, the actual terrain, and the interpretations of other historians. In the light of that evidence, he would try to frame an explanation. Or a literary critic who wanted to understand why a certain novelist often used certain themes would study the facts of the novelist's life as found in whatever sources were available (letters, memoirs, public records, biographies), the kind of education he received, the kind of ideas current in his particular place and time, and so forth. Such material would be his evidence. The researcher might discover new facts, and new facts can easily upset old theories. But he might have to depend on facts that were already available but were available only in scattered sources. Then his task would be to collect these facts and shape them into a new pattern of interpretation.

The professional historian or literary critic writing a book and the student writing a term paper use the same basic method: they collect the facts and interpret them. The term paper can be intelligent, well informed, interesting, and original. To make it so, the student must be systematic.

The first step toward making his paper systematic is to learn how to investigate his subject. There are two kinds of sources that he can use: primary and secondary. The historian going to the order book of a general or the terrain of a battlefield, the anthropologist observing the Indian tribe, or the literary scholar studying the manuscripts or letters of an author are using what are called *primary sources;* that is, firsthand information, the original documents. The college student must usually use *secondary sources;* that is, secondhand information, a report on, or analysis of, the original documents. He reads the report of the anthropologist or he studies an edition of a poet prepared by a scholar. There are also *tertiary sources*— the digest of, or commentary on, the anthropologist's report (e.g., *The Reader's Digest* and *The Book Review Digest*). The student should not use these unless he cannot get access to the secondary or primary sources. Even when he has no choice but to cite a tertiary source, he should do so with great caution. Get as close to the facts as possible. No matter how good your reasoning is, it is useless if the facts on which it works are not dependable.

Bibliography

The research paper, we have said, draws its material from many sources. It is not a digest of one book or article. But how do you get at the useful sources?

Reference books are a good starting point. Some of the more important reference books are listed below (with abbreviated entries).

GENERAL DICTIONARIES (UNABRIDGED)

Dictionary of American English. 4 vols. 1936–44.
Funk & Wagnalls New Standard Dictionary. 1964.
Oxford English Dictionary. 12 vols. and supplement. 1933.
Webster's Third New International Dictionary. 1966

SPECIAL DICTIONARIES

Evans, Bergen and Cornelia. *A Dictionary of Contemporary American Usage.* 1957.
Fowler, H. W. *Dictionary of Modern English Usage.* 2nd ed. rev. 1965.
Horwill, H. W. *Dictionary of Modern American Usage.* 2nd ed. 1944.
Partridge, Eric, ed. *Dictionary of Slang and Unconventional English.* 1961.
Roget's Thesaurus of Words and Phrases. 3rd ed. 1962.
Webster's Dictionary of Synonyms. 1951.

GENERAL ENCYCLOPEDIAS

Encyclopedia Americana. 30 vols. 1955.
Encyclopedia Britannica. 24 vols. 1954.

Note: Each of these encyclopedias publishes an annual supplement, which should be consulted for additional, recent information.

Americana Annual. 1923–.
Britannica Book of the Year. 1938–.
New International Year Book. 1907–.

ATLASES AND GAZETTEERS

Atlas of World History (Palmer). 1957.
Chamber's World Gazetteer. 1954.

Collier's World Atlas and Gazetteer. 1953.
Columbia Atlas. John Bartholomew, ed. 1954.
Columbia Lippincott Gazetteer of the World. 1952.
Encyclopedia Britannica World Atlas. 1954.
Goode's World Atlas. 12th ed. 1964.
Hammond's Ambassador World Atlas. 2nd ed. 1961.
Rand McNally *Cosmopolitan World Atlas*. 1964.
Times (London) *Atlas of the World*. 5 vols. 1955–59.
Webster's Geographical Dictionary. 1962.

YEARBOOKS—CURRENT EVENTS

American Yearbook. 1910–19, 1925–50.
Information Please Almanac. 1947–.
Statesman's Year-Book. 1864–.
Statistical Abstract of the United States. 1878–.
World Almanac. 1868–.
Yearbook of World Affairs. 1947–.

GENERAL GUIDES

Besterman, Theodore. *A World Bibliography of Bibliographies*. 3rd ed.
    rev. 4 vols. 1955–56.
Books in Print, an index to the *Publishers' Trade List Annual*. 1957–.
Publishers' Trade List Annual. 1873–.
Textbooks in Print. 1956–.
United States Catalog: Books in Print. 4th ed. 1928.
    Supplement: *Cumulative Book Index*. A World List of Books in the
    English Language. 1898–.
Winchell, Constance M. *Guide to Reference Books*. 8th ed. 1967. Sup-
    plements.

GENERAL PERIODICAL INDEXES

Book Review Digest. 1905–.
Book Review Index. 1965–.
International Index to Periodicals. 1963–64.
New York Public Library Index. 1942.
New York Times Index. 1913–.
Poole's Index to Periodical Literature. 1802–1907. 2 vols.
Reader's Guide to Periodical Literature. 1900–.
Standard Periodical Directory. 1964/65–.
Ulrich's Periodicals Directory, a classified guide to a selected list of current
    periodicals, foreign and domestic. 10th ed. 1963.

SPECIAL REFERENCES

Agriculture

Agricultural Index. 1916–64.
Bailey, L. H. *Cyclopedia of American Agriculture.* 4 vols. 1917.
U. S. Department of Agriculture. *Yearbook of Agriculture.* 1894–.

Art and Architecture

Art Index. 1929–.
Chamberlain, Mary Walls. *Guide to Art Reference Books.* 1959.
Fletcher, Banister. *A History of Architecture.* 17th ed. rev. 1961.
Gardner, Helen. *Art Through the Ages.* 5th ed. 1970.
Janson, H. W. *History of Art.* 1962.
Penguin Dictionary of Architecture. 1966.
Year's Art. 1880–1947. Annual.

Biography

Biography Index. 1947–.
Contemporary Authors. 1962–.
Current Biography. 1940–.
Dictionary of American Biography. 20 vols. 1928–37.
Dictionary of National Biography (British). 22 vols. 1885–1949.
Directory of American Scholars. 5th ed. 1969.
Webster's Biographical Dictionary. 1962.
Who's Who. 1849–.
Who's Who in America. 1899–.

Business

Munn, Glenn G. *Encyclopedia of Banking and Finance.* 6th ed. 1962.
Prentice-Hall *Encyclopedic Dictionary of Business Finance.* 1960.
Schwartz, Robert J. *The Dictionary of Business and Finance.* 1954.
U. S. Department of Commerce Publications. 1952.

Classical Literature and Mythology

Avery, C. B., ed. *New Century Classical Handbook.* 1962.
Feder, Lillian. *Crowell's Handbook of Classical Literature.* 1964.
Harvey, Sir Paul. *Oxford Companion to Classical Literature.* 2nd ed. 1937.
Oxford Classical Dictionary. 1949.
Peck, Harry Thurston. *Harper's Dictionary of Classical Literature and Antiquities.* 1962.

Education

Education Index. 1929–.
Education Abstracts. 1949–65.
Harris, Chester W. *Encyclopedia of Educational Research.* 3rd ed. 1960.
Monroe, P. *Cyclopedia of Education.* 5 vols. 1911–13.

History

Adams, J. T. *Dictionary of American History*. 6 vols. 1942–61.
A New Cambridge Modern History. 1957–.
Cambridge Ancient History. Rev. 12 vols. 1961–65.
Cambridge Medieval History. 8 vols. 1911–36.
Cambridge Modern History. 2nd ed. 14 vols. 1926.
Cole, Donald B. *Handbook of American History*. 1968.
Langer, William L. *An Encyclopedia of World History*. Rev. ed. 1952.

Literature

Bartlett's Familiar Quotations. 1955.
Brewer's Dictionary of Phrase and Fable. 1953.
Cambridge History of American Literature. 4 vols. 1917–21.
Cambridge History of English Literature. 15 vols. 1907–33.
Cassell's Encyclopedia of World Literature. 2 vols. 1953.
English Association. *Year's Work in English Studies*. 1920–.
Hart, James D. *Oxford Companion to American Literature*. 3rd ed. 1956.
Harvey, Sir Paul. *Oxford Companion to English Literature*. 3rd ed. 1946.
New Century Handbook of English Literature. 1956.
Oxford History of English Literature. 12 vols. 1945–63.
Reader's Encyclopedia of American Literature. 1962.
Smith, Horatio, ed. *Columbia Dictionary of Modern European Literature*. 1947.
Spiller, R. E. and others. *Literary History of the United States*. 3rd ed. rev. 2 vols. 1963
Stevenson, B. E. *Home Book of Quotations*. 9th ed. rev. 1964.

Music

Apel, Willi. *Harvard Dictionary of Music*. 2nd ed. rev. and enlarged. 1969.
Baker, Theodore. *Biographical Dictionary of Musicians*. 5th ed. 1958.
Grove's Dictionary of Music and Musicians. 5th ed. 9 vols. 1954. Supplement, 1961.
Music Index. 1949–.
Scholes, P. A. *Oxford Companion to Music*. 9th ed. 1955.
Thompson, O. *International Cyclopedia of Music and Musicians*. 9th ed. 1964.
Ulrich, Homer, and Pisk, Paul. *A History of Music and Musical Style*. 1963.

Psychology

Drever, James. *A Dictionary of Psychology*. 1964.
Psychological Abstracts. 1927–.
Psychological Index. 42 vols. 1894–1935.

Religion

Catholic Encyclopedia. 17 vols. 1907–22. Supplement, 1950.

Cross, F. L. *The Oxford Dictionary of the Christian Church.* 1961.

Hastings, James. *Dictionary of the Bible.* 5 vols. 1898–1904.

Hastings, James, ed. *Encyclopedia of Religion and Ethics.* 12 vols. 1908–27.

Universal Jewish Encyclopedia. 10 vols. 1939–44.

Science and Technology

American Men of Science. Jaques Cattell, ed. 11th ed. 1968.

Applied Sciences and Technology Index. 1913–.

Engineering Index. 1884–.

Handbook of Chemistry and Physics (Chemical Rubber Company). 45th ed. 1964.

Hawkins, R. R. *Scientific, Medical, and Technical Books Published in the United States of America.* A selected list of titles in print with annotations. 1930–44. Supplements, 1950, 1953.

Henderson, I. F., and Henderson, W. D. *Dictionary of Scientific Terms in Biology, Botany, Zoology, Anatomy, Cytology, Embryology, Physiology.* 8th ed. 1963.

The McGraw-Hill *Encyclopedia of Science and Technology.* 15 vols. 1960.

Van Nostrand's Scientific Encyclopedia. 3rd ed. 1958.

Reference books are so numerous and sometimes so specialized that it is often helpful to consult the *Guide to Reference Books,* by Constance M. Winchell, to know where to go in the first place.

The reference book will give an introduction to a subject and certain basic facts. Best of all for the student, it will usually offer a bibliography, a list of other works on the subject—books or articles less limited in scope than the treatment in the reference book itself. With this as a starting point the student can make up his own *working bibliography* for his subject. As he reads more about his subject he will encounter references to other works, and can gradually extend the range of his working bibliography. The subject catalogue of the library will also provide new items.

The working bibliography should be kept on convenient cards of uniform size, with only one entry to a card. This allows the student to arrange them in alphabetical or other order (by topics, for example), according to his need. The entry on the card should contain all the basic information about a book or article: the author's name with the last name first, the title of the work, the volume number, if any, the place of publication, the publisher, the date of publication. If the work appears in a periodical or collection, that fact should be indicated with the volume number, the date, and the pages occupied by the work.

This form of card entry is to be retained in making up the final bibliography to be attached to your finished paper. There the order will be alphabetical by authors. Your final bibliography may be shorter than your working bibliography, for the final bibliography should contain no entry from which you have not taken material for the actual paper, whereas certain items in your working bibliography may have been dropped as more valuable items came to light.

ENTRY FOR A BOOK

```
Strachey, Lytton.  Elizabeth and Essex.  London:
  Chatto and Windus, 1928.
```

ENTRY FOR AN ARTICLE

```
Barrington, Margaret.  "The Censorship in Eire,"
  Commonweal, XLVI (August 15, 1947) 429-32.
```

What items should be included in the student's working bibliography? The professional scholar may want to work through all the material on his subject, but the student preparing a term paper scarcely has the time for such a program. Many items in the bibliographies he encounters are antiquated or trivial. So to save his time and energy, he should try to select the items that will best repay his attention. There is no rule for selecting a bibliography. The student, however, can sometimes get ideas from a similarly selected bibliography in a textbook or other book on his subject. Sometimes an author will refer with special respect to certain other works on his subject. The student can also take his working bibliography to his instructor and ask for comment.

■ **APPLICATIONS**

I Perhaps the instructor in one of your courses has already assigned a general topic for a research paper. If not, choose a general topic. The lists of topics on pp. 16, 63, and 68, may give you some ideas.

II Having chosen your topic, make a preliminary bibliography for it.

Notes

Unless you take notes on your reading you will probably not be able to remember much of the relevant material and will certainly not be able to organize it well when you write your paper. If you have taken your notes carefully, you will be able to lay out before you the whole subject and put it in order. In this way the paper will almost write itself. If the notes are to give you the most help, they must have a convenient mechanical form. Notes can be put on note cards (usually 4″ x 6″ or 5″ x 7″). Not more than one note, however brief, should be on a card. This rule should be strictly adhered to, even when the notes are on the same topic; for when you take the notes, you cannot be sure in what order you will eventually use them. Only if each note is independent can you arrange them in the order desired when you write your paper. Each note should carry at the top, at the left, or toward the center, some indication of the precise content—not the general subject of your investigation, but some subtopic. And at the top right or at the bottom, the note should carry an adequate reference to the source from which it is drawn. Presumably the full bibliographical information about that source is already in your working bibliography, and so some skeleton notation will be adequate here. (When you are taking notes not related to a working bibliography—when, for example, you are doing general reading—you should record full bibliographical information with the note.) See specimen card below.

```
American success worship              Chesterton, What I
                                      Saw in America,
                                      pp.  107-10.

American worship of success not materialistic.  Fact
of worship means a mystic rather than a materialist.
Frenchman who saves money to retire and enjoy his ome-
let more of a materialist.  American does not work for
the enjoyment of things, but for some ideal vision of
success.  He does not want the dollar for what it will
buy but as a symbol.  Phrase "making good" illustrates
the fact; carries a moral connotation by a "sort of
ethical echo in the word" good  (p. 108).  Not neces-
sarily an admirable morality, but a morality implied,
and idealism of a kind.
```

When we look at the actual note on the card we see that several other phrases might have been used to indicate the topic discussed; for instance, "American business mysticism," or "American materialism." All that is needed is a word or phrase that will remind the note-taker of the content.

We notice, too, that after the direct quotation there is a parenthesis with the page number. The note-taker apparently feels that this is a telling phrase worth remembering and perhaps using. If he quotes it, he will want the exact page reference.

As for the bibliographical indication at the upper right, he might have reduced it simply to "Chesterton" if there was no Chesterton other than G. K. Chesterton in his bibliography and no other book by that author. This, like the topic indication, is for his own convenience and need tell no more than he himself has to know to identify the source.

So much for the mechanics of note-taking. As for the process, you should make your notes relevant, accurate, and clear. To make them relevant you must keep constantly in mind the main purpose of your investigation. You are studying a particular subject with particular limits. (Remember in this connection what was said on pages 12–15 with regard to a "true subject.") You are not concerned with anything only casually associated with the subject. If, for instance, you are reading a general history to find information on the subject of the economic background of the American Revolution, you should not be distracted by the military strategy of the French and Indian War or an analysis of Puritan theology. Your job is to follow your main purpose through a body of various materials, and often what is major for you will be minor in the work you are investigating.

It is possible to take notes prematurely. Therefore, it is always best to become acquainted with a work before you take notes from it. In your first reading you may indicate material for possible notes and pass on. When you have finished the work, or those parts relevant to your interest, you can then better assess the material for possible notes. In this way you will get from any particular work only the most pertinent notes, and you will avoid duplication.

The note itself may be direct quotation or summary. If direct quotation is used, it is sometimes valuable to record the context of the quotation. What leads the author to make his statement? What point does he try to establish by it? You do not want to misinterpret your author by implication. For instance, suppose a critic should write:

> Although Herman Melville has created in Captain Ahab of *Moby Dick* a character of intense interest and monumental proportions, he has in general little sense of the shadings of personality and motive. Most of his creations are schematic, mere outlines without flesh. He lacks that basic gift of the novelist, a sense of character.

If you, assembling material for a paper on Melville as a novelist, should merely quote, "Herman Melville has created in Captain Ahab of *Moby Dick* a character of intense interest and monumental proportions," you would have a misleading note. An accurate note would run something like this:

Even though this critic believes that Melville in general lacks a sense of character, he admits that Captain Ahab is a "character of intense interest and monumental proportions."

This principle of context holds good for both the note by summary and the note by quotation.

When you are taking notes by summary, the kind of summary to be used depends on the special case. In one case, the author's method of reasoning may be very important, and then the summary should be of a form to indicate the logical structure of the original text. In another case, where mere facts or scattered opinions are involved, the summary need record merely these facts and opinions. As for the scale of the summary, there is no guiding principle except the note-taker's need. Try to forecast what you will need when you actually come to write your paper; not merely what you will want to incorporate in the paper, but what you will need in order to understand your subject fully.

Once your notes are taken, how do you use them? [2] This again depends on the kind of subject with which you are dealing. Some subjects suggest a chronological order, others a logical order. For instance, if you are doing a paper on Keats's development as a poet you might first arrange your notes chronologically—notes on early poems, notes on middle poems, notes on late poems. But if your subject is an analysis of the themes of Keats's poems, you might try to arrange your notes by themes, trying various classifications until you have one that seems to make sense. Or you might find, sometimes, that two levels of organization are necessary. For instance, certain themes of Keats's poems might be characteristic of certain periods. Then having established one type of classification (by theme), you might run another type (by chronology). Notes are flexible. You can use them as a device to help your thinking or to help you organize your material.

Notes record questions and issues. The different authors you have consulted have had individual approaches to the general subject, different interests, different conclusions. As you work over your cards you can locate these differences and try to see what they mean to you in your special project. Ask yourself if there is any pattern of disagreement among the authors you have consulted. List the disagreements. Are they disagreements of fact or of interpretation? Compare the evidence and reasoning offered by the authors who are in disagreement. Can you think of any new evidence or new line of reasoning on disputed points? Can you think of any significant points not discussed by your authors? What bearing would such points have on their conclusions? Again, use your notes as a device to help your thinking.

---

[2] At this point it might be useful for you to look back over Chapter 3, Organizing the Composition, pp. 31–51.

The Outline

The outline has two uses. It can help the writer to organize his own thoughts and lay a plan for his work before he begins the actual paper. And it can help the reader to define the basic meaning and structure of what he reads. The two uses have much in common, for both mean that the maker of the outline is dealing with the structure of a discourse. In fact, once an outline is completed, an observer might not be able to tell whether it was designed by a writer or a reader.

Types of outlines

There are several common types of outlines: (1) the suggestive, or scratch, outline, (2) the topic outline, (3) the sentence outline, and (4) the paragraph outline. Variations may be worked out for special purposes.

1 **The Scratch Outline** The scratch outline is a set of notes and jottings that may be useful either for writing or for understanding and remembering what one has read. It is probably not highly organized. For instance, the student, in making a preliminary survey of his notes, may simply put down the various topics and ideas that come to him in the order in which they come. As some line of thought begins to emerge he may indicate this, too. But his primary purpose is not to define the form and order from the beginning. It is to assemble suggestive material from his notes. He may not use some of it because, in the end, it may seem superfluous or irrelevant. The scratch outline embodies the early exploration of a subject and may be meaningless to everybody except the maker of the outline. (For examples of scratch outlines see pp. 533–34 and 549–50.)

2 **The Topic Outline** The topic outline does indicate the order of treatment of individual topics and does indicate in a systematic fashion, by heads and subheads, the relation among the parts in degree of importance. But as the name indicates, it proceeds, not by sentences, but by listing topics. There is, however, one exception: the outline should be introduced by a statement of the theme of the paper in the form of a fully rounded sentence. Let us set up a topic outline based on an essay by Louis D. Brandeis called "True Americanism."

> *Statement:* True Americanism is defined as the rights to life, liberty, and the pursuit of happiness, for both individuals and nations.
> I. Motto of United States, *E pluribus unum*
>   A. Union through federation of many states
>   B. Nation created through mixture of many peoples
>   1. Immigration important in growth of nation
>   2. Immigrants Americanized through liberty
> II. Nature of Americanization
>   A. Adoption of language, manners, and customs

B. Development of affection for and interests in United States
C. Harmonization with American ideals
III. American ideals
  A. Development of the individual through liberty
  B. Attainment of common good through democracy and social justice
  C. Achievement of American standard of living
    1. Good working conditions
    2. Education throughout life
    3. Industrial freedom for the individual
    4. Financial security through social insurance
  D. Inclusive brotherhood
    1. Equality of individual accepted by other countries
    2. Equality of nationalities and races accepted only by United States

The student should understand that the headings in this outline do *not* correspond to paragraph divisions. Heading I, for example, may correspond to only one paragraph; heading II may cover several paragraphs. That is, the outline is not by paragraphs but by topics. Not infrequently we find that a topic that looms very important in the outline will correspond to only part of a paragraph in the text. The outline indicates the relative importance of a topic and not the amount of space devoted to it.

3 **The Sentence Outline** The sentence outline is the most complete and formal type. Here, every entry is in the form of a complete sentence. As with the topic outline, the entries in the sentence outline should correspond to the content and the order of arrangement in the text. The sentence outline differs from the topic outline in indicating more fully the content of each item and the relation among the items. To fulfill these requirements, the sentences should be very precise and to the point. Vague statements defeat the very purpose of the sentence outline and make such an outline look like merely an inflated topic outline. For the sentence outline should really take us deeper into the subject, defining the items more closely and indicating the structure more fully. By and large, the topic outline will serve for fairly simple material, the sentence outline for more complicated material. In setting up a sentence outline, main heads should be given Roman numerals; the subdivisions, scaling down in importance, should be marked *A, 1, a*. A dummy form will make the system clear:

  I. ....
    A. ....
      1. ....
        a. ....
        b. ....
      2. ....
        a. ....
        b. ....
    B. ....
      1. ....

```
          a.  ....................................................................................
          b.  ....................................................................................
      2.  ....................................................................................
  II.  ....................................................................................
      A.  etc.
```

It is important to keep the indentations on the left margin consistent in each class and to be sure that a class of lower importance is more deeply indented than the class just above it. If more subdivisions are needed than are indicated here, the system can be begun over again with the key numerals and letters in parentheses. For instance, if subdivisions are needed under *a,* we can use *(1), (A), (1),* and so forth. But for ordinary purposes such an extension is rarely necessary.

Here is an example of a sentence outline made up from the first six paragraphs of Schlesinger's "On the Inscrutability of History" (pp. 826–28):

> *Statement:* A knowledge of history is important for the statesman, but it must be used with full awareness of history's inscrutability.
> I. All public policy decisions are based on history.
>   A. It is difficult to determine how history is used to make policy.
>   1. Does history provide reasons for policy or arguments to favor predetermined policy?
>   2. The ambiguity of history can supply rationalizations for more than one policy.
>   B. The central problem is to decide how successfully history can be used as a means of prediction.
>   1. Many historians do not believe in its value for prediction.
>   2. Public figures who were also historians were not necessarily influenced by history.
>   3. Some historians do believe that knowledge of the past can provide guidance for the future.
>   C. The value of history in policy-making lies in the uniformities and recurrences of events.

4 **The Paragraph Outline** In the paragraph outline each sentence corresponds to a paragraph in the text. In dealing with a very obviously organized piece of writing, the paragraph outline may be composed of the topic sentences, or adaptations of the topic sentences, of the paragraphs. (It is possible, of course, to make a paragraph outline of entries that are not complete sentences, but such a paragraph outline would have little utility. It would consist of little more than suggestive notes for paragraphs.) In dealing with other kinds of writing, however, it is necessary to summarize for each paragraph the content and intention. The paragraph outline has a very limited utility. On the one hand, in dealing with work composed by someone else, the paragraph outline often misses the real logical organization; for, as we have seen, paragraphs do not necessarily represent logical stages. On the other hand, in dealing in a preliminary way with material about which one intends to write oneself, not only may the outline fail to indicate the

logical organization desired, but it may be arbitrary and misleading. It is very hard to predict the paragraph-by-paragraph development of any relatively extensive or complicated piece of work. To try to do so sometimes cramps and confuses the writer in the actual process of composition. The paragraph outline is chiefly valuable as a check on your own writing. In trying to make a paragraph outline of one of your own compositions, you may discover that some of your paragraphs have no proper center or function, and thus you may be led to revise.

Here is a sample of a paragraph outline designed to schematize the first three paragraphs of an essay by B. F. Skinner on "Freedom and the Control of Men" (pp. 644–45):

    I. The democratic philosophy that made possible the rise of modern science has prevented the full application of scientific principles to the conduct of human affairs.

    II. Science can explain human behavior by conditions outside the individual, and hence, it can produce desired behavior in men.

    III. The science of behavior is similar to the optimistic eighteenth- and nineteenth-century doctrines of human perfectibility, which democracy has lately lost sight of.

Outlining the research paper

By working over your notes and thinking about ideas suggested in them you will probably strike on some vague general plan for your paper. But do not commit yourself to the first plan that comes into your head. Consider various possibilities. Then when you have chosen the most promising, try to work up an outline on that basis. You will undoubtedly start with a scratch outline, the barest shadow of the paper you want to write. By checking back on your material you can begin to fill in the outline and determine the relation among the facts and ideas you wish to present. Perhaps a topic outline will serve your purpose, but at some stage a sentence outline will probably be helpful, for to make it you will have to state clearly and exactly what you mean.

Once you have an outline prepared, you can begin the actual composition. Use your outline as a guide, but do not consider yourself bound by it. As you write, new ideas will probably come to you, and if they are good ideas you should revise your outline to accommodate them. The outline is not sacred. Like your notes, it is simply a device to help you think. And remember that your paper should be a fully rounded composition, unified and coherent, emphasizing matters according to the scale of their importance. The outline is, in fact, only a start toward creating a fluent, well-proportioned discussion.

Your paper should be more than a tissue of facts and quotations from your notes. It should represent your handling of a subject and not a mere report on what other writers have said. Naturally, a large part of your material will be derived from other writers, but you should always ask yourself just what a fact or idea means in relation to your own purpose. If there is no proper place for it in your pattern, it should be excluded. A writer who has studied his subject well always has more material than he can use.

The Form of Footnotes and Bibliography

Full credit should be given for the source of every fact or idea derived from another writer. In your own text you will want to acknowledge any important item as a matter of help to your reader. It is easy to introduce a statement or a quotation by a clear explanatory phrase or sentence such as:

> Charles A. Beard has proved that . . .
> James Truslow Adams maintains that . . .
> An excellent statement of this view is given by James Truslow Adams in his *Epic of America:* . . .
> As Sinclair Lewis shows in *Main Street,* the culture of the American town is . . .
> On the other hand, a liberal economist such as Paul Douglas holds that . . .
> As Thomas Wolfe observed . . .

Some facts or ideas can simply be stated in your text if the fact or idea is not especially to be associated with the particular writer from whom you derived it. But in all cases, authority should be given in a footnote.

Exactly what must be footnoted? First, every direct quotation is identified in a footnote. Second, every statement of fact is referred to its source in a footnote. The student must use his discretion about documenting commonly known facts that are available in many sources. It is not necessary, for example, to cite an authority for the fact that the world is round. But it is probably necessary to document an assertion that the world is actually the shape of a grapefruit or a slightly squishy cantaloupe, the account given by present-day scientists. Third, every opinion or interpretation drawn from another writer should be referred to its source in a footnote, *even if the opinion or interpretation is one that you have independently come upon in your own thinking.* In cases where a group of facts or opinions treated together in one paragraph is drawn from the same source, one note at the end of the paragraph will serve for all the material. In cases where more than one source is involved for a single item in the text, one note will serve to acknowledge the several sources.

Footnotes

Variation in certain details is permissible in the form of footnotes—as we shall see in the discussion to follow—*but not* within the same paper.

Learn one of the standard forms and use it consistently in all your work.[3]
Here are a few general principles:

1 The author's name appears in direct form, not with the last name first as in the bibliography.

2 The title of a book or periodical is underlined in typescript or writing. This corresponds to italics in print. Even a relatively short piece of writing that has independent publication is considered a book. Sometimes a piece of writing, a poem for instance, first appears independently as a little book and is later included in a collection of the author's work. Practice varies in treating such items, but it is permissible to treat it as a book. Thus, we would underscore the title of T. S. Eliot's Four Quartets, but we might quote "Burnt Norton" (which is one of the four poems included) or we might underscore it.

3 The title of an item in a periodical appears in quotation marks.

4 When an item is first mentioned in a footnote, full bibliographical information is given. Later references use a brief identifying form, to be described later.

Here are examples of various types of footnotes. Observe carefully the form of punctuation, the nature of the material included, and the order of the items presented.

FOOTNOTES FOR BOOKS

One author

[1] Gay Talese, *The Kingdom and the Power* (New York and Cleveland, 1969), p. 17.

More than one author

[1] James L. Steffensen, Jr., and Lawrence Handel, *Europe This Way* (New York, 1968), p. 20.

[1] Mark Schorer and others, *Harbrace College Reader:* Second Edition (New York, 1964), p. 542. [When a book has two authors, both names are given. When there are more than two authors, only the name listed first on the title page is given.]

Translation

[1] Anton Chekhov, *The Party and Other Stories,* trans. Constance Garnett (London, 1919), p. 43.

Work in more than one volume

[1] Morris Bishop, ed., *A Survey of French Literature* (New York, 1955), II, 77. [Here the abbreviation *ed.* is for editor.]

Edited work

[1] Edgar Allan Poe, *Short Stories,* ed. Killis Campbell (New York, 1927), p. xxiii.

---

[3] The forms for footnotes and bibliography given in this and the following chapter are based on those in the Style Sheet published by the Modern Language Association.

FOOTNOTES FOR ITEMS FROM COLLECTIONS

[1] Ann Saddlemyer, "The Cult of the Celt," in *The World of W. B. Yeats,* ed. Robin Skelton and Ann Saddlemyer (Victoria, B. C., 1965), p. 24.

FOOTNOTES FOR ITEMS FROM PERIODICALS

[1] Eric F. Goldman, "The White House and the Intellectuals," *Harper's Magazine,* CCXXXVIII (January 1969), 43. [Here the Roman numerals give the volume number of the periodical. The last number, 43, is the page reference. Notice that the abbreviation *p.* is omitted for periodicals after the volume number.]

[2] Walter Sullivan, "Shell Collecting Tied to Spread of Starfish," *New York Times,* September 30, 1969, p. 38. [When no volume number is given, the abbreviation *p.* (or *pp.*) is used.]

[3] "Model VI," *The New Yorker,* XLV (September 20, 1969), 35. [An unsigned article. When certain items of information are missing, as in a government document or newspaper account that has no author, put the items in the same order, simply omitting any unavailable information.]

FOOTNOTES FOR ITEMS FROM THE BIBLE

[1] Psalms 23:6–8. [Here the first number is for chapter, the others for verses, inclusive.]

[2] II Cor. 6:9. [Here the abbreviation *II Cor.* stands for Second Corinthians. Certain books of the Bible have such standard abbreviations.]

When material is not drawn directly from its original source but from some intermediary source, acknowledgment should be made to both sources. For instance, the following note indicates that the writer has used a quotation from Stephen Spender that appeared in a book by Moody E. Prior:

[1] Stephen Spender, *The Destructive Element,* p. 11, quoted by Moody E. Prior, *The Language of Tragedy* (New York, 1947), p. 343.

All the forms given above indicate the first reference to a work. For subsequent references, three forms may be used. When the source in a footnote is the same as that indicated in the footnote immediately preceding, the abbreviation *ibid.* (for *ibidem*: in the same place) is used, with a new page reference if that is needed. For example:

[1] Loren Eiseley, "Science and the Unexpected Universe," *The American Scholar,* XXXV (Summer 1966), 423.

[2] *Ibid.,* 424.

When the reference to be repeated does not immediately precede, either of two basic forms may be used. If only one work by a particular author is referred to in the footnotes, his last name may be used, followed by the page reference, or his last name with the abbreviation *op. cit.* (for *opere citato:* in the work cited), with the page reference. The first practice is simpler, and is becoming more common than the other. For example:

¹ Loren Eiseley, "Science and the Unexpected Universe," *The American Scholar,* XXXV (Summer 1966), 423.
² Sir John Summerscale, ed., *The Penguin Encyclopedia* (Baltimore, 1965), p. 255.
³ Eiseley, 424.

If the author has more than one work referred to in the footnotes, then his last name will not be enough, and an abbreviated title will be necessary.

¹ Eiseley, "Science," 464. *Or:* Talese, *Power,* p. 22. [Notice that the abbreviation *p.* is omitted in the Eiseley reference, for the reference is to a periodical, while it is used in the Talese reference, which is to a book. In other words, the short form follows the practice of the long form in this respect.]

We have already referred to the abbreviations *ibid.* and *op. cit.* But there are a number of other abbreviations found in notes and bibliographical forms. You will not find a use for all of them in your own writing, but you will sooner or later encounter them in works that you read. Some of the Latin abbreviations are now commonly replaced by English forms or may be omitted altogether (as with *op. cit.*). In using such abbreviations, the main thing is to be consistent: use either Latin or English throughout any composition.

anon. Anonymous.
c. or *ca. (circa)* About a certain date (to be used to indicate an approximate date, when the real date cannot be determined).
cf. (confer) Compare.
ch. or **chs.** Chapter(s).
col. or **cols.** Column(s).
ed. Edited by, editor, or edition.
et al. (et alii) And others (when a book has several authors, the name of the first author followed by *et al.* may replace the full list).
f. or **ff.** One or more pages following the page indicated.
ibid. (ibidem) In the same work (referring to a work cited in a note immediately preceding).
idem Exactly the same reference, title, and page as that given above.
infra Below (indicating a later discussion).
l. or **ll.** Line(s).
loc. cit. (loco citato) In the place cited (when there is an earlier reference to the source).
MS., MSS. Manuscript, manuscripts.
n.d. No date (when publication date cannot be determined).
no. Number (as when listing the number of the issue of a periodical or series).
n.p. No place (when place of publication cannot be determined).
op. cit. (opere citato) In the work cited (used with author's name to indicate source already referred to).

p. or pp.   Page(s).

passim   In various places (used when the topic referred to appears in several places in a work cited).

q.v. (quod vide)   Which see (English form: see).

rev.   Revised.

see   Used to suggest that the reader consult a certain work referred to.

seq. (sequentia)   Following (English form: f. or ff.).

supra   Above (when the topic referred to has already been discussed).

tr. or trans.   Translated by, translator, or translation.

vide   See (English form: see).

vol. or vols.   Volume(s) (but "vol." and "p." are not used if figures for both are given, as in listing a periodical reference; in such cases, use Roman numerals for volume and Arabic for page: II, 391).

Bibliography

After you have prepared a draft of your paper and established all your footnotes, you are ready to set up your final bibliography. This may differ from your working bibliography, as was pointed out above, in that it contains only items that are actually referred to in your paper, not items that have been consulted but not used.

The form for such a bibliography permits certain minor variations. For instance, the name of the publisher is sometimes omitted; and there may be differences in punctuation. For example, the following entry can be punctuated in two ways:

> Barnes, Harry Elmer. *The Genesis of the World War.* New York: Alfred A. Knopf, 1926.

or:

> Barnes, Harry Elmer, *The Genesis of the World War,* New York, Alfred A. Knopf, 1926.

But in all forms the author's name comes first (with the last name first) followed by the full title of the work, the periodical or series if any, the place of publication, the publisher (if this form is used), and the date of publication. The items may be arranged in either of two ways. First, in a straight alphabetical order, according to the last name of the author or, if there is no author, by the main word of the title. Second, alphabetically within certain groups determined by the material dealt with: "Books," "Periodicals," "Documents," and so forth. Here are some examples of entries as they might appear in the bibliography of a paper on Woodrow Wilson:

> (PERIODICAL)   Baker, Ray Stannard. "Our Next President and Some Others," *American Magazine,* LXXIV (June 1912), 131–43.

(BOOK)	Barnes, Harry Elmer. *The Genesis of the World War*. New York: Alfred A. Knopf, 1926.
(DOCUMENT)	*Congressional Record,* XLIX–LI. Washington: Government Printing Office, 1913–14.
(BOOK)	McAdoo, Eleanor R. W. *The Woodrow Wilsons*. New York: The Macmillan Company, 1937.
(BOOK)	Wilson, Woodrow. *The Public Papers of Woodrow Wilson*. Edited by Ray Stannard Baker and William Edward Dodd, 3 volumes. New York: Harper and Bros., 1925–27.
(PERIODICAL)	Wilson, Woodrow. "Democracy and Efficiency," *Atlantic Monthly,* LXXXVII (March 1901), 289–99.

Notice that an overall alphabetical order is given, by author when an author is specified, and by leading word when there is no author ("Congressional"). In this short bibliography all types of sources are grouped together —books, collections, periodicals, and documents. In a long bibliography each type might be set up separately, with each group in alphabetical order.

CHAPTER 15

The Final Version: Writing and Rewriting

Throughout this book we have been insisting that in good writing all the elements are interrelated. There is no such thing as "good" diction apart from the context in which it occurs, or "correct" tone abstracted from a specific occasion. In good writing the principles of unity, coherence, and emphasis apply at all levels—not only to the larger blocks of the composition, but to the individual phrases and even the individual words.

Though this principle of interrelation, if clearly understood by the student, can illuminate the problems of writing, it can also be inhibiting. Confronted with the demand that every item in his composition be ultimately related to everything else, the student writer may not know where to start. He may feel that in a fabric so intricately interwoven, there are no seams— no natural divisions with which to begin. It may be well, therefore, in this last chapter to do two things. The first will be to review the typical methods by which one builds up a composition. The second thing will be to point out the importance of *rewriting*. Even professional writers rarely achieve an adequate unification of elements in the first draft. In this chapter we shall want to examine very carefully—and with concrete examples—what is involved in the process of rewriting.

Writing a Term Paper

Let us assume that the student has been assigned a term paper that is to deal with some aspect of American history [1]—political, economic, cultural,

---

[1] Later in the chapter we will discuss the problems involved in writing a literary paper.

or military. He may, if he likes, write about early movies or the development of the steel industry or the exploits of John Paul Jones. He happens to be interested, however, in the American Civil War, particularly as that war revealed the adaptation to warfare of the new machines and techniques of the dawning industrial age. He first thinks about treating the use in the Civil War of balloons for military observation, but decides that this topic is rather limited. He then seriously considers discussing the development of the ironclad ship as exemplified by the *Merrimac* and the *Monitor*. Finally, it occurs to him that the role of the railroads in the Civil War might offer him not only a topic in which he has a particular interest (his uncle is an official of a railroad) but one which would allow him a good deal of scope.

On reflection, he begins to fear that the topic offers him too much scope. In an important sense the whole of the war was, he realizes, a fight for control of means of communication—railroads and navigable rivers. He is up against the problem we dealt with earlier in this book (pp. 12–15), the problem of finding a "true subject." Discussion of the total strategy of the war would be more than he wants to attempt, but he feels that in the process of research and writing he may be able to grasp his true subject. At any rate, he goes to the library and sets to work to make an exploration of the subject of the role of the railroad in the Civil War.

Bibliography

By using the card catalogue in his library and some of the general aids referred to on pages 511–15 with some help from the reference librarian, he comes up with the following list of books and articles:

BOOKS

Primary Sources

Haupt, Herman. *Reminiscences of General Herman Haupt*. Milwaukee: Wright and Joys Co., Limited Autograph Edition, July, 1901.

Jacobs, M. *Notes on the Rebel Invasion of Maryland and Pennsylvania and the Battle of Gettysburg*. Gettysburg: Times Printing House, 1909.

Order Book. Civil War. Military Railroads. General Orders, Instructions, and Reports. n.p., n.d. (found at the Library Bureau of Railway Economics, Association of American Railroads, Washington, D.C.). Cited as "Order Book."

The War of the Rebellion. Official Records of Union and Confederate Armies. Washington: Government Printing Office, 1902, Series 1, 53 vols.

Secondary Sources

Freeman, Douglas S. *R. E. Lee*. 4 volumes. New York: Charles Scribner's Sons, 1934–36.

Turner, George Edgar. *Victory Rode the Rails*. Indianapolis: Bobbs-Merrill Company, Inc., 1953.

PERIODICALS

Weber, Thomas. Book review of *Victory Rode the Rails,* in *Mississippi Valley Historical Review,* XL, No. 4 (March 1954), 742.

MAPS

Map of United States Military Railroads, 1866 (to accompany reports of D. C. McCallum, 1861–66). Located at the Library Bureau of Railway Economics, Association of American Railroads, Washington, D.C.

(The student found many more books and articles, but these were the ones he actually sampled or read through carefully. Note that he did not use all these sources in his complete draft.)

Note-taking

Here are some sample notes taken by our student:

```
Haupt urged Burnside to cross        War of the
the Rappahannock                     Rebellion
                                     Vol. 33, 789.

1.  Supplies could be brought by water.
2.  He would have an established rail center to
    fall back on at Falmouth or
3.  to use for communication with Washington
    if he reached Richmond.
```

```
Haupt supplies Meade at        Turner, Victory Rode
Gettysburg                     the Rails, p. 280.

Haupt supplied enough materials to Meade in
four days to allow him to take the offensive.
The South was unable to do this for Lee in the
winter of 1862-1863.
```

```
┌─────────────────────────────────────────────────────────────┐
│                                                               │
│   Ewell's route to        Freeman, Douglas Southall,          │
│   Gettysburg              Lee's Lieutenants, New York:        │
│                           Charles Scribner's Sons,            │
│                           1944, 3 vols., III, 36.             │
│                                                               │
│   "To Heidlersburg, on the road to Gettysburg,                │
│   'Dick' Ewell made his way before sundown on                 │
│   June 30."                                                   │
│                                                               │
│                                                               │
│                                                               │
│                                                               │
└─────────────────────────────────────────────────────────────┘
```

(Note that on this third card there is full bibliographical information. The first two cards could omit it, for they refer to works already mentioned in the bibliography, where full information is given.)

■ APPLICATION

If you have already done the exercise on page 516, Chapter 14, you are ready to reduce your topic to a true subject. If you have not done this exercise, turn back to it now; select a topic and make a preliminary bibliography.

1   Take notes on your subject, following the suggestions outlined in Chapter 14, pages 517–19.

2   With the help of the notes you have assembled, fix upon the limited subject on which you will write.

Outline

When our student had finished his research in books and magazines, he had decided to narrow his subject to a discussion of the importance of railroads in one particular campaign, that which culminated at Gettysburg. So he jotted down the following scratch outline:

SCRATCH OUTLINE

The importance of the railroads in the Civil War can be illustrated by the Battle of Gettysburg and the events leading up to it.
Haupt's part in the Battle of Fredericksburg.
The Confederate army is forced to remain on the defensive because of the inefficiency of its railroad communications.
The next Federal offensive and the Battle of Chancellorsville.

Lee reorganizes his army and takes the offensive.
Lee's plan to cut the railroads connecting Washington with the rest of the Union.
Events that lead up to the Confederate failure at Gettysburg.
The problem of supplying Meade by railroads.
Haupt solves the problem.
Summary of Haupt's accomplishment.

First draft

Our student was aware that his scratch outline did not give him as clear an idea of the organization of the paper as might be desired. Still the scratch outline got down on paper many of the ideas that he wanted to deal with, and he still hoped that in the actual process of writing his ideas would become adequately clarified. At any rate, he decided to begin writing without going farther with his outline. Here are the first ten paragraphs of his paper.

RAILROADS IN THE CIVIL WAR

Railroads were used in the Crimean War, but the American Civil War was the first railroad war. Many historians studying the war ignore the significance of the railroads. They get bogged down in battles, by which I mean the actual fighting, or if they include them at all they include them in their passing mention of the industrial capacity of the North and South. The theme of this paper, on the other hand, is to discuss the strategic and tactical importance of the railroads in the campaigns of the Civil War by outlining their significance in the important period from the Battle of Fredericksburg to the Battle of Gettysburg. We live in an age of technology, but we did not invent it, it is well to remember.

The story of Gettysburg begins in the fall of 1862 when General Ambrose E. Burnside, who replaced General McClellan after the Battle of Antietam, moved his army to Stratford Heights and Falmouth on the north bank of the Rappahannock River overlooking Fredericksburg. In shifting position, Burnside was following the advice of his transportation chief, Herman Haupt. Even though it had to be rebuilt, Haupt favored using the Richmond, Fredericksburg, and Potomac Railroad to supply Burnside because it was a more protected road. On November 22, Haupt further advised Burnside to cross the Rappahannock, suggesting that supplies then could be carried by water, he would still have the railroad center at Falmouth to fall back on, and he would have an open means of communication with Washington if he reached Richmond.[1] It is not known to what extent this dispatch influenced Burnside, but on December 13 he attacked Lee at Fredericksburg and was defeated. The two armies spent the rest of the winter watching each other across the river.

Burnside was able to attack because Haupt had provided him with

---

[1] *The War of the Rebellion. Official Records of Union and Confederate Armies* (Washington, 1902), Series 1, XXXIII, 789.

enough supplies. On the other hand, Lee was unable to take the offensive during the winter of 1862–63, even after the victory at Fredericksburg, because his men were too weak from lack of food and the animals lacked forage. Fifty miles away at Richmond there were plenty of supplies, but they could not be brought forward because of the inefficiency of the railroads.[2] Yet Lee was being supplied by the same railroad, a different section, as Burnside.

The Confederates were consequently forced to take the defensive; and in the spring of 1863 General Hooker, who had replaced Burnside, began to prepare for an offensive. Haupt, in addition to meeting the daily demands of the Army of the Potomac, landed and made ready seventy cars of supplies, material, and prefabricated bridge trusses for the "on to Richmond" movement.[3]

The ensuing Battle of Chancellorsville was a stalemate, but the Union forces suffered more physically and moralewise. The time was opportune for an offensive by the South, but again the transportation corps could not provide the necessary supplies, and forage was running out in the area of Fredericksburg. Lee concluded his best alternative was to invade Pennsylvania, for he could gather his own supplies and forage there and he might be able to isolate Washington and give encouragement to the Peace Party, which was gaining strength in the North.[4]

After the Battle of Chancellorsville and the death of Jackson, Lee reorganized his army into three corps with James Longstreet, Richard Ewell, and A. P. Hill in command of the first, second, and third corps, respectively. Lee entered his most important battle with an untested, reorganized army. The objective of the invasion of Pennsylvania was railroad centers whose destruction would cut Washington off from the north and south and this again ties into the main idea. Ewell's corps was to move up the Shenandoah from Fredericksburg with Longstreet following him and with Stuart to the right of Longstreet as a screen. Hill, by remaining at Fredericksburg, would screen the rear, but when Ewell reached the Potomac River, Hill was to follow him, and Longstreet was to move westward into the Valley and then proceed northward leaving Stuart to defend the mountain passes and screen the right.[5]

Once into Maryland, Ewell was to destroy the Baltimore and Ohio Railroad and then split up his force, part heading to Harrisburg to destroy the Cumberland Valley Railroad and part moving toward York to destroy the Northern Central. Longstreet was then to push forward to Havre de Grace and destroy the Pennsylvania Railroad main line and the great bridges over the Susquehanna River. Washington would then be isolated.[6]

Lee advanced according to schedule and on June 28, when General Meade replaced Hooker as commander of the Army of the Potomac, Ewell

---

[2] Douglas S. Freeman, *R. E. Lee* (New York, 1934–36), II, 493–94.

[3] Haupt's dispatch to Stanton, September 9, 1863, *Order Book* (n.p., n.d.).

[4] M. Jacobs, *Notes on the Rebel Invasion of Maryland and Pennsylvania and the Battle of Gettysburg* (Gettysburg, 1909), p. 1.

[5] Freeman, II, 33.

[6] George Edgar Turner, *Victory Rode the Rails* (Indianapolis, 1953), p. 273.

was only eighteen miles from Harrisburg and the Army of the Potomac was still around Frederick, Maryland. Unfortunately Stuart became separated from Lee, who then did not know where the Army of the Potomac was, and when Meade began to move after Lee, the two armies unknowingly converged on Gettysburg. Both armies were reorganized and untested; and Lee, who had given up his communications with Richmond, was living off the land. Meade did not give up his lines of communication, but he had to move so fast it became difficult to supply his army. When the two armies met July 1, 2, and 3, they were in some ways evenly matched, and a writer like Douglas Freeman seems to argue that the main difference at Gettysburg was the tactical errors made.

Perhaps the most telling fact was the reorganization of the Confederate Army and the attitude of the commanding generals. Lee was used to giving discretionary orders to Jackson, but the new commanders were used to explicit orders and lacked initiative. Several times they failed to act at crucial moments or failed to use their initiative. On July 1, Ewell and his division commanders were unwilling, after driving the enemy off Seminary Ridge, to attack Cemetery Hill, which could have been easily taken since the Union Army had not yet arrived in full force. Even more disastrous, Longstreet delayed the assault ten hours, and the next day during that time the ridge was fully fortified by forces that were just arriving. The delay was due mainly to Longstreet's disgruntled mood caused by Lee's rejection of a flanking movement he had planned. Yet Lee should have been able to shock Longstreet out of his insubordination.[7]

Another factor in the outcome was that Lee had no reconnaissance without Stuart.[8] He was like a blind man at times. Another minor factor was the poor use of Confederate artillery. The principle of converging lines of fire was ignored as were several advantageous positions and vulnerable targets.[9]

---

[7] Freeman, III, 147–50.
[8] *Ibid.,* p. 147.
[9] *Ibid.,* p. 152.

Rewriting

When the student had gotten this far, he stopped. He had become aware that his paper had lost direction. The last three paragraphs that he had written did not pertain to the thesis that he had meant to develop. A sentence like "Yet Lee should have been able to shock Longstreet out of his insubordination" touches upon a matter of interest to anyone concerned with the Battle of Gettysburg, but it really has nothing to do with the role of the railroads. At this point, therefore, the student decided to go back and rethink his paper. To this end, he resolved to make a careful outline, in this instance, a sentence outline. He hoped that the process of working out a fairly elaborate and precise outline would enable him to see how much space he should give to the Confederate difficulties of command—if any— and how to relate this matter to his general thesis.

Before working out his sentence outline, however, our student turned back to the chapter on exposition and reread the various sections, including that on expository narration, for it was apparent that a discussion of the importance of the railroads in the Civil War would make use of expository methods, and that if he discussed a particular military campaign, narrative methods would also be involved. Here follows the student's sentence outline:

SENTENCE OUTLINE

Proposition: A consideration of the Battle of Gettysburg and the events leading up to it reveals how important were the railroads in determining the strategy and the outcome of the Civil War.

I. The role of the railroads in the Civil War, a role that the historians have tended to slight, may be illustrated with the Gettysburg campaign.

II. The chief events leading up to Gettysburg were powerfully determined by problems of rail supply.

    A. Burnside and Lee fought at Fredericksburg in December, 1862, because Burnside's transportation chief, Haupt, had favored using the Richmond, Fredericksburg, and Potomac Railroad.

        1. He argued that this rail line was better protected, and that

        2. If Burnside could break through to Richmond, he would have an open means of communication with Washington.

    B. Though victorious at Fredericksburg, Lee's inefficient rail supply prevented him from going over to the offensive.

    C. When in the spring of 1863 Lee defeated Hooker at Chancellorsville, lack of supplies and forage hampered his taking the offensive.

        1. Supplies were low in the vicinity of Fredericksburg, and

        2. Inefficient rail service prevented them from being brought from more distant areas.

III. The railroads were important in shaping Lee's plan to invade Pennsylvania.

    A. He hoped, by living off the country in Pennsylvania, to ease his own problem of supply.

    B. He hoped to isolate Washington by cutting its rail connection.

        1. Ewell was first to destroy the Baltimore and Ohio Railroad, and then to destroy the Cumberland Valley Railroad and the Northern Central.

        2. Longstreet was to destroy the main line of the Pennsylvania Railroad at Havre de Grace and the bridges over the Susquehanna River.

    C. Lee followed his plan and on June 28 when Meade replaced Hooker, Lee was to the west and Meade to the east of Gettysburg, where the two forces eventually met and brought on the battle.

IV. The contribution made by Haupt's management of the railroads becomes clear when one realizes how close the Confederates came, in spite of costly mistakes, to winning at Gettysburg.

    A. Various reasons have been alleged for Lee's failure, including
        1. His lack of adequate reconnaissance because of Stuart's absence.
        2. The use of vague and discretionary orders that allowed lags and failures on the part of the corps commanders.
        3. Longstreet's tardiness in carrying out Lee's orders to attack.
        4. Other tactical mistakes of various kinds.
    B. In spite of piecemeal rather than unified attack, the Confederate forces mounted an intense offensive that came close to winning.
    C. Since none of Meade's forces had supplies to fight a three-day battle, Meade's success in holding his ground depended heavily on Haupt's ability to keep him supplied with food, ammunition, and equipment.

  V. Haupt's problem in supplying Meade's army in Pennsylvania was a difficult one.
    A. He first had to make the proper diagnosis of Lee's intentions.
    B. The one direct rail route from Baltimore to Gettysburg had been destroyed by Ewell.
    C. The closest available rail route stopped at Westminster.
        1. The distance from Westminster to Gettysburg would have to be covered by wagon.
        2. The rail route lacked sidings, turntables, and watering stations.
        3. It could handle only four trains a day, whereas thirty were required.

  VI. Haupt's success in organizing railroad supply lines was the result not only of forethought but of brilliant improvisation.
    A. He had previously stockpiled materials and tools for just such an emergency.
    B. On the Western Maryland he used such expedients as
        1. Running the trains in convoys of five each.
        2. Running the trains backwards on the return trip.
        3. Replenishing water from streams by bucket brigades.
    C. So successful was Haupt that by July 3, the Western Maryland's capacity had been increased tenfold.
    D. Haupt also had his construction crews immediately start repairs on alternate rail lines to Gettysburg.
    E. On July 5 Meade was actually being supplied beyond his daily needs.

  VII. The North was indeed fortunate in having in its service a man of Haupt's special genius.

■ **APPLICATION**

Write a sentence outline of the paper for which you have taken notes. (See pp. 521–22.) If you have been assigned a paper in literary criticism, you may want to take into account pages 546–49 as well.

With his sentence outline before him, the student proceeded to redraft the first part of his paper and to go on to complete it. He was happy to find, as he began to write, that the sentence outline substantially justified the first four paragraphs of his first draft. He did make a number of changes, however, as you will see by comparing the first four paragraphs of the two drafts. (Most of the added matter and also of the transposed matter has been put in italics so that the reader can more easily locate the changes.) Note also the changes made in paragraphs 5 through 9. Here the student had felt the need to compress material that was not really very relevant to his thesis. He was also attempting in these paragraphs to strengthen the argument for the importance of the railroads, and to find a better transition to his account of Haupt's extraordinary feat at Gettysburg. As you read the revised paper (which follows), observe the changes.

RAILROADS IN THE CIVIL WAR

(1) *Although* railroads had been used in the Crimean War, the American Civil War was the first railroad war. *It was the first time each side utilized an extensive rail system in a total war effort.* Many historians studying the war ignore the significance of the railroads or include them in their passing mention of the industrial capacity of the North and South. The theme of this paper asserts the strategic and tactical importance of the railroads in the campaigns of the Civil War by outlining their significance in the important period from the Battle of Fredericksburg to the Battle of Gettysburg.

(2) The story of Gettysburg *really* begins in the fall of 1862 when General Ambrose E. Burnside, who *had* replaced General McClellan after the Battle of Antietam, moved his army to Stratford Heights and Falmouth on the north bank of the Rappahannock River overlooking Fredericksburg. In shifting *his* position, Burnside was following the advice of his transportation chief, Herman Haupt. *Because the Richmond, Fredericksburg, and Potomac Railroad was relatively easy to protect,* Haupt favored using it to supply Burnside *even though it had to be rebuilt.* On November 22 Haupt advised Burnside to cross the Rappahannock, suggesting that supplies then could be carried by water, *that if unsuccessful, Burnside* would still have the railroad center at Falmouth to fall back on, and *that if he did break through to Richmond,* he would have an open means of communication with Washington.[1] It is not known to what extent this dispatch influenced Burnside, *but in any case it was the duty of Burnside to judge Haupt's advice in the overall military situation. Burnside must take the responsibility for the brutal defeat he suffered when, on December 13, he attacked Lee at Fredericksburg.* The two armies spent the rest of the winter watching each other across the river.

(3) Burnside was able to attack because Haupt had provided him with enough supplies. Lee, *on the other hand,* was unable to take the offensive during the winter of 1862–1863, even after the victory at Fredericksburg,

---

[1] *The War of the Rebellion. Official Records of Union and Confederate Armies* (Washington, 1902), Series 1, XXXIII, 789.

because his men were too weak from lack of food and the animals lacked forage. *Only* fifty miles away at Richmond there were plenty of supplies, but they could not be brought forward because of the inefficiency of the rail *lines.*[2] Yet Lee was being supplied by the same railroad—*though* a different section *of it, of course*—as *that which served* Burnside.

(4) The Confederates were consequently forced to *remain upon* the defensive; and in the spring of 1863, General Hooker, who had replaced Burnside, began to prepare *another* offensive. Haupt, in addition to meeting the daily demands of the Army of the Potomac, landed and made ready seventy cars of supplies, material, and prefabricated bridge trusses for the "on to Richmond" movement.[3] *Hooker advanced, and was badly mauled by Lee and Jackson at* the Battle of Chancellorsville. The time was *again* opportune for an offensive by the South, but again the transportation corps could not provide the necessary supplies, and forage was running out in the area of Fredericksburg. *The rich countryside of Pennsylvania looked like a promising source of supplies.*

(5) *Lee's choice of route for the invasion was thus to a considerable extent dictated to him by the poor shape of the railroads on which he depended for much of his supplies. But railroads also figured in another way in his plans. He meant to achieve the isolation of Washington by severing the railroad lines that connected it with the north, west, and south. To cut off and seize the Northern capital would have immediate political advantage, by giving* encouragement to the Peace Party which was then gaining strength in the North.[4]

(6) *The plan was for Lee's army, which had been reorganized after the Battle of Chancellorsville, to make the invasion in three corps:* Ewell's corps was to move up the Shenandoah Valley from Fredericksburg with Longstreet's *corps* following him, and with Stuart *and his cavalry flanking* the right of Longstreet *and acting* as a screen. Hill's *corps,* by remaining at Fredericksburg, would *protect* the rear; but when Ewell reached the Potomac River, Hill was to follow him, and Longstreet was to move westward into the *Shenandoah* Valley and then proceed northward, leaving Stuart's *cavalry* to defend the mountain passes and *to furnish* a screen *to the* right *flank.*[5]

(7) Once into Maryland, Ewell was to destroy the Baltimore and Ohio Railroad and then split up his force, *one* part heading *for* Harrisburg to destroy the Cumberland Valley Railroad and *the other* moving toward York to destroy the Northern Central. Longstreet was then to push forward to Havre de Grace and destroy *the main line of* the Pennsylvania Railroad and the great bridges over the Susquehanna River. Washington would then be isolated.[6]

(8) Lee advanced according to schedule and when General Meade replaced Hooker on June 28, *Lee's forces were well up into Pennsylvania*

---

[2] Douglas S. Freeman, *R. E. Lee* (New York, 1934–36), II, 493–94.

[3] Haupt's dispatch to Stanton, September 9, 1863, *Order Book* (n.p., n.d.).

[4] M. Jacobs, *Notes on the Rebel Invasion of Maryland and Pennsylvania and the Battle of Gettysburg* (Gettysburg, 1909), p. 1.

[5] Freeman, II, 33.

[6] George Edgar Turner, *Victory Rode the Rails* (Indianapolis, 1953), p. 373.

to the west and north of Gettysburg while the main Federal army was still around Frederick, Maryland, *to the east, between Lee and his ultimate objective, Washington. Neither force had a clear notion of where the other was and small detachments, accidentally coming into contact at Gettysburg, brought on the battle there. The battle began blind.*

(9)   *The Battle of Gettysburg has for nearly a century held the interest of military historians. Various reasons have been advanced to account for Lee's repulse in this great struggle, which probably proved to be the turning point of the whole war. In advancing the notion here that Haupt's ability to supply Meade was a decisive factor, I am not trying to come up with the full answer to a difficult question. I am not forgetting that Stuart's absence with the cavalry put out Lee's eyes,[7] or that Lee's army in its new organization was largely untested, or that Lee's orders were too vague or left too much to the discretion of field commanders, or that Longstreet's notorious delay in launching the attack Lee had ordered almost amounted to insubordination.[8] In fact, so much went wrong that the remarkable thing is that the Confederates were able to mount so intensive an offensive and come so close to victory. But the very narrowness of the margin between victory and defeat itself stresses the importance of Haupt's contribution. Had Meade's army been seriously weakened by a lack of supplies, it might not have managed to hold firm.*

[From this point on the treatment is new.]

(10)   General Haupt took charge of the railroads in Maryland and Pennsylvania on June 28, the same day that Meade replaced Hooker. The problem that confronted him was a formidable one. Meade's army had moved in four days from the Potomac to Gettysburg and some of the troops arrived on Cemetery Ridge after long hours of marching. For an unexpected, intense, three-day battle Haupt had to supply Meade's army in a position picked by accident and over rail lines the enemy had already damaged. To cap the climax, just as he was about to go to Pennsylvania, he was unexplainably delayed by the War Department.[9]

(11)   When he was released from Washington, he hurried to Harrisburg but was detoured through Philadelphia because Ewell had already destroyed part of the direct route. He arrived there the evening of June 30, and Tom Scott, district manager for the Pennsylvania Railroad, reported the enemy had withdrawn from the region of Harrisburg toward Gettysburg. Scott, who had organized his own company of railroad scouts to protect his lines, thought the Army of Northern Virginia was withdrawing; but Haupt realized they were concentrating their forces to meet Meade and that there would probably be a battle at Gettysburg unless Meade altered his course. Late that night Haupt headed for Baltimore. The one rail route that went directly to Gettysburg had been destroyed by Ewell. The closest available rail route was from Baltimore to Westminster and thence by wagon to Gettysburg. The road was only twenty-eight miles long, but unfortunately there were no sidings, no turntables, no watering

---

[7] Freeman, III, 147.
[8] *Ibid.,* pp. 147–50.
[9] Turner, p. 276.

stations, and little wood available. Thirty trains would be needed a day; and the road could only handle four at the most, two each way.[10]

(12)   On July 1, Haupt arrived in Westminster and found chaos. Supplies were trickling in and hundreds of Meade's wagons were collecting there. Haupt had, literally, to hide from the crowd, but in several minutes he had devised a plan and before returning to Baltimore had sent several hurried telegrams. Within a few hours his construction corps began to arrive in Baltimore from Alexandria, with buckets, tools, material, and wood, supplies that Haupt had stockpiled in Alexandria for just such an emergency. Impressed rolling stock also began to accumulate in the Baltimore yards.[11]

(13)   On July 1, trains began to roll over the Western Maryland line to Westminster, the day Meade was hurrying to reinforce the two corps who then were holding Cemetery Ridge. None of Meade's forces had supplies to fight a three-day battle. The supply trains ran in convoys of five each, at eight-hour intervals. Each convoy had time to cover the distance, unload supplies, and return with wounded before the next convoy, loaded and waiting in the Baltimore yards, pulled out. Haupt had persuaded the Quartermaster Department to supply enough men so that when the trains arrived in Westminster every car was unloaded simultaneously and then reloaded with wounded. The trains were run backwards and filled with water from streams by bucket brigades. In addition to these crews, repair crews were placed at intervals along the route to check for and repair weak places, for the road bed and track were not strong enough to handle the increased load of traffic. Haupt's men were aware of the crisis and worked like beavers; so by July 3, fifteen hundred tons were being carried daily. The capacity of the road had been increased tenfold.[12]

(14)   The great number of men involved in this operation had been supplied by Haupt, as had all the material. He even supplied the train crews. However, he did not limit his activity to the Western Maryland. He assigned a number of men from his construction corps to work on the Northern Central and York and Cumberland, which ran directly to Gettysburg. Ewell had destroyed nineteen bridges and miles of track on this route.[13] Haupt, however, realized that while the road could not be made ready for the immediate battle, it might be needed later. If the Union forces were victorious, it could easily be able to provide enough supplies for an offensive against the demoralized forces of Lee and could remove the wounded so the army could move forward quickly. In case of defeat it would facilitate retreat. Haupt's crews began work on the afternoon of July 1; and by the afternoon of July 4, the day Lee was retreating, the road was open to within fifteen miles of Gettysburg and completed just after midnight.[14] The wounded were now carried out by this route and supplies brought in through Westminster.

---

[10] Haupt's dispatch to Stanton.
[11] Turner, p. 279.
[12] *Ibid.*
[13] Haupt's dispatch to Stanton.
[14] Turner, p. 280.

(15)   On July 5, Haupt was supplying Meade with supplies beyond his daily needs, and it was on this day that Haupt urged Meade to follow up his advantage. The Army of the Potomac now had an established supply line, and back in Virginia the rail lines would be badly damaged. Meade would not advance and Haupt returned to Washington and tried to get a pre-emptory order.[15] This attempt failed, and by July 14 Lee was back in the Shenandoah.

(16)   General Haupt had performed an amazing feat at Gettysburg. It is further from Baltimore to Gettysburg than from Richmond to Fredericksburg, but Haupt had done in four days of battle what the South could not do in four months of peace before Chancellorsville: to supply the army with enough provisions and material to take the offensive.[16]

(17)   The North was fortunate to find a man of Haupt's caliber who had the ability to utilize the potential of railroads in wartime. In one and three quarter years Haupt developed precedents for the operation of railroads in time of war, a problem never before faced by anyone, which still form the basis for the operation of railroads in war by the United States almost a hundred years later.

> Haupt was an engineering genius who helped sustain mediocre Union commanders in Virginia and who performed an outstanding feat of transportation on the Western Maryland Railroad during the Gettysburg campaign.[17]

A study of the operations of General Haupt or of the use of railroads in other campaigns and under other men would show clearly that the railroads had a decisive effect in many of the campaigns of the Civil War.

---

[15] Herman Haupt, *Reminiscences of General Herman Haupt* (Milwaukee, 1901), Limited Autograph Edition, p. 73.
[16] Turner, p. 280.
[17] Thomas Weber, book review of *Victory Rode the Rails,* in *Mississippi Valley Historical Review,* XL (March 1954), 742.

At this point the student has before him a completed draft of his paper. The first section of it actually represents, as we have seen, a rewriting—a second draft. Let us stop and review that part that is a second draft, and try to follow the logic of some of the changes.

The main change has already been mentioned—the reorganization to correct the diffuse analysis of the causes of the Confederate defeat and to put the focus back on the subject of the railroads. In paragraph 9 we can see how competently the student has done this. The military aspects of the occasion are finally related to the point of the paper: "But the very narrowness of the margin between victory and defeat itself stresses the importance of Haupt's contribution"—and, of course, the importance of the railroad.

To turn to smaller concerns, we can see clear improvements in the first paragraph. The rewriting of the first sentence, with the remark about the Crimean War now put into an introductory subordinate clause introduced by the concessive *although,* sharpens the focus on the Civil War. The new second paragraph makes precise what had been vaguely implied by the phrase "railroad war" in the original first sentence. The student has also sharpened his meaning by getting rid of the sentence beginning "They [the historians] get bogged down in battles . . ." (p. 534). The metaphor of "bogging down" in battles is a poor one, both trite and inaccurate, and the fumbling explanation beginning "by which I mean . . ." doesn't help matters. In the rewriting, the student has compressed and stated more accurately his view of the historians. And he has dropped the last sentence of the paragraph, which had set up a distraction from the main idea of the paper.

If we jump ahead to paragraph 5 (p. 540) we see some clear gains in clarity of organization. But there are gains of another sort in the revision of the clause "but the Union forces suffered more physically and morale-wise" (first draft, p. 535). It is not quite clear what the student means by "suffered more physically." Does he mean that the Union army endured more casualties? Probably, but there is still a confusing margin of other possibilities of meaning. As for the word *moralewise,* it is an example of the current practice of tacking *wise* on to any word—*insurancewise, healthwise, housewise*—to make a series of barbarous and superfluous coined words.

In the *final* draft of the paper, which is not given here, the student made several further revisions. Among them was a revision of paragraph 13. Quite properly he was dissatisfied with the structure of that paragraph. On reflection he saw that the first two sentences do not belong to a paragraph dealing with the details of the supply system. So he rewrote them and attached them to the previous paragraph as a kind of climax:

> . . . rolling stock also began to accumulate in the Baltimore yards. On July 1, the very day when Meade was hurrying reinforcements to the two corps then holding Cemetery Ridge, the first train rolled over the Western Maryland line to Westminster. It was none too soon, for none of Meade's forces had supplies for the bitter three-day contest which lay ahead.
>
> The supply trains ran in convoys. . . .

■ APPLICATIONS

I Reread the brief comments above on the student's revision of his paper. Can you account for the changes that have not been discussed there? Has the theme anywhere been altered for the worse? Can you suggest further changes?

1 In paragraph 9 we find the sentence: "In fact, so much went wrong that the remarkable thing is that the Confederates were able to mount so intensive an offensive and come so close to victory." In his final version the student made two changes in the sentence. Can you guess why? What changes would you make?

2 Near the end of paragraph 13 occurs the sentence: "Haupt's men were aware of the crisis and worked like beavers; so by July 3, fifteen hundred

tons were being carried daily." What do you think of this sentence? If you do not like it, how would you revise it?

3 Does paragraph 14 exhibit unity? Is there material in it that should go back into the previous paragraph? If you think so, try to revise the end of paragraph 13 and the beginning of the next. Keep in mind the question of transition.

4 Go back to paragraph 1 of the second version (p. 539). What is the promised subject of the paper? Now look at the last paragraph. Is it properly geared to the subject, or does it dwell too much on the personal achievement of General Haupt? Try to revise the paragraph.

II Write the first draft of the paper for which you have made an outline.[2] (See p. 538.) Now begins the really serious work: revision. Study your paper with reference to the following considerations:

1 Have you stated the thesis or proposition of your paper? If not, is it clear by implication?

2 Does the body of the paper form a logical sequence? That is, does it present evidence and argument, if such are appropriate, in an orderly fashion? Does it give narrative, if its business is to give narrative, in such a way as to indicate cause and effect, and to give an impression of meaningful climax? And so on. Does the logical sequence, of whatever sort it happens to be, lead continuously from the first paragraph to the last? Are there any distracting digressions?

3 Are there clearly defined transitions from paragraph to paragraph?

4 Are the paragraphs organized so that they exhibit unity and coherence?

5 Check the sentence structure, the agreement of subjects and verbs, the reference of pronouns, the sequence of tenses, the position of modifiers. Check punctuation.

6 Have you any examples of metaphorical language? If so, are they fresh and apt? If not, try again. Do you find any points where some comparison might help?

7 To whom are you addressing your paper? What is your attitude toward your audience? What do you expect to be the attitude of the audience to your subject? What is your own attitude? In the light of these questions, do you feel that the tone of your paper is satisfactory?

8 Read your paper out loud—or better, have someone read it to you. Do you find any rhythms that are jarring or monotonous? If so, try to determine the reason. Perhaps your sentences tend to be of the same length and structure. Or perhaps they are so sprawling that the ear cannot grasp them. Try shifting the elements for variety and emphasis. Try to relate the logic of what you are saying to what your ear instinctively indicates about the rhythm.

---

[2] If you have chosen or been assigned a literary topic, you may—unless you have already done so—want to study pages 547–49 before you embark on a first draft of that paper.

After the first complete revision put the paper down for a day or two. Then come back to it. Try again to improve it. The writer, whether novice or veteran, must not become weary in well doing. Good writing is mostly re-writing. The sweat is worth as much as the inspiration.

Writing a Literary Paper

Let us assume that the student has been assigned a paper in literature—a paper that treats of a particular author or a literary work or a literary genre such as, say, comedy or propaganda novels. The *general* problems that are involved are the same as those already discussed and illustrated in the student paper on "Railroads in the Civil War." But papers in literature do tend to present some special problems, and it may be well to illustrate these by a concrete example, a student paper on the poetry of the great twentieth-century poet, William Butler Yeats.

This student—for ease of subsequent reference let us call her Susan—had become very much interested in Yeats's poetry. After encountering some ten or twelve of his poems in an anthology, she immediately bought a paperback selection of his poems. This further acquaintance with his poetry soon decided her to do her term paper on Yeats.

Clearly her first task was to master (as nearly as she could) Yeats's poetry; but she obviously needed also to read a life of Yeats, and she thought she ought to learn something about what the established Yeats authorities had said about the man and his work. When, however, she consulted the card catalogue in her college library, she was appalled at the number of books and articles on Yeats. In fact, she was overawed by the sheer number of plays, essays, letters, and other autobiographical documents written by Yeats himself.

Susan's difficulty here is one frequently met by a student who is planning to write on any well-known writer. Our age produces a vast number of books and articles. (Some would say that it overproduces them.) If all the books and articles that achieve print were good, one could speak of an embarrassment of riches. But the true situation is different. Though there are, to be sure, many excellent books and essays, there are also many mediocre ones, there is much duplication, and there is even some trash.

What is the student to do? He cannot read everything. How is he to know what is worth reading? Susan sensibly went first to her instructor for advice; she then made a list of works based on his suggestions and on the bibliography in her copy of the selected poems, which, her instructor said, had been edited by a sound Yeats authority. Finally, she did some vigorous sampling of each work before committing herself to reading it through.

Here is the list of books and articles that Susan drew up. Some she used in her paper and others she simply consulted casually. To see which works she actually used, check the bibliography that appears at the end of the revised draft (p. 584).

LIST OF WORKS CONSULTED

Baker, Howard. "Domes of Byzantium," *The Southern Review,* VII (1941–42), 639–52.

Berryman, Charles. *W. B. Yeats: Design of Opposites.* New York: Exposition, 1967.

Blackmur, R. P. "The Later Poetry of W. B. Yeats," *The Southern Review,* II (1936–37), 339–62.

Donoghue, Denis, and J. R. Mulryne, editors. *An Honored Guest.* New York: St. Martin's Press, 1948.

Ellmann, Richard. *Yeats: The Man and the Masks.* New York: Macmillan, 1948.

Henn, T. R. *The Lonely Tower.* London: Methuen, 1950.

Hone, Joseph. *W. B. Yeats, 1865–1939.* London: Macmillan, 1942.

Jarrell, Randall. "The Development of Yeats's Sense of Reality," *The Southern Review,* VII (1941–42), 653–66.

Jeffares, A. Norman. *W. B. Yeats: Man and Poet.* New Haven: Yale University Press, 1949.

Kermode, Frank. "The Artist in Isolation," in *Yeats: A Collection of Critical Essays.* Edited by John Unterecker. Englewood Cliffs, N.J.: Prentice-Hall, 1963.

Kermode, Frank. *Romantic Image.* London: Routledge and Kegan Paul, 1957.

Menon, V. K. Narayana. *The Development of William Butler Yeats.* Edinburgh: Oliver and Boyd, 1942.

Mizener, Arthur. "The Romanticism of W. B. Yeats," *The Southern Review,* VII (1941–42), 601–23.

Polletta, Gregory. "The Progress in W. B. Yeats's Theories of Poetry," *Dissertation Abstracts,* XXII (Jan.–Mar. 1962), 2399–400.

Rosenthal, M. L., editor. *Selected Poems and Two Plays of William Butler Yeats.* New York: Collier Books, 1966.

Saddlemyer, Ann. "The Cult of the Celt: Pan-Celtism in the Nineties," in *The World of W. B. Yeats: Essays in Perspective.* Edited by Robin Skelton and Ann Saddlemyer. Victoria, B. C.: University of Victoria Press, 1965.

Stauffer, Donald A. "W. B. Yeats and the Medium of Poetry," *ELH,* XV (1948), 227–46.

Tate, Allen. "Yeats's Romanticism: Notes and Suggestions," *The Southern Review,* VII (1941–42), 591–600.

Unterecker, John. *A Reader's Guide to William Butler Yeats.* New York: Noonday Press, 1959.

Yeats, W. B. *Autobiographies.* London: Macmillan, 1955.

———. *Collected Poems.* New York: Macmillan, 1951.

———. *Essays and Introductions.* New York: Macmillan, 1961.

———. *Explorations.* London: Macmillan, 1962.

———. *Mythologies.* New York: Macmillan, 1959.

———. *On the Boiler.* Dublin: Cuala Press, 1939.

Choosing a subject

On page 14, and earlier in this chapter, we discussed the need to discover one's true subject. With a literary topic, the problem of locating the true subject may present special difficulties. The reason is easy to see: in a literary paper the interpretative element is large, and the problems of interpretation may take subtle forms. It is much easier to evaluate the strategy in a military campaign than the literary strategy employed in a sonnet or a novel. The importance to an army of an excellent line of supply is obvious and easily stated. The importance to a poet of a certain kind of imagination is harder to make clear to a reader.

It was Susan's deep interest in Yeats's poetry that had induced her to choose it for her topic. But she wanted to do more in her paper than say over and over how much she admired Yeats's poetry. Even if she tried to tell the reader how much a particular poem—like "The Second Coming" or "A Prayer for My Daughter"—had meant to her, she feared that her merely personal response would not exert much of a claim on any reader's attention. In very skillful hands, a highly personal response might lead to a fine piece of impressionistic criticism. But Susan, in her modesty, was well aware that in her case it might simply lead to gush.

It might be worth remarking just at this point that most literary discussions may be usefully divided into three general categories: (1) Discussion that has to do with the *effects* of the literary work; for example, on the reader, as in Susan's delighted response to Yeats's poetry, or on other readers, as Yeats's influence on other modern poets or on the Irish people. (2) Discussion of the *make-up* of the work—what it means and "how" it means—its arrangement of parts, use of language, choice of metaphors, development of symbols, complications of tone, and so forth. In this category would come an analysis of a particular Yeats poem or play or of a group of his poems. (3) Discussions of the background and "causes" of the literary work. Into this category would fall essays on the various factors, historical and personal, conscious and unconscious, that had shaped Yeats's poetry. In this area of interest, the student of Yeats might write about the way in which Yeats's unhappy love affair with Maud Gonne had affected his poetry or how the climate of ideas in which he had grown up made it possible for him to write a certain kind of poetry, and so on.

Though it is true that one cannot make a rigid separation of the three areas of interest (the effects of, the make-up of, and the genesis of, a work of literature), and though the literary critics and scholars quite properly move back and forth across the boundaries between them, an awareness of these differences of interest may clarify certain problems and even help the student—as it helped Susan—to choose his true subject when he is assigned to write a literary paper.

In her search for a true subject, Susan jotted down such topics as "Yeats as an Irish Poet," "Yeats as a Modern Poet," "The Development of Yeats's

Poetry," "How Yeats Became a Poet of Reality," and "What the Abbey Theatre Taught Yeats."

Susan immediately realized that the last topic, for one, was entirely too restrictive for her purposes. Yeats's practical struggles with an Irish theater and his disappointment with the way in which the Irish people responded to it may well have had a profound effect on this poetry. But Susan was not primarily interested in Yeats as a playwright, and she felt that she didn't know enough (and wouldn't have time to learn enough) about the workings of the Abbey Theatre to be able to make much of this rather special material.

As she looked again at this list of topics, she noticed that one basic idea seemed to be trying to emerge: the fact of a significant development in Yeats's poetry. At her very first reading of Yeats, she had been struck with the difference between his early, rather charmingly dreamy, lyrics and the powerfully muscled poems that came as he approached middle age. Susan soon discovered that most authorities on Yeats took some such development for granted, though they proceeded to account for it in rather different ways. At any rate, their corroboration of what she had discovered for herself gave her confidence. She would try to explore and document in her own way Yeats's development toward realism. (Perhaps *realism* wasn't the best term, but it would do until she found a better one.)

Thus, Susan's paper would fall primarily in the third area of interest described above. Yet at every point, of course, she would need to deal with the second area (the make-up of Yeats's poetry). Otherwise, she wouldn't be able to say how his early, dreamy poetry differed in quality from the tough-minded poetry of his maturity.

Outline and first draft

Susan put down as a tentative title: "The Poet and the Poem: W. B. Yeats's Concept of Poetry and Life." It was too long and probably too general, and might have to be modified later, but she felt that it was something with which she could begin work. With this title in mind, she went back over her reading in and about Yeats, making notes on cards (pp. 517–19) and searching the bibliographies for books and articles that concerned themselves especially with Yeats's development. In taking notes, Susan was particularly careful to set down such quotations from Yeats as she thought might serve to document the observations she would be making about the stages of his development.

After she had assembled a good number of such note cards, she began to jot down her ideas on paper, arranged and rearranged them, and finally developed the following scratch outline:

> Yeats believed that poetry was nourished by reality and not by abstractions from reality. Therefore, the poet must not run away from life.
> Yet Yeats began his poetic career by trying to escape into a dream world. See his early lyrics and his long poem "The Wanderings of Oisin."

Even the "escapist" Yeats, however, shows an affectionate regard for some
  aspects of earthly life, and even in his early poetry one feels a tension
  between the claims of reality and the imagination.
Yeats's interest in Ireland's heroic past. By recalling it to his countrymen,
  Yeats hoped to strengthen the modern Irishman's sense of his unique
  cultural identity. Yeats helps to found the Abbey Theatre.
Yeats not an activist in politics; rather, wished to give his countrymen
  spiritual inspiration.
Failure of Yeats's attempt to revive legends about the ancient gods and
  heroes of Ireland. Yeats's disappointment with modern Ireland.
Modern Irish impress Yeats as timid shopkeepers and not passionate men
  of action.
Yeats's unhappy love affair with Maud Gonne.
Yeats's failure and disappointments bring him to a more realistic view of
  things and change his conception of what his own poetry ought to be.
  His poetry becomes "cold" and "hard" and sometimes angry.
Poetry becomes for Yeats no longer an escape from life but the real busi-
  ness of his life, and Yeats becomes a philosophical and prophetic poet.
Summary of the argument.

Then Susan proceeded to write the following paper:

THE POET AND THE POEM: W. B. YEATS'S CONCEPTS OF POETRY AND LIFE

(1)   William Butler Yeats realized that a poet often lives a mental
existence. In his mind the poet contemplates ideas, and this contemplation
necessitates withdrawal from the world of men. Yeats questioned this withdrawal: "Can a man of genius make that complete renunciation of the
world necessary to the full expression of himself without some vice or
some deficiency?" [1] "No" was Yeats's answer; if the poet renounces the
world, both his poetry and his life will be deficient.

> The poet must not seek for what is still and fixed, for that has no
> life for him; and if he did, his style would become cold and monoto-
> nous, and his sense of beauty faint and sickly . . . , but be content
> to find his pleasure in all that is for ever passing away that it may
> come again, in the beauty of woman, in the fragile flowers of spring,
> in momentary heroic passion, in whatever is most fleeting, most
> impassioned . . . . [2]

Imagined, "fixed," abstract images are inferior to the reality of this world
  as matter for poetry.

> Art bids us touch and taste and hear and see the world, and shrinks
> from what Blake calls mathematic form, from every abstract thing,

---

[1] W. B. Yeats, *Autobiographies* (London, 1955), p. 512.
[2] W. B. Yeats, "The Cutting of an Agate," in *Essays and Introductions* (New York, 1961), p. 287.

from all that is of the brain only, from all that is not a fountain jetting from the entire hopes, memories, and sensations of the body.[3]

The poet must avoid isolation in a mental world of abstractions; he must experience the world and write about mundane life. This Yeats believed, so he sought to live vigorously in the real world and to express his experiences in his poetry. The older he became and the more experiences he gathered, the more his poetry reflected and illumined his experiences: poetry became for Yeats the clarifier of his life, not an escape from life.

(2) However, Yeats's poetry evolved to this state of nonescapism; it did not begin there. His early poems praise escape into the imagination, away from this real world of sorrow. Thus in "The Song of the Happy Shepherd" (1889) Yeats sympathizes with the "sick children of the world" who endure "all the many changing things/In dreary dancing past us whirled."[4] "Words alone are certain good," the young shepherd declares and the young Yeats would like to sing his songs and dream by the grave of the faun. But even here the stuff of poetry is human experience.

> Go gather by the humming sea
> Some twisted, echo-harbouring shell,
> And to its lips thy story tell,
> And they thy comforters will be,
> Rewording in melodious guile
> Thy fretful words a little while,
> Till they shall singing fade in ruth
> And die a pearly brotherhood;
> For words alone are certain good:
> Sing, then, for this is also sooth.[5]

The poet's fretful words about life are transformed by his imagination (the seashell) into pearly poetic words.

(3) "The Wanderings of Oisin" (1887) also contains some of Yeats's youthful escapism. Yeats exalts the imaginary land of faeries, where love and youth last forever, and the dead Fenian warriors of Irish legends—both so opposite from modern-day, Christian Irishmen who are an unheroic, a "small and feeble populace stooping with mattock and spade/Or weeding or ploughing."[6] As in "The Song of the Happy Shepherd," Yeats dreams of escape but at the same time recognizes the dreadful state of life in the real world.

(4) The theme of escape to the land of faeries pervades Yeats's poetry written before 1900. These faeries were the gods of ancient Ireland; they are called the Tuatha de Danaan or the Sidhe.[7] They are supernatural beings who seek to entice mortals to their kingdom. To the young Yeats they represent a haven from worldly cares.

---

[3] *Ibid.,* p. 293.
[4] W. B. Yeats, *Collected Poems* (New York, 1951), p. 7.
[5] *Ibid.,* p. 8.
[6] *Ibid.,* p. 378.
[7] M. L. Rosenthal, ed., *Selected Poems and Two Plays of William Butler Yeats* (New York, 1962), p. 211.

Away with us he's going,
The solemn-eyed:
He'll hear no more the lowing
Of the calves on the warm hillside
Or the kettle on the hob
Sing peace into his breast,
Or see the brown mice bob
Round and round the oatmeal-chest.
For he comes, the human child,
To the waters and the wild
With a faery, hand in hand,
From a world more full of weeping than he can understand.[8]

The world is a place of weeping from which a man can flee to the faeries and dance and forget earthly woes. But even in his anticipation of this escape, Yeats recognizes the pleasures of life—the kettle that can "sing peace into his breast." There are some parts of earthly life that Yeats does not want to escape.

(5) This tension between the real world and the faery world, between reality and the imagination, is one of the basic themes in Yeats's poetry ("The Man Who Dreamed of Faeryland," "To the Rose Upon the Rood of Time," "All Things Can Tempt Me"). The poet must live in both worlds, and he must balance them.

> An art may become impersonal because it has too much circumstance or too little, because the world is too little or too much with it, because it is too near the ground or too far up among the branches.[9]

Circumstance and the world are the raw material of poetry, but the artist must transform them into beauty.

> I have desired, like every artist, to create a little world out of the beautiful, pleasant, and significant things of this marred and clumsy world . . . .[10]

Creating beautiful and pleasant things requires thinking about living instead of living.

> Our fire must burn slowly, and we must constantly turn away to think, constantly analyse what we have done, be content even to have little life outside our work. . . . Only then do we learn to conserve our vitality, to keep our mind enough under control and to make our technique sufficiently flexible for expression of the emotions of life as they arise.[11]

In his early poetry, Yeats often strays from the life outside his work. "To an Isle in the Water," "A Faery Song," "The Lake Isle of Innisfree,"

---

[8] "The Stolen Child," in *Collected Poems,* p. 19.

[9] "The Cutting of an Agate," in *Essays,* p. 272.

[10] *The Celtic Twilight* (1893) as quoted by Ann Saddlemyer, "The Cult of the Celt," in *The World of W. B. Yeats,* ed. Robin Skelton and Ann Saddlemyer (Victoria, B. C., 1965), p. 24.

[11] Yeats, *Autobiographies,* p. 318.

"The Hosting of the Sidhe," "Into the Twilight"—all of these pre-1900 poems contain the dream of escape from worldly cares and actions. Yeats wants a better world and seeks it in his imagination.

(6) Yet even during this time (1890–1900) Yeats did not solely dream about escape. He had a plan for uniting Ireland and so helping her gain the mental strength for fighting Britain. The plan for unity had two aspects: religious and literary. Yeats wanted to revive the Druid traditions, combine them with his Hermetic Society mysticism, and initiate a new Irish cult.[12] The second aspect was literary and entailed writing plays, reviving Irish legends, and with Lady Gregory, founding the Abbey Theatre (1904). Yeats's absorption in Irish legends was not an unusual interest, because many other people were studying Irish folklore during this period known as the Celtic Revival.[13] The Irish legends about Fergus and Cuchulain, Finn and Oisin, emerged in poetry and prose, with "renewed emphasis on the virtues of the peasant and the glamour of the remote past."[14] Yeats used the legends not to escape reality but to mold a new reality, a new Ireland.

> Might I not, with health and good luck to aid me, create some new
> *Prometheus Unbound;* Patrick or Columcille, Oisin or Finn, in
> Prometheus' stead; and, instead of Caucasus, Cro-Patrick or Ben
> Bulben? Have not all races had their first unity from a mythology
> that marries them to rock and hill? We had in Ireland imaginative
> stories, which the uneducated classes knew and even sang, and
> might we not make those stories current among the educated classes,
> rediscovering for the work's sake what I have called 'the applied
> arts of literature,' the association of literature, that is, with music,
> speech, and dance; and at last, it might be, so deepen the political
> passion of the nation that all, artist and poet, craftsman and day-
> laborer would accept a common design?[15]

The "common design" was to be the emancipation of Ireland from England's rule.

(7) However, Yeats's involvement in politics was more mystical than militant. He espoused the freedom movement partly because of his love for Maud Gonne, a rabid revolutionist. Yeats's more impassioned involvement was not politics but building a "mystical order" or religious cult for Ireland. For ten years he worked to establish mysteries for it.

> I had an unshakable conviction, arising how or whence I cannot
> tell, that invisible gates would open as they opened for Blake, as

---

[12] Richard Ellman, *Yeats: The Man and the Masks* (New York, 1948), pp. 115–27.
[13] Saddlemyer, pp. 19–21. Saddlemyer gives specific publications that presented Celtic literature, beginning in the year 1856. Old Irish manuscripts were exhumed and translated by German scholars; "by the end of the century innumerable scholars, organizations and periodicals were devoted to the recovery of the Celt" (p. 20). The Pan-Celtic Society was founded in 1899; *Celtic: a Pan-Celtic Magazine* published its first number in 1901.
[14] Saddlemyer, p. 21.
[15] Yeats, *Autobiographies*, pp. 193–94.

they opened for Swedenborg, as they opened for Boehme, and that this philosophy would find its manuals of devotion in all imaginative literature, and set before Irishmen for special manual an Irish literature which, though made by many minds, would seem the work of a single mind, and turn our places of beauty or legendary association into holy symbols.[16]

This new Irish cult would give Irishmen "spiritual inspiration" and fortification.[17] Thus Yeats, working in literature, worked for Irishmen. He was very much involved in the real problem of Irish independence, and he sought to involve his art in it.

(8) As has been shown, Yeats's use of Irish folklore had a practical goal—the spiritual unification of Irishmen to fight the English. More importantly, he hoped that the association of literature, music, speech and dance would give Ireland Unity of Culture—"philosophy and a little passion."[18] This goal failed: "the dream of my early manhood, that a modern nation can return to Unity of Culture, is false; though it may be we can achieve it for some small circle of men and women, and there leave it till the moon bring round its century."[19] But even though Yeats failed, the fact remains that he was writing for real men about real life. He stated his goals explicitly:

> My work in Ireland has continually set this thought before me: "How can I make my work mean something to vigorous and simple men whose attention is not given to art but to a shop, or teaching in a National School, or dispensing medicine? . . .
>
> They must go out of the theatre with the strength they live by strengthened from looking upon some passion that could, whatever its chosen way of life, strike down an enemy, fill a long stocking with money or move a girl's heart. . . . Their legs will tire on the road if there is nothing in their hearts but vague sentiment, and though it is charming to have an affectionate feeling about flowers, that will not pull the cart out of the ditch.[20]

Clearly Yeats wanted to affect his audience, to strengthen their hearts and minds and help them live active heroic lives in the real world. He did not want to just show them an Elysium of faeries and folk heroes.

(9) The way to give Ireland Unity of Culture was to give all Irishmen

---

[16] *Ibid.*, p. 254.
[17] Ellman, p. 122. Ellman goes on to write: "Maud Gonne thought that the order might work for separation of Ireland from Britain in the same way as the Masonic lodges in the north of Ireland were, she believed, working for union. It would use Masonic methods against the Masons, as another nationalistic organization, the Clan na Gael, had done. Yeats, less political in his objectives, vaguely anticipated that the order would be able to aid the movement for national independence by its magical powers. . . . Driven almost frantic by loving in vain 'the most beautiful woman in the world,' he thought that in collaboration with Maud Gonne in this spiritual conspiracy their minds would be so united that she would consent to become his."
[18] Yeats, *Autobiographies*, p. 195.
[19] *Ibid.*, p. 295.
[20] "The Cutting of an Agate," in *Essays*, pp. 265–66.

Unity of Being—a life of intellect and emotion, contemplation and action. But Yeats knew that Irishmen were not unified beings. They were primarily dullards—not heroic men of action like their ancestors had been.

> What need you, being come to sense,
> But fumble in a greasy till
> And add the halfpence to the pence
> And prayer to shivering prayer, until
> You have dried the marrow from the bone?
> For men were born to pray and save:
> Romantic Ireland's dead and gone,
> It's with O'Leary in the grave.[21]

Modern Irishmen spend their time praying, hoarding their money, and keeping their shops. They have no appreciation of art and therefore refused to build a museum for Hugh Lane's pictures.[22] But he still hopes that the "Ireland of priest, merchant, and politician might [come to] resemble 'an Ireland/The poets have imagined, terrible and gay,' might, in fact, resemble Cuchulain's Ireland, a land of reckless heroes. . . ."[23]

(10)   Yeats now wanted to make his poetry too the opposite of all that his earlier poetry had been. No longer did he seek images of bright colors or of ethereal shapes but cold and austere images.

> . . . as I look backward upon my own writing, I take pleasure alone in those verses where it seems to me I have found something hard and cold, some articulation of the Image which is the opposite of all that I am in my daily life, and all my country is. . . .[24]

Yeats's hard, cold Image and its hard poetic form represented the opposite of his real tender-hearted self. This remarkable shift in poetic temperament had definite causes: Maud Gonne married John MacBride (1903); Dublin rejected the Hugh Lane pictures (1912–13); Synge's *Playboy of the Western World* was violently rejected by the Irish (1907). Yeats was angry and disappointed with Ireland. The real world had jolted his mind and heart, and his thoughts and feelings found a voice in his poetry. Gone are the dreams of faeries and Innisfree. Now Yeats writes about thwarted love ("Adam's Curse," "No Second Troy"), about his theater work ("The Fascination of What's Difficult"—"My curse on plays/That have to be set up in fifty ways,/On the day's war with every knave and dolt,/Theatre business, management of men"), and about his petty countrymen ("September 1913," "Paudeen").

(11)   Poetry was Yeats's life, his work, and his business. "I thought it was my business in life to be an artist and a poet, and that there could be

---

[21] "September 1913," in *Collected Poems*, p. 106.
[22] Hugh Lane was the nephew of one of Yeats's friends, Lady Gregory. For an account of the incident, see A. Norman Jeffares, *W. B. Yeats: Man and Poet* (New Haven, 1949), pp. 169–70.
[23] John Unterecker, *A Reader's Guide to William Butler Yeats* (New York, 1959), p. 17.
[24] Yeats, *Autobiographies*, p. 274.

no business comparable to that."[25] Yeats's attitude toward his business changed as he got older. His anger and hatred (seen in *Responsibilities,* 1914) softened, especially after his marriage to George Hyde-Lees in 1917. In *The Wild Swans at Coole* (1919), Yeats philosophically reminisces about his past youth ("The Wild Swans at Coole"), his dead friends ("In Memory of Major Robert Gregory"), and regretful events ("The Fisherman" with its lines about "The beating down of the wise/And great Art beaten down."). Moreover, Yeats began a new role in his business as poet— that of poetic prophet. His wife's automatic writing revealed a system for classifying men, nations, and periods of history into lunar phases of certain degrees of objectivity and subjectivity. So Yeats begins writing about the system—"The Phases of the Moon," "The Saint and the Hunchback," "The Double Vision of Michael Robartes." In these philosophical poems, Yeats seeks to understand his world. His system as presented in *A Vision* (1925) was for Yeats "not reality but the pattern of reality."[26] The system clarified reality; it was not a realm fabricated by Yeats for the purpose of escaping from the real world.

(12) Yeats's poems continued to reflect the real events around him. In "Easter 1916" he praises the patriots—Constance Markiewicz, Patrick Pearse, Thomas MacDonagh, John MacBride—who led the abortive Easter Rising. Yeats revered and supported the fighters for Irish freedom, yet he disliked their disdain for the old, aristocratic traditions and feared the hatred "peddled in the thoroughfares" ("A Prayer for My Daughter"). The year 1922 brought civil war to Ireland, and Yeats writes about the violence in "Meditations in Time of Civil War" and in "Nineteen Hundred and Nineteen." At the same time he continues to systematize reality and predict the future in such poems as "The Second Coming," "Two Songs from a Play," and "Leda and the Swan." Nostalgia for the aristocracy and the peasants ("Under Ben Bulben"), laments for old age ("The Tower"), exhortations about Unity of Being ("Among School Children"), memories of dead friends ("The Municipal Gallery Revisited"), the immortality of art ("Sailing to Byzantium" and "Byzantium")—these themes dominate the poems written by the elder Yeats.

(13) Yeats was a sensitive man who reacted strongly to reality and recorded his reactions in his poetry. He also tried to understand reality— history and men—by formulating systems and writing poetry about the systems. His poetry helped him understand himself.

> I might have found more of Ireland if I had written in Irish, but I have found a little, and I have found all myself. I am persuaded that if the Irishmen who are painting conventional pictures or writing conventional books on alien subjects . . . would do the same, they, too, might find themselves.[27]

Furthermore, he strove to understand the real world and men in order to write better poetry.

---

[25] *Ibid.,* p. 188.
[26] Unterecker, p. 24.
[27] "Ireland and the Arts," in *Essays,* p. 208.

All my life I have been haunted with the idea that the poet should know all classes of men as one of themselves, that he should combine the greatest personal realization with the greatest possible knowledge of speech and circumstances of the world.[28]

Knowledge of worldly circumstances, knowledge of other men, and "personal realization" are the sources of meaningful poetry, according to Yeats. He strove to be "preoccupied with life"—not aloof from it.[29] He wanted to express in his poetry "the normal active man" instead of the "traditional poet."[30] He believed that the necessary ingredient for a "great poet" was an "interesting" life.[31] Although Yeats's early poetry deals primarily with escapism and secondarily with his interesting life, reality increasingly invades his poems until it eventually consumes them: the reality of his life becomes art. Yeats is always aware of reality, even in his dreamiest poems, and likewise his earthiest poems have imaginative wanderings into Anima Mundi or faeryland. Yeats's thoughts roamed in both worlds—the real and the fictional, but he chose to root his life and his poetry predominantly in the real.

---

[28] Yeats, *Autobiographies,* p. 470.
[29] *Ibid.,* p. 188.
[30] *Ibid.,* p. 492.
[31] *Ibid.,* p. 103. Yeats would have subscribed to his father's dictum: "All art is *reaction from life,* but never, when it is vital and great, an *escape....*" (See Frank Kermode, "The Artist in Isolation," in *Yeats: a Collection of Critical Essays,* ed. John Unterecker [Englewood Cliffs, N.J., 1963], p. 39.)

Revising the first draft

Susan handed her paper to her roommate, Jane, to look over. Jane read it with care but, after paying Susan some rather general compliments, confessed that certain things in the paper were not clear to her. The conversation between the two students went like this:

SUSAN: Do you mean that you don't get the drift of the general argument? I thought I had made it clear that Yeats began his career as a rather dreamy, escapist poet but later became more and more involved in the real world.

JANE: No, my difficulty isn't with your general argument. That is plain enough. But I am confused by your account of Yeats's development. For example, you write in paragraph 4 that "The world is a place of weeping from which a man can flee to the faeries and dance and forget earthly woes"—that is, you are saying that Yeats found the real world so sorrowful that he wanted to escape from it. So when you write in paragraph 10 that "The real world had jolted his mind and heart," I expect you to go on to say that Yeats was confirmed in his rejection of the painful world of reality; but instead you write: "Gone are [his] dreams of faeries and Innisfree." Yet if, as he grew older, the world became even less satisfactory, why didn't he reject it still more violently?

SUSAN: Oh, but by this time Yeats had become involved in the world around him and that involvement had its effect on his poetry.

JANE: That's not the point that bothers me. [As sometimes happens in criticizing literary works, Jane was having difficulty in explaining exactly what she found unclear in Susan's paper.] I agree that you stress Yeats's growing interest in contemporary Irish culture and politics. You date that interest as early as the 1890's. In paragraph 6 you write that even in this period "Yeats did not solely dream about escape."

SUSAN: I make that point as early as paragraph 4, and in paragraph 5 I say flatly that "one of the basic themes" of Yeats's poetry is a "tension between the real world and the faery world, between reality and the imagination."

JANE: Hold on! What you just said—that last phrase, "between reality and the imagination"—marks precisely the spot where I get lost. You imply that reality and the imagination are opposed. Yet if they are, how can the poetry of the mature Yeats—or any other work of the imagination—reflect the world of reality?

SUSAN: But Yeats's great imaginative work—the poetry of his maturity—does encompass reality. That's just what my paper——

JANE: Wait! I'm sorry to keep interrupting. But you're missing my point: Just what do you mean by *imagination?* You are not using that word consistently, and that's why your paper is confusing. Let me illustrate. I've always understood that a poet is a man of powerful imagination and that therein lies his poetic gift. But in your second paragraph you say that Yeats's "early poems praise escape *into* the imagination."

SUSAN: Aren't you quibbling about a term? Surely——

JANE: It may sound like nit-picking, but it isn't. There's an important issue at stake. When you write "escape into the imagination," presumably you mean "escape into a dreamy unreal world," and yet a little further along—let's see, yes, in paragraph 6—you quote Yeats's remark that the traditional Irish "imaginative stories" could be used to "deepen the political passion of the nation" and (in paragraph 7) that Ireland might find its new "manuals of devotion" in "imaginative literature." These remarks sound as if Yeats thought of the imagination not as a means of escaping from reality but as a means of revealing, and perhaps even molding, it. Your various uses of the word *imagination* just aren't consistent, and this inconsistency confuses your discussion of Yeats's development.

SUSAN: Well, I'm not fully convinced, but it's plain that I had better rethink my use of this term.

Susan did so. She discovered that her use of the word *imagination* was indeed ambiguous, and that at a number of points in her paper she had been guilty of fuzzy thinking and an imprecise use of terms. Papers involving literary criticism frequently involve difficulties of this kind. We lack a consistent critical vocabulary, and some literary concepts are in themselves difficult to grasp. But the student, like Susan, should not be overawed by such difficulties. Common sense and some care in rewriting will take care of most of them.

Let us now look at a few of the specific problems that Susan uncovered and follow her line of reasoning as she uncovered them. To return to *imagination,* she had to decide whether imagination, as she and Yeats used the term, was a "good thing," the essential resource of a great poet, or whether it was a means for evading reality. She decided to limit her use of *imagination* to the former meaning and to revise the sentence challenged by Jane to read something like this: "The contest between the claims of the workaday world and a yearning to escape into the timeless world of the faeries is one of the basic themes of Yeats's early poetry." (Perhaps this sentence might be revised even further in terms of a changed context.)

Another use of vague language was related to her earlier ambiguous use of *imagination.* Thus, in paragraph 5 she had written that "The poet must live in both worlds [that is, the world of reality and that of the imagination], and he must balance them." But what, she had to ask herself, did her sentence mean? When the poet is eating his breakfast or waiting for a bus, is he living in the real world? But *not* living in it when he is using his imagination and creating a poem? If her sentence could be taken to imply the latter notion—and in the context, she had to admit to herself, it might—then it falsified the relation of the imagination to reality.

Yet even if she altered the sentence in paragraph 5 to make it clear that the two things to be balanced by the poet were matter-of-fact and make-believe, was *balance* the right word? The poet doesn't balance these elements, measuring out so many ounces of fantasy into one pan of the scales in order to balance so many ounces of factuality in the other. That is not the way in which any poet works. Susan had put the real situation much more accurately when she wrote, further down in the same paragraph, that "Circumstance and the world are the raw material of poetry, but the artist must transform them into beauty." The transforming agent, as she herself had suggested in paragraph 2, is the imagination.

So, instead of "The poet must live in both worlds," and so on, Susan decided to substitute some such statement as the following: "As a young poet, Yeats gave rather direct expression to his yearnings, dreams, and aspirations: his earlier poems thus tend to be fantasies of escape from the limitations of human reality rather than an imaginative transformation of it."

Susan's reinspection of her third and fifth paragraphs and her sharpened awareness of the need to distinguish between imagination (which can transform reality) and mere daydreaming (which usually means an escape from reality) prompted her to review very carefully her opening paragraphs. In her very first paragraph she had noted the mature Yeats's repudiation of escapism. She had substantiated this point by three quotations from Yeats's own writings, one from his *Autobiographies* and two from "The Cutting of an Agate." She had read the latter work in a collection called *Essays and Introductions,* published in 1961.

Suddenly it occurred to her that she ought to check the date of first publication of "The Cutting of an Agate," for *Essays and Introductions* included quite early as well as late writings by Yeats. A little research disclosed that "The Cutting" was first published in 1906, and so was therefore perhaps too early to provide solid evidence of the views of the mature poet.[3] This discovery prompted her to give a careful rereading to the two passages she had quoted from "The Cutting," and she quickly found even better reasons for dropping them. The first is a warning, not against escapism but against the "still and fixed," and also as the second (and related) passage makes abundantly clear, a warning against abstraction in general—"mathematic form" and "every abstract thing, all that is from the brain only." In these two passages Yeats is not repudiating the legends of ancient Ireland or even the dreamy world of "The Happy Shepherd," for Yeats regarded neither the Shepherd nor the Sidhe as bloodless beings, devoid of passion. On the contrary, it was with the contemporary world that he associated "mathematic form" and "mechanic process." Clearly Susan would have to seek out better quotations to support her claim that in his later poetry Yeats had made a realistic acceptance of the world. She decided to search some of his last poems for appropriate quotations. (See p. 565 for her revised first paragraph.)

Susan suspected that the basic distinction between the imagination as yielding an insight into reality and reverie as an escape from it might offer a way out of some of the other tangles in which she was involved. For example, she had begun her paper by writing that "a poet often lives a mental existence." (What a truism! How else could he write at all?) And in her next sentence she had written that "Contemplation necessitates withdrawal from the world of men," a withdrawal that she said Yeats "questioned" (see p. 550). Some such withdrawal is of course necessary if the poet is to do more than make brainless noises, but she was implying that the poet permanently disassociated himself. Her way of putting matters had set up a not very useful distinction between physical action and mental action. The pertinent distinction, as Susan now saw, was between fruitful meditation and irresponsible reverie. It was what you did in your mind that counted—not the withdrawal from physical action in order to meditate.

To make sure that she had handled this distinction properly in paragraph

---

[3] Students who use collected works, whether of poetry or prose, should be careful to ascertain when the work they cite was first published—better still, when first written. Such care is particularly necessary if the student uses the work to document opinions held at a particular time.

5, Susan went over that paragraph once more and looked carefully at the passages that she had quoted as documentation. She had illustrated the appeal exerted on Yeats by the world of the faeries by a quotation from his *Celtic Twilight*. Reconsideration indicated that her choice had been apt. *The Celtic Twilight* is an early work (first published in 1893) of Yeats's escapist period and, in the passage Susan had quoted, Yeats does talk as if art, which he says is made out of "beautiful" and "pleasant" and "significant" things, can serve as a substitute for "this marred and clumsy world." But Susan decided that her comment on this passage ("Creating beautiful and pleasant things requires thinking about living instead of living") required alteration. If she intended her sentence as a summary of what the youthful Yeats thought about art, then she needed to make clear that the notion was Yeats's, for it did not represent her own judgment. The creation of exalted and tragic things also requires "thinking and living."

Susan thought she had chosen poorly in quoting the sentence about an "impersonal" art from "The Cutting of an Agate." What is the relation of an "impersonal" art to either realistic or escapist poetry? What would her reader make of the quotation? Not much of anything, Susan feared. She looked back at the context in which the sentence occurred to see whether by enlarging the quotation she could make Yeats's meaning clearer. She was lucky: in the process of exploring the context, she found, a few pages further along, just the right passage: see paragraph 6 of her revised paper (pp. 570–71). The new passage was a warning against an art too far removed from life, and it provided a solid basis—as the earlier quotation had not—for the comment with which Susan had immediately followed it: "Circumstances and the world are the raw material of poetry, but the artist must transform them into beauty." [4]

It was particularly useful to get a suitable passage from a piece of work so early as "The Cutting of an Agate" (see p. 571 above), for in her fourth paragraph Susan insists that even the young Yeats was not wholly escapist, and that his early poetry reveals his appreciation of the real world. Thus, she had justified her use of the word *tension* (see the first sentence of paragraph 5) by being able to illustrate, from writings of the same general period, the power of the two counterattractions. (Susan decided that the third quotation in her fifth paragraph was too vague, was somewhat off the point, and in general didn't pay its own way. She dropped it; see paragraph 6 of her revised paper.)

By this time Susan had convinced herself that a drastic revision of her paper was in order. On inspection, the first draft of her paper was simply not good enough to turn in. She did not feel, however, that her review of her terms and concepts had called in question her basic thesis. Yet obviously a

---

[4] The student working on a literary topic may resent the tedium of looking up relevant passages for quotation. But diligence here is nearly always rewarding. Truly apposite quotations do more than anything else to convince the reader that the author of the paper has mastered his subject and knows what he is writing about.

great deal of revision was required to clarify her argument. The beginning of the paper in particular would have to be substantially changed. She must try to eliminate every bit of fuzzy thinking, and she resolved to look very carefully at all the passages that she quoted from Yeats by way of documentation. If a passage in question didn't really illustrate the point, she would simply have to keep looking.

Susan decided to make a sentence outline for the revised paper. In her anxiety to get her paper started right, she exercised particular care with the first sections of the outline, and Sections I–IV of the outline below amount, in fact, to a paragraph outline (pp. 522–23).

I. Yeats bade farewell to life in a poem celebrating life and passion.
   A. He celebrated, from Ireland's past, men of action and passion with traits like
      1. The recklessness of the country gentry,
      2. The holiness of monks, and
      3. The laughter of the drunkard.
   B. He challenged Irishmen of the future to fulfill such ideals of passionate life.
II. Yet Yeats began his career by writing a very different kind of poetry.
   A. It expressed a wish to escape the limitations of our modern world.
   B. It looked back to a simple, idyllic world.
   C. It celebrated dream, preferring it to the "Grey Truth" of science.
III. Even in Yeats's "The Song of the Happy Shepherd," however, the speaker hints that he cannot take refuge in a personal dream.
   A. By the very act of writing a poem, he shows his need to share his sorrow with someone.
   B. He expresses his belief that his sorrow can be given a permanent form and thus achieve the status of enduring truth.
IV. Though Yeats's "Wandering of Oisin" tells a story out of the heroic past about a man who tried to escape the human world, it also testifies to the fact that man cannot really escape the human condition.
   A. Oisin, even in the land of the faeries, could not put aside human sorrow, and longed to return to humankind.
   B. In the end Oisin is compelled to lose his immortality and become a mere human being once more.
V. Even in his early poetry, Yeats takes some account of the "other side" of an issue:
   A. Though "The Stolen Child" stresses the human world as a place of sorrow, it mentions some of the earth's homely joys.
   B. Other early poems reveal a similar tension between the claims of the human world and the world of the faeries.
   C. Yet, like many other poets of the 1890's, essentially Yeats was a poet in retreat from the world.
VI. Yeats hoped to recover for modern Irishmen a sense of their heroic past (including legends of the Sidhe) through ritual and literature.

A. He planned to create a new Irish cult for which he devised a special ritual.
B. He encouraged the writing of stories, poems, and plays based on Irish legends.
   1. The stories and poems would draw upon the recent wave of scholarly interest in Celtic history and literature.
   2. The plays were to be produced in the Abbey Theatre, which had been founded by Yeats and Lady Angela Gregory for this purpose.
VII. Yeats, however, was not a political activist and quarreled with Maud Gonne, who was.
A. Yeats had no relish for violence.
B. He scorned to write propaganda.
C. He felt that modern Ireland could achieve freedom only through a spiritual regeneration.
VIII. Yeats believed that modern Irishmen had succumbed to the ills of modernity.
A. They had lost contact with the heroic life of their ancestors.
B. They had become bourgeois in their outlook.
C. They were essentially divided men who needed to recover what Yeats called "Unity of Being."
IX. Yeats's increasing concern with the problems of contemporary Ireland was reflected by a change in his own poetry.
A. Yeats stripped his poetry of ornament and made it muscular and spare.
B. He cultivated in his poetry an "Image" of himself that was the opposite of all that he was in his daily life.
C. He employed a harsher and more realistic subject matter than in his earlier verse.
D. In sum, he sought to achieve the poetic effect through clarifying and intensifying the realistic, and sometimes even sordid, circumstance of the world.

(This outline does not cover the last three paragraphs of the revised paper; see pp. 582–83.)

Susan then developed her outline into a revised paper and in the process altered her title to read "From Dream to Reality: The Poetic Development of W. B. Yeats." Susan's revised paper follows on pages 564–84.

From Dream to Reality:

The Poetic Development of W. B. Yeats

by

Susan Blank

Middlewestern State University

June, 1969

Properly, the title page is
followed by a sentence
or topic outline of the
paper. In this instance,
however, we have given
the outline above. Hence,
it is omitted here.

From Dream to Reality:

The Poetic Development of W. B. Yeats

(1) William Butler Yeats, in his valedictory
poem, "Under Ben Bulben," praises the types
of men whom he had come to value during his
lifetime. He celebrates the poet, the artist,
the peasant,

> Hard-riding country gentlemen,
> The holiness of monks, and after
> Porter-drinkers' randy laughter....[1]

It is a curious and interesting company: it
includes no bankers, file clerks, or real
estate salesmen. Yeats urges the Irish poets
who are to succeed him to

> Sing the lords and ladies gay
> That were beaten into the clay
> Through seven heroic centuries;
> Cast your mind on other days
> That we in coming days may be
> Still the indomitable Irishry.[2]

These lines pulse with a tremendous concern
for a life of action and heroic endeavor and
passion--both the monk's passion and the
drunkard's. Such a concern is typical of
Yeats's later poetry. It reflects and illuminates the experiences of his lifetime. In-

---

[1] W. B. Yeats, Collected Poems (New York,
1951), p. 343.
[2] Ibid., p. 343.

If one is to begin the paper with Yeats's mature conception of poetry, why not dramatize the issue by quoting from his last great poem?

The two quotations from "The Cutting of an Agate" in first draft dropped because not pertinent to the issue here.

deed, poetry had become for Yeats not a prettification of life nor an escape from life, but a clarification of the very meaning of life.

(2) Yet Yeats did not begin his career with this tough-minded conception of poetry, nor could he, at the beginning of his career, have written poetry of this character. As a young poet Yeats tended to express rather directly his yearnings, dreams, and aspirations: his earlier poems thus tend to be fantasies of escape from the limitations of human reality rather than imaginative transformations of it. Thus, in "The Song of the Happy Shepherd" (1889) Yeats sympathizes with the "sick children of the world" who have to endure "all the many changing things/ In dreary dancing past us whirled."[3] In the present world of meaningless change, it seems to him that "Words alone are certain good." The ancient world of fauns and shepherds and pastoral poetry has passed away. Yeats's "happy shepherd" is not really very happy. He laments that though "Of old the world on dreaming fed,/Grey Truth is now her painted toy." But dreaming is also truth, so the shepherd argues, and constitutes a more rewarding truth than that offered by science.

[3] Ibid., p. 7.

With the second sentence in this paragraph, compare the second sentence of paragraph 2 of Susan's original draft (p. 551) and also Susan's first attempt to correct and improve it, the sentence beginning "The contest between . . ." (p. 559).

Note that the reference to "The Song of the Happy Shepherd" has been developed,

③ Yet even in this poem, which celebrates the romantic past and the poetic dreaming associated with it, the poet is not able to divorce himself entirely from human experience. Consider, for example, some further lines from "The Song of the Happy Shepherd."

> Go gather by the humming sea
> Some twisted, echo-harbouring
>   shell,
> And to its lips thy story tell,
> And they thy comforters will be,
> Rewording in melodious guile
> Thy fretful words a little while,
> Till they shall singing fade in
>   ruth
> And die a pearly brotherhood;
> For words alone are certain good:
> Sing, then, for this is also
>   sooth.[4]

The meaning of the passage as quoted is not altogether clear, but a number of things do emerge plainly enough: the speaker needs comfort and needs to tell his sorrows to someone or something. His fretful complaining words about life will, he asserts, if spoken into the lips of the shell, be transformed—does the shell stand for the imagination here?—into a "pearly brotherhood." (What is meant by their fading "in ruth" or how they can "die" into a "pearly brother-

and expanded: the poem can illustrate more of Yeats's earlier attitude than it was made to do in paragraph 2 of the original version. Note that reference to the grave of the faun has been dropped as being no more than an incidental detail.

[4]Ibid., p. 8.

hood" is not made altogether clear.) But
that the words of complaint become "pearls"
does suggest a permanence that sets them
off from the "many changing things / In
dreary dancing past us whirled." Perhaps the
poet is saying that poetry is the only enduring truth.

(4) "The Wanderings of Oisin" (1887) is
another poem that exhibits some of Yeats's
youthful escapism. Indeed, the plot of the
poem has to do with an attempt to escape
from human sorrow. The hero, Oisin, abandons
human kind and goes away to live a heroic
life in the land of the faeries. These faeries were the gods of ancient Ireland; they
are called the Tuatha de Danaan or the Sidhe.
They were supernatural beings, living lives
of passionate activity. With them love and
youth last forever. They stand in sharp opposition to the Christianized Irishmen of a
later time who impress Oisin, when he returns, as puny and unheroic, a "small and
feeble populace stooping with mattock and
spade, / Or weeding or ploughing. . . ."[5]
Yet it is significant that though Oisin, because of his love for the faery Niamh, had
lived for three hundred years among the
Sidhe, he was never able to eradicate from
his heart a sense of kinship with the mortals

[5]*Ibid*., p. 378.

The account of "The Wanderings of Oisin" has been expanded, and the reference to the Sidhe in paragraph 4 of the first draft moved up to this paragraph where the Sidhe are an important part of Oisin's story.

who live under the menace of time. The poem
suggests that the youthful Yeats recognized
that it was not easy and perhaps was indeed
impossible to evade the penalties of the
human lot. Man is mortal, and much as he may
long to become a god, he cannot in fact do
so.

(5) The theme of escape to the land of the
faeries is to be found in many other poems
written by Yeats before 1900. For example,
note the following lines from a poem entitled
"The Stolen Child" (first published in December 1886).[6]

> Away with us he's going,
> The solemn-eyed:
> He'll hear no more the lowing
> Of the calves on the warm hillside
> Or the kettle on the hob
> Sing peace into his breast,
> Or see the brown mice bob
> Round and round the oatmeal-chest.
> For he comes, the human child,
> To the waters and the wild
> With a faery, hand in hand,
> From a world more full of
>   weeping than he can understand.[7]

Yeats is employing here the ancient superstition that held that the faeries liked to steal

---

[6] A. Norman Jeffares, W. B. Yeats: Man and
Poet (New Haven, 1949), p. 38
[7] Yeats, Collected Poems, p. 19.

away to their realm children and brides on
their wedding night. The source of the faeries' power to win the human being lay in the
fact that mortals dread the unhappiness of
the world as it is. Yet even in this poem,
Yeats recognizes that human life has its own
pleasures, and he enumerates lovingly a number of them--the kettle that can "Sing peace
into [the child's] breast" or the "lowing /
Of the calves on the warm hillside...." It
should be noted that Yeats was willing, even
in his early period, to present the "other
side" of a situation, and this honesty was a
source of strength for his poetry. In his mature work in particular, Yeats rarely shows
himself to be opinionated or cranky: he is
nearly always wonderfully fair to the complexities and even contradictions of human
experience.

(6) From the beginning, a basic theme in
Yeats's poetry (see, for example, "The Man
Who Dreamed of Faeryland," "To the Rose upon
the Rood of Time," "All Things Can Tempt Me")
is the tug of war between the claims of the
world of faery and the counter-claims of the
real world--between reverie and reality. If,
as we have already observed, the youthful poet
too often yielded to reverie, by the turn of
century there were signs to indicate that he
was becoming aware of the weakness of vague
and dreamy poetry. In a rather early essay

Yeats observes that art will probably suffer
if it is divorced from the everyday world.
Thus he writes in "The Cutting of an Agate"
(1906):

This quotation from "The Cutting of an Agate" has been substituted for that in the original paragraph 5 as more directly applicable.

> All art is sensuous, but when a man puts
> only his contemplative nature and his
> more vague desires into his art, the
> sensuous images through which it speaks
> become broken, fleeting, uncertain, or
> are chosen for their distance from gen-
> eral experience, and all grows unsub-
> stantial and fantastic. (italics supplied)[8]

Circumstance and the world are the raw material of poetry, but the artist must transform
them into beauty. The transformation depends
for its success, however, on some resistance
in the materials to be transformed: one can
bend wood into a bow or forge steel into a
sword, but how could one "transform" a mere
cloud or a wavering band of mist into anything
at all!

(7) It is useful to compare the observation
just quoted with a passage taken from a much
earlier book, The Celtic Twilight (1893). Here
Yeats voices a much more naive view of artistic creation and one that accords with the
notion of art as an escape from the drab and
humdrum world around us. Yeats writes:

The importance of the date and the implication for Yeats's poetry of this quotation from *The Celtic Twilight* were insufficiently emphasized in the first draft.

> I have desired, like every artist,
> to create a little world out of

---

[8] W. B. Yeats, Essays and Introductions (New
York, 1961), p. 293.

> the beautiful, pleasant, and signifi-
> cant things of this marred and clumsy
> world....[9]

In this passage, clearly the assumption is
that the artist sorts out for his artistic
use what is beautiful or pleasant or significant in this marred and clumsy world and dis-
cards what is ugly or unpleasant or insignificant. Such a view of art was not of course
confined to the young Yeats. It is part of
the artistic credo of the 1890's. The poets
of that period tended to assume that "poetry"
was determined by the nature of the materials rather than by the creativity of the
artist. Brought up on such a theory, the
young Yeats naturally tends to run away from
the streets of the city to the woodland paths
of nature, from the new-fangled and "modern"
to the old and familiar, from the complex to
the simple. As we have observed earlier, the
theme of escape comes out quite directly in
a number of the earlier poems. Significantly,
"The Lake Isle of Innisfree" begins "I will
arise and go now, and go to Innisfree...."
and "The Hosting of the Sidhe" ends with the
words "<u>Away, come away</u>." It is not too much

The passage quoted from Yeats's *Autobiographies* in the original paragraph 5 has been dropped because it is not really pertinent to Yeats's "escapism." It comes from a later period of Yeats's life and refers to the general problem of a poet's need to meditate.

---

[9] As quoted by Ann Saddlemyer, "The Cult of
the Celt" in <u>The World of W. B. Yeats</u>, ed.
Robin Skelton and Ann Saddlemyer (Victoria,
B.C., 1965), p. 24.

9

to say that the Yeats of the 'nineties was a
poet in retreat from the world.

(8) Yet even during the decade from 1890 to
1900, Yeats did not solely dream about escape.
He wished to see Ireland unified by a cultural
ideal and hoped that his own poetry might give
her the spiritual strength to stand firm
against England and English culture. His plan
for uniting and spiritualizing Ireland had
two aspects: religious and literary. As for
the first, Yeats wanted to revive the ancient
Druidic traditions and by combining them with
his Hermetic Society for Mysticism, initiate
a new Irish cult.[10] Yeats even went so far as
to devise a ritual for his religious cult.

> I had an unshakeable conviction, arising
> how or whence I cannot tell, that invis-
> ible gates would open as they opened for
> Blake, as they opened for Swedenborg, as
> they opened for Boehme, and that this
> philosophy would find its manuals of de-
> votion in all imaginative literature,
> and set before Irishmen for special man-
> ual an Irish literature which, though
> made by many minds, would seem the work
> of a single mind, and turn our places of
> beauty or legendary association into
> holy symbols.[11]

The phrase "fighting Britain" in the original paragraph 6 softened to "stand firm against England and English culture" in view of what will be said in paragraph 10 below.

Material from paragraph 7 of the first draft has been moved here, where it may directly illustrate the first aspect of Yeats's plan.

[10] Richard Ellmann, Yeats: The Man and the Masks (New York, 1948), pp. 115-27.
[11] W. B. Yeats, Autobiographies (London, 1955), p. 254.

Yeats believed that this new Irish cult could give Irishmen "spiritual inspiration" and fortification.[12]

This second aspect of Yeats's plan is here given a separate paragraph.

(9) The literary aspect of Yeats's plan had to do with reviving the Irish legends and embodying them in poems, fiction, and plays. In order to provide means for producing such plays, Yeats joined with Lady Angela Gregory in founding the Abbey Theater in Dublin in 1904. Yeats was not alone, however, in becoming interested in Irish legend. He took advantage of a general trend. Many other people were studying Irish folklore during this period.[13] The revival of the Irish

Relevant (but not essential) material reduced to a footnote (as in the first draft).

---

[12]Ellmann, p. 122. "Maud Gonne thought that the order might work for separation of Ireland from Britain in the same way as the Masonic lodges in the north of Ireland were, she believed, working for union. It would use Masonic methods against the Masons, as another nationalistic organization, the Clan na Gael, had done. Yeats, less political in his objectives, vaguely anticipated that the order would be able to aid the movement for national independence by its magical powers.... Driven almost frantic by loving in vain 'the most beautiful woman in the world,' he thought that in collaboration with Maud Gonne in this spiritual conspiracy their minds would be so united that she would consent to become his."

[13]Saddlemyer, pp. 19-21. Miss Saddlemyer lists specific publications that presented Celtic

(cont'd)

stories about such heroes as Fergus and
Cuchulain, Finn and Oisin, would serve to
call attention to Ireland's heroic past. It
was indeed a very remote past: Cuchulain was
thought to have lived in the first century of
the Christian era; Finn and Oisin, in the
third. But Yeats sought to use the legends
not to escape from the present into mythical
times but to mold a new reality by changing
the spiritual climate in present-day Ireland.

> Might I not, with health and good luck
> to aid me, create some new Prometheus
> Unbound; Patrick or Columcille, Oisin
> or Finn, in Prometheus' stead; and, in-
> stead of Caucasus, Cro-Patrick or Ben
> Bulben? Have not all races had their
> first unity from a mythology that mar-
> ries them to rock and hill? We had in
> Ireland imaginative stories, which the
> uneducated classes knew and even sang,
> and might we not make those stories
> current among the educated classes, re-
> discovering for the work's sake what I
> have called "the applied arts of litera-
> ture," the association of literature,
> that is, with music, speech, and dance;
> and at last, it might be, so deepen the

------

literature, beginning in the year 1856. Old
Irish manuscripts were exhumed and translated by German scholars; "by the end of
the century innumerable scholars, organizations and periodicals were devoted to the
recovery of the Celt" (p. 20). The Pan-
Celtic Society was founded in 1899; Celtic:
a Pan-Celtic Magazine published its first
number in 1901.

political passion of the nation that all,
artist and poet, craftsman and day
labourer would accept a common design?[14]

Comment added here to
point up the implications
of Yeats's reference to the
uneducated Irishman's
knowledge of these
stories.

As the foregoing comment makes plain, Yeats
saw in the use of Ireland's "imaginative
stories," a way of making common cause between the educated classes of Ireland and the
uneducated classes in whose memories and imagination these stories still lingered.

(10) It is plain that Yeats's involvement in
politics was more mystical than militant. Indeed, he quarreled with Maud Gonne, the woman
with whom he had fallen passionately in love,
because Maud wanted to liberate Ireland by
direct action--demonstrations, violent protests, and even the use of dynamite. Yeats
refers to these disagreements in a number of
his poems about Maud. For example, in "No
Second Troy" he writes

Added to clarify Maud
Gonne's differences with
Yeats.

> Why should I blame her that she
>   filled my days
> With misery, or that she would of
>   late
> Have taught to ignorant men most
>   violent ways
> Or hurled the little streets upon
>   the great....[15]

More was involved, however, in Yeat's distaste for such violence than mere squeamish-

---

[14] Yeats, _Autobiographies_, pp. 193-94.
[15] Yeats, _Collected Poems_, p. 89.

ness. Yeats believed Ireland could not be freed
from foreign control unless and until she possessed her own soul. Until she had recovered
her own identity and had come to terms with
her own past, any freeing her from outside
domination would be superficial and mechanical. Besides, Yeats scorned to write propaganda: great poetry was much more than an
incitement to a particular action or political commentary on a topical event.

(11) Yet in spite of the qualifications just
made, Yeats's attempt to use poetry and drama
to give Irishmen "spiritual inspiration" and
to revive Irish mythology and ancient legends
in order to bring about the spiritual unification of the Irish did mean involvement in
the modern world. What possibly may have begun as an escape into the past and as an
aesthetic indulgence in mythological glories
eventually issued in a commitment to the
present. Yeats had become intensely interested
in the cultural life of the people around him.
How intense that interest had become is
revealed in some comments that he made later
in his Autobiographies. He tells us that he
had hoped the association of literature and
music, speech and dance, would give Ireland
Unity of Culture--"philosophy and a little
passion."[16] What Yeats may have had in mind

---

[16] Yeats, Autobiographies, p. 195.

is suggested by a passage from "The Cutting of an Agate," published in 1906:

> My work in Ireland has continually set this thought before me: "How can I make my work mean something to vigorous and simple men whose attention is not given to art but to a shop, or teaching in a National School, or dispensing medicine?... They must go out of the theatre with the strength they live by strengthened from looking upon some passion that could, whatever its chosen way of life, strike down an enemy, fill a long stocking with money or move a girl's heart....Their legs will tire on the road if there is nothing in their hearts but vague sentiment, and though it is charming to have an affectionate feeling about flowers, that will not pull the cart out of the ditch.[17]

(12) Yeats hoped to give Ireland Unity of Culture by creating in all Irishmen a "Unity of Being"--a life of intellect _and_ emotion, contemplation _and_ action. For Yeats knew that Irishmen were divided beings. They had lost their hold on the high-hearted life of their ancient ancestors. They had lost the ancient aristocracy's sense of noblesse oblige and the peasantry's folk imagination and folk wit. Many of them had adopted bourgeois values along with the bourgeois mode of life. This at least is the force of the taunt embodied in Yeats's poem "September 1913."

Material added to give needed context for an understanding of the passage quoted from "September 1913."

------

[17]Yeats, Essays, pp. 265-66.

> What need you, being come to sense,
> But fumble in a greasy till
> And add the halfpence to the pence
> And prayer to shivering prayer,
>   until
> You have dried the marrow from the
>   bone?
> For men were born to pray and save:
> Romantic Ireland's dead and gone,
> It's with O'Leary in the grave.[18]

Modern Irishmen spent their time in "shivering prayer," hoarding their money, and in keeping their shops. Yet Yeats had hoped that the "Ireland of priest, merchant and politician," might come to "resemble 'an Ireland / The poets have imagined, terrible and gay,' might, in fact, resemble Cuchulain's Ireland, a land of reckless heroes."[19] Yeats later was to admit he had failed to attain his dream. He writes: "the dream of my early manhood, that a modern nation can return to Unity of Culture is false; though it may be we can achieve it for some small circle of men and women, and there leave it till the moon bring round its century."[20] But even if he had not succeeded in carrying out his dream, he had come to write for his own people living at his own time.

Material moved from paragraph 9 in first draft; placed here it serves as a summary of and comment on Yeats's earlier hopes.

[18] Yeats, Collected Poems, p. 106
[19] John Unterecker, A Reader's Guide to William Butler Yeats (New York, 1959), p. 19.
[20] Yeats, Autobiographies, p. 295.

(13) As Yeats came, more and more, to write
poems about the world of contemporary Ireland
and less and less indulged himself in day-
dreaming about a world free from human cares,
he developed a new poetic style. He stripped
his own poetry of ornament and made it more
spare and muscular, harder and colder and
more austere. A look at such volumes as The
Green Helmet (1910), Responsibilities (1914),
and The Wild Swans at Coole (1919) will make
this new quality fully evident. In his Autobiographies Yeats makes direct mention of his
changing notion of what he had come to aim at
in his own verse. He writes:

> I take pleasure alone in those verses
> where it seems to me I have found some-
> thing hard and cold, some articulation
> of the Image which is the opposite of
> all that I am in my daily life, and all
> my country is. . . .[21]

Yeats is correct in describing this new
"image" as the opposite of all that he was
in his daily life. This new, hard, cold
image and the poetic form that he developed
to accommodate it do represent the opposite
of his real tender-hearted self. They certainly represent the opposite of all that
people have taken Ireland to be. Yet one
must be careful to see that Yeats's austere

----

[21]Ibid., p. 274.

Compare the opening of
this paragraph with the
corresponding paragraph
10 of first draft. Note also
specific reference to
Yeats's transitional
volumes.

style does not represent another special means
to escape from life but rather a successful
way to penetrate to the inner reality of life.
The proof that this is so is shown by the
kinds of material that fill this new, harder,
colder poetry. There are poems about thwarted
love ("Adam's Curse," "No Second Troy"), about
Yeats's work with the Abbey Theater ("The Fascination of What's Difficult")[22] and about
the pettiness of some of his countrymen ("September 1913," "Paudeen").

(14) One may sum up by saying that Yeats's
more austere style is a way of putting into
judged and ordered perspective the circumstances of the world that flowed around him.
The poems are not, however, mere photocopies
of life's circumstance, nor are they, on the
other hand, ways of denying and evading it.
Rather it is as if Yeats has found a special
lens through which to view the world about
him in all of its earthiness and ugliness and
squalor, but his is a lens that gives the
cluttered scene depth and clarity and aesthetic distance: what is revealed is not mean-

---

[22] My curse on plays
That have to be set up in fifty ways,
On the day's war with every knave and
    dolt,
Theatre business, management of men....
(Collected Poems, p. 91)

Note the addition of the summarizing paragraph.

Quotation reduced to a footnote: compare more awkward treatment in paragraph 10 of first draft.

ingless clutter or sordid detail but a scene
heightened, clarified, intensified, and given
the special radiance of great poetry.

(15) This remarkable shift in Yeats's style
probably had its relation to definite causes:
Maud Gonne married John MacBride in 1903;
Dublin neglected the arts and showed scant
enthusiasm in raising funds to provide a gallery to house the gift of Hugh Lane's pictures (1912-13); in 1907 Synge's Playboy of
the Western World was violently rejected at
its first performance at the Abbey Theater.
Yeats was angry and disappointed with Ireland,
but he had begun to find a way to deal with
this disorderly world. He did not run away
from it nor ignore it, but he did find a way
to heighten it into poetry.

(16) If we understand the connection between
Yeats's own life and personality and the
poetry of his middle and final periods, we
shall be able to see the folly of charging
that Yeats's poetry is an escape from life.
Poetry had become Yeats's life, his world,
and his business. He says in his Autobiographies, "I thought it was my business in
life to be an artist and a poet, and that
there could be no business comparable to
that."[23]

---

[23]p. 188.

Note that the statement in paragraph 11 of the first draft about softening of Yeats's "anger and hatred" has been dropped. Someone had pointed out to Susan that "The Fisherman," for instance, shows plenty of anger.

(17) Yeats's poems continued to reflect the
events going on around him. In "Easter 1916"
he praises the patriots--Constance Markiewicz,
Patrick Pearse, Thomas MacDonough, John Mac-
Bride--who led the abortive Easter rising.
Though Yeats disliked their disdain for the
old aristocratic tradition and though he
feared the hatred as "Peddled in the thoroughfares" by Maud Gonne,[24] among others, and
though he hated John MacBride for marrying
the woman with whom he was hopelessly in love
--he was now able to praise the patriots, including MacBride himself. Yeats had by this
time become wiser, more sensitive, more complex, and in short, more mature, and he had
developed a style in which he could do justice
to the real complexities of the world. In one
of the great passages in his Per Amica Silen-
tia Lunae, Yeats had written: "We make out of
the quarrel with others, rhetoric, but of the
quarrel with ourselves, poetry."[25] There is
another great though brief passage in the
Autobiographies that ought to be set beside
that just quoted. There Yeats remarks: "We
begin to live when we have conceived life as
tragedy."[26]

> Note attempt here to interpret Yeats's quarrel with the world as a positive force in his later poetry.

------

[24]See "A Prayer for My Daugher," Collected
Poems, p. 187.
[25]Yeats, Mythologies (New York, 1959), p. 331.
[26]Yeats, Autobiographies, p. 189.

Bibliography

Ellmann, Richard. <u>Yeats: The Man and Masks</u>. New York: Macmillan, 1948.

Jeffares, A. Norman. <u>W. B. Yeats: Man and Poet</u>. New Haven: Yale University Press, 1949.

Saddlemyer, Ann. "The Cult of the Celt: Pan-Celtism in the Nineties," in <u>The World of W. B. Yeats: Essays in Perspective</u>. Edited by Robin Skelton and Ann Saddlemyer. Victoria, B. C.: University of Victoria Press, 1965.

Unterecker, John. <u>A Reader's Guide to William Butler Yeats</u>. New York: Noonday Press, 1959.

Yeats, W. B. <u>Autobiographies</u>. London: Macmillan, 1955.

_____ <u>Collected Poems</u>. New York: Macmillan, 1951.

_____ <u>Essays and Introductions</u>. New York: Macmillan, 1961.

_____ <u>Mythologies</u>. New York: Macmillan, 1959.

Note that this bibliography includes only the works that Susan actually referred to in the final draft of her paper. The complete bibliography of works consulted is given above.

THE INSTRUCTOR'S COMMENT

This is a very thoughtful paper, well organized and rather carefully written. But in paragraph 3, in which you try to show that even in "The Song of the Happy Shepherd" Yeats reveals a concern for reality, I think that your argument is a bit forced. If you are trying to say that the poet, through his very need to communicate his emotions and through his desire to find an imperishable form for them, reveals that he has a stake in the world about him, you need to make this point more specifically. I find some repetition: paragraph 8, for example, tends to repeat a point first made in paragraph 3. Yet these are minor matters. There is actually very little waste motion in your paper.

I particularly like your handling of some fairly tricky concepts— imagination as distinguished from fantasy or reverie or daydreaming. You've evidently tried to choose your terms with care and to use them responsibly.

Your choice of quotations from Yeats's writings deserves commendation. On the whole, they seem very apt and they underscore your various points quite effectively. You show a thorough knowledge of Yeats's poetry and a more than adequate knowledge of his prose writing.

I also appreciate your not leaning unduly on secondary sources but trying to establish your thesis by a direct appeal to Yeats's own work. Your thesis about Yeats is not new, but I find it to be worked out rather freshly. And you have brought your paper to a very neat conclusion.

P.S. Your metaphor of the lens in paragraph 14 is quite effective. Is it original with you?

■ APPLICATIONS

I Do you agree with the instructor's comment? Has he been too generous with Susan? Do you find difficulties in the revised paper that he has not noted? Has he, on the other hand, failed to mention features of this paper that you think have merit? (Since the instructor presumably had not seen Susan's first draft, you may be in a somewhat better position than he to see what is right and what is wrong with her paper. Don't, therefore, be too timid to disagree with him or to go beyond his comments.)

II Make a detailed examination of the differences between the original and the revised forms of this paper. In comparing the first and revised drafts, you will find the side notes to the revised form helpful, but they by no means deal with all the changes Susan made. They take no special notice of some of her important revisions. Make your own notes on the significance of Susan's various revisions, and if you think that sometimes her revisions are for the worse, indicate why you think so.

Some general notes on literary papers

1 In writing a literary paper, it is very wise to try to determine as early as possible the primary area of interest with which one is concerned. As we noted on page 548 above, there are at least three different fields of critical and scholarly interest, and whereas the student need not try to keep strictly within the bounds of any one of them, he will find it helpful to decide at the outset the principal critical emphasis that his paper will take.

2 Even a paper stressing literary history or reader response requires that the writer possess a thorough knowledge of the character and value of the particular literary work or works examined. This is not the place to discuss such matters, for *Modern Rhetoric* does not pretend to be an introduction to the study of literature: its purpose is to train the student to write rather than to read. Yet the two processes obviously interact, and a number of the chapters in this book—notably those on description, narration, diction, metaphor, and tone—do bear quite directly on the problem of reading and judging literature.

3 One of the special problems that comes up in writing a literary paper of any kind is the definition of terms, for literary terms, as we have already noted (p. 559), are particularly difficult. Be sure that you know clearly what you mean by the terms that you are using. In rereading your paper, be on the alert for contradictory statements: they constitute good evidence that something has gone wrong. (It was Jane's calling attention to such contradictions that set Susan to work rethinking her paper.)

4 Make sure that the passage you quote from an author really illustrates the point that you are making about his work. If the passage quoted does not support your statement, then keep looking until you find one that does. If, on the other hand, you cannot find a passage that really illustrates your generalization, perhaps it is your generalization that is at fault. Be prepared to revise it.

5 Try to date accurately any illustrative quotations. For example, an essay written in 1900 may not necessarily express what the writer came to feel twenty years later. (There are some instances of this fault in the first draft of Susan's paper.)

6 Be careful of what you borrow from scholars, critics, and other literary authorities. Perhaps you do not feel yourself in a position to judge which of them are really authoritative and which are not; but you can at least determine whether the statement that you are borrowing makes sense in the context in which you are using it.

● CAUTION

Do you really understand the critic's special terminology, the meaning of the context in which the passage you mean to quote occurs, and the drift of the critic's general argument? If you don't, maybe you'd best not lean on this critic or scholar for support.

7   Don't bite off more than you can chew. In saying this, we are not necessarily urging brevity, and we are certainly not urging the student to settle for an easy subject. But the effectiveness of any literary paper is seriously compromised if the writer crams in a great deal more material than is necessary to make his point, or if he presents his reader with ill-digested material which, though it may seem at a hasty reading rather learned and profound, turns out to be, when carefully inspected, pretentious nonsense.

■ APPLICATIONS

Susan faced the problem of excess material in the rewriting of her paper. Paragraph 13 of her first draft, it may be noted, does not appear in her revised paper at all, though some of the material in this paragraph is interesting and bears on the general topic that Susan is discussing. But when Susan had got through paragraph 17 of her revised version, she decided that she had really established the thesis of her paper and that she might properly conclude it there, simply discarding the concluding paragraph (13) of her original draft. This kind of problem comes up constantly in the writing of research papers and particularly in those on literary topics.

The importance of making the proper cuts and exclusions, and the difficulty of doing so (for one is usually reluctant to leave out already assembled material) is perhaps worth a little further concrete illustration. Hence these two applications.

I   Do you think that Susan was right to exclude paragraph 13 of her first draft from the revised paper? Indicate why or why not.

II   Whatever your answer to I, let us suppose that Susan had been given a minimum length for her paper, one that left room for, and even demanded, the use of additional material. How would you go about incorporating this additional paragraph into the rewritten version? Before you start the process of doing such rewriting as will be necessary to incorporate this additional material, you might read the following notes, which will indicate some of your options.

It is possible that you may want to retain paragraph 17 of the revised paper as the conclusion of the amplified paper. (Much will depend upon whether you think that it constitutes an effective conclusion.) In that case you would have to try to find a way to insert the additional material into paragraphs 16 and 17 of the revised paper or even somewhere *before* paragraph 16. On the other hand, you may prefer to try to develop a conclusion out of the material in paragraph 13 of the first draft. If you choose either of these alternatives, you will have the problem of working out a proper line of development from the revised paper on through the additional paragraph, and you will have to make the proper connections and transitions.

A third possibility is to take the material in paragraph 13 and in paragraphs 16 and 17 of the revised draft and work it into a totally new conclusion for the paper. If you undertake to follow this procedure, you must be sure to include all of Susan's main points. Be prepared to justify the omission of any material.

Before you begin any rewriting, it might be useful to make a sentence outline of paragraph 13 of the first draft. Note that what we are suggesting here is a sentence outline and not a paragraph outline (see pp. 521–23). Because "paragraphs do not necessarily represent logical stages" (p. 522), the sentence outline will be more useful here, for you need to see clearly what the logical structure is. It will also be useful to make a sentence outline of the last three paragraphs of the revised paper. A carefully prepared outline may suggest ways in which the additional material can be articulated with the closing paragraphs of the revised paper. Such an outline would also serve to expose any contradiction that might possibly be lurking within paragraph 13 of the first draft. Remember that Susan had *not* revised this paragraph.

APPENDIXES

Causal Analysis

There are four methods that are helpful when investigating a situation to determine a cause. They are called the methods of *agreement,* of *difference,* of *agreement and difference,* and of *variation.* After examining them the student may feel that he has always been acquainted with them, for they merely describe how his mind works when it is dealing with problems of this kind. But studying the methods may sharpen his awareness of the processes of his own reasoning.

1 Agreement If we have two or more situations from which we get the effect X, and find that these situations have only one constant factor, E, then that constant factor may be taken as the cause of X. Let us set this up as a chart:

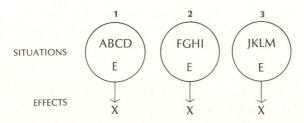

CASE I

Here E is the cause of X.

The method here stated is sound in theory but in some cases is difficult to apply. Even in the laboratory, where the experimenter can create his situation with a degree of control, it is hard to be sure that only one factor, E, is constant. But it is especially difficult to apply this method to a complicated event outside of the laboratory. The investigator rarely finds a set of situations in which *only* one factor is constant. Ordinarily he will encounter a set of situations such as may be indicated by the following chart:

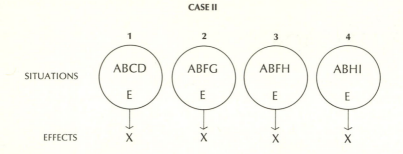

CASE II

We can notice two things about this set of situations.

First, several factors occur in more than one situation. For instance, factor F occurs in situations 2 and 3; factor H occurs in situations 3 and 4.

Second, three factors (A, B, and E) occur in all situations.

When the investigator sees that certain factors are repeated, as is true of F and H, he must inquire whether they are repeated in *all* situations. If they are not repeated in all situations, he can discard them. So F and H can be discarded. When the investigator sees that two or more factors, as is true of A, B, and E, are repeated in all situations, there are two lines of thought open to him.

First, he may explore the possibility that A, B, and E are to be taken as components of the cause—that no one by itself would be sufficient to bring about the effect.

Second, he may explore the possibility that one or two of the factors that are present in all of his available instances might not occur in other instances when the effect does occur and therefore are not relevant to the effect.

At this point the investigator has to make a judgment as to which of the two lines of thought he will follow. He must judge whether or not all of the constant factors (A, B, and E) are relevant to the effect. He can do this only in terms of his knowledge of the field that he is investigating.

Let us take an example. Suppose we wish to learn why a certain school lost most of its football games over a period of years. We find certain things true every year. Most of the players every year are Catholic, for it is a Catholic school. Let us call this constant factor A. The same coach has been employed for a number of years (factor B). The school has very high academic standards, and no one is permitted to participate in any athletic event who does not have an average grade of "fair" (factor E). The question is: Do we have a complex of factors here (A, B, and E) that are all necessary components of the cause?

Common sense and our experience with athletics at once make us rule out factor A—for we know that Catholicism bears no relation to the matter of football losses. But we cannot so readily rule out factors B and E, the matter of the coach and the matter of the high academic average required. At this point we have to investigate further. We have to look into the coach's previous record, we have to pass a judgment on the type of instruction he gives now, and so forth. Or we must try to learn how many good players have been disqualified by the rule requiring a certain scholastic average, and so forth. We may satisfy ourselves that both of these factors (B and E) contribute to the defeats. Or we may decide that only one is the cause.

In any event, this is not a foolproof formula. Knowledge and experience are required to apply it. Even when it is applied we cannot be absolutely sure that we have determined the cause of X. We have merely indicated a certain degree of probability.

2 Difference If we have two situations, identical save that one involves the factor E and the effect X, and the other does not involve the factor E and the effect X, then E may be taken as the cause of X or an indispensable factor in the cause. Let us put it as a chart:

CASE III

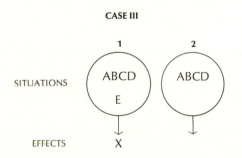

If we can be quite sure that the first situation resembles the second in all significant factors except E and X, then we may take E as the cause of X or an indispensable factor in the cause. But it is often difficult to find such clear-cut instances, and we have to draw on our judgment and experience to decide what factors are relevant.

CASE IV

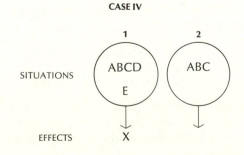

Here D as well as E is missing from the second situation. The following possibilities suggest themselves. First, D may be irrelevant, and E is the cause. Second, D may be relevant and in conjunction with E constitutes the cause. If we can control the situation, we may test the second possibility by setting up the factors ABCE. If we still get X, then we know that D is irrelevant. But if we cannot control the situation, we must consult our judgment and experience in deciding about the relevance of D.

3 Agreement and Difference This is, of course, a combination of the two previous methods. Therefore the method involves both *positive* and *negative* instances. In the positive instances we apply the method of agreement and then check the negative instances against the positive instances by the method of difference.

CASE V

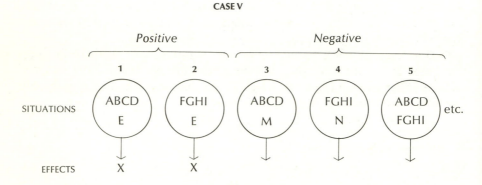

In situations 1 and 2 we have the ordinary method of agreement. But when we come to the negative situations, we notice that there is none that fulfills the requirement of the strict method of difference; that is, the negative situation differing from the positive situation only in that it does not have the factor that appears to be the cause. Though situation 3 has all the factors of situation 1 except E, the factor of cause, it also has a new factor, M. And so on with the other cases: they involve, in differing combinations and sometimes with new factors, the various factors, except E, that were present when X took place.

We can set up a simple example of the method. Let us assume that in a family of five people three suffer from an attack of food poisoning. The problem is to determine what item of the restaurant meal was the cause. John, Mary, and Sue are ill.

> John ate beans, potatoes, beef, and ice cream.
> Mary ate a salad, soup, and ice cream.
> Sue ate sweet potatoes, broccoli, ham, and ice cream.

So much for the positive cases. Since ice cream is the only item common to the meals eaten by the victims, there is a strong probability that it is the cause. But we can check this against the negative cases, that is, cases of persons who were *not* ill.

Mildred ate beans, potatoes, beef, and lemon pie.

Thomas ate a salad, sweet potatoes, and ham, with no dessert.

These negative cases include most of the dishes eaten by the victims— with the exception of ice cream. So the argument for ice cream becomes even stronger. Few situations, however, are as simple as the one given above, and in making an analysis we are often called upon to rule out many common factors that we judge to be unrelated to the effect (for instance, we might rule out the color of the plates used in all the above meals).

4 Variation If one factor in a situation varies whenever a certain other factor varies, there is a causal connection between the factors.

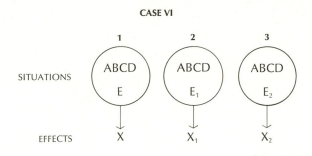

CASE VI

For instance, as the temperature rises, mercury expands; as the supply of a commodity increases, its price goes down; or as the amount of advertising of a product increases, its sales increase. These are illustrations of the principle, but in them are great differences in the degree of complication. In the first instance, the relation between the variation in temperature and the variation in the mercury is regular and constant. We depend on the fact, and our thermometers operate on that principle. But an economist cannot depend on the relation between supply and price with the same certainty, nor can a sales manager be sure that an increase in his advertising appropriation will pay off in the market. Here, too many unpredictable factors may be involved in the situation.

We must remember that it does not matter whether the variation is direct or inverse. For instance, we have direct variation with temperatures and mercury: as the temperature increases, the mercury increases in volume. And we have inverse variation with supply and price: as the supply increases, the price decreases.

■ **APPLICATION**

Make up incidents to illustrate each of the above methods in operation.

The Book Report, Summary, and Précis

The Book Report

Your instructor may occasionally assign a book report. A book report is to be sharply distinguished from a research paper, for it deals with one book in its entirety—not with certain aspects of several books and documents as, for example, in the model research paper "Railroads in the Civil War" (pp. 533–44). The book report is also to be clearly distinguished from a book review or a critical essay, for it merely reports on a book without undertaking to compare it with other books or to pass judgment on its value. Note that even a brief review such as Nigel Dennis's "Lordships Observed" (pp. 784–86) ranges far beyond the strict limits of a report on the book with which it formally concerns itself and that an essay like Santayana's "Dickens" (pp. 771–81) compares the novels of Dickens with novels by other writers, relates them to the social and intellectual scene in nineteenth-century England, and makes judgments about their value as reflections of life in Victorian times and of universal human nature.

We have said that a book report does not undertake to make comparative judgments, but it may very well include a certain amount of background material. This may have to do with the author himself, his other work, his reputation, or the circumstances under which the book was written. The presentation of such material, however, should not be allowed to become an end in itself. In scope and proportion it should be kept subordinate to the presentation of the book itself and, we may note, some book reports can dispense with it altogether.

To write a good book report you need to answer the following questions:

1 Who is the author? (What are his nationality and origins? When did he write?)
2 What other work has he done?
3 What is his reputation?
4 Are there any important or enlightening circumstances connected with the composition of this book?
5 What kind of book is this? (Is it fiction, history, literary criticism, biography, poetry, drama, or what?)
6 What is the subject of this book?
7 What material does it treat?
8 What is the theme of the book—the author's basic interpretation of the material?
9 What method of organization does he employ?
10 What are the tone and style of the book?

Note that questions 1 through 4 concern themselves with background information. If such information is needed for your book report, and is not available in the book itself or on the book jacket, consult a few standard reference works to obtain the basic facts, or look into one or two good biographies of the author or historical or critical works about him. There is no need to do a full research job (though you may find it wise to take your notes as if for a research paper so that your material will be conveniently available and easily put into proper order). Different kinds of books obviously require different handling in a book report. Here follow a few suggestions for treating three types of books:

Report on a biography

If you are reporting on a biography, identify the subject of the work, summarize the subject's career as given by the biographer (including the basic pieces of evidence that the biographer employs to support his interpretation of the life he is writing), give some notion of the biographer's method of organization, and comment on his tone and style.

With regard to tone and style, you may want to ask yourself such questions as these: Is the book a scholarly treatise or a popular biography? Is the book well adapted to the audience that the biographer evidently has in mind? Does he give any interesting anecdotes and colorful touches, or does he confine himself to facts and to historical or psychological analysis?

Report on a novel

A book report on a novel should define the kind of world that the author is interested in. Does he write of drawing rooms or village parlors or farms or battlefields? What kinds of characters and issues interest him? What is the outline of his plot? How do the motivations of his characters fit the plot? What is the theme of his novel? In a novel, questions of tone and style obviously are also very important.

Report on a book dealing with international affairs

If you are dealing with a book on, say, Russian influence in the Middle East, your primary concern will be to present the author's account of the situation provoking his discussion, to set forth the policy that he recommends, and to present the arguments that he uses to support that policy. You might even be led to present the philosophical or political assumptions that provide the basis for his policy. The kind of audience to whom he addresses his book will be an important consideration, and you ought to try to define it. But, in general, with books of this type, questions of tone and style—except in so far as mere clarity is involved—would be somewhat less important. In general, accommodate the shape and emphasis of your report to the kind of book on which you are reporting.

The Summary

The book report can be regarded as a kind of summary since it tells us in compact form what a particular book is about and what it says. Yet a "summary," technically considered, differs from the book report in one very important way. There is no introductory or background material on the author or the circumstances that bear on his composition of the work under consideration. *In short, there is nothing in a summary that is not actually in the work summarized.* The summary gives us in compact form the main points of the longer work; moreover, it undertakes to give *all* the main points and in their proper relation to each other.

Yet a summary is not merely a digest of a longer discourse; considered rhetorically, it is a piece of discourse in its own right. This means that it is no mere collection of words and phrases, but is composed of complete sentences, and that a person writing a summary must observe the principles of unity, coherence, emphasis, and proportion. The relation of one sentence to another must be obvious or else indicated by a suitable transition. Furthermore, if the summary extends beyond one paragraph, then the connection between the paragraphs must be made clear.

Organization of a summary

The organization of a summary is determined by the purpose that a summary is to serve. For instance, the summary may follow the order of the original text and thus give some notion of the approach used by its author. On the other hand, the summary may make use of a mode of organization quite different from that according to which the author organized the original discourse. Take, for example, an article agitating for the reform of the public school system of a certain city. The article begins with an illustrative anecdote, then moves forward by analyzing certain particular situations that obtain in the city, and concludes with an appeal for a reorganization of the school system. Yet an adequate summary might employ a very different method of organization. The summary might well begin by making an appeal for reform, then proceed to analyze the particular situation in such a way as to indicate cogent reasons for the reform. The summary might read as follows:

Summary of
"DO WE GIVE OUR CHILDREN A BREAK?"
by William Becker

The conditions in our public schools are deplorable on several accounts. It is well known that the record in college of graduates of our high schools falls below the average for graduates of schools in cities of comparable size. Local businessmen, industrialists, and editors are not satisfied with the general or vocational training of job-holders from our schools. And the schools are not doing their part in maintaining the moral health of the young, as is witnessed by the alarming and disproportionate increase in juvenile delinquency. It is time to have a general overhauling of our system.

Before we can remedy the situation, however, we must diagnose the causes. First, the school system has become a political football: members of the school board are chiefly concerned with building their political fences, and many appointments to supervisory and teaching positions are not made on merit. Second, parents have been uninterested in the schools, and many with influence have been more concerned to get special favors for their children than to raise the educational level. Third, local salaries are deplorably low, below the national average, and far below those paid in neighboring cities. No one of these causes can be taken as *the* cause, and any serious attempt to improve our schools must attempt to deal with all of them.

The author of the original article was probably right in beginning with an illustrative anecdote calculated to catch the attention of its general audience. This attention-catching device is not, however, needed in the summary, and the method used in the summary is, in fact, more systematic and states the logic of the case in a clearer form. The point is to organize your summary in the way that will best serve your purpose. At times you may want to follow the way in which the author put his article or his speech together. At other times, however, the author's way of doing this may prove quite irrelevant to your purposes.

Scale of the summary

The scale of the summary, like its organization, is determined by the purpose the summary is to serve. The real question is how much information do you need to pack into your abbreviated form? Sometimes, and for some purposes, a brief paragraph will give you an adequate digest of a whole book. On the other hand, if you are working on a finer scale, with very rich and interesting material, you may require a number of paragraphs to make a proper digest of a fairly short essay. In general, remember that a summary must summarize: unless you can squeeze down the book or article to much smaller size, then your labor has hardly been worth the trouble.

The Précis

What we call a précis (pronounced *pray-see*) is also a kind of summary, but it is more specialized than the kind that we have just been discussing. The précis retains the basic order of the original text, keeps the same proportions of part to part, and maintains the same tone. Thus, the précis has a much closer relation to the original text than do looser kinds of summary. This closer relation, however, does not mean that we should use much direct quotation or very close paraphrase. Material in the original discourse can be, and often should be, restated for economy and emphasis. Moreover, the degree of reduction, as in looser forms of summary, will be greater or smaller, depending on the purpose that the précis is to serve. But since the précis is committed to maintain the relative proportions of the original discourse, the reduction in a précis can never be so drastic as that in a "summary."

Here follows a précis of the first *three* paragraphs of "On the Inscrutability of History," by Arthur Schlesinger, Jr. (pp. 826–27), the first *six* paragraphs of which have already been outlined (p. 522).

> As a professional historian and occasional government official, I have been fascinated and perplexed by the interaction of history and public decisions. A public decision in rational politics always implies a guess about the future derived from experience of the past. Thus it involves a historical judgment. Yet when we ask what specific judgments underlie the adoption of specific policies, we realize that a statesman's appeal to history may sometimes be a mere rationalization for an action really undertaken for other reasons. Moreover, the same lesson of history can be interpreted to justify different and even opposed policies.

Here the original passage contains about 375 words and the précis about 95 words. The précis might be reduced even further if that seemed desirable.

APPENDIX **3**

Description of Feelings and States of Mind

In the chapter on description we were concerned with the rendering of the world outside ourselves—objects, scenes, conditions, actions. But description, in some of its more subtle applications, is concerned with rendering our own inner states—or the inner states of other people as we can imagine them to be.

In our earlier discussion we saw how a description may evoke in the reader a certain mood or attitude that the writer wishes to communicate. There is some relation, then, between the physical details of the object described and human feelings. This relationship leads us to another kind of description, not of objects or persons, but of feelings or states of mind. How can such an intangible, without physical existence and with no possible appeal to our senses, be described?

Strictly speaking, the literal feeling or state of mind cannot be described because it cannot be perceived through the senses. But we have seen how character, which is also intangible, can be indicated through description. By a kind of parallel process we can *indicate* a state of mind, that of the writer himself or of some person about whom he is writing.

Our common speech recognizes the principle behind this process. For instance, if a man has an evil nature we may say that he has a "black heart," or if a man is cheerful and optimistic we may say that he has a "sunny disposition." The abstract, general words *evil* and *cheerful* are replaced by the concrete words *black* and *sunny,* which properly belong to the physical world.

Here is an example of the description, not of a personality, but of a state of feeling, the feeling at the moment of passing from sleep to waking:

"I was not asleep," I answered as I awoke.

I said this in good faith. The great modification which the act of awakening effects in us is not so much that of introducing us to the clear life of consciousness, as that of making us lose all memory of that other, rather more diffused light in which our mind has been resting, as in the opaline depths of the sea. The tide of thought, half veiled from our perception, over which we were drifting still a moment ago, kept us in a state of motion perfectly sufficient to enable us to refer to it by the name of wakefulness. But then our actual awakenings produce an interruption of memory. A little later we describe these states as sleep because we no longer remember them. And when shines that bright star which at the moment of waking illuminates behind the sleeper the whole expanse of his sleep, it makes him imagine for a few moments that this was not a sleeping but a waking state; a shooting star, it must be added, which blots out with the fading of its light not only the false existence but the very appearance of our dream, and merely enables him who has awoken to say to himself: "I was asleep."

—MARCEL PROUST: *The Guermantes Way*.

The same use of physical description to indicate a mental state appears in the following passage:

Sterne's discovery was made. It was repugnant to his imagination, shocking to his ideas of honesty, shocking to his conception of mankind. This enormity affected one's outlook on what was possible in this world: it was as if, for instance, the sun had turned blue, throwing a new and sinister light on men and nature. Really in the first moment he had felt sickish, as though he had got a blow below the belt: for a second the very color of the sea seemed changed—appeared queer to his wandering eye; and he had a passing, unsteady sensation in all his limbs as though the earth had started turning the other way.

—JOSEPH CONRAD: "The End of the Tether," *Youth: A Narrative*.

We notice in the above quotation how the author begins by making a general statement: the discovery is repugnant, is shocking, changes Sterne's outlook. But we notice how quickly these generalities shade over into concrete presentations that are intended to evoke in us a direct sense of Sterne's sensation: the blue sun, a blow below the belt, the sudden reversal of the earth's motion.

In the following passage we find a slightly different application of the same principle. Above we have been dealing with the description of a momentary feeling; here we shall be dealing with the description of a protracted situation, a state of being. A wife has discovered that her husband's conception of life, his "mansion," is oppressive and deadening for her:

But when, as the months had elapsed, she had followed him further and he had led her into the mansion of his own habitation, then, *then* she had seen where she really was.

She could live it over again, the incredulous terror with which she had taken the measure of her dwelling. Between those four walls she had lived ever since; they were to surround her for the rest of her life. It was the house of darkness, the house of dumbness, the house of suffocation. Osmond's beautiful mind gave it neither light nor air; Osmond's beautiful mind indeed seemed to peep down from a small high window and mock at her. Of course it had not been physical suffering; for physical suffering there might have been a remedy. She could come and go; she had her liberty; her husband was perfectly polite. He took himself so seriously; it was perfectly appalling. Under all his culture, his cleverness, his amenity, under his good-nature, his facility, his knowledge of life, his egotism lay hidden like a serpent in a bank of flowers.

—HENRY JAMES: *The Portrait of a Lady.*

The descriptions of the states of feeling just considered are direct in treatment. That is, we are introduced as fully as may be into the consciousness of the person who has the feeling or experiences the state of mind, the seaman Sterne or the disappointed wife. But there is an indirect way of using description to portray feeling or state of mind, a way that presents the symptoms but does not endeavor to describe the feeling or the state of mind itself. This way is analogous, of course, to the use of description of a person's physical appearance to indicate his character, without giving any general statements about the character.

If we describe a person as having shifty eyes and a flabby mouth, the reader is very apt to draw certain conclusions about that person's character. And by the same token, if we describe a person at the moment when his lips whiten, the blood flushes his cheeks, his eyes flash, and his respiration is rapid, the reader is apt to conclude that the person is laboring under great rage or other excitement. Such descriptions of the symptoms, as it were, of a state of feeling can be very effective in giving the reader a sense of the reality of the situation being presented. Here is an example from a student theme:

Then the policeman made us all five stand up in front of Mr. Evans, while Mr. Evans asked us some questions. He asked me first, if I had done it, and then some questions supposed to trip me up. I really didn't know a thing about how it had happened, and said so. When he stopped asking me questions, I began watching the other boys. Alex was the most nervous of the lot and he could scarcely put words together. Jack was the least nervous. When they got to him, he began answering very calmly almost before a question could be spoken. But then I began to notice a vein in his neck which gave a peculiar little jumping motion. And I noticed how the edges of his nostrils were twitching just a little bit. The nostrils, too, looked white right at the bottom. As I noticed this I wasn't following much what he was saying. Then it dawned on me. Everything he was saying was indicating in a very clever way that I was the one.

Then I saw the sweat running down under the hair back of his ears, just a drop or two coming out on the bare skin. I don't know what made me do it. I jumped in front of him, and pointed at him.

"Look," I yelled at him, "look how you're sweating! It's running down your neck, you're sweating so. Why don't you say it was you?"

He put his hands to his neck, then jerked them back to look at them. He was, all at once, white as a sheet.

■ **APPLICATIONS**

I Make a list of physical symptoms that you might use to indicate the following states: (1) fear, (2) rage, (3) disgust, (4) drowsiness, and (5) despair.

II Describe briefly, say in 250 words, a person experiencing one of the above states.

Figurative Language in the Description of Feelings and States of Mind

It should be obvious from the examples given above that when a writer comes to describe a feeling or a state of mind he is often forced to use figurative language. For instance, when Henry James wishes to describe the feeling of the wife who discovers that her husband is unsympathetic and egotistical (p. 603), he resorts to figurative language: the wife feels she has been imprisoned in the "house of dumbness," the "house of suffocation," and most of the passage is an elaboration of this comparison of her condition to an imprisonment. The whole question of figurative language has been discussed at some length before in this book (pp. 435–65) but the question is of so much importance for description that we must at least touch upon it here.

We may say, for the sake of convenience, that such comparisons have two functions in description—to enrich and to interpret. First, they may make for vividness and immediacy—the sensation of the scene unfolding before our eyes. Second, they may serve to interpret the object described or an attitude toward it.

If we write of a girl's hair that it is very black and glossy, we do little to stir the imagination of the reader to a full sense of the quality of the hair. But if we write that the girl's hair is like a raven's wing, then we have done something to set the imagination of the reader to work. The comparison just used is, unfortunately, a rather trite one; it has been used so often that its power to stir the imagination is almost gone. But when Thomas Hardy writes of the hair of one of his heroines, that "a whole winter did not contain darkness enough to form its shadow," or that it "closed over her forehead like nightfall," the imagination is stirred, and the image of the woman is evoked.

We often find that the function of a comparison is merely to increase vividness, to help the reader to grasp the object, or that the interpretative value of the comparison is very slight. For instance, in Stevenson's comparison of the atoll to a basin almost submerged in water (p. 304), we have almost as pure an example as it would be possible to find of a comparison which works to aid in vividness without any interpretative force. When Faulkner describes Miss Emily (p. 293): "Her eyes, lost in the fatty ridges of her face, looked like two small pieces of coal pressed into a lump of dough," the chief effect is to startle us, by this caricature of a face, into visualizing Miss Emily. But, here, if we are acquainted with the story in which the sentence appears, we realize that some interpretation may also be involved—the pallor, the pasty quality of the flesh, the unhuman quality of the comparison, are appropriate for this house of decay and death.

We can find many passages in which the interpretative value of the comparisons is more important than the value of vividness. For instance, when Melville says the vast volcanic islands "present a most Plutonian sight" (p. 276), the function is primarily interpretative. At that point in the passage we have already been given a very strong visual impression of the islands, and we are not likely to have a clear picture of the underworld in our minds. But the comparison does strongly suggest the idea of waste and desolation —the interpretative aspect.

Let us look at the end of the following paragraph to see how the comparison there sums up the whole impression of the city described:

> Except for the Marabar Caves—and they are twenty miles off—the city of Chandrapore presents nothing extraordinary. Edged rather than washed by the river Ganges, it trails for a couple of miles along the bank, scarcely distinguishable from the rubbish it deposits so freely. There are no bathing-steps on the river front, as the Ganges happens not to be holy here; indeed there is no river front, and bazaars shut out the wide and shifting panorama of the stream. The streets are mean, the temples ineffective, and though a few fine houses exist they are hidden away in gardens or down alleys whose filth deters all but the invited guest. Chandrapore was never large or beautiful, but two hundred years ago it lay on the road between Upper India, then imperial, and the sea, and the fine houses date from that period. The zest for decoration stopped in the eighteenth century, nor was it ever democratic. There is no painting and scarcely any carving in the bazaars. The very wood seems made of mud, the inhabitants of mud moving. So abased, so monotonous is everything that meets the eye, that when the Ganges comes down it might be expected to wash the excrescence back into the soil. Houses do fall, people are drowned and left rotting, but the general outline of the town persists, swelling here, shrinking there, like some low but indestructible form of life.
>
> —E. M. FORSTER: *A Passage to India.*

Here we have an excellent example of the interpretative emphasis in a comparison: the Indian city is like "some low but indestructible form of life."

A good comparison cannot be purely arbitrary. When T. E. Lawrence describes his arrival at an Arabian port, saying, "the heat of Arabia came out like a drawn sword and struck us speechless" (p. 290), we have nothing that corresponds as far as shape is concerned with the sword, but we do have the metallic glitter of sea and sand, the suddenness and violence of the heat after days at sea; and then, at the level of interpretation, we have the notion of ferocity and deadliness—the pitiless heat and the drawn blade. Or in Proust's comparison of various depths of the sea and of various kinds of light to describe the process of waking (p. 602), there is no object that corresponds to those things; but the vague shadings and confusions of dawning consciousness provide the basis for comparison.

It does not matter on what basis the comparison is established—by what senses or feelings—but there must be some primary connection if interpretation is to be established. A comparison, even if it does carry an appropriate interpretation, must not be so far-fetched that the reader cannot accept it. At the same time, the comparison that is too trite or too obvious does not stir the imagination. There is no rule for establishing these limits. The writer must simply depend on observation of the practice of others and on his own experience. (See Metaphor, pp. 435–65.)

■ APPLICATIONS

I   From the examples of description given above and from the group at the end of Chapter 12, select ten comparisons that are effective. Try to state in your own words what each comparison implies. Try to determine what the basis of the comparison is; that is, what do the two things involved in the comparison have in common.

II   Write a brief description of some feeling you have experienced—a sudden grief, shock at betrayal by a friend, the distress of a sleepless night, joy at unexpected good fortune.

APPENDIX **4**

Special Problems
in Narration

Here we shall discuss certain special problems in narration, problems that find their greatest importance, perhaps, in formal fiction, but that are of some importance in all narration.

Scale

By *scale* we mean the degree of fullness with which an event is treated. Here we can think in terms of extremes of method—*summary rendering* and *full rendering*. The tendency in narration is to use summary rendering for parts that are necessary only for continuity or, as it were, scaffolding, and to use full rendering for those parts that present the more significant moments. The following selection, which concludes Guy de Maupassant's celebrated story "The Necklace," illustrates the principle clearly. The main character, Mathilde Loisel, has been a vain, frivolous woman, who lived in daydreams of a rich and fashionable life. When she is finally invited to a ball, she borrows what she understands to be a diamond necklace from a friend, Madame Forestier. The necklace is lost at the ball, and Mathilde and her husband buy one to replace it, getting the money from usurers. At this point our selection picks up the story:

> She learned the heavy cares of a household, the odious work of a kitchen. She washed the dishes, using her rosy nails upon the greasy pots and the bottoms of the stewpans. She washed the soiled linen, the chemises and

dishcloths, which she hung on the line to dry; she took down the refuse to the street each morning and brought up the water, stopping at each landing to breathe. And, clothed like a woman of the people, she went to the grocer's, the butcher's, and the fruiterer's, with her basket on her arm, shopping, haggling to the last sou her miserable money.

Every month it was necessary to renew some notes, thus obtaining time, and to pay others.

The husband worked evenings, putting the accounts of some merchant in order, and at night he often copied manuscript at five sous a page.

And this life lasted ten years.

At the end of ten years, they had restored all, all, with interest of the usurers, and the compound interest besides.

Mme. Loisel looked old now. She had become a strong, hard woman, the rough woman of the poor household. Her hair tangled, her skirts awry, her hands red, she talked in loud tones, and washed the floors with a great swishing of water. But sometimes, when her husband was at the office, she would sit by the window and remember that evening of the ball, where she had been so beautiful and so happy.

What would have happened if she had not lost the necklace? Who knows? Who knows? How life is strange and changeful! How little is needed to ruin one or to save one!

One Sunday, as she was walking in the Champs Élysées, to restore herself after the work of the week, she suddenly saw a woman with a child. It was Madame Forestier, still young, still beautiful, still charming. Madame Loisel was moved. Should she speak to her? Yes, certainly. Now that she had paid, she would tell her all. Why not?

She approached her. "Good morning, Jeanne."

Her friend did not recognize her, and was surprised to be addressed by this woman of the people. She stammered: "But, Madame—I do not know—you must be mistaken——"

"No, I am Mathilde Loisel."

Her friend uttered a cry of surprise: "Oh, my poor Mathilde! How you are changed——"

"Yes, I have seen some hard days since I saw you—some miserable ones —and all because of you——"

"Because of me? How?"

"You remember the diamond necklace you loaned me to wear to the Minister's ball?"

"Yes, very well."

"Well, I lost it."

"How is that, since you returned it to me?"

"I returned one like it. And it has taken us ten years to pay for it. You can understand that it was not easy for us who have nothing. But it is finished, and I am very glad."

Madame Forestier stopped. She said: "You say that you bought a diamond necklace to replace mine?"

"Yes. You did not know it then? They were very like."

And she smiled with a joy that was proud and naïve.

Madame Forestier was touched, and seized both her hands as she said:

"Oh, my poor Mathilde! My necklace was false. It was not worth over five hundred francs!" —GUY DE MAUPASSANT: "The Necklace."

We notice here that the first half of the passage covers a time of ten years, the second half a time of three or four minutes. The ten years are summarized. The meeting in the park is rendered fully, word for word, instant by instant. We can readily see the reason why the writer summarized the ten years: they are all alike, a dreary grind of misery, and what is important is their result, Mathilde's new energy and fortitude, not the single events within them. As for the last scene, we can see that it is important in itself: it is dramatic, it is the moment when Mathilde realizes her situation, it is the result of all her past experience.

In the half of the selection rendered by summary we observe, however, that certain details do give us the impression of the quality and movement of life—Mathilde's bargaining, the coarseness of her voice, the way she scrubs the floor with great swishing sweeps of the wet mop. Narrative summary differs from the mere summary of ideas: when successful it still gives some hint of the quality and movement of life.

Dialogue

Narration often involves the use of dialogue—not only fictional narration but historical writing, biography, and other types. Dialogue sometimes seems to be an easy way to get a story told. The writer—especially an inexperienced writer—thinks that he knows how people talk. He thinks that to set down talk will be easier than to present material in the straight narrative form that he himself will have to compose. But the problem is not so simple as that. First, to compose effective dialogue is not easy, and second, to use dialogue constantly is monotonous.

On the first point it can be said that dialogue that is effective on the page is rarely a direct transcript of what people would say in conversation. Conversation is often stumbling, wandering, diffuse. The real point at issue in an actual conversation frequently becomes lost in mere wordiness or in the distractions of side issues and matters of incidental interest. The writer of dialogue cannot afford to duplicate such a conversation; if he does so, the reader will not be readily able to follow the line of significance. So the writer must organize the material to permit the reader to follow the development of the issue at stake. There must be an impression of give-and-take and a forward thrust of idea.

Let us examine a piece of unsatisfactory dialogue:

> Gertrude collapsed into her chair, helpless with amusement; giving herself up to her laughter, she made him feel suddenly ashamed of that remembered delight.

"Oh—oh—oh—oh!" she cried. "That is the most ridiculous thing I ever heard of. You call that girl a shy arbutus. And at your age, too. You certainly are silly."

"Well! I don't think it is so funny. You don't know the girl the way I do, and furthermore she is very modest and appealing. All sorts of people think so. For example, I have heard Mrs. Buckley say——"

"The shy arbutus! As I said, it is perfectly ridiculous. I don't want to be impolite, but she isn't exactly an arbutus, and as for Mrs. Buckley's opinion, you know what a sentimental old biddy she is, and how she gushes over everything. A shy arbutus. Forgive me, Harry, but that's too funny. How old *are* you?"

He flung his cigarette at the back-log and grinned.

"I knew it was no use," he grumbled amiably. "I can't make you see her, and it's no use trying. I know Mrs. Buckley is sentimental and does gush, but I don't think I am gushy, and I have also heard Tom Barker comment on the girl. Very favorably, too. And he is a hard-headed sort of fellow. Why, you remember, don't you, how he always brings a conversation right down to common sense. There was that time we were talking about the performance of that pianist—you know, the one who played at the Murdocks' house—last November—and everybody said how good she was, but Tom just said, 'Nuts, all she's got is ten quite ordinary fingers and a very extraordinary figure—but it is the fingers that have to play the piano!' That's just like old Tom. But to come back to the subject, Tom may understand the girl, but I can't make you see her, and it's no use trying."

"I heard that pianist, and she was rather good, I thought. Whatever Tom Barker thought. But the trouble with you is, you're in love with this girl. It is a well-known fact that a man in love is not able to exercise his best judgment. But it's precisely when you're in love that you need to keep your wits about you. Or the wits of your friends. Now I've come to the conclusion that you *mustn't* marry her, Harry. There are very good reasons."

"Well—I don't know. I don't think that being in love has done anything to my judgment."

"*No!* It is certainly my considered opinion that to marry that girl would be ruinous for you. You must think about your career. And more important, about your happiness. Won't she bore you to death in three years? She is quite dull. Now the kind of girl you want is somebody with spirit and mischief. A girl who has got some smartness, and who could amuse your friends. Think of the dull parties with this girl in the saddle."

The trouble here is that the dialogue is loaded with irrelevant material. People do load their conversations with irrelevant material, but dialogue in narrative cannot afford that weight. It kills the forward thrust.

Let us now look at the same piece of dialogue as it actually occurs in a story, stripped to the essentials:

"Oh—oh—oh—oh!" she cried.
"Well!"

"The shy arbutus! . . . Forgive me, Harry, but that's too funny. How old *are* you?"

He flung his cigarette at the back-log and grinned.

"I knew it was no use," he grunted amiably. "I can't make you see her, and it's no use trying."

"Well—I can see this much. You *are* in love with her.. Or you couldn't possibly be such a fool. But it's precisely when you're in love that you need to keep your wits about you. Or the wits of your friends. . . . You *mustn't* marry her, Harry."

"Well—I don't know."

"No! . . . It would be ruinous."

           —CONRAD AIKEN: "Spider, Spider," *Costumes by Eros.*

In the passage above, the line of interest is clear, and the collision between Gertrude and Harry is quite definite. In the expanded version there is a blurring of the effect. This blurred effect might actually result from a conversation of a Gertrude and Harry in real life, but that fact has no final bearing on the case here. The problem of the writer of dialogue is a problem of selection and logical organization.

There is, furthermore, the problem of giving dialogue a realistic surface. There must be, in addition to the logical organization, an impression of real life, a sense of the pauses, the changes, the waverings of conversation. But this must be an *impression* and not a word-for-word recording. There is no rule for giving this impression, but there are certain considerations that may help a writer to give it.

First, we can notice, as in the example above, that the breaks and the italicized words are of some use in this respect. We get the impression of the sudden shift of idea or the hesitancy of a speaker. And from the italicized words we get the impression of Gertrude's voice, with its slightly satirical emphasis. But these are devices that would not always apply, and in any case should be used sparingly.

Second, and more important, the writer can try to indicate the fact that each speaker has his own way of phrasing and his own rhythm of voice. Expertness in giving such an impression can only come from close observation—an awareness of the little catch phrases a person tends to repeat, of the type of sentence structure he tends to use, of the mannerisms of speech.

Third, in addition to the individual qualities of speech, we can note that there are qualities dependent on cultural background, race, geographical origin, and so forth, qualities that are shared by members of a group. The commonest way to indicate these qualities is by mere dialectal peculiarities, when such exist. But mere peculiarity of spelling is a crude device, and in the end usually becomes monotonous. It is better for the writer to use such a device sparingly, and to focus his attention on the vocabulary, idiom, and rhythm of the group to which his speaking character belongs.

Here are some examples in which the language used by a speaker gives some impression of his social group and of his individuality:

A BOY WHO IS THE SON OF A JOCKEY:

I guess looking at it, now, my old man was cut out for a fat guy, one of
those regular little roly fat guys you see around, but he sure never got that
way, except a little toward the last, and then it wasn't his fault, he was
riding over the jumps only and he could afford to carry plenty of weight
then. I remember the way he'd pull on a rubber shirt over a couple of jerseys
and a big sweat shirt over that, and got me to run with him in the forenoon
in the hot sun.
—ERNEST HEMINGWAY: "My Old Man," *Three Stories and Ten Poems.*

A PRETENTIOUS, SERVILE WOMAN:

"Well, now, that is so like you," returned Miss Knag. "Ha! ha! ha! Of
club feet! Oh very good. As I often remark to the young ladies, 'Well I
must say, and I do not care who knows it, of all the ready humor—hem—
I ever heard anywhere'—and I have heard a good deal; for when my dear
brother was alive (I kept house for him, Miss Nickleby), we had to supper
once a week two or three young men, highly celebrated in those days for
their humor, Madame Mantalini—Of all the ready humor,' I say to the
young ladies, '*I* ever heard, Madame Mantalini's is the most remarkable
—hem. It is so gentle, so sarcastic, and yet so good-natured (as I was observing to Miss Simmonds only this morning), that how, or when, or by
what means she acquired it, is to me a mystery indeed.'"
Here Miss Knag paused to take breath, and while she pauses it may be
observed—not that she was marvellously loquacious and marvellously def-
erential to Madame Mantalini, since these are facts which require no comment; but that every now and then, she was accustomed, in the torrent of
her discourse, to introduce a loud, shrill, clear, "hem!" the import and
meaning of which was variously interpreted by her acquaintance. . . .
—CHARLES DICKENS: *Nicholas Nickleby.*

A FATHERLY PROFESSOR:

"You may be right, and then you may have a one-sided view. When I
say that your prejudice is literary, I mean that you have read what universities are like and applied that reading here. You have condemned
without participating. You know, there may be good things, even in this
town. Why, I sometimes think you even like me a bit." Dr. Whitlock
smiled. "You see, there is indifference, intellectual servility, a vague attempt at education. But to know these things is not enough. You have to
go deeper, you must understand; your conviction must be intellectual as
well as emotional. There are more than economic reasons at stake, and
there may be greater social injustice in this small university town than in
the smashing of a miners' strike by hired bullies."
—MICHAEL DE CAPITE: *No Bright Banner.*

We have said that logical organization, the development of the point
at issue in a dialogue, is extremely important. But occasionally there is
little or no point at issue, and then the intended significance of a passage may

be the exhibition of the speaker's character, as in the speech by Miss Knag from *Nicholas Nickleby,* quoted above. There the wandering sentences, the interpolations, and the characteristic "hem!" indicate the quality of her mind, just as some of the remarks themselves indicate her mixture of vanity, pretentiousness, and servility.

In some instances, of course, a piece of dialogue may develop a point and at the same time contain elements that are irrelevant to that point but indicate the character of the speaker. Here is the famous passage between Falstaff and Mistress Quickly, who is trying to remind Falstaff that he had promised to marry her. Her talkativeness and fuzzy-mindedness appear here in the very way she presents the argument, the point, to Falstaff:

> Marry, if thou wert an honest man, thyself and the money too. Thou didst swear to me upon a parcel-gilt goblet; sitting in my Dolphin Chamber, at the round table, by a sea-coal fire, upon Wednesday in Wheeson week, when the Prince broke thy head for liking his father to a singing man of Windsor—thou didst swear to me then, as I was washing thy wound, to marry me and make me my lady thy wife. Canst thou deny it? Did not goodwife Keech, the butcher's wife, come in then and call me Gossip Quickly? Coming in to borrow a mess of vinegar, telling us she had a good dish of prawns, whereby thou didst desire to eat some, whereby I told thee they were ill for a green wound? And didst thou not, when she was gone down stairs, desire me to be no more so familiarity with such poor people, saying that ere long they would call me madam? And didst thou not kiss me and bid me fetch thee thirty shillings?
>
> —WILLIAM SHAKESPEARE: *Henry IV, Part II*

Characterization

Early in the discussion of narration we pointed out the relation between persons and action. Most narratives, from news stories to novels, are about people. Things happen to people and people make things happen. To understand an action we must understand the people involved, their natures, their motives, their responses, and to present an action so that it is satisfying we must present the people. This process is called *characterization*.

A news story gives a minimum of characterization. It merely identifies the persons involved—"Adam Perkins, age thirty-three, of 1217 Sunset Drive"—and then proceeds to give the bare facts of the event. If it deals with motive it does so in the barest possible way. If Adam Perkins has committed suicide, the news story may report that he had been in ill health and had, according to his wife, been worrying about financial reverses, but it will give no detail. On the other hand, a novel or biography usually gives very full characterization. It seeks to make us understand thoroughly the relationship between the character and the events and the effects of events on character. In between the news story and the novel or biography, there are all sorts of narratives that present more or less fully the relationship between character and event and that try to answer the fundamental questions: Why does the character do what he does to cause the event? Why does he respond as he does to the event?

To answer these questions, the writer of a narrative must characterize the person. This is as important for narratives dealing with matters of fact, such as biography or history, as it is for narratives dealing with imaginary persons, such as novels or short stories. The difference between the two types is simply this: the biographer must interpret the facts in order to understand the character and present him, and the writer of fiction must create the details in order to present the character.

Whether the details of a character are drawn from fact or from imagination, it is important to remember that a character cannot be effectively presented as a mere accumulation of details. The details must be related to one another to build up a unified impression and to convey the sense of an individual personality. As this impression of an individual personality relates to an action, we are concerned with motive or response. What is the main motive of a character? What is his main response? We must be sure that we have an answer to these questions before we can give an effective characterization. Then we must be sure that we have given a clear indication of this main fact of the character.

Once the main fact of the character is established in the writer's mind, he must relate other details of the character to it. That is, the character must be consistent. We know that real people are often very complicated and therefore often do things that seem inconsistent. The same person does good things and bad things, generous things and selfish things, wise things and stupid things, but even so, we usually feel that there is an explanation for such inconsistency, that the very inconsistencies can be understood in relation to a deeper consistency of character. And the object of the writer should be to contribute to this deeper understanding of character. He may present the inconsistent details, but at the same time he wants to present them as part of a comprehensible whole. There is no formula for accomplishing this, and the only way we can learn to do it is by studying human nature as we can observe it in life and in books.

Once the conception of a character is clear, we can, however, think systematically about methods of presenting it. Generally speaking, character can be presented by means of five different methods: by appearance and mannerisms, by analysis, by speech, by reactions of other persons, or by action.

Appearance and mannerisms really involve description, considered independently or as absorbed into narration, but description as an indication of the inner nature of persons. We have already seen in Dickens's description of Chadband (pp. 291–92) how the physical oiliness of the man is taken as a lead to his "oily" personality, and how his mannerism of lifting a hand before speaking gives the suggestion of false piety and vanity, of a hypocritical preacher.

As the method of description suggests the character, that of analysis states it and explains it. This is really a kind of exposition drawn into the service of narration. It may be very obvious and systematic, as when we write:

> Jack Staple's character is marked by what seems, at first inspection, to be a fundamental inconsistency: on some occasions he is kind and generous even to a fault, and at the same time he is capable of extreme cruelty. But the inconsistency disappears into a frightening consistency once we realize that the spring of his every action is a profound egotism, an egotism which can express itself as well through good as through evil. Both gratitude and fear can flatter his ego.

But in the following example, drawn from a student theme, we see a rather successful attempt to absorb the analysis into the narrative itself.

> When Mr. Hinks came into the geometry class that day, there was some kind of ripple round the room. It wasn't anything you could put your finger on, and as soon as it was over you felt you had been kidding yourself. It was like when you are out in a boat on an absolutely still day, and a breath of air just ripples the water, then stops. But later on I heard some of the fellows say they had felt something funny that first minute he came in.
>
> To look at, Mr. Hinks was not out of the ordinary. He was a sort of pudgy middle-aged man, with a round face, and a twinkle in his eye. No, it wasn't a twinkle. It was just that it was the sort of face that ought to have had a twinkle. It was the glitter of his spectacles that fooled you. When, about two months later, that day it happened—the thing I am writing about—he took his spectacles off and looked at me, it was the shock of my life. There certainly wasn't any twinkle. His eyes were the color of oysters, and looked about as cold.
>
> Today he began his talk as pleasant as anybody. He introduced himself, and made a joke about being an old hand at squaring the circle. It wasn't much of a joke, but we all laughed, out of a sense of duty, or the way you do to an older person who is trying to be funny at your level and doesn't know how. You know how you get somewhat embarrassed and sorry for such a person, and tend to laugh too much. We were laughing, all but Jack Purvess, who was sitting way over at the end of the front row. I then saw Mr. Hinks giving Jack a sidewise look. It wasn't the sort of thing that seemed to mean much at the time, but you notice something and the fact you noticed it must be a signal. Anyway, I remembered the fact, and two days later, when he asked Jack what the study of geometry was, I remembered again. You couldn't put your finger on what Mr. Hinks did. When Jack bumbled around a little, each question that Mr. Hinks asked him, in his nicest tone of voice, seemed to be aimed at helping him. But every time Jack got in deeper. Then Jack began to flush up. He knew he was making a big fool of himself. Somebody tittered. Mr. Hinks turned very

sternly, and said: "I want no one to laugh at Jack's expense. He is doing the very best he can. Aren't you, Jack?"

If Jack said yes to that he was admitting he was the biggest idiot in town. If he said no, he was admitting something else. Mr. Hinks was very patient. He kept waiting for the answer.

Under the topic of dialogue we have already discussed some of the ways by which speech indicates character: Miss Knag's habit of saying "hem" or the professor's special, somewhat stilted vocabulary and turn of phrase. But further, we must distinguish between what a person says and how he says it. The ideas or attitudes expressed should spring from the character and exhibit it, and the vocabulary, rhythm, and mannerisms (if there are mannerisms) should be significant.

It is difficult to find a brief example of the method of indicating character by the reactions of other people, for usually a fully developed scene is required to make such a point. But in the passage of narrative above, the "ripple" in the class when Mr. Hinks enters and Jack's behavior tell us something about the man. The principle is simple, and we can observe it constantly in real life: the feelings and behavior of those around a person act as a mirror of that person's character. And we often encounter it in narratives, sometimes with some such obvious signal as the ripple in the class when Mr. Hinks enters; but the method may be used without the signal. The reactions may form part of the narrative itself.

The method that most concerns the writer of narrative is, of course, the exhibiting of character through action. Again it is difficult to illustrate this method by a brief extract, for we can be sure that a single act is properly expressive of character only if we test that act against the other acts in the narrative. Any good short story or novel or biography will illustrate this method. But in general terms, we must ask if the particular incident is vivid, significant in itself, and consistent with other incidents. Our final test here is human nature, and thorough observation is the best teacher.

■ APPLICATIONS

I In the Readings, study the selections by Mailer (pp. 672–82), Podhoretz (pp. 847–58), Baldwin (pp. 858–67), and Lowell (pp. 867–76). Do you find any effective examples of rendering character by description, by analysis, by speech, by reactions of others, or by action?

II Write a piece of characteristic dialogue on any subject illustrating the speech of some member of a special group such as college students, lawyers, hippies, rock musicians, ranch hands, or clergymen.

III Take a person, real or imaginary, and write an analysis of his character, in some 150 or 200 words. Then compose a narrative of 500 words in which this person exhibits his character in action and speech.

PART FIVE

A BOOK
OF READINGS

1 / ARTICLES OF INFORMATION
AND OBSERVATION

The Method of Scientific Investigation

T. H. Huxley

Thomas Henry Huxley (1825–95) was not only a distinguished British biologist but a lucid expositor. He gave powerful support to the cause of Darwinism in Victorian England. His books include *The Physical Basis of Life* (1868), *Science and Culture* (1881), and *Science and Morals* (1886). "The Method of Scientific Investigation" is typical of his subject matter and his style.

The method of scientific investigation is nothing but the expression of the necessary mode of working of the human mind. It is simply the mode at which all phenomena are reasoned about, rendered precise and exact. There is no more difference, but there is just the same kind of difference, between the mental operations of a man of science and those of an ordinary person, as there is between the operations and methods of a baker or of a butcher weighing out his goods in common scales, and the operations of a chemist in performing a difficult and complex analysis by means of his balance and finely graduated weights. It is not that the action of the scales in the one

THE METHOD OF SCIENTIFIC INVESTIGATION: From *Collected Essays*, "Darwiniana," by T. H. Huxley.

case, and the balance in the other, differ in the principles of their construction or manner of working; but the beam of one is set on an infinitely finer axis than the other, and of course turns by the addition of a much smaller weight.

You will understand this better, perhaps, if I give you some familiar example. You have all heard it repeated, I dare say, that men of science work by means of induction and deduction, and that by the help of these operations, they, in a sort of sense, wring from Nature certain other things, which are called natural laws, and causes, and that out of these, by some cunning skill of their own, they build up hypotheses and theories. And it is imagined by many, that the operations of the common mind can be by no means compared with these processes, and that they have to be acquired by a sort of special apprenticeship to the craft. To hear all these large words, you would think that the mind of a man of science must be constituted differently from that of his fellow men; but if you will not be frightened by terms, you will discover that you are quite wrong, and that all these terrible apparatus are being used by yourselves every day and every hour of your lives.

There is a well-known incident in one of Molière's plays, where the author makes the hero express unbounded delight on being told that he had been talking prose during the whole of his life. In the same way, I trust that you will take comfort, and be delighted with yourselves, on the discovery that you have been acting on the principles of inductive and deductive philosophy during the same period. Probably there is not one here who has not in the course of the day had occasion to set in motion a complex train of reasoning, of the very same kind, though differing of course in degree, as that which a scientific man goes through in tracing the causes of natural phenomena.

A very trivial circumstance will serve to exemplify this. Suppose you go into a fruiterer's shop, wanting an apple—you take up one, and on biting it, you find it is sour; you look at it, and see that it is hard and green. You take up another one and that too is hard, green, and sour. The shopman offers you a third; but, before biting it, you examine it, and find that it is hard and green, and you immediately say that you will not have it, as it must be sour, like those that you have already tried.

Nothing can be more simple than that, you think; but if you will take the trouble to analyse and trace out into its logical elements what has been done by the mind, you will be greatly surprised. In the first place you have performed the operation of induction. You found that, in two experiences, hardness and greenness in apples went together with sourness. It was so in the first case, and it was confirmed by the second. True, it is a very small basis, but still it is enough to make an induction from; you generalise the facts, and you expect to find sourness in apples where you get hardness and greenness. You found upon that a general law that all hard and green apples are sour; and that, so far as it goes, is a perfect induction. Well, having got your natural law in this way, when you are offered another apple which you find is hard and green, you say, "All hard and green apples are sour; this apple is hard and green, therefore this apple is sour." That train of reasoning is what logicians call a syllogism, and has all its various parts and terms—its major premiss, its minor premiss, and its conclusion. And, by the help of further reasoning, which, if drawn out, would have to be exhibited in two or three other syllogisms, you arrive at your final determination, "I will not have that apple." So that, you see, you have, in the first place, established a law by induction, and upon that you have founded a deduction, and reasoned out the special particular case. Well now, suppose, having got your conclusion of the law, that at some time afterwards, you are discussing the qualities of apples with a friend: you will say to him, "It is a very curious thing, but I find that all hard and green apples are sour!" Your friend says to you, "But how do you know that?" You at once reply, "Oh, because I have tried them over and over again, and have always found them to be so." Well, if we were talking science instead of common sense, we should call that an experimental verification. And, if still opposed, you go further, and say, "I have heard from the people in Somersetshire and Devonshire, where a large number of apples are grown, that they have observed the same thing. It is also found to be the case in Normandy, and in North America. In short, I find it to be the universal experience of mankind wherever attention has been directed to the subject." Whereupon, your friend, unless he is a very unreasonable man, agrees with you, and is convinced that you are quite right in the conclusion you have drawn. He believes, although perhaps he does not know he believes it, that the more extensive verifications are—that the more frequently experiments have been made, and results of the same kind arrived at—that the more varied the conditions under which the same results are attained, the more certain is the ultimate conclusion, and he disputes the question no further. He sees that the experiment has been tried under all sorts of conditions, as to time, place, and people, with the same result; and he says with you, therefore, that the law you have laid down must be a good one, and he must believe it.

In science we do the same thing—the philosopher exercises precisely the same faculties, though in a much more delicate manner. In scientific inquiry it becomes a matter of duty to expose a supposed law to every possible kind of verification, and to take care, moreover, that this is done intentionally, and not left to a mere accident, as in the case of the apples. And in science, as in common life, our confidence in a law is in exact proportion to the absence of variation in the result of our experimental verifications. For instance, if you let go your grasp of an article you may have in your hand, it will immediately fall to the ground. That is a very common verification of one of the best established laws of nature—that of gravitation. The method by which men of science establish the existence of that law is exactly the same as that by which we have established the trivial proposition about the sourness of hard and green apples. But we believe it in such an extensive, thorough, and unhesitating manner because the universal experience of mankind verifies it, and we can verify it ourselves at any time; and that is the strongest possible foundation on which any natural law can rest.

So much, then, by way of proof that the method of establishing laws in science is exactly the same as that pursued in common life. Let us now turn to another matter (though really it is but another phase of the same question), and that is, the method by which, from the relations of certain phenomena, we prove that some stand in the position of causes towards the others.

I want to put the case clearly before you, and I will therefore show you what I mean by another familiar example. I will suppose that one of you, on coming down in the morning to the parlour of your house, finds that a tea-pot and some spoons which had been left in the room on the previous evening are gone—the window is open, and you observe the mark of a dirty hand on the window-frame, and perhaps, in addition to that, you notice the impress of a hob-nailed shoe on the gravel outside. All these phenomena have struck your attention instantly, and before two seconds have passed you say, "Oh, somebody has broken open the window, entered the room, and run off with the spoons and the tea-pot!" That speech is out of your mouth in a moment. And you will probably add, "I know there has; I am quite sure of it!" You mean to say exactly what you know; but in reality you are giving expression to what is, in all essential particulars, an hypothesis. You do not *know* it at all; it is nothing but an hypothesis rapidly framed in your own mind. And it is an hypothesis founded on a long train of inductions and deductions.

What are those inductions and deductions, and how have you got at this hypothesis? You have observed in the first place, that the window is open; but by a train of reasoning involving many inductions and deductions, you have probably arrived long before at the general law—and a very good one it is—that windows do not open of themselves; and you therefore conclude that something has opened the window. A second general law that you have arrived at in the same way is, that tea-pots and spoons do not go out of a window spontaneously, and you are satisfied that, as they are not now where you left them, they have been removed. In the third place, you look at the marks on the window-sill, and the shoe-marks outside, and you say that in all previous experience the former kind of mark has never been produced by anything else but the hand of a human being; and the same experience shows that no other animal but man at present wears shoes with hob-nails in them such as would produce the marks in the gravel. I do not know, even if we could discover any of those "missing links" that are talked about, that they would help us to any other conclusion! At any rate the law which states our present experience is strong enough for my present purpose. You next reach the conclusion that, as these kinds of marks have not been left by any other animal than man, or are liable to be formed in any other way than by a man's hand and shoe, the marks in question have been formed by a man in that way. You have, further, a general law, founded on observation and experience, and that, too, is I am sorry to say, a very universal and unimpeachable one—that some men are thieves; and you assume at once from all these premises—and that is what constitutes your hypothesis—that the man who made the marks outside and on the window-sill, opened the window, got into the room, and stole your tea-pot and spoons. You have now arrived at a *vera causa*—you have assumed a cause which, it is plain, is competent to produce all the phenomena you have observed. You can explain all these phenomena only by the hypothesis of a thief. But that is a hypothetical conclusion, of the justice of which you have no absolute proof at all; it is only rendered highly probable by a series of inductive and deductive reasonings.

I suppose your first action, assuming that you are a man of ordinary common sense, and that you have established this hypothesis to your own satisfaction, will very likely be to go off for the police, and set them on the track of the burglar, with the view to the recovery of your property. But just as you are starting with this object, some person comes in, and on learning what you are about, says, "My good friend, you are going on a great deal too fast. How do you know that the man who really made the marks took the spoons? It might have been a monkey that took them, and the man may have merely looked in afterwards." You would probably reply, "Well, that is all very well, but you see it is contrary to all experience of the way tea-pots and spoons are abstracted; so that, at any rate, your hypothesis is less probable than mine." While you are talking the thing over in this way, another friend arrives, one of the good kind of people that I was talking of a little while ago. And he might say, "Oh, my dear sir, you are certainly going on a great deal too fast. You are most presumptuous. You admit that all these occurrences took place when you were fast asleep, at a time when you could not possibly have known anything about what was taking place. How do you know that the laws of Nature are not suspended during the night? It may be that there has been some kind of supernatural interference in this case." In point of fact, he declares that your hypothesis is one of which you cannot at all demonstrate the truth, and that you are by no means sure that the laws of Nature are the same when you are asleep as when you are awake.

Well, now, you cannot at the moment answer that kind of reasoning. You feel that your worthy friend has you somewhat at a disadvantage. You will feel perfectly convinced in your own mind, however, that you are quite right, and you say to him, "My good friend, I can only be guided by the natural probabilities of the case, and if you will be kind enough to stand aside and permit me to pass, I will go and fetch the police." Well, we will suppose that your journey is successful, and that by good luck you meet with a policeman; that eventually the burglar is found with your property on his person, and the marks correspond to his hand and to his boots. Probably any jury would consider those facts a very good experimental verification of your hypothesis, touching the cause of the abnormal phenomena observed in your parlour, and would act accordingly.

Now, in this supposititious case, I have taken phenomena of a very common kind, in order that you might see what are the different steps in an ordinary process of reasoning, if you will only take the trouble to analyse it carefully. All the operations I have described, you will see, are involved in the mind of any man of sense in leading him to a conclusion as to the course he should take in order to make good a robbery and punish the offender. I say that you are led, in that case, to your conclusion by exactly the same train of reasoning as that which a man of science pursues when he is endeavouring to discover the origin and laws of the most occult phenomena. The process is, and always must be, the same; and precisely the same mode of reasoning was employed by Newton and Laplace in their endeavours to discover and define the causes of the movements of the heavenly bodies, as you, with your own common sense, would employ to detect a burglar. The only difference is, that the nature of the inquiry being more abstruse, every step has to be most carefully watched, so that there may not be a single crack or flaw in your hypothesis. A flaw or crack in many of the hypotheses of daily life may be of little or no moment as affecting the general correctness of the conclusions at which we may arrive; but, in a scientific inquiry, a fallacy, great or small, is always of importance, and is sure to be in the long run constantly productive of mischievous if not fatal results.

Do not allow yourselves to be misled by the common notion that an hypothesis is untrustworthy simply because it is an hypothesis. It is often urged, in respect to some scientific conclusion, that, after all, it is only an hypothesis. But what more have we to guide us in nine-tenths of the most important affairs of daily life than hypotheses, and often very ill-based ones? So that in science, where the evidence of an hypothesis is subjected to the most rigid examination, we may rightly pursue the same course. You may have hypotheses, and hypotheses. A man may say, if he likes, that the moon is made of green cheese: that is an hypothesis. But another man, who has devoted a great deal of time and attention to the subject, and availed himself of the most powerful telescopes and the results of the observations of others, declares that in his opinion it is probably composed of materials very similar to those of which our own earth is made up: and that is also only an hypothesis. But I need not tell you that there is an enormous difference in the value of the two hypotheses. That one which is based on sound scientific knowledge is sure to have a corresponding value; and that which is a mere hasty random guess is likely to have but little value. Every great step in our progress in discovering causes has been made in exactly the same way as that which I have detailed to you. A person observing the occurrence of certain facts and phenomena asks, naturally enough, what process, what kind of operation known to occur in Nature, applied to the particular case, will unravel and explain the mystery? Hence you have the scientific hypothesis; and its value will be proportionate to the care and completeness with which its basis had been tested and verified. It is in these matters as in the commonest affairs of practical life; the guess of the fool will be folly, while the guess of the wise man will contain wisdom. In all cases, you see that the value of the result depends on the patience and faithfulness with which the investigator applies to his hypothesis every possible kind of verification.

The Colors That Animals Can See

H. Munro Fox

H. Munro Fox (1889–1967) was educated at Cambridge University, where he was later a fellow of Gonville and Caius College. From 1941 to 1954 he was Professor of Zoology at the University of London (from 1954 until his death, Professor Emeritus). He served a term as President of the International Union of Biological Sciences.

What colors can animals see? Is the world more brightly colored or duller to animals than it is to us? To find out the answers to these questions scientists have used a method of training the animals to come to different colors, which is similar in principle to the method used in studying the sense of hearing in animals.

Let us take bees first of all, partly because more exact scientific research has been done on the color-sense of bees than of almost any other animal. It is especially interesting to know what colors bees can see because these insects visit flowers to get sweet nectar from them to make honey, and in so doing the bees incidentally carry pollen from flower to flower. On the face of it, it would seem very likely that bees are attracted to flowers by their bright colors. But possibly it is the scents that attract the bees, or perhaps it is both color and scent. So, among other things, we want to know whether bees can really see the colors of flowers, and if so, what colors they can see. Exactly how is this found out?

A table is put in a garden, and on the table a piece of blue cardboard is placed, on which there is a watch-glass containing a drop of syrup. After a short while bees come to the syrup and suck up some of it. The bees then fly to their hive and give the syrup to other bees in the hive to make honey.

THE COLORS THAT ANIMALS CAN SEE: From *The Personality of Animals* by H. Munro Fox. Reprinted by permission of Penguin Books Ltd.

Then they return to the feeding-place which they have discovered. We let the bees go on doing this for a while, after which we take away the blue cardboard with the syrup on it. Instead of this card we now put on the table a blue card on the left side of the first feeding-place, and a red card to the right of the first feeding-place. These new cards have no syrup on them but only an empty watch-glass lying on each. Thus, the blue card is on the left, the red card on the right, and there is nothing where the first blue feeding-card used to be. After we have arranged these new cards, we have not long to wait. Very soon bees arrive again, and it can be seen that they fly straight on to the blue card; none go to the red card.

This behavior of the bees seems to indicate two things. The first is that the bees remember that blue means syrup and so they fly to the blue. Since they did not go to the place on the table where the syrup used to be, but flew to the blue card which had been placed on the left, it really was the blue card that attracted them, not the place where the syrup had previously been. We have trained the bees to come to the blue card. And the second thing our experiment seems to mean is that bees can tell blue from red.

But can they? This is not yet quite certain. The reason for our doubt is as follows. It is well known that there are a few people in the world, very few, who cannot see colors at all. These people are totally color-blind. To them all colors look like different shades of grey. They may be able to tell red from blue, because red will perhaps look darker and blue lighter in shade, but the colors are not red or blue. It might be, then, that bees are really color-blind, and that in the experiment they came to the blue card not because they saw it as blue but just because it appeared lighter in shade than the red card. Perhaps they had really been trained to come not to blue, but to the lighter of two shades. We can find out quite simply if this is so by another training experiment.

On our table in the garden we put a blue card, and all around this blue card we put a number of different grey cards. These grey cards are of all possible shades of grey, from the extremes of white to black. On each card a watch-glass is placed. The watch-glass on the blue card has some syrup in it; all the others are empty. After a short time bees find the syrup as before, and they come for it again and again. Then, after some hours, we take away the watch-glass of syrup which was on the blue card and put an empty one in its place. Now what do the bees do? They still go straight to the blue card, although there is no syrup there. They do not go to any of the grey cards, in spite of the fact that one of the grey cards is of exactly the same brightness as the blue card. Thus the bees do not mistake any shade of grey for blue. In this way we have proved that they really do see blue as a color.

We can find out in just the same way what other colors bees can see. It turns out that bees see various colors, but these insects differ from us as regards their color-sense in two very interesting ways. Suppose we train bees to come to a red card, and having done so we put the red card on the table in the garden among the set of different grey cards. This time we find that the bees mistake red for dark grey or black. They cannot distinguish between them. Thus it appears that red is not a color at all for bees; for them it is just dark grey or black. In reality further experiments have shown that bees can see red as a color but only when it is brilliantly illuminated: They are relatively insensitive to red.

That is one strange fact: here is the other. A rainbow is red on one edge, violet on the other. Outside the violet of the rainbow there is another color which we cannot see at all. The color beyond the violet, invisible to us, is called the ultra-violet. Although invisible, we know that the ultra-violet is there because it affects a photographic plate. Now, although we are unable to see ultra-violet light, bees can do so; for them ultra-violet is a color. Thus bees see a color which we cannot even imagine. This has been found out by training bees to come for syrup to various different parts of a spectrum, or artificial rainbow, thrown by a quartz prism on a table in a dark room. In such an experiment the insects can be taught to fly to the ultra-violet, which for us is just darkness.

We will leave the bees now and turn to birds. Cocks have striking colors in their plumage—striking to us, at any rate—while hens only possess dull tints. But can hens see the colors of the cock as we can see them? Can the peahen, for instance, see the wonderful colors of the peacock? To answer this question we must know what colors a bird can actually see. This has been studied in the following manner. A lamp and prism are set up to throw a spectrum of rainbow colors on the floor of a dark room. On the different colors of the spectrum grains of corn are sprinkled, and then a hen is brought in. She pecks at the grains of corn and gobbles up all she can see. After a time we remove the hen and take note of what grains are left untouched by her. We find that the hen has eaten nearly all the grains which were in the red, in the yellow, and in the green regions of the spectrum. We find that she has taken a few of the grains in the blue light, but the hen leaves the grains in the violet untouched. This means that she cannot see the grains which are in the violet light, and she is not able to see those in the blue very well either, for she did not pick up many of them. So violet is just like black to the hen, and blue is not a very bright color.

This has been confirmed with homing pigeons on which colored spectacles were fitted; with red and yellow specs the birds flew home normally, but with green, and especially blue, they were unable to do so. A human being could see clearly through the blue celluloid of which the spectacles were made, but evidently blue is like a black-out to the bird, and it is well known that homing pigeons cannot find their way in dim light or darkness.

Other birds are like this, too, which seems strange at first, because some birds are themselves blue. The kingfisher, for instance, is blue. Are we to conclude that the kingfisher is unable to see the beautiful color of its mate? This does not follow; the kingfisher can probably see his mate's blue plumage, for our experiments do not show that birds are unable to see blue at all. Birds just do not see this color very well; for them to see blue, the blue must be intense. And indeed the color of the kingfisher is very bright. Yet it is not all birds that have such difficulty in seeing blue; owls, on the contrary, are more sensitive than we ourselves to the blue end of the spectrum.

And what can dogs see? The answer to this question is disappointing: dogs apparently see no colors. The answer is disappointing because many owners of dogs will naturally be sorry that their dogs cannot see colors which to them are beautiful. But then, they may reflect that dogs have an extraordinarily keen sense of smell. The dogs' world is rich in enjoyable smells, even if it may be colorless.

How do we know if dogs are color-blind? This has been tested in the same way that it has been discovered what dogs can hear. The attempt has been made to train dogs to salivate when they are shown certain different colors, just as they were trained so that their mouths watered when definite musical notes were sounded. Such experiments have turned out failures; it has been found impossible to make dogs distinguish colors from one another as signals for their dinner. This question requires further testing with other techniques, but so far as the available scientific evidence goes, dogs seem to be color-blind. Many dog-owners will disagree with this, being convinced that their dogs know, for instance, the color of a dress. But the evidence given for this has never been sufficiently rigid for a scientist, who is not certain that the dog did not really respond to some other clue or sign than the color—to a smell, for instance, or to the particular behavior of the wearer of the dress.

Experiments have been made, too, to test the color-sense of cats; although these experiments may not yet be conclusive, they have indicated, so far, that cats are color-blind. Different cats were trained to come for their food in response to signals of each of six different colors. But the cats always confused their particular color with one of a number of shades of grey, when these were offered at the same time as the color.

Monkeys, on the other hand, are able to distinguish colors. They have been trained successfully to go for their meal to a cupboard, the door of which was painted in a certain color, and to ignore other available cupboards with differently colored doors, in which there was no food. Apart from monkeys and apes, however, most mammals seem to be color-blind, at any rate those which have been scientifically tested. Even bulls have been shown not to see red as a color. In spite of popular belief they are not excited by red, and they cannot distinguish red from dark grey. No doubt any bright waving cloth excites a high-spirited bull.

Color-blindness in mammals, other than monkeys, is comprehensible when one considers the lives of the animals in a wild state. For nearly all wild mammals are nocturnal or crepuscular. Wolves and lions hunt mostly at night, while antelopes and wild cattle graze at night, or in the evening when colors are dim. But monkeys, in the forests where they live, are awake and about in the daytime, and there are abundant colors for them to see in the bright tropical light.

Moreover, the color-blindness of mammals other than monkeys accords with the fact that the animals themselves are more or less dull colored; their coats are brown or yellow, black or white. Only in monkeys are greens, bright reds, and blues found. These are colors which recall the brilliant tints of birds and of fish, animals which also possess color-vision.

Jackdaws

Konrad Lorenz

> Konrad Lorenz (b. 1903), Austrian-born biologist, is the author of *King Solomon's Ring* (1952), *Man Meets Dog* (1954), *Evolution and Modification of Behavior* (1965), and *On Aggression* (1966). Since 1967 he has been the Director of the Max-Planck-Institut for Physiology of Behavior.

Twenty-five years have passed since the first jackdaw flew round the gables of Altenberg, and I lost my heart to the bird with the silvery eyes. And, as so frequently happens with the great loves of our lives, I was not conscious of it at the time when I became acquainted with my first jackdaw. It sat in Rosalia Bongar's pet shop, which still holds for me all the magic of early childhood memories. It sat in a rather dark cage and I bought it for exactly four shillings, not because I intended to use it for scientific observations, but because I suddenly felt a longing to cram that great, yellow-framed red throat with good food. I wished to let it fly as soon as it became independent and this I really did, but with the unexpected consequence that even to-day, after the terrible war, when all my other birds and animals are gone, the jackdaws are still nesting under our roof-tops. No bird or animal has ever rewarded me so handsomely for an act of pity.

Few birds—indeed few of the higher animals (the colony-building insects come under a different heading) possess so highly developed a social and family life as the jackdaws. Accordingly, few animal babies are so touchingly helpless and so charmingly dependent on their keeper as young jackdaws. Just as the quills of its primary feathers became hard and ready for flight, my young bird suddenly developed a really childlike affection for my person. It refused to remain by itself for a second, flew after me from one room to another and called in desperation if ever I was forced to leave it alone. I christened it "Jock" after its own call-note, and to this day we preserve the tradition that the first young bird of a new species reared in isolation is christened after the call-note of its kind.

Such a fully fledged young jackdaw, attached to its keeper by all its youthful affection, is one of the most wonderful objects for observation that you can imagine. You can go outside with the bird and, from the nearest viewpoint, watch its flight, its method of feeding, in short all its habits, in perfectly natural surroundings, unhampered by the bars of a cage. I do not think that I have ever learned so much about the essence of animal nature from any of my beasts or birds as from Jock in that summer of 1925.

It must have been owing to my gift of imitating its call that it soon preferred me to any other person. I could take long walks and even bicycle rides with it and it flew after me, faithful as a dog. Although there was no doubt that it knew me personally and preferred me to anybody else, yet it would desert me and fly after some other person if he was walking much faster than me, particularly if he overtook me. The urge to fly after an object moving away from it is very strong in a young jackdaw and almost takes the form of a reflex action. As soon as he had left me, Jock would notice his error and correct it, coming back to me hurriedly. As he grew older, he learned to repress the impulse to pursue a stranger, even one walking very fast indeed. Yet even then I would often notice his giving a slight start or a movement indicative of flying after the faster traveller.

Jock had to struggle with a still greater mental conflict when one or more hooded crows, common in this district, flew up in front of us. The sight of those beating black wings disappearing rapidly into the distance released in the jackdaw an irresistible urge to pursue which it never, in spite of bitter experience, learned to resist. It used to rush blindly after the crows which repeatedly lured it far away and it was only by good luck that it did not get lost altogether. Most peculiar was its reaction when the crows alighted: the moment that the magic of those flapping black wings ceased to work, Jock entirely lost interest! Though a flying crow had such an overwhelming attraction for him, a sitting one evidently did not, and as soon as the crows landed he had had enough of them, was seized with loneliness and began to call for me in that strange, complaining tone with which young, lost jackdaws call for their parents. As soon as he heard my answering call, he rose and flew towards me with such determination that he frequently drew the crows with him and came flying to my side as the leader of their troop. So blindly would the crows follow him in such cases that they were almost upon me before they noticed me at all. When finally they became conscious of my presence, they were struck with terror and darted away in such a panic that Jock—infected by the general consternation—once again flew away after them. When I had learned to recognize this danger, I was able to avoid complications by making myself as conspicuous as possible and thus warding off the approaching crows early enough to prevent a panic.

Like the stones of a mosaic, the inherited and acquired elements of a young bird's behaviour are pieced together to produce a perfect pattern. But, in a bird that has been reared by hand, the natural harmony of this design is necessarily somewhat disturbed. All those social actions and reactions whose object is not determined by inheritance, but acquired by individual experience, are apt to become unnaturally deflected. In other words, they are directed towards human beings, instead of fellow-members of the bird's species. As Rudyard Kipling's Mowgli thought of himself as a wolf, so Jock, had he been able to speak, would certainly have called himself a human being. Only the sight of a pair of flapping black wings sounded a hereditary note: "Fly with us." As long as he was walking, he considered himself a man, but the moment he took to wing, he saw himself as a hooded crow, because these birds were the first to awaken his flock instinct. . . .

It was entirely due to Jock that, in 1927, I reared fourteen young jackdaws in Altenberg. Many of her remarkable instinctive actions and reactions towards human beings, as substitute objects for fellow-members of her species, not only seemed to fall short of their biological goal, but remained incomprehensible to me and therefore aroused my curiosity. This awakened in me the desire to raise a whole colony of free flying tame jackdaws, and then study the social and family behaviour of these remarkable birds.

As it was out of the question that I should act as substitute for their parents and train each of these young jackdaws as I had done Jock the previous year, and as, through Jock, I was familiar with their poor sense of orientation, I had to think out some other method of confining the young birds to the place. After much careful consideration, I arrived at a solution which subsequently proved entirely satisfactory. In front of the little window of the loft where Jock had now dwelt for some time, I built a long and narrow aviary, consisting of two compartments which rested upon a stone-built gutter a yard in width, and stretched almost the entire breadth of the house.

Jock was, at first, somewhat upset by the building alterations in the near neighbourhood of her home and it was some time before she became reconciled to them and flew in and out freely through the trap-door in the roof of the front compartment of the aviary. It was only then that I proceeded to instal the young birds, each of which had been made recognizable by coloured rings on one or both legs. From these rings the young jackdaws also derived their names. When the birds were all well settled in their new quarters, I lured them into the rear compartment of the cage, leaving only Jock and the two tamest of the young birds, Blueblue and Redblue, in the front compartment, the one with the trap-door. Thus separated, the birds were again left to themselves for a few days. What I hoped to attain by these measures was that the birds destined for free flight should be held back by their social attachment to those who were still imprisoned in the hindmost part of the aviary. At this time, as I have already mentioned, Jock had begun to mother one of the young jackdaws, Leftgold, and this was very fortunate indeed as it brought about her return home at the right moment for the experiments I am about to describe. I did not choose Leftgold as one of the first subjects for release, because I hoped that, for his sake, Jock would remain in the precincts of our house, otherwise there was a risk of her flying off with Leftgold who was now fully fledged, to live with my . . . housemaid in the next village.

My hopes that the young jackdaws would fly after Jock as she had followed me, were only partly fulfilled. When I opened the trap-door, Jock was outside in a flash and, making one dive for liberty, within a few seconds had disappeared. It was a long time before the young jackdaws, mistrustful of the unaccustomed aspect of the open trap-door, dared to fly through it. At last, both of them did so simultaneously, just as Jock came whizzing past again outside. They tried to follow her but soon lost her as neither could imitate her sharply banked turns and her steep dives. This lack of consideration for the limited flying abilities of the young is not shown by good parent jackdaws, who meticulously avoid such flying stunts while guiding their offspring. Later, when Leftgold was freed, Jock also behaved in this manner, flying slowly and refraining from all difficult manoeuvring, looking back over her shoulder constantly to see whether the young bird was still following. Not only did Jock pay no attention to the other young jackdaws, but they, for their part, obviously did not realize that she was equipped with a most desirable local knowledge which they lacked and that she would have been a more reliable guide than one of their own companions. These silly children sought leadership among themselves, each one trying to fly after the other. In such cases, the wild, aimless circling of the birds impels them higher and higher into the sky, and as, at this age, they are quite incapable of descending in a bold dive, these antics invariably result in their getting lost, because the higher they mount, the farther they will be from home when they ultimately succeed in coming down again. Several of the fourteen young jackdaws went astray in this fashion. An old and experienced jackdaw, particularly an old male, would have prevented such a thing happening, as will be explained later on, but at this stage no such bird was present in the colony.

This lack of leadership revealed itself in another and even more serious way. Young jackdaws have no innate reactions against the enemies which threaten them, whereas a good many other birds, such as magpies, mallards or robins, prepare at once for flight at their very first sight of a cat, a fox or even a squirrel. They behave in just the same way, whether reared by man or by their own parents. Never will a young magpie allow itself to be caught by a cat and the tamest of hand-reared mallards will instantly react to a red-brown skin, pulled along the back of the pond on a string. She will treat such a dummy exactly as if she realized all the properties of her mortal enemy, the fox. She becomes anxiously cautious and, taking to the water, never for a moment averts her eyes from the enemy. Then, swimming, she follows it wherever it goes, without ceasing to utter her warning cries. She knows, or rather her innate reacting mechanisms know, that the fox can neither fly, nor swim quickly enough to catch her in the water, so she follows it around to keep it in sight, to broadcast its presence and, in this way, to spoil the success of its stalking.

Recognition of the enemy—which in mallards and many other birds is an inborn instinct—must be learned personally by the young jackdaws. Learned through their own experience? No, more curious still: by actual tradition, by the handing-down of personal experience from one generation to the next!

Of all the reactions which, in the jackdaw, concern the recognition of an enemy, only one is innate: any living being that carries a black thing, dangling or fluttering, becomes the object of a furious onslaught. This is accompanied by a grating cry of warning whose sharp, metallic, echoing sound expresses, even to the human ear, the emotion of embittered rage. At the same time the jackdaw assumes a strange forward leaning attitude and vibrates its half-spread wings. If you possess a tame jackdaw, you may, on occasion, venture to pick it up to put it into its cage or, perhaps, to cut its overgrown claws. But not, if you have *two!* Jock, who was as tame as any dog, had never resented the occasional touch of my hand, but when the young jackdaws came to our house, it was a different story altogether: on no account would she allow me to touch one of these small, black nestlings. As all unsuspecting, I did so for the first time, I heard behind me the sharp satanic sound of that raucous rattle, a black arrow swooped down from above, over my shoulder and on to the hand which held the jackdaw baby— astonished, I stared at a round, bleeding, deeply pecked wound in the back of my hand! That first observation of this type of attack was, in itself, illuminating as to the instinctive blindness of the impulse. Jock was, at this time, still very devoted to me and hated these fourteen young jackdaws most cordially. (Her adoption of Leftgold took place later on.) I was forced to protect them from her continually: she would have destroyed them, at one fell swoop, if she had been left alone with them for a few minutes. Nevertheless she could not tolerate my taking one of the babies into my hand. The blind reflex nature of the reaction became even clearer to me through a coincidental observation later that summer. One evening, as dusk fell, I returned from a swim in the Danube and, according to my custom, I hurried to the loft to call the jackdaws home and lock them up for the night. As I stood in the gutter, I suddenly felt something wet and cold in my trouser pocket into which, in my hurry, I had pushed my black bathing drawers. I pulled them out—and the next moment was surrounded by a dense cloud of raging, rattling jackdaws, which hailed agonizing pecks upon my offending hand.

It was interesting to observe the jackdaws' reaction to other black objects which I carried in my hands. My large, old, naturalist's camera never caused a similar commotion, although it was black and I held it in my hands, but the jackdaws would start their rattling cry as soon as I pulled out the black paper strips of the pack film which fluttered to and fro in the breeze. That the birds knew me to be harmless, and even a friend, made no difference whatever: as soon as I held in my hand something black and moving, I was branded as an "eater of jackdaws." More extraordinary still is the fact that the same thing may happen to a jackdaw itself: I have witnessed a typical rattling attack on a female jackdaw who was carrying to her nest the wing feather of a raven. On the other hand, tame jackdaws neither emit their rattling cry, nor make an attack, if you hold in your hand one of their own young whilst it is still naked and, therefore, not yet black. This I proved experimentally with the first pair of jackdaws which nested in my colony. The two birds, Greengold and Redgold—two of the aforementioned fourteen—were completely tame, perched on my head and shoulders and were not in the least upset if I handled their nest and watched all their activities at close quarters. Even when I took the babies from the nest and presented them to their parents on the palm of my hand, it left them quite unmoved. But the very day that the small feathers on the nestling burst through their quills, changing their colour into black, there followed a furious attack by the parents on my outstretched hand. . . .

Do animals thus know each other among themselves? They certainly do, though many learned animal psychologists have doubted the fact and indeed denied it categorically. Nevertheless, I can assure you, every single jackdaw of my colony knew each of the others by sight. This can be convincingly demonstrated by the existence of an order of rank, known to animal psychologists as the "pecking order." Every poultry farmer knows that, even among these more stupid inhabitants of the poultry yards, there exists a very definite order, in which each bird is afraid of those that are above her in rank. After some few disputes, which need not necessarily lead to blows, each bird knows which of the others she has to fear and which must show respect to her. Not only physical strength, but also personal courage, energy, and even the self-assurance of every individual bird are decisive in the maintenance of the pecking order. This order of rank is extremely conservative. An animal proved inferior, if only morally, in a dispute, will not venture lightly to cross the path of its conqueror, provided the two animals remain in close contact with each other. This also holds good for even the highest and most intelligent mammals. A large Nemestrinus monkey bursting with energy, owned by my friend, the late Count Thun-Hohenstein, possessed, even when adult, a deeply rooted respect for an ancient Javanese monkey of half his size who had tyrannized him in the days of his youth. The deposing of an ageing tyrant is always a highly dramatic and usually tragic event, especially in the case of wolves and sledge dogs, as has been observed and graphically described by Jack London in some of his arctic novels.

The rank order disputes in a jackdaw colony differ in one important way from those of the poultry yard, where the unfortunate cinderellas of the lower orders eke out a truly miserable existence. In every artificial conglomeration of less socially inclined animals, such as in the poultry yard and the song bird aviary, those higher in the social scale tend to set upon their comrades of lower rank, and the lower the standing of the individual, the more savagely will he be pecked at by all and sundry. This is often carried so far that the wretched victim, bullied from all sides, is never able to rest, is always short of food and, if the owner does not interfere, may finally waste away altogether. With jackdaws, quite the contrary is the case: in the jackdaw colony, those of the higher orders, particularly the despot himself, are not aggressive towards the birds that stand far beneath them; it is only in their relations towards their immediate inferiors that they are constantly irritable; this applies especially to the despot and the pretender to the throne—Number One and Number Two. Such behaviour may be difficult for a casual observer to understand. A jackdaw sits feeding at the communal dish, a second bird approaches ponderously, in an attitude of self-display, with head proudly erected, whereupon the first visitor moves slightly to one side, but otherwise does not allow himself to be disturbed. Now comes a third bird, in a much more modest attitude which, surprisingly enough, puts the first bird to flight; the second, on the other hand, assumes a threatening pose, with his back feathers ruffled, attacks the latest comer and drives him from the spot. The explanation: the latest comer stood in order of rank midway between the two others, high enough above the first to frighten him and just so far beneath the second as to be capable of arousing his anger. Very high caste jackdaws are most condescending to those of lowest degree and consider them merely as the dust beneath their feet; the self-display actions of the former are here a pure formality and only in the event of too close approximation does the dominant bird adopt a threatening attitude, but he very rarely attacks.

The degree of animosity of the higher orders towards the lower is in direct proportion to their rank, and it is interesting to note that this essentially simple behaviour results in an impartial levelling-up of the disputes between individual members of the colony. The gestures of anger and attack may also stimulate those against whom they are not directed. I myself, when I hear two people cursing each other in an overcrowded tramcar, have to suppress an almost uncontrollable desire to box the ears of both parties soundly. High ranking jackdaws evidently feel the same emotion, but, as they are in no way inhibited by the horror of making a scene, they interfere vigorously in the quarrel of two subordinates, as soon as the argument gets heated. The arbitrator is always more aggressive towards the higher ranking of the two original combatants. Thus a high-caste jackdaw, particularly the despot himself, acts regularly on chivalrous principles—where there's an unequal fight, always take the weaker side. Since the major quarrels are mostly concerned with nesting sites (in nearly all other cases, the weaker bird withdraws without a struggle), this propensity of the strong male jackdaws ensures an active protection of the nests of the lower members of the colony.

Once the social order of rank amongst the members of a colony is established it is most conscientiously preserved by jackdaws, much more so than by hens, dogs or monkeys. A spontaneous re-shuffling, without outside influence, and due only to the discontent of one of the lower orders, has never come to my notice. Only once, in my colony, did I witness the dethroning of the hitherto ruling tyrant, Goldgreen. It was a returned wanderer who, having lost in his long absence his former deeply imbued respect for his rules, succeeded in defeating him in their very first encounter. In the autumn of 1931, the conqueror, "Double-aluminium"—he derived this strange name from the rings on his feet—came back, after having been away the whole summer. He returned home strong in heart and stimulated by his travels, and at once subdued the former autocrat. His victory was remarkable for two reasons: first, Double-aluminium, who was unmated and therefore fighting alone, was opposed in the struggle by both the former ruler and his wife. Secondly, the victor was only one and a half years old, whereas Goldgreen and his wife both dated back to the original fourteen jackdaws with which I started the settlement in 1927.

The way in which my attention was drawn to this revolution was quite unusual. Suddenly, at the feeding tray, I saw, to my astonishment, how a little, very fragile, and, in order of rank, low-standing lady sidled ever closer to the quietly feeding Goldgreen, and finally, as though inspired by some unseen power, assumed an attitude of self-display, whereupon the large male quietly and without opposition vacated his place. Then I noticed the newly returned hero, Double-aluminium, and saw that he had usurped the position of Goldgreen, and I thought, at first, that the deposed despot, under the influence of his recent defeat, was so subdued that he had allowed himself to be intimidated by the other members of the colony, including the aforesaid young female. But the assumption was false: Goldgreen had been conquered by Double-aluminium only, and remained forever the second in command. But Double-aluminium, on his return, had fallen in love with the young female and within the course of two days was publicly engaged to her! Since the partners in a jackdaw marriage support each other loyally and bravely in every conflict, and as no pecking order exists between them, they automatically rank as of equal status in their disputes with all other members of the colony; a wife is therefore, of necessity, raised to her husband's position. But the contrary does not hold good—an inviolable law dictates that no male may marry a female that ranks above him. The extraordinary part of the business is not the promotion as such but the amazing speed with which the news spreads that such a little jackdaw lady, who hitherto had been maltreated by eighty per cent of the colony, is, from to-day, the "wife of the president" and may no longer receive so much as a black look from any other jackdaw. But more curious still—the promoted bird knows of its promotion! It is no credit to an animal to be shy and anxious after a bad experience, but to understand that a hitherto existent danger is now removed and to face the fact with an adequate supply of courage requires more sense. On a pond, a despot swan rules with so tyrannical a rule that no other swan, except the wife of the feared one, dares to enter the water at all. You can catch this terrible tyrant and carry him away before the eyes of all the others, and expect that the remaining birds will breathe an audible sigh of relief and at once proceed to take the bath of which they have been so long deprived. Nothing of the kind occurs. Days pass before the first of these suppressed subjects can pluck up enough courage to indulge in a modest swim hard against the shores of the pond. For a much longer time, nobody ventures into the middle of the water.

But that little jackdaw knew within forty-eight hours exactly what she could allow herself, and I am sorry to say that she made the fullest use of it. She lacked entirely that noble or even blasé tolerance which jackdaws of high rank should exhibit towards their inferiors. She used every opportunity to snub former superiors, and she did not stop at gestures of self-importance, as high-rankers of long standing nearly always do. No—she always had an active and malicious plan of attack ready at hand. In short, she conducted herself with the utmost vulgarity.

You think I humanize the animal? Perhaps you do not know that what we are wont to call "human weakness" is, in reality, nearly always a prehuman factor and one which we have in common with the higher animals? Believe me, I am not mistakenly assigning human properties to animals: on the contrary, I am showing you what an enormous animal inheritance remains in man, to this day. . . .

The Reach of Imagination

Jacob Bronowski

Jacob Bronowski (b. 1908) is a scientist who is also very much interested in the processes of artistic creation. His concern for both science and literature is reflected in the titles of his books, such as *The Poet's Defense* (1939), *William Blake* (1944), *The Common Sense of Science* (1951) and *Science and Human Values* (1958). He is an Honorary Fellow of Jesus College, Cambridge, and a Senior Fellow and Trustee of the Salk Institute for Biological Studies at San Diego, California.

For three thousand years, poets have been enchanted and moved and perplexed by the power of their own imagination. In a short and summary essay I can hope at most to lift one small corner of that mystery; and yet it is a criti-

THE REACH OF IMAGINATION: Reprinted by permission of Jacob Bronowski and The American Academy of Arts and Letters from *The American Scholar*, Spring 1967.

cal corner. I shall ask, What goes on in the mind when we imagine? You will hear from me that one answer to this question is fairly specific: which is to say, that we can describe the working of the imagination. And when we describe it as I shall do, it becomes plain that imagination is a specifically *human* gift. To imagine is the characteristic act, not of the poet's mind, or the painter's, or the scientist's, but of the mind of man.

My stress here on the word *human* implies that there is a clear difference in this between the actions of men and those of other animals. Let me then start with a classical experiment with animals and children which Walter Hunter thought out in Chicago about 1910. That was the time when scientists were agog with the success of Ivan Pavlov in forming and changing the reflex actions of dogs, which Pavlov had first announced in 1903. Pavlov had been given a Nobel prize the next year, in 1904; although in fairness I should say that the award did not cite his work on the conditioned reflex, but on the digestive glands.

Hunter duly trained some dogs and other animals on Pavlov's lines. They were taught that when a light came on over one of three tunnels out of their cage, that tunnel would be open; they could escape down it, and were rewarded with food if they did. But once he had fixed that conditioned reflex, Hunter added to it a deeper idea: he gave the mechanical experiment a new dimension, literally—the dimension of time. Now he no longer let the dog go to the lighted tunnel at once; instead, he put out the light, and then kept the dog waiting a little while before he let him go. In this way Hunter timed how long an animal can remember where he has last seen the signal light to his escape route.

The results were and are staggering. A dog or a rat forgets which one of three tunnels has been lit up within a matter of seconds—in Hunter's experiment, ten seconds at most. If you want such an animal to do much better than this, you must make the task much simpler: you must face him with only two tunnels to choose from. Even so, the best that Hunter could do was to have a dog remember for five minutes which one of two tunnels had been lit up.

I am not quoting these times as if they were exact and universal: they surely are not. Hunter's experiment, more than fifty years old now, had many faults of detail. For example, there were too few animals, they were oddly picked, and they did not all behave consistently. It may be unfair to test a dog for what he *saw,* when he commonly follows his nose rather than his eyes. It may be unfair to test any animal in the unnatural setting of a laboratory cage. And there are higher animals, such as chimpanzees and other primates, which certainly have longer memories than the animals that Hunter tried.

Yet when all these provisos have been made (and met, by more modern experiments) the facts are still startling and characteristic. An animal cannot recall a signal from the past for even a short fraction of the time that a man can—for even a short fraction of the time that a child can. Hunter made comparable tests with six-year-old children, and found, of course, that they were incomparably better than the best of his animals. There is a striking and basic difference between a man's ability to imagine something that he saw or experienced, and an animal's failure.

Animals make up for this by other and extraordinary gifts. The salmon and the carrier pigeon can find their way home as we cannot; they have, as it were, a practical memory that man cannot match. But their actions always depend on some form of habit: on instinct or on learning, which reproduce by rote a train of known responses. They do not depend, as human memory does, on calling to mind the recollection of absent things.

Where is it that the animal falls short? We get a clue to the answer, I think, when Hunter tells us how the animals in his experiment tried to fix their recollection. They most often pointed themselves at the light before it went out, as some gun dogs point rigidly at the game they scent—and get the name *pointer* from the posture. The animal makes ready to act by building the signal into its action. There is a primitive imagery in its stance, it seems to me; it is as if the animal were trying to fix the light in its mind by fixing it in its body. And indeed, how else can a dog mark and (as it were) name one of three tunnels, when he has no such words as *left* and *right,* and no such numbers as *one, two, three?* The directed gesture of attention and readiness is perhaps the only symbolic device that the dog commands to hold on to the past, and thereby to guide himself into the future.

I used the verb *to imagine* a moment ago, and now I have some ground for giving it a meaning. *To imagine* means to make images and to move them about inside one's head in new arrangements. When you and I recall the past, we imagine it in this direct and homely sense. The tool that puts the human mind ahead of the animal is imagery. For us, memory does not demand the preoccupation that it demands in animals, and it lasts immensely longer, because we fix it in images or other substitute symbols. With the same symbolic vocabulary we spell out the future—not one but many futures, which we weigh one against another.

I am using the word *image* in a wide meaning, which does not restrict it to the mind's eye as a visual organ. An image in my usage is what Charles Peirce called a *sign,* without regard for its sensory quality. Peirce distinguished between different forms of signs, but there is no reason to make his distinction here, for the imagination works equally with them all, and that is why I call them all images.

Indeed, the most important images for human beings are simply words, which are abstract symbols. Animals do not have words, in our sense: there is no specific center for language in the brain of any animal, as there is in the human brain. In this respect at least we know that the human imagination depends on a configuration in the brain that has only evolved in the last one or two million years. In the same period, evolution has greatly enlarged the front lobes in the human brain, which govern the sense of the past and the future; and it is a fair guess that they are probably the seat of our other images. (Part of the evidence for this guess is that damage to the front lobes in primates reduces them to the state of Hunter's animals.) If the guess turns out to be right, we shall know why man has come to look like a highbrow or an egghead: because otherwise there would not be room in his head for his imagination.

The images play out for us events which are not present to our senses, and thereby guard the past and create the future—a future that does not yet exist, and may never come to exist in that form. By contrast, the lack of symbolic ideas, or their rudimentary poverty, cuts off an animal from the past and the future alike, and imprisons him in the present. Of all the distinctions between man and animal, the characteristic gift which makes us human is the power to work with symbolic images: the gift of imagination.

This is really a remarkable finding. When Philip Sidney in 1580 defended poets (and all unconventional thinkers) from the Puritan charge that they were liars, he said that a maker must imagine things that are not. Halfway between Sidney and us, William Blake said, "What is now proved was once only imagin'd." About the same time, in 1796, Samuel Taylor Coleridge for the first time distinguished between the passive fancy and the active imagination, "the living Power and prime Agent of all human Perception." Now we see that they were right, and precisely right: the human gift is the gift of imagination—and that is not just a literary phrase.

Nor is it just a literary gift; it is, I repeat, characteristically human. Almost everything that we do that is worth doing is done in the first place in the mind's eye. The richness of human life is that we have many lives; we live the events that do not happen (and some that cannot) as vividly as those that do; and if thereby we die a thousand deaths, that is the price we pay for living a thousand lives. (A cat, of course, has only nine.) Literature is alive to us because we live its images, but so is any play of the mind—so is chess: the lines of play that we foresee and try in our heads and dismiss are as much a part of the game as the moves that we make. John Keats said that the unheard melodies are sweeter, and all chess players sadly recall that the combinations that they planned and which never came to be played were the best.

I make this point to remind you, insistently, that imagination is the manipulation of images in one's head; and that the rational manipulation belongs to that, as well as the literary and artistic manipulation. When a child begins to play games with things that stand for other things, with chairs or chessmen, he enters the gateway to reason and imagination together. For the human reason discovers new relations between things not by deduction, but by that unpredictable blend of speculation and insight that scientists call induction, which—like other forms of imagination—cannot be formalized. We see it at work when Walter Hunter inquires into a child's memory, as much as when Blake and Coleridge do. Only a restless and original mind would have asked Hunter's questions and could have conceived his experiments, in a science that was dominated by Pavlov's reflex arcs and was heading toward the behaviorism of John Watson.

Let me find a spectacular example for you from history. What is the most famous experiment that you had described to you as a child? I will hazard that it is the experiment that Galileo is said to have made in Sidney's age, in Pisa about 1590, by dropping two unequal balls from the Leaning Tower. There, we say, is a man in the modern mold, a man after our own hearts: he insisted on questioning the authority of Aristotle and St. Thomas Aquinas, and seeing with his own eyes whether (as they said) the heavy ball would reach the ground before the light one. Seeing is believing.

Yet seeing is also imagining. Galileo did challenge the authority of Aristotle, and he did look hard at his mechanics. But the eye that Galileo used was the mind's eye. He did not drop balls from the Leaning Tower of Pisa— and if he had, he would have got a very doubtful answer. Instead, Galileo made an imaginary experiment in his head, which I will describe as he did years later in the book he wrote after the Holy Office silenced him: the *Discorsi . . . intorno à due nuove scienze,* which was smuggled out to be printed in the Netherlands in 1638.

Suppose, said Galileo, that you drop two unequal balls from the tower at the same time. And suppose that Aristotle is right—suppose that the heavy ball falls faster, so that it steadily gains on the light ball, and hits the ground first. Very well. Now imagine the same experiment done again, with only one difference: this time the two unequal balls are joined by a string between them. The heavy ball will again move ahead, but now the light ball holds it back and acts as a drag or brake. So the light ball will be speeded up and the heavy ball will be slowed down; they must reach the ground together because they are tied together, but they cannot reach the ground as quickly as the heavy ball alone. Yet the string between them has turned the two balls into a single mass which is heavier than either ball—and surely (according to Aristotle) this mass should therefore move faster than either ball? Galileo's imaginary experiment has uncovered a contradiction; he says trenchantly,

> You see how, from your assumption that a heavier body falls more rapidly than a lighter one, I infer that a (still) heavier body falls more slowly.

There is only one way out of the contradiction: the heavy ball and the light ball must fall at the same rate, so that they go on falling at the same rate when they are tied together.

This argument is not conclusive, for nature might be more subtle (when the two balls are joined) than Galileo has allowed. And yet it is something more important: it is suggestive, it is stimulating, it opens a new view—in a word, it is imaginative. It cannot be settled without an actual experiment, because nothing that we imagine can become knowledge until we have translated it into, and backed it by, real experience. The test of imagination is experience. But then, that is as true of literature and the arts as it is of science. In science, the imaginary experiment is tested by confronting it with physical experience; and in literature, the imaginative conception is tested by confronting it with human experience. The superficial speculation in science is dismissed because it is found to falsify nature; and the shallow work of art is discarded because it is found to be untrue to our own nature. So when Ella Wheeler Wilcox died in 1919, more people were reading her verses than Shakespeare's; yet in a few years her work was dead. It had been buried by its poverty of emotion and its trivialness of thought: which is to say that it had been proved to be as false to the nature of man as, say, Jean Baptiste Lamarck and Trofim Lysenko were false to the nature of inheritance. The strength of the imagination, its enriching power and excitement, lies in its interplay with reality—physical and emotional.

I doubt if there is much to choose here between science and the arts: the imagination is not much more free, and not much less free, in one than in the other. All great scientists have used their imagination freely, and let it ride them to outrageous conclusions without crying "Halt!" Albert Einstein fiddled with imaginary experiments from boyhood, and was wonderfully ignorant of the facts that they were supposed to bear on. When he wrote the first of his beautiful papers on the random movement of atoms, he did not know that the Brownian motion which it predicted could be seen in any laboratory. He was sixteen when he invented the paradox that he resolved ten years later, in 1905, in the theory of relativity, and it bulked much larger in his mind than the experiment of Albert Michelson and Edward Morley which had upset every other physicist since 1881. All his life Einstein loved to make up teasing puzzles like Galileo's, about falling lifts and the detection of gravity; and they carry the nub of the problems of general relativity on which he was working.

Indeed, it could not be otherwise. The power that man has over nature and himself, and that a dog lacks, lies in his command of imaginary experience. He alone has the symbols which fix the past and play with the future, possible and impossible. In the Renaissance, the symbolism of memory was thought to be mystical, and devices that were invented as mnemonics (by Giordano Bruno, for example, and by Robert Fludd) were interpreted as magic signs. The symbol is the tool which gives man his power, and it is the same tool whether the symbols are images or words, mathematical signs or mesons. And the symbols have a reach and a roundness that goes beyond their literal and practical meaning. They are the rich concepts under which the mind gathers many particulars into one name, and many instances into one general induction. When a man says *left* and *right,* he is outdistancing the dog not only in looking for a light; he is setting in train all the shifts of meaning, the overtones and the ambiguities, between *gauche* and *adroit* and *dexterous,* between *sinister* and the sense of right. When a man counts *one, two, three,* he is not only doing mathematics; he is on the path to the mysticism of numbers in Pythagoras and Vitruvius and Kepler, to the Trinity and the signs of the Zodiac.

I have described imagination as the ability to make images and to move them about inside one's head in new arrangements. This is the faculty that is specifically human, and it is the common root from which science and literature both spring and grow and flourish together. For they do flourish (and languish) together; the great ages of science are the great ages of all the arts, because in them powerful minds have taken fire from one another, breathless and higgledy-piggledy, without asking too nicely whether they ought to tie their imagination to falling balls or a haunted island. Galileo and Shakespeare, who were born in the same year, grew into greatness in the same age; when Galileo was looking through his telescope at the moon, Shakespeare was writing *The Tempest;* and all Europe was in ferment, from Johannes Kepler to Peter Paul Rubens, and from the first table of logarithms by John Napier to the Authorised Version of the Bible.

Let me end with a last and spirited example of the common inspiration of literature and science, because it is as much alive today as it was three hundred years ago. What I have in mind is man's ageless fantasy, to fly to the moon. I do not display this to you as a high scientific enterprise; on the contrary, I think we have more important discoveries to make here on earth than wait for us, beckoning, at the horned surface of the moon. Yet I cannot belittle the fascination which that ice-blue journey has had for the imagination of men, long before it drew us to our television screens to watch the tumbling of astronauts. Plutarch and Lucian, Ariosto and Ben Jonson wrote about it, before the days of Jules Verne and H. G. Wells and science fiction. The seventeenth century was heady with new dreams and fables about voyages to the moon. Kepler wrote one full of deep scientific ideas, which (alas) simply got his mother accused of witchcraft. In England, Francis Godwin wrote a wild and splendid work, *The Man in the Moone,* and the astronomer John Wilkins wrote a wild and learned one, *The Discovery of a New World.* They did not draw a line between science and fancy; for example, they all tried to guess just where in the journey the earth's gravity would stop. Only Kepler understood that gravity has no boundary, and put a law to it—which happened to be the wrong law.

All this was a few years before Isaac Newton was born, and it was all in his head that day in 1666 when he sat in his mother's garden, a young man of twenty-three, and thought about the reach of gravity. This was how he came to conceive his brilliant image, that the moon is like a ball which has been thrown so hard that it falls exactly as fast as the horizon, all the way round the earth. The image will do for any satellite, and Newton modestly calculated how long therefore an astronaut would take to fall round the earth once. He made it ninety minutes, and we have all seen now that he was right; but Newton had no way to check that. Instead he went on to calculate how long in that case the distant moon would take to round the earth, if indeed it behaves like a thrown ball that falls in the earth's gravity, and if gravity obeyed a law of inverse squares. He found that the answer would be twenty-eight days.

In that telling figure, the imagination that day chimed with nature, and made a harmony. We shall hear an echo of that harmony on the day when we land on the moon, because it will be not a technical but an imaginative triumph, that reaches back to the beginning of modern science and literature both. All great acts of imagination are like this, in the arts and in science, and convince us because they fill out reality with a deeper sense of rightness. We start with the simplest vocabulary of images, with *left* and *right* and *one, two, three,* and before we know how it happened the words and the numbers have conspired to make a match with nature: we catch in them the pattern of mind and matter as one.

from Freedom and the Control of Men

A PSYCHOLOGIST PRESENTS THE CASE FOR THE BEHAVIORAL SCIENCES

B. F. Skinner

B. F. Skinner (b. 1904) has been since 1948 a professor of psychology at Harvard University and, since 1958, holder of the Edgar Pierce Chair in that subject. His books include *Behavior of Organisms* (1938), *Walden Two* (1948), and *Science and Human Behavior* (1953).

The second half of the twentieth century may be remembered for its solution of a curious problem. Although Western democracy created the conditions responsible for the rise of modern science, it is now evident that it may never fully profit from that achievement. The so-called "democratic philosophy" of human behavior to which it also gave rise is increasingly in conflict with the application of the methods of science to human affairs. Unless this conflict is somehow resolved, the ultimate goals of democracy may be long deferred.

1

Just as biographers and critics look for external influences to account for the traits and achievements of the men they study, so science ultimately explains behavior in terms of "causes" or conditions which lie beyond the individual himself. As more and more causal relations are demonstrated, a

From FREEDOM AND THE CONTROL OF MEN: Reprinted by permission of B. F. Skinner from *The American Scholar,* Winter 1955–56.

practical corollary becomes difficult to resist: it should be possible to *produce* behavior according to plan simply by arranging the proper conditions. Now, among the specifications which might reasonably be submitted to a behavioral technology are these: Let men be happy, informed, skillful, well behaved, and productive.

This immediate practical implication of a science of behavior has a familiar ring, for it recalls the doctrine of human perfectibility of eighteenth- and nineteenth-century humanism. A science of man shares the optimism of that philosophy and supplies striking support for the working faith that men can build a better world and, through it, better men. The support comes just in time, for there has been little optimism of late among those who speak from the traditional point of view. Democracy has become "realistic," and it is only with some embarrassment that one admits today to perfectionistic or utopian thinking.

The earlier temper is worth considering, however. History records many foolish and unworkable schemes for human betterment, but almost all the great changes in our culture which we now regard as worthwhile can be traced to perfectionistic philosophies. Governmental, religious, educational, economic, and social reforms follow a common pattern. Someone believes that a change in a cultural practice—for example, in the rules of evidence in a court of law, in the characterization of man's relation to God, in the way children are taught to read and write, in permitted rates of interest, or in minimal housing standards—will improve the condition of men: by promoting justice, permitting men to seek salvation more effectively, increasing the literacy of a people, checking an inflationary trend, or improving public health and family relations, respectively. The underlying hypothesis is always the same: that a different physical or cultural environment will make a different and better man.

The scientific study of behavior not only justifies the general pattern of such proposals; it promises new and better hypotheses. The earliest cultural practices must have originated in sheer accidents. Those which strengthened the group survived with the group in a sort of natural selection. As soon as men began to propose and carry out changes in practice for the sake of possible consequences, the evolutionary process must have accelerated. The simple practice of making changes must have had survival value. A further acceleration is now to be expected. As laws of behavior are more precisely stated, the changes in the environment required to bring about a given effect may be more clearly specified. Conditions which have been neglected because their effects were slight or unlooked for may be shown to be relevant. New conditions may actually be created, as in the discovery and synthesis of drugs which affect behavior.

This is no time, then, to abandon notions of progress, improvement, or, indeed, human perfectibility. The simple fact is that man is able, and now as never before, to lift himself by his own bootstraps. In achieving control of the world of which he is a part, he may learn at last to control himself.

Timeworn objections to the planned improvement of cultural practices are already losing much of their force. Marcus Aurelius was probably right in advising his readers to be content with a haphazard amelioration of mankind. "Never hope to realize Plato's republic," he sighed, ". . . for who can change the opinions of men? And without a change of sentiments what can you make but reluctant slaves and hypocrites?" He was thinking, no doubt, of contemporary patterns of control based upon punishment or the threat of punishment which, as he correctly observed, breed only reluctant slaves of those who submit and hypocrites of those who discover modes of evasion. But we need not share his pessimism, for the opinions of men can be changed. The techniques of indoctrination which were being devised by the early Christian Church at the very time Marcus Aurelius was writing are relevant, as are some of the techniques of psychotherapy and of advertising and public relations. Other methods suggested by recent scientific analyses leave little doubt of the matter.

The study of human behavior also answers the cynical complaint that there is a plain "cussedness" in man which will always thwart efforts to improve him. We are often told that men do not want to be changed, even for the better. Try to help them, and they will outwit you and remain happily wretched. Dostoievsky claimed to see some plan in it. "Out of sheer ingratitude," he complained, or possibly boasted, "man will play you a dirty trick, just to prove that men are still men and not the keys of a piano. . . . And even if you could prove that a man is only a piano key, he would still do something out of sheer perversity—he would create destruction and chaos—just to gain his point. . . . And if all this could in turn be analyzed and prevented by predicting that it would occur, then man would deliberately go mad to prove his point." This is a conceivable neurotic reaction to inept control. A few men may have shown it, and many have enjoyed Dostoievsky's statement because they tend to show it. But that such perversity is a fundamental reaction of the human organism to controlling conditions is sheer nonsense.

So is the objection that we have no way of knowing what changes to make even though we have the necessary techniques. That is one of the great hoaxes of the century—a sort of booby trap left behind in the retreat before the advancing front of science. Scientists themselves have unsuspectingly agreed that there are two kinds of useful propositions about nature—facts and value judgments—and that science must confine itself to "what is," leaving "what ought to be" to others. But with what special sort of wisdom is the nonscientist endowed? Science is only effective knowing, no matter who engages in it. Verbal behavior proves upon analysis to be composed of many different types of utterances, from poetry and exhortation to logic and factual description, but these are not all equally useful in talking about cultural practices. We may classify useful propositions according to the degrees of confidence with which they may be asserted. Sentences about nature range from highly probable "facts" to sheer guesses. In general, future events are less likely to be correctly described than past. When a scientist talks about a projected experiment, for example, he must often resort to statements having only a moderate likelihood of being correct; he calls them hypotheses.

Designing a new cultural pattern is in many ways like designing an experiment. In drawing up a new constitution, outlining a new educational program, modifying a religious doctrine, or setting up a new fiscal policy, many statements must be quite tentative. We cannot be sure that the practices we specify will have the consequences we predict, or that the consequences will reward our efforts. This is in the nature of such proposals. They are not value judgments—they are guesses. To confuse and delay the improvement of cultural practices by quibbling about the word *improve* is itself not a useful practice. Let us agree, to start with, that health is better than illness, wisdom better than ignorance, love better than hate, and productive energy better than neurotic sloth.

Another familiar objection is the "political problem." Though we know what changes to make and how to make them, we still need to control certain relevant conditions, but these have long since fallen into the hands of selfish men who are not going to relinquish them for such purposes. Possibly we shall be permitted to develop areas which at the moment seem unimportant, but at the first signs of success the strong men will move in. This, it is said, has happened to Christianity, democracy, and communism. There will always be men who are fundamentally selfish and evil, and in the long run innocent goodness cannot have its way. The only evidence here is historical, and it may be misleading. Because of the way in which physical science developed, history could until very recently have "proved" that the unleashing of the energy of the atom was quite unlikely, if not impossible. Similarly, because of the order in which processes in human behavior have become available for purposes of control, history may seem to prove that power will probably be appropriated for selfish purposes. The first techniques to be discovered fell almost always to strong, selfish men. History led Lord Acton to believe that power corrupts, but he had probably never encountered absolute power, certainly not in all its forms, and had no way of predicting its effect.

An optimistic historian could defend a different conclusion. The principle that if there are not enough men of good will in the world the first step is to create more seems to be gaining recognition. The Marshall Plan (as originally conceived), Point Four, the offer of atomic materials to power-starved countries—these may or may not be wholly new in the history of international relations, but they suggest an increasing awareness of the power of governmental good will. They are proposals to make certain changes in the environments of men for the sake of consequences which should be rewarding for all concerned. They do not exemplify a disinterested generosity, but an interest which is the interest of everyone. We have not yet seen Plato's philosopher-king, and may not want to, but the gap between real and utopian government is closing.

3

But we are not yet in the clear, for a new and unexpected obstacle has arisen. With a world of their own making almost within reach, men of good will have been seized with distaste for their achievement. They have uneasily rejected opportunities to apply the techniques and findings of science in the service of men, and as the import of effective cultural design has come to be understood, many of them have voiced an outright refusal to have any part in it. Science has been challenged before when it has encroached upon institutions already engaged in the control of human behavior; but what are we to make of benevolent men, with no special interests of their own to defend, who nevertheless turn against the very means of reaching long-dreamed-of goals?

What is being rejected, of course, is the scientific conception of man and his place in nature. So long as the findings and methods of science are applied to human affairs only in a sort of remedial patchwork, we may continue to hold any view of human nature we like. But as the use of science increases, we are forced to accept the theoretical structure with which science represents its facts. The difficulty is that this structure is clearly at odds with the traditional democratic conception of man. Every discovery of an event which has a part in shaping a man's behavior seems to leave so much the less to be credited to the man himself; and as such explanations become more and more comprehensive, the contribution which may be claimed by the individual himself appears to approach zero. Man's vaunted creative powers, his original accomplishments in art, science, and morals, his capacity to choose and our right to hold him responsible for the consequences of his choice—none of these is conspicuous in this new self-portrait. Man, we once believed, was free to express himself in art, music, and literature, to inquire into nature, to seek salvation in his own way. He could initiate action and make spontaneous and capricious changes of course. Under the most extreme duress some sort of choice remained to him. He could resist any effort to control him, though it might cost him his life. But science insists that action is initiated by forces impinging upon the individual, and that caprice is only another name for behavior for which we have not yet found a cause.

In attempting to reconcile these views it is important to note that the traditional democratic conception was not designed as a description in the scientific sense but as a philosophy to be used in setting up and maintaining a governmental process. It arose under historical circumstances and served political purposes apart from which it cannot be properly understood. In rallying men against tyranny it was necessary that the individual be strengthened, that he be taught that he had rights and could govern himself. To give the common man a new conception of his worth, his dignity, and his power to save himself, both here and hereafter, was often the only resource of the revolutionist. When democratic principles were put into practice, the same doctrines were used as a working formula. This is exemplified by the notion of personal responsibility in Anglo-American law. All governments make certain forms of punishment contingent upon certain kinds of acts. In democratic countries these contingencies are expressed by the notion of responsible choice. But the notion may have no meaning under governmental practices formulated in other ways and would certainly have no place in systems which did not use punishment.

The democratic philosophy of human nature is determined by certain political exigencies and techniques, not by the goals of democracy. But exigencies and techniques change; and a conception which is not supported for its accuracy as a likeness—is not, indeed, rooted in fact at all—may be expected to change too. No matter how effective we judge current democratic practices to be, how highly we value them, or how long we expect them to survive, they are almost certainly not the *final* form of government. The philosophy of human nature which has been useful in implementing them is also almost certainly not the last word. The ultimate achievement of democracy may be long deferred unless we emphasize the real aims rather than the verbal devices of democratic thinking. A philosophy which has been appropriate to one set of political exigencies will defeat its purpose if, under other circumstances, it prevents us from applying to human affairs the science of man which probably nothing but democracy itself could have produced.

4

Perhaps the most crucial part of our democratic philosophy to be reconsidered is our attitude toward freedom—or its reciprocal, the control of human behavior. We do not oppose all forms of control because it is "human nature" to do so. The reaction is not characteristic of all men under all conditions of life. It is an attitude which has been carefully engineered, in large part by what we call the "literature" of democracy. With respect to some methods of control (for example, the threat of force), very little engineering is needed, for the techniques or their immediate consequences are objectionable. Society has suppressed these methods by branding them "wrong," "illegal," or "sinful." But to encourage these attitudes toward objectionable forms of control, it has been necessary to disguise the real nature of certain indispensable techniques, the commonest examples of which are education, moral discourse, and persuasion. The actual procedures appear harmless enough. They consist of supplying information, presenting opportunities for action, pointing out logical relationships, appealing to reason or "enlightened understanding," and so on. Through a masterful piece of misrepresentation, the illusion is fostered that these procedures do not involve the control of behavior; at most, they are simply ways of "getting someone to change his mind." But analysis not only reveals the presence of well-defined behavioral processes, it demonstrates a kind of control no less inexorable, though in some ways more acceptable, than the bully's threat of force.

Let us suppose that someone in whom we are interested is acting unwisely—he is careless in the way he deals with his friends, he drives too fast, or he holds his golf club the wrong way. We could probably help him by issuing a series of commands: don't nag, don't drive over sixty, don't hold your club that way. Much less objectionable would be "an appeal to reason." We could show him how people are affected by his treatment of them, how accident rates rise sharply at higher speeds, how a particular grip on the club alters the way the ball is struck and corrects a slice. In doing so we resort to verbal mediating devices which emphasize and support certain "contingencies of reinforcement"—that is, certain relations between behavior and its consequences—which strengthen the behavior we wish to set up. The same consequences would possibly set up the behavior without our help, and they eventually take control no matter which form of help we give. The appeal to reason has certain advantages over the authoritative command. A threat of punishment, no matter how subtle, generates emotional reactions and tendencies to escape or revolt. Perhaps the controllee merely "feels resentment" at being made to act in a given way, but even that is to be avoided. When we "appeal to reason," he "feels freer to do as he pleases." The fact is that we have exerted *less* control than in using a threat; since other conditions may contribute to the result, the effect may be delayed or, possibly in a given instance, lacking. But if we have worked a change in his behavior at all, it is because we have altered relevant environmental conditions, and the processes we have set in motion are just as real and just as inexorable, if not as comprehensive, as in the most authoritative coercion.

"Arranging an opportunity for action" is another example of disguised control. The power of the negative form has already been exposed in the analysis of censorship. Restriction of opportunity is recognized as far from harmless. As Ralph Barton Perry said in an article which appeared in the Spring, 1953, *Pacific Spectator,* "Whoever determines what alternatives shall be made known to man controls what that man shall choose *from.* He is deprived of freedom in proportion as he is denied access to *any* ideas, or is confined to any range of ideas short of the totality of relevant possibilities." But there is a positive side as well. When we present a relevant state of affairs, we increase the likelihood that a given form of behavior will be emitted. To the extent that the probability of action has changed, we have made a definite contribution. The teacher of history controls a student's behavior (or, if the reader prefers, "deprives him of freedom") just as much in *presenting* historical facts as in suppressing them. Other conditions will no doubt affect the student, but the contribution made to his behavior by the presentation of material is fixed and, within its range, irresistible.

The methods of education, moral discourse, and persuasion are acceptable not because they recognize the freedom of the individual or his right to dissent, but because they make only *partial* contributions to the control of his behavior. The freedom they recognize is freedom from a more coercive form of control. The dissent which they tolerate is the possible effect of other determiners of action. Since these sanctioned methods are frequently ineffective, we have been able to convince ourselves that they do not represent control at all. When they show too much strength to permit disguise, we give them other names and suppress them as energetically as we suppress the use of force. Education grown too powerful is rejected as propaganda or "brainwashing," while really effective persuasion is decried as "undue influence," "demagoguery," "seduction," and so on.

If we are not to rely solely upon accident for the innovations which give rise to cultural evolution, we must accept the fact that some kind of control of human behavior is inevitable. We cannot use good sense in human affairs unless someone engages in the design and construction of environmental conditions which affect the behavior of men. Environmental changes have always been the condition for the improvement of cultural patterns, and we can hardly use the more effective methods of science without making changes on a grander scale. We are all controlled by the world in which we live, and part of that world has been and will be constructed by men. The question is this: Are we to be controlled by accident, by tyrants, or by ourselves in effective cultural design?

The danger of the misuse of power is possibly greater than ever. It is not allayed by disguising the facts. We cannot make wise decisions if we continue to pretend that human behavior is not controlled, or if we refuse to engage in control when valuable results might be forthcoming. Such measures weaken only ourselves, leaving the strength of science to others. The first step in a defense against tyranny is the fullest possible exposure of controlling techniques. A second step has already been taken successfully in restricting the use of physical force. Slowly, and as yet imperfectly, we have worked out an ethical and governmental design in which the strong man is not allowed to use the power deriving from his strength to control his fellow men. He is restrained by a superior force created for that purpose—the ethical pressure of the group, or more explicit religious and governmental measures. We tend to distrust superior forces, as we currently hesitate to relinquish sovereignty in order to set up an international police force. But it is only through such countercontrol that we have achieved what we call peace—a condition in which men are not permitted to control each other through force. In other words, control itself must be controlled.

Science has turned up dangerous processes and materials before. To use the facts and techniques of a science of man to the fullest extent without making some monstrous mistake will be difficult and obviously perilous. It is no time for self-deception, emotional indulgence, or the assumption of attitudes which are no longer useful. Man is facing a difficult test. He must keep his head now, or he must start again—a long way back.

from The Abolition of Man

C. S. Lewis

> C. S. Lewis (1898–1963) was a distinguished British scholar in medieval studies and a powerful Christian apologist. He was for many years a fellow of Magdalen College, Oxford. Later in life, he accepted a professorship in medieval studies at Cambridge University, a post that he held until his death. Perhaps his two best-known scholarly books are *The Allegory of Love* (1936) and *English Literature in the Sixteenth Century* (1954), a volume in the Oxford History of English Literature. As a Christian apologist he is most widely known for his *Screwtape Letters* (1942), but his Christian interests also pervade his science-fiction novels such as *Out of the Silent Planet* (1938), *Perelandra* (1943), and *That Hideous Strength* (1945). *The Abolition of Man* (from which the selection that follows is taken) is his most pointed contribution to the discussion of science and its relation to human values. His last book was *Grief Observed* (1963).

Human nature will be the last part of Nature to surrender to Man. The battle will then be won. We shall have "taken the thread of life out of the hand of Clotho" and be henceforth free to make our species whatever we wish it to be. The battle will indeed be won. But who, precisely, will have won it?

For the power of Man to make himself what he pleases means, as we have seen, the power of some men to make other men what *they* please. In all ages, no doubt, nurture and instruction have, in some sense, attempted to exercise this power. But the situation to which we must look forward will be novel in two respects. In the first place, the power will be enormously increased. Hitherto the plans of educationalists have achieved very little of what they attempted and indeed, when we read them—how Plato would have every infant "a bastard nursed in a bureau," and Elyot would have the boy see no men before the age of seven and, after that, no women,[1]

[1] *The Boke Named-the Governour*, I. iv: "Al men except physitions only shulde be excluded and kepte out of the norisery." I. vi: "After that a childe is come to seuen yeres of age . . . the most sure counsaile is to withdrawe him from all company of women."

and how Locke wants children to have leaky shoes and no turn for poetry [2] —we may well thank the beneficent obstinacy of real mothers, real nurses, and (above all) real children for preserving the human race in such sanity as it still possesses. But the man-moulders of the new age will be armed with the powers of an omnicompetent state and an irresistible scientific technique: we shall get at last a race of conditioners who really can cut out all posterity in what shape they please. The second difference is even more important. In the older systems both the kind of man the teachers wished to produce and their motives for producing him were prescribed by the *Tao* [3]—a norm to which the teachers themselves were subject and from which they claimed no liberty to depart. They did not cut men to some pattern they had chosen. They handed on what they had received: they initiated the young neophyte into the mystery of humanity which over-arched him and them alike. It was but old birds teaching young birds to fly. This will be changed. Values are now mere natural phenomena. Judgments of value are to be produced in the pupil as part of the conditioning. Whatever *Tao* there is will be the product, not the motive, of education. The conditioners have been emancipated from all that. It is one more part of Nature which they have conquered. The ultimate springs of human action are no longer, for them, something given. They have surrendered— like electricity: it is the function of the Conditioners to control, not to obey them. They know how to *produce* conscience and decide what kind of conscience they will produce. They themselves are outside, above. For we are assuming the last stage of Man's struggle with Nature. The final victory has been won. Human nature has been conquered—and, of course, has conquered, in whatever sense those words may now bear.

The Conditioners, then, are to choose what kind of artificial *Tao* they will, for their own good reasons, produce in the Human race. They are the motivators, the creators of motives. But how are they going to be motivated themselves? For a time, perhaps, by survivals, within their own minds, of the old "natural" Tao. Thus at first they may look upon themselves as servants and guardians of humanity and conceive that they have a "duty" to do it "good." But it is only by confusion that they can remain in this state. They recognize the concept of duty as the result of certain processes which they can now control. Their victory has consisted precisely in emerging from the state in which they were acted upon by those processes to the state in which they use them as tools. One of the things they now have to

---

[2] *Some Thoughts concerning Education,* 7: "I will also advise his *Feet to be wash'd* every Day in cold Water, and to have his Shoes so thin that they might leak and *let in Water,* whenever he comes near it." 174: "If he have a poetick vein, 'tis to me the strangest thing in the World that the Father should desire or suffer it to be cherished or improved. Methinks the Parents should labour to have it stifled and suppressed as much as may be." Yet Locke is one of our most sensible writers on education.

[3] [The Chinese term *Tao* means Reality, Nature, the Road, the Way—the way in which the universe goes on and things emerge into space and time. It is also the way which men should tread in imitation of this progression. It is a harmony of Man with the Universe. Ed.'s note.]

decide is whether they will, or will not, so condition the rest of us that we can go on having the old idea of duty and the old reactions to it. How can duty help them to decide that? Duty itself is up for trial: it cannot also be the judge. And "good" fares no better. They know quite well how to produce a dozen different conceptions of good in us. The question is which, if any, they should produce. No conception of good can help them to decide. It is absurd to fix on one of the things they are comparing and make it the standard of comparison.

To some it will appear that I am inventing a factitious difficulty for my Conditioners. Other, more simple-minded, critics may ask "Why should you suppose they will be such bad men?" But I am not supposing them to be bad men. They are, rather, not men (in the old sense) at all. They are, if you like, men who have sacrificed their own share in traditional humanity in order to devote themselves to the task of deciding what "Humanity" shall henceforth mean. "Good" and "bad," applied to them, are words without content; for it is from them that the content of these words is henceforward to be derived. Nor is their difficulty factitious. We might suppose that it was possible to say, "after all, most of us want more or less the same things—food and drink and sexual intercourse, amusement, art, science, and the longest possible life for individuals and for the species. Let them simply say, 'This is what we happen to like,' and go on to condition men in the way most likely to produce it. Where's the trouble?" But this will not answer. In the first place, it is false that we all really like the same things. But even if we did, what motive is to impel the Conditioners to scorn delights and live laborious days in order that we, and posterity, may have what we like? Their duty? But that is only the *Tao,* which they may decide to impose on us, but which cannot be valid for them. If they accept it, then they are no longer the makers of conscience but still its subjects, and their final conquest over Nature has not really happened. The preservation of the species? But why should the species be preserved? One of the questions before them is whether this feeling for posterity (they know well how it is produced) shall be continued or not. However far they go back, or down, they can find no ground to stand on. Every motive they try to act on becomes at once a *petitio.* It is not that they are bad men. They are not men at all. Stepping outside the *Tao,* they have stepped into the void. Nor are their subjects necessarily unhappy men. They are not men at all: they are artefacts. Man's final conquest has proved to be the abolition of Man.

Yet the Conditioners will act. When I said just now that all motives fail them, I should have said all motives except one. All motives that claim any validity other than that of their felt emotional weight at a given moment have failed them. Everything except the *sic volo, sic jubeo* has been explained away. But what never claimed objectivity cannot be destroyed by subjectivism. The impulse to scratch when I itch or to pull to pieces when I am inquisitive is immune from the solvent which is fatal to my justice, or honour, or care for posterity. When all that says "it is good" has been debunked, what says "I want" remains. It cannot be exploded or "seen through" because it never had any pretensions. The Conditioners, therefore, must come to be motivated simply by their own pleasure. I am not here speaking of the corrupting influence of power nor expressing the fear that under it our Conditioners will degenerate. The very words *corrupt* and *degenerate* imply a doctrine of value and are therefore meaningless in this context. My point is that those who stand outside all judgments of value cannot have any ground for preferring one of their own impulses to another except the emotional strength of that impulse. We may legitimately hope that among the impulses which arise in minds thus emptied of all "rational" or "spiritual" motives, some will be benevolent. I am very doubtful myself whether the benevolent impulses, stripped of that preference and encouragement which the *Tao* teaches us to give them and left to their merely natural strength and frequency as psychological events, will have much influence. I am very doubtful whether history shows us one example of a man who, having stepped outside traditional morality and attained power, has used that power benevolently. I am inclined to think that the Conditioners will hate the conditioned. Though regarding as an illusion the artificial conscience which they produce in us their subjects, they will yet perceive that it creates in us an illusion of meaning for our lives which compares favourably with the futility of their own: and they will envy us as eunuchs envy men. But I do not insist on this, for it is mere conjecture. What is not conjecture is that our hope even of a "conditioned" happiness rests on what is ordinarily called "chance"—the chance that benevolent impulses may on the whole predominate in our Conditioners. For without the judgement "Benevolence is good"—that is, without re-entering the *Tao*—they can have no ground for promoting or stabilizing their benevolent impulses rather than any others. By the logic of their position they must just take their impulses as they come, from chance. And Chance here means Nature. It is from heredity, digestion, the weather, and the association of ideas, that the motives of the Conditioners will spring. Their extreme rationalism, by "seeing through" all "rational" motives, leaves them creatures of wholly irrational behaviour. If you will not obey the *Tao,* or else commit suicide, obedience to impulse (and therefore, in the long run, to mere "nature") is the only course left open.

At the moment, then, of Man's victory over Nature, we find the whole human race subjected to some individual men, and those individuals subjected to that in themselves which is purely "natural"—to their irrational impulses. Nature, untrammelled by values, rules the Conditioners and, through them, all humanity. Man's conquest of Nature turns out, in the moment of its consummation, to be Nature's conquest of Man. Every victory we seemed to win has led us, step by step, to this conclusion. All Nature's apparent reverses have been but tactical withdrawals. We thought we were beating her back when she was luring us on. What looked to us like hands held up in surrender was really the opening of arms to enfold us for ever. If the fully planned and conditioned world (with its *Tao* a mere product of the planning) comes into existence, Nature will be troubled no more by the restive species that rose in revolt against her so many millions of years ago, will be vexed no longer by its chatter of truth and mercy and beauty and happiness. *Ferum victorem cepit:* and if the eugenics are efficient enough there will be no second revolt, but all snug beneath the Conditioners, and the Conditioners beneath her, till the moon falls or the sun grows cold.

My point may be clearer to some if it is put in a different form. Nature is a word of varying meanings, which can best be understood if we consider its various opposites. The Natural is the opposite of the Artificial, the Civil, the Human, the Spiritual, and the Supernatural. The Artificial does not now concern us. If we take the rest of the list of opposites, however, I think we can get a rough idea of what men have meant by Nature and what it is they oppose to her. Nature seems to be the spatial and temporal, as distinct from what is less fully so or not so at all. She seems to be the world of quantity, as against the world of quality: of objects as against consciousness: of the bound, as against the wholly or partially autonomous: of that which knows no values as against that which both has and perceives value: of efficient causes (or, in some modern systems, of no causality at all) as against final causes. Now I take it that when we understand a thing analytically and then dominate and use it for our own convenience we reduce it to the level of "Nature" in the sense that we suspend our judgements of value about it, ignore its final cause (if any), and treat it in terms of quantity. This repression of elements in what would otherwise be our total reaction to it is sometimes very noticeable and even painful: something has to be overcome before we can cut up a dead man or a live animal in a dissecting room. These objects *resist* the movement of the mind whereby we thrust them into the world of mere Nature. But in other instances too, a similar price is exacted for our analytical knowledge and manipulative power, even if we have ceased to count it. We do not look at trees either as Dryads or as beautiful objects while we cut them into beams: the first man who did so may have felt the price keenly, and the bleeding trees in Virgil and Spenser may be far-off echoes of that primeval sense of impiety. The stars lost their divinity as astronomy developed, and the Dying God has no place in chemical agriculture. To many, no doubt, this process is simply the gradual discovery that the real world is different from what we expected, and the old opposition to Galileo or to "body-snatchers" is simply obscurantism. But that is not the whole story. It is not the greatest of modern scientists who feel most sure that the object, stripped of its qualitative properties and reduced to mere quantity, is wholly real. Little scientists, and little unscientific followers of science, may think so. The great minds know very well that the object, so treated, is an artificial abstraction, that something of its reality has been lost.

From this point of view the conquest of Nature appears in a new light.

We reduce things to mere Nature *in order that* we may "conquer" them. We are always conquering Nature, because "Nature" is the name for what we have, to some extent, conquered. The price of conquest is to treat a thing as mere Nature. Every conquest over Nature increases her domain. The stars do not become Nature till we can weigh and measure them: the soul does not become Nature till we can psycho-analyse her. The wresting of powers *from* Nature is also the surrendering of things *to* Nature. As long as this process stops short of the final stage we may well hold that the gain outweighs the loss. But as soon as we take the final step of reducing our own species to the level of mere Nature, the whole process is stultified, for this time the being who stood to gain and the being who has been sacrificed are one and the same. This is one of the many instances where to carry a principle to what seems its logical conclusion produces absurdity. It is like the famous Irishman who found that a certain kind of stove reduced his fuel by half and thence concluded that two stoves of the same kind would enable him to warm his house with no fuel at all. It is the magician's bargain: give up our soul, get power in return. But once our souls, that is, our selves, have been given up, the power thus conferred will not belong to us. We shall in fact be the slaves and puppets of that to which we have given our souls. It is in Man's power to treat himself as a mere "natural object" and his own judgements of value as raw material for scientific manipulation to alter at will. The objection to his doing so does not lie in the fact that this point of view (like one's first day in a dissecting room) is painful and shocking till we grow used to it. The pain and the shock are at most a warning and a symptom. The real objection is that if man chooses to treat himself as raw material, raw material he will be: not raw material to be manipulated, as he fondly imagined, by himself, but by mere appetite, that is, mere Nature, in the person of his dehumanized Conditioners.

2 / REPORTAGE

Slouching Towards Bethlehem [1]

Joan Didion

Joan Didion (b. 1934) lives in California, is the author of a novel, *Run River* (1963), and of numerous essays and articles on such subjects as contemporary California, life in literary New York, the mansions of Newport, and so forth. They have appeared in *Holiday*, *Vogue*, *Mademoiselle*, *The Saturday Evening Post*, and other magazines.

The center was not holding. It was a country of bankruptcy notices and public-auction announcements and commonplace reports of casual killings and misplaced children and abandoned homes and vandals who misspelled even the four-letter words they scrawled. It was a country in which families routinely disappeared, trailing bad checks and repossession papers. Adolescents drifted from city to torn city, sloughing off both the past and the

[1] [The title and the first sentence of this piece of reportage are borrowed from W. B. Yeats's celebrated poem, "The Second Coming":

Things fall apart: the center cannot hold;
Mere anarchy is loosed upon the world. . . .
And what rough beast, its hour come round at last,
Slouches towards Bethlehem to be born?]

future as snakes shed their skins, children who were never taught and would never now learn the games that had held the society together. People were missing. Children were missing. Parents were missing. Those left behind filed desultory missing-persons reports, then moved on themselves.

It was not a country in open revolution. It was not a country under enemy siege. It was the United States of America in the cold late spring of 1967, and the market was steady and the G.N.P. high and a great many articulate people seemed to have a sense of high social purpose and it might have been a spring of brave hopes and national promise, but it was not, and more and more people had the uneasy apprehension that it was not. All that seemed clear was that at some point we had aborted ourselves and butchered the job, and because nothing else seemed so relevant I decided to go to San Francisco. San Francisco was where the social hemorrhaging was showing up. San Francisco was where the missing children were gathering and calling themselves "hippies." When I first went to San Francisco in that cold late spring of 1967 I did not even know what I wanted to find out, and so I just stayed around awhile, and made a few friends.

A sign on Haight Street, San Francisco:

> *Last Easter Day*
> *My Christopher Robin wandered away.*
> *He called April 10th*
> *But he hasn't called since*
> *He said he was coming home*
> *But he hasn't shown.*
>
> *If you see him on Haight*
> *Please tell him to wait*
> *I need him now*
> *I don't care how*
> *If he needs the bread*
> *I'll send it ahead.*
>
> *If there's hope*
> *Please write me a note*
> *If he's still there*
> *Tell him how much I care*
> *Where he's at I need to know*
> *For I really love him so!*
>
> > *Deeply,*
> > *Marla*
>
> *Marla Pence*
> *12702 NE. Multnomah*
> *Portland, Ore. 97230*
> *503/252–2720.*

I am looking for somebody called Deadeye and I hear he is on the Street this afternoon doing a little business, so I keep an eye out for him and pretend to read the signs in the Psychedelic Shop on Haight Street when a kid, sixteen, seventeen, comes in and sits on the floor beside me.

"What are you looking for," he says.

I say nothing much.

"I been out of my mind for three days," he says. He tells me he's been shooting crystal, which I already pretty much know because he does not bother to keep his sleeves rolled down over the needle tracks. He came up from Los Angeles some number of weeks ago, he doesn't remember what number, and now he'll take off for New York, if he can find a ride. I show him a sign offering a ride to Chicago. He wonders where Chicago is. I ask where he comes from. "Here," he says. I mean before here. "San Jose, Chula Vista, I dunno. My mother's in Chula Vista."

A few days later I run into him in Golden Gate Park when the Grateful Dead are playing. I ask if he found a ride to New York. "I hear New York's a bummer," he says.

Deadeye never showed up that day on the Street, and somebody says maybe I can find him at his place. It is three o'clock and Deadeye is in bed. Somebody else is asleep on the living-room couch, and a girl is sleeping on the floor beneath a poster of Allen Ginsberg, and there are a couple of girls in pajamas making instant coffee. One of the girls introduces me to the friend on the couch, who extends one arm but does not get up because he is naked. Deadeye and I have a mutual acquaintance, but he does not mention his name in front of the others. "The man you talked to," he says, or "that man I was referring to earlier." The man is a cop.

The room is overheated and the girl on the floor is sick. Deadeye says she has been sleeping for twenty-four hours now. "Lemme ask you something," he says. "You want some grass?" I say I have to be moving on. "You want it," Deadeye says, "it's yours." Deadeye used to be an Angel around Los Angeles but that was a few years ago. "Right now," he says, "I'm trying to set up this groovy religious group—'Teenage Evangelism.' " . . .

There are always little girls around rock groups—the same little girls who used to hang around saxophone players, girls who live on the celebrity and power and sex a band projects when it plays—and there are three of them out here this afternoon in Sausalito where the Grateful Dead rehearse. They are all pretty and two of them still have baby fat and one of them dances by herself with her eyes closed.

I ask a couple of the girls what they do.

"I just kind of come out here a lot," one of them says.

"I just sort of know the Dead," the other says.

The one who just sort of knows the Dead starts cutting up a loaf of French bread on the piano bench. The boys take a break and one of them talks about playing the Los Angeles Cheetah, which is in the old Aragon Ballroom. "We were up there drinking beer where Lawrence Welk used to sit," Jerry Garcia says.

The little girl who was dancing by herself giggles. "Too much," she says softly. Her eyes are still closed. . . .

A new group is supposed to play in the Panhandle today but they are having trouble with the amplifier and I sit in the sun listening to a couple of little girls, maybe seventeen years old. One of them has a lot of makeup and the other wears Levi's and cowboy boots. The boots do not look like an affectation, they look like she came up off a ranch about two weeks ago. I wonder what she is doing here in the Panhandle trying to make friends with a city girl who is snubbing her but I do not wonder long, because she is homely and awkward and I think of her going all the way through the consolidated union high school out there where she comes from and nobody ever asking her to go into Reno on Saturday night for a drive-in movie and a beer on the riverbank, so she runs. "I know a thing about dollar bills," she is saying now. "You get one that says '1111' in one corner and '1111' in another, you take it down to Dallas, Texas, they'll give you $15 for it."

"Who will?" the city girl asks.

"I don't know."

"There are only three significant pieces of data in the world today," is another thing Chet Helms told me one night. We were at the Avalon and the big strobe was going and the colored lights and the Day-Glo painting and the place was full of high-school kids trying to look turned on. The Avalon sound system projects 126 decibels at 100 feet but to Chet Helms the sound is just there, like the air, and he talks through it. "The first is," he said, "God died last year and was obited by the press. The second is, fifty percent of the population is or will be under twenty-five." A boy shook a tambourine toward us and Chet smiled benevolently at him. "The third," he said, "is that they got twenty billion irresponsible dollars to spend." . . .

Deadeye's old lady, Gerry, meets us at the door of their place. She is a big, hearty girl who has always counseled at Girl Scout camps during summer vacations and was "in social welfare" at the University of Washington when she decided that she "just hadn't done enough living" and came to San Francisco. "Actually the heat was bad in Seattle," she adds.

"The first night I got down here," she says, "I stayed with a gal I met over at the Blue Unicorn. I looked like I'd just arrived, had a knapsack and stuff." After that, Gerry stayed at a house the Diggers were running, where she met Deadeye. "Then it took time to get my bearings, so I haven't done much work yet."

I ask Gerry what work she does. "Basically I'm a poet," she says, "but

I had my guitar stolen right after I arrived, and that kind of hung up my thing."

"Get your books," Deadeye orders. "Show her your books."

Gerry demurs, then goes into the bedroom and comes back with several theme books full of verse. I leaf through them but Deadeye is still talking about helping people. "Any kid that's on speed," he says, "I'll try to get him off it. The only advantage to it from the kids' point of view is that you don't have to worry about sleeping or eating."

"Or sex," Gerry adds.

"That's right. When you're strung out on crystal you don't need *nothing*."

"It can lead to the hard stuff," Gerry says. "Take your average Meth freak, once he's started putting the needle in his arm, it's not too hard to say, well, let's shoot a little smack."

All the while I am looking at Gerry's poems. They are a very young girl's poems, each written out in a neat hand and finished off with a curlicue. Dawns are roseate, skies silver-tinted. When Gerry writes "crystal" in her books, she does not mean Meth.

"You gotta get back to your writing," Deadeye says fondly, but Gerry ignores this. She is telling about somebody who propositioned her yesterday. "He just walked up to me on the Street, offered me six hundred dollars to go to Reno and do the thing."

"You're not the only one he approached," Deadeye says.

"If some chick wants to go with him, fine," Gerry says. "Just don't bum my trip." She empties the tuna-fish can we are using for an ashtray and goes over to look at a girl who is asleep on the floor. It is the same girl who was sleeping on the floor the first day I came to Deadeye's place. She has been sick a week now, ten days. "Usually when somebody comes up to me on the Street like that," Gerry adds, "I hit him for some change."

When I saw Gerry in the Park the next day I asked her about the sick girl, and Gerry said cheerfully that she was in the hospital, with pneumonia.

Max tells me about how he and Sharon got together. "When I saw her the first time on Haight Street, I flashed. I mean flashed. So I started some conversation with her about her beads, see, but I didn't care about her beads." Sharon lived in a house where a friend of Max's lived, and the next time he saw her was when he took the friend some bananas. "It was during the great banana bubble. You had to kind of force your personality and the banana peels down their throats. Sharon and I were like kids—we just smoked bananas and looked at each other and smoked more bananas and looked at each other."

But Max hesitated. For one thing he thought Sharon was his friend's girl. "For another I didn't know if I wanted to get hung up with an old lady." But the next time he visited the house, Sharon was on acid.

"So everybody yelled 'Here comes the banana man,'" Sharon interrupts, "and I got all excited."

"She was living in this crazy house," Max continues. "There was this one kid, all he did was scream. His whole trip was to practice screams. It was too much." Max still hung back from Sharon. "But then she offered me a tab, and I knew."

Max walked to the kitchen and back with the tab, wondering whether to take it. "And then I decided to flow with it, and that was that. Because once you drop acid with somebody you flash on, you see the whole world melt in her eyes."

"It's stronger than anything in the world," Sharon says.

"Nothing can break it up," Max says. "As long as it lasts."

No milk today—
My love has gone away . . .
The end of my hopes—
The end of all my dreams—
is a song I heard every morning in the
cold late spring of 1967 on KFRC, the
Flower Power Station, San Francisco.

Deadeye and Gerry tell me they plan to be married. An Episcopal priest in the District has promised to perform the wedding in Golden Gate Park, and they will have a few rock groups there, "a real community thing." Gerry's brother is also getting married, in Seattle. "Kind of interesting," Gerry muses, "because, you know, his is the traditional straight wedding, and then you have the contrast with ours."

"I'll have to wear a tie to his," Deadeye says.

"Right," Gerry says.

"Her parents came down to meet me, but they weren't ready for me," Deadeye notes philosophically.

"They finally gave it their blessing," Gerry says. "In a way."

"They came to me and her father said, 'Take care of her,' " Deadeye reminisces. "And her mother said, 'Don't let her go to jail.' "

Barbara baked a macrobiotic apple pie and she and Tom and Max and Sharon and I are eating it. Barbara tells me how she learned to find happiness in "the woman's thing." She and Tom had gone somewhere to live with the Indians, and although she first found it hard to be shunted off with the women and never to enter into any of the men's talk, she soon got the point. "That was where the *trip* was," she says.

Barbara is on what is called the woman's trip to the exclusion of almost everything else. When she and Tom and Max and Sharon need money, Barbara will take a part-time job, modeling or teaching kindergarten, but she dislikes earning more than ten or twenty dollars a week. Most of the time she keeps house and bakes. "Doing something that shows your love that way," she says, "is just about the most beautiful thing I know." Whenever I hear about the woman's trip, which is often, I think a lot about nothin'-

says-lovin'-like-something-from-the-oven and the Feminine Mystique and how it is possible for people to be the unconscious instruments of values they would strenuously reject on a conscious level, but I do not mention this to Barbara.

It is a pretty nice day and I am just driving down the Street and I see Barbara at a light.
What am I doing, she wants to know.
I am just driving around.
"Groovy," she says.
It's a beautiful day, I say.
"Groovy," she agrees.
She wants to know if I will come over. Sometime soon, I say.
"Groovy," she says.
I ask if she wants to drive in the Park but she is too busy. She is out to buy wool for her loom.

Arthur Lisch gets pretty nervous whenever he sees me now because the Digger line this week is that they aren't talking to "media poisoners," which is me. So I still don't have a tap on Chester Anderson, but one day in the Panhandle I run into a kid he says he is Chester's "associate." He has on a black cape, black slouch hat, mauve Job's Daughters sweatshirt and dark glasses, and he says his name is Claude Hayward, but never mind that because I think of him just as The Connection. The Connection offers to "check me out."
I take off my dark glasses so he can see my eyes. He leaves his on.
"How much you get paid for doing this kind of media poisoning?" he says for openers.
I put my dark glasses back on.
"There's only one way to find out where it's at," The Connection says, and jerks his thumb at the photographer I'm with. "Dump him and get out on the Street. Don't take money. You won't need money." He reaches into his cape and pulls out a Mimeographed sheet announcing a series of classes at the Digger Free Store on How to Avoid Getting Busted, Gangbangs, VD, Rape, Pregnancy, Beatings, and Starvation. "You oughta come," The Connection says. "You'll need it."
I say maybe, but meanwhile I would like to talk to Chester Anderson.
"If we decide to get in touch with you at all," The Connection says, "we'll get in touch with you real quick." He kept an eye on me in the Park after that but never called the number I gave him.

It is twilight and cold and too early to find Deadeye at the Blue Unicorn so I ring Max's bell. Barbara comes to the door.
"Max and Tom are seeing somebody on a kind of business thing," she says. "Can you come back a little later?"

I am hard put to think what Max and Tom might be seeing somebody about in the way of business, but a few days later in the Park I find out.

"Hey," Max calls. "Sorry you couldn't come up the other day, but *business* was being done." This time I get the point. "We got some great stuff," he says, and begins to elaborate. Every third person in the Park this afternoon looks like a narcotics agent and I try to change the subject. Later I suggest to Max that he be more wary in public. "Listen, I'm very cautious," he says. "You can't be too careful."

By now I have an unofficial taboo contact with the San Francisco Police Department. What happens is that this cop and I meet in various late-movie ways, like I happen to be sitting in the bleachers at a baseball game and he happens to sit down next to me, and we exchange guarded generalities. No information actually passes between us, but after a while we get to kind of like each other.

"The kids aren't too bright," he is telling me on this particular day. "They'll tell you they can always spot an undercover, they'll tell you about 'the kind of car he drives.' They aren't talking about undercovers, they're talking about plainclothesmen who just happen to drive unmarked cars, like I do. They can't tell an undercover. An undercover doesn't drive some black Ford with a two-way radio."

He tells me about an undercover who was taken out of the District because he was believed to be overexposed, too familiar. He was transferred to the narcotics squad, and by error was sent immediately back into the District as a narcotics undercover.

The cop plays with his keys. "You want to know how smart these kids are?" he says finally. "The first week, this guy makes forty-three cases."

The Jook Savages are supposed to be having a May Day party in Larkspur and I go by the Warehouse and Don and Sue Ann think it would be nice to drive over there because Sue Ann's three-year-old, Michael, hasn't been out lately. The air is soft and there is a sunset haze around the Golden Gate and Don asks Sue Ann how many flavors she can detect in a single grain of rice and Sue Ann tells Don maybe she better learn to cook *yang,* maybe they are all too *yin* at the Warehouse, and I try to teach Michael "Frère Jacques." We each have our own trip and it is a nice drive. Which is just as well because there is nobody at all at the Jook Savages' place, not even the Jook Savages. When we get back Sue Ann decides to cook up a lot of apples they have around the Warehouse and Don starts working with his light show and I go down to see Max for a minute. "Out of sight," Max says about the Larkspur caper. "Somebody thinks it would be groovy to turn on five hundred people the first day in May, and it would be, but then they turn on the last day in April instead, so it doesn't happen. If it happens, it happens. If it doesn't, it doesn't. Who cares. Nobody cares."

Some kid with braces on his teeth is playing his guitar and boasting that he got the last of the STP from Mr. O. himself and somebody else is talking about how five grams of acid will be liberated within the next month and you can see that nothing much is happening this afternoon around the *San Francisco Oracle* office. A boy sits at a drawing board drawing the infinitesimal figures that people do on speed, and the kid with the braces watches him. *"I'm gonna shoot my wo–man,"* he sings softly. *"She been with a–noth–er man."* Someone works out the numerology of my name and the name of the photographer I'm with. The photographer's is all white and the sea ("If I were to make you some beads, see, I'd do it mainly in white," he is told), but mine has a double death symbol. The afternoon does not seem to be getting anywhere, so it is suggested that we go over to Japantown and find somebody named Sandy who will take us to the Zen temple.

Four boys and one middle-aged man are sitting on a grass mat at Sandy's place, sipping anise tea and watching Sandy read Laura Huxley's *You Are Not the Target.*

We sit down and have some anise tea. "Meditation turns us on," Sandy says. He has a shaved head and the kind of cherubic face usually seen in newspaper photographs of mass murderers. The middle-aged man, whose name is George, is making me uneasy because he is in a trance next to me and stares at me without seeing me.

I feel that my mind is going—George is *dead,* or we *all* are—when the telephone rings.

"It's for George," Sandy says.

"George, *tele*phone."

"George."

Somebody waves his hand in front of George and George finally gets up, bows, and moves toward the door on the balls of his feet.

"I think I'll take George's tea," somebody says. "George—are you coming back?"

George stops at the door and stares at each of us in turn. "In a *mo*ment," he snaps.

> *Do you know who is the first eternal spaceman of this universe?*
> *The first to send his wild wild vibrations*
> *To all those cosmic superstations?*
> *For the song he always shouts*
> *Sends the planets flipping out . . .*
> *But I'll tell you before you think me loony*
> *That I'm talking about Narada Muni . . .*
> *Singing*
> HARE KRISHNA   HARE KRISHNA
> KRISHNA KRISHNA HARE HARE
> HARE RAMA   HARE RAMA

RAMA RAMA   HARE HARE
is a Krishna song. Words by
Howard Wheeler and music by
Michael Grant.

Maybe the trip is not in Zen but in Krishna, so I pay a visit to Michael
Grant, the Swami A.C. Bhaktivedanta's leading disciple in San Francisco.
Michael Grant is at home with his brother-in-law and his wife, a pretty girl
wearing a cashmere pullover, a jumper, and a red caste mark on her forehead.

"I've been associated with the Swami since about last July," Michael
says. "See, the Swami came here from India and he was at this ashram in
upstate New York and he just kept to himself and chanted a lot. For a
couple of months. Pretty soon I helped him get his storefront in New York.
Now it's an international movement, which we spread by teaching this
chant." Michael is fingering his red wooden beads and I notice that I am
the only person in the room with shoes on. "It's catching on like wildfire."

"If everybody chanted," the brother-in-law says, "there wouldn't be
any problem with the police or anybody."

"Ginsberg calls the chant ecstasy, but the Swami says that's not exactly
it." Michael walks across the room and straightens a picture of Krishna as
a baby. "Too bad you can't meet the Swami," he adds. "The Swami's in
New York now."

"Ecstasy's not the right word at all," says the brother-in-law, who has
been thinking about it. "It makes you think of some . . . mun*dane* ecstasy."

The next day I drop by Max and Sharon's, and find them in bed smoking a little morning hash. Sharon once advised me that half a joint even of
grass would make getting up in the morning a beautiful thing. I ask Max
how Krishna strikes him.

"You can get a high on a mantra," he says. "But I'm holy on acid."

Max passes the joint to Sharon and leans back. "Too bad you couldn't
meet the Swami," he says. "The Swami was the turn-on."

> Anybody who thinks this is all about drugs has his head in a bag.
> It's a social movement, quintessentially romantic, the kind that re-
> curs in times of real social crisis. The themes are always the same.
> A return to innocence. The invocation of an earlier authority and
> control. The mysteries of the blood. An itch for the transcendental,
> for purification. Right there you've got the ways that romanticism
> historically ends up in trouble, lends itself to authoritarianism. When
> the direction appears. How long do you think it'll take for that to
> happen? is a question a San Francisco psychiatrist asked me.

At the time I was in San Francisco the political potential of what was
then called the movement was just becoming clear. It had always been clear

to the revolutionary core of the Diggers, whose every guerrilla talent was not bent toward open confrontations and the creation of a summer emergency, and it was clear to many of the straight doctors and priests and sociologists who had occasion to work in the District, and it could rapidly become clear to any outsider who bothered to decode Chester Anderson's call-to-action communiqués or to watch who was there first at the street skirmishes which now set the tone for life in the District. One did not have to be a political analyst to see it; the boys in the rock groups saw it, because they were often where it was happening. "In the Park there are always twenty or thirty people below the stand," one of the Dead complained to me. "Ready to take the crowd on some militant trip."

But the peculiar beauty of this political potential, as far as the activists were concerned, was that it remained not clear at all to most of the inhabitants of the District, perhaps because the few seventeen-year-olds who are political realists tend not to adopt romantic idealism as a life style. Nor was it clear to the press, which at varying levels of competence continued to report "the hippie phenomenon" as an extended panty raid; an artistic avant-garde led by such comfortable YMHA regulars as Allen Ginsberg; or a thoughtful protest, not unlike joining the Peace Corps, against the culture which had produced Saran-Wrap and the Vietnam War. This last, or they're-trying-to-tell-us-something approach, reached its apogee in a *Time* cover story which revealed that hippies "scorn money—they call it 'bread' " and remains the most remarkable, if unwitting, extant evidence that the signals between the generations are irrevocably jammed.

Because the signals the press was getting were immaculate of political possibilities, the tensions of the District went unmarked upon, even during the period when there were so many observers on Haight Street from *Life* and *Look* and CBS that they were largely observing one another. The observers believed roughly what the children told them: that they were a generation dropped out of political action, beyond power games, that the New Left was just another ego trip. *Ergo,* there really were no activists in the Haight-Ashbury, and those things which happened every Sunday were spontaneous demonstrations because, just as the Diggers say, the police are brutal and juveniles have no rights and runaways are deprived of their right to self-determination and people are starving to death on Haight Street, a scale model of Vietnam.

Of course the activists—not those whose thinking had become rigid, but those whose approach to revolution was imaginatively anarchic—had long ago grasped the reality which still eluded the press: we were seeing something important. We were seeing the desperate attempt of a handful of pathetically unequipped children to create a community in a social vacuum. Once we had seen these children, we could no longer overlook the vacuum, no longer pretend that the society's atomization could be reversed. This was not a traditional generational rebellion. At some point between 1945 and 1967 we had somehow neglected to tell these children the rules of the game we happened to be playing. Maybe we had stopped believing in the rules ourselves, maybe we were having a failure of nerve about the game. Maybe there were just too few people around to do the telling. These were children who grew up cut loose from the web of cousins and great-aunts and family doctors and lifelong neighbors who had traditionally suggested and enforced the society's values. They are children who have moved around a lot, *San Jose, Chula Vista, here.* They are less in rebellion against the society than ignorant of it, able only to feed back certain of its most publicized self-doubts, *Vietnam, Saran-Wrap, diet pills, the Bomb.*

They feed back exactly what is given them. Because they do not believe in words—words are for "typeheads," Chester Anderson tells them, and a thought which needs words is just one more of those ego trips—their only proficient vocabulary is in the society's platitudes. As it happens I am still committed to the idea that the ability to think for one's self depends upon one's mastery of the language, and I am not optimistic about children who will settle for saying, to indicate that their mother and father do not live together, that they come from "a broken home." They are sixteen, fifteen, fourteen years old, younger all the time, an army of children waiting to be given the words.

Peter Berg knows a lot of words.
"Is Peter Berg around?" I ask.
"Maybe."
"Are you Peter Berg?"
"Yeh."
The reason Peter Berg does not bother sharing too many words with me is because two of the words he knows are "media poisoning." Peter Berg wears a gold earring and is perhaps the only person in the District on whom a gold earring looks obscurely ominous. He belongs to the San Francisco Mime Troupe, some of whose members started the Artist's Liberation Front for "those who seek to combine their creative urge with sociopolitical involvement." It was out of the Mime Troupe that the Diggers grew, during the 1966 Hunter's Point riots, when it seemed a good idea to give away food and do puppet shows in the streets making fun of the National Guard. Along with Arthur Lisch, Peter Berg is part of the shadow leadership of the Diggers, and it was he who more or less invented and first introduced to the press the notion that there would be an influx into San Francisco during the summer of 1967 of 200,000 indigent adolescents. The only conversation I ever have with Peter Berg is about how he holds me personally responsible for the way *Life* captioned Henri Cartier-Bresson's pictures out of Cuba, but I like to watch him at work in the Park.

Janis Joplin is singing with Big Brother in the Panhandle and almost everybody is high and it is a pretty nice Sunday afternoon between three and six o'clock, which the activists say are the three hours of the week when something is most likely to happen in the Haight-Ashbury, and who turns up but Peter Berg. He is with his wife and six or seven other people, along with Chester Anderson's associate The Connection, and the first peculiar thing is, they're in blackface.

I mention to Max and Sharon that some members of the Mime Troupe seem to be in blackface.

"It's street theater," Sharon assures me. "It's supposed to be really groovy."

The Mime Troupers get a little closer, and there are some other peculiar things about them. For one thing they are tapping people on the head with dime-store plastic nightsticks, and for another they are wearing signs on their backs. "HOW MANY TIMES YOU BEEN RAPED, YOU LOVE FREAKS?" and "WHO STOLE CHUCK BERRY'S MUSIC?", things like that. Then they are distributing communication company fliers which say:

> & this summer thousands of un-white un-suburban boppers are going to want to know why you've given up what they can't get & how you get away with it & how come you not a faggot with hair so long & they want haight street one way or the other. IF YOU DON'T KNOW, BY AUGUST HAIGHT STREET WILL BE A CEMETERY.

Max reads the flier and stands up. "I'm getting bad vibes," he says, and he and Sharon leave.

I have to stay around because I'm looking for Otto so I walk over to where the Mime Troupers have formed a circle around a Negro. Peter Berg is saying if anybody asks that this is street theater, and I figure the curtain is up because what they are doing right now is jabbing the Negro with the nightsticks. They jab, and they bare their teeth, and they rock on the balls of their feet and they wait.

"I'm beginning to get annoyed here," the Negro says. "I'm gonna get mad."

By now there are several Negroes around, reading the signs and watching.

"Just beginning to get annoyed, are you?" one of the Mime Troupers says. "Don't you think it's about time?"

"Nobody *stole* Chuck Berry's music, man," says another Negro who has been studying the signs. "Chuck Berry's music belongs to *every*body."

"Yeh?" a girl in blackface says. "Everybody *who*?"

"Why," he says, confused. "Everybody. In America."

"In *America*," the blackface girl shrieks. "Listen to him talk about *America*."

"Listen," he says helplessly. "Listen here."

"What'd *America* ever do for you?" the girl in blackface jeers. "White kids here, they can sit in the Park all summer long, listening to the music they stole, because their bigshot parents keep sending them money. Who ever sends you money?"

"Listen," the Negro says, his voice rising. "You're gonna start something here, this isn't right—"

"You tell us what's right, black boy," the girl says.

The youngest member of the blackface group, an earnest tall kid about nineteen, twenty, is hanging back at the edge of the scene. I offer him an apple and ask what is going on. "Well," he says, "I'm new at this, I'm just beginning to study it, but you see the capitalists are taking over the District, and that's what Peter—well, ask Peter."

I did not ask Peter. It went on for a while. But on that particular Sunday between three and six o'clock everyone was too high and the weather was too good and the Hunter's Point gangs who usually come in between three and six on Sunday afternoon had come in on Saturday instead, and nothing started. While I waited for Otto I asked a little girl I knew slightly what she had thought of it. "It's something groovy they call street theater," she said. I said I had wondered if it might not have political overtones. She was seventeen years old and she worked it around in her mind awhile and finally she remembered a couple of words from somewhere. "Maybe it's some John Birch thing," she said.

When I finally find Otto he says "I got something at my place that'll blow your mind," and when we get there I see a child on the living-room floor, wearing a reefer coat, reading a comic book. She keeps licking her lips in concentration and the only off thing about her is that she's wearing white lipstick.

"Five years old," Otto says. "On acid."

The five-year-old's name is Susan, and she tells me she is in High Kindergarten. She lives with her mother and some other people, just got over the measles, wants a bicycle for Christmas, and particularly likes Coca-Cola, ice cream, Marty in the Jefferson Airplane, Bob in the Grateful Dead, and the beach. She remembers going to the beach once a long time ago, and wishes she had taken a bucket. For a year now her mother has given her both acid and peyote. Susan describes it as getting stoned.

I start to ask if any of the other children in High Kindergarten get stoned, but I falter at the key words.

"She means do the other kids in your class turn on, *get stoned,*" says the friend of her mother's who brought her to Otto's.

"Only Sally and Anne," Susan says.

"What about Lia?" her mother's friend prompts.

"Lia," Susan says, "is not in High Kindergarten."

Sue Ann's three-year-old Michael started a fire this morning before anyone was up, but Don got it out before much damage was done. Michael burned his arm though, which is probably why Sue Ann was so jumpy when she happened to see him chewing on an electric cord. "You'll fry like rice," she screamed. The only people around were Don and one of Sue Ann's macrobiotic friends and somebody who was on his way to a commune in the Santa Lucias, and they didn't notice Sue Ann screaming at Michael because they were in the kitchen trying to retrieve some very good Moroccan hash which had dropped down through a floorboard damaged in the fire.

1967

from The Armies of the Night

Norman Mailer

Norman Mailer (b. 1923) saw service in World War II and made a great early reputation with his war book, *The Naked and the Dead* (1948). He has since published poems, novels, and essays. He has written accounts of the antidraft and peace march on the Pentagon in October, 1967, and of the Democratic National Convention at Chicago in August, 1968. The story of the Pentagon march was published in 1968 under the title *The Armies of the Night*.

Mailer begins his story by quoting from *Time* magazine (October 27, 1967).

> Washington's scruffy Ambassador Theater, normally a pad for psychedelic frolics, was the scene of an unscheduled scatological solo last week in support of the peace demonstrations. Its anti-star was author Norman Mailer, who proved even less prepared to explain Why Are We in Vietnam? than his current novel bearing that title.
>
> Slurping liquor from a coffee mug, Mailer faced an audience of 600, most of them students, who had kicked in $1,900 for a bail fund against Saturday's capers. "I don't want to grandstand unduly," he said, grandly but barely standing.

Mailer goes on to quote the rest of *Time*'s account and adds, "Now we may leave *Time* in order to find out what happened."

The first excerpts from *The Armies of the Night* is part of Mailer's story about what happened on the steps of the Department of Justice. The second excerpt is from Mailer's account of how he got arrested.

JUSTICE

Well, they were now at the steps—one of the set of steps in any case. It all seemed a hint undramatic. When he had first heard of the action from Mitch Goodman, pictures had crossed his mind of charged disagreeable encounters with FBI men in the corridors of the Department of Justice, now instead there was not a government man in sight if one did not count the number of FBI and CIA agents doubtless circulating among the press as photographers, newsreel men, TV cameramen, and newspapermen, there to mug and map every subversive face in sight. The nearest representative of any potential violence face to face was a stand of five American Nazis wearing swastikas for armbands, and kept by the police off to one side of the proceedings. All through the afternoon the Nazis kept chanting slogans. "We want dead Reds," was the clearest.

Here was the disposition of bodies: on a corner of the steps of the Department of Justice were gathered about fifteen men, most of whom were going to speak for a minute or two. Facing them, just below the steps, was a phalanx of mass-media representatives, and they were going through a preliminary boxing out and jockeying in for position between newsreel, still and television cameras. To the sides of them, and behind them, was a group of four or five hundred people who for the most part cheered politely although with distinct well-bred fervor at remarks they particularly liked.

Coffin gave the main address. He began by speaking of the procedure to be followed. After a few short speeches, those students representing themselves or organizations of students who might wish to turn in their draft cards, would come forward one by one and deposit their cards in a bag. Then, any individuals in the audience, student, faculty, or onlookers who thought to hand in their draft cards as well could join. At that point, Mitch Goodman, Coffin, Dr. Spock, and seven other demonstrators would "disappear for a while and enter the Department of Justice Building. Once inside," said Coffin, "we will proceed to the Office of the Attorney General and there hand over the cards and notify him of our intention which is that we hereby publicly counsel these young men to continue in their refusal to serve in the Armed Forces as long as the war in Vietnam continues, and we pledge ourselves to aid and abet them in all the ways we can." There were cheers. "At that point," Coffin went on, "depending on how we are received, we shall either leave, and rejoin you here to report our conversation, or if there are difficulties, we may be delayed." It was impossible to tell if he was hinting they might be arrested. "If we do not reappear quickly, I would ask you all to wait and divert yourselves with speeches"—small titter—"or song." More amusement. "If it takes too long, and we are not able to send word out, I would then suggest you disperse and those interested can come together tonight at the meeting already signified, for a full account."

Then he gave his prepared speech. It was reasonable in length, the points clearly made, his indignation kept nicely in leash but nonetheless vibrant.

His sentences had a nonpoetic bony statement of meaning which made them exactly suitable for newspaper quotation.

". . . in our view it is not wild-eyed idealism but clear-eyed revulsion that brings us here. For as one of our number put it: 'If what the United States is doing in Vietnam is right, what is there left to be called wrong?'

"Many of us are veterans, and all of us have the highest sympathy for our boys in Vietnam. They know what a dirty, bloody war it is. But they have been told that the ends justify the means, and that the cleansing water of victory will wash clean their hands of all the blood and dirt. No wonder they hate us who say 'There must be no cleansing water.' But what they must strive to understand, hard as it is, is that there can be no cleansing water if military victory spells moral defeat.

"We have the highest sympathy also for those who back the war because their sons or lovers or husbands are fighting or have died in Vietnam. But they too must understand a very basic thing—that sacrifice in and of itself confers no sanctity. Even if half a million of our boys were to die in Vietnam that would not make the cause one whit more sacred. Yet we realize how hard that knowledge is to appropriate when one's husband is numbered among the sacrificed."

Had he, Mailer was ready to wonder, come from a long line of New England ministers whose pride resided partly in their ability to extract practical methods from working in the world? It was a Protestant discipline of which our Participant knew little, and it had made in his opinion for a great deal of waste in the world, since America's corporations were in Mailer's opinion more guilty than the Communists at polluting the air, fields, and streams, debasing the value of manufactured products, transmuting faith into science, technology, and medicine, while all embarked on scandalous foreign adventures with their eminently practical methods—yes, all that might have come by panning the homely practical silt out of the tumultuous rivers of Christian experience in the world. What was fascinating to Mailer is that the Yale Chaplain had one of those faces you expected to see on the cover of *Time* or *Fortune,* there as the candidate for Young Executive of the Year, he had that same flint of the eye, single-mindedness in purpose, courage to bear responsibility, that same hard humor about the details in the program under consideration, that same suggestion of an absolute lack of humor once the line which enclosed his true Wasp temper had been breached. He was one full example of the masculine principle at work in the cloth.

"As the law now stands, for a man to qualify as a conscientious objector he must believe in God. Could anything be more ethically absurd? Have humanists no conscience? Why,—and as a Christian I say this with contrition—some of the most outstanding humanists I know would think they were slipping from their high ideals were they to take steps towards conversion. As a Christian I am convinced it is a gross misfortune not to believe in God, but it is not automatically an ethical default.

"Then despite numerous appeals by numerous religious bodies, Congress last spring chose to provide alternative service only for the absolute pacifist. This too is absurd, for the rights of a man whose conscience forbids him to participate in a particular war are as deserving of respect as the rights of a man whose conscience forbids him to participate in any war at all."

This drew the largest applause of his speech. Just as in the thirties when the success of every Communist meeting was absolutely dependent upon the victory talk being given by a man with a fine Irish brogue—"Down with the doorty capitalist system say I!"—so the conscientious objection of the non-religious would be advanced consummately in the hands of a minister. Indeed, who else?

"The law of the land is clear. Section 12 of the National Selective Service Act declares that anyone 'who knowingly counsels, aids, or abets another to refuse or evade registration or service in the armed forces . . . shall be liable to imprisonment for not more than five years or a fine of ten thousand dollars or both.'

"We hereby publicly counsel these young men to continue in their refusal to serve in the armed forces as long as the war in Vietnam continues, and we pledge ourselves to aid and abet them in all the ways we can. This means that if they are now arrested for failing to comply with a law that violates their consciences, we too must be arrested, for in the sight of that law we are now as guilty as they."

There were a few more speeches, all short. Mitch Goodman made one, Dr. Spock made one, and then three or four other people whose names Mailer did not recognize and to whose speeches he hardly listened. It was turning cold, the sun had gone back of a cloud, and his hangover had settled in for a bout. It would not leave now until the proceedings were over, and he could go somewhere to get a drink. He had no idea if they would call upon him in a little while to speak, although he judged not. Probably Mitch Goodman had passed word that Mailer was attending, but with no especial good grace.

In the middle of these speakers, Robert Lowell was called up. He had been leaning against a wall in his habitual slumped over position, deep in revery at the side of the steps—and of course had been photographed as a figure of dejection—the call for him to say a few words caught him partly by surprise. He now held the portable hand microphone with a delicate lack of intimacy as if it were some valuable, huge, and rare tropical spider which he was obliged to examine but did not have to enjoy. "I was asked earlier today," he began in his fine stammering voice which gave the impression that life rushed at him like a series of hurdles and some he succeeded in jumping and some he did not, "I was asked earlier this afternoon by a reporter why I was not turning in my draft card," Lowell said with the beginnings of a pilgrim's passion, "and I did not tell him it was a stupid question, although I was tempted to. I thought he should have known that I am now too old to have a draft card, but that it makes no difference. When some of us pledge ourselves to counsel and aid and abet any young men who wish to turn in their cards, why then you may be certain we are aware of the possible consequences and do not try to hide behind the technicality of whether we literally have a draft card or not. So I'm now saying to the gentlemen of the press that unlike the authorities who are running this country, we are not searching for tricks, we try to think of ourselves as serious men, if the press, that is, can comprehend such an effort, and we will protest this war by every means available to our conscience, and therefore not try to avoid whatever may arise in the way of retribution."

It was said softly, on a current of intense indignation and Lowell had never looked more dignified nor more admirable. Each word seemed to come on a separate journey from the poet's mind to his voice, along a winding route or through an exorbitant gate. Each word cost him much—Lowell's fine grace was in the value words had for him, he seemed to emit a horror at the possibility of squandering them or leaving them abused, and political speeches had never seemed more difficult for him, and on the consequence, more necessary for statement.

So Mailer applauded when Lowell was done. And suddenly liked him enormously for his speech, and decided he liked him truly. Beneath all snobbery, affectations of weariness, literary logrollermanship, neutralsmanship, and whatever other fatal snob-infested baggage of the literary world was by now willy-nilly in the poet's system, worked down intimately close to all his best and most careful traditions and standards, all flaws considered, Lowell was still a fine, good, and honorable man, and Norman Mailer was happy to be linked in a cause with him.

But now much began to happen to Mailer on the aftermath of this speech. For shortly afterward students began to file up the steps to deposit their solitary or collective draft cards in the bag, and this procession soon became a ceremony. Each man came up, gave his name, and the state or area or college he represented, and then proceeded to name the number of draft cards he had been entrusted to turn in. The numbers were larger than one might have expected. There were almost two hundred from New York, there were much more than two hundred from Boston, and a good number from Yale. As these numbers were announced, the crowd being when all is said, good Americans, gave murmurs of pleasure, an academic distance from the cry they had given as children to the acrobats of the circus, but not entirely unrelated, for there was something of the flying trapeze in these maneuvers now; by handing in draft cards, these young men were committing their future either to prison, emigration, frustration, or at best, years where everything must be unknown, and that spoke of a readiness to take moral leaps which the acrobat must know when he flies off into space—one has to have faith in one's ability to react with grace en route, one has ultimately, it may be supposed, to believe in some kind of grace.

On the *a fortiori* evidence, then, they were young men with souls of interesting dimension, and their faces did nothing to disprove this. None of them looked alike; they had a surprising individuality in their appearance. Some were scholarly and slight, dressed conservatively, and looked like clerks; others were in dungarees, and possessed, like Dickie Harris, the Negro on the grass, that private élan reminiscent of the old cavaliers of SNCC; a few were sports and looked to have eight hobbies, custom cars, pot, draft cards, skiing, guitar, surfboard, chicks, and scuba—not many of these, but Mailer had been expecting none. One tall student from the West, California no doubt, even looked like one's image of the President of the Young Republicans at Stanford, he was handsome enough in conventional measure to have been Number 1 Deke in Delta Kappa Eps. After he dropped his card in the bag, he gave a little talk to the effect that many of these students had been scared when first they burned their cards, months ago—they had said goodbye to their girls and family and waited for the clang of the jail gate. But the jail gate never came. "Now we think the government might be afraid to go near us. That gets around. A lot of kids who were afraid to join us last year won't be afraid this year. So every bit helps. If we get arrested, we make our point, and people won't forget it—our point being that with good careers ahead of us, we still hate this war so much that we go to jail—if they show they're reluctant to arrest us, then others are in more of a hurry to join us." He was almost too good to be true. The suspicion came up for a moment that the CIA had doubtless not stopped their recruiting in colleges, and would certainly be happy to infiltrate here, an unpleasant thought, but then (1) Mailer came from New York where unpleasant thoughts were common, and (2) the writer in him was intrigued at the thought of a short novel about a young American leading a double life in college as a secret policeman. What a good novel that could make! About once a week Mailer by-passed wistfully around the excitements of the new book which had just come into his head. He would leave it to his detractors to decide that the ones he did not write were better than the ones he did.

Another student came by, then another. One of them, slight, with a sharp face, wearing a sport shirt and dark glasses had the appearance of a Hollywood hustler, but that was misleading; he wore the dark glasses because his eyes were still weak from the Mace squirted in them by police at Oakland. This student had a Berkeley style which Mailer did not like altogether: it was cocky, knowledgeable, and quick to mock the generations over thirty. Predictably, this was about the first item on which the kid began to scold the multitude. "You want to come along with us," he told the Over-Thirties, "that's okay, that's your thing, but we've got our thing, and we're going to do it alone whether you come with us or not." Mailer always wanted to give a kick into the seat of all reflection when he was told he had his thing—one did not look forward to a revolution which would substitute "thing" for better words.

Still, the boy from Berkeley proved to have a fair wit. He had begun to tell about Mace. To correct the hint of self-pity in his voice (which had an adenoidal complacency reminiscent of any number of old-line Party speakers who were never so unbearable as when bona fide martyrs) he made the little point that while the suffering was great, the reporting, for once, had also been great. "You see," he said, "the reporters were on our side." He looked down boldly now on the fifty or more assorted media men in front of him, and said, "They didn't want to be particularly, but the cops were so dumb they couldn't tell the reporters from the demonstrators, so the reporters got the Mace in their eyes too. For once, instead of putting down our big threat to the American flag, the cops were the villains, that is: the cops were the villains as soon as the reporters could see well enough to go back and write their story, which took a couple of hours, I can assure you. That Mace is rough on the eyes."

On they came, twenty-four to thirty of them, one by one, making for the most part short dry single sentences for statement, as for example, "I am ready to turn in my draft card, but can't because I burned it in Kansas City several months ago so am here submitting an affidavit with my name and address so the government can find me."

In a little more than a half hour, the students were done. Now began the faculty. They too came up one by one, but now there was no particular sense offered of an internal organization. Unlike the students, they had not debated these matters in open forum for months, organized, proselyted, or been overcome by argument, no, most of them had served as advisers to the students, had counseled them, and been picked up, many of them, and brought along by the rush of this moral stream much as a small piece of river bank might separate from the shore and go down the line of the flood. It must have been painful for these academics. They were older, certainly less suited for jail, aware more precisely of how and where their careers would be diverted or impeded, they had families many of them, they were liberal academics, technologues, they were being forced to abdicate from the machines they had chosen for their life. Their decision to turn in draft cards must have come for many in the middle of the night; for others it must have come even last night, or as they stood here debating with themselves. Many of them seemed to stand irresolutely near the steps for long periods, then move up at last. Rogoff, standing next to Mailer, hugging his thin chest in the October air, now cold, finally took out his card and, with a grin at Mailer, said, "I guess I'm going to turn this in. But you know the ridiculous part of it is that I'm 4-F." So they came up one by one, not in solidarity, but as individuals, each breaking the shield or the fence or the mold or the home or even the construct of his own security. And as they did this, a deep gloom began to work on Mailer, because a deep modesty was on its way to him, he could feel himself becoming more and more of a modest man as he stood there in the cold with his hangover, and he hated this because modesty was an old family relative, he had been born to a modest family, had been a modest boy, a modest young man, and he hated that, he loved the pride and the arrogance and the confidence and the egocentricity he had acquired over the years, that was his force and his luxury and the iron in his greed, the richest sugar of his pleasure, the strength of his competitive force, he had lived long enough to know that the intimation one was being steeped in a new psychical condition (like this oncoming modest grace) was never to be disregarded, permanent new states could come into one on just so light a breeze. He stood in the cold watching the faculty men come up, yes always one by one, and felt his hangover which had come in part out of his imperfectly swallowed contempt for them the night before, and in part out of his fear, yes now he saw it, fear of the consequences of this weekend in Washington, for he had known from the beginning it could disrupt his life for a season or more, and in some way the danger was there it could change him forever. He was forty-four years old, and it had taken him most of those forty-four years to begin to be able to enjoy his pleasures where he found them, rather than worry about those pleasures which eluded him—it was obviously no time to embark on ventures which could eventually give one more than a few years in jail. Yet, there was no escape. As if some final cherished rare innocence of childhood still preserved intact in him was brought finally to the surface and there expired, so he lost at that instant the last secret delight he retained in life as a game where finally you never got hurt if you played the game well enough. For years he had envisioned himself in some final cataclysm, as an underground leader in the city, or a guerrilla with a gun in the hills, and had scorned the organizational aspects of revolution, the speeches, mimeograph machines, the hard dull forging of new parties and programs, the dull maneuvering to keep power, the intolerable obedience required before the over-all intellectual necessities of each objective period, and had scorned it, yes, had spit at it, and perhaps had been right, certainly had been right, such revolutions were the womb and cradle of technology land, no the only revolutionary truth was a gun in the hills, and that would not be his, he would be too old by then, and too incompetent, yes, too incompetent said the new modesty, and too showboat, too lacking in essential judgment—besides, he was too well-known! He would pay for the pleasures of his notoriety in the impossibility of disguise. No gun in the hills, no taste for organization, no, he was a figurehead, and therefore he was expendable, said the new modesty—not a future leader, but a future victim: *there* would be his real value. He could go to jail for protest, and spend some years if it came to it, possibly his life, for if the war went on, and America put its hot martial tongue across the Chinese border, well, jail was the probable perspective, detention camps, dissociation centers, liquidation alleys, that would be his portion, and it would come about the time he had learned how to live.

The depth of this gloom and this modesty came down on Mailer, and he watched the delegation take the bag into the Department of Justice with 994 cards contained inside, and listened to the speeches while they waited, and was eventually called up himself to make a speech, and made a modest one in a voice so used by the stentorian demonstrations of the night before that he was happy for the mike since otherwise he might have communicated in a whisper. He said a little of what he had thought while watching the others: that he had recognized on this afternoon that the time had come when Americans, many Americans, would have to face the possibility of going to jail for their ideas, and this was a prospect with no cheer because prisons were unattractive places where much of the best in oneself was slowly extinguished, but it could be there was no choice. The war in Vietnam was an obscene war, the worst war the nation had ever been in, and so its logic might compel sacrifice from those who were not so accustomed. And, out of hardly more than a sense of old habit and old anger, he scolded the press for their lies, and their misrepresentation, for their guilt in creating a psychology over the last twenty years in the average American which made wars like Vietnam possible; then he surrendered the mike and stepped down and the applause was pleasant.

After a period, Coffin came out from the Department of Justice with his delegation. He made a short announcement. The draft cards had not been accepted. A game of bureaucratic evasion had been played. In fact, the Attorney General had not even been there, instead his assistant. "The assistant simply refused to take our cards," said Coffin. "Consider this! Here was an officer of the law facing clear evidence of an alleged crime, and refusing to accept that evidence. He was derelict in his duty." There was a contained anger in Coffin, much like lawyer's anger, as if some subtle game had been played in which a combination had been based on a gambit, but the government had refused the gambit, so now the combination was halted.

Further reports were given by Dr. Spock, and one or two other members of the delegation. Then the meeting dispersed. Macdonald, Lowell, and Mailer going off for well-earned drinks at the nearest bar, ended up having dinner together. For all his newly inherited modesty, Mailer had nonetheless a merry meal. Liquor, it seemed, was still given special dispensation by the new regime of discipline, asceticism, moderation and self-sacrifice. Yet before dinner was over, the three men had agreed they would go out together tomorrow on the March to the Pentagon, and that they would probably—all consideration given—seek to get arrested. Mailer's hangover was now about gone. The evening went its agreeable way. . . .

A CONFRONTATION BY THE RIVER

It was not much of a situation to study. The MPs stood in two widely spaced ranks. The first rank was ten yards behind the rope, and each MP in that row was close to twenty feet from the next man. The second rank, similarly spaced, was ten yards behind the first rank and perhaps thirty yards behind them a cluster appeared, every fifty yards or so, of two or three U.S. Marshals in white helmets and dark blue suits. They were out there waiting. Two moods confronted one another, two separate senses of a private silence.

It was not unlike being a boy about to jump from one garage roof to an adjoining garage roof. The one thing not to do was wait. Mailer looked at Macdonald and Lowell. "Let's go," he said. Not looking again at them, not pausing to gather or dissipate resolve, he made a point of stepping neatly and decisively over the low rope. Then he headed across the grass to the nearest MP he saw.

It was as if the air had changed, or light had altered; he felt immediately much more alive—yes, bathed in air—and yet disembodied from himself, as if indeed he were watching himself in a film where this action was taking place. He could feel the eyes of the people behind the rope watching him, could feel the intensity of their existence as spectators. And as he walked forward, he and the MP looked at one another with the naked stricken lucidity which comes when absolute strangers are for the moment absolutely locked together.

The MP lifted his club to his chest as if to bar all passage. To Mailer's great surprise—he had secretly expected the enemy to be calm and strong, why should they not? they had every power, all the guns—to his great surprise, the MP was trembling. He was a young Negro, part white, who looked to have come from some small town where perhaps there were not many other Negroes; he had at any rate no Harlem smoke, no devil swish, no black, no black power for him, just a simple boy in an Army suit with a look of horror in his eye, "Why, why did it have to happen to me?" was the message of the petrified marbles in his face.

"Go back," he said hoarsely to Mailer.

"If you don't arrest me, I'm going to the Pentagon."

"No. Go back."

The thought of a return—"since they won't arrest me, what can I do?"—over these same ten yards was not at all suitable.

As the MP spoke, the raised club quivered. He did not know if it quivered from the desire of the MP to strike him, or secret military wonder was he now possessed of a moral force which implanted terror in the arms of young soldiers? Some unfamiliar current, now gyroscopic, now a sluggish whirlpool, was evolving from that quiver of the club, and the MP seemed to turn slowly away from his position confronting the rope, and the novelist turned with him, each still facing the other until the axis of their shoulders was now perpendicular to the rope, and still they kept turning in this psychic field, not touching, the club quivering, and then Mailer was behind the MP, he was free of him, and he wheeled around and kept going in a half run to the next line of MPs and then on the push of a sudden instinct, sprinted suddenly around the nearest MP in the second line, much as if he were a back cutting around the nearest man in the secondary to break free—that was actually his precise thought—and had a passing perception of how simple it was to get past these MPs. They looked petrified. Stricken faces as he went by. They did not know what to do. It was his dark pinstripe suit, his vest, the maroon and blue regimental tie, the part in his hair, the barrel chest, the early paunch—he must have looked like a banker himself, a banker gone ape! And then he saw the Pentagon to his right across the field, not a hundred yards away, and a little to his left, the marshals, and he ran on a jog toward them, and came up, and they glared at him and shouted, "Go back."

He had a quick impression of hard-faced men with gray eyes burning some transparent fuel for flame, and said, "I won't go back. If you don't arrest me, I'm going on to the Pentagon," and knew he meant it, some absolute certainty had come to him, and then two of them leaped on him at once in the cold clammy murderous fury of all cops at the existential moment of making their bust—all cops who secretly expect to be struck at that instant for their sins—and a surprising force came to his voice, and he roared, to his own distant pleasure in new achievement and new authority—"Take your hands off me, can't you see? I'm not resisting arrest," and one then let go of him, and the other stopped trying to pry his arm into a lock, and contented himself with a hard hand under his armpit, and they set off walking across the field at a rabid intent quick rate, walking parallel to the wall of the Pentagon, fully visible on his right at last, and he was arrested, he had succeeded in that, and without a club on his head, the mountain air in his lungs as thin and fierce as smoke, yes, the livid air of tension on this livid side promised a few events of more interest than the routine wait to be free, yes he was more than a visitor, he was in the land of the enemy now, he would get to see their face.

A Dictionary Looks Up Grammarians

Israel Shenker

Israel Shenker (b. 1925) is a reporter for the *New York Times*. Until 1968 he was a correspondent for *Time*, having served as bureau chief in The Hague, Paris, Moscow, and Rome.

A dictionary should be an embarrassment of riches, not a richness of embarrassments, but nowadays it is a little of both.

In 1961, Webster's Third New Unabridged Dictionary was praised and damned as permissive. By the time Random House published its dictionary, in 1966, it was harder to tell permissiveness from strict construction. In the American Heritage Dictionary (to be published jointly with Houghton Mifflin on Sept. 15), the distinction will be approached even more warily.

Since democracy is part of the American heritage, the dictionary's editors set up a "usage panel" of 104 writers, editors, professors, and public figures to vote on specific expressions and general usage.

On occasion the panelists on whom the burden fell were surprisingly permissive. Thus Dwight Macdonald, the author-critic, wrote: "I favor dropping 'whom' altogether as a needless refinement."

But Katherine Anne Porter, the novelist, would not hear of allowing "who" for "whom." She said it was "Acceptable in speech, if you don't mind who hears you." Acceptable no matter who's listening, ruled the panel, but unacceptable in writing.

'SYMBOL OF GENTILITY'

The split infinitive was welcomed cautiously. Banning it, said Morris Bishop, author and a past president of the Modern Language Association, is a "mere symbol of gentility, like the prohibition of cutting lettuce with a fork." The panel voted to more or less accept split infinitives, with each use to be separately examined.

"It is me" won 60 per cent of the votes for use in speech, but only 22 per cent for use in writing. Joseph A. Brandt, a professor emeritus of journalism at the University of California at Los Angeles, called it "grammatical incest."

The panel reached unanimity only once—when it examined "simultaneous" as an adverb, as in "the referendum was conducted simultaneous with the election." Nobody voted yes.

On the use of "above" as an adjective (as in "the above figures") and as a noun (as in "the above is incorrect"), Red Smith, the sports columnist, commented: "It's business-letter English, meaning acceptable and undesirable." A majority agreed to accept "above" as an adjective, but not as a noun.

Did the panel object to "gift" as a transitive verb? Mr. Smith observed: "If he gifts her wisely, she should host him warmly, which could be immoral." Six per cent were ready to accept such a gift, and 18 per cent were prepared to go along with Mr. Smith's use of "host."

The verb "escalate," used transitively in the sense of stepping up an effort, provoked forceful rejoinders, but three-quarters of the panel voted for it. Richard H. Rovere of The New Yorker magazine said: "This one has been settled by force of arms and may as well be accepted as a useful term."

"Yes, dammit!" agreed Russell Lynes of Harper's magazine, while Bruce Catton, the historian, said: "No, but I suppose nothing can be done about it." Mr. Lynes confronted with the suffix "-wise," as in "population-wise," replied, "Nowise!"

Prof. Jacques Barzun of Columbia University decried "descalate" for "de-escalate." "I would deprecate it," he said, and so would 93 per cent of the panel.

Isaac Asimov, a biochemist who writes history and science-fiction, refused to see "finalize" in any of his pasts or futures. John Bainbridge, the author, was more tolerant: "To be used only facetiously, except by bureaucrats and generals." (It was Asimov, 9 to 1.)

Professor Barzun flailed at "flaunt" as a substitute for "flout" (defy with contempt): "This is an appalling question, for if latitude is given in this case, all malapropisms are justified. Just cut the dictionary in half and double the synonyms." Only 9 per cent opposed his view.

UPSET FOR BARZUN

There was no one like Dr. Barzun when it came to antilatitudinarianism. On "regime" as a synonym for "administration," as in "Kennedy regime," he said: "No, and cut out 'dynasty' in the same contexts: these are technical terms, you blasted non-historians!" (72 per cent took no offense, and voted against Dr. Barzun's view.)

On "premiere" as a verb ("the conductor will premiere two works") Professor Barzun asked: "And derrière them at the same time?" (86 per cent turned their backs on that.)

Confronted by "enthuse," Mr. Macdonald declared: "By God, let's hold the line on this one!" John Fischer, of Harper's, said simply: "There is no such word." Only a quarter of his colleagues disagreed.

When Mr. Macdonald faced "fortuitous" as a substitute for "fortunate" he dug in his cleats: "Users of a language must learn it before they can change it; simple illiteracy is no basis for linguistic evolution." (15 per cent voted for such illiteracy.)

David Ogilvy, an adman—or rather, advertising executive, was optimistic about ending "hopefully," as in, "Hopefully, I'll get a raise this year."

"If your dictionary could kill this horror, and do nothing else," Mr. Ogilvy wrote, "it would be worth publishing." (56 per cent of the panel joined his plea for capital punishment.)

A SLIP OF FOOLS

Miss Porter decided that "O.K." was a slip of fools: "Any form, any spelling is a detestable vulgarity, entirely offensive to the ear. I have never spoken the word in my life, and I loathe the sound of it." But the expression as a noun was O.K.'d by 57 per cent, as an adjective by 23 per cent, as a verb by 42 per cent and as an adverb by 20 per cent.

"Personality," in the sense of well-known person, squeezed through with 57 per cent. "Very common and bad," insisted William K. Zinsser, the humorous personality and critic. "Help stamp out 'personality'!"

Berton Roueché of The New Yorker was ready to send "senior citizen" into permanent retirement, but 47 per cent were not. "I'd as soon use 'underprivileged' for 'poor,'" he remarked, "or any other social-science Choctaw."

John Ciardi, the author, asserted that the use of "shall" was "pretentious" and that "will" was "the natural response of the American voice box."

"Hear, Hear!" cried 62 per cent.

A correct appraisal of the first person's role was crucial to the whole exercise. Said Dr. Asimov: "My own neologisms are perfectly acceptable. It is those of others to which I object."

Wallace Stegner, author, noted: "My objections, as well as my approvals, strike me as nearly totally irrational."

"You are still going strong," Sheridan Baker, professor of English at the University of Michigan, told the pollsters encouragingly. "Or is it strongly?"

3 / ARTICLES OF PROPAGANDA
AND OPINION

How to Detect Propaganda

Institute for Propaganda Analysis

> The Institute for Propaganda Analysis was a nonprofit, educational corporation, with headquarters in New York City, which from 1938 through 1942 issued pamphlets and articles of the sort printed below.

If American citizens are to have clear understanding of present-day conditions and what to do about them, they must be able to recognize propaganda, to analyze it, and to appraise it.

But what is propaganda?

As generally understood, *propaganda is expression of opinion or action by individuals or groups deliberately designed to influence opinions or actions of other individuals or groups with reference to predetermined ends.* Thus propaganda differs from scientific analysis. The propagandist is trying to "put something across," good or bad, whereas the scientist is trying to discover truth and fact. Often the propagandist does not want careful scrutiny and criticism; he wants to bring about a specific action. Because the action may be socially beneficial or socially harmful to millions of people,

HOW TO DETECT PROPAGANDA: From *Propaganda Analysis,* November 1937. Copyright 1937 by The Institute for Propaganda Analysis, Inc.

it is necessary to focus upon the propagandist and his activities the search-light of scientific scrutiny. Socially desirable propaganda will not suffer from such examination, but the opposite type will be detected and revealed for what it is.

We are fooled by propaganda chiefly because we don't recognize it when we see it. It may be fun to be fooled but, as the cigarette ads used to say, it is more fun to know. We can more easily recognize propaganda when we see it if we are familiar with the seven common propaganda devices. These are:

1. The Name Calling Device
2. The Glittering Generalities Device
3. The Transfer Device
4. The Testimonial Device
5. The Plain Folks Device
6. The Card Stacking Device
7. The Band Wagon Device

Why are we fooled by these devices? Because they appeal to our emotions rather than to our reason. They make us believe and do something we would not believe or do if we thought about it calmly, dispassionately. In examining these devices, note that they work most effectively at those times when we are too lazy to think for ourselves; also, they tie into emotions which sway us to be "for" or "against" nations, races, religions, ideals, economic and political policies and practices, and so on through automobiles, cigarettes, radios, toothpastes, presidents, and wars. With our emotions stirred, it may be fun to be fooled by these propaganda devices, but it is more fun and infinitely more to our own interests to know how they work.

Lincoln must have had in mind citizens who could balance their emotions with intelligence when he made his remark: "... but you can't fool all of the people all of the time."

NAME CALLING

"Name Calling" is a device to make us form a judgment without examining the evidence on which it should be based. Here the propagandist appeals to our hate and fear. He does this by giving "bad names" to those individuals, groups, nations, races, policies, practices, beliefs, and ideals which he would have us condemn and reject. For centuries the name "heretic" was bad. Thousands were oppressed, tortured, or put to death as heretics. Anybody who dissented from popular or group belief or practice was in danger of being called a heretic. In the light of today's knowledge, some heresies were bad and some were good. Many of the pioneers of modern science were called heretics; witness the cases of Copernicus, Galileo, Bruno. Today's bad names include: Fascist, demagogue, dictator, Red, financial oligarchy, Communist, muckraker, alien, outside agitator, economic royalist, Utopian, rabble-rouser, troublemaker, Tory, Constitution wrecker.

"Al" Smith called Roosevelt a Communist by implication when he said in his Liberty League speech, "There can be only one capital, Washington or Moscow." When "Al" Smith was running for the presidency many called him a tool of the Pope, saying in effect, "We must choose between Washington and Rome." That implied that Mr. Smith, if elected President, would take his orders from the Pope. Likewise Mr. Justice Hugo Black has been associated with a bad name, Ku Klux Klan. In these cases some propagandists have tried to make us form judgments without examining essential evidence and implications. "Al Smith is a Catholic. He must never be President." "Roosevelt is a Red. Defeat his program." "Hugo Black is or was a Klansman. Take him out of the Supreme Court."

Use of "bad names" without presentation of their essential meaning, without all their pertinent implications, comprises perhaps the most common of all propaganda devices. Those who want to *maintain* the status quo apply bad names to those who would change it. . . . Those who want to *change* the status quo apply bad names to those who would maintain it. For example, the *Daily Worker* and the *American Guardian* apply bad names to conservative Republicans and Democrats.

GLITTERING GENERALITIES

"Glittering Generalities" is a device by which the propagandist identifies his program with virtue by use of "virtue words." Here he appeals to our emotions of love, generosity, and brotherhood. He uses words like truth, freedom, honor, liberty, social justice, public service, the right to work, loyalty, progress, democracy, the American way, Constitution defender. These words suggest shining ideals. All persons of good will believe in these ideals. Hence the propagandist, by identifying his individual group, nation, race, policy, practice, or belief with such ideals, seeks to win us to his cause. As Name Calling is a device to make us form a judgment to *reject and condemn,* without examining the evidence, Glittering Generalities is a device to make us *accept and approve,* without examining the evidence.

For example, use of the phrases "the right to work" and "social justice" may be a device to make us accept programs for meeting labor-capital problems, which, if we examined them critically, we would not accept at all.

In the Name Calling and Glittering Generalities devices, words are used to stir up our emotions and to befog our thinking. In one device "bad words" are used to make us mad; in the other "good words" are used to make us glad.

The propagandist is most effective in the use of these devices when his words make us create devils to fight or gods to adore. By his use of the "bad words," we personify as a "devil" some nation, race, group, individual, policy, practice, or ideal; we are made fighting mad to destroy it. By use of "good words," we personify as a godlike idol some nation, race, group, etc. Words which are "bad" to some are "good" to others, or may be made so. Thus, to some the New Deal is "a prophecy of social salvation" while to others it is "an omen of social disaster."

From consideration of names, "bad" and "good," we pass to institutions and symbols, also "bad" and "good." We see these in the next device.

TRANSFER

"Transfer" is a device by which the propagandist carries over the authority, sanction, and prestige of something we respect and revere to something he would have us accept. For example, most of us respect and revere our church and our nation. If the propagandist succeeds in getting church or nation to approve a campaign in behalf of some program, he thereby transfers its authority, sanction, and prestige to that program. Thus we may accept something which otherwise we might reject.

In the Transfer device, symbols are constantly used. The cross represents the Christian Church. The flag represents the nation. Cartoons like Uncle Sam represent a consensus of public opinion. Those symbols stir emotions. At their very sight, with the speed of light, is aroused the whole complex of feelings we have with respect to church or nation. A cartoonist by having Uncle Sam disapprove a budget for unemployment relief would have us feel that the whole United States disapproves relief costs. By drawing an Uncle Sam who approves the same budget, the cartoonist would have us feel that the American people approve it. Thus the Transfer device is used both for and against causes and ideas.

TESTIMONIAL

The "Testimonial" is a device to make us accept anything from a patent medicine or a cigarette to a program of national policy. In this device the propagandist makes use of testimonials. "When I feel tired, I smoke a Camel and get the grandest 'lift.' " "We believe the John L. Lewis plan of labor organization is splendid; C.I.O. should be supported." This device works in reverse also; counter-testimonials may be employed. Seldom are these used against commercial products like patent medicines and cigarettes, but they are constantly employed in social, economic, and political issues. "We believe that the John L. Lewis plan of labor organization is bad; C.I.O. should not be supported."

PLAIN FOLKS

"Plain Folks" is a device used by politicians, labor leaders, businessmen, and even by ministers and educators to win our confidence by appearing to be people like ourselves—"just plain folks among the neighbors." In election years especially do candidates show their devotion to little children and the common, homey things of life. They have front porch campaigns. For the newspapermen they raid the kitchen cupboard, finding there some of the good wife's apple pie. They go to country picnics; they attend service at the old frame church; they pitch hay and go fishing; they show their belief in home and mother. In short, they would win our votes by showing that they're just as common as the rest of us—"just plain folks"—and, therefore, wise and good. Businessmen often are "plain folks" with the factory hands. Even distillers use the device. "It's our family's whiskey, neighbor; and neighbor, it's your price."

CARD STACKING

"Card Stacking" is a device in which the propagandist employs all the arts of deception to win our support for himself, his group, nation, race, policy, practice, belief, or ideal. He stacks the cards against the truth. He uses under-emphasis and over-emphasis to dodge issues and evade facts. He resorts to lies, censorship, and distortion. He omits facts. He offers false testimony. He creates a smoke screen of clamor by raising a new issue when he wants an embarrassing matter forgotten. He draws a red herring across the trail to confuse and divert those in quest of facts he does not want revealed. He makes the unreal appear real and the real appear unreal. He lets half-truth masquerade as truth. By the Card Stacking device, a mediocre candidate, through the "build-up," is made to appear an intellectual titan; an ordinary prize fighter, a probable world champion; a worthless patent medicine, a beneficent cure. By means of this device propagandists would convince us that a ruthless war of aggression is a crusade for righteousness. Some member nations of the Non-Intervention Committee send their troops to intervene in Spain. Card Stacking employs sham, hypocrisy, effrontery.

THE BAND WAGON

The "Band Wagon" is a device to make us follow the crowd, to accept the propagandist's program en masse. Here his theme is: "Everybody's doing it." His techniques range from those of medicine show to dramatic spectacle. He hires a hall, fills a great stadium, marches a million men in parade. He employs symbols, colors, music, movement, all the dramatic arts. He appeals to the desire, common to most of us, to "follow the crowd." Because he wants us to "follow the crowd" in masses, he directs his appeal to groups held together by common ties of nationality, religion, race, environment, sex, vocation. Thus propagandists campaigning for or against a program will appeal to us as Catholics, Protestants, or Jews; as members of the Nordic race or as Negroes; as farmers or as school teachers; as housewives or as miners. All the artifices of flattery are used to harness the fears and hatreds, prejudices, and biases, convictions and ideals common to the group; thus emotion is made to push and pull the group on to the Band Wagon. In newspaper article and in the spoken word this device is also found. "Don't throw your vote away. Vote for our candidate. He's sure to win." Nearly every candidate wins in every election—before the votes are in.

PROPAGANDA AND EMOTION

Observe that in all these devices our emotion is the stuff with which propagandists work. Without it they are helpless; with it, harnessing it to their purposes, they can make us glow with pride or burn with hatred, they can make us zealots in behalf of the program they espouse. As we said at the beginning, propaganda as generally understood is expression of opinion or action by individuals or groups with reference to predetermined ends. Without the appeal to our emotion—to our fears and to our courage, to our selfishness and unselfishness, to our loves and to our hates—propagandists would influence few opinions and few actions.

To say this is not to condemn emotion, an essential part of life, or to assert that all predetermined ends of propagandists are "bad." What we mean is that the intelligent citizen does not want propagandists to utilize his emotions, even to the attainment of "good" ends, without knowing what is going on. He does not want to be "used" in the attainment of ends he may later consider "bad." He does not want to be gullible. He does not want to be fooled. He does not want to be duped, even in a "good" cause. He wants to know the facts and among these is included the fact of the utilization of his emotions.[1]

Keeping in mind the seven common propaganda devices, turn to today's newspapers and almost immediately you can spot examples of them all. At election time or during any campaign, Plain Folks and Band Wagon are common. Card Stacking is hardest to detect because it is adroitly executed or because we lack the information necessary to nail the lie. A little practice with the daily newspapers in detecting these propaganda devices soon enables us to detect them elsewhere—in radio, news-reel, books, magazines, and in expressions of labor unions, business groups, churches, schools, political parties.

---

[1] For better understanding of the relationship between propaganda and emotion see Chapter One of *Folkways* by William Graham Sumner. This shows why most of us tend to feel, believe, and act in traditional patterns. See also *The Mind in the Making* by James Harvey Robinson. This reveals the nature of the mind and suggests how to analyze propaganda appealing to traditional thought patterns.

The Age of Overkill

Benjamin DeMott

> Benjamin DeMott (b. 1924), professor of English at Am-
> herst College, has written a column for *Harper's Maga-
> zine* and for *The American Scholar*. He has published
> two novels and has contributed many articles and es-
> says to various magazines on both sides of the Atlantic.
> "The Age of Overkill" originally appeared in the *New
> York Times Magazine* for May 19, 1968. The version
> printed below is from DeMott's recent collection of
> essays entitled *Supergrow* (1969).

he Spirit of Overkill was everywhere in this period. Drifting sluggishly
over the land from the international power struggle, a dense, polluting wave,
it penetrated the very marrow of the culture. Journalism, conversation,
manners, the arts—the innermost thoughts and feelings of men—all were
touched or tainted.

At first the influence appeared only in certain small changes of accent
and idiom, hints of the habitual irascibility to come. The emergence of
anger as the normal Anglo-American tone of voice was scarcely noticed.
But in the sequel the whole age was caught up in verbal ferocity, and at the
climax, in the late sixties, the fury turned compulsive. In speech and song,
poem and proclamation, fiercely, ceaselessly, a weird, inexplicable "assault"
was pressed—not at new "enemies" but at old ones already in tatters.
There was no breaking out of the mindless cycle of supertaunts; long after
the target institutions lay in lifeless ruin at their feet, men continued to
rain down abuse upon them, locked in the rage to rage. And at the end,
crazed by hatred that could find no standing object to destroy, they beat
and tore at themselves.

As might be guessed, the movement at its height was marked by epi-
sodes of uncommon vulgarity and tastelessness. One periodical of the
day—its motto was "Irreverence is our only sacred cow"—published a
"report" on President Lyndon Johnson's behavior on the Air Force plane
that bore him back to Washington from Dallas after the assassination of
President Kennedy; it asserted that the President, before taking the oath,
had mounted the casket and reached sexual climax in the throat wound of
his dead predecessor (*The Realist*, 1967). Another—a Methodist church

---

THE AGE OF OVERKILL: From the book *Supergrow: Essays and Reports on Imagination in
America* by Benjamin DeMott. Copyright © 1969 by Benjamin DeMott. Reprinted by per-
mission of E. P. Dutton & Co., Inc. Reprinted by permission of Harold Ober Associates
Incorporated.

magazine, which lusted, like the secular organs of the time, after new modes of mockery—another invented a news-story framework for the nineteenth-century Nietzschean cry that "God is dead," and "quoted" the reactions of the crude and witless great to the "item." The Pope: ". . . it is difficult to imagine how we shall proceed without Him." DeGaulle: "God is dead! Long live France!" President Truman: "I'm always sorry to hear somebody is dead. It's a damn shame." President Eisenhower: "He will be missed" (*Motive*, 1966).

More interesting than the vulgarity at full tide, however, was the power of Overkill throughout its span to draw together ill-sorted minds. The decade's steady hounding of people "over thirty" was led, for the most part, by public entertainers, "rock groups," and the like. Beatle Harrison spoke against "all these old fools who are governing us and . . . bombing us and doin' all that. . . ." Stone Jagger laid it down: "Politics, like the legal system, is dominated by old men. Old men who are also bugged by religion." Leary of Milbrook, a guru, told undergraduates at Yale: "Your legislators, your President, and your Defense Department are for the most part impotent old men who are riding on youth. They don't want you to be free. Laws are made by old people who don't want young people to do exactly those things young people were meant to do—to make love, turn on, and have a good time"(*Friday*, 1968).

But in the very season that Stones and Beatles and gurus were thus baying the aged, a respected Nobel Prize winner himself elected to run with the pack. At the time I did my best work, said Dr. James Watson to an undergraduate audience of hundreds at Harvard (the time was the spring of 1968), "I thought of people over forty as at the end of their lives . . . and that was the right attitude to take—not too much reverence for the big boys. If they knew what to do, they'd be doing it."

And Professor Watson was but one of hundreds of distinguished figures from the world of mind who lent weight to the Overkill cause. From the first, indeed, that cause was a favorite with artists as well as intellectuals. James Baldwin, the novelist and essayist, spoke authentic Overkill whenever he appeared in public. (The author of *Another Country* was given to describing his country as "the Fourth Reich": *New York Times*, 1968.) Susan Sontag, a writer well known in that day, was no less fiercely ignorant in her essays on history and race: "The white race is the cancer of history," she said flatly. "It is the white race and it alone—its ideologies and inventions—which eradicates autonomous civilization wherever it spreads, which has upset the ecological balance of the planet, which now threatens the very existence of life itself" (*Partisan Review*, 1967).

Given leadership of this order, youth inevitably responded with explosions of its own—student editorials calling for guerrilla bands to roar through "college campuses burning books, burning degrees and exams, burning school records, busting up classrooms, and freeing our brothers from the prison of the university . . ." The Berkeley *Barb* continued: "The universities cannot be reformed. They must be abandoned or closed down. They should be used as bases for actions against society, but never taken seriously. The professors have nothing to teach. . . . We can learn more from any jail than we can from any university." And the result was, to repeat, that by the end of the sixties the entire articulate Anglo-American community—young, middle-aged, and aged people alike—was transformed into a monster-chorus of damnation-dealers, its single voice pitched ever at hysterical level, its prime aim to transform every form of discourse into a blast.

There were Overkill aphorisms in that period ("The world belongs to politics, which is to say the world belongs to death": Theodore Roszak), and Overkill definitions ("The family is the American fascism": Paul Goodman). There were Overkill toppers, comebacks, and sneers. (When a television interviewer in England told the novelist Mary McCarthy that she appeared to be "accusing [the American] people of stupidity, not wickedness," the author stoutly replied, "I think they are wicked, too.") There were Overkill critical assessments (Thomas Wolfe was a "professional hillbilly": Alfred Kazin), and Overkill letters to the editor, especially in the Manhattan weeklies of the day. "We are rats in a laboratory maze," the letter writers regularly wrote in. "The Government is feeding us frustration, bringing us to the verge of madness." (Replies to these letters were themselves similarly tinged. One columnist for a suburban paper called *Newsday* answered his mail by stamping the letters with an obscenity—special oversized rubber stamp—and returning them straight to their senders.) There was Overkill in public speaking, sometimes in rhetorical questions ("You call yourselves revolutionaries?" shouted Rap Brown. "How many white folks you killed today?"), sometimes in hymns of praise ("All the people at the Pentagon!" shouted the poet Allen Ginsberg, honoring the turned-on tastes of a group of peace marchers. "They were all heads!"), sometimes in historical analogies ("Reading a speech of Andrew Jackson's . . . the other day," said Robert Bly, declining a prize at the 1968 National Book Awards, "I realized he was the Westmoreland of 1830").

And there were reams—floods—oceans of Overkill poetry. New chants were reported in newspapers. ("Dean Rusk is a murderer!" shouted four hundred in unison outside a West Coast hotel.) Simple Overkill refrains were "socko" Off Broadway. ("The middle class/Are just like pigs . . . The middle class/Are just like pigs": Jacques Brel.) Old-style blues underwent sea changes: "My Baby Done Left Me and I Feel Like Homemade Shit": The Fugs.

And prose poems of immeasurable putridity took art straight to its borders—witness the garbage epic by a Mrs. Hentoff, columnist for a paper called *The Village Voice*. The theme of the work—New York *as* garbage—was a response to a lengthy strike by city garbage collectors early in 1968. The opening strains sang softly and with satisfaction of Manhattan sans sanitation. (". . . almost as if [the city] had become what we knew it was all along. There was garbage on the sidewalks, garbage in the gutters, garbage lining the walls of buildings, garbage blowing in the wind . . .") Then, to a moving ripe air, the voice rose in a plea that the strike never be ended, that it go "on and on until the garbage fill[s] the canyons and the rats leap from mound to mound." And finally, at the close, a gentle self-loving cadence celebrated the poet's "truthful image" of the town.[1]

Contemporary observers who maintained critical detachment from the new fashion, and sought to define its relations with the past, turned up several notions that still possess interest. One writer theorized that Overkill was an extension of the American tall-tale tradition. Another traced its genesis to the post-nineteenth-century expansion of literacy and general education, developments that intensified a threat to the elite. (According to this view, men who considered themselves to belong to the elite were obliged to speak and write in extravagant terms in order to establish their position. In ages of limited literacy, this was unnecessary; a man possessing the ability to order his thoughts cogently on paper was an aristocrat by virtue of that ability. But once cogency was brought within Everyman's reach, it ceased to be a distinction: wildness had to come in.)

Still other theorists sought to connect the advent of Overkill with the new educational theories of the time. "Think," wrote one observer, "think of the uphill fifty-year struggle waged by educators on behalf of 'immediacy' and 'relevance' as against knowledge and the sense of the past. Is no measure of credit owing here? Suppose for a moment that, in place of new-style utter nowsense, children were still immersed in the dreary stuff of history: could the thrust of a story of Western Civilization like Miss Sontag's [see above] ever then have been felt?"

But though a few contemporary theses or "explanations" retain an edge of usefulness, most were error-strewn. It was usual, for instance, to date abuse-escalation in the late sixties, coincident with the Southeast Asian wars, and to ignore the embryonic states, as well as sudden prophetic outbursts like Lord Russell's against Macmillan and Kennedy:

> We used to call Hitler wicked for killing off the Jews, but Kennedy and Macmillan are much more wicked than Hitler. . . . We cannot obey these murderers. They are wicked. They are abominable. They are the wickedest people who ever lived in the history of man and it is our duty to do what we can against them.[2]

---

[1] Another Overkill salute, by an American poet, to New York filth can be found in the Russian poet Yevgeny Yevtushenko's poem "Smog," which detailed a trip to America in the 1960s. Yevtushenko quoted Robert Lowell as having explained city soot as "a vengeance from heaven for depravity and moral collapse." It is worth nothing, perhaps, as a curiosity, that the Russian poet appears to have picked up a taste for Overkill idiom during the trip in question. In the same poem he saw a likeness between his accommodations at the Chelsea Hotel on Eighth Avenue and Twenty-third Street and a concentration camp. ("In the cell-like room," he wrote, "there is a smell of Dachau.")

[2] In 1961. Lord Russell's name is another reminder of a point worth stressing: many foreigners learned to speak Overkill with ease. Not least notable of them was Fidel Castro, who produced much classic work—including a jibe (at the 1968 International Cultural Congress at Havana) at population-control programs. Such programs, the Cuban premier asserted, were proof of "imperialism's lack of faith in the future."

Again: a standard practice was to associate verbal extravagance and apocalyptic expression primarily with the political left—new militants, student activists, Filthy Speech chiefs, and the rest. It was an understandable mistake: many public events that attracted notice were reported in ways that nourished acceptance of the equation. A writer for *The New Yorker* magazine attending a young people's political convention in Chicago in 1967 observed that, for a whole week, the word *revolution* was used "for every nuance of dissent."

Yet even so it must remain mystifying that, on the basis of slim evidence like this, men could conclude that Overkill was an identifying mark of the left. Before Berkeley there were the so-called Birchers, radical rightists apt at every form of verbal excess. ("The whole country is one vast insane asylum and they're letting the worst patients run the place": Robert Welch, founder of the Birch Society.) And could it really have been believed that, say, Norman Mailer (another writer well regarded in this period) on the American narcosis was in any significant sense different from the 1967 Christian Crusade's Dean Noebel, who held forth as follows on the "Commie-Beatle Pact"? ". . . the Communists have contrived an elaborate, calculating and scientific technique directed at rendering a generation of American youth useless through nerve-jamming, mental deterioration and retardation. . . . The destructive music of the Beatles . . . reinforces . . . mental breakdown. . . ."

The truth that should have been plain even then was that Overkill was larger than politics: Overkill masters cared far more for style than for views. The issue of *The Realist* that carried the report on the behavior of President Johnson also contained an account—equally slanderous—of President Kennedy as a client of Dallas call girls. And there was the celebrated Kopkind case, involving a correspondent in Washington for an English leftist weekly. Though yielding to no man in his detestation of President Johnson, the correspondent Kopkind was haunted (apparently) by an even deeper passion—that for Overkill—and he spoke the tongue continually, even when no one hateful was by. ("Senator [Eugene] McCarthy is one of the Senate's few intellectuals," wrote this pundit, "and . . . one of its most obvious hypocrites: the two go hand in hand.")

And if the movement was larger than politics, it was also—dare we say?—more complex than the conventional wisdom of our own day even yet allows. "Despondent over their inability to alter the course of national affairs, men turned in helpless fury to a vocabulary of imprecation which they themselves knew to be useless, but that at least permitted an expression of agony, of fierce frustration, of certainty that apocalypse was near." Here is the genetic thesis in favor just now; it is attractive, and when pressed in connection with certain literary heroes of that time—rare men whose integrity matched their intensity—it may be held to contain a piece of the truth.

But surely we oversimplify if we consider impotence to be the single key. The route to satisfactory accounts of broad cultural movements passes invariably through thickets of complication. And in travelling that path, there is some point always in attending to primary meanings. In the time of which we speak, the term *Overkill* referred to surplus obliterative power—mega-weapons capable of killing ten times the human population and turning the earth to ashes thrice. And implicit in the surplus, as in certain usages of the word, was the assumption that lives destroyed still await destruction and are thus in some inexpressible sense unreal. (A man's third death can be counted as well as his first.) Putting it another way: When obliterative power is adjusted to the sum of the obliterable, that adjustment constitutes an acknowledgement of the reality of existence. But when there is no such adjustment, when men ignore the sum of the obliterable, when men manufacture destruction beyond what is "needed," it is a sign of a weakened sense of the hard, substantial, objective world.

And precisely that weakness figured, as we must now recognize, in Overkill as a *cultural* phenomenon. It is in fact possible that this element alone—the loss of belief in a substantive outer reality—separated the Overkillers of the sixties from premodern titans of abuse. The heroic scorners of earlier times—Dante on to Swift—had no more energy of contempt than late twentieth-century man. But they did have a far stronger conviction that beyond them lay living targets, villains whose substance words could touch and wound. ("Vilify! Vilify!" went Beaumarchais's famous aphorism. "At least some of the dirt *will stick*.") Even the cooler arguefiers of the pre-Overkill past dwelt on the substantiality of the world inhabited by their enemies, and upon the necessity of imaginatively penetrating that world in order to hurt. William James, for one, never tired of quoting a contemporary who insisted that the first duty of men with the pacifist conscience was to "enter the point of view of the militarist and seek to move the point." Everywhere in former days the clearly held assumption was that the "opponent" did exist.

But in the sixties—to say once again—a frail sense of outer reality had become the rule: a disbelief in counterunderstandings of events that pit themselves over against mine. The disbelief showed itself not only in Overkill spectaculars—the notorious fits of fury that plucked out eyes from severed heads. It appeared also in the frequency of theatrical metaphor in Overkill masters' chat. All England is an empty music hall, cried the playwright John Osborne, as the curtain rose on the Overkill age. "On the Vietnam stage," said the editor of the *New Statesman* at the end of the decade, "the West enacts a travesty of itself, spoken in Newspeak, performed by fake heroes and real buffoons. . . ." And these writers only echoed the common American line. "The stars of Vietnam," wrote a critic on *The Village Voice,* "are LBJ and Ho, Westmoreland and Giap . . . they are all playing the parts. . . . Senator Eugene McCarthy, waiting in the wings for a piece of scenery to fall on the actor he is understudying . . . Senator Robert F. Kennedy . . . in his dressing room . . . this multi-billion dollar superproduction . . ." Ceaselessly the Voice of Overkill chanted to itself that there was nothing substantial Out There. The bad men were shadows, not substances; mere actors, figures in shows, not penetrable, imaginable bodies, not men who thought and felt their way into their mistakes. The likelihood is, in sum, that the Overkill phenomenon is best thought of as part of a seamless cultural whole embracing even the astrophysics of that day— that incredible world view wherein, as one critical contemporary (Hannah Arendt) wrote, "instead of objective qualities . . . we find instruments, and instead of nature or the universe . . . [the investigator] encounters only himself."

But, as must be added, the latter is of course only "a likelihood"— not a certainty. The historian's voice speaks confidently, bent on establishing once more that no corridor of the past is beyond reach, no puzzle beyond solution. But questions nag. Mysteries remain. The age we study was not, after all, composed of innocents. Scholars then were no less aware than ourselves that in periods of strife violence is done upon language. Then, as now, sober heads could read Thucydides on the confusions of meaning and the transformation of terms during social upheavals. (During the Corcyrean Revolution, said the great man, "reckless audacity became courage . . . prudent hesitation, specious cowardice, ability to see all sides of a question, inaptness to act on any. Frantic violence became the attribute of manliness; safe plotting, a justifiable means of self-defense.") And there were writers closer to the sixties in time—the Englishman Orwell, for one—who insisted on the obligation of men of mind to guard against pollution of meaning traceable either to political flatulence or intensity.

Yet in the sixties men of mind were heedless. Why so? Can any of our confidently advanced explanations finally tell us much? What were the sacred texts that misled thinkers in that day? Was it that they believed, perhaps, with the aesthete Cyril Connolly, that henceforth there would be no more means of judging a man save by "the quality of his despair"? Did they therefore drive themselves into fury because fury—however abstract, frustrating, unfocused—seemed a possible substitute for moral clarity and worth? Or are we simply to conclude that verbal dementia was only the other side of the coin of physical violence—a mere necessitous counterpart to assassination, riot, arson?

If we cannot know the answers—history has cunning passages—we can at least pause to ponder our ignorance. And it will not be amiss if, as we do so, we turn again, with a freshly grateful eye, to those never sufficiently praised architects of the Great Disengagement at the century's end. But for their genius, their determination to negotiate a defusing of The Words as well as of The Bombs, what would our future now be? Who among us, reader or writer, can doubt—given the truth of what nearly happened in the sixties—that it is to their decision to lay down the lash of language that we today owe the breath of our life?

Conflict of Generations

Lewis S. Feuer

Lewis S. Feuer (b. 1912) is a professor of sociology at the University of Toronto. Some of his books are *Psychoanalysis and Ethics* (1955), *Spinoza and the Rise of Liberalism* (1958), and *The Scientific Intellectual* (1963). "Conflict of Generations" is adapted from Chapters 1 and 10 of a book by the same title, published in 1969.

"As David wept for Absalom, many later generations were to weep for their sons. If the fathers were forbidden to send their children into the fires of Moloch, the children sometimes seemed to seek the flames themselves in obedience to a demon within."

Generational conflict, generational struggle, has been a universal theme of history. Unlike class struggle, however, the struggle of generations has been little studied and little understood. Labor movements have a continuous and intelligible history. Student movements, by contrast, have a fitful and transient character, and even seem lacking in the substantial dignity which a subject of political sociology should have. The student status, unlike that of the workingman, is temporary; a few brief years, and the quantum-like experience in the student movement is over. Nevertheless, the history of our contemporary world has been basically affected by student movements. Social revolutions in Russia, China, and Burma sprang from student movements, while governments in Korea, Japan, and the Sudan have fallen in recent years largely because of massive student protest. Here, then, is a recurrent phenomenon of modern times which challenges our understanding.

Generational struggle demands categories of understanding unlike those of the class struggle. Student movements are born of vague, undefined emotions which seek for some issue, some cause, to which to attach themselves. A complex of urges—altruism, idealism, revolt, self-sacrifice, and self-destruction—searches the social order for a strategic avenue of expression. Labor movements have never had to search for issues in the way stu-

CONFLICT OF GENERATIONS: This article is adapted from Chapters 1 and 10 of *The Conflict of Generations* by Lewis S. Feuer, © 1969 by Lewis S. Feuer, Basic Books, Inc., Publishers, New York. Copyright 1969 by Saturday Review, Inc. Reprinted by permission of Heinemann Educational Books Ltd.

dent movements do. The wage demands and the specific grievances of work-ingmen are born directly of their conditions of life. But the conflict of generations derives from deep, unconscious sources, and the outlook and philosophy of student movements are rarely materialistic. If labor seeks to better its living conditions as directly as possible, student movements sacrifice their own economic interests for the sake of a vision of a nobler life for the lowliest. If historical materialism is the ideology of the working class, then historical idealism is the ideology of student movements. If "exploitation" is the master term for defining class conflict, then "alienation" does similar service for the conflict of generations.

We may define a student movement as a congregation of students inspired by aims which they try to explicate in a political ideology, and moved by an emotional rebellion in which there is always present a disillusionment with and rejection of the values of the older generation. Moreover, the members of a student movement have the conviction that their generation has a special historical mission to fulfill where the older generation, other elites, and other classes have failed.

To their own consciousness, students in student movements have been the bearers of a higher ethic than the surrounding society. Certainly they are at odds with the "social system." As Walter Weyl said: "Adolescence is the true day for revolt, the day when obscure forces, as mysterious as growth, push us, trembling, out of our narrow lives into the wide throbbing life beyond self." No society altogether succeeds in molding the various psychological types which comprise it to conform to its material, economic requirements. If there were a genuine correspondence between the material economic base and the psychological superstructure, then societies would be static, and basic social change would not take place. In every society, those psychological types and motivations which the society suppresses become the searching agents of social change. Thus psycho-ethical motives, which are not only independent of the socioeconomic base but actually contrary to the economic ethics that the social system requires, become primary historical forces.

The Russian revolutionary student movement is the classic case of the historic workings of the ethical consciousness. When in the 1860s and 1870s several thousand student youth, inspired by feelings of guilt and responsibility for the backward people, embarked on their "back-to-the-people" movement, it was a collective act of selfless idealism.

The students' ethical consciousness was utterly independent of class interests and class position. The largest single group among those who were arrested in the back-to-the-people movement from 1873 to 1877 were children of the nobility. They could have availed themselves of the ample openings in the governmental bureaucracy. Instead, many of them chose a path of self-sacrifice and suffering. Rebuffed by the peasants, the revolutionary student youth later gave themselves to the most extreme form of individual terrorism. And when terrorism failed to produce the desired social change, circles of student intellectuals provided the first nuclei of the Social Democratic party. Lenin aptly said that the intellectuals brought a socialist consciousness to the workers, who by themselves would not have gone beyond trade union aspirations. The intellectuals Lenin referred to were indeed largely the self-sacrificing revolutionary students.

The universal themes of generational revolt, which cut across all societies, produced in Russia a "conflict of generations" of unparalleled intensity because of special social circumstances. The Russian students lived their external lives in a social reality which was absolutist, politically tyrannical, and culturally backward; internally, on the other hand, they lived in a milieu imbued with Western cultural values. Their philosophical and idealistic aims transcended the social system, and were out of keeping with it. The Government opened universities to provide recruits for its bureaucracy. Some students followed the appointed path, but the universities became the centers not only for bureaucratic education but for revolutionary dedication. The idealistic student as a psychological type rebelled against the specifications of the social system.

The civil rights movement in the United States has likewise owed much to students as the bearers of an ethical vocation in history. A wave of sit-ins which spread through Negro college towns began in February 1, 1960, when four freshmen from the all-Negro Agricultural and Technical College at Greensboro, North Carolina, sat down at the lunch counter of the local Woolworth dime store. The surrounding community was puzzled that it was precisely the best educated, the most disciplined and cultured—and essentially middle-class—Negro students who took the self-sacrificing initiative. In the next years came movements which resembled even more the "back-to-the-people" movement of the Russian studentry. The freedom riders of 1961, the several hundred white students in the Mississippi summer project of 1964 risking their lives to establish freedom schools among the Negroes, were descendants in spirit of the Russian students of the preceding century.

Nonetheless, the duality of motivation which has spurred student movements has always borne its duality of consequence. On the one hand, student movements during the past 150 years have been the bearers of a higher ethic for social reconstruction, of altruism, and of generous emotion. On the other hand, with all the uniformity of a sociological law, they have imposed on the political process a choice of means that are destructive both of self and of the goals which presumably were sought. Suicidalism and terrorism have both been invariably present in student movements. A youth-weighted rate of suicide is indeed characteristic of all countries in which large-scale revolutionary student movements are found. In what we might call a "normal" country or one in which there is a "generational equilibrium," suicide, as Louis Dublin said, "is much more prevalent in advanced years than during youth." But a "normal" country is one without a revolutionary student movement. Where such movements have existed, where countries are thus characterized by a severe conflict of generations, the rate of suicide has been highest for the youthful group. Nihilism has tended to become the philosophy of student movements not only because it constitutes a negative critique of society but because it is also a self-critique moved by an impulse toward self-annihilation.

Every historical era tends to have its own most significant choices, but the double-edged choice which confronts student movements is perhaps best expressed in the title of an essay by Ivan Turgenev, *Hamlet and Don Quixote,* written as the Russian student movement was being born. For Hamlet, with his negation, destructive doubt, and intellect turned against himself, was indeed the suicidal pole in the Russian student character, whereas Don Quixote, with his undoubting devotion to an ideal, his readiness to fight for the oppressed and to pit himself against all social institutions, represented the messianic, back-to-the-people component. The Russian student activist, like his successor, oscillated between these polar impulses; rejected by the people, he would often find in terrorism a sort of synthesis, for thereby he could assail a social institution in a personalized form and hurl against it all the aggressive passions which menaced himself. Don Quixote thus became a student terrorist. When his ventures in terror miscarried, his passions turned against himself; in the last act, he was Hamlet destroying himself. Yet Turgenev believed that if there were no more Don Quixotes the book of history would be closed.

A student movement thus is founded upon a coalescence of several themes and conditions. It tends to arise in societies which are gerontocratic—that is, where the older generation possesses a disproportionate amount of economic and political power and social status. Where the influences of religion, ideology, and the family are especially designed to strengthen the rule of the old, an uprising of the young will be most apt to occur. A gerontocratic order, however, is not a sufficient condition for the rise of a student movement. Among other factors, there must also be a feeling that the older generation has failed. We may call this experience the process of the "de-authoritization" of the old. A student movement will not arise unless there is a sense that the older generation has discredited itself and lost its moral standing. The Japanese student movement which arose after the Second World War was based on the emotional trauma which the young students had experienced in the defeat of their country. Traditional authority was discredited as it never had been before; their fathers, elders, teachers, and rulers were revealed as having deceived and misled them. Japan in 1960 was far more technologically advanced than it had been in the Twenties, and also far more democratic. Yet because in 1960 the psychological hegemony of the older generation was undermined, there arose a large student movement where there had been none previously.

A student movement, moreover, tends to arise where political apathy or a sense of helplessness prevails among the people. The young feel that the political initiative is theirs, especially in countries where the people are illiterate. The educated man has an inordinate prestige in a society of illiterates. Throughout human history, whenever people of a society have been overwhelmingly illiterate and voiceless, the intellectual elite has been the sole rival of the military elite for political power.

This brings us to what is most significant for the theory of social change— namely, the consequences of the superimposition of a student movement on a nationalistic, peasant, or labor movement. Every student movement tries to attach itself to a "carrier" movement of much more major proportions— such as a peasant, labor, nationalist, racial, or anti-colonial movement. We may call the latter the "carrier" movements, analogous to the harmonic waves superimposed on the carrier wave in physics. But the superimposition of waves of social movements differs in one basic respect from that of physical movements. The student movement gives a new qualitative character and direction to social change. It imparts to the carrier movement a quality of emotion, dualities of feeling, which would otherwise have been lacking. Emotions issuing from the students' unconscious, and deriving from the conflict of generations, impose or attach themselves to the underlying political carrier movement, and channel it in strange directions. Given a set of alternative paths—rational or irrational—for realizing a social goal, the direction of a student movement will tend toward the most irrational means to achieve the end.

In the case of the Russian student movement, it was the opinion of the most distinguished anarchist, Peter Kropotkin, that "the promulgation of a constitution was extremely near at hand during the last few months of the life of Alexander II." Kropotkin greatly admired the idealism of the Russian students, yet he felt their intervention had been part of an almost accidental chain of circumstances that had defeated Russia's hopes. Bernard Pares, the historian, who had witnessed the masochist terrorist characteristics of the Russian students at first hand, wrote: "The bomb that killed Alexander II put an end to the faint beginnings of Russian constitutionalism." A half-hour before the Czar set out on his last journey on March 1, 1881, he approved the text of a decree announcing the establishment of a commission likely to lead to the writing of a constitution. Instead, the students' act of Czar-killing and self-killing brought into Russian politics all the psychological overtones of sons destroying their fathers; their dramatic idealism projected on a national political scale the emotional pattern of "totem and taboo," the revolt and guilt of the primal sons Freud described.

Student revolutionary leaders made their debut in world literature in the novel *Les Miserables* by Victor Hugo. The traits of the student activist, this new psychological type, were delineated there for all time. With a few changes, the characters of the Parisian student movement of the 1830s are identical with those of the Russian movement of the 1890s, the Chinese movement of 1917, and the Berkeley movement of 1964. The psychological types in history are universal; in diverse eras the same cast of characters acts out eternal human drives. Thus Victor Hugo describes the student revolutionary activists in their secret circle, the Friends of A.B.C.:

> It was a secret society, in a state of embryo, and we might almost call it a coterie, if coteries produced heroes ... Most of the Friends of the A.B.C. were students who maintained a cordial understanding with a few workmen. . . . These young men formed a species of family through their friendship. . . .
>
> [Their leader, Enjolras, twenty-two years old, the scion of a wealthy family] was angelically beautiful, and looked like a stern Antinous. You might have fancied that he had gone through the revolutionary apocalypse in some previous existence. He knew the traditions of it like an eyewitness. . . . He was of a pontifical and warlike nature, strange in a young man; he was a churchman and a militant; from the immediate point of view a soldier of democracy, but, above the contemporary movement, a priest of the ideal ... He was serious, and did not appear to know that there was on the earth a being called woman. He had only one passion, justice, and only one thought, overthrowing the obstacle. On the Mons Arentinus, he would have been Gracchus; in the Convention, he would have been Saint-Just ... He was severe in his pleasures, and before all that was not the Republic he chastely lowered his eyes ...

Saint-Just, the *enfant terrible* of the French Revolution, was indeed, as Victor Hugo perceived, the precursor of the revolutionary student leaders. Twenty-four years old in 1793, the youngest man in the Convention, he overawed it as "an idea energized by a passion," deporting himself as one above humanity. Only a short time earlier, he had run away to Paris with his mother's silver and written an epic of pornopolitics, the *Organt,* in twenty cantos, which interspersed its critique of kings and priests with long scenes of passion, "the raping of nuns, and discourses on the right to pleasure." The university students at Rheims, where he studied law, were drawn to the character and leadership of Saint-Just, and took him as their hero. He evidently had a passion for equality, the back-to-the-people spirit of the student activist, and was said to walk the roads in all weathers to bring help to needy families.

Young Saint-Just had the austerity of death-seeking. "I am going to get myself killed," he said as he left Paris for the armies, and he voiced his sense of alienation: "The man who is compelled to isolate himself from his fellow-beings, and even from his own thoughts, finds anchorage in time to be." A skeptic at twenty, an idealist at twenty-two, an executioner at twenty-five—and himself executed the next year—the student leader Saint-Just, who declared, *"Formons la cité"* ("Let us found the city"), became instead the symbol for inflexible terrorist dictatorship.

From the combination of youth, intellectuality, and altruistic emotion, arise certain further basic traits of student movements. In the first place, a student movement, unlike a labor movement, has at its inception only a vague sense of its immediate goals. It emerges from a diffused feeling of opposition to things as they are. It is revolutionary in emotion to begin with, and because its driving energy stems largely from unconscious sources, it has trouble defining what it wants. A Japanese student leader of many years' standing, Shigeo Shima, remarked: "One cannot understand the student movement if one tries to understand it in terms of the labor movement. The strength of the student movement lies in its energy of consciousness trying to determine existence, instead of the other way around." An intellectual has been defined as a person whose consciousness determines his existence; in the case of the young intellectuals of a student movement, we might add that their ideological consciousness is founded on the emotional unconscious of generational revolt.

To the young student of a backward country whose mind is filled with the most advanced ideas, there is a heightened sense of the contradictions, the unfitness of things. In the stagnant world of Russia after the Decembrist defeat of 1825, Alexander Herzen wrote, "children were the first to raise their heads." Around them was a people, "frightened, weak, distracted" with its bureaucracy of "cringing officials." Not so the children. What impressed them was the complete *contradiction* of the words they were taught with the facts of life around them. Their teachers, their books, their *university* spoke one language and that language was intelligible to heart and mind. Their father and mother, their relations and all their surroundings spoke another with which neither mind nor heart was in agreement—but with which the dominant authorities and financial interests were in accord.

This contradiction between education and ordinary life nowhere reached such proportions as among the nobility of Russia. It is important to bear in mind that the culture of the student movements, of the intellectual elite, is the one genuinely international culture. Students at any given time throughout the world tend to read the same books. We might call this the law of the universality of ideas, or the law of universal intellectual fashions, or the maximum rate of diffusion for intellectual culture. At any rate, the Chinese students of 1917, like their counterparts in America and Britain, were reading Bertrand Russell, John Dewey, and later Lenin and Marx; earlier they had read Ibsen, Tolstoy, and Spencer. Kwame Nkrumah as a university student in America and Britain studied Marx and logical positivism; Jomo Kenyatta sank himself in the writings of Marx and Malinowski. Today in Africa the young students, like their fellows in France, the United States, and Japan, read Marx, Camus, and the existentialist writers. In the Soviet Union, young university students try to find copies of Camus and Freud, and, overcoming the obstacles imposed by the Government against the free flow of books and ideas, have succeeded in maintaining a bond with the world intellectual community.

In this sphere of the intellect, historical materialism is clearly invalid, for the mode of production of the given society does not determine its mode of reading. Whatever the economic conditions, no matter how they vary from country to country, intellectuals tend to adopt the same ideas everywhere. In this sense, ideas resemble fashions: like the dress designs set in Paris, they diffuse rapidly throughout the rest of the world. Thus, an international intellectual culture arises, and a world-wide community of intellectuals. The aftermath of World War I set Japanese students reading the socialistic works of Bernard Shaw and Henri Barbusse. The Thirties brought Eliot, Hemingway, and Steinbeck; and after the Second World War, Camus, Sartre, Beauvoir, Arthur Miller, Norman Mailer, and Graham Greene. The intellectual is what he reads, and in all societies his world of books, with its moral imperatives, has seemed more real to him than the world of men.

Every student movement, however, also has a populist ingredient. A student movement always looks for some lowly oppressed class with which to identify psychologically. Whether it be to the peasantry, the proletariat, or the Negro, the students have a tremendous need to offer themselves in a self-sacrificial way, to seek out an exploited group on whose behalf their sacrifices will be made. Conceiving of themselves as deceived, exploited sons, they feel a kinship with the deceived and exploited of society as a whole.

The Russian revolutionary student movement—the classical case— was periodically returning to the people, first the peasantry, later the proletariat, beginning in the 1860s with Herzen's cry, *"V narod!"* ("To the people!"). This Populist stage answers that vague emotional need for identification which is felt in advance of any political ideology. The identification with the people assuages the students' own sense of guilt. For theirs is then not simply a generational uprising, a rebellion against the fathers, but a movement on behalf of the people sanctified by the very ethic which the fathers themselves have professed but betrayed. The people, the proletariat, the peasantry, become a kind of projective alternative conscience which supersedes the fathers. Moreover, they are a source of untold physical strength still untapped, and they give to the young student intellectuals a feeling of being close to the physical sources of life. The students by themselves feel too weak to alter the structure of a society ruled by the older generation. Perhaps, in the psychoanalytical metaphor, this identification with a lower class assuages the castrational fears aroused by the students' revolt against their fathers.

The populist and elitist moods in student movements can merge into a morbid self-destructive masochism, as they did, for instance, among the Russian students. The burden of guilt which a generation in revolt takes upon itself is immense, and it issues in perverse, and grotesque ways. Nevertheless, something would be lost in our understanding of student movements if we were to see in them solely a chapter of history written on an abnormal theme. For student movements, let us remember, are the most sincerely selfless and altruistic which the world has seen. A student is a person who, midway between childhood and maturity, is imbibing the highest ideals and hopes of the human cultural heritage; moreover, he lives in comradeship with his fellow-students, usually the last communal fellowship he will experience. The student feels that he will then enter into a maelstrom of competitive and bureaucratic pseudo-existence; he has a foreboding that he will become alienated from the self he now is. Articulate by education, he voices his protest. No edict in the world can control a classroom. It is everywhere the last free forum of mankind. Students meet together necessarily, think together, laugh together, and share a common animus against the authorities.

Curiously, generational consciousness was not clearly recognized as a mainspring of social change in modern times until the first stirrings of the Russian student movement. It was in Russia that men became dated by their generations; one was a man of the "Forties," the "Sixties," the "Eighties." Rudin, in Turgenev's novel of that name, as Kropotkin says "was a man of the 'forties,' nurtured upon Hegel's philosophy, and developed under the conditions which prevailed under Nicholas I, when there was no possibility whatever for a thinking man to apply his energy, unless he chose to become an obedient functionary of an autocratic, slave-owning state."

Often a generation's consciousness is shaped by the experience of what we might call the "generational event." To the Chinese Communist students of the early Thirties, for instance, the "Long March" with Mao Tse-tung was what one writer called their "unifying event." More than class origin, such a historical experience impresses itself on the consciousness of a student movement. The Depression, the struggle against fascism, the ordeals of the civil rights agitation—all these were generational events, they marked a generation in its coming of age.

But the character of the historical experience was most important. What keeps generational consciousness most intense is the sense of generational martyrdom, the experience of seeing one's fellow-students assaulted, killed, imprisoned, by armed deputies of the elder generation. Whether in Russian, Chinese, or Latin American universities, or at Berkeley, the actual physical clash made students frenzied with indignation. The youthful adolescent resents the elders' violence, especially for its assault upon his new manhood. Student movements make of their martyrs the high symbols of a common identity. The Iranian Students' Association, for example, published a leaflet in their exile to commemorate "Student Day" for three of their comrades. Its language was that of the martyrology of generational consciousness:

> The three students died but their memory and their heroic sacrifice will forever remain with us to guide the student movement of Iran. To honor their memories and to rededicate ourselves to the cause for which they gave their lives, this day will always be honored. . . .

Every student movement has cherished similar memories of brothers whom their fathers destroyed.

The generational struggle in politics, as a universal theme in human history, was naturally recorded by the earliest masters of political science, Plato and Aristotle, both of whom recognized its primacy as an independent factor in political change. To Plato, generational struggle constituted virtually the basic mechanism in political change, the always disequilibrating factor in systems of government, the prime agent in the alternation of political forms. To Aristotle, the psychological sources of generational conflict made for its universality. Generational conflict, in Aristotle's view, basically stemmed from the structure of the generations. The young, he wrote, love honor and victory "more than they love money, which indeed they love very little, not having yet learnt what it means to be without it. . . ." Political revolutions, according to Aristotle, were caused not only by the conflict of rich and poor but by the struggle between fathers and sons. He documented the embittered strain between the generations as revealed in their proverbs and maxims: "Nothing is more foolish than to be the parent of children"; "Never show an old man kindness."

Indeed, the concept of wisdom as it was first formulated in antiquity by the Egyptian and Hebrew sages, was precisely cross-generational in purpose. Wisdom was a warning against generational pride and rebellion; the son was to be his father's good pupil. Thus, history's first document on the principles of right conduct, the Maxims of Ptahhotep, were already concerned with the conflict of generations. As Ptahhotep, a man of the Establishment, evidently Grand Vizier to the Pharaoh Isesi of the Fifth Dynasty in the twenty-seventh century b.c., set down the wisdom of a lifetime, he bade youth listen to their fathers: "How worthy it is when a son hearkens to his father! If the son of a man receives what his father says, none of his projects will miscarry. . . ." The Hebrew Proverbs echoed Ptahhotep's wisdom, yet wisdom proved feeble against the forces of generational uprising. As David wept for Absalom, many later generations were to weep for their sons. If the fathers were forbidden to send their children into the fires of Moloch, the children sometimes seemed to seek the flames themselves in obedience to a demon within.

One can have generational equilibrium as well as a generational struggle; we must ask, therefore, what accounts for the breakdown of generational equilibrium and the emergence of overt struggle. Age differences in and of themselves do not necessitate the outbreak of generational conflict and the heightening of generational consciousness.

There can be little doubt that the French Revolution and its Napoleonic aftermath were the prime factors in the disruption of the generational equilibrium in Europe. In their wake came not only the German movement of Karl Follen but also the Young Italy of Giuseppe Mazzini. No previous age in European history would have so honored the word "young"; youth, with its romantic enthusiasm, displaced the old with its conceived mission to rule. Secret societies of the young appeared; they brooded on death and suicide. Mazzini's work and its movement showed indeed all the traits which later student movements more fully exhibited. At the Royal College of Genoa which he attended, the students "were principally preoccupied with the problem of how to overthrow authority." They learned they could do so "if only they were bold enough." A day before he was sixteen years old, in 1820, at the University of Geneva, Giuseppe helped organize a disturbance in the University Church over some trivial question of seating arrangements; he enjoyed his first arrest. The next year, in a more back-to-the-people spirit, he and his fellow-students demonstrated on behalf of the Carbonari revolt in Piedmont.

Mazzini and his fellow-students read Byron and Rousseau; he wept at the sorrows of Goethe's suicidal hero Werther. But self-destruction was more than romantic fantasy for the young student activists. Mazzini's close friend, the student Jacopo Ruffini, killed himself in disillusionment over the betrayal of comrades in Young Italy; his eldest brother too committed suicide as a student at Geneva. Young Italy drew its barrier between the generations; it excluded those over forty from its ranks and avowed that its sense of mission was not only to liberate the Italian people from foreign oppression but to liberate themselves from the old. They took to conspiracy and terrorism. Mazzini told Charles Albert of Sardinia, "Blood calls for blood, and the dagger of the conspirator is never so terrible as when sharpened upon the touchstone of a martyr." Thus the student movement was impelled to superimpose the irrational patterns of its general revolt on the movement for an independent Italian nation.

It was during the political reaction after the French Revolution that generational consciousness first became pronounced. The chronicles of the Old Testament had made use of the concept "generation," but theirs was primarily a static image: "And so-and-so begat so-and-so. . . ." The "generation of 1830," wrote George Brandes, "had heard in their childhood of the great events of the Revolution, had known the Empire, and were sons of heroes or victims." Now they saw the new order, bourgeois, timid, colorless, middle-class. An earlier youth had gone through Europe creating with its armies a new Europe and a new dream of freedom. Now the bourgeoisie ruled, with its omnipotence of economic interests, the pursuit of money. The romantic "school" emerged, and it was indeed a school, for it issued out of the feelings of protest on the part of students against the social environment. The young found themselves speaking a common language "unknown to the rest of their contemporaries." They lived with enthusiasm, and with an awe and reverence for each other, unlike their bourgeois elders. "These young Romanticists," says Brandes, "felt like brothers, like fellow-conspirators; they felt that they were the sharers in a sweet and invigorating secret. . . ." They were generation-conscious; their aim was to overturn tradition, conformity, order, formalism; they wanted passion, life, blood.

The conflict of generations is a universal theme in history; it is founded on the most primordial facts of human nature, and it is a driving force of history, perhaps even more ultimate than that of class struggle. Yet its intensity fluctuates. Under fortunate circumstances, it may be resolved within a generational equilibrium. Under less happy circumstances, it becomes bitter, unyielding, angry, violent; this is what takes place when the elder generation, through some presumable historical failure, has become de-authoritized in the eyes of the young.

Thus student movements have been the chief expression of generational conflict in modern history. As intellectual elites of the younger generation, they have had their special ethic of redemption, self-sacrifice, and identification. They have attained the greatest heights of idealistic emotion even as they have been enthralled by compulsions to destruction.

These student movements are more than an episode in the "modernization" of developing nations, for they can affect advanced industrial societies as well as traditional or transitional ones. They arise wherever social and historical circumstances combine to cause a crisis in loss of generational confidence, impelling the young to resentment and uprising. The unconscious ingredient of generational revolt in the students' idealism has tended to shape decisively their political expression. The will to revolt against the de-authoritized father has evolved into a variety of patterns of political action. This hegemony of the unconscious has differentiated student movements from the more familiar ones of class and interest groups. The latter are usually conscious of their psychological sources and aims, whether they be material economic interests or enhanced prestige and power. Student movements, on the other hand, resist the psychological analysis of their emotional mainspring; they wish to keep unconscious the origins of their generational revolt. A politics of the unconscious carries with it untold dangers for the future of civilization.

When generational struggle grows most intense, it gives rise to generational theories of truth. Protagorean relativism is translated into generational terms; only youth, uncorrupted, is held to perceive the truth, and the generation becomes the measure of all things. This generational relativism in the Sixties is the counterpart of the class relativism which flourished in the Thirties; where once it was said that only the proletariat had an instinctive grasp of sociological truth, now it is said that only those under thirty, or twenty-five, or twenty, are thus privileged. It would be pointless to repeat the philosophical criticisms of relativist ideology. This generational doctrine is an ideology insofar as it expresses a "false consciousness"; it issues from unconscious motives of generational uprising, projects its youthful longings onto the nature of the cosmos, sociological reality, and sociological knowledge, but represses precisely those facts of self-destruction and self-defeat which we have documented.

The reactionary is also a generational relativist, for he believes that the old have a privileged perspective upon reality, that only the old have learned through experience the recalcitrance of facts to human desire. But the philosophical truth is that no generation has a privileged access to reality; each has its projective unconscious, its inner resentments, its repressions and exaggerations. Each generation will have to learn to look at itself with the same sincerity it demands of the other. The alternative is generational conflict, with its searing, sick emotions, and an unconscious which is a subterranean house of hatred.

The substance of history is psychological—the way human beings have felt, thought, and acted in varying circumstances—and the concept of generational struggle which we have used is a psychological one. There are those who see the dangers of "reductionism" in our psycho-historical method; they feel that the genesis of student movements in generational conflict has no bearing on the validity of their programs, goals, objectives. Of what import, they ask, is the psychology of student movements so long as they work for freedom, liberating workers and peasants and colored races, university reform, and the end of alienation? To such critics we reply that the psychological origin of student movements puts its impress on both their choice of political means and underlying ends. Wherever a set of alternative possible routes toward achieving a given end presents itself, a student movement will usually tend to choose the one which involves a higher measure of violence or humiliation directed against the older generation. The latent aim of generational revolt never surrenders its paramountness to the avowed patent aims. The assassination of an archduke, for instance, may be justified by an appeal to nationalistic ideals which are said to have a sanctity overriding all other consequences; actually the sacred cause, the nationalistic ideal, becomes too easily a pseudo-end, a rationalization, a "cause" which affords the chance to express in a more socially admired way one's desire to murder an authority figure.

When all our analysis is done, however, what endures is the promise and hope of a purified idealism. I recall one evening in 1963 when I met with a secret circle of Russian students at Moscow University. There were twelve or thirteen of them drawn from various fields but moved by a common aspiration toward freedom. Among them were young physicists, philosophers, economists, students of languages. Their teachers had been apologists for the Stalinist repression, and the students were groping for truthful ideas, for an honest philosophy rather than an official ideology. Clandestine papers and books circulated among them—a copy of Boris Pasternak's *Dr. Zhivago,* George Orwell's *1984,* reprints of Western articles on Soviet literature, a revelation of the fate of the poet Osip Mandelstamm. The social system had failed to "socialize" them, had failed to stifle their longing for freedom. The elder generation was de-authoritized in their eyes for its pusillanimous involvement in the "cult of personality." Here on a cold March night in a Moscow academic office I was encountering what gave hope to the future of the Soviet Union. The conflict of generations, disenthralled of its demonry, becomes a drama of sustenance and renewal which remains the historical bearer of humanity's highest hopes.

Adolescence: Self-Definition and Conflict

Edgar Z. Friedenberg

> Edgar Z. Friedenberg (b. 1921) has been since 1964 a professor of sociology at the University of California at Davis. His publications include *Coming of Age in America* (1965), *The Dignity of Youth and Other Atavisms* (1965), and *The Vanishing Adolescent* (1959) from which the selection that follows is taken.

One of the most precise clues to what is actually going on psychologically in a culture is its use of language. People only bother to name those aspects of their experience that mean something to them. Those who share the language, therefore, share to some extent a common situation and a common concern.

If a people have no word for something, either it does not matter to them or it matters too much to talk about. If they *do* have a word for something, it is worth asking why they have included in their concept just what they have, and not other aspects which might, from a slightly different point of view, easily have been included. And if they cannot use the words they have without becoming arch, coy, or diffuse—if they cannot discuss a subject of apparent importance to them with vigor and precision—they are clearly in some kind of trouble about it. When experience is deformed by conflict or anxiety, language no longer quite fits. The personal needs of those who are trying to discuss a problem come between their experience and their common symbols, and they find it difficult or impossible to speak about it normally.

Adolescence is one of the topics which is subject to all these difficulties and which is correspondingly difficult to discuss intelligibly in English. Despite our exaggerated concern for and almost prurient interest in the "teen-ager," we have no neutral term for persons between the ages of, say, fourteen and twenty-one. "Adolescent" has overtones at once pedantic and erotic, suggestive of primitive fertility rites and of the orgies of classical antiquity. "Young person" meets the requirements of British jurisprudence in referring precisely to a portion of this age range, but is too poor in connotations to be a useful phrase in ordinary speech. "Teen-ager" remains the choice for popular usage. It is patronizing, and sounds rather uneasy and embarrassed; but these qualities may add to its appeal, for many of us do indeed respond to adolescence with forced joviality.

There is no English noun which simply identifies precisely persons between the ages of fourteen and twenty-one, leaving the reader free to feel what he pleases about them. This is odd. We have neutral nouns for persons and things that arouse feeling in nearly everyone: child, adult, hangman, cancer, mother, mistress, senator. These are exact; they mean what they mean. They can be dissociated from their connotations if the context demands it. "Teen-ager" cannot be. What does one call an eighteen-year-old girl if one wishes to note that she has triumphed as Joan of Arc or Anne Frank, or written another successful novel? What does one call an eighteen-year-old boy in reporting that he has been killed in a training maneuver at boot camp? Such things do not happen to "teen-agers," absorbed as they are in delinquency and in endless telephone discussions of rock and roll.

Yet, if we have no convenient language for discussing adolescence we seem equally unable to dismiss it. And this too is rather odd. What is there about these eight or so years that lingers so in the psyche? Granted that puberty is a notable event, that the onset of sexual maturity and the bodily changes which ensue are dramatic, and that no language applies its word for "child" to persons beyond the early teens. Nothing so conspicuous demarcates the adolescent from the young adult; yet adults who are no longer young are likely to feel much more at ease with a young man of twenty-five than a boy of eighteen. They place the two in different classes of humanity, while allotting thirty years, more or less, to middle age. These thirty years also bring changes in personality and body build, but we see them as gradual and have not divided them up with conceptual barriers.

This conception of an upper limit to adolescence is by no means universal. In most primitive cultures—variable as these are—young people are usually initiated into adult life shortly after puberty. They are conducted through *rites de passage* of varying degrees of harshness designed to "separate the men from the boys"; the separation is not a genuine period of adolescence but a brief *interregnum*. Essentially, in such societies, one is either a child or an adult, though adult society is marked by status differences quite as complex and elaborate as ours.

Adolescence is conceived as a distinct stage of life in societies so complicated and differentiated that each individual's social role and function takes years to define and learn. When years of special preparation for adult life are required, these years become a distinguishable period with its own rules, customs, and relationships. The ordeal of the classical British preparatory and public school, for example, could not simply be sweated out in a burst of adolescent pluck; the initiation became a way of life. To instill into youth the complex code of the empire-builder and gentleman so thoroughly that this would be maintained in loneliness and isolation, and even under conditions in which it had become something of a nuisance to all concerned, took time and more than time. It took experience, under discipline, in relating to many different kinds of people whose status with respect to oneself varied sharply. In this way, the schoolboy learned to respond with spontaneous and often deep personal feeling to some of the people and events in his life, while limiting the *range* of his response to persons and situations he had learned to regard as worth noticing.

The British public school, at its most imposing, made adolescence much more than an interregnum. It made it an epoch. Its austerity could be relieved by a sensitive husbanding of sparse human resources; its heroes became myths, and in turn clichés, but the schoolboy had strong feelings about them. The prefect who caned you for specific offenses might, at other times, offer brusque understanding when you seriously needed it. He might also be a sadistic bully, or simply a rather stupid boy who was good at games. There were classmates with whom you could share brief, vivid perceptions and long, comfortable silences, though there were many more with whom you could share nothing. There were masters who had some respect for scholarship and for boys, and there were others who respected neither. All these defined themselves through the years as individuals as well as parts of a system. They could be fought, but there was no getting away from them or erasing your experience with them. At best, they helped the adolescent make himself into a strongly characterized human being who was ready to go on to something more: at worst, their impact made adolescence interminable and their victims permanently fixated "old boys." In any case, they defined the content of adolescence; they gave the adolescent something to be adolescent about.

In a society that sets up special institutions for inducting the young into it, and takes several years doing it, the developmental process that we call adolescence can occur. This institutional provision need not, however, be formal or intentionally planned. A delinquent gang is such an institution. And even institutions as formal and coercive as the classical British public school or the old-fashioned military school influenced their students most strongly in ways that were not consciously planned, though they were certainly the consequence of powerful unconscious intentions.

The unconscious and conscious intentions that dominate a society are, of course, expressed through all its institutions, including those that deal with adolescents. The institutions which mold the adolescence of most young people in technically developed countries today are the instruments of a very different society from that which created the British public school or the military school. They are intended to yield young people predisposed to very different social behavior. They are seldom coercive or immediately painful, but rather informal, democratic, and apparently mild in operation. They make use of sanctions that hardly hurt at all when applied, but that often make their victims ill much later.

The kind of character these institutions—whether the school, the TV, or even the modern army and navy—tend to develop is in many ways the very opposite of that which the British public school, or the old-fashioned school of any kind, sought consciously and unconsciously to produce. All the contemporary institutions that bear on the young, diverse as they seem to be, are united in their insistence on cultivating sensitivity and pliability to the demands and expectations of other persons. Other-direction, adaptability, adjustment, conformity—call it what you will, the idea is familiar enough—is a trait of great short-run, social usefulness in today's relatively open and rootless society; and that society has done a formidable job of creating institutions which mold other-directed and adjustable character structure.

One might expect that the general increase in blandness and good humor which has resulted would also have sweetened the relationship between adults and adolescents; and in many ways it has. There are real friendships between adolescents and adults in contemporary society, especially in America; it is taken for granted that there should be. This would not have been possible earlier, and it is still most unusual in many European or Latin-American countries. It is a basic development in human relations, scarcely less important than the simultaneous improvement in relations among different racial groups, which is resulting from quite similar social changes.

But the modern emphasis on cooperation and group adjustment has also injured the relationship between adolescents and adults in two very significant ways. These are not very widely recognized, but they lie, I believe, at the root of our difficulty in considering adolescence without self-consciousness or conflict. The first of these is rather superficial; the second is much more serious.

The tolerant, reasonable, democratic approach to "teen-agers"—like the comparable approach to formerly discriminated racial groups—is based on a premise of greater respect for them than the earlier attitude of coercive, if paternalistic, dominance. This much is valuable. But the same difficulty arises as in the improvement of interracial relations. In order for this to occur smoothly, the members of the dominant group must like and respect the subordinate group a good deal in the first place. If adults dislike or fear adolescents, the change will make those adults more frightened and more hostile, because it is a very real threat to their continued domination. In today's society they will probably have to be "nice to the kids" despite their fear and hostility; but they will most certainly try to maintain by seduction and manipulation the dominance they previously achieved by coercion and punishment.

This, it seems to me, is what usually does happen. Certainly, there are many exceptions, and the proportion seems to be growing nicely; but I think a detached observer of the behavior and attitudes of school personnel, juvenile court officials, and so forth would probably conclude that, on the whole, these individuals dislike and distrust youngsters more often than they like them. They are often disturbed at the prospect of being involved with young people in any situation that is not under their quite complete control; a dean who has grown accustomed to functioning as a rather fair-minded though rigid martinet is likely to become unscrupulous and conspiratorial if changes in his school force him to act as "adviser" to an ostensibly self-governing student disciplinary committee. Such officials are usually willing to abandon coercive techniques of control in favor of manipulative ones, since these help them preserve a more favorable image of themselves as guides who are liked and accepted by their charges; and, in any case, manipulative techniques work better than coercive ones with modern youngsters, who are usually quite skilled themselves at making tyrants feel guilty. But the teacher, dean, or probation officer who genuinely sees youngsters as persons of dignity equal to himself and who is satisfied to have purely rational authority over them is still rather the exception. The point can be overstressed, and I do not mean to suggest that the planet has become a sort of Madison Avenue streamlined version of Dotheboy's Hall. But the perception of the orientation of the world of adults toward adolescents so well and movingly expressed by Holden Caulfield in *The Catcher in the Rye* seems to me almost wholly valid.

Much of the ambivalence of adults toward "teen-agers" is, I should judge, simply a kind of repressed panic-response to the liquidation of authority over them. It must be understood, however, that the loss of authority is real; the adult empire is tottering. All empires are; this is the era of skepticism about the relationship between authority and status. It is an error, I believe, to interpret what is happening as a decline in respect for authority as such. American youngsters today are generous in according respect to parents, teachers, and other adults who earn it as individuals; and they are far more perceptive of individual quality in their elders than they could possibly have been when all adults were regarded as potentially or actually hostile and dangerous. But it is true that they are less likely to respect an adult today simply because he occupies a position of authority. It is also true that a boy who can be punished for insulting you is far less frightening—even if he is *very* insulting—than a boy who offers out of sheer kindness to share his analyst with you because he has noticed, correctly, that you need help worse than he does.

Adults who do not basically like and respect adolescents—and this includes a large proportion of those who make a career of working with them—are badly frightened by the increasingly democratic relationships between adolescents and adults that are coming to prevail in our society. They have become more tense in their attitude toward youngsters, and contribute greatly to the difficulties of young people in our society. Their manipulative and covert hostility demoralizes adolescents and forms the basis of real personal and social problems. It is easier, and less damaging, for a youngster to face bad grades, disappointment at being passed over for a team or a club, or formal punishment, than it is for him to deal with gossip about his character or his manners, with teachers who pass the word along that he is a troublemaker or that he needs special patience and guidance because his father drinks.

Nevertheless, this is probably not too serious a matter, for it is pretty certain to work itself out in the course of time. Newer and better trained teachers and social workers tend to be of a somewhat different stamp. The youngsters themselves grow more accustomed to respectful handling and more confident of it; they become less rebellious but also less easily diverted from their own moral judgments and decisions. When they *do* nevertheless have to deal with a hostile or tricky adult, they are more likely to know what they want and what they are doing, and can face him coolly. He, in turn, is *not* really confident of himself or his authority, and rapidly becomes more anxious. He may stubbornly refuse to listen; he may lose his temper and really try to hurt them, and this time he may succeed. But he also finds that his efforts to dominate the young cause him more anxiety than he can easily bear. Unless his superiors support him in a counterattack, he is likely to withdraw gradually behind a barrage of indignant complaint. Ultimately, he becomes picturesque; the young may grow quite fond of him.

What is far more serious is that the emphasis on cooperation and group adjustment characteristic of modern life interferes specifically with the central developmental task of adolescence itself. *This task is self-definition. Adolescence is the period during which a young person learns who he is, and what he really feels. It is the time during which he differentiates himself from his culture, though on the culture's terms. It is the age at which, by becoming a person in his own right, he becomes capable of deeply felt relationships to other individuals perceived clearly as such.* It is precisely this sense of individuality which fails to develop, or develops only feebly, in most primitive cultures or among lower-status social groups. A successful initiation leads to group solidarity and a warm sense of belonging; a successful adolescence adds to these a profound sense of self—of one's own personality.

Personalization is the métier of adolescence. Of all persons, adolescents are the most intensely personal; their intensity is often uncomfortable to adults. As cooperation and group adjustment become pervasive social norms; as tolerance supersedes passion as the basis for social action; as personalization becomes false-personalization, adolescence becomes more and more difficult. Conceivably, it might become again a rather rare event, having no function in the new world of glad-handing primitives happy among their electronic trinkets. But, for the present at least, the old norms of individual character, personal devotion, particular love and hate retain enough authority to make those who remain faithful to them, as adolescents tend to do, extremely troublesome to their contemporaries.

Adolescents often behave much like members of an old-fashioned aristocracy. They maintain private rituals, which they often do not really understand themselves. They are extremely conservative in their dress and tastes, but the conventions to which they adhere are purely those of their own social group; they try to ignore the norms of the larger society if these conflict with their own. They can be extravagantly generous and extravagantly cruel, but rarely petty or conniving. Their virtues are courage and loyalty; while the necessity for even a moderate degree of compromise humiliates them greatly. They tend to be pugnacious and quarrelsome about what they believe to be their rights, but naïve and reckless in defending them. They are shy, but not modest. If they become very anxious they are likely to behave eccentrically, to withdraw, or to attack with some brutality; they are less likely to blend themselves innocuously into the environment with an apologetic smile. They are honest on occasions when even a stupid adult would have better sense.

They are therefore at a considerable disadvantage in many relationships of modern life. Modern life is hostile to the aristocratic social principle. Aristocratic attitudes and modes of action snarl its very mainsprings. They interfere with the conduct of practical affairs and impede administrative action. In busy, anxious, and ambitious people, they arouse anger and resentment; but beneath the anger and resentment there is shame and guilt.

Adolescents insult us by quietly flaunting their authenticity. They behave as if they did not even know that passion and fidelity are expensive, but merely assumed that everyone possessed them. This, certainly, is inexcusably valorous; and it is not excused. But it makes us awkward in their presence, and embarrassed in our approach to them.

Not all adolescents, by any means, retain this quality. There are many who learn to soothe adults ruffled by encounters with their more ardent and challenging peers, and charm them on suitable occasions by an ingratiating youthfulness. When a boy or girl is needed for display, they are available; in the same clothes all the others wear, they look a little—not too much—neater. Having them in charge of the school paper and the student government saves a good deal of wear and tear all around; they are described in their school records as having qualities of leadership.

At certain times and places—perhaps here and now—such boys and girls predominate. Processes comparable to natural selection almost insure that they will. Schools nudge them into the pathways believed to lead to success in adult life and rehearse them for it in carefully designed facsimiles of adult institutions. Student life in the modern high school is now conducted through a veritable rat-maze of committees. The big man on campus is a perfectly executed scale model of a junior executive. It may therefore seem either inconsistent or willfully sentimental that I have described my heuristic model of an adolescent as a knight in shining chino pants.

But I think it is valid to maintain this, not just because I have encountered a goodly few such errant defenders of the faith in the course of half a lifetime, but because I am concerned here with a process of growth rather than with a statistical norm. There is certainly no doubt that modern society has power to corrupt, and that it starts early. But the function of adolescence is growth and individuation, and these can be fruitful only if a reasonable and increasing degree of integrity is maintained.

A youngster who has abandoned the task of defining himself in dialectical combat with society and becomes its captive and its emissary may be no rarity; but he is a casualty. There is not much more to be said about him: one can only write him off and trust that the world will at least feed him well if it cannot keep him warm. The promise of maturity must be fulfilled by those who are strong enough to grow into it at their own rate as full bargaining members.

Must there be conflict between the adolescent and society? The point is that adolescence *is* conflict—protracted conflict—between the individual and society. There are cultures in which this conflict seems hardly to occur; but where it does not, the characteristic development of personality which we associate with adolescence does not occur either.

There are cultures, as in Margaret Mead's classic description of coming of age in Samoa, where the young pass delicately as Ariel through puberty into adulthood. But their peoples do not seem to us like adults; they are charming people, but they are from our point of view insufficiently characterized. There is not much difference between them, and they do not seem to make much difference to one another.

In other simple cultures, in which the role of the adult is likewise thoroughly familiar to the child by the time he reaches puberty, the young are initiated into adult life much more harshly. Sometimes the process is more loving than it appears to be, though the very fact that adults find it necessary to inflict it is conclusive evidence of some hostility toward the young. In any case, it is comparatively brief. Some of these cultures are primitive; others are relatively stable subcultures of the Western world like that of British coal miners whose sons are hazed into adult status by their elders when they first enter the mines themselves. But in these as well, the adults seem curiously indistinguishable by our criteria of personality. Differences of temperament and of attitude toward life may be very conspicuous indeed. But they stop short of what we regard as normal variation of human personality; the range is as wide, but not as deep.

And there are other cultures in which there is no conflict because conflict is thoroughly repressed. Not by externally applied brutality—this suppresses; it does not effectively repress. There are adolescents even in totalitarian countries, as the Polish and Hungarian authorities discovered in 1956. But where totalitarianism really sinks in, even the young will be so intensely anxious that no conflict will arise. Only those feelings and attitudes approved by society will then even occur to them as possibilities. There can be no adolescence in *1984.*

Conflict between the individual and society, as Lionel Trilling has so clearly stated in *Freud and the Crisis of Our Culture,* is inherent in the development of personality by the standards of Western man. Freud is still the source of our most tough-minded psychodynamic system, and this point is basic to it. And it is in adolescence that this conflict is critical to individual development. Or to put it another way, and perhaps more truly, adolescence *is* this conflict, no matter how old the individual is when it occurs. Adolescent conflict is the instrument by which an individual learns the complex, subtle, and precious difference between himself and his environment. In a society in which there is no difference, or in which no difference is permitted, the word "adolescence" has no meaning.

But conflict is not war; it need not even involve hostile action. It must, to be sure, produce some hostile feelings, among others. But there need be no intent to wound, castrate, or destroy on either side. Conflict between the adolescent and his world is dialectical, and leads, as a higher synthesis, to the youth's own adulthood and to critical participation in society as an adult. Some of the experiences of adolescence which turn out to be most beneficial to growth are, it is true, painful at the time. Looking for your first job, among strangers; learning that your first love is the girl she is but not the girl you need; getting soundly beaten in your first state-wide track meet when you are used to being the fastest runner in town—none of this is fun. But such experiences are not sickening, heartbreaking, or terrifying because, even at the time, they can be felt as bringing you in closer touch with reality. The pain they produce is somehow accepted as benign, like soreness following unaccustomed physical exercise or the pain of normal childbirth. Growth is more satisfying, and far more reassuring, than comfort; though normal growth is comfortable most of the time.

One cannot, therefore, use the inevitability of conflict in adolescence as a justification for actions which hurt adolescents on the pretext of "toughening them up." If "growing pains" are never sickening, heartbreaking, or terrifying, it is equally true that heartbreak, terror, and a sense of insult and violation contribute nothing to growth. They stunt it or twist it, and the grower is more or less deformed. Perhaps the commonest deformation which these cause in persons too young to know how to handle themselves in pain is apathy.

In their encounters with society, youngsters are frequently badly hurt, and there is no mistaking this kind of agony for growing pains. They are sickened and terrified; they feel their pride break, cringe from the exposure of their privacy to manipulation and attack, and are convulsed with humiliation as they realize that they cannot help cringing and that, in fact, their responses are now pretty much beyond their control. Control once regained is consolidated at a less humane level; there will be no more love lost or chances taken on the adversary.

A number of psychological and social dynamisms can take over at this juncture; none of them is a part of the process of healthy growth, though some at least give time for scars to form so that growth may be resumed later. But most of these defense mechanisms are dangerous in their total context, although they make perfectly good sense in the light of the victim's immediate emotional condition. This is the fundamental dilemma of organism. A severe heart attack is not such a bad idea from the immediate viewpoint of the exhausted heart, if only the rest of the body and the heart itself, as a muscle, were not so thirsty for blood. Somehow, however it has been insulted, the heart must be kept in action, for its own sake as well as for that of the body as a whole; though a wise physician knows when to keep demands on it to a minimum, and also knows that the minimum may still be more than can be borne.

Growth, too, must continue. Apathy, a fawning acceptance of authority, or a hard-eyed campaign of organized delinquency with enough real violence to show you mean business, may all be understood as functional for adolescents bearing certain kinds of wounds. But understandable or not, functional or not, these are dangerous expedients for the young. They may provide cover for the processes of healing, and facilitate the formation of strong emotional scar tissue. But they not only lead to more trouble with society; they lead away from the kinds of relationships by which growth continues, and from the kind of self-perception of which growth consists.

Delinquency, apathy, and seductive fawning are not aspects of the essential conflict between youth and society which constitutes adolescence. They are the consequences of the conflict having gone terribly wrong, and a corresponding wisdom and patience—more than is usually available under actual working conditions—are needed to restore it as a fruitful process. For most young people, of course, things do not go terribly wrong. They go moderately wrong, but we nevertheless grow up, more or less, and conduct ourselves toward the next generation in its need with such humanity as we can muster. For the result, no blame attaches. Adam and Eve, at the time that Cain was born, had no opportunity to read the works of Gesell.

I know of no reason to suppose that, at the present time, there is a crisis in our relationship to youth; and, in any case, this is certainly not a book of instructions to be supplied with adolescents. But if the function of adolescence is self-definition, one would expect it to be very difficult in a society which suffers from a dearth of individuality and in which alienation is a crucial problem. And if the instrument of self-definition is the conflict between the adolescent and a basically humane society—which nevertheless has purposes of its own, and more to do than take care of kids—one would expect the self-defining process to break down as that society became less humane and more manipulative. A society which has *no purposes* of its own, other than to insure domestic tranquillity by suitable medication, will have no use for adolescents, and will fear them; for they will be among the first to complain, as they crunch away at their benzedrine, that tranquilizers make you a square. It will set up sedative programs of guidance, which are likely to be described as therapeutic, but whose apparent function will be to keep young minds and hearts in custody till they are without passion.

We have by no means gone so far as yet; but the sort of process of which I speak is already discernible. . . .

Politics of the Non-political

Stephen Spender

> Stephen Spender (b. 1909) is best known as a poet, but he is also a translator and an editor, and he has written criticism and essays on literature, culture, and politics. He lives in London but has often lectured in the United States and has served as Consultant in Poetry at the Library of Congress. The excerpt printed below is taken from his recent book, *The Year of the Young Rebels,* 1969.

One can only compare what seems, to the militant students, to have happened in the external world of the society in which they live, to a kind of crystallisation, like the surface of a pond suddenly freezing and becoming covered with ice. They feel their inner world of personal values to be frozen over by the events taking place in the external public world of politics. The external world seems to threaten actually to disrupt the values of the inner world. To realise and even to retain his own values the student has to convert the most personal values of his own being into political counteraction. The non-political finds himself in a world where suddenly everything is explained in terms of politics.

When this happens the student appears in the eyes of his elders to have changed, and to become another person—with his odious Midas touch which turns everything to politics.

It is in such a situation that the kind of controversy occurs which is to be seen in a book called *Democracy and the Student Left,* which consists of an essay of that name by George Kennan, followed by replies from students and teachers. To understand the confrontation, you must think of Mr Kennan standing like an antique Roman, quite the noblest of them all, on one side of that institution, Princeton University, and today's militant students standing on the other. The institution has been a good deal altered by the fact that the student population has been multiplied perhaps tenfold since Mr Kennan's day and that there are a great many disturbances blowing like a typhoon through the campus. So Mr Kennan from his side of time sees a quite different university from that which the students see from theirs. To Mr Kennan the university is a place where 'there is a certain detachment and seclusion, a certain voluntary withdrawal and renunciation of participation in contemporary life in the interests of a better perspective on that life when the period of withdrawal is over.' It is brooded over by the ghost of another antique Roman, Woodrow Wilson, from whom Mr Kennan quotes, with austere fervour:

> I have had sight of the perfect place of learning in my thought: a free place, and a various, where no man could be and not know with how great a destiny knowledge had come into the world; but not perplexed, living with a singleness of aim not known without; the home of sagacious men, hard-headed and with a will to know, debaters of the world's questions every day and used to the rough ways of democracy; and yet a place removed—calm Science seated there, recluse, ascetic like a nun; not knowing that the world passes, not caring, if the truth but come in answer to her prayer. ... A place where to hear the truth about the past and hold debate about the affairs of the present, with knowledge and without passion. ...[1]

etc., etc., it goes on like this. Doubtless to the militant students at Columbia, it would sound like a description of a nun ripe for raping.

As a good many correspondents pointed out, the demands on today's students implicit in Mr Kennan's description would have had more weight had they not been addressed to students many of whom had little chance of voluntary withdrawal. For hanging over them was the threat of being drafted to take part in the war in Vietnam. But Mr Kennan says they exaggerate the extent of this threat.

Mr Kennan goes on to criticise the militant students for their ignorance and he objects to the destructive violence of their protests. He thinks that if the young find the political structure objectionable they should 'put forward a programme of constitutional amendment or political reform' and promote it 'with reasoned argument and discussion,' instead of their having no programme and indulging in 'violence for violence's sake' and 'in attempts to frighten or intimidate an administration into doing things for which it can itself see neither the rational nor the electoral mandate.' Mr Kennan also takes exception to those who protest by violating the law, even though they are prepared to accept the legal consequences of doing so.

Mr Kennan invites the young to try and change the constitution before protesting about Vietnam. This seems like asking them to wait a very long time before acting about something of the most immediate urgency.

The volume contains a great many answers—some of them abusive—to Mr Kennan. One of the best is a polite and well reasoned letter written with a courtesy and distinction almost the equal of Mr Kennan's own, by David King, a Harvard freshman. He regards Mr Kennan as 'the personification of the balance between idealism and realism that I would like, eventually, to attain.' Nevertheless he disagrees profoundly with him. His letter goes to show, I think, that it is not a change in the mentality of generations that

---

[1] From *Democracy and the Student Left* by George F. Kennan, by permission of Atlantic-Little, Brown and Co. Copyright © 1968 by George F. Kennan.

has caused the division between old and young but a situation which has put the old on the side of what the young regard as immorality, the young on the side of what the old see correctly as rebellion. Mr King declares that he is not against the draft, which he regards as an odious necessity, but nevertheless he supports those who consider that when it involves their being sent to Vietnam the draft 'constitutes a violation of their personal morality.' He compares the draft to a tax applied to raise not money but manpower for 'enforcing the policies of the government.'

> In this situation the law is reaching into the personal domain of a man's soul. . . . In the end, every individual is responsible to a higher authority than the government and whether it is religious or personal it is sacrosanct. The United States itself held this view in the Nuremberg trials when it found that 'following orders' does not excuse one from the consequences of his actions.[2]

He considers that one is justified in 'resisting the government's attempt to subvert his morals.'

Partly I have given this example to show that a young student who is not a Hippie, or an *enragé,* may nevertheless feel that what a much respected member of the older generation considers political complexity, he considers moral outrage. Mr King finds American policy so immoral that he compares it with the actions for which Nazi leaders were tried at Nuremberg. And what this quiet-mannered freshman who so admires Mr Kennan asks for is the politics of a different morality. In asking this, Mr King is of course attempting to reduce immensely tangled political problems to simple either/or propositions. One can sympathise with Mr Kennan writing:

> Never has there been an era when the problems of public policy even approached in their complexity those by which our society is confronted today, in this age of technical innovation and the explosion of knowledge. The understanding of these problems is something to which one could well give years of disciplined and restrained study, years of the scholar's detachment, years of readiness to reserve judgement while evidence is being accumulated. And this being so, one is struck to see such massive certainties already present in the minds of people who not only *have not* studied very much but presumably *are not* studying a great deal because it is hard to imagine that the activities to which this aroused portion of our student population gives itself are ones readily compatible with quiet and successful study.[3]

Yet if the students whom Mr Kennan addresses oversimplify issues Mr Kennan does the reverse. Or perhaps Mr Kennan, with all his subtlety

---

[2] From *Democracy and the Student Left* by George F. Kennan, by permission of Atlantic-Little, Brown and Co. Copyright © 1968 by Little, Brown and Company (Inc.).

[3] From *Democracy and the Student Left* by George F. Kennan, by permission of Atlantic-Little, Brown and Co. Copyright © 1968 by George F. Kennan.

is *not,* after all, complex enough. For what he fails to see is that complex though an international problem such as the position of America in Asia may be, war itself is a simplification. I may have immensely complex reasons for hating my neighbour and grievances against him which anyone who devoted ten years to studying the matter would admit to be just, but if I murder him I have simplified the issue to the method and fact of murder, and although study of the complex situation might mitigate the offence, I have murdered just the same.

I know that this answer is not conclusive, unless for a pacifist, because we do not in all circumstances condemn war, but it goes a long way. Napalm bombs iron out the complexities of politics. Even if going to war is accepted as a 'necessary crime' the fighting can, if protracted, and the methods used can, if excessively horrible, render the decision to fight a mistake. This is especially true, I think, of colonial wars which are usually 'interventions' by an external power in a civil war, rather than direct invasions. The intervention ceases to be justified—just as colonialism—and the colonialist— ceases to be justified if too many people on the spot do not want the intervener, or if the side against which he intervenes resists for an indefinite period. I agree that the whole history of colonial wars goes to show that intervention is an immensely complicated strategic and political operation. But these complexities do not invalidate the position of a person who simply thinks that intervention is wrong; nor of one who comes to think that the operation by its extent and horror has been proved to be wrong. There is virtue of course in knowing as much as possible about the complexities of the situation—it is admirable to do so—but the person who objects on moral grounds is not answered by saying that he knows too little about it.

These observations, I know, breed further complexities. It will be argued that if the Americans were not in Vietnam, the Chinese or the Russians or the local Communists would be there and in neighbouring parts of south-east Asia. The arguments are certainly very involved but here again, given the methods used or excused, there is a clash between considerations of complex strategy and those of simple morality. If someone considers that it is morally wrong to defend one position because of the hypothetical possibility of failure to defend it leading to the loss of other positions, and he refuses to enter into complicated studies and calculations about the wrong, there is not much point in rebuking him for ignoring complexities.

But it is true that unless a conflict between morals and policy had arisen, there would be no question of such simplification. The student would be studying, playing games or writing a poem.

Mr Kennan, who is civilised, intelligent and Christian, nevertheless seems almost congenitally disposed to think that if there is a conflict between a hypothetically correct (because 'realistic') policy and a moral one, the first is bound to be right and the second wrong. He produces against the students who object, perhaps over-officiously, to universities having investments in South Africa, the following *témoignage:*

I myself recently spent some time in South Africa, and I know of no one familiar with the situation there who does not see in the continued rapid development of the South African economy the greatest single impediment to the realisation of the official concept of *apartheid* and the greatest hope, accordingly, for advancement of the country's black and 'coloured' inhabitants. It is further evident that every intensification of the isolation of that country from the world community plays into the hands of the regime in its efforts to impose the policies of 'separate development.' Whoever is sincerely interested in the breakdown of the existing racial restrictions there ought normally to be interested in encouraging both the development of South African industry as such and the maximum participation of foreign capital in the process.[4]

I feel that Mr Kennan ought not to have advanced this argument without mentioning the names of some of the people he did—and did not—meet (how many blacks, for example) in South Africa. Not to have done so lays him open to reminder that there were people who went to Germany in the mid-Thirties and who were very willing to produce similar bland arguments. They came back saying that all the businessmen they met assured them that nothing would help the Jews more than support for the German economy. They may have been right and Mr Kennan may be right but the note of bland assurance is not really quite all it pretends to be: good sense and the consensus of everyone met who is open to reason.

Mr Kennan does not answer the point implicitly made in Mr King's words about 'the law reaching into the domain of a man's soul'—that the 'draft resister is resisting the government's attempts to subvert his morals'—unless he does so by drawing attention to the fact that the whole thing is greatly exaggerated—very few students are going to be drafted anyway. But Mr Kennan and Mr King are really at cross purposes. Mr Kennan's basic assumption is that if the students had really studied the matters under discussion they would not protest or burn their draft cards. After years of study they would undertake a long-term operation to alter the American constitution. Mr King's position is that the war is wicked and should be resisted by every possible means, legal or illegal.

The point I am concerned with making is that on one level, that of politeness, there is no quarrel between Mr King and Mr Kennan. On another level, that of political tactics versus morality, there is total disagreement. Politeness may not seem of major importance here, but it is symptomatic. Mr King's letter is the exception that proves the rule of the students' tone which is one of studied rudeness, insolence and boorishness. The reason for this is that most students evidently no longer think they are addressing the authorities as 'persons.' If they address them as such, they do so jeeringly, mockingly, striking a note of false conviviality, as though both parties, the insulter and the insulted, should agree that the older man only

---

[4] From *Democracy and the Student Left* by George F. Kennan, by permission of Atlantic-Little, Brown and Co. Copyright © 1968 by George F. Kennan.

pretends to be a person. He is really inhuman authority incarnate. The political leaders, college presidents, etc., tend to disappear into patterns of power and governmental or business interest—the realities behind the carnival masks (Nixon and Humphrey) which grotesquely caricature the human. On the other hand, if someone appears on the public stage who has claims to be human—for example, Senator McCarthy—he is immensely welcomed and supported by some students, while others—the more radical —try to prove that his human look is just as much a pretence as that of the others. They take off the mask of the real personality to show that of the false personality behind.

Thus the situation that Mr Kennan and his critics demonstrate is one of complex politics confronted by the simplicist morality. Somewhere between the two, the democracy, if not the forms to which Mr Kennan attaches a justifiable importance, is endangered. For if there are reasons so complicated that they cannot be explained to the people to justify the politics that the most intelligent and thoughtful of the young find immoral, then politics becomes a mystery which can only be played by the most powerful and astute, and only understood by the most learned. This makes democratic processes irrelevant and mischievous, the intrusion of ignorant people into the affairs of knowledgeable ones. But if the government of a democracy is so wicked that the young are justified in disregarding its processes and refusing to obey its laws, then democracy will go by the board before some form of revolution, probably leading first to anarchy and next to dictatorship.

This is the situation, in which, on the one hand there seems to be nothing but unscrupulous power politics, on the other, no choice but revolution in the name of morals.

Hipsters Unleashed

David McReynolds

> In *The Beats* (1960), a collection of essays from which "Hipsters Unleashed" is taken, Seymour Krim, the editor, provided the following introduction for David McReynolds: "McReynolds is 30, responsible, has a long socialist-pacifist background, was actually Socialist Party candidate for Congress in 1958, is one of the few knowing bridges between tough politics and the beat mutiny. He'll speak to an audience at the drop of a topic and writes a brainy straightforward prose. A good man to have on your side. Out of California."

Liberals and radicals, remembering with nostalgia the political movements of their youth, are confused by the present student generation. They ask themselves what has gone wrong with young people—where is that old fire to build a new world, that naive but glorious idealism once so characteristic of students? They are dismayed to find that most young people seem intent only on their own security—and to hell with the hungry, sick and oppressed peoples of the earth. Those youths who do not conform are even harder to understand—for the nonconformists today are the "beat generation" seemingly composed of delinquents, sexual perverts, drug addicts, and confused writers of bad poetry—a generation of irresponsible, irrational, and incomprehensible nihilists.

As someone sympathetic to the beat generation—and to its most swinging member, the hipster—I believe that the juvenile delinquents, the noisy young poets, and the unkempt crew of jazz hipsters represent a vital force in our society—a force which, if understood, will throw considerable light on the crisis of our times. To understand why many of our most talented and creative young people have "disaffiliated" from society, we must look at the society they have rejected.

The first factor to consider is the Bomb. The advent of nuclear weapons has changed the meaning of two important concepts—"future" and "death." "Future" has become a tentative concept. It is not a question of whether the future will be good or bad, but whether there will be *any* future. And "death" has assumed a finality it never had before.

Up to the present we have believed that men must die, but that man would live on through his children, through his works of art, through his

---

HIPSTERS UNLEASHED: From *The Beats*, Seymour Krim, ed. Reprinted by permission of Seymour Krim and David McReynolds.

heroic deeds in battle—*through the survival of the race*. But now the race may not survive, and our individual death becomes a collective and final death. Allen Ginsberg writes of those who sit "listening to the crack of doom on the hydrogen juke-box"; and proceeds, in another poem, to ask Americans "When will you look at yourself through the grave?" Lawrence Ferlinghetti writes about "any stray assinine action by any stray assinine second lieutenant pressing any strange button anywhere far away over an arctic ocean thus illuminating the world once and for all." Faced by this sudden new "finality" of death, it is very important to understand what life itself is about, and to experience life as deeply as possible. If we knew we had but one week to live, would there be time for politics? Or would we do those things we had somehow never found time for in our crisis-ridden lives? Would love become important? Would we walk through the park? Would we put a dime in the blind man's cup?

The second factor is the revolution now occurring in human culture. This is a revolution far more profound than any contemporary political movement. There are rare points in human history where such basic shifts occur. There is no precedent for our present industrial-technological revolution—except other *equally unprecedented* social changes in the past (such as the shift from a nomadic to an agricultural way of life).

This is a revolution that subjects society to constant and shattering changes. There is only one thing about modern society which does not change—and that is the relentless process of change itself. No sooner does the Model T Ford take us out of our homes (revolutionizing our sexual mores in the process) than television brings us back into them (destroying the art of conversation in the process). We have not planned these changes and culturally we are too immature to know how to control them.

There are no stable institutions to which the individual can turn. The son cannot follow his father's trade even if he wants to, for technology destroys old trades one day and creates new ones the next. Cultural patterns are eroded by a system of mass production and mass communication in which we all become like one another, speaking the same language, wearing the same clothes, reading the same magazines. But instead of creating a sense of community, this only creates a crowd of faceless and anonymous men.

How is a man to know who he is today? By what does he identify himself? Not by a relationship to the soil on which he was born—for we have left the land for the city, where we flit like harried vagrants from one apartment to another. Nor can a person find his identity in the family—for that institution is breaking down. By winning the right to enter the labor market women have found a degree of economic freedom that makes marriage less necessary—our high divorce rate is one price we pay for technological progress. The sudden equality of the sexes creates tension in both men and women as they realize that their old roles are destroyed but are uncertain what their new ones should be.

This is the society of the mass. We know everyone by his first name—

trying to imply a relationship which doesn't exist. Families living in an apartment house are more isolated from their neighbors a few feet away than were families on the American frontier who lived twenty miles apart. The individual is never able to feel that he is an important part of some meaningful whole. Our hearts ache with loneliness, but we don't know how to talk to one another. "Society" is a word from which all content has been drained. Society doesn't mean community—there is no community, only what David Riesman calls "the lonely crowd."

The third factor influencing youth is the loss of values we have experienced. Medieval man had a set of values centering around the Church— a belief in God gave meaning to life. Rationalist philosophy, emerging triumphant from the French Revolution, destroyed the medieval concept of God, but substituted the concept of the inherent rationality and perfectibility of man. We might not go to heaven, but the human race was on its way to utopia. God was dead, but so was the Devil—we didn't need redemption, we just needed education. When education failed to produce the desired miracles, Marxists argued that the problem lay in the "system," that man could still make his own utopia, but that he would need a revolution first.

The liberal hope for utopia died of poison gas in World War I. The revolutionary hope for utopia was shot in the back of the head during the Soviet purge trials. After Dachau and Buchenwald, all that was left of our faith in the ultimate goodness and rationality of man was a bar of soap and some lampshades made of human flesh.

We emerged from World War II without any sense of basic moral values. Words like "freedom" and "peace" became masks for conformity and violence and the death of individual spontaneity. Both the Soviet and the American blocs speak of themselves as defenders of peace and democracy. Yet what student can forget or ignore the realities of dead men and women in the streets of Budapest, or the harried flight of the Dalai Lama? The bright collective banners of Communism can no longer hide its treason against the concept of a society where the individual man would be liberated (not simply where the working class would be liberated, for one never liberates "groups"—*if freedom is not experienced by the individual there is no freedom*).

And can we make any defense at all of the "free nations of the West"? There is no more ardent or inflexible defender of freedom than the United States—freedom for the people of Russia, of Hungary, of Tibet. But the concern for freedom is betrayed by the United States in precisely those areas where it has power to make the ideal a reality. In Algeria it supplies the French with NATO arms. In Formosa it overlooks the tyranny of Chiang Kai-shek over the native population. In Latin America it supported Batista and supplied him with military equipment until he was overthrown. The ultimate expression of America's disregard for any concept of "truth" was contained in those statements of the Administration favoring nuclear tests in order "to give humanity a Clean Hydrogen Bomb." Youth senses intuitively that a set of relative "values" which not only permits but *demands* the building of hydrogen bombs and guided missiles is not a set of values at all, but a rationale for insanity.

Young people disaffiliate from society because they see it as phoney—it is not "real" enough to bother changing. I remember how well this alienation was brought home to me as I was talking to a juvenile delinquent who belonged to a gang, stole cars and got drunk on weekends. He was a smart kid from a good family, but he saw society as absolutely phoney—the only way he knew to assert himself against society was to break as many of its rules as he could. At one point he said: "The guys I really can't stand are the 'clubbies' at school—they still believe in the system." The 'clubbies' he was talking about were the members of the leading social clubs on campus. He didn't envy them. They hadn't rejected him—he had rejected them. The tragic fact is that many of our best young people, our potential leaders, have turned to crime as a rebellion against a society they do not understand and do not trust. With a great deal of justification, they believe that anyone who is socially responsible to an irresponsible and dishonest society is being played for a sucker.

But the beat generation is in the process of growth—having rejected society because it lacks real values, the individual finds himself compelled to search out the meaning of life and of reality. This search must, by its very nature, be individual. Without a set of values social action is impossible. This generation is not "silent," nor has it been bludgeoned into conformity —it is simply functioning outside of society altogether.

It is this concern for understanding reality—for experiencing all possible levels of reality—that accounts for the wide use of drugs like marijuana and peyote. Most of the poets and hipsters take these drugs to help unlock the doors of the other levels of reality and experience, not "just for the kicks." (Neither marijuana nor peyote is habit forming; marijuana usually has a mild effect which is different with each individual, while peyote is stronger. Both drugs seem to have the ability to erase the barrier between the conscious and unconscious mind. Neither drug is particularly harmful physically—probably not as dangerous as alcohol—but use of either may result in a psychotic break with reality.)

In his sexual behavior also, the hipster seeks new levels of experience. One writer asked me if I didn't think it was terrible that there is so much homosexuality among the beats. This is nonsense. There is no more exclusively homosexual behavior among the beat generation than there is in "normal" society and perhaps there is less. But there is a lot of bisexual behavior and a greater freedom in having sexual relations. This is not because the hipster is trying to turn life into one long orgy, but because he believes in carrying relationships with people as far and as deep as possible. One of the beatest characters I ever knew was a girl who told me she felt it was terrible to go to bed with someone you didn't like very much. She couldn't understand how people could make such a big thing of sex itself. At the same time she felt that if you liked someone very much you ought to sleep with him or her at least once, because sex helped bring you closer to the person. I don't put this forward as ideal sexual morality, but it is a lot healthier than the sexual morality of many "un-beat" squares, for whom the sexual partner is only a means of gratifying their own physical needs, and not a human being to be loved and respected.

Thus far we have discussed the obvious reasons for the existence of the beat generation. But there is a fourth reason at work which is the real dynamite of the movement. This is the rebellion against rationality—the attempt by the hipster to establish a sense of meaning and of community by accepting the irrational and intuitive aspect of his personality.

And here, if we are to understand the hipster, we must discuss the role of jazz. Jazz is the international language of the beat generation. Whenever you find the beats, there also you will find jazz. The British Isles are awash with young kids playing in "skiffle" bands (a form of early New Orleans jazz produced on washboards, jugs, kazoos, etc.). Russians tell American tourists that the most popular programs on the "Voice of America" are the jazz programs. Recently in Yugoslavia three thousand five hundred youth waited six hours for a concert by Louis Armstrong.

It is superficial to say that youth has adopted jazz because it is a music of protest. True, jazz music contains an element of protest—particularly early jazz, which grew from Negroes alienated from a white culture. But it is hard to accept this "obvious" explanation as the real one. The real explanation, I think, is that jazz is irrational music. It is music of spontaneity, of improvisation. A good jazz group does not need written music, a rehearsal or even a discussion. Starting with some tune the group knows, and working out from a steady beat, the musicians can create their music on the spot—directly out of themselves.

Jazz appears as something of a mass social movement in a society which fears the unconscious as a seething maelstrom of incest, murder and the death wish; a society terrified that the unconscious may burst forth and overwhelm the "rational" mind. It is natural that a culture based on science and rationality must fear the intuitive, must try to deny and repress it. Rather than accepting the intuitive (i.e., the irrational) as a necessary part of ourselves and the source of all our creative impulses, we have tried to cut it off altogether.

This breakthrough of irrationality is not confined to jazz and the hipsters. We find it also in modern art, and in the theater. It is natural to find the beat writers, the jazz musicians and the abstract painters in voluntary association—they share a common affirmation of the intuitive as opposed to the rational. Nor is it surprising that this group has met with such intense hostility from so many quarters. The antagonism is based on the fear which a rational culture has for something it cannot understand and therefore cannot control.

The beat generation, in embracing jazz, is also acting to create its own community. For many hipsters jazz is a kind of a religious experience, demanding the participation of the listener. To quote from a letter that I recently received from a young jazz musician: "You grab the fistfulls of notes by the balls or rather they grab you. You hold on and you stay on top, riding, flying. You know you are alive. You become the notes and the sound. Everything becomes one and your personality ceases to exist as a personality—it becomes what you blow."

This description applies to a jazz audience as well as to the musician. A hip crowd listening to a good jazz group will interrupt with shouts of "Go Man Go— Go! Go! Go! Go!" and will greet the end of the number with shouts and applause, for it was more than a piece of music being played —it was a group experience shared, a ritual of community in which the individual could lose himself and thus identify with the whole group.

In embracing the intuitional element of man, the beat generation may point toward basic cultural change. Science has reached a dead end—hard as it may try, it cannot give us a set of values. It cannot tell us "why"— only "how." If man is to live in peace with his technology, then I think he will have to make peace with his intuitional self. (This assumption, that a set of values may be based on the intuitional aspect of personality, raises, of course, certain basic questions of a religious nature, including the possibility that "God" is not as dead as we had assumed. It seems possible to me that the beat generation may herald a rebirth of a religious movement— but if so, a religious movement quite unlike any of the major religions in the West, as they are now practiced.)

When people refer to the beat generation and the hipsters as passing fads they could not be more mistaken. The terms will change—they always do—and the slick magazines will move on to find some new interest. But the hipster was there long before *Time* discovered him. And the beat generation, by whatever name it is called, is the natural expression of our times, international in character and deeply rooted in the chaos of our society.

For all his faults, the hipster is a hero of our times because he has rebelled against a society which is only rational *but no longer sane,* a society which, because it has divorced man from his intuitive self, can talk calmly of waging nuclear war. The hipster's ability to act spontaneously in a society which demands conformity is in itself an affirmation of the ability of the human being to will his own actions.

There is a final point to make, concerning those of us who are liberals and radicals. We must understand that many of our best youth will not return to political action until politics assumes an existential value. This is to say that our means must be compatible with our ends. In a world where the human race may die at any moment the wise man will not sell his soul in hope that his present evil may purchase future good. He will insist that each act have positive meaning in itself.

Our politics must have integrity, which means that it must be based on the one absolute value left in our world—the individual human being as a unique and valuable object that we will not shoot or jail or hate. Let us shape our dogmas to fit the living reality of individual persons instead of trying to shape people to fit the sterile framework of abstract theories. Through direct action on a community level—politics based on people—we must establish that sense of community which is so terribly absent from contemporary life.

I believe in the human race and in its future. I am convinced that the hipster also wants desperately to believe—that the one great weakness of the beat generation is its inability to affirm life. A real affirmation of life means a great deal more than what Gary Snyder calls "a kind of mindless enthusiasm"—it means the joy and the agony of involvement in life itself, as a participant and not merely as an observer. But before the hipster will participate he must see in action an ideal worth the involvement. It is a Gandhi, not a Stevenson, that the hipster will follow. The only way to give meaning to politics or to life in this troubled and uncertain world is to recognize that, whatever the "future" may hold, politics will have value only if we are committed to act with integrity in the present.

The Anatomy of Academic Discontent

Bruno Bettelheim

Bruno Bettelheim (b. 1903) was born in Vienna, came to the United States in 1939, and became a naturalized citizen in 1944. He teaches psychology and psychiatry at the University of Chicago, where he is Rowley Professor of Education. His publications include *Love Is Not Enough: The Treatment of Emotionally Disturbed Children* (1950), *Truants from Life* (1955), *The Empty Fortress* (1967), and *Children of the Dream* (1969).

While history does not repeat itself, and while the present situation in the United States is radically different from that of pre-Hitler Germany, some similarities between the present student rebellion in this country and what happened in the German universities to spearhead Hitler's rise to power are nevertheless striking. Politically, of course, the German student rebels embraced the extreme right, while here the dissenters embrace the extreme

THE ANATOMY OF ACADEMIC DISCONTENT: Reprinted by permission of Bruno Bettelheim and *Change* magazine, from *Change* magazine, May–June 1969.

left, but what is parallel is the determination to bring down the establishment. In Germany the philosophy which gained the rebels a mass following
was racist and directed against a discriminated minority (the Jews), while
here the radical students intend to *help* a discriminated minority. This is
an important difference, but it does not change the parallel that universities
then and now were forced to make decisions with respect to the race of students, rather than on the basis of disregard of racial origin. To use only one
example, German universities began to cave in when students coerced
faculties to appoint professorships in *Rassenwissenschaft;* that is, professorships devoted to teaching the special aspects, merits and achievements
of one race as opposed to others, rather than teaching the contributions to
knowledge, whatever the origins of the contributors.

Professor Walter Z. Laqueur (*Young Germany,* Basic Books, 1962)
says, "National Socialism came to power as the party of youth." Its cult
of youth was as pronounced as that of Italian fascism whose very hymn was
called "Youth" (Giovinezza). Hitler insisted all along that his movement
was a revolt "of the coming generation against all that was senile and rotten with decay in German democratic society." Professor Peter Gay (*Weimar Culture: The Outsider as Insider,* Harper and Row, 1968) stresses the
prevalence in pre-Hitler days of an ideology that pitted sons against fathers
and insisted that the generations cannot understand each other, that they
are deadly enemies; in short, an ideology that said exactly the same thing
in this respect that our rebellious students, who insist that nobody over
thirty is trustworthy, say today. Then, as now, the student rebels were pictured as the new generation, disgusted with the complacency of their parents, fighting courageously for a better world. And what were then the mass
media often depicted them as idealists, as young people concerned with
the real issues of society. They were, in their time, the wave of the future.
And leftist student activists in 1968 burned books they did not like in the
same manner and at the same place—Berlin—as did Hitler's youthful followers in 1933.

Then, as now, these youthful followers of the extremists were anti-
intellectual, resting their case on convictions based on their emotions. They
were fascinated with violence. Their favorite technique was to disrupt meetings, not just because they were not to their liking, but more as a demon-
stration of their power; and they created disorder which then was claimed
to demonstrate that the establishment was unable to function, and hence
had to be replaced by one based on their creed.

Having stressed these parallels, one must also recognize the vast differences between the present American student rebelliousness and that of
pre-Hitler Germany. It is these differences which should permit us to work
toward an entirely different outcome. If I read the signs of the time correctly,
I do not think that the rebellious students in and by themselves are a serious
danger to this country, although they are a real danger to the universities.
The danger, I fear, is rather an opposite one: that the disgusting behavior

of a very small group of students—the overwhelming majority of our students are sound and wish nothing more than to take advantage of the opportunities higher education offers them—will arouse a severe counterreaction, so much so that their leftist radicalism may lead to a fascist type of backlash. This is the greatest danger inherent in their efforts to create chaos. To prevent chaos, and in desperation—and the rebels do succeed in creating desperation—repressive measures might be embraced which would be dangerous to our democratic institutions. Because of this danger, student rebellions must be dealt with in the best interest of all society, including that of the rebelling students themselves. But they can be dealt with intelligently and constructively only if the measures adopted are designed to eliminate the causes of the widespread discontent.

To understand this discontent, one has to realize first that many more young people go to college today than ever before, and hence many more are much less prepared for it. Taking advantage of college and being satisfied with the experience, rather than being defeated by it, requires a considerable amount of self-discipline and a high degree of satisfaction with developing one's intellect. Present-day education, both at home and in school, teaches very little self-discipline compared to even very recent times. The expectation now is that education can hand over knowledge and skills, and nearly instantly; and there is a widespread feeling that if students do not do well in school, then this is the failing of the educational system, not the result of a lack of personal application. With each year in school, this feeling becomes stronger in those who do not do well academically. And with it, the system becomes the enemy which deliberately withholds from them what they believe it could so easily give; hence their hatred of the system.

To understand why pressures erupt in adolescence on a growing scale nowadays, and why society's controls seem to grow weaker, we must recognize that adolescent revolt is not a stage of development that follows automatically from our natural makeup. What makes for adolescent revolt is the fact that our society keeps the younger generation too long dependent in terms of mature responsibility and a striving for independence. Years ago, when formal schooling ended for the vast majority at the age of fourteen or fifteen and thereafter one became self-supporting, married and had children, there was no need for adolescent revolt. Because while puberty is a biological given, adolescence as we know it with its identity crises is not. All children grow up and become pubertal; but by no means do they all become adolescents. To be adolescent means that one has reached, and even passed, the age of puberty, is at the height of physical development—healthier, stronger, even handsomer than one has been or will be for the rest of one's life; but to be adolescent also means that one must nevertheless postpone full adulthood long beyond what any other period in history has considered reasonable. And the educational experiences in home and school prepare well only a small minority of young people for such a prolonged waiting, for being able to control their angry impatience while waiting.

It is this waiting for the real life that creates a climate in which a sizeable segment of college students can at least temporarily be seduced into following the lead of small groups of militants. It seems to give them a chance to prove themselves as real men. Thus it is the empty wait for real life which makes for student rebellions. This can be seen from the fact that most of the rebellious students, here and abroad, are either undergraduates, are studying the social sciences and the humanities, or both. There are few militants among students of medicine, engineering, the natural sciences; they are busy doing things that are important to them: they are working in the laboratory and at their studies. It is those students who do not quite know what they are preparing themselves for and why, those students who sit around waiting for examinations rather than doing active work, who form the cadres of the student rebellion.

One example may stand for many. In a class I am presently teaching, a student who was close to the activists gave me, at first, a very hard time in class. Two months later he was one of my most interested, cooperative students. I asked him what happened. He answered: "A few weeks ago I got a job which interests me, and I also began to be interested in my classes; that did it."

There are today far too many students in college who essentially have no business there. Some are there to evade the draft; many others are there out of a vague idea that it will help them to find better paying jobs, although they do not know what jobs they want. And many go to college simply because they do not know what better to do and because it is expected of them. Their deep dissatisfaction with themselves and their inner confusion is projected first against the university, and second against all institutions of society, which are blamed for their own inner weakness.

To make matters worse, our institutions of higher learning have expanded much too rapidly; under public pressure for more education for everybody, they have increased enrollment beyond reason. The result is classes which are too large, and which are often taught in our large universities by teaching assistants, some of whom, out of their own inner dissatisfaction and insecurity, tend to side with the rebellion. All this leads to the anonymity, the impersonal nature of student-faculty contacts, about which many students rightly complain. And since many of them are essentially not interested in the intellectual adventure, the knowledge which the faculty can convey to them is not what they want. What they do want, essentially, is group therapeutic experiences to help them to mature, to be secure, to find themselves. But since colleges are not mass therapeutic institutions, they disappoint the students where their greatest need lies.

Because of the vast expansion in numbers, moreover, the old methods to lend coherence to the college experience, and to offer students a life geared to the needs of late adolescence, have disintegrated. This the fraternities and sororities used to do by offering group homes to ease the transition from family to society at large. But they no longer can contain the large proportion of students. The demand of some black students for separate black housing should therefore be understood, at least in part, as the consequence of their feeling lost in the anonymous mass of students. Indeed, most white students are similarly lost until they find themselves in their work and study experiences. The old rituals which enhanced student life and bound students both to each other and to their college—the football rallies, the homecomings—have lost most of their meaning and have been replaced by nothing equalling the excitement which the sit-ins and protests provide. The spirit of intimate comradeship—important as at no other time in life—that used to prevail in the fraternity house is now found by all too many students in their demonstrations, where they feel closely bound together, doing things which they deep down know they do also for the emotional satisfaction of simply being together, whatever high sounding issues they think are motivating their actions. Nor should the symbolic meaning of students invading the dean's or president's office, whether violently or non-violently, be overlooked; big in age and size, they inwardly feel like little boys, and hence they need to play big by sitting in papa's big chair. They want to have a say in how things are run, want to sit in the driver's seat, not because they feel competent to do so, but because they cannot bear to feel incompetent.

It is unnatural to keep large numbers of young people in dependency and attending school for some twenty years. This was the way of life for that small elite which always in the past went to universities, but never did they represent more than a small percentage of the youth population, the vast majority of which actively met life early and proved itself as men and women, as real and strong human beings. Now, however, the tremendous push to send everybody to college has brought into the university an incredibly large number of young people who do not find their self-realization through study, or through the intellectual adventure. Yet, still needing to find their early manhood, they try to change the university into something in which they can find it by engaging in an active, sometimes violent, battle against the existing order or all of society. Their victory would change the university into an institution no longer dedicated to the intellectual virtues, to the frontiers of knowledge, but dedicated, rather, to the belligerent reshaping of society; and this is exactly what the militants want—not to engage in study and research, but in political battles. The reason we didn't have student revolts of this kind and this scope before is partly because only those went to college who wanted to be educated, and partly because those students who had to put themselves through school proved their early manhood—at least to some degree—by the very fact that they could do so. I think many of the rebellious students today are essentially guilt-ridden individuals. They feel terribly guilty about all their advantages, including their exemption from the draft, which is a serious guilt. Unable to bear living with their inner guilt, they try to destroy society or certain of its institutions rather than deal with it.

Since all too many students who now go to college have little interest, ability and use for what constitutes a college education, they would be better off with a high-level vocational education closely linked to a work program to give scope to their needs for physical activity and visible, tangible achievement. The complaint of many of these students is that nobody needs them. They view themselves as parasites of society, and therefore come to hate the society which they think makes them feel this way. Here we should learn from the communist countries where studies are combined with work in factories and in the fields. This, I believe, would be a much better arrangement for those students who do not feel a deep commitment to the intellectual enterprise (that is, study and research), and those who are so committed will never constitute more than a relatively small segment of youth.

I would, in fact, urge the creation of a government program of a couple of years' duration—a civilian Peace Corps—in which young people would work on socially significant projects while earning pay for it, and simultaneously receive higher vocational training. After such service and training, only those who really wish to do so would enter the universities, while the rest would feel a much greater stake in a society they helped to rebuild; at the least, they would be well-prepared for permanent jobs. Such a program should be an alternative to the draft. Only those young men who volunteer should serve in the armed forces. And I am convinced that if every able-bodied person were required to serve two years in national service of some kind, there would be no scarcity of volunteers for the armed forces, particularly if military servicemen received advantages in pay or other special advantages at the end of their service. This would also eliminate the draft exemption of college students which, in connection with the war in Vietnam, is behind so much of the student unrest. *If I am exempt from service when others are not, I can live in peace with myself only if convinced this is a vile war.*

In calming the dissent that is so widespread on our campuses now, we should concentrate our efforts on separating the ready followers from the small group of rebellion leaders. Were it not for the widespread discontent, protest leaders would find a scant following, and if they should break the law without such followers, they could be readily dealt with. It is the mass following they can arouse because of the widespread malaise which alone makes them dangerous.

There has always been a small percentage of persons bent on destroying society and on fomenting revolution. In earlier generations there were the Wobblies; later there were the campus communists. But the present brand of campus revolutionaries, who are of anarchist and nihilist persuasion, are much more dangerous because they can point to success after success with their disrupting tactics. And nothing succeeds like success. Two hundred years ago Immanuel Kant warned that we shall never be able to control violence if it is rewarded. "It is far more convenient," he wrote, "to commit an act of violence, and afterwards excuse it, than laboriously to consider convincing arguments and lose time in listening to objections. This very boldness itself indicates a sort of conviction of the legitimacy of the action, and the God of success is afterwards the best advocate."

The greatest danger presently, then, is the readiness with which violence is excused, and the seemingly convincing arguments which are brought forth to justify it before and after the act. Worst and most dangerous of all, there seems to be a tendency in our society to legitimize the results of violence so that, as Kant put it, the God of success afterwards serves as advocate for the violent action that preceded it, and suggests its future use. On our campuses, those committed to violence (to quote Kant again) "lose no time on considering arguments, or on listening to objections." They refuse to be rational about their grievances and, by violent means, insist on having their way, no matter what. And if they get it, as Kant knew, their success then legitimizes their disruptive actions.

The rebels gain their success by arousing a sizeable number of students through the tactic of confrontation, and by the universities' fear of confrontation. Confrontation has one important aim—to use the reaction of the provoked to generate a new unity among the demonstrators. In its most direct form, militants have stood in front of policemen and denounced them as pigs until the men in uniform hit out. The art of demonstrating then lies in ensuring that the blows are directed against the less-committed demonstrators and, if possible, against completely uninvolved persons. This provides the mass following required for success.

Of the small group of leaders of the radical left, it has been observed that most come from well-educated, very liberal families. Of those whom I know, I would say, too, that they have had their intellectual abilities developed very highly at much too early an age, at the expense of their emotional development. Although often very bright, emotionally some of them remained fixated at the age of the temper tantrum. It is this discrepancy between great intellectual maturity and utter emotional immaturity which is so baffling, often even to the universities, where some members of the faculty fail to see behind the obvious intelligence the inability to act rationally, and most of all, the inability to act responsibly. It is one of the weaknesses of university professors that, as persons committed to value intellectual ability most highly, they are captivated by the intelligence of these students to the degree that they are ready to excuse or brush aside the students' disruptiveness and intellectual arrogance.

As for the discontented students themselves, psychologically I always found them hating themselves as intensely as they hate the establishment, a self-hatred they try to escape by fighting *any* establishment. They need help in overcoming their emotional difficulties, and punishment is hardly the answer. If we bring them to the universities, we should provide facilities for helping them. It is their emotional immaturity that explains both their call for immediate action, and the retreat of the dropout and the hippy into utter non-action; each masks the inability of very intelligent young people to take time to think things out. The militants must want to destroy the universities because they do not want to be students, for to be a student means to prepare oneself to do something more worthwhile in the future. The militant student's cry is for action now, not preparation for action later. In this sense, he is no longer a student at all, since he clearly rejects knowledge as a precondition of meaningful activity. Truth, moreover, is no longer sought but "revealed"; the contempt for free speech and free thought is demonstrated as much by his actions as by his words. Were he ever to capture the university, it would cease to be a university.

In their inability to delay action for thought, both right and left extremists, the militants of all colors, are brothers under the skin. This is among the reasons why historically it has happened before that the young followers of the extreme right have become those of the extreme left, or the other way around. The mainspring of the rebels' action is more their wish to prove themselves strong—and less any particular political conviction—superimposed on self-doubt and hatred of a society which they feel has left them out in the cold. In Germany the National Socialists and the Communists voted together and worked together to bring down the democratic Weimar government, and in the same context, it is not so surprising that former Nazis easily involved themselves in the communistic government of East Germany.

But there are also good reasons why it is mainly the children of leftist parents who become hippies or student revolutionaries in our society, just as in other places and other times the children of conservative parents, under similar emotional conditions, spearheaded rightwing radicalism. It was the children of conservative German parents, for example, who first embraced the Emperor's War and enthusiastically went to their death because they felt a need to lay their bodies on the line for ideas their parents had only lukewarmly held; for thus they proved themselves strong, while at the same time proving their parents weak, wishy-washy and unworthy of true respect. They felt, too, that this was a means of rebirth, a way to revitalize an ossified society, to create a new society; with little patience for the voice of reason, they asked for authenticity and confrontation. All these were the main tenets of Hitler's academic youth, as they are now those of our own student left.

Thus, while the emotional constellations which make for very different student revolts are strangely similar, the specific political content of a student revolt depends to a large degree on the beliefs of the students' parents. For in many ways rebellion represents a desperate wish by youth to do better than their parents in exactly those beliefs in which parents seem weakest. In this sense, rebellion also represents a desperate desire for parental approval, but even more it represents a desperate wish that parents had been stronger in their convictions. So many of our radicals embrace Maoism and chant "Ho, Ho, Ho Chi Minh" much as another generation chanted at football rallies. These are strong father-figures with strong convictions who powerfully coerce their "children" to follow their commands. While consciously the students demand freedom and participation, unconsciously their commitment to Mao and other dictatorships suggests their desperate need for controls from the outside, since without them they are unable to bring order into their inner chaos. Such controls, however, must not be imposed punitively, nor for the benefit of others. They must be controls that clearly and definitely benefit the individual, so that he will eventually make them his own.

The inability of militant students to wait and work hard for long-range goals marks them as emotionally disturbed; so does their hatred for their parents who failed to give them direction and set them against the world by exposing their immature minds to criticism of all that could have given meaning to their lives. Indeed, it is their hatred of society that makes it so easy for the militant student leaders to make common cause with another small group that provides temporary leadership for some of the rebellions: outright paranoid individuals. The proportion of paranoids among students is no greater than in any comparable group of the population. But they are more dangerous because of their high intelligence, which permits them to conceal more successfully the degree of their disturbance. And student revolt permits them to act out their paranoia to a degree that no other position in society permits. How understandable, then, that all paranoids who can, do flock into the ranks of the militants. Unfortunately, most non-experts do not know how persuasive paranoids can be, at least until they are recognized. The persuasiveness of a Hitler or a Stalin is now regarded as the consequence of his own paranoia and his unconscious appeal to the vague paranoid tendencies among the immature and disgruntled. I have no doubt that the ranks of today's militants contain some would-be Hitlers and Stalins.

Paranoids make a persuasive appeal to any group in the population which rightly or wrongly feels persecuted, and they seek out such groups because they are most likely to view their own paranoia as true understanding of a persecuted group's particular predicament. Which brings me to the special problems of some of our black students who, fortunately, seem to recognize more and more that SDS is using them rather than helping them. (They are not quite as successfully seeing through the motives of some of the paranoid student leaders.)

The overwhelming majority of black students desires exactly the same as does the overwhelming majority of white students: a rightful place in society. Only a very small minority of black and white students wishes to destroy it. Thus if the blacks could be convinced that there is a good place for them in society, their attitude would change and they would part ways with SDS, as many of them have already done. But the difficulty is that many black students, because of the nature of the commitment of the university, do not feel that being a student is necessarily the best way for them to find their rightful place in society. It is here that our wish and theirs, that they should become part of the elite, runs afoul of what for many of them is their reality. Many black students in our colleges are often ill-prepared academically and lacking in the skills required for academic success. At the same time, they have been imbued with the notion that it is the fault of the establishment that they are disadvantaged. While this is true to some degree, awareness of such truth offers an easy way out if one does not succeed. All students find the transition from home to college difficult. In past times the student placed the blame for this on himself, and most students therefore tried to do something about themselves and sooner or later succeeded. Today both white and black students tend to blame the faculty for the difficulties they encounter in adjusting to a different way of life and study. The demand for black-study programs originated, not only in the justified feeling that one must be familiar and proud of one's own background, but to a large degree in the feeling that such studies would be easier, and that the faculty would have greater understanding.

The fact is that the preparation of some black students who are induced to go to college is inferior to that of the white majority of the college population. While the faculty is ready to make allowances for this, compensation runs counter to the self-respect of the black student, who rightly does not wish to be treated as a second-class citizen. But if he cannot compete successfully with his fellow students who have had so many educational and social advantages, he is in a terrible conflict. Brought to college to do as well as the others, when he fails his background does not permit him to accept the fact of failure because of his lack of preparation; to do so would make him feel second-class, a position he is seeking to escape by obtaining a college education. Although intellectually able, he has difficulty in adjusting, and he comes to feel that the very place which promised to make him equal fails to do so. Disappointed, he rages against the institution which once more makes him feel inferior, and special programs of assistance only make his feelings of inferiority even deeper. The many black students who are well able to hold their own with the best feel they must not desert their fellow black comrades, and in times of protest, they make their comrades' burden their own.

If we want to bring a large number of black students into our universities, as we should, we must start much earlier than college. From high school on, it will be necessary to educate a larger number of blacks, together with white youngsters from culturally deprived backgrounds, in true prep schools to permit them to enter college as well prepared academically and socially as the more advantaged students.

There is today a fascination in society with sex and violence, with drugs and insanity, which both influences the student militants and provides them with a noteworthiness which they exploit to the full. If students protest in an orderly and rational fashion, they receive little public attention. But if they shed their clothes and walk around naked, this makes news all over the nation, whatever case they may or may not have had; it is part of a dangerous fascination with youth and its extreme positions. What passes for modern literature which these youngsters read in junior high school intoxicates their minds with the appeal of drug-induced madness, with sexual acting out and with violence.

The universities, because of their intellectual prestige, give the student activists a platform for their revolutionary claims which they otherwise would never have. For example, for days not more than some twenty to thirty students recently occupied the administration building of the University of Chicago. They got headlines every day and were prominently featured on radio and television. Had thirty people demonstrated in any other place, they would have received no attention whatever. This SDS knows, and this is why it aims at the universities. The contrast between an institution devoted to the highest achievements of reason, and the obscenity and violence perpetrated there, makes it all the more fascinating, a fascination on which SDS tries to build its revolutionary success.

An idea in itself may amount to next to nothing, but it becomes news by interfering with something else which is considered to be of public importance. In themselves, a couple of hundred demonstrators somewhere in New York or Chicago would amount to very little; but when fifty students march into a lecture hall, seize control of the podium and broadcast their claims and philosophy to people who came to hear something quite different—then they have made news. If someone advocates urinating on graves (as the Fugs did), or if a few girls dress up as witches and put curses on professors (as they did in Chicago), if they did so without reference to politics, people would rightly wonder about their sanity. But when they do so as a condemnation of the Vietnam war or in the name of some progressive cause, they win the support of many older liberals and enlightened radicals who invariably consider it all very socially significant. When a teen-ager wrestles with the police for the sake of the moral superiority of a future social order, he cannot fail to obtain the sympathetic attention of radio and television editors, if not psychiatrists. The ritualistic invocation of ideology is thus both an alibi and a defense.

Perhaps it all has made too many headlines, perhaps it has been talked about too much for people to accept the fact, but the truth of the matter is that these rebellions can and do paralyze our universities. Not only are classes interrupted and buildings occupied, but faculty members must devote their energies to calming things down. Even more importantly, the time and energy which should be devoted to more lasting achievements are drained away on plans to forestall new confrontations. A last comparison with pre-Hitler days: In Germany at that time, as Professor George L. Mosse (*The Crisis of German Ideology,* Grosset and Dunlap, 1964) puts it, "professors tended to be either scholars who withdrew into their own specialty, taking scant notice of the world around them, or men who attempted to play the role of prophets. The first kind of academic wanted only to be left in peace. . . . The professor as prophet, with very few exceptions indeed, was to be found on the side of the revolting students." Of the students of that time he says, "They had found a basis for action that opposed existing authority yet remained independent of any political movement directed by their elders." And the faculties, he says, "failed to provide any opposition, failed to use administrative powers and failed to organize effective alternative groups of students. At best they displayed a detached passivity . . . at worst they joined in the harassment."

In our universities today we have faculty members who are trying to remain aloof from it all, and others who are trying to anticipate even the most radical student demands so as to avoid confrontations. Worse, though, there are few efforts being made to organize effective alternative groups of students. Worst of all, many professors are so intimidated that they cave in even before the students exercise pressure. It is the continuous worry about what the militant students may do next, the anxious efforts to give them no offense, which saps the universities of their strength to the point of paralysis. And this anxious avoidance of taking a firm stand gives not only these militants, but also many non-committed students, the feeling that they have the faculty on the run.

If the colleges and universities would take a determined stand against coercion and intimidation—though always open to, indeed inviting, reasonable and non-coercive discussion about much-needed reform—then student rebellions could be reduced to the point where they would no longer threaten either the universities or society. The university must strengthen its will to resist disruption and coercion. If it succeeds, it will have little need to take recourse to punitive measures, beyond setting into practice the principle that those who do not wish to have any part of our universities should have their will: they should not be permitted to be, live or work in a place they hate, not as a punishment, but because to remain in a place they hate and despise serves no good purpose and is detrimental to their emotional well-being.

4 / ESSAYS FORMAL AND INFORMAL

The World That Books Have Made

W. H. Auden

> W. H. Auden (b. 1907) is one of the most distinguished poets of our time. He (with Chester Kallman) has supplied the libretti for a number of operas. He has also contributed numerous essays and articles to magazines on both sides of the Atlantic. A selection of these appeared in 1962 under the title *The Dyer's Hand.* His most recent book is *Secondary Worlds* (1968).

"**O**f the making of books there is no end," sighed the Preacher more than two thousand years ago. "We read many books because we cannot know enough people," said Mr. Eliot wryly only a few years ago. "They are so right," I say to myself this morning. But how is it that I am able to agree with them? Because I have bought and read their books. There is a real case to be made out against reading, but the prosecutor has to have had direct experience of what he is talking about, which puts him in the paradoxical position of Carlyle, who is said to have extolled the virtues of silence in nineteen volumes.

The principal charges brought against books are two. The first is the psychologist's assertion that all imaginative literature, fiction or verse,

THE WORLD THAT BOOKS HAVE MADE: Reprinted from the *New York Times Book Review,* December 2, 1951, by permission of W. H. Auden. Copyright © 1951 by The New York Times Company. Reprinted by permission.

indulges day-dreaming and makes it difficult for its devotees to adjust to the demands of reality. There is a small grain of sense in this position, but only a small one. Let us, however, swallow it whole; it still betrays a false identification of human weakness with a particular means of indulging it; like all puritanical reformers, the ascetic preacher of the Reality Principle argues that, if the means of indulgence are cut off, the desire will wither away, a doubtful proposition. I often spend time reading detective stories when I ought to be answering letters, but, if all detective stories were suppressed, I see no reason to believe that I should not find some other device for evading my duty.

The second, and more serious, objection to the printed word is that the language, sensibility and wisdom of literate persons are, in so many cases, inferior to that of the illiterate—the D. H. Lawrence pro-peasant position. How much substance is there in this? It is nonsense to talk of the "second-hand" experience gained from books in contrast to the "firsthand" experience gained from the bookless life, for human beings are not born, like the insects, fully equipped for life, but have to learn almost everything secondhand from others. If we were limited to our firsthand, that is, our sensory experience, we should still be living in trees on a diet of raw vegetables. If a literate person seems inferior to an illiterate, this means that the quality of experience he is gaining from his reading is inferior to that which a peasant gains from talking to his father or his neighbors. The remedy is not to stop him reading but to persuade him to read better books.

The pro-illiteracy position confuses symptom and cause. The real disease in our technological civilization is the ever-widening gap between the size and nature of the social organization required for the mass production of cheap consumer goods, and the size and nature of a psychologically and politically healthy community. When Aristotle asserted that a variable community is one in which everybody can recognize the faces of his neighbors, and when Plato set the population figure of the ideal community at 5,040, they based their conclusions on an estimate of man's spiritual and political nature which history has, till now, confirmed. How the problem of cheap goods versus a civilized community is to be solved, few would dare to pretend that they know; I only know that the abolition of books would solve nothing.

The what-would-happen-if game is always amusing to play. Suppose, then, our society exactly as it is except for the printed word, an industrial society without printing presses, typewriters or mimeograph machines. Two things would certainly vastly improve, our memory and our handwriting. From our earliest years we should be trained to learn great masses of material by heart, and the person whose hand was illegible would be at a grave economic disadvantage. Skilled occupations would become more and more specialized and probably hereditary. The necessity of either keeping all the knowledge requisite to one's job in one's head or of having access to rare and costly manuscripts would narrow the field in which anyone could hope to be an expert, and the personal intimacy between teacher and pupil which the oral transmission of knowledge demands would have to be so close and last so long that it would inevitably tend to become a family affair.

Mass entertainment, movies, radio, television, would not be immediately much affected, but, in the long run, the same symptoms would appear and there would grow up a caste of professional storytellers with very rigid and conservative conventions. Politically, whatever the form of state in theory, we should, in practice, be governed by a small conservative oligarchy. Indeed, every would-be dictator must dream of a world in which the means of entertainment and popular instruction are restricted to the screen and the loudspeaker. Movies require a lot of apparatus, time and money to make and exhibit, an opposition radio station can readily be jammed, a street-corner orator cannot attract a following without the knowledge of the police, but books and pamphlets are relatively cheap to produce and easy to carry and conceal. In an industrialized society, no printing press, no minority, is an axiom.

Thank God, then, for the printing press, and thank God for books, even for the publishers' free copies which keep piling up in my closet and on which I can never give an opinion because I shall never read them, just as I shall never read *Kalevala, The Anatomy of Melancholy* or *Pamela*. The annual tonnage of publications is terrifying if I think about it, but I don't have to think about it. That is one of the wonderful things about the written word; it cannot speak until it is spoken to. (Imagine the horror of life if bars had literary equivalents to Muzak and the juke-box.) In theory I may feel that there are too many books, but in practice I complain that there are not enough—when, for instance, I try to obtain the collected works of some favorite author and find that half of them are out of print, or when I try to find exactly the right book as a gift to a friend. Of course a great many of the books I do read are mediocre or dull, but life, as Henry James remarked, is, luckily for us, only capable of splendid waste, and every now and then I am rewarded by one which gives such happiness and excitement that the memory of every wasted or tedious hour is soon obliterated.

Finally, and most fervently of all, thank God for books as an alternative to conversation. People may say all they like about the plethora of books, their low quality and the damage they do, but the same charges, only ten times more strongly, can be brought against that unruly member, the human tongue. What has been said of youth applies, unfortunately, to most of us: "How wonderful we should be if we could not hear what we said." Luckily we forget 99 per cent of it immediately; otherwise we should very soon find ourselves restricted to the company of our cats and dogs. I have what I believe is an invaluable suggestion to offer to any hostess. Buy a stack of writing pads and pencils and then throw a dumb cocktail party. Even the most hardened bore who thinks nothing of trapping an unfortunate fellow guest in a corner and asking him "What do you think of Modern Poetry?" would lose his nerve, I think, if he had to commit himself on paper.

The Written Word

Marshall McLuhan

> Marshall McLuhan (b. 1911) is a professor of English at the University of Toronto. His many publications include *The Mechanical Bride* (1951), a satiric examination of advertising, *The Gutenberg Galaxy* (1962), and *Understanding Media* (1964). It is interesting to compare Auden's account of what McLuhan calls the "Age of Gutenberg" with that contained in the chapter from *Understanding Media* printed below.

Prince Modupe wrote of his encounter with the written word in his West African days:

> The one crowded space in Father Perry's house was his bookshelves. I gradually came to understand that the marks on the pages were *trapped words*. Anyone could learn to decipher the symbols and turn the trapped words loose again into speech. The ink of the print trapped the thoughts; they could no more get away than a *doomboo* could get out of a pit. When the full realization of what this meant flooded over me, I experienced the same thrill and amazement as when I had my first glimpse of the bright lights of Konakry. I shivered with the intensity of my desire to learn to do this wondrous thing myself.

In striking contrast to the native's eagerness, there are the current anxieties of civilized man concerning the written word. To some Westerners the written or printed word has become a very touchy subject. It is true that there is more material written and printed and read today than ever before, but there is also a new electric technology that threatens this ancient technology of literacy built on the phonetic alphabet. Because of its action in extending our central nervous system, electric technology seems to favor the inclusive and participational spoken word over the specialist written word. Our Western values, built on the written word, have already been considerably affected by the electric media of telephone, radio, and TV. Perhaps that is the reason why many highly literate people in our time find it difficult to examine this question without getting into a moral panic. There is the further circumstance that, during his more than two thousand years of literacy, Western man has done little to study or to understand the effects of the phonetic alphabet in creating many of his basic patterns of culture. To begin now to examine the question may, therefore, seem too late.

THE WRITTEN WORD: From *Understanding Media: The Extensions of Man* by Marshall McLuhan. Copyright © 1964 by Marshall McLuhan. Used with permission of McGraw-Hill Book Company. Reprinted by permission of Routledge and Kegan Paul Ltd.

Suppose that, instead of displaying the Stars and Stripes, we were to write the words "American flag" across a piece of cloth and to display that. While the symbols would convey the same meaning, the effect would be quite different. To translate the rich visual mosaic of the Stars and Stripes into written form would be to deprive it of most of its qualities of corporate image and of experience, yet the abstract literal bond would remain much the same. Perhaps this illustration will serve to suggest the change the tribal man experiences when he becomes literate. Nearly all the emotional and corporate family feeling is eliminated from his relationship with his social group. He is emotionally free to separate from the tribe and to become a civilized individual, a man of visual organization who has uniform attitudes, habits, and rights with all other civilized individuals.

The Greek myth about the alphabet was that Cadmus, reputedly the king who introduced the phonetic letters into Greece, sowed the dragon's teeth, and they sprang up armed men. Like any other myth, this one capsulates a prolonged process into a flashing insight. The alphabet meant power and authority and control of military structures at a distance. When combined with papyrus, the alphabet spelled the end of the stationary temple bureaucracies and the priestly monopolies of knowledge and power. Unlike pre-alphabetic writing, which with its innumerable signs was difficult to master, the alphabet could be learned in a few hours. The acquisition of so extensive a knowledge and so complex a skill as pre-alphabetic writing represented, when applied to such unwieldy materials as brick and stone, insured for the scribal caste a monopoly of priestly power. The easier alphabet and the light, cheap, transportable papyrus together effected the transfer of power from the priestly to the military class. All this is implied in the myth about Cadmus and the dragon's teeth, including the fall of the city states, the rise of empires and military bureaucracies.

In terms of the extensions of man, the theme of the dragon's teeth in the Cadmus myth is of the utmost importance. Elias Canetti in *Crowds and Power* reminds us that the teeth are an obvious agent of power in man, and especially in many animals. Languages are filled with testimony to the grasping, devouring power and precision of teeth. That the power of letters as agents of aggressive order and precision should be expressed as extensions of the dragon's teeth is natural and fitting. Teeth are emphatically visual in their lineal order. Letters are not only like teeth visually, but their power to put teeth into the business of empire-building is manifest in our Western history.

The phonetic alphabet is a unique technology. There have been many kinds of writing, pictographic and syllabic, but there is only one phonetic alphabet in which semantically meaningless letters are used to correspond to semantically meaningless sounds. This stark division and parallelism between a visual and an auditory world was both crude and ruthless, culturally speaking. The phonetically written word sacrifices worlds of meaning and perception that were secured by forms like the hieroglyph and the

Chinese ideogram. These culturally richer forms of writing, however, offered men no means of sudden transfer from the magically discontinuous and traditional world of the tribal word into the cool and uniform visual medium. Many centuries of ideogrammic use have not threatened the seamless web of family and tribal subtleties of Chinese society. On the other hand, a single generation of alphabetic literacy suffices in Africa today, as in Gaul two thousand years ago, to release the individual initially, at least, from the tribal web. This fact has nothing to do with the *content* of the alphabetized words; it is the result of the sudden breach between the auditory and the visual experience of man. Only the phonetic alphabet makes such a sharp division in experience, giving to its user an eye for an ear, and freeing him from the tribal trance of resonating word magic and the web of kinship.

It can be argued, then, that the phonetic alphabet, alone, is the technology that has been the means of creating "civilized man"—the separate individuals equal before a written code of law. Separateness of the individual, continuity of space and of time, and uniformity of codes are the prime marks of literate and civilized societies. Tribal cultures like those of the Indian and the Chinese may be greatly superior to the Western cultures, in the range and delicacy of their perceptions and expression. However, we are not here concerned with the question of values, but with the configurations of societies. Tribal cultures cannot entertain the possibility of the individual or of the separate citizen. Their ideas of spaces and times are neither continuous nor uniform, but compassional and compressional in their intensity. It is in its power to extend patterns of visual uniformity and continuity that the "message" of the alphabet is felt by cultures.

As an intensification and extension of the visual function, the phonetic alphabet diminishes the role of the other senses of sound and touch and taste in any literate culture. The fact that this does not happen in cultures such as the Chinese, which use nonphonetic scripts, enables them to retain a rich store of inclusive perception in depth of experience that tends to become eroded in civilized cultures of the phonetic alphabet. For the ideogram is an inclusive *gestalt,* not an analytic dissociation of senses and functions like phonetic writing.

The achievements of the Western world, it is obvious, are testimony to the tremendous values of literacy. But many people are also disposed to object that we have purchased our structure of specialist technology and values at too high a price. Certainly the lineal structuring of rational life by phonetic literacy has involved us in an interlocking set of consistencies that are striking enough to justify a much more extensive inquiry than that of the present chapter. Perhaps there are better approaches along quite different lines; for example, consciousness is regarded as the mark of a rational being, yet there is nothing lineal or sequential about the total field of awareness that exists in any moment of consciousness. Consciousness is not a verbal process. Yet during all our centuries of phonetic literacy we have favored the chain of inference as the mark of logic and reason. Chinese writing, in contrast, invests each ideogram with a total intuition of being and reason that allows only a small role to visual sequence as a mark of mental effort and organization. In Western literate society it is still plausible and acceptable to say that something "follows" from something, as if there were some cause at work that makes such a sequence. It was David Hume who, in the eighteenth century, demonstrated that there is no causality indicated in any sequence, natural or logical. The sequential is merely additive, not causative. Hume's argument, said Immanuel Kant, "awoke me from my dogmatic slumber." Neither Hume nor Kant, however, detected the hidden cause of our Western bias toward sequence as "logic" in the all-persuasive technology of the alphabet. Today in the electric age we feel as free to invent nonlineal logics as we do to make non-Euclidean geometries. Even the assembly line, as the method of analytic sequence for mechanizing every kind of making and production, is nowadays yielding to new forms.

Only alphabetic cultures have ever mastered connected lineal sequences as pervasive forms of psychic and social organization. The breaking up of every kind of experience into uniform units in order to produce faster action and change of form (applied knowledge) has been the secret of Western power over man and nature alike. That is the reason why our Western industrial programs have quite involuntarily been so militant, and our military programs have been so industrial. Both are shaped by the alphabet in their technique of transformation and control by making all situations uniform and continuous. This procedure, manifest even in the Graeco-Roman phase, became more intense with the uniformity and repeatability of the Gutenberg development.

Civilization is built on literacy because literacy is a uniform processing of a culture by a visual sense extended in space and time by the alphabet. In tribal cultures, experience is arranged by a dominant auditory sense-life that represses visual values. The auditory sense, unlike the cool and neutral eye, is hyper-esthetic and delicate and all-inclusive. Oral cultures act and react at the same time. Phonetic culture endows men with the means of repressing their feelings and emotions when engaged in action. To act without reacting, without involvement, is the peculiar advantage of Western literate man.

The story of *The Ugly American* describes the endless succession of blunders achieved by visual and civilized Americans when confronted with the tribal and auditory cultures of the East. As a civilized UNESCO experiment, running water—with its lineal organization of pipes—was installed recently in some Indian villages. Soon the villagers requested that their pipes be removed, for it seemed to them that the whole social life of the village had been impoverished when it was no longer necessary for all to visit the communal well. To us the pipe is a convenience. We do not think of it as culture or as a product of literacy, any more than we think of literacy as changing our habits, our emotions, or our perceptions. To nonliterate people, it is perfectly obvious that the most commonplace conveniences represent total changes in culture.

The Russians, less permeated with the patterns of literate culture than Americans, have much less difficulty in perceiving and accommodating the Asiatic attitudes. For the West, literacy has long been pipes and taps and streets and assembly lines and inventories. Perhaps most potent of all as an expression of literacy is our system of uniform pricing that penetrates distant markets and speeds the turn-over of commodities. Even our ideas of cause and effect in the literate West have long been in the form of things in sequence and succession, an idea that strikes any tribal or auditory culture as quite ridiculous, and one that has lost its prime place in our own new physics and biology.

All the alphabets in use in the Western world, from that of Russia to that of the Basques, from that of Portugal to that of Peru, are derivatives of the Graeco-Roman letters. Their unique separation of sight and sound from semantic and verbal content made them a most radical technology for the translation and homogenization of cultures. All other forms of writing had served merely one culture, and had served to separate that culture from others. The phonetic letters alone could be used to translate, albeit crudely, the sounds of any language into one-and-the-same visual code. Today, the effort of the Chinese to use our phonetic letters to translate their language has run into special problems in the wide tonal variations and meanings of similar sounds. This has led to the practice of fragmenting Chinese mono-syllables into polysyllables in order to eliminate tonal ambiguity. The Western phonetic alphabet is now at work transforming the central auditory features of the Chinese language and culture in order that China can also develop the lineal and visual patterns that give central unity and aggregate uniform power to Western work and organization. As we move out of the Gutenberg era of our own culture, we can more readily discern its primary features of homogeneity, uniformity, and continuity. These were the characteristics that gave the Greeks and Romans their easy ascendancy over the nonliterate barbarians. The barbarian or tribal man, then as now, was hampered by cultural pluralism, uniqueness, and discontinuity.

To sum up, pictographic and hieroglyphic writing as used in Babylonian, Mayan, and Chinese cultures represents an extension of the visual sense for storing and expediting access to human experience. All of these forms give pictorial expression to oral meanings. As such, they approximate the animated cartoon and are extremely unwieldy, requiring many signs for the infinity of data and operations of social action. In contrast, the phonetic alphabet, by a few letters only, was able to encompass all languages. Such an achievement, however, involved the separation of both signs and sounds from their semantic and dramatic meanings. No other system of writing had accomplished this feat.

The same separation of sight and sound and meaning that is peculiar to the phonetic alphabet also extends to its social and psychological effects.

Literate man undergoes much separation of his imaginative, emotional, and sense life, as Rousseau (and later the Romantic poets and philosophers) proclaimed long ago. Today the mere mention of D. H. Lawrence will serve to recall the twentieth-century efforts made to by-pass literate man in order to recover human "wholeness." If Western literate man undergoes much dissociation of inner sensibility from his use of the alphabet, he also wins his personal freedom to dissociate himself from clan and family. This freedom to shape an individual career manifested itself in the ancient world in military life. Careers were open to talents in Republican Rome, as much as in Napoleonic France, and for the same reasons. The new literacy had created an homogeneous and malleable milieu in which the mobility of armed groups and of ambitious individuals, equally, was as novel as it was practical.

The Dog That Bit People

James Thurber

> James Thurber (1894–1961) began his career as a journalist. Later he became managing editor of *The New Yorker,* and later still, a staff writer and contributor. He is well known for his cartoons, many of which appeared in *The New Yorker,* as well as for his essays. Collections of these include *The Seal in the Bedroom* (1932), *My Life and Hard Times* (1933), *Men, Women and Dogs* (1943), *Alarms and Diversions* (1957), and *Let Your Mind Alone* (1960).

Probably no one man should have as many dogs in his life as I have had, but there was more pleasure than distress in them for me except in the case of an Airedale named Muggs. He gave me more trouble than all the other fifty-four or -five put together, although my moment of keenest embarrassment was the time a Scotch terrier named Jeannie, who had just had six puppies in the clothes closet of a fourth floor apartment in New York, had the unexpected seventh and last at the corner of Eleventh Street and Fifth Avenue during a walk she had insisted on taking. Then, too, there was the prize winning French poodle, a great big black poodle—none of your little, untroublesome white miniatures—who got sick riding in the rumble seat of a car with me on her way to the Greenwich Dog Show. She had a red rubber bib tucked around her throat and, since a rain storm came up when we were half way through the Bronx, I had to hold over her a small green umbrella, really more of a parasol. The rain beat down fearfully and suddenly the driver of the car drove into a big garage, filled with mechanics. It happened so quickly that I forgot to put the umbrella down and I will always remember, with sickening distress, the look of incredulity mixed with hatred that came over the face of the particular hardened garage man that came over to see what we wanted, when he took a look at me and the poodle. All garage men, and people of that intolerant stripe, hate poodles with their curious hair cut, especially the pom-poms that you got to leave on their hips if you expect the dogs to win a prize.

But the Airedale, as I have said, was the worst of all my dogs. He really wasn't my dog, as a matter of fact: I came home from a vacation one summer to find that my brother Roy had bought him while I was away. A big, burly, choleric dog, he always acted as if he thought I wasn't one of the family. There was a slight advantage in being one of the family, for he didn't bite the family as often as he bit strangers. Still, in the years that we had him he bit everybody but mother, and made a pass at her once but missed. That was during the month when we suddenly had mice, and Muggs refused to do anything about them. Nobody ever had mice exactly like the mice we had that month. They acted like pet mice, almost like mice somebody had trained. They were so friendly that one night when mother entertained at dinner the Friraliras, a club she and my father had belonged to for twenty years, she put down a lot of little dishes with food in them on the pantry floor so that the mice would be satisfied with that and wouldn't come into the dining room. Muggs stayed out in the pantry with the mice, lying on the floor, growling to himself—not at the mice, but about all the people in the next room that he would have liked to get at. Mother slipped out into the pantry once to see how everything was going. Everything was going fine. It made her so mad to see Muggs lying there, oblivious of the mice—they came running up to her—that she slapped him and he slashed at her, but didn't make it. He was sorry immediately, mother said. He was always sorry, she said, after he bit someone, but we could not understand how she figured this out. He didn't act sorry.

Mother used to send a box of candy every Christmas to the people the Airedale bit. The list finally contained forty or more names. Nobody could understand why we didn't get rid of the dog. I didn't understand it very well myself, but we didn't get rid of him. I think that one or two people tried to poison Muggs—he acted poisoned once in a while—and old Major Moberly fired at him once with his service revolver near the Seneca Hotel in East Broad Street—but Muggs lived to be almost eleven years old and even when he could hardly get around he bit a Congressman who had called to see my father on business. My mother had never liked the Congressman—she said the signs of his horoscope showed he couldn't be trusted (he was Saturn with the moon in Virgo)—but she sent him a box of candy that Christmas. He sent it right back, probably because he suspected it was trick candy. Mother persuaded herself it was all for the best that the dog had bitten him, even though father lost an important business association because of it. "I wouldn't be associated with such a man," mother said. "Muggs could read him like a book."

*Nobody knew exactly what
was the matter with him.*

We used to take turns feeding Muggs to be on his good side, but that didn't always work. He was never in a very good humor, even after a meal. Nobody knew exactly what was the matter with him, but whatever it was it made him irascible, especially in the mornings. Roy never felt very well in the morning, either, especially before breakfast, and once when he came downstairs and found that Muggs had moodily chewed up the morning paper he hit him in the face with a grapefruit and then jumped up on the dining room table, scattering dishes and silverware and spilling the coffee. Muggs' first free leap carried him all the way across the table and into a bronze fire screen in front of the gas grate but he was back on his feet in a moment and in the end he got Roy and gave him a pretty vicious bite in the leg. Then he was all over it; he never bit anyone more than once at a time. Mother always mentioned that as an argument in his favor; she said he had a quick temper but that he didn't hold a grudge. She was forever defending him. I think she liked him because he wasn't well. "He's not strong," she would say, pityingly, but that was inaccurate; he may not have been well but he was terribly strong.

One time my mother went to the Chittenden Hotel to call on a woman mental healer who was lecturing in Columbus on the subject of "Harmonious Vibrations." She wanted to find out if it was possible to get harmonious vibrations into a dog. "He's a large tan-colored Airedale," mother explained. The woman said that she had never treated a dog but she advised my mother to hold the thought that he did not bite and would not bite. Mother was holding the thought the very next morning when Muggs got the iceman but she blamed that slip-up on the iceman. "If you didn't think he would bite you, he wouldn't," mother told him. He stomped out of the house in a terrible jangle of vibrations.

One morning when Muggs bit me slightly, more or less in passing, I reached down and grabbed his short stumpy tail and hoisted him into the air. It was a foolhardy thing to do and the last time I saw my mother, about six months ago, she said she didn't know what possessed me. I don't either, except that I was pretty mad. As long as I held the dog off the floor by his tail he couldn't get at me, but he twisted and jerked so, snarling all the time, that I realized I couldn't hold him that way very long. I carried him to the kitchen and flung him onto the floor and shut the door on him just as he crashed against it. But I forgot about the backstairs. Muggs went up the backstairs and down the frontstairs and had me cornered in the living room. I managed to get up onto the mantelpiece above the fireplace, but it gave way and came down with a tremendous crash throwing a large marble clock, several vases, and myself heavily to the floor. Muggs was so alarmed by the racket that when I picked myself up he had disappeared. We couldn't find him anywhere, although we whistled and shouted, until old Mrs. Detweiler called after dinner that night. Muggs had bitten her once, in the leg, and she came into the living room only after we assured her that Muggs had run away. She had just seated herself when, with a great growling and scratching of claws, Muggs emerged from under a davenport where he had been quietly hiding all the time, and bit her again. Mother examined the bite and put arnica on it and told Mrs. Detweiler that it was only a bruise. "He just bumped you," she said. But Mrs. Detweiler left the house in a nasty state of mind.

Lots of people reported our Airedale to the police but my father held a municipal office at the time and was on friendly terms with the police. Even so, the cops had been out a couple of times—once when Muggs bit Mrs. Rufus Sturtevant and again when he bit Lieutenant-Governor Malloy—but mother told them that it hadn't been Muggs' fault but the fault of the people who were bitten. "When he starts for them, they scream," she explained, "and that excites him." The cops suggested that it might be a good idea to tie the dog up, but mother said that it mortified him to be tied up and that he wouldn't eat when he was tied up.

Muggs at his meals was an unusual sight. Because of the fact that if you reached toward the floor he would bite you, we usually put his food plate on top of an old kitchen table with a bench alongside the table. Muggs would stand on the bench and eat. I remember that my mother's Uncle Horatio, who boasted that he was the third man up Missionary Ridge, was splutteringly indignant when he found out that we fed the dog on a table because we were afraid to put his plate on the floor. He said he wasn't

*Lots of people reported
our dog to the police.*

afraid of any dog that ever lived and that he would put the dog's plate on the floor if we would give it to him. Roy said that if Uncle Horatio had fed Muggs on the ground just before the battle he would have been the first man up Missionary Ridge. Uncle Horatio was furious. "Bring him in! Bring him in now!" he shouted. "I'll feed the —— on the floor!" Roy was all for giving him a chance, but my father wouldn't hear of it. He said that Muggs had already been fed. "I'll feed him again!" bawled Uncle Horatio. We had quite a time quieting him.

In his last year Muggs used to spend practically all of his time outdoors. He didn't like to stay in the house for some reason or other—perhaps it held too many unpleasant memories for him. Anyway, it was hard to get him to come in and as a result the garbage man, the iceman, and the laundryman wouldn't come near the house. We had to haul the garbage down to the corner, take the laundry out and bring it back, and meet the iceman a block from home. After this had gone on for some time we hit on an ingenious arrangement for getting the dog in the house so that we could lock him up while the gas meter was read, and so on. Muggs was afraid of only one thing, an electrical storm. Thunder and lightning frightened him out of his senses (I think he thought a storm had broken the day the mantelpiece fell). He would rush into the house and hide under a bed or in a clothes closet. So we fixed up a thunder machine out of a long narrow piece of sheet iron with a wooden handle on one end. Mother would shake this vigorously when she wanted to get Muggs into the house. It made an excellent imitation of thunder, but I suppose it was the most roundabout system for running a household that was ever devised. It took a lot out of mother.

A few months before Muggs died, he got to "seeing things." He would rise slowly from the floor, growling low, and stalk stiff-legged and menacing toward nothing at all. Sometimes the Thing would be just a little to the right or left of a visitor. Once a Fuller Brush salesman got hysterics. Muggs came wandering into the room like Hamlet following his father's ghost. His eyes were fixed on a spot just to the left of the Fuller Brush man, who stood it until Muggs was about three slow, creeping paces from him. Then he shouted. Muggs wavered on past him into the hallway grumbling to himself but the Fuller man went on shouting. I think mother had to throw a pan of cold water on him before he stopped. That was the way she used to stop us boys when we got into fights.

Muggs died quite suddenly one night. Mother wanted to bury him in the family lot under a marble stone with some such inscription as "Flights of angels sing thee to thy rest" but we persuaded her it was against the law. In the end we just put up a smooth board above his grave along a lonely road. On the board I wrote with an indelible pencil "Cave Canem." Mother was quite pleased with the simple classic dignity of the old Latin epitaph.

The Decline of the Graces

Max Beerbohm

Max Beerbohm (1872–1956) drew witty caricatures of many prominent British figures in literature and politics. These have been collected in *Twenty-five Gentlemen* (1896), *The Poet's Corner* (1904), and *Rossetti and His Circle* (1922). Beerbohm is also the author of a celebrated novel about Oxford, *Zuleika Dobson* (1911). But he is probably best known for his informal essays collected under such titles as *The Happy Hypocrite* (1897), *Yet Again* (1909), and *And Even Now* (1920). The student may be amused to compare the instructions in rhetoric provided for "Fair Russell" with those contained in this textbook.

Have you read *The Young Lady's Book?* You have had plenty of time to do so, for it was published in 1829. It was described by the two anonymous Gentlewomen who compiled it as "A Manual for Elegant Recreations, Ex-

---

THE DECLINE OF THE GRACES: From *Yet Again* by Max Beerbohm.

ercises, and Pursuits." You wonder they had nothing better to think of? You suspect them of having been triflers? They were not, believe me. They were careful to explain, at the outset, that the Virtues of Character were what a young lady should most assiduously cultivate. They, in their day, laboring under the shadow of the eighteenth century, had somehow in themselves that high moral fervor which marks the opening of the twentieth century, and is said to have come in with Mr. George Bernard Shaw. But, unlike us, they were not concerned wholly with the inward and spiritual side of life. They cared for the material surface, too. They were learned in the frills and furbelows of things. They gave, indeed, a whole chapter to "Embroidery." Another they gave to "Archery," another to "The Aviary," another to "The Escrutoire." Young ladies do not now keep birds, nor shoot with bow and arrow; but they do still, in some measure, write letters; and so, for sake of historical comparison, let me give you a glance at "The Escrutoire." It is not light reading.

> For careless scrawls ye boast of no pretence;
> Fair Russell wrote, as well as spoke, with sense.

Thus is the chapter headed, with a delightful little wood-engraving of "Fair Russell," looking preeminently sensible, at her desk, to prepare the reader for the imminent welter of rules for "decorous composition." Not that pedantry is approved. "Ease and simplicity, an even flow of unlabored diction, and an artless arrangement of obvious sentiments" is the ideal to be striven for. "A metaphor may be used with advantage" by any young lady, but only "if it occur naturally." And "allusions are elegant," but only "when introduced with ease, and when they are well understood by those to whom they are addressed." "An antithesis renders a passage piquant"; but the dire results of a too-frequent indulgence in it are relentlessly set forth. Pages and pages are devoted to a minute survey of the pitfalls of punctuation. But when the young lady of that period had skirted all these, and had observed all the manifold rules of calligraphy that were laid down for her, she was not, even then, out of the wood. Very special stress was laid on "the use of the seal." Bitter scorn was poured on young ladies who misused the seal. "It is a habit of some to thrust the wax into the flame of the candle, and the moment a morsel of it is melted, to daub it on the paper; and when an unsightly mass is gathered together, to pass the seal over the tongue with ridiculous haste—press it with all the strength which the sealing party possesses—and the result is, an impression which raises a blush on her cheek."

Well! The young ladies of that day were ever expected to exhibit sensibility, and used to blush, just as they wept or fainted, for very slight causes. Their tears and their swoons did not necessarily betoken much grief or agitation; nor did a rush of color to the cheek mean necessarily that they were overwhelmed with shame. To exhibit various emotions in the drawing-room was one of the Elegant Exercises in which these young ladies were drilled thoroughly. And their habit of simulation was so rooted in sense of duty that it merged into sincerity. If a young lady did not swoon at the breakfast-table when her Papa read aloud from *The Times* that the Duke of Wellington was suffering from a slight chill, the chances were that she would swoon quite unaffectedly when she realized her omission. Even so, we may be sure that a young lady whose cheek burned not at sight of the letter she had sealed untidily—"unworthily" the Manual calls it—would anon be blushing for her shamelessness. Such a thing as the blurring of the family crest, or as the pollution of the profile of Pallas Athene with the smoke of the taper, was hardly, indeed, one of those "very slight causes" to which I have referred. The Georgian young lady was imbued through and through with the sense that it was her duty to be gracefully efficient in whatsoever she set her hand to. To the young lady of today, belike, she will seem accordingly ridiculous—seem poor-spirited, and a pettifogger. True, she set her hand to no grandiose tasks. She was not allowed to become a hospital nurse, for example, or an actress. The young lady of today, when she hears in herself a "vocation" for tending the sick, would willingly, without an instant's preparation, assume responsibility for the lives of a whole ward at St. Thomas's. This responsibility is not, however, thrust on her. She has to submit to a long and tedious course of training before she may do so much as smooth a pillow. The boards of the theatre are less jealously hedged in than those of the hospital. If your young lady have a wealthy father, and retain her schoolroom faculty for learning poetry by heart, there is no power on earth to prevent her from making her debut, somewhere, as Juliet—if she be so inclined; and such is usually her inclination. That her voice is untrained, that she cannot scan blank-verse, that she cannot gesticulate with grace and propriety nor move with propriety and grace across the stage, matters not a little bit—to our young lady. "Feeling," she will say, "is everything"; and, of course, she, at the age of eighteen, has more feeling than Juliet, that "flapper," could have had. All those other things—those little technical tricks—"can be picked up," or "will come." But no; I misrepresent our young lady. If she be conscious that there are such tricks to be played, she despises them. When, later, she finds the need to learn them, she still despises them. It seems to her ridiculous that one should not speak and comport oneself as artlessly on the stage as one does off it. The notion of speaking or comporting oneself with conscious art in real life would seem to her quite monstrous. It would puzzle her as much as her grandmother would have been puzzled by the contrary notion.

Personally, I range myself on the grandmother's side. I take my stand shoulder to shoulder with the Graces. On the banner that I wave is embroidered a device of prunes and prisms.

I am no blind fanatic, however. I admit that artlessness is a charming idea. I admit that it is sometimes charming as a reality. I applaud it (all the more heartily because it is rare) in children. But then, children, like the young of all animals whatsoever, have a natural grace. As a rule, they begin to show it in their third year, and to lose it in their ninth. Within that span of six years, they can be charming without intention; and their so frequent failure in charm is due to their voluntary or enforced imitation of the ways of their elders. In Georgian and Early Victorian days the imitation was always enforced. Grown-up people had good manners, and wished to see them reflected in the young. Nowadays, the imitation is always voluntary. Grown-up people have no manners at all; whereas they certainly have a very keen taste for the intrinsic charm of children. They wish children to be perfectly natural. That is (aesthetically, at least) an admirable wish. My complaint against these grown-up people is, that they themselves, whom time has robbed of their natural grace as surely as it robs the other animals, are content to be perfectly natural. This contentment I deplore, and am keen to disturb.

I except from my indictment any young lady who may read these words. I will assume that she differs from the rest of the human race, and has not, never had, anything to learn in the art of conversing prettily, of entering or leaving a room or a vehicle gracefully, of writing appropriate letters, *et patati et patata*. I will assume that all these accomplishments came naturally to her. She will now be in a mood to accept my proposition that of her contemporaries none seems to have been so lucky as herself. She will agree with me that other girls need training. She will not deny that grace in the little affairs of life is a thing which has to be learned. Some girls have a far greater aptitude for learning it than others; but, with one exception, no girls have it in them from the outset. It is a not less complicated thing than is the art of acting, or of nursing the sick, and needs for the acquirement of it a not less laborious preparation.

Is it worth the trouble? Certainly the trouble is not taken. The "finishing school," wherein young ladies were taught to be graceful, is a thing of the past. It must have been a dismal place; but the dismalness of it—the strain of it—was the measure of its indispensability. There I beg the question. Is grace itself indispensable? Certainly it has been dispensed with. It isn't reckoned with. To sit perfectly mute "in company," or to chatter on at the top of one's voice; to shriek with laughter; to fling oneself into a room and dash oneself out of it; to collapse on chairs or sofas; to sprawl across tables; to slam doors; to write, without punctuation, notes that only an expert in handwriting could read, and only an expert in misspelling could understand; to hustle, to bounce, to go straight ahead—to be, let us say, perfectly natural in the midst of an artificial civilization, is an ideal which the young ladies of today are neither publicly nor privately discouraged from cherishing. The word "cherishing" implies a softness of which they are not guilty. I hasten to substitute "pursuing." If these young ladies were not in the aforesaid midst of an artificial civilization, I should be the last to discourage their pursuit. If they were Amazons, for example, spending their lives beneath the sky, in tilth of stubborn fields, and in armed conflict with fierce men, it would be unreasonable to expect of them any sacrifice to the Graces. But they are exposed to no such hardships. They have really a very comfortable sort of life. They are not expected to be useful. (I am writing all the time, of course, about the young ladies in the affluent classes.) And it seems to me that they, in payment of their debt to Fate, ought to occupy the time that is on their hands by becoming ornamental and increasing the world's store of beauty. In a sense, certainly, they are ornamental. It is a strange fact, and an ironic, that they spend quite five times the annual amount that was spent by their grandmothers on personal adornment. If they can afford it, well and good: let us have no sumptuary law. But plenty of pretty dresses will not suffice. Pretty manners are needed with them, and are prettier than they.

I had forgotten men. Every defect that I had noted in the modern young woman is not less notable in the modern young man. Briefly, he is a boor. If it is true that "manners makyth man," one doubts whether the British race can be perpetuated. The young Englishman of today is inferior to savages and to beasts of the field in that they are eager to show themselves in an agreeable and seductive light to the females of their kind, whilst he regards any such effort as beneath his dignity. Not that he cultivates dignity in demeanor. He merely slouches. Unlike his feminine counterpart, he lets his raiment match his manners. Observe him any afternoon, as he passes down Piccadilly, sullenly, with his shoulders humped, and his hat clapped to the back of his head, and his cigarette dangling almost vertically from his lips. It seems only appropriate that his hat is a billycock, and his shirt a flannel one, and that his boots are brown ones. Thus attired, he is on his way to pay a visit of ceremony to some house at which he has recently dined. No; that is the sort of visit he never pays. (I must confess I don't myself.) But one remembers the time when no self-respecting youth would have shown himself in Piccadilly without the vesture appropriate to that august highway. Nowadays there is no care for appearances. Comfort is the one aim. Any care for appearances is regarded rather as a sign of effeminacy. Yet never, in any other age of the world's history, has it been regarded so. Indeed, elaborate dressing used to be deemed by philosophers an outcome of the sex-instinct. It was supposed that men dressed themselves finely in order to attract the admiration of women, just as peacocks spread their plumage with a similar purpose. Nor do I jettison the old theory. The declension of masculine attire in England began soon after the time when statistics were beginning to show the great numerical preponderance of women over men; and is it fanciful to trace the one fact to the other? Surely not. I do not say that either sex is attracted to the other by elaborate attire. But I believe that each sex, consciously or unconsciously, uses this elaboration for this very purpose. Thus the over-dressed maiden of today and the ill-dressed youth are but symbols of the balance of our population. The one is pleading, the other scorning. "Take me!" is the message borne by the furs and the pearls and the old lace. "I'll see about that when I've had a look round!" is the not pretty answer conveyed by the billycock and the flannel shirt.

I dare say that fine manners, like fine clothes, are one of the stratagems of sex. This theory squares at once with the modern young man's lack of manners. But how about the modern young woman's not less obvious lack? Well, the theory will square with that, too. The modern young woman's gracelessness may be due to her conviction that men like a girl to be thoroughly natural. She knows that they have a very high opinion of themselves; and what, thinks she, more natural than that they should esteem her in proportion to her power of reproducing the qualities that are most salient in themselves? Men, she perceives, are clumsy, and talk loud, and have no drawing-room accomplishments, and are rude; and she proceeds to model herself on them. Let us not blame her. Let us blame rather her parents or guardians, who, though they well know that a masculine girl attracts no man, leave her to the devices of her own inexperience. Girls ought not to be allowed, as they are, to run wild. So soon as they have lost the natural grace of childhood, they should be initiated into that course of artificial training through which their grandmothers passed before them, and in virtue of which their grandmothers were pleasing. This will not, of course, ensure husbands for them all; but it will certainly tend to increase the number of marriages. Nor is it primarily for that sociological reason that I plead for a return to the old system of education. I plead for it, first and last, on aesthetic grounds. Let the Graces be cultivated for their own sweet sake.

The difficulty is, how to begin. The mothers of the rising generation were brought up in the unregenerate way. Their scraps of oral tradition will need to be supplemented by much research. I advise them to start their quest by reading *The Young Lady's Book*. Exactly the right spirit is therein enshrined, though of the substance there is much that could not be well applied to our own day. That chapter on "The Escrutoire," for example, belongs to a day that cannot be recalled. We can get rid of bad manners, but we cannot substitute the Sedan-chair for the motor-car; and the penny post, with telephones and telegrams, has, in our own beautiful phrase, "come to stay," and has elbowed the art of letter-writing irrevocably from among us. But notes are still written; and there is no reason why they should not be written well. Has the mantle of those anonymous gentlewomen who wrote *The Young Lady's Book* fallen on no one? Will no one revise that "Manual of Elegant Recreations, Exercises, and Pursuits," adapting it to present needs? ... A few hints as to Deportment in the Motor-Car; the exact Angle whereat to hold the Receiver of a Telephone, and the exact Key wherein to pitch the Voice; the Conduct of a Cigarette.... I see a wide and golden vista.

Prof 'Understanding' Right Up to the End

Art Buchwald

> Art Buchwald (b. 1925) is a syndicated columnist whose
> work appears in newspapers in this country and abroad.
> He has published several books, among them *Art Buch-
> wald's Paris* (1954), *Is It Safe to Drink the Water?* (1962),
> *I Chose Capitol Punishment* (1963), *Son of the Great
> Society* (1966), and *Have I Ever Lied to You?* (1968).

One of the things that impresses people about the student demonstrations
is the strong stand that some members of the faculty are taking on the issues.

I was on the campus of Northamnesty University and ran into a professor who was trying to stop his nose from bleeding.

"What happened, Professor?" I asked.

"The militant students just took over my office and threw me down
the stairs."

"Why, that's terrible," I said.

"From my point of view it is, but I think we have to look at it from their
point of view. Where have we, as faculty, failed them?"

"Are you going to press charges?"

"On the contrary. If I pressed charges, I would only be playing into the
hands of the repressive forces outside the university who would like nothing better than to see the students arrested for assault."

"But they did assault you?"

"Yes. But there was one heartening note. As they threw me down the
stairs, one of the students yelled, 'It isn't you, Professor. It's the system.' "

"Say, isn't that the philosophy building going up in flames?"

"I believe it is. Now, why did they have to go and set fire to the philosophy building?"

"I was going to ask you that."

"I'm not quite sure. My guess is that it probably has to do with something the administration and the students are at odds about."

"But that's a terrible thing to do."

"I would say burning down a philosophy building could be interpreted
as an unlawful act. At the same time, there are moments when an unlawful
act can bring about just reforms."

"Shouldn't we at least call the fire department?"

"I don't believe the fire department should be called until the faculty

PROF 'UNDERSTANDING' RIGHT UP TO THE END: Reprinted by permission of Art Buchwald,
from the *New Orleans Times-Picayune*, April 24, 1969, © 1969 the *Washington Post*. Reprinted by permission of Art Buchwald.

has met and voted on what course of action should be taken. There are times when a fire department can only inflame a situation. We should also hear from the students and get their side of it. After all, they have as much stake in the university as anyone else, and if they don't want a philosophy building, we should at least listen to their arguments."

"I never thought of it that way," I admitted. "Professor, I believe the militant students over at the quadrangle are building a scaffold. They wouldn't hang anyone, would they?"

"They haven't before," the professor said. "But it's quite possible that this is their way of seeking a confrontation with the establishment."

A group of students rushed up and grabbed the professor. "We got one here," the ringleader shouted. "Get the rope."

"Don't worry, Professor," I shouted as I was pushed away by the mob. "I'll get the police."

"I wish you wouldn't," he said calmly, as the students led him toward the scaffold. "If we don't let the students try new methods of activism, they'll never know for themselves which ones work and which ones are counterproductive."

Love in Paris and Red Tape Too

Art Buchwald

Of all the men I worked with on the Paris *Herald,* the one I admired the most was Milliken. Let me say right now that Milliken was not his real name, and I am using a false one only to protect the guilty, which Milliken certainly was.

Milliken was an American in his late twenties. He had a beard; he usually wore blue jeans and a torn sweater; he lived in a cold-water flat on the Left Bank; he was usually broke. And yet Milliken was always in the company of the most beautiful girls in Paris. They used to call him every day on my phone; they waited for him in front of the Paris *Herald* until midnight; they cooked breakfast for him; they let him use their bathtubs, and they lent him money until pay day. Milliken's cup was constantly running over.

I couldn't understand it and it drove me crazy. There had to be an an-

LOVE IN PARIS AND RED TAPE TOO: Reprinted by permission of The World Publishing Company from *I Chose Capitol Punishment* by Art Buchwald. Copyright © 1962 and 1963 by Art Buchwald.

swer somewhere. Finally after six months of taking his messages and watching him in operation, I could stand it no longer.

So one afternoon while we were having a drink at Fouquet's, on the Champs Elysées, I said, "Damn it all, Milliken, what's your secret? How do you get away with it?"

"Get away with what?" he said innocently.

"Get away with all these girls. You're not handsome, you're not rich, you don't even own a car. What right do you have to attract all these American women? What do they see in you?"

"It's quite simple," he said calmly. "No mystery about it at all. I promise to marry them."

"You what?"

"I promise to marry them. Once I promise to marry them, everything else comes easily."

"I don't get it," I said.

"All right, I'll explain it to you. Where did you get married?"

"In London."

"Why?" he asked.

"Because there is too much red tape for a foreigner who wants to get married in France. I waited four months and finally gave up."

"Exactly," said Milliken. "It's almost impossible for a foreigner to get married in France, so when I propose to a girl and we go down to the Prefect of Police to make an application for a marriage license, I know we'll never get it. But the girl doesn't know that, and while we're waiting for our papers to be processed, which they never will be, we're officially 'engaged.' And since I have proved I intend to marry the girl, she has no choice but to treat me as she would her future husband."

"Milliken, you're a rat," I said, trying to hide the awe in my voice.

"I am not a rat. The French bureaucrats are the rats. I am only taking advantage of an impossible governmental situation. I didn't make the loophole, but as with taxes, I have every right to make the most of it."

"But when does the girl wise up that you aren't going to marry her?"

"One month, maybe two months, maybe three, depending on how many times we visit the Prefect of Police. The more times we go down, the more discouraged she gets. But I must say I've never been blamed by any of them. They know I have no control over the French attitude toward foreigners getting married in France."

"It's an unbeatable system." I whistled.

"Too bad you went to London" was all he said to me.

During the next six months Milliken proposed to at least five girls that I know of, and I watched him with the envy of a man who sees someone rolling nothing but sevens at a crap table.

But then one day Milliken came rushing into the office, his face white, his hands shaking, stark fear in his eyes. "You've got to help me," he cried.

"What happened?"

"I proposed to this girl, a mousy one at that, last night, and this morning we went down to the Prefect of Police to apply for permission to get married and they're going to give it to us."

"It's impossible," I said.

"No, it isn't. The lady behind the counter said she didn't believe in red tape and if two people wanted to get married it was all she cared about. She's a crazy romantic."

"What can I do to help you?"

"Don't you know someone at the Prefect of Police who can stop it?"

"No, I don't."

"Well, come down with me this afternoon and tell them I'm married already, or I'm a deserter from the Army, or anything. You've got to save me."

I felt so sorry for Milliken I went down with him and his mousy fiancée to the Prefect.

"*Voilà*, Monsieur," the lady said. "I have all your papers."

The mouse screeched with joy.

"But I don't have my birth certificate," Milliken protested.

"Your passport will do."

"I better take a health examination."

"You look very healthy to me," the lady said.

"I'm married already," Milliken cried.

"Will you swear to that under oath?"

"No," said Milliken, "but he will." He pointed to me.

"The devil I will," I said.

"Then let's have no more nonsense, Monsieur," said the lady. "Marriage is a serious business and I have risked my job to see your papers were approved. Usually it would take months to get the permissions, but because you are both young and Americans, I have made an exception. Perhaps when they find out what I have done they will transfer me. But love is more important than the government."

Milliken was in a state of shock during the following week so I made all the arrangements at the local city hall for the wedding. I was Milliken's best man, my wife stood witness for the mouse. The mayor of the *arrondissement* made a beautiful speech in French about marriage and both my wife and the mouse cried.

After that there was no reason for Milliken to stay in Paris, and he moved back to the United States where he bought a house in Levittown, shaved off his beard, and got a job doing public relations for the Long Island Railroad. It's not a very pleasant picture and I try to drive it out of my mind. I always want to remember Milliken as the guy who almost broke the bank at Monte Carlo.

The Miniature Adults

Russell Baker

Russell Baker (b. 1925) is a newspaperman and columnist. Since 1954 he has been a member of the Washington bureau of the New York *Times* and his column appears regularly in the *Times*. His collections of short essays include *An American in Washington* (1961), *No Cause for Panic* (1964), and *All Things Considered* (1965).

A great deal is being thought and written nowadays about the problems of the aged, but there is no realistic agreement about who these aged are.

It is not enough to define them as the people over sixty-five, or "our senior citizens," to use the unctuous euphemism. Everyone knows of the over-forty group, which is too young for Social Security but too old to be hired, and of the over-forty-five group inside industry, which is too young to be retired but too old to start up the management ladder.

But there are many aged who are even younger than these. There is the whole generation of parents between the ages of thirty and forty who have come home one afternoon, to discover their children practicing teen-age-ism.

Teen-age-ism. It is a terrible thing, not to be confused with adolescence. No one can help being an adolescent; it is a natural stage of man. Being a teen-ager, on the other hand, is the youngest profession, an artificial condition imposed upon youth by peculiar forces in the society.

These forces compel the poor adolescent to behave according to the precepts of teen-age-ism, a curious philosophy which holds that youth is a terrible thing to happen to the young. To help them through this miserable period, the theory goes, the old folks (in the thirty-to-forty bracket) must humor them in the conceit that they are really little underdeveloped adults.

This may be very nice for the adolescents (although it probably isn't), but it places an enormously unfair burden on the parents. If a twelve-year-old starts thinking of himself as adult, he is naturally going to start thinking of his parents as senescent ("square" is the word in common usage) and start treating them accordingly.

A mother of thirty-five years who finds herself being treated like an old woman, or a square, is bound to start feeling self-conscious about her age, no matter how frisky she may feel at the cocktail hour. Intimations of mortality will inevitably begin to intrude into her carefree moments.

"Drinking again, Mother!" the miniature adult may say, with only the slightest hint of censure, poisoning the moment and opening views onto a future of gray hair and failed liver.

"But you're too young for a Tony Curtis haircut!" the father may protest to his eleven-year-old boy. And the boy's "Oh, Dad! Get with it!" is a veiled threat to have the old gentleman committed to a rocking chair.

In these moments of despair, the old folks may occasionally remind the miniature adults that it hasn't been long since they learned to do the Jitterbug on the drugstore corner. A terrible mistake. Anyone old enough to remember Elvis Presley is ancient, and all before that is Egyptology.

The result on the parents is shocking. One day they are rocking contentedly along, thinking of themselves as "young marrieds," the stars of the American advertising drama; the next, they are simply "the folks" to a pack of cunning little adults, or, in really acute cases, "the old man" and "the old lady."

Can this premature aging be avoided? Probably not any longer in the United States nor in Western Europe. Teen-age-ism, which originated here, is traveling the earth like a plague. There is no reason to think that the children like it, but they have no way to escape it.

It is drilled into them by movies, television, disk jockeys, newspapers, magazines, authors, lecturers and merchandisers. All have combined to create the awful trial known as "teen-age" and to teach the wretched young how to survive it.

Aside from the strain on the children, the terrible part of all this is the way it lowers the threshold of old age into the thirties. Some heretics say that a false sense of youth can be preserved if parents will occasionally lay about them with a strap, but the prophets of teen-age-ism regard this as unwholesome and warn that the teen-agers may retaliate by going into an expensive neurosis. The bills for analysis usually age the old folks very rapidly indeed.

5 / CRITICISM

Dickens

George Santayana

George Santayana (1863–1952) was a philosopher, poet, novelist, and critic. He was born in Spain but was brought as a child of nine to live in the United States. For many years he was a professor of philosophy at Harvard. In 1912 he resigned to spend the rest of his life in travel and study. His last years were spent in Rome. Santayana's one novel, *The Last Puritan,* appeared in 1935. His best-known philosophical works are *The Sense of Beauty* (1896), *The Life of Reason* (1905–06), and *Scepticism and Animal Faith* (1923). *Soliloquies in England and Later Soliloquies,* from which "Dickens" is taken, appeared in 1925 and reflects his deep and abiding interest in England and English culture.

If Christendom should lose everything that is now in the meltingpot, human life would still remain amiable and quite adequately human. I draw this comforting assurance from the pages of Dickens. Who could not be happy in

DICKENS: "Dickens" is reprinted with the permission of Charles Scribner's Sons from *Soliloquies in England and Later Soliloquies* by George Santayana. Reprinted by permission of Constable & Co. Ltd.

his world? Yet there is nothing essential to it which the most destructive revolution would be able to destroy. People would still be as different, as absurd, and as charming as are his characters; the springs of kindness and folly in their lives would not be dried up. Indeed, there is much in Dickens which communism, if it came, would only emphasize and render universal. Those schools, those poorhouses, those prisons, with those surviving shreds of family life in them, show us what in the coming age (with some sanitary improvements) would be the nursery and home of everybody. Everybody would be a waif, like Oliver Twist, like Smike, like Pip, and like David Copperfield; and amongst the agents and underlings of social government, to whom all these waifs would be entrusted, there would surely be a goodly sprinkling of Pecksniffs, Squeerses and Fangs; whilst the Fagins would be everywhere commissioners of the people. Nor would there fail to be, in high places and in low, the occasional sparkle of some Pickwick or Cheeryble Brothers or Sam Weller or Mark Tapley; and the voluble Flora Finchings would be everywhere in evidence, and the strong-minded Betsy Trotwoods in office. There would also be, among the inefficient, many a Dora and Agnes and Little Emily—with her charm but without her tragedy, since this is one of the things which the promised social reform would happily render impossible; I mean, by removing all the disgrace of it. The only element in the world of Dickens which would become obsolete would be the setting, the atmosphere of material instrumentalities and arrangements, as travelling by coach is obsolete; but travelling by rail, by motor, or by airship will emotionally be much the same thing. It is worth noting how such instrumentalities, which absorb modern life, are admired and enjoyed by Dickens, as they were by Homer. The poets ought not to be afraid of them; they exercise the mind congenially, and can be played with joyfully. Consider the black ships and the chariots of Homer, the coaches and riverboats of Dickens, and the aeroplanes of today; to what would an unspoiled young mind turn with more interest? Dickens tells us little of English sports, but he shares the sporting nature of the Englishman, to whom the whole material world is a playing-field, the scene giving ample scope to his love of action, legality, and pleasant achievement. His art is to sport according to the rules of the game, and to do things for the sake of doing them, rather than for any ulterior motive.

It is remarkable, in spite of his ardent simplicity and openness of heart, how insensible Dickens was to the greater themes of the human imagination—religion, science, politics, art. He was a waif himself, and utterly disinherited. For example, the terrible heritage of contentious religions which fills the world seems not to exist for him. In this matter he was like a sensitive child, with a most religious disposition, but no religious ideas. Perhaps, properly speaking, he had no *ideas* on any subject; what he had was a vast sympathetic participation in the daily life of mankind; and what he saw of ancient institutions made him hate them, as needless sources of oppression, misery, selfishness, and rancour. His one political passion was philanthropy, genuine but felt only on its negative, reforming side; of positive utopias or enthusiasms we hear nothing. The political background of Christendom is only, so to speak, an old faded back-drop for his stage; a castle, a frigate, a gallows, and a large female angel with white wings standing above an orphan by an open grave—a decoration which has to serve for all the melodramas in his theatre, intellectually so provincial and poor. Common life as it is lived was varied and lovable enough for Dickens, if only the pests and cruelties could be removed from it. Suffering wounded him, but not vulgarity; whatever pleased his senses and whatever shocked them filled his mind alike with romantic wonder, with the endless delight of observation. Vulgarity—and what can we relish, if we recoil at vulgarity?—was innocent and amusing; in fact, for the humorist, it was the spice of life. There was more piety in being human than in being pious. In reviving Christmas, Dickens transformed it from the celebration of a metaphysical mystery into a feast of overflowing simple kindness and good cheer; the church bells were still there—in the orchestra; and the angels of Bethlehem were still there—painted on the back curtain. Churches, in his novels, are vague, desolate places where one has ghastly experiences, and where only the pew-opener is human; and such religious and political conflicts as he depicts in *Barnaby Rudge* and in *A Tale of Two Cities* are street brawls and prison scenes and conspiracies in taverns, without any indication of the contrasts in mind or interests between the opposed parties. Nor had Dickens any lively sense for fine art, classical tradition, science, or even the manners and feelings of the upper classes in his own time and country: in his novels we may almost say there is no army, no navy, no church, no sport, no distant travel, no daring adventure, no feeling for the watery wastes and the motley nations of the planet, and—luckily, with his notion of them—no lords and ladies. Even love of the traditional sort is hardly in Dickens's sphere—I mean the soldierly passion in which a rather rakish gallantry was sobered by devotion, and loyalty rested on pride. In Dickens love is sentimental or benevolent or merry or sneaking or canine; in his last book he was going to describe a love that was passionate and criminal; but love for him was never chivalrous, never poetical. What he paints most tragically is a quasi-paternal devotion in the old to the young, the love of Mr. Peggotty for Little Emily, or of Solomon Gills for Walter Gay. A series of shabby little adventures, such as might absorb the interest of an average youth, were romantic enough for Dickens.

I say he was disinterested, but he inherited the most terrible negations. Religion lay on him like the weight of the atmosphere sixteen pounds to the square inch, yet never noticed nor mentioned. He lived and wrote in the shadow of the most awful prohibitions. Hearts petrified by legality and falsified by worldliness offered, indeed, a good subject for a novelist, and Dickens availed himself of it to the extent of always contrasting natural goodness and happiness with whatever is morose; and his morose people were wicked, not virtuous in their own way; so that the protest of his temperament against his environment never took a radical form nor went back to first principles. He needed to feel, in his writing, that he was carrying the sympathies of every man with him. In him conscience was single, and he could not conceive how it could ever be divided in other men. He denounced scandals without exposing shams, and conformed willingly and scrupulously to the proprieties. Lady Dedlock's secret, for instance, he treats as if it were the sin of Adam, remote, mysterious, inexpiable. Mrs. Dombey is not allowed to deceive her husband except by pretending to deceive him. The seduction of Little Emily is left out altogether, with the whole character of Steerforth, the development of which would have been so important in the moral experience of David Copperfield himself. But it is not public prejudice alone that plays the censor over Dickens's art; his own kindness and even weakness of heart act sometimes as marplots. The character of Miss Mowcher, for example, so brilliantly introduced, was evidently intended to be shady, and to play a very important part in the story; but its original in real life, which was recognized, had to be conciliated, and the sequel was omitted and patched up with an apology—itself admirable—for the poor dwarf. Such a sacrifice does honour to Dickens's heart; but artists should meditate on their works in time, and it is easy to remove any too great likeness in a portrait by a few touches making it more consistent than real people are apt to be; and in this case, if the little creature had been really guilty, how much more subtle and tragic her apology for herself might have been, like that of the bastard Edmund in *King Lear!* So, too, in *Dombey and Son,* Dickens could not bear to let Walter Gay turn out badly, as he had been meant to do, and to break his uncle's heart as well as the heroine's; he was accordingly transformed into a stage hero miraculously saved from shipwreck, and Florence was not allowed to reward the admirable Toots, as she should have done, with her trembling hand. But Dickens was no free artist; he had more genius than taste, a warm fancy not aided by a thorough understanding of complex characters. He worked under pressure for money and applause, and often had to cheapen in execution what his inspiration had so vividly conceived.

What, then, is left, if Dickens had all these limitations? In our romantic disgust we might be tempted to say, Nothing. But in fact almost everything is left, almost everything that counts in the daily life of mankind, or that by its presence or absence can determine whether life shall be worth living or not; because a simple good life is worth living, and an elaborate bad life is not. There remains in the first place eating and drinking; relished not bestially, but humanly, jovially, as the sane and exhilarating basis for everything else. This is a sound English beginning; but the immediate sequel, as the England of that day presented it to Dickens, is no less delightful. There is the ruddy glow of the hearth; the sparkle of glasses and brasses and well-scrubbed pewter; the savoury fumes of the hot punch, after the tingle of the wintry air; the coaching scenes, the motley figures and absurd incidents of travel; the changing sights and joys of the road. And then, to balance this, the traffic of ports and cities, the hubbub of crowded streets, the luxury of shop windows and of palaces not to be entered; the procession of the passers-by, shabby or ludicrously genteel; the dingy look and musty smell of their lodgings; the labyrinth of back-alleys, courts, and mews, with their crying children, and scolding old women, and listless, half-drunken loiterers. These sights, like fables, have a sort of moral in them to which Dickens was very sensitive; the important airs of nobodies on great occasions, the sadness and preoccupation of the great as they hasten by in their mourning or on their pressing affairs; the sadly comic characters of the tavern; the diligence of shop-keepers, like squirrels turning in their cages; the children peeping out everywhere like grass in an untrodden street; the charm of humble things, the nobleness of humble people, the horror of crime, the ghastliness of vice, the deft hand and shining face of virtue passing through the midst of it all; and finally a fresh wind of indifference and change blowing across our troubles and clearing the most lurid sky.

I do not know whether it was Christian charity or naturalistic insight, or a mixture of both (for they are closely akin) that attracted Dickens particularly to the deformed, the half-witted, the abandoned, or those impeded or misunderstood by virtue of some singular inner consecration. The visible moral of these things, when brutal prejudice does not blind us to it, comes very near to true philosophy; one turn of the screw, one flash of reflection, and we have understood nature and human morality and the relation between them.

In his love of roads and wayfarers, of river-ports and wharves and the idle or sinister figures that lounge about them, Dickens was like Walt Whitman; and I think a second Dickens may any day appear in America, when it is possible in that land of hurry to reach the same degree of saturation, the same unquestioning pleasure in the familiar facts. The spirit of Dickens would be better able to do justice to America than was that of Walt Whitman; because America, although it may seem nothing but a noisy nebula to the impressionist, is not a nebula but a concourse of very distinct individual bodies, natural and social, each with its definite interests and story. Walt Whitman had a sort of transcendental philosophy which swallowed the universe whole, supposing there was a universal spirit in things identical with the absolute spirit that observed them; but Dickens was innocent of any clap-trap, and remained a true spirit in his own person. Kindly and clear-sighted, but self-identical and unequivocally human, he glided through the slums like one of his own little heroes, uncontaminated by their squalor and confusion, courageous and firm in his clear allegiances amid the flux of things, a pale angel at the Carnival, his heart aflame, his voice always flute-like in its tenderness and warning. This is the true relation of spirit to existence, not the other which confuses them; for this earth (I cannot speak for the Universe at large) has no spirit of its own, but brings forth spirits only at certain points, in the hearts and brains of frail living creatures, who like insects flit through it, buzzing and gathering what sweets they can;

and it is the spaces they traverse in this career, charged with their own moral burden, that they can report on or describe, not things rolling on to infinity in their vain tides. To be hypnotized by that flood would be a heathen idolatry. Accordingly Walt Whitman, in his comprehensive democratic vistas, could never see the trees for the wood, and remained incapable, for all his diffuse love of that human herd, of ever painting a character or telling a story; the very things in which Dickens was a master. It is this life of the individual, as it may be lived in a given nation, that determines the whole value of that nation to the poet, to the moralist, and to the judicious historian. But for the excellence of the typical single life, no nation deserves to be remembered more than the sands of the sea; and America will not be a success, if every American is a failure.

Dickens entered the theatre of this world by the stage door; the shabby little adventures of the actors in their private capacity replace for him the mock tragedies which they enact before a dreaming public. Mediocrity of circumstances and mediocrity of soul forever return to the centre of his stage; a more wretched or a grander existence is sometimes broached, but the pendulum soon swings back, and we return, with the relief with which we put on our slippers after the most romantic excursion, to a golden mediocrity—to mutton and beer, and to love and babies in a suburban villa with one frowsy maid. Dickens is the poet of those acres of yellow brick streets which the traveller sees from the railway viaducts as he approaches London; they need a poet, and they deserve one, since a complete human life may very well be lived there. Their little excitements and sorrows, their hopes and humours are like those of the Wooden Midshipman in *Dombey and Son;* but the sea is not far off, and the sky—Dickens never forgets it— is above all those brief troubles. He had a sentiment in the presence of this vast flatness of human fates, in spite of their individual pungency, which I think might well be the dominant sentiment of mankind in the future; a sense of happy freedom in littleness, an open-eyed reverence and religion without words. This universal human anonymity is like a sea, an infinitive democratic desert, chock-full and yet the very image of emptiness, with nothing in it for the mind, except, as the Moslems say, the presence of Allah. Awe is the counterpart of humility—and this is perhaps religion enough. The atom in the universal vortex ought to be humble; he ought to see that, materially, he doesn't much matter, and that morally his loves are merely his own, without authority over the universe. He can admit without obloquy that he is what he is; and he can rejoice in his own being, and in that of all other things in so far as he can share it sympathetically. The apportionment of existence and of fortune is in Other Hands; his own portion is contentment, vision, love, and laughter.

Having humility, that most liberating of sentiments, having a true vision of human existence and joy in that vision, Dickens had in a superlative degree the gift of humour, of mimicry, of unrestrained farce. He was the perfect comedian. When people say Dickens exaggerates, it seems to me they can have no eyes and no ears. They probably have only *notions* of what things and people are; they accept them conventionally, at their diplomatic value. Their minds run on in the region of discourse, where there are masks only and no faces, ideas and no facts; they have little sense for those living grimaces that play from moment to moment upon the countenance of the world. The world is a perpetual caricature of itself; at every moment it is the mockery and the contradiction of what it is pretending to be. But as it nevertheless intends all the time to be something different and highly dignified, at the next moment it corrects and checks and tries to cover up the absurd thing it was; so that a conventional world, a world of masks, is superimposed on the reality, and passes in every sphere of human interest for the reality itself. Humour is the perception of this illusion, the fact allowed to pierce here and there through the convention, whilst the convention continues to be maintained, as if we had not observed its absurdity. Pure comedy is more radical, cruder, in a certain sense less human; because comedy throws the convention over altogether, revels for a moment in the fact, There take that! That's what you really are! At this the polite world pretends to laugh, not tolerantly as it does at humour, but a little angrily. It does not like to see itself by chance in the glass, without having had time to compose its features for demure self-contemplation. "What a bad mirror," it exclaims; "it must be convex or concave; for surely I never looked like that. Mere caricature, farce, and horse play. Dickens exaggerates; *I* never was so sentimental as that; *I* never saw anything so dreadful; *I* don't believe there were ever any people like Quilp, or Squeers, or Serjeant Buzfuz." But the polite world is lying; there *are* such people; we are such people ourselves in our true moments, in our veritable impulses; but we are careful to stifle and to hide those moments from ourselves and from the world; to purse and pucker ourselves into the mask of our conventional personality; and so simpering, we profess that it is very coarse and inartistic of Dickens to undo our life's work for us in an instant, and remind us of what we are. And as to other people, though we may allow that considered superficially they are often absurd, we do not wish to dwell on their eccentricities nor to mimic them. On the contrary, it is good manners to look away quickly, to suppress a smile, and to say to ourselves that the ludicrous figure in the street is not at all comic, but a dull ordinary Christian, and that it is foolish to give any importance to the fact that its hat has blown off, that it has slipped on an orange-peel and unintentionally sat on the pavement, that it has a pimple on its nose, that its one tooth projects over its lower lip, that it is angry with things in general, and that it is looking everywhere for the penny which it holds tightly in its hand. That may fairly represent the moral condition of most of us at most times; but we do not want to think of it; we do not want to see; we gloss the fact over; we console ourselves before we are grieved, and reassert our composure before we have laughed. We are afraid, ashamed, anxious to be spared. What displeases us in Dickens is that he does not spare us; he mimics things to the full; he dilates and exhausts and repeats; he wallows. He is too intent on the passing experience to look over his shoulder, and consider whether we have not already understood, and had enough. He is not thinking of us; he is obeying the impulse of the passion, the person, or the story he is enacting. This faculty, which renders him a consummate comedian, is just what alienated from him a later generation in which people of taste were aesthetes and virtuous people were higher snobs; they wanted a mincing art, and he gave them copious improvisation, they wanted analysis and development, and he gave them absolute comedy. I must confess, though the fault is mine and not his, that sometimes his absoluteness is too much for me. When I come to the death of Little Nell, or to What the Waves were always Saying, or even to the incorrigible perversities of the pretty Dora, I skip. I can't take my liquor neat in such draughts, and my inner man says to Dickens, Please don't. But then I am a coward in so many ways! There are so many things in this world that I skip, as I skip the undiluted Dickens! When I reach Dover on a rough day, I wait there until the Channel is smoother; am I not travelling for pleasure? But my prudence does not blind me to the admirable virtue of the sailors that cross in all weathers, not even to the automatic determination of the seasick ladies, who might so easily have followed my example, if they were not the slaves of their railway tickets and of their labelled luggage. They are loyal to their tour, and I to my philosophy. Yet as wrapped in my great-coat and sure of a good dinner, I pace the windy pier and soliloquize, I feel the superiority of the bluff tar, glad of breeze, stretching a firm arm to the unsteady passenger, and watching with a masterful thrill of emotion the home cliffs receding and the foreign coasts ahead. It is only courage (which Dickens had without knowing it) and universal kindness (which he knew he had) that are requisite to nerve us for a true vision of this world. And as some of us are cowards about crossing the Channel, and others about "crossing the bar," so almost everybody is a coward about his own humanity. We do not consent to be absurd, though absurd we are. We have no fundamental humility. We do not wish the moments of our lives to be caught by a quick eye in their grotesque initiative, and to be pilloried in this way before our own eyes. For that reason we don't like Dickens, and don't like comedy, and don't like the truth. Dickens could don the comic mask with innocent courage; he could wear it with a grace, ease, and irresistible vivacity seldom given to men. We must go back for anything like it to the very greatest comic poets, to Shakespeare or to Aristophanes. Who else, for instance, could have penned this:

> "It was all Mrs. Bumble. She *would* do it," urged Mr. Bumble; first looking around to ascertain that his partner had left the room.
> "That is no excuse," replied Mr. Brownlow. "You were present on the occasion of the destruction of these trinkets, and indeed are the more guilty of the two, in the eye of the law; for the law supposes that your wife acts under your direction."
> "If the law supposes that," said Mr. Bumble, squeezing his hat emphati-

cally in both hands, "the law is a ass, a idiot. If that's the eye of the law, the law is a bachelor; and the worst I wish the law is, that his eye may be opened by experience—by experience."

Laying great stress on the repetition of these two words, Mr. Bumble fixed his hat on very tight, and putting his hands in his pockets, followed his helpmate downstairs.

This is high comedy; the irresistible, absurd, intense dream of the old fool, personifying the law in order to convince and to punish it. I can understand that this sort of thing should not be common in English literature, nor much relished; because pure comedy is scornful, merciless, devastating, holding no door open to anything beyond. Cultivated English feeling winces at this brutality, although the common people love it in clowns and in puppet shows; and I think they are right. Dickens, who surely was tender enough, had so irresistible a comic genius that it carried him beyond the gentle humour which most Englishmen possess to the absolute grotesque reality. Squeers, for instance, when he sips the wretched dilution which he has prepared for his starved and shivering little pupils, smacks his lips and cries: "Here's a richness!" It is savage comedy; humour would come in if we understood (what Dickens does not tell us) that the little creatures were duly impressed and thought the thin liquid truly delicious. I suspect that English sensibility prefers the humour and wit of Hamlet to the pure comedy of Falstaff; and that even in Aristophanes it seeks consolation in the lyrical poetry for the flaying of human life in the comedy itself. Tastes are free; but we should not deny that in merciless and rollicking comedy life is caught in the act. The most grotesque creatures of Dickens are not exaggerations or mockeries of something other than themselves; they arise because nature generates them, like toadstools; they exist because they can't help it, as we all do. The fact that these perfectly self-justified beings are absurd appears only by comparison, and from outside; circumstances or the expectations of other people, make them ridiculous and force them to contradict themselves; but in nature it is no crime to be exceptional. Often, but for the savagery of the average man, it would not even be a misfortune. The sleepy fat boy in *Pickwick* looks less foolish; but in himself he is no more foolish, no less solidly justified, than a pumpkin lying on the ground. Toots seems ridiculous; and we laugh heartily at his incoherence, his beautiful waistcoats, and his extreme modesty; but when did anybody more obviously grow into what he is because he couldn't grow otherwise? So with Mr. Pickwick, and Sam Weller, and Mrs. Gamp, and Micawber, and all the rest of this wonderful gallery; they are ridiculous only by accident, and in the context in which they never intended to appear. If Oedipus and Lear and Cleopatra do not seem ridiculous, it is only because tragic reflection had taken them out of the context in which, in real life, they would have figured. If we saw them as facts, and not as emanations of a poet's dream, we should laugh at them till doomsday; what grotesque presumption, what silly whims, what mad contradiction of the simplest realities! Yet we should not laugh at them without feeling how real their griefs were; as real and terrible as the griefs of children and dreams. But facts, however serious inwardly, are always absurd outwardly; and the just critic of life sees both truths at once, as Cervantes did in *Don Quixote*. A pompous idealist who does not see the ridiculous in *all things* is the dupe of his sympathy and abstraction; and a clown, who does not see that these ridiculous figures are living quite in earnest, is the dupe of his egotism. Dickens saw the absurdity, and understood the life; and I think he was a good philosopher.

It is usual to compare Dickens with Thackeray, which is like comparing the grape with the gooseberry; there are obvious points of resemblance, and the gooseberry has some superior qualities of its own; but you can't make red wine with it. The wine of Dickens is of the richest, the purest, the sweetest, the most fortifying to the blood; there is distilled in it, with the perfection of comedy, the perfection of morals. I do not mean, of course, that Dickens appreciated all the values that human life has or might have; that is beyond any man. Even the greatest philosophers, such as Aristotle, have not always much imagination to conceive forms of happiness or folly other than those which their age or their temperament reveals to them; their insight runs only to discovering the *principle* of happiness, that it is the spontaneous life of any sort harmonized with circumstances. The sympathies and imagination of Dickens, vivid in their sphere, were no less limited in range; and of course it was not his business to find philosophic formulas; nevertheless I call his the perfection of morals for two reasons: that he put the distinction between good and evil in the right place, and that he felt this distinction intensely. A moralist might have excellent judgement, he might see what sort of life is spontaneous in a given being and how far it may be harmonized with circumstances, yet his heart might remain cold, he might not suffer nor rejoice with the suffering or joy he foresaw. Humanitarians like Bentham and Mill, who talked about the greatest happiness of the greatest number, might conceivably be moral prigs in their own persons, and they might have been chilled to the bone in their theoretic love of mankind, if they had had the wit to imagine in what, as a matter of fact, the majority would place their happiness. Even if their theory had been correct (which I think it was in intention, though not in statement) they would then not have been perfect moralists, because their maxims would not have expressed their hearts. In expressing their hearts, they ought to have embraced one of those forms of "idealism" by which men fortify themselves in their bitter passions or in their helpless commitments; for they do not wish mankind to be happy in its own way, but in theirs. Dickens was not one of those moralists who summon every man to do himself the greatest violence so that he may not offend them, nor defeat their ideals. Love of the good of others is something that shines in every page of Dickens with a truly celestial splendour. How entirely limpid is his sympathy with life—a sympathy uncontaminated by dogma or pedantry or snobbery or bias of any kind! How generous is this keen, light spirit, how pure this open heart! And yet, in spite of this extreme sensibility, not the least wobbling; no deviation from a just severity of judgement, from an uncompromising distinction between white and black. And this happens as it ought to happen; sympathy is not checked by a flatly contrary prejudice or commandment, by some categorical imperative irrelevant to human nature; the check, like the cheer, comes by tracing the course of spontaneous impulse and circumstances that inexorably lead it to success or to failure. There is a bed to this stream, freely as the water may flow; when it comes to this precipice it must leap, when it runs over these pebbles it must sing, and when it spreads into that marsh it must become livid and malarial. The very sympathy with human impulse quickens in Dickens the sense of danger; his very joy in joy makes him stern to what kills it. How admirably drawn are his surly villains! No rhetorical vilification of them, as in a sermon; no exaggeration of their qualms or fears; rather a sense of how obvious and human all their courses seem from their point of view; and yet no sentimental apology for them, no romantic worship of rebels in their madness or crime. The pity of it, the waste of it all, are seen not by a second vision but by the same original vision which revealed the lure and the drift of the passion. Vice is a monster here of such sorry mien, that the longer we see it the more we deplore it; that other sort of vice which Pope found so seductive was perhaps only some innocent impulse artificially suppressed, and called a vice because it broke out inconveniently and displeased the company. True vice is human nature strangled by the suicide of attempting the impossible. Those so self-justified villains of Dickens never elude their fates. Bill Sikes is not let off, neither is Nancy; the oddly benevolent Magwitch does not escape from the net, nor does the unfortunate young Richard Carstone, victim of the Circumlocution Office. The horror and ugliness of their fall are rendered with the hand of a master; we see here, as in the world, that in spite of the romanticists it is not virtue to rush enthusiastically along any road. I think Dickens is one of the best friends mankind has ever had. He has held the mirror up to nature, and of its reflected fragments has composed a fresh world, where the men and women differ from real people only in that they live in a literary medium, so that all ages and places may know them. And they are worth knowing, just as one's neighbours are, for their picturesque characters and their pathetic fates. Their names should be in every child's mouth; they ought to be adopted members of every household. Their stories cause the merriest and the sweetest chimes to ring in the fancy, without confusing our moral judgement or alienating our interest from the motley commonplaces of daily life. In every English-speaking home, in the four quarters of the globe, parents and children will do well to read Dickens aloud of a winter's evening; they will love winter, and one another, and God the better for it. What a wreath that will be of ever-fresh holly, thick with bright berries, to hang to this poet's memory—the very crown he would have chosen!

Sandburg's "The Cool Tombs"

Robert Graves and Laura Riding

Robert Graves (b. 1895) is a poet, critic, novelist, and essayist. He began his literary career as a poet and regards poetry as his real vocation, but in the course of a lifetime he has written on almost everything and usually with verve and grace. His historical novels, such as *I, Claudius* (1934), *Claudius the God* (1934), and *Hercules My Shipmate* (1945), are distinguished representatives of that genre. In 1928 he and Laura Riding issued *A Pamphlet Against Anthologies,* a lively and irreverent treatment of anthology pieces, "best poems" and "the perfect modern lyric." Their account of Sandburg's "The Cool Tombs" (printed below) is a characteristic example of their critical standards and strategy of attack.

Laura Riding (b. 1901) is a poet and essayist. Her *Collected Poems* appeared in 1938.

Modern American anthology-pieces are not quite so successful as their British counterparts, because the Free Verse movement has made it difficult to use worn-out material in quite so hypnotic a manner, and the true bad-vigour quality only comes with rhyme. Still, Mr. Sandburg manages successfully enough in his 'Cool Tombs.'

'When Abraham Lincoln was shovelled into the tombs, he forgot the copperheads and the assassin . . . in the dust, in the cool tombs.'

'Shovelled' is intended as a confidential colloquialism, 'tombs' as a poetical enlargement of singular into plural. But the colloquial and the poetical obstruct each other: the verse reads as though poor President Lincoln had been assassinated with dynamite and had to be distributed with a shovel among the different state-cemeteries. There, such as it is, the poem really ends, but it is protracted as an anthology-piece by the old ballad device of three parallel statements and a conclusion—'I said it once, I say it again, what I say three times' (in slightly different ways) 'is true.'

'And Ulysses Grant lost all thought of con men and Wall Street, cash and collateral turned ashes . . . in the dust, in the cool tombs.'

SANDBURG'S "THE COOL TOMBS": Reprinted from *A Pamphlet Against Anthologies* by Robert Graves and Laura Riding with permission of Robert Graves, Laura Riding, and A. P. Watt & Son.

Sandburg here cites a second typical American citizen who has undergone multiple burial. To complete the mystic trinity we must search out an inevitable third to this great-hearted and hard-headed pair. John Brown? Virginia Dare? Barbara Frietchie? Uncle Remus? Who else is a dead American?

'Pocahontas' body, lovely as a poplar, sweet as a red haw in November or a pawpaw in May, did she wonder? does she remember? . . . in the dust, in the cool tombs?'

Evidently Pocahontas' body (since Mr. Sandburg puts it as a question) has a possible sense of memory which Lincoln and Grant (or their bodies) lack. Is it because she was a woman and, though respectably married, of middle age, and a mother, beautiful still? Or because she was buried not in America but in a London church? It is interesting to note as an example of the practical effect of the bad poem that there has been a patriotic movement started for exhuming Pocahontas and transferring her to America. Will she wonder? Will she hell! By this time Carl Sandburg himself no longer remembers. Though he has not yet been shovelled into the cool tombs.

'Take any streetful of people buying clothes and groceries, cheering a hero or throwing confetti and blowing tin horns . . . tell me if the lovers are losers . . . tell me if any get more than the lovers . . . in the dust . . . in the cool tombs.'

The question 'Are the lovers losers?' means just what? Losers in comparison with the hero-cheerers and the grocery-buyers? Or losers in comparison with Lincoln, Grant and Pocahontas? Or losers in regard to love? The supplementary question is equally indistinct. Does it mean 'Do any others get more than the lovers get when the lovers are in the cool tombs?' Or does it mean 'Do any others get more than the lovers get when they themselves are in the cool tombs?' But the anthology reader doesn't mind; he is fagged out by his own cash and collaterals, he is too weary to remember his Country's heroes or even that women are beautiful. In fact, he too might just as well be . . . in the dust . . . in the cool tombs . . . like Pocahontas, Carl Sandburg, and everybody else.

Lordships Observed

Nigel Dennis

> Nigel Dennis (b. 1912) is a playwright, critic, and editor.
> His *Boys and Girls Come Out to Play* was published in
> 1949 and his *Dramatic Essays,* in 1962. Since 1967 he
> has been a joint editor of the magazine *Encounter.*

Aristocrats are on the way out, of course, but as long as long books are
written about them they will bide a wee. In *The Last of the Best* ("The Aristocracy of Europe in the Twentieth Century"), Andrew Sinclair agrees with
the best authorities that to be an aristocrat, a man should have lots of land.
Well, bags of attention and Press-cuttings are worth at least one acre of
London and 100,000 of Scotland.

Like their pedigrees, aristocrats exist only in the imagination. Left to
themselves, they would wither away, but the common man sees to it that
they are not left to themselves. His common mind leaps up when he reads:
DUKE'S SON ON FRAUD CHARGE; EARL BEAT MODEL, SAYS
CONSTABLE. "There, but for the grace of God, go I," he mutters en-
viously.

Let's face it. Film stars only shine a few years before declining into
hollow bores. Millionaires have only millions to offer—and rarely do.
Sportsmen get fat. Cricketers become clergymen. Prime Ministers deflate
like gas-bags. But princes mature like port and counts like claret. WITTELS-
BACH (88) WEDS BEATLE'S WIDOW—always hot and strong like
mother made it.

Mr. Sinclair has a lot to say about the well-known adaptability of the
British aristocrat—his readiness to exhibit himself for money, his fondness
for being paid to sit on directors' boards, his aptitude for many kinds of
remunerative work, his respect for the supposed equality of others. But
are these the characteristics we expect from aristocrats? Surely we ask a
little more?

There is, as Mr. Sinclair hints, something just a little selfish about aristocratic behaviour in Britain. Here is a minority sect that is counting on
us to see it through and is really concerned with nothing but its own survival.
Is not this very wrong? Where is the sense of duty that old-fashioned aristocrats used to talk about so much? Where is the desire to do or die that we
like to associate with men—and women, too, of course—of rank?

It makes a fellow lick his lips to hear about the *dolce vita* that Italian
aristocrats enjoy. Here are Neapolitan noblemen who care not a straw for

LORDSHIPS OBSERVED: Reprinted from the *Daily Telegraph*, March 30, 1969, by permission of
the *Daily Telegraph.*

democracy and equality and simply devote their lives to delicious beach-parties and Roman carnivals. When the government sequesters their estates (as it occasionally does), they just snatch the compensation lolly with a hearty laugh, and rush off to spend it on more vice. While our noblemen are reading *The Financial Times,* Italy's are getting into *Oggi.* What a world of difference!

The British aristocracy has never really made the transition from the grouse-moor to the beach-party. Indeed, it has tended to shun the latter in order to retain the former. The fact that a handful of peers have plunged recklessly into photography, interior decoration, and ancient motor-cars does not alter the situation. One swallow does not make a summer.

What, then, is wrong with our peers? Mr. Sinclair remarks the fact that most of them are still brought up by nannies—but, heaven knows, a man can be brought up by a nanny and still have a bit of vice in him. Many foreign noblemen have had British nannies from time immemorial, but it has had no more effect on their adult behaviour than eating Oxford Vintage Marmalade and using Pear's Soap. No, we must look deeper.

When we do so, we see that nothing is a greater handicap to an aristocracy than to live in a monarchy. Aristocrats can only do their stuff properly in the free air of a republic, where the need for status and privilege cannot fail to be infinitely stronger in the populace. But for the French Republic, France's aristocrats would never have developed their amazing talent for rich marriages and the orchidaceous atmosphere of rich cohesion that has followed these. On the other hand, it brings tears to one's eyes to read what Mr. Sinclair has to say about the aristocrats of monarchical Holland: who would not rather be a democrat than a Dutch gentleman?

The Vatican has gone so far as to abolish Papal titles. This has meant that even the nobleman's handle—thought by many to be the very keystone of aristocracy, if only because of what it has to offer the ambitious wife—has been sent to pot. No wonder the pious nobles fought back like lions. At stake, as Mr. Sinclair points out, were the earthly dibs that went with the Heavenly titles—"tax-exempt car licences, cigarettes, petrol, liquor, and imported food."

Dictatorship can be a very good thing for an aristocracy. All dictators frown on aristocrats, but make their daughters marry them. General Franco does not parade his aristocrats, but he keeps a few on the boards of banks and hundreds more up his sleeve. If there were a popular insurrection, he would have something to lean over backwards on.

The present German set-up is a pretty poor show. Here is a republic that was once as rich in aristocrats as June is in roses—but where are they now, all those double-barrelled Vons and Zus? Apparently, they have been swamped by Germany's economic miracle—trampled to death in the triumphant pursuit of the *deutschmark.* Let us all pray that no such miracle be worked in our own dear country.

Mr. Sinclair's book is serious and comprehensive and will be welcomed by all thoughtful peers. But he could have done better with his illustrations, which are far from glamorous. Many of the noblemen look quite common, particularly when they are out shooting. Nor is there any excuse for "Lady Angela St. Clair Erskine with a Hottentot" and "Lady Angela St. Clair Erskine with her first trout." If breeding cannot do better than that, why should we lend our snobbery to supporting it?

Not that it will make any difference, says Mr. Sinclair. "For the meritocracy has already taken over from the aristocracy. . . . Privilege exists and will continue to exist in every society; but that privilege is no longer to be inherited by blood, but won by brains."

Brains, sir? Pass me your tiny hand! I want to pat it.

Homage to Hemingway

John Peale Bishop

> John Peale Bishop (1892–1944) is the author of *Many Thousands Gone* (1931), a fiction collection, and *Act of Darkness* (1935), a novel; but he is better known for his poetry: *Now with His Love* (1933), and *Minute Particulars* (1936). In 1922 he was living in Paris as one of the group of young American writers, which included F. Scott Fitzgerald, Archibald MacLeish, and Ernest Hemingway, to whose art he pays tribute in the essay that follows. This essay was written in 1936 when Hemingway was at the height of his career.

I

Ernest Hemingway had the chance to become the spokesman of the war generation, or, more particularly, he came to be regarded as the spokesman of that generation by those who had not, in their own persons, known the experience of war. The phrase which he had culled from one of his many conversations with Gertrude Stein and printed opposite the title page of *The Sun Also Rises*—"You are all a lost generation"—was destined to *faire fortune.* And to this he appended another quotation from the aged and charming cynic of Ecclesiastes, which not only pointed the title of his book, but linked its own disillusionment with another so old and remote in time as to seem a permanent proclamation of the vanity of things.

His own generation admired him, but could also appraise how special his experience had been. It was a still younger generation, those who were schoolboys at the time of the War, who were infatuated with him. Hemingway not only supplied them with the adventures they had missed; he offered them an attitude with which to meet the disorders of the postwar decade. It was they who accepted the Hemingway legend and by their acceptance gave it a reality it had not had.

It is as one who dictated the emotions to contemporary youth that Hemingway has been compared to Lord Byron. The comparison is in many ways an apt one. The years of Byron's fame were not unlike the decade after the last war. The hopes raised by the French Revolution had been frustrated and all possibilities of action were being rapidly destroyed by those in power. In the 1920's, the disintegration of the social fabric which began before the War became apparent to almost anyone. Here and there were new faces in politics, but Hemingway, who had worked on a Midwestern paper in his youth, gone abroad shortly after the War as a correspondent to a Canadian newspaper, come into contact with the literary diplomats at the Quai d'Orsay, followed the French troops of M. Poincaré into the Ruhr, known Mussolini when he too was a journalist, seen war and government from both sides in the Turkish-Greek conflict, was not likely to rate the new gangsters above the old gangs. It should have been obvious to a disinterested observer in 1922 that there was no longer much prospect of immediate revolution in the countries of Europe. It was in 1922 that Hemingway seriously began his career as a writer.

He was to become, like Byron, a legend while he was still in his twenties. But when I first met him in the summer of 1922 there could be no possibility of a legend. I had just come abroad and, calling on Ezra Pound, had asked him about American writers of talent then in Paris. Pound's answer was a taxi, which carried us with decrepit rapidity across the Left Bank, through the steep streets rising toward Mont Saint-Geneviève, and brought us to the Rue du Cardinal Lemoine. There we climbed four flights of stairs to find Ernest Hemingway. He had then published nothing except his newspaper work, none of which I had ever seen; so that my impressions could be only personal. From that time until 1930 I saw Hemingway fairly constantly. Since then he has retired to Florida, and I have seen him but once. Any later impressions I have are gathered entirely from his books. I say this to make clear what I shall have to say about the legendary figure.

The legend is, in some ways, astounding. Nothing is more natural than that the imaginative man should at times envy the active one. Stendhal would have liked to be a handsome lieutenant of hussars. But the born writer is, by his very imagination, cut off from the satisfactions of the man of action; he can emulate him only by a process of deliberate stultification. Hemingway, as he then appeared to me, had many of the faults of the artist, some, such as vanity, to an exaggerated degree. But these are faults which from long custom I easily tolerate. And in his case they were compensated for by extraordinary literary virtues. He was instinctively intelligent, disinterested and not given to talking nonsense. Toward his craft, he was humble, and had, moreover, the most complete literary integrity it has ever been my lot to encounter. I say the most complete, for while I have known others who were not to be corrupted, none of them was presented with the opportunities for corruption that assailed Hemingway. His was that innate and genial honesty which is the very chastity of talent; he knew that to be preserved it must constantly be protected. He could not be bought. I happened to be with him on the day he turned down an offer from one of Mr. Hearst's editors, which, had he accepted it, would have supported him handsomely for years. He was at the time living back of the Montparnasse cemetery, over the studio of a friend, in a room small and bare except for a bed and table, and buying his midday meal for five sous from street vendors of fried potatoes.

The relation of a living writer to his legend may become curiously complicated. If we take the account that Mr. Peter Quennell has recently given us in *Byron: The Years of Fame,* it would seem that superficially the poet had at twenty-two only a very slight resemblance to the picture which the public presently began to compose of him. On the contrary, he seemed to his friends a personable, gay young man, an excellent drinking companion; there was, of course, the limp; and he had, as they may not have known, the consciousness of a bad heredity. *Childe Harold* was made of emotions only latent in Byron. It was a corollary of his fame that the poet should be identified with Childe Harold in the minds of his admirers. But it was not long before in his own imagination he became Childe Harold. And presently Lord Byron is committing incest with his sister. His conscience required that he complete the fiction by a private action. Byron's public stood as panders beside Augusta's bed.

In attempting to say what has happened to Hemingway, I might suggest that, for one thing, he has become the legendary Hemingway. He appears to have turned into a composite of all those photographs he has been sending out for years: sunburned from snows, on skis; in fishing get-up, burned dark from the hot Caribbean; the handsome, stalwart hunter crouched smiling over the carcass of some dead beast. Such a man could not have written Hemingway's early books; he might have written most of *Green Hills of Africa.* He is proud to have killed the great kudu. It is hard not to wonder whether he has not, hunting, brought down an even greater victim.

Byron's legend is sinister and romantic, Hemingway's manly and lowbrow. One thing is certain. This last book is hard-boiled. If that word is to mean anything, it must mean indifference to suffering and, since we are what we are, can signify a callousness to others' pain. When I say that the young Hemingway was among the tenderest of mortals, I do not speak out of private knowledge, but from the evidence of his writings. He could be, as any artist must in this world, if he is to get his work done, ruthless. He wrote courageously, but out of pity; having been hurt, and badly hurt, he could understand the pain of others. His heart was worn, as was the fashion of the times, up his sleeve and not on it. It was always there and his best tricks were won with it. Now, according to the little preface to *Green Hills of Africa,* he seems to think that, having discarded that half-concealed card, he plays more honestly. He does not. For with the heart the innate honesty of the artist is gone. And he loses the game.

II

The problem of style is always a primary one, for to each generation it is presented anew. It is desirable, certainly, that literature reflect the common speech; it is even more necessary that it set forth a changed sensibility, since that is the only living change from one generation to another. But to an American who, like Hemingway, was learning the craft of prose in the years that followed the War, that problem was present in a somewhat special way. He must achieve a style that could record an American experience, and neither falsify the world without nor betray the world within.

How difficult that might be, he could see from his immediate predecessors; they had not much else to teach. On the one side there was Mr. Hergesheimer, whose style falsified every fact he touched. On the other was Mr. Dreiser, a worthy, lumbering workman who could deliver the facts of American existence, all of them, without selection, as a drayman might deliver trunks. Where, then, to start? To anyone who felt there was an American tradition to be carried on, there was but one writer who was on the right track: Sherwood Anderson. When he was in his stride, there was no doubt about it, he was good. The trouble with Anderson was there was never any telling just how long he could keep up his pace. He had a bad way of stumbling. And when he stumbled he fell flat.

So did Mark Twain, who loomed out of the American past. All authentic American writing, Hemingway has said, stems from one book: *Huckleberry Finn.* How much was he prepared to learn from it may be ascertained by comparing the progress of the boy's raft down the Mississippi with the journey of Jake and his friend from France to Spain in *The Sun Also Rises.* Mark Twain is the one literary ancestor whom Hemingway has openly acknowledged; but what neither he nor Sherwood Anderson, who was Hemingway's first master, could supply was a training in discipline.

It was here that chance served. But it was a chance from which Hemingway carefully profited. There was one school which for discipline surpassed all others: that of Flaubert. It still had many living proponents, but none more passionate than Ezra Pound. In Paris, Hemingway submitted much of his apprentice work in fiction to Pound. It came back to him blue-penciled, most of the adjectives gone. The comments were unsparing. Writing for a newspaper was not at all the same as writing for a poet.

Pound was not the young American's only critical instructor. If Hemingway went often to 70 bis, Rue Nôtre Dame des Champs, he was presently to be found also at 12, Rue de Fleurus. There he submitted his writings to the formidable scrutiny of Gertrude Stein. It was of this period that Hemingway said to me later: "Ezra was right half the time, and when he was wrong, he was so wrong you were never in doubt about it. Gertrude was always right."

Miss Stein, for all her long residence abroad, was American. As she sat in one of the low chairs in the pavilion of the Rue de Fleurus, she was as unmistakably American as Mark Hanna; the walls were covered with Picassos; but with her closely clipped masculine head and old-fashioned dress, she might have been an adornment to the McKinley era. And if the problem was to combine Mark Twain and Gustave Flaubert—to convert a common American speech to the uses of the French tradition—it could hardly be doubted that Miss Stein had done it. She had taken up, in her *Three Lives,* where Flaubert left off. In *Un Coeur Simple,* he had presented the world through the eyes of a servant girl; but the words through which her vision is conveyed are not her own, but Flaubert's. Miss Stein had rendered her servant girls in an idiom which, if not exactly theirs, is supposed to be appropriate to their mentality. It is, so to speak, a transcript of dumb emotions. Having made it, Miss Stein discovered that she had arrived at a curious formalization of the common speech, which, she presently decided, might be put to other uses than the one for which it was originally intended.

If Gertrude Stein is always interesting in what she sets out to do, the result, once her writing is done, is all too often unsurpassed for boredom. She has told us in her *Autobiography of Alice B. Toklas* that she is a genius. We would have preferred that the statement had been made by someone else, but it happens to be true. Miss Stein has a mature intelligence; her genius, unfortunately, has not yet arrived at the age of three years. Ernest Hemingway, at the time he came under her influence, was a young man of twenty-four. But he was all of that. Miss Stein had developed a literary medium; but she had no material, at least none that was available to that strangely infantile genius of hers. She had at last realized that proud jest of Villiers de l'Isle-Adam; she had had, quite literally, to let her servants live for her. The relation between a writer and his material is much more mysterious than most critics would like to admit. Miss Stein has led, in Paris and elsewhere, what anyone would call an interesting life. She could never write of it until, leaving the genial baby behind, she assumed the proportions of Miss Alice B. Toklas, her companion, and began writing as an intelligent being of her own years.

Hemingway had an abundance of material. There was a boyhood in the Midwest, with summers in the forests of Michigan, where he had come in contact with the earliest American way of life. There were the love affairs of a young man. There was not one war, but two. He had known in his own person an experience for which Gertrude Stein had vainly sought a substitute in words.

What she taught Hemingway must be in part left to conjecture. Like Pound, she undoubtedly did much for him simply by telling him what he must not do, for a young writer perhaps the most valuable aid he can receive. More positively, it was from her prose he learned to employ the repetitions of American speech without monotony. (I say this quite aware that Miss Stein's repetitions are monotonous in the extreme.) She also taught him how to adapt its sentence structure, inciting in him a desire to do what Hemingway calls "loosening up the language." She did not teach him dialogue. The Hemingway dialogue is pure invention. He does not talk like his characters and neither does Miss Stein. And it was not until they had read Hemingway's books that the two ladies of the Rue de Fleurus acquired those dramatic tricks of speech.

They are brilliant. But they have deafened Hemingway to the way people talk. In *The Sun Also Rises,* each of the characters has his own particular speech, but by the time we reach *Death in the Afternoon* and the extraordinary conversations with the Old Lady, there is no longer even the illusion that there is more than one way of talking. It is a formula, in that book employed with great dexterity and no small power; but it is dramatic only in words; in terms of character it is not dramatic at all.

There is no space here to appraise Hemingway's style with accuracy. It is enough to say that, as no one before him had done, he made Midwestern speech into a prose, living and alert, capable of saying at all times exactly what he wanted it to say. It is no longer the lean unlovely thing it was. Just as Eliot, in such a poem as "Sweeney Among the Nightingales," had shown how by controlling the sound apart from the sense the most prosaic statements could be turned to poetry, Hemingway made this American speech into prose by endowing it with a beauty of accurate motion. It is changed, as a gawky boy may change in a few years to an accomplished athlete; its identity is not destroyed. And here I am reminded of a remark of Hemingway's that it was Napoleon who taught Stendhal how to write. It may be that more than one of the best qualities of this prose were acquired from a careful watching of Spanish bullfighters.

III

We were in the garden at Mons. Young Buckley came in with his patrol from across the river. The first German I saw climbed up over the garden wall. We waited until he got one leg over and then potted him. He had so much equipment on and looked awfully surprised and fell down in the garden. Then three more came over further down the wall. We shot them. They all came just like that.

It is easy to see how a story like this could convey the impression that Hemingway is indifferent alike to cruelty and suffering. And yet this tale is a precise record of emotion. What we have here is not callousness, but the Flaubertian discipline carried to a point Flaubert never knew—just as in the late war military control was brought to such perfection that dumb cowed civilians in uniform, who cared nothing for fighting and little for the issues of battle, could be held to positions that the professional soldiers of the nineteenth century would have abandoned without the slightest shame. Flaubert describing an incident, despite his pretending to be aloof, or even absent throughout, is continually intent on keeping his emotions implicit within the scene. The reader is never left in the slightest doubt as to what he is supposed to feel from the fiction. But in this account of the Germans coming over the wall and being shot, one by one, all emotion is kept out, unless it is the completely inadequate surprise of the victims. The men who kill feel nothing. And yet what Hemingway was doing in the summer of 1922, lying on a bed in a room where the old Verlaine had once had lodging, was first remembering that he had been moved, and then trying to find out what happened to cause the emotion. It is the bare happening that is set down, and only the happening that must arouse in the reader whatever emotion he is capable of according to his nature: pity, horror, disgust.

But this was a point beyond which Hemingway himself could not go. And in the stories that follow the first little volume, published in Paris and called *In Our Time,* he is almost always present in one guise or another. That is not to say, as might be assumed, that these stories are necessarily autobiographical. Wounded in the War, Hemingway was a very apprehensive young man. Indeed, his imagination could hardly be said to exist apart from his apprehension. I should not call this fear. And yet he could hardly hear of something untoward happening to another that he did not instantly, and without thought, attach this event to himself, or to the woman he loved. The narration is still remarkably pure. But there is always someone subject to the action.

For this is another distinction. In Flaubert, people are always planning things that somehow fail to come off—love affairs, assignations, revolutions, schemes for universal knowledge. But in Hemingway, men and women do not plan; it is to them that things happen. In the telling phrase of Wyndham Lewis, the "I" in Hemingway's stories is "the man that things are done to." Flaubert already represents a deterioration of the romantic will, in which both Stendhal and Byron, with the prodigious example of Napoleon before them, could not but believe. Waterloo might come, but before the last battle there was still time for a vast, however destructive, accomplishment of the will. Flaubert had before him Louis Philippe, whose green umbrella and thrifty bourgeois mind would not save him from flight; Louis Napoleon, whose plans were always going astray. But even Sedan was a better end than Woodrow Wilson had, with his paralytic chair and his closed room on a side street in Washington. And in Hemingway, the will is lost to action. There are actions, no lack of them but, as when the American lieutenant shoots the sergeant in *A Farewell to Arms,* they have only the significance of chance. Their violence does not make up for their futility. They may be, as this casual murder is, shocking; they are not incredible; but they are quite without meaning. There is no destiny but death.

It is because they have no will and not because they are without intelligence that the men and women in Hemingway are devoid of spiritual being. Their world is one in time with the War and the following confusion, and is a world without traditional values. That loss has been consciously set down.

IV

It is the privilege of literature to propose its own formal solutions for problems which in life have none. In many of the early stories of Hemingway the dramatic choice is between death and a primitive sense of male honor. The nineteen-year-old Italian orderly in "A Simple Enquiry" is given to choose between acceding to his major's corrupt desires and being sent back to his platoon. Dishonor provides no escape, for in "The Killers" the old heavyweight prizefighter who has taken that course must at last lie in his room, trying to find the courage to go out and take what is coming to him from the two men who are also waiting in tight black overcoats, wearing gloves that leave no fingerprints. One can make a good end, or a bad end, and there are many deaths besides the final one. In "Hills Like White Elephants," love is dead no matter what the lovers decide. "I don't feel any way," the girl says. "I just know things." And what she knows is her own predicament.

The Spaniards stand apart, and particularly the bullfighters, not so much because they risk their lives in a spectacular way, with beauty and skill and discipline, but because as members of a race still largely, though unconsciously, savage, they retain the tragic sense of life. In *The Sun Also Rises,* the young Romero, courteous, courageous, born knowing all the things that the others—wise-cracking Americans, upper-class British or intellectual Jews—will never learn, is a concentration of contrast. And yet the character in that novel who most nearly represents the author is aware, as soon as he has crossed the border back into France, that it is here that he belongs, in the contemporary world. He is comfortable only where all things have a value that can be expressed and paid for in paper money.

The best one can do is to desert the scene, as every man and woman must do sooner or later, to make, while the light is still in the eyes, a separate peace. And is this not just what Hemingway has done? Is there a further point to which he can retire than Key West? There he is still in political America, but on its uttermost island, no longer attached to his native continent.

His vision of life is one of perpetual annihilation. Since the will can do nothing against circumstance, choice is precluded; those things are good which the senses report good; and beyond their brief record there is only the remorseless devaluation of nature, which, like the vast blue flowing of the Gulf Stream beyond Havana, bears away of our great hopes, emotions and ambitions only a few and soon disintegrating trifles. Eternity—horribly to paraphrase Blake—is in love with the garbage of time.

What is there left? Of all man's activities, the work of art lasts longest. And in this morality there is little to be discerned beyond the discipline of the craft. This is what the French call the sense of the *métier* and their conduct in peace and war has shown that it may be a powerful impulse to the right action; if I am not mistaken, it is the main prop of French society. In "The Undefeated," the old bullfighter, corrupt though he is with age, makes a good and courageous end, and yet it is not so much courage that carries him as a proud professional skill. It is this discipline, which Flaubert acquired from the traditions of his people and which Pound transmitted to the young Hemingway, that now, as he approaches forty, alone sustains him. He has mastered his *métier* as has no American among his contemporaries. That is his pride and his distinction.

Ernest Hemingway

Dwight MacDonald

> Dwight MacDonald (b. 1906) has been for many years a critic of American society and culture. Among his books are *Fascism and the American Scene* (1938), *Memoirs of a Revolutionist* (1957), *The Ford Foundation: The Men and the Millions* (1956), and *Against the American Grain* (1962). He has been an editor of *The Partisan Review* and *Politics, a Monthly Review.* (He is the MacDonald referred to by Norman Mailer in *The Armies of the Night;* see p. 680.)

He was a big man with a bushy beard and everybody knew him. The tourists knew him and the bar-tenders knew him and the critics knew him too. He enjoyed being recognised by the tourists and he liked the bar-tenders but he never liked the critics very much. He thought they had his number. Some of them did. The hell with them. He smiled a lot and it should have been a good smile, he was so big and bearded and famous, but it was not a good smile. It was a smile that was uneasy around the edges as if he was not sure he deserved to be quite as famous as he was famous.

He liked being a celebrity and he liked celebrities. At first it was Sherwood Anderson and Ezra Pound and Gertrude Stein. He was an athletic young man from Oak Park, Illinois, who wanted to write and he made

ERNEST HEMINGWAY: From *Against the American Grain,* by Dwight MacDonald. Copyright © 1962 by Dwight MacDonald. Reprinted by permission of Random House, Inc. and Victor Gollancz Ltd.

friends with them. He was always good at making friends with celebrities. They taught him about style. Especially Gertrude Stein. The short words, the declarative sentences, the repetition, the beautiful absence of subordinate clauses. He always worked close to the bull in his writing. In more senses than one, *señor*. It was a kind of inspired baby-talk when he was going good.[1] When he was not going good, it was just baby-talk.[2] Or so the critics said and the hell with them. Most of the tricks were good tricks and they worked fine for a while especially in the short stories. Ernest was fast and stylish in the hundred-yard dash but he didn't have the wind for the long stuff. Later on the tricks did not look so good. They were the same tricks but they were not fresh any more and nothing is worse than a trick that has gone stale. He knew this but he couldn't invent any new tricks. It was a great pity and one of the many things in life that you can't do anything about. Maybe that was why his smile was not a good smile.

After 1930, he just didn't have it any more. His legs began to go and his syntax became boring and the critics began to ask why he didn't put in a few subordinate clauses just to make it look good. But the bar-tenders still liked him and the tourists liked him too. He got more and more famous and the big picture magazines photographed him shooting a lion and catching a tuna and interviewing a Spanish Republican militiaman and fraternising with bullfighters and helping liberate Paris and always smiling bushily and his stuff got worse and worse. Mr. Hemingway the writer was running out of gas but no one noticed it because Mr. Hemingway the celebrity was such

---

[1] "And what if she should die? She won't die. People don't die in childbirth nowadays. That was what all husbands thought. Yes, but what if she should die? She won't die. She's just having a bad time. The initial labor is usually protracted. She's only having a bad time. Afterwards we'd say what a bad time, and Catherine would say it wasn't really so bad. But what if she should die? She can't die. Yes, but what if she should die? She can't, I tell you. Don't be a fool. It's just a bad time. It's just nature giving her hell. It's only the first labor, which is almost always protracted. Yes, but what if she should die? She can't die. Why should she die? What reason is there for her to die? . . . But what if she should die? She won't. She's all right. But what if she should die? She can't die. But what if she should die? Hey, what about that? What if she should die?" *A Farewell to Arms* (pp. 245–6, Penguin ed.). [Reprinted by permission of Charles Scribner's Sons from *A Farewell to Arms* (Copyright 1929 Charles Scribner's Sons; renewal copyright © 1957 Ernest Hemingway). Reprinted by permission of the Executors of the Ernest Hemingway Estate and Jonathan Cape Ltd.]

[2] I remember waking in the morning. Catherine was asleep and the sun was coming in through the window. The rain had stopped and I stepped out of bed and across the floor to the window. . . .
"How are you, darling?" she said. "Isn't it a lovely day?"
"How do you feel?"
"I feel very well. We had a lovely night."
"Do you want breakfast?"
She wanted breakfast. So did I and we had it in bed, the November sunlight coming in through the window, and the breakfast tray across my lap.
"Don't you want the paper? You always wanted the paper in the hospital."
No," I said. "I don't want the paper now." *A Farewell to Arms* (p. 193). [Reprinted by permission of Charles Scribner's Sons from *A Farewell to Arms* (Copyright 1929 Charles Scribner's Sons; renewal copyright © 1957 Ernest Hemingway). Reprinted by permission of the Executors of the Ernest Hemingway Estate and Jonathan Cape Ltd.]

good copy. It was all very American and in 1954 they gave him the Nobel Prize and it wasn't just American any more. The judges were impressed by "the style-forming mastery of the art of modern narration" he had shown in *The Old Man and the Sea,* which he had published in *Life* two years earlier. *Life* is the very biggest of the big picture magazines and *Life* is exactly where *The Old Man and the Sea* belonged. Literary prize judges are not always clever. This is something you know and if you don't know it you should know it. They gave him the prize and he went to Stockholm and the King of Sweden put the medal around his neck and they shook hands. Mr. Hemingway meet Mr. Bernadotte.

After 1930 his friends were not named Anderson or Pound or Stein. They are named Charles Ritz and Toots Shor and Leonard Lyons and Ava Gardner and Marlene Dietrich and Gary Cooper. He almost had a fight with Max Eastman because he thought Max Eastman had questioned his virility and he almost fought a duel with someone he thought might have insulted the honor of Ava Gardner but he didn't have the fight and he decided that Ava Gardner's honor had not been insulted after all. It is often difficult to tell about honor. It is something you feel in your *cojones.* Or somewhere. He liked Marlene Dietrich very much. They had good times together. He called her "The Kraut" and she called him "Papa." His wife called him "Papa" too. Many other people called him "Papa." He liked being called "Papa."

He wrote a novel called *Across the River and Into the Trees.* It was not a good novel. It was a bad novel. It was so bad that all the critics were against it. Even the ones who had liked everything else. The trouble with critics is that you can't depend on them in a tight place and this was a very tight place indeed. They scare easy because their brains are where their *cojones* should be and because they have no loyalty and because they have never stopped a charging lion with a Mannlicher double-action .34 or done any of the other important things. The hell with them. Jack Dempsey thought *Across the River* was OK. So did Joe Di Maggio. The Kraut thought it was terrific. So did Toots Shor. But it was not OK and he knew it and there was absolutely nothing he could do about it.

He was a big man and he was famous and he drank a great deal now and wrote very little. He lived in Havana and often went game fishing and *Life* photographed him doing it. Sometimes he went to Spain for the bullfights and he made friends with the famous bullfighters and wrote it up in three instalments for *Life.* He had good times with his friends and his admirers and his wife and the tourists and the bar-tenders and everybody talked and drank and laughed and was gay but it all went away when he was alone. It was bad when he was alone. Nothing helped then. He knew he had been very good once, he knew he had been as good as they come at the special kind of thing he was good at, and he knew he had not been good for a long time. He talked to interviewers: "I trained hard and I beat Mr. De Maupassant. I've fought two draws with Mr. Stendhal, but nobody is going to

get me in any ring with Mr. Tolstoy unless I'm crazy or keep getting better."
But he knew he was getting worse, and not better. He was a writer and his
writing had gone soft a long time ago and he knew this no matter what the
Nobel Prize judges and the editors of *Life* told him and he was a writer and
nothing else interested him much. He took shock treatments for depression
at the Mayo Clinic. He went twice and he stayed there a long time but they
didn't work. He was overweight and his blood pressure was high and his
doctor made him cut down on the eating and drinking. Last spring his friend
Gary Cooper died. He took it hard. The position is outflanked the lion can't
be stopped the sword won't go into the bull's neck the great fish is breaking
the line and it is the fifteenth round and the champion looks bad.

Now it is that morning in the house in Ketchum, Idaho. He takes his
favourite gun down from the rack. It is a 12-gauge double-barrelled shotgun
and the stock is inlaid with silver. It is a very beautiful gun. He puts the end
of the gun-barrel into his mouth and he pulls both triggers. There is nothing much left above the chin.

That week his great shaggy head looks down from the covers of the picture magazines on the news-stands and the graduate students smile thinly
as they realise that a definitive study of the complete *œuvre* of Ernest Hemingway is now possible.

II

A professor of English in North Carolina State College recently called
Hemingway "essentially a philosophical writer." This seems to me a foolish statement even for a professor of literature. It is true that Hemingway
originated a romantic attitude which was as seductive to a whole generation, and as widely imitated, as Byron's had been. (It is still attractive:
Norman Mailer, for instance, is a belated Hemingway type, though his
prose style is different.) But Hemingway was no more a philosopher than
Byron was; in fact, he was considerably less of one. A feeling that loyalty
and bravery are the cardinal virtues and that physical action is the basis of
the good life—even when reinforced with the kind of nihilism most of us
get over by the age of twenty—these don't add up to a philosophy. There
is little evidence of thought in Hemingway's writing and much evidence of
the reverse—the kind of indulgence in emotion and prejudice which the
Nazis used to call "blood-thinking." For all the sureness of his instinct as
a writer, he strikes one as not particularly intelligent. Byron wrote *Manfred*
but he also wrote *Don Juan* and the letters and journals; underneath the romantic pose there was a tough, vigorous, and sceptical mind, a throwback
to the 18th century and the Age of Reason. There were two Byrons but there
was (alas) only one Hemingway. He was hopelessly sincere. His life, his
writing, his public personality and his private thoughts were all of a piece.
Unlike Byron, he believed his own propaganda. I hate to think what his letters and journals must be like. I suspect he kept no journals, since to do so
implies reflection and self-awareness; also that one has a private life as

apart from one's professional and public existence; I don't think Hemingway did—indeed I think it was this lack of private interests which caused him to kill himself when his professional career had lost its meaning.

We know what his conversation was like, in his later years at least, from Lillian Ross's minute account of two days spent with Hemingway and his entourage *(The New Yorker,* May 13th, 1950). The article presents a Hemingway who sounds as fatuous and self-consciously he-man as his general in *Across the River.* At least that is how it sounds to me. But Miss Ross has a different ear. She insists, and I believe her, that (a) she simply reported what Hemingway said and did, and (b) that she liked and respected him (and what he said and did). She also states that she showed advance proofs to Hemingway and that he made no objections to the article and in fact was pleased with it. One can only admire his objectivity and good nature. But perhaps his reaction was a little *too* objective. Perhaps it shows an alienation from himself that is neurotic—one should feel a certain amount of prejudice in favour of one's self, after all. Or perhaps, worse, it means that Hemingway by then had accepted the public personality that had been built up for him by the press—a well-trained lion, he jumped through all the hoops—and even gloried in the grotesque (but virile) philistine Miss Ross had innocently depicted. This latter possibility is suggested by a letter from Hemingway which Miss Ross quoted in *The New Republic* of August 7th last when she protested against Irving Howe's assumption that she had been out to "smear" Hemingway in her *New Yorker* piece. "The hell with them," Hemingway wrote her after the piece had been published, apropos of people who had found it "devastating" (as I must confess I still do). "Think one of the 'devastating' things was that I drink a little in it and that makes them think I am a rummy. But of course if they (the devastated people) drank what we drink in that piece they would die or something. Then (I should not say it) there is a lot of jealousy around and because I have fun a lot of the time and am not really spooky and so far always get up when they count over me some people are jealous. They can't understand you being a serious writer and not solemn." This seems to me, taken in conjunction with Miss Ross's reportage, to indicate the opposite to what the writer intended to indicate.

III

Hemingway's importance, I think, is almost entirely as a stylistic innovator. I have just reread *A Farewell to Arms* and *Men Without Women* and what strikes me most is their extreme mannerism. I don't know which is the more surprising, after twenty years, the virtuosity of the style or its lack of emotional resonance to-day. Consider the opening paragraphs of *In Another Country:*

> In the fall the war was always there, but we did not go to it any more. It was cold in the fall in Milan and the dark came very early. Then the electric lights came on, and it was pleasant along the streets looking in the

windows. There was much game hanging outside the shops, and the snow powdered in the fur of the foxes and the wind blew their tails. The deer hung stiff and heavy and empty, and small birds blew in the wind and the wind turned their feathers. It was a cold fall and the wind came down from the mountains.

We were all at the hospital every afternoon, and there were different ways of walking across the town through the dusk to the hospital. Two of the ways were alongside canals, but they were long. Always, though, you crossed a bridge across a canal to enter the hospital. There was a choice of three bridges. On one of them a woman sold roasted chestnuts. It was warm, standing in front of the charcoal fire, and the chestnuts were warm afterwards in your pocket. The hospital was very old and very beautiful, and you entered through a gate on the other side. There were usually funerals starting from the courtyard. Beyond the old hospital were the new brick pavilions, and there we met every afternoon and were all very polite and interested in what was the matter, and sat in the machines that were to make so much difference.[3]

This is a most peculiar way to begin a story. Nothing "happens" until the last sentence of the second paragraph. Up to then everything is simply atmosphere but not atmosphere as it was generally known before Hemingway, except for the wonderful two sentences about the game hanging outside the shops. It is an original mixture of the abstract and the concrete, as in the first sentence, and the effect is to describe not a particular state of mind but rather a particular way of looking at experience, one which makes as sharp a break with previous literary methods as Jackson Pollock made with previous ways of painting. The primitive syntax is the equivalent of Pollock's "drip and dribble" technique and, like it, is a declaration of war against the genteel and academic style. There is also a parallel with the architecture of Mies Van Der Rohe, whose "Less is more" applies to Hemingway's style, which gets its effect from what it leaves out. (Maybe this is the characteristic 20th-century manner in the arts: I'm told that in the music of Webern and the jazz of Thelonius Monk one should listen not to the notes but to the silences between them.) Because Van Der Rohe's buildings are simple in form and without ornamentation many people think they are functional, but in fact they are as aggressively unfunctional as the wildest baroque. The same goes for Hemingway's style which is direct and simple on the surface but is actually as complexly manneristic as the later James.

"Refinements in the use of subordinate clauses are a mark of maturity in style," writes Albert C. Baugh in *A History of the English Language*. "As the loose association of clauses (parataxis) gives way to more precise indications of logical relationship and subordination (hypotaxis), there is need for a greater variety of words effecting the union." Hemingway was

---

[3] [Reprinted by permission of Charles Scribner's Sons from "In Another Country" (Copyright 1927 Charles Scribner's Sons; renewal copyright © 1955). Reprinted by permission of the Executors of the Ernest Hemingway Estate and Jonathan Cape Ltd.]

a most paratactical writer. Not because he was primitive but because he was stylistically sophisticated to the point of decadence. Supremely uninterested in "precise indications of logical relationship," he needed very few words; his vocabulary must be one of the smallest in literary history.

I can see why, in the 'twenties, the two paragraphs quoted above were fresh and exciting, but in 1961 they seem as academically mannered as *Euphues* or *Marius the Epicurean*. This is, of course, partly because Hemingway's stylistic discoveries have become part of our natural way of writing, so that they are at once too familiar to cause any excitement and at the same time, in the extreme form in which Hemingway used them, they now sound merely affected. This kind of writing is lost unless it can create a mood in the reader, since it deliberately gives up all the resources of logic and reason. But I was, in 1961, conscious of the tricks—and impatient with them. *Why* must we be told about the two ways of walking to the hospital and the three bridges and the chestnut seller? The aim is probably to create tension by lingering over the prosaic—writers of detective stories, a highly artificial literary form, have learned much from Hemingway—just as the purpose of stating that it is warm in front of a fire and that newly roasted chestnuts feel warm in one's pocket is to suggest the coldness of Milan that fall. But these effects didn't "carry" with me, I just felt impatient.

IV

A Farewell to Arms is generally considered Hemingway's best novel. It has aged and shrivelled from what I remembered. I found myself skipping yards and yards of this sort of thing:

> "We could walk or take a tram," Catherine said.
> "One will be along," I said. "They go by here."
> "Here comes one," she said.
> The driver stopped his horse and lowered the metal sign on his meter. The top of the carriage was up and there were drops of water on the driver's coat. His varnished hat was shining in the wet. We sat back in the seat and the top of the carriage made it dark.
> (Half a page omitted)
> At the hotel I asked Catherine to wait in the carriage while I went in and spoke to the manager. There were plenty of rooms. Then I went out to the carriage, paid the driver, and Catherine and I walked in together. The small boy in buttons carried the package. The manager bowed us towards the elevator. There was much red plush and brass. The manager went up in the elevator with us.[4]

There is a great deal of paying cab drivers and finding it dark at night inside a closed carriage.

---

[4] [Reprinted by permission of Charles Scribner's Sons from *A Farewell to Arms* (Copyright 1929 Charles Scribner's Sons; renewal copyright © 1957 Ernest Hemingway). Reprinted by permission of the Executors of the Estate of Ernest Hemingway and Jonathan Cape Ltd.]

I found both the military part and the love-story tedious except at moments of ordeal or catastrophe. The wounding of the narrator, Lieutenant Henry, and his escape after Caporetto are exciting, and the chapters on the retreat from Caporetto are as good as I remembered, especially the four pages about the shooting of the officers by the battle police. As long as the lieutenant and Catherine Baker are making love and having "a good time" together, one is bored and sceptical. To my surprise, I found that Catherine was like the heroines of *For Whom the Bell Tolls* and *Across the River and Into the Trees,* not a person but an adolescent day dream utterly beautiful and utterly submissive and utterly in love with the dreamer: "You see I'm happy, darling, and we have a lovely time. . . . You are happy, aren't you? Is there anything I do you don't like? Can I do anything to please you? Would you like me to take down my hair? Do you want to play?" "Yes and come to bed." "All right. I'll go and see the patients first." The conversation of these lovers is even more protracted and boring than that of real lovers. (It is curious how verbose Hemingway's laconic style can become.) But at the end when Catherine dies in childbed, the feeling comes right and one is moved—just as the preceding ordeal of the escape to Switzerland by rowing all night is well done. This deathbed scene is one of the few successful ones in literary history; it is the stylistic antithesis to Dickens' Death of Little Nell (of which Oscar Wilde remarked, "One must have a heart of stone to read it without laughing").

The fact is Hemingway is a short-story writer and not a novelist. He has little understanding of the subject-matter of the novel: character, social setting, politics, money matters, human relations, all the prose of life. Only the climactic moments interest him, and of those only ordeal, suffering, and death. (Except for a lyrical feeling about hunting and fishing.) In a novel he gets lost, wandering around aimlessly in a circle as lost people are said to do, and the alive parts are really short stories, such as the lynching of the fascists and the blowing up of the bridge in *For Whom the Bell Tolls.* In the short story he knows just where he is going and his style, which becomes tedious in a novel, achieves the intensity appropriate to the shorter form. The difference may be seen in comparing the dialogue in *A Farewell to Arms* with that in the little short story, "Hills Like White Elephants." The former is often aimlessly repetitious because the writer sees nowhere to go (except at peak moments of crisis) but the latter is directed with superb craftsmanship to the single bitter point the story makes. Every line of this apparently random conversation between a man and a girl waiting at a Spanish railway station—she is going to Madrid for an abortion he wants but she doesn't—develops the theme and when towards the end she asks, "Would you do something for me now?" and he replies, "I'd do anything for you," and she says "Would you please please please please please please stop talking?"—then one feels that tightening of the scalp that tells one an artist has made his point.

Dwight MacDonald **801**

V

"Hemingway's tragedy as an artist," Cyril Connolly writes in *Enemies of Promise,* "is that he has not had the versatility to run away fast enough from his imitators. . . . A Picasso would have done something different; Hemingway could only indulge in invective against his critics—and do it again." The list of Hemingwayesque writers includes James M. Cain, Erskine Caldwell, John O'Hara, and a whole school of detective fiction headed by Dashiell Hammett and Raymond Chandler. It also includes Hemingway. Connolly wrote before Hemingway had begun to parody himself in *The Old Man and the Sea*—which is simply his early short story, "The Undefeated," perhaps the best thing he ever did, re-told in terms of fishing instead of bullfighting and transposed from a spare, austere style into a slack, fake-biblical style which retains the mannerisms and omits the virtues—and above all in *Across the River and Into the Trees,* an unconscious self-parody of almost unbelievable fatuity. The peculiar difficulty American creative writers have in maturing has often been commented on. Emotionally, Hemingway was adolescent all his life; intellectually, he was a Philistine on principle. His one great talent was æsthetic—a feeling for style, in his writing and in his life, that was remarkably sure. But the limits of æstheticism unsupported by thought or feeling are severe. Hemingway made one big, original stylistic discovery—or rather he worked it out most consciously with the aid of Gertrude Stein—but when he had gotten everything there was to be gotten out of it (and a bit more) he was unable, as Connolly notes, to invent anything else. He was trapped in his style as a miner might be trapped underground; the oxygen is slowly used up without any new air coming in.

Hemingway's opposites are Stendhal and Tolstoy—interesting he should feel especially awed by them—who had no style at all, no effects. Stendhal wrote the way a police sergeant would write if police sergeants had imagination—dry, matter-of-fact style. Tolstoy's writing is clear and colourless, interposing no barrier between the reader and the narrative, the kind of direct prose, businesslike and yet Olympian, that one imagines the Recording Angel uses for entries in *his* police blotter. There is no need for change or innovation with such styles, but the more striking and original a style is, obviously the greater such necessity. Protean innovators like Joyce and Picasso invent, exploit, and abandon dozens of styles; Hemingway had only one; it was not enough. But he did write some beautiful short stories while it was working. Perhaps they are enough.

6 / HISTORY

It Was a Stable World

Robert Graves

For a biographical note on Robert Graves see page 782.

The world was stable—a compact world of manageable size, centrally governed—a Mediterranean world with Imperial Rome as the hub, the smoke of sacrifice reeking from a thousand altars and the heavenly bodies circling in foreseeable fashion overhead. True, there was another world that began at the River Euphrates, the Eastern world into which Alexander the Great had freakishly broken three centuries before. But the Romans had left it alone since losing 30,000 men at Carrhae in an attempt to advance their frontiers at Parthian expense. Oriental luxury goods—jade, silk, gold, spices, vermillion, jewels—had formerly come overland by way of the Caspian Sea and now that this route had been cut by the Huns, a few daring Greek sea-captains were sailing from Red Sea ports, catching the trade winds and loading up at Ceylon. But commercial relations were chancy.

Northward, dense forests swarming with uncivilised, red-haired, beer-swilling Germans; and foggy Britain with its chariot fighters who seemed to have stepped from the pages of Homer; and the bleak steppes of Russia peopled by mare-milking nomad Scythians. Westward, the Ocean, supposedly extending to the point where it spilt over into nothingness. Nobody had thought it worth while to test the truth of the Greek legend that far out lay a chain of islands where coconuts grew on palms and life was indolent and merry. Southward, marvellous Africa, of which only the nearest regions had been explored; from beyond came rumours of burning deserts, pigmies, camel-leopards and marshes full of cranes. Though the Greek scientist Eratosthenes had calculated the distance of the sun from the earth, and the earth's circumference at the Equator, with only a small error, his theory of a global world was received with polite scorn by men of common sense: how could there be a Southern Hemisphere? An Egyptian admiral had once been sent out from Suez as a punishment for insubordination, with orders to follow the African coast as far as it went; after three years he had returned by way of Gibraltar claiming to have circumnavigated the continent. But that was centuries back, and the fellow had been put to death for an impious report that at the Southern Cape the sun had been rising in the wrong quarter of the sky. For the ordinary Roman citizen, the earth was still as flat as the palm of his hand.

"Midmost is safest," the Romans said—a dull, unadventurous, home-loving race, who hated the sea, preferred walking to riding, and thought banishment from their country scarcely preferable to death. They had become masters of the world against their real inclinations: the incentive to expand had not been patriotism or a self-imposed civilising mission, as was later alleged, but family rivalry sharpened by greed. The Republican institution of the "triumph" was to blame. While there was a Sacred King at Rome he won his title by marrying the queen's daughter or younger female relative, not by being the former king's eldest son; but in a prolonged struggle for the succession at the death of King Tullius all the royal princesses were either defiled or killed. This unfortunate accident—not "a burning love of freedom"—ended the monarchy. However, in the Republic that took its place, the Senate might decree one great privilege of the former king to honour commanders-in-chief who conquered an enemy state: to ride in triumph through Rome, with the captured gods—that is, their sacred statues—carried on carts behind him, himself impersonating and possessed by, the scarlet-faced Oak-god Mars, patron of shepherds. Republican commanders-in-chief, who were also judges of the Supreme Court, could be appointed only from the nobility, and it was rivalry between these noble families as to which could secure most triumphs that started Roman imperialism. For the commoners who did the fighting the rewards were loot, glory, decorations for valour and farm-lands in the conquered country upon their discharge.

The technique of expansion was simple. *Divide et impera:* enter into solemn treaty with a neighbouring country, foment internal disorder, intervene in support of the weaker side on the ground that Roman honour was involved, replace the legitimate ruler with a puppet, giving him the status of subject ally; later, goad him into rebellion, seize and sack the country, burn down the temples and carry off the captive gods to adorn a triumph. Conquered territories were put under the control of a provincial governor-general, an ex-commander-in-chief, who garrisoned it, levied taxes, set up courts of summary justice, and linked the new frontiers with the old by so-called Roman roads—usually built up by Greek engineers and native forced labour. Established social and religious practices were permitted so long as they did not threaten Roman administration or offend against the broad-minded Roman standards of good taste. The new province presently became a spring-board for further aggression.

Rome was now a great jackdaw's nest, with temples and mansions newly built in solid vulgar, imitation-Greek architectural style—much of it con-crete with a thin marble facing—stuffed with loot from more ancient and beautiful cities. Typical scenes of "the grandeur that was Rome" at the sack of Corinth. A group of smoke-blackened Roman infantrymen squatting on a priceless old master—Aristides's *The God Dionysus*—and shooting craps for possession of sacred chalices looted from Dionysus's temple. Others hacking souvenirs from the most famous relic of antiquity, the stern of the ship *Argo* which had brought back the Golden Fleece from the Caucasus more than a thousand years before. The Army commander impressing on the transport captains detailed to convey unique works of art back to Rome —"Mind you, my men, anything you lose you'll have to replace."

The prisoners captured in these wars became slaves. The chief cause of Rome's industrial backwardness was not lack of inventiveness but the remarkable cheapness of highly skilled slave labour. A first-class smith or weaver or potter could often be bought for about the same price that a good dairy cow would fetch nowadays, and was not much more expensive to keep. (For that matter, a Greek schoolmaster or a qualified doctor could be bought for only a few pounds more.) In the Mediterranean the winter, in general, is short and mild, and the Romans could import unlimited cheap grain from Egypt, Libya and Tripoli—it was not for some centuries that overcultivation made a dust-bowl of the whole North African coast. Olive-oil, dried fish, chickpeas, wine, and fruit were also in plentiful supply. Corn-mills driven by water power had been known for some generations, yet were little used: it was a principle of industrial economy to keep one's slaves, especially women, in good physical condition by making them do their daily pull at the lever of a hand-mill. And though the carpenter had developed into a highly skilled cabinet-maker, three more centuries passed before the principle of the water-mill was combined with that of the saw. Still more remarkable, the steam-engine had been invented by one Ctesibius—who also invented a water-clock and a hydraulic organ—and a working model had long been on show in the lighthouse at Alexandria where it was used as a donkey-engine. Capitalists were unimpressed: "Introduce mechanical hauling into industry and encourage laziness in the workers." In the same spirit the Emperor Tiberius, Augustus's successor, put to death an inventor who brought him a specimen of unbreakable and malleable glass: the discovery would have thrown the jewelry trade into disorder and depreciated the value of gold bullion.

On the whole, slaves were treated well and encouraged to hard work and obedience by being given occasional tips and allowed to earn money in their off hours. Eventually they could hope to buy themselves free, though still owing certain duties as freedmen to their masters; and their children would be free-born. It was dangerous to starve slaves or flog them too freely; indeed, gross cruelty to a slave was now a penal offence. This lesson had been learned in the great Slave Revolt under the gladiator Spartacus two generations before, which had all but succeeded in making the slaves their masters' masters. Slavery was now regarded by industrialists as a safeguard against the pretensions of the free-born working classes, who could not compete in price against well-organised and highly financed slave labour. Strikes of working-men were exceptional: as when the Levite bakers in the Temple of Jerusalem walked out on being refused a 100 per cent rise in pay. The High Priest tried to break the strike by importing bakers from the rival Jewish Temple at Leontopolis in Egypt, but their shewbread was not up to Jerusalem standard and the strikers gained their demands.

At the apex of the social pyramid, which was still nominally Republican, stood the Emperor Augustus. As leader of the winning side in the Civil Wars, caused by murderous rivalry between noble families, he had been invested with temporary dictatorial powers, religious as well as civil, which he often undertook to relinquish when the time should be ripe; but it never was. Under him in descending order of importance came the remains of the nobility, who formed a rubber-stamp Senate and from whom all high-ranking Army officers and Government officials were drawn; next, the Knights, merchant families eligible for less distinguished offices; next, the free-born Roman citizens with full civil rights, including that of voting at the free democratic elections which no longer took place, and exemption from the servile punishment of crucifixion. After these, free-born foreigners with more limited right; then freedmen; lastly, slaves.

In the higher income groups the birth-rate fell steadily despite bachelor taxes and personal appeals for fertility by the Emperor. Few society women could be bothered to bear children in any quantity and preferred to let their husbands amuse themselves in sporting-houses or with Greek mistresses. The society woman's day was a full one: "Madam, your warm cinnamon milk, and the bath is ready." "Madam, the masseuse, the chiropodist, the hair-dresser." "The jeweller has called to show madam the Indian emeralds." "The chief chef wishes to ask madam's advice about the wild-boar steaks. He is of opinion that they should hang a day or two longer." "Has madam decided after all to attend the wedding of her third cousin, the Lady Metalla? It is today." "Madam's pet monkey has, I regret to report, been at his tricks again in the master's study. Yes, madam, I have squared the master's secretary and, please, he has undertaken to procure madam a copy of the charming bawdy little Greek novel that she picked up at Corbulo's yesterday." "My Lady Lentula's compliments and will madam confirm last night's bet of one thousand gold pieces to three hundred against Leek Green in the second race tomorrow?"

There was constant recruitment of the nobility from the merchant class, and rich commoners went up into the merchant class and were privileged to wear a gold thumb-ring and sit in seats reserved for them at the theatre immediately behind the nobility. Morals among the less fortunately born were based largely on social ambition. Conviction for petty felonies disqualified a man from membership of the social clubs of his class; serious felony degraded him. There was also a vague fear that crimes, even when successfully concealed, might be punished in a shadowy Hell with perpetual tortures. Belief in the islands of Elysium, where virtue was rewarded with a life of perpetual bliss, was still vague; besides, Homer had made it clear that these abodes were reserved for royalty. Ordinary citizens became twittering ghosts and went down to Hell, and stayed there except for an annual ticket-of-leave holiday between owl-cry and cock-crow, when their pious descendants put food out for them to lick at, and themselves kept carefully indoors.

Among the governing classes superstitious fear of evil omens, ghosts, and bogeys contrasted with the fashionable scepticism about the gods. However, the majesty of Law and the sanctity of treaties depended in theory on the official Olympian cult, and so did the complicated system of national holidays and popular entertainments. Jokes at the expense of cross, lecherous old Father Jupiter, his shrewish wife Juno, and his clever unmarried daughter Minerva—the Roman trinity—were confined to intimate gatherings. But gods and goddesses, so far from being jealous guardians of family morals, permitted and even demanded periodical orgies of drunkenness and sexual promiscuity as healthy vents for popular emotion. Their images also presided at the wild-beast shows, chariot races, gladiatorial fights, dances, plays, musical entertainments and displays of juggling and contortionism, arranged in their honour by endowed priesthoods.

There was no system of public education even for the free-born except in Greek cities that still prided themselves on their high standard of culture, and among the Jews everywhere, for whom attendance at the synagogue school was now a religious obligation. Elsewhere, reading, writing, and arithmetic were luxuries reserved for the governing and mercantile classes with their stewards, secretaries, accountants, and agents. The Jews were at once a comfort and a worry to the central government. Though industrious, law-abiding and peaceful wherever they were left alone, they were not merely a nation of perhaps three and a half millions settled in Palestine under the rule of Herod the Great, a petty king appointed by the Emperor, with a tribal god, a Temple, and established festivals. They were also a huge religious fraternity, including a great many converts of non-Jewish race, whose first article of faith was that there was only one God, and the intimate contact with Goddess-worshippers was disgusting and sinful. Far more Jews lived outside Palestine than in it, spread about in small or large communities from one end of the world to another and over the edge of the world in Babylonia. They constituted a serious obstacle to the Imperial policy of encouraging provincials to pay divine honours to the Emperor, but were still allowed perfect religious freedom. The distinction between Semites and Europeans had not yet been drawn; for the Spartans who were pure Greeks, officially claimed cousinship with the Jews in virtue of a common descent from Abraham. There was, however, strong local jealousy of Jews who had broken into Greek commercial spheres, with which went resentment of them as over-righteous spoilsports.

Colour was no problem. If the question had even arisen—but it never did—whether the black races were inferior to the white the answer would immediately have been found in Homer, who was quoted as an inspired authority in all matters of general morality: "Homer relates that the blessed gods themselves used to pay complimentary visits to the Blameless Ethiopians." Colour was not popularly associated with slavery, since slaves were for the most part white, and nothing prevented coloured monarchs from owning white slaves if honestly come by. Nor was miscegenation frowned upon. Augustus rewarded his ally King Juba, a Moor, with the hand of Selene, the beautiful daughter of Cleopatra, the Greek queen of Egypt, and his own late brother-in-law Mark Antony.

The Romans were oddly backward in military development, except in the arts of entrenchment, siege warfare and infantry drill with javelin and stabbing-sword. They never practised archery even for sport, or formed their own cavalry units, but relied for flank protection of their solid, slow-moving infantry masses on allied lancers and horse-archers, including many coloured squadrons. To join the Army usually meant staying with one's regiment until the age of sixty, and campaigning was arduous, especially against active and light-armed foresters or mountaineers. The soldier's load weighed more than eighty pounds, which he had to hump for fifteen or twenty miles a day in all weathers; rations were poor, comforts few, pay irregular, floggings frequent. But peacetime garrison duty in big frontier camps was pleasant enough. A regiment kept the same station for generations, and the camp gradually developed into a city as camp-followers set up general stores under the protection of the fortifications, and soldiers married native women and built permanent huts. In remote outposts of the Empire time dragged. Last year an inscription was found on the site of a small Roman camp on the Libyan frontier to this effect "The Company commander fears that it will be a long time before their promised relief arrives from Rome; meanwhile the company have made the best of a bad job and hereby dedicate this commodious swimming-pool to the Goddess of Army Welfare."

The swimming-pool was a Greek institution. It was from the Greeks that the Romans had learned practically all they knew: law, literary technique, public speaking, philosophy, engineering, music, medicine, mathematics, astronomy, stagecraft and acting, domestic and industrial science, sanitation, and athletics. But, with a few notable exceptions, they were all barbarians at heart, and in athletics, for example, showed no innate sense of sportsmanship or any appreciation of the finer points of play. In the public ring they abandoned the Greek style of boxing with light leather gloves in favour of Mack Sennett knuckle-dusters studded with iron points with which outsize heavy-weights slogged great chunks off one another.

No great epidemics of plague, typhus, and cholera, such as ravaged Europe in the Middle Ages, are recorded in this epoch. Well-regulated water supply and sewage system in cities, official supervision of foodstuffs and wine exposed for sale, and a great determination to enjoy life to the full while it lasted: all this increased popular resistance to disease. Medicine, too, was in a saner state than it reached again before the nineteenth century: cures were effected by tried herbal remedies, fomentations, dieting, exercise, massage, and spa waters. Greek surgeons following in the wake of Roman armies had got a better knowledge of the interior of the human body from battlefield observation than hitherto from dissection of Egyptian mummies in the Alexandrian medical school; and dentists undertook fillings and complicated bridge work as well as extractions. Mail and transport services ran smoothly throughout the Empire; the insurance rate for shipping was low, now that piracy had been suppressed, and losses by burglary and fire were infrequent. Bureaucracy had just begun rearing its anonymous head: the Emperor Augustus, grown too old and weary to undertake all the official business that falls to a dictator, allowed his ex-slave secretariat to issue minutes, demands, and routine orders under his seal.

Typical success story: M. Fullanus Atrox, grandson of a Sicilian slave, has made money in hogs, invested it in a suburban tile-factory and tenement-rents in a central block at Rome. He now sells a half interest in the factory, which is placing heavy orders in Spain and North Africa, buys a villa near Naples with central heating, baths, a picture gallery, formal gardens, stabling, twenty acres of good land and accommodation for fifty slaves—the very villa where his father once stoked the furnace. He marks the happy occasion by presenting a solid gold salver engraved with poplar leaves to the nearby temple of Hercules—it will create a good impression locally. At the same time he sends his son to the university of Athens.

It was a stable world. But the farther from the hub one went the uglier grew the scene, especially after Augustus's succession by less humane and energetic Emperors. When the poorly paid Roman armies of occupation were quartered in the provinces of Asia Minor and Syria, the rich man was bled but the poor man was skinned. Banditry, beggary, blackmail, and squalor abounded. Conditions were as bad after the death of Herod the Great in the Protectorate of Judaea, where communism was already in operation among the ascetic communities of the Dead Sea area, and in the Native State of Galilee. The cost of living in Galilee, during Jesus' Ministry, was excessively high. Everything was taxed separately: houses, land, fruit trees, cattle, carts, fishing-boats, market produce, salt. There was also a poll-tax, a road tax, and taxes on exports and imports. Worse: the collection of taxes was leased to private financiers and sub-leased by them to contractors who had to buy police protection at a high cost. The Disciples were poor working-men with dependents. When they were on the road their annual out-of-pocket account—apart even from money handed out to the distressed—can hardly have grossed less than £3,000. But out they went, two by two, deploring the instability of a world that was based on greed, lovelessness, and the power of the sword. Unexpectedly, St. Luke mentions among their financial backers the wife of a high finance officer of the rapacious Native Court.

from This Hallowed Ground

Bruce Catton

Bruce Catton (b. 1899) began his writing career as a journalist, serving on newspapers in Cleveland, Boston, and Washington. After World War II, in which he served as a government official, he devoted himself more and more to history and has become one of our leading authorities on the American Civil War. Some of his books are *Mr. Lincoln's Army* (1951), *A Stillness at Appomattox* (1953), which in 1954 won the Pulitzer prize, *Grant Moves South* (1959), *Glory Road* (1959), *Grant Takes Command* (1969), and *This Hallowed Ground* (1956), from which the following excerpt is taken.

It came to an end at last on Palm Sunday—April 9, 1865—when Sheridan and his cavalry and a whole corps of infantry got squarely across the road in Lee's front. The nearest town was the village of Appomattox Court House, and the last long mile had been paced off. Lee had armed Yankees in his front, in his rear, and on his flank. There was a spatter of fighting as his advance guard tried the Yankee line to see if it could be broken. It could not. The firing died down, and Lee sent a courier with a white flag through the lines carrying a letter to U. S. Grant.

Until this Palm Sunday of 1865 the word Appomattox had no meaning. It was a harsh name left over from Indian days, it belonged to a river and to a country town, and it had no overtones. But after this day it would be one of the haunted possessions of the American people, a great and unique word that would echo in the national memory with infinite tragedy and infinite promise, recalling a moment in which sunset and sunrise came together in a streaked glow that was half twilight and half dawn.

The business might almost have been stage-managed for effect. No detail had been overlooked. There was even the case of Wilmer McLean, the Virginian who once owned a place by a stream named Bull Run and who found his farm overrun by soldiers in the first battle of the war. He sold out and moved to southern Virginia to get away from the war, and he bought a modest house in Appomattox Court House; and the war caught up with him finally, so that Lee and Grant chose his front parlor—of all the rooms in America—as the place where they would sit down together and bring the fighting to an end.

Lee had one staff officer with him, and in Mr. McLean's front yard a Confederate orderly stood by while the war horse Traveler nibbled at the spring grass. Grant came with half a dozen officers of his own, including the famous Sheridan, and after he and Lee had shaken hands and taken their seats these trooped into the room to look and to listen. Grant and Lee sat at two separate tables, the central figures in one of the greatest tableaus of American history.

It was a great tableau not merely because of what these two men did but also because of what they were. No two Americans could have been in greater contrast. (Again, the staging was perfect.) Lee was legend incarnate—tall, gray, one of the handsomest and most imposing men who ever lived, dressed today in his best uniform, with a sword belted at his waist. Grant was—well, he was U. S. Grant, rather scrubby and undersized, wearing his working clothes, with mud-spattered boots and trousers and a private's rumpled blue coat with his lieutenant general's stars tacked to the shoulders. He wore no sword. The men who were with them noticed the contrast and remembered it. Grant himself seems to have felt it; years afterward, when he wrote his memoirs, he mentioned it and went to some lengths to explain why he did not go to this meeting togged out in dress uniform. (In effect, his explanation was that he was just too busy.)

Yet the contrast went far beyond the matter of personal appearance. Two separate versions of America met in this room, each perfectly embodied by its chosen representative.

There was an American aristocracy, and it had had a great day. It came from the past and it looked to the past; it seemed almost deliberately archaic, with an air of knee breeches and buckled shoes and powdered wigs, with a leisured dignity and a rigid code in which privilege and duty were closely joined. It had brought the country to its birth and it had provided many of its beliefs; it had given courage and leadership, a sense of order and learning, and if there had been any way by which the eighteenth century could possibly have been carried forward into the future, this class would have provided the perfect vehicle. But from the day of its beginning America had been fated to be a land of unending change. The country in which this leisured class had its place was in powerful ferment, and the class itself had changed. It had been diluted. In the struggle for survival it had laid hands on the curious combination of modern machinery and slave labor, the old standards had been altered, dignity had begun to look like arrogance, and pride of purse had begun to elbow out pride of breeding. The single lifetime of Robert E. Lee had seen the change, although Lee himself had not been touched by it.

Yet the old values were real, and the effort to preserve them had nobility. Of all the things that went to make up the war, none had more poignance than the desperate fight to preserve these disappearing values, eroded by change from within as much as by change from without. The fight had been made and it had been lost, and everything that had been dreamed and tried and fought for was personified in the gray man who sat at the little table in the parlor at Appomattox and waited for the other man to start writing out the terms of surrender.

The other man was wholly representative too. Behind him there was a new society, not dreamed of by the founding fathers: a society with the lid taken off, western man standing up to assert that what lay back of a person mattered nothing in comparison to what lay ahead of him. It was the land of the mudsills, the temporarily dispossessed, the people who had nothing to lose but the future; behind it were hard times, humiliation and failure, and ahead of it was all the world and a chance to lift oneself by one's bootstraps. It had few standards beyond a basic unformulated belief in the irrepressibility and ultimate value of the human spirit, and it could tramp with heavy boots down a ravaged Shenandoah Valley or through the embers of a burned Columbia without giving more than a casual thought to the things that were being destroyed. Yet it had its own nobility and its own standards; it had, in fact, the future of the race in its keeping, with all the immeasurable potential that might reside in a people who had decided that they would no longer be bound by the limitations of the past. It was rough and uncultivated and it came to important meetings wearing muddy boots and no sword, and it had to be listened to.

It could speak with a soft voice, and it could even be abashed by its own moment of triumph, as if that moment were not a thing to be savored and enjoyed. Grant seems to have been almost embarrassed when he and Lee came together in this parlor, yet it was definitely not the embarrassment of an underling ill at ease in a superior's presence. Rather it was simply the diffidence of a sensitive man who had another man in his power and wished to hurt him as little as possible. So Grant made small talk and recalled the old days in the Mexican War, when Lee had been the polished staff officer in the commanding general's tents and Grant had been an acting regimental quartermaster, slouching about like the hired man who looked after the teams. Perhaps the oddest thing about this meeting at Appomattox was that it was Grant, the nobody from nowhere, who played the part of gracious host, trying to put the aristocrat at his ease and, as far as might be, to soften the weight of the blow that was about to come down. In the end it was Lee who, so to speak, had to call the meeting to order, remarking (and the remark must have wrenched him almost beyond endurance) that they both knew what they were there for and that perhaps they had better get down to business. So Grant opened his orderly book and got out his pencil. He confessed afterward that when he did so he had no idea what words he was going to write.

He knew perfectly well what he was going to say, however, and with a few pauses he said it in straightforward words. Lee's army was to be surrendered, from commanding general down to humblest private. All public property would be turned over to the United States Army—battle flags, guns, muskets, wagons, everything. Officers might keep their side arms (Grant wrote this after a speculative glance at the excellent sword Lee was wearing) and their horses, but the army and everything it owned was to go out of existence.

It was not, however, to go off to a prison camp. Throughout the war Lincoln had stressed one point: the people of the South might have peace whenever they chose just by laying down their arms and going home. Grant made this official. Officers and men, having disarmed themselves, would simply give their paroles. Then they could go to their homes . . . and here Grant wrote one of the greatest sentences in American history, the sentence that, more than any other thing, would finally make it impossible for any vengeful government in Washington to proceed against Confederate veterans as traitors. Having gone home, he wrote, officers and men could stay there, "not to be disturbed by the United States authorities so long as they observe their paroles and the laws in force where they may reside." When the powerful signature, "U. S. Grant," was signed under that sentence, the chance that Confederate soldiers might be hanged or imprisoned for treason went out the window.

Having written all of this, Grant handed it over for Lee to read.

Lee's part was not easy. He made a business of getting out his glasses, polishing them carefully, crossing his legs, and adjusting himself. Once he borrowed a lead pencil to insert a word that Grant had omitted. When he had finished he raised a point. In the Confederate army, he said, horses for cavalry and artillery were not government issue; the soldiers themselves owned them. Did the terms as written permit these men to take their horses home with them? Grant shook his head. He had not realized that Confederate soldiers owned their steeds, and the terms he had written were explicit: all such animals must be turned in as captured property. Still—Grant went on to muse aloud; the last battle of the war was over, the war itself was over except for picking up the pieces, and what really mattered was for the men of the South to get back home and become civilians again. He would not change the written terms, but he supposed that most of Lee's men were small farmers anxious to return to their acres and get a crop in, and he would instruct the officers in charge of the surrender ceremonies to give a horse or a mule to any Confederate soldier who claimed to own one, so that the men would have a chance "to work their little farms." And in those homely words the great drama of Appomattox came to a close.

The draft of the terms having been agreed on, one of Grant's staff officers took the document to make a fair copy. The United States Army, it appeared, lacked ink, and to write the copy the officer had to borrow a bottle of ink from Lee's staff officer; a moment later, when the Confederate officer sat down to write Lee's formal acceptance, it developed that the Confederate army lacked paper, and he had to borrow from one of Grant's men. The business was finally signed and settled. Lee went out on the porch, looked off over the hills and smote his hands together absently while Traveler was being bridled, and then mounted and started to ride away. Grant and his officers saluted, Lee returned the salute, and there was a little silence while the man in gray rode off to join the pathetic remnant of an army that had just gone out of existence—rode off into mist and legend, to take his place at last in the folklore and the cherished memories of the nation that had been too big for him.

The American Civilization Puzzle

George F. Carter

> George Carter (b. 1912) has been, since 1967, Distinguished Professor of Geography at the Agricultural and Mining College of Texas. His books include *Plant Geography and Culture History in the American Southwest* (1945), *Pleistocene Man at San Diego* (1957), and *Man and the Land* (1964).

Why, people ask, do professors like me study the things we do? Of course, they tell me, Indians are interesting—but are they important? Even if we do manage to find out when and how they developed their civilizations, is the knowledge really worth our working so hard to acquire it?

To such questions I give an emphatic Yes.

THE AMERICAN CIVILIZATION PUZZLE: Reprinted by permission of *The Johns Hopkins Magazine*, from *The Johns Hopkins Magazine*, February, 1957.

We need to know a good deal about the origin of civilization in general. We must know *how* civilization arose. And to answer the "how" we must know when and where. Did civilization arise just once, or several times? What part, if any, did climate and soil and landform and race play in its growth or growths? To give it a modern application: if we get careless with our super-bombs and wipe out civilization, what is the likelihood of a new civilization springing up? How soon? What kind? And where?

Behind these questions lies a further set of questions. Is man largely controlled or directed or influenced by his physical environment, or is he relatively independent of it? And another: Is man predominantly inventive or retentive? There have been whole schools of thought, and still are, that take one side or another on these questions. And we still know little, with any certainty, about how civilization arose, spread, and grows.

The growth of the American Indian civilizations has come to be of crucial importance to the whole problem. For some, it is an example of the inventiveness of man. For others it is an example of the overwhelming force of the physical environment in the molding of man. For still others, it is an example of how uninventive man really is, of how extremely retentive he is, and of the complete dominance of the *spread* of ideas—or "diffusion"—over the *invention* of ideas.

Great battles—really fierce battles—have raged over such things. The current battleground, the current testing-ground, is America.

And, in these battles, I find myself in the thick of things.

In the area from southern Mexico to northern Chile, civilization apparently began rather suddenly, possibly about 1000 B.C. and probably not earlier than 2000 or 3000 B.C.

The peopling of America had been accomplished very much earlier, most probably by small bands of rather primitive people who wandered across from northeastern Asia into Alaska and then wandered slowly southward into the open, unpopulated continents that spread before them. They did not "discover" America. They simply drifted in. They did not "migrate" through the Americas. They simply multiplied and each generation moved a few miles. In such a manner it would take only a few thousand years for such people to reach all parts of North and South America. We know they had plenty of time: by the most advanced methods of measuring past time, we now know that man was here more than thirty-eight thousand years ago. If my current research is right, he was here far earlier than that.

Our present problem, however, is not with this original peopling, but with what happened once these people had settled down. They entered with simple cultures, lacking domestic animals except the dog, lacking the bow and arrow, lacking any knowledge of pottery-making. When we Europeans discovered them many thousands of years later, the Indian peoples in Middle America were practicing agriculture, making pottery, raising some domesticated animals, practicing metallurgy, using practically all the known techniques of weaving, living in organized city states and even empires, and having great capitals that would rival Rome or Athens or Thebes or Babylon.

Just how did all of this come about? Did they do all of it by themselves, with no help? Or did ideas dribble across the great watery moats of the seas? Or, perhaps, did whole floods of ideas reach them from overseas?

On the answers, scholars violently disagree. This is the Diffusion controversy, and for more than one hundred years it has rustled the ivy on academic halls. Some professors, "Diffusionists," think the evidence indicates that man crossed the oceans carrying ideas with him. Others, "Independent Inventionists," fiercely defend the doctrine that nothing of the sort ever happened. They believe that, lacking strong evidence that such transmission of knowledge took place, it is more likely that groups of men all over the world, faced with similar problems, reached similar solutions—even though these groups never had contact with one another.

Gradually, the Independent Inventionists have had to retreat. Gradually, diffusion has been demonstrated over wider and wider areas, through greater and greater time depths, and for more and more things. In the Old World, agriculture, metallurgy, architecture, and the alphabets tended to arise in one center or another and spread to the others. Each area took the basic ideas and wove them into its own particular way of life, giving them a special local flavor. But fundamentally, most of the basic ideas used in this great area of civilization's early growth had their origins in one center or the other. It has been clear for some time now that the growth of civilization in the Old World was a closely interrelated phenomenon.

The New World was the Independent Inventionist's last great stronghold. Here, he could point out, the American Indians developed *in isolation* from the culture growths of the Old World. And in this isolation they had developed nearly everything that the Old World had. They had invented agriculture, but none of the plants were like the domestic plants of the Old World. They had domesticated a few animals: ducks, turkeys, camels (llamas), guinea pigs. And while these might seem uncomfortably close to ducks, chickens, camels, and rabbits of the Old World, the Indians never domesticated any cow-like animal such as the buffalo. They never used any animal for draft purposes, never milked an animal, never made animal domestication an important part of their lives. So, said the Independent Inventionist (with obvious relief), the seeming similarities are not really significant, after all.

The Old World-New World similarities kept piling up, however. In Middle America (a convenient term to designate the area from southern Mexico to northern Chile) the Indian people built pyramids somewhat as some of the people in the Old World did. But the pyramids were built primarily as commanding locations for temples, rather than for the burial of kings as in Egypt. The Independent Inventionists tended to overlook the presence of just such pyramids in Southeast Asia, with temples on *their* truncated tops. Some of the Diffusionists were equally guilty, and played right into the Independent Inventionists' hands, by insisting that nearly all ideas came from Egypt, where of course the pyramids were royal tombs.

The list of men who have entered the debate over the separateness of the Americas from Asia and Eurafrica, and the mountains of evidence and nonsense that have been presented, could be fitted into a doctoral dissertation only with difficulty. Almost from the beginning there were rumblings of Asiatic contacts with America. The Spaniards learned from the Incas of Peru that they had legends of people coming from across the Pacific to trade. And the Incas insisted that they had sent out a great fleet of balsa-log rafts that were gone for two years and finally returned with stories of lands across the sea. This strange tale was believed by the Spaniards, and there followed a series of intrigues over who should head the expedition that would discover another source of wealth like Mexico or Peru. In the political maneuvering, the wrong man ended up in the job. He followed the wrong directions, and the Spaniards found themselves in the impoverished, Negro-populated islands of the southwest Pacific. The Incas' tale was discredited.

The sequel has been written in this decade of the twentieth century. The intrepid Thor Heyerdahl has demonstrated that the Incas could have done just what they said they did; that balsa rafts *can* be sailed across the Pacific. And Heyerdahl has since learned enough about such rafts that, should he wish to, he could now sail one to Asia and then turn around and sail back. By studies in the Galápagos Islands he has shown that the Incas used these islands, six hundred miles offshore, as a base for their fishing fleet—no mean bit of navigation for people using rafts. But it was long denied that the Indians possessed such ability.

The evidence was difficult to throttle. It was pointed out that the game of parchesi, which we got from India, was practically the national pastime in Mexico when the Spanish reached there. There was no mistaking the game. All the rules, and the shape of the board on which it was played, were as we know the game today. In addition, it had special meanings that were duplicated in India.

In America, the Indians blew on pipes of Pan. The pipes blew the identical notes, in the same scale, on both sides of the Pacific. As if this were not enough, in Peru they were played in pairs. Two people stood facing each other, connected by a string that led from one set of pipes to the other. One set of pipes was called Mama and the other Father. The same thing was done in Southeast Asia.

Surely this is stretching coincidence extremely far. Is it really reasonable that the same scale, the same notes, and the identical customs would all be reinvented? There is nothing in the climate or in the soil or in man himself that compels such detailed parallels.

Mathematical and recording systems showed similar strange parallels. In Peru, records of taxes, populations, and histories were kept by tying knots in strings. The system for numbers was a decimal one. A knot tied in one string stood for one, in the next string for ten, in the next for one hundred, and so on.

This is a remarkable invention. It involves the idea that the value of a number is established by its position, and this includes the idea of a decimal place and a zero. It leads directly into negative numbers. All of these concepts we of the Western World received from India.

But when one begins tracing the distribution of such systems as the Peruvian knots in strings, one finds them in the islands of the Pacific and, anciently, in China, Tibet, and India. The Chinese say that they recorded their history by tying knots in strings, before writing was invented.

Thus we have one of the most difficult of mathematical ideas, associated with a particular way of recording it, with a continuous distribution from the probable source, India, to the exact part of America that has a whole host of other parallels to the Southeast Asian center.

The material is formidable in extent. A partial list of further parallels appears below.

COINCIDENCE?

Here is a sampling of ideas, inventions, and legends suggesting varied contacts between America and the Old World:

MATHEMATICAL

The zero: Used in India, Peru, and Mexico.
Place numeral systems: India to China; Peru and Mexico.
Knot-in-string records: Peru, Polynesia, China (before script).
The zodiac: Asia and Mexico.

TECHNOLOGICAL

The loom: In Peru, with all its Old-World parts.
Cloth: In Peru, all known Old-World weaves.
The wheel: On toys, only, in America.
Alcoholic beverages: Close parallels in Polynesia and Peru.
Metals: Elaborate smelting, casting, and alloying techniques duplicated in Old World and Middle America.
Seamanship: Centerboards used for sailing in Peru and China.
Obsidian mirrors: Polynesia and Peru.

RACIAL

Vivid portraits in stone, clay, and paint, showing Indian, Mongolian, and bearded European types.
Legends giving emphatic, clear-cut descriptions of blond, bearded, learned visitors.
Chinese palm prints among the Maya.

ARTISTIC

Jade emphasized in Mexico, Peru, and China.
Trefoil arch: Maya and India.
Sacred tree design: Maya and India.
Tiger thrones: Maya and Southeast Asia.
Lotus staff, lotus stone, lotus panels: detailed similarities between Maya and India.
Serpent columns, balustrades: Mexico and Southeast Asia.
The diving god: Mexico and Bali.
Copper bells: Made by same technique and with same designs in Mexico and Indochina.
Featherwork cloaks: Peru and Polynesia.

Peruvian tales of an expedition across the Pacific.

Chinese document, possibly describing a Buddhist missionary effort in America about 500 A.D.

Polynesian legends of voyages to and from America.

Explicit stories of tall, bearded men who came and taught the Indians.

Serpent deities in Asia and Middle America.

Corn Mother myth (and others) common to Southeast Asia and Middle America.

AGRICULTURAL

Sweet potato: Surely carried across seas, probably from America.

Coconut: Most probably carried to America.

Bottle gourd: Probably carried to America.

Cotton: Most probably carried to America.

Pineapple: Probably carried from America.

Terracing of mountainsides.

Specialized irrigation techniques.

A long list of possible (unconfirmed) plant transfers.

MUSICAL

Panpipe: Identical scale, notes, and ceremonial use in Middle America and Southeast Asia.

Nose flute.

Gourd whistle.

Conch-shell trumpet with similar names in both America and Polynesia. (One Polynesian shell trumpet found in Peru.)

Hollowed log with slit: Used both for music and for signaling in Africa, Middle America, and Polynesia.

One would think from all this that it would quickly be agreed that ideas were indeed carried in some quantity directly from Asia to America. But such has not been the case. Instead, it has been claimed that such transoceanic voyages were impossible, especially for such landlubbers as Chinese or Hindus. The Polynesians were discounted as people with only wooden dugouts totally incapable of such voyages. The Incas were pictured as comical fellows possessed of the world's clumsiest shipping—rafts that could not stay afloat more than a week or so before they had to be pulled out and dried in order to maintain their buoyancy.

The Inca raft, built of great logs of balsa, is now revealed as an excellent ocean-going vessel, capable of voyaging across the Pacific and back, of sailing before the wind or, by ingenious use of centerboards, of sailing into the wind, and of tacking and performing all the maneuvers of the square-rigged vessels of the days of sail. The Polynesian dugouts were often one hundred feet long, more than twice the length of Columbus's smallest ship and fully capable of making great sea voyages. The Hindus and the Chinese had large ocean-going ships when written history began in that area, and we have no evidence of how long they had had them before that.

Still, we could *prove* nothing one way or the other. I could argue that the pipes of Pan and parchesi and the system of recording things decimally by tying knots in strings are most unlikely to be independently reinvented. But the opposition could well reply that this was only my opinion. In *their* opinion there was nothing unusual about such independent invention on two sides of the vast ocean. And so there it would rest—unless there were other ways to determine which opinion was more likely right. Fortunately, there is other evidence—and evidence of such nature that opinion plays no part in it.

Man invents pottery, mathematics, pyramids, and metallurgy. And, in a very real sense, man invents agriculture.

But he does not invent plants.

Plants are natural creations. Man may modify them, and he most certainly did so in developing wild plants into the useful ones of today. But plants have definite homelands. We know for certain that oranges came from Southeast Asia, that wheat came from the Near East, and that olives came from the Mediterranean. We also know that all pumpkins and squashes, tomatoes, potatoes, and chocolate, came from America. No one, not even the Independent Inventionists, has ever claimed that men independently created identical or even similar plants in different parts of the world. Here, then, were markers that offered an opportunity to test the separateness of the two worlds.

This knowledge could not be used immediately. We did not know until rather recently just where our domestic plants came from. One of the pioneers in gathering that information was Alphonse De Candolle, who wrote his great work in 1884. At that time there was still uncertainty about such ultra-American crops as squashes and pumpkins, and their American origin was finally established as late as 1931.

About the turn of the century, O. F. Cook became interested in the coconut. He found that practically all the palms of the coconut family were American. He thought it strange indeed that only the domesticated member of this family should be non-American and concluded that it would be more natural for the domestic coconut to come *from* America.

Cook then went on to investigate a number of other plants. He found that there was considerable evidence that coconuts were not the only foreigners on the pre-Columbian American shores. Further, he found that a few American plants had strayed overseas, also. Of these, two seemed to have carried their names with them. One was the sweet potato; the other was the hibiscus. The names were the same both in parts of Middle America and in Polynesia, the island world of the mid-Pacific. On this and other evidence, Cook built the idea that agriculture had originated in America and spread across the Pacific Ocean to Southeast Asia. He was an early Diffusionist, and a pretty extreme one at that.

His ideas were attacked very sharply. Should they stand, whole schools of thought about the independent growth of civilizations, the psychic unity of mankind, the nature of the growth of culture, the nature of man, the influence of the physical environment on man, and many other beloved theories would have to be discarded. This was a grave threat to academic peace of mind. It was all the more serious because it was backed by an expert in a science.

The way out of this type of difficulty is to get another expert in the same science to counteract the first. (This is a well-known maneuver in more professions than the academic one, by the way.) The Independent Inventionists soon found a champion in the late E. D. Merrill, of Harvard. Merrill assured them that Cook was a very poor expert, indeed. The evidence of pre-Columbian coconuts was not valid. Besides, coconuts could float, so that even if they had been in America in pre-Columbian times it would not mean that men had carried them across the Pacific. The seeds of some hibiscus varieties can also float and stay alive. And as for the sweet potato—well, that was just a case of poor historical research. Merrill was a devastating critic, and he demonstrated to the utter satisfaction of the Independent Inventionists, and to the considerable discomfiture of the Diffusionists, that Cook could be ignored. The botanical evidence was destined to be let alone for a few decades.

Meanwhile another champion of diffusion, a most interesting man, entered the battle. G. Elliot Smith was a physician and surgeon. He worked for many years in Egypt and, among other things, became interested in the Egyptian mummies. This is a fascinating subject, and particularly intriguing to a surgeon. In the preparation of the body for embalming, certain parts had to be removed. This was a professional problem, and Dr. Smith took a keen professional interest in the problem of the removal of the viscera and the brain, the closing of the openings so created, the problem of retaining the fingernails during the pickling process. It was enough to make an inquiring doctor wish that he could have been right there to discuss stitches and incisions, and to inquire into just why some of the operations were performed in such deucedly awkward and stylized ways. Dr. Smith was interested enough to read all that he could get his hands on concerning the funerary arts, processes, and rituals of the Egyptians.

Dr. Smith was also a great traveler. He visited the Trobriand Islanders, in the island world north of Australia. Here, to his astonishment, he found people practicing practically the identical embalming techniques: the incisions in the same awkward places, the same sort of stitches, and even some of the same rituals. His interest was aroused, and he began to trace other spreads of ideas from Egypt. Soon he was tracing everything imaginable to Egypt. Eventually he was tracing things even farther, for he had begun to look at Inca mummies. Here again he found the same improbably surgical procedures. (I hesitate to discuss the details of the preparation of a body for mummification, for it is a grisly subject to those not used to dealing rather offhandedly with cadavers. The resemblances are specific and detailed, however, and entail such singular solutions of the problem as to leave little doubt of their singular origin, if I may be allowed an apt pun.)

G. Elliot Smith marshaled vast amounts of evidence. However, he destroyed his case by insisting that *everything* came from Egypt. (It seems only fair to record that his critics have been equally extreme in discarding his evidence because of flaws in his presentation of it. This technique is known in best scientific parlance as throwing the baby out with the bathwater. It is probably the major contributor to the high infant mortality in the world of ideas, especially of those ideas that run counter to the notions held by powerful and vocal critics.)

Plant evidence was in disrepute due to the efforts of E. D. Merrill, who had overly brilliantly picked the flaws in Cook's arguments. Cook had opened the door to attack on himself by some uncritical work, and by his enthusiasm's leading him to think that the origin of agriculture, *the* origin of agriculture, was in America. Smith had made the same mistakes. He became too enthused with his Egyptian origins. The battle went to the critics. The Independent Inventionists ruled in peace. All the textbooks and all the lectures assured the rising generation that there had been no contact between America and Asia. The Pacific was a vast and impregnable moat.

But this was an uneasy peace. For facts are a bit like the fires of a volcano. They may lie dormant, but actually they are smoldering away, awaiting only the touch of an investigator's hand to spring into life, capable of destroying the most elaborate of philosophical structures.

In the world of knowledge there is utterly no way of knowing where a given piece of research will lead. The work that was to reopen the Diffusionist controversy began with an attempt by a group of botanists to untangle the relationships of the cottons of the world. Hutchinson, Silow, and Stevens teamed up on this job, using the modern techniques of genetics. They soon found that they could divide the cottons of the world into three groups: the wild and domestic cottons of the Old World, the wild cottons of the New World, and the domestic cottons of the New World. The New World domestic cottons particularly interested them. When they studied cells under high-powered microscopes they found that they contained twice as many hereditary units (chromosomes) as did the other cottons. Further, they could tell that there were two sets of chromosomes there, one the Old World type and the other the New World type. The most probable explanation they could find was that man had brought a domestic cotton from the Old World into the New, and that the two cottons had crossed, combined the full sets of chromosomes from both plants, and created this new plant.

They then did a very interesting thing. They examined the New World domestic cotton and carefully catalogued all its characteristics. Next they searched the cottons of the world to see just what two cottons, if combined, would give them these characteristics. They found the answer in an Asiatic domestic cotton and in a Peruvian wild cotton. They then succeeded in crossing these two plants and producing a near-duplicate of the American domesticated cotton.

We cannot get much nearer to proof than this. Thus the whole question of voyages to America was again wide open. Cotton seeds are not particularly tough. Plant men do not believe that they can float around the ocean and remain alive. To have got to America they must have been carried by someone. (Just how cotton got to America *and* the Old World in the first place is quite another problem of an utterly different time, and I will not try to deal with it here.)

It was at this point that I entered the controversy. Having been "properly" educated in the field of anthropology, I knew that once the American Indians entered America, they had been sealed off and had developed entirely on their own. They were of stupendous interest as the living examples of how inevitable the growth and development of cultures and civilization really were. They were the final answer to the Diffusionist. "Why just look, even the minute details are alike! Weaving, casting of metals, the shape of helmets, feathered robes for royalty. Name it and you can have it. There was almost nothing in the Old World that had not been independently reinvented in the New World. This certainly proves independent invention, doesn't it?"

Ah, yes. But *did* it prove it? Or did it prove just the opposite? Those mischievous geneticists were threatening to lift the lid of Pandora's box. If someone had brought cotton to the New World, how could we be sure that other things, such as zeros, Panpipes, metallurgy, and parchesi hadn't been brought in, also? Obviously this required looking into.

Since I had just finished a doctoral thesis in which I had used plants as tracers for determining the spread of peoples and ideas within America, it was quite natural for me to turn to the plant evidence to see just what there was to this controversy. To begin with, I knew the classical position. There were, in pre-Columbian times, no domestic plants from the Old World in the Americas, and conversely there were no American plants in the Old World. To be specific, the Indians had no wheat or rice, and the peoples of the Old World had no corn, American beans, or squash.

Work began with a review of the cotton situation. Stevens sent me a manuscript discussing the cultural implications of what he and his colleagues had done. It was a disturbing document for a man thoroughly indoctrinated with the idea of the separateness of the Old and New Worlds. I took it to a Johns Hopkins geneticist to have it read from a geneticist's point of view. (In retrospect I must secretly have been hoping that there was a gross error in the work. Otherwise there was an awful lot of reading and thinking ahead of me.) The reply was that the genetics was sound, the conclusions from the data reasonable, and the probability quite good that Hutchinson, Silow, and Stevens had drawn the right conclusion. This left me no alternative but to dive into the problem and see what more evidence there was. The results were shocking.

Cotton was not the only plant involved. The sweet potato had been investigated by a professor hostile to the idea of voyages to and from America. But he had shown that the sweet potato had been in the Pacific area before any possible European spread. Further, there was positive proof in the form of a letter written by one of Cortes's lieutenants that coconuts were in America when Cortes landed there. Still further, tests on the ability of coconuts to survive a long period of drifting in the ocean currents had raised considerable doubts that the coconut could get across the Pacific in that way. And when I applied my knowledge of ocean currents and wind directions, it seemed to me that these chances vanished. Further there were other plants. The bottle gourd was present in America in the earliest levels, and very ancient in the Old World. (I was later to prove by experiments in the Chesapeake Bay that these gourds *could* have floated to America.) But there were American weeds in the islands of the Pacific that certainly could not have blown or drifted there. There *were* American plants that had got out of America and there *were* Asiatic plants that had got into America. Someone *had* crossed the Pacific both ways. Pandora's box was open. The moat was crossed. The Independent Inventionists' vessel had sprung a leak.

This was not a leak that could be readily repaired by referring to the similarity of men's minds and claiming that the zero concept, wheels, pyramids, and games of chance are so natural to man that they prove nothing when they reappear in similar forms in distant parts of the world. Man does not invent plants. To quote O. F. Cook, "The same plant does not originate twice, and varieties dependent everywhere for their very existence on human care must also have been distributed by human agency." And again: "For the present purposes it suffices to remember that the actual introduction of plants by human agency discounts in advance all objections on the ground of distances and difficulties of communication, and justifies the fullest use of biological or other data in tracing the origin and dissemination of agricultural civilization in the tropics of both hemispheres." The plant evidence was an iceberg that in one rending crash ripped the bottom out of the isolation of pre-Columbian America.

The sequels to the plant story are of interest. The list of plants possibly carried is quite extensive, and almost nothing is now safe from question. It is suspected that Indian corn was known in Africa and in Southeast Asia before Columbus. (The reason that the Europeans first called Indian corn "Turkish wheat" is again being examined, and the old answers no longer satisfy.) Questions are being asked about the time of appearance of the American peanut in Asia, and of the Old World bananas in the Americas. The chicken from Southeast Asia is strongly suspected of being in America in pre-Columbian times, and no one claims that it could either fly or swim the Pacific.

The plant evidence is unshakable, and it is now admitted, at least in part, by its bitterest foes. They tend to retreat firing such Parthian shots as "unimportant in number," "probably a few unimportant accidental landings," "not important to the story of the growth and development of the American Indian civilizations." But I like the simile of Pandora's box. The lid has been lifted and all sorts of ideas have escaped to buzz about our heads.

Quite independently a further line of attack has been reopened. This is the investigation of art resemblances on the two sides of the Pacific. This work has been done by Professor Robert Heine-Geldern of Austria and Dr. Gordon Ekholm of the American Museum of Natural History in New York.

Comparison of the art and architecture of Southeast Asia with that of some parts of the Americas led to the discovery of some remarkable parallels. Not only were there truncated pyramids in Cambodia with temples on top of them, just as there were in Yucatán and in Peru, but they were sometimes almost identical down to small architectural details. The dragons on Chou-dynasty bronze vases were duplicated in minute detail in Mayan Indian art. And these details were multiplied. Criticism immediately centered on the fact that the similarities were picked more or less at random over a considerable range of time and space. This has since been met with a vengeance. Heine-Geldern's latest work names the individual Asiatic city states and points out their art influence in specific times and places in the Americas.

Such thoughts are met with some skepticism. If the people of Southeast Asia actually did such things, why do we have no records of all this? How could such a discovery ever be lost? My reply is to point out that the Norse discovered America about 1000 A.D. and maintained colonies in Greenland until about 1400 A.D. This is in the full light of modern European history. Yet most people are surprised to hear of this, and the effective discovery of America was left to Columbus. Further there is at least one Chinese document that probably refers to a Chinese voyage to America and return.

There are all sorts of strange bits of other evidence. The palm prints of the Maya are specifically like those of the Chinese. The Polynesian legends tell of reaching America, and the American Indian told the Spaniards that people from the Pacific came to them for trading purposes. Then there are the plants, the mathematics, the games, the arts and architecture, and all the other clues.

In capsule form, what we have learned, or are in the process of learning, is this: all the Old World civilizations were interconnected and drew on each other for ideas and inspiration. We do not know just where and how this civilization began. It seems to have started in that area we call the Near East. It is not too difficult to make a case for the single origin of civilization there. The New World civilizations seem to be to some as-yet-unknown degree dependent on the Old World growth of civilization.

Peering into the future, guessing at things to come, I would estimate that the American Indians had made some very modest advances toward agriculture and the beginnings of settled village life. The peoples of the Old World, sometime after 3000 B.C. and before 500 B.C., discovered the New World. They maintained contact over a long period of time. During this time they colonized parts of America, introduced arts, crafts, science, and governmental forms, and carried some domestic plants back and forth. It was this impact that set off the civilizations of Middle America.

We cannot say that civilization would never have been achieved by the

American Indians had they been left alone. Neither do we know that they ever would have. The natives of Australia, Africa, America north of Mexico, and south and east of Peru and Bolivia certainly never did.

The interesting by-product of all this is that we are faced with the possibility that civilization has but one beginning. One could seriously argue for this view. We do not know that any particular people or any particular geography gave rise to it. Nor would we know how to start the process over again should the present civilization be extinguished. It appears to me from such studies as these that the civilization that we carry today is a unique growth.

If this is true, then man is certainly to be viewed as basically noninventive. He proves, rather, to be a splendid copyist, infinitely more able to borrow an idea than to invent a new one. To answer one of our earlier questions: man is retentive and not particularly inventive. Civilization, once the germ is implanted, can flourish in desert or jungle, on mountain plateau or lowland plain. It is not the physical environment that is all-important; it is the cultural environment.

These are important things to know, and it is the pursuit of this type of knowledge that underlies the professional passion for study of such seemingly exotic things as the long-dead civilizations of the American Indians.

On the Inscrutability of History

Arthur Schlesinger, Jr.

> Arthur Schlesinger, Jr. (b. 1917) became a professor at Harvard in 1954. His *Age of Johnson* (1945) won the Pulitzer prize for history in 1946. He has written *The Age of Roosevelt,* with volumes on *The Crisis of the Old Order* (1957), *The Coming of the New Deal* (1958), and *The Politics of Upheaval* (1960). In 1961 he became a special consultant to President John F. Kennedy. His *A Thousand Days: John F. Kennedy in the White House* was published in 1965.

My subject is the way statesmen use history—or are used by it. As one who is by profession an historian and has been by occasion a government official, I have long been fascinated and perplexed by the interaction between history and public decision: fascinated because, by this process, past history becomes an active partner in the making of new history; perplexed because the role of history in this partnership remains both elusive and tricky.

It is elusive because, if one excludes charismatic politics—the politics of the prophet and the medicine man—one is bound to conclude that all thought which leads to decisions of public policy is in essence historical. Public decision in rational politics necessarily implies a guess about the future derived from the experience of the past. It implies an expectation, or at the very least a hope, that certain actions will produce tomorrow the same sort of results they produced yesterday. This guess about the future may be based on a comprehensive theory of historical change, as with the Marxists; or it may be based on specific analogies drawn from the past; or it may be based on an unstated and intuitive sense of the way things happen. But, whatever it is based on, it involves, explicitly or implicitly, an historical judgment.

And the problem is tricky because, when explicit historical judgments intervene, one immediately encounters a question which is, in the abstract, insoluble: is the history invoked really the source of policies, or is it the source of arguments designed to vindicate policies adopted for antecedent reasons? Moreover, even when history is in some sense the source of policies, the lessons of history are generally so ambiguous that the antecedent reasons often determine the choice between alternative historical interpretations. Thus, in France between the wars Reynaud and Mandel drew one set of conclusions from the First World War, Bonnet and Laval another. Yet one cannot, on the other hand, reduce the function of history in public policy to that of mere rationalisation, for historical models acquire a life of their own. Once a statesman begins to identify the present with the past, he may in time be carried further than he intends by the bewitchments of analogy.

However hard it may be to define with precision the role of history in public policy, it is evident that this role must stand or fall on the success of history as a means of prediction. This is a point, it should immediately be said, on which professional historians, on the whole, have few illusions among themselves. They privately regard history as its own reward; they study it for the intellectual and aesthetic fulfilment they find in the disciplined attempt to reconstruct the past and, perhaps, for the ironic aftertaste in the contemplation of man's heroism and folly, but for no more utilitarian reason. They understand better than outsiders that historical training confers no automatic wisdom in the realm of public affairs. Guizot, Bancroft, Macaulay, Thiers, Morley, Bryce, Theodore Roosevelt, Woodrow Wilson: one cannot say that their training as historians deeply influenced their practice as politicians; and the greatest of them—Roosevelt and Wilson—were harmed as politicians by exactly the moralism from which the study of history might have saved them. But then neither was a particularly good historian.[1]

---

[1] Churchill is a different matter; but he was a politician who turned to history, not an historian who turned to politics. So too was Kennedy.

Yet historians, in spite of their candour within the fellowship, sometimes invoke arguments of a statelier sort in justifying themselves to society: particularly the argument that one should study history because knowledge of yesterday can provide guidance for tomorrow. Thus Raleigh:

> We may gather out of History a policy no less wise than eternal; by the comparison and application of other men's fore-passed miseries with our own errours and ill-deservings.

Or Burke:

> In history, a great volume is unrolled for our instruction, drawing the materials of future wisdom from the past errors and infirmities of mankind.

In what sense is this true? Why should history help us foresee the future? Because presumably history repeats itself enough to make possible a range of historical generalisation; and because generalisation, sufficiently multiplied and interlaced, can generate insight into the shape of things to come.

Many professional historians—perhaps most—reject the idea that generalisation is the goal of history. We all respond, in Marc Bloch's phrase, to "the thrill of learning singular things." Indeed, it is the commitment to concrete reconstruction as against abstract generalisation—to life as against laws—which distinguishes history from sociology. Yet, on the other hand, as Crane Brinton once put it, "the doctrine of the absolute uniqueness of events in history seems nonsense." Even historians who are skeptical of attempts to discern a final and systematic order in history acknowledge the existence of a variety of uniformities and recurrences. There can be no question that generalisations about the past, defective as they may be, are possible—and that they can strengthen the capacity of statesmen to deal with the future.

So historians have long since identified a life-cycle of revolution which, if properly apprehended, might have spared us misconceptions about the Russian Revolution—first, about its goodwill and, later, when we abandoned belief in its goodwill, about the fixity and permanence of its fanatical purpose—and which, if consulted today, might save us from the notion that the Chinese Revolution will be forever cast in its present mould. Historical generalisations in a number of areas—the processes of economic development, for example, or the impact of industrialisation and urbanisation or the effect of population growth, or the influence of climate or sea power or the frontier, or the circulation of political élites or entrepreneurial innovation—will enlarge the wisdom of the statesman, giving his responses to the crises of the moment perspective, depth, and an instinct for the direction and flow of events. Sometimes this wisdom may even lead to what Bloch called "the paradox of prevision"—to the point when men, sufficiently warned by historical extrapolation of horrid eventualities, may take action to avert them, which means that prevision may be destroyed by prevision.

The result is historical insight: that is, a sense of what is possible and probable in human affairs, derived from a feeling for the continuities and discontinuities of existence. This sense is comparable not to the mathematical equations of the physicist but to the diagnostic judgments of the doctor. It is this form of historical insight which has led in recent years to Bertrand de Jouvenel's *L'Art de la Conjecture* and to the stimulating intellectual exercise involved in the search for *futuribles*. But *futuribles* are speculative constructions of possible long-range futures, useful perhaps to those who may be Presidents and Prime Ministers in 2000, hardly to their predecessors in 1970.

Still every day around the planet great decisions are being made (or at least rationalised) in terms of short-run historical estimates. The whole Marxist world, of course, is sworn to a determinist view of the future, according to which fixed causes produce fixed effects and mankind is moving along a predestined path through predestined stages to a single predestined conclusion. For the Marxists, history has become a "positive model": it prescribes not only for the long but for the short run, not only strategy but tactics—the immediate policies to be favoured, courses pursued, action taken. It is a tribute to the devotion of Marxists, if hardly to their intelligence, that they have remained so indefatigably loyal to their metaphysic in spite of the demonstrated limits of Marxism as a system of prediction.

For, if any thesis was central to the Marxist vision of history, it was that the process of modernisation, of industrialisation, of social and economic development, would infallibly carry every nation from feudalism through capitalism to communism: that the communist society was the inevitable culmination of the development process. Thus Marx contended that, the more developed a country was, the more prepared it was for communism, and that communism in consequence must come first to the most industrialised nations. In fact, communism has come only to nations in a relatively early stage of development, like Russia and China, and it has come to such nations precisely as a means to modernisation, not as a consequence of it. Instead of being the climax of the development process, the end of the journey, communism is now revealed as a technique of social discipline which a few countries in early stages of development have adopted in the hope of speeding the pace of modernisation. Instead of the ultimate destination towards which all societies are ineluctably moving, communism now appears an epiphenomenon of the transition from stagnation to development. Modernisation, as it proceeds, evidently carries nations not towards Marx but away from Marx—and this would appear true even of the Soviet Union itself.

History thus far has refuted the central proposition in Marx's system of prediction. It has also refuted important corollary theses—notably the idea that the free economic order could not possibly last. Far from obeying dogma and perishing of its own inner contradictions, free society in the developed world has rarely displayed more creativity and vitality. It is casting as powerful a spell on the intellectuals and the youth of the communist world as the communist world cast on us during the Depression thirty years ago.

Why did Marx go wrong here? His forecast of the inevitable disintegration of free society was plausibly based on the *laissez-faire* capitalism of the mid-19th century. This devil-take-the-hindmost economic order did very likely contain the seeds of its own destruction—especially in those tendencies, pronounced irreversible by Marx, towards an ever-widening gap between rich and poor (alleged to guarantee the ultimate impoverishment of the masses) and towards an ever-increasing frequency and severity of structural economic crisis (alleged to guarantee the progressive instability of the system). This may indeed be a salient example of the "paradox of prevision"; for the Marxist forecast unquestionably stimulated progressive democrats to begin the reform of classical capitalism through the invention of the affirmative state. "The more we condemn unadulterated Marxian Socialism," Theodore Roosevelt used to say, "the stouter should be our insistence on thoroughgoing social reforms. . . ." The combination of the affirmative state with the extraordinary success of the free economic order as an engine of production—a success which, contrary to *laissez-faire* dogma, government intervention increased rather than hampered—eventually thwarted the Marxist prophecy.

In the end, the Marxists were undone by Marxism. Ideology told them that those who owned the economy *must* own the state, and the state could therefore never act against their desires or interests. Yet fifteen years before the *Communist Manifesto* an American President, Andrew Jackson, had already suggested that the state in a democratic society, far from being the instrument of the possessors, could well become the means by which those whom Jackson called the "humble members of society" might begin to redress the balance of social power against those whom Hamilton had called the "rich and well-born." Thus, in the 20th-century developed world, the economic machine drowned the revolution in consumers' goods, while the affirmative state, with its policies of piece-meal intervention in the economy, brought about both a relative redistribution of wealth (defeating Marx's prediction of the immiseration of the poor) and a relative stabilisation of the economy (defeating Marx's prediction of ever-deepening cyclical crisis). The last place to look for a Marxist victory is precisely the place where Marx said it would come first—*i.e.,* in the most developed countries.

So the Marxist prophecy of a single obligatory destiny for mankind has missed in both its parts: in its prediction of the irresistible breakdown of the free economy, and in its prediction of the irresistible triumph of communism as the fulfilment of the development process. In spite of many subsidiary insights and successes, Marxism must surely stand in our time as the spectacular flop of history as prophecy. The failure, indeed, has been so complete that contemporary Marxists revile each other in seeking the true meaning of the most elementary doctrines; the more fanatical stand Marx on his head, rejecting his basic theory and arguing that communism will come "out of the countryside," not the city.

Yet the democratic world is hardly in a position to take too much satisfaction from the intellectual collapse of Marxism. It is true that our philosophical heritage—empirical, pragmatic, ironic, pluralistic, competitive—has happily inoculated us against rigid, all-encompassing, absolute systems of historical interpretation. But, though we may reject the view of history as metaphysically set and settled, we seem at times to embrace our own forms of historical fatalism—even if we invoke history less as theology than as analogy. This is only a marginal advantage. The argument by metaphor can generate a certitude almost as mischievous as the argument by determinism.

For democratic policy-makers, history generally appears as a "negative" rather than a "positive" model. It instructs us, not like Marxism, in the things we must do, but in the things we must *not* do—unless we wish to repeat the mistakes of our ancestors. The traumatic experience of World War I thus dominated the diplomacy of World War II, at least as far as the United States was concerned. So the American insistence on the doctrine of "unconditional surrender" in 1943 sprang from the belief that the failure to get unconditional surrender in 1918 had made possible the stab-in-the-back myth and guaranteed the revival of German nationalism. The American obsession with the United Nations came from the conviction that the failure to join the League of Nations had opened the way to the second World War. The American readiness to make concessions to the Soviet Union (as Professor E. R. May has suggested) was based, in part, on an analogy with Clemenceau's France. The American President viewed the Soviet Union as a nation which, having lived in permanent insecurity, could be expected, like France twenty-five years earlier, to value security above almost anything else.

> Roosevelt [Professor May has perceptively written] was determined to see Stalin's point of view as Wilson had not seen Clemenceau's. He was determined that, in so far as possible, the Soviet Union should have the guarantees it wanted and should not be forced into the sullen self-preoccupation of the France of Poincaré.

The second World War, then, provided a new traumatic experience. In the years since, the consciousness of policy-makers has been haunted by the Munich and Yalta analogies—the generalisation, drawn from attempts to accommodate Hitler in 1938, and Stalin in 1945, that appeasement always assures new aggression. Of these analogies, Munich, as the more lucid in its pattern and the more emphatic in its consequence, has been the more powerful; Yalta, indeed, figures rather as a complicated special case. I trust that a graduate student some day will write a doctoral essay on the influence of the Munich analogy on the subsequent history of the 20th century. Perhaps in the end he will conclude that the multitude of errors committed in the name of "Munich" may exceed the original error of 1938.

Certainly Munich was a tragic mistake, and its lesson was that the appeasement of a highly wound-up and heavily-armed totalitarian state in the context of a relatively firm and articulated continental equilibrium of power was likely to upset the balance and make further aggression inevitable. But to conclude from this that all attempts to avert war by negotiation must always be "Munichs" goes beyond the evidence. No one understood this better than the greatest contemporary critic of Munich. An historian himself, Winston Churchill well understood the limits of historical analogy. So he defined the issue in his chapter on Munich in *The Gathering Storm:*

> It may be well here to set down some principles of morals and action which may be a guide in the future. No case of this kind can be judged apart from its circumstances.
>
> Those who are prone by temperament and character to seek sharp and clear-cut solutions of difficult and obscure problems, who are ready to fight whenever some challenge comes from a foreign power, have not always been right. On the other hand, those whose inclination is to bow their heads, to seek patiently and faithfully for peaceful compromise, are not always wrong. On the contrary, in the majority of instances, they may be right, not only morally but from a practical standpoint. . . .
>
> How many wars have been precipitated by fire-brands! How many misunderstandings which led to war could have been removed by temporising! How often have countries fought cruel wars and then after a few years of peace found themselves not only friends but allies!

Sixteen years after Munich President Eisenhower wrote Churchill, "If . . . Indochina passes into the hands of the Communists, the ultimate effect on our and your global strategy and position . . . could be disastrous. . . . We failed to halt Hirohito, Mussolini and Hitler by not acting in unity and in time. That marked the beginning of many years of stark tragedy and desperate peril. May it not be that our nations have learned something from that lesson?" Eisenhower was invoking the Munich analogy to persuade the British to join the Americans in backing the French in Indochina. Churchill remained unmoved by Eisenhower's argument. He saw no useful parallel between Hitler, the man on the bicycle who could not stop, a madman commanding vast military force and requiring immediate and visible success, and the ragged bands and limited goals of Ho Chi-Minh. Nor could he see any useful parallel between Europe—a developed continent with well-defined national frontiers, interests, and identities and a highly-organised equilibrium of power—and South-East Asia, an underdeveloped sub-continent filled with fictitious states in vague, chaotic, and unpredictable revolutionary ferment. Churchill rejected Eisenhower's analogy—which did not, of course, prevent Churchill's successor as Prime Minister two years later from seeing Nasser and the Middle East in terms of 1938 and committing his nation to the Suez adventure. This time it was Eisenhower who rejected the Munich analogy.

Today the same analogy pursues us again, echoing in the corridors of Washington, with China now cast in the role of Nazi Germany.

"In the 'forties and 'fifties," President Johnson has said, "we took our stand in Europe to protect the freedom of those threatened by aggression. Now the centre of attention has shifted to another part of the world where aggression is on the march. Our stand must be as firm as ever." The instrument of this aggression, we are told, is the communist-instigated war of national liberation. If this technique is permitted to succeed in Viet Nam, it will be tried elsewhere. If it is defeated in Viet Nam, the Chinese will know that we will not let it succeed in other countries and they will have to reconsider their policies.

"If aggression succeeds," Secretary of State Rusk recently said (as quoted by Stewart Alsop),

> it invites larger and more dangerous aggression, possibly leading step by step to world war. That's a lesson we learned, or ought to have learned, thirty years ago. I'm not the village idiot. I know Hitler was an Austrian and Mao is a Chinese. I know all the other differences between this situation and the situation in the 'thirties. But what is common between the two situations is the phenomenon of aggression.

The Secretary of State had even the imagination to compare an exhortation made last year by the Chinese Defence Minister, Marshal Lin Piao, with Hitler's *Mein Kampf.*

This is not the place to comment on the Viet Nam riddle—except to suggest that it is not to be solved by bad historical analogies. It may seem a little forced, for example, to equate a civil war in what was up to a dozen years ago the single country of Viet Nam with Hitler's invasion of Austria and Czechoslovakia across well-established national frontiers. And if Mao rather than Ho has now become the equivalent of Hitler, the U.S. State Department has yet to produce evidence that the Viet Cong of South Viet Nam are only the spearhead of a premeditated and co-ordinated conspiracy of Chinese aggression. Nor do the Chinese themselves have the overwhelming military power nor, evidently, the pent-up mania for immediate expansion which would substantiate the Hitler parallel. As for the Lin Piao document, a reasonably careful reading shows that, far from being Mao's *Mein Kampf,* a Chinese master-plan for revolution around the earth, it is a prudent signal to guerrilla movements in other lands, including Viet Nam, that they are on their own and cannot expect direct Chinese support.

The fact that the Munich analogy is invalid does not necessarily invalidate the Viet Nam policy. There is much to be said for the proposition that a negotiated settlement in Viet Nam will be impossible so long as the other side thinks it can win; and this offers a strong argument for a holding action in South Viet Nam, though hardly for widening the war in the north. The point here, however, is not to assess American Viet Nam policy but to illustrate the depressing persistence of the mentality which makes policy through stereotype—through historical generalisation wrenched illegitimately out of the past and imposed mechanically on the future. Santayana's aphorism must be reversed: too often it is those who *can* remember the past who are condemned to repeat it.

"No case of this kind," Churchill said, "can be judged apart from its circumstances."

I well remember President Kennedy expressing to me after the Cuban missile crisis in 1962 his fear that people would conclude from his victory that all we would have to do thereafter in dealing with the communists was to be tough and they would collapse. The missile crisis, he pointed out, had three distinctive features: it took place in an area where we enjoyed local conventional superiority, where Soviet national security was not directly engaged, and where the Russians lacked a case which they could convincingly sustain before the world. Things would be different, he said, if the situation were one where the communists had the local superiority, where their national security was directly engaged, and where they could persuade themselves and others they were in the right.

Kennedy, who, like Churchill, had the mind of a first-class historian, was without illusion about the infallibility of historical analogy. The point is not terribly complicated, even for village idiots. Burke long ago warned against the practice of viewing an object "as it stands stripped of every relation, in all the nakedness and solitude of metaphysical abstraction. Circumstances (which with some gentlemen pass for nothing) give in reality to every political principle its distinguishing colour and discriminating effect." Even Toynbee, the magician of historical analogy, has remarked that historians are

> never in a position to guarantee that the entities which we are bringing into comparison are properly comparable for the purpose of our investigation. . . . However far we may succeed in going in our search for sets of identical examples on either side, we shall never be able to prove that there is not some non-identical factor that we have overlooked, and this non-identical factor is not the decisive factor that accounts for the different cases of what has looked to us like an identical situation but may not have been this in truth.

Or, as Mark Twain put it, somewhat more vividly, in *Following the Equator:* "We should be careful to get out of an experience only the wisdom that is in it—and stop there; lest we be like the cat that sits down on a hot stove lid. She will never sit down on a hot stove lid again—and that is well; but also she will never sit down on a cold one. . . ."

One cannot doubt that the study of history makes people wiser. But it is indispensable to understand the limits of historical analogy. Most useful historical generalisations are statements about massive social and intellectual movements over a considerable period of time. They make large-scale, long-term prediction possible. But they do not justify small-scale, short-term prediction. For short-run prediction is the prediction of detail and, given the complex structure of social events, the difficulty of anticipating the intersection or collision of different events and the irreducible mystery, if not invincible freedom, of individual decision, there are simply too many variables to warrant exact forecasts of the immediate future. History, in short, can answer questions, after a fashion, at long range. It cannot answer questions with confidence or certainty at short range. Alas, policy makers are rarely interested in the long run—"in the long run," as Keynes used to say, "we are all dead"—and the questions they put to history are thus most often the questions which history is least qualified to answer.

Far from offering a short-cut to clairvoyance, history teaches us that the future is full of surprises and outwits all our certitudes. For the study of history issues not in scientific precision nor in moral finality but in irony. If twenty-five years ago, anyone had predicted that before the end of the decade of the 'forties Germany and Japan would be well on the way to becoming close friends and allies of Britain and the United States, he would have been considered mad. If fifteen years ago, as the Russians and Chinese were signing their thirty-year pact of amity and alliance, anyone predicted that by the end of the 'fifties they would be at each other's throats, he too would have been considered mad. The chastening fact is that many of the pivotal events of our age were unforeseen: from the Nazi-Soviet pact and the Tito-Stalin quarrel of years ago to such events in today's newspapers as the anti-communist upsurge in Indonesia and the overthrow of Nkrumah in Ghana (and his resurrection in Guinea).

Occasionally one reads in the U.S. press that leading political figures in Washington are shaping their actions today by calculations with regard to the Democratic presidential nomination in 1972. I am sure that the men mentioned in such stories are themselves under no delusion about the hopelessness of such an undertaking. 1972 is today as far away from us as 1960, and no one reflecting on the unpredictability of the last six years in the United States could sensibly suppose that the next six are going to be any more predictable. I have often thought that a futurist trying to forecast the next three American Presidents in early 1940 would hardly have named as the first President after Franklin D. Roosevelt an obscure back-bench senator from Missouri, anticipating defeat by the governor of his state in the Democratic primaries; as the second, an unknown lieutenant-colonel in the United States Army; and, as the third, a kid still at college. Yet that sequence began to unfold in less time than between now and 1972.

The salient fact about the historical process, so far as the short run is concerned, is its inscrutability. One must bear this in mind, I believe, when asked to accept drastic decisions now on the basis of someone's speculation as to what the behaviour of Communist China will be a dozen years from now. In its coarsest form, this is the argument that "we must have a show-down with China before it gets the bomb." Here is the old preventive-war thesis we used to hear so often in the late 'forties: yet I do not think anyone can rationally contend that the world would be better off today had we dropped the bomb on Russia twenty years ago. Having been wrong so often in the past, how can we be sure we have achieved such infallibility now that we would risk the future of mankind on a guess?

Who can possibly predict the course the Chinese Revolution will take in the years ahead? The study of revolution has shown us that the emotional and doctrinal pitch of revolutions waxes and wanes; that, while revolutions at first may devour their children, in the end the children sometimes devour the revolutions; that even totalitarian revolutions fail at total mass indoc-trination; that a successful revolution begins to develop a stake in the *status quo;* that post-revolutionary generations have their own identities and aspirations; that the possession of a major nuclear arsenal has thus far had a sobering effect on the possessor; that nations follow their historic inter-ests rather more faithfully than they do their ideologies; and that there is no greater error than to try and deduce the policy of future from the rhetoric of the present. Nor does the example of Hitler and *Mein Kampf* change this. Hitler was indeed the man on the bicycle; he had to keep moving. The Nazi revolution never got beyond the first messianic phase; its nature condemned it to *Götterdämmerung.* We must not forget that the Chinese revolutionary régime has already lasted five years longer than the whole life of the Third Reich. And we have seen in the case of the Soviet Union the permutation and erosion time and national interest have worked on what were once thought to be final motives and permanent objectives. With an equation so overflowing with variables, how can anyone forecast now the behaviour of China twenty years from now?

History, in short, does not furnish the statesman with a detailed scenario of particular relationships or policies. Too often it equips his decisions with good rather than real reasons, holding out a mirror in which he fatuously sees his own face. This is not an argument against the knowledge of history: it is an argument against the superficial knowledge of history. The single analogy is never enough to penetrate a process so cunningly compounded not only of necessity but of contingency, fortuity, ignorance, stupidity and chance. The statesman who is surest that he can divine the future most urgently invites his own retribution. "The hardest strokes of heaven," Her-bert Butterfield has written, "fall in history upon those who imagine that they can control things in a sovereign manner, playing providence not only for themselves but for the far future—reaching out into the future with the wrong kind of farsightedness, and gambling on a lot of risky calculations in which there must never be a single mistake."

What then has history to offer the statesman? Let me suggest first that the way to protect the policy maker from the misuse of history is not to deprive him of historical knowledge altogether. This is the practice customarily adopted in totalitarian states, and the results invariably show the melancholy consequence when politicians believe their own propaganda. Can one infer from this that it is short-sighted for democratic governments, as, for example, in Great Britain, to withhold from its Parliament and people cautionary tales of governmental folly? Happily, we have had in the United States the full benefit of the Bay of Pigs—an event which took place five years after the British adventure in Suez but which has been discharged a good deal earlier from the cosy bondage of official secrecy. Does the British government really regard the protection of the reputation of politicians as the primary function of history? Naturally such a theory has a strong bi-partisan appeal, but it is surely injurious not only to history but to democracy itself. The acquiescence of the British people in the denial to themselves of facts indispensable to the judgment of their masters is one of the masochistic curiosities of our age.

The only antidote to a shallow knowledge of history is a deeper knowledge—the knowledge which produces not dogmatic certitude but diagnostic skill, not clairvoyance but insight. It offers the statesman a sense, at once, of short-run variables and long-run tendencies, and an instinct for the complexity of their intermingling, including the understanding that (as Rousseau once put it), "the ability to foresee that some things cannot be foreseen is a very necessary quality." Indeed, half the wisdom of statecraft, to borrow a phrase from Richard Goodwin, is "to leave as many options open as possible and decide as little as possible.... Since almost all important policy judgments are speculative, you must avoid risking too much on the conviction you are right."

Of course keeping too many options open too long may paralyse the lobe of decision and lose the game. There *does* come a time when accommodation turns into appeasement. This is the other half of the wisdom of statecraft: to accept the chronic lubricity and obscurity of events without yielding, in Lincoln's words, firmness in the right as God gives us to see the right. In deciding when to decide the criterion must be the human consequences—the results for people, not for doctrine.

Randolph Churchill's forthcoming life of his father reproduces an extraordinary letter written seventy years ago by the young Winston Churchill to a New York politician of the time, Bourke Cockran.

> The duty of government [Churchill said] is to be first of all practical. I am for makeshifts and expediency. I would like to make the people who live on

this world at the same time as I do better fed and happier generally. If incidentally I benefit posterity—so much the better—but I would not sacrifice my own generation to a principle however high or a truth however great.

Such an approach may seem too modest, even, perhaps, too cynical, for those theological statesmen whose self-righteousness has almost sunk our age. Most of these confident moralists have been high priests of one or another totalitarian faith (though some, alas, have been American Secretaries of State); but all have been prepared in the best conscience and in the name of history to sacrifice their generations on the altars of their own metaphors. It can only be said that, whether they see history as ideology or as analogy, they see it wrong. Far from unveiling the secret of things to come, history bestows a different gift: it makes us—or should make us—understand the extreme difficulty, the intellectual peril, the moral arrogance of supposing that the future will yield itself so easily to us.

"I returned," *Ecclesiastes* reminds us, "and saw under the sun that the race is not to the swift, nor the battle to the strong, neither yet bread to the wise nor riches to men of understanding, but time and chance happeneth to them all." The Old Testament carries the case against historical generalisation to the extreme. But, without going so far, we can agree that history should lead statesmen to a profound and humbling sense of human frailty— to a recognition of the fact, so insistently demonstrated by experience and so tragically destructive of our most cherished certitudes, that the possibilities of history are far richer and more various than the human intellect is likely to conceive. This, and the final perception that while the tragedy of history implicates us all in the common plight of humanity, we are never relieved, despite the limits of our knowledge and the darkness of our understanding, from the necessity of meeting our obligations.

7 / BIOGRAPHY

Alf

Laurie Lee

> Laurie Lee (b. 1914) is a well-known English poet. For a number of years he worked in films. As a young man he tramped the roads of Great Britain during the Great Slump. In his portrait of Alf, he is drawing on the experience of those years. In 1969 he published *As I Walked Out One Midsummer Morning*.

. . . I was not the only one on the road; I soon noticed there were many others, all trudging northward in a sombre procession. Some, of course, were professional tramps, but the majority belonged to that host of unemployed who wandered aimlessly about England at that time.

One could pick out the professionals; they brewed tea by the roadside, took it easy, and studied their feet. But the others, the majority, went on their way like somnambulists, walking along and seldom speaking to each other. There seemed to be more of them inland than on the coast—maybe the police had seen to that. They were like a broken army walking away from a war, cheeks sunken, eyes dead with fatigue. Some carried bags of tools, or shabby cardboard suitcases; some wore the ghosts of city suits; some, when they stopped to rest, carefully removed their shoes and polished them vaguely with handfuls of grass. Among them were carpenters, clerks, engineers from the Midlands; many had been on the road for months, walking up and down the country on the jobless treadmill of the middle nineteen-thirties.

Then, for a couple of days, I got a companion. I was picked up by the veteran Alf. I'd turned off the road to set up camp for the night when he came filtering through the bushes.

I'd seen him before; he was about five feet high and was clearly one of the brotherhood. He wore a deerstalker hat, so sodden and shredded it looked like a helping of breakfast food, and round the waist of his mackintosh, which was belted with string, hung a collection of pots and spoons.

Rattling like a dustbin, he sat down beside me and began pulling off his boots.

"Well," he said, "you're a poor little bleeder, 'ent you?"

Rummaging through the hardware round his waist, he produced a battered can, the kind of thing my uncles brought home from the war—square, with a triangular handle. It was a miniature cauldron, smoke-blackened outside and dark, tannin-stained within.

"'Ere, take it," he said. "You make me miserable." He started to build a fire. "I'm goin' to boil you a bit of tea and taters." And that is what he did.

We stayed together as far as Guildford, and I shared more of his pungent brews—screws of tea, sugar, scraps of meat and cake, which he'd then boil up in one awful mess. He was a tramp to his bones, always wrapping and unwrapping himself, and picking over his bits and pieces. He wasn't looking for work; this was simply his life, and he carefully rationed his energies—never passing a patch of grass that looked good for a shakedown, nor a cottage that seemed ripe for charity. He said his name was Alf, but one couldn't be sure, as he called me Alf, and everyone else.

Alf talked all day, but was garrulously secretive, and never revealed his origins. As for his own technique of roadwork, he wasn't slow out of laziness but because he moved to a deliberate timetable, making his professional grand tour in a twelvemonth's rhythm, which seemed to him fast enough. During the winter he'd hole up in a London doss house, then restart his leisurely cycle of England, turning up every year in each particular district with the regularity of the seasons. Thus he was the spring tramp of the Midlands, the summer bird of the South, the first touch of autumn to the Kentish Weald—indeed, I think he firmly believed that his constancy of motion spread a kind of reassurance among the housewives, so that he was looked for and welcomed as one of the recurring phenomena of nature, and was suitably rewarded therefore.

At Guildford, we parted, Alf turning east for the Weald, which for him still lay three months away.

"So long, Alf," I said.

"So long, Alf," he answered. "Try not to be too much of a nuisance."

Pierre Auguste Renoir

René Gimpel

René Gimpel (1881–1944) became one of the great art dealers of the twentieth century. His *Diary of an Art Dealer* (first published in France in 1963) was issued in English translation in this country in 1966. It is a fascinating record of Gimpel's association with other art dealers such as Lord Duveen, who was his brother-in-law, and American millionaire collectors like Rockefeller, Frick, and Huntington. Most valuable of all for the history of art are some of his intimate pictures of great French painters such as Monet, Degas, and Bracques. The portrait of Renoir printed below is a short section of the *Diary*. Gimpel was seized by the Germans when they occupied Paris in 1940 and taken to a German labor camp, where he died four years later.

AT RENOIR'S, AT CAGNES

"Can M. Renoir receive us?"

"He didn't sleep last night," answered the servant. "I'll go and see. Shall I take your card?"

Renoir didn't know me; I was counting on the description the servant would give him of the carriage and pair, the hacks from Grasse. When she returned she said: "If you would be so kind as to bring madame into the dining room, we shall get monsieur down." Get monsieur down? Whatever did she mean?

The garden resembles a poverty-stricken farmyard, and the doors and windows have the shoddy lozenges of those pseudo-Louis XVI villas thrown up in haste and by the dozen on beaches created overnight by speculators, the Dufayel type. The view of the sea and countryside is beautiful.

Renoir lost his wife three years ago; the house shows the effect of it: last night's crumbs hadn't been swept up.

On a table in a corner, near a window, there were some brushes, a box of water colors, and small ceramic squares decorated with flowers and with childlike designs of boats and pastoral trees; also some plates with his eternal nude woman, her knees crossed. I recognized the master's style and colors. Was Renoir doing ceramics?

Through the partly open door I caught sight of him: they were bringing him down, two women carrying him in a kind of litter. Georges Bernheim, the dealer in modern painting, said to me in Paris, "He's doddering." And that's how it seemed. I wondered what on earth I was doing there. Before me was a shell of a man. They lifted him out of the chair, holding him firmly by the shoulders to keep him from collapsing. But his bent-up knees didn't give. He was all unyielding angles, like the unhorsed knights in a set of tin soldiers. He rested on one foot, the other being huge, all swaddled. They sat him down again by tipping him backward.

Seated, he is a frightful spectacle, elbows clamped to his sides, forearms raised; he was shaking two sinister stumps dangling with threads and very narrow ribbons. His fingers are cut almost to the quick: the bones jut out, with barely some skin on them. Ah, no, he has his fingers—pressed in and spread against the palms of his hands, his pitiful fleshless hands like the claws of a chicken plucked and trussed ready for the spit.

But I still had not seen his head: it was sunk on a curved, humped back. He was wearing a large, tall English traveling cap. His face is pale and thin; his white beard, stiff as a gorse, hangs sideways as if wind-blown. How has it managed that crazy angle? As to his eyes—well, it's hard to say.

Could I really expect this amorphous being to answer me? What intelligence could still exist there? I had to say something. I ventured on something like: "As admirers of your work, my wife and I have come to pay homage to the great painter. We salute the master."

He motioned to us to be seated and then to the servant to give him a cigarette.

She put it in his mouth and lit it for him.

Then Renoir raised his voice and said: "I have all the vices, even that of painting."

I stopped holding my breath. This jest, uttered clearly and in an animated tone, reassured me. I laughed. He smiled. His eyes, so dim just a moment ago, suddenly brightened. I told him: "On that table in the corner I noticed some ceramics in which I recognized your hand."

"Yes, ceramics were my first calling, and I'm teaching the art to my grandson who is sixteen and lives with me. Everyone needs an occupation, and this one seems to suit him. It's very difficult. The same color applied by two different hands gives two different tones."

"I've been told that you tried to mix your colors to keep them from changing later on."

"Yes, but will I succeed? I remember seeing, sixty years ago, the great Troyon in the Louvre, *The Return of the Herd*, with the steam from the bullocks' nostrils brilliant with the sun. But when I saw the picture again, several years ago, the sun on the animals' snouts had gone. That's why we have to search endlessly."

My wife asked him if he was fond of landscapes.

"Very much, but it's too difficult. I am classified as a painter of figures, and quite rightly. My landscapes are nothing but accessories. Just now I'm striving to blend them with the people I paint. The old masters didn't attempt that."

"What about Giorgione?"

Renoir didn't answer. He disapproved. Then I mentioned Corot, and he said: "There you have the great genius of the century, the greatest landscape artist who ever lived. He was called a poet. What a misnomer! He was a naturalist. I have studied ceaselessly without ever being able to approach his art. I have often gone to the places where he painted: Venice, La Rochelle. I've never come anywhere near him. The towers of La Rochelle, ah, what trouble they've given me! It was his fault, Corot's, that I wanted to emulate him. The towers of La Rochelle—he got the color of the stones exactly, and I never could do it."

Throwing his cigarette into a bowl at his feet, he motioned again to his servant to give him another, and continued: "Landscapes are the painter's stumbling block. You think it's gray; but what colors there are in a gray landscape! If you only knew, monsieur, how hard it is to anatomize a tree with a brush."

"It's extraordinary," I said to him, "that at a time when nearly all the masters of 1830 were still alive, when that school was at its zenith of glory and admiration—its decline scarcely foreseeable—and when you admired their work so deeply—that you and your friends could create a rival school that is not only altogether different but is even a direct opposite."

"It was chance. There was a Swiss in Paris, Gleyre, who had a very cheap class in drawing, ten francs a month. I hadn't any money, which is what took me there. And there I met Monet, Sisley, Bazille. It was our mutual poverty that brought us together and thus made it possible for us, having formed a group, to bring into being the impressionist school. Each of us on his own wouldn't have had the strength or courage, or even the idea. The impressionist school had its origin too in our friendship and discussions. We had to struggle apace and stand by one another. In 1872 Berthe Morisot joined us, and to raise some money for ourselves, we all had a sale at the Hôtel Drouot which caused a riot. A man named Chocquet did us a lot of good. He was an old habitué of public sales, one of those people who like breathing in that dust, with its very special odors. He came into our gallery, spied a friend passing in the corridor, and called to him: 'Come and see the horrors being shown here.' The effect was altogether different from what Chocquet had expected. His friend admired our pictures. Chocquet was furious: 'They're obscenities.' He called in others. In no time, two rival factions sprang up, and came to blows. The police were called, passers by rushed in from the street, the Hôtel Drouot was invaded, absolute mayhem. The doors had to be shut until peace could be restored. But after that, we had our supporters."

Recalling these memories of youth and strife kindled Renoir's eyes till they sparkled. Doddering? Far from it! Georges Bernheim was exaggerating.

Had he never looked at Renoir's eyes? The chair-bound cripple with his quivering stumps: it all vanished when you saw those eyes. Those eyes, what animation and vivacity, what youth in them still!

I asked to see some paintings, and he instructed the servant to accompany us.

She took us along to a bedroom where two rows of canvases not on stretcher frames were fixed with drawing pins on the wall. Others were lying on the eiderdown on the bed. Sometimes, on the same canvas he had painted three or four subjects in all different directions; sometimes, pieces were missing, cut off at the corners. Pictures worth twenty, thirty, forty thousand francs left there like laundry hung out to dry. Many portraits. In the Midi sun, his last works lack the bricklike aspect, often so unpleasant, to which he has been partial for some years now; his heads also seem more distinguished. I was surprised. This was like a cluster of precious stones. Nonetheless these canvases aren't up to those of his youth. "But how can he paint?" we asked the woman.

"I place the brushes between his fingers and fasten them with the strings and ribbons you saw. Sometimes they fall and I put them back— but what's so astonishing about M. Renoir are those lynx eyes of his. Sometimes he calls me and tells me to remove a hair that's come off the brush and got stuck on the canvas. I look and see nothing till monsieur shows it to me: minuscule, hidden in a daub of paint."

"Does he paint much?"

"A great deal, ceaselessly. Many of his pictures he gives to charities, or to old friends or their children fallen on hard times."

The good woman has been in his service for sixteen years and she is disconsolate at not being able to talk about art, his sole pleasure, and so be anything more to him than a nurse. She took us into a little studio off in the garden and showed us the canvas on which the master was then working —a nude woman, with her back meticulously studied. The stretcher frame, instead of being held on the easel by a shelf, is hung and kept up by a counterweight, allowing Renoir to raise and lower his canvas easily by himself.

We rejoined the old man; I was rhapsodizing over the marvels I had seen, and I confessed my astonishment at the wealth of work in his studio. He informed me that he had sold more than three thousand paintings in his lifetime. I asked him if he would spare me one, and he replied: "No, not at the moment. I haven't enough to leave my children; in a year's time I'll see."

I didn't press the point but said: "It must be a great joy to you to realize how enormous the influence of your school has been in the world—your influence has been so strong that it's even overridden the faculty of different peoples to develop along national lines. Whether in America, Canada, Sweden, Norway, or even Germany, everywhere it's the French school they follow."

"Everywhere," he said, "and even in Germany, where everything has remained Gothic. They live as in the Middle Ages in their taverns; their architecture is still of that time. The Kaiser speaks like an old fossil: his sword and his God. By the way, have you seen the Degas exhibition?"

"Yes, at Durand-Ruel's." And I repeated to him what I had told Miss Cassatt.

"What a brute he was, that Degas! What a sharp tongue and what *esprit!* All his friends felt obliged to desert him in the end: I was one of the last to stand by him, but I couldn't hold out. What is incomprehensible is that Manet, who was so mild and gentle, was always controversial, while Degas, bitter, violent and intractable as he was, was from the start recognized by the Institute, the public, and the revolutionaries."

"He was feared," I suggested.

"Yes, that's it. For my part, I kept his friendship for a long time by teasing him. One day he said to me: 'Renoir, I have a terrible, an invincible enemy.' 'Who is it?' I asked. 'You old fool,' he replied, tapping his chest, 'you ought to know that enemy of mine—it's myself.'"

from Tolstoy

Henri Troyat

> Henri Troyat (b. 1911) is a member of the French Academy. His novel *L'Asaigne* won the Prix Goncourt in 1936. He has written biographies of the great Russian novelists: Pushkin, Dostoevski, and Tolstoy. From the last of these comes the vignette of Tolstoy's grandmother printed below.

Winter evenings also had their charm. The entire family shut itself up, shivering, into the main house, isolated by snow and silence. The tile stoves crackled. Time passed with delectable slowness. Numb with contentment, little Leo told himself that no house in the whole world was more beautiful than the one in which he had been born. Yet the amenities here were primitive; apart from a few mahogany stands and one or two winged armchairs, all the furniture had been hewn and put together by the muzhiks; the only note of luxury was the gilt of the frames around the mirrors and paintings. Even the children's shoes were made by the village cobbler.

Before going to bed they said good-night to the grownups and kissed their hands. If they had been good, they were allowed a few extra minutes in the drawing room. Grandmother, with a ruched bonnet on her head, laid out her eternal "traveler's solitaire" on a little table. Beside her on the divan sat the wife of a Tula gunsmith whom she had adopted for a friend and who wore cartridge belts over her jacket. The gunsmith's wife spun wool and, now and then, she would knock her spindle against the wall, in which she had finally gouged a hole. One aunt read aloud, the other knitted or did needlepoint; Papa, his pipe between his teeth, stared absently at the cards and, curled up on a chair, Milka, his whippet, blinked and yawned.

When the grownups gave the children the order to retire, the fun was not yet over for at least one of them: it was the custom in the family for them to take turns spending the night with their grandmother, Pelagya Nikolayevna. The instant he entered her room, Leo fell into a state of ecstasy. He watched her—corpulent and white, in her nightdress and white cap—as she washed her hands. To amuse him she made soap bubbles between her wrinkled yellow fingers. An old man sat in the window bay: Leo Stepanovich, whom Prince Volkonsky had bought long ago for his gifts as a storyteller. He was blind, which was why he was also allowed to be present during Her Highness' toilette. A bowl containing some scraps from the master's meal was brought to him there. When Pelagya Nikolayevna had completed her ablutions she climbed up into her bed, Leo jumped into his, and a maid put out the candles, leaving only a vigil light burning in the corner in front of the icons. In this eerie light the matriarch, leaning back against her pillows, her head upright under her white nightcap, looked down on the world as from a throne of snow. Her shadow wavered on the wall. The blind man began his tale in a drawling voice: "Once there was a powerful king who had an only son . . ."

Leo, fascinated by this hieratic grandmother, did not listen: was she asleep, or did she hear everything that was said? He could not tell. Sometimes the bard, draped in his cloak, deferentially asked, "Do you command me to proceed?" The reply snapped down, dictatorial, from the summit of the bed: "Yes; go on." And he resumed his tale, mixing Russian folklore with tales from Scheherazade. Lulled by the monotonous murmur, Leo's eyes closed, and he carried away into his dreams a mask of an ancient queen under a beribboned lace cap.

In the morning Grandmother made more soap bubbles between her fingers without losing a whit of her majesty. Sometimes she took the children to gather hazelnuts. She would climb into the famous yellow cabriolet and two servants—Petrushka and Matyusha—would harness themselves to the shafts and pull her along the paths. In the woods they reverently bent down the branches for their mistress, who chose the ripest nuts and stuffed them in a bag. Her grandsons raced around her, scavenging and squabbling. "I remember Grandmother," Tolstoy later wrote, "the hazel grove, the pungent smell of its leaves, the servants, the yellow cabriolet, the sun, and they all melt together into a single impression of radiance." In reality, Pelagya Nikolayevna was a narrow-minded woman, capricious and despotic, hard on those who served her but indulgent to the point of spinelessness with her son and grandchildren.

Making It: The Brutal Bargain

Norman Podhoretz

> Normal Podhoretz (b. 1930) was born in Brooklyn. In 1960 he became editor-in-chief of the magazine *Commentary.* In 1964 he published *Doings and Undoings: The Fifties and After in American Writing.* His most recent publication is *Making It* (1968). It is from this book that we have chosen a selection about his boyhood.

One of the longest journeys in the world is the journey from Brooklyn to Manhattan—or at least from certain neighborhoods in Brooklyn to certain parts of Manhattan. I have made that journey, but it is not from the experience of having made it that I know how very great the distance is, for I started on the road many years before I realized what I was doing, and by the time I did realize it I was for all practical purposes already there. At so imperceptible a pace did I travel, and with so little awareness, that I never felt footsore or out of breath or weary at the thought of how far I still had to go. Yet whenever anyone who has remained back there where I started—remained not physically but socially and culturally, for the neighborhood is now a Negro ghetto and the Jews who have "remained" in it mostly reside in the less affluent areas of Long Island—whenever anyone like that happens into the world in which I now live with such perfect ease, I can see that in his eyes I have become a fully acculturated citizen of a country as foreign to him as China and infinitely more frightening.

That country is sometimes called the upper middle class; and indeed I am a member of that class, less by virtue of my income than by virtue of the way my speech is accented, the way I dress, the way I furnish my home, the way I entertain and am entertained, the way I educate my children—the way, quite simply, I look and I live. It appalls me to think what an immense transformation I had to work on myself in order to become what I have become: if I had known what I was doing I would surely not have been able to do it, I would surely not have wanted to. No wonder the choice had to be blind; there was a kind of treason in it—treason toward my family, treason toward my friends. In choosing the road I chose, I was pronouncing a judgment upon them, and the fact that they themselves concurred in the judgment makes the whole thing sadder but no less cruel.

When I say that the choice was blind, I mean that I was never aware—obviously not as a small child, certainly not as an adolescent, and not even as a young man already writing for publication and working on the staff of an important intellectual magazine in New York—how inextricably my "noblest" ambitions were tied to the vulgar desire to rise above the class into which I was born; nor did I understand to what an astonishing extent these ambitions were shaped and defined by the standards and values and tastes of the class into which I did not know I wanted to move. It is not that I was or am a social climber as that term is commonly used. High society interests me, if at all, only as a curiosity; I do not wish to be a member of it; and in any case, it is not, as I have learned from a small experience of contact with the very rich and fashionable, my "scene." Yet precisely because social climbing is not one of my vices (unless what might be called celebrity climbing, which very definitely *is* one of my vices, can be considered the contemporary variant of social climbing), I think there may be more than a merely personal significance in the fact that class has played so large a part both in my life and in my career.

But whether or not the significance is there, I feel certain that my long-time blindness to the part class was playing in my life was not altogether idiosyncratic. "Privilege," Robert L. Heilbroner has shrewdly observed in *The Limits of American Capitalism,* "is not an attribute we are accustomed to stress when we consider the construction of *our* social order." For a variety of reasons, says Heilbroner, "privilege under capitalism is much less 'visible,' especially to the favored groups, than privilege under other systems" like feudalism. This "invisibility" extends in America to class as well.

No one, of course, is so naïve as to believe that America is a classless society or that the force of egalitarianism—powerful as it has been in some respects—has ever been powerful enough to wipe out class distinctions altogether. There was a moment during the 1950s, to be sure, when social thought hovered on the brink of saying that the country had to all intents and purposes become a wholly middle-class society. But the emergence of the civil-rights movement in the 1960s and the concomitant discovery of the poor—to whom, in helping to discover them, Michael Harrington interestingly enough applied, in *The Other America,* the very word ("invisible") that Heilbroner later used with reference to the rich—has put at least a temporary end to that kind of talk. And yet if class has become visible again, it is only in its grossest outlines—mainly, that is, in terms of income levels—and to the degree that manners and style of life are perceived as relevant at all, it is generally in the crudest of terms. There is something in us, it would seem, which resists the idea of class. Even our novelists, working in a genre for which class has traditionally been a supreme reality, are largely indifferent to it—which is to say, blind to its importance as a factor in the life of the individual.

In my own case, the blindness to class always expressed itself in an outright and very often belligerent refusal to believe that it had anything to do with me at all. I no longer remember when or in what form I first discovered that there was such a thing as class, but whenever it was and whatever form the discovery took, it could only have coincided with the recognition that criteria existed by which I and everyone I knew were stamped as inferior: we were in the *lower* class. This was not a proposition I was willing to accept, and my way of not accepting it was to dismiss the whole idea of class as a prissy triviality.

Given the fact that I had literary ambitions even as a small boy, it was inevitable that the issue of class would sooner or later arise for me with a sharpness it would never acquire for most of my friends. But given the fact also that I was on the whole very happy to be growing up where I was, that I was fiercely patriotic about Brownsville (the spawning ground of so many famous athletes and gangsters), and that I felt genuinely patronizing toward other neighborhoods (especially the "better" ones like Crown Heights and East Flatbush which seemed by comparison colorless and unexciting)— given the fact, in other words, that I was not, for all that I wrote poetry and read books, an "alienated" boy dreaming of escape, my confrontation with the issue of class would probably have come later rather than sooner if not for an English teacher in high school who decided that I was a gem in the rough and took it upon herself to polish me to as high a sheen as she could manage and I would permit.

I resisted—far less effectively, I can see now, than I then thought, though even then I knew that she was wearing me down far more than I would ever give her the satisfaction of admitting. Famous throughout the school for her altogether outspoken snobbery, which stopped short by only a hair (and sometimes did not stop short at all) of an old-fashioned kind of patrician anti-Semitism, Mrs. K. was also famous for being an extremely good teacher; indeed, I am sure that she saw no distinction between the hopeless task of teaching the proper use of English to the young Jewish barbarians whom fate had so unkindly deposited into her charge and the equally hopeless task of teaching them the proper "manners." (There were as many young Negro barbarians in her charge as Jewish ones, but I doubt that she could ever bring herself to pay very much attention to them. As she never hesitated to make clear, it was punishment enough for a woman of her background—her family was old-Brooklyn and, she would have us understand, extremely distinguished—to have fallen among the sons of East European immigrant Jews.)

For three years, from the age of thirteen to the age of sixteen, I was her special pet, though that word is scarcely adequate to suggest the intensity of the relationship which developed between us. It was a relationship right out of *The Corn Is Green,* which may, for all I know, have served as her model; at any rate, her objective was much the same as the Welsh teacher's in that play: she was determined that I should win a scholarship to Harvard. But whereas (an irony much to the point here) the problem the teacher had in *The Corn Is Green* with her coal-miner pupil in the traditional class society of Edwardian England was strictly academic, Mrs. K.'s problem with me in the putatively egalitarian society of New Deal America was strictly social. My grades were very high and would obviously remain so, but what would they avail me if I continued to go about looking and sounding like a "filthy little slum child" (the epithet she would invariably hurl at me whenever we had an argument about "manners")?

Childless herself, she worked on me like a dementedly ambitious mother with a somewhat recalcitrant son; married to a solemn and elderly man (she was then in her early forties or thereabouts), she treated me like a cruelly ungrateful adolescent lover on whom she had humiliatingly bestowed her favors. She flirted with me and flattered me, she scolded me and insulted me. Slum child, filthy little slum child, so beautiful a mind and so vulgar a personality, so exquisite in sensibility and so coarse in manner. What would she do with me, what would become of me if I persisted out of stubbornness and perversity in the disgusting ways they had taught me at home and on the streets?

To her the most offensive of these ways was the style in which I dressed: a T-shirt, tightly pegged pants and a red satin jacket with the legend "Cherokees, S.A.C." (social-athletic club) stitched in large white letters across the back. This was bad enough, but when on certain days I would appear in school wearing, as a particular ceremonial occasion required, a suit and tie, the sight of those immense padded shoulders and my white-on-white shirt would drive her to even greater heights of contempt and even lower depths of loving despair than usual. *Slum child, filthy little slum child.* I was beyond saving; I deserved no better than to wind up with all the other horrible little Jewboys in the gutter (by which she meant Brooklyn College). If only I would listen to her, the whole world could be mine: I could win a scholarship to Harvard, I could get to know the best people, I could grow up into a life of elegance and refinement and taste. Why was I so stupid as not to understand?

II

In those days it was very unusual, and possibly even against the rules, for teachers in public high schools to associate with their students after hours. Nevertheless, Mrs. K. sometimes invited me to her home, a beautiful old brownstone located in what was perhaps the only section in the whole of Brooklyn fashionable enough to be intimidating. I would read her my poems and she would tell me about her family, about the schools she had gone to, about Vassar, about writers she had met, while her husband, of whom I was frightened to death and who to my utter astonishment turned out to be Jewish (but not, as Mrs. K. quite unnecessarily hastened to inform me, *my* kind of Jewish), sat stiffly and silently in an armchair across the room squinting at his newspaper through the first pince-nez I had ever seen outside the movies. He spoke to me but once, and that was after I had read Mrs. K. my tearful editorial for the school newspaper on the death of Roosevelt—an effusion which provoked him into a full five-minute harangue whose blasphemous contents would certainly have shocked me into insensibility if I had not been even more shocked to discover that he actually had a voice.

But Mrs. K. not only had me to her house; she also—what was even more unusual—took me out a few times, to the Frick Gallery and the Metropolitan Museum, and once to the theater, where we saw a dramatization of *The Late George Apley,* a play I imagine she deliberately chose with the not wholly mistaken idea that it would impress upon me the glories of aristocratic Boston.

One of our excursions into Manhattan I remember with particular vividness because she used it to bring the struggle between us to rather a dramatic head. The familiar argument began this time on the subway. Why, knowing that we would be spending the afternoon together "in public," had I come to school that morning improperly dressed? (I was, as usual, wearing my red satin club jacket over a white T-shirt.) She realized, of course, that I owned only one suit (this said not in compassion but in derision) and that my poor parents had, God only knew where, picked up the idea that it was too precious to be worn except at one of those bar mitzvahs I was always going to. Though why, if my parents were so worried about clothes, they had permitted me to buy a suit which made me look like a young hoodlum, she found it very difficult to imagine. Still, much as she would have been embarrassed to be seen in public with a boy whose parents allowed him to wear a zoot suit, she would have been somewhat less embarrassed than she was now by the ridiculous costume I had on. Had I no consideration for her? Had I no consideration for myself? Did I want everyone who laid eyes on me to think that I was nothing but an ill-bred little slum child?

My standard ploy in these arguments was to take the position that such things were of no concern to me: I was a poet and I had more important matters to think about than clothes. Besides, I would feel silly coming to school on an ordinary day dressed in a suit. Did Mrs. K. want me to look like one of those "creeps" from Crown Heights who were all going to become doctors? This was usually an effective counter, since Mrs. K. despised her middle-class Jewish students even more than she did the "slum children," but probably because she was growing desperate at the thought of how I would strike a Harvard interviewer (it was my senior year), she did not respond according to form on that particular occasion.

"At least," she snapped, "they reflect well on their parents."

I was accustomed to her bantering gibes at my parents, and sensing, probably, that they arose out of jealousy, I was rarely troubled by them. But this one bothered me; it went beyond banter and I did not know how to deal with it. I remember flushing, but I cannot remember what if anything I said in protest. It was the beginning of a very bad afternoon for both of us.

We had been heading for the Museum of Modern Art, but as we got off the subway, Mrs. K. announced that she had changed her mind about the museum. She was going to show me something else instead, just down the street on Fifth Avenue. This mysterious "something else" to which we proceeded in silence turned out to be the college department of an expensive clothing store, De Pinna. I do not exaggerate when I say that an actual physical dread seized me as I followed her into the store. I had never been inside such a store; it was not a store, it was enemy territory, every inch of it mined with humiliations. "I am," Mrs. K. declared in the coldest human voice I hope I shall ever hear, "going to buy you a suit that you will be able to wear at your Harvard interview." I had guessed, of course, that this was what she had in mind, and even at fifteen I understood what a fantastic act of aggression she was planning to commit against my parents and asking me to participate in. Oh no, I said in a panic (suddenly realizing that I *wanted* her to buy me that suit), I can't, my mother wouldn't like it. "You can tell her it's a birthday present. Or else I will tell her. If I tell her, I'm sure she won't object." The idea of Mrs. K. meeting my mother was more than I could bear: my mother, who spoke with a Yiddish accent and whom, until that sickening moment, I had never known I was so ready to betray.

To my immense relief and my equally immense disappointment, we left the store, finally, without buying a suit, but it was not to be the end of clothing or "manners" for me that day—not yet. There was still the ordeal of a restaurant to go through. Where I came from, people rarely ate in restaurants, not so much because most of them were too poor to afford such a luxury—although most of them certainly were—as because eating in restaurants was not regarded as a luxury at all; it was, rather, a necessity to which bachelors were pitiably condemned. A home-cooked meal was assumed to be better than anything one could possibly get in a restaurant, and considering the class of restaurants in question (they were really diners or luncheonettes), the assumption was probably correct. In the case of my own family, myself included until my late teens, the business of going to restaurants was complicated by the fact that we observed the Jewish dietary laws, and except in certain neighborhoods, few places could be found which served kosher food; in midtown Manhattan in the 1940s, I believe there were only two and both were relatively expensive. All this is by way of explaining why I had had so little experience of restaurants up to the age of fifteen and why I grew apprehensive once more when Mrs. K. decided after we left De Pinna that we should have something to eat.

The restaurant she chose was not at all an elegant one—I have, like a criminal, revisited it since—but it seemed very elegant indeed to me: enemy territory again, and this time a mine exploded in my face the minute I set foot through the door. The hostess was very sorry, but she could not seat the young gentleman without a coat and tie. If the lady wished, however, something could be arranged. The lady (visibly pleased by this unexpected —or was it expected?—object lesson) did wish, and the so recently defiant but by now utterly docile young gentleman was forthwith divested of his so recently beloved but by now thoroughly loathsome red satin jacket and provided with a much oversized white waiter's coat and a tie—which, there being no collar to a T-shirt, had to be worn around his bare neck. Thus attired, and with his face supplying the touch of red which had moments earlier been supplied by his jacket, he was led into the dining room, there to be taught the importance of proper table manners through the same pedagogic instrumentality that had worked so well in impressing him with the importance of proper dress.

Like any other pedagogic technique, however, humiliation has its limits, and Mrs. K. was to make no further progress with it that day. For I had had enough, and I was not about to risk stepping on another mine. Knowing she would subject me to still more ridicule if I made a point of my revulsion at the prospect of eating non-kosher food, I resolved to let her order for me and then to feign lack of appetite or possibly even illness when the meal was served. She did order—duck for both of us, undoubtedly because it would be a hard dish for me to manage without using my fingers.

The two portions came in deep oval-shaped dishes, swimming in a brown sauce and each with a sprig of parsley sitting on top. I had not the faintest idea of what to do—should the food be eaten directly from the oval dish or not?—nor which of the many implements on the table to do it with. But remembering that Mrs. K. herself had once advised me to watch my hostess in such a situation and then to do exactly as she did, I sat perfectly still and waited for her to make the first move. Unfortunately, Mrs. K. also remembered having taught me that trick, and determined as she was that I should be given a lesson that would force me to mend my ways, she waited too. And so we both waited, chatting amiably, pretending not to notice the food while it sat there getting colder and colder by the minute. Thanks partly to the fact that I would probably have gagged on the duck if I had tried to eat it—dietary taboos are very powerful if one has been conditioned to them—I was prepared to wait forever. And, indeed, it was Mrs. K. who broke first.

"Why aren't you eating?" she suddenly said after something like fifteen minutes had passed. "Aren't you hungry?" Not very, I answered. "Well," she said, "I think we'd better eat. The food is getting cold." Whereupon, as I watched with great fascination, she deftly captured the sprig of parsley between the prongs of her serving fork, set it aside, took up her serving spoon and delicately used those two esoteric implements to transfer a piece of duck from the oval dish to her plate. I imitated the whole operation as best as I could, but not well enough to avoid splattering some partly congealed sauce onto my borrowed coat in the process. Still, things could have been worse, and having more or less successfully negotiated my way around that particular mine, I now had to cope with the problem of how to get out of eating the duck. But I need not have worried. Mrs. K. took one bite, pronounced it inedible (it must have been frozen by then), and called in quiet fury for the check.

Several months later, wearing an altered but respectably conservative suit which had been handed down to me in good condition by a bachelor uncle, I presented myself on two different occasions before interviewers from Harvard and from the Pulitzer Scholarship Committee. Some months after that, Mrs. K. had her triumph: I won the Harvard scholarship on which her heart had been so passionately set. It was not, however, large enough to cover all expenses, and since my parents could not afford to make up the difference, I was unable to accept it. My parents felt wretched but not, I think, quite as wretched as Mrs. K. For a while it looked as though I would wind up in the "gutter" of Brooklyn College after all, but then the news arrived that I had also won a Pulitzer Scholarship which paid full tuition if used at Columbia, and a small stipend besides. Everyone was consoled, even Mrs. K. Columbia was at least in the Ivy League.

The last time I saw her was shortly before my graduation from Columbia and just after a story had appeared in the *Times* announcing that I had been awarded a fellowship which was to send me to Cambridge University. Mrs. K. had passionately wanted to see me in Cambridge, Massachusetts, but Cambridge, England, was even better. We met somewhere near Columbia for a drink, and her happiness over my fellowship, it seemed to me, was if anything exceeded by her delight at discovering that I now knew enough to know that the right thing to order in a cocktail lounge was a very dry martini with lemon peel, please.

III

Looking back now at the story of my relationship with Mrs. K. strictly in the context of the issue of class, what strikes me most sharply is the astonishing rudeness of this woman to whom "manners" were of such overriding concern. (This, as I have since had some occasion to notice, is a fairly common characteristic among members of the class to which she belonged.) Though she would not have admitted it, good manners to Mrs. K. meant only one thing: conformity to a highly stylized set of surface habits and fashions which she took, quite as a matter of course, to be superior to all other styles of social behavior. But in what did their superiority consist? Were her "good" manners derived from or conducive to a greater moral sensitivity than the "bad" manners I had learned at home and on the streets of Brownsville? I rather doubt it. The "crude" behavior of my own parents, for example, was then and is still marked by a tactfulness and a delicacy that Mrs. K. simply could not have approached. It is not that she was incapable of tact and delicacy; in certain moods she was (and manners apart, she was an extraordinarily loving and generous woman). But such qualities were neither built into nor expressed by the system of manners under which she lived. She was fond of quoting Cardinal Newman's definition of a gentleman as a person who could be at ease in any company, yet if anything was clear about the manners she was trying to teach me, it was that they operated—not inadvertently but by deliberate design—to set one at ease *only* with others similarly trained and to cut one off altogether from those who were not.

While I would have been unable to formulate it in those terms at the time, I think I must have understood perfectly well what Mrs. K. was attempting to communicate with all her talk about manners; if I had not understood it so well, I would not have resisted so fiercely. She was saying that because I was a talented boy, a better class of people stood ready to admit me into their ranks. But only on one condition: I had to signify by my general deportment that I acknowledged them as *superior* to the class of people among whom I happened to have been born. That was the bargain—take it or leave it. In resisting Mrs. K. where "manners" were concerned—just as I was later to resist many others—I was expressing my refusal to have any part of so brutal a bargain.

But the joke was on me, for what I did not understand—not in the least then and not for a long time afterward—was that in matters having to do with "art" and "culture" (the "life of the mind," as I learned to call it at Columbia), I was being offered the very same brutal bargain and accepting it with the wildest enthusiasm.

I have said that I did not, for all my bookishness, feel alienated as a boy, and this is certainly true. Far from dreaming of escape from Brownsville, I dreaded the thought of living anywhere else, and whenever my older sister, who hated the neighborhood, began begging my parents to move, it was invariably my howls of protest that kept them from giving in. For by the age of thirteen I had made it into the neighborhood big time, otherwise known as the Cherokees, S.A.C. It had by no means been easy for me, as a mediocre athlete and a notoriously good student, to win acceptance from a gang which prided itself mainly on its masculinity and its contempt for authority, but once this had been accomplished, down the drain went any reason I might earlier have had for thinking that life could be better in any other place. Not for nothing, then, did I wear that red satin jacket to school every day. It was my proudest possession, a badge of manly status, proving that I was not to be classified with the Crown Heights "creeps," even though my grades, like theirs, were high.

And yet, despite the Cherokees, it cannot be that I felt quite so securely at home in Brownsville as I remember thinking. The reason is that something extremely significant in this connection had happened to me by the time I first met Mrs. K.: without any conscious effort on my part, my speech had largely lost the characteristic neighborhood accent and was well on its way to becoming as neutrally American as I gather it now is.

Now whatever else may be involved in a nondeliberate change of accent, one thing is clear: it bespeaks a very high degree of detachment from the ethos of one's immediate surroundings. It is not a good ear alone, and perhaps not even a good ear at all, which enables a child to hear the difference between the way he and everyone else around him sound when they talk, and the way teachers and radio announcers—as it must have been in my case—sound. Most people, and especially most children, are entirely insensitive to such differences, which is why anyone who pays attention to these matters can, on the basis of a man's accent alone, often draw a reasonably accurate picture of his regional, social, and ethnic background. People who feel that they belong in their familiar surroundings—whether it be a place, a class, or a group—will invariably speak in the accent of those surroundings; in all likelihood, indeed, they will never have imagined any other possibility for themselves. Conversely, it is safe to assume that a person whose accent has undergone a radical change from childhood is a person who once had fantasies of escaping to some other world, whether or not they were ever realized.

But accent in America has more than a psychological or spiritual significance. "Her kerbstone English," said Henry Higgins of Eliza Doolittle, "will keep her in the gutter to the end of her days." Most Americans probably respond with a sense of amused democratic superiority to the idea of a society in which so trivial a thing as accent can keep a man down, and it is a good measure of our blindness to the pervasive operations of class that there has been so little consciousness of the fact that America itself is such a society. While the broadly regional accents—New England, Midwestern, Southern—enjoy more or less equal status and will not affect the economic or social chances of those who speak in them, the opposite is still surely true of any accent identifiably influenced by Yiddish, Italian, Polish, Spanish—that is, the languages of the major post-Civil War immigrant groups (among which may be included American-Irish). A man with such an accent will no longer be confined, as once he would almost automatically have been, to the working class, but unless his life, both occupational and social, is lived strictly within the milieu in whose tone of voice he speaks, his accent will at the least operate as an obstacle to be overcome (if, for example, he is a schoolteacher aspiring to be a principal), and at the most as an effective barrier to advancement (if, say, he is an engineer), let alone to entry into the governing elite of the country. (For better or worse, incidentally, these accents are not a temporary phenomenon destined to disappear with the passage of the generations, no more than ethnic consciousness itself is. I have heard third-generation American Jews of East European stock speaking with thicker accents than their parents.)

Clearly, then, while fancying myself altogether at home in the world into which I was born, I was not only more detached from it than I realized; I was also taking action—and of a very fundamental kind—which would eventually make it possible for me to move into some other world. Yet I still did not recognize what I was doing—not in any such terms. My ambition was to be a great and famous poet, not to live in a different community, a different class, a different "world." If I had a concrete image of what greatness would mean socially, it was probably based on the famous professional boxer from our block who had moved to a more prosperous neighborhood but still spent his leisure time hanging around the corner candy store and the local poolroom with his old friends (among whom he could, of course, experience his fame far more sharply than he could have done among his newly acquired peers).

But to each career its own sociology. Boxers, unlike poets, do not undergo a cultural change in the process of becoming boxers, and if I was not brave enough or clever enough as a boy to see the distinction, others who knew me then were. "Ten years from now, you won't even want to talk to me, you won't even recognize me if you pass me on the street," was the kind of comment I frequently heard in my teens from women in the neighborhood, friends of my mother who were fond of me and nearly as proud as she was of the high grades I was getting in school and the prizes I was always winning. "That's crazy, you must be kidding," I would answer. They were not crazy and they were not kidding. They were simply better sociologists than I.

As, indeed, my mother herself was, for often in later years—after I had become a writer and an editor and was living only a subway ride away but in a style that was foreign to her and among people by whom she was intimidated—she would gaze wistfully at this strange creature, her son, and murmur, "I should have made him for a dentist," registering thereby her perception that whereas Jewish sons who grow up to be successes in certain occupations usually remain fixed in an accessible cultural ethos, sons who grow up into literary success are transformed almost beyond recognition and distanced almost beyond a mother's reach. My mother wanted nothing so much as for me to be a success, to be respected and admired. But she did not imagine, I think, that she would only purchase the realization of her ambition at the price of my progressive estrangement from her and her ways. Perhaps it was my guilt at the first glimmerings of this knowledge which accounted for my repression of it and for the obstinacy of the struggle I waged over "manners" with Mrs. K.

For what seemed most of all to puzzle Mrs. K., who saw no distinction between taste in poetry and taste in clothes, was that I could see no connection between the two. Mrs. K. knew that a boy from Brownsville with a taste for Keats was not long for Brownsville, and moreover would in all probability end up in the social class to which she herself belonged. How could I have explained to her that I would only be able to leave Brownsville if I could maintain the illusion that my destination was a place in some mystical country of the spirit and not a place in the upper reaches of the American class structure?

Saint Paul, who was a Jew, conceived of salvation as a world in which there would be neither Jew nor Greek, and though he may well have been the first, he was very far from the last Jew to dream such a dream of transcendence—transcendence of the actual alternative categories with which reality so stingily presents us. Not to be Jewish, but not to be Christian either; not to be a worker, but not to be a boss either; not—if I may be forgiven for injecting this banality out of my own soul into so formidable a series of fantasies—to be a slum child but not to be a snob either. How could I have explained to Mrs. K. that wearing a suit from De Pinna would for me have been something like the social equivalent of a conversion to Christianity? And how could she have explained to me that there was no socially neutral ground to be found in the United States of America, and that a distaste for the surroundings in which I was bred, and ultimately (God forgive me) even for many of the people I loved—and so a new taste for other kinds of people—how could she have explained that all this was inexorably entailed in the logic of a taste for the poetry of Keats and the painting of Cézanne and the music of Mozart?

from The Fire Next Time

James Baldwin

> James Baldwin (b. 1924) was born in New York City. The section reprinted below, from *The Fire Next Time* (1963), is an account of his growing up in Harlem. Baldwin has written a play, *Blues for Mister Charlie* (1964), several novels, two of which are *Another Country* (1961) and *Tell Me How Long the Train's Been Gone* (1968), and polemical and autobiographical essays: *Notes of a Native Son* (1955) and *Nobody Knows My Name* (1961).

I underwent, during the summer that I became fourteen, a prolonged religious crisis. I use the word "religious" in the common, and arbitrary, sense, meaning that I then discovered God, His saints and angels, and His blazing Hell. And since I had been born in a Christian nation, I accepted this Deity as the only one. I supposed Him to exist only within the walls of a church—in fact, of *our* church—and I also supposed that God and safety were synonymous. The word "safety" brings us to the real meaning of the word "religious" as we use it. Therefore, to state it in another, more accurate way, I became, during my fourteenth year, for the first time in my life, afraid—afraid of the evil within me and afraid of the evil without. What I saw around me that summer in Harlem was what I had always seen; nothing had changed. But now, without any warning, the whores and pimps and racketeers on the Avenue had become a personal menace. It had not before occurred to me that I could become one of them, but now I realized that we had been produced by the same circumstances. Many of my comrades were clearly headed for the Avenue, and my father said that I was headed that way, too. My friends began to drink and smoke, and embarked—at first avid, then groaning—on their sexual careers. Girls, only slightly older than I was, who sang in the choir or taught Sunday school, the children of holy parents, underwent, before my eyes, their incredible metamorphosis, of which the most bewildering aspect was not their budding breasts or their rounding behinds but something deeper and more subtle, in their eyes, their heat, their odor, and the inflection of their voices. Like the strangers on the Avenue, they became, in the twinkling of an eye, unutterably different and fantastically *present*. Owing to the way I had been raised, the abrupt discomfort that all this aroused in me and the fact that I had no idea what my voice or my mind or my body was likely to do next caused me to consider myself one of the most depraved people on earth. Matters were not helped by the fact that these holy girls seemed rather to enjoy my terrified lapses, our grim, guilty, tormented experiments, which were at once as chill and joyless as the Russian steppes and hotter, by far, than all the fires of Hell.

Yet there was something deeper than these changes, and less definable, that frightened me. It was real in both the boys and the girls, but it was, somehow, more vivid in the boys. In the case of the girls, one watched them turning into matrons before they had become women. They began to manifest a curious and really rather terrifying singlemindedness. It is hard to say exactly how this was conveyed: something implacable in the set of the lips, something farseeing (seeing what?) in the eyes, some new and crushing determination in the walk, something peremptory in the voice. They did not tease us, the boys, any more; they reprimanded us sharply, saying, "You better be thinking about your soul!" For the girls also saw the evidence on the Avenue, knew what the price would be, for them, of one misstep, knew that they had to be protected and that we were the only protection there was. They understood that they must act as God's decoys, saving the souls of the boys for Jesus and binding the bodies of the boys in marriage. For this was the beginning of our burning time, and "It is better," said St. Paul—who elsewhere, with a most unusual and stunning exactness described himself as a "wretched man"—"to marry than to burn." And I began to feel in the boys a curious, wary, bewildered despair, as though they were now settling in for the long, hard winter of life. I did not know then what it was that I was reacting to; I put it to myself that they were letting themselves go. In the same way that the girls were destined to gain as much weight as their mothers, the boys, it was clear, would rise no higher than their fathers. School began to reveal itself, therefore, as a child's game that one could not win, and boys dropped out of school and went to work. My father wanted me to do the same. I refused, even though I no longer had any illusions about what an education could do for me; I had already encountered too many college-graduate handymen. My friends were now "downtown," busy, as they put it, "fighting the man." They began to care less about the way they looked, the way they dressed, the things they did; presently, one found them in twos and threes and fours, in a hallway, sharing a jug of wine or a bottle of whiskey, talking, cursing, fighting, sometimes weeping: lost, and unable to say what it was that oppressed them, except that they knew it was "the man"—the white man. And there seemed to be no way whatever to remove this cloud that stood between them and the sun, between them and love and life and power, between them and whatever it was that they wanted. One did not have to be very bright to realize how little one could do to change one's situation; one did not have to be abnormally sensitive to be worn down to a cutting edge by the incessant and gratuitous humiliation and danger one encountered every working day, all day long. The humiliation did not apply merely to working days, or workers; I was thirteen and was crossing Fifth Avenue on my way to the Forty-second Street library, and the cop in the middle of the street muttered as I passed him, "Why don't you niggers stay uptown where you belong?" When I was ten, and didn't look, certainly, any older, two policemen amused themselves with me by frisking me, making comic (and terrifying) speculations concerning my ancestry and probable sexual prowess, and for good measure, leaving me flat on my back in one of Harlem's empty lots. Just before and then during the Second World War, many of my friends fled into the service, all to be changed there, and rarely for the better, many to be ruined, and many to die. Others fled to other states and cities—that is, to other ghettos. Some went on wine or whiskey or the needle, and are still on it. And others, like me, fled into the church.

For the wages of sin were visible everywhere, in every wine-stained and urine-splashed hallway, in every clanging ambulance bell, in every scar on the faces of the pimps and their whores, in every helpless, newborn baby being brought into this danger, in every knife and pistol fight on the Avenue, and in every disastrous bulletin: a cousin, mother of six, suddenly gone mad, the children parcelled out here and there; an indestructible aunt rewarded for years of hard labor by a slow, agonizing death in a terrible small room; someone's bright son blown into eternity by his own hand; another turned robber and carried off to jail. It was a summer of dreadful speculations and discoveries, of which these were not the worst. Crime became real, for example—for the first time—not as *a* possibility but as *the* possibility. One would never defeat one's circumstances by working and saving one's pennies; one would never, by working, acquire that many pennies, and, besides, the social treatment accorded even the most success-ful Negroes proved that one needed, in order to be free, something more than a bank account. One needed a handle, a lever, a means of inspiring fear. It was absolutely clear that the police would whip you and take you in as long as they could get away with it, and that everyone else—housewives, taxi-drivers, elevator boys, dishwashers, bartenders, lawyers, judges, doctors, and grocers—would never, by the operation of any generous human feeling, cease to use you as an outlet for his frustrations and hostili-ties. Neither civilized reason nor Christian love would cause any of those people to treat you as they presumably wanted to be treated; only the fear of your power to retaliate would cause them to do that, or to seem to do it, which was (and is) good enough. There appears to be a vast amount of confusion on this point, but I do not know many Negroes who are eager to be "accepted" by white people, still less to be loved by them; they, the blacks, simply don't wish to be beaten over the head by the whites every instant of our brief passage on this planet. White people in this country will have quite enough to do in learning how to accept and love themselves and each other, and when they have achieved this—which will not be tomorrow and may very well be never—the Negro problem will no longer exist, for it will no longer be needed.

People more advantageously placed than we in Harlem were, and are, will no doubt find the psychology and the view of human nature sketched above dismal and shocking in the extreme. But the Negro's experience of the white world cannot possibly create in him any respect for the standards by which the white world claims to live. His own condition is overwhelming proof that white people do not live by these standards. Negro servants have been smuggling odds and ends out of white homes for generations, and white people have been delighted to have them do it, because it has assuaged a dim guilt and testified to the intrinsic superiority of white people. Even the most doltish and servile Negro could scarcely fail to be impressed by the disparity between his situation and that of the people for whom he worked; Negroes who were neither doltish nor servile did not feel that they were doing anything wrong when they robbed white people. In spite of the Puritan-Yankee equation of virtue with well-being, Negroes had excellent reasons for doubting that money was made or kept by any very striking adherence to the Christian virtues; it certainly did not work that way for black Christians. In any case, white people, who had robbed black people of their liberty and who profited by this theft every hour that they lived, had no moral ground on which to stand. They had the judges, the juries, the shotguns, the law—in a word, power. But it was a criminal power, to be feared but not respected, and to be outwitted in any way whatever. And those virtues preached but not practiced by the white world were merely another means of holding Negroes in subjection.

It turned out, then, that summer, that the moral barriers that I had supposed to exist between me and the dangers of a criminal career were so tenuous as to be nearly nonexistent. I certainly could not discover any principled reason for not becoming a criminal, and it is not my poor, God-fearing parents who are to be indicted for the lack but this society. I was icily determined—more determined, really, than I then knew—never to make my peace with the ghetto but to die and go to Hell before I would let any white man spit on me, before I would accept my "place" in this republic. I did not intend to allow the white people of this country to tell me who I was, and limit me that way, and polish me off that way. And yet, of course, at the same time, I *was* being spat on and defined and described and limited, and could have been polished off with no effort whatever. Every Negro boy—in my situation during those years, at least—who reaches this point realizes, at once, profoundly, because he wants to live, that he stands in great peril and must find, with speed, a "thing," a gimmick, to lift him out, to start him on his way. *And it does not matter what the gimmick is.* It was this last realization that terrified me and—since it revealed that the door opened on so many dangers—helped to hurl me into the church. And, by an unforeseeable paradox, it was my career in the church that turned out, precisely, to be my gimmick.

For when I tried to assess my capabilities, I realized that I had almost none. In order to achieve the life I wanted, I had been dealt, it seemed to me, the worst possible hand. I could not become a prize-fighter—many of us tried but very few succeeded. I could not sing. I could not dance. I had been well conditioned by the world in which I grew up, so I did not yet dare take the idea of becoming a writer seriously. The only other possibility seemed to involve my becoming one of the sordid people on the Avenue, who were not really as sordid as I then imagined but who frightened me terribly, both because I did not want to live that life and because of what they made me feel. Everything inflamed me, and that was bad enough, but I myself had also become a source of fire and temptation. I had been far too well raised, alas, to suppose that any of the extremely explicit overtures made to me that summer, sometimes by boys and girls but also, more alarmingly, by older men and women, had anything to do with my attractiveness. On the contrary, since the Harlem idea of seduction is, to put it mildly, blunt, whatever these people saw in me merely confirmed my sense of my depravity.

It is certainly sad that the awakening of one's senses should lead to such a merciless judgment of oneself—to say nothing of the time and anguish one spends in the effort to arrive at any other—but it is also inevitable that a literal attempt to mortify the flesh should be made among black people like those with whom I grew up. Negroes in this country—and Negroes do not, strictly or legally speaking, exist in any other—are taught really to despise themselves from the moment their eyes open on the world. This world is white and they are black. White people hold the power, which means that they are superior to blacks (intrinsically, that is: God decreed it so), and the world has innumerable ways of making this difference known and felt and feared. Long before the Negro child perceives this difference, and even longer before he understands it, he has begun to react to it, he has begun to be controlled by it. Every effort made by the child's elders to prepare him for a fate from which they cannot protect him causes him secretly, in terror, to begin to await, without knowing that he is doing so, his mysterious and inexorable punishment. He must be "good" not only in order to please his parents and not only to avoid being punished by them; behind their authority stands another, nameless and impersonal, infinitely harder to please, and bottomlessly cruel. And this filters into the child's consciousness through his parents' tone of voice as he is being exhorted, punished, or loved; in the sudden, uncontrollable note of fear heard in his mother's or his father's voice when he has strayed beyond some particular boundary. He does not know what the boundary is, and he can get no explanation of it, which is frightening enough, but the fear he hears in the voices of his elders is more frightening still. The fear that I heard in my father's voice, for example, when he realized that I really *believed* I could do anything a white boy could do, and had every intention of proving it, was not at all like the fear I heard when one of us was ill or had fallen down the stairs or strayed too far from the house. It was another fear, a fear that the child, in challenging the white world's assumptions, was putting himself in the path of destruction. A child cannot, thank Heaven, know how vast and how merciless is the nature of power, with what unbelievable cruelty people treat each other. He reacts to the fear in his parents' voices because his parents hold up the world for him and he has no protection without them. I defended myself, as I imagined, against the fear my father made me feel by remembering that he was very old-fashioned. Also, I prided myself on the fact that I already knew how to outwit him. To defend oneself against a fear is simply to insure that one will, one day, be conquered by it; fears must be faced. As for one's wits, it is just not true that one can live by them—not, that is, if one wishes really to live. That summer, in any case, all the fears with which I had grown up, and which were now a part of me and controlled my vision of the world, rose up like a wall between the world and me, and drove me into the church.

As I look back, everything I did seems curiously deliberate, though it certainly did not seem deliberate then. For example, I did not join the church of which my father was a member and in which he preached. My best friend in school, who attended a different church, had already "surrendered his life to the Lord," and he was very anxious about my soul's salvation. (I wasn't, but any human attention was better than none.) One Saturday afternoon, he took me to his church. There were no services that day, and the church was empty, except for some women cleaning and some other women praying. My friend took me into the back room to meet his pastor—a woman. There she sat, in her robes, smiling, an extremely proud and handsome woman, with Africa, Europe, and the America of the American Indian blended in her face. She was perhaps forty-five or fifty at this time, and in our world she was a very celebrated woman. My friend was about to introduce me when she looked at me and smiled and said, "Whose little boy are you?" Now this, unbelievably, was precisely the phrase used by pimps and racketeers on the Avenue when they suggested, both humorously and intensely, that I "hang out" with them. Perhaps part of the terror they had caused me to feel came from the fact that I unquestionably wanted to be *somebody's* little boy. I was so frightened, and at the mercy of so many conundrums, that inevitably, that summer, *someone* would have taken me over; one doesn't, in Harlem, long remain standing on any auction block. It was my good luck—perhaps—that I found myself in the church racket instead of some other, and surrendered to a spiritual seduction long before I came to any carnal knowledge. For when the pastor asked me, with that marvellous smile, "Whose little boy are you?" my heart replied at once, "Why, yours."

The summer wore on, and things got worse. I became more guilty and more frightened, and kept all this bottled up inside me, and naturally, inescapably, one night, when this woman had finished preaching, everything came roaring, screaming, crying out, and I fell to the ground before the altar. It was the strangest sensation I have ever had in my life—up to that time, or since. I had not known that it was going to happen, or that it could happen. One moment I was on my feet, singing and clapping and, at the same time, working out in my head the plot of a play I was working on then; the next moment, with no transition, no sensation of falling, I was on my back, with the lights beating down into my face and all the vertical saints above me. I did not know what I was doing down so low, or how I had got there. And the anguish that filled me cannot be described. It moved in me like one of those floods that devastate counties, tearing everything down, tearing children from their parents and lovers from each other, and making everything an unrecognizable waste. All I really remember is the pain, the unspeakable pain; it was as though I were yelling up to Heaven and Heaven would not hear me. And if Heaven would not hear me, if love could not descend from Heaven—to wash me, to make me clean—then utter disaster was my portion. Yes, it does indeed mean something—something unspeakable—to be born, in a white country, an Anglo-Teutonic, antisexual country, black. You very soon, without knowing it, give up all hope of communion. Black people, mainly, look down or look up but do not look at each other, not at you, and white people, mainly, look away. And the universe is simply a sounding drum; there is no way, no way whatever, so it seemed then and has sometimes seemed since, to get through a life, to love your wife and children, or your friends, or your mother and father, or to be loved. The universe, which is not merely the stars and the moon and the planets, flowers, grass, and trees, but *other people,* has evolved no terms for your existence, has made no room for you, and if love will not swing wide the gates, no other power will or can. And if one despairs— as who has not?—of human love, God's love alone is left. But God—and

I felt this even then, so long ago, on that tremendous floor, unwillingly—is white. And if His love was so great, and if He loved all His children, why were we, the blacks, cast down so far? Why? In spite of all I said thereafter, I found no answer on the floor—not *that* answer, anyway—and I was on the floor all night. Over me, to bring me "through," the saints sang and rejoiced and prayed. And in the morning, when they raised me, they told me that I was "saved."

Well, indeed I was, in a way, for I was utterly drained and exhausted, and released, for the first time, from all my guilty torment. I was aware then only of my relief. For many years, I could not ask myself why human relief had to be achieved in a fashion at once so pagan and so desperate—in a fashion at once so unspeakably old and so unutterably new. And by the time I was able to ask myself this question, I was also able to see that the principles governing the rites and customs of the churches in which I grew up did not differ from the principles governing the rites and customs of other churches, white. The principles were Blindness, Loneliness, and Terror, the first principle necessarily and actively cultivated in order to deny the two others. I would love to believe that the principles were Faith, Hope, and Charity, but this is clearly not so for most Christians, or for what we call the Christian world.

I was saved. But at the same time, out of a deep, adolescent cunning I do not pretend to understand, I realized immediately that I could not remain in the church merely as another worshipper. I would have to give myself something to do, in order not to be too bored and find myself among all the wretched unsaved of the Avenue. And I don't doubt that I also intended to best my father on his own ground. Anyway, very shortly after I joined the church, I became a preacher—a Young Minister—and I remained in the pulpit for more than three years. My youth quickly made me a much bigger drawing card than my father. I pushed this advantage ruthlessly, for it was the most effective means I had found of breaking his hold over me. That was the most frightening time of my life, and quite the most dishonest, and the resulting hysteria lent great passion to my sermons—for a while. I relished the attention and the relative immunity from punishment that my new status gave me, and I relished, above all, the sudden right to privacy. It had to be recognized, after all, that I was still a schoolboy, with my schoolwork to do, and I was also expected to prepare at least one sermon a week. During what we may call my heyday, I preached much more often than that. This meant that there were hours and even whole days when I could not be interrupted—not even by my father. I had immobilized him. It took rather more time for me to realize that I had also immobilized myself, and had escaped from nothing whatever.

The church was very exciting. It took a long time for me to disengage myself from this excitement, and on the blindest, most visceral level, I never really have, and never will. There is no music like that music, no drama like the drama of the saints rejoicing, the sinners moaning, the tambourines racing, and all those voices coming together and crying holy unto the Lord. There is still, for me, no pathos quite like the pathos of those multicolored, worn, somehow triumphant and transfigured faces, speaking from the depths of a visible, tangible, continuing despair of the goodness of the Lord. I have never seen anything to equal the fire and excitement that sometimes, without warning, fill a church, causing the church, as Leadbelly and so many others have testified, to "rock." Nothing that has happened to me since equals the power and the glory that I sometimes felt when, in the middle of a sermon, I knew that I was somehow, by some miracle, really carrying, as they said, "the Word"—when the church and I were one. Their pain and their joy were mine, and mine were theirs—they surrendered their pain and joy to me, I surrendered mine to them—and their cries of "Amen!" and "Hallelujah!" and "Yes, Lord!" and "Praise His name!" and "Preach it, brother!" sustained and whipped on my solos until we all became equal, wringing wet, singing and dancing, in anguish and rejoicing, at the foot of the altar. It was, for a long time, in spite of—or, not inconceivably, because of—the shabbiness of my motives, my only sustenance, my meat and drink. I rushed home from school, to the church, to the altar, to be alone there, to commune with Jesus, my dearest Friend, who would never fail me, who knew all the secrets of my heart. Perhaps He did, but I didn't, and the bargain we struck, actually, down there at the foot of the cross, was that He would never let me find out.

He failed His bargain. He was a much better Man than I took Him for. It happened, as things do, imperceptibly, in many ways at once. I date it—the slow crumbling of my faith, the pulverization of my fortress—from the time, about a year after I had begun to preach, when I began to read again. I justified this desire by the fact that I was still in school, and I began, fatally, with Dostoevski. By this time, I was in a high school that was predominantly Jewish. This meant that I was surrounded by people who were, by definition, beyond any hope of salvation, who laughed at the tracts and leaflets I brought to school, and who pointed out that the Gospels had been written long after the death of Christ. This might not have been so distressing if it had not forced me to read the tracts and leaflets myself, for they were indeed, unless one believed their message already, impossible to believe. I remember feeling dimly that there was a kind of blackmail in it. People, I felt, ought to love the Lord *because* they loved Him, and not because they were afraid of going to Hell. I was forced, reluctantly, to realize that the Bible itself had been written by men, and translated by men out of languages I could not read, and I was already, without quite admitting it to myself, terribly involved with the effort of putting words on paper. Of course, I had the rebuttal ready: These men had all been operating under divine inspiration. *Had* they? *All* of them? And I also knew by now, alas, far more about divine inspiration than I dared admit, for I knew how I worked myself up into my own visions, and how frequently—indeed, incessantly—the visions God granted to me differed from the visions He granted to my father. I did not understand the dreams I had at night, but I knew that they were not holy. For that matter, I knew that my waking hours were far from holy. I spent most of my time in a state of repentance for things I had vividly desired to do but had not done. The fact that I was dealing with Jews brought the whole question of color, which I had been desperately avoiding, into the terrified center of my mind. I realized that the Bible had been written by white men. I knew that, according to many Christians, I was a descendant of Ham, who had been cursed, and that I was therefore predestined to be a slave. This had nothing to do with anything I was, or contained, or could become; my fate had been sealed forever, from the beginning of time. And it seemed, indeed, when one looked out over Christendom, that this was what Christendom effectively believed. It was certainly the way it behaved.

from "91 Revere Street"

Robert Lowell

> Robert Lowell (b. 1912) was born in Boston. His first volume of poems, *Land of Unlikeness* (1944), drew immediate attention. It was followed by *Lord Weary's Castle* (1946), which won the Pulitzer prize, *Life Studies* (1960), *For the Union Dead* (1964), and *Notebook 1967–68* (1969). In *Life Studies,* the poems of which contain many references to Lowell's family, he included a prose section entitled "91 Revere Street," describing his childhood and boyhood. The excerpt printed below is taken from these reminiscences of Revere Street.

In 1924 people still lived in cities. Late that summer, we bought the 91 Revere Street house, looking out on an unbuttoned part of Beacon Hill bounded by the North End slums, though reassuringly only four blocks away from my Grandfather Winslow's brown pillared house at 18 Chestnut Street. In the decades preceding and following the First World War, old Yankee families had upset expectation by regaining this section of the Hill from the vanguards of the lace-curtain Irish. This was bracing news for my parents in that topsy-turvy era when the Republican Party and what were called "people of the right sort" were no longer dominant in city elections. Still, even in the palmy, laissez-faire '20s, Revere Street refused to be a straightforward, immutable residential fact. From one end to the other, houses kept being sanded down, repainted, or abandoned to the flaking of decay. Houses, changing hands, changed their language and nationality. A few doors to our south the householders spoke "Beacon Hill British" or the flat *nay nay* of the Boston Brahmin. The parents of the children a few doors north spoke mostly in Italian.

My mother felt a horrified giddiness about the adventure of our address. She once said, "We are barely perched on the outer rim of the hub of decency." We were less than fifty yards from Louisburg Square, the cynosure of old historic Boston's plain-spoken, cold roast elite—the Hub of the Hub of the Universe. Fifty yards!

As a naval ensign, Father had done postgraduate work at Harvard. He had also done postgraduate work at M.I.T., preferred the purely scientific college, and condescended to both. In 1924, however, his tone began to change; he now began to speak warmly of Harvard as his second alma mater. We went to football games at the Harvard Stadium, and one had the feeling that our lives were now being lived in the brutal, fashionable expectancy of the stadium: we had so many downs, so many minutes, and so many yards to go for a winning touchdown. It was just such a winning financial and social advance that my parents promised themselves would follow Father's resignation from the Navy and his acceptance of a sensible job offered him at the Cambridge branch of Lever Brothers' Soap.

The advance was never to come. Father resigned from the service in 1927, but he never had a civilian *career;* he instead had merely twenty-two years of the civilian *life.* Almost immediately he bought a larger and more stylish house; he sold his ascetic, stove-black Hudson and bought a plump brown Buick; later the Buick was exchanged for a high-toned, as-good-as-new Packard with a custom-designed royal blue and mahogany body. Without drama, his earnings more or less decreased from year to year.

But so long as we were on Revere Street, Father tried to come to terms with it and must have often wondered whether he on the whole liked or disliked the neighborhood's lack of side. He was still at this time rather truculently democratic in what might be described as an upper middle-class, naval, and Masonic fashion. He was a mumbler. His opinions were almost morbidly hesitant, but he considered himself a matter-of-fact man of science and had an unspoiled faith in the superior efficiency of northern nations. He modeled his allegiances and humor on the cockney imperialism of Rudyard Kipling's swearing Tommies, who did their job. Autochthonous Boston snobs, such as the Winslows or members of Mother's reading club, were alarmed by the brassy callousness of our naval visitors, who labeled the Italians they met on Revere Street as "grade-A" and "grade-B wops." The Revere Street "grade-B's" were Sicilian Catholics and peddled crummy second-hand furniture on Cambridge Street, not far from the site of Great-

great-grandfather Charles Lowell's disused West Church, praised in an old family folder as "a haven from the Sodom and Gomorrah of Trinitarian orthodoxy and the tyranny of the letter." Revere Street "grade-A's," good North Italians, sold fancy groceries and Colonial heirlooms in their shops near the Public Garden. Still other Italians were Father's familiars; they sold him bootleg Scotch and *vino rosso* in teacups.

The outside of our Revere Street house was a flat red brick surface unvaried by the slightest suggestion of purple panes, delicate bay, or triangular window-cornice—a sheer wall formed by the seamless conjunction of four inseparable façades, all of the same commercial and purgatorial design. Though placed in the heart of Old Boston, it was ageless and artless, an epitome of those "leveler" qualities Mother found most grueling about the naval service. 91 Revere Street was mass-produced, *regulation-issue,* and yet struck Boston society as stupidly out of the ordinary, like those white elephants—a mother-of-pearl scout knife or a tea-kettle barometer—which my father used to pick up on sale at an Army-Navy store.

The walls of Father's minute Revere Street den-parlor were bare and white. His bookshelves were bare and white. The den's one adornment was a ten-tube home-assembled battery radio set, whose loudspeaker had the shape and color of a Mexican sombrero. The radio's specialty was getting programs from Australia and New Zealand in the early hours of the morning.

My father's favorite piece of den furniture was his oak and "rhinoceros hide" armchair. It was ostentatiously a masculine, or rather a bachelor's, chair. It had a notched, adjustable back; it was black, cracked, hacked, scratched, splintered, gouged, initialed, gunpowder-charred and tumbler-ringed. It looked like pale tobacco leaves laid on dark tobacco leaves. I doubt if Father, a considerate man, was responsible for any of the marring. The chair dated from his plebe days at the Naval Academy, and had been bought from a shady, shadowy, roaring character, midshipman "Beauty" Burford. Father loved each disfigured inch.

My father had been born two months after his own father's death. At each stage of his life, he was to be forlornly fatherless. He was a deep boy brought up entirely by a mild widowed mother and an intense widowed grandmother. When he was fourteen and a half, he became a deep young midshipman. By the time he graduated from Annapolis, he had a high sense of abstract form, which he beclouded with his humor. He had reached, perhaps, his final mental possibilities. He was deep—not with profundity, but with the dumb depth of one who trusted in statistics and was dubious of personal experience. In his forties, Father's soul went underground: as a civilian he kept his high sense of form, his humor, his accuracy, but this accuracy was henceforth unimportant, recreational, *hors de combat.* His debunking grew myopic; his shyness grew evasive; he argued with a fumbling languor. In the twenty-two years Father lived after he resigned from the Navy, he never again deserted Boston and never became Bostonian.

He survived to drift from job to job, to be displaced, to be grimly and literally that old cliché, a fish out of water. He gasped and wheezed with impotent optimism, took on new ideals with each new job, never ingeniously enjoyed his leisure, never even hid his head in the sand.

Mother hated the Navy, hated naval society, naval pay, and the triphammer rote of settling and unsettling a house every other year when Father was transferred to a new station or ship. She had been married nine or ten years and still suspected that her husband was savorless, unmasterful, merely considerate. Unmasterful—Father's specialized efficiency lacked utterly the flattering bossiness she so counted on from her father, my Grandfather Winslow. It was not Father's absence on sea-duty that mattered; it was the eroding necessity of moving *with* him, of keeping in step. When he was far away on the Pacific, she had her friends, her parents, a house to herself—Boston! Fully conscious of her uniqueness and normality she basked in the refreshing stimulation of dreams in which she imagined Father as suitably sublimed. She used to describe such a sublime man to me over tea and English muffins. He was Siegfried carried lifeless through the shining air by Brunnhilde to Valhalla, and accompanied by the throb of my Great Aunt Sarah playing his leitmotif in the released manner taught her by the Abbé Liszt. Or Mother's hero dove through the grottoes of the Rhine and slaughtered the homicidal and vulgar dragon coiled about the golden hoard. Mother seemed almost lightheaded when she retold the romance of Sarah Bernhardt in *L'Aiglon,* the Eaglet, the weakling! She would speak the word *weakling* with such amused vehemence that I formed a grandiose and false image of L'Aiglon's Father, the *big* Napoleon: he was a strong man who scratched under his paunchy little white vest a torso all hair, muscle, and manliness. Instead of the dreams, Mother now had the insipid fatigue of keeping house. Instead of the *Eagle,* she had a twentieth-century naval commander interested in steam, radio, and "the fellows." To avoid naval yards, steam, and "the fellows," Mother had impulsively bought the squalid, impractical Revere Street house. Her marriage daily forced her to squander her subconsciously hoarded energies.

"Weelawaugh, we-ee-eeelawaugh, weelawaugh," shrilled Mother's high voice. *"But-and, but-and, but-and!"* Father's low mumble would drone in answer. Though I couldn't be sure that I had caught the meaning of the words, I followed the sounds as though they were a movie. I felt drenched in my parents' passions.

91 Revere Street was the setting for those arthritic spiritual pains that troubled us for the two years my mother spent in trying to argue my father into resigning from the Navy. When the majestic, hollow boredom of the second year's autumn dwindled to the mean boredom of a second winter, I grew less willing to open my mouth. I bored my parents, they bored me.

"Weelawaugh, we-ee-eelawaugh, weelawaugh!" "But-and, but-and, but-and!"

During the week ends I was at home much of the time. All day I used to look forward to the nights when my bedroom walls would once again vibrate, when I would awake with rapture to the rhythm of my parents arguing, arguing one another to exhaustion. Sometimes, without bathrobe or slippers, I would wriggle out into the cold hall on my belly and ambuscade myself behind the banister. I could often hear actual words. "Yes, yes, yes," Father would mumble. He was "backsliding" and "living in the fool's paradise of habitual retarding and retarded do-nothing inertia." Mother had violently set her heart on the resignation. She was hysterical even in her calm, but like a patient and forbearing strategist, she tried to pretend neutrality. One night she said with murderous coolness, "Bobby and I are leaving for Papá's." This was an ultimatum to force Father to sign a deed placing the Revere Street house in Mother's name.

I writhed with disappointment on the nights when Mother and Father only lowed harmoniously together like cows, as they criticized Helen Bailey or Admiral De Stahl. Once I heard my mother say, "A *man* must make up his *own* mind. Oh Bob, if you are going to resign, do it *now* so I can at least plan for your son's *survival* and education on a single continent."

About this time I was being sent for my *survival* to Dr. Dane, a Quaker chiropractor with an office on Marlborough Street. Dr. Dane wore an old-fashioned light tan druggist's smock; he smelled like a healthy old-fashioned drugstore. His laboratory was free of intimidating technical equipment, and had only the conservative lay roughness and toughness that was so familiar and disarming to us in my Grandfather Winslow's country study or bedroom. Dr. Dane's rosy hands wrenched my shoulders with tremendous éclat and made me feel a hero; I felt unspeakable joy whenever an awry muscle fell back into serenity. My mother, who had no curiosity or imagination for cranky occultism, trusted Dr. Dane's clean, undrugged manliness—so like home. She believed that chiropractic had cured me of my undiagnosed asthma, which had defeated the expensive specialists. . . .

My parents' confidences and quarrels stopped each night at ten or eleven o'clock, when my father would hang up his tuxedo, put on his commander's uniform, and take a trolley back to the naval yard at Charlestown. He had just broken in a new car. Like a chauffeur, he watched this car, a Hudson, with an informed vigilance, always giving its engine hair-trigger little tinkerings of adjustment or friendship, always fearful lest the black body, unbeautiful as his boiled shirts, should lose its outline and gloss. He drove with flawless, almost instrumental, monotony. Mother, nevertheless, was forever encouraging him to walk or take taxis. She would tell him that his legs were growing vestigial from disuse and remind him of the time a jack had slipped and he had broken his leg while shifting a tire. "Alone and at night," she would say, "an amateur driver is unsafe in a car." Father sighed and obeyed—only, putting on a martyred and penny-saving face, he would keep his self-respect by taking the trolley rather than a taxi. Each night he shifted back into his uniform, but his departures from Revere Street were so furtive that several months passed before I realized what was happening—we had *two* houses! Our second house was the residence in the Naval Yard assigned to the third in command. It was large, had its own flagpole, and screen porches on three levels—yet it was something to be ashamed of. Whatever pomp or distinction its possession might have had for us was destroyed by an eccentric humiliation inflicted on Father by his superior, Admiral De Stahl, the commandant at Charlestown. De Stahl had not been consulted about our buying the 91 Revere Street house. He was outraged, stormed about "flaunting private fortunes in the face of naval tradition," and ordered my father to sleep on bounds at the Yard in the house provided for that purpose.

On our first Revere Street Christmas Eve, the telephone rang in the middle of dinner; it was Admiral De Stahl demanding Father's instant return to the Navy Yard. Soon Father was back in his uniform. In taking leave of my mother and grandparents he was, as was usual with him under pressure, a little evasive and magniloquent. "A woman works from sun to sun," he said, "but a sailor's watch is never done." He compared a naval officer's hours with a doctor's, hinted at surprise maneuvers, and explained away the uncommunicative arrogance of Admiral De Stahl: "The Old Man has to be hush-hush." Later that night, I lay in bed and tried to imagine that my father was leading his engineering force on a surprise maneuver through arctic wastes. A forlorn hope! "Hush-hush, hush-hush," whispered the snowflakes as big as street lamps as they broke on Father—broke and buried. Outside, I heard real people singing carols, shuffling snow off their shoes, opening and shutting doors. I worried at the meaning of a sentence I had heard quoted from the *Boston Evening Transcript:* "On this Christmas Eve, as usual, the whole of Beacon Hill can be expected to become a single old-fashioned open house—the names of mine host the Hill, and her guests will read like the contents of the Social Register." I imagined Beacon Hill changed to the snow queen's palace, as vast as the north pole. My father pressed a cold finger to his lip: "hush-hush," and led his surprise squad of sailors around an altar, but the altar was a tremendous cash register, whose roughened nickel surface was cheaply decorated with trowels, pyramids, and Arabic swirls. A great drawer helplessly chopped back and forth, unable to shut because choked with greenbacks. "Hush-hush!" My father's engineers wound about me with their eye-patches, orange sashes, and curtain-ring earrings, like the Gilbert and Sullivan pirates' chorus. . . . Outside on the streets of Beacon Hill, it was night, it was dismal, it was raining. Something disturbing had befallen the familiar and honorable Salvation Army band; its big drum and accordion were now accompanied by drunken voices howling: *The Old Gray Mare, she ain't what she used to be, when Mary went to milk the cow.* A sound of a bosun's whistle. Women laughing. Someone repeatedly rang our doorbell. I heard my mother talking on the telephone. "Your inebriated sailors have littered my doorstep with the dregs of Scollay Square." There was a gloating panic in her voice that showed she enjoyed the drama of talking to Admiral De Stahl. "Sir," she shrilled, "you have compelled my husband to leave me alone and defenseless on Christmas Eve!" She ran into my bedroom. She hugged me. She said, "Oh Bobby, it's such a comfort to have a man in the house." "I am not a man," I said, "I am a boy." . . .

New England winters are long. Sunday mornings are long. Ours were often made tedious by preparations for dinner guests. Mother would start airing at nine. Whenever the air grew so cold that it hurt, she closed the den windows; then we were attacked by sour kitchen odors winding up a clumsily rebuilt dumb-waiter shaft. The windows were again thrown open. We sat in an atmosphere of glacial purity and sacrifice. Our breath puffed whitely. Father and I wore sleeveless cashmere jerseys Mother had bought at Filene's Basement. A do-it-yourself book containing diagrams for the correct carving of roasts lay on the arm of Father's chair. At hand were Big Bill Tilden on tennis, Capablanca on chess, newspaper clippings from Sidney Lenz's bridge column, and a magnificent tome with photographs and some American's nationalist sketch of Sir Thomas Lipton's errors in the Cup Defender races. Father made little progress in these diversions, and yet one of the authors assured him that mastery demanded only willing readers who understood the meaning of English words. Throughout the winter a gray-whiteness glared through the single den window. In the apoplectic brick alley, a fire escape stood out against our sooty plank fence. Father believed that churchgoing was undignified for a naval man; his Sunday mornings were given to useful acts such as lettering his three new galvanized garbage cans: R. T. S. LOWELL—U.S.N.

Our Sunday dinner guests were often naval officers. Naval officers were not Mother's sort; very few people *were* her sort in those days, and that was her trouble—a very authentic, human, and plausible difficulty, which made Mother's life one of much suffering. She did not have the self-assurance for wide human experience; she needed to feel liked, admired, surrounded by the approved and familiar. Her haughtiness and chilliness came from apprehension. She would start talking like a *grande dame* and then stand back rigid and faltering, as if she feared being crushed by her own massively intimidating offensive.

Father's old Annapolis roommate, Commander Billy "Battleship Bilge" Harkness, was a frequent guest at Revere Street and one that always threw Mother off balance. Billy was a rough diamond. He made jokes about his "all-American family tree," and insisted that his name, pronounced H*ark*ness, should be spelled H*erk*ness. He came from Louisville, Kentucky, drank whisky to "renew his Bourbon blood," and still spoke with an accent that sounded—so his colleagues said—"like a bran-fed stallion." Like my father, however, Commander Billy had entered the Naval Academy when he was a boy of fourteen; his Southernisms had been thoroughly rubbed away. He was teased for knowing nothing about race horses, mountaineers, folk ballads, hams, sour mash, tobacco . . . Kentucky Colonels. Though hardly an officer and a gentleman in the old Virginian style, he was an unusual combination of clashing virtues: he had led his class in the sciences and yet was what his superiors called "a *mathmaddition* with the habit of command." He and my father, the youngest men in their class, had often been shipmates. Bilge's executive genius had given color and direction to Father's submissive tenacity. He drank like a fish at parties, but was a total abstainer on duty. With reason Commander Harkness had been voted the man most likely to make a four-star admiral in the class of '07.

Billy called his wife *Jimmy* or *Jeems,* and had a rough friendly way of saying, "Oh, Jimmy's bright as a penny." Mrs. Harkness was an unpleasant rarity: she was the only naval officer's wife we knew who was also a college graduate. She had a flat flapper's figure, and hid her intelligence behind a nervous twitter of vulgarity and toadyism. "Charlotte," she would almost scream at Mother, "is this mirAGE, this MIRacle your *own* dining room!"

Then Mother might smile and answer in a distant, though cosy and amused, voice, "I usually manage to make myself pretty comfortable."

Mother's comfort was chic, romantic, impulsive. If her silver service shone, it shone with hectic perfection to rebuke the functional domesticity of naval wives. She had determined to make her *ambiance* beautiful and luxurious, but wanted neither her beauty nor her luxury unaccompanied. Beauty pursued too exclusively meant artistic fatuity of a kind made farcical by her Aunt Sarah Stark Winslow, a beauty too lofty and original ever to marry, a prima donna on the piano, too high-strung ever to give a public recital. Beauty alone meant the maudlin ignominy of having one's investments managed by interfering relatives. Luxury alone, on the other hand, meant for Mother the "paste and fool's-gold polish" that one met with in the foyer of the new Statler Hotel. She loathed the "undernourishment" of Professor Burckhard's Bauhaus modernism, yet in moments of pique she denounced our pompous Myers mahoganies as "suitable for politicians at the Bellevue Hotel." She kept a middle-of-the-road position, and much admired Italian pottery with its fresh peasant colors and puritanical, clean-cut lines. She was fond of saying, "The French *do* have taste," but spoke with a double-edged irony which implied the French, with no moral standards to support their finish, were really no better than naval yahoos. Mother's beautiful house was dignified by a rich veneer of the useful.

"I have always believed carving to be *the* gentlemanly talent," mother used to proclaim. Father, faced with this opinion, pored over his book of instructions or read the section on table carving in the Encyclopaedia Britannica. Eventually he discovered among the innumerable small, specialized Boston "colleges" an establishment known as a carving school. Each Sunday from then on he would sit silent and erudite before his roast. He blinked, grew white, looked winded, and wiped beads of perspiration from his eyebrows. His purpose was to reproduce stroke by stroke his last carving lesson, and he worked with all the formal rightness and particular error of some shaky experiment in remote control. He enjoyed quiet witticisms at the expense of his carving master—"a philosopher who gave himself all the airs of a Mahan!" He liked to pretend that the carving master had stated that "No two cuts are identical," *ergo:* "each offers original problems for the *executioner.*" Guests were appeased by Father's saying, "I am just a plebe at this guillotine. Have a hunk of my roast beef hash."

What angered Father was Mrs. Harkness's voice grown merciless with excitement, as she studied his hewing and hacking. She was sure to say something tactless about how Commander Billy was "a stingy artist at carving who could shave General Washington off the dollar bill."

Nothing could stop Commander Billy, that born carver, from reciting verses:

> *"By carving my way*
> *I lived on my pay;*
> *This reeward, though small,*
> *Beats none at all . . .*
>
> *My carving paper-thin*
> *Can make a guinea hin,*
> *All giblets, bones, and skin,*
> *Canteen a party of tin."*

And I, furious for no immediate reason, blurted out, "Mother, how much does Grandfather Winslow have to fork up to pay for Daddy's carving school?"

These Sunday dinners with the Harknesses were always woundingly boisterous affairs. Father, unnaturally outgoing, would lead me forward and say, "Bilge, I want you to meet my first coupon from the bond of matrimony."

Commander Billy would answer, "So this is the range-finder you are raising for future wars!" They would make me salute, stand at attention, stand at ease. "Angel-face," Billy would say to me, "you'll skipper a flivver."

"Jimmy" Harkness, of course, knew that Father was anxiously negotiating with Lever Brothers' Soap, and arranging for his resignation from the service, but nothing could prevent her from proposing time and again her "hens' toast to the drakes." Dragging Mother to her feet, Jimmy would scream, "To Bob and Bilgy's next battleship together!"

What Father and Commander Billy enjoyed talking about most was their class of '07. After dinner, the ladies would retire to the upstairs sitting room. As a special privilege I was allowed to remain at the table with the men. Over and over, they would talk about their ensigns' cruise around the world, escaping the "reeport," gunboating on the upper Yangtse during the Chinese Civil War, keeping sane and sanitary at Guantanamo, patroling the Golfo del Papayo during the two-bit Nicaraguan Revolution, when water to wash in cost a dollar a barrel and was mostly "alkali and wrigglers." There were the class casualties: Holden and Holcomb drowned in a foundered launch off Hampton Roads; "Count" Bowditch, killed by the Moros and famous for his dying words to Commander Harkness: "I'm all right. Get on the job, Bilge."

Reveries over Childhood

W. B. Yeats

> William Butler Yeats (1865–1939) is universally regarded as one of the very great poets of the twentieth century. Of his prose works, one of the most interesting is the collection called *Autobiographies*. We print below a short portion of Yeats's account of his childhood memories of his grandfather and grandmother in Ireland. The section of *Autobiographies* from which it is taken, *Reveries*, was first published in 1916.

One day some one spoke to me of the voice of conscience, and as I brooded over the phrase I came to think that my soul, because I did not hear an articulate voice, was lost. I had some wretched days until being alone with one of my aunts I heard a whisper in my ear, "What a tease you are!" At first I thought my aunt must have spoken, but when I found she had not, I concluded it was the voice of my conscience and was happy again. From that day the voice has come to me at moments of crisis, but now it is a voice in my head that is sudden and startling. It does not tell me what to do, but often reproves me. It will say perhaps, "That is unjust" of some thought; and once when I complained that a prayer had not been heard, it said, "You have been helped." I had a little flagstaff in front of the house and a red flag with the Union Jack in the corner. Every night I pulled my flag down and folded it up and laid it on a shelf in my bedroom, and one morning before breakfast I found it, though I knew I had folded it up the night before, knotted round the bottom of the flagstaff so that it was touching the grass. I must have heard the servants talking of the faeries, for I concluded at once that a faery had tied those four knots and from then on believed that one had whispered in my ear. I have been told, though I do not remember it myself, that I saw, whether once or many times I do not know, a supernatural bird in the corner of the room. Once too I was driving with my grandmother a little after dark close to the Channel that runs for some five miles from Sligo to the sea, and my grandmother showed me the red light of an outward-bound steamer and told me that my grandfather was on board, and that night in my sleep I screamed out and described the steamer's wreck. The next morning my grandfather arrived on a blind horse found for him by grateful passengers. He had, as I remember the story, been asleep when the Captain aroused him to say they were going on the rocks. He said, "Have you tried sail on her?" and judging from some answer that the captain was demoralised, took over the command and, when the ship could not be saved, got the crew and passengers into the boats. His own boat was upset and he saved himself and some others by swimming; some women had drifted ashore, buoyed up by their crinolines. "I was not so much afraid of the sea as of that terrible man with his oar," was the comment of a schoolmaster who was among the survivors. Eight men were, however, drowned and my grandfather suffered from that memory at intervals all his life, and if asked to read family prayers never read anything but the shipwreck of St. Paul.

I remember the dogs more clearly than any one except my grandfather and grandmother. The black hairy one had no tail because it had been sliced off, if I was told the truth, by a railway train. I think I followed at their heels more than they did at mine, and that their journeys ended at a rabbit-warren behind the garden; and sometimes they had savage fights, the black hairy dog, being well protected by its hair, suffering least. I can remember one so savage that the white dog would not take his teeth out of the black dog's hair till the coachman hung them over the side of a water-butt, one outside and one in the water. My grandmother once told the coachman to cut the hair like a lion's hair and, after a long consultation with the stable-boy, he cut it all over the head and shoulders and left it on the lower part of the body. The dog disappeared for a few days, and I did not doubt that its heart was broken.

There was a large garden behind the house, full of apple trees, with flower-beds and grass-plots in the centre, and two figureheads of ships, one among the strawberry plants under a wall covered with fruit trees and one among the flowers. The one among the flowers was a white lady in flowing robes, while the other, a stalwart man in uniform, had been taken from a three-masted ship of my grandfather's called the *Russia,* and there was a belief among the servants that the stalwart man represented the Tsar and had been presented by the Tsar himself. The avenue, or as they say in England the drive, that went from the hall door through a clump of big trees to an insignificant gate and a road bordered by broken and dirty cottages, was but two or three hundred yards, and I often thought it should have been made to wind more, for I judged people's social importance mainly by the length of their avenues. This idea may have come from the stable-boy, for he was my principal friend. He had a book of Orange rhymes, and the days when we read them together in the hay-loft gave me the pleasure of rhyme for the first time. Later on I can remember being told, when there was a rumour of a Fenian rising, that rifles had been served out to the Orangemen; and presently, when I had begun to dream of my future life, I thought I would like to die fighting like the Fenians. I was to build a very fast and beautiful ship and to have under my command a company of young men who were always to be in training like athletes and so become as brave and handsome as the young men in the story-books, and there was to be a big battle on the sea-shore near Rosses and I was to be killed. I collected little bits of wood and piled them in the corner of the yard, and there was an old rotten log in a distant field I often went to look at because I thought it would go a long way in the making of the ship. All my dreams were of ships; and one day a sea-captain who had come to dine with my grandfather put a hand on each side of my head and lifted me up to show me Africa, and another day a sea-captain pointed to the smoke from the pern mill on the quays rising up beyond the trees of the lawn, as though it came from a mountain, and asked me if Ben Bulben was a burning mountain.

Once every few months I used to go to Rosses Point or Ballisodare to see another little boy, who had a piebald pony that had once been in a circus and sometimes forgot where it was and went round and round. He was George Middleton, son of my great-uncle William Middleton. Old Middleton had bought land, then believed a safe investment, at Ballisodare and at Rosses, and spent the winter at Ballisodare and the summer at Rosses. The Middleton and Pollexfen flour mills were at Ballisodare, and a great salmon weir, rapids and a waterfall, but it was more often at Rosses that I saw my cousin. We rowed in the river-mouth or were taken sailing in a heavy slow schooner yacht or in a big ship's boat that had been rigged and decked. There were great cellars under the house, for it had been a smuggler's house a hundred years before, and sometimes three loud raps would come upon the drawing-room window at sun-down, setting all the dogs barking: some dead smuggler giving his accustomed signal. One night I heard them very distinctly and my cousins often heard them, and later on my sister. A pilot had told me that, after dreaming three times of a treasure buried in my uncle's garden, he had climbed the wall in the middle of the night and begun to dig but grew disheartened "because there was so much earth." I told somebody what he had said and was told that it was well he did not find it, for it was guarded by a spirit that looked like a flat iron. At Ballisodare there was a cleft among the rocks that I passed with terror because I believed that a murderous monster lived there that made a buzzing sound like a bee.

It was through the Middletons perhaps that I got my interest in country stories, and certainly the first faery stories that I heard were in the cottages about their houses. The Middletons took the nearest for friends and were always in and out of the cottages of pilots and of tenants. They were practical, always doing something with their hands, making boats, feeding chickens, and without ambition. One of them had designed a steamer many years before my birth and, long after I had grown to manhood, one could hear it—it had some sort of obsolete engine—many miles off wheezing in the Channel like an asthmatic person. It had been built on the lake and dragged through the town by many horses, stopping before the windows where my mother was learning her lessons, and plunging the whole school into candle-light for five days, and was still patched and repatched mainly because it was believed to be a bringer of good luck. It had been called after the betrothed of its builder *Janet,* long corrupted into the more familiar *Jennet,* and the betrothed died in my youth, having passed her eightieth year and been her husband's plague because of the violence of her temper. Another Middleton who was but a year or two older than myself used to shock me by running after hens to know by their feel if they were on the point of dropping an egg. They let their houses decay and the glass fall from the windows of their greenhouses, but one among them at any rate had the second sight. They were liked but had not the pride and reserve, the sense of decorum and order, the instinctive playing before themselves that belongs to those who strike the popular imagination.

Sometimes my grandmother would bring me to see some old Sligo gentlewoman whose garden ran down to the river, ending there in a low wall full of wallflowers, and I would sit up upon my chair, very bored, while my elders ate their seed-cake and drank their sherry. My walks with the servants were more interesting; sometimes we would pass a little fat girl and a servant persuaded me to write her a love-letter, and the next time she passed she put her tongue out. But it was the servants' stories that interested me. At such and such a corner a man had got a shilling from a drill sergeant by standing in a barrel and had then rolled out of it and shown his crippled legs. And in such and such a house an old woman had hid herself under the bed of her guests, an officer and his wife, and on hearing them abuse her beaten them with a broomstick. All the well-known families had their grotesque or tragic or romantic legends, and I often said to myself how terrible it would be to go away and die where nobody would know my story. Years afterwards, when I was ten or twelve years old and in London, I would remember Sligo with tears, and when I began to write, it was there I hoped to find my audience. Next to Merville where I lived, was another tree-surrounded house where I sometimes went to see a little boy who stayed there occasionally with his grandmother, whose name I forget and who seemed to me kind and friendly, though when I went to see her in my thirteenth or fourteenth year I discovered that she only cared for very little boys. When the visitors called I hid in the hay-loft and lay hidden behind the great heap of hay while a servant was calling my name in the yard.

I do not know how old I was (for all these events seem at the same distance) when I was made drunk. I had been out yachting with an uncle and my cousins and it had come on very rough. I had lain on deck between the mast and the bowsprit and a wave had burst over me and I had seen green water over my head. I was very proud and very wet. When we got into Rosses again, I was dressed up in an older boy's clothes so that the trousers came down below my boots and a pilot gave me a little raw whiskey. I drove home on an outside car and was so pleased with the strange state in which I found myself that for all my uncle could do, I cried to every passer-by that I was drunk, and went on crying it through the town and everywhere until I was put to bed by my grandmother and given something to drink that tasted of black currants and so fell asleep.

INDEXES

Author-Title Index

Baker, John R., "Missing Links," from *Science in a Changing World,* 459–60, 505

Baker, Russell, "The Miniature Adults," 483, 505, and Readings, 769–70

Baldwin, James, *The Fire Next Time,* 286, 291, 296, 318, 345, 465, 616, and Readings, 858–67

Bates, Arlo, "Reading on the Run," from *Talks on the Study of Literature,* 459

Beach, Joseph Warren, rewriting of paragraph by John Dewey, from *Outlook for American Prose,* 427–28, 497

Becker, Carl, "The Marxian Philosophy of History," 404

Bedford, Sybille, *The Sudden View,* 300–01

Beerbohm, Max, on Algernon Swinburne, 379–80, altered 380; "Decline of the Graces, The," 480–81, and Readings, 759–64; *Yet Again,* 358

"Bee's Knees, The," Charles D. Stewart, 459

Belloc, Hilaire, *Economics for Young People,* 117–19; "The Mowing of a Field," from *Hills and the Sea,* 279–80

Bellow, Saul, "Skepticism and the Depth of Life," 480

Benét, Stephen Vincent, *The Devil and Daniel Webster,* 462

Bettelheim, Bruno, "The Anatomy of Academic Discontent," 29, 68, 236, 393, 470, and Readings, 734–45

Between the Thunder and the Sun, Vincent Sheean, 327–28, 343, 345, 346, 350, 367

Bishop, John Peale, "Homage to Hemingway," 371, and Readings, 786–94

Bismarck, Otto von, on experience, 212

"Black and White," from *Back Home,* Irvin S. Cobb, 452

"Black America's African Heritage," Jack Shepherd, 28

"Black-White: Can We Bridge the Gap?" Patricia Coffin, 27–28

Bleak House, Charles Dickens, 249, 287–88, 291–92, 360

Bouvet, Marguerite, *A Little House in Pimlico,* 485–86

Bronowski, Jacob, "The Reach of Imagination," 3 *note,* 23, 25, 73, 129, 186, 465, and Readings, 637–44

Brown, Claude, *Manchild in the Promised Land,* 339–40

Browne, Sir Thomas, *Religio Medici,* 493

Brustein, Robert, "America's New Culture Hero," from *The Third Theatre,* 78, 139–41

Buchwald, Art, on grounding airline hostesses, 478; "Love in Paris and Red Tape Too," 484, and Readings, 766–68; "Prof 'Understanding' Right Up to the End," 505, and Readings, 765–66; "Son Off to Campus Wars; Parents Sob," 470–71

"'Bugs' Baer Says," 450–51, 462

Bunyan, John, *Pilgrim's Progress,* 377

Burke, Edmund, "On Conciliation with America," 382

Burke, Kenneth, *A Grammar of Motives,* 240

Burns, Robert, excerpt, 113

Burns, Walter Noble, *The Saga of Billy the Kid,* 81–82, 360

"Burnt Norton," T. S. Eliot, 253

Burroughs, John, *Leaf and Tendril,* 290–91, 367

Butler, Samuel, "Hudibras," 453

C

Caesar and Cleopatra, George Bernard Shaw, 306

Cape Cod, Henry David Thoreau, 303

Carter, George F., "The American Civilization Puzzle," 29, 145, 461, and Readings, 814–26

Catton, Bruce, *This Hallowed Ground,* 351, and Readings, 810–14

"Causation of Ice Ages," David B. Ericson and Goesta Wollin, 20

"Causes of the Texas Revolution," student theme, 159

Chase, Mary Ellen, *The White Gate,* 438

Chesterton, G. K., *Heretics,* 382–83; "On the Wit of Whistler," from *Heretics,* 358, altered 364

Churchill, Winston, address to House of Commons, 247, 252–53

Clark, Blake, "America's Greatest Earthquake," 502–03

Clark, John B., *The Philosophy of Wealth,* 116–17

Clemens, Samuel L., *The Adventures of Huckleberry Finn,* 302; *Life on the*

"Getting Engaged," student theme, 283–85, 332, 488

"Gettysburg Address," Abraham Lincoln, 257–58

Gibbon, Edward, excerpt, 393

Gimpel, René, "Pierre Auguste Renoir," 351, and Readings, 841–45

"Gold-Bug, The," Edgar Allan Poe, 43

Golden Bowl, The, Henry James, 311–12

Grammar of Motives, A, Kenneth Burke, 240

Graves, Robert, "It Was a Stable World," 29, 370, 416, 505, and Readings, 803–10; *Reader Over My Shoulder,* 443

Graves, Robert, and Laura Riding, "Sandburg's 'The Cool Tombs,'" 484, and Readings, 782–83

Gray, George W., "Little Drops of Water," 479

"Great Man, A," student theme, 88–89

"Great Society Is a Sick Society, The," J. W. Fulbright, 45

Guermantes Way, The, Marcel Proust, 309–10, 602

Gulliver's Travels, Jonathan Swift, 89, 397

H

"Haircut," Ring Lardner, 346

Haldane, J. B. S., "On Being the Right Size," from *Possible Worlds,* 447

Hamlet, William Shakespeare, 71

Hamlet, The, William Faulkner, 295–96

Han Suyin, *The Crippled Tree,* 495

"Happy Warrior, The," John Dos Passos, 500

Hardy, Thomas, *The Dynasts,* 309; "The Withered Arm," 294, 362

Harper's Magazine, 433

Harte, Bret, "The Luck of Roaring Camp," 462; "The Outcasts of Poker Flat," 484

Hawkes, Jacquetta, *Man on Earth,* 59

Hawthorne, Nathaniel, *The Marble Faun,* 309

Hemingway, Ernest, *A Farewell to Arms,* 346, 386; *For Whom the Bell Tolls,* 301–02; "My Old Man," from *Three Stories and Ten Poems,* 612

Henry IV, Part II, William Shakespeare, 613

Henry, O., "The Furnished Room," from *Strictly Business,* 463

Heretics, G. K. Chesterton, 382–83

Hero in America, The, Dixon Wecter, 59

Hero in History, The, Sidney Hook, 10, altered 35

"Herring, The," T. H. Huxley, 79–80, 360

Hichens, Robert, *The Garden of Allah,* 505–06

Hidden Persuaders, The, Vance Packard, 248–49, 254–55

"Hipsters Unleashed," David McReynolds, 29, 126, 127, 470, and Readings, 728–34

History of England, G. M. Trevelyan, 359–60

Hoffer, Eric, *The Temper of Our Time,* 42, 175; *The True Believer,* 425–26, altered 426, 428

Hogben, Lancelot, *Mathematics for the Million,* 432–33

Holmes, Oliver Wendell, *Abrams versus United States,* 213–14; on truth, 15; *Town versus Eisner,* 397 and *note*

"Homage to Hemingway," John Peale Bishop, 371, and Readings, 786–94

Hook, Sidney, *Academic Freedom and Academic Anarchy,* 122–25, 129; *The Hero in History,* 10, altered 35

"How Beautiful with Shoes," Wilbur Daniel Steele, 294

"How I Write," Eudora Welty, 458

"How to Detect Propaganda," Institute for Propaganda Analysis, 198, 225, and Readings, 686–91

"How to Get That Good 'Media Image,'" 266–67

"Hudibras," Samuel Butler, 453

Hughes, Richard, *The Fox in the Attic,* 60

Human Nature and Conduct, John Dewey, 427, altered 427–28, 497

Huxley, Aldous, on advertising, 265; editor of D. H. Lawrence's *Letters,* 307 and *note;* "Propaganda in a Democratic Society," from *Brave New World Revisited,* 268 and *note;* "Wordsworth in the Tropics," from *Do What You Will,* 24–25

Huxley, Sir Julian, on Konrad Lorenz, 467; on religion, 128

Huxley, T. H., "The Herring," 79–80,

Phillips, M. Ogden and J. Russell Smith, *North America*, 275–76

Philosophy of Wealth, The, John B. Clark, 116–17

Pictures from an Institution, Randall Jarrell, 455

Pierce, Charles S., excerpt, 393

"Pierre Auguste Renoir," René Gimpel, 351, and Readings, 841–45

Pilgrim's Progress, John Bunyan, 377

Plato, 264

Platt, Rutherford, *A Pocket Guide to the Trees,* 134

Pocket Guide to the Trees, A, Rutherford Platt, 134

Podhoretz, Norman, "The Know-Nothing Bohemians," 127; "Making It: The Brutal Bargain," 23, 39, 318, 332, 616, and Readings, 847–58

Poe, Edgar Allan, "The Fall of the House of Usher," 346; "The Gold-Bug," 43

Poetics of Music, Igor Stravinsky, 383

"Point of No Return, The," George McGovern, 258–64

"Politics of the Non-political," Stephen Spender, 129, 189, 470, and Readings, 722–27

Porter, Katherine Anne, excerpt, 393; *The Days Before,* 481; "Flowering Judas," 294–95; "The Jilting of Granny Weatherall," 464

Portrait of a Lady, The, Henry James, 603

Portrait of the Artist as a Young Man, A, James Joyce, 464

Price, Reynolds, *Love and Work,* 462–63, 463–64

Priestly, J. B., *Midnight on the Desert,* 359

Problem of Heart Disease, The, Louis I. Dublin, 135

Problems of Philosophy, The, Bertrand Russell, 151–52

"Prof 'Understanding' Right Up to the End," Art Buchwald, 505, and Readings, 765–66

"Propaganda in a Democratic Society," from *Brave New World Revisited,* Aldous Huxley, 268 and *note*

Propaganda: The Formation of Men's Attitudes, Jacques Elluel, 268

Prose Style of Samuel Johnson, The, W. K. Wimsatt, Jr., 388 and *note*

Proust, Marcel, *The Guermantes Way,* 309–10, 602

Psalms 1:3–4, 463

Q

Queen Victoria, Lytton Strachey, 390

"Quiz Kids Denounce 'Bloated Plutocrats,'" Howard Jacobs, 422–23

R

Randolph, John, on aristocracy, 212; on Edward Livingston, 250

"Reach of Imagination, The," Jacob Bronowski, 3 *note*, 23, 25, 73, 129, 186, 465, and Readings, 637–44

Reader Over My Shoulder, Robert Graves, 443

"Reading on the Run," from *Talks on the Study of Literature,* Arlo Bates, 459

"Red-bloods and Mollycoddles," from *Appearances,* G. Lowes Dickinson, 76–78, 361

Religio Medici, Sir Thomas Browne, 493

Religion: Matthew Arnold on, 128; Sir James Frazer on, 128; Sir Julian Huxley on, 128; Saint James on, 128; Karl Marx on, 128; Paul Tillich on, 128; E. B. Tylor on, 128

Reporter, The, 424

"Reveries over Childhood," W. B. Yeats, Readings, 876–80

Rhetoric, Aristotle, 240, 241–42

Riding, Laura, and Robert Graves, "Sandburg's 'The Cool Tombs,'" 484, and Readings, 782–83

Right & Wrong, Paul Weiss and Jonathan Weiss, 174

Robber Bridegroom, The, Eudora Welty, 9

Robinson Crusoe, Daniel Defoe, 310, 326, 346, 401

Romeo and Juliet, William Shakespeare, 324, 325, 338

"Roosevelt: An Autopsy," H. L. Mencken, 500–01

"Rose for Emily, A," William Faulkner, 293, 401

Roswell *Dispatch,* 378

Ruesch, Hans, *Top of the World,* 83–86

Ruskin, John, *The Stones of Venice,* 299, 400

Subject Index

Authority: opinion of, as evidence, 195–98

B

Begging the question: 221–22
Beginning: of a narrative, 323–24; problem of making a, 11–30; *see also* Discourse, Introduction
Bibliography: and footnote, the form of, 524–29; research paper, 511–16, 524, 528–29, 547; specimen index cards in a, 516, 517
Book report: 596–98

C

Caricature: 291–92
Causal analysis: 146–60, 591–95
Cause: 146–47; circumstances controlling, 152–54; complex, 155; conditions controlling, 147–49; reasoning about, 149–50; rules of connection and, 147–50; *see also* Causal analysis, Event
Characteristics: in classification, 91; in definition, 108–10
Characterization: as a problem in narration, 613–16
Clarity: and rhythm, as aspects of style, 491–97
Class: and area of interest in exposition, 71–72; deductive reasoning by, 206–18; diagrammatically illustrated, 72; for illustration, 79–83; *see also* Classification, Reasoning
Classification: and analysis and structure, 130–31; characteristics as determinants of, 91; cross-ranking in, 93–94; in definition, 104; exhaustive, 97–100; as a method of exposition, 90–100; schematized examples of, 91–94; systems, simple and complex, 92–93; uses of, in exposition, 94–100; *see also* Class, Genus, Reasoning, Species
Clichés: 420
Coherence: cautions for use of controls in, 43–44; distinguished from unity, 35; logical order in, 36–39; space order in, 41–42; time order in, 39–40; and unity, in paragraph, 363–65
Common ground: in argument, 167–70
Communication: importance of language in, 3–4; importance of tone in, 479–84
Comparison and contrast: interest a fac-

tor in significant, 71–72; metaphorical, 453–54; as a method of exposition, 69–79; ways of organizing material for, 73–79, 361
Complication: as middle of narrative, 324–25, 328, 330–31
Composition: organizing principles in, 31–51
Conclusion: 16, 29–30; of a narrative, 325; in reasoning, 206, 210; in syllogism, 361; two things to avoid in, 30
Concrete words: 398–99, 402–04
Conflict: in argument, 161–62
Connotation: and denotation, 396–97, 415
Context: paragraph function determined by, 371
Contrast: *see* Comparison and contrast
Coordination and subordination: 385
Cross-ranking: in classification, 93–94

D

Dangling modifiers: 380
Data: 163 *note;* 168 *note*
Deduction: and extended argument, 228–37; and reasoning by classes, 206–18; *see also* Argument, Induction, Reasoning
Definition: circular, caution against, 114; classifying process in, 104–08; and common ground, 111–13; as dictionary meaning, 100 and *note,* 406–10; as an equation of convertible terms, 101–03; extended, 115–29; and generalization, 109–10; and metaphorical language, 113–14; as a method of exposition, 100–30; necessary and sufficient characteristics of, 108–09; structure of, 104–07; supportive characteristics of, 109–10; *see also* Identification
Demand: the immediate practical and beyond, 5
Denotation: and connotation, 396–97, 415
Denouement: as narrative end, 325, 328, 331
Description: 275–312; choice of words in, 293–96; dominant impression as, 286–88; of feelings and states of mind, 601–16; figurative language in, 604–06; generalized, 134; impressionistic style in, 300–01; intention of, 57; and interpretation, 134; as a kind of dis-

Description (cont.)
course, 57; motivation for use of, 278; and other kinds of discourse, 282–86; perception in, 281; suggestive, 132–33, 276, 277; suggestive, and the senses, 279–81; technical (or expository) and analysis, 132–36, 275–76, 277; texture and pattern in, 296–305
Dialogue: a problem in narration, 609–13
Diction: 396–434; abstract and concrete, 398–99, 402–04; as clichés, 420; as creator of tone, 467; dictionary explanations of, 406–09; general and specific, 398–99, 402–04; informal (colloquial) and formal, 410–14; as jargon, 423–31, 493; as slang, 397–98, 411, 421–23; as stereotypes, 421–23; and style, 497–98; see also Language, Words
Dictionary: a record of meanings, 100 and note, 107, 406–10; sample derivations in a typical, 406, 407, 409
Difference: methods of, and of agreement, in causal analysis, 591–95
Differentia (ae): in refining the defining process, 105, 107, 108, 114, 116, 117
Discourse: argument as a kind of, 57, 161–237; description as a kind of, 57, 275–312; as determined by intention, 57; exposition as a kind of, 56–57, 61–160; form and function of, 55; four kinds of, 56–58; main divisions of, 16–30; narration as a kind of, 57, 313–51; research paper as a form of, 509; special problems of, 353–506
Discussion: 16, 29; occasion of the, 178–79
Dominant impression: 286–88
Doubt: in argument, 161–62

E

Either-or reasoning: 218–19; fallacy of, 222–24
Elaboration: in extended definition, 122
Emotions: in persuasion, 246–55; and reason, 164
Emphasis: devices for achieving, 44–46; faulty devices of, 46; by flat statement, 45; as an organizing principle, 44–51; in paragraph, 365–67; by paragraph isolation, 46; by position, 45; by proportion, 45; see also Definition, Description, Exposition, Organization

Equivocation: 221
Etymology: samples of, from dictionary: 406, 407, 409
Euphemisms: 417
Event: and cause, rules of connection between, 147–50; movement of, in time, 320–21; natural and narrative orders of, 321; relevance and selection of, in narration, 344–45; summary and full rendering of, 607–09; see also Action, Time
Evidence: 163 note, 168 note; in argument, 193–99; fact as, 193–95; opinion as, 195–98
Expletive construction: 374–75
Exposition: 61–160; by analysis, 130–59; by classification, 90–100; by comparison and contrast, 69–79; by definition, 100–30; focus of interest in, 62–63; general and abstract words in, 403; by identification, 69; by illustration, 79–90; as a kind of discourse, 56–57; and logic, in argument, 164–65; methods of, 61–160; in narration, 324, 329–30; question and proposition in, 63; research paper as a form of, 509; thinking by classes, 71 note
Expository narration: 142–43
Extended definition: 115–29; elaboration in, 122–26; frame for, 116–19; variety in, 126–29

F

Fact: analysis and propositions of, 188–89; as evidence, 193–95; propositions of action or of, 176–77; see also Cause, Event
Fallacies: 211 note, 221–28; in persuasion, 255; in reasoning about cause, 149–50; and refutation, 225
False enthusiasm: 489
Feeling: atmosphere and, in description, 289–90; and language, thinking and rhetoric, 3–10; order of, 36
Feelings and states of mind: description of, 601–06
Fiction: as one type of narration, 313 note
Figurative language: 604–06
Final version: writing and rewriting the, 530–88
Flat statement: emphasis by, 45
Footnotes: and bibliography, form of, 524–28

Form: and function, in composition, 55
Frame formula: in definition, 116–19
Frame image: in description, 302–03

G

General words: 398–99, 402–04
Generalization: and definition, 109–10; in induction, 199–202; and uniformity, 151–52
Generalized description: 134
Generalized narration: 143, 145
Genus: defined in relation to species, 105, 108, 116; illustrated diagrammatically, 106; *see also* Class, Differentia
Gobbledygook: 423, 493
Grammar: and rhetoric of the sentence, 371–95

H

History of the question: 178–79
Humor: 87–90, 469–70
Hypotheses: 153–54

I

Identification: logic versus psychology in, 245–46; as a method of exposition, 69; in persuasion, 240–46
If-then reasoning: 219–20
Ignoring the question: 122
Illustration: metaphor as, 445–46; as method of exposition, 79–90; as method of paragraph organization, 360; in narrative presentation, 82–87; relevant and irrelevant qualities in, 80–81; use of, for humor and satire, 87–90
Image: 265–66
Imagery: 300–01
Impression: principle of the dominant, in description, 286–88
Impressionistic style: in visual description, 300–01
Induction: by analogy, 202–04; as generalization, 199–202
Inductive leap: 200
Insult: 250 and *note*
Intention: the main, 55–60; in narration, 145, 314–17
Interest: action determined by, 343–45; area of, in comparison and contrast, 71–72; as a condition of cause, 147; dominant, in paragraph organization, 363; in illustration, 80–81; and method, in analysis, 131; and method in

narration, 317–18; multiple, 66; and pattern, in description, 301–02; true subject determined by, 12, 62; value of, for exposition, tested, 62–63
Interpretation: in narration, 336–39; in technical description, 134
Introduction: 16; absence of a formula for, 28; reverse process for, 28–29; and what it must accomplish, 20–29
Irony: 479–84
Issues: in argument, 186–88

J

Jargon: 423–31, 493; antidotes for, 429–31; and worn-out metaphor, 439–41

K

Key point: 256–57
Key words: 268–69

L

Language: figurative, in the description of feelings and states of mind, 604–06; growth of, by extension of meaning, 404–10; importance of, in communication, 3–4; importance of metaphor in, 436–44; metaphorical, and definition, 113–14; shifts in meaning of, 398; and thinking, feeling and rhetoric, 3–10; *see also* Diction, Meaning, Persuasion
Literary paper: 546–63, 586
Logic: and causality, in narration, 321–23; and exposition, in argument, 164–65; order of, in coherence, 36–39; in persuasion (rationalization), 253–55; versus psychology, in identification, 245–46
Loose sentences: 389–90

M

Meaning: clarity of, and rhythm, 491–97; control of, by association, 414–20; dictionary as record of, 406–10; language growth by extension of, 404–10; in narrative, 333–36; primary and secondary, 398; shifts in, 398; tone as qualification of, 474–89; transfer of, in metaphor, 435–36
Metaphor: 435–65; caution against, in definition, 113–14; comparison and contrast in, 453–54; confused, 441–43; and context, 458–65; criteria for

Metaphor (cont.)
good, 453–59; as essential statement, 448–49; as expository illustration, 445–46; function of, 444–52; importance of, in everyday language, 436–44; in language growth, 405; and metonymy, 435 *note;* not necessary in notational statement, 444–45; and simile, 435 *note;* as slang, 439; and tone, 466, 467; worn-out, and jargon, 439–41; *see also* Imagery, Language, Meaning

Metonymy: 435 *note*

Modifiers: adjectival, 377–78; adverbial, 378–79; dangling, 380

Monotony: controls for avoiding, 39

Mood: in paragraph organization, 363

Motivation: in use of description, 278

N

Narration: 313–51; and absorbed forms of discourse, 318; action in, determined by interest, 343–44; expository, 142–43; generalized, 143–45; in illustration, 82–87; intention in, 57, 145, 314–17; interest and method in, 317–18; as a kind of discourse, 57; meaning in, 333–36; pattern in, 326–33; point of view in, 345–50; relevance in, 344; selection in, 344; special problems in, 607–16; time, the basic order of, 40; *see also* Action, Event

Non sequitur: 224

Note-taking: and research paper preparation, 509–30, 532–33

Nouns: derivation of, 406, 407, 409; in description, 294

O

Observer: in causal analysis, 154–55; in description, 297–300

Officialese: 423

Omniscient point of view: in narration, 347

Opinion: as evidence, 195–98

Oratory: 238–39

Organization: coherence through, 31, 35–44; for comparison and contrast, 73–79; of the composition, 31–51; emphasis as a principle of, 44–51; of paragraph, 360–63; through précis, 600; through summary, 598–600; unity in, 31–34; *see also* Classification, Outline, Research paper

Originality: as adjunct of style, 499

Outline: paragraph, 522–23; research paper, 520–24, 549–50; scratch, 520, 533–34; sentence, 18–19, 521–22, 537–38; topic, 520–21

Overstatement: and understatement, effect of, on tone, 484–89

P

Panoramic point of view: in narration, 347

Paragraph: as a convenience to reader, 355–57; emphasis in, 46, 365–67; linking one with another, 367–70; organization of, 360–63; and the sentence, 355–95; of specialized function, 370–71; structure of, 357–60; transition, 367–68; unity and coherence in, 363–65

Parallelism: as rhetorical device, 381–84; violations of, 384–85

Particular, the: and its irrelevant qualities in illustration, 80–81

Passive voice: 374

Pattern: and interest, 301–02; mixing of, in description, 303–05; in narration, 326–33; and point of view, 297–301; and texture, in description, 296–305

Perception: massiveness of, 281

Periodic sentences: 389–90

Personality: impress of, in originality, 499

Perspective: individual, 269; social, 265–69

Persuasion: 238–74; and argument, differences between, 239–40; Aristotle's three modes of, 240, 242, 246, 253, 254; common ground in, 240; and emotions, 246–55; and ethics, 264–70; fallacies in, 255; perspective in, 265–69; and power, 238–39; rationalization in, 253–55; and reasoning, relation between, 255–64; and rhetoric, 269–70; slanting and suggestion in, 250–51; tone in, 467

Point of view: illustrated diagrammatically, 347; in narration, 345–50; panoramic, 347; and pattern, in description, 297–301

Position: for emphasis, 45

Power: and persuasion, 238–39

Précis: 600

Premise: 163 *note,* 168 *note,* 361; in reasoning, 206, 210, 214

Preparation and note-taking: 509–30, 532–33

Pronouns: demonstrative, use of, in linking paragraphs, 369–70

Propaganda: 223–24, 265

Proportion: of parts, for emphasis, 45–46; and pattern, in narration, 326

Proposition: the clear, 177–78; and dramatic content, 14; illustrated diagrammatically, 185; main, and supporting points, 182–86; as premise in reasoning, 206, 210; and question, in exposition, 63; single, 179–81; statement of, as basis for argument, 172–74; and true subject, 14; two kinds of, 175–76; *see also* Class, Premise, Reasoning

Propositions of action: and analysis, 190–92

Propositions of fact: and analysis, 188–89

Psychology: versus logic, in identification, 245–46

Purpose: three types of, for comparison and contrast, 70

Q

Question: begging the, 121–22; forcing the, in argument, 171 *note;* history of the, 178–79; ignoring the, 122; and proposition, in exposition, 63

R

Rationalization: 253–55; distinguished from reasoning, 254

Reader: hostile, 27–29; uninterested, 25–27

Reason: and argument, 162–64, 199

Reasoning: deductive, 206–18; by either-or, 218–19; fallacious, 149–50, 221–28, 255; by if-then, 219; inductive, 199–205; and persuasion, relation between, 255–64; rationalization distinguished from, 254; slips in, 215–17; for truth and for assent, 255–64; *see also* Argument, Class, Classification, Proposition

Relevance: in narration, 344–45

Repetition: of idea, 46, 388; jingling, and word echo, 387–88; of key word in paragraph, 268–69

Research paper: 509–88; bibliography for, 511–16, 524, 528–29, 531–32; final version of, writing and rewriting, 530–88; first draft, 534–36, 550–57; footnotes, 524–29; literary paper, 546–63, 586; outline, 520–24, 533–34, 537–38, 549; preparation and note-taking, 509–30, 532–33; revision, 539–44, 557–63; rewriting, 536–37; rewritten, 564–84; sample, 539–44; sources for, primary and secondary, 510–11; term paper, 530–31

Rewriting: and writing, 530–88

Rhetoric: definition, 6; and grammar of the sentence, 371–95; and language, thinking and feeling, 3–10

Rhythm: and clarity, as aspects of style, 491–97

S

Sarcasm: 479–80

Satire: 87–90

Scale: a problem in narration, 607–09

Selection: in description, 290–91; in narration, 344

Sentence: fixed word order of normal, 372–75; length and variation of, 390–93; loose and periodic, 389–90; and the paragraph, 355–95; parts of, 373, 381; rhetoric and grammar of the, 371–95; rhythmic inflection of, 492; special patterns in structure of, 381–90; topic, 357–58; *see also* Organization, Rhetoric

Sentimentality: caution against, 489

Sequence: action and, in narration, 319–32; time order in, 39–50

Sharp focus: in narration, 348

Simile: 435 *note*

Slang: 387–98, 411; and jargon, 421–23; and metaphor, 439

Slanting: and suggestion, in persuasion, 250–51

Sociological style: 424

Sources: primary and secondary, for research paper, 510–11

Space: arrangements of objects in, as method of paragraph organization, 362; order of, in coherence, 41

Special problems: of discourse, 353–506; in narration, 607–16

Species: defined in relation to genus, 105, 108, 116; illustrated diagrammatically, 106

Specific words: 398–99, 402–04

States of mind: and feelings, description of, 601–06

Stereotypes: including slang, 421–23

A 0
B 1
C 2
D 3
E 4
F 5
G 6
H 7
I 8
J 9